3rd EDITION

The Press and America

An Interpretative History of the Mass Media

EDWIN EMERY

Professor of Journalism and Mass Communication
University of Minnesota

PRENTICE-HALL, INC., *Englewood Cliffs, New Jersey*

Library of Congress Cataloging in Publication Data

Emery, Edwin.
The press and America, an interpretative history of the mass media.

Includes bibliographies.
1. Press—U. S. 2. American newspapers. I. Title.
PN4855.E6 1972 071.3 77-38634
ISBN 0-13-697961-0

PRENTICE-HALL, INC.
Englewood Cliffs, N. J.

10 9 8 7 6 5 4 3 2 1

Printed in the United States of America

PRENTICE-HALL INTERNATIONAL, INC., *London*
PRENTICE-HALL OF AUSTRALIA, PTY. LTD., *Sydney*
PRENTICE-HALL OF CANADA, LTD., *Toronto*
PRENTICE-HALL OF INDIA PRIVATE LIMITED, *New Delhi*
PRENTICE-HALL OF JAPAN, INC., *Tokyo*

Foreword

Journalism history is the story of man's long struggle to communicate freely with his fellow men—to dig out and interpret news, and to offer intelligent opinion in the market place of ideas. Part of the story has as its theme the continuing efforts by men and women to break down the barriers that have been erected to prevent the flow of information and ideas, upon which public opinion is so largely dependent. Another aspect of the story is concerned with the means, or media, by which this essential news and opinion reached the public, from the days of the handwritten "newes letter" to the printed page, radio, and television. Just as important to this story are the heroes and villains, as well as the bit actors, who made the press (meaning all media of communication) what it is today. Finally, all this becomes more meaningful when the development of our journalistic tradition is related to the political, economic, and social progress of our people.

The title, *The Press and America,* reflects the emphasis placed upon correlation of journalism history with political, economic, and social trends. In this interaction, the press has had its influence upon the course taken by our country. Conversely, the conditions and influences present in each historical era have cumulatively determined the shape of the press. Within this framework emerges the story of the men and women of journalism, and of the institutions and traditions they created.

In the opening chapters, beginning with the European roots of American journalism and covering the long time-span ending with the Civil War, the primary concern is with an exposition of the principles upon which the American Fourth Estate was founded. The remaining chapters examine the modern mass media—newspapers, television, radio, magazines, press associations—and their role in an increasingly complex society. For this edition, there have been many extensive revisions, particularly in enlarging coverage of the broadcast media. The concluding chapters analyze the controversial role of television during the 1960s and the crisis of credibility arising from conflict between government and press. Among new sections of the book are those treating the Vietnam War, the Kerner and Walker reports, the Pentagon Papers case, the black press, and the underground press.

Thanks are due to many persons who have aided in this venture during two decades. For this edition, comprehensive criticisms of the manuscript and many valuable suggestions came from Professors Richard A. Schwarzlose of Northwestern University, William H. Taft of the University of Missouri, and Michael C. Emery of San Fernando Valley State College. Extending aid in their specialized areas were Sam Kuczun of the University of Colorado; William A. Hachten, University of Wisconsin; Donald M. Gillmor and Randall L. Murray, University of Minnesota; Harvey Saalberg, Kent State University; Roland E. Wolseley, Syracuse University; Henry G. La Brie III, University of Iowa; John D. Stevens, University of Michigan; Paul V. Peterson, Ohio State University; Robert V. Hudson, Michigan State University; William E. Ames, University of Washington; and Donald L. Shaw, University of North Carolina.

My debt to Henry Ladd Smith, co-author for the first edition, remains great, particularly for graceful writing in the early chapters. I also wish to thank again three journalism professors who gave counsel and criticism during the preparation of the original manuscript: Ralph D. Casey, University of Minnesota; Frederick B. Marbut, Pennsylvania State University; and the late Kenneth E. Olson, Northwestern University. Harold L. Nelson, University of Wisconsin, gave invaluable assistance during the preparation of the original index and has offered many suggestions for text revisions, particularly for the colonial period. Recognition is due the late Warren C. Price, University of Oregon, and Calder M. Pickett, University of Kansas, for their extensive work in journalism bibliography.

Information on special areas has come from many, including Ralph O. Nafziger, University of Wisconsin; Fredrick S. Siebert, Michigan State University; Quintus C. Wilson, Northern Illinois University; Robert W. Desmond, University of California; J. Edward Gerald, Raymond B. Nixon, R. Smith Schuneman, and the late Edwin H. Ford, University of Minnesota; and the late Jacob Scher of Northwestern University. I also wish to thank the many others whose comments have aided and encouraged me. To my wife, Mary M. Emery, I express appreciation for assistance and patient support.

Finally, I acknowledge my debt to the many scholars and writers whose contributions to journalism history are listed in the footnotes and bibliographies.

EDWIN EMERY

Contents

1

The Heritage of the American Press 1

2

The Birth of the American Newspaper 21

3

The Press Wins a Beachhead 37

4

Rise of the Fourth Estate 53

5

The Seeds of Revolution 69

6

The Press and Revolution 85

7

The Press and the Second Revolution 99

8

The Tocsin of a Nation 117

9

The Press and the Expanding Nation 129

10

Coonskin Democracy and the Press 149

11

A Press for the Masses 165

12

The Race for News 191

13

The Press and the Rise of Sectionalism 207

14

The Irrepressible Conflict 231

15

The Press at a Watershed 259

16

A Revolution in National Life 279

17

The New Journalism 307

18

The Modern Newspaper Emerges 325

19

The Age of Yellow Journalism 349

20

The People's Champions 379

21

The Great and the Colorful 413

22

Media Consolidation Begins 441

23

The Common Denominators 465

24

The Press in Modern War 507

25

From Jazz Journalism to Interpretative Reporting 553

26

Radio and Television: Revolution in Communication 587

27

Economic Pressures Shape the Mass Media 617

28

The Surviving Newspaper Press 653

29

Government, Publishers, and Guild 677

30

The Challenge of Criticism 695

31

A Crisis of Credibility 739

Index 763

Illustrations

The Daily Courant of London (1702)	*facing* 1
Publick Occurrences (1690) and order banning it	20
Boston News-Letter (1704)	30
New England Courant (1722)	36
English Common Press	48
Colonial cartoon	51
Pennsylvania Gazette (1735)	52
Trial of John Peter Zenger	62
John Dickinson, James Rivington, Samuel Adams, Isaiah Thomas	68
Stamp Act issue of *Pennsylvania Journal* (1765)	72
Tom Paine's first Crisis paper in *Pennsylvania Packet* (1776)	84
Philip Freneau, Benjamin Russell, William Cobbett	98
Report of signing of the Constitution	115
Cartoon of Lyon-Griswold duel	116
National Intelligencer (1820) reporting Missouri Compromise	128
"Personals" from *National Intelligencer* (1823) and *Argus of Western America* (1836)	147
Argus of Western America (1824)	148
Morning Courier and Enquirer (1830)	156
Early cylinder press	161
Horace Greeley, James Gordon Bennett Sr.	164
New York Herald (1836)	171
Samuel Bowles III (from *Harper's Weekly*)	184
First illustrated front page	189
The Californian (1849)	190
Type-revolving press	202

Freedom's Journal (1827), first black newspaper 206
William Lloyd Garrison's *Liberator* (1837) 212
Frederick Douglass 220
Early full-page illustration 229
New York Herald (1865), Civil War ends 230
Henry J. Raymond (from *Harper's Weekly*) 235
Charles A. Dana, E. L. Godkin, Harvey W. Scott, Henry Watterson 258
Tammany Tiger cartoon in *Harper's Weekly* (1871) 266
Leslie's Illustrated Newspaper (1858) 278
Henry W. Grady 295
Melville E. Stone, William Rockhill Nelson 299
Joseph Pulitzer 306
New York World (1883) 316
Advertising page in *Chicago Times-Herald* (1898) 324
Page of ads from *Harper's Magazine Advertiser* (1901) 347
William Randolph Hearst 348
The "Yellow Kid" of the *New York World* (1896) 356
"Maine" edition, *New York Journal* (1898) 368
"Maine" edition, *New York World* 370
"Maine" edition, *New York Post* 372
Edward Wyllis Scripps 378
Josephus Daniels 399
Joseph Medill 400
McClure's Magazine (1903) 402
Early trademarks and brand advertising 411
"Titanic" edition, *New York Times* (1912) 412
Adolph S. Ochs, Carr Van Anda 419
William Allen White 427
New York Herald (1904) 434
Wright brothers' "Flying Machine" 439
Frank Munsey, Cyrus H. K. Curtis 440
Montage of comic strips from 1890s to present 464
Kent Cooper, Wes Gallagher (AP) 473
Hugh Baillie, Roger Tatarian (UPI) 476
Walter Duranty 486
Columnists: Thomas L. Stokes, Marquis Childs, Walter Lippmann, Mary McGrory, Joseph Kraft, Art Buchwald 492
Cartoons by Rollin Kirby, Jay (Ding) Darling, Daniel Fitzpatrick, Edmund Duffy, Herbert L. Block, Bill Mauldin 495
Cartoons by Patrick Oliphant, Paul Conrad, Thomas F. Darcy, John Fischetti 497
St. Louis Post-Dispatch (1970) reporting Cambodian invasion 506

Armistice Day edition, *New York Times* (1918) 514
Pearl Harbor edition, *San Francisco Chronicle* (1941) 523
Ernie Pyle 530
Korean War opens, *New York Herald Tribune* (1950) 534
Marguerite Higgins 535
Chicago Daily News (1966) reporting Vietnam War 543
Vietnam War correspondents: Neil Sheehan, Malcolm Browne, David Halberstam, Harrison Salisbury 545
New York Daily News (1928) 552
Erwin D. Canham, Bernard Kilgore 568
Henry R. Luce, Harold Ross 577
Uses of radio, "Wonder Science of the Century" 585
Walter Cronkite, Chet Huntley and David Brinkley 586
Radio: David Sarnoff, H. V. Kaltenborn, Elmer Davis, Edward R. Murrow 598
The "Great Debate," *Christian Science Monitor* (1960) 605
Television: Eric Sevareid, Dan Rather, John Chancellor, Frank McGee, Howard K. Smith, Harry Reasoner 608
Man on the moon, *Washington Post* (1969) 612
Media leaders: William S. Paley, Lord Thomson, John H. Johnson, Henry Luce III 616
Group owners: Samuel I. Newhouse, Paul Miller, John S. Knight, John H. Sengstacke, John Cowles, Jr., Marshall Field V 628
Afro-American (1971) 636
Muhammad Speaks (1971), *La Raza* (1971) 643
Village Voice (1971), *Los Angeles Free Press* (1971) 646
Page from final issue of *Look* 651
Assassination of JFK, *New York Herald Tribune* (1963) 652
Publishers: Arthur Hays Sulzberger, Mrs. Helen Rogers Reid, Katharine Graham, Otis Chandler, Barry Bingham, Joseph Pulitzer III 659
Editors: O. K. Bovard, Harry J. Grant, James B. Reston, Nick B. Williams, Benjamin C. Bradlee, Lee Hills 665
FDR's first fireside chat, *New York Herald Tribune* (1933) 676
Heywood Broun 680
Nixon's China trip, *Chicago Tribune* (1971) 694
William Randolph Hearst Jr., Robert R. McCormick 707
Roy W. Howard, Edward W. Scripps II 713
Chicago riots, *Chicago Sun-Times* (1968) 720
Pentagon Papers victory, *New York Times* (1971) 738
Cartoon by Paul Conrad (Vietnam War) 745
Cambodia-Kent State parallel, *Los Angeles Times* (1970) 747

The Daily Courant.

Wednesday, March 11. 1702.

From the Harlem Courant, Dated March 18. N. S.

Naples, Feb. 22.

ON Wednesday last, our New Viceroy, the Duke of Escalona, arriv'd here with a Squadron of the Galleys of Sicily. He made his Entrance drest in a French habit; and to give us the greater Hopes of the King's coming hither, went to Lodge in one of the little Palaces, leaving the Royal one for his Majesty. The Marquis of Grigni is also arriv'd here with a Regiment of French.

Rome, Feb. 25. In a Military Congregation of State that was held here, it was Resolv'd to draw a Line from Ascoli to the Borders of the Ecclesiastical State, thereby to hinder the Incursions of the Transalpine Troops. Orders are sent to Civita Vecchia to fit out the Galleys, and to strengthen the Garrison of that Place. Signior Casali is made Governor of Perugia. The Marquis del Vasto, and the Prince de Caserta continue still in the Imperial Embassador's Palace; where his Excellency has a Guard of 50 Men every Night in Arms. The King of Portugal has desir'd the Arch-Bishoprick of Lisbon, vacant by the Death of Cardinal Sousa, for the Infante his second Son, who is about 11 Years old.

Vienna, Mar. 4. Orders are sent to the 4 Regiments of Foot, the 2 of Cuirassiers, and to that of Dragoons, which are broke up from Hungary, and are on their way to Italy, and which consist of about 14 or 15000 Men, to hasten their March thither with all Expedition. The 6 new Regiments of Hussars that are now raising, are in so great a forwardness, that they will be compleat, and in a Condition to march by the middle of May. Prince Lewis of Baden has written to Court, to excuse himself from coming thither, his Presence being so very necessary, and so much desir'd on the Upper-Rhine.

Francfort, Mar. 12. The Marquiss d' Uxelles is come to Strasburg, and is to draw together a Body of some Regiments of Horse and Foot from the Garisons of Alsace; but will not lessen those of Strasburg and Landau, which are already very weak. On the other hand, the Troops of His Imperial Majesty, and his Allies, are going to form a Body near Germeshein in the Palatinate, of which Place, as well as of the Lines at Spires, Prince Lewis of Baden is expected to take a View, in three or four days. The English and Dutch Ministers, the Count of Frise, and the Baron Vander Meer; and likewise the Imperial Envoy Count Lowenstein, are gone to Nordlingen, and it is hop'd that in a short time we shall hear from thence of some favourable Resolutions for the Security of the Empire.

Liege, Mar. 14. The French have taken the Cannon de Longie, who was Secretary to the Dean de Mean, out of our Castle, where he has been for some time a Prisoner, and have deliver'd him to the Provost of Maubeuge, who has carry'd him from hence, but we do not know whither.

Paris, Mar. 13. Our Letters from Italy say, That most of our Reinforcements were Landed there; that the Imperial and Ecclesiastical Troops seem to live very peaceably with one another in the Country of Parma, and that the Duke of Vendome, as he was visiting several Posts, was within 100 Paces of falling into the Hands of the Germans. The Duke of Chartres, the Prince of Conti, and several other Princes of the Blood, are to make the Campaign in Flanders under the Duke of Burgundy; and the Duke of Maine is to Command upon the Rhine.

From the Amsterdam Courant, Dated Mar. 18.

Rome, Feb. 25. We are taking here all possible Precautions for the Security of the Ecclesiastical State in this present Conjuncture, and have desir'd to raise 3000 Men in the Cantons of Switzerland. The Pope has appointed the Duke of Berwick to be his Lieutenant-General, and he is to Command 6000 Men on the Frontiers of Naples: He has also settled upon him a Pension of 6000 Crowns a year during Life.

From the Paris Gazette, Dated Mar. 18. 1702.

Naples, Febr. 17. 600 French Soldiers are arrived here, and are expected to be follow'd by 3400 more. A Courier that came hither on the 14th. has brought Letters by which we are assur'd that the King of Spain designs to be here towards the end of March; and accordingly Orders are given to make the necessary Preparations against his Arrival. The two Troops of Horse that were Commanded to the Abruzzo are posted at Pescara with a Body of Spanish Foot, and others in the Fort of Montorio.

Paris, March. 18. We have Advice from Toulon of the 5th instant, that the Wind having long stood favourable, 22000 Men were already sail'd for Italy, that 2500 more were Embarking, and that by the 15th it was hoped they might all get thither. The Count d' Estrees arriv'd there on the Third instant, and set all hands at work to fit out the Squadron of 9 Men of War and some Fregats, that are appointed to carry the King of Spain to Naples. His Catholick Majesty will go on Board the *Thunderer*, of 110 Guns.

We have Advice by an Express from Rome of the 18th of February, That notwithstanding the pressing Instances of the Imperial Embassadour, the Pope had Condemn'd the Marquis del Vasto to lose his Head and his Estate to be confiscated, for not appearing to Answer the Charge against him of Publickly Scandalizing Cardinal Janson.

ADVERTISEMENT.

IT will be found from the Foreign Prints, which from time to time, as Occasion offers, will be mention'd in this Paper, that the Author has taken Care to be duly furnish'd with all that comes from Abroad in any Language. And for an Assurance that He will not, under Pretence of having Private Intelligence, impose any Additions of feign'd Circumstances to an Action, but give his Extracts fairly and Impartially; at the beginning of each Article he will quote the Foreign Paper from whence 'tis taken, that the Publick, seeing from what Country a piece of News comes with the Allowance of that Government, may be better able to Judge of the Credibility and Fairness of the Relation: Nor will he take upon him to give any Comments or Conjectures of his own, but will relate only Matter of Fact, supposing other People to have Sense enough to make Reflections for themselves.

This Courant (as the Title shews) will be Publish'd Daily: being design'd to give all the Material News as soon as every Post arrives: and is confin'd to half the Compass, to save the Publick at least half the Impertinences, of ordinary News-Papers.

LONDON. Sold by *E. Mallet*, next Door to the *King's-Arms* Tavern at *Fleet-Bridge*.

Facsimile of the first daily newspaper in the English language.

1

The Heritage of the American Press

Give me but the liberty of the press and I will give to the minister a venal House of Peers . . . and servile House of Commons . . . I will give him all the power that place can confer upon him to purchase up submission and overawe resistance—And yet, armed with liberty of the press . . . I will attack the mighty fabric he has reared . . . and bury it amidst the ruins of the abuses it was meant to shelter.

—Richard Brinsley Sheridan

We might begin our story with the appearance of the first newspaper in colonial America—surely that would appear to be the beginning of American journalism. But the colonial newspaper was so closely patterned after the British product that to understand the function of the press at that time, it is necessary to explain a little about the English influence. Many able writers, including Bleyer and Shaaber, have started their histories of the American press with the appearance of the "corantos," or primitive newspapers printing foreign news, in the early seventeenth century.

But the English coranto was, in turn, traceable to similar publications on the continent. It is now generally conceded that the modern press is the gift of no one nation, and that it was already in the process of development in other parts of the world long before the corantos began to be read in London.

THE EARLIEST NEWSPAPERS

The oldest known and preserved copies of a primitive newspaper were published in Germany in 1609, but the existing copies do not indicate the city, printer, or publisher. From an analysis of paper, type, printing technique, political content, and religious coloring, experts conceded that the site of this earliest known newspaper had to be in North Germany. According to Dr. Ralph O. Nafziger, who has made a lengthy study of the evidence produced by German researchers, the 1609 *Aviso* was located in Wolfenbüttel rather than in Bremen as earlier thought.[1]

Painstaking research has established other early newspaper publication in Strasbourg, also in 1609, and in Cologne in 1610. By 1620 it had spread to Frankfurt, Berlin, Hamburg, Basel, Vienna, Amsterdam, and Antwerp. Amsterdam printers were publishing papers in the English and French languages in 1620, but the first London publication appeared in 1621 and the first Paris paper in 1631. A court newspaper begun in Stockholm in 1645 still appears and is the world's oldest known continuously published newspaper.[2]

Other countries also contributed to the development of the press. In 1566 the Venetian Magistracy ordered accounts of the war in Dalmatia to be read and posted in public places. Persons interested in this news paid a small coin, called a *gazetta,* for the privilege of obtaining it. Thirty volumes of these "Gazettes" have been preserved in the Maggliabecchi Library in Florence.[3] Even before this the Italian peninsula was noted for its advances in the publication of current events; as far back as 59 B.C., news sheets known as *Acta Diurna* were posted in public places in Rome. These were filed each succeeding day in a special building housing records, where they were available to anyone wishing to make use of them.

During the European Middle Ages, the Chinese made important contributions to the art of printing. In A.D. 868, Wang Chieh published a book printed from blocks. Copies of it survive as man's oldest printed book. The first known use of movable type was by another Chinese, Pi Shêng, around 1045. Although the influence of the Chinese craftsmen on Western pioneers would be difficult to establish, it is known that Marco Polo described Chinese printing methods when he returned to Venice from the East in 1295. It was in the same area that paper was first used in printing. The court gazette at Peking set a record for continuous publication by appearing for more than 1,000 years, but disappeared in 1911.

THE CONCEPT OF NEWS

The point to all this is that England had no special claim as the home of the modern press, even though it advanced beyond all other countries journalistically. And in England, as in other lands, news was exchanged long

[1] Dr. Nafziger, director emeritus of the University of Wisconsin School of Journalism, is himself a scholar in German press history.

[2] Folke Dahl, ed., *The Birth of the European Press* (Stockholm: The Royal Library, 1960), summarizes much of this research. Dahl found local news emphasized in a Viennese paper of 1629—an unusual development. The oldest known Swedish paper was printed at Strängnäs in 1624.

[3] Venice and Florence were early news centers in Italy, but Genoa is credited with the first continuously titled paper, begun in 1645.

before there was even the most primitive form of newspaper. One of the great attractions at the country fairs of the Middle Ages was the opportunity to exchange gossip and information. Countrymen and gentry traveled annually to Bartholomew, Donnybrook, or Stourbridge as much to swap news as to buy yearly supplies of staples. Newspapers did not create news; news created newspapers.

It has been said that the true newspaper must meet these qualifications: (1) it must be published at least once a week; (2) it must be produced by mechanical means (to distinguish it from the handwritten "newes letters"); (3) it must be available to anyone willing to pay the price, regardless of class or special interests; (4) it must print anything of interest to a general public, as contrasted with some of the religious and business publications; (5) it must have an appeal to a public of ordinary literary skill; (6) it must be timely, or at least relatively so, in the light of technical development; and (7) it must have stability, as contrasted to the fly-by-night publications of more primitive times.[4]

Any publication that could meet all these qualifications was indeed an innovation. It might even be said that the newspaper was the most significant contribution of the printing press. There were extensive libraries of books long before there was a printing press. The so-called "cradle books," produced immediately after Johann Gutenberg introduced movable type to Europe around 1440 at Mainz and printed his famous Bible in the 1450s, were not essentially different from the handwritten volumes common before that date. Both the longhand and printed books contained information bound between permanent covers. Illustrations, format, materials, and even letter characters were similar in appearance.

The newspaper, on the other hand, was something new. Not until movable type had been perfected was it possible to produce literature and printed reports cheap enough to reach the masses. The revolution was not so much in the medium, perhaps, as in the audience. At any rate, the newspaper was the most novel product of the printing press.

With a publication of this type, there was some incentive for gathering and processing information of interest to the general public—news. News thereupon became a commodity, like food or merchandise, produced for profit to meet a demand. It is significant that there was little use of the word "news" until after the invention of printing made possible the periodical of the masses. Up to about 1500, "Tydings" was the usual word to describe reports of current events. The word "news" was coined to differentiate between the casual dissemination of information and the deliberate attempt to gather and process the latest intelligence.[5]

Almost everything in the modern newspaper can be traced back far be-

[4] Eric W. Allen, "International Origins of the Newspapers: The Establishment of Periodicity in Print," *Journalism Quarterly,* VII (December 1930), 314; quoting from Otto Groth, *Ein System der Zeitungskunde (Journalistik)* (Mannheim: J. Bensheimer, 1928), V. I, pp. 21 ff.

[5] One example was the widespread collection of news by the great commercial house of Fugger, whose sixteenth-century news letters are famous.

yond the beginning of printing, with the possible exception of advertising. What we call "feature stuff" today can be traced back at least 300 years. Illustrations were common long before the newspaper appeared.[6] Comics, sports articles, political columns, and something like the modern editorial were already known. In the sixteenth century as today, the unusual and exciting furnished the bulk of the text. The only innovation of the printing press was to expand the availability of this material. By fulfilling that one function—making news more available to a larger public—the press exerted a tremendous impact upon history.

How could movable type make such a change in thinking and habits accepted for centuries? We take the press so much for granted today that we are likely to be unaware of its significance. By going back into the early days of journalism, when issues were not so confused as they are now, we can see what the press has meant to our society.

THE IMPACT OF PRINTING

In the first place, printing lowered the cost of education. News letters, book manuscripts, and written materials were beyond the reach of the common man before printing, even if such a public had had the literacy skill to make use of them. The cost of a handwritten news letter was directly proportional to the number of copies produced by the copyists. Each additional copy in longhand cost about as much as the previous issue. The main expense of printing was setting the type. Thereafter, every copy produced by the press reduced the unit cost. That meant that literary forms, such as the newspaper, could be tried out at slight financial risk. Reading was thus offered to a much broader base of the population. Illiteracy was then the main barrier between the publisher and his public.

Cheap publication offered the illiterate an incentive to learn to read. The more readers, the lower the cost of such material. The lower the cost, the more readers. This was a chain reaction that was certain to cause an explosion; and it did. Learning to read is likely to make a man or woman curious, simply because matters are brought into focus that have never been imagined before. As the Middle Ages ended, various tendencies broke the crust of fixed custom and ushered in the "age of discussion," which is progressive, inasmuch as it gives a premium to intelligence.[7]

The printing press also made a record for all to see. It offered a more responsible report of transactions, as compared with word-of-mouth information. After the invention of the printing press, people could begin to check

[6] In 1643, before the publication of the first true English newspaper, *Mercurius Civicus* was luring the reader through the use of pictures, much as the tabloids were to do 300 years later. In Antwerp, Abraham Verhoeven was using woodcut illustrations in his newspaper during the 1620s.

[7] Paraphrased from Walter Bagehot, as quoted by Allan Nevins, *Gateway to History* (Boston: D. C. Heath and Co., 1938), p. 245.

the failures and accomplishments of their rulers more effectively. They could pin down responsibility for public policy. It is true that pamphlets were more important than newspapers in this respect, but in time the newspaper took over this function, too.

FIRST ENGLISH PRESS

It is significant that the newsaper first flourished in areas where authority was weak, as in Germany, at that time divided into a patchwork of small principalities; or where rulers were more tolerant, as in the low countries. This explains why the development of the press lagged in England. True, William Caxton set up the first press in England in 1476, but nearly two centuries elapsed before the country had a genuine newspaper.

Caxton learned about printing on the continent, where it had been a craft since the middle of the fifteenth century. He had been governor of a chartered association of "adventurers," or merchants interested in foreign enterprise. Caxton was a learned man, the author and translator of several volumes, and a collector of fine books. He believed that it was his mission to bring the culture of the continent to his countrymen. His king, Edward IV, encouraged these ideas. Edward had just come to power, following a long civil war that had split the country. Not until 1471 was he safely in control of his government.[8] At once he began to repair the ravages of the internal conflict. Edward was responsible for progress in law, industry, and culture. It was under such circumstances that Caxton set up his tiny press "at the Sign of the Red Pale" in the almonry of the abbey at Westminster in 1476.[9]

THE TUDOR REIGN: LICENSING

The Battle of Bosworth Field in 1485 brought a new dynasty into being. Henry Tudor, the victor, ended the long feud between the royal houses of York and Lancaster, thereby bringing the country back to the stability it so desperately needed. A Lancastrian by blood and a Yorkist by marriage, he emerged from the Wars of the Roses, as the civil strife was called, with powers

[8] Relatively speaking, that is. The wars continued after his death in 1483, when his heir was pushed aside by Richard of Gloucester. Gloucester was ultimately defeated by young Henry Tudor at Bosworth Field. There was a period under Edward IV when England was peaceful, however, and it is to this time that the above passage refers.

[9] It is not absolutely established where Caxton set up his press, but the consensus is that it was in the abbey. In 1660, one Richard Atkyns, a Stuart supporter tried to prove that the first press was established by royal grant in 1468. Atkyns was trying to show precedent for royal control of printing. Caxton apparently began printing on his own initiative and without sanction. Most authorities on the subject now agree there is no validity to the Atkyns claims. See Fredrick Seaton Siebert, *Freedom of the Press in England, 1476–1776* (Urbana: University of Illinois Press, 1952), pp. 22–24.

that were eventually to make the Tudors as nearly absolute in power as English monarchs could be. The nobility, which had previously restrained the powers of the English kings, was decimated by the long years of fighting. The Tudor monarchs took full advantage of the situation. Most of them were brilliant and able administrators. Under Tudor leadership England experienced a golden age. It was not conducive to the progress of the press, however.

Caxton enjoyed relative freedom from royal interference, mostly because he never tried to test his status. Printing was not a social force for about 50 years after its establishment in England. Under the Tudors, however, the press became a matter of kingly concern, for that strong dynasty was noted for its attempts to grasp all possible power. Henry VIII started the control of the press with a list of prohibited books. This was in 1529, and the purpose was to set up a bulwark against the rising tide of Protestantism. The first licensing system under government control was established a year later, and by a proclamation on Christmas day, 1534, Henry VIII required printers to have royal permission before setting up shop. Thus the concept of "prior restraint" became law.

During this period the powers of the Privy Council were also increased, at the expense of Parliament and the older courts, but to the advantage of the crown. The Council supervised the administration of laws, regulated trade, kept an eye on the courts, and controlled the press. Beginning in 1542 the records of the Council show a continuous report of proceedings against individuals for "unfitting worddes," seditious utterances, and the like. As early as 1540 the Council made arrests for the printing of street ballads about political matters. The proclamation (ordinance) was the tool employed by the king or his Council to give legality and force to the regulation of the press. By later standards there was no legality to such royal ordinances, but they were enforced as law by the strong Tudors.[10]

Despite these repressive measures, a kind of literary black market supplied the forbidden information and entertainment. We know, for example, that Henry VIII was angered in the thirty-sixth year of his reign by accounts of a battle in Scotland. The news was peddled by London "broadsheet" vendors, a broadsheet being a paper printed specifically to describe a certain event. The king's complaint was not so much that the reports were false, but that the news had been printed without his permission. Apparently, even the absolute powers of the king could not throttle the press, but the climate was not healthy for the steady growth of journalism.

THE STATIONERS COMPANY

One way to control an industry is to make it a monopoly and then to hold the directors of it responsible for abuses. The Tudors did that with the print-

[10] Siebert, *Freedom of the Press in England,* Chapter 1, describes the situation admirably.

ing industry in 1557 when Queen Mary established the Stationers Company. This organization had existed since 1357 as a society of court and text writers, to which the "limners," or illustrators, were admitted after 1404. By 1500 the printers had also been admitted, but by Mary's time the word "stationer" was applied to the publishers and dealers in books, as distinct from the printers.[11] It was a kind of printing trust, and it made it easier for authorities to run down rebel printers not members of the elite group, or sanctioned by it. Queen Elizabeth supplemented this control by her "Injunctions," which gave the religious hierarchy a measure of control over printing. Until the upheavals of the mid-seventeenth century the Stationers Company exerted one of the most powerful controls over the press. In 1576, for example, the Stationers adopted an order for weekly search of London printing houses (where almost all printing was concentrated). Pairs of searchers reported on work in progress, the number of orders on hand, identity of customers, number of employees, and wages paid. That was an effective check on extensive bootleg printing.

THE STAR CHAMBER

The infamous Star Chamber court, originally set up to protect the public, but later the symbol of repression, was another barrier to free expression during the long period preceding the appearance of the English newspaper. By edict of the Privy Council in 1566 and of the Star Chamber in 1586, the pattern of restrictions for the next hundred years was outlined. Severe penalties were prescribed for printers foolish enough to defy the authorities. Strange as it may seem, there were printers willing to run that risk. There was William Carter, who was hanged for printing pamphlets favorable to the Catholic cause. Arrested and tortured in 1580, he was executed in 1584.[12] Puritan rebels against the Established Church included Hugh Singleton, Robert Waldegrave, John Stroud, and John Hodgkins. The attack on the monopoly control was led by John Wolfe, Roger Ward, William Holmes, and John Charlewood. Waldegrave was the printer of the first "Martin Marprelate" tracts, the Puritan arguments published surreptitiously against the Established Church. Hodgkins carried on when Waldegrave was hounded from the country.

The Tudor control of the press was maintained in the interest of public safety. From Henry VIII to Elizabeth, the Crown acted on the principle that peace demanded the suppression of unwarranted dissent. The Tudors were able, and even brilliant, administrators on the whole. Sensitive to public opinion, they understood their people so well that they knew just how far to push their arbitrary rule. Ruthless and erratic as they were at times, their subjects admired them, with some exceptions. Under the Tudors the country had de-

[11] See *ibid.*, Chapter 3, for a detailed discussion of the Stationers Company. Siebert has found that some of these dates have been incorrectly reported.

[12] It was the only execution of this type under the Tudors, however.

veloped great national pride. The Tudors "had the feel" of the country and more often than not were interested in the general welfare. Resistance to them was negligible, therefore, at least from the journalistic standpoint.

THE STUARTS AND TURMOIL

The upheaval came when a new dynasty came to power. James I (he was James VI of Scotland) was sincere and well-meaning, but he was never in tune with the times, or with his subjects. He was the son of the unfortunate Mary Queen of Scots, whose life had been marked by scandal and violence. As the son of Mary, he was early suspected of "Papist" sympathies, in a day when that was religious jargon for treason. It was also his misfortune to succeed one of England's great rulers, Elizabeth—"Good Queen Bess." He suffered badly in comparison with this astute and able monarch. Under the Stuarts, beginning with James, the opposing factions formed battle lines. And since the press thrives in such a climate, if restraints break down, perhaps this partially explains the rapid development of journalism during the seventeenth century.

During the early part of that century news became of great importance to the English people. The religious disputes, the rise of England as a maritime power, the struggles between King and Parliament, and the changing social conditions made the public more interested in events beyond its local sphere. The balladeers and broadsheet vendors could not meet the demand. Prose pamphlets were much more effective, as evidenced by the success of the Marprelate tracts, but such publications were not regular enough. The news letter writers, or "intelligencers," as the publishers of handwritten sheets were called, were capable journalists, but the average man could not afford their products.[13] The time was ripe for a new type of publication.

FIRST ENGLISH CORANTOS

In the summer of 1621, nearly a century and a half after Caxton introduced printing to England, the very rudimentary prototypes of the modern newspaper appeared on the streets of London. These primitive news sheets were called "corantos." They lacked the regularity that is a necessary of the true newspaper, and they were too specialized in content, but they did fulfill a need.

In 1620 the English were interested in continental developments. The popular Princess Elizabeth had married Frederick, Elector of the Palatinate,

[13] As Siebert points out, the first real English reporters were the "intelligencers" John Chamberlain, John Pory, William Locke, and the Reverends Larkin and Mead.

in 1613. He was a Protestant, highly favored by nonconformists, both on the Continent and in England. When he decided to accept the crown of Bohemia against the wishes of the Holy Roman Emperor, he precipitated the Thirty Years' War.

Printers in the Netherlands were quick to capitalize on this interest. At least 25 English-language corantos reporting war news were produced, nearly all at Amsterdam, by George Veseler and Broer Jonson. These single sheets, now in the British Museum, were dated December 2, 1620, to September 18, 1621. Nathaniel Butter, a bookseller, was the English distributor. Sales were so brisk that in the summer of 1621 Butter decided to do the publishing himself, pirating his news from Dutch news sheets. Thomas Archer, a printer, was probably his partner. Copies of their sheets printed in the summer of 1621 do not survive. Six similar corantos,[14] dated September 24 to October 22, do. But by that time printer Archer had run afoul of the law.

When Frederick, the newly elected king of Bohemia, led his forces to defeat in revolt against the Hapsburgs at a battle near Prague, English sentiment favored intercession by James I for his son-in-law. James could not make up his mind, however. The corantos were critical of his foreign policy, and in retaliation the king cracked down on the editors, using the old rules of the Tudors. In December of 1620 and again in July of 1621 the king issued proclamations against "the great liberty of discourse concerning matters of state." He followed this up with an order suppressing corantos, but apparently some of the printers flouted his orders, for there is a record of the Stationers Company calling up Archer for a hearing in August. He was imprisoned.

Nicholas Bourne now enters the picture. He was a respected member of his craft and it is possible that Butter teamed up with him because of his prestige. Their first coranto was authorized in September of 1621 and undoubtedly bore the legend "Published With Authority" at the top of the page, as did later issues. The earliest surviving coranto of this press is dated May 23, 1622. Archer, now out of prison, was the printer. Butter was probably the editor and Bourne was the publisher, or responsible promoter. The paper was printed on one side only, and the sheet was somewhat smaller than a page of modern typewriter paper.

It was not until 1624 that the corantos began to be identified by name, thus supplying something of the continuity required of a true newspaper. The earliest known coranto published by title was *The Continuation of Our Weekly Newes,* from the office of Bourne and Butter. Because this title appeared on at

[14] These six corantos, bearing only the initials "N.B." as publisher, have perplexed English historians. They probably were issued by Nicholas Bourne (see below) but they could have been a continuation of Nathaniel Butter's summer series. The account here of the first London corantos is based upon Siebert, who found evidence in records and correspondence going beyond that offered by the surviving corantos. See also Matthias A. Shaaber, *Some Forerunners of the Newspaper in England, 1476–1622* (Philadelphia: University of Pennsylvania Press, 1929), pp. 314–18.

least 23 consecutive issues, the offering marks another step in the development of the newspaper.

The earliest corantos printed nothing but foreign news. The first domestic reports can be traced back to the publication by the Westminster clerks of Parliamentary proceedings dated about 1628. Out of these accounts developed the "diurnals," or daily reports of local events. The diurnals flourished during the struggle between King and Parliament, when it was safe to comment on local news because neither side was strong enough to take punitive measures, and when both factions were seeking public support. Many of the restrictions on the press were modified by the Long Parliament, and after 1640 diurnals appeared by the score. Oldest known paper of this type is John Thomas' *Diurnall Occurrences,* which first appeared November 29, 1641.

MILTON'S *AREOPAGITICA*

The interim of the first decade of the revolution beginning in 1640 was a period of great development for the press. The Long Parliament abolished the dreaded Star Chamber in 1641. Voices began to be raised in favor of a greater freedom of expression. On November 24, 1644, the poet John Milton published his famous *Areopagitica,* probably the best known of the great pleas for a free press.[15] Milton spoke eloquently for the right of discussion and declared that

> . . . though all the winds of doctrine were let loose to play upon the earth, so truth be in the field, we do injuriously by licensing and prohibiting to misdoubt her strength. Let her [truth] and falsehood grapple; who ever knew truth put to the worse, in a free and open encounter? [16]

Milton gave the most perfect expression to the idea of a free press, but just as courageous and articulate were such journalistic heroes as William Walwyn, who argued for liberty of the press following his studies on religious toleration; Henry Robinson, who based his theory of a free press on economic principles and free enterprise; Richard Overton, the Tom Paine of his day, who expanded his Separatist views on religion into principles of democracy; and John Lilburne, who did more than any of his compatriots in making his countrymen conscious of their right of discussion.[17] As a matter of fact, Milton had very

[15] His ideas and even some of his phrases had already been expressed by Peter Wentworth, who made a speech in Parliament in 1571 on freedom of discussion. Milton's Parliament speech, later published as *Areopagitica,* arose out of his difficulties with the Stationers Company after Milton published a series of licensed and unlicensed pamphlets on divorce.

[16] Quoted from Rufus Wilmot Griswold, ed., *The Prose Works of John Milton,* Vol. I (Philadelphia: J. W. Moore, 1856), p. 189. Milton's glory is dimmed somewhat by the fact that he himself was serving as licenser and censor only seven years later.

[17] The Separatists, one of many dissenting sects, were strong believers in the separation of church and state. The Lilburne thesis was that Englishmen had a birthright in speaking out fearlessly on all measures, and that restrictions were usurpation of power.

little effect in bringing about any improvement. His words were not widely disseminated at the time. The ideas expressed in *Areopagitica* were picked up nearly a hundred years later by people all over the world, notably in America, struggling to obtain even greater freedom than they already enjoyed. Milton is mentioned here because he fits into the chronological pattern, but he really belongs to the rebels of a century later.

With the execution of Charles I in 1649 and the rise of the Commonwealth under Oliver Cromwell, the press again fell upon evil days. Cromwell's "Roundheads" had taken over the royal prerogatives, which had at times so restricted Puritan writers and publishers, but the new regime was no more tolerant of the press than the Crown had been. Cromwell permitted only administration organs to be published, such as *Mercurius Politicus,* censored by the great Milton, *A Perfect Diurnall,* also controlled for a time through Milton, and later the *Publick Intelligencer* (1655). All unauthorized publications were treated roughly.

The restoration of Charles II in 1660 resulted in the establishment of an exclusive patent, or monopoly, system under Henry Muddiman and Roger L'Estrange. For a time the ancient, handwritten news letters were the only means of disseminating information with any degree of freedom. Printed newspapers could be liquidated by confiscating presses, whereas news letters could be produced as long as scribes could find a hideaway, or were willing to defy authorities. During this period ultimate control was divided between Crown and Parliament. Regulations and restrictions were fewer, but they were clearly stated and enforcement was effective under the Surveyor of the Press.

It was under Charles that a new era of journalism was ushered in with the publication of the *Oxford Gazette* in 1665. Edited by Muddiman while the royal court was fleeing from the London plague, it was, strictly speaking, the first periodical to meet all the qualifications of a true newspaper. It was printed twice a week, by royal authority. After 24 issues, the publication became the *London Gazette* when the court moved back to the capital. It continued to be published right on up through the twentieth century as the official court organ.

LICENSING ENDS

The old licensing powers appeared to be crumbling as the Restoration period drew to a close. This was through no choice of the authorities, but more likely because of the growing tendency for class and political alignments. In 1679 Parliament allowed the Licensing Act of 1662 to lapse. It was revived from time to time, but with the increasing tension between Crown and Parliament, each side sought to protect its own spokesmen. The so-called Regulation of Printing, or Licensing, Act expired in 1694, not because authorities were convinced as to the injustice of licensing, but because it was politically unsound. From 1694 to the passage of the first Stamp Act of 1712, the only controls were the laws of treason and seditious libel, and regulations against reporting proceedings of Parliament. Prior restraint had ended.

One last victim under Charles was Benjamin Harris, a brash and somewhat reckless journalist. Harris was convicted of violating the King's laws. He was fined and pilloried. Unable to pay the fine, he spent two years in prison. When his office was again raided in 1686, Harris fled to Bristol with his family and took passage for America. He appears again soon in these pages as the publisher of one of the first newspapers in America.

After the Revolution of 1688, which brought a change in the monarchical institution, journalists were accorded considerable freedom. William and Mary were rulers by right of public opinion and they had the common sense not to antagonize printers and publishers, who were factors in the development of public opinion. There are no serious persecutions in their reign. By 1694 the old Licensing Act died of senility and neglect. With the rise of the two-party system during the reign of William and Mary, it was difficult to maintain licensing. Without the decisive action of the old monarchs, it was impossible to continue such an archaic system. The attack on the Act in Commons centered around the commercial unfairness of the monopoly system, the restrictions on the printing industry, the tendency of suspected violators to use bribery, and the inadequacy of censorship. But as Macaulay declared in his *History of England,* "on the great question of principle, on the question whether the liberty of unlicensed printing be, on the whole, a blessing or a curse to society, not a word is said." [18]

RISE OF A MIDDLE CLASS

Journalistic progress was speeded up by the development of the party system of government. It is significant that parties emerged at the very time that the newspaper began to be a force in the political and social affairs of a people interested more and more in government. The corantos were printed during the death throes of an outworn social system. England was moving steadily from feudalism, whose economic manifestation was production for use, to capitalism, translated economically into production for profit. The change brought social strains as power was grasped by one class at the expense of another.

A new type of citizen began to assert himself. He was the commercial man—the trader, merchant, and (later) the manufacturer. A great middle class was arising. Standing between the producer and the consumer, it profited from the processing and distribution of goods. In doing so, it helped to raise living standards to the highest level. And the wealth accumulated during this process was inevitably translated into power.

[18] Siebert, *Freedom of the Press in England,* p. 262, from T. B. Macaulay, *History of England* (London: J. M. Dent and Sons, Ltd., 1906), III, 328.

Feudalism had no provision for the middle class. The ancient system provided a stability and an effective adjustment to living during a stage of human development. But it gave the Church, the landowner, the aristocrat, and the military special spheres of privilege and power. The emerging middle class could win recognition and influence only by acquiring some of the ancient privileges and powers of the traditional classes.

The language of this period must be understood as ambiguous—the words were often religious, although the meaning might be social or political. Religion had been the great unifying force of the Middle Ages. The emerging middle class tended to be disruptive of old authorities, and it posed new problems in the field of religion. It is significant that the rise of Protestantism and the rise of capitalism were integrated. Both were disruptive of the established order, and the religio-politico jargon employed during this process is confusing to the contemporary reader.

Many of the issues that concerned the people of the seventeenth century appear to have been met with what sounds today like religious bickering. Implicit in the religious arguments, however, were problems still facing us today. Three groups struggled for power. They could have been designated almost equally as well under religious, political, and even social titles. One group was largely Anglican in religion, Tory in politics, and aristocratic as a class. The second group was likely to be Presbyterian, Whig, and middle class. The third was made up of religious dissenters, radicals, and people of more lowly station. All three classes produced newspapers and journalists; perhaps inevitably the Whig middle class would provide the capital and the printing equipment for writers and editors emerging from the working class, dissenters or radicals though they might be.

EIGHTEENTH-CENTURY JOURNALISM

The eighteenth century of British journalism overlaps the infant years of the American press, as described in the next chapter, but because colonial editors were influenced by their British contemporaries, it is pertinent to mention some of the later press developments abroad. The first half of the eighteenth century produced some great journalists in England. Defoe, Swift, Addison, Steele, Fielding, and Samuel Johnson edited newspapers, or wrote essays and other pieces for the popular prints at one time or another. The standard set by them was widely imitated in the American colonies. While this material cannot be classed as news, it served to entertain and elevate the reader. And it did meet the craving for more popular literary fare. The newspapers were the medium for such expression, just as in modern times the popular press offers non-news material in great quantities to meet a demand. The ordinary citizen was also beginning to participate in journalism. Much of the newspaper content was contributed by readers during the eighteenth century.

FIRST ENGLISH DAILY

The popularity of the newspaper was so great that publishers were encouraged to print daily issues. On March 11, 1702, the *Daily Courant* appeared on the streets of London. It was the first daily newspaper printed in the English language. It was produced and "sold by E. Mallet" and authorities differ on the sex of the founder—Elizabeth or Edward? Whichever, the initial venture lasted only a few days.

The real hero of the *Daily Courant* was Samuel Buckley, who revived the daily and made it into a remarkable newspaper. Buckley insisted on a standard of journalism quite unheard of at the time.[19] It was a *news* paper, not a rumor-mill. He insisted upon reporting factual news, rather than opinion. He was impartial in his publication of these facts. He was careful to dateline the articles, ". . . that the Publick, seeing from what Country a piece of News comes with the Allowance of that Government, may be better able to Judge of the Credibility and Fairness of the Relation. . . ."[20] He practiced what he preached. Although Buckley was a Whig, he did not manipulate news of that party to its favor, even when the Whigs were engaged in desperate struggle for power. Printing on a single sheet of paper, with the reverse largely devoted to profitable advertising, except on exceptional news days, he had little opportunity for experimentation in makeup. Occasionally, however, Buckley used maps and tabulated figures to clarify his reports. Much of the advertising was spurious by modern standards, but Buckley made money from it. Undoubtedly this revenue made possible his excellent coverage of foreign news.

The high literary quality of eighteenth-century journalism is indicated by the "essay papers," read by students on both sides of the Atlantic even today. The *Tatler* (1709–11) and the *Spectator* (1711–12, 1714) were the products of, first, Richard Steele, and then of Steele and Joseph Addison. Printed on one side of a sheet, and selling for a penny, this type of paper was enormously popular. The *Spectator* was issued daily and at one time reached 60,000 readers, its promoters boasted. Moreover, its literary form was widely imitated, even in America.

Greatest English journalist of the period was Daniel Defoe, who edited *Mist's Journal* from 1717 through 1720. Steele probably got the idea of his *Tatler* series from reading Defoe's brilliant offerings in earlier papers. Some authorities go so far as to hold that Defoe was the father of the modern editorial. He discussed all manner of topics in a most charming and persuasive style. He, too, was widely copied by American journalists.

19 An excellent description of the paper is given by Marvin Rosenberg, "The Rise of England's First Daily Newspaper," *Journalism Quarterly*, XXX (Winter 1953), 3–14.

20 Rosenberg, *op. cit.*, p. 4.

CATO'S LETTERS

In the great controversy between Tories and Whigs, Dean Swift wrote some of his greatest satire. That was while he was editing the *Examiner* (1710). The conflict brought out other great writers, whole ideas were conveyed to the masses mostly through the newspapers. Influential both in England and America were the so-called "Cato Letters," written by John Trenchard and Thomas Gordon over the pen name, "Cato." The series appeared between 1720 and 1723 in the *London Journal,* later called the *British Journal.*[21] In convincing, readable form, they discussed theories of liberty, representative government, and freedom of expression. In 1724 this series was collected and published in four volumes. Copies were in great demand in the colonies, where the first stirrings of revolution were beginning to be felt. Through American newspapers and pamphlets the influence of "Cato" can be seen right up to the signing of the Declaration of Independence.

Such progress came at great cost, however. Although party conflict raised the voices of free expression, a reactionary government in control was able to force new restrictions. In 1712 the Tories succeeded in imposing a tax on newspapers and advertisements. These "taxes on knowledge" tended to curb the press by economic sanction. Even worse, they kept the price of papers high, so that the masses did not have as ready access to such publications—which was certainly one of the intentions of the authorities. The stamp tax on news sheets and advertisement taxes were not fully removed for another 140 years. The British newspaper, as a result, was low in circulation and small in size until the 1850s. Thanks to the satire of Dr. Samuel Johnson and the courage of newspaper publisher John Wilkes, whose jailing for sedition in the 1760s aroused widespread public reaction, the ban on reporting proceedings of the Commons was dropped in 1771. But threat of trial for seditious libel still hung over those who defied authority.

It is clear from a study of this period that modern journalists can learn much from the experiences of the past. The progress of press freedom shows that the press belongs to those who rule. If power is concentrated in the hands of a monarch, or an elite group, there is no need for the public to receive information and ideas pertaining to political or social matters. Indeed, providing the public with intelligence (news) may actually constitute a threat to national security and stability, and hence the press must be confined strictly to entertainment or innocuous comment under such a system. On the other

[21] The letters were written by John Trenchard and Thomas Gordon. The first series appeared in the *Independent Whig* between January 20, 1720 and January 4, 1721. Much of the text in the 53 essays was concerned with religious liberty. After the financial crash known as the "South Sea Bubble," the authors wrote 144 more letters on the responsibilities of government in protecting citizens. These appeared in the *London Journal* and the succeeding *British Journal* between November 12, 1720 and December 7, 1723.

hand, if the public participates in government, it must have access to information in direct ratio to its place in the political scheme.

Another lesson to be learned from this period is that the more secure a government is, the less it fears undermining, and the more freedom it accords its press. This is true right up to the present moment. During and after wars, when political leaders and their followers are apprehensive about national safety, liberty of speech and press is in danger of restrictions. Henry VIII's insecurity after his establishment of the English church resulted in strict enforcement of press regulations. Elizabeth cracked down on the press when her claim to the throne was in some doubt. On the other hand, the stability of the government from the end of the seventeenth century was accompanied by press freedom such as the world had never seen before. As Siebert says, "It is axiomatic that government does not exert itself in its own protection unless it is attacked, or believes itself to be seriously threatened." [22]

In the next chapter we shall see the process carried over to America, where the concept of a free press was eventually to prevail as it had in no other country. The philosophy providing the stimulus for this progress developed from the English spokesmen, however, and the American debt to English press traditions is incalculable.

Annotated Bibliography

Bibliographies

Indispensable references for students of American journalism are Warren C. Price, *The Literature of Journalism: An Annotated Bibliography* (Minneapolis: University of Minnesota Press, 1959), with 3,147 entries, and Warren C. Price and Calder M. Pickett, *An Annotated Journalism Bibliography 1958–1968* (Minneapolis: University of Minnesota Press, 1970), with 2,172 entries including some from pre-1958. Entries are particularly full in the areas of general journalism histories, specialized and individual histories, biographies, and narratives of journalists at work. Other sections cover press appraisals, press law, international communication, magazines, radio and television, public opinion and propaganda, communication theory, techniques of journalism, journalism education, periodicals of the press, bibliographies, and directories. British and Canadian journalism is well covered. Also useful is Eleanor Blum, *Basic Books in the Mass Media* (Urbana: University of Illinois Press, 1972), a selected book list.

For listings of American newspapers, Clarence S. Brigham's *History and Bibliography of American Newspapers, 1690–1820* (Worcester, Mass.: American Anti-

[22] Siebert, *Freedom of the Press in England*, p. 10. For a scholarly proof of Siebert's proposition ("The area of freedom contracts and the enforcement of restraints increases as the stresses on the stability of the government and of the structure of society increase") see Donald L. Shaw and Stephen W. Brauer, "Press Freedom and War Constraints: Case Testing Siebert's Proposition II," *Journalism Quarterly*, XLVI (Summer 1969), 243, an analysis of the threats against a North Carolina Civil War editor.

quarian Society, 1947) is the guide to surviving early newsprint. Winifred Gregory's *American Newspapers, 1821–1936: A Union List of Files Available in the United States and Canada* (New York: Wilson, 1936) has diminished usefulness since libraries began to discard their more recent bound volumes in favor of microfilm. The Library of Congress publishes *Newspapers on Microfilm,* updating periodically, listing microfilm holdings of libraries newspaper by newspaper. The largest single newspaper collection for the entire period of American history is at the Library of Congress; the largest for the colonial period at the American Antiquarian Society. Ranking high in overall strength are the libraries of the Wisconsin State Historical Society and Harvard University, with the Bancroft Library of University of California famous for its western collections as well. Strong in importance for their regions are the New York Historical Society, New York Public Library, Chicago Historical Society, University of Chicago, Pennsylvania Historical Society, and Boston Public Library. Noteworthy for general collections are University of Missouri, University of Minnesota, Yale University, University of Washington, and UCLA.

Two major bibliographies for the study of American history are *A Guide to the Study of the United States of America* (Washington: Library of Congress, 1960) and the *Harvard Guide to American History* (Cambridge, Mass.: Harvard University Press, 1954). The first named, while less voluminous, carries extensive annotations lacking in the second and has a far better selection of journalistic titles.

For well-balanced discussions of recent trends in American historiography—involving the progressive, consensus, and New Left schools—see Richard Hofstadter, *The Progressive Historians: Turner, Beard, Parrington* (New York: Knopf, 1968), by a onetime consensus advocate; John Higham, *Writing American History* (Bloomington: Indiana University Press, 1970), by a critic of the newer schools; and C. Vann Woodward, ed., *The Comparative Approach in American History* (New York: Basic Books, 1968). Bibliographies in this volume will identify leading exponents of these various approaches to American history.

For historiography in journalism and mass communications, see Ronald T. Farrar and John D. Stevens, eds., *Mass Media and the National Experience* (New York: Harper & Row, 1971). Essays on communications history techniques and subject areas are written by the editors and by William E. Ames, Dwight L. Teeter, Donald L. Shaw, Richard F. Hixson, John M. Harrison, R. Smith Schuneman, Richard C. Burke, William H. Taft, and Robert K. Thorp. A good discussion linking newspaper history and public affairs is William H. Taft's *Newspapers as Tools for Historians* (Columbia, Mo.: Lucas Brothers, 1970).

Books

Blagden, Cyprian, *The Stationers Company.* London: Allen & Unwin, 1960. A scholarly account of licensing and control of printing.

Bleyer, Willard Grosvenor, *Main Currents in the History of American Journalism.* Boston: Houghton Mifflin, 1927. Chapter One is a good description of early English journalism, to about 1750.

Clyde, William M., *The Struggle for the Freedom of the Press from Caxton to Cromwell.* New York: Oxford University Press, 1934. This excellent study is now largely superseded by Siebert (see below).

Cranfield, G. A., *The Development of the Provincial Newspaper, 1700–1760.* London: Oxford University Press, 1962. Researched story of eighteenth-century British printers.

Dahl, Folke, ed., *The Birth of the European Press.* Stockholm: The Royal Library, 1960. A 36-page brochure cataloguing an exhibition of early papers from the library's famous collection.

Ford, Edwin H., and Edwin Emery, eds., *Highlights in the History of the American Press: A Book of Readings.* Minneapolis: University of Minnesota Press, 1954. Selected articles from magazines; the first four discuss sixteenth-century ballads, journalism of the Civil War (1640) period, the eighteenth-century British press, and Daniel Defoe.

Frank, Joseph, *The Beginnings of the English Newspaper.* Cambridge, Mass.: Harvard University Press, 1961. Carries the story through the Restoration of 1660.

Hart, Jim Allee, *Views on the News: The Developing Editorial Syndrome, 1500–1800.* Carbondale: Southern Illinois University Press, 1970. An overview of the origins of the newspaper editorial and development of the opinion-giving function.

Herd, Harold, *The March of Journalism: The Story of the British Press from 1622 to the Present Day.* London: Allen & Unwin, 1952. A condensed, readable history of British newspapers and magazines.

McMurtrie, Douglas C., *The Book: The Story of Printing and Bookmaking.* New York: Oxford University Press, 1943. Tells the Gutenberg story, and traces the spread of printing in Europe and the New World.

Moore, John Robert, *Daniel Defoe: Citizen of the Modern World.* Chicago: University of Chicago Press, 1958. Defoe's ideas and role in early press development.

Morison, Stanley, *The English Newspaper: Some Account of the Physical Development of Journals Printed in London between 1622 and the Present Day.* Cambridge, England: Cambridge University Press, 1932. One of the recognized histories in its field, well illustrated.

Shaaber, Matthias A., *Some Forerunners of the Newspaper in England, 1476–1622.* Philadelphia: University of Pennsylvania Press, 1929. An authoritative, detailed study of the pre-coranto period of journalism.

Siebert, Fredrick Seaton, *Freedom of the Press in England, 1476–1776.* Urbana: University of Illinois Press, 1952. The outstanding study of the subject. Corrects many inaccuracies of older histories.

Steinberg, S. H., *Five Hundred Years of Printing.* London: Faber and Faber, 1959. A brief account of the history of printing, emphasizing the relationships of technical developments and ideas.

Strauss, Victor, *The Printing Industry.* New York: R. R. Bowker, 1967. A history of printing from Gutenberg to computers.

The Tatler and The Spectator. London: G. A. Aitken, ed., 1898–99. The complete file of the famous Addison and Steele literary papers.

von Klarwill, Victor, ed., *The Fugger News Letters,* first series. New York: G. P. Putnam's Sons, 1924. Second series, 1926. An interesting study of the content of news before the days of newspapers.

Werkmeister, Lucyle, *The London Daily Press, 1772–1792.* Lincoln: University of Nebraska Press, 1963. Only detailed history of late eighteenth-century press.

Williams, Francis, *Dangerous Estate: The Anatomy of Newspapers.* New York: Macmillan, 1958. History of the British press since 1702 with emphasis on the press as a social institution.

Periodicals and Monographs

Allen, Eric W., "International Origins of the Newspapers: The Establishment of Periodicity in Print," *Journalism Quarterly,* VII (December 1930), 307. Discusses qualifications of the true newspaper.

Baker, Harry T., "Early English Journalism," *Sewanee Review,* XXV (October 1917), 396. Nathaniel Butter and Sir Roger L'Estrange are highlighted in this detailed account.

Bleyer, Willard G., "The Beginnings of English Journalism," *Journalism Quarterly,* VIII (September 1931), 317. A study of foreign news in early English corantos, showing ties with the continent.

Lowenthal, Leo, and Marjorie Fiske, "Reaction to Mass Media Growth in 18th-Century England," *Journalism Quarterly,* XXXIII (Fall 1956), 442. How literary tastes were lowered by mass consumption.

Rosenberg, Marvin, "The Rise of England's First Daily Newspaper," *Journalism Quarterly,* XXX (Winter 1953), 3. An excellent description of Samuel Buckley's *Daily Courant.*

Numb.—1.

PUBLICK
OCCURRENCES
Both FORREIGN and DOMESTICK.

Boſton, Thurſday Sept. 25th. 1690.

IT is deſigned, that the Countrey ſhall be furniſhed once a moneth (or if any Glut of Occurrences *happen, oftener,) with an Account of ſuch conſiderable things as have arrived unto our Notice.*

In order hereunto, the Publiſher will take what pains he can to obtain a Faithful Relation *of all ſuch things; and will particularly make himſelf beholden to ſuch Perſons in* Boſton *whom he knows to have been for their own uſe the diligent Obſervers of ſuch matters.*

That which is herein propoſed, is, Firſt, *That* Memorable Occurrents *of* Divine Providence *may not be neglected or forgotten, as they too often are.* Secondly, *That people every where may better underſtand the Circumſtances of Publique Afairs both abroad and at home; which may not only direct their* Thoughts *at all times, but at ſome times alſo to aſſiſt their* Buſineſſes *and* Negotiations.

Thirdly, *That ſome thing may be done towards the* Curing, *or at leaſt the* Charming *of that* Spirit of Lying, *which prevails amongſt us, wherefore nothing ſhall be entered, but what we have reaſon to believe is true, repairing to the beſt fountains for our Information. And when there appears any* material miſtake *in any thing that is collected, it ſhall be* corrected *in the* next.

Moreover, the Publiſher of theſe Occurrences *is willing to engage, that whereas, there are many* Falſe Reports, *maliciouſly made, and ſpread among us, if any well-minded perſon will be at the pains to trace any ſuch* falſe Report *ſo far as to find out and Convict the* Firſt Raiſer *of it, he will in this Paper (unleſs juſt Advice be given to the contrary) expoſe the Name of ſuch perſon, as* A malicious Raiſer of a falſe Report. *It is ſuppos'd that none will diſlike this Propoſal, but ſuch as intend to be guilty of ſo villanous a Crime.*

THE Chriſtianized *Indians* in ſome parts of *Plimouth*, have newly appointed a day of Thankſgiving to God for his Mercy in ſupplying their extream and pinching Neceſſities under their late want of Corn, & for His giving them now a proſpect of a very *Comfortable Harveſt*. Their Example may be worth Mentioning.

'Tis obſerved by the Huſbandmen, that altho' the With draw of ſo great a ſtrength from them, as what is in the Forces lately gone for *Canada*, made them think it eſtimoſt impoſſible for them to get well through the Affairs of their Husbandry at this time of the year, yet the Seaſon has been ſo unuſually favourable that they ſca ce find any want of the many hundreds of hands, that are gone from them; which is looked upon as a Merciful Providence

While the barbarous *Indians* were lurking about *Chelmsford*, there were miſſing about the beginning of this month a couple of Children belonging to a man of that Town, one of them aged about eleven the other aged about nine years, both of them ſuppoſed to be fallen into the hands of the *Indians*.

A very *Tragical Accident* happened at *Water-Town*, the beginning of this Month an *Old man*, that was of ſomewhat a Silent and Moroſe Temper, but one that had long Enjoyed the reputation of a *Sober* and a *Pious Man*, having newly buried his Wife, The Devil took advantage of the Melancholy which he thereupon fell into, his Wives diſcretion and induſtry had long been the ſupport of his Family, and he ſeemed hurried with an impertinent fear that he ſhould now come to want before he dyed, though he had very careful friends to look after him who kept a ſtrict eye upon him, leaſt he ſhould do himſelf any harm. But one evening eſcaping from them into the Cow-houſe, they there quickly followed him found him *hanging by a Rope*, which they had uſed to tye their *Calves* withal, he was dead with his feet near touching the Ground.

Epidemical *Fevers* and *Agues* grow very common, in ſome parts of the Country, whereof, tho' many dye not, yet they are ſorely unfitted for their imployments; but in ſome parts a more *malignant Fever* ſeems to prevail in ſuch ſort that it uſually goes thro' a Family where it comes, and proves *Mortal* unto many.

The *Small-pox* which has been raging in *Boſton*, after a manner very Extraordinary is now very much abated. It is thought that far more have been ſick of it then were viſited with it, when it raged ſo much twelve years ago, nevertheleſs it has not been ſo Mortal, The number of them that have

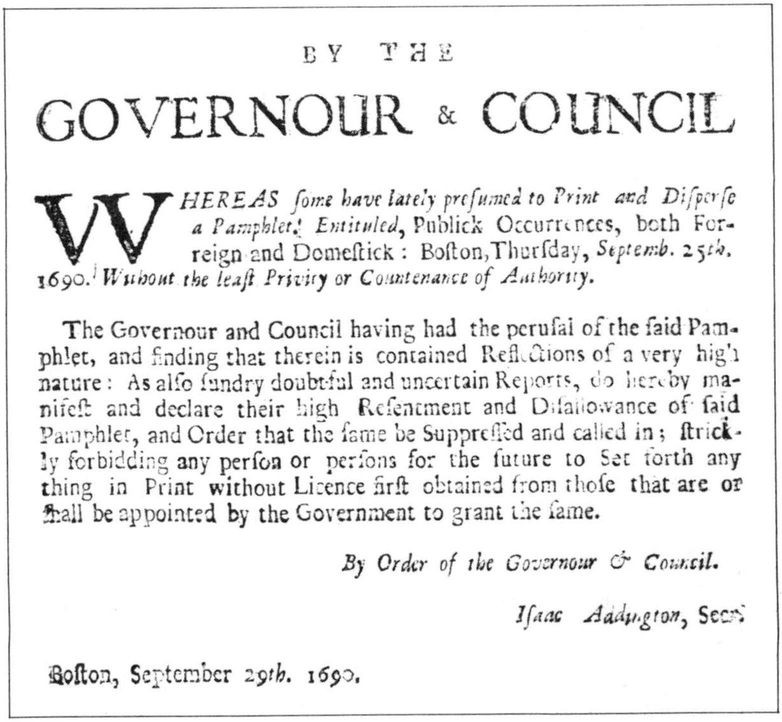

BY THE
GOVERNOUR & COUNCIL

WHEREAS ſome have lately preſumed to Print and Diſperſe a Pamphlet, Entituled, Publick Occurrences, both Forreign and Domeſtick: Boſton, Thurſday, *Septemb. 25th.* 1690. *Without the leaſt Privity or Countenance of Authority.*

The Governour and Council having had the peruſal of the ſaid Pamphlet, and finding that therein is contained Reflections of a very high nature: As alſo ſundry doubtful and uncertain Reports, do hereby manifeſt and declare their high Reſentment and Diſallowance of ſaid Pamphlet, and Order that the ſame be Suppreſſed and called in; ſtrickly forbidding any perſon or perſons for the future to Set forth any thing in Print without Licence firſt obtained from thoſe that are or ſhall be appointed by the Government to grant the ſame.

By Order of the Governour & Council.

Iſaac Addington, Secr.

Boſton, September 29th. 1690.

The first effort at a colonial newspaper, and the order banning it.

2

The Birth of the American Newspaper

The way to get at the nature of an institution, as of anything else that is alive, is to see how it has grown.
—A. G. Keller [1]

New England was the birthplace of the American newspaper, but it was not until 1704, or 84 years after the establishment of the first successful colony in that area, that a publication meeting all the qualifications of a true newspaper appeared. Printers were available from the very beginning. William Brewster and Edward Winslow, two of the "elders," or leaders, of the Pilgrims who came to Plymouth in December of 1620, were printers. They had published religious tracts for the Separatists, the more radical offshoot of English Protestantism, and they had lived for a time near George Veseler, who was printing the first English coranto in the Netherlands while the Pilgrims were on the way to the New World in the "Mayflower." Despite this background, the Plymouth colony existed nearly a century before it enjoyed a newspaper or popular periodical.

Ten years after the arrival of the Pilgrims, another group of religious exiles settled around Boston, a day's sail to the north of Plymouth. This Massachusetts Bay Colony, as it was then known, was to be the cradle of American journalism. Many of its members were prosperous. The educational level was high, and some of the settlers were respected scholars. Unlike the Plymouth settlement, which grew slowly, the Massachusetts Bay Colony increased rapidly in population and area of influence. From the beginning it had a high degree of self-government. The charter of the organization had been brought to America, where it served as a kind of constitution beyond the tampering of

[1] Famous in his time as a great teacher and lecturer on sociology at Yale University.

jealous officials in the home government. In effect, the colony had a form of autonomy, or at least of participating home rule, that was to be of great significance in the political development of New England.

THE NEW ENGLAND ENVIRONMENT

These colonists were concerned about the education of their children. Having enjoyed educational advantages themselves, they wished to pass on the heritage to succeeding generations. Six years after the founding of the settlement, they established Harvard College (1636). In the larger towns there were "grammar schools," which prepared boys for Harvard. As part of this educational process, the authorities established the first press in the English colonies at Cambridge in 1638. Its function was to produce the religious texts needed in school and college. Other presses were set up not long after. Later, these presses printed cultural material, including the first history of the colony and some poetry.

It was this interest in education and cultural dissemination that made Boston famous as the intellectual capital of the New World. Here were all the ingredients for the development of a newspaper—high literacy, interest in community matters, self-government, prosperity, and cultural leadership—yet no successful newspaper appeared until the fourth generation.

There was good reason for the lag. At first, the wilderness absorbed the energies of the colonists. Any demand for news was satisfied well enough by the English papers, which arrived on every ship from home. For the colonists had few ties with other communities in the New World. Years after he arrived, the settler was still oriented toward the homeland, not toward his neighbors.

So there was no demand for the type of news that had fostered early newspapers in Europe. Nor was there any visible means of supporting a popular press. There was little to sell and little to advertise. Yet during this period the area was producing a breed of citizen that was to expand the frontiers of social and political freedom in America, aided by an aggressive and powerful press. It took time, that is all.

The New Englander was a product of glaciation, rugged climate, and Calvinism. Glaciers had scored the country into a land of narrow valleys, swiftly flowing streams, and thin soil. The endless field stone fences of New England are evidences of the toil involved in scratching a living from such a land. It was difficult for one family to care for many backbreaking acres, and so the individual farms tended to be small. The narrow valleys and the small farms brought people closer together. This suited the New Englander, who preferred to live in towns, where he could attend church and the meetinghouse. In the South, where broad rivers drained the wide savannahs, people lived more spaciously. It is significant that here the gatherings were more in the nature of social events. A southerner met to enjoy himself. A New Englander met to improve himself—and others.

It was fortunate for later generations of Americans that the New England settlers had great appreciation for property, especially in the form of land. Land had been the symbol of prestige and standing in England. The decline of feudalism and the emergence of the capitalist class brought many dispossessed British farmers to America. Driven from the land by the manor lord who had turned from subsistence farming to wool raising, which required much less help; sick of the stinking slums which were the only refuge of the dispossessed; unwanted—large numbers of these ex-plowmen fled to America. The country needed them, and that alone is enough to start strong loyalties. In America they could not only work the land they loved, but they could even acquire property, the mark of a superior person.[2]

The New England woman was another significant factor in the development of the region. Women came over with the original settlers. They reared large families, and the group kept its identity. In South America, and to some extent in French Canada, colonists tended to be absorbed by the native populations, because Europeans in those regions did not generally bring women along with them. The New England pioneer preserved the traditions of an old race and the characteristics of a great culture. This solidarity was even more secure in New England than in other American colonies because of the rejection of Negro slavery there. In the South, slavery was to be disruptive of homogeneity in years to come. The New Englander was saved from the curse of slavery not just because he was opposed to the system, but because it was uneconomical.

COMMERCE: FORERUNNER OF THE PRESS

The commercial stimulation that encourages the development of a popular press was brought to New England in a curious way. Because farming paid such a small return on the energy invested in it, the New England Yankee early turned to fishing as an easier way of earning a living. Surrounding waters teemed with fish. Soon Yankee fishermen were the main suppliers of fish to the Mediterranean basin, where a combination of religions and diet provided a ready market. The South might just as well have developed a fishing industry, but plantation life was more satisfactory to the southerner than spending cold weeks in pitching vessels on the Grand Banks fishing grounds.

Fishing made New Englanders into great seafarers. Soon they were building their own vessels, designed for special purposes, and superior to anything under sail up to then. The forests provided the raw material for a thriving industry. The region abounded in excellent harbors. Shipbuilding and ocean commerce stimulated the growth of lumbering, wood manufacture, and other small industries, for which there was abundant water power. As a result, a

[2] True, the farm colonist might have settled in other areas, but New England had its share, along with its middle-class émigrés.

class of shrewd, tough, independent businessmen began to win renown for New England. Many of them became wealthy and were ready to help support a publication that could advertise wares and spread pertinent information.

For a time the coffeehouses had sufficed as a news medium, even as the market places and fairs had served Europe in previous centuries. Here men of congenial interests met to exchange gossip and useful information. Buyers, as well as retailers, were interested in the arrival and departure of ships. Businessmen were curious about conditions in areas largely ignored by the British papers. Commerce along the American coast was slowly increasing, for example, and there was a thriving trade with the West Indies. What was being done to disperse local pirates? Was it true that a new postal system was about to be established by His Majesty's Government? Finally, as rivalry spurred trade in the growing communities, the merchant discovered he could move his goods to the local customer faster if he printed notices, or advertisements, in a publication read by his customers. The emphasis on this aspect of journalism is indicated by the number of early newspapers with the word "Advertiser" in the name plate. The development of commerce, then, had an important bearing on the establishment of the first newspaper, and all the early publications appeared in commercial centers.

Commerce and Calvinism, the religion of the Yankee, fitted well together. The New Englander was usually a believer in the doctrine of John Calvin, the sixteenth-century reformer who had set up a theocratic government in Geneva. The essence of Calvinism is "predestination." The Calvinist believed that the world and its people followed a plan of God. Man's salvation or damnation was thus already predetermined according to this pattern. Prosperity was a sign that God had looked upon a man with favor. A successful businessman could think of himself as having passed through the eye of the needle into the circle of the elect. So, of course, every good Calvinist tried to look prosperous to show the world that he had been marked by God for salvation.

THE SOUTHERN AND MIDDLE COLONIES

The New England "Puritan" made many important contributions to the culture and society that were to prepare the way for the American experiment in self-rule and eventual independence. Other areas fortunately infused some of the more human qualities into the product, however. The South, for example, was in strong contrast to New England. Life was easier and more relaxed on the wide plantations. The general viewpoint remained agrarian, rather than commercial. Communications develop slowly in such a society. Although Virginia, the "Old Dominion," was settled 13 years before the Pilgrims landed at Plymouth, it lagged far behind in press progress. But the South contributed great ideas and spokesmen, essential to the development of democracy, with which the press was to be so closely integrated. The graciousness of the South was a fortunate leavening for the tough-mindedness of the Yankee, when the time came for the colonies to cooperate.

The South could even teach a few lessons on democracy in the earliest days of colonization. The New England Puritan was not noted for his tolerance. Intellectual misfits, such as Anne Hutchinson, the first great American feminist, and Roger Williams were driven into exile by the intransigent theocrats of Massachusetts because of ideas unacceptable to the leaders. It took a little while for Americans to learn the lesson that it takes ideas to keep democracy dynamic—that is, adjustable to changing conditions. The institutions of the South were not necessarily more democratic, but the areas of intolerance were different. At least the southerner appeared to have a more human outlook on life.

The Middle Atlantic, or "bread," colonies helped to fuse the regional characteristics of the colonies. Philadelphia and New York were the great commercial centers. In this respect the middle colonies resembled the New England of Boston, Salem, and Providence in this first century of colonial history. But the inhabitants tended to live more spaciously, like the southerner. Young Ben Franklin, hiding out in Philadelphia, found it to be as bustling as Boston, but more congenial to a man of his inquisitive nature. And it is significant that Philadelphia was the second American city to support a successful newspaper.

The middle colonies attracted settlers of various national and religious backgrounds. Along the Delaware river the Swedes had established communities dating from the early seventeenth century. The Dutch West India Company in 1621 established New Netherland colony, later to be renamed by the English successors New York. Later many other groups moved into the area. Areas in Pennsylvania became almost as Germanic as the cities in the Palatinate whence the "Pennsylvania Dutch" (Deutsch) had come. The region also absorbed religious expatriates, such as Catholics, Lutherans, Quakers, and Dutch Reformers.

By the end of the seventeenth century there were about 250,000 inhabitants of European extraction in the American colonies. Massachusetts had grown from about 100 in 1620 to 45,000 by 1700. Virginia had a white population of about 50,000. Maryland was next, with 20,000. The others were much smaller, but were growing fast. A few families had accumulated respectable fortunes by this time, but the general income level was relatively low.

POLITICAL UNREST

The colonies reflected the religious and political troubles of the mother country. Many Americans had emigrated because of differences in beliefs, and they brought their problems with them. The restoration of Charles II after the revolution of 1640 was a period of political reaction. Once again the king exerted his old powers—or tried to. James II, who succeeded Charles, should have learned that it was dangerous to flout the good will of his subjects, but James was even more unpopular than his predecessors. Under James, revolt seethed. The unrest was reflected in the colonies.

In 1664 the British conquered the Dutch and took as one of the spoils of war the New Netherland colony. In the next few years the king tried to strengthen his power in England. It is not surprising that the same process was apparent in the colonies. The General Court of Massachusetts, for example, passed the first formal act restricting the press in 1662. The only printing plant in the colony at the time was the one at Harvard, consisting of two presses, but the authorities were taking no chances with possible subversive literature, and the law provided for rigorous censorship.[3]

One of the governors sent out to the colonies about this time was Sir Edmund Andros. He first took over the seat of government in New York in 1674. It was his understanding that his commission gave him jurisdiction over the area between the Delaware and Connecticut rivers. This was interpreted by colonial leaders as proof that the Crown wished to establish a more effective control of this area by means of centralization of authority. The charters of the New England colonies were declared invalid, and Andros believed he had a mandate to take over this region, too. By 1686 he was in control of most of the populated and prosperous colonies.

Two years later (1688) Parliament deposed James II in the "Glorious Revolution." The crown was then offered jointly to his eldest daughter, Mary, and her husband, William of Orange. William and Mary were wise rulers. Aware of the circumstances under which they had been offered the crowns, they tended to be conciliatory. The counterpart of these events in America was the revolt against royal authority in the guise of Andros. He was sent back to England in 1689 for trial.[4]

BENJAMIN HARRIS, PRINTER

It was at this very time that an ex-London bookseller and publisher decided to offer a periodical that the ordinary person could afford and could understand. Boston then had a population of nearly 7,000 and was the largest city in America. It offered sufficient sales potential for the type of publication the promoter had in mind. Cultural and literacy levels were sufficient to warrant the financial risk. There was a demand by the commercial interests for such an organ, and they could offer the essential support. The situation was made to order for a newspaper, and the man of the hour was at hand, although he never did quite achieve the honor of producing the first American newspaper.

The hero of this episode was the exiled printer, Benjamin Harris, who was

[3] One of the best discussions of this period will be found in Clyde A. Duniway, *The Development of Freedom of the Press in Massachusetts* (New York: Longmans, Green & Company, 1906).

[4] He was never tried. Indeed, he was soon returned to favor, and came back to America as governor of Virginia.

last seen fleeing from the law. Harris arrived in Boston in 1686. Already he had had considerable experience in the London publishing business. Unfortunately, Harris was a troublemaker, and shortly after he had started his London newspaper in 1679, he was arrested for having seditious literature in his possession. He was sentenced to the pillory, which was erected in front of his own office. Friends kept passersby from throwing refuse at the prisoner, but they could not help him pay the stiff fine imposed, and Harris had to go to jail. From his cell he continued to edit his paper. In 1686 his shop was again raided. Officers seized a quantity of pamphlets connecting Harris with subversive organizations, and a warrant was issued for his arrest. Warned of the danger, Harris fled with his family to America. In the fall of 1686 he opened a combined coffee and book shop in Boston at the corner of State and Washington streets.

The shop was a favorite meeting place for some of Boston's most interesting citizens. Judge Sewall, chronicler of his times and a former publisher, was a regular customer. Most of the local wits and writers made the shop their headquarters. The progressive views of the proprietor are indicated by the fact that his was the only coffee shop in the city where respectable women were welcome.

Harris was a shrewd businessman. He succeeded against formidable opposition. There were seven booksellers in the neighborhood when Harris set up shop. He sat down and wrote a spelling book that was a best seller in the country for many years. He published books for a distinguished clientele, and thus acquired a respect and prestige that some of his rivals lacked. He was not a printer at this time, but rather the promoter of literary works. The downfall of Andros gave Harris the opportunity to go back to his first love, the publication of a newspaper.

PUBLICK OCCURRENCES, 1690

On September 25, 1690, the printing shop of R. Pierce issued a four-page newspaper. It was printed on only three sides. The fourth page was blank so the reader could add his own news items before passing it on. The pages measured only 6 x 10¼ inches. There was very little attempt at makeup. This was Harris' *Publick Occurrences, Both Foreign and Domestick,* called by some authorities the first American newspaper. It might very well have been, except that it was banned after the first issue, and one of the qualifications of a newspaper is periodicity, or continuity. If continuity is ignored, a publication printed the year before might just as logically be called the first American newspaper. This was *The Present State of the New-English Affairs.* It was printed in 1689 as a report from the Rev. Increase Mather to Governor Broadstreet of Massachusetts. The Reverend Mather was representing the colony in London, and the publication was designed to let the public know what progress had been made in colonial problems. This was certainly news, and was printed as such.

There are even earlier examples of broadsheets and reprints of big new events. The characteristic that set *Publick Occurrences* apart was that it looked like a newspaper, it read like a newspaper, and it was intended as a permanent news organ, unlike the others.[5] Harris was a good reporter for his time. His style was concise—"punchy," the modern editor would call it. The paper included both foreign and local news—another distinction from earlier news publications. Indeed, his "occurrences" covered a multitude of interests. Thus, we find at the bottom of the outside column on page one:

> The *Small-pox* which has been raging in *Boston*, after a manner very Extraordinary is now very much abated. It is thought that far more have been sick of it than were visited with it, when it raged so much twelve years ago, nevertheless it has not been so Mortal. The number of them that have dyed in *Boston* by this last Visitation is about three hundred and twenty, which is not perhaps half so many as fell by the former. . . .[6]

Harris knew what would interest his readers. He included intelligent comment, but he knew that most of his readers would be attracted more by appeals to basic emotions and by reference to familiar persons and places. Conflict and fear were two such emotions emphasized in this early paper. The pattern has been used successfully right up to modern times, which is not to say that this is the *only* means for winning subscribers.

Harris got into trouble with the local authorities, not because he printed libels, but because he printed the truth as he saw it. He had also violated licensing restrictions first imposed in 1662. One of Harris' items reported that Indian allies of the "English Colonies & Provinces of the West" had forced an army under General Winthrop to postpone an attack on the French. The Indians, Harris wrote, had failed to provide "canoo's" for the transportation of the forces into enemy territory. War chiefs had explained that the redmen were too weakened from smallpox to fulfill their commitments, and that was probably true. They were not too weak to make individual raids, however. From one of these raids, Harris reported, they "brought home several *Prisoners*, whom they used in a manner too barbarous for any English to approve."[7] The journalist referred to these Indian allies as "miserable savages, in whom we have too much confided."

All these remarks could be taken as criticism of colonial policy, which at that moment was concerned with winning, not alienating, Indian neighbors. Harris was also accused of bad taste. He had spiced up his paper by reporting that the French king had been taking immoral liberties with the prince's wife, for which reason the prince had revolted. Judge Sewall wrote in his diary that

[5] Even on this count it would fail to qualify technically as a newspaper, according to the criteria listed on page 3, because Harris intended to issue the paper only once a month, unless an "unusual glut of occurrences" made greater frequency of publication practicable.

[6] From a facsimile filed in the London Public Office (1845), as reprinted in Willard G. Bleyer, *Main Currents in the History of American Journalism* (Boston: Houghton Mifflin, 1927), p. 45.

[7] *Loc. cit.*

the Puritan clergy was scandalized by this account in a publication reaching the Boston public.

It was the Massachusetts licensing act that ended Harris' career as an American newspaper publisher, however. How he expected to get around that restriction is not at all clear. Harris eventually returned to England, where he fades out of the scene as the penurious vendor of quack medicines.

Not for another 14 years was there a newspaper in the American colonies, and when one did appear, it operated alone for 15 years. The example of *Publick Occurrences* may have warned away any journalistic promoters during this interim. When the next newspapers did appear, they were inclined to be stodgy and dull, partly because the publishers lacked Harris' color and boldness, and partly because all news had to be "safe" to pass the licensers. Each of the successful Boston publishers in the next 30 years was careful to notify his public that he printed "by authority." More important, they had the protection of an important office—for the journalists who followed immediately after Harris were all postmasters.

In Europe there had been a long tradition of affiliation between the postal service and journalism. Many of the early continental newspapers had been published by postmasters. There was good reason for this. Postmasters were especially interested in disseminating information. That was their principal business. They had access to most of the intelligence available to the community. They broke the seals of official pouches and delivered important dispatches. Postmasters then, as today, heard much of the local gossip. They were "in the know." And in colonial times, as in modern times, the postmaster was likely to be an important political figure. That was how he usually earned his office.

But such advantages do not necessarily produce good newspapers. Softness and safety never beget great journalism—then or now. Newspapers have progressed farthest in times of strife. Yet the early postmaster-publishers contributed much to American journalism. At least they understood that the main problem was survival, which is more than could be said of Harris. It was the ability to adjust to conditions that enabled a postmaster to produce the first genuine newspaper in America. And if he lagged 14 years behind Harris, the fault was not all his. Until 1692 there had been no official postal service in the colonies. In that year the British government authorized an intercolonial mail system—an indication that the respective colonies were beginning to take note of each other.

JOHN CAMPBELL'S *NEWS-LETTER*, 1704

One of the postmasters appointed by the Crown for the new intercolonial service was John Campbell. He took over the Boston post office in 1700. From the very beginning he made use of the postal service to supply information to special correspondents in other colonies. He issued this intelligence in the form

N. E. Numb. 3.

The Boſton News-Letter.

Publiſhed by Authority.

From Monday May 1. to Monday May 8. 1704.

London Gazette, from *Novemb.* 8 to 11. 1703.

Weſtminſter, *Novemb.* 9.

THE Parliament met here this day, and Her Majeſty being come to the Houſe of Peers, and ſeated on the Throne in Her Royal Robes, with the uſual Solemnity, the Gentleman Uſher of the Black Rod, was ſent with a Meſſage to the Houſe of Commons, requiring their Attendance in the Houſe of Peers, whither they came accordingly, and Her Majeſty was pleaſed to make a moſt Gracious Speech to both Houſes, which follows.

My Lords and Gentlemen,

I Have Called you together aſſoon as I thought you could conveniently Come out of your Countries, that no Time may be loſt in making Our Preparations for Carrying on the Preſent War, in which I do not Doubt of your Cheerful Concurrence, ſince you can't but be ſenſible, that on the Succeſs of it depends Our Own Safety and Happineſs and that of all *Europe*.

I Hope I have Improved the Confidence you Repoſed in Me laſt Year, to your Satisfaction and the Advantage of Us and Our Allies, by the Treaty with the King of *Portugal*, and the Declaration of the Duke of *Savoy*, which in great Meaſure may be Imputed to the Cheerfulneſs with which you Supported Me in this War, and the Aſſurance with which you Truſted Me in the Conduct of it: And We cannot ſufficiently Acknowledge the Goodneſs of Almighty God, who is pleaſed to Afford Us ſo far a Proſpect as We now have, of bringing it to a Glorious and Speedy Concluſion.

I muſt therefore Deſire you, *Gentlemen of the Houſe of Commons*, to Grant Me ſuch Supplies as ſhall be requiſite to Defray the Neceſſary Charge of the War in the next Year, with regard, not only to all Our former Engagements, but particularly to Our Alliance lately made with the King of *Portugal* for recovering the Monarchy of *Spain* from the Houſe of *Bourbon*, and Reſtoring it to the Houſe of *Auſtria*, which Treaty being in it ſelf of the higheſt Importance imaginable, and requiring all poſſible Diſpatch in the Execution of it, has Neceſſarily Occaſion'd a great Expence even in this preſent Year, tho' not ſo much as it will Require, and for which, I hope, We ſhall be amply Recompenſed in the next.

The Subſidies which will now be immediately Required for the Aſſiſtance of the Duke of *Savoy*, will likewiſe Occaſion a further Neceſſary Charge.

I muſt take Notice to you, That tho' no particular Proviſion was made in the laſt Seſſion, either for the Charge of Our preſent Expedition to *Portugal*, or for that of the Augmentation Troops deſired by the *States General*, yet the Fonds given by Parliament have held out ſo well, and the Produce of the Prizes has Prov'd ſo Conſiderable, that you will find the Publick will not be in Debt by Reaſon of either of theſe Additional Services.

I may further obſerve to you, That tho' the Fonds for the Civil Government are diminiſht by the War I have, in Conjunction with the *States General*, Contributed out of My Own Revenue towards ſome Publick Services, and particularly the Support of the Circle of *Suabia*, whoſe firm Adherence to the Intereſt of the Allies under the greateſt Preſſures, did very well Deſerve our Seaſonable Aſſiſtance: And I ſhall ſtill be Careful not to engage My Self in any Unneceſſary Expence of My Own, that I may have the more to Spare towards the Eaſe of My Subjects.

My Lords and Gentlemen,

I Heartily Wiſh ſome eaſie and leſs-chargeable Method could be found for the Speedy and Effectual Manning of the Fleet.

I muſt alſo Recommend to you to make ſome Regulation for Preventing the Exceſſive Price of Coals, I have Examined this Matter, and taken particular Care to appoint Convoys for that Service; but the Price has not been in the leaſt Abated notwithſtanding a very conſiderable quantity has been Imported ſince that time; This gives great ground of Suſpicion there may be a Combination of ſome Perſons to Enrich themſelves by a general Oppreſſion of others, and particularly the Poor: 'Twill deſerve your Conſideration how to Remedy this great Inconvenience.

And in all your Affairs, I muſt Recommend to you as much Diſpatch as the Nature of them will admit; This is Neceſſary to make Our Preparations early, on which in great Meaſure Depends the good Succeſs of all Our Enterprizes.

I want Words to Expreſs to you My earneſt Deſires of Seeing all My Subjects in perfect Peace and Union among themſelves: I have nothing ſo much at Heart as their general Welfare and Happineſs; Let Me therefore Deſire you all That you would Carefully Avoid any Heats or Diviſions that may Diſappoint Me of that Satisfaction, and Give Encouragement to the Common Enemies of Our Church and State.

London, December 9.

ON Monday the Marqueiſe *de Hencourt*, a French Proteſtant Refugee, departed this Life, in the 72 year of his Age, leaving behind him a very good Name, for his great Piety and other Vertues, truly becoming a Noble-man. As he had cheerfully made a Sacrifie of a great Eſtate to his Religion, he lived in his Exile after ſo Exemplary a manner, that juſtly gained him the eſteem of all that knew him.

By His Excellency JOSEPH DUDLEY Eſq. Captain General and Governour in Chief, in and over Her Majeſties Province of the *Maſſachuſetts-Bay* in *New-England*.

A PROCLAMATION for a General FAST.

UPon Conſideration of the troubleſome Sate of Europe, *by reaſon of the Calamitous Wars wherein thoſe Nations are Engaged amongſt themſelves, and of Her Majeſties Great and Juſt Intereſt therein: As alſo the preſent*

The first successful newspaper to be printed in America, by John Campbell.

of a news letter—the primitive, handwritten report that had been the common medium of communication in Europe before the invention of printing. Most of the information sent out by Campbell was concerned with commercial and governmental matters. Boston was the most important city in the colonies then, and the postmaster's information was therefore highly pertinent all along the Atlantic seaboard. Meetings, proclamations, complaints, legal notices, actions in court, available cargo space, and the arrivals of Very Important Persons provided the grist for Campbell's news mill. There was such a demand for his news letter that Campbell began to look around for some way of relieving the pressure upon his time and energy. He got his brother, Duncan, to help, but even together they could not supply the demand for news. They just couldn't write longhand fast enough. A shrewd Scotsman, Campbell decided there must be an easier way to earn a living. He set out one afternoon to make a call on Bartholomew Green. Green was one of the few printers in the area. That day the two struck a bargain.

In Green's shop on Newbury Street there was printed on the morning of April 24, 1704, the first genuine American newspaper. It was called the *Boston News-Letter,* an appropriate title, since it was merely a continuation of the publication the Campbells had been producing since 1700. The *News-Letter* was printed on both sides of a sheet just a little larger than the dimensions of Harris' paper—that is, slightly larger than a sheet of typewriter paper.

The news in the first issue was not very startling. The publisher-editor-postmaster had simply clipped the incoming London newspapers, already weeks old, and had inserted the items as foreign exchanges. Since he did not have space for all the European dispatches, he put aside excess information for future use. As a result, some of his news was months old before it reached the reader. On the other hand, local news was fairly timely. It was terse, but surprisingly informative. For example:

> Boston, April 18. Arrived Capt. Sill from Jamaica, about four Weeks Passage, says, they continue there very sickly.
>
> Mr. Nathaniel Oliver, a principal Merchant of this place dyed April 15 & was decently inter'd. April 18, Aetatis 53. . . .
>
> The 20 the R'd Mr. Pemberton Preached an Excellent Sermon on 1 Thes. 4:11. "And do your own business"; Exhorting all Ranks & Degrees of Persons to do their own work, in order to a REFORMATION; which His Excellency has ordered to be printed.
>
> The 21 His Excellency Dissolved the Gen. Assembly. . . .[8]

But it was savorless journalism, after Harris' reports on bloodthirsty savages and lustful kings. Campbell cleared all the copy with the Governor, or with his secretary. That made his paper libel-proof, censor-proof, and well-nigh reader-proof. Though we have noted that it was the only newspaper in the

[8] From a facsimile in the Wisconsin State Historical Society Library.

colonies for 15 years, Campbell never had enough subscribers to make his venture profitable. The first advertisement in an American newspaper was concerned with this problem of circulation. It was what the trade would call a "blind ad," or piece of promotion. Campbell discovered, as many another editor-publisher was to find out later, that the public is never willing to pay the full price for the information it must have to exert its rights. The postmaster was frantic on several occasions because so many subscribers were in arrears. His circulation seldom exceeded 300. Twice Campbell was saved from bankruptcy by a government subsidy. The paper was valuable for the publication of official notices, which could be reproduced cheaper in the *News-Letter* than by private printing. Despite this support, the publisher had to suspend publication for eight months at one critical period for lack of funds.

Even Campbell's embryonic journal contributed to the traditions of an honorable craft. He had a strong sense of responsibility to his public. That is proved by his determination to print the news in spite of public apathy and financial distress. It was also evidenced by his sincere policy of printing "for a Publick Good, to give a true Account of all Foreign & Domestick Occurrences, and to prevent a great many false reports of the same"—a policy still respected by honest publishers.

Despite his clumsiness at news gathering and news writing, Campbell tried his best to be fair and accurate. In one issue he apologized for misplacing a comma in a preceding number, although this was only a drop in the sea of other errors. An uninspired minor bureaucrat in an unpopular administration, he still had the good editor's sense of decency and kindness for his fellow men. Of a suicide involving a poor woman, he wrote that "he hoped the Inserting of such an awful Providence here may not be offensive, but rather a Warning to all others to watch against the Wiles of our Grand Adversary." He obviously regretted having to print the account of a prisoner's whipping, but the culprit had cheated the public by selling tar mixed with dirt. The news, Campbell explained sadly, "is here only Inserted to be a caveat to others, of doing the like, least a worse thing befal them." Clearly, Campbell deserves better of history.

Unimpressive as it was, the *Boston News-Letter* was like the Biblical mustard seed. From it stemmed the mighty American Fourth Estate, a force no single person could ignore.

Annotated Bibliography

Books

The most useful books for the general reader from among histories of American journalism earlier than this volume are those by Mott, Bleyer, A. M. Lee, and Payne, listed below. The earliest attempt at a general account was that by Isaiah

Thomas in 1810 (see bibliography for Chapter 3). Next were those by Frederic Hudson in 1873 and by S. N. D. North in 1884 (see bibliographies for Chapters 12 and 16, respectively). These three books remain of special use to journalism historians. Other general histories of lesser quality have been those by James Melvin Lee, *History of American Journalism* (Boston: Houghton Mifflin, 1917); Robert W. Jones, *Journalism in the United States* (New York: Dutton, 1947); Edith M. Bartow, *News and These United States* (New York: Funk & Wagnalls, 1952); John W. Tebbel, *The Compact History of the American Newspaper* (New York: Hawthorn, 1963), a readable but quick survey of high points; and Sidney Kobre, *Development of American Journalism* (Dubuque, Iowa: Wm. C. Brown Company, 1969), a compiling of earlier works that adds details about many regional papers but lacks balance. For analyses of the subject see the annotations in Price, *The Literature of Journalism*, pp. 3–7, and Allan Nevins, "American Journalism and Its Historical Treatment," *Journalism Quarterly*, XXXVI (Fall 1959), 411.

Especially recommended for background reading in American history are the interpretive histories by the Beards and Boorstin and the studies of American thought by Parrington and Curti, listed below. Other excellent general histories include John D. Hicks and George E. Mowry, *A History of American Democracy*, 4th ed. (Boston: Houghton Mifflin, 1970); Richard Hofstadter, William Miller, and Daniel Aaron, *The United States: The History of a Republic*, 2nd ed. (Englewood Cliffs, N.J.: Prentice-Hall, 1967); Samuel Eliot Morison and Henry Steele Commager, *The Growth of the American Republic*, 6th ed. (New York: Oxford University Press, 1969); and Henry Bamford Parkes, *The United States of America, a History* (New York: Knopf, 1968).

Two good ready references for historical facts are the *Encyclopaedia of American History* and the *Dictionary of American History*. Biographies of many journalists are found in the *Dictionary of American Biography*. The *Encyclopaedia Britannica* and the *Encyclopaedia of the Social Sciences* contain articles on newspapers, magazines, press laws, printing, advertising, radio and television, and other journalistic subjects.

Beard, Charles A., and Mary R. Beard, *The Rise of American Civilization*. New York: Macmillan, 1930. A stimulating and provocative history of the United States, with much economic, social, and intellectual detail incorporated into a brilliant general narrative.

Bleyer, Willard Grosvenor, *Main Currents in the History of American Journalism*. Boston: Houghton Mifflin, 1927. One of the standard histories of journalism—reliable and detailed. Places emphasis on leading editors after the 1830s.

Boorstin, Daniel, *The Americans: The Colonial Experience*. New York: Random House, 1958. A major voice of the consensus school of historians, stressing "togetherness" and continuity rather than conflict.

Channing, Edward, *History of the United States*, Vol. II. New York: Macmillan, 1927. A learned and readable summary of events and forces significant in colonial social and political development.

Curti, Merle, *The Growth of American Thought*, 3rd ed. New York: Harper & Row, 1964. One of the most scholarly studies of the American social and literary heritage by a Pulitzer Prize historian.

Duniway, Clyde A., *The Development of Freedom of the Press in Massachusetts.* New York: Longmans, Green & Company, 1906. A detailed and invaluable contribution to the history of early American journalism.

Emery, Michael C., R. Smith Schuneman, and Edwin Emery, eds., *America's Front Page News 1690–1970.* New York: Doubleday, 1971. Some 300 newspaper pages reproduced to trace main themes of U.S. political history, wars, popular movements, triumphs and tragedies. See also Edwin Emery's *The Story of America as Reported by Its Newspapers 1690–1965* (New York: Simon & Schuster, 1965).

Lee, Alfred McClung, *The Daily Newspaper in America.* New York: Macmillan, 1937. A topical history with a sociological approach, especially useful for its discussions of economic factors.

Miller, Perry, *The New England Mind: The Seventeenth Century.* New York: Macmillan, 1939.

———, *The New England Mind: From Colony to Province.* Cambridge, Mass.: Harvard University Press, 1953. The first volume, covering to 1660, is a readable interpretation of the Puritan character. The second volume discusses society and thought to 1730.

Mott, Frank Luther, *American Journalism.* New York: Macmillan, 1941, rev. eds. 1950, 1962. The most detailed general reference book by an outstanding scholar of American journalism. The revisions add sections for the 1940s and 1950s.

Nettels, Curtis P., *The Roots of American Civilization.* New York: Appleton-Century-Crofts, 1938. Study of economic factors leading to colonial self-development and conflict with Britain.

Parrington, Vernon Louis, *Main Currents in American Thought,* Vol. I "The Colonial Mind." New York: Harcourt Brace Jovanovich, 1927. A Pulitzer Prize winning study of the social, economic, and political backgrounds of American literature, in three volumes, which ranks as a classic work for history students.

Payne, George H., *History of Journalism in the United States.* New York: Appleton-Century-Crofts, 1920. An old history, but accurate and detailed, particularly useful for the period up to 1800.

Wertenbaker, Thomas Jefferson, *The Founding of American Civilization: The Middle Colonies.* New York: Scribner's, 1938. Describes contributions of region to cultural development of the country.

Wish, Harvey, *Society and Thought in Early America.* New York: Longmans, Green & Company, 1950. An excellent background study of the period under discussion. First of a two-volume work (Vol. 2, New York: McKay, 1962).

Wright, Louis B., *The Cultural Life of the American Colonies, 1607–1763.* New York: Harper & Row, 1957. A study focusing on the aristocracies of the plantations and the trade centers.

Periodicals and Monographs

"The First American Newspaper and the 'New England Primer,'" *Bookman,* LXXVI (January 1933), 103. A brief account of the life of Benjamin Harris.

Kobre, Sidney, "The First American Newspaper: A Product of Environment,"

Journalism Quarterly, XVII (December 1940), 335. Social and economic factors leading to the founding of the press.

Parkes, H. B., "New England in the Seventeen-Thirties," *New England Quarterly*, III (July 1930), 397. A valuable appraisal of the Puritan traditions, which also discusses effect of British essay papers.

Shaaber, Matthias A., "Forerunners of the Newspaper in America," *Journalism Quarterly*, XI (December 1934), 339. Describes predecessors of *Publick Occurrences*. Reprinted in Ford and Emery, *Highlights in the History of the American Press*.

THE [No 58

New-England Courant.

From MONDAY September 3. to MONDAY September 10. 1722.

Quod eſt in corde ſobrii, eſt in ore ebrii.

To the Author of the New-England Courant.

SIR, [No XII.

IT is no unprofitable tho' unpleaſant Purſuit, diligently to inſpect and conſider the Manners & Converſation of Men, who, inſenſible of the greateſt Enjoyments of humane Life, abandon themſelves to Vice from a falſe Notion of *Pleaſure* and *good Fellowſhip.* A true and natural Repreſentation of any Enormity, is often the beſt Argument againſt it and Means of removing it, when the moſt ſevere Reprehenſions alone, are found ineffectual.

I WOULD in this Letter improve the little Obſervation I have made on the Vice of *Drunkeneſs*, the better to reclaim the *good Fellows* who uſually pay the Devotions of the Evening to *Bacchus*.

I DOUBT not but *moderate Drinking* has been improv'd for the Diffuſion of Knowledge among the ingenious Part of Mankind, who want the Talent of a ready Utterance, in order to diſcover the Conceptions of their Minds in an entertaining and intelligible Manner. 'Tis true, drinking does not *improve* our Faculties, but it enables us to *uſe* them; and therefore I conclude, that much Study and Experience, and a little Liquor, are of abſolute Neceſſity for ſome Tempers, in order to make them accompliſh'd Orators. *Dic. Ponder* diſcovers an excellent Judgment when he is inſpir'd with a Glaſs or two of *Claret*, but he paſſes for a Fool among thoſe of ſmall Obſervation, who never ſaw him the better for Drink. And here it will not be improper to obſerve, That the moderate Uſe of Liquor, and a well plac'd and well regulated Anger, often produce this ſame Effect; and ſome who cannot ordinarily talk but in broken Sentences and falſe Grammar, do in the Heat of Paſſion expreſs themſelves with as much Eloquence as Warmth. Hence it is that my own Sex are generally the moſt eloquent, becauſe the moſt paſſionate. "It has been ſaid in the Praiſe of ſome Men, "(ſays an ingenious Author,) that they could talk "whole Hours together upon any thing; but it "muſt be owned to the Honour of the other Sex, "that there are many among them who can talk "whole Hours together upon Nothing. I have "known a Woman branch out into a long extempore Diſſertation on the Edging of a Petticoat, and "chide her Servant for breaking a China Cup, in all "the Figures of Rhetorick."

BUT after all it muſt be conſider'd, that no Pleaſure can give Satisfaction or prove advantageous to a *reaſonable Mind*, which is not attended with the *Reſtraints of Reaſon.* Enjoyment is not to be found by Exceſs in any ſenſual Gratification; but on the contrary, the immoderate Cravings of the Voluptuary, are always ſucceeded with Loathing and a palled Appetite. What Pleaſure can the Drunkard have in the Reflection, that, while in his Cups, he retain'd only the Shape of a Man, and acted the Part of a Beaſt; or that from reaſonable Diſcourſe a few Minutes before, he deſcended to Impertinence and Nonſenſe?

I CANNOT pretend to account for the different Effects of Liquor on Perſons of different Diſpoſitions, who are guilty of Exceſs in the Uſe of it. 'Tis ſtrange to ſee Men of a regular Converſation become rakiſh and profane when intoxicated with Drink, and yet more ſurprizing to obſerve, that ſome who appear to be the moſt profligate Wretches when ſober, become mighty religious in their Cups, and will then, and at no other Time addreſs their Maker, but when they are deſtitute of Reaſon, and actually affronting him. Some ſhrink in the Wetting, and others ſwell to ſuch an unuſual Bulk in their Imaginations, that they can in an Inſtant underſtand all Arts and Sciences, by the liberal Education of a little vivifying *Punch*, or a ſufficient Quantity of other exhilerating Liquor.

AND as the Effects of Liquor are various, ſo are the Characters given to its Devourers. It argues ſome Shame in the Drunkards themſelves, in that they have invented numberleſs Words and Phraſes to cover their Folly, whoſe proper Significations are harmleſs, or have no Signification at all. They are ſeldom known to be *drunk*, tho they are very often *boozey, cogey, tipſey, fox'd, merry, mellow, fuddl'd, groatable, Confoundedly cut, See two Moons*, are *Among the Philiſtines, In a very good Humour, See the Sun*, or, *The Sun has ſhone upon them*; they *Clip the King's Engliſh*, are *Almoſt froze, Feavouriſh, In their Altitudes, Pretty well enter'd*, &c. In ſhort, every Day produces ſome new Word or Phraſe which might be added to the Vocabulary of the *Tiplers*: But I have choſe to mention theſe few, becauſe if at any Time a Man of Sobriety and Temperance happens to *cut himſelf confoundedly*, or is *almoſt froze*, or *feavouriſh*, or accidentally *ſees the Sun*, &c. he may eſcape the Imputation of being *drunk*, when his Misfortune comes to be related.

I am SIR,
Your Humble Servant,

SILENCE DOGOOD.

FOREIGN AFFAIRS.

Berlin, May 8. Twelve Pruſſian Batallions are ſent to Mecklenburg, but for what Reaſon is not known. 'Tis ſaid, the Emperor, ſuſpecting the Deſigns of the Czar, will ſecure all the Domains of the Duke of Mecklenburg. His Pruſſian Majeſty, to promote the intended Union of the Reformed and Lutherans in his Dominions, has charged the Miniſters of thoſe two Communions, not to make the leaſt mention in the Pulpits of the religious Differences about ſome abſtruſer Points, particularly the Doctrine of Predeſtination, and to forbear all contumelious Expreſſions againſt one another.

Hamburg, May 8. The Imperial Court has order'd the Circles of Lower Saxony, to keep in Rea-

Ben Franklin's "Silence Dogood" essay on drunkenness, in the *New England Courant*.

3

The Press Wins a Beachhead

They that can give up essential liberty to obtain a little temporary safety deserve neither liberty nor safety.
—Benjamin Franklin

Colonial readers had a choice of newspapers for the first time after December 21, 1719, when Campbell fell from political favor. William Brooker won the appointment as postmaster. He was encouraged by his sponsors to continue publication of a semiofficial newspaper. Campbell refused to relinquish the *News-Letter,* however, so Brooker had to start a new publication. And so, after 15 years of monopoly, the pioneer American newspaper faced "opposition." The new rival was the *Boston Gazette.*

Competition did not noticeably improve either the semiofficial *Gazette* or the free-enterprise *News-Letter*. The *Gazette* started out as an imitator, and a stodgy one at that. Except for a market page, it offered nothing that Campbell had not given his readers. Brooker had one great advantage, however. As postmaster, he could distribute his publication at lower cost.

Five successive postmasters continued the *Gazette* until 1741, when it was merged with another rival that had appeared in the meantime—the *New England Weekly Journal.* The merger was the first such transaction in the history of American journalism. These early newspapers were all rather dull. Campbell, Brooker, and their successors, as minor bureaucrats, were careful not to offend officials upon whom they were dependent for privileges and subsidies. Every issue of the papers was approved by a government representative before publication, even though formal licensing laws had lapsed.

THE *NEW ENGLAND COURANT*, 1721

This safe policy was brought to an abrupt end with the establishment in 1721 of the *New England Courant*. This vigorous little sheet was published by James Franklin, elder brother of the more famous Benjamin, but a notable American in his own right. James had been printer of the *Gazette* when Brooker was postmaster. When the publisher lost his appointment, and the *Gazette* passed on to the succeeding postmaster, the paper was printed in another shop. Franklin was irked by this turn of events, and when a group of leading citizens opposed to the governing group encouraged him to start another paper, he agreed to the proposal.

The spirit of rebellion was manifest in the *Courant* from the start. Although it lasted only five years, it exerted a great influence upon the American press. It was a fresh breeze in the stale journalistic atmosphere of Boston. The *Courant* was the first American newspaper to supply readers with what they liked and needed, rather than with information controlled by self-interested officials. Its style was bold and its literary quality high. James Franklin had one of the best libraries in the city. He was also familiar with the best of the London literary publications. Here was a publisher who knew how to interest readers. He lightened his pages by poking fun at rivals. His personality sketches appealed to local interests.

James Franklin was also the first to use a device that was almost an essential of the newspaper at a much later date. This was the "crusade" type of journalism, involving an editorial campaign planned to produce results by presenting news in dramatic form. A crusading editor is not content with the mere reporting of events, but knows how to generate stories of interest to the public. Franklin was an expert in the use of this device.

James Franklin was much more than just a tough and independent newspaperman. The *Courant* also filled a great literary vacuum. Literature of a high standard for popular consumption was rare in Colonial America in the first quarter of the eighteenth century. Now and then a peddler sold a copy of some such classic as Hakluyt's *Voyages*, but most of the available reading of that day was heavily larded with moral lessons and religious doctrine. James Franklin was a cultured man, for his day and society, and while learning the printing trade in England he had enjoyed the essay papers that were then so popular.

Franklin, and many editors who followed him, offered a starved reading public something new in literary fare. Most of the *Spectator* and *Guardian* essays were reprinted in colonial newspapers. Addison and Steele were introduced to hundreds of Americans through such papers as the *Courant*. Such writers were imitated in the colonies, and some of this local material was very good. The young Benjamin Franklin, apprenticed to his brother James at an early age, secretly authored such essays for publication in his brother's newspaper. Indeed, Ben Franklin's "Silence Dogood" essays rank as about the best of the American imitations.

The literature in the *Courant* was witty, pertinent, and even brilliant at times. But the colonial press after the appearance of the *Courant* also offered more solid cultural contributions. Daniel Defoe's great book, *Robinson Crusoe,* was printed serially in many colonial papers as fast as installments could be pirated from abroad. Not every reader could discern the significance of Defoe's work, which expressed in the novel form his criticism of the existing social structure. Those who missed the social message could still enjoy the excellent narrative, and indeed it is still read for this purpose alone, as any youth can testify. In thus broadcasting the new literature, the American newspaper made another contribution to the culture of a new society.[1]

JAMES FRANKLIN, REBEL

But the most important contribution of James Franklin was his unshackling of the American press from the licenser. All the other publishers had bowed to official pressures to print "by authority" despite the end of actual licensing. Franklin printed his paper not "by authority," but in spite of it. He thus helped establish the tradition of editorial independence, without which no press can be called free. Nor was Franklin cautious in the use of this new power. The pompous and restrictive religious and political leaders of the community were the particular targets of his editorial shafts.

The restrictive authorities were both spiritual and temporal. Censorship was supervised by government officials, of course, but the influences of the church leaders was nearly as great, if less direct. Puritan thought dominated the region, and the hierarchy was directed by two brilliant and strong-willed clergymen, Increase Mather and his son, Cotton. Many citizens of the region secretly detested the stern discipline imposed by the Mathers and their followers, but few dared challenge the dominant theocrats. This situation changed when Franklin began to publish the *Courant.*

A man of James Franklin's intellectual independence was certain to be irked by the type of restraint imposed by the Mathers. He began his attack at once. One wishes that Franklin might have selected some other issue to contest with the Mathers, however, because in this case he actually obstructed medical progress.

The issue was smallpox inoculation. The disease took an enormous toll of life in those days, and sometimes reached the proportions of a plague. Around 1720 Dr. Zabdiel Boylston of Boston injected blood from recovered smallpox

[1] An excellent account of this literary phase is given in Elizabeth C. Cook, *Literary Influences in Colonial Newspapers, 1704–1750* (New York: Columbia University Press, 1912).

patients into the bodies of other persons. There was no doubt that an immunity could be achieved this way, but the risks were great and most physicians of the period frowned on the practice. It was almost 80 years before the great scientist, Edward Jenner, introduced the safer vaccination method.

Cotton Mather encouraged Dr. Boylston in his researches. There was considerable controversy over the subject, and because of the positions of the protagonists, the issue became political and social, as well as medical. James Franklin used the inoculation quarrel as a means of attacking the Mathers. What he did, although he did not know it at the time, was to launch the first newspaper crusade in America. He developed an issue by dramatic treatment until everyone in the area was aware of the fight. Around Franklin gathered the rebels against Increase and Cotton Mather. They contributed articles to the *Courant,* some of them so vindictive as to be libelous. The insufferable Mathers [2] discovered that the tide of public opinion was strong against them. They defended themselves in vain in the rival *Gazette* and *News-Letter;* it was the *Courant* that won the sympathy of the public.

The *Courant* was admired because Franklin said what many a reader had dreamed of saying to the stern Puritan leaders. For a time the Mathers had virtually dictated policies. When Increase returned from England at the end of the seventeenth century he had even won the right to nominate the governor. His judgment was not particularly good, however, and his political power was waning as Franklin began the inoculation crusade. The governing authorities undoubtedly welcomed the *Courant* as an ally, even if it did end the tradition of a licensed press in America.

But when the spunky journalist turned around and fired a fusillade at the administration, the authorities believed it was time to swat this gadfly. Franklin accused the government of ineffective defense against pirates in the vicinity. Called before the Council in 1722 on a charge of contempt, Franklin was as outspoken as he had been in the columns of his paper. For such impertinence the editor-publisher was thrown into jail.

BENJAMIN FRANKLIN, APPRENTICE

James showed not the slightest remorse for his rude appraisal of the administration, and jail had no effect upon him in this way. Once free, he stepped up his criticism of authorities—both religious and political. By the end of the

[2] The Mathers were insufferable in the sense that their righteousness made them too sure of themselves, but that does not detract from their important place in colonial history. Increase was licenser of the press after 1674, in addition to his duties as the leading minister of the dominant Puritans. He was president of Harvard and was a respected agent of Massachusetts in London. Cotton opposed the arrogant Sir Edmund Andros, ousted from New England after the Revolution of 1688. The Mathers were prolific writers of considerable merit. They were also outstanding historians. In later life they became more tolerant. In all, they contributed much to the development of their community.

year both factions agreed on one thing, at least: James Franklin was too troublesome to be allowed in the community without restriction. At this point the General Court declared that "James Franklin be strictly forbidden . . . to print or publish the *New-England Courant* or any Pamphlet or paper of the like Nature, Except it be first Supervised, by the Secretary of this Province." [3] This, of course, was a reaffirmation of the old licensing power.

James evaded the order by making his brother, Ben, the official publisher of the paper. No such restriction had been imposed upon the younger Franklin. But in carrying out this evasion, James eventually lost the services of his essential brother. James ostensibly cancelled Ben's apprenticeship in order to name the boy as publisher. At the same time, he made Ben sign secret articles of reapprenticeship, to be put into effect as soon as the restrictive pressure was relaxed.

This was the chance Ben had been awaiting. True, the secret articles were binding, and under the law James could return his brother if Ben tried to run away. But if James did so, after assuring the General Court that he had relinquished his paper to his brother, he would thereby acknowledge that he had flouted the Court's order. Young Ben was clever enough to size up the situation. The next time we meet him is as a printer in his own right in Philadelphia.

The *Courant* declined in popularity and influence after that. Five and a half years after he had established the paper, James abandoned it. Later he accepted the position of government printer for Rhode Island. At Newport, in 1732, he founded the *Rhode Island Gazette,* first newspaper in that colony. It survived only a short time, and James never did achieve his former eminence in journalism.[4] If he did nothing else but establish the principle in America of printing "without authority," he would deserve a high place in America's journalistic hall of fame. He had accomplished much more, however. He had shown that when a newspaper is aggressive and readable in serving the public cause, it will elicit support sufficient to protect it from powerful foes.

PHILADELPHIA'S JOURNALISM BEGINS

The second largest city in the colonies at this time was Philadelphia. Two years after the founding of that city in 1683, William Bradford set up the first printing press in the colony. At first he printed only pamphlets and religious tracts for Quaker patrons, but because he had the only press in the region, he was also useful to the administration. Soon he was devoting much of his time

[3] As quoted in Frank Luther Mott, *American Journalism* (New York: Macmillan, 1950), p. 20. Colonial writing style called for use of many hyphens, such as in New-England, which are not used here for reasons of simplicity in identifying newspapers.

[4] His widow, two daughters, and a son carried on the printing business in Newport. In 1758, James, Jr., with the help of his rich uncle Benjamin, established the *Newport Mercury,* which survived until 1934. Its name was then retained in a small weekly edition of the *Newport News.*

to the printing of government documents. Unfortunately, he quarreled with his Quaker superiors, and in 1693 he moved his printing shop to New York, where he established the first newspaper in that city many years later, in 1725. We shall meet him again in the next chapter.

William Bradford's son, Andrew, published the first newspaper in Philadelphia. It was also the first newspaper outside Boston. His *American Weekly Mercury* first appeared on December 22, 1719, the day after Brooker published the first issue of the *Gazette,* Boston's first rival to the *News-Letter.* The *Mercury* was another postmaster paper, but it was a little more outspoken than the usual safe, semiofficial publications of that type that were to appear in the next two decades. On occasion the *Mercury* criticised the administration. It defended James Franklin when the Boston journalist was jailed by angry authorities. It printed the controversial "Cato Letters," which had first appeared in London as popular manifestations of the movement for civil and religious liberties. As a pioneer newspaper publisher, Andrew Bradford deserves an honorable niche in a history of the press. He, too, will appear again in the following chapter, which describes the development of press freedom in colonial America. But in the period with which this chapter is concerned, Bradford was overshadowed in Philadelphia by the greatest printer-journalist of the period.

BENJAMIN FRANKLIN'S GREATNESS

He was Benjamin Franklin, who arrived almost penniless in the City of Brotherly Love after running away from his apprenticeship to brother James. Within five years he was a successful and prosperous citizen of the town. Ben Franklin's whole career was one of success, color, and usefulness. There has never been another American quite like him. He was "the complete man," like DaVinci, Michelangelo, or Roger Bacon. Everything he did, he did well, and he did many things. He was an unusual person, but he so perfectly summed up the characteristics for which Americans were becoming known that it is pertinent to discuss him at this point.

Franklin's greatness resulted as much from his open mind as from his genius. Brought up in a Calvinist environment, he lost all trace of that narrow ideology by the time he had become important in Philadelphia. A product of the emerging middle class, he refused to be bound by the petty prejudices of the commercial group. He was equally at ease before his local Board of Trade, or before the most lavish court in Europe. A good husband, he held his wife ("dear Debby") in great affection, and some of his most charming letters were penned to keep her informed of the French fashions he knew would interest her; but he was also human clay, after all, if his numerous love affairs right up into his seventies are admissible evidence. Indeed, these very weaknesses in an acknowledged great man only endeared him the more to those who knew him well.

Franklin was respected because he excelled in activities the American esteemed highly. He was an idealist, but he made more money than most of his "hard-headed" rivals and associates. He was rich, but he understood, respected, and represented the poor. He could talk familiarly with the dilettante on almost any subject, but he was strictly "old shoe" with simple people. Children adored him. He was as direct as his own literary child, "Poor Richard," whose sayings are quoted to this day, but he could carry to successful conclusions the most devious diplomatic negotiations. The gentry admired him for his scientific accomplishments in a day when science was a fad of the privileged class, but he was equally respected by the stodgy burghers, who knew that he worked constantly for civic improvements. He was noted for his drawing-room conversation, but he was also the careful scholar. He was a pioneer American sociologist and economist. The insurance company he founded is still thriving.

He was all this and much more—but first of all, Ben Franklin was a printer and journalist. That is how he began his rise to fame. That is the base upon which he built his fortune. He had concluded at the very beginning of his career that the quickest way to acquire influence was to gain wealth. There was nothing new in that idea, except that Franklin chose to make the press his medium for reaching that estate. That *was* a new idea. And when he achieved his goal, he showed others that journalism merited the attention of the prudent and ambitious. Franklin's later honors overshadowed his journalistic success, but it should be remembered that he did not leave the printing business until he was 42—only a few years short of the average life expectancy of that day.

THE *PENNSYLVANIA GAZETTE*, 1729

Franklin took over the management of the *Pennsylvania Gazette* in October, 1729. He did not establish the paper. Instead, he obtained it from its founder by shrewd negotiations that spread his fame as a businessman and printer. The publishing picture in Philadelphia must have appeared bleak to most young printers of the time. The city was far below the cultural standard it was later to achieve. Few books were sold, and almost none were printed, except for an occasional theological tract. The only oasis in this literary desert was the disordered printing shop of Samuel Keimer.[5]

Keimer has not fared well in history. He never lived down the fact that he had been the target of a famous man's jibes. But it was Keimer who started Franklin on his career in Philadelphia. And Keimer certainly had some pretensions to culture. His history of the Quakers, published in 1728, was the most important book to be printed in Pennyslvania up to that time. In 1729 he published *Epictetus*, the first translation of a classic writer offered by an American

[5] Andrew Bradford published a few books, but they were mostly theological, rather than literary, in content. At the time, Bradford operated a general store, an apothecary shop, and a post office, in addition to the *American Weekly Mercury*.

printer. On the other hand, he was erratic, a shoddy craftsman, and a miserable businessman.

Keimer could not compete successfully with Bradford, who could distribute newspapers cheaply as postmaster of the area, and who also had a backlog of ballots, notices, orders, minutes, and laws as official printing for the colony. Franklin was not at all impressed by this formidable rival, however. And so we find Franklin and his friend, Hugh Meredith, opening their printing shop in the spring of 1728. Already they were planning a newspaper. They were delayed by a jealous rival. A friend of the young partners disclosed the plans to Keimer, who was irked because Franklin had left his shop to set up one of his own. Keimer saw a way to get even. He at once announced his own plans for a newspaper, intending thereby to thwart Franklin. In December of 1728 Keimer published the first number of *The Universal Instructor in All Arts and Sciences: and Pennsylvania Gazette.* The paper was about as readable as the rival *Mercury*—until a new feature began to appear in that publication. A series of clever essays in the Addison and Steele style soon brought delighted patrons to Bradford's shop for copies of the *Mercury.* The series came to be known as the "Busy-Body Papers." The anonymous author was actually Benjamin Franklin, and his most frequent target of satire was none other than Samuel Keimer. In the end, Keimer gave up the struggle. On October 2, 1729, Ben Franklin took over the good will and liabilities of Keimer's paper and began his career as a newspaper publisher.

He shortened the title to the *Pennsylvania Gazette,* dropped the encyclopaedia, and substituted news and literary material of a more popular type. Franklin had little difficulty winning public acceptance, and with it came a volume of profitable advertising. In addition to being a readable paper, it was a bold one. Franklin's experience in Boston, plus his innate common sense, kept him from getting into serious trouble with the authorities. But he took a stand on issues, just the same. Men have many opinions, he explained to his readers, and printers publish these opinions as part of their business.

"They are educated in the belief," he added, "that when men differ in opinion, both sides ought equally to have the advantage of being heard by the public; and that when truth and error have fair play, the former is always an overmatch for the latter [shades of Milton and his *Areopagitica*]. . . . If all printers were determined not to print anything till they were sure it would offend nobody," said he, "there would be very little printed." [6]

FRANKLIN'S BUSINESS SUCCESS

With Keimer out of the way, Andrew Bradford remained as Franklin's only serious rival. He had what amounted to a government subsidy through his contract for official printing. Franklin met that challenge by writing up an

[6] As quoted in Carl Van Doren, *Benjamin Franklin* (New York: Viking, 1938), p. 100.

important legislative address, which he then sent to every member of the Assembly at his own expense. The same report appeared in the *Mercury*, but the *Gazette* story was so much better that Franklin made a great impression on the lawmakers. He continued this reporting. Within a year Franklin had won away the government printing contract.[7]

He now bought out his partner, Meredith, with money loaned to him by influential businessmen he had cultivated in his short career in Philadelphia. Thus, at the age of 24, we see him as the sole proprietor of the best newspaper in the American colonies. It soon had the largest circulation, most pages, highest advertising revenue, most literate columns, and liveliest comment of any paper in the area. Retiring from publishing 18 years later, he had made a fortune in a business that usually offered a bare subsistence to its promoters.

During this time Franklin established what amounted to the first chain of newspapers. True, each unit was independent in policy and direction since Franklin exercised only a fatherly control over them. It was his custom to watch worthy apprentices, and then to help them set up shop when the articles of service had been fulfilled. Franklin let these young journalists pay him back out of earnings. It was Franklin, too, who helped establish the first foreign-language paper at Germantown, near Philadelphia. It was also Franklin who first planned to publish a magazine on this side of the Atlantic. Again, as in his newspaper venture, he was outmaneuvered by a jealous rival who learned of the plans. Andrew Bradford's *American Magazine* appeared in 1741 three days before the first issue of Franklin's *General Magazine*. Neither was successful, although Franklin's survived the longer.

But Franklin's greatest contribution to American journalism was that he made it respectable. Campbell, Brooker, the Bradfords, and Keimer were dull fellows, on the whole. Some, like Campbell, lived and died in their communities without achieving more than casual recognition. James Franklin was too tactless to win the respect of "solid" citizens. Most of the printer-journalists had trouble meeting expenses, as their frequent pleas to delinquent subscribers indicate. Franklin showed that a good journalist and businessman could make money in the publishing field. That was, and is, an effective way of making any business respectable. When intelligent and industrious youths saw the possibilities of journalism, as developed by the grand old man of the press, they began to turn more often to this calling. Getting this improved type of personnel into the craft was the best possible tonic for American journalism.

PAPERS IN OTHER COLONIES

After 1725, newspapers sprouted all over the colonies. In Boston, Samuel Kneeland established the *New England Weekly Journal* on March 20, 1727.

[7] Some time before, Franklin had visited London, where great progress was being made in the printing industry. Partly as a result of this trip, he became an expert typographer and engraver.

It is worth a mention because it was the first newspaper to have correspondents in nearby communities whose duty it was to send in pertinent information about the neighborhood, a practice still followed by newspaper publishers. Another important Boston paper was the *Weekly Rehearsal,* founded in 1731 by Jeremy Gridley, a lawyer. A year later he turned over the publication to Thomas Fleet, James Franklin's old printer. Fleet changed the name to the *Evening Post* a few years later. Under him, it became the best and most popular paper in Boston. It lasted until Revolutionary War times. Gridley, the founder, eventually returned to journalism in 1743 as the editor of the first magazine to win public support, and the third monthly magazine to appear in the colonies. This was the *American Magazine and Historical Chronicle,* which survived until 1746.

Maryland was the fourth colony to have a newspaper.[8] William Parks, a former English editor, set up the *Maryland Gazette* at Annapolis in 1727. His paper reflected good taste, literary skill, and pride in the craft he had learned so well under the best English masters. Later, in 1736, he founded the *Virginia Gazette,* first newspaper in Virginia, at Williamsburg. That little shop has been restored, and is now one of the interesting exhibits at the old colonial capital.[9] Because it tells us what the printing business must have been like in colonial days, it might be worth a moment to look into this quaint building.

THE ENGLISH COMMON PRESS

The office is on the ground floor of a small brick building. In the center stands the English Common Press, shipped over in pieces from the mother country, for no presses were to be had in America until Isaac Doolittle of Connecticut began turning them out in 1769. Close at hand are the accessories: the imposing stones, upon which the type is gathered; the "horse" and "bank" tables, from which the paper is fed to the press; the wetting trough, for the preparation of the paper; an ink grinding stand; and the matrix punches, made in England by William Caslon himself, for cutting the beautiful type that bears his name. The press stands seven feet high and weighs about 1,500 pounds. It is firmly braced to floor and ceiling by heavy oak beams to insure rigidity when heavy pressure is applied to the type forms.

From this clumsy apparatus colonial printers such as the Bradfords, Greens,

[8] The other colonies: Massachusetts, Pennsylvania, and New York.

[9] Other firsts in their respective colonies: *Rhode Island Gazette* and *South Carolina Gazette,* 1732; *North Carolina Gazette,* 1751; *Connecticut Gazette,* 1755; *New Hampshire Gazette,* 1756; *Georgia Gazette,* 1763; *New Jersey Gazette,* 1777; *Vermont Gazette,* 1780; and *Delaware Gazette,* 1785. James Parker, one of Ben Franklin's protégés, founded the Connecticut paper. Another of Franklin's "boys" established the South Carolina paper, although there is some doubt as to which one of two has the more valid claim.

Sowers, Parks, and Franklins produced letterpress work of the highest quality.[10] There was much bad printing during this period, too, but that was often the fault of poor craftsmanship and worn equipment. There is abundant proof that the colonial printing press was capable of turning out superb work, under the supervision of a skilled printer. He had to know his business, however. A single impression, or "token," required 13 distinct operations. Two expert craftsmen and an apprentice working under the best of conditions might turn out about 200 tokens an hour. The usual four-page paper had to be "pulled" twice—the pull being the application of pressure when a stout man put his weight on the lever to print a token.

Let us watch the colonial printer as he works. The bed of the press is rolled out by means of a wheel and pulley arrangement. The type, all set by hand, is locked tight in the form and placed on the bed. A young apprentice, or "devil," applies the homemade ink to the type, using a doeskin dauber on a stick for this purpose. The paper is then moistened in a trough so that it will take a better impression. It is placed carefully over the type. The bed is rolled back under the press. The "platen," or upper pressure plate, is then pressed against the type by means of a screw or lever device. The platen is then released; the bed is wheeled out; the sheet is hung on a wire to dry before it is ready for its second "run" for the reverse side; and the printers get ready to prepare another token.

The usual colonial paper consisted of four pages, often about ten by fifteen inches in dimension. The paper was rough foolscap. There were no headlines, as we know them, until after 1750, and even then they were uncommon. The only illustrations were the colophons, or printers' trade marks, on the title page, and an occasional woodcut to embellish an advertisement. The Greens and Sowers made their own paper, but most of it was imported from England. It

[10] There were two great Bradford printing families. William Bradford was founder of the Pennsylvania line and was a pioneer printer in Philadelphia and New York. His son, Andrew, established the first newspaper in Philadelphia. William Bradford III was the famous soldier-editor of the Revolution and publisher of the *Pennsylvania Journal* in Philadelphia. His son, Thomas, succeeded the father as editor. John Bradford, no relative of the Pennsylvania clan, was a surveyor who founded the first paper in Kentucky, at Lexington. His brother, Fielding, was also active in journalism. James, another member of this branch, founded the first newspaper in Louisiana, and may have been the first American war correspondent, according to Mott (p. 196). The Greens were prominent in New England. Bartholomew and Samuel were pioneers in the Boston-Cambridge area; the former as printer of the first successful newspaper in America. From Samuel Green of Cambridge descended a long line of printer-journalists. Timothy Jr. founded the New London, Conn., *Summary* in 1758. His son, Timothy III, changed the name to the *Gazette,* after the death of the father. Samuel and Thomas founded the first paper in New Haven in 1767. Thomas, the brother of Timothy III, founded the *Connecticut* (now *Hartford*) *Courant* in 1764. Timothy IV was co-founder of the first Vermont paper. The Sowers were Germans who settled near Philadelphia. First in the printing dynasty was Christopher, who, with the encouragment of Benjamin Franklin, established one of the earliest foreign language newspapers, the Germantown *Zeitung.* A mechanical genius, he constructed his own press and made his own ink and paper. His sons carried on the business, but Christopher III was a Tory during the Revolution and his journalistic career was ruined by the American victory. The Franklin influence in Massachusetts, Rhode Island, and Pennsylvania has been described.

Drawing of a colonial wooden hand press.

was made of rags and was of surprising durability, despite its mottled appearance.

With this primitive equipment the printer-journalist not only produced fine graphic art, but he had at hand an implement that was soon to make the press truly a Fourth Estate. At times it was more powerful than the government itself. In half a century times had changed the role of the journalist. No longer did he wait in the governor's outer office, cap in hand, while a representative of the administration checked his copy for statements disapproved by the authorities. Even the most obstinate bureaucrat had been forced to concede that this new engine of public opinion was not to be abused with impunity. Eighteenth-century journalists had learned a lesson that apparently has to be re-learned at regular intervals—that when the public supports them, no power is strong enough to throttle press freedom. They learned that when editors are identified with the public cause, putting responsibility to the people above whims and personal convenience, they not only win the essential backing, but help to generate other forces for freedom within the community.

Annotated Bibliography

Books

Andrews, Charles M., *Colonial Folkways.* New Haven: Yale University Press, 1921. A small volume in the Chronicle of America series, giving eighteenth-century background, by the noted author of the four-volume *The Colonial Period of American History.*

Brigham, Clarence S., *History and Bibliography of American Newspapers, 1690–1820,* 2 vols. Worcester, Mass.: American Antiquarian Society, 1947. Gives brief descriptions of all newspapers up to 1820. An indispensable tool of the colonial press historian.

———, *Journals and Journeymen.* Philadelphia: University of Pennsylvania Press, 1950. Fifteen essays on the colonial press; one particularly interesting one on advertising.

Cambridge History of American Literature, I. New York: Putnam's, 1917–21. Volume I of this four-volume work discusses Franklin (pp. 90–110) and colonial newspapers and magazines (pp. 111–23).

Cook, Elizabeth C., *Literary Influences in Colonial Newspapers, 1704–1750.* New York: Columbia University Press, 1912. Describes the role of the press in supplying the craving for popular literature.

De Armond, Anna Janney, *Andrew Bradford: Colonial Journalist.* Newark, Del.: University of Delaware Press, 1949. Well-documented.

Franklin, Benjamin, *The Autobiography of Benjamin Franklin,* edited by Leonard W. Labaree. New Haven: Yale University Press, 1964. A new text, restored to Franklin's original.

Kobre, Sidney, *The Development of the Colonial Newspaper.* Pittsburgh: The Colonial Press, Inc., 1944. A short, but classic, study of the integration of political, social, and economic forces in the development of the American press.

McMurtrie, Douglas C., *The Beginnings of the American Newspaper.* Chicago: Black Cat Press, 1935. A 36-page description of colonial newspapers, including a few facsimiles.

———, *A History of Printing in the United States.* New York: R. R. Bowker Company, 1936. McMurtrie planned a four-volume history of the press during the pioneer period of each state in the union. Only the second volume, on the Middle and South Atlantic states, was completed. Well-documented and illustrated, it treats in detail Franklin, the Philadelphia press, and the early German press in Pennsylvania.

Mott, Frank L., and Ralph D. Casey, eds., *Interpretations of Journalism.* New York: Appleton-Century-Crofts, 1936. Contains an excellent word portrait of Franklin, the printer, reprinting some of Franklin's own comments; see pages 101–12.

The Papers of Benjamin Franklin, Vol. I. New Haven: Yale University Press, 1959. Covers period to 1734, including Silence Dogood and Busy-Body letters. Extensive introduction by editor Leonard W. Labaree.

Parrington, Vernon L., *Main Currents in American Thought,* Vol. 1. Excellent background material and interesting comment on Franklin.

Thomas, Isaiah, *History of Printing in America,* 2 vols. Worcester, Mass.: Isaiah Thomas, Jr. (first printing), 1810; Albany, N.Y.: Joel Munsell, 1874. The standard authority on colonial journalism; contains biographies of printers and accounts of newspapers in all colonies and in some states after independence.

Van Doren, Carl, *Benjamin Franklin.* New York: Viking, 1938. The most readable account of a great printer-journalist by a prize-winning biographer.

Wroth, Lawrence C., *The Colonial Printer.* Portland, Me.: Southworth-Anthoensen Press, 1938. An excellent study of the printing craft.

Periodicals and Monographs

Fogel, Howard H., "Colonial Theocracy and a Secular Press," *Journalism Quarterly,* XXXVII (Autumn 1960), 525. A study of how the colonial press won its freedom from interference by religious authorities.

Ford, Edwin H., "Colonial Pamphleteers," *Journalism Quarterly,* XIII (March 1936), 24. A scholarly discussion of the journalistic contributions of such colonial leaders as Increase and Cotton Mather, and Samuel Sewall. Reprinted in Ford and Emery, *Highlights in the History of the American Press.*

King, Marion Reynolds, "One Link in the First Newspaper Chain, the South Carolina Gazette," *Journalism Quarterly,* IX (September 1932), 257. Describes the arrangement by which Franklin financed his apprentices in setting up printing shops.

White, William, "The Maryland Gazette: America's Oldest Newspaper?," *Journalism Quarterly,* XXXV (Fall 1958), 439. The answer is "no" to this claim to the title of America's oldest continuously published newspaper, more properly claimed by the *Hartford Courant,* founded as the weekly *Connecticut Courant* in 1764 and a daily since 1837. See Frank Luther Mott, "What is the Oldest U.S. Newspaper?," *Journalism Quarterly,* XL (Winter 1963), 95.

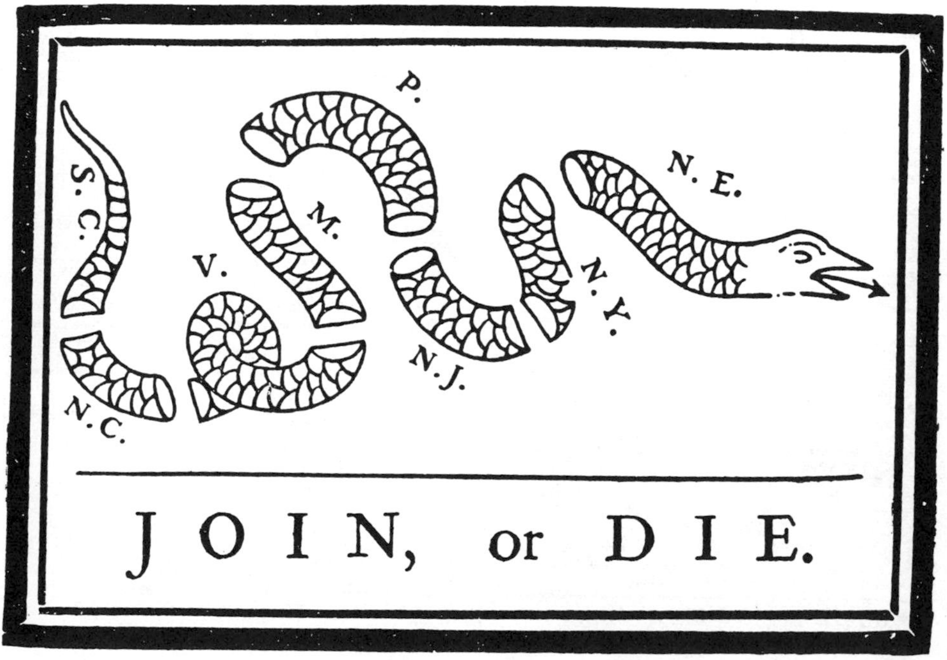

Facsimile from *Pennsylvania Gazette*

THE
Pennſylvania GAZETTE.

Containing the freſheſt Advices Foreign and Domeſtick.

From July 24. to July 31. 1735.

TO BE SOLD,
At the Houſe of the Widow Richardſon in Front-Street, near the North-Eaſt Corner of Market-Street.

A LIKELY Negroe Wench about 16 or 18 Years old. ſingle and double refin'd Loaf-Sugar, Barbadoes white and muſcovado Sugar. Alſo Choice Barbadoes Limes in Barrels at reaſonable Rates.

Juſt Imported from London and Briſtol,
And to be SOLD by JOHN INGLIS, at his Store below the Draw-Bridge, in Front-Street, Philadelphia:

BRoad-Cloths, Kerſeys and Plains, Ruggs, Blankets, Oznabrigs, Checks, London Shalloons, Tammies, Calimancoes, ſeven eighths and yard wide Garlix, Men and Womens worſted Stockings, Men and Womens Shammy Gloves, Pinns, Baladine Silk, ſilk Laces, faſhionable Fans, Paduaſoys, Ribbons, ſilk Ferrits, Gartering, Caddis, Buttons and Mohair, cotton Romals, linnen Handerchiefs, Chiloes, Mens worſted Caps, Bunts, fine Bed-Ticks made up in Suits, India Taffities, Damasks and Perſians, ſix quarter Muſlins, Suits of ſuper fine Broad-Cloth, with Lining and Trimmings, London double refin'd Sugar, Bird, Pidgeon, Duck, Gooſe and Swan Shot, Bar Lead, 8, 10 and 20 penny Nails, Window Glaſs, Patterns of Chintz for Beds, ſarſnet Handkerchiefs, Briſtol quart Bottles; and ſundry other Goods, for ready Money, or the uſual Credit.

WHereas George Carter, a thick ſhort Man, with light buſhy Hair, about 40 Years old, born in White Pariſh, ſix Miles from New-Sarum, in Wiltſhire, by Trade a Baker, went on board a Ship at Briſtol, bond to Penſilvania, about the Year 1722: Theſe are to deſire the ſaid George Carter (if living) to return to his native Country, or to give Notice where he lives to John Atkinſon, at the White Lyon Tavern, on Cornhil, London, or to Iſrael Pemberton, jun. of Philadelphia, who can inform him of ſomething conſiderable to his Advantage: If he be deceas'd, Information is deſir'd when and where he died. And if any of his Children be living they may have the ſame Advantage, by applying as aforeſaid.

TO BE SOLD,

BY James Oſwald in Front-Street, at the Houſe of Mr. Joſeph Turner, and by William Wallace, at the Upper-End of Second-Street, Sugar Bakers, Choice double refin'd LOAF-SUGAR at Eighteen-pence the Pound, ſingle refin'd, Sugar Candy, Mollaſſes, &c. at reaſonable Prices.

RUN away from the Subſcriber, the 4th Day of November laſt, a Servant Woman, aged about 28 Years, fair Hair'd, wants ſome of her Teeth before, a little deafiſh, named Suſannah Wells, born near Biddeford, in England: She had on when ſhe went away, a Callico Gown, with red Flowers, blue Stockings, with Clocks, new Shoes, a quilted Petticoat, Plat Hat. Whoever ſecures ſaid Servant, and delivers her to ſaid Subſcriber at Wilmington, or to Robert Dixſon in Philadelphia, ſhall have Twenty-five Shillings Reward, and reaſonable Charges paid by Robert Dixon, or Thomas Downing.

Philad. December 4. 1740.

N. B. It's believed the ſaid Servant was carried from New-Caſtle in the Ship commanded by Capt. Lawrence Dent, now lying at Philadelphia.

Juſt Publiſhed.

POOR Richard's ALMANACKS, for the Year 1741. Alſo, Jerman's Almanacks, and Pocket and Sheet Almanacks. Printed and Sold by B. Franklin.

ALL Perſons are hereby deſired to take Notice, That the Bills of Credit of the Province of Pennſylvania, bearing Date any time before the Year 1739, are by an Act of Aſſembly of the ſaid Province, made in the Year aforeſaid, declared to be null and void, ſince the tenth Day of the Month called Auguſt laſt paſt: And that the ſame ſhould be no longer the current Bills of the ſaid Province. Therefore all Perſons who are poſſeſſed of any of the ſaid Bills, are deſired forthwith to bring them in to the General Loan-Office of the ſaid Province at Philadelphia, where Attendance will be given to Exchange them for New-Bills. J. KINSEY.

RUN away from the Subſcriber the 3d Inſt. a Servant Man named Thomas Wenn, by trade a Barber, appears by his looks to be at leaſt 40 Years old, but pretends he is not 30, middle Stature, well ſet, ſore ey'd, and near ſighted: Had on when he went away, a ſmall Hat but good, a ſmall black Wig, but may have taken another of ſome other colour, a kerſey Coat almoſt new of a mixt colour rediſh and white, lin'd through with a red half thick or ſerge, large flat metal Buttons, old white dimity Jacket, a pair of ſtout buckſkin Breeches almoſt new with braſs Buttons, a pair of new thick mill'd Stockings of a bluiſh colour, Shoes about half worn. Whoever ſecures the ſaid Servant ſo that he may be had again, ſhall have if twenty Miles off this City Twenty Shillings, if thirty, thirty Shilings, and if forty, forty Shillings Reward, paid by

Philad. January 5. 1740. William Crofthwaite.

TO BE SOLD
By ELIZABETH COMBS, at her Houſe over the Draw-Bridge,

ALL kinds of white and check Linnens, Dimities, Callimancoes, Frizes, Hankerchiefs, Cotton Gowns, ſortable Shot, Sail Cloth, and ſeveral other Goods, for ready Money or ſhort Credit.

For SOUTH-CAROLINA directly,
The Ship Loyal-Judith, LOVELL PAYNTER, Commander,

WILL Sail when the Weather permits. For Freight or Paſſage agree with the ſaid Maſter on board the ſaid Ship, now lying at Mr. Samuel Auſtin's Wharff; or with Benjamin Shoemaker, Merchant, in High-Street Philadelphia.

Juſt Imported,

A Parcel of likely Negro Men, Women, and Children: As alſo, choice London double and ſingle refin'd, clay'd and Muſcovado SUGARS, and GINGER; to be ſold by Joſeph Marks, at the Corner of Walnut and Second-Street, Philadelphia.

Juſt Imported,
And to be Sold very reaſonably by Peter Turner, at his Store over againſt the Poſt-Office in Market-Street, Philadelphia;

A Large Sortment of Kerſeys, napt and fine Drab Kerſeys, Broad-Cloths, London Shalloons, Embos'd Flannens, Womens Shoes and Cloggs, Hat Lineings, fine Gulic and Hingham Holland, Seven-eights Garlix, Callicoes, Writing Paper, crimſon, blue and green harateens for Beds, fine half Ell crimſon, blue and green worſted Damasks, 3, 4, 8 penny Nails, London Steel, Scyths, Wool-Cards, Shot and Lead, fine and coarſe Bolting Cloths, Hungary Water, fine Green Tea, fine lacker'd Sconces, ell wide Perſians, black and coloured Taffitys, with ſundry other Goods.

PHILADELPHIA: Printed by B. FRANKLIN, POST-MASTER, at the NEW PRINTING-OFFICE, near the Market. Price 10 s. a Year.

The *Pennsylvania Gazette* advertises sales of Negroes, *Poor Richard's Almanack*.

4

Rise of the Fourth Estate

The question before the court . . . is not [just] the cause of the poor printer. . . . No! It may in its consequence affect every freeman . . . on the main of America. It is the best cause; it is the cause of Liberty . . . the liberty both of exposing and opposing arbitrary power . . . by speaking and writing Truth.
—Andrew Hamilton's defense in the Zenger trial

In the second quarter of the eighteenth century the newspaper became a force to be feared by arrogant administrators. True, the infant newspaper mortality rate was high, usually as a result of financial malnutrition. For example, more than half of the 2,120 newspapers established between 1690 and 1820 expired before they were two years old.[1] Only 34 lasted a generation. Nevertheless, by 1750 most literate Americans had access to some journal of information. In that year there were 14 weekly newspapers in the six most populous colonies, and soon the increase in such publications was to be rapid, as we shall see in the next chapter.

The product was better, too. Semiweekly and even triweekly newspapers were available after the mid-century, and had first appeared even earlier. Circulation was rising. A few publishers had won fame and fortune in the business. Rapid increase in population, better transportation and communication facilities, and rising political tensions partly explain the growth of the press. Many colonials had become prosperous and were looking around for ways of investing capital. Ports, such as New York, began to achieve world importance.

[1] Clarence S. Brigham, *History and Bibliography of American Newspapers, 1690-1820* (Worcester, Mass.: American Antiquarian Society, 1947), p. x (Intro.).

About a third of the ships in the British merchant fleet were launched by New England shipwrights. There were 360 whalers operating from American ports. There were skillful artisans in the towns. The famous "Pennsylvania Rifle," one of the great weapons of the time, was a product of such craftsmen, for example. Despite the restrictions of the mother country, manufacture of finished articles continued to furnish employment for many hands. In one year alone during this period New Englanders shipped out 13,000 pairs of shoes.[2]

The press was useful to the ambitious trader and businessman. Advertising was the cheapest way to move goods offered for sale by the rising commercial class. Business intercourse between the colonies increased, and accordingly there was need for information only American journalists could provide quickly and cheaply.

Better roads led to better communications. Early editor-postmasters had a double reason for improving roads. Franklin, who reversed the process by being appointed postmaster *after* taking up journalism, was named as deputy postmaster of all the colonies, along with William Hunter of Virginia, another printer-journalist. When Franklin took office, it required six weeks to bring the posts regularly from Boston to Philadelphia by land, and there was a mail pickup only fortnightly. Franklin, who took over most of the postal responsibility because of Hunter's ill-health, cut the travel time in half and established weekly service.

There was also improvement in education, always a factor in developing publics favorable to the newspaper. Many parents could now afford to send their children to school, and seminaries and academies were available in the urban centers. Colleges in many colonies produced not only teachers and ministers, effective foes of illiteracy, but writers and political spokesmen of the people.

The great technical advances in printing were far in the future, but better type was available during this period. About 1720 William Caslon began modifying Nicolas Jenson's fifteenth-century type into a more readable form. Caslon type was adopted by American printers soon after, and it is still popular. The best standard press was the invention of Willem Janszon Blaeu, a Dutch craftsman of the seventeenth century. Not until around 1800, when Adam Ramage and the Earl of Stanhope came out with the iron press, was there any great improvement in this essential equipment.

THE FIRST ADVERTISING MESSAGES

The development of commerce led to progress in the advertising field. Advertising and printing had been closely associated almost from the beginning. William Caxton, who set up the first press in England, issued a broadside

[2] These aspects of development are admirably presented in Sidney Kobre, "The Revolutionary Colonial Press—A Social Interpretation," *Journalism Quarterly*, XX (September 1943), 193–97.

advertising his service (religious) book, *The Pyes of Salisbury Use,* in 1480. Number 62 of the *London Gazette,* first complete newspaper in the English language, included an announcement of a special advertising supplement in June, 1666. An interesting use of advertising is shown in Number 94 of the same paper. After the great fire of London in the fall of 1666 the paper opened its columns to those seeking word of missing loved ones. There were also advertisements concerning salvaged furniture, addresses of scattered families, and houses offering shelter to the homeless.

Presbrey calls John Houghton the father of modern advertising.[3] Houghton was an apothecary; merchant of coffee, tea, and chocolate; book critic; Fellow of the Royal Society; and publisher. He established a newspaper for commercial readers in 1692. This prototype of the *Wall Street Journal* was the first newspaper to emphasize the role of advertising. Houghton had an appreciation of advertising ethics, in an age when the margin between quackery and professional knowledge was narrower than it is today. He was willing to advertise almost any product, but he would not give his seventeenth-century "seal of approval" to statements he believed to be dangerously dishonest. That advertising was a topic for debate and criticism two hundred years ago, as it is today, is implied by a comment of that famous pundit, Dr. Samuel Johnson, in the *Idler* of January 20, 1758:

> . . . Advertisements are now so numerous that they are very negligently perused, and it is therefore become necessary to gain attention by magnificence of promises and by eloquence sometimes sublime and sometimes pathetick. Promise—large promise—is the soul of advertising. . . . The trade of advertising is now so near perfection that it is not easy to propose any improvement.[4]

Advertising in the eighteenth century emphasized the fundamental drives of human beings to make them buy goods or services. Thus, a merchant of 1750 offered tooth cleansers not only for the purpose of polishing teeth, which was the utilitarian value, but to beautify, and thus to act as an ally of love, social prestige, or business appeal. Then, as today, rival merchants knew the effectiveness of turning universal desires into sales stimulations. The advertiser of 1750 was as aware as his modern counterpart that emotional appeals bring a more positive response than logic from the general public. The more immediate the response, the more effective the sales campaign. Advertising copy writers of the eighteenth century used every device to arouse such a response, carrying novelty and imagination to fantastic limits.

The advertiser could teach the journalist some important lessons on the subject of reader response. For example, the advertiser quickly discovered that his message must be simply stated to reach the most people. It took the

[3] Frank Presbrey, *The History and Development of Advertising* (Garden City, N.Y.: Doubleday, 1929), p. 56.

[4] *Ibid.,* p. 70.

news writer a long time to learn this lesson. Advertisers also understood the value of attractive presentation. They led the way in experimentation with type, illustrations, makeup, and legibility. The press owes much to these practical psychologists and literary showmen.

RISING POLITICAL TENSION

The greatest stimulus to the development of the American press of this period was the rising political tension that was to culminate in the war for independence. The press had an essential role in the drama about to unfold. The newspaper thrives on controversy, providing it is able to take part in the discussions with any degree of freedom. The great development of the press during the first half of the eighteenth century was its victory over the forces that would have restricted that liberty. This victory made the press the most powerful weapon of the American revolutionaries.

Even Milton, perhaps the most eloquent of the pioneers for liberty of expression, admitted there was a need for some limitation on press freedom. The publication of his speech to Parliament in 1644 (*Areopagitica*) enunciated a concept that was largely ignored at the time, but which became a battle cry a hundred years later in America. Milton had no patience with "superstitions," but he insisted that the publication of truth should be protected as a right, since "who ever knew truth put to the worse, in a free and open encounter [with falsehood]?" Milton was arguing for the right to express himself in print without having to have that expression approved in advance. Almost forgotten today are the battles and sacrifices by which this concept won general acceptance.

WILLIAM AND ANDREW BRADFORD

In 1692, before the first successful newspaper had yet been born in America, a Philadelphia printer boldly stated one of the cardinal principles of a free press. He was William Bradford, founder of a remarkable printing dynasty. Bradford had to placate both a jealous government and a sensitive Quaker hierarchy when he set up his little shop. Every now and then he was threatened by one or the other because of ideas expressed in pamphlets he turned out at regular intervals. Arrested in 1692 for a minor infraction, Bradford declared he was tired of such interference, and notified the authorities he was taking his press to a more congenial community. Officials were alarmed by this threat, for they depended upon Bradford for the dissemination of governmental, religious, and commercial information. The General Assembly therefore quashed the charge and induced Bradford to remain by granting him a yearly retainer of 40 pounds and all the printing he could handle by himself.

Because of the disposition of this case, Bradford's defense was not widely known, but it is worth a mention here because it brought up an issue that was hotly debated a generation later. For the printer had insisted that the jury in such cases was responsible for judging both the *law* and the *fact*. Now courts had held that when seditious libel (criticism of government) was charged, it was the duty of the jury only to establish the authorship of the statement. This was a point of *fact*. It was up to the judges to determine whether the statement was punishable. This was a point of *law*. Bradford objected to this. Some 40 years later, the issue that Bradford had successfully pressed in 1692 was to become a principal point in the trial of John Peter Zenger.

Bradford's son, Andrew, jousted regularly with the authorities on the right to express himself freely. He criticised the financial policy of the government and was brought before the magistrate for reprimand. He was ordered to print nothing about the Pennsylvania administration—or any other colonial government—unless he had express permission to do so. This was the old principle of "previous restraint" before publication, and Andrew objected. Sometime later the younger Bradford printed an essay in his newspaper. The subject was liberty versus tyranny. Andrew was not the author, but again he was hailed into court as publisher of the *Mercury*. This time the printer carried his arguments to the people. Authorities were so uncertain of popular backing that they dropped the trial. From then on, the *Mercury* appeared regularly with statements critical of the administration.

The Franklins also fought for the cause of free expression, long before that cause was generally recognized and protected by the courts. James Franklin was the first American publisher to flout the licenser. In his bouts with the authorities he argued that he had the duty to tell his readers everything he believed to be news. Benjamin Franklin also spoke, if prudently, for a free press. He quoted *Areopagitica* on occasion and believed there was much more danger in what printers left unsaid out of fear, than in what they said. Ben Franklin seldom tangled with the authorities, but he discovered he could print almost anything with impunity, so long as public opinion sustained him. He won that support by making people respect him.

THE ZENGER CASE: BACKGROUND

But the most celebrated case involving freedom of the press was the Zenger trial of 1734–35. It has been much overrated for its effect on legal reform, and it settled nothing because of the dubious circumstances under which it was conducted. Its inspirational impact was tremendous, however, and the space given to it in these pages is justified.

At this point we meet again our old friend, William Bradford, late of Philadelphia. The senior Bradford had moved to New York when he was offered the position of government printer there. As a subsidized businessman, Bradford printed nothing that would antagonize his patrons. On November 8,

1725, he printed the first newspaper in the colony—the *New York Gazette*. Of course it favored the administration on all issues. Like many an editor who followed, Bradford rebelled when persecuted, as in Philadelphia, but conformed when offered special privileges and inducements by the same group he might have fought under different circumstances.

By 1734, New York was experiencing a mild revolution. A group of wealthy merchants and landowners insisted upon a greater share of control in the colony's affairs. This was an American manifestation of the situation in seventeenth-century England described in Chapter 1. A new commercial class was rising in the new world, as it had in the old. It demanded repeal of laws that restricted commerce. It insisted upon a devaluation of royal power and a greater emphasis upon the role of the king's (and governor's) advisers, representing the new class. In England this activity culminated in the "Glorious Revolution" and the eventual triumph of the Whig, or commercial, party. This development was a little slower in America, but the issue came up shortly after Bradford began issuing his paper from his little office on Hanover Square in the fall of 1725.

The rising capitalist class in New York had no way of communicating its ideas. Bradford had the only newspaper, and he was firmly committed to the administration faction. However, Bradford's former partner was fit, willing, and able to take over this function. He was John Peter Zenger, an immigrant from the German Palatinate, whose family had found relief from religious persecution when they were offered asylum in the new world. Zenger had been apprenticed to Bradford as a youth of 13. The master appears to have been a bit strict with his protégé, for Zenger left his shop after a few years and went to Maryland.

Eventually returning to New York, Zenger still had some trouble with the language, and his writing shows it, but he was a good enough craftsman to be in demand. Bradford forgave his former apprentice and even offered Zenger a partnership in the *Gazette* shop. The partners soon disagreed, however, and Zenger ended up with his own shop just around the corner from the *Gazette*. Here a small delegation waited upon him late in the summer of 1733. They were leaders of the commercial faction, and they asked Zenger if he would be willing to edit a paper that would be a medium for expressing their aspirations and policies.

The situation which prompted this meeting had a long and complex history. Governor Montgomerie of New York had died in 1731. Appointed as his successor was William Cosby. He was unable to sail from England immediately, and it was August of 1732 before he arrived at his new post. During this time the executive functions had been performed by Rip Van Dam, a 72-year-old Dutch colonial merchant of considerable means and prestige, although not identified with the "aristocracy." He had been on the governor's council for 30 years, and as senior member he was acting governor for the 13 months preceding Cosby's arrival. Van Dam was tough and powerful. He was a leader of the rising class that was becoming restless under an arrogant Tory ruling group.

Governor Cosby demanded a division of fees collected by Van Dam during the interval that the Dutchman was acting governor. Van Dam was willing to make some concessions, but Cosby stood upon his rights and refused to compromise. There was much more involved, however. In the litigation that followed, the governor demanded that the case be heard in the court of chancery—a court of special law—which he controlled. All money matters were to be tried in a regular court, however, and here Van Dam would most certainly have won. The struggle to take the case out of the hands of the governor's court involved Lewis Morris, chief justice of the highest colonial court. For his siding with Van Dam, Morris was removed by the governor. Van Dam thereupon filed a complaint against Governor Cosby and Justice Morris sailed for England to press the charges against the governor. Morris had more to complain of than the fee case. Governor Cosby was accused of demanding one-third the sale of all public lands sold under his jurisdiction. There were also suspected transactions involving illegal acquisition of land around what is now Utica, N. Y. Finally, there was evidence that the governor had rigged the elections so as to stack his council with his own puppets.[5] In the meantime, Governor Cosby had replaced Justice Morris with one of his own henchmen, young James Delancey.[6] The new chief justice had not been approved by the council, as required under the charter, and Van Dam added this to the list of complaints against the governor. There is evidence that Governor Cosby realized he had a powerful faction seeking his removal for abusing prerogatives, and perhaps this is why he acted so ruthlessly in the Zenger case.

The leaders of the anti-administration forces were articulate and able citizens. They included men like Van Dam; Justice Morris; James Alexander, a member of the council and also surveyor general for the colonies of New York and New Jersey; and William Smith, noted for his *History of the Colony of New York From Its Founding to 1762,* and a well-known public figure at the time of the trial. These, and other important citizens, were interested in having Zenger start a newspaper which would express the views of the opposition party.

THE *NEW YORK WEEKLY JOURNAL,* 1733

The first issue of Zenger's *New York Weekly Journal* appeared on November 5, 1733. From the very first day, the *Journal* clashed with the administration. Bradford at the *Gazette* was no match for Zenger and the brains

[5] Warren C. Price, "Reflections on the Trial of John Peter Zenger," *Journalism Quarterly,* XXXII (Spring 1955), 161, provides much new data on the Zenger case and points to the land-grabbing episode as one reason why public opinion swung to the Zenger-Morris side so heavily. "Cosby Manor" at Utica, 20 miles by 10 miles in extent, was an example of the governor's greed.

[6] "Henchman" is perhaps too strong a word to apply to Delancey. Delancey was young, and he was eager to get himself established in the colony. He was actually ill-equipped to take on such an important case. Later, he became lieutenant governor of New York and served with distinction and honor.

behind his venture. At once other rebellious elements gathered around the standard raised by the *Journal.* Smith and, more particularly, Alexander apparently were the hidden gunners of this journalistic ambuscade, and they laid down a continual barrage until the harassed governor and his party were driven into a desperate route.

On December 3, 1733, a story appeared in Zenger's paper attacking Governor Cosby for permitting French warships to spy out defenses in the lower bay. In the same issue were several derogatory statements about the administration. The governor was accused of letting only his favorites attend council meetings, for example. An irate New Jersey correspondent who wrote very much like Alexander denounced the colonial bureaucracy for incompetence. Indeed, the entire tone of the paper that day was critical.

The public enjoyed this show, and Zenger had to run off extra editions to satisfy customers. The governor was not so enthusiastic about such journalistic enterprise. Charging Zenger with "Scandalous, Virulent and Seditious Reflections upon the Government," Cosby ordered his handpicked chief justice, Delancey, to obtain an indictment against the brash editor. But the grand jury called to consider the matter refused to return a true bill. The Assembly likewise balked at filing any charges. Finally, a selected group of the governor's council agreed to start an action against Zenger, but only after much prodding by the governor, and after the original accusation had been considerably watered down. On a Sunday afternoon, November 17, 1734, Zenger was arrested on a charge of "raising sedition."

He was bound over to the grand jury, but the case was not called at the end of the term, and the defense therefore demanded and obtained his release. It was up to Richard Bradley, the attorney general, and a Cosby man, to file an "information" against the prisoner, since the grand jury would not act. This he did, and Zenger was returned to jail to await the next term of court. During this time, the *Journal* continued to appear. The editorial attacks on the administration were intensified, if anything. One account has it that Zenger's wife deserves credit for this chapter of the story. Others believe that Alexander and Smith were responsible for the content of the paper, with Mrs. Zenger and an old retainer doing the actual printing. In any case, the *Journal* appeared regularly while the publisher was in jail, and his paper was known far and wide.

ZENGER'S TRIAL, 1735

In July, 1735, Zenger at last faced his judges. They were Cosby's man, Delancey, and Frederick Philipse. Bradley, the Cosby appointee who had filed the information against Zenger, was prosecutor. Alexander and Smith, who were to have defended the printer, had been disbarred when they had disputed the information, or prosecutor's warrant, filed against Zenger. One John

Chambers was appointed by the court to defend the accused. Chambers demanded postponement until August, so he could prepare the case. Fortunately for Zenger, this plea was granted as was customary in all English courts.

The trial began August 4, 1735. The process of impaneling the jury, and the preliminaries to the presentaton of testimony indicated that there was little hope for the accused. Zenger was 38 years old then, but long months in prison had made him look older. He was pale and tired. On the bench the justices, Delancey and Philipse, glowered at the spectators crowding the room. In their black robes and elaborate wigs the judges looked stern and implacable. It is not difficult to reconstruct the scene:

The court listens attentively as Attorney General Bradley recites the offenses alleged in his own "information" (the equivalent of a grand jury indictment). Chambers, the defense counsel, arises at the end to enter a plea of "not guilty," but he does not appear to be very sure of himself. The spectators sit quietly. Most of them are members of the rebel group, and they are aware that their champion is in danger of defeat.

ANDREW HAMILTON, ZENGER'S LAWYER

But while Chambers enters his plea, an old man stands watching from the rear of the room. His long, white hair falls to his shoulders, but his body is muscular and erect. The keen old eyes take in the scene. He bows with old-school elegance, as all eyes turn in his direction. It is Andrew Hamilton of Philadelphia, a famed lawyer now in his eighties, who has risked the vicissitudes of travel to offer his services in behalf of the accused.

Striding majestically to the bar, he asks permission to present his credentials and to make his request. The bench must recognize such an eminent authority. He is granted the right to act in defense of Zenger. Turning half around so that both the judges and the jury can hear him clearly, he opens his remarks in a resonant, clear voice—a voice famous through the colonies. This is the "Philadelphia lawyer" in the original, favorable meaning of the term.

"I cannot think it proper to deny the Publication of a Complaint which I think is the right of every free born Subject to make," he declares, "and therefore I'll save Mr. Attorney the trouble of examining his Witness to that point; and I do confess (for my Client) that he both printed and published the two Papers set forth in the Information. I do hope in so doing he has committed no Crime." [7]

The courtroom is hushed in amazement. Is Hamilton deliberately throwing his case away? The only thing for the jury to decide is whether or not the accused is responsible for the publications, and Hamilton has now admitted

[7] The descriptive parts of the trial are taken from "Freedom of the Press Vindicated," *Harper's New Monthly Magazine* (July 1878), 296.

Bettmann Archive

A somewhat inaccurate artist's version of the Zenger trial.

that. Bradley, his eyes beaming with delight at this apparent easy victory, arises to address the judges:

"Then, if Your Honors please, since Mr. Hamilton has confessed the Fact, I think our Witnesses may be discharged; we have no further Occasion for them."

The court functionaries must make the next step. Bradley remarks that since publication of the offending articles has been admitted by the defense, there is nothing more for the jury to do but bring in a verdict of guilty. To this Hamilton replies calmly, but firmly:

"Not so, neither, Mr. Attorney. There are two Sides to that Bargain. I hope it is not our bare printing or publishing a Paper that will make it a Libel. You will have something more to do before you make my client a libeller. For the Words themselves must be libelous—that is, FALSE, MALICIOUS, AND SEDITIOUS—or else we are not guilty."

Bradley approaches the bench and renews his arguments. One by one Hamilton demolishes them. He goes back to the Magna Carta and the abolishing of the Star Chamber to prove that the concept he upholds—freedom to express justifiable truth—has long been accepted in the older courts, and that colonial New York is behind the times. His arguments are worded in decisive language, but his manner is so courtly, and his voice so mild, that the fascinated judges listen as though hypnotized. When the spectators begin to cheer during a lull, however, the prosecution objects to Hamilton's statements, and when Hamilton insists that "the *Falsehood* makes the *Scandal,* and both the *Libel,*" and then offers to "prove these very Papers that are called Libel to be *True,*" Justice Delancey remonstrates.

"You cannot be admitted, Mr. Hamilton," says the judge sternly, "to give the Truth of a Libel in evidence . . . The Court is of the Opinion you ought not to be permitted to prove the Facts in the Papers," and he cites a long list of supporting authorities.

"These are Star Chamber Cases," answers Hamilton patiently, "and I was in hopes that Practice had been dead with that Court."

Angered by this veiled criticism of his legal knowledge, the youthful Delancey cries out angrily:

"The Court have delivered their Opinion, and we expect you will use us with good Manners. You are not permitted to argue against this Court."

HAMILTON'S GREAT PLEA TO THE JURY

Hamilton pauses a moment. He looks at the jury; then at the audience; and then at Zenger, like a great actor sensing the mood of his public. Now he turns to the judges and bows courteously.

"I thank you," he replies without a trace of rancor. Then, turning his back upon the judges as though they no longer were to be considered, he acknowledges the jury with a courtly flourish. He speaks to the jurymen directly, in a voice loud enough to carry to all parts of the room.

"Then it is to you, Gentlemen, we must now appeal for Witnesses to the Truth of the Facts we have offered, and are denied the Liberty to prove. . . ."

Now Hamilton is talking as though the judges were not even in the room. He exhorts the jury to act like freemen, and to follow their own consciences, without fear of official reprisals, as guaranteed under the English system of law. He ends:

". . . old and weak as I am, I should think it my Duty if required, to go to the utmost Part of the Land, where my Service could be of any Use in assisting to quench the Flame of Prosecutions upon Informations, set on Foot by the Government, to deprive a People of the Right of Remonstrating (and complaining too), of the arbitrary Attempts of Men in Power. *Men who injure and oppress the People under their Administration provoke them to cry out and complain; and then make that very Complaint the Foundation for new Oppressions and Prosecutions.*

". . . But to conclude; the Question before the Court and you Gentlemen of the Jury, is not of small nor private Concern. It is not the Cause of the poor Printer, nor of *New York* alone, which you are now trying; No! It may in its Consequence, affect every Freeman that lives under a British Government on the main of *America.* It is the best Cause. It is the Cause of Liberty; and I make no Doubt but your upright Conduct, this Day, will not only entitle you to the Love and Esteem of your Fellow-Citizens; but every Man who prefers Freedom to a Life of slavery will bless and honour You, as Men who have baffled the Attempt of Tyranny; and by an impartial and uncorrupt Verdict, have laid a Noble Foundation for securing to ourselves, our Posterity and our Neighbors, That, to which Nature and the Laws of our Country have given us a Right,—the Liberty—both of exposing and opposing arbitrary Power (in these Parts of the World, at least) by speaking and writing—Truth."

On that note, Hamilton won his case. The jury returned a verdict of "not guilty" and Zenger was freed. He has now become a hero of American journalism, and on the two-hundredth anniversary of the trial considerable attention was again given to the case by newspapers, radio, and movies. Less known, but equally as heroic, was Andrew Hamilton, who argued the cause of Liberty so ably.

THE ZENGER TRIAL ANALYZED

But there are some negative aspects of the case. The verdict had no effect on libel law for more than half a century. Pennsylvania was the first state to recognize the principles of truth as a defense and the right of the jury to decide both the law and the fact, by including them in its 1790 constitution. New York accepted them in 1805. It was 1792 in England before Fox's Libel Act gave the jury power of decision, and it was 1843 before Lord Campbell's Act recognized truth as a defense.

It is very possible that expediency, rather than principle, guided the authorities after trial. They admitted no new legal precedent in the Zenger case. It is quite probable that Zenger would have been rearrested for his very next offense, except for circumstances. Governor Cosby was cautious for a time after the trial ended, because Justice Morris was in England arguing for Cosby's dismissal, and the governor had no wish to achieve any further notoriety for himself. Then he fell desperately ill during the winter of 1735–36 and died the following March. Had he lived, he might not have accepted defeat so easily.

Again, all the reports of the trial are one-sided. The only complete account of the trial is in Zenger's own newspaper. The Crown never did issue a report, giving its side of the verdict. Since the accused had good reason to paint the picture in black and white, the Crown arguments and principles have been largely ignored. O'Callaghan's *Documents Relative to the Colonial History of New York* (Albany, 1849, V) include statements of Governor Cosby to the Lords of Trade, and they are the nearest thing to a presentation of the other side of the argument. But the "internal evidence" (facts that appear from close reading) indicate that the British view has never been fairly presented.

For example, Justice Delancey, who has always been portrayed as an arrogant judge, showed great restraint in refusing to set aside the verdict and in not overruling Hamilton. He might even have had the old lawyer arrested for his contempt of the bench. The British government in this case, as in many others, including the Stamp Act of 1765, did not use its powers to curb opinion, but backed down in the face of overwhemling public dissatisfaction.

This is an important point. The courts as much as the press guard the freedom so jealously maintained by a democratic people. To flout the law for the sake of expedience in a press case is dangerous precedent. Hamilton said the jury had the right to determine both the law and the fact, and that is what readers of the Zenger episode assume to be true. But the courts did not recognize that principle, either before the trial, or for more than 50 years thereafter. The jury in the Zenger case had only to determine the fact—that is, whether or not Zenger had printed the articles on exhibit. They knew, as everyone knew, that the editor was responsible for the offending stories. To turn in a verdict of "not guilty," therefore, was a direct contradiction of the evidence. It may have been a good verdict for the accused and for American press freedom, but when defendants are acquitted because of political feelings, rather than a calm appraisal of the known facts, that is a threat to a system every bit as important to our freedom as the liberty of the press. Admittedly, court procedure changes with the times, and the Zenger trial coincided with one of these transition periods. But at least two reputable colonial lawyers of the day agreed that the Zenger verdict was a perilous one for the overall cause of justice.[8]

Justice Delancey appears to be somewhat ridiculous today in his opinion that truth could not be offered as a defense in this type of libel action. The fact is, he had considerable precedent to back him up. For the principle recognized by the courts of that day was "the greater the truth, the greater the libel." The logic behind this doctrine was this: Public accusations, or criticisms of those in authority, might upset the entire community and cause a serious breach of the public peace. In Zenger's case, popular opinion was behind him, but this did not sway colonial writers on the subject of seditious libel. Almost all of them remained agreed that government could be libeled and that to do so was properly to be considered a crime. And many responsible citizens agreed with them. The threat of punishment—under the common law of seditious libel or under the power of a legislature to punish for contempt—for those who criticised officials remained strong until the close of the eighteenth century when the struggle over the Sedition Act of 1798 brought the issue to a climax.[9]

These negative aspects of the case are counteracted by the inspirational

[8] Warren C. Price (see p. 59 fn.) cites these reports from Howell's *State Trials,* published in 1783. The right of the jury to determine both the law and the fact had been exercised in England at least as early as 1649 in the trial of John Lilburne, one of Cromwell's soldiers. See *Notes and Queries,* Vol. 1, second series (London: Bell and Baldy, 1856), p. 355.

[9] Leonard W. Levy, *Legacy of Suppression* (Cambridge: Harvard University Press, 1960), develops this thesis of colonial adherence to the concept of seditious libel except as it could be turned against one's own faction. Levy traces this attitude as prevailing as late as the 1790s.

contributions of Zenger and Hamilton and the psychological effects of the trial. For the trial did enunciate a principle—even if it did not establish legal precedent—and this principle is vital to our libertarian philosophy of today in matters of free speech and press. The right to criticise officials is one of the main pillars of press freedom.[10] Psychologically, the Zenger trial advanced this goal, for no other colonial court trial of a printer for seditious libel after 1735 has come to light. Some were found to be in contempt by their own colonial legislatures or governor's councils, but none was tried by the Crown.[11] Popular opinion had proved its power. The Zenger case thus merits its place in history, as a forerunner of what was to follow.

Annotated Bibliography

Books

Adams, James Truslow, *Provincial Society, 1690–1763,* A History of American Life, Vol. III. New York: Macmillan, 1927. This series was the first large-scale attempt at social history and remains highly usable. Other volumes will be cited later. The series was edited by Arthur M. Schlesinger and Dixon Ryan Fox.

Alexander, James, *A Brief Narrative of the Case and Trial of John Peter Zenger, Printer of the New York "Weekly Journal,"* edited by Stanley N. Katz. Cambridge, Mass.: Harvard University Press, 1963. Scholarly reprint with annotations of document by Zenger's lawyer.

Bridenbaugh, Carl, *Cities in the Wilderness: the First Century of Urban Life in America, 1625–1742* and *Cities in Revolt: Urban Life in America, 1743–1776.* New York: Knopf, 1955. Cities studied are Boston, Newport, New York, Philadelphia, and Charleston.

Buranelli, Vincent, ed., *The Trial of Peter Zenger.* New York: New York University Press, 1957. Reprint of the text of the trial, with biographical information about participants and an analysis of its meaning.

Duniway, Clyde A., *The Development of Freedom of the Press in Massachusetts.* New York: Longmans, Green & Company, 1906. An early and scholarly study of colonial press freedom.

Levy, Leonard W., ed., *Freedom of the Press from Zenger to Hamilton.* Indianapolis: Bobbs-Merrill, 1966. A collection of documents tracing theories of freedom of the press from Zenger trial to Jeffersonian period and rise of libertarianism.

———, *Legacy of Suppression.* Cambridge, Mass.: Harvard University Press, 1960. A prize-winning study of the English and colonial roots of freedom of expression,

[10] The others: (1) The right to publish without official license, established in America by James Franklin; (2) The right to report matters of public interest, a right not widely recognized until well into the nineteenth century, and still contested by reluctant public officials.

[11] Harold L. Nelson, "Seditious Libel in Colonial America," *American Journal of Legal History, III* (April 1959), 160–72. Professor Nelson finds the colonial assembly more effective than the courts in disciplining printers, and cites available evidence that Zenger's trial was the last.

which documents a thesis that only a narrow concept of such freedom was held before 1800.

Mott, Frank L., ed., *The Case and Tryal of John Peter Zenger.* Columbia, Mo.: Press of the Crippled Turtle, 1954. An exact reprint of Zenger's original pamphlet on his trial.

Osgood, Herbert L., *The American Colonies in the Eighteenth Century,* Vol. II. New York: Columbia University Press, 1924. Pages 443–82 give the political background for the Zenger trial, examining the Cosby administration.

Ould, Harmon, ed., *Freedom of Expression.* London: Hutchinson International Authors, Ltd., 1945. A memoriam on the tercentenary of Milton's *Areopagitica.* Contributors are important British and foreign thinkers, writers, journalists, and lawyers. A very interesting discussion of press freedom from early days to the present.

Presbrey, Frank, *The History and Development of Advertising.* Garden City: Doubleday, 1929. The best known and most complete history of advertising. Especially useful because of its numerous illustrations.

Rutherfurd, Livingston, *John Peter Zenger.* New York: Peter Smith, 1941. Reprints the text of the trial, with a biographical study of Zenger and an analysis of the political setting. The above edition is a reprint from a 1904 edition published by Dodd, Mead and Company.

Schuyler, Livingston R., *The Liberty of the Press in the American Colonies Before the Revolutionary War.* New York: Thomas Whittaker, 1905. A short history of an important period in press development.

Wood, James Playsted, *The Story of Advertising.* New York: Ronald Press, 1958. Less extensive but more readable than Presbrey. Relatively brief in its coverage of the period before 1850.

Periodicals and Monographs

"Freedom of the Press Vindicated," *Harper's New Monthly Magazine,* LVII (July 1878), 296. A colorful and fascinating description of the Zenger trial, set forth with a realism lacking in most of the reports of that event.

Kobre, Sidney, "The Revolutionary Colonial Press—A Social Interpretation," *Journalism Quarterly,* XX (September 1943), 193. A digest of a more detailed study by the same author. Especially useful for its background information.

Nelson, Harold L., "Seditious Libel in Colonial America," *American Journal of Legal History,* III (April 1959), 160. Establishes thesis that after the Zenger trial, printers were disciplined by legislatures or governor's councils, rather than by trial courts. The colonial assembly became the major force in limiting press freedom.

Price, Warren C., "Reflections on the Trial of John Peter Zenger," *Journalism Quarterly,* XXXII (Spring 1955), 161. Deals with the negative aspects of Hamilton's appeal insofar as legal status was concerned, and examines Cosby's land-grabbing operations.

Steiner, Bernard C., "Andrew Hamilton and John Peter Zenger," *Pennsylvania Magazine,* XX (Summer 1896), 405. Since Hamilton is as much a hero of this period as is Zenger, this description of the lawyer's place in history is very useful.

Pennsylvania Magazine of History and Biography

JOHN DICKINSON, the Colonial Whig

Magazine of American History

JAMES RIVINGTON, leading Tory editor

Bettmann Archive

SAMUEL ADAMS, propagandist of the Revolution

C. K. Shipton and American Antiquarian Society

ISAIAH THOMAS, Patriot editor

5

The Seeds of Revolution

The United Voice of all His Majesty's free and loyal *Subjects in America— Liberty and Property, and no Stamps.*
—Motto of various colonial newspapers

Many believe today that the American Revolution was strictly a struggle by freedom-loving people for independence from a tyrannical British king. Actually, the reasons for the revolution were much more complex. The clash of debtor and creditor was a factor. The weakness of British policy, inept leadership, and overemphasis of the mercantile system (by which Europeans exploited colonies) were all involved in the dispute. Colonists resented restraints on American development of commerce and industry. They complained that their frontier was being denied to them after the hard-won victory over the French, which they had expected to open up vast new areas to expansion. Refusal of the British to grant home rule was another point of dispute.

But these are not sufficient *reasons* for the war. All the above disputes might have been settled peaceably, some historians say. Other British colonies had similar grievances at the time, yet they did not have to resort to war. Nor can it be held that the issue was confined to Britain and her colonies. In other parts of the world the same issues were being raised. France and South America were soon to be embroiled in revolution, indicating that the War for Independence was a regional manifestation of world unrest.

Many students of the period maintain that the war was unnecessary. The American shipper might quarrel over British denial of certain markets, but he knew that the British navy made it possible for him to sail the high seas with reasonable safety from seizure. Certainly the little Atlantic seaboard communities in America could not have provided such essential protection—

not by themselves, at least. Merchants resented the trade restrictions, but they knew full well that they also enjoyed great benefits through monopolies and bounties that only a great trading nation, such as Great Britain, could make possible. Frontiersmen might curse such measures as the Quebec Act, which limited westward expansion, but the same complainants were aware that the motherland provided the roads by which the frontier was developed and tamed. They knew, also, that British troops garrisoning forts up and down the colonies were the main bulwarks against Indian retaliation.

CAUSES OF THE REVOLUTION

How, then, did the American colonies find themselves at war with the homeland in 1775? Perhaps it can be explained that the war was as much a class struggle—a domestic rebellion, even—as it was a struggle for political separation. The fight for freedom was both internal and external, if we see it as a class conflict. This class struggle was directed by an able and articulate group of "agitators"—one of the best proofs, indeed, of the nature of the conflict. It is even possible that there might have been no shooting war, had it not been for these class leaders. Sam Adams was a typical leader of this movement. He was a spokesman for a class insisting upon a greater share of control. Having aroused his public, he proceeded to win his goals. For that reason, it is pertinent to study this period in terms of public opinion, and through the eyes of those who manipulated public support leading to war.

It is significant that the Stamp Act of 1765 alienated two very influential groups—the lawyers and the journalists. The new law placed a heavy duty on paper used in publishing newspapers. There was also a heavy tax on all legal documents. Thus, the lawyer, who swayed people by the spoken word, and the journalist, who had an even wider influence through the written word, were both turned against those who favored the unpopular act.

Yet one can scarcely blame the British for proposing some such law. After the Seven Years' War, which saw the British triumphant over the French in North America and India, Great Britain emerged as a great empire—one of the greatest of all time. On the other hand, victory found the British nearly bankrupt. Some way had to be found to pay the cost of defending the wide frontiers. Since the Americans had gained so much from the victory over the French, they should be willing to pay a small share of the defense costs, the statesmen in London insisted.

The colonists were indeed willing to offer help—in their own fashions. Colonial legislatures were ready to raise levies, but they did not raise enough, and they did not exert themselves enough to turn over such funds when needed. Since the legislatures controlled the colonial purse strings, not much could be done when levies were in arrears. Empire leaders believed the solution was the imposition of special taxes that could be collected more effectively for this purpose. The Stamp Act was one such attempt. The British themselves paid such a tax. George Grenville, sponsor of the hated measure, pointed out that even Massachusetts had imposed a similar tax in 1755. A little later New York did the same.

The colonists replied that the local stamp acts were imposed by the people paying the tax. As Sam Adams brought out in his resolutions of 1765, the colonies had no direct representation in Parliament. He recognized that this would be impracticable, considering the distance apart of the two areas. That was why he insisted that the colonies be given home rule under a common king.[1] But that was no solution to the immediate problem.

The opposition of the editors took many forms. Some suspended publication. Some publications appeared without title or masthead, which technically took them out of the newspaper classification. A few appeared without the required stamp, but with the notice that none could be procured, which may have been true, since mobs prevented the sale of stamps in every colony. Several publications satirized the event. On the day before the tax was to be enforced, the *Pennsylvania Journal and Weekly Advertiser* appeared with heavy black column margins, or "turned rules," the traditional symbol of journalistic mourning, but this time in the shape of a tombstone.

The Stamp Act agitation was actually only an episode in a long conflict between Great Britain and her colonies. The British were leading exponents of the "mercantile system." Under this program, colonies were to be developed for raw materials, and again as markets for finished products. Essential to the system was a favorable balance of trade for Great Britain, meaning that the value of exports must exceed that of imports. This policy was fostered by whatever party gained control. That was why the British Government had imposed restrictions on trade, industry, and finances in the colonies beginning in 1651. Scarcity of money in the colonies became a serious matter, for example, but the refusal of British creditors to ease the debt burden embittered many a colonial.[2] An Act of 1751, specifically, denied the printing of paper money secured by land, which would have made money less dear. Sam Adams, often called "The Father of the Revolution," never forgot that his father had been ruined by these restrictive laws, and that he had been cheated of his patrimony thereby.

The colonists did not make violent objection, however, until after the victory over the French. Smuggling went on openly, engaged in by respected citizens as a legitimate way around measures believed to be unsound by local consensus. But after 1763, the British began to enforce old laws and to impose new ones. A royal proclamation closed all the frontier west of the mountains to settlement and expansion, thereby raising land values in the older areas.

[1] "Resolutions of the House of Representatives of Massachusetts, October 29, 1765," in Harry R. Warfel, Ralph H. Gabriel, and Stanley Williams, eds., *The American Mind* (New York: American Book, 1937), p. 138.

[2] Curtis P. Nettels, "The Money Supply of the American Colonies Before 1720," *University of Wisconsin Studies* No. 20 (1934), pp. 279–83.

Thursday, October 31, 1765. THE NUMB. 1195.

PENNSYLVANIA JOURNAL; AND WEEKLY ADVERTISER.

EXPIRING: In Hopes of a Resurrection to LIFE again.

I AM sorry to be obliged to acquaint my Readers, that as The STAMP-ACT, is fear'd to be obligatory upon us after the *First of November* ensuing, (the *fatal To-morrow*) the Publisher of this Paper unable to bear the Burthen, has thought it expedient to STOP awhile, in order to deliberate, whether any Methods can be found to elude the Chains forged for us, and escape the insupportable Slavery; which it is hoped, from the just Representations now made against that Act, may be effected. Mean while, I must earnestly Request every Individual of my Subscribers, many of whom have been long behind Hand, that they would immediately Discharge their respective Arrears, that I may be able, not only to support myself during the Interval, but be better prepared to proceed again with this Paper, whenever an opening for that Purpose appears, which I hope will be soon. WILLIAM BRADFORD.

Remember, O my friends! the Laws, the Rights,
The generous plan of power deliver'd down,
From age to age, by your renown'd forefathers,
O let it never perish in your hands!
But piously transmit it to your children.
Do thou, great Liberty, inspire our souls,
And make our lives in thy possession happy;
Or our deaths glorious in thy defence. ADDISON's Cato.

LIBERTY is one of the greatest Blessings, which human beings can possibly enjoy: When we are deprived of this earthly happiness, we are fettered with the Chains of inimical servitude. Nations, who are born for the mutual support of each other, should preserve a steady attachment to the welfare and happiness of that nation with whom they are united, that their mutual alliance of friendship might be sincere and permanent. When this union is separated by the illegal encroachments on that Liberty, which is the Soul of Commerce, and the support of Life, it degenerates into implacable Enmity, which in time grows inveterate, and finally recoils upon those who have been the means of its unhappy dissolution. *The Liberty of the Press* has very justly been esteemed one of the main Pillars of the Liberty of the People. While this is maintained, the first Steps to Oppression are detected, and the Attention of the People seasonably awakened. When this is suppressed, the Suspicion of the People, and their Ruin may admit of so sudden a transition, as renders the Success of the first unpracticable, and the Miseries attending the latter unavoidable. So dangerous is this to lawless Power, that the farthest approaches to it are resolutely opposed, or rigorously punished. So essential is this to Freedom, Property, and Happiness, that the most plausible Attempts to curtail it even in the smallest Degree, have always been most strenuously opposed by the virtuous, free, and unbiassed Patriot. It is the Priviledge of Britons to speak Truth with impunity, and even to fear no Danger from speculative Error whether in Religion or Politicks. The want of attending to this has produced needless Enquiries, and unjustifiable Censures of what is true in Fact or no more than false in Speculation.---But how unhappily is it to be debarr'd from this last Relief in a dangerous and sickly State! How melancholly to pine and die while no kind Physician is allowed to explore the Cause, or prescribe the Cure of our manifold Disorders? The love of Ease, and absence of Pain in some Distempers, is a fatal symptom of the desperate Circumstances of the Patient. And in all political Disorders the more contented we are under them, so much the worse are they, and so much the worse are we for them. It is a very happy Circumstance attending public Virtue and public Spirit, that the more it is vilified, the more illustrious it always appears. No Falshood formed against it can prosper, for it at once detects and confutes the darkest and most inveterate Calumny. But although public Virtue cannot be affected by the Indulgence of the most unlimited Freedom of speaking or writing, yet Oppression and Tyranny as it derives all its Influence from its Secrecy, may be extremely benefited by the Reverse. For this reason, in Countries subjected to the insatiable Demands of Power and Avarice, the first Attempts to inspire People with a just Sense of their Condition, are commonly nipt in the Bud. It is of the last Importance to the Views of designing Men to shut up the most successful and universal Channel of Information from the People, when they are forming such Schemes as need only to be known in order to be Opposed. Besides the Deprivation of our whole Liberty may be justified on the same Principles as the Deprivation of any individual Part, such as the Liberty of the Press undoubtedly is.

How amiable is the Enjoyment of Liberty! But how detestable are the Bonds of Servitude! 'Tis therefore sincerly to be hoped, that the old *New-England* Spirit so exemplarily free in former Times, will never condescend to Submission to new and unwarrantable Restrictions.

A Day, an Hour of virtuous Liberty,
Is worth a whole Eternity in Bondage.

May we all as loyal Subjects, and free born Britons exert our utmost to preserve the Rights and Liberties of our Country, in a Manner that shall add Honour to our Endeavours; that future Posterity may reap the Benefit, and bless the Hands which were the Instruments of procuring it.---

That Glory then, the brightest Crown of Praise,
Which every Lover of his Country's Wealth,
And every Patron of Mankind deserves,
Will gracefully adorn such Patriot's Deeds,
And leave behind an Honour that will last
With Praise immortal to the End of Time.

Thursday last arrived here the ship Philadelphia Packet, Capt. Budden, from London, by whom we have the following advices.

ROME, *July 24.*

THE harvest in this country hath not proved so good as we hoped. This event hath engaged the congregation established for inspecting into the supplies of provisions for this capital, to seek all possible means to prevent a fresh scarcity.

St James's, August 17. The king has been pleased to appoint the most honourable the Marquis of Rockingham to be lord lieutenant of the west-ridings of the county of York, and of the city of York, and county of the same city; and also Custos Rotulorum of the north and west ridings in the said county of York and of the city of York, and county of the same city; and Ainsty, otherwise Aynstry, of York.

The king has been pleased to appoint the right hon. William Earl of Dartmouth, Soam Jenyns, Edward Eliot, John York, George Rice, John Roberts, Jeremiah Dyson, and William Fitzherbert, Esqrs; to be commissioners of trade, and for inspecting and improving his majesty's plantations in America, and elsewhere.

The king has been pleased to grant unto the right hon. Richard Viscount How, the office of treasurer of his Majesty's navy.

St James's, August 27. By the last letters from Col Desmaretz, his majesty's commissary at Dunkirk, we are assured, that orders were given by the French ministry, for immediately setting about the demolition of the Jettees, which are the support of the harbour of Dunkirk.

Warsaw, August 1. The tribunal of Great Poland held at Polnania, has granted permission to the Lutherans at Lobsentz to open their church, which has been shut near twenty years, to provide a minister, and to perform divine service in public.

Corunna, July 27. The detachment of one hundred men drafted for Louisiana, are on the march for Ferrol, where they are to embark on board the Unicorn frigate with a governor, two capuchin friars, a commissionary at war, and some civil officers.

Cadiz, July 23. Letters brought by the last post from Gibralter say, the report before spread, that the Algerines have killed their Dey, and declared war against all the European powers except England and France, proves not true.

LONDON.

August 17. On Thursday at the king's arms tavern in Cornhill, an elegant entertainment was given by the committee of North-American merchants to Richard Glover, and Charles Garth, Esqrs; when those gentlemen received the thanks of that body, for their endeavours to prevent the soldiery from being billeted upon the private houses of their fellow-subjects in America.

Part of a letter from an officer in the East-India service, dated from the Arictur camp, January 8, 1765.

"In my last I acquainted you that we did at last reduce Madure. The army has since conquered the Arictur country for the Nabob, of 100,000l. revenue a year. We are now under orders to attack another chief, or polygor contiguous to this country; both chiefs have mutually maintained an independency of the Nabob till now; meerly on account of the impenetrable woods they are possessed of. You certainly have heard before of the memorable battle Major Munro gained at Bengal over Suja Dowla, one of the most formidable powers of India: The consequence of this battle gives the company the command of trade in the greatest part of the Mogul's dominions; and, without exaggeration, the East-India company at present may be brought in comparison with Alexander the Great, whose command, from the river Indus to the river Ganges, was not so much respected as their's."

It is said the new m----y, taking into consideration the present deplorable situation of the Canadians, have determined to take up all the Canada bills at par, with interest to the present time; and afterwards to demand, in the most spirited terms, *immediate* and *full* payment of France, under pain of all the consequences that can result from a refusal.

The new lords of trade and plantations will hold a board on Monday next, for the first time, at the Cockpit Whitehall.

We hear the rent rolls of the several proprietary estates in America, obtained by former grants under the crown are ordered to be made out, as also an estimate of the annual produce of their land tax, in order to introduce a more equitable form of levying his majesty's revenues in that part of the world.

They write from Gibralter, that English officers and seamen are engaging both there and at Minorca by foreign agents, to serve on board his Sardinian majesty's ships of war in the Mediterranean.

August 20. The right honourable the Earl Cornwallis, lieutenant colonel to the 24 regiment of foot, is appointed one of his majesty's aids de camp, with the rank of colonel of foot in the army.

We are informed, that a gentleman lately very popular in this country, is soon to reside at Lousanne, in Switzerland, where he intends publishing his friend Mr. Churchill's poems, with explanatory notes; and we are likewise informed, that he has an intention of publishing, at the same place, a history of England wrote by himself.

By a vessel arrived at Guernsey from Belleisle there is advice, that the French are erecting several batteries at Sandy Bay, on the south east of the island, and in the great road where the descent was made in the late war by the seamen and troops under Admiral Keppel and General Hodgson.

Aug. 23. We hear lord Viscount Spencer is shortly to be created an earl.

All thoughts of any farther changes are said to be entirely laid aside.

It is reported, that a person of high rank, on being lately offered a great employment, refused it, saying, "that he could not possibly accept of it, consistently with the love he bore to the British nation, which would ever be the object of his care and attention."

Monday some dispatches said to be of importance, were received here from Holland, but the subject has not yet transpired.

Private letters from Paris mention that the true realm

An Emblem of the Effects of the STAMP.

O! the fatal STAMP.

Adieu, Adieu to the LIBERTY of the PRESS.

Facsimile of the famed "Tombstone Edition" protesting the 1765 Stamp Act.

Smuggling was reduced by an effective amendment to an old law of 1733. Currency restrictions were tightened. Commodities never before taxed were now enumerated. And just to rub it in, the home government asserted the right of Parliament to make all laws for the colonies.

The reaction to the trend is seen in the colonial attempts to present their grievances peaceably at first, and then by more direct action when this policy failed. The Stamp Act Congress, which succeeded in bringing about the repeal of the hated law, showed the colonies what could be accomplished by united, decisive action. Granted all this—one must still conclude that economics were only a factor in the coming revolution. For ideas were stirring men, too. Indeed, it can be said that the revolution was completed by 1775, if ideas are the criteria, in which case the war was only the means of defending them against those who could not subscribe to the new thought.

Here is where the press of the time played such an important part. In newspaper and pamphlet (often reprints of weekly journals) appeared the literature of this revolution. Here it was that the passions and arguments of the revolutionaries found expression. As Beard has said:

> . . . Unlike France of the Old Regime, provincial America did not produce, long before the struggle commenced, great treatises such as the *Encyclopedia* or the ringing calls for revolt such as Rousseau's *Social Contract*.
>
> The reasons were not difficult to find: the colonists already had textbooks of revolution in the writings of Englishmen who defended and justified the proceedings of the seventeenth century—above all, John Locke's writings, wherein was set forth the right of citizens to overthrow governments that took their money or their property without their consent. . . . All that editors and publicists had to do was to paraphrase, decorate, and repeat. . . .[3]

The conflicting ideas as the revolution progressed can be followed conveniently by studying the products of three journalists who represented their respective classes or groups. They were James Rivington, the Tory spokesman, John Dickinson, "the penman of the revolution," representing the Whig philosophy, and Samuel Adams, evangelist of democracy and leader of the "agitators" or Radicals.

JAMES RIVINGTON, THE TORY SPOKESMAN

We are likely to think of the American Tory as something of a traitor because of his refusal to bear arms against his king in the War for Independence. Actually, it was the Tory who remained loyal to his country when others

[3] Charles A. and Mary R. Beard, *The Rise of American Civilization*, Vol. I (New York: Macmillan, 1930), p. 187.

rebelled. Only defeat in war made the Tory a traitor. Readers of Kenneth Roberts' historical novel, *Oliver Wiswell,* can understand that there were many sincere and honest Americans who believed in the Tory cause in the middle of the eighteenth century.

The goal of the Tory, apparently, was to retain the basic structure of colonial society. He wished to continue governing by right of property, heredity, position, and tradition—which would appear to be the attributes of a nobility. This seems a strange and distasteful desideratum, by democratic standards, but it had its persuasive proponents. Such a one was Rivington.

"Jemmy" Rivington came to the colonies in 1762, after he had lost his fortune at the race track—not the last newspaperman to suffer in this way, it might be added. Despite this preoccupation with the king of sports, Rivington was a credit to journalism and to his class. One can hardly blame him for his Tory views. For generations his family had been official publishers of religious books for the Church of England—the Established Church, and therefore the one that had the most general appeal to most good Tories. King and Bishop represented authority, by which order could be maintained most effectively, the Tory argued. Thus, an attack on the authority of the state was also a threat to the authority of the church, men like Rivington insisted, and history of revolution has shown that this is indeed the usual consequence. It was the duty of all citizens, therefore, to help the forces of law and order against anarchistic elements.

Rivington was influential in America, and could do much for the Tory cause. He was proprietor of the first chain of book stores in America, with branches in Boston, New York, and Philadelphia. He had been so successful in this venture that he decided to publish a newspaper. In 1773, on the eve of the revolt in the colonies, he founded *Rivington's New York Gazetteer or the Connecticut, New Jersey, Hudson's River and Quebec Weekly Advertiser,* a local paper, despite its impressive, regional title. The paper was well edited and skillfully printed. It was also very profitable, as shown by the fact that it averaged about 55 per cent advertising.

Rivington merited respect for his venture because he was willing to discuss both sides of political questions—an objectivity that was not the standard in his era. Such objectivity was just what the "patriot" rivals resented, however. They were not interested in fair and accurate reports. That was no way to fight for a cause, they believed, and so we find Rivington complaining in his issue of April 20, 1775:

> The Printer is bold to affirm that his press has been open to publication from ALL PARTIES. . . . He has considered his press in the light of a public office, to which every man has a right to have recourse. But the moment he ventured to publish sentiments which were opposed to the dangerous views and designs of certain demagogues, he found himself held up as an enemy of his country.

Rivington's complaint was a common one for Tories in the decade preceding outbreak of war. Power was slipping away from the English authorities, into the hands of the colonial assemblies. In their eyes, criticism of the Crown was no longer seditious libel. But criticism of the assemblies, or of the "patriot" cause, might well be seditious or contemptuous. Freedom of expression meant largely freedom for your side—and the Tory was on the losing side.

The troubles of the Tory printers came largely from public pressures generated by such Radical "agitators" as Sam Adams rather than from official actions. An organized campaign of threats and economic coercion was reinforced at times by mob action against printers who were not all-out for the Radical cause. The Tories, or Loyalists, were nearly all hounded out of business; those who tried to be neutral were either forced into the Radical camp or into suspension.[4]

In Boston, for example, the well-organized Radical group used threats to persuade some reluctant printers to use their propaganda, and to mute Tory voices. When John Mein's stoutly Tory *Chronicle* refused to cower, but instead attacked the Radical leaders, Mein was hanged in effigy, attacked on the street, and finally mobbed. He had to flee to England and his paper was suspended in 1770. Thomas Fleet's *Evening Post,* which tried to print both sides of the argument, closed down in 1775, as did the Tory *Post-Boy.* The last Tory voice, the *News-Letter,* died early in 1776. In Philadelphia, William Goddard was roughed up for publishing pro-Crown materials in his *Pennsylvania Chronicle.* Rivington thus could complain about the experiences of others, as well as his own, in opposing the Radical-generated tide of public opinion.

After Lexington and Concord Rivington ceased to be objective. During the war he was as partisan as his "patriot" rivals. His wartime paper, renamed the *Royal Gazette,* reeked with unfounded charges against American leaders. He appeared to relish vicious rumors that might harm the rebels—but this was in time of war, whose first casualty is objectivity. And he had little reason to feel charitable toward his political and social enemies. He had been burned in effigy by mobs for expressing his views. Twice his shop had been raided—the type destroyed on one occasion. He had been forced to sign a humiliating public apology for merely voicing his opinions. He had even been driven back to England for a while. Even so, it should be pointed out that Rivington's most malicious writings were produced while the British general, Lord Howe, was breathing down the editor's neck. For the general had hoped that a bloody war might be averted if the colonists could be turned from the error of their ways. Rivington suited his purposes as an instrument for persuasion.

Tories such as Rivington stood for government "by the better sort." There are always those who, perhaps unconsciously, believe in this philosophy. They

[4] See Arthur M. Schlesinger, *Prelude to Independence: The Newspaper War on Britain, 1764–1776* (New York: Knopf, 1958), for the story of the use of the press by the Radical propagandists.

see their communities largely populated by illiterate and inexperienced citizens. The alternatives are either to place government in abler hands, or to let such citizens choose their own leaders. In many times and places the choice has been made in favor of the former. To allow the ignorant a voice in government is to bring charlatans in as officials. Rivington understood this. Such a system was the worst type of tyranny, he believed. It was much more dangerous than Tory control at its very worst. At least the Tory could argue that he had education, leisure for the study of government, long experience as an administrator, a sense of responsibility as a governor which would tend to keep the mob from wishing to revolt, and the *noblesse oblige* that comes from generations of duty to one's position.

JOHN DICKINSON, THE WHIG PHILOSOPHER

Spokesmen for other groups disputed these views—some mildly, and some violently. The American Tory was opposed by a rising capitalist faction—it could not as yet be called a party—often referred to as the Colonial Whigs. An articulate Whig was John Dickinson of Pennsylvania, sometimes called "The Penman of the Revolution."

Although not a publisher or printer, Dickinson deserves to be ranked with the great journalists of the period. By newspaper and pamphlet he spread the gospel of his political faith. The gist of his philosophy appeared in a series of articles entitled "Letters From a Farmer In Pennsylvania." The first such letter was printed in the *Pennsylvania Chronicle* in 1767. Eleven others followed on into 1768. They were widely reprinted up and down the seaboard. The letters not only discussed American foreign policy; they actually *were* the policy of the colonials at the time. Dickinson had no wish to bring on a war of independence, but he, more than any other writer except Sam Adams, prepared public opinion for the Revolution.

The subject matter of his writings makes him appear to be dangerously radical in his views. We recall that he was the author of the *Declaration of Rights of the Stamp Act Congress;* that he wrote the two *Petitions to the King;* and that he was coauthor of the Articles of Confederation. Actually, Dickinson was not at all the firebrand intimated above. He was as conservative as the class he represented, this mild Quaker, who had married a wealthy girl, and who recognized property as the basis of sound government.

Dickinson was as contemptuous of rabble-rousers as were Rivington and the rest of the Tories. For the Whig had rather narrow ideas of liberty. The great battle cry of the Whig, for example, was "no taxation without representation," which is strictly an economic aspect of the struggle. The Whig had no great interest in the rise of the common man. He had only the vaguest of ideas regarding the "natural rights" philosophy of social reform, for he thought more in terms of property, rather than in terms of human rights. Yet he, too, was fighting for a principle, and in the conflict he brought liberties to others less able to fight on fair terms. The curious twist to all this was that the worst enemy of the American Whig was his counterpart in England. The British Whig imposed commercial restrictions that were considered harmful to American business interests. The American argued that if British businessmen in control of the government both at home and abroad could impose taxes arbitrarily without colonial representation, then American business rivals could be driven into oblivion.

But note that the American Whig is always the conciliationist. Says "Farmer" Dickinson in one of his letters:

> . . . The cause of liberty is a "cause of too much dignity, to be sullied by turbulence and tumults." It ought to be maintained in a manner suitable to her nature. Those who engage in it, should breathe a sedate yet fervent spirit, animating them to actions of prudence, justice, modesty, bravery, humanity and magnanimity.[5]

And again:

> . . . I hope, my dear countrymen, that you will in every colony be upon your guard against those who may at any time endeavor to stir you up, under pretenses of patriotism, to any measures disrespectful to our sovereign and our mother country. . . .
> . . . If once *we* are separated from our mother country, what new form of government shall we accept, or shall we find another *Britain* to supply our loss? Torn from the body to which we are united by religion, liberty, laws, affections, relations, language and commerce, we must bleed at every vein. . . .
> The *constitutional* modes of obtaining relief, are those which I would wish to see pursued. . . .

When the Revolution had to be defended by arms, the American Whig had to choose between loyalty to the crown, which provided the law and order he so prized; or loyalty to his local government, which held the promise of the unrestricted enterprise he coveted. The dilemma forced the Whig into becoming either a Loyalist or a Patriot during the shooting war, for there was by that time no place for the compromiser. Dickinson himself had to make this choice. He could not bring himself to stand for outright independence from his beloved motherland, and he refused to sign the Declaration of Independence. But neither could he accept the role of the Loyalist. When the

[5] All the quotations on this page are from Letter Number Three, "Letters From a Farmer In Pennsylvania," in Harry R. Warfel, Ralph H. Gabriel, and Stanley Williams, eds., *The American Mind* (New York: American Book, 1937), pp. 142–44.

Radicals persuaded the colonies to break away from Great Britain, Dickinson would have no part in the public demonstrations. He was roundly abused by his colleagues and had to give up honored positions. True, he carried a musket during the war in defense of his home, but his heart was not in the fighting. We hear very little of him during this unhappy interlude. Afterward, he emerges again, when the Federalist party offers an outlet for his conservative views.

Dickinson was influential because he was respected by the propertied class—a group generally regarded as hardheaded, practical, and unemotional. Once convinced, the businessman could do more than anyone else in swinging his neighbors in favor of a cause. For his neighbors reasoned that if a "sound" businessman believed in proposed changes, there must be good reason for his attitude. Dickinson reached this group by articles geared to their interests. His letters were brilliant, convincing, and readable. They were widely printed. All but three of the newspapers of the period carried the complete series by the "Pennsylvania Farmer." Ideas expressed in these contributions were reflected in the press for weeks, and even for years.

SAMUEL ADAMS, THE RADICAL PROPAGANDIST

The weakest group at the beginning of the struggle, and the most important at the end of the conflict, was the so-called "Radical" or "Patriot"—words not at all synonymous at a later date. The Tory had great interest in hereditary rights; the Whig was preoccupied with economic issues; but the Radical carried on into a very different field. The Radicals were the only ones seriously interested in social change. They might have been overcome, as they had been in England, however, had it not been for the very effective leadership in America. Probably the best example of the Radical leader was Samuel Adams, one of the most prolific journalists of his time.

As a propagandist, Adams was without peer. He understood that to win the inevitable conflict, he and his cohorts must achieve five main objectives. They must justify the course they advocated. They must advertise the advantages of victory. They must arouse the masses—the real shock troops—by instilling hatred of enemies. They must neutralize any logical and reasonable arguments proposed by the opposition. And finally, they must phrase all the issues in black and white, so that the purposes might be clear even to the common laborer. Adams was able to do all this, and his principal tool was the colonial newspaper.

Adams believed that the American colonies were justified in repudiating the mother country because Parliament continued to ignore basic rights. It was the British who broke the contract, he argued, and hence the obligations of the colonials no longer applied. (The theory of the law of contracts was, and still is, that violation by one party releases all other contractors from obligations.) Adams made it appear as though his class and party fought for the traditional rights, now ignored by the British Parliament. Technically, then, it was the British who were in revolt—the colonists were the people maintaining the traditional ways.

Sam Adams was not the only propagandist of the revolution, but he was the greatest of them all. He was truly the "master of the puppets," as his enemies dubbed him. He was perfectly fitted for the role. Adams had turned away from the ministry, from law, and from teaching, although he was familiar with all these professions. As a young Radical, Adams met regularly with the Caucus Club, founded by his father and other aggressive Boston spirits. The club sponsored a newspaper, the *Independent Advertiser,* and in 1748, at the age of 26, Sam Adams became editor of that publication. Later, he was a regular contributor to the *Boston Gazette and Country Journal,* descendant of the second newspaper published in the colonies.

Adams made a strike for liberty in May, 1764, when he was appointed one of a committee of five to instruct his town's representative to the legislature. Included was a denial of Parliament's right to impose Grenville's hated Stamp Act. A final paragraph of the document also suggested a union of all the colonies for the most effective expression of grievances.[6] These instructions were printed by the *Gazette,* and since this paper was closely followed as the mouthpiece of the "patriot" element, the stirring message was broadcast up and down the seaboard.

EDES AND GILL'S *BOSTON GAZETTE*

At once Adams was recognized as leader of a small but vociferous group. Two of this band were Benjamin Edes and John Gill, boyhood friends and now proprietors of the *Gazette.* By the end of 1764 the newspaper was the nerve center of the Boston Radicals. Many famous Americans wrote for the paper, especially after the passage of the obnoxious Townshend Acts of 1767, levying new duties on colonial imports, but none was more effective than Sam Adams.

He was more than a writer, he was an expert news gatherer. His Committees of Correspondence, organized in 1772, kept him alert to every movement and sentiment throughout the colonies. His agents "covered" every important meeting as ably as modern reporters gather information for the press services today. In a remarkably short time all such news reached Adams' local

[6] William V. Wells, *The Life and Public Services of Samuel Adams,* Vol. I (Boston: Little, Brown, 1865), p. 48.

committee, which then processed it for effective dissemination where such information was needed. This primitive news service was highly efficient, yet no one in the colonies had thought of such a device until Adams came along.

He was just as successful at instilling his enthusiasm for the cause into the hearts of useful helpers. Since a man's greatness can be measured by the caliber of his associates, we must assume that Adams was a great man indeed. Cousin John, who later became second president of the United States, sometimes disappointed Sam, as in John's defense of the British soldiers involved in the "Boston Massacre," but on the whole, the two respected each other, as indicated by the fact that Sam used his influence in John's behalf even while the two argued. They were both honest men. John was useful in enlisting the more dignified members of the community, especially the legal fraternity, disdainful of Sam's noisier methods.

Another associate was Josiah Quincy, who understood what some organizers now refer to as "solidarity." Quincy argued that to think justly was not enough; citizens must also think *alike* before there could be a united force of public opinion strong enough to make warriors of the cause invincible. Still another great co-worker was Joseph Warren, the charming and kindly physician, who spoke with great logic for the patriot cause. Warren insisted upon taking direct action when the shooting began. He lost his life as a high-ranking officer in the first pitched battle of the war at Breed's (Bunker) Hill. James Otis was the spellbinder of the group—one of the great orators of his day. The British feared Otis most of all, because of his persuasive powers.

But none of these leaders ever equaled the old master in the art of mass manipulation.

Day after day Adams pressed his foes through newspaper and through pamphlet. He emphasized the need for a realignment of class power. Tory doctrine, which was made to sound so noble by newspaper editors such as Rivington, was only window dressing, said Adams. It could fool only the gullible. He appealed to the self interest of every type of American, shifting his style with his quill. At least 25 pen names have been recognized as in his hand. Late at night passersby looked up at the lighted window of the Adams home, and they knew the veteran revolutionary was still at work, writing a piece for the *Gazette*, perhaps, making it hot for the Tories. His neighbors could not help but be impressed. Many of his loyal followers may not have known just what all the furor was about, but they knew that Adams spoke for them, and they were certain that "whatever the old man wanted" must be all right.

Granted all this, is a public writer justified in smearing men's characters, even for a cause? The question is pertinent right on up to modern times. Adams believed that his technique was essential to victory. For years the laborer and clerk had shown inordinate deference to aristocratic "superiors." This attitude was less marked in America than in England, but the attitude had to be completely changed, if the masses were to make the big push for liberty and popular sovereignty. For if one class were to be treated with special deference, then the words and ideas of these "superior" persons would have weight all out of proportion to merit and numbers. Somehow, Adams had to whittle the aristocrat down to size. Until the common man was raised, and the aristocrat was brought down to a common level, the majority of workers was clearly at a disadvantage. Adams knew how to find the soft spots in the Tory shell. The weakness of the Tory was his arrogance. Adams' weapon was his quill, dipped into the venom of vituperation. His skill in conducting a smear campaign has never been surpassed.

The ways of the idol wrecker may not be pretty. Governor Hutchinson was correct when he called Adams an assassin of reputations. The governor knew whereof he spoke, for the last British administrator was a favorite target for the caustic rebel journalist. In the end, Hutchinson, who traced his ancestry back to the illustrious and independent Anne (first outstanding woman in American public life), was forced to leave his native land for England. No wonder Hutchinson was so bitter. But Adams was playing a desperate game. His smear attacks were one way of helping to bring down the odds.

The "Master of the Puppets" did his work well. No one had more to do with the outcome than Adams. On the morning of April 19, 1775, the "shot heard 'round the world" was fired at the battle of Lexington and Concord. From then on, the country was in arms, fighting for the ultimate victory that Adams had helped to engineer.

Annotated Bibliography

Books

Bailyn, Bernard, *The Ideological Origins of the American Revolution*. Cambridge, Mass.: Harvard University Press, 1967. A structured study, utilizing the Harvard Library pamphlet collection, that exhibits feeling for the radical nature of the Revolution. See also his *Origins of American Politics* (1968).

Becker, Carl L., *The Eve of the Revolution*. New Haven: Yale University Press, 1918. An excellent one-volume summary of this period by an eminent authority.

Beer, George L., *British Colonial Policy*. New York: Macmillan, 1907. Presents the British point of view in a way that may not be familiar to the average college student.

Bowen, Catherine D., *John Adams and the American Revolution*. New York: Little, Brown, 1950. Following the school of historical writing which allows the author to describe the feelings of his subjects, this book nevertheless gives a very real picture of the times.

Davidson, Philip, *Propaganda and the American Revolution*. Chapel Hill: University of North Carolina Press, 1941. Reveals the tremendous impact of pamphlets, broadsides, newspapers, and books in conditioning the public to rebellion.

Gipson, Lawrence H., *The Coming of the Revolution, 1763–1775.* New York: Harper & Row, 1954. Stresses colonial resistance to more efficient English administration. Part of the New American Nation series.

Greene, Evarts B., *The Revolutionary Generation, 1763–1790.* A History of American Life, Vol. IV. New York: Macmillan, 1943. Source for social history.

Miller, John C., *Sam Adams: Pioneer in Propaganda.* Boston: Little, Brown, 1936. A "debunking" treatment of Adams; sometimes vague, but useful. See also Miller's *Origins of the American Revolution* (Boston: Little, Brown, 1943).

Miner, Ward L., *William Goddard, Newspaperman.* Durham, N.C.: Duke University Press, 1962. Detailed study of a colonial editor.

Morgan, Edmund S., and Helen M. Morgan, *The Stamp Act Crisis.* Chapel Hill: University of North Carolina Press, 1953. A scholarly study of the 1765 crisis as a "prologue to revolution."

Parrington, Vernon L., *Main Currents in American Thought,* Vol. I. New York: Harcourt Brace Jovanovich, 1927. John Dickinson and Samuel Adams are commented upon.

Rossiter, Clinton, *Seedtime of the Republic.* New York: Harcourt Brace Jovanovich, 1953.

———, *The Political Thought of the American Revolution.* New York: Harcourt Brace Jovanovich, 1963. Written with consensus theory approach, emphasizing unity and continuity in U.S. experience.

Schlesinger, Arthur M., *Prelude to Independence: The Newspaper War on Britain, 1764–1776.* New York: Knopf, 1958. An excellent detailed study of the role of the newspaper in promoting revolution, and a history of the press for the period.

Wells, William V., *The Life and Public Services of Samuel Adams,* 3 vols. Boston: Little, Brown, 1865. Useful for the documents published verbatim.

Wood, Gordon S., *The Creation of the American Republic, 1776–1787.* Chapel Hill: University of North Carolina Press, 1969. An analysis of political and social thought and the institutions shaping it.

Periodicals and Monographs

Adams, Samuel, "The Right of the Colonists," *Old South Leaflets,* VII (1906), general series. This is the report of the Committee of Correspondence to the Boston Town Meeting, November 20, 1772. It is a good example of the type of activity in which Adams was engaged.

Cullen, Maurice R., Jr., "The Boston Gazette: a Community Newspaper," *Journalism Quarterly,* XXXVI (Spring 1959), 204. Tells how the *Gazette* reflected Boston life in the 1760s and 1770s.

"The Father of the Revolution," *Harper's New Monthly Magazine,* LIII (July 1876), 185. A good summary of the influence of Adams.

Lawson, John L., "The 'Remarkable Mystery' of James Rivington, 'Spy,' " *Journalism Quarterly,* XXXV (Summer 1958), 317. Disposes of myth that Rivington was a secret spy for George Washington.

Schlesinger, Arthur M., "The Colonial Newspaper and the Stamp Act," *New England Quarterly,* VIII (March 1935), 63. An outstanding Harvard historian describes the influence of the newspaper medium.

Teeter, Dwight L., " 'King' Sears, the Mob and Freedom of the Press in New York, 1765–76," *Journalism Quarterly,* XLI (Autumn 1964), 539. The mob, disrespectful of freedom of ideas, drove James Rivington out of business.

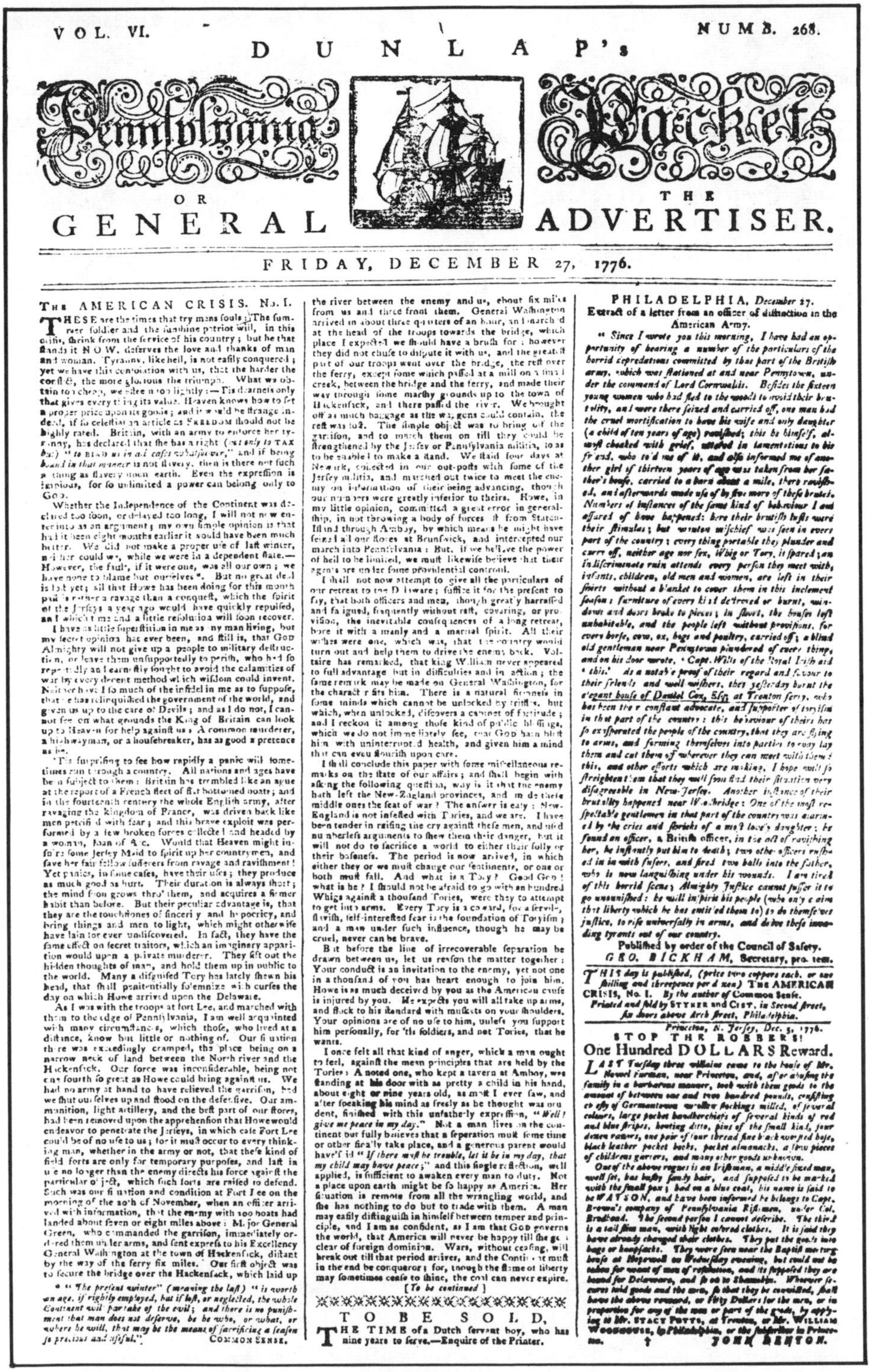

VOL. VI. NUMB. 268.

DUNLAP's

Pennsylvania Packet

OR THE

GENERAL ADVERTISER.

FRIDAY, DECEMBER 27, 1776.

THE AMERICAN CRISIS. No. I.

THESE are the times that try mens souls: The summer soldier and the sunshine patriot will, in this crisis, shrink from the service of his country; but he that stands it NOW, deserves the love and thanks of man and woman. Tyranny, like hell, is not easily conquered; yet we have this consolation with us, that the harder the conflict, the more glorious the triumph. What we obtain too cheap, we esteem too lightly:—'Tis dearness only that gives every thing its value. Heaven knows how to set a proper price upon its goods; and it would be strange indeed, if so celestial an article as FREEDOM should not be highly rated. Britain, with an army to enforce her tyranny, has declared that she has a right (*not only to* TAX *but*) "*to* BIND *us in all cases whatsoever*," and if being *bound in that manner* is not slavery, then is there not such a thing as slavery upon earth. Even the expression is impious, for so unlimited a power can belong only to GOD.

Whether the Independence of the Continent was declared too soon, or delayed too long, I will not now enter into as an argument; my own simple opinion is that had it been eight months earlier it would have been much better. We did not make a proper use of last winter, neither could we, while we were in a dependent state.—However, the fault, if it were one, was all our own; we have none to blame but ourselves*. But no great deal is lost yet; all that Howe has been doing for this month past is rather a ravage than a conquest, which the spirit of the Jerseys a year ago would have quickly repulsed, and which time and a little resolution will soon recover.

I have as little superstition in me as any man living, but my secret opinion has ever been, and still is, that GOD Almighty will not give up a people to military destruction, or leave them unsupportedly to perish, who had so repeatedly and earnestly sought to avoid the calamities of war by every decent method which wisdom could invent. Neither have I so much of the infidel in me as to suppose, that he has relinquished the government of the world, and given us up to the care of Devils; and as I do not, I cannot see on what grounds the King of Britain can look up to Heaven for help against us: A common murderer, a highwayman, or a housebreaker, has as good a pretence as he.

'Tis surprising to see how rapidly a panic will sometimes run through a country. All nations and ages have been subject to them: Britain has trembled like an ague at the report of a French fleet of flat bottomed boats; and in the fourteenth centery the whole English army, after ravaging the kingdom of France, was driven back like men petrified with fear; and this brave exploit was performed by a few broken forces collected and headed by a woman, Joan of Arc. Would that Heaven might inspire some Jersey Maid to spirit up her countrymen, and save her fair fellow sufferers from ravage and ravishment! Yet panics, in some cases, have their uses; they produce as much good as hurt. Their duration is always short; the mind soon grows thro' them, and acquires a firmer habit than before. But their peculiar advantage is, that they are the touchstones of sincerity and hypocricy, and bring things and men to light, which might otherwise have lain for ever undiscovered. In fact, they have the same effect on secret traitors, which an imaginery apparition would upon a private murderer. They sift out the hidden thoughts of man, and hold them up in public to the world. Many a disguised Tory has lately shewn his head, that shall penitentially solemnize with curses the day on which Howe arrived upon the Delaware.

As I was with the troops at Fort Lee, and marched with them to the edge of Pennsylvania, I am well acquainted with many circumstances, which those, who lived at a distance, know but little or nothing of. Our situation there was exceedingly cramped, the place being on a narrow neck of land between the North river and the Hackensack. Our force was inconsiderable, being not one fourth so great as Howe could bring against us. We had no army at hand to have relieved the garrison, had we shut ourselves up and stood on the defensive. Our ammunition, light artillery, and the best part of our stores, had been removed upon the apprehension that Howe would endeavor to penetrate the Jerseys, in which case Fort Lee could be of no use to us; for it must occur to every thinking man, whether in the army or not, that these kind of field forts are only for temporary purposes, and last in use no longer than the enemy directs his force against the particular object, which such forts are raised to defend. Such was our situation and condition at Fort Lee on the morning of the 20th of November, when an officer arrived with information, that the enemy with 200 boats had landed about seven or eight miles above: Major General Green, who commanded the garrison, immediately ordered them under arms, and sent express to his Excellency General Washington at the town of Hackensack, distant by the way of the ferry six miles. Our first object was to secure the bridge over the Hackensack, which laid up the river between the enemy and us, about six miles from us and three from them. General Washington arrived in about three quarters of an hour, and marched at the head of the troops towards the bridge, which place I expected we should have a brush for: however they did not chuse to dispute it with us, and the greatest part of our troops went over the bridge, the rest over the ferry, except some which passed at a mill on a small creek, between the bridge and the ferry, and made their way through some marshy grounds up to the town of Hackensack, and there passed the river. We brought off as much baggage as the waggons could contain, the rest was lost. The simple object was to bring off the garrison, and to march them on till they could be strengthened by the Jersey or Pennsylvania militia, so as to be enabled to make a stand. We staid four days at Newark, collected in our out-posts with some of the Jersey militia, and marched out twice to meet the enemy on information of their being advancing, though our numbers were greatly inferior to theirs. Howe, in my little opinion, committed a great error in generalship, in not throwing a body of forces off from Staten-Island through Amboy, by which means he might have seized all our stores at Brunswick, and intercepted our march into Pennsylvania: But, if we believe the power of hell to be limited, we must likewise believe that their agents are under some providential controul.

I shall not now attempt to give all the particulars of our retreat to the Delaware; suffice it for the present to say, that both officers and men, though greatly harrassed and fatigued, frequently without rest, covering, or provision, the inevitable consequences of a long retreat, bore it with a manly and a martial spirit. All their wishes were one, which was, that the country would turn out and help them to drive the enemy back. Voltaire has remarked, that king William never appeared to full advantage but in difficulties and in action; the same remark may be made on General Washington, for the character fits him. There is a natural firmness in some minds which cannot be unlocked by trifles, but which, when unlocked, discovers a cabinet of fortitude; and I reckon it among those kind of public blessings, which we do not immediately see, that GOD hath blest him with uninterrupted health, and given him a mind that can even flourish upon care.

I shall conclude this paper with some miscellaneous remarks on the state of our affairs; and shall begin with asking the following question, why is it that the enemy hath left the New-England provinces, and made these middle ones the seat of war? The answer is easy: New-England is not infested with Tories, and we are. I have been tender in raising the cry against these men, and used numberless arguments to shew them their danger, but it will not do to sacrifice a world to either their folly or their baseness. The period is now arrived, in which either they or we must change our sentiments, or one or both must fall. And what is a Tory? Good GOD! what is he? I should not be afraid to go with an hundred Whigs against a thousand Tories, were they to attempt to get into arms. Every Tory is a coward, for a servile, slavish, self-interested fear is the foundation of Toryism; and a man under such influence, though he may be cruel, never can be brave.

But before the line of irrecoverable separation be drawn between us, let us reason the matter together: Your conduct is an invitation to the enemy, yet not one in a thousand of you has heart enough to join him. Howe is as much deceived by you as the American cause is injured by you. He expects you will all take up arms, and flock to his standard with muskets on your shoulders. Your opinions are of no use to him, unless you support him personally, for 'tis soldiers, and not Tories, that he wants.

I once felt all that kind of anger, which a man ought to feel, against the mean principles that are held by the Tories: A noted one, who kept a tavern at Amboy, was standing at his door with as pretty a child in his hand, about eight or nine years old, as most I ever saw, and after speaking his mind as freely as he thought was prudent, finished with this unfatherly expression, "*Well! give me peace in my day.*" Not a man lives on the continent but fully believes that a seperation must some time or other finally take place, and a generous parent would have said "*If there must be trouble, let it be in my day, that my child may have peace;*" and this single reflection, well applied, is sufficient to awaken every man to duty. Not a place upon earth might be so happy as America. Her situation is remote from all the wrangling world, and she has nothing to do but to trade with them. A man may easily distinguish in himself between temper and principle, and I am as confident, as I am that GOD governs the world, that America will never be happy till she gets clear of foreign dominion. Wars, without ceasing, will break out till that period arrives, and the Continent must in the end be conqueror; for, though the flame of liberty may sometimes cease to shine, the coal can never expire.

[*To be continued*]

* "*The present winter*" (*meaning the last*) "*is worth an age, if rightly employed, but if lost, or neglected, the whole Continent will partake of the evil; and there is no punishment that man does not deserve, be he who, or what, or where he will, that may be the means of sacrificing a season so precious and useful.*" COMMON SENSE.

TO BE SOLD,

THE TIME of a Dutch servant boy, who has nine years to serve.—Enquire of the Printer.

PHILADELPHIA, *December* 27.

Extract of a letter from an officer of distinction in the American Army.

"*Since I wrote you this morning, I have had an opportunity of hearing a number of the particulars of the horrid depredations committed by that part of the British army, which was stationed at and near Pennytown, under the command of Lord Cornwallis. Besides the sixteen young women who had fled to the woods to avoid their brutality, and were there seized and carried off, one man had the cruel mortification to have his wife and only daughter (a child of ten years of age) ravished; this he himself, almost choaked with grief, uttered in lamentations to his friend, who told me of it, and also informed me of another girl of thirteen years of age was taken from her father's house, carried to a barn about a mile, there ravished, and afterwards made use of by five more of these brutes. Numbers of instances of the same kind of behaviour I am assured of have happened: here their brutish lusts were their stimulus; but wanton mischief was seen in every part of the country; every thing portable they plunder and carry off, neither age nor sex, Whig or Tory, is spared; an indiscriminate ruin attends every person they meet with, infants, children, old men and women, are left in their shirts without a blanket to cover them in this inclement season; furniture of every kind destroyed or burnt, windows and doors broke to pieces; in short, the houses left unhabitable, and the people left without provisions, for every horse, cow, ox, hogs and poultry, carried off; a blind old gentleman near Pennytown plundered of every thing, and on his door wrote, 'Capt. Wills of the Royal Irish did 'this.' As a notable proof of their regard and favour to their friends and well wishers, they yesterday burnt the elegant house of Daniel Cox, Esq; at Trenton ferry, who has been their constant advocate, and supporter of toryism in that part of the country: this behaviour of theirs has so exasperated the people of the country, that they are flying to arms, and forming themselves into parties to way lay them and cut them off wherever they can meet with them: this, and other efforts which are making, I hope will so streighten them that they will soon find their situation very disagreeable in New-Jersey. Another instance of their brutality happened near Woodbridge: One of the most respectable gentlemen in that part of the country was alarmed by the cries and shrieks of a most lovely daughter; he found an officer,* a British officer, *in the act of ravishing her, he instantly put him to death; two other officers rushed in in with fusees, and fired two balls into the father, who is now languishing under his wounds. I am tired of this horrid scene; Almighty Justice cannot suffer it to go unpunished: he will inspirit his people (who only claim that liberty which he has entitled them to) to do themselves justice, to rise universally in arms, and drive these invading tyrants out of our country.*

Published by order of the Council of Safety.

GEO. BICKHAM, Secretary, pro tem.

THIS *day is published, (price two coppers each, or one shilling and threepence per dozen)* THE AMERICAN CRISIS, No. I. *By the author of* Common Sense.

Printed and sold by STYNER and CIST, *in Second street, six doors above Arch street, Philadelphia.*

Princeton, N. Jersey, Dec. 5, 1776.

STOP THE ROBBERS!

One Hundred DOLLARS Reward.

L*AST Tuesday three villains came to the house of Mr. Nowel Furman, near Princeton, and, after abusing the family in a barbarous manner, took with them goods to the amount of between one and two hundred pounds, consisting of fifty of Germantown worsted stockings milled, of several colours, large pocket handkerchiefs of several kinds of red and blue stripes, hooting ditto, pins of the small kind, four dozen razors, one pair of four thread fine black worsted hose, black leather pocket books, pocket almanacks, a few pieces of childrens garters, and many other goods unknown.*

One of the above rogues is an Irishman, a middle sized man, well set, has bushy sandy hair, and supposed to be marked with the small pox; had on a blue coat, his name is said to be WATSON, *and have been informed he belongs to Capt. Brown's company of Pennsylvania Riflemen, under Col. Brodhead. The second person I cannot describe. The third is a tall slim man, with light colored clothes. It is said they have already changed their clothes. They put the goods into bags or knapsacks. They were seen near the Baptist meeting house at Hopewell on Wednesday evening, but could not be taken for want of men of resolution, and its supposed they are bound for Delaware, and so on to Shamokin. Whoever secures said goods and the men, so that they be convicted, shall have the above reward, or Fifty Dollars for the men, or in proportion for any of the men or part of the goods, by applying to Mr.* STACY POTTS, *at Trenton, or Mr.* WILLIAM WOODHOUSE, *in Philadelphia, or the subscriber in Princeton.*

JOHN DENTON.

Tom Paine's first *Crisis* paper, opening: "These are the times that try men's souls."

6

The Press and Revolution

Should the liberty of the press be once destroyed,
farewell the remainder of our invaluable rights
and privileges! We may next expect padlocks
on our lips, fetters on our legs, and only our hands
at liberty to slave for our worse than EGYPTIAN
TASKMASTERS, OR—FIGHT OUR WAY TO
CONSTITUTIONAL FREEDOM.
—Isaiah Thomas

Printers, publishers, and editors were important influences in preparing the public for revolution, and in maintaining the fighting spirit during the War for Independence. Edes and Gill, mentioned in the previous chapter as proprietors of the Radical *Boston Gazette,* were examples of the patriot-journalist. William Bradford III, grandson of the founder of a famous printing dynasty, wielded both the pen and the sword during the war. It was he who first printed Thomas Paine's original *Crisis* essay. His *Pennsylvania Journal* was dedicated to the patriot ideology. But the greatest journalist of the period was Isaiah Thomas, one of the important pioneers of the American Fourth Estate.

ISAIAH THOMAS, PATRIOT EDITOR

Thomas began his career when he was only six, as an apprentice printer. He had to help support his widowed mother and therefore missed the advantages of formal education. Later, he became a great scholar; owner of one of the finest private libraries in the country; first president of the learned Antiquarian Society; and historian of the colonial press.

Thomas once wrote that he owed his education to the type case over which he worked so long as a lad. He learned to spell from setting type. He broadened his knowledge from studying galley proof. Zechariah Fowle, Thomas' master, was an inconsiderate employer, who turned over much of the actual operation of the shop to his apprentice without appropriate recognition of the young man's worth. The resentful Thomas ran away to Halifax. In 1766, at the age of 17, Thomas was aroused by the agitation over the Stamp Act. He was so outspoken in his views that his new master had to discharge him. After a time as an itinerant printer's-helper, Thomas returned to Boston in 1770. Fowle welcomed his runaway apprentice and offered to take him into partnership. Together they founded the *Massachusetts Spy,* a newspaper that lived until 1904.

THE *MASSACHUSETTS SPY,* 1770

Thomas soon bought out his shiftless partner. Under his proprietorship the *Spy* became one of the most successful newspapers in the colonies. It was nominally nonpartisan, but it followed the Whig philosophy for the most part in its early days. Thomas tried to be fair, however. A line under the name plate advertised that the *Spy* was: "A Weekly Political and Commercial Paper —Open to All Parties, but *influenced* by None." Until hostilities began, this was a successful formula, for at 21, the handsome publisher owned a paper exceeded only by Rivington's in circulation and bulk.

Thomas found it increasingly difficult to remain nonpartisan as war loomed. He began to shift his Whig doctrine as it became apparent that conciliationists like Dickinson were ineffective. Eventually he had to make the choice all Whigs had to make—to remain loyal, or to side with the Radicals. Thomas chose the latter course. Soon he was the acknowledged spokesman for the Independence group in his area. When British troops arrived in Boston to enforce laws formerly flouted by the colonials, Thomas became a leader of the underground movement. It was they who flashed the signal light from the steeple of Old North Church warning the Minutemen couriers of the impending British raid on Lexington and Concord.[1]

Next day Thomas was an eyewitness of the first battle in the War for Independence. If he did not hear "the shot heard 'round the world," he at least understood its significance. His report of the encounter remains today as the most notable war reporting of that conflict. He would have been the first to deny that his "story" of the fight was objective. By that time he was committed to the use of his press as an instrument of war, and his report is therefore highly colored with propaganda favorable to his compatriots. Even so, his word picture of the event was probably accurate in its main theme, and

[1] Rider Paul Revere was an influential member of the patriot group and made engravings for their publications. A major mission of the riders was to warn Samuel Adams and John Hancock, asleep in an inn, that General Gage had ordered their arrests.

there is so much color and vigor in his writing that the account deserves mention here. According to Thomas' report:

> About ten o'clock on the night of the eighteenth of April, the troops in Boston were disclosed to be on the move in a very secret manner, and it was found they were embarking on boats (which they privately brought to the place in the evening) at the bottom of the Common; expresses set off immediately to alarm the country, that they might be on their guard. When the expresses got about a mile beyond Lexington, they were stopped by about fourteen officers on horseback, who came out of Boston in the afternoon of that day, and were seen lurking in by-places in the country till after dark. One of the expresses immediately fled, [this was probably Dr. Samuel Prescott] and was pursued two miles by an officer, who, when he had got up with him presented a pistol, and told him he was a dead man if he did not stop, but he rode on till he came up to a house, when stopping of a sudden his horse threw him off, having the presence of mind to holloo [the rider, of course, not the horse] to the people in the house,
>
> "Turn out. Turn out. I have got one of them."
>
> The officer immediately retreated and fled as fast as he had pursued. The other express, [Paul Revere] after passing through a strict examination, by some means got clear.
>
> The body of troops in the meantime, under the command of Lieutenant Colonel Smith, had crossed the river and landed at Phipp's Farm. They immediately, to the number of 1000, proceeded to Lexington, about six miles below Concord, with great silence. A company of militia, of about eighty men, mustered near the meeting house; the troops came in sight of them just before sunrise. The militia, upon seeing the troops, began to disperse. The troops then set out upon the run, hallooing and hussaing, and coming within a few rods of them, the commanding officer accosted the militia, in words to this effect,
>
> "Disperse, you damn'd rebels—Damn you, disperse."
>
> Upon which the troops again hussaed and immediately one or two officers discharged their pistols, which were instantaneously followed by the firing of four or five of the soldiers; and then there seemed to be a general discharge from the whole body. Eight of our men were killed and nine wounded. . . .[2]

The war was hard on patriot editors and publishers. They had committed themselves to the cause so wholeheartedly that it was impossible to stay in business under British occupation. Both the *Gazette* and the *Spy* printing plants had to be smuggled out of Boston, if these two patriot organs were to continue beating the drums for the American cause. The *Gazette* was moved at night across the Charles river to Watertown, where it was published until

[2] *Massachusetts Spy*, May 3, 1775. This appeared on the inside (page 3) of the paper under a Worcester dateline. After moving to Worcester, Thomas described his paper in a page-one skyline as "THE MASSACHUSETTS SPY, or American ORACLE of Liberty."

the British were forced out of Boston in 1776. Thomas had his press sent by trusted employees to Worcester on the eve of the Lexington battle, and he made that city his permanent home thereafter.

THOMAS, THE PUBLISHER AND SCHOLAR

Once firmly established in Worcester, Thomas again began to thrive as a journalist and publisher. By the time his fellow patriots emerged from war triumphant, he was the leading publisher of his day. Seven presses and 150 employees kept his shop at Worcester humming. He established his own paper mill and bindery. In eight other cities his former apprentices operated branch publishing houses, with Thomas providing advice and some financial backing. And in the midst of the war Thomas found time to launch one of the earliest magazines.

He was one of the most skillful and prolific printers of his day. Under his imprint appeared more than 400 books on law, medicine, agriculture, and science. He was the first American to publish Blackstone's *Commentaries,* Bunyan's *Pilgrim's Progress,* and Defoe's *Robinson Crusoe* (in book form—it had already appeared serially in several colonial newspapers). He printed the first Greek grammar in America; the first printed music; and the first novel by a native author—William Hill Brown's *Power of Sympathy.* It was Thomas who brought out the first American dictionary, by William Perry, and more than 50,000 copies were sold. This was something of a publishing record until the same author wrote a speller, published by Thomas, whose various editions aggregated 300,000 copies. In addition to these feats of publication enterprise, Thomas produced more than a hundred children's books, including the first American versions of *Mother Goose* and *Little Goody Two-Shoes.*

It is getting ahead of the story, but the accomplishments of Thomas in his later life might just as well be mentioned here. When he retired from business in 1802 to devote his declining years to scholarly research, he was a wealthy man and the owner of a priceless store of books. This material was useful in gathering information for his two-volume *History of Printing in America* (1810), still the outstanding authority on the early days of the industry. He had enough energy left over to serve as postmaster of Worcester for 25 years and to found the American Antiquarian Society, whose Worcester building today houses the leading collection of colonial printing.

TOM PAINE, THE RADICAL WRITER

Thomas did much to *prepare* the public for the conflict. Another effective journalist of the war was a penniless and somewhat disreputable stranger to these shores.[3] He was Tom Paine, the Thetford Quaker, who arrived on the eve of the war. He was then 37 years old and his life up to that point had been anything but inspiring. He is sometimes represented as lacking in education. It is true that his meager schooling stopped when he went to work as a youth of 13, but it could be pointed out that he was once offered a position in an English school, and that his original purpose in coming to America was to establish, of all things, a girl's seminary.

His early career is not impressive. His father was a Norfolk farmer and corset maker, who subscribed to the Quaker faith. His mother, whom the boy disliked, belonged to the Established Church. Apparently there was philosophical friction between parents and son from the beginning. After an unsuccessful attempt to work in the corset-making business, young Tom Paine was appointed an exciseman. He was soon accused of incompetency and neglect of duty. Reinstated, he was discharged again for what we would now call "unionization." He had been chosen by the excisemen of his district to represent them in their agitation for higher pay, and it was partly because of his failure as an agitator that he left his homeland.

By a fortunate coincidence, he met Benjamin Franklin, then at the height of his career as our spokesman in Europe. Franklin, a shrewd judge of men, saw enough in Paine to write a letter of recommendation. Paine was advised to go to America, where Franklin's son-in-law, Richard Bache, would offer helpful advice. Paine arrived in Philadelphia sick in mind and body. He later said that the very air of America was his tonic. With every breath of freedom he grew stronger. He spoke wonderingly of being able to sit in the same coffeehouses with the "gentry." Paine's first contributions were to Robert Aitken's *Pennsylvania Magazine,* one of several such periodical ventures that flowered and withered during this period. Aitken's magazine was one of the better ones. It did not survive, but Paine wrote for it long enough to establish a reputation as a stimulating commentator. Already he was arguing against the institution of Negro slavery, British arrogance, and in favor of universal suffrage and education.

PAINE'S PAMPHLET, *COMMON SENSE*

His fame as a writer was achieved by means of a pamphlet copied by many of the colonial newspapers of 1776. This was *Common Sense,* which helped to bring the lukewarm patriots into the revolutionary movement. *Common Sense* appeared in January, 1776, just a little more than a year after the

[3] Paine is usually identified as a writer, or political philosopher. In this book the journalist is defined as one who acts as the transmission belt carrying ideas, information, and inspiration to the general public, dependent upon such resources for rational opinion. This was Paine's prime function during the American Revolution. His work for Aitken on the *Pennsylvania Magazine,* often ignored in sketches about him, also qualifies him for consideration as a journalist, in the broad sense.

arrival of the uncouth English immigrant. Its popularity was instantaneous and amazing. More than 120,000 copies were sold in the first three months. "I challenge the warmest advocate for reconciliation to show a single advantage that this continent can reap by being connected with Great Britain," he wrote. This challenge was hurled at the Dickinsonian Whigs, who shuddered at the word "independence," and they replied in the local newspapers with condemnation of this upstart. In a matter of weeks, however, Paine's views in *Common Sense* were known to virtually every literate American, and it is significant that only six months later, the Declaration of Independence committed the former colonies to this doctrine. Although *Common Sense* was a "best seller," Paine would accept no remuneration for his writing. His work was strictly for the cause.

After the fighting broke out Paine offered to serve in what amounted to a foreign legion. When the unit was cut to pieces by the British at Amboy, Paine made his way to Washington's headquarters at Fort Lee, where the defeated Americans were licking their wounds preparatory to withdrawal to the Delaware River line. His curious status as a foreigner, which was neither that of an officer, nor of an enlisted man, gave him access to both groups. He talked with all types of Americans as he marched along the wintry roads. Actually, the season was unusually mild, but for the ill-clad troops the nightly bivouac brought only misery. The tattered companies were breaking up fast. In 1776 the ideology of the conflict was still vague. Many of the soldiers had only a hazy notion of what the shooting was all about.

PAINE'S *CRISIS* PAPERS

At this crucial moment, Paine wrote his first *Crisis* paper. Whether or not he wrote it at Washington's direction, by candlelight on a drum head, is inconsequential. There is no doubt, however, that it was written from the heart, and under pressure. There was nothing new in what he said, but like a poet, he expressed what others could only feel. His work was rough, but that made it all the more appealing to the common man for whom it was written. The foot-slogging militiamen understood that one of their own was speaking.

And who can overestimate the power of words in arousing the will to fight? Down through history hopeless wars and battles have been won when words have doubled the force of arms. So it was with Paine's *Crisis*. His style had a kind of Biblical resonance and rhythm. Like Winston Churchill's "We shall fight them on the beaches" speech of World War II, the words rallied weary men by that most potent of spiritual tonics—dedication to a cause. They are words that have lived through the generations. In the bleak days of World War II, when there were no victories to report, the conquered peoples, despairing of freedom, listened with kindling hope as these words, written December 19, 1776, came through the ether to their secret radio receivers:

> These are the times that try men's souls. The summer soldier and the sunshine patriot will, in this crisis, shrink from the service of his country; but he that stands it NOW, deserves the love and thanks of man and woman. Tyranny, like hell, is not easily conquered; yet we have this consolation with us, that the harder the conflict the more glorious the triumph. What we obtain too cheap, we esteem too lightly—Tis dearness only that gives every thing its value. Heaven knows how to put a proper price upon its goods; and it would be strange indeed if so celestial an article as FREEDOM should not be highly rated.[4]

The first *Crisis* paper exceeded *Common Sense* in popularity. Printed on one side of a sheet and folded in half to make a pamphlet, the clarion call was echoed from patriot newspapers throughout the colonies. Washington had the *Crisis* papers read to his numb troops as the words emerged fresh from Paine's pen. It is significant that the week after Paine made his first plea to the dejected, they turned on the foe and won a needed victory at Trenton. Morale rose to the point where Washington, given the troops the niggardly Continental Congress refused to supply, might have won the war before the year was out.[5]

Other *Crisis* papers appeared as the need demanded. Most of them were reprinted in the newspapers of the period. More than any other writer of the war, Paine caught the significance of the American Revolution. While others confined the issues to political and economic arguments, Paine advocated social revolt as well. In many ways, he was not an American at all, but an internationalist temporarily caught up in the American movement because it fitted his pattern. "The world is my country, all mankind are my brethren, to do good is my religion . . ." he said later in his *Rights of Man,* and this self-appraisal sums up his creed. His place was wherever the plain people needed a tribune. It is significant, for example, that he went to France after the victory in America. There he used the same weapons to arouse the laggards. For a time he served as a member of the French National Assembly. He not only carried the spirit of the American Revolution to France, but as we shall see in a later chapter, he brought that spirit back home after it nearly died out in the postwar reaction here.

Such a man of course drew attack from all sides. The Tories hunted him

[4] As printed in *Dunlap's Pennsylvania Packet, or the General Advertiser,* December 27, 1776. "The Crisis. No. 1" was the heading; the byline was "by the author of *Common Sense,*" in an adjoining advertisement for reprints. See Michael C. Emery *et al., America's Front Page News 1690–1970,* p. 27.

[5] Charles and Mary Beard, *The Rise of American Civilization,* Vol. I (New York: Macmillan, 1930), p. 241.

in packs. Stalwart Whigs, such as John Dickinson and William Smith, provost of the college that later became the University of Pennsylvania, challenged his ideas on property. The latter group insisted that Paine was merely an opportunist. They said he argued as he did because he had nothing to risk for his cause. Usually the revolutionary is pictured by his critics as a madman or as a visionary, with his head in the clouds and his hands in the pockets of his betters. Paine was no exception to this stereotype. His enemies eventually conquered him, not by frontal assault, but by infiltration.

In the end, he was disgraced not by the formidable foes he had attacked on both sides of the Atlantic, but by a group whose influence he had sadly underestimated. Following the publication of his *Age of Reason,* Paine was attacked by clergyman of most denominations as an atheist. Actually, the book was an attempt to explain God in rational, rather than in supernatural, terms. The author was technically a Deist, a far cry from an atheist. What he did attack was religious organization, including churches of every faith, sect, and denomination. The Protestant clergy, particularly, turned upon him. By the turn of the century, Paine had been driven to cover by forces he had heretofore ignored. But his great work had by then been accomplished. He died almost forgotten in 1809 in a land he had helped to free.

THE REVOLUTIONARY PRESS

The skill and energy of Revolutionary journalists, propagandists, and popular political writers amaze historians. Editors used every known trick to win public support for the revolutionary movement. The first shot of the war was still echoing around the world when the battle of words began. Each side tried to race its version of Lexington and Concord back to the people of Great Britain, where the colonial stand was respected by a sizable public. General Gage's report placed all the blame for the shooting upon the treasonous minutemen. He sent this report to London by the fastest sloop at his command. Four days later the patriots had prepared their statement, which reversed the blame for the bloodshed. Captain John Darby of Salem, Massachusetts, agreed to carry the message to the mother country. Of course the British sloop had no chance of outrunning a Salem skipper who knew how to crowd sail. Captain Darby arrived 11 days ahead of his rival. His report, handed to Benjamin Franklin, the American agent in Europe, was disseminated in papers throughout the land, thanks to Franklin's skill as a publicist. General Gage's belated account was an anticlimax. The contemptible rebels had scored one of the most impressive scoops of the period.[6] On the whole, the "ragged Continentals" were alert to the importance of news and propaganda. They used communications effectively.

[6] An inspiring account of such activities is given in Lynn Montross, *Rag, Tag and Bobtail* (New York: Harper & Row, 1952).

Only 20 of the 35 newspapers being published at the beginning of the war survived. Considering the vicissitudes of the times, that was not a bad record. Many would have disappeared had there been no war. And 35 new papers were established during the six years of fighting. Enough of these survived to bring the total number of papers at the end of the war up to the prewar figure. All were weeklies, and most of them were patriot in sentiment. Where the British held strategic bases, Tory papers continued to be printed, but by the end of the war they had succumbed to public pressure.

Revolutionary newspapers went into about 40,000 homes, but each issue had a larger number of readers per copy than would be true in modern times. Every word was read, even to the small "liners" and advertisements. Many an American first learned of the Declaration of Independence through his newspaper. It first appeared publicly in the *Pennsylvania Evening Post* of July 6, 1776, but others soons published the document.

Such enterprise is impressive. On the other hand, any student of the times becomes aware very soon of the primitive communications facilities of the period. It took six weeks for the account of Lexington and Concord to reach Savannah. Often the reporting of war events was of the most haphazard type. "The Hartford Post tells us," Hugh Gaine, the turncoat patriot editor wrote in the February 2, 1778, issue of his *New York Gazette and Mercury,* "That he saw a Gentleman in Springfield, who informed him that he (the Gentleman) saw a letter from an Officer in Gen. Howe's Army to another in Gen. Burgoyne's, giving him to understand, war was declared on the sides of France and Spain against the MIGHTY Kingdom of Britain." The news had actually come from a Boston paper already a month old, and the story was not true, in any case.[7] Some of the news was high in reporting quality, however. Often it was printed verbatim, which added to its charm and authenticity. That was how the details of the battle of Yorktown reached the office of the *Freeman's Journal* in Philadelphia:

> *BE IT REMEMBERED*
>
> That on the 17th day of October, 1781, Lieut. Gen. Charles Earl Cornwallis, with about 5,000 British troops, surrendered themselves prisoners of war to His Excellency, Gen. George Washington, Commander-in-Chief of the allied forces of France and America. LAUS DEO.[8]

That was all the paper had to tell of the greatest, and final, victory of the war. The account should have been authentic, because the reporter was none other than General Washington. The editor had printed verbatim the dispatch sent out by the general.

[7] Frank Luther Mott, *American Journalism,* rev. ed. (New York: Macmillan, 1950), p. 100.

[8] From *America Goes to Press,* by Laurence Greene, copyright 1936, used by special permission of the publishers, Bobbs-Merrill.

Some of the most popular items in the war newspapers were columns of names the Sons and Daughters of the American Revolution might find it embarrassing to read today. These items were lists of deserters and "bounty jumpers"—men who had enlisted just long enough to collect their volunteer bonuses before disappearing from the ranks. The papers were full of such information. Sometimes notices were printed in the press asking authorities to pick up entire squads and companies of men who had deserted. The temptation for men to leave the battlefields was great. Soldiers often could not collect their pay. When they did get it, it might be in the form of scrip, which declined rapidly in value. Many of the troops were underfed, underclothed, and underarmed. No wonder the war was too much for some of the "sunshine patriots," as Paine called them.

A serious problem was the shortage of printing supplies. Paper, ink, and type had come from Europe before the war, for the most part. Not until 1769 was an American press sold commercially. American paper mills could not begin to supply the demand for stock. Paper at that time was made of linen, and cloth of any kind was scarce, especially in wartime. That was why Washington did not put it beneath his dignity to issue a plea, asking patriot women to save all available material that might be converted into printing paper. That shows how important the Commander-in-Chief considered the press to be. In this connection, it is interesting to note that he contributed his prestige to encourage the founding by the Quaker printer Isaac Collins of the *New Jersey Gazette*, which, for a time, served as a kind of army newspaper.

An example of journalistic prosperity in wartime was the *Connecticut Courant*. By 1781 it had the then amazing circulation of 8,000 subscribers each issue. It was full of advertising. Few London papers could boast of such success. The *Courant* printed on paper from its own mill. It was one of the best-printed papers in America. On the other hand, patriot John Holt had to leave his *New York Journal*'s printing equipment behind in New York in 1776 when the British came, settled down in Kingston only to be routed again by British troops, finally reestablished the *Journal* in Poughkeepsie, and returned to New York in 1783—only to die the following year a worn-out man.

Visitors to this country, including the many who came to help us win our war, were impressed by the popularity of the American press. Although editors did not hesitate to print rumor, opinion, and even deliberate lies, most of the journalists were closely identified with their readers. Their very partisanship provided a comradeship with their publics that modern objectivity tends to discourage. If the news was not accurate, at least readers understood the editor's attitude. Each paper was spokesman for a particular public. That public willingly excused journalistic abuses on the ground that the editor, in prosecuting his case, had to use exaggeration to strengthen and to emphasize his arguments, as did lawyers in court. At least the reader of a particular paper, be it Tory or Patriot, believed that the editor was on his side. In this period, the press, the public, and the government were all working together for a common cause, once the Tories were driven to cover.

Annotated Bibliography

Books

Aldridge, Alfred O., *Man of Reason: The Life of Thomas Paine*. Philadelphia: Lippincott, 1959. The best study of Paine since Moncure D. Conway's two-volume *Life of Thomas Paine* (London: Putnam's, 1892). See also Mary A. Best, *Thomas Paine* (New York: Harcourt, Brace & Jovanovich, 1927).

Channing, Edward, *History of the United States,* Vol. III. New York: Macmillan, 1927. The high literary quality and thoughtful comments make this volume of Channing particularly useful as background reading of the period.

Commager, Henry Steele, ed., *Documents of American History*. New York: Appleton-Century-Crofts, 1934; Hawthorn Books, 1969. Contains writings of Dickinson, the Adamses, Madison, Jefferson, etc. Very useful in checking the original sources of information. The comment preceding each document is helpful in explaining the circumstances involved.

Curti, Merle, and Willard Thorp, *American Issues,* Vol. I, "The Social Record." Philadelphia: Lippincott, 1941. Excellent appraisals of Dickinson, Paine, and leaders of Federalist party.

East, Robert, *Business Enterprise in the American Revolutionary Era.* New York: Columbia University Press, 1938. A scholarly review of the capitalistic development during this period.

Fast, Howard M., *Citizen Tom Paine*. New York: Duell, Sloan and Pearce, 1943. Not strictly a biography, but a more romantic interpretation of Paine.

Greene, Laurence, *America Goes to Press*. Indianapolis; Bobbs-Merrill, 1936. Goes to source materials to describe how the news of important events reached the people through the press.

Hixson, Richard F., *Isaac Collins: A Quaker Printer in 18th Century America.* New Brunswick, N.J.: Rutgers University Press, 1968. The scholarly biography of a patriot printer-editor.

Jensen, Merrill, *Founding of the New Nation: A History of the American Revolution*. New York: Oxford University Press, 1968. A major new study.

Marble, Annie R., *From 'Prentice to Patron—The Life Story of Isaiah Thomas.* New York: Appleton-Century-Crofts, 1935. The standard biography.

Montross, Lynn, *Rag, Tag and Bobtail.* New York: Harper & Row, 1952. Demonstrates that the people's army and government operated remarkably effectively, despite many mistakes. Public opinion and its manipulators are seen to have been highly important.

Paine, Thomas, *The Life and Major Writings of Thomas Paine,* edited by Philip S. Foner. New York: Citadel Press, 1961. Annotated texts of Paine's major works.

Snyder, Louis L., and Richard B. Morris, eds., *A Treasury of Great Reporting.* New York: Simon & Schuster, 1962. This book contains excerpts from outstanding journalistic writings between colonial times and post-World War II.

Trevelyan, Sir George Otto, *The American Revolution,* Part III. New York: Longmans, Green & Company, 1907. The epoch viewed from the standpoint of a great British historian.

Van Tyne, Claude H., *The War of Independence; American Phase.* Boston: Houghton Mifflin, 1929. Volume two of a study by one of the leading authorities on the period.

Periodicals and Monographs

Batchelder, Frank R., "Isaiah Thomas, the Patriot Printer," *New England Magazine, N.S.,* XXV (November 1901), 284. An excellent short sketch of the great publisher.

Benjamin, S. G. W., "Notable Editors Between 1776 and 1800—Influence of the Early American Press," *Magazine of American History,* XVII (February 1887), 97. Colorful description of early personal journalism, including Royalist publications.

Jensen, Merrill, "The American People and the American Revolution," *Journal of American History,* LVI (June 1970), 5. Excellent example of newspaper, pamphlet, broadside use.

Lorenz, Alfred L., Jr., "Hugh Gaine: Colonial Printer-Editor, 1752–1783," Ph.D. thesis, Southern Illinois University, 1968. Economic self-interest made him a "turn-coat."

Mott, Frank Luther, "The Newspaper Coverage of Lexington and Concord," *New England Quarterly,* XVII (December 1944), 489. A day-by-day analysis of how the news was spread. Reprinted in Ford and Emery, *Highlights in the History of the American Press.*

Parker, Peter J., "The Philadelphia Printer: A Study of an 18th Century Businessman," *Business History Review,* XL (Spring 1966), 24. The colonial artisan becomes a fledgling capitalist.

Siebert, Fred S., "The Confiscated Revolutionary Press," *Journalism Quarterly,* XIII (June 1936), 179. Describes how British used captured equipment to produce counterrevolutionary propaganda.

Teeter, Dwight L., "A Legacy of Expression: Philadelphia Newspapers and Congress During the War for Independence, 1775–1783," Ph.D. thesis, University of Wisconsin, 1966. A perceptive and scholarly study; the existence of contending factions enabled press to freely criticize. See also his "Press Freedom and the Public Printing: Pennsylvania, 1775–1783," *Journalism Quarterly,* XLV (Autumn 1968), 445.

Thomas, Charles M., "The Publication of Newspapers During the American Revolution," *Journalism Quarterly,* IX (December 1932), 358. Describes the three political classifications of editors and appraises their wartime contributions.

"Tom Paine's First Appearance in America," *Atlantic Monthly,* IV (November 1859), 565. Describes Paine's propaganda activities and journalistic contributions. Reprinted in Ford and Emery, *Highlights in the History of the American Press.*

Philip Freneau

Benjamin Russell

William Cobbett

Philip Freneau, as an Anti-Federalist editor, helped stimulate the "Second Revolution" that put Thomas Jefferson into the White House. Benjamin Russell, editor of the *Columbian Centinel,* was a pillar of the Federalist party and a noted journalist of his time. William Cobbett, better known as "Peter Porcupine," came from Britain to become a rabid Federalist editor who perhaps has never been exceeded in the art of invective. (*Magazine of American History*)

7

The Press and the Second Revolution

Men who distrust the people and the future may overwhelm us with their learning, but they do not impress us with their wisdom—thank God.
—Gerald Johnson

During the war the Tory had disappeared as a political factor in America, but two other groups now struggled for control of the Government. One of the elements was conservative in tone. It consisted, for the most part, of citizens engaged in commerce, banking, manufacturing, and property management. Generally, this group was more interested in preserving and extending its economic advantages than in risking social experiments. The other element was largely made up of the agrarian, small-farmer class, increasingly strengthened by the city wage-earner, or "mechanic," as he was called then; but with a significant leavening of intellectuals and political philosophers interested in social reform.

At the end of the American Revolution, the people of the United States had a choice to make. They might continue to experiment with social change, endorsing the ideals which had been their battle cries. Or they might consolidate strength by making right of property the fundamental consideration. Or they might work out some arrangement completely satisfactory to neither, but warranting mutual support. The record of the Confederation gave the conservatives hope that public opinion might be swung to their side. The opportunity was the proposal to draft a new national charter.

State legislatures sent the delegates to the Constitutional Convention at Philadelphia. The state assemblies were dominated by the property group. This was because the big commercial centers were strongholds of the conservatives, where land and voting qualifications disfranchised many "mechanics," or laborers. It was therefore the men of means and community standing who brought about the fundamental change in government under the Constitution. They succeeded in placing financial power in the hands of a strong, central government, and otherwise protected the position of property against attacks within individual states. But they could not have their way entirely. They could not have obtained acceptance of the new charter by the people, unless the authors had made concessions. The document they produced is a marvel of balanced forces.

THE BILL OF RIGHTS AND PRESS FREEDOM

One of the concessions offered by the conservatives was the Bill of Rights. Offered as the first ten amendments, these articles have since been considered part of the Constitution, in the sense that they were the price paid by the authors for the liberal consent that made the document practicable. The first article of the Bill of Rights is of special interest to journalists. It provides that: "Congress shall make no law . . . abridging the freedom of speech or of the press . . ." This is the cornerstone of our press liberty, but there is evidence that the authors of the Constitution spent little time discussing this issue. Madison's careful minutes of the convention show only casual and infrequent mention of the press.

But there was long precedent for the protection that finally was provided the press. British Common Law, as used in the various states, provided great freedom of expression for the times, even though it still recognized seditious libel laws. The same basic principles were stated in the Declaration of Rights written by John Dickinson when the First Continental Congress convened in 1774. Nine of the 13 states had already provided such constitutional protection by 1787. The Virginia Bill of Rights, of 1776, stated: "That freedom of the press is one of the great bulwarks of liberty, and can never be restrained but by despotick governments. . . ." Article XVI of the Massachusetts Bill of Rights, of 1780, expressed similar sentiments, and other states used variations of this theme to establish the principle.[1]

This probably explains why the authors of the new national charter ignored the press issue. They assumed that full protection was already granted under the states. Charles Pinckney of South Carolina did present a draft of a constitution with a clause similar to the one eventually adopted, but apparently little attention was paid to his suggestion at that time.

It soon was clear, however, that the Constitution could not possibly succeed without concessions to public sentiment. Delegates from Massachusetts reported it would be impossible to win ratification of the Constitution in that state without a clause concerning freedom of expression. Virginia could not

[1] Henry Steele Commager, ed., *Documents of American History* (New York: Appleton-Century-Crofts, 1934), p. 104, Article XII; and p. 109, Article XVI.

muster enough votes for ratification until Governor Edmund Randolph called upon the framers to add the Bill of Rights. A constitutional committee was appointed to draft such a bill. The resolution was a modification of the Virginia document. Delegates were then told to return to their respective states, and to use all influence available in mustering support for ratification of the main document on the promise that the Rights clauses would be included in the charter. It was on this understanding that New York finally approved the Constitution, but even so, it was not an easy victory for the Federalists.

Because of promises given, the Bill of Rights was an important issue in the first session of Congress. Madison headed the committee charged with drafting the amendments. When his first draft was read out of committee, it stated: ". . . no state shall violate the equal rights of conscience or of freedom of speech. . . ." The select committee to which the report was referred added ". . . or of the press." Modified by House and Senate, the clause became the first amendment, as ratified in 1791.

It should be noted that freedom of the press is part of our fundamental law, regardless of how it came to be included. In Great Britain, Parliament provides the protection granted by our Constitution, and presumably, Parliament could also take away that right. In the United States, such freedom could not be restricted legally without submitting the question to Constitutional amendment. Neither the President nor Congress could abridge freedom of the press without running into resistance from the courts. In Great Britain, the courts have no such check. Furthermore, the specific mention of press freedom in our Constitution *in addition* to our recognition of the common law on the subject, which the British have depended upon as a safeguard, showed that liberty of the press was more advanced on this side of the Atlantic in 1791 than it was in the freest state in Europe.

THE FEDERALIST SERIES

Curiously, the press, which had to be protected as a concession to the public sentiment, was the most effective weapon of the conservatives in winning support for the charter they grudgingly admitted was the best document they could obtain in favor of their interests. The best exposition of the conservative doctrine was a series of articles which first appeared in the semi-weekly *New York Independent Journal* from October, 1787 to April, 1788. Reprinted throughout the country, and later published in pamphlet and (with six new essays) book form, these articles are known collectively as *The Federalist.*

They were written for mass consumption, and they were so effective that they gave their name to the party that was actually nationalist in doctrine, rather than federalist. The Federalists, as they came to be known during the publication of the 85 offerings, won their fight with this journalistic effort.

Written hastily, much as daily editorials were written later on, these are still read, not only as revealing political studies, but as good literature. Alexander Hamilton wrote the largest number of *Federalist* articles over the pen name, "Publius." James Madison is believed to have written 29, some of which are the best in the series. John Jay, a noted New York state political leader, probably wrote a half-dozen. In clear, concise style, *The Federalist* explained the philosophy of the Constitutional party. The gist of this doctrine is described in the tenth, supposedly written by Madison. Madison stood somewhere between the two opposing leaders. He disapproved of Hamilton's financial and autocratic ideas, but he veered from his mentor, Jefferson, in sponsoring a stronger national government. Madison had attended all the meetings of the constitutional committee and had engineered many of the modifications in the document. Said he, in describing the form of government prescribed by the framers of the national charter: ". . . justice must prevail [even] over a majority," to prevent the whims of an unstable public from wrecking the ship of state. This control would be accomplished through a republican form of government, offering protection to the masses, without direct control by them, as under the true "democratic" system.

ALEXANDER HAMILTON, LEADER OF THE FEDERALISTS

The Federalist firmly established Alexander Hamilton as leader of the party that took the title of the series as its label. He saw himself as the St. George of the anarchist dragon, for the radicalism and disorganization of the liberals could lead only to this, he reasoned. "We should be rescued from democracy," Hamilton insisted, and he looked forward to a restoration of an aristocracy, according to at least one of his biographers.[2] It has been suggested that Hamilton's respect for the aristocracy, and his continual seeking of recognition by those who valued heredity most highly, may have depended upon the uncertainty of his paternity. Why was he a patriot in the Revolution, instead of a Tory, then? Born and reared to young manhood in the British West Indies, Hamilton became an American not so much out of hatred of the British social and political structure, as out of contempt for British corruption and mismanagement.

That is why he fought for home rule, and there can be no doubt that he had strong feelings on the subject before the cause of revolution was generally endorsed. His war record was excellent. General Washington, who recognized Hamilton's virtues and who understood the youngster's faults (he was 18 at the time of Lexington and Concord) had a hard time keeping the fiery patriot out of battle and behind the ledgers, where he was much more useful.

[2] Claude G. Bowers, *Jefferson and Hamilton* (Boston: Houghton Mifflin, 1925), p. 31.

This was the man who led the Federalists. One cannot speak of him without indicating bias, one way or the other. In his day he was one of the most respected and reviled men in government. He had little knowledge of social forces. Never having lived the life of toil, he tended to dismiss the problems of the working people. He was quick to see that a government of fine phrases and glittering shibboleths was certain to be ineffective. He believed that the way to make government work was to let those with special interests in it control it, since they had most to lose by inept rule. Let those qualified take command, insisted Hamilton, who always imagined himself as the ideal soldier, ruling by command, rather than by consultation.

Hamilton believed it his duty to establish the credit of the country by drastic financial measures, regardless of the luckless victims of an inadequate monetary system. He had no compassion for popular leaders such as Daniel Shays, the Massachusetts war veteran who led a hopeless revolt in 1786 against a taxation and hard money policy that threatened the very livelihood, to say nothing of the freedoms, of the small farmer. Hamilton saw the danger in such uprisings of the common man, and that was one reason he wished to rush through the Constitution, which he correctly predicted would solve many problems. But he would have taken care of the Shayses by force, rather than by placating the aggrieved. He admired military efficiency. Yet his life was to prove his genius not as a soldier, but as a writer and political thinker. As Bowers says:

> He was a natural journalist and pamphleteer—one of the fathers of the American editorial. His perspicacity, penetration, powers of condensation, and clarity of expression were those of a premier editorial writer. These same qualities made him a pamphleteer without peer. That he would have shown with equal luster in the reportorial room of a modern paper is shown in his description of the hurricane and in his letter to Laurens picturing vividly the closing hours of Major Andre. From the moment he created a sensation with "A Farmer Refuted" in his eighteenth year, until in the closing months of his life he was meeting Coleman surreptitiously in the night to dictate vigorous editorials for the New York *Evening Post* he had established, he recognized his power. No man ever complained more bitterly of the attacks of the press; none ever used the press more liberally and relentlessly to attack . . . Nowhere in the literature of invective is there anything more vitriolic than the attack on a war speculator and profiteer, under the signature of "Publius." . . . But usually he appealed to reason, and then he was at his best. . . . It will be impossible to comprehend the genius of Hamilton, his domination of his party, and his power, despite his unpopularity with the masses, without a foreknowledge of his force with the pen. It was his scepter and his sword.[3]

[3] Bowers, *Jefferson and Hamilton,* p. 26. Bowers, it should be pointed out, is a respecter, but no admirer, of Hamilton.

That was how the biographer, Bowers, answers those who underestimate Hamilton's journalistic role. This was the man who led the forces working for the ratification of the Constitution. Curiously, Hamilton did not like the document. It was a "shilly-shally thing of milk and water which could not last and was good only as a step to something better," he once said.[4] Although the Constitution was supposedly the product of the conservatives, it was all too liberal for an admirer of aristocracy, such as Hamilton. He sponsored it, however, by facing what he believed to be the facts. The document offered a means of drawing together the type of person Hamilton believed should control government. And although he disapproved of its populist concessions, he was shrewd enough to see that such compromise was essential, if any protection of property were to be imposed. When, on a summer day, he drifted slowly down the Hudson River on the New York packet and thereupon decided to subordinate his personal preferences in writing the first of *The Federalist* papers, he reached the height of his greatness. Had he accomplished nothing else in his lifetime, his services as a journalist that day would have justified his niche in the memory of his countrymen.

Hamilton led his forces so brilliantly that he won all his early battles against the vastly larger army of "unimportant men" opposing his policies. Under his generalship, the Federalists succeeded with the ratification of the Constitution. As first Secretary of the Treasury, he began grouping his cohorts even before the first Congress convened. Two months before the head of the Treasury was scheduled to make his report to Congress, the recommendations of Hamilton's "Report on the Public Credit" leaked out in some way. Public securities went up 52 per cent after the word got out that the Government would "fund" the public debt.

Hamilton's plan was to consolidate war debts and then to pay them off at face value. Few honest men could object to this program. It would help to establish national credit among nations. The domestic debt was something else. The face value of securities was about 42 million dollars. They had depreciated to about 20 cents on the dollar. Hamilton now proposed to pay at face value. His recommendations, discovered by speculators long before the Treasury report was made public, allowed the unscrupulous to reap a golden harvest. By fast ship and by speedy horse the speculators raced to the hinterlands, where news of Hamilton's plans had not yet penetrated. Thousands of original creditors sold their securities at the depreciated price. Many of the swindled were war veterans who had earned these securities in exchange for hazardous service. When they discovered they had been cheated by speculators and that these vultures were now to be paid in full by taxes collected from their victims, the resentment against Hamilton produced a violent reaction. The hatred was fanned when the same exploitation was repeated in Hamilton's program for the assumption of state debts.

[4] As quoted in Wilfred E. Binkley, *American Political Parties: Their Natural History* (New York: Knopf, 1943), p. 32.

THE FEDERALIST EDITORS: FENNO, WEBSTER, COBBETT, RUSSELL

The outstanding Federalist newspaper in the lush days of the party was the *Gazette of the United States.* Sponsored and supported by Hamilton, it was edited by John Fenno, who issued the first edition at the national capital, then in New York, April 15, 1789. Fenno had been a school teacher, and it is noteworthy that we are already beginning to see the development of the specialized journalist. Most of the previous editors and publishers had come up through the print shop. Fenno established his reputation as a journalist without benefit of mechanical apprenticeship. Soon his paper was the acknowledged mouthpiece of the Federalist party and it moved with the government when Philadelphia became the national capital in 1791.

Another powerful Federalist voice was that of Noah Webster, remembered for his dictionary, but a man of many parts. Lawyer, pioneer weatherman, translator, historian, economist, and scientific farmer, Webster was recognized in his day as a great editor. He started out as a lawyer and teacher. He was fascinated by words. His avocation resulted in a three-part *Grammatical Institute of the English Language.* The first part, the speller, appeared in 1784, and enjoyed a phenomenal sale—eventually 60 million copies were sold (not all within the author's lifetime, of course). Webster came back to New York in 1793 to edit the daily *Minerva* and the semiweekly *Herald* (after 1797 the *Commercial Advertiser* and *Spectator,* respectively), as a supporter of Hamilton.

Webster was an articulate and intelligent interpreter of the Federalist program. He defended President Washington against the smear tactics of such editors as Freneau and Bache, and stood firm for the party against opposition attacks. Webster was no mere party hack, however. He resented what he called the "betrayal" of President Adams by Hamilton, the circumstances of which will be described later. At any rate, the *Minerva* was an important organ in the Federalist attempt to regain control. Eventually Webster tired of politics, however, and returned to his old love—linguistics. He is remembered now for his dictionary, which appeared in preliminary form in 1803 and as a great contribution to lexicography in 1828.

Another great Federalist editor was William Cobbett, who never was an American at all, but who offered severe criticism of the (Jeffersonian) Republicans and who defended the Federalists between 1794 and 1800. Cobbett was a refugee in this country after exposing graft and corruption in the British army. He first showed his writing abilities in an attack on Joseph Priestley, whose scientific views were curiously related to his political views, which were leftist. Encouraged by the success of his writing, and sponsored by friends of the Federalist party, Cobbett gave up his modest tutoring position in 1797 to edit *Porcupine's Gazette and Daily Advertiser* in Philadelphia.

In the short span of three years, Cobbett made a name for himself throughout the new country. He made no pretense of objectivity. His purpose was to expose his enemies, and his weapon was his vitriolic pen. Few editors in history have surpassed the British exile in sustained vituperation. His general theme was alliance with Britain, war against France, and perdition for Republicans. Tom Paine was his special target, and his biography of the Revolution's penman was all the more readable because Cobbett never let himself be restrained by the facts. In short, he had a marvelous time lampooning his enemies and their ideas. His pseudonym, "Peter Porcupine," appeared regularly after he "told off" a magazine editor in a pamphlet entitled *A Kick for a Bite.* A reviewer of the piece likened Cobbett to a porcupine, a creature with bristles erect against those who sought to manhandle it. That was just the creature Cobbett fancied himself as being, and he gloried in the name.

The oldest Federalist paper was Major Benjamin Russell's *Massachusetts* (later *Columbian*) *Centinel,* published at Boston. Russell fought at Lexington as a lad of 13. He learned the printing trade under Isaiah Thomas and after serving his time as a journeyman, founded his paper in 1784. His first big crusade was his attempt to push his state toward ratification of the Constitution. That put him in the forefront of the forces that eventually rallied under the Federalist banner. Russell was pro-British, anti-French, an advocate of an American nobility, and later a hater of Jefferson. His paper followed the Federalist line 100 per cent, but in addition, it had excellent news coverage, and it enjoyed great prosperity.

THE FRENCH REVOLUTION

With such journalistic big guns trained upon their hapless opponents, the Federalists rapidly consolidated their power. Had it not been for the French Revolution, they might have annihilated the ideas for which many an American had fought. As Colonel Thomas W. Higginson wrote in his voluminous notes of the period, the French Revolution "drew a red hot plow share through the history of America." [5] Whereas America had triggered the French upheaval after its own fight for freedom, the French were now repaying in kind—and just in time. The French influence stopped the American monarchists in their tracks. It destroyed the last hope of the aristocrats and it changed the trend toward realliance with the British. It also provided the literature and philosophy needed as ammunition against the skillful journalistic batteries defending the Federalist citadel. All that was needed was a great leader. As usual in such emergencies, a great one emerged.

[5] Quoted from Vernon L. Parrington, *Main Currents in American Thought,* I (New York: Harcourt, Brace & Jovanovich, 1927), p. 321.

THOMAS JEFFERSON, ANTI-FEDERALIST

He was Thomas Jefferson, then Secretary of State in Washington's cabinet. Jefferson was the antithesis of his colleague, Hamilton, both in temperament and in ideology. The American yeoman, rather than the commercial man, was Jefferson's ideal of the sovereign citizen. He was convinced that no other people of the world were so well off as the independent, rural landowners of the United States. Having seen the wretchedness of European cities, he was all the more certain that the benefits of the American yeoman must be maintained. It should be pointed out, however, that Jefferson did not stand as tribune for all the groups made up of the common man. He distrusted the proletariat—the workers in the cities. The slum was his measurement of a sick society.

It is commonly believed that Jefferson was an idealist, as opposed to Hamilton, the hardfisted realist. Actually, an argument could be presented to show that just the reverse was true. If we assume that a realist is one who would make the best of the situation facing him, and the idealist is the proponent of things as they should be, then Jefferson emerges more and more as the realist. Jefferson and Hamilton lived before the age of great industrial development in this country. Jefferson based his political philosophy on an existing agrarian economy. He faced conditions as they were, and sought to make the best of them. Under the above definition, that would make him a realist. Hamilton did everything he could to gear America for a capitalist, industrial future. He was so far ahead of his time that we can only conclude that he was an idealist.

The two clashed on every point. For Jefferson's purposes, a decentralized, States' rights government was sufficient. Since credit, commerce, and manufacturing were subordinate matters, Jefferson would have been content with no more government than was necessary to preserve internal order. Hamilton stood for exactly the opposite. Thus, the Federalist leader insisted upon a *responsible* government—one that could protect property and aid commerce—whereas Jefferson was much more interested in a *responsive* government, and was more concerned with the current needs of the people than in security.

The two champions inevitably clashed openly, as they had privately since their appointments as cabinet officers. The issue came to a head in 1791. Jefferson returned from a tour through New England with Madison to find himself the center of controversy. The two had already been mentioned in the *Maryland Journal* as potential anti-Federalist leaders. At this point, Edmund Burke in England had launched an attack upon those who defended the French Revolution. Paine had replied in his brilliant defense of democracy, *Rights of Man*. The Federalists saw to it that Burke's charges were widely reprinted in America. Paine's reply was slow in coming. Jefferson had obtained a copy from Madison, however, and it elated him; here was the answer to the Federalist gospel, he believed. Jefferson was stimulated into making some move against the Hamiltonians.

He encouraged the American publication of Paine's book. Unfortunately, Jefferson had to return the only copy of the *Rights of Man* before he had finished it, so that it could be set up in type. To save time, he sent it directly to the printer, and he enclosed a note explaining the reason for the delay: "I am extremely pleased to find it will be reprinted here," he wrote, "and that something is at length to be publicly said against the political heresies which have sprung up among us. I have no doubt our citizens will rally a second time round the standard of *Common Sense*."

Jefferson maintained that he was surprised when he discovered the printer had used this note as a preface to the book. The general reader could only assume that the Secretary of State meant that the "political heresies" applied to such leaders as Vice President John Adams, whose tedious "Discourses of Davilla" were being accepted as holy writ by Federalists as the essays appeared serially in John Fenno's *Gazette of the United States*. This was of course a serious breach of official family etiquette. Cabinet members were not supposed to bicker publicly. As a result, a storm of abuse broke over Jefferson. His friends rose to defend him. Another result was that thousands rushed to buy copies of the Paine book. Thus, the political battle was joined, and Jefferson found himself thrust into the van as leader. He accepted the responsibility.

PHILIP FRENEAU, JEFFERSON'S EDITOR

Philip Freneau, who helped to start the second internal revolution, was a lifelong rebel. It is significant that he was of Huguenot extraction. The Huguenots had suffered for generations in the cause of religious freedom. Freneau was graduated from Princeton in 1771. At that time the college was a hotbed of sedition. Among the students who gathered in the room Freneau shared with James Madison were such "Radicals" as Harry Lee, Aaron Burr, and William Bradford, later a member of Washington's cabinet. Freneau was the most zealous patriot of the lot. Long before the Revolution he was writing newspaper contributions and fierce poems on liberty. After Lexington and Concord, he took an active part in the conflict—a rather pathetic little man, pitting his feeble efforts uselessly, as it turned out, against the enemy. For Freneau was far ahead of his time. While he was arguing for independence, most of his colleagues were still thinking in terms of home rule and reform. In disgust, he took to the sea in one of his father's ships.

He was in Bermuda when news arrived of the Declaration of Independence. Here was Revolution he could understand. Freneau hurried home to take an active part in the movement. With Letters of Marque (license for a civilian to wage war) from the Continental Congress, he put his available resources into a privateer, a vessel he called the "Aurora." The ship had to strike its colors in the first battle, and Freneau spent weary weeks in the notorious British prison hulks anchored in New York harbor—an experience that left him physically shattered, and which made him an even more implacable hater of the British. At length he was exchanged. Returning to New York sick and penniless, he turned to his last resource—his pen. Freneau's poem, "The Prison Ship," whipped apathetic patriots into renewed efforts against the enemy. His account of the exploits of John Paul Jones instilled pride into a dejected nation.

He is not a heroic figure—this seedy wisp of a man, his pockets stuffed with poetry written on any scrap of paper he could find. Yet he did as much to fire up the morale of the patriots by poetry as Paine had through prose. His title, "Poet of the Revolution," is indeed valid. Had this been his only contribution, he would more appropriately be discussed in a history of literature, rather than in a story of journalism. His greatest work still lay ahead, however.

By the end of the war he had given his health, his fortune, and all his soul to the cause of liberty. As he saw it, the sacrifice had been in vain. He charged his old leaders—Washington included—with failure to carry out the promises of 1776. He saw Jeffersonian Republicanism as a movement to carry on the original drives of the Revolution over the opposition of the Federalists.

It was Madison, Freneau's classmate, who brought the little rebel to Jefferson's attention. Madison had told the Anti-Federalist leader that Freneau was just the man to engage in journalistic jousting with such champions as Fenno or Russell. Jefferson was always considerate of the ideas of Madison, who was like a son to the master of Monticello. He offered Freneau a small subsidy as State Department translator if he would found an Anti-Federalist paper. It was not money that lured Freneau to the capital at Philadelphia, however. He saw himself as a journalistic crusader striving to fix the attention of the public on the prize of Revolutionary victory, which he believed had been denied by the Federalist counterrevolution.

FRENEAU VS. FENNO: VITUPERATIVE PARTISANSHIP

And so it was that Freneau became editor of the *National Gazette* (often called the "Federal Gazette") in 1791. The early editions were mild enough, but there were hints of what was to come. Fenno, his rival, would never have tolerated a phrase like "public opinion sets the bounds to every government, and is the real sovereign of every free one." [6] The four short columns of comment on page one of the *National Gazette* looked innocuous in those first few months, but while Fenno was ridiculing the right of plain citizens to complain against government officials, Freneau was telling his readers that "perpetual jealousy of the government" was necessary against "the machinations of ambition," and he warned that "where that jealousy does not exist in a reasonable degree, the saddle is soon prepared for the back of the people." [7] But these

[6] *National Gazette,* December 19, 1791.
[7] *National Gazette,* February 9, 1792.

were mere ripples in the placid pool heretofore dominated by the Federalist frogs. Freneau, the poet, had yet to adopt fully the vitriolic language of the political partisan.

Then one day Freneau discharged both barrels at Hamilton over the injustices of the funding system. He used the pen name "Brutus" that day, and at once the Federalist leader discovered he had a journalistic foe worthy of his steel. Day by day Freneau sent succeeding volleys after the first one, and his brashness encouraged other articulate voices to sound the call to battle stations. Even the less gifted Anti-Federalist editors could arouse readers now, by picking up *National Gazette* "exchanges." The alarm of the Federalists was indicated by the torrent of abuse flowing from their editorial pens, but this, too, Freneau could return in double measure.

Freneau was so dangerous to Hamilton's plans that the Secretary of the Treasury made the mistake of taking up the cudgels personally. Convinced that the "Federal Gazette" had been established by his arch-rival, Jefferson, for the sole purpose of wrecking all that he had built so carefully, Hamilton tossed aside the dignity of his office to engage in public bickering. His contribution to Fenno's paper was over the signature "T.L.," but the word soon got around that Hamilton was the author. He charged that Freneau had no right to criticise the government that paid him his subsidy as a translator. Freneau answered:

> The above is beneath reply. It might be queried, however, whether a man who receives a small stipend for services rendered as a French translator to the Department of State, and as editor of a free newspaper admits into his publication impartial strictures on the proceedings of government, is not more likely to act an honest and distinterested part toward the public, than a vile sycophant, who obtaining emoluments from government, far more lucrative than the salary alluded to [a reference to Fenno's printing contract with the Senate and Treasury, and his alleged business connections with the Bank of the United States], finds his interest in attempting to poison the minds of the people by propaganda and by disseminating principles and sentiments utterly subversive of the true republican interests of the country, and by flattering and recommending every and any measures of government however pernicious and destructive its tendency might be to the great body of the people. The world is left to decide the motive of each. . . .[8]

PRESIDENT WASHINGTON'S INVOLVEMENT

Such exchanges explain why the relations of Hamilton and Jefferson became more and more strained. They made cabinet meetings difficult for President Washington. The President performed one of his greatest services to his country when he tolerated such dissension within his official family. Washing-

[8] *National Gazette,* July 28, 1792.

ton knew how to draw out the best in each of his brilliant protégés. In the light of history it is apparent that the country profited by the fight. Jefferson took some of the conceit and arrogance out of Hamilton, and Hamilton made Jefferson test his concepts on the solid ground of public opinion. But in the summer of 1792 even the Father of His Country could not control the cabinet foes. Hamilton publicly charged that Jefferson was the real author of the *National Gazette*'s vilifications, which, of course, was also an insult to Freneau. The editor replied with an affidavit denying that the Secretary of State had ever written a line for the paper, which is more than Fenno could say about the Secretary of the Treasury.

Although Jefferson, so far as is known, never did write directly for the Anti-Federalist organ, Washington called him on the carpet, along with Hamilton. Before his chief Hamilton admitted authorship of the embarrassing newspaper pieces, but he said he had been driven to desperation by his rival's political deceit. Jefferson, on the other hand, admitted that he had no faith in the party of Hamilton (and Washington), and he added that he resented Hamilton's interference in State Department matters. As to the articles written by Freneau, he said he could see no reason to censor an editor for attempting to uncover "aristocratic and monarchial principles."

Both Freneau and Fenno were rivals for public favor, Jefferson later wrote the President. Fenno courted by flattery, and the other by censure, he added, and ". . . the one has been as servile as the other has been severe." Referring to Hamilton, the Secretary of State continued: "But is not the dignity and even decency of government committed when one of its principal ministers enlists himself as an anonymous writer . . . for either one or the other of them?" As for the objections that had been made to Freneau's criticism of governmental measures, Jefferson answered with feeling that ". . . no government ought to be without censors; and where the press is free, no one ever will. If [the government is] virtuous, it need not fear the free operation of attack and defense. Nature has given to man no other means of sifting out the truth, either in religion, law, or politics. . . ." [9]

There could be no resolving of differences between leaders of two such opposite views. Freneau and his increasing corps of imitators swung into the fray all the more furiously after this attempt at mediation. Freneau even had the audacity to swing at Washington and Vice President Adams. This helps to explain the reputation he established in history. The Federalists, who controlled the leading colleges, saw to it that Freneau lost all claim to his former recognition as the "Father of American Poetry."

It must be said that he gained nothing personally for his pains. His paper was widely read and exerted great influence, but it produced little revenue. Nor did his position bring him power or prestige. And certainly the arousing

[9] This exchange can be followed in more detail in Bowers, *Jefferson and Hamilton*, pp. 168–74. The quotation is from Saul K. Padover, *Thomas Jefferson on Democracy* (New York: Penguin, 1939), p. 93. Copyright 1939, D. Appleton-Century Company, Inc., by permission of the publishers, Appleton-Century-Crofts, New York.

of hate was not pleasant to him. He did enjoy a fight, it is true, but only for a purpose. "How oft has rugged nature charged my pen with gall," he once lamented, remembering all the enemies he had made. But if his personal war was grim and onerous, it was warfare for a cause. He was fighting with every weapon at his command for an ideal, and against a foe that offered no quarter. The victory he sought was the survival of the democratic spirit.

That was why he dared attack such demigods as Washington and Adams. He knew very well that the first President was great-souled. Anyone who had served with the Commander-in-Chief during the War of Independence, as had Freneau, understood that. But Washington appeared to Freneau to be a "front" for the Federalists. The editor believed that the old war hero was being used unfairly by the opposition. The only solution Freneau could suggest was to turn the hero back to human clay again. It was the same motivation mentioned in the discussion of Samuel Adams in an earlier chapter. Freneau smeared his old chief so that the words of a hero would not have undue weight with those who opposed his party. This, of course, is no *excuse* for such motives, but it is a *reason* for Freneau's policy.

We cannot blame Washington for cursing "that rascal Freneau," when the editor wrote such impudent items as: "The first magistrate of a country . . . seldom knows the real state of the nation, particularly if he be buoyed up by official importance to think it beneath his dignity to mix occasionally with the people." That was a low blow, indeed, to the man who had led his ragged army from Valley Forge to victory.

In the end, it was neither the opposition nor the government that defeated Freneau. The *National Gazette* simply died of financial malnutrition. There were no "angels" to come to the rescue, as there had been for Fenno under Hamilton's sponsorship. Jefferson could offer some help, but when he left the cabinet in 1793, Freneau had virtually no financial support. By that time, the editor was nearly bankrupt. When yellow fever drove his workmen out of the city, Freneau closed the office. He never reopened it. The paper had lasted only two years, but it is doubtful if any other publication had ever accomplished so much in that time. The end of the paper was just about the end of Freneau as a journalist, too. He tried his hand for a time in New Jersey and New York, but eventually he returned to the sea. Later, he was rediscovered as a poet.

Annotated Bibliography

Books

Axelrad, Jacob, *Philip Freneau: Champion of Democracy*. Austin: University of Texas Press, 1967. Carefully researched biography.

Bailey, Thomas A., *A Diplomatic History of the American People*. New York:

Appleton-Century-Crofts, 1969. Eighth edition of a leading account of foreign policy.

Binkley, Wilfred E., *American Political Parties: Their Natural History.* New York: Knopf, 1963. A clear and thoughtful study of the topic. The chapters on the early party era are good background reading.

Boorstin, Daniel, *The Americans: The National Experience.* New York: Random House, 1965. Consensus history; traces social history to the Civil War, minimizing political conflicts, clashes of ideas.

Bowers, Claude G., *Jefferson and Hamilton.* Boston: Houghton Mifflin, 1925. This book is particularly interesting to the student of journalism because the author draws heavily upon newspaper sources for much of his documentation. Strongly Anti-Federalist.

Cobbett, William, *Selections.* Oxford: Clarendon Press, 1923. These excerpts from the journalist's detailed *Works* demonstrate the style and content of Cobbett's best contributions.

Faÿ, Bernard, *Notes on the American Press at the End of the Eighteenth Century.* New York: Grolier Club, 1927. A brief study, with facsimiles of leading papers.

Hartz, Louis, *The Liberal Tradition in America.* New York: Harcourt Brace Jovanovich, 1955. An interpretation of political thought since the Revolution; leading effort to generalize the idea of an American consensus—a liberal community which developed no proletariat, but a victorious middle class.

Jensen, Merrill, *The New Nation.* New York: Knopf, 1950. A brilliant refutation of the dreary picture of the confederation period, as painted by such classic historians as John Fiske.

Krout, John Allen, and Dixon Ryan Fox, *The Completion of Independence, 1790–1830,* A History of American Life, Vol. V. New York: Macmillan, 1944. Social history.

Leary, Lewis, *That Rascal Freneau.* New Brunswick: Rutgers University Press, 1941. The standard "life" of the Anti-Federalist editor.

Lipset, Seymour, *The First New Nation: The United States in Historical and Comparative Perspective.* New York: Basic Books, 1963. Application of the comparative approach to U.S. history.

Lodge, Henry Cabot, *Alexander Hamilton.* Boston: Houghton Mifflin, 1882. A sympathetic treatment of the great Federalist.

McMaster, John Bach, *A History of the People of the United States from the Revolution to the Civil War.* 8 vols. New York: Appleton-Century-Crofts, 1883–1913. McMaster is chosen from among some of the best historians who wrote of this period, because he depended upon newspaper sources to bring out the flavor and the temper of the times.

Nevins, Allan, *American Press Opinion, Washington to Coolidge.* Boston: Heath, 1928. This book is a fairly complete journalistic history, using short comment, followed by verbatim documentation. An excellent reference.

Osborne, John W., *William Cobbett: His Thought and His Times.* New Brunswick, N.J.: Rutgers University Press, 1966. Biography of the Federalist editor of *Porcupine's Gazette.*

Pollard, James E., *The Presidents and the Press.* New York: Macmillan, 1947. The attitude of the Chief Executive regarding the press is an indicator of journalistic prestige and power, decade by decade. This book is useful as a supplementary text.

Rutland, Robert Allen, *The Birth of the Bill of Rights, 1776–1791.* Chapel Hill: University of North Carolina Press, 1955. A documented study of the origins and passage of the 10 amendments.

Schachner, Nathan, *Alexander Hamilton.* New York: Appleton-Century-Crofts, 1946. A middle-of-the-road interpretation.

Scudder, H. E., *Noah Webster.* Boston: Houghton Mifflin, 1882. An adequate, concise biography of a versatile and interesting personality, who, among his other accomplishments, was a noted journalist.

Stewart, Donald H., *The Opposition Press of the Federalist Period.* Albany: State University of New York Press, 1969. A scholarly study of the partisan press with much new detail.

Van Doren, Carl, ed., *The Federalist.* New York: Heritage Press, 1945. An annotated edition of the famous series of political editorials.

Periodicals and Monographs

"Cobbett," *Fraser's Magazine,* XII (August 1835), 207. A personality sketch, which brings out the journalist's wit and pugnacity.

Coll, Gary, "Noah Webster: Journalist, 1783–1803," Ph.D. thesis, Southern Illinois University, 1971. Assesses his contributions to both form and content of the newspaper and magazine.

Reitzel, William, "William Cobbett and Philadelphia Journalism," *Pennsylvania Magazine,* LIX (July 1935), 223. An excellent interpretation of the journalist. Reprinted in Ford and Emery, *Highlights in the History of the American Press.*

"William Cobbett," *Littell's Living Age,* XLI (Spring 1854), 61. A short but surprisingly complete biographical sketch, with an interesting section on Cobbett's career in America.

Done in Convention, by the unanimous consent of the States present, the seventeenth day of September, in the year of our Lord, one thousand seven hundred and eighty-seven, and of the Independence of the United States of America the twelfth. In witness whereof we have hereunto subscribed our names.

GEORGE WASHINGTON, President,

And Deputy from Virginia.

New-Hampshire. { *John Langdon, Nicholas Gilman.*

Massachusetts. { *Nathaniel Gorham, Rufus King.*

Connecticut. { *William Samuel Johnson, Roger Sherman.*

New-York. *Alexander Hamilton.*

New-Jersey. { *William Livingston, David Brearly, William Paterson, Jonathan Dayton.*

Pennsylvania. { *Benjamin Franklin, Thomas Mifflin, Robert Morris, George Clymer, Thomas Fitzsimons, Jared Ingersoll, James Wilson, Gouverneur Morris.*

Delaware. { *George Read, Gunning Bedford, junior. John Dickinson, Richard Bassett, Jacob Broom.*

Maryland. { *James Mc Henry, Daniel of St. Tho. Jenifer. Daniel Carrol.*

Virginia. { *John Blair, James Madison, junior.*

North-Carolina. { *William Blount, Richard Dobbs Spaight, Hugh Williamson.*

South-Carolina. { *John Rutledge, Charles C. Pinckney, Charles Pinckney, Pierce Butler,*

Georgia. { *William Few, Abraham Baldwin.*

Attest, *William Jackson,* SECRETARY.

In CONVENTION, Monday, September 17th, 1787

PRESENT

The States of New-Hampshire, Massachusetts, Connecticut, Mr. *Hamilton* from New-York, New-Jersey, Pennsylvania, Delaware, Maryland, Virginia, North-Carolina, South-Carolina and Georgia:

RESOLVED,

THAT the preceding Constitution be laid before the United States in Congress assembled, and that it is the opinion of this Convention, that it should afterwards be submitted to a Convention of Delegates, chosen in each State by the People thereof, under the recommendation of its Legislature, for their assent and ratification; and that each Convention assenting to, and ratifying the same, should give notice thereof to the United States in Congress assembled.

Resolved, *That it is the opinion of this Convention, that as soon as the Conventions of nine States shall have ratified this Constitution, the United States in Congress assembled should fix a day on which Electors should be appointed by the States which shall have ratified the same, and a day on which the Electors should assemble to vote for the President, and the time and place for commencing proceedings under this Constitution. That after such publication the Electors should be appointed, and the Senators and Representatives elected: That the Electors should meet on the day fixed for the Election of the President, and should transmit their votes certified, signed, sealed and directed, as the Constitution requires, to the Secretary of the United States in Congress assembled, that the Senators and Representatives should convene at the time and place assigned; that the Senators should appoint a President of the Senate, for the sole purpose of receiving, opening and counting the votes for President; and, that after he shall be chosen, the Congress, together with the President, should, without delay, proceed to execute this Constitution.*

By the unanimous Order of the Convention,

GEORGE WASHINGTON, President.

William Jackson, Secretary.

Boston Gazette

Bettmann Archive

Cartoon of the Lyon-Griswold duel in the hall of Congress.

8

The Tocsin of a Nation

The press [is] the only tocsin of a nation.
—Jefferson to Thomas Cooper

One of the leading journalists who carried the torch of Anti-Federalism dropped by Freneau was Benjamin Franklin Bache, the grandson of Benjamin Franklin. Bache was just 21 when he founded the *Philadelphia General Advertiser*, better known as the *Aurora* (the name appeared in small print around the name plate). Bache was a mercurial young man—impetuous, brilliant, and often intemperate in expression. He was influenced by the style of Freneau, and his paper was even more violently partisan than the *National Gazette* had been. Too often he was downright vicious.

BACHE AND THE *AURORA*

Not that the Federalists did not give him cause for his editorial mudslinging. He had seen the statue of his grandfather—one of the great men of the country—desecrated by hoodlums inspired to acts of vandalism by those opposed to the principles so ably enunciated by "Poor Richard" in Franklin's famous *Almanac*. Brought up in France and Switzerland by his doting grandfather, young Bache was sympathetic to the French cause from the beginning of his journalistic career. That put him in opposition to President Washington when the old war hero backed up the anti-French party headed by Hamilton and others. Like Freneau, Bache resorted to personal attack in his campaign to wreck the Federalist party. He even tried to besmirch the character of "The Father of His Country."

"If ever a nation was debauched by a man, the American nation has been debauched by Washington," he wrote in the December 23, 1796, issue of the *Aurora.*

Federalists wrecked the *Aurora* office and beat the editor in retaliation. Fenno caned Bache in the street and Cobbett wrote of him in *Porcupine's Gazette:*

> This atrocious wretch (worthy descendant of old Ben) knows that all men of any understanding put him down as an abandoned liar, as a tool and a hireling, . . . He is an ill-looking devil. His eyes never get above your knees. He is of a sallow complexion, hollow-cheeked, dead eyed, and has *a toute ensemble,* just like that of a fellow who has been about a week or ten days in a gibbet.[1]

Some historians have called this period the "Dark Ages of Journalism," because of the scurrility of the press. This was a transition period, however, and perhaps violent partisanship, as reflected in the press, was a means of expending some of the venom stored up against the British after the war.[2] Adding to the tension was the war between Great Britain and Napoleonic France. It was not easy for Americans to take the advice of Washington, who warned against entangling foreign alliances in the last hours of his administration.[3] The new nation had little to gain by taking sides, but unfortunately, the war was forced upon the attentions of Americans by the belligerents.

The French and the British were about equally callous regarding American foreign policy. The "paper" blockades imposed by Napoleon violated international precedent, and American shipping interests were infuriated by unlawful seizure of their vessels by the French. But the British were annoying, too. They had fallen back upon the "Rule of 1756," which forbade neutrals from trading in wartime with nations not ordinarily regular customers. This made sense to the British, for it was clear to them that the enemy otherwise could supply himself through adjoining neutral countries, despite the blockade, but the enforcement of this rule threatened the development of American commerce.

THE ISSUE OF FRANCE

But the Federalists saw evil only in France. They were repelled by the excesses of the French Revolution, and by the success of Napoleon. Since the Federalists were in firm control of the government, they could manipulate for-

[1] *Porcupine's Gazette,* November 16, 1797.

[2] See, for example, B. E. Martin, "Transition Period of the American Press," *Magazine of American History,* XVII (April 1887), 273–94.

[3] It is remarkable all during these critical years how all roads to safety eventually led right back to Washington. He was not a political genius, but he appeared to know instinctively the policies that would offer the greatest security to the nation he had saved in wartime.

eign policy to favor the British. The Anti-Federalists argued that America had the duty of siding with France in the name of Rochambeau, Lafayette, and DeGrasse, who had come from France to help us win our war with Britain. Federalists answered that our promises of assistance to France in time of trouble had been made to a government since overthrown by a regime to which we had no binding ties.[4] The fact is, Federalists and Anti-Federalists were in conflict over the issue not because of persuasive logic, but because of partisan bitterness.

Both sides found ammunition for their cause in the European issue. There was, for example, the case of "Citizen" Edmond Charles Genêt, minister to the United States from the French Republic. Genêt arrived in Charleston in the spring of 1793. Had he arrived in Boston he might have been sent home packing, but the South was Anti-Federalist territory, and on the Frenchman's month-long trip north, it was roses, roses all the way. By that time he was so certain he had public opinion behind him that when President Washington brushed off suggestions that the French be allowed to use American ports for refitting damaged war vessels, Genêt went right ahead with his plans. Washington was correct in slapping down such a presumptuous guest of the country, and the people, as a whole, approved. The Federalists used the incident to discredit their pro-French opponents.

Even more embarrassing to the Anti-Federalists was the so-called "XYZ Affair," in which it appeared that the unscrupulous French foreign minister, Talleyrand, had informed our diplomats that he would receive them as accredited ministers only after they had paid him a bribe. It was very difficult to defend pro-French sentiment in the face of such raw insults to national pride.

On the other hand, the Anti-Federalists were collecting a few rocks to throw at their enemies, too. Genêt's mistake hurt the Anti-Federalist cause in one way, but it did show how many countrymen were opposed to Federalist policy. Many a timid Republican was thus encouraged to enlist in Jefferson's party. The treaty signed by John Jay in 1794 was also used against the Federalists. "Jay's Treaty" was an attempt to get the British to meet agreements negotiated during the Treaty of Paris, which ended the War for Independence. It did get the British out of the frontier forts that they had promised to evacuate, but nothing was settled about impressment of American seamen, which irritated many Americans, especially those doomed to the harsh life of the British Navy. The Federalist leaders had no intention of forcing the British at this time, and the scorn of the people for Jay, one of the authors of *The Federalist* papers, was violent. At that, Jay did about as well as he could, what with Hamilton notifying the British authorities secretly that the administration had no wish to press its claims at that point—a policy that reduced Jay's bargaining power to zero.

Partisan feeling was running high when John Adams took the oath of

[4] Just as commitments to Chiang Kai-shek in World War II did not bind the United States to the succeeding Chinese Communist government.

office as the second president of the United States, after the election of 1796. With the Federalists in firm control, the administration began to prepare for war with France. Congress dutifully authorized an army of 35,000, which was a larger force than Washington had ever had at his disposal during the Revolution. Two new superfrigates, the "United States" and the "Constitution," were laid down as part of the war program. To pay for these items Congress levied a tax that fell particularly heavily upon the small landowner, who was least interested in foreign wars.

The result was a political and journalistic battle that passed all the bounds of decency. Even during the Revolution, when Tory and patriot clawed at each other, there had never been such a caterwaul. Bache and Fenno carried their personal feud beyond the pages of their papers by engaging in a street brawl. "Peter Porcupine" (William Cobbett) brought invective to finest flower by attacking well-known Anti-Federalists, living and dead.

THE ALIEN AND SEDITION ACTS OF 1798

This was the situation when the administration tried to throttle such violent opposition in the summer of 1798. In June and July of that year, Congress passed the Alien and Sedition Acts. One was a law aimed at troublesome foreigners living in the country; the other concerned the muzzling of irritating editors.

There were then about 25,000 aliens in the United States. Many of them were refugees from stern authorities in their home lands, and they therefore tended to be on the side of the Jeffersonians, who believed in as little government as possible. Others were poor, or at least propertyless, and again such persons were more likely to gravitate into the ranks of the Anti-Federalists. Groups such as the Irish immigrants were by tradition opposed to the British, and so could not possibly see any good in the Hamiltonian policy of British appeasement. There were also many intellectuals in this category. Dr. Joseph Priestley, the discoverer of oxygen and seven other gases, was a British expatriate noted for his leftist views. The Du Ponts, at that time aggressive backers of liberalism, brought French ideas into the platform of the Anti-Federalists. And there was Albert Gallatin, destined to be a great Secretary of the Treasury under Jefferson, who was already making a name for himself in Pennsylvania, despite the difficulty of adjusting to a country so different from his native Switzerland. Men like these were almost certain to be opposed to the administration. The Alien Act, it was hoped, would reduce the ranks of these threatening foreigners.

One provision of the law was an extension of the naturalization period from five to fourteen years. Another clause empowered the President to deport aliens judged by him to be subversive (a power Adams did not actually employ). Some foreign-born Americans, such as John Burk, publisher of the Anti-

Federalist *Time Piece* in New York, went underground until the trouble blew over. Anyone could see that the alien section applied only to enemies of the administration. Peter Porcupine (William Cobbett) was not only a foreigner who held Americans in contempt, but he was becoming obnoxious, even to some of the Federalist leaders, as the editor of a paper that attacked Vice President Jefferson in almost every issue. But the Sedition Act did not protect the office of Vice President against false criticism.

The Sedition Act was an obvious attempt to control the journalistic spokesmen of the Anti-Federalists. It declared: "That if any person shall write, print, utter, or publish . . . any false, scandalous and malicious writing . . . against the government of the United States, or either house of the Congress . . . or the said President . . . or to excite against them the hatred of the good people of the United States . . . or to resist or oppose, or defeat any such law . . . shall be punished by a fine not exceeding two thousand dollars, and by imprisonment not exceeding two years." [5] The laws were to stand for two years.

One of the cornerstones of press freedom is the right to express criticism of government and its administrators freely. The Alien and Sedition laws reversed a process that had made America the envy of the oppressed. And yet there were important contributions in the laws. Nor have the repressive features been properly appraised in many accounts of the period. The original bill called for a declaration of war with France. The clauses that followed imposed penalties on all who gave any aid or comfort to this enemy. At the last minute, the war declaration was defeated by a narrow margin, but the following clauses concerning aliens and the press were allowed to stand. That was why all pro-French sentiment was so ruthlessly attacked by the administration.

And in some ways the Sedition Act can be called a *milestone* on the road to freedom of the press. The law did not forbid criticism of the government. It only attempted to curb malicious and false statements published to defame officials. And it provided a pair of safeguards: truth could be offered as a defense, and the jury could determine both the law and the fact. This was the twin argument made by Andrew Hamilton in the John Peter Zenger trial. Now it was enacted into the law of 1798.[6]

At first glance the Sedition Act may appear to merit support. But experience has shown us time and again that the party in power will inevitably abuse such controls in the interests of expediency. It was so in 1798. Even Alexander Hamilton, the father of the Federalist party, was apprehensive of the measure. The ailing and retired General Washington rose from his bed to warn against the abuses he foresaw. President Adams, an honest man despite his political

[5] *U. S. Statutes at Large*, "The Sedition Act," I, Sec. 2, p. 596.

[6] The key votes in the House of Representatives on the Sedition Act were almost entirely on party lines. There were 47 Federalists, 39 Anti-Federalists. The bill passed 44–41, with 43 Federalist votes. Six Federalists joined in the modifications involving truth as a defense. The jury provision, however, was backed by all 39 Anti-Federalists and 28 Federalists. See John D. Stevens, "Constitutional History of the 1798 Sedition Law," *Journalism Quarterly*, XLIII (Summer 1966), 247.

ineptitude, did what he could to modify the bill. Unfortunately, the leaders who had made the Federalist party dominant in all branches of government no longer had the power to impede the machine they had set in motion. Extremists had taken over control, and they were intent upon revenge for all the indignities heaped upon them by opposition editors.

THE VIRGINIA AND KENTUCKY RESOLUTIONS

The Alien and Sedition Acts gave the Anti-Federalists the unifying force their party needed. Jefferson himself began the counterattack, using the repressive laws as the battle line. He was aided in his fight by James Madison, father of the Constitution, but now concerned about the turn of events that had given the Federalists so much control. In the fall of 1798 Jefferson called his party leaders to his home at Monticello. They agreed that little could be accomplished for the time being in persuading Congress to repeal the acts. The Federalists were too strong in both houses of Congress. The hope lay in the State governments, especially in the South, and it was on this basis that the Monticello junta proceeded.

The result was the Virginia and Kentucky Resolutions. The two resolutions emphasized the essential role of a free press in a democracy. But in suggesting the means for restoring rights abused by the Alien and Sedition Acts, the resolutions questioned the very nature of the federal union. The documents affirmed that the federal government was created by the states, and that the states must logically be superior, therefore. On that basis, a state might repudiate, or nullify, a federal law when such a measure was clearly opposed by public opinion in a state. In giving up some of their sovereignty to the federal government, it was argued, the states had thereby entered into a contract. If the federal government violated that contract, then the states involved were no longer bound by it.

Here was a concept that later was to lead to a bloody contest between states' rights and federal authority, but it should be pointed out that in 1798 nullification was used as a weapon to return to the people a freedom threatened by an arrogant party. It is only fair to say that in this period such a principle was certain to be proposed sooner or later. In 1798 there was no such safety valve as "judicial review," or the right of the United States Supreme Court to declare a legislative act unconstitutional. Not until 1803 did John Marshall establish that function of the court in the case of *Marbury v. Madison.*

The Virginia and Kentucky Resolutions were widely reprinted in newspapers up and down the seaboard. Press reaction was generally unfavorable. Some of the editors no doubt saw that the seeds of national disintegration were implanted in the documents. But since the press was predominantly Federalist in policy, much of the opposition was strictly partisan. But in any case, the public had a chance to discuss this important issue, and there is no doubt that the cause of the Anti-Federalists was helped thereby. Jefferson sat back to await the next step.

SEDITION ACT PROSECUTIONS

The Adams administration played right into his hands. The Federalists abused the new laws so openly that for a time freedom of the press was seriously threatened in America. It was far from being the "reign of terror" charged by the opposition, but the record is not one of which Americans can be proud. Timothy Pickering, the Secretary of State, spent half his time reading Anti-Federalist papers so that he could ferret out violators of the law.

One of the victims of the Sedition Act was Matthew Lyon of Vermont. Born in Ireland, Lyon had landed in America as an indentured servant. He had worked his way up to a position of respect and prestige in his community, and was Representative to Congress from his state. Lyon was one of the famous "Green Mountain Boys" in the War for Independence. Cashiered from the army for an act that should have earned him a medal, he was later reinstated and promoted to the rank of colonel.

One afternoon in the House of Representatives, Roger Griswold, a leading Federalist from that citadel of Federalism, Connecticut, made insulting remarks about Lyon's war record. The Vermonter ignored Griswold at first, but when his colleague grasped his coat and repeated the insult, Lyon replied in the uncouth but effective manner of the frontier—he spat in Griswold's eye. Next day Griswold walked up to Lyon's desk in the House and began beating him with a cane. Lyon grabbed a handy pair of fire tongs and beat back his adversary. The Federalists tried to expel Lyon from the House, but failed to muster the needed two-thirds vote.

The Sedition Act was used to settle scores with such persons. The crime charged against Lyon under the Act was the publication of a letter to an editor accusing President Adams of "ridiculous pomp, foolish adulation, and selfish avarice." For such remarks, Lyon was hailed before a Federalist judge, who sentenced the defendant to four months in jail and a fine of a thousand dollars. The vindictiveness of the judge was indicated by the fact that although the trial was held in Rutland, Vermont, where there was a passable jail, Lyon was condemned to a filthy cell at Vergennes, some 40 miles distant. Thousands of local citizens signed a petition requesting parole for the prisoner. It was ignored. When Editor Anthony Haswell printed an advertisement in his *Vermont Gazette* announcing a lottery to raise money for paying the fine, he, too, was hustled off to jail for abetting a "criminal."

The Federalists should have heeded the warning. For the public reaction to such injustice was positive and immediate. Lyon was jailed in October, 1798, convicted by what he called a packed jury of political opponents. In December he was reelected to the House by a two-to-one vote over his closest opponent.

Freed in February, 1799, after money had flowed in to pay his fine, the Vermonter returned in triumph to the capital at Philadelphia. At one time the procession behind his carriage was 12 miles long. In 1801 he was to play a crucial role in making Jefferson president.[7]

Other editors also had felt the lash of the Federalist masters. James Callender was one. He edited the *Richmond Examiner*. For criticising the President, Callender was brought to trial. He probably deserved what he got, for the man was an unprincipled political opportunist. The Federalists were not attacking him on principle, however, but on technicalities, and his case is just as significant as though he were a man of high character. Callender was defended by William Wirt, the South's leading lawyer and man of letters. The judge was Samuel Chase, who had said before he had even arrived in Virginia that he was going to give the Anti-Federalists a lesson. Just as predicted, Callender was found guilty. He was sentenced to nine months in jail.

A Connecticut editor was imprisoned because he criticised the Army and the military policies of Congress. A New York editor wrote an uncomplimentary article about the President, and was promptly jailed. Then the general public began to see through the hypocrisy of the repressive laws. It was noticed that whereas the slightest criticism of President Adams resulted in penalties, violent abuse of Anti-Federalist officials passed unpunished. Bache, for example, was indicted for criticism of Adams and others, while Fenno, who was just as violent, went unscathed.

The persecutions under the Alien and Sedition Acts have sometimes been described as insignificant. In all, there were 14 indictments under the Sedition Act. Eleven trials resulted, with 10 convictions. During the same time span there were at least five other convictions for seditious libel under the provisions of British Common Law in state or federal courts. Eight of the convictions involved newspapers.[8] Whatever the numbers, the uproar over the prosecutions was enough to make it clear that the states had erred in enacting laws during the Revolution perpetuating the concept of seditious libel. What caught a Tory then caught a Republican now. There were a few more seditious libel cases after 1800 but the example of the Sedition Act proved conclusive. People saw that the test of tyranny is not necessarily the number of prosecu-

[7] The 1800 election brought out a flaw in the political machinery. Jefferson was clearly the popular choice for President, but he and his running mate, Aaron Burr, both received 73 electoral votes under the indirect system of election. This threw the election into the House of Representatives, with 16 states having one vote each. The Federalists, despite Hamilton's opposition, voted for Burr. For 35 ballots Jefferson had eight states, one short of a majority. Burr had six and two state delegations were split. One was Vermont. On the final ballot the Federalist from Vermont abstained, thus allowing Lyon to cast the decisive vote. Lyon had not run again in 1800, but he was to serve in the House from 1803 to 1811 as congressman from Kentucky.

[8] James M. Smith, *Freedom's Fetters: The Alien and Sedition Laws and American Civil Liberties* (Ithaca, N.Y.: Cornell University Press, 1956), verifies 14 indictments under the Sedition Act. Other totals are from Mott, *American Journalism*, p. 149.

tions, but the number of men and women restrained from speaking freely because of fear.

But the tide was turning. President Adams would have been undone in any case by the perfidy of his cabinet members, such as Pickering, Wolcott (Treasury), and McHenry (War), but the Alien and Sedition laws had completed the undermining of the top-heavy Federalist party. By 1800 the ponderous edifice, built so carefully by the high priests of property, collapsed of its own weight through insufficient support at the base. The biggest blunder of the Federalists was the passage of the repressive laws.

THE END OF THE BATTLE

By 1800 the battle was over. Fenno and Bache both died in the terrible yellow fever epidemic that scourged Philadelphia in the summer of 1798 while Bache was still under indictment. Freneau, driven out by the fever, never reestablished his *Gazette*. Cobbett had left the country, following a libel suit that forced him into bankruptcy.

On the whole, the press improved after the outstanding character assassins were silenced in one way or the other. The widow Bache married her husband's assistant, William Duane, whose wife had died of the fever. Duane made a decent woman of the *Aurora*. The *Aurora* continued to back Jefferson and his party, but it was much more reasonable in tone under Duane. He was as courageous as Freneau, without Freneau's shrillness and bad taste. He was as colorful in his writing as Cobbett, but without the Englishman's recklessness. Duane suffered for the cause, along with other Anti-Federalists. He was beaten up by hoodlums set upon him by his foes. He also was arrested under the Sedition Act.

The party battle in the House over the Sedition Act continued after the close 44–41 passage vote in 1798. Attempts were made to amend or repeal it in 1799 and again in 1800. In February, 1801, a Federalist effort to extend it two more years was defeated 53–49, with 6 Federalists from the South deserting the party to join all 47 supporters of the new President, Jefferson. The law expired March 3, 1801, under its own terms and was the last federal sedition law until the wartime law of 1917. Jefferson promptly pardoned all those in jail and cancelled remaining trials.[9]

The removal of the national capital from Philadelphia to Washington ended an epoch, and began a new one. There had been a complete change in party and administration control, too. For by 1800 Jefferson's scorned "unimportant men" had risen in wrath to throw out the Federalists who had held them in such contempt. In the election year of 1800, Federalists were dom-

[9] Stevens, *op. cit.*, p. 254.

inant in the House, the Senate, the Presidency, the cabinet, the courts, the churches, business, and education. Up to four-fifths of the newspapers opposed Jefferson and his party.

Against this seemingly invincible army stood the obscure men of farm, workbench, and counter. True, more and more of them were winning the right to vote, and that was to be important in the outcome. On the other hand, they were so disorganized and so individually helpless that their cause appeared to be hopeless. They had only one weapon, but it was enough. That weapon was a free press. For although most newspapers were Federalist organs, enough editorial comment and information was offered under the free press concept to rally public opinion for the ultimate overthrow of the Federalists.

Jefferson understood the function of the press, and he used newspapers effectively. He knew that one feeble publication carrying a message of hope and encouragement could rally the aggrieved and discontented, no matter how much brilliant journalism the opposition had at its command. The little men and the little papers trounced a tightly organized coalition of powerful interests, teaching them that arrogance, force, and misrepresentation are no defenses against an aroused public opinion. The Federalists had intended and used the Alien and Sedition laws to bolster their selfish designs, but these same laws were largely instrumental in damaging the Federalist party so badly that it was more than a generation before members of its persuasion regained political control.

As the historian, Arthur M. Schlesinger, Jr., has written: "When a party starts out by deceiving the people, it is likely to finish by deceiving itself." [10] Since there is good evidence that this statement is true, the press, as demonstrated in this chapter, is more than ever essential in its role of disclosing party deceptions, for without such disclosures the vast majority of the public would not long remain free. Unfortunately, men had to suffer before this was generally understood—men like Lyon, Bache, Duane, and Thomas Adams of the *Boston Independent Chronicle.* Adams and his brother, Abijah, refused to be intimidated by their Federalist persecutors, although prison and worse confronted them. Sick and near death, they answered their detractors in double-space, double-measure Caslon bold type: "The Chronicle is destined to persecution. . . . It will stand or fall with the liberties of America, and nothing shall silence its clarion but the extinction of every principle which leads to the achievement of our independence." [11]

[10] *The Age of Jackson* (Boston: Little, Brown, 1945), p. 282.

[11] Thomas Adams was the first important editor to be indicted under the Sedition Act. Before he could be tried, he was indicted under the common law for criticising the Massachusetts legislature. He was too sick to stand trial, but his brother, Abijah, was convicted and jailed for a month, although he too was ailing. The defiant Thomas, faced with both federal and state sedition trials, sold the *Chronicle* in May, 1799, two weeks before he died.

Annotated Bibliography

Books

Commager, Henry Steele, *Documents of American History.* New York: Appleton-Century-Crofts, 1934; Hawthorn Books, 1969. An interesting history course could be given with this book as a text. Most of the important documents of American history are described briefly and then are printed in original form, including the Alien and Sedition Acts and the Virginia and Kentucky Resolutions, and the replies to them.

Faÿ, Bernard, *The Two Franklins.* Boston: Little, Brown, 1933. A contrast between Benjamin Franklin and his grandson, Benjamin Franklin Bache.

Levy, Leonard W., ed., *Freedom of the Press from Zenger to Jefferson.* Indianapolis: Bobbs-Merrill, 1966. Contains documents and essays related to the Sedition Act, the rise of a Libertarian outlook toward the press, and Jefferson's philosophy.

Miller, John C., *Crisis in Freedom: The Alien and Sedition Acts.* Boston: Little, Brown, 1951. A relatively brief account of passage of the laws and details of the trials.

Nevins, Allan, *American Press Opinion, Washington to Coolidge.* Boston: Heath, 1928. An excellent selection of the partisan editorials of the period is included.

Smith, James M., *Freedom's Fetters: The Alien and Sedition Laws and American Civil Liberties.* Ithaca, N.Y.: Cornell University Press, 1956. Detailed and documented analysis of the laws and court cases.

Periodicals and Monographs

Conway, Moncure D., "An Unpublished Letter of Thomas Paine," *Nation,* LXII (February 6, 1896), 118. Describes French feeling during Washington's administration, and charges the American President with being a hypocrite. Conway is the best known biographer of Paine.

Goldsmith, Adolph O., "The Roaring Lyon of Vermont," *Journalism Quarterly,* XXXIX (Spring 1962), 179. The stormy career of the congressman reelected while in jail for Sedition Act conviction.

Padover, Saul K., "Wave of the Past," *New Republic,* CXVI (April 21, 1947), 14. A concise description of the effect of the Alien and Sedition laws on the Federalist defeat of 1800.

Stevens, John D., "Congressional History of the 1798 Sedition Law," *Journalism Quarterly,* XLIII (Summer 1966), 247. A detailed report of the partisan battle in the House, with analysis of votes.

"Thomas Paine in England and in France," *Atlantic Monthly,* IV (December 1859), 690. Describes the post-Revolutionary influence of Paine, here and abroad.

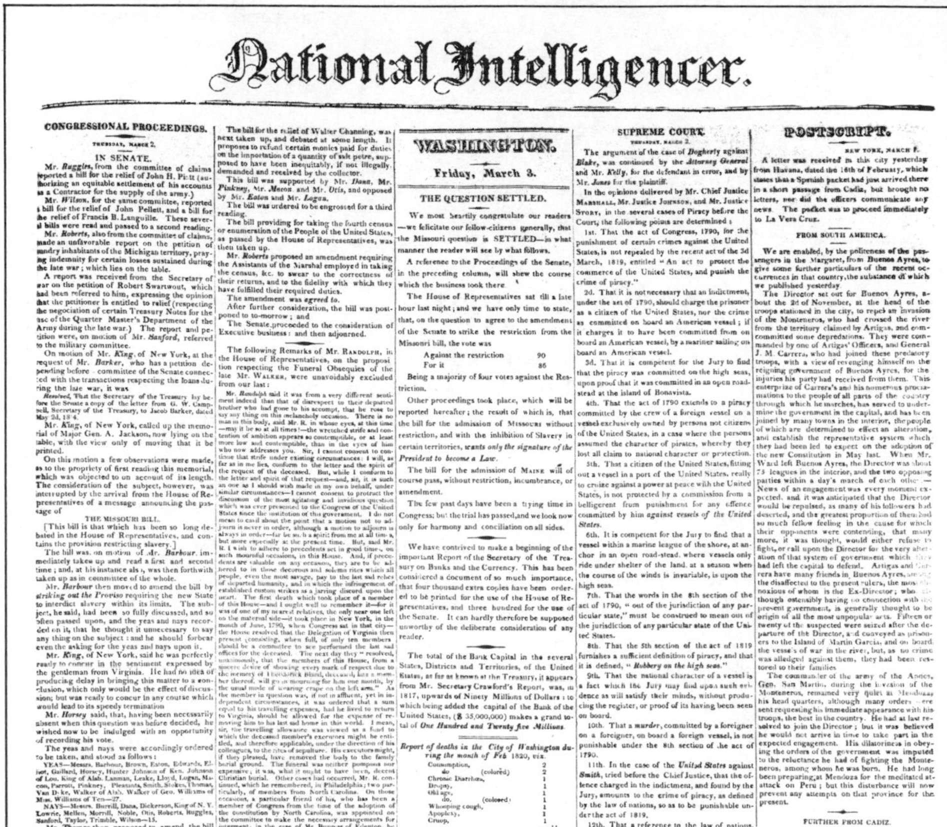
National Intelligencer.

CONGRESSIONAL PROCEEDINGS.

THURSDAY, MARCH 2.

IN SENATE.

Mr. *Ruggles*, from the committee of claims reported a bill for the relief of John H. Piatt (authorizing an equitable settlement of his accounts as a Contractor for the supply of the army.)

Mr. *Wilson*, for the same committee, reported a bill for the relief of John Pellett, and a bill for the relief of Francis B. Languille. These several bills were read and passed to a second reading.

Mr. *Roberts*, also from the committee of claims, made an unfavorable report on the petition of sundry inhabitants of the Michigan territory, praying indemnity for certain losses sustained during the late war; which lies on the table.

A report was received from the Secretary of war on the petition of Robert Swartwout, which had been referred to him, expressing the opinion that the petitioner is entitled to relief (respecting the negociation of certain Treasury Notes for the use of the Quarter Master's Department of the Army during the late war.) The report and petition were, on motion of Mr. *Sanford*, referred to the military committee.

On motion of Mr. *King*, of New York, at the request of Mr. *Barker*, who has a petition depending before committee of the Senate connected with the transactions respecting the loans during the late war, it was

Resolved, That the Secretary of the Treasury be before the Senate a copy of the letter from G. W. Campbell, Secretary of the Treasury, to Jacob Barker, dated May 2d, 1814.

Mr. *King*, of New York, called up the memorial of Major Gen. A. Jackson, now lying on the table, with the view only of moving that it be printed.

On this motion a few observations were made, as to the propriety of first reading this memorial, which was objected to on account of its length. The consideration of the subject, however, was interrupted by the arrival from the House of Representatives of a message announcing the passage of

THE MISSOURI BILL.

[This bill is that which has been so long debated in the House of Representatives, and contains the provision restricting slavery.]

The bill was, on motion of Mr. *Barbour*, immediately taken up and read a first and second time; and, at his instance also, was then forthwith taken up as in committee of the whole.

Mr. *Barbour* then moved to amend the bill by *striking out the Proviso* requiring the new State to interdict slavery within its limits. The subject, he said, had been so fully discussed, and so often passed upon, and the yeas and nays recorded on it, that he thought it unnecessary to say any thing on the subject: and he should forbear even the asking for the yeas and nays upon it.

Mr. *King*, of New York, said he was perfectly ready to concur in the sentiment expressed by the gentleman from Virginia. He had no idea of producing delay in bringing this matter to a conclusion, which only would be the effect of discussion; but was ready to concur in any course which would lead to its speedy termination.

Mr. *Horsey* said that, having been necessarily absent when this question was before decided, he wished now to be indulged with an opportunity of recording his vote.

The yeas and nays were accordingly ordered to be taken, and stood as follows:

YEAS—Messrs. Barbour, Brown, Eaton, Edwards, Elliot, Gaillard, Horsey, Hunter, Johnson of Ken. Johnson of Lou. King of Alab. Lanman, Leake, Lloyd, Logan, Macon, Parrott, Pinkney, Pleasants, Smith, Stokes, Thomas, Van Dyke, Walker of Alab. Walker of Geo. Williams of Miss. Williams of Ten—27.

NAYS—Messrs. Burrill, Dana, Dickerson, King of N. Y. Lowrie, Mellen, Morrill, Noble, Otis, Roberts, Ruggles, Sanford, Taylor, Trimble, Wilson—15.

Mr. *Thomas* then proposed to amend the bill by inserting therein a section declaring the inhibition of slavery in the *Territories* of the United States North of 36 degrees 30 minutes North Latitude (the same as was previously proposed by the Senate to be added to the Maine Bill)

This motion was agreed to, without debate.

The amendments were then reported from the committee of the whole, and the first of them was concurred in without a division.

To the second (Mr. *Thomas's*) Mr. *Trimble* proposed an amendment, which was, to strike out the part thereof descriptive of the territory from which slavery is to be excluded, and in lieu thereof, to insert the following:

"All that part of Louisiana West of the Mississippi, ceded by France to the United States, except the state of Louisiana, the territory included in the proposed state of Missouri and the Arkansaw territory East of the 17th or 94th degree of longitude agreeably to Mellish's map."

Mr. *Trimble* said he would not have offered this amendment, but with the hope that some agreement might take place between the two houses, and in the belief that that amendment embraced principles on which the two houses might unite on this subject. When we go into the territory which was uninhabited at the date of the Louisiana treaty, and is yet uninhabited, very law, he believed, entertained scruples as to the constitutionality of the restriction. For his part, he did not see on what principle the constitution could be brought to bear on the subject. He had offered this amendment with a view, should it succeed, to vote for the bill in its present form. He had little doubt that it contained principles on which, were it agreed to, the bill would pass the other House; and he was under the impression that it would not succeed on the principle of the amendment of the gentleman from Illinois, as it now stood.

The question was then taken, without debate, on Mr. Trimble's motion to amend the amendment, as above stated, and decided as follows:

YEAS—Messrs. Burrill, Dana, Dickerson, King, of N. Y. Lanman, Mellen, Morril, Otis, Ruggles, Sanford, Trimble, Wilson—12.

NAYS—Messrs. Barbour, Brown, Eaton, Edwards, Elliot, Gaillard, Horsey, Johnson, of Ken. Johnson, of Lou. Leake, Lloyd, Logan, Lowrie, Macon, Noble, Palmer, Parrott, Pinkney, Pleasants, Roberts, Smith, Stokes, Taylor, Thomas, Van Dyke, Walker, of Alab. Walker, of Geo. Williams, of Miss. Williams, of Ten.—30.

Mr. *Thomas's* amendment was then concurred in, as agreed to in committee of the whole.

And the amendments were then ordered to be engrossed, and with the bill to be read a third time: it was read a third time accordingly, passed, and sent to the House of Representatives, requesting their concurrence in the amendments.

The engrossed bill for the relief of F. Goetz and others, was read a third time, passed, and sent to the House of Representatives.

The resolution offered yesterday by Mr. *Trimble*, for *enquiring* into the expediency of abolishing the system of trading-houses with the Indian tribes, was agreed to, *nem. con.*

The bill for the relief of Walter Channing, was next taken up, and debated at some length. It proposes to refund certain monies paid for duties on the importation of a quantity of salt petre, supposed to have been inequitably, if not illegally, demanded and received by the collector.

This bill was supported by Mr. *Dana*, Mr. *Pinkney*, Mr. *Macon*, and Mr. *Otis*, and opposed by Mr. *Eaton* and Mr. *Logan*.

The bill was ordered to be engrossed for a third reading.

The bill providing for taking the fourth census or enumeration of the People of the United States, as passed by the House of Representatives, was then taken up.

Mr. *Roberts* proposed an amendment requiring the Assistants of the Marshal employed in taking the census, &c. to swear to the correctness of their returns, and to the fidelity with which they have fulfilled their required duties.

The amendment was *agreed to*.

After further consideration, the bill was postponed to to-morrow; and

The Senate proceeded to the consideration of Executive business: and then adjourned.

The following Remarks of Mr. RANDOLPH, in the House of Representatives, on the proposition respecting the Funeral Obsequies of the late Mr. WALKER, were unavoidably excluded from our last:

[illegible]

FOR SALE.

A HOUSE and LOT, elegantly situated on the bank of the Potomac, in the city of Washington, a few hundred yards south of Major Davidson's wharf. There is a handsome view from the premises of the river, the surrounding country, Mason's island, and Georgetown. The house is substantially built, of brick, two stories high, with six rooms and a passage on each floor, and is now in good repair. The Lot contains 21,330 square feet, bounding on the river. The terms of payment will be easy, and possession given on the 1st of June next. The property formerly belonged to Mr N. G. Maxwell, who built the House, and is now occupied by M. John Gardiner.

Apply to S. M. M'Kean, corner of north I and 17th streets.

mar 3—dtf

WASHINGTON.

Friday, March 3.

THE QUESTION SETTLED.

We most heartily congratulate our readers—we felicitate our fellow-citizens generally, that the Missouri question is SETTLED—in what manner the reader will see by what follows.

A reference to the Proceedings of the Senate, in the preceding column, will shew the course which the business took there.

The House of Representatives sat till a late hour last night; and we have only time to state, that, on the question to agree to the amendment of the Senate to strike the restriction from the Missouri bill, the vote was

Against the restriction	90
For it	86

Being a majority of four votes against the Restriction.

Other proceedings took place, which will be reported hereafter; the result of which is, that the bill for the admission of MISSOURI without restriction, and with the inhibition of Slavery in certain territories, *wants only the signature of the President to become a Law*.

The bill for the admission of MAINE will of course pass, without restriction, incumbrance, or amendment.

The few past days have been a trying time in Congress; but the trial has passed, and we look now only for harmony and conciliation on all sides.

We have contrived to make a beginning of the important Report of the Secretary of the Treasury on Banks and the Currency. This has been considered a document of so much importance, that four thousand extra copies have been ordered to be printed for the use of the House of Representatives, and three hundred for the use of the Senate. It can hardly therefore be supposed unworthy of the deliberate consideration of any reader.

The total of the Bank Capital in the several States, Districts and Territories, of the United States, as far as known at the Treasury, it appears from Mr. Secretary Crawford's Report, was, in 1817, upwards of Ninety Millions of Dollars: to which being added the capital of the Bank of the United States, ($35,000,000) makes a grand total of *One Hundred and Twenty five Millions*.

Report of deaths in the City of Washington during the month of Feb 1820, viz.

Consumption,	2
do. (colored)	2
Chronic Diarrhœa,	1
Dropsy,	1
Old age,	1
do. (colored)	1
Whooping cough,	1
Apoplexy,	1
Croup,	1
	—11
Adults,	8
Children,	3
	—11

HENRY HUNTT, Health Officer.

March 1st 1820.

FOR LIVERPOOL,

The fine coppered Ship Eagle, Capt. Merrill—expected to sail in about 15 days.

For passage, having excellent accommodations, apply to the Master on board, or to

Georgetown, March 3—d2w W. SMITH.

ROBERT LITTLE

HAS just opened an assortment of fine cotton Hosiery, consisting of Ladies' white and black cotton Stockings, ... [fine print partly illegible] ... Articles, have lately been added to his stock.

Pennsylvania avenue, March 3—3t

ROBERT LITTLE

RESPECTFULLY acquaints gentlemen and families residing in this city, and members of Congress, that at his store they may suit themselves with almost every article of fine silver plated goods, and cutlery of the best description; ... [fine print partly illegible] ... march 3—3t

SUPREME COURT.

THURSDAY, MARCH 2.

The argument of the case of *Dogherty* against *Blake*, was continued by the *Attorney General* and Mr. *Kelly*, for the defendant in error, and by Mr. *Jones* for the plaintiff.

In the opinions delivered by Mr. Chief Justice MARSHALL, Mr. Justice JOHNSON, and Mr. Justice STORY, in the several cases of Piracy before the Court, the following points are determined:

1st. That the act of Congress, 1790, for the punishment of certain crimes against the United States, is not repealed by the recent act of the 3d March, 1819, entitled "An act to protect the commerce of the United States, and punish the crime of piracy."

2d. That it is not necessary that an indictment, under the act of 1790, should charge the prisoner as a citizen of the United States, nor the crime as committed on board an American vessel; if it charges it to have been committed from on board an American vessel, by a mariner sailing on board an American vessel.

3d. That it is competent for the Jury to find that the piracy was committed on the high seas, upon proof that it was committed in an open roadstead at the island of Bonavista.

4th. That the act of 1790 extends to a piracy committed by the crew of a foreign vessel on a vessel exclusively owned by persons not citizens of the United States, in a case where the persons assumed the character of pirates, whereby they lost all claim to national character or protection.

5th. That a citizen of the United States, fitting out a vessel in a port of the United States, really to cruise against a power at peace with the United States, is not protected by a commission from a belligerent from punishment for any offence committed by him *against vessels of the United States*.

6th. It is competent for the Jury to find that a vessel within a marine league of the shore, at anchor in an open road-stead, where vessels only ride under shelter of the land, at a season when the course of the winds is invariable, is upon the high seas.

7th. That the words in the 8th section of the act of 1790, "out of the jurisdiction of any particular state," must be construed to mean out of the jurisdiction of any particular state of the United States.

8th. That the 5th section of the act of 1819 furnishes a sufficient definition of piracy, and that it is defined, "*Robbery on the high seas*."

9th. That the national character of a vessel is a fact which the Jury may find upon such evidence as will satisfy their minds, without producing the register, or proof of its having been seen on board.

10th. That a *murder*, committed by a foreigner on a foreigner, on board a foreign vessel, is not punishable under the 8th section of the act of 1790.

11th. In the case of the *United States* against *Smith*, tried before the Chief Justice, that the offence charged in the indictment, and found by the Jury, amounts to crime of piracy, as defined by the law of nations, so as to be punishable under the act of 1819.

12th. That a reference to the law of nations, as contained in the act of 1819, to define the crime of piracy, is such a definition as the constitution of the United States requires.

13th. In the case of the *United States* against *Klintock*, that Aury's commission does not exempt the prisoner from the charge of piracy.

That, although the fraud practised on the Dane may not, in itself, support the charge of piracy, the whole transaction, as stated in the indictment, and in the facts stated in the record, does amount to piracy.

That the prisoner is punishable under the provisions of the 8th section of the act of 1790.

And that the act of 1790 does extend to all persons, on board all vessels which throw off their national character by cruizing piratically, and committing piracy on other vessels.

MARRIED,

On Wednesday evening, at the residence of James Davidson, Esq. by the Revd. Mr. Hawley, Mr. JOHN STOVER, to Mrs. CHARLOTTA JULIA DELNENT, all of this place.

On the 27th instant, by the Rev. Mr. M'Cormick, Mr. ROBERT MARSHALL, to Mrs. ANN BERRY, both of Prince Georges county.

FRANCIS DORMONS, *Tobacconist*,

RESPECTFULLY acquaints his friends, and the citizens of Washington and Georgetown in general, that he has removed from Alexandria to Washington, on Pennsylvania avenue, opposite the Patriotic Bank, where he intends to carry on his business, and will keep a constant supply of the best articles in his line, viz: Spanish Segars, first quality; American, do; Harris's large Twist, first quality, and Barclay's small Twist, do; Lorrilard's Maccaboy, and Rappee and Scotch Snuff; and Smoking Tobacco in papers, &c. &c.

Which he will sell cheap for cash, wholesale and retail.

N. B. He wishes to purchase Country Tobacco, for which cash will be paid. Two or three steady hands will meet with constant employment.

mar 3—dtf

PINE APPLES.

A FEW Pine Apples of superior quality just received and for sale at the Confectionary opposite Davis' Hotel, Pennsylvania Avenue.

march 3—3t

MORE NEW BOOKS.

JUST received, and for sale, at G. DAVIS's Book Store and Lottery Office, the following new Books, &c.

The Forlge Family in Washington; a new supply.

The Red Book of Baltimore, complete. Also, several extra copies of Nos. 1 and 6, to complete sets heretofore purchased.

Ivanhoe, a Romance, by the author of Waverly, &c. &c.

The Munster Cottage Boy, by Regina Maria Roche, author of the Children of the Abbey, &c.

Tales of the Hall, by the Rev George Crabb.

Conversations of Natural Philosophy.

Giovanni Sbogarra, a Venetian Tale, taken from the French, by Percival G——.

Travels of my Landlord.

Sketch Book, complete

mar 3—

POSTSCRIPT.

NEW YORK, MARCH 1.

A letter was received in this city yesterday from Havana, dated the 16th of February, which states that a Spanish packet had just arrived there in a short passage from Cadiz, but brought no letters, nor did the officers communicate any news. The packet was to proceed immediately to La Vera Cruz.

FROM SOUTH AMERICA.

We are enabled, by the politeness of the passengers in the Margaret, from Buenos Ayres, to give some further particulars of the recent occurrences in that country, the substance of which we published yesterday.

The Director set out for Buenos Ayres, about the 2d of November, at the head of the troops stationed in the city, to repel an invasion of the Montoneros, who had crossed the river from the territory claimed by Artigas, and committed some depredations. They were commanded by one of Artigas' Officers, and General J. M. Carrera, who had joined these predatory troops, with a view of revenging himself on the reigning government of Buenos Ayres, for the injuries his party had received from them. This enterprize of Carrera's and his numerous proclamations to the people of all parts of the country through which he marches, has served to undermine the government in the capital, and has been joined by many towns in the interior, the people of which are determined to effect an alteration, and establish the representative system which they had been led to expect on the adoption of the new Constitution in May last. When Mr. Ward left Buenos Ayres, the Director was about 75 leagues in the interior, and the two opposing parties within a day's march of each other. News of an engagement was every moment expected, and it was anticipated that the Director would be repulsed, as many of his followers had deserted, and the greatest proportion of them had so much fellow feeling in the cause for which their opponents were contending, that many more, it was thought, would either refuse to fight, or call upon the Director for the very alteration of that system of government which they had left the capital to defend. Artigas and Carrera have many friends in Buenos Ayres, among the disaffected to the present rulers, the most obnoxious of whom is the Ex-Director; who, although ostensibly having no connection with the present government, is generally thought to be origin of all the most unpopular acts. Fifteen or twenty of the suspected were seized after the departure of the Director, and conveyed as prisoners to the Island of Martin Garcia, and on board the vessels of war in the river; but, as no crime was alleged against them, they had been restored to their families.

The commander of the army of the Andes, Gen. San Martin, during the invasion of the Monteneros, remained very quiet at Mendoza his head quarters, although many orders were sent requesting his immediate appearance with his troops, the best in the country. He had at last resolved to join the Director; but it was believed he would not arrive in time to take part in the expected engagement. His dilatoriness in obeying the orders of the government was imputed to the reluctance he had of fighting the Monteneros, among whom he was born. He had long been preparing, at Mendoza for the meditated attack on Peru; but this disturbance will now prevent any attempts on that province for the present.

FURTHER FROM CADIZ.

Extract of a letter dated "Cadiz, Jan. 6.

"It would appear that a strong division of the Grand Army, originally destined against Buenos Ayres, had orders to march for Cadiz, where a detachment to consist of 6000 men were to be sent to succour Morillo. The day before yesterday, 2000 men entered the Isla, and at the bridge the Marine Guards attempted to oppose their entrance. The result was, that the commander of the guards and the colonel were shot by the approaching troops. On their entering the town they disarmed the Marine Guards, took the captain general of marines prisoner, and proceeded for this place; but the ships of war in the bay having learnt what had taken place at Isla, sent about 400 Marine soldiers and officers to the "Corto Dura,"* who, on the approach of the Insurgents, fired on them from the Fort and killed about 13 on the spot.

The troops then retired to the Isla, and then the commander (a colonel) issued a proclamation styling themselves the advance guard of the "Constitutional army." Other commanders, it is said, have gone with their respective divisions, which consist of the whole of the army of the expedition, to different departments of the kingdom, and that the plot is of magnitude there is no doubt. I will write you soon and more fully, via Gibraltar."—*Phil. Gaz.*

*A strong fort on the Narrow Pass.

PUBLIC SALES.

This Day, at 11 o'clock, a. m.

By John Peabody, Auctioneer.

AT the Bridge street Auction Rooms will be sold an extensive variety of seasonable dry goods and fancy articles: 4-4 and 3-4 white and unbleached domestics; 1 case 4-4 and 6-4 cambrics; Irish linens; bedtickings; vestings; pattinett laces; threads; cotton balls; silk handkerchiefs; cassimere; Canton silk and cotton shawls; Marseilles vestings; boot webbings; umbrellas; 20 dozen high top combs; snuff boxes; 1 case pins; gilt frame looking glasses; tea caddies; dressing glasses; candlesticks; tea boards; steel chains; watches, chains, and seals; an elegant assortment of eight day time-pieces, &c; 106 pair women's welted shoes; 80 pair women's pumps.

At 1 o'clock,

6 setts handsome fancy chairs

2 bureaus

2 sofas; house mats

4 trunks

2 mahogany tables

4 barrels Susquehannah shad.

And at early candlelight,

Dry goods and fancy articles, in lots to suit purchasers.

Georgetown, march 3—

PUBLIC SALE.

By David Bates, Auctioneer.

ON Saturday the 4th at 11 o'clock, A. M. at his store, a parcel of furniture, beds, tables, chairs, &c. looking glass, keg of nails, keg of tobacco, a parcel of port bottles, one barrel vinegar, all without reserve, for cash.

March 3—

The *National Intelligencer* reports the passage of the 1820 Missouri Compromise.

9

The Press and the Expanding Nation

I have lent myself willingly as the subject of a great experiment . . . to demonstrate the falsehood of the pretext that freedom of the press is incompatible with orderly government.
—Jefferson to Seymour

Jefferson's victory in 1800 made his party subject to the same type of attack that had so recently been launched against the Federalists while they were in power. The Jeffersonian "Republicans" had gained control of the administration, but the President estimated that up to three-fifths of the editors continued to support Federalist policies. In some areas Federalist newspapers outnumbered their political rivals by as much as five to one. The rank and file voter was not impressed by this "one-party" press, apparently, for he continued to return to office a long succession of candidates representing the Republican party (as the Anti-Federalists became known before eventually adopting the name, Democratic party).

The disparity between public and editorial opinion in the periods of Jefferson, Jackson, and even in the administration of Franklin D. Roosevelt, has concerned students of our press. They point to the occasions when overwhelming popular mandates coincided with preponderant press opposition to the popular cause, and critics sometimes wonder if the American press is the power the journalists say it is. This history will indicate that the power of the press is not in its persuasion by opinion, but in its dissemination of information and its arousal of interest in important issues hitherto submerged in public apathy.

THE *NEW YORK EVENING POST,* 1801

One of the important Federalist organs was founded by Alexander Hamilton a year after the defeat of his party in 1800. The Federalist leader believed that a reputable party paper was needed more than ever to stem the tide of Republican popularity. This was the *New York Evening Post,* destined to become the city's oldest newspaper. Hamilton chose William Coleman as the first editor. Coleman was a lawyer and former court reporter, again indicating the trend of journalism since the days when the printer-editor was the rule. He was an able editor, but while "The General," as Hamilton liked to be called, was around, it was plain to all that Coleman was subordinate in the office.

Coleman was a writer of some literary pretensions. He could express his convictions in a slashing style that often cut down wavering opposition within and without the party. He also had great personal charm and courage. Eventually, he broke with Hamilton because of Coleman's loyalty to Aaron Burr,[1] but in the founding days of the *Post,* Coleman did not make an editorial move without consulting his sponsor. It is significant that Coleman was a shorthand expert, and that was one reason he had been selected by Hamilton. Late at night Coleman could have been seen in the empty streets hurrying to the home of the Federalists' great leader to take dictation for the next day's editorial. These editorials needed no reworking. They were the work of Hamilton at his journalistic best. Picked up by Federalist editors around the country, they exerted an important party influence.

The victorious party in 1800 needed opposition, as does any party in power. Jefferson had committed himself frequently as a believer in press freedom. His party had fought against the Alien and Sedition Acts in accordance with this doctrine. He had sponsored and encouraged the Virginia and Kentucky Resolutions as an attack on press restrictions by the Federalists. He had helped Freneau and Thomas Ritchie establish newspapers to help stem the tide of Federalist dominance.[2] Now he found himself after the party victory accused of press restrictions by the Federalists. This is a pattern commonly found in the history of American journalism—the reversal of free expression policies, once a group wins power.

JEFFERSON'S VIEW OF THE PRESS

Jefferson appears to have been sincere in his defense of a free press. Even when the press humiliated him, he defended its freedom. Wrote Jefferson to his friend, Carrington, in 1787:

[1] Coleman was a great admirer of Burr and remained loyal even after Hamilton was killed by Burr in a duel in 1804. By that time the editor of the *Post* was expressing himself independently.

[2] In 1804 the President helped Thomas Ritchie found the *Richmond Enquirer,* soon the most influential paper in Virginia. Ritchie was political boss of his state, and his views were therefore of significance throughout the South, and were widely reprinted there.

I am persuaded that the good sense of the people will always be found to be the best army. They may be led astray for a moment, but will soon correct themselves. The people are the only censors of their governors; and even their errors will tend to keep these to the true principles of their institution. To punish these errors too severely would be to suppress the only safeguard of the public liberty. The way to prevent these irregular interpositions of the people, is to give them full information of their affairs through the channel of the public papers, and to contrive that those papers should penetrate to the whole mass of the people. The basis of our government being the opinion of the people, the very first object should be to keep that right; and were it left to me to decide whether we should have a government without newspapers, or newspapers without a government, I should not hesitate a moment to prefer the latter.

This part of Jefferson's letter to Carrington is widely quoted. It is bandied about particularly when press moguls fear various degrees of restriction or inconvenience from any quarter. But the second part of Jefferson's letter is not so well known, though it is a qualification essential to the above statement. For the great statesman went on to say:

But I should mean that every man should receive those papers, and be capable of reading them.

Later, when the Federalist editors had made life miserable for him, he wrote in exasperation to a friend:

The newspapers of our country by their abandoned spirit of falsehood, have more effectually destroyed the utility of the press than all the shackles devised by Bonaparte.[3]

But that was in 1813, when he was very tired. His more considered views of the vicious opposition press are better summed up in the following letter:

They [Federalists] fill their newspapers with falsehoods, calumnies, and audacities. . . . We are going fairly through the experiment of whether freedom of discussion, unaided by coercion, is not sufficient for the propagation and protection of truth, and for the maintenance of an administration pure and upright in its actions and views. No one ought to feel under this experiment, more than myself. Nero wished all the necks of Rome united in one, that he might sever them at a blow. So our ex-federalists, wishing to have a single representative of all the objects of their hatred, honor me with that post and exhibit against me such atrocities as no nation has ever before heard or endured. I shall protect them in the right of lying and calumniating, and still go on to

[3] From the *Letters*. The above is quoted from Saul K. Padover, *Thomas Jefferson on Democracy* (New York: Penguin, 1939), pp. 92–93. Copyright 1939, D. Appleton-Century Company, Inc. By permission of the publishers, Appleton-Century-Crofts, New York.

> merit the continuance of it, by pursuing steadily my object of proving that a people, easy in their circumstances as ours are, are capable of conducting themselves under a government founded not in the fears and follies of man, but on his reason, on the predominance of his social over his dissocial passions, so free as to restrain him in no moral right, and so firm as to protect him from every moral wrong, which shall leave him, in short, in possession of all his natural rights.[4]

But although Jefferson's views on the press were well known to his followers, and although he wielded strong control over his party, he could not keep his subordinates from trying to impose restrictions on opposition editors, now that the Jeffersonians were in power. Much has been made of this inconsistency. Actually, the victorious Republicans were rather restrained, considering their former persecution. Moreover, the preponderant Federalist press continued to spread vindictive libels against the administration. With Republican victory there came the understandable temptation to even up old scores. Granted all this, however, the prosecutions brought by the Republicans against Federalist editors did not square with the earlier statements regarding freedom of expression in the preceding period.

An example of this vindictiveness was the prosecution of Joseph Dennie for remarks deemed by Republican party leaders to be seditious. Dennie, a grandson of Bartholomew Green, Jr., onetime printer of the *Boston News-Letter,* was one of the ablest editors of his day. His *Farmer's Weekly Museum,* published at Walpole. New Hampshire, was so popular that it achieved national recognition. Later, Dennie took over the editorial direction of the *Port Folio,* an outspoken Federalist magazine published in Philadelphia. Shortly after Jefferson moved into the unfinished White House, Dennie wrote a series of editorials pointing out the weaknesses of popular rule. Although he did not attack the American Government specifically, he made it clear that he believed democracy to be futile. These remarks were declared by government officials to be seditious, and the editor was indicted on that charge. After all that Jefferson had written about the press as a rightful censor of its government, the administration action appeared to be highly hypocritical. The jury must have thought so, too, for after a brilliant defense by Joseph Hopkinson, composer of the patriotic song, "Hail, Columbia," Dennie was acquitted.

On the other hand, some measures had to be taken to make vindictive editors more responsible for injuries to public reputations. Jefferson himself declared that for all his love of press freedom, a few convictions for libel might have a salutary effect. He held that this could be done safely by bringing action under the various State laws. In other words, he advocated a "selected" prosecution of notorious and malicious offenders, rather than a wholesale throttling of an opposition press, as the Federalists had imposed under the infamous Sedition Act.

[4] To Volney, 1802. New York Public Library, Manuscript II, 199, as reprinted in Padover, *op. cit.,* p. 95.

THE CROSWELL SEDITIOUS LIBEL CASE

The most celebrated case involving the press during this period was prosecuted under a state law, as recommended by the President. The defendant was Harry Croswell, editor of a Federalist paper at Hudson, New York. Croswell called his little weekly *The Wasp,* and it was an appropriate name. It was so vicious and annoying that respectable Federalists disdained it. *The Wasp* stung political opponents in every column. One day Croswell printed an "exchange" from the *New York Evening Post,* Hamilton's personal mouthpiece. The article reported that Jefferson had paid James Callender, the Richmond editor, to spread the word that George Washington had been a robber, traitor, and perjurer, and that other Federalist leaders were equally reprehensible. This was a serious charge against Jefferson and the dignity of his office. *The Wasp,* rather than the *Post,* was prosecuted because Croswell's paper was the type of scandal sheet Jefferson had in mind when he suggested smoking out the worst of the Federalist editors under State law.

Croswell was indicted in 1804. He was found guilty, but appealed the case. When the trial was called, a titan arose to argue for the defense. He was Alexander Hamilton, Jefferson's arch rival, and more bitter than ever, after the defeat of his party. Hamilton was the most important political figure in the state, whether or not he held office. His words were therefore followed closely. It was acknowledged that he might well "make law" in the celebrated case. The transcript of the proceedings has been lost, but Hamilton's notes indicate that this was one of the greatest speeches of his entire career.

The four judges listened with obvious respect as the brilliant pleader stated a principle as applicable today as it was in 1804. The press, Hamilton argued, had "the right to publish with impunity truth, with good motives, for justifiable ends, though reflecting on Government, Magistracy, or individuals." Since the "good motives" and "justifiable ends" would have to be disproved by the complainant, Hamilton was essentially saying that truth, and truth alone, was a defense in a libel action. In his arguments against the need for a Bill of Rights covering press freedom, Hamilton had not appeared as very sympathetic to the cause of liberty of written expression. But when he stood up at the Croswell trial and insisted upon the "right" of submitting truth as a full defense, Hamilton won his place alongside the great fighters for press freedom.

It so happened that Hamilton lost the case, when the four judges were evenly divided in their opinions. The New York state laws still adhered to the old policy, "the greater the truth, the greater the libel." Truth had been recognized as a defense in the Sedition Act, but the law had lapsed four years before, and the precedent had not been accepted in the courts. Hamilton also insisted on the right of a jury to determine both the law and the fact. Both issues had been raised in the Zenger case, but only in Pennsylvania had they been recognized in law (in 1790).

The significance of the Croswell trial can be seen in legislation immediately following Hamilton's plea. Even before the judges had handed down the verdict, a bill was engrossed in the New York Legislature providing that truth thereafter was to be admitted in defense. The same bill gave the jury the right to determine both the law and the fact. By 1805, these principles had become law in New York—70 years after Zenger's trial. Soon other states followed suit and the shadow of the British common law of seditious libel was lifted. In 1812 the Supreme Court held that the federal government could not prosecute under the old common law.

The great pioneer in press freedom did not live to see his eventual triumph; ironically, it was another libel episode that brought about Hamilton's violent death. A remark attributed to Hamilton which appeared in an Albany newspaper while the Croswell case was being tried angered New York's second most imposing political figure—Aaron Burr. Burr's prestige was by this time slipping, which probably made him especially sensitive to insults, real or imagined. He challenged Hamilton to a duel. Hamilton might have declined with no great blackening of his honor, but he accepted the gage. On July 11, 1804, his seconds rowed him across the Hudson river to the grassy bank near Weehawken where his son had been killed in a duel several months before. Burr was an expert marksman, and in the exchange of shots he wounded Hamilton so critically that the great leader died the next day. If Hamilton had contributed nothing else in his life except his successful battle for a freer press, he would still be remembered.

GROWTH OF THE PRESS: FIRST DAILIES

The first daily newspaper in America was established by Benjamin Towne at Philadelphia in 1783. His *Pennsylvania Evening Post* was as characterless as its publisher. Towne was a patriot in 1776, and was one of the first to print the Declaration of Independence for the public. Later, he became a Tory. After the surrender he confessed his sins and resumed a partial state of grace in his community. However his shoddy little daily lasted only 17 months.

It was succeeded by a very good daily, the *Pennsylvania Packet and Daily Advertiser*, published by the partnership of John Dunlap and David C. Claypoole. Like the *Evening Post* owned by Towne, the *Packet* was originally a weekly publication that had been founded by Dunlap in 1771. Switching from triweekly to daily status in 1784, the Dunlap and Claypoole venture was successful from the beginning.

By 1800, most big ports and commercial centers were supporting daily papers. Philadelphia had six; New York, five; Baltimore, three; and Charleston, two. But for some curious reason Boston, the home of the American newspaper, had no daily paper at this time. Many of these publications had been forced into the daily field to meet the competition of the coffeehouses, where the London papers were available, and where news was freely exchanged. The American journalists met the challenge by issuing first semiweekly, then triweekly, and finally daily editions containing commercial information not elsewhere readily obtained.

Philadelphia even had an all-day newspaper for a time. It was the *New World*, published by Samuel Harrison Smith in morning and evening editions. It was not successful, but it indicated the growing interest in fresh news presentation. Of 512 papers being printed in 1820, 24 were dailies, 66 were semiweeklies or triweeklies, and 422 were weeklies. They were still generally slanted toward the more prosperous citizen, for the price was more than the average man could afford. Circulations were not impressive, either, by present standards. A circulation of 1,500 was considered adequate in all but the largest centers. But because the bulk of circulation was among the prosperous class who tended to gravitate to the conservative political party, most editors patterned their products accordingly. With the rising pressure of the masses for greater political recognition, the pages of these papers began to be filled more and more with political information and opinion.

In the hinterlands the press was also booming. The number of newspapers beyond the urban fringe increased sixfold during this period.[5] Advertising helped to support this newspaper boom. For although most families tended to buy their supplies in wholesale lots for seasonal storage, there was already some development of the retail trade that was to sustain the press in later years. The development of the postal system also accounted for some of this expansion. By postal acts of 1782 and 1792, educational and informational matter could be mailed at very low rates.

THE PRESS MOVES WESTWARD

The expansion of the press reflected the spirit of the country. It had taken 150 years to settle the seaboard colonies, and on the basis of the past record, it should have taken another 200 years to push the frontier to the Mississippi river. But once the Appalachian mountains were conquered, the lands to the west were rapidly taken up. Jefferson, who had always opposed national imperialism, had a chance in 1803 to purchase the vast Louisiana territory, and the bargain was too good to turn down out of principle. When this domain was added to the United States as a vast territory for exploitation, settlers poured in from the East. The lust for western lands is indicated by the numer-

[5] Most of the newspaper figures and comments in this section are based on Clarence S. Brigham, *History and Bibliography of American Newspapers, 1690–1820,* 2 vols. (Worcester, Mass.: American Antiquarian Society, 1947).

ous petitions for statehood during this period. Between 1790 and 1820, nine new States were admitted to the Union.

The waterways were the highways into these frontier regions. Along the Ohio, the Kanawha, and the Cumberland, tiny communities began to appear that would some day become teeming cities. By present standards they were mere hamlets, but each served a wide trading area. They were thus far more important as markets and social centers than their populations would indicate. If they were county seats, with courts, law enforcing agencies, and land offices, they were even more important. And usually one of the first to set up shop in such communities was the frontier printer-editor. He was the enthusiastic promoter of the village that he was certain would one day rival London. He was a leading businessman. But most of all he was the man who, more than anyone else, knit the community into an organization that could begin to bring civilization to the remote areas. On flat boats and on ox carts he brought his few cases of type and his printing furniture. The local carpenter and blacksmith might help to install the primitive hand press, but sometimes he did that work, too. And not long after the main street began to take form, according to the plats in the surveyor's office, the first edition of the *Argus, Gazette, Gem of the Prairie*—or whatever its name—was ready to serve the various interests so interdependent in the midst of a savage country.

The first newspaper west of the mountains was John Scull's venture of 1786, the *Pittsburgh Gazette,* still thriving as the *Post-Gazette.* A year later, John Bradford, who bore a name well known in the printing industry, although he was only indirectly related to the famous Philadelphia publishing family, set up his shop in Lexington, Kentucky. His *Kentucky Gazette* might have been the first paper in the West, had his equipment not been wrecked in transit the year before the establishment of the Pittsburgh enterprise. The Ohio river was the most important artery of commerce in this early period, but there were also important settlements along the Wabash, and where lesser streams, such as the Muskingum, Scioto, Maumee, and Cuyahoga, opened up avenues to the hinterlands. By 1800, 21 newspapers had been started west of the mountains.

There was little local news in these early frontier newspapers, for like the first of the colonial publications, content was lifted from the papers back home. Advertising was rarely adequate to support the news business, but fortunately there needed to be some means of publishing legal information in this new area, and that was often sufficient inducement to start up a paper. Elihu Stout, for example, himself poled up the Wabash with his press to found the *Indiana Gazette* at Vincennes in 1804. He had been induced to give up his business in Frankfort, Kentucky, on the promise that he would be awarded the territorial legal printing contract, which was enough of a stake for him to establish a paper.

The northern route to the frontier was along the Mohawk valley, straight across New York state from the Hudson river. This was the route of the Erie

Canal, which was soon to make New York City the largest metropolis in the land, but even before that, it was an important highway. At the end of the valley, the Great Lakes served as transportation and communication routes between the vast wilderness and the East. Detroit, one of the outer bastions of the frontier then, had a newspaper, the *Gazette,* by 1817. Soon other communities in the area could boast the same. A Congressional Act of 1814 provided that all federal laws must be printed in two (later, three) newspapers in each state and territory. This was a logical way of letting electors know what their representatives were doing, but it also encouraged the founding of pioneer papers in communities not quite ready to support such ventures.[6]

By the end of the first decade of the nineteenth century, the western press was lusty and influential. Editors began to depend less on "exchanges" and to speak out for themselves on matters pertinent to readers. Editors and politicians who understood their constituencies saw that the region had its special problems. They tended to side with the Jeffersonians on the rights of the common man, but their dependence upon the federal government for defense of their sparse settlements against the Indian threat made them favor strong, centralized administration.

THE INFLUENCE OF THE FRONTIER

The new states also turned to the federal government for the development of transportation, so essential to their growth and prosperity. Again, the great land companies, organized to promote colonization at a profit, were dependent upon the national administrations, rather than upon the territorial or parent-state politicians. There was a tendency, then, for the westerner to demand local and statewide autonomy to work out the destiny he believed to be peculiar to his region, but he was less touchy about state sovereignty because of his need of strong, centralized government. He insisted upon solid representation in the administration of that government, as indicated by the impatience of territories for statehood. But he visualized that government as a kind of public service corporation, not a dispenser of privileges for the wealthy and powerful. Under the Northwest Ordinances, land was set aside to be sold for educational revenue, and the pattern was generally followed in other areas. Suffrage was likely to be broader than in the more settled regions; property might be a voting requisite, but it was easy to acquire.

The West was to have a profound influence upon the development of the new nation. The importance of that influence has been disputed since Professor Frederick Jackson Turner suggested that the frontier was a political and social

[6] Regulations such as this and the law requiring publication at state cost of letters uncalled for at the post office were also a means of rewarding pro-administration editors. As administrations changed, political rivals found ready-made organs of expression.

laboratory which had produced a distinctive American character.[7] His studies had convinced him that climate alone had as much to do with political traditions as established philosophies. He argued that regions, rather than boundaries, identified peoples. Weather might be responsible for great social change. A severe drought in a wheat area might cause a migration to more prosperous communities. Turner pointed out that the poor and underprivileged were more interested in popular rule than were the wealthy, because it gave them a chance to even up the opportunities. Carried to its conclusion, the Turner theory would hold that "radicalism" is only the political expression of economic maladjustment. Those who are satisfied do not desire change or experimentation. But the men and women who moved across the mountains usually accepted the perils and discomforts of pioneer life because they were dissatisfied with the older community life.[8] On the frontier these pioneers lived roughly and dangerously. When people suffer and face dangers together, they tend to act together, regardless of past background, customs, privileges, or attitudes. Such people begin to make demands. They blame those in control for failing to consider their problems. When they become strong enough politically and economically, they tend to force the older society to adopt measures that have proved to be effective under the exacting tests of the wilderness. Thus, the frontier has been responsible for much of the social and political experimentation that helped to distinguish the American character and organization, the Turner school maintains.

THE WAR OF 1812

The War of 1812 will serve as an example of how the frontier had come to influence American thought and politics. This disgraceful conflict reflects little on either of the belligerents. We do not like to be reminded of General William Hull's abject surrender to an inferior British and Indian force at De-

[7] The Turner theory, first suggested by the Wisconsin historian in 1893 and elaborated by him and an entire school of historians, is explained in his own *The Significance of Sections in American History* (New York: Holt, Rinehart & Winston, 1933), in Walter Prescott Webb's *The Great Plains* (Boston: Ginn, 1931), and with a modified updating in Ray Billington's *America's Frontier Heritage* (New York: Holt, Rinehart & Winston, 1967). It is opposed in Henry Nash Smith's *The Virgin Land* (Cambridge, Mass.: Harvard University Press, 1950), by Fred A. Shannon in "Critiques of Research in the Social Sciences," *Social Science Research Council Bulletin*, No. 46 (New York: The Council, 1940), and by Louis M. Hacker in "Sections or Classes," *Nation*, CXXXVII (July 26, 1933), 108. For two well-balanced discussions of Turner's influence on American historiography see Richard Hofstadter, *The Progressive Historians: Turner, Beard, Parrington* (New York: Knopf, 1968) and John Higham, *Writing American History* (Bloomington: Indiana University Press, 1970).

[8] Studies have shown that by no means all of the pioneers were of this type. It took some capital to head west, otherwise the slums would have been the reservoirs of the frontier society, which they were not. But dissatisfaction can take many forms, and the statement would appear to be true, in general.

troit, or the burning of our national capitol. There were heroic episodes, too, such as Commodore Oliver Hazard Perry's useless naval victory on Lake Erie;[9] the courageous, but futile, sea battles of American naval vessels and privateersmen against the world's greatest sea power; and General Andrew Jackson's victory at New Orleans, two weeks after the peace had been signed at Ghent.[10] But for better or for worse, the force of public opinion in the West was largely responsible for that war.

Generations of Americans believed that the War of 1812 resulted from American resentment over British abuses of free transit on the high seas, and the "impressment," or forcible return, of former British naval ratings by methods insulting to our national pride. If these were major causes for war, then New England should have been preponderantly in favor of the conflict. The big shipping interests were centered in that area, and the commercial interests there suffered most from British naval arrogance. The fact is, New Englanders emphatically voiced disapproval of the war. It was the West that forced military action. Western newspapers offer the evidence on this point.

In 1810 the Indians went on the warpath under a great leader and statesman, Tecumseh, and his brother, Teuskwatawa, "The Prophet." Frontiersmen discovered that the Indians were killing Americans with weapons supplied by the British through Canada. The leaders of the West were in favor of war to settle the dispute. These were the men who became known as the "War Hawks." They were not interested in the plight of the seamen, or the Napoleonic blockades, or the shipping embargoes imposed by the United States to boycott the arrogant Europeans at such great sacrifice to the commercial interests. It is significant that Henry Clay, perhaps the most vehement of the War Hawks, was elected Speaker of the House by the western bloc.

And poor Madison, best known for his constructive contributions to the American experiment, found himself in the role of a war President, thanks to the pressure of western public opinion. Clay controlled enough votes by 1812 to swing the election against Madison, if that great American did not go along with the War Hawks. Madison's opponent, Governor DeWitt Clinton of New York, was opposed to war, so the issue was clear in 1812. It was Madison and war, or Clinton and peace. Thus, it is easy to read the influence of the West by examining the records. The electral vote of the Northeast, where the shipping and commercial men were important, was unanimous for Clinton and peace. Madison, who was presented to the voters as protector of the shipping interests, received not a single vote from the electors of New England. But the electoral vote of the West was unanimous for Madison and war. The

[9] A useless victory, because the armies to be supplied by the Great Lakes route, such as Hull's command, were ineffective by the time Commodore Perry cleared the enemy from the lake.

[10] The treaty was signed December 24, 1814. Jackson won his remarkable victory January 8, 1815. News of the battle reached Washington January 28; news of the treaty reached New York by ship February 11. As a result, many Americans believed that Jackson's victory had much to do with the successful negotiations.

middle and southern states were more evenly divided, but there was enough war sentiment in those areas to endorse the western stand, and from then on, it was "Mr. Madison's War."

THE FRONTIER NEWSPAPER

The flimsy little weeklies of the isolated villages and booming river towns had much to do in the crystallization of public opinion that made the West a new factor in American politics. What were they like, these newspapers that exerted such influence in the West? They were small, hand-set, scrubby publications, on the whole. It is apparent that there was no place on them for large staffs, regular correspondents, or columnists furnishing opinions for readers too busy to form their own. There was plenty of opinion, of course, but most of it was contributed by readers. Usually there was a column or two of local news, printed sometimes as scattered items, without benefit of headlines. There might be half a column of exchanges, or news gleaned from other newspapers arrived by the last post. The remaining material, exclusive of the notices, or advertisements, was very likely submitted by readers. Every subscriber who could wield a pen sooner or later appeared in the columns. All the aggrieved wrote out their pet complaints for the pages of the local mercury. Even government officials participated in this exchange, not always openly, true, but with sufficient identity to warrant spirited replies. Ofter this material was strident and in bad taste. "Straight news" tended toward distortion, flamboyance, and vindictiveness. But whatever its faults, it was a robust, colorful press. The great French observer, de Tocqueville, described the institution at a somewhat later period, but his remarks then were pertinent to this decade. He was impressed by the virility of the American press even while repelled by its provincialism. Western crudeness shocked him, but he was amazed at the success of the democratic experiment, and he conceded that the press had been an important implement in this development. De Tocqueville found a close relationship between the press and its public, fostered, no doubt, by the active participation of readers in the local journalistic effort. The public appeared to respect the Fourth Estate, he reported, and this was manifest in the great freedom accorded the institution.

WARTIME ATTACKS ON THE FEDERALIST PRESS

As in most wars, the press suffered to some extent in the 1812 period. The most notorious attempt to muzzle an editor was in Baltimore, a shipping center with a strong faction opposed to administration war policies. Especially critical of the President was the *Federal Republican*, published by Jacob Wagner and Alexander Hanson. Some of their statements, made while an enemy was threatening our shores, no doubt merited censorship, but editors and contributors of the paper were charged by the opposition as traitors, although two of the staff members were Generals James Lingan and "Light Horse Harry" Lee, heroes of the War of Independence. When the mob descended on the office, the journalists held out until the irate citizens set up a cannon to blow the building down. At this point cooler heads negotiated a truce, including safe conduct of the besieged to the jail for protection. After the mob destroyed the press and building, its leaders ordered an assault on the jail. Some of the prisoners escaped, but nine were beaten and thrown to the mob. General Lingan was killed. General Lee was maimed for life.

The wonder is that more Federalist editors were not held up to scorn. It was one thing to criticise administration policy in peacetime, but another to condemn the government while the enemy was threatening our shores. Even such a reputable Federalist as Major Benjamin Russell of the *Columbian Centinel* in Boston appeared to be more interested in administration discomfiture than in British defeat. Major Russell was a spearhead of New England hostility to a government desperately waging a war. There was actually a revolt in the area against continuing the war, and Russell went so far as to endorse a movement for the secession of his region from the rest of the Union.[11] During the dark days of 1814 a group of disgruntled New Englanders met at Hartford to discuss withdrawal from the Federal Union and perhaps return to British sovereignty. If this was not treason, while the British were pillaging our shores, at least one can scarcely blame members of Madison's party for feeling so bitter toward journalistic spokesmen of the Federalists. In the end, the Hartford Convention fizzled out as a mere rebuke of the administration, but that was only because the war was about over. It should be pointed out, however, that the South was not the first to advocate secession from the Union. Major Russell must have known the ultimate purpose of the Hartford Convention, but possible secession did not worry him.

By the election of 1816, which put James Monroe into office with no opposition from the Federalists, much of the wartime rancor appeared to be dying out. On the surface, the country seemed to enjoy peace and prosperity. There was a kind of political truce while the forces realigned themselves. "The era of good feeling," Major Russell called it.[12] Actually, partisan rivalry had been substituted by other controversies. Sectional and economic disputes were soon to resound, but between 1816 and 1820 some of the former bitter

[11] *Columbian Centinel,* January 13, 1813.

[12] One of Russell's many colorful phrases, which were widely quoted. Another had its birth in 1812, when a man named Gerry was governor. The Republican legislature of Massachusetts had divided a political district into a weird shape in order to gain voting power. According to one account, Gilbert Stuart called Russell's attention to the new district's resemblance to a salamander. "Better say a Gerrymander!" replied the Federalist editor, although in truth the governor had had no part in the original "gerrymandering."

factionalism disappeared. As a result, it was a dull period, journalistically speaking.

GOVERNMENT REPORTING: THE *NATIONAL INTELLIGENCER*

The most important press development at this time was in government reporting. The right to report meetings of interest to the general public is one of the tests of a free press, by the English-American concept. Reporters had access to the national House of Representatives from April 8, 1789, two days after it was established. For a time the Senate was more secretive, since it excluded not only reporters, but also members of the House, from its debates. By December 9, 1795, the Senate had completed a gallery for reporters, however. When the capital was transferred from New York to Philadelphia, the gallery was too far from the rostrum for the reporters to hear clearly, but on January 2, 1802, the Senate (now in Washington) voted the reporters access to the floor. There was some squabbling between reporters and the House over arrangements. In Philadelphia, reporters were assigned "four seats on the window sill," and in Washington, after some agitation, they won the right to report the debates.[13]

One of the most effective reports of government was provided by the *National Intelligencer,* an outstanding newspaper of the period. Its founder was Samuel Harrison Smith, only 28 when Jefferson induced him to give up a promising publishing venture in Philadelphia to start a newspaper in the new capital at Washington. The President was head of the learned American Philosophical Society of Philadelphia (founded by Franklin), and Smith had been secretary of the organization. Jefferson was much impressed with the young man. The *National Intelligencer* soon became the semiofficial organ of the administration, but it served papers of all factions outside Washington with its remarkably objective reporting of Congressional debates.

Smith retired from the paper in 1810, but his work was carried on ably by the partners who succeeded him, Joseph Gales, Jr., and William W. Seaton. One reported proceedings in the House, while the other covered the Senate. Both were experts in a recently-perfected shorthand technique, and they were able to offer complete, accurate reports of the debates. Actually, they served as the semiofficial recorders of Congress, until the *Congressional Globe,* predecessor of the *Congressional Record,* was established in 1834. Gales and Seaton made the *National Intelligencer* a daily when they assumed control (it had been a triweekly up to then). It is gratifying to learn that the paper was a success, financially and editorially, proving that a newspaper did not have to be partisan, noisy, or scandalous to meet competition.

[13] See Elizabeth Gregory McPherson, "Reporting the Debates of Congress," *Quarterly Journal of Speech,* XXVIII (April 1942) pp. 141–48.

MAGAZINES GAIN A FOOTHOLD

But the *National Intelligencer* was not typical of the press of the "era of good feeling." Few other newspapers won historical recognition at this time. On the other hand, there was an interesting development in the magazine field during the period. Efforts to publish magazines had been made occasionally since 1741, when Benjamin Franklin was thwarted in his plans by Andrew Bradford, who published the first periodical three days before Franklin's magazine appeared.

Five magazines were established in the Revolutionary period. By that time there was some indication that the magazine might one day be self-supporting. It was the *Pennsylvania Magazine,* published in Philadelphia by Robert Aitken, that offered the American public its first taste of Tom Paine. This periodical was well edited. It was full of interesting political information, literary contributions of good quality, and discussions of important issues. Eventually it failed, but it showed that the magazine had possibilities.

An interesting publication started in the period of the party press was the *Farmer's Weekly Museum,* printed at Walpole, on the New Hampshire side of the Connecticut river. Founded by Isaiah Thomas, who retained his interest in it, it gained its greatest fame under the same Joseph Dennie who later got into trouble for his attacks on democracy printed in the *Port Folio,* during Jefferson's first administration. Dennie was so witty, critical, and readable that his paper was in demand all over the nation. It was actually a forerunner of the news magazine.

Other magazines at the end of the eighteenth century are now valuable sources of information for the historian. The *Columbian Magazine,* founded in 1786, was elaborately illustrated (with copperplate engravings), thus pointing the way to the picture magazine. Mathew Carey's *American Museum,* founded a year later, was the best-edited periodical of its day, according to Frank Luther Mott, the leading authority on magazine history in this country. It has been a mine of information on political, social, and economic history for students of the period. Some issues ran to more than a hundred pages.

The war with Britain ended in 1815, but magazines of that period continued to present views both favorable and unfavorable to the British. One of the anti-British publications was the *North American Review,* founded in 1815 under the auspices of the Anthology Club of Boston. It became a quarterly after three years as a bimonthly magazine, and was published until 1940. It was closely associated with Harvard, after its first few years. Jared Sparks and Edward Everett, foremost scholars of the day, were regular contributors. Although circulation was small, the magazine was read by thoughtful men and women who wielded influence in their communities.

NILES' WEEKLY REGISTER

Mott estimates that several hundred quarterly, monthly, and weekly magazines were printed at one time or another in the first third of the nineteenth century. Most of them have long since been forgotten. One that deserves special mention, however, was *Niles' Weekly Register.* Edited by Hezekiah Niles, a printer with common sense, integrity, and a flare for concise reporting on current trends, the *Register* is known to every historian of the period. It was published in Baltimore, but was read in every state in the Union. The *Register* was the early nineteenth-century equivalent of the modern news magazine. Niles started his publication in 1811. There was a minimum of opinion in it at first. Most of the material was a weekly roundup of speeches, important documents, and statements of leaders everywhere concerning current problems. Niles was an objective journalist. He was conservative in his views but he was also honest in his evaluation of events. Thus, both sides of a controversy found space in the *Register,* and the material was indexed for ready reference, much to the delight of the later researchers. Its files were so important to historians that the entire publication has been reprinted, issue by issue, for libraries all over the world needing an authoritative chronicle of the first half of the nineteenth century. Probably no day passes without some researcher digging into the information supplied with so much care and responsibility by Hezekiah Niles, a journalist who deserves the honorable recognition of his craft.

Annotated Bibliography

Books

Adams, Henry, *History of the United States of America During the Administration of Thomas Jefferson.* New York: A. & C. Boni, 1930. The first two volumes of Adams' brilliant history; the next two cover the Madison administration. Adams' first six chapters portray magnificently the United States of 1800. The nine-volume work first appeared in 1889–91.

Ames, William E., *A History of the National Intelligencer.* Chapel Hill: University of North Carolina Press, 1971. Intensive use of files, other documentary materials; covers Smith, Gales, Seaton, other editors of the outstanding paper. See also his "Samuel Harrison Smith Founds the *National Intelligencer,*" *Journalism Quarterly,* XLII (Summer 1965), 389.

Billington, Ray, *America's Frontier Heritage.* New York: Holt, Rinehart & Winston, 1967. Brings the case for the frontier up to date, with a modified Turner-theory approach.

Bowers, Claude G., *Jefferson in Power*. Boston: Houghton Mifflin, 1936. A continuation of the author's *Jefferson and Hamilton*. Bowers uses newspaper sources heavily.

Ford, Worthington C., *Jefferson and the Newspaper, 1785–1830*. New York: Columbia University Press, 1936. Gives examples of how the great statesman regarded the journalists and their media.

Luxon, Norval Neil, *Niles' Weekly Register*. Baton Rouge: Louisiana State University Press, 1947. This doctoral dissertation is the best available information on this influential publication.

Malone, Dumas, *Jefferson and the Ordeal of Liberty*. Boston: Little, Brown, 1962.

———, *Jefferson the President: First Term, 1801–5*. Boston: Little, Brown, 1970. Third and fourth volumes of *Jefferson and His Time*, a monumental biographic effort.

Mott, Frank Luther, *History of American Magazines, 1741–1850*. New York: Macmillan, 1930. Volume one of a series by the outstanding authority on the subject. The author won a Pulitzer award for his study.

———, *Jefferson and the Press*. Baton Rouge: Louisiana State University Press, 1943. An excellent monograph.

Nelson, Harold L., ed., *Freedom of the Press from Hamilton to the Warren Court*. Indianapolis: Bobbs-Merrill, 1967. A collection of documents, cases, essays, with a lucid introduction by the editor summarizing press freedom trends since 1800.

Padover, Saul K., *Thomas Jefferson on Democracy*. New York: Penguin, 1939. Excerpts from his letters and speeches. One section is concerned with the press.

Peterson, Merrill D., *Thomas Jefferson and the New Nation*. New York: Oxford University Press, 1970. Biography by a leading Jeffersonian scholar covering entire life.

Pollard, James E., *The Presidents and the Press*. New York: Macmillan, 1947. Describes relationships of Jefferson, Madison, and Monroe with the press during this period.

Smith, Henry Nash, *The Virgin Land*. Cambridge, Mass.: Harvard University Press, 1950. Turner theory fails to take account of industrial revolution.

William Winston Seaton. Boston: James R. Osgood and Company, 1871. The biography of the great Washington editor of the *National Intelligencer*, with notes of family and friends.

Wood, James Playsted, *Magazines in the United States*. New York: Ronald Press, 1956. A study of the influence of magazines on American society. Fairly comprehensive in its coverage of general magazines, but far less detailed than Mott (above).

Periodicals and Monographs

Clark, Carlisle, "The Old Corner Printing House," *Granite Monthly*, XXX (August 1901), 91. Describes the *Farmer's Weekly Museum*, started by Isaiah Thomas, and later a pioneer national magazine.

Glicksberg, Charles, "Bryant and the United States Review," *New England Quarterly*, VII (December 1934), 687. Describes early nineteenth-century periodicals and the movement to establish a national literature through such magazines as the *North American Review*.

Lee, Alfred McClung, "Dunlap and Claypoole: Printers and News-Merchants of the Revolution," *Journalism Quarterly*, XI (June 1934), 160. The story of the men who founded the first successful American daily.

Martin, Benjamin Ellis, "Transition Period of the American Press—Leading Editors in This Century," *Magazine of American History*, XVII (April 1887), 273. Describes battles between Federalist and Republican journalists. Includes interesting facsimile examples of papers.

Murphy, Lawrence W., "John Dunlap's 'Packet' and Its Competitors," *Journalism Quarterly*, XXVIII (Winter 1951), 58. The story of the struggle for survival among the first dailies.

Plasterer, Nicholas N., "The Croswell Case: Paradox of History," *Journalism Quarterly*, XLIV (Spring 1967), 125. Argues that Croswell case deserves more attention than Zenger's.

WINE, LIQUOR, AND CIGAR STORE.

Opposite Strother's Hotel, Pennsylvania Avenue.

RECEIVED, This Day, from Boston, per the schooner Alfred, a most choice and extensive selection of old and pure Wines and Liquors, to wit:

Old Cognac Brandy
Do Weesp Anchor Holland Gin } both in Wood, Demijohns, & Bottles
Do Jamaica Spirits
Do Irish Whiskey
Do London Particular Madeira Wine } both in Wood & bottles, and warranted to have been a voyage to India
Do Sherry
Do Teneriffe
Do Sicily
Do Pico
St. Estephe, St. Julian, and other Claret Wines
Old South Hampton Port in Bottles
Superior Hermitage Wine, in boxes of 25 bottles each
Sauterne and Burgundy Wine
J. C. Dinet, Ruin Art and J. H. G. Sparking Champaigne
Hibbert's best double Brown Stout, in quart and pint bottles
A few dozen very superior Old Arrack

Also, on hand, and for sale,
Choice old Rye Whiskey
Cabanas, Flint, Woodville, Zamora, Delpino, Deservenine, and Dosamycos Cigars, in wholes, halves, quarters, and eighths of boxes, of the first quality.
Chewing Tobacco, &c.

dec 3—eotf WILLIAM COX.

BARGAINS AT THE NEW STORE.

WILLIAM W. WHITE & Co. have, in addition to their former stock, just received a new and seasonable supply of staple and fancy Dry Goods, which they are now opening at their cheap Cash Store, on the south side of Pennsylvania avenue, three doors east of the Centre Market, for which, if early application be made, they can be had cheap, wholesale or retail, or by the piece. Shop and tavern-keepers, heads of families, &c will find it to their interest to call and examine. The articles are such as

Cloths	Lineas
Cassimeres	Hosiery
Cassinetts	Shirting
Venetian Carpeting	Cambric Muslins
Ingrain do	Mull do
Scotch do	Book do

Domestics
Cashmere Shawls and Scarfs
Merino do do
Imitation do do
Super elegant French Chints
Figured black Silks
Do Mandarin Robes
Do Pekin do
Superfine black Bombazine
do Plaid do
Do Circassian Plaids
Ladies' party colored Hdkfs.
Velvetine and Rob Roy do
Gentlemen's Military Cravats

And many other articles, comprising almost every other article in the dry good line.

dec 3—3t

REMEDY FOR THE PILES.

THE medicine now offered to the public is one which has been fully subjected to the infallible test of experience, and, in every instance where it has been fairly tried, it has been attended with the most complete success. In some of the cases, the patients have been laboring under this disease for years, and, during that period, had received the best medical advice, and had even undergone a painful surgical operation, without permanent advantage. It is not like those usually advertised and offered as an infallible cure for a long catalogue of diseases; but those afflicted with this complaint, for which alone it is recommended, may rely with confidence upon obtaining relief, even in its worst forms, in a short time, and they themselves are the best judges of the importance of such a remedy. Price 50 cents per box, with directions, signed by the proprietor. If the case is severe, and of long standing, more than one box may be necessary. Prepared and sold at James A. Austin's Drug and Chemical Store, No. 263, North 3d street, Philadelphia.

The proprietor has appointed Lewis Johnson, at the Snuff Store, corner of 12th street and Pennsylvania avenue, sole agent for the sale of this medicine, in Washington City.

dec 3—3teo

BUGGY FOR SALE.

A NEW complete Buggy Gig, with new good Harness, for sale, at JAMES SMITH'S Livery Stable.

dec 3—3t

From *National Intelligencer* (1823)

STRAYED,

FROM the residence of the subscriber, in Frankfort, in September 1835, a red COW, horns bored, crop in one ear and a slit in the other. Any person finding said Cow, or giving such information that I may get her, will be liberally rewarded.

BATHSHEBA LONG.

March 6th, 1836.—7-3w.

IMPORTED HORSE SWISS,

WILL stand the present season at the Franklin association Race Course, 3½ miles East of Frankfort, on the Georgetown Road, and will be let to mares at $50 the season. His Pedigree and performance, and the performance of his Colts may be seen by reference to his Bills.

PEN. LUCKETT.

March 30th, 1836.—6.–10w.

Dr. J. O. T. HAWKINS,

WILL continue to practice his profession in the town of Frankfort, and its vicinity. His residence and office, is at the brick house of Mrs. Bryant, near the east end of the Market House, on Broad Way, where he solicits patronage and promises fidelity and attention to all who may employ him, and where he may be always found except when absent on professional business.

March 30th, 1836.—6–tf.

Mr. JOHN KERSEY.

YOU are hereby notified, that on the 10th day of June next, at the house of Edward Lewis, Esq. in the county of Green, I shall proceed to take the depositions of Freborn G. Grayham, William Hanks and others, to be read as evidence in the suit of myself against you, for a divorce now pending in the Green Circuit court in Chancery, and if all of said depositions be not taken on said day, I will continue from day to day, Sundays excepted, until all are taken, when and where if you choose, you can attend.

ELIZABETH KERSEY.

March 19th, 1836.—6–5w.

JAMES HENRY,

DOMESTIC DRY GOODS, COMMISSION MERCHANT, AND AGENT FOR THE SALE OF WOLCOTT'S STEUBENVILLE JEANS,

Wall Street, Louisville, Ky.

LIBERAL advances will be made on consignments of negro clothing, linsey and socks, all of which articles ought to be in this market by the middle of June. On hand and for sale—having just received 16 cases by steamer Wacausta—1000 pieces of Wolcott's Steubenville Jeans, which will be sold on liberal terms to responsible houses. Buyers will please to call and examine these goods.

JAMES HENRY,
Wall Street.

The following papers in Kentucky will publish the above advertisement, weekly, for 2 months, and charge Lou. Adv.—Gazette, Lexington; Enquirer, Covington; paper at Princeton; Argus, Frankfort; Gazette, Hopkinsville; Gazette, Greensburgh; Register, Elizabethtown, paper at Russellville; Citizen, Paris; paper at Richmond; Olive Branch, Danville; Whig, Mount Sterling; Monitor, Maysville; Sentinel, Georgetown; paper at Shelbyville; Gazette, Bowlinggreen.

March 3, 1836. —6–2m.

$100 Reward.

RANAWAY from the farm whereon Dr. Samuel B. Crockett resides, about the middle of July last, a negro man, named ISAAC. Said man is about 30 years of age, pleasant countenance, rather chunky built. He had on when he went away, a cassinet frock coat, linnen pantaloons, and a white hat. The above reward of $100 DOLLARS, will be given for said Isaac, if taken out of the State, or FIFTY DOLLARS if taken in the State, and delivered to me, or secured, so that I get him.

JOHN M'KEE.

Franklin County, Dec. 3, 1835.—tf.

From *Western America* (1836)

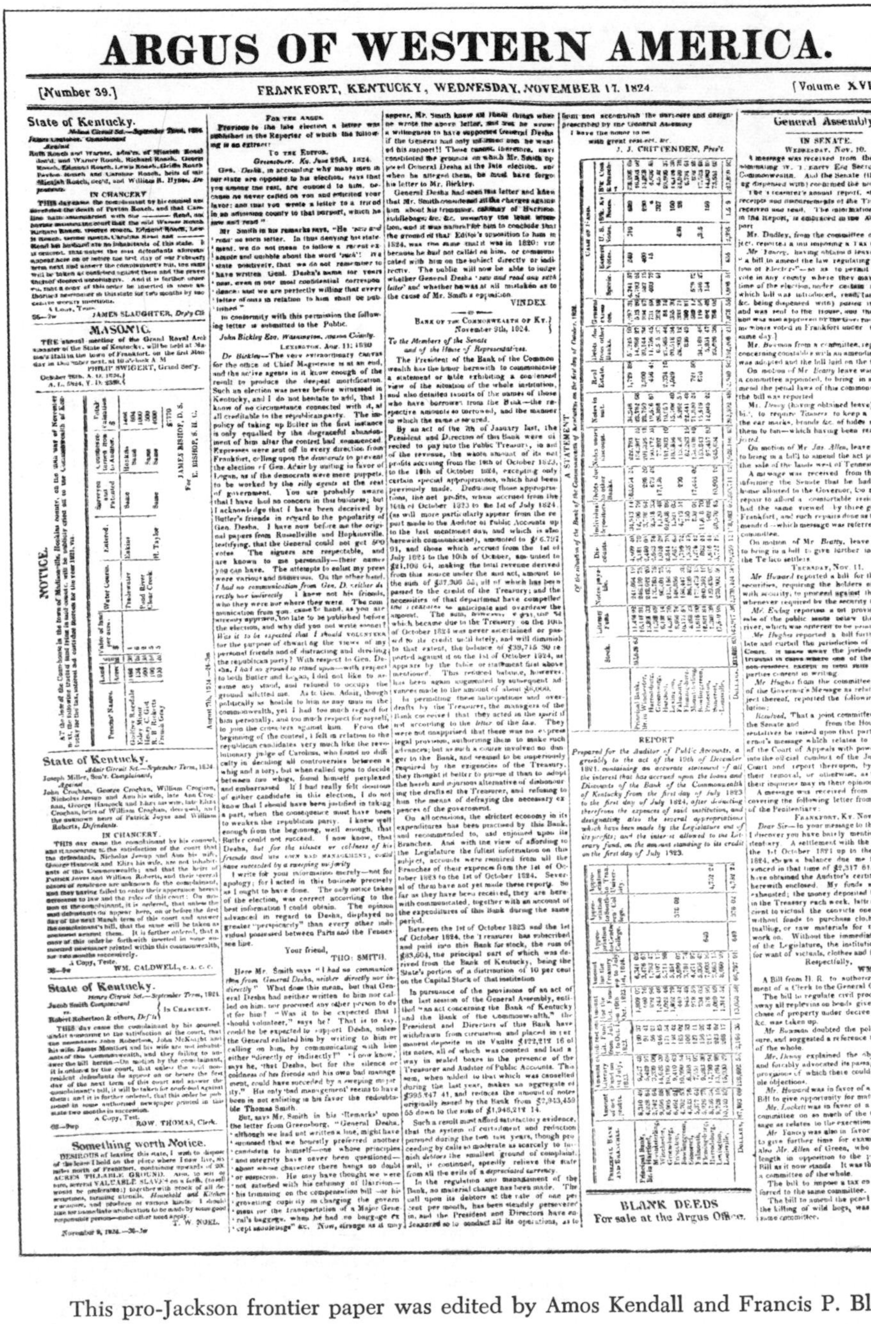
ARGUS OF WESTERN AMERICA.

[Number 39.] FRANKFORT, KENTUCKY, WEDNESDAY, NOVEMBER 17. 1824. [Volume XVII.]

State of Kentucky.

IN CHANCERY.

JAMES SLAUGHTER, Dep'y Clk

MASONIC.

PHILIP SWIGERT, Grand Sec'y.

NOTICE.

JAMES BISHOP, D. S.

State of Kentucky.

IN CHANCERY.

WM. CALDWELL, c. a. c. c.

State of Kentucky.

ROW. THOMAS, Clerk.

Something worth Notice.

T. W. NOEL.

FOR THE ARGUS.

TO THE EDITOR.

Your friend,

THO: SMITH.

VINDEX

BANK OF THE COMMONWEALTH OF KY. November 9th, 1824.

J. J. CRITTENDEN, Pres't

A STATEMENT

REPORT

BLANK DEEDS
For sale at the Argus Office.

General Assembly.

IN SENATE.

WM HARDIN.

This pro-Jackson frontier paper was edited by Amos Kendall and Francis P. Blair.

10

Coonskin Democracy and the Press

A country, like an individual, has dignity and power only in proportion as it is self-informed.
—William Ellery Channing

America in the 1820's was still largely rural, but industry was beginning to exert the influence that was to be so profoundly felt by society in the near future. All the new states followed the Vermont pattern in providing suffrage for all white males. After 1810, state after state in the East dropped restrictive voting qualifications, not always peaceably. The enfranchisement of the common man was to bring about what amounted to a bloodless revolution, but in the 1820s the significance of the first farm-labor movement was not generally recognized. The so-called "common man" was not yet fully aware of the new power he had won. Until 1828, federal administration of government was still largely by "gentlemen," like Madison, Monroe, and John Quincy Adams. Yet it was in this period that the pressures for popular sovereignty began to be exerted, and the press was to play an important role in this drama.

AN EXPANSION OF THE PRINTED WORD

Indeed, the press was more and more counted upon to supply the information, inspiration, agitation, and education of a society often unable to keep up with its need for schools. Newspapers, books, and magazines increased so fast in this period that presses could not meet the craving for such material. There were 375 printing offices in 1810. By 1825 there were three times as many. Between 1820 and 1830, publication of books alone increased 10 per cent, and still did not supply the need, for Americans continued to buy 70 per cent of their books from European publishers. Despite this literary dependence upon the Old World, Americans were offering every encouragement to journalist promoters. It is significant that by 1820 more than 50,000 titles, including books, magazines, and newspapers, were listed as American. Sale of such products increased by more than a million dollars in the decade beginning in 1820, when publications grossed about two and a half million dollars.[1]

True, much of this American material was extremely shallow and provincial. The *Port Folio,* one of the most literate of the magazines, rarely exceeded 2,000 subscribers. The authoritative *North American Review* had a normal circulation of about 3,000 copies. The biggest New York newspapers printed up to 4,000 copies an issue, but 1,500 to 2,500 was much more common. Only in the religious field was circulation impressive. The Methodist *Christian Journal and Advocate,* for example, had about 25,000 subscribers by its own estimate in 1826. But although circulations were small, popular publications were reaching more and more citizens, and their numbers increased yearly.

Unfortunately, most ordinary citizens could not afford to pay five or ten dollars a year in advance for such publications. The prevailing wage scale gave many workers only about eight dollars a week, which put virtually all magazines, and most newspapers, out of their reach. Even so, enough circulation reached the common man to give the United States the highest per capita newspaper readership in the world. In 1826, newspaper circulation in America exceeded that of Great Britain by more than three million annually. In 1810 there were 376 newspapers in the United States. By 1828, at the time of Jackson's election, there were nearly 900 (mainly weeklies). Nevertheless, what the nation needed was a newspaper press that could reach deeper into the masses.

In many communities, newspapers were the only literature available for the bulk of the citizenry. They served as the main educational device until other cultural institutions could take up the slack caused by rapid migrations. European visitors often did not realize the obstacles to cultural progress in such a new land. They sometimes failed to see that the United States was at a stage where rudimentary education fulfilled the needs of much of the population. What had Americans, other than Franklin, contributed to science, literature, the arts, or philosophy, the Rev. Sydney Smith asked rhetorically in an article from the *Edinburgh Review* reprinted in an American newspaper. Actually, the United States was beginning to fill this vacuum. In the field of letters the country could offer Washington Irving, James Fenimore Cooper, William Cullen Bryant, Margaret Fuller, Nathaniel Hawthorne, and Ralph Waldo Emerson, all of whom would soon be recognized even in Europe.

[1] Merle Curti, *The Growth of American Thought* (New York: Harper & Row, 1943), p. 215.

JOHN MARSHALL'S COURT DECISIONS

The trend toward a more enlightened age was noticeable by the end of the 1820s. By that time there were 49 colleges in the United States. The increase in endowed institutions of learning was appreciable after the decision of the Supreme Court in the Dartmouth College case of 1819. Until then, the trend had been toward state control of such educational establishments. The apathy of the philanthropist in supporting universities is therefore understandable. The Court held in the Dartmouth College case that a state had no right to change contracts; specifically, to make a private institution into a State university. Potential patrons of endowed education had hesitated to make donations to educational institutions threatened by State control.

The Dartmouth College decision was one of a series by which Chief Justice John Marshall guided the Supreme Court in establishing a philosophy of government. Two famous decisions, *McCulloch v. Maryland* (1819) and *Gibbons v. Ogden* (1824), asserted the supremacy of the national government over the States. Other decisions limited the States in their restriction of the rights of property-holders. They were indicative of the general attitude regarding the superiority of private controls. This was the heyday of unrestricted enterprise. The attitude on this subject is also reflected in the philosophies of Justice Joseph Story of Massachusetts, author of *Commentaries on the Constitution,* and of James (Chancellor) Kent of New York, who wrote *Commentaries on American Law.* The two eminent and influential jurists interpreted laws so as to make them fit the needs of an increasingly commercial nation. They had no sympathy for any extension of government regulation that might curb the individual businessman, but they were willing to let the government come to the help of the commercial interests when such aid was convenient.

This was what Senator Thomas Hart Benton of Missouri had in mind when he argued at the end of the decade that the "East," the symbol of business and banking, saw to it that western demands for the homestead laws were obstructed in order to maintain a cheap labor supply for the eastern businessman. Another instance of this philosophy in action was the passage of the tariff of 1828—the "tariff of abominations"—which protected the business promoter at the expense of other interests.

AMERICA OF THE 1820s

But this turn to the right had brought social and political strains. As the businessman assumed a more dominant place in federal control, and as he began to exert his influence to his own advantage, there was an equal and opposite reaction. It is significant that labor unions and a labor press emerge about this time. The cries of anguish over the "tariff of abominations," especially in the agrarian areas, were a prelude to the battle cries of the War Between the States. And yet, curiously, American writers had little to say about the forces shaping the destiny of our country at this time. We can learn more by reading the reports of foreign observers who visited our shores during the first 30 years of the century.

Many, such as Basil Hall and Mrs. Frances Trollope, were devastating in their contempt for American culture and materialism. Others, such as Harriet Martineau, a trained journalist with an understanding heart, saw through the American veneer. In between were reporters, such as Charles Dickens, who were generally severe, but reasonably accurate.[2] They were appalled, for the most part, by American provincialism, unmindful that the American was preoccupied with hacking a nation from a wilderness. This complete absorption in the development of our own resources had resulted in a strong nationalism obnoxious to the foreign observer. Earlier visitors had confined their observations to the more sophisticated East, but the European reporters of the 1820–30s were more interested in the western regions. They were disgusted by the boastfulness, the smugness, superior attitudes, and ill-mannered ignorance of the type of American about to step into control of the government. Most of these observers carried home a great disdain for the American concept of popular rule. One who did not was the French observer, Alexis de Tocqueville, whose *Democracy in America* reflects his observations of 1831–32.

The full consequence of the industrial revolution in America was not apparent until a later date, but the trend was already started in the 1820s. The opening of the Erie Canal in 1825 was to make New York truly the "Empire State" and its metropolis one of the world's great commercial centers. In 1830, only about 7 per cent of the people lived in cities, but the influence of industry was manifested by the obsession of political leaders in such problems as tariffs and the recognition of the working man's vote.

On the whole, the new class emerging out of the industrial revolution was at first inarticulate. The so-called "common man" appeared to be unaware of his new power. But as early as 1820 there was the beginning of populist revolt in Massachusetts, where workers were insisting upon a greater voice in government. New York experienced the same thing in 1821. In Rhode Island, where the worker was less successful at first, pressure built up into actual violence (Dorr's Rebellion), although the denouement dragged out into a later period. The issue was the rights of property versus the rights of the individual. The issue was pointed up by the provision of manhood suffrage. Slowly control began to slip from the landowner and capitalist to the farmer and mechanic. The trend brought new groups into opposition to each other. The

[2] See Godfrey T. Vique, "Six Months in America"; Thomas Hamilton, "Men and Manners in America"; Harriet Martineau, "Society in America"; reprinted in Allan Nevins, ed., *American Social History* (New York: Holt, Rinehart & Winston, 1923).

western farmer, in debt to the eastern capitalist, tended to blame his troubles upon the men of the metropolis. The city mechanic, as the urban worker was called at that time, resented exploitation by what he believed to be a privileged class. He resented being paid in wildcat banknotes that sometimes depreciated to less than half of his contracted wage. It is significant that in 1829 about 75,000 men were jailed for debt. More than half of these victims owed less than $20. Conditions of labor, especially for women and children, brought out a long line of social reformers who insisted upon protective legislation.

Slowly the common man began to realize his power at the polls. In 1824, only six states still chose presidential electors through the legislators, heretofore the frequent tools of the property group. By 1832, only South Carolina maintained this system, and it was in that year that the party convention took at least some of the power away from "King Caucus"—the selection of candidates by secret conclave of political leaders.

THE JACKSONIAN REVOLUTION

By 1824 the emergence of the common man as a power was well under way, although few probably knew it at the time. The popular vote went to Andrew Jackson, darling of the masses. There were four candidates, however, and none had sufficient popular support to carry the election. Henry Clay, with the fewest votes, swung his support to John Quincy Adams, who was declared winner by the House of Representatives. Jackson was convinced that he had been sold out, particularly after Adams selected Clay as his secretary of state. The old hero of New Orleans was therefore all the more determined to lead his followers to victory. In the melee, the old parties were shaken to pieces. The Whigs succeeded the Federalists, after some readjustments, as the party of the right, but the realignment brought greater emphasis to the business element of society. Federalism had strong roots in the aristocratic tradition. It was especially strong in the seaboard North and East. The Whig was a party member more from economic than from social pressure. The opposition group called itself the Democratic party, and its development from the older Jeffersonian components will appear in the following pages.

Jackson became the seventh president of the United States in 1828, following a period of depression and social discontent that did much to build up his popular support. His election was such a victory for new and vigorous elements that his administration has sometimes been called the "Jacksonian Revolution." By 1828, each section of the country had problems only a federal government could hope to solve. Westerners believed they were hampered in their expansion by selfish eastern interests, and it is significant that they helped elect a man who was the very personification of the "western type."

Just as significant was the support of Jackson by the industrial areas, however. He carried both New York and Pennsylvania in 1824, and was overwhelmingly favored by the laborer in eastern commercial centers in 1828. Working men saw that any relief they hoped to gain must come from the federal government. But the South also demanded attention to its troubles. Southern planters accused northern industrialists of trying to wreck the agrarian control, long acknowledged by the political economists. The "tariff of abominations," which threatened to split the regions wide open, heralded this growing rebellion against the growing power of the northern commercial interests.

Henry Clay believed he had found a way to satisfy all the dissident elements. Why Clay, the old western War Hawk of 1812, should now be a Whig leader would take too long to explain here, but his scheme may make his political affiliations appear less inconsistent. A century before anyone ever heard of "economic planning," Clay had worked out a way to make all regions and all groups happy, or so he believed. He called his plan the American System. It was based primarily upon a high protective tariff, which would assure safety to the capitalist, profit to the industrialist, and prosperity to the laborer through high wages. This economy would mean that industry would buy more from the farmer at higher prices. Unfortunately, the farmer had never been able to tap this rich urban market because of the exorbitant price he had to pay to get his goods transported to the big centers. Clay had provided for that. All the proceeds of the tariff would be devoted to improving highways, canals, and railroads. Thus, both the western and southern agrarian, and the eastern commercial interests would profit from each other and would forget their growing differences.

The plan sounded fine, but by 1828 a large part of the population began to suspect that the American System was like a deck of marked cards. They saw very clearly who would win all the big pots. And so voters turned to more direct relief. They listened to such men as Thomas Hart Benton, Senator from Missouri, who cried the loudest against eastern perfidy. Then Old Hickory threw his hat in the presidential ring, and at last common men had a leader around whom they could rally. In 1828 the populist movement swept all before it. For the first time the farm-labor coalition put its own man in the White House. The common man expected results, and Jackson did not let him down.

JACKSON'S "COMMON MAN"

Amos Kendall, the mouthpiece of the Jacksonian administration, saw the conflict clearly. He described it as a fight between the "producing" classes—farmers, laborers, and craftsmen—and the "nonproducing" capitalist, middleman, and landlord. Although outnumbered, this nonproducing class remained dominant through control of banks, education, most of the churches, and the bulk of the press. Thus, Kendall pointed out, "those who produce all the wealth are themselves left poor." [3] Even an old Whig like Horace Greeley had to admit

[3] Arthur M. Schlesinger, Jr., *The Age of Jackson* (Boston: Little, Brown, 1945), p. 306.

the validity of the charge, although that journalistic genius insisted he had better remedies than Kendall had to offer.

At any rate, this was "radical" thinking. The Whig party, digging in for the long battle against the invincible Democrats, was just as far to the right in its thinking. The sanctity of property was explained very comfortably by the ultra-Whig *American Quarterly Review,* published in Philadelphia, which reported just after the end of the decade: "The lowest orders of society ordinarily mean the poorest—and the highest the richest. Sensual excess, want of intelligence, and moral debasement distinguish the former—knowledge, intellectual superiority, and refined, social and domestic affections the latter." As the Pulitzer Prize historian of this period remarks: "Property, in [Whig] reflexes, became almost identified with character." Nicholas Biddle, who as head of the powerful Second Bank of the United States, believed he was the leader of a class too strong for any attempted restraint by the Jacksonians, smugly summed up the opposition Democrats as a party made up of "men with no property to assess and no character to lose." [4]

Fortunately for the Democrats, they were not so easily squelched. The complacency of the Whigs, indeed, accounted for their continued defeat. They could not believe that anything more than their own criticism of the administration was necessary to bring about a victory for them. The pompous Biddle was utterly astounded when, in the summer of 1832, Jackson vetoed a bill for rechartering the Bank of the United States. "Biddled, diddled, and undone," Charles Gordon Greene of the *Boston Post* wrote of Jackson's veto. Unconcerned about their lack of character, the Democrats tracked their muddy boots across the White House floors, just as though they were as good as anyone else. And despite their crudeness and governmental inexperience, they began to accomplish some of their objectives. They won these goals through the combined efforts of the obscure lawmakers, in most cases. The fame of Webster and Clay has come down to us through history as they rolled their armies of purple rhetoric against the thin, gray replies of the little men. But Webster and Clay invariably were on the losing side.

FIRST LABOR PAPERS

A direct result of the industrial revolution and the growing need for recognition of the new type of citizen was the development of the labor press. Some means had to be found to answer the Biddles and the Websters. The depression during the terrible winter of 1828–29, and the rising cost of living, fostered the beginning of a labor revolt long overdue. The appearance of the first labor paper in 1827—the *Journeyman Mechanic's Advocate* of Philadel-

[4] All quoted from *ibid.,* p. 14.

phia—was a clear signal that the laboring man intended to fight for his advantage, as the property man had long fought for his. The first labor paper lasted only a year. The times were too difficult for workers to provide sufficient support. It was a significant "first," however, for in conjunction with the success of the populists at the polls in 1828, the attempt of labor to express itself was prophetic. Two months before Jackson's election, the first working man's party was organized. It was sponsored by the Mechanic's Union of Trade Associations. In the same year the *Mechanic's Free Press* was established as the first successful labor newspaper. Until the depression of 1837 killed it, the *Free Press* had an average weekly circulation of around 1,500—very good for a period when even the biggest New York papers rarely exceeded 4,000.

In many ways, the early labor papers were superior to modern labor organs. Their functions were primarily to counteract prejudices against the working man, to supply labor information that the commercial press ignored, and to offer inspiration to the dispirited. The *Free Press* actually had much less propaganda and biased reporting than would be found in the typical modern labor paper. It offered thoughtful articles on pertinent legislation. The reports were concise, reasonably factual for the standards of that day, and well writ-

Morning Courier and Enquirer.

New-York.

WEDNESDAY, MAY 26, 1830.

Great Public Meeting of the Workingmen at the North American Hotel.—The meeting which is called to-night at the North American Hotel, Bowery, of the Mechanics and Workingmen, will probably be very tumultuously attended, and as probably may end in something very disgraceful to the character of the city. Called together by a majority of the self styled Executive Committee, for the purpose of opposing a minority of twenty-five, who have been playing the dictators, we should not be surprised if the good sense and energy of the Workingmen were to depose the whole Committee, and put into their places a new set of men who would not bring the good character of the Workingmen of New-York into the disgrace which the present impudent club has done since its organization in last December.

It is now about six months since the members of the present Executive Committee assumed the power of dictating to the whole Workingmen of New-York what opinions they should adopt—what doctrines avow, and what measures support. Having originally constituted themselves the keepers of the consciences of the whole of this city, their conduct has corresponded with that daring usurpation. Acting under the impulses, & co-operating with the views of Fanny Wright and Robert Dale Owen, and two or three miserable hack politicians, they have promulgated reports, advanced doctrines, and dictated opinions of the most dangerous character to society, to the stability of our state constitutions, to the safety of the city, and to the interests of the true Workingmen. It was but last Sabbath evening that Miss Fanny Wright boldly avowed before a crowded auditory, the success which has already attended the efforts of the Executive Committee, and the labours of herself and her coadjutors. "How great" said she "is the change wrought in this city within the last six months! In that short time we have witnessed the breaking up of parties, the stirring of mechanics, the alarm of politicans, and the anathemas of the bigot. The Workingmen of this city have turned their attention to republican education. Yes, continued she, WE *have drawn their eyes from the clouds and directed their attention to the realities of life around them.* In vain have they been denounced as agrarians, and in vain has the press sought to link opprobium with the title of Infidel." In her paper called the "Free Enquirer" of last Saturday, under her own signature, the same boast is made—the same denunciations fulminated upon all the benevolent and religious societies of the city—upon all our banks and bankers—and upon all those men who are the benefactors of the age, and the pride of the state and nation.

And most truly has the Executive Committee acted up to the principles of Miss Wright. During the last session of the legislature, this impudent political club had a *corps* of lobby members at Albany, deceiving the unsuspecting country members—playing upon the easy temper of Gen. Root—throwing the legislature into difficulty in relation to our city banks—producing as much mischief as possible, and circulating their principles and doctrines in every way, and by every means. Some of them having been practised in roguery and charlatanism, under the famous coffin hand-bill committee in the Arcade, in 1828, but abandoned by the respectable portion of the friends of Mr. Adams, they became, all at once, the friends of Mechanics, and assumed the right to govern and direct them in all their movements. At one period, lobby members—at another, disciples of Miss Wright—now nominating candidates for Governor—anon spreading infidel principles, this impudent political association has at length, like a band of robbers, or a tribe of banditti, quarrelled among themselves, and are now divided into two parties, both of which are equally unprincipled—equally dangerous to society, and equally insulting to Mechanics and Workingmen. Each of the two divisions is now lustily contending which shall lord it over the Workingmen, and make them their stepping stones to office and power. To attain this great object, the atrocious conduct—the impudent threats—the disgraceful principles of the Marat and Robesperian clubs in Paris, during the horrors of the French revolution, did not deserve the contempt and indignation of a free, moral, and religious people in a greater degree, than does this association, which styles itself the Executive Committee of the Mechanics and Workingmen of New York. The honest Mechanics and Workingmen of this city never gave it existence, and never could have given existence to such a miserable squad of foreign radicals. It is a self appointed and self sustained conclave, composed of the vilest and most worthless materials. Whatever consideration it may have received from a few deluded men, either here or at Albany, there is not a man in this city that is not now satisfied that it ought to be put out of existence, at once—the whole committee, and nothing but the committee. It has disgraced the cause of the Workingmen, and ought not that disgrace to be wiped off?

Let the Mechanics and Workingmen now come forward in their strength—let them throw off the tyranny and usurpation of a synod of old lobby members, ex-coffin handbill pedlers, hack politicians, and Brummagen Radicals—let them choose to-night and install to-night a new committee of sensible men—new from the stump, with not a single rotten branch of the present club to corrupt them—let there be a fair trial made to purge this city from the disgraceful nest of jacobins and Brummagen Radicals, who have for the last six months impudently pretended to represent their interests and direct their votes and energies. Let them do this, and then discreet and independent men will support them in what is right, and advocate their cause, in what is worth advocating. As for ourselves we consider that this press has done the Mechanics and Workingmen of New York, one of the greatest pieces of service by hunting down the infamous Executive Grand & their myrmidons until they have found themselves in their present state of confusion, disorder and despair. We have exposed their machinations—their fantastic tricks—their dangerous principles—their impudent pretensions—their ridiculous assumptions, until they now stand before the whole Workingmen of New

The militant Fanny Wright is denounced by the conservative *Courier and Enquirer.*

ten. Such papers helped to develop labor unity, and it should be noted that labor was solidly behind Jackson.

This agitation led to the organization of the first national labor association—the National Trades Union—founded in 1834. A strong supporter of the labor organization movement was the *Working Man's Advocate,* founded in New York in 1829 by George H. Evans, an English printer. Another important publication supporting labor's cause (along with other social issues) was the *Free Enquirer,* edited in New York by the charming and talented Frances "Fanny" Wright. Fanny Wright, who came to the United States from Scotland in 1818, became a power in the New Harmony utopian experiment conducted by Robert Dale Owen. She had helped put out the *New Harmony Gazette,* published in New York from 1829 as the *Free Enquirer.* Among Miss Wright's many admirers was a young carpenter who was a great believer in democracy, and whose poems began to sing of the people. The poet was Walt Whitman, himself a journalist a little later.

Most of the standard newspapers had scant regard for this labor movement, but one or two helped the cause. William Cullen Bryant, the poet and editor of the *New York Evening Post,* pleaded the case of the working man. The stand of the *Post* indicated how far it had veered since its establishment by the father of Federalism, Alexander Hamilton. Bryant had been employed in 1825 by Coleman, the militant Federalist editor of the paper. Four years later Bryant was in full charge of the *Post,* and remained with the paper, except for a few lapses, for half a century. Under Bryant, the *Post* cast off much of its Federalist tradition. On many issues the paper sided with the Jacksonian Democrats. Thus, denouncing what it believed to be an unjust verdict against a "criminal conspiracy" (strike) by the Society of Journeyman Tailors, the *Post* said:

> They were condemned because they determined not to work for the wages offered them . . . If this is not SLAVERY, we have forgotten its definition. Strike the right of associating for the sale of labour from the privileges of a freeman, and you may as well at once bind him to a master.[5]

William Leggett, part owner of the *Post,* and interim editor after Bryant went abroad in 1834, was even more pro-labor than was Bryant. He was so outspoken, indeed, that the more temperate Bryant had to cool him down on occasion. Later, as we shall see, the cause of the working man was taken up by another famous editor, Horace Greeley. There were magazines, too, fighting for labor during this period. One was the *Democratic Review,* edited by the fiery John L. O'Sullivan. Despite these editorial champions of the underprivileged, the press in general took a dim view of such Jacksonian policies.

[5] *New York Evening Post,* June 13, 1836.

JACKSON'S "KITCHEN CABINET"

Equally obnoxious to the haters of the new order was the so-called "Kitchen Cabinet" of the President. The driving energy of any reform or revolution usually comes from a small group of like-minded leaders. That was true after 1828. Jackson depended upon a little band of men bound together by common zeal for the cause. Normally, they should have made up his official cabinet, but they were not known to the general public, and even an independent like the President had to bow to tradition in the selection of his official family. He chose important men for the ranking positions, but he paid them little heed. The President needed men around him who were closer to him ideologically and temperamentally. Therefore, he turned for advice not to the men chosen by protocol, but to an inner circle of "cronies," as the opposition called them derisively. This was the Kitchen Cabinet.

Some of the most influential members of this inner circle were journalists. Duff Green, the editor of the party paper in Washington, was one of the cronies until his endorsement of Calhoun lost him Jackson's support. Isaac Hill, the crippled, rebellious, and vituperative New Hampshire editor, was another intimate of the President. The two most important powers behind the party, however, were Amos Kendall and Francis Preston Blair.

KENDALL AND BLAIR

Amos Kendall was the most important member of the group. Reared on a New England farm, he was too frail for such rugged work. He had a passion for scholarship, and his family recognized this bent. After he was graduated from Dartmouth College, Kendall headed for the frontier, where opportunities were better for inexperienced lawyers. He hung up his shingle in Lexington, Kentucky.

As a lawyer, Kendall easily turned his energies to politics. He was a protégé of a regional political chieftain, Colonel Richard M. Johnson, who insisted that the erudite New Englander take over the editorship of the Democratic party organ. The newspaper was the *Argus of Western America*, published at Frankfort. Kendall made it the party voice of the entire region. His position was achieved not without great risk, politically as well as physically. For a time he carried a pistol and a bowie knife for protection against those he had scorched in his *Argus* articles. An able, honest, and articulate journalist, his fame as a party spokesman eventually came to the attention of the party's supreme commander, General Jackson. Kendall fought courageously for the debtor's relief system which split Kentucky wide open during Adams' administration. After the voters of Kentucky were cheated of their victory in the "Relief War," he put all his energies into the election of Jackson and came to Washington.

Perhaps their physical ills gave them a common bond. The President was old and full of the miseries. Kendall was something of a hypochondriac, but he had always been frail, so perhaps his attitude was justified. At any rate, there was a strong bond between the two men. Jackson was not a polished writer, and he was happy to have Kendall edit his important statements. Time and again Kendall took down the dictation of the wan warrior. Jackson would lie on a faded sofa beneath the portrait of his beloved Rachel, while Kendall skillfully interpreted his chief's rough ideas and put them into presentable form. Jackson spoke forcefully, but there was too much of the western uncouthness in his diction. Kendall would smooth away the crudeness and read back the paragraph to the President. Perhaps they would have to try again, but eventually the old general would nod approval. Kendall was often surprised at the effectiveness of the speech as it appeared in print.

When Jackson first moved into the White House, the administration organ at Washington was the *United States Telegraph*, founded in 1826.[6] Duff Green was editor of the paper. He had worked hard to elect Jackson, but his other hero was John C. Calhoun, Jackson's party rival. The split in loyalty cost Green the support of the President. The Jacksonian faction decided to make Francis P. Blair Green's successor. Blair had taken over the editorship of the *Argus* after Kendall went to Washington. He had proved to be a very able journalist, but he had to be cleared of $40,000 in debts before he could accept the Washington proposal.

Blair's paper, the *Washington Globe*, appeared at the end of 1830. By that time Jackson and Blair were on the best of terms. "Give it to Bla-ar," the President used to say when he had a particularly trenchant statement requiring journalistic finesse. From Blair's pencil, on scraps of paper held on his knee, came the fighting editorials that helped to knit the party even closer. In 1832, John C. Rives became Blair's assistant. Rives, a shaggy giant, quite in contrast to his colorless associates, also came to enjoy the confidences of the inner guard.

But Kendall was the most important of them all. As one of Jackson's rivals put it, Kendall was ". . . the President's *thinking* machine, and his *writing* machine—ay, and his *lying* machine. . . . He was chief overseer, chief reporter, amanuensis, scribe, accountant general, man of all work—nothing was well done without the aid of his diabolical genius."[7] And ex-President Adams, not given to exaggeration, once stated of Van Buren and Jackson, "Both . . . have been for twelve years the tool of Amos Kendall, the ruling mind of their dominion."[8] Kendall became Postmaster General in 1835.

[6] The *electric* telegraph had not been invented at that time. The name probably derived from the semaphore signal.

[7] Schlesinger, *The Age of Jackson*, p. 73.

[8] *Loc. cit.*

INVENTIONS FOR A PEOPLE'S PRESS

But where were the publications for the masses? Surely all this democratic ferment must have had its consequences in developing a newspaper the man in the street could afford and could enjoy. As a matter of fact, the same forces that brought about the emergence of the common man also accounted for the establishment of a people's press. The industrial revolution, which resulted in cheaper goods, also made it possible to produce a cheaper paper. All the social pressures mentioned in the preceding pages shared in making possible the newspaper for the masses. There was a vast, untapped public tempting the promoter, if only the product could be made attractive. And by 1833, the technical progress had reached the point where this was possible.

In 1822, Peter Smith, connected with R. Hoe and Company, printing-press makers, invented a hand press with a much faster lever action. Five years later Samuel Rust of New York put out the Washington hand press, still seen in some offices. It had many automatic devices—a platen raised and lowered by springs; an ingenious toggle device for quick impressions; a faster-moving bed; and later, automatic ink rollers.

The next step was to harness power to the press. This was the Age of Steam, and at once inventors set themselves to the problem. Daniel Treadwell of Boston had partial success in 1822. A steam book press was developed by Isaac Adams of Boston in 1830 and was popular for many years, but it was a European who perfected the process for speedy power printing. He was Friedrich Koenig, of Saxony, who, after many delays, produced the first of his presses in London in 1811. It had a movable bed which carried the type back and forth to be inked after each impression. Paper was fed into the top of a cylinder. Three years later Koenig invented a two-cylinder press that printed both sides of the paper—the so-called "perfecting press." The *Times* of London was the first to use this press for newspaper work late in 1814. The paper proudly stated that it could outstrip all rivals by printing papers at the unbelievable rate of 1,100 an hour.

In 1830 David Napier of England perfected the Koenig steam press so as to triple the speed of printing. America's R. Hoe and Company, which was to become a byword in newspaper plants, chose the Napier press as the prototype of a new product for American printers. The new Hoe was actually a great improvement over the Napier, and it could produce four thousand double impressions an hour. Such technical progress was essential to the production of a cheap paper that the masses could afford to buy.

By 1833 all the ingredients were available for the establishment of such a venture. It was possible to print a paper that would sell for one cent, in contrast to the six cents charged by the average commercial dailies. To a workman, six cents was the equivalent of a quarter-pound of bacon, or a pint of

R. Hoe & Co., Inc.

An American adaptation of Koenig's power press.

local whisky. In England, Henry Hetherington had published two periodicals for the masses. He failed, not because of the price he charged, but because he was caught evading the so-called "taxes on knowledge," which kept the price of British newspapers out of the hands of the common man, as intended. John Wight, the Bow Street police reporter, had also demonstrated by 1820 the type of news that would make the presses of the masses successful.

In 1829, Seba Smith founded a daily paper at Portland, Maine, that was smaller than a standard newspaper, but cheaper by half than the usual daily. It cost four dollars a year, payable in advance. A year later, Lynde M. Walter, a Boston brahmin, bought an existing paper and made it into the daily *Transcript,* offered at four dollars a year. More popular because it offered spicier items, perhaps, was the *Boston Morning Post,* founded as a four-dollar daily by Charles G. Greene in 1831. Two years later Captain John S. Sleeper founded the *Boston Mercantile Journal,* offered at the same price. All were successful, but they were sold by subscription, which took them out of the reach of the usual laboring man, who could not pay a lump sum in advance.

In Philadelphia, Dr. Christopher Columbus Conwell established a penny paper, *The Cent,* in 1830. Although interesting as a forerunner of the press for the masses, it survived such a short time that it is of little significance to the present summary. A serious and nearly-successful attempt to put out a genuine penny paper for the masses, to be sold by the issue, and not entirely by subscription, was made by Horace Greeley in partnership with Dr. H. D. Shepard, a dentist, in January, 1833. This was the *New York Morning Post.* A violent snow storm kept so many citizens indoors the first few days of its appearance that the promoters had to give up the venture.

The time was ripe for a successful penny paper, however. Indeed, the next attempt to produce a penny paper was to bring such a significant change to American journalism as to warrant the description "revolutionary."

Annotated Bibliography

Books

The volumes by the Beards, Parrington, Curti, and Boorstin, previously cited, are basic references for this period. Others are:

Brooks, Van Wyck, *The World of Washington Irving.* New York: Dutton, 1944. An interpretation of the period through the literary contributions of American writers.

Brown, Charles H., *William Cullen Bryant.* New York: Scribner's, 1971. A comprehensive study of the editor of the *New York Evening Post.*

Cambridge History of American Literature, II. New York: Putnam's, 1917–21. Pages 160–75 describe magazines during 1783–1850; pages 176–95 describe the general newspaper picture from 1775 to 1860. Book publishing is surveyed in Volume 4 (pp. 533–53).

Commons, John R., ed., *Documentary History of American Industrial Society,* IV. Cleveland: A. H. Clark Company, 1910. Basic source.

Fish, Carl Russell, *The Rise of the Common Man, 1830–1850,* A History of American Life, Vol. VI. New York: Macmillan, 1927. Social history, and a standard appraisal of the period.

Forsyth, David P., *The Business Press in America, 1760–1865.* Philadelphia: Chilton, 1964. A prize-winning history of business journalism.

Gabriel, Ralph H., *The Course of American Democratic Thought.* New York: Ronald Press, 1956. Intellectual history since 1815.

Nevins, Allan, *American Social History.* New York: Holt, Rinehart & Winston, 1923. Includes a description of American manners and culture as seen by various British observers of the period.

Schlesinger, Arthur M., Jr., *The Age of Jackson.* Boston: Little, Brown, 1945. A penetrating study of the political background by a Pulitzer Prize winner. Includes a chapter on the press.

Tocqueville, Alexis de, *Democracy in America.* New York: Doubleday, 1969. Editions have been appearing since 1835 of this famous French observer's study of American democracy and its effect upon the social system.

Turnbull, Arthur T., and Russell N. Baird, *The Graphics of Communication.* New York: Holt, Rinehart & Winston, 1968. Standard reference, with account of letterpress printing.

Tyler, Alice Felt, *Freedom's Ferment: Phases of American Social History to 1860.* Minneapolis: University of Minnesota Press, 1944. Emphasizes effects of religious and reform movements.

Periodicals and Monographs

Hage, George S.,"Anti-Intellectualism in Press Comment: 1828 and 1952," *Journalism Quarterly,* XXXVI (Fall 1959), 439. Comparison of newspaper content in two presidential elections. A full study is in his doctoral dissertation, "Anti-Intellectualism in Newspaper Comment in the Elections of 1828 and 1952," University of Minnesota, 1957.

Miller, Alan R., "America's First Political Satirist: Seba Smith of Maine," *Journalism Quarterly,* XLVII (Autumn 1970), 488. The creator of Major Jack Downing at the *Portland Courier.*

Myers, Donald James, "The Birth and Establishment of the Labor Press in the United States," Master's thesis, University of Wisconsin, 1950. An authoritative study of the labor press up to 1880.

Smith, Elbert B., "Francis P. Blair and the Globe," *Register of the Kentucky Historical Society,* LVII (October 1959), 340. Blair's role as editor of the Jackson party paper in Washington.

Smith, William E., "Francis P. Blair, Pen-Executive of Andrew Jackson," *Mississippi Valley Historical Review,* XVII (March 1931), 459. A vivid portrait of the *Washington Globe* and its editor. Reprinted in Ford and Emery, *Highlights in the History of the American Press.*

Bettmann Archive

JAMES GORDON BENNETT of the *Herald*

From _Harper's Weekly_

HORACE GREELEY of the *Tribune*

11

A Press for the Masses

But the world does move, and its motive power under God is the fearless thought and speech of those who dare to be in advance of their time—who are sneered at and shunned through their days of struggle as lunatics, dreamers, impracticables and visionaries; men of crotchets, vagaries, and isms. They are the masts and sails of the ship to which conservatism answers as ballast. The ballast is important—at times indispensable—but it would be of no account if the ship were not bound to go ahead.
—Horace Greeley

Whenever a mass of people has been neglected too long by the established organs of communication, agencies eventually have been devised to supply that want. Invariably this press of the masses is greeted with scorn by the sophisticated reader because the content of such a press is likely to be elemental and emotional. Such scorn is not always deserved. Just as the child ordinarily starts his reading with Mother Goose and fairy stories before graduating to more serious study, so the public first reached by a new agency is likely to prefer what the critics like to call "sensationalism," which is the emphasis on emotion for its own sake. This pattern can be seen in the periods when the most noteworthy developments in popular journalism were apparent. In 1620, 1833, the 1890s, or 1920, this tapping of a new, much-neglected public started with a wave of sensationalism.

The phenomenon is clearly exhibited in the period of the 1830s and 1840s covered by this chapter. For it was in 1833 that the first successful penny newspaper tapped a reservoir of readers collectively designated "the common man."

The first offerings of this poor man's newspaper tended to be highly sensational. This was only a developmental phase, however. Before long some of the penny newspapers began to attract readers from other social and economic brackets. And the common man, as his literacy skill improved, also demanded a better product. Within a decade after the appearance of the first penny paper, the press of the common man included respectable publications that offered significant information and leadership.

Before the appearance of the penny papers, publishers charged from six to ten dollars a year in advance for a newspaper subscription. That was more than most skilled workmen earned in a week, and in any case, the man of limited means could not pay that much in a lump sum. The standard newspapers usually were edited for people of means, and that partially accounted for the preponderance of conservatism in the press. It also was a factor in keeping circulations small, although mechanical limitations certainly had a similar effect. In 1833 the largest dailies in New York were the morning *Courier and Enquirer,* published by the colorful and irascible Colonel James Watson Webb, and the *Journal of Commerce,* founded by Arthur Tappan in 1827, but soon taken over by Gerard Hallock and David Hale.[1] The largest afternoon paper was William Cullen Bryant's *Post.* These and the other eight city papers sold for six cents a copy, and most of them were distributed by subscription, rather than by the street sale which was to characterize the penny press.

DAY'S *NEW YORK SUN,* 1833

Journalism began a new epoch on September 3, 1833, with the appearance of a strange little newspaper, the *New York Sun* ("It Shines for ALL"). Its founder was Benjamin H. Day, who arrived in New York as a lad of 20, after an apprenticeship on Massachusetts' excellent *Springfield Republican.* That was in 1831. For two years he operated a printing shop without much success; there were financial disturbances, and in 1832 a plague further cut into the city's prosperity. In desperation, Day decided to publish a paper in an effort to take up some of the slack in his declining job-printing business. He had watched the early attempts to establish penny papers in Boston, Philadelphia, and New York, and it appeared to him that such a publication would be successful if it could be sold and financed on a per-issue basis. He discussed the proposal with two friends, Arunah S. Abell and William M. Swain. They warned him against the undertaking, a bit of advice they had to eat sometime later, when they founded their own successful penny papers in Philadelphia and Baltimore. Day decided to go ahead with his plans anyway.

[1] The paper had strong religious undertones, but it was aggressive in its news policies and business coverage. It will receive more attention in a later discussion on the development of cooperative news gathering.

The appearance of the *Sun* that September day did not give the impression that it would soon outshine all rivals in circulation.[2] It was printed on four pages, each about two-thirds the area of a modern tabloid page. The front page was four columns wide and devoid of any display devices. Emphasis was on local happenings and news of violence. Most of the material was trivial, flippant—but highly readable. Most important, it was cheap. Within six months the *Sun* had a circulation of around 8,000, which was nearly twice that of its nearest rival.

The reporting of George Wisner accounted for some of this success. Remembering the popularity of the Bow Street police-station news in the London forerunners of the penny press, Day hired Wisner, a Bow Street veteran, to write for the *Sun.* He was an instant success. Wisner received four dollars a week for covering the courts, plus a share in the profits of the paper. Within a year he had become co-owner of the paper.

"Human interest" news was a specialty of the *Sun.* Here is a sample of the *Sun* technique taken from a typical issue after the paper was firmly established:

> Some six years ago a young gentleman, the oldest son of a distinguished baronet in England, after completing his course in education, returned home to pay his respects to his parents, and to participate in the pleasures of their social circle.[3]

The account goes on to describe how the handsome youth fell in love with a girl his father had adopted as a ward. Eventually the couple ran off together because such marriages were forbidden, and the scion was disinherited by the angry baron. On the death of the father, however, the son was declared heir to the title. A younger son tried to wrest the estate by charging his elder brother with incest. This part of the story fills all of the *Sun*'s first page for that day. No names are used. It could have been complete fabrication, except that the word "recent" is used to give a news flavor to the piece. The fate of the heir is never determined, although the account is embellished by such passages as:

> . . . And while our hero was unsuspiciously reposing on the soft bosom of his bride, a brother's hand, impelled by a brother's hate, was uplifted with fratricidal fierceness for destruction.

A half column on the following page headed "Shocking Accident" described how a 19-year-old New Hampshire youth had been buried alive in a well cave-in. This had been picked out of the exchanges, apparently because

[2] By 1837 the *Sun* was printing 30,000 copies a day, which was more than the total of all New York daily newspapers combined when the *Sun* had first appeared.

[3] *New York Sun,* January 3, 1835.

of the twist to the story. It seems the poor chap was to have been wed the following week, which was the type of tear-jerker the *Sun* editors loved. There was humor of a sort mixed up in all this rubbish. Under a standing head, "Police Office—Yesterday," there was an item about the night watch being called to foil a desperate jail break, only to find that a pet squirrel in a cage was the source of the suspicious riot sounds. A Negro woman before the police magistrate made a whimsical remark based on the confusion of the words "prosecute" and "prostitute." All good, rich fare for the sensation-hungry *Sun* reader.

The only concession to the commercial interests of the community in this typical issue was a column of shipping news on the third page. Obviously, the paper was not printed for the property class. And yet anyone could see that the paper was bringing in plenty of advertising revenue. The back page was solid advertising, and about half the third page was devoted to classified notices, including "Want Ads." Even page one contained advertising, such as the one about Robert Hoe and Son, the printing-press maker at 29 Gold Street, who had just installed a new cylinder press for the *Sun* that was the fastest in the city—1,500 complete papers an hour.

A PENNY PRESS FOR THE COMMON MAN

The appearance of the penny press and the rise of the common man were closely integrated. The newspaper for the masses arrived just as the labor class began to win recognition under the Jacksonian democracy. Politics for the masses had some of the flaws corresponding to the faults of the factory system. Too often majority rule encouraged the spoils system, bossism, and mediocrity in government. Too often the early penny papers provoked criticism in striving to reach the public by lowering standards. The *Sun*, for example, was ready to sacrifice truth, if that would bring in more customers. The fact is, it nearly trebled in circulation in 1835 when one of its reporters, a descendant of John Locke, the political philosopher, wrote a series of articles purporting to describe life on the moon. The so-called "moon hoax" of Richard Adams Locke may not have increased public confidence in the paper, but readers did not appear to resent the journalistic trick that had been played on them.

And yet there was much that was revealed as good in the sunrise of a new journalism, despite all the vulgarity, cheapness, and spuriousness of the first penny paper. The *Sun* was a recognition of the common man on the communications level. The working man had already won the right to vote. Now the penny papers could reach out to him as no other medium could. It did not take the politician long to discover this fact. The student of journalism will look in vain for any profound expressions of political philosophy in the early editions of the penny press, but after the first wave of sensationalism, the editors of these publications began to offer information of a more significant type.

At the same time, readers began to show a little more interest in the government they had the power to control.

But of course it took a little time to win them away from the outright emotionalism with which they had been lured into the journalistic fold. Even in later stages of his development the common man showed little interest in the complicated and erudite opinions comprising the main fare of the orthodox press. The newly-recognized public was more interested in *news* than in *views*. The penny papers concentrated on supplying this type of intelligence—in readable form. The *Sun* and its galaxy of imitators proved that news was a valuable commodity, if delivered in a sprightly manner.

Another person began to take a special interest in the newspaper for the masses. This was the advertiser, who was impressed by the amazing circulations of the new medium. He saw that readership of the cheap daily cut through political interests, so that the paper reached a broad base of people, instead of a mere political faction. Putting an ad in every publication bought by small splinter groups was expensive and ineffective sales promotion. The large circulations of the penny papers now made it feasible to publicize articles for sale that formerly would not have warranted advertising expense.

On the other hand, advertising revenue made it possible for editors and publishers to expand and to experiment with new methods of news gathering. Since advertising flowed to the circulation leaders, and since news appeared to be the most popular type of literature, publishers began to invest heavily in various devices for improving news coverage. The full scope of this development will be described in the next chapter, but the relation between advertising and the penny press deserves mention at this point. As publishers began to understand the technique of obtaining mass circulations, they had to have better presses. Moses Y. Beach, Ben Day's brother-in-law, who took over the *Sun* in 1837, used part of his profits to buy a new steam-driven Hoe cylinder press capable of producing 4,000 papers an hour. It was the most advanced printing equipment of its day.

The penny papers also brought changes in distribution methods. Commercial and standard newspapers had been sold on the subscription basis. Workmen not only could not pay a large sum in advance, but many also moved around too much to subscribe regularly. There were times when the worker could not read at all, because of his job, or because of his poverty. The penny papers reached such readers by depending primarily upon street sales, under the so-called "London Plan." Vendors bought the papers from the publisher at the rate of a hundred copies for 67 cents, to be sold for one cent each. This put a premium on individual initiative, as indicated by the shrill cries of the vendors on street corners. The distribution system also inevitably changed the appearance of the paper, as editors tried to lure readers from rival publications through the use of better makeup and more readable type.

The raw product of the press was also changed by the newspaper of the masses. When the *views*paper became a *news*paper, the style of the writer also changed. Editors were less interested in opinion, and were more concerned with reporting straight news. This was less a development toward objectivity than it was a shift away from political partisanship.

BENNETT'S *NEW YORK HERALD*, 1835

One of the most successful promoters of a newspaper cutting through the partisanship of the times was James Gordon Bennett.[4] Bennett was strictly a reporter and editor, in contrast to the printer-publishers who have figured so prominently in this history. He had gained valuable experience as a Washington correspondent, which was to stand him in good stead when he began to develop national news as a commodity. As editor for Colonel James Watson Webb, he had engineered the 1829 merger of the *Courier* and the *Enquirer*, to make it the largest newspaper in New York. Twice he had tried to found a paper of his own, but without success. The newspaper he produced on the morning of May 6, 1835, changed this picture.

Bennett was 40 years old, disillusioned, and deep in debt when he founded the *New York Morning Herald*. His capital was five hundred dollars, plus some credit from his printers. His office was a cellar in the basement of a building at 20 Wall Street. Equipment consisted of a desk made from a plank spanning two dry goods boxes, a secondhand chair, and a box for files. His entire staff consisted of himself. On this basis Bennett built one of the most profitable newspaper properties of his time.

There was a month's delay after the first appearance of the *Herald*, but from June, 1835, the paper boomed. The *Herald* was an imitator of the *Sun*, in using sensational material, but Bennett added many tricks of his own. When it came to crime reporting the *Herald* knew no equal. The issue of June 4, 1836, a year after regular publication of the paper, will show the typical *Herald* treatment of such news. The whole front page, unrelieved by headlines, was devoted to the Robinson-Jewett case. This involved the murder of a prostitute in a brothel by a notorious man-about-town, and Bennett gave the sordid murder all the resources of his paper. He stirred up so much interest in the case that the court could not continue hearing testimony when the defendant was up for trial. The tone of *Herald* reporting is indicated by this "precede" to the main story of the trial and the disturbances in the court room:

> The mayor—the sheriff, all endeavored to restore order—all in vain. A terrible rain storm raged out doors—a mob storm indoors. The Judges

[4] It would be ridiculous to maintain that the penny press avoided partisanship. Papers like the *Herald* took up issues every day, and often fought for them as violently as in the old partisan-press days. But that was not the purpose of these papers, as it had been when papers reflected factions and parties. The newspaper was a little more impersonal than the viewspaper, but the development of objectivity had barely started, and the goal had not been reached more than a hundred years later. All such progress must be measured relatively.

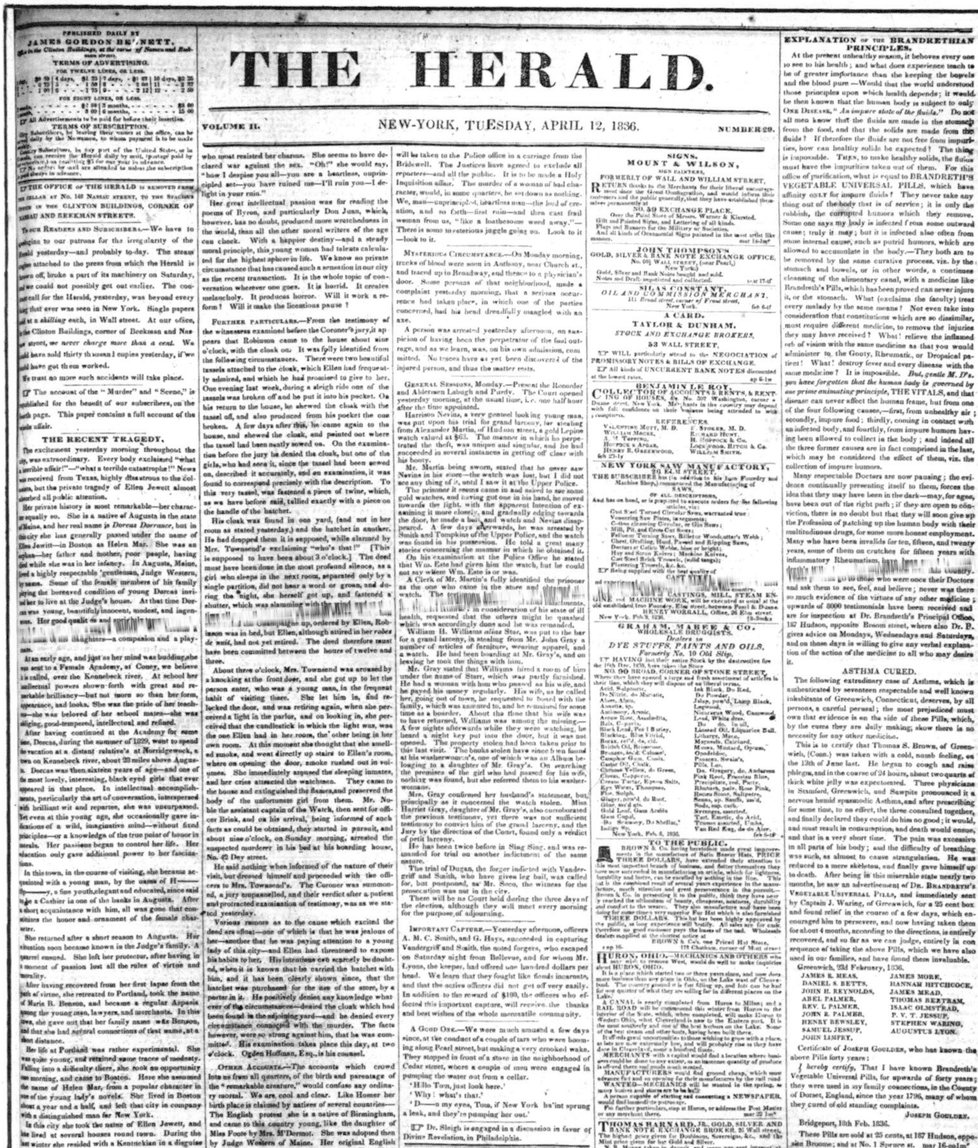

THE HERALD.

VOLUME II. NEW-YORK, TUESDAY, APRIL 12, 1836. NUMBER 29.

Bennett runs a three-column, second-day analysis of the Ellen Jewett murder case.

> and the Officers left the hall. Robinson was carried out of court, and the Public Authorities were trying to clear the hall of the mob, when this extra went to press.
>
> Why is not the militia called?
>
> We give the additional testimony up to the latest hour. . . . The mystery of the bloody drama increases—increases—increases.[5]

The "extra" feature of this news coverage (an "extra" is a special edition) was typical of Bennett's aggressive style of journalism. Soon this type of news treatment gave way to an increasing interest in more significant news. Bennett himself had no qualms about using violent news, for he was certain his paper was getting better every day. He got out of the penny-paper category in the summer of 1836 and defended his policy by stating that his readers were getting more for their money—the new price was two cents—than they could get anywhere else.

Year by year the *Herald* branched out into other fields of journalism. The paper appealed to the business class by developing the best financial section of any standard journal. Bennett, a former teacher of economics, wrote what he called the "money page." He had had experience in such reporting, and he took a special interest in this phase of journalism. When administrative duties at last forced him to give up this work, he saw to it that his best staff men were assigned to the Wall Street run. In the meantime, he was offering more serious background material than his rivals on the *Sun*. His editorial comment was seldom profound, but it was decisive, reasoned, and informative. The *Herald* led the pack in hounding news from all areas, local, foreign, and national, as we shall see in the next chapter. Bennett built up an interesting "letters" column, where readers could comment on the paper, as well as upon events. He helped develop the critical review column and society news. Long before other editors recognized the appeal of the subject, Bennett was offering sports news. Thus it was all along. The great contribution of the *Herald* was as an innovator and perfecter.

This aggressive policy paid big dividends. The *Herald* was full of advertising and was on its way to circulation leadership. It had 20,000 readers in 1836 and would be the world's largest daily, at 77,000, by 1860. Such success for a disliked rival brought a movement to boycott the *Herald*. The attack by Bennett's critics was started in May, 1840, by Park Benjamin of the *New York Signal*. Colonel James Watson Webb, Bennett's onetime employer, joined in the fray (he once administered a caning to the editor of the *Herald*), and soon all the opposition papers joined the "moral war" against the upstart journalist. Bennett was accused of blasphemy (he had carried his saucy style into the coverage of religious news) and some of the leading clergymen used their influence to make the boycott effective. Advertisers who feared to offend the

[5] *New York Herald*, June 4, 1836 ("Morning" was dropped from the nameplate in 1835).

moral experts withdrew their accounts. There is no doubt that Bennett offended decent members of the community with his bad taste, quackery, and sensationalism, but the real cause of the moral war was resentment over Bennett's amazing success. He had made his rivals appear stuffy and outdated.

Bennett solved the problem confronting the *Herald* in characteristic manner. He sent his best reporters out to cover the church beats, including all religious meetings of any consequence. A man of little religious feeling, he had the news sense to understand that here was another neglected public worth cultivating. He also toned down some of the obvious charlatanism that had made the *Herald* the symbol of publicized wickedness. The result was victory for Bennett.

Bennett put some needed ingredients into American journalism. He added spice and enterprise and aggressive news coverage. He proved that a publisher devoted to the continual improvement of his product could expect rich rewards. It cost a large fortune to provide all the machinery and personnel that put the *Herald* ahead of its rivals, but the investment paid huge dividends. Bennett left a valuable property to his son, and he died a rich man. But the *Herald* was remembered not so much for *what* it said, as for *how* it said it. Bennett's contributions were largely technical.

PENNY-PRESS EXPANSION: PHILADELPHIA, BALTIMORE

Other publishers spread the gospel of penny-press journalism to other cities. Benjamin Day's printer friends, William M. Swain and Arunah S. Abell, saw the *Sun* thrive despite the pessimistic advice they had offered, but they fully admitted their errors when they founded the *Philadelphia Public Ledger* in March, 1836, with Azariah H. Simmons as partner. Philadelphia had already been introduced to penny-press journalism by Dr. Christopher Columbus Conwell, who had experimented unsuccessfully with a penny paper, *The Cent,* in 1830. In 1835 William L. Drane founded the *Daily Transcript,* and was operating successfully when the three partners founded the *Public Ledger.* But the new paper was soon to become one of the great American dailies. It was a cleaned up version of the *Herald*—full of sensational news, but without the extreme bad taste of the New York paper. It was an effective policy. Within two years after its founding, the *Public Ledger* had absorbed its rival, the *Transcript,* and was printing more than 20,000 copies a day. Like the *Herald,* the *Public Ledger* made full use of the most modern technical and news coverage developments.

Swain was the dominant figure on the *Public Ledger,* and after an interval, Abell decided to strike out for himself. He selected Baltimore as a likely city. It was second only to New York as a trade center, and was then third in population. Swain and Simmons were not enthusiastic about the undertaking at first.

Eventually they underwrote the investment, but Abell promoted the Baltimore publication pretty much by himself. The *Baltimore Sun* first rose May 17, 1837. Its appearance coincided with a depression that had already closed the banks. The first issue of the paper played up the story of a city council meeting the day before, at which $100,000 worth of fractional currency ("shinplasters") was authorized to meet the financial crisis. This was scarcely the appropriate time to found a new paper, it would seem, but the *Sun* prospered, like its New York namesake, and appeared to be safely established at the end of the first year with a circulation of 12,000. Like its Philadelphia affiliate, the *Sun* was always noted for its enterprise and technical progress. It was a pioneer in the development of telegraph news. Both the Baltimore and Philadelphia penny papers worked with the *New York Herald* in exchanging the latest news. The arrangement accounted for numerous scoops, especially during the Mexican war. But the *Baltimore Sun* made a contribution of its own. It developed the Washington bureau of correspondence in its first year of operation. Soon other papers came to value the Baltimore publication for complete and accurate coverage of national news. Government officials also began to follow the paper closely for trends in political development.

The success of the penny-paper pioneers encouraged other publishers to follow the pattern. There were 35 penny papers started in New York in the 1830s. All but the *Sun* and *Herald* succumbed, but in other cities the promoters fared better. By 1840, the four largest American cities had penny papers. Most of them had similar news policies: much local news, great attention to human interest stories, and a fat budget for entertainment material. But more and more significant news was creeping into the columns, and the penny papers led in aggressive news gathering.

GREELEY'S *NEW YORK TRIBUNE*, 1841

The maturing of the press for the masses was best indicated by the newspaper founded at the very beginning of the fifth decade of the century. The paper was the *New York Tribune,* and its founder was Horace Greeley, soon to become one of the most influential editors in the history of American journalism. More books have been written about him than about any other American of the period, except Lincoln.

Horace Greeley was like a character from a Dickens novel—so real that he appeared to be a caricature. He had the angularity of the Vermonter (which he was); a stiff, homespun personality, coupled with the shyness which makes the New England breed so difficult for others to understand. His inconsistencies were legendary. A professed Whig (the party opposed to popular rule), he worked all his life to bring a greater share of material and political benefits to the common man. A leader of the group standing for a continuance of the *status quo,* he was one of the most "radical" men of his age. At a time when the democratic process was under great stress, Greeley "put his faith in the unshackled mind."

He saw the ample resources of the United States, and he was certain that every American could enjoy the abundant life, if only simple justice could be made to prevail. He believed in what he called "beneficent capitalism." The practical application of this theory was the American System, sponsored by Henry Clay. Clay was Greeley's great hero. Until death ended the career of the Great Compromiser, Greeley devoted a column of his paper to discussions of current issues under the standing headline, "Henry Clay." Greeley, like Clay, honestly believed that if the proceeds of the protective tariff could be used to develop markets for the farmers, all the workers of the country would be prosperous. Because Greeley advocated the high tariff, he was sometimes suspected by the masses of opposing their interests. Because he had scant regard for agrarian dominance in an age of expanding industrialism, he was accused by the farmer of hypocrisy. Because he believed in the organization of unions to prevent exploitation by the privileged, he was frequently attacked by the property interests. Actually, his idea was to direct the forces of capitalism so that industry, labor, and agriculture could complement each other in improving the common lot. The day Greeley had in mind was one in which opportunity, work, and education would be available to all. Women would be paid at the same rate as men, for similar services, and would have equal civil rights. Temperance would prevail in all things. Labor would be well organized for its own protection. Capital would reap the benefits of a prosperous community, but would feel responsible for better living standards. Slavery, and imprisonment for debt, would be abolished.

The man who proposed these revolutionary ideas was hardly messianic in appearance. He looked as though he had stepped out of a modern comic strip. He walked with a shambling, uncertain gait, as though he were feeling his way in the dark. His usual garb was a light-gray "duster," or gown, which he had purchased from an immigrant for $3, and which he wore winter and summer over his ill-fitting, nondescript suits. His guileless, baby-blue eyes were set in a moonlike face fringed with wispy whiskers sprouting out of his collar like reeds around a mossy stone. A high-pitched, whiny voice added nothing to this unimpressive ensemble. Yet this was the man who was to capture the loyalties of newspaper readers as few editors have in the history of American journalism.

Greeley began his career at the age of 15 as an apprentice to a printer whose business soon failed. He traveled around New York State as a tramp printer for five years, reading voraciously all the while. When he arrived in New York in 1831 he had just ten dollars to his name. After part-time work as a compositor, he finally landed a permanent position on the *Evening Post*.

Soon he and a partner, Francis Story, set up a shop of their own. They printed a small weekly on contract, but the main revenue was from lottery advertising, a circumstance his foes and rivals never let him forget later on.

The attempt of the partners to found a penny paper in the winter of 1833 has already been described. In 1834, Greeley founded the *New Yorker*, a stimulating and well-edited publication mainly devoted to literary fare. While publishing this paper he wrote editorials for the *Daily Whig* and had entire charge of a political paper published at Albany by the Whig party leaders. For six months during the presidential campaign of 1840 he edited and published a campaign paper, the *Log Cabin*. He was an experienced journalist, therefore, when he announced in the *Log Cabin* that beginning April 10, 1841, he would publish a daily penny paper, the *New York Tribune*.

His political activities had made Greeley one of the New York Whig triumvirate, which included state party boss Thurlow Weed, the Albany journalist, and Governor William H. Seward. Now was the time to found a newspaper that could carry the Whig message to the common man. It is significant that the *Tribune* appeared just a month after President William Henry Harrison's inauguration following the Whig victory of 1840. Greeley must have been aware that the climate was right for his undertaking. His influence in state and federal political circles must certainly have been a factor in the establishment of the paper. It should be pointed out, too, that Henry Clay, Greeley's hero, expected to be a key figure in the new administration, and was confident that the American System, also promoted by Greeley, would be pushed through at once. But the President died a month after his inauguration, and many ambitions were cut short thereby. Not Greeley's, however.[6]

With a thousand dollars of borrowed money, about that much of his own, plus a mortgage on his shop—a total capitalization of not more than three thousand dollars—Greeley issued the first *Tribune* as a penny paper. It was not much to look at. Its four pages were five columns wide and about the dimensions of a modern tabloid. The printing was good, however, and so was the content, apparently. At least it attracted readers, for Greeley boasted of a circulation in excess of 11,000 after the second month. This was about one-fourth the print order of the *Sun*, then the most popular paper in America, but it was enough to establish the *Tribune* firmly. Greeley was a good editor but a poor manager. He himself never shared in the fortune that his paper was to make for others. Indeed, the paper might have failed, had not the very able Thomas McElrath purchased a half interest for $2,000. The paper was then losing money. At the end of the second year the price was raised to two cents (weekly subscribers paid 1½ cents an issue) and the *Tribune* began to make money.

The *Tribune* always trailed both the *Sun* and the *Herald* in daily circulation, but part of its great reputation was to rest upon its weekly edition, which was a phenomenal success. It first appeared September 2, 1841. Offered at two dollars a year, or one dollar a year when "clubs" of 20 members bought it (which was very common) the weekly *Tribune* largely established Greeley's

[6] Harrison's running mate, John Tyler of Virginia, proved as President to be more southern than Whig and vetoed Clay's pet bills. In the 1844 presidential year the Whigs ditched Tyler for Clay, but Democrat James K. Polk won.

reputation as the greatest editor of his day. It was said to have been read in the midwestern states areas "next to the Bible."

ESTIMATES OF GREELEY'S STATURE

Many able critics have declared that Horace Greeley does not deserve the acclaim that has been given to him. Victor Lawson, the great editor of the *Chicago Daily News*, knew Greeley personally. Lawson considered the *Tribune* editor to be the most overrated journalist in American history.[7] The younger Schlesinger apparently thinks of Greeley as a humbug. Says he:

> Greeley's reputation (apart from his strong, if belated, stand on slavery) rests mainly on his feverish advocacy of sideshow reforms. He (Greeley) was eminently a "safe" radical. When he devoutly fought for the American System, what did it matter if he allowed Albert Brisbane to pay him a hundred dollars a week for printing a column on Fourierism? [see p. 179] Brisbane was . . . a cheap price for a progressive reputation . . .[8]

But equally reliable students say that Greeley was of heroic proportions. John R. Commons, the great authority on the labor movement, called the *Tribune* "the first and only great vehicle this country has known for the ideas and experiments of constructive democracy."[9] E. L. Godkin, one of the great journalists of the late nineteenth century, who is often misquoted on Greeley, actually had great respect for the editor of the *Tribune*. Godkin ridiculed Greeley's whimsies, but in his *Life and Letters* wrote: "The Tribune in particular excited my warm admiration. . . . The influence of such a journal was deservedly high. Greeley . . . sacrificed everything—advertisers, subscribers, and all else—to what he considered principle."[10] This was indeed an endorsement, coming from such a severe critic as E. L. Godkin. Joseph Bishop, who succeeded Godkin as editor of the influential *New York Evening Post*, wrote in his autobiography: "The 'Tribune' was a tremendous force in the country because of the personal faith of the plain people in the honesty of its editor. Every word the 'Tribune' printed was believed implicitly because he was the

[7] This statement was made after the bitter campaign of 1872, however, when Lawson opposed Greeley as the leader of a coalition party seeking to put Greeley into the White House in place of President Grant.

[8] Arthur M. Schlesinger, Jr., *The Age of Jackson* (Boston: Little, Brown, 1945), pp. 295–96.

[9] John R. Commons, "Horace Greeley and the Working Class Origins of the Republican Party," *Political Science Quarterly*, XXIV (September 1909), 472.

[10] Rollo Ogden, ed., *Life and Letters of Edwin Lawrence Godkin*, Vol. I (New York: Macmillan, 1907), pp. 166–67. Godkin's better-known appraisal of Greeley as a "trader in politics" was made during and after the Civil War, when Godkin's brand of liberalism could not square with Greeley's philosophies.

man behind it. The power he wielded was not equaled by any editor of his time—neither has it been equaled by any editor since."[11]

On the other hand, William Cullen Bryant, one of the great *Post* editors, had nothing but contempt for Greeley and refused to nod or speak to the *Tribune* editor even when they were brought together at social functions not connected with journalism or politics.

Perhaps the best way to evaluate such a controversial figure is to ignore his critics and to consider his record. The early issues of his paper offer no clue as to his greatness. The three pages of fine print describing the details of the President's funeral contain none of the stimulation and challenge for which Greeley was to become famous. And yet the very first issue indicates the significance of the *New York Tribune*. It sold for one cent, in competition with the other penny papers, and therefore was plainly intended for mass readership. But instead of pandering to emotionalism, the entire issue was devoted to serious discussion and reportage. The *Tribune* could offer its public murder stories just as sensational as those of its rivals, but that type of journalism was not the hallmark of the paper. Greeley had the curious faith that the masses could be attracted by reason as well as by emotionalism. He did not insult the common man by trying to "write down" to him. There is nothing that can raise the dignity of the scorned more effectively than honest recognition, and this appeal undoubtedly was a factor in the *Tribune*'s success.

GREELEY'S ROLE IN OPINION LEADERSHIP AND SOCIAL CHANGE

Admittedly, much of the *Tribune's* later content was rational only in the broad sense. Any crackpot social philosopher could express himself in the paper, if he wrote forcefully. The common criticism of Greeley, indeed, was that he was utterly irrational. But some of his "idealism" was founded on sound reasoning. He saw that Jeffersonian ideas, based on an agrarian society, were not applicable to a nation fast becoming an industrial power. He also realized the dangers of unrestricted industrialism. The slums of Europe warned of that. Allowing selfish business interests and rugged individualism to dominate American society could only lead to anarchy, Greeley reasoned. The duty of the statesman, as he understood it, was to reduce social friction between classes and economic interests. That could be done only when the state had strong regulatory powers.

So Greeley groped for the way out. Lacking formal education, he knew little about social and political philosophers. He preferred to learn by experimentation. That is why he allowed Albert Brisbane the use of his columns.

[11] Joseph Bucklin Bishop, *Notes and Anecdotes of Many Years* (New York: Scribner's, 1925), p. 24. By permission of the publishers.

Brisbane was the American prophet of Fourierism, a scheme for curing the ills of capitalism by a form of collective living he called "associationism." In the 1850s the *Tribune* spent many pages explaining Socialism, and Greeley himself debated the issue publicly with brilliant opponents, including Henry Raymond of the *New York Times*. For a decade one of the London correspondents for the *Tribune* was Karl Marx, so-founder of Communism. Greeley fought steadily for agrarian reforms, including the Homestead Bill, offering land in the West that immigrants could afford to develop. All this completely violated Whig doctrine, and yet Greeley was one of the leaders of the party. No wonder his critics were confused.

But it should be clear that Greeley did not endorse all the opinions expressed in the *Tribune*. He was aware that most of the suggestions were impractical. But he was also aware that America was still groping toward a goal, and that it would have to continue experimenting, if democracy were to be kept dynamic. His readers appeared to understand. They saw Greeley was intent upon producing a better world—and a better press. If his experiments were ineffectual, they were no more so than those of a scientist who keeps working with test tubes to find solutions.

Despite all criticism, Greeley was read by all types of persons. Whether he wrote on politics, farming, labor, education, the horror of debt, the rights of women, temperance, marriage, the frontier, or slavery, all classes of society took note of the *Tribune*. He upbraided a nation for its whisky consumption —and the liquor-loving public kept right on reading the Tribune. He denounced the tobacco smokers and chewers—they, too, remained regular readers. He criticised the speculator and financier—they fumed and fussed, and read on.

Why should such persons, many of whom resented all this "radicalism," not only have tolerated Greeley's paper, but have supported it loyally? There was no doubt of its success. It was full of advertising—its front page was usually solid with commercial notices—universally read, and highly respectable. The weekly edition had more readers than any other publication of the period. Many of its 200,000 subscribers were farmers in the Middle West, who had no sympathy with many of Greeley's ideas on industrial society. The daily lagged behind the *Sun* and the *Herald*, but the circulation was always high. Could such a paper succeed today? It had more inflammatory material in it than even the labor papers of the time. Was it popular because the reader trusted the sincerity of its editor?

The secret of Greeley's popularity was his consciousness of responsibility to the reader. His flights into socialistic fancy were erratic and irresponsible, perhaps, but the average reader appeared to understand that the motives were sincere. That was why the farmers, who often disagreed violently with Greeley's views, read the "Try-bune," as they usually called it, "next to the Bible." How could anyone doubt the sincerity of a man who advocated a fairer distribution of weath and who lived up to his advice by giving away to his employees all but a few shares of the gold mine he had made out of the *Tribune*? He changed the press of the masses from the vulgar level of sensationalism to a promoter of culture and stimulating ideas, and made it pay dividends. His protégés also raised the standards of the Fourth Estate. For many years Charles A. Dana, who will appear again in these pages, was Greeley's assistant, and much of the early success of the *Tribune* has been ascribed to Dana. Henry J. Raymond, soon to establish the *New York Times,* started out under Greeley. Margaret Fuller, one of the truly great literary figures of the period, wrote regularly for the *Tribune.* Carl Schurz, John Hay, Whitelaw Reid, Henry James, William Dean Howells, George Ripley, and Richard Hildreth, who made names for themselves in various fields of literature, journalism, and history, served under "Uncle Horace."

The identification of Greeley with his paper is brought out by an anecdote told by Joseph Bishop in his *Notes,* written after Bishop had left the editorship of the *Post.* The editor was in Vermont a year or so after Greeley's death in 1872, and made some remark about an article that had recently appeared in the *Tribune.* "Does the Try-bune still print?" asked a farmer in the audience. "Why, I thought Greeley was dead." [12]

RAYMOND'S *NEW YORK TIMES,* 1851

A thesis was advanced at the beginning of this chapter that when a new public is first tapped by the mass media, the appeal is invariably upon an emotional plane. The result is a "sensational" vehicle of communication. Readers of the *Sun* first bought it primarily for its police reports. Many of these readers matured with the years, however, for as time went on, cheap papers competing successfully with the *Sun* offered more nourishing fare. Greeley proved that a publisher could reach the masses without resorting to sensationalism. Even the *Sun* and the *Herald* offered more substantial material as time went on. They had to, to keep up with the increasing skills of their readers. Eventually, such papers left the semiliterate public behind, and another wave of sensational papers had to be established (as in the 1890s) to take up the slack. The completion of this cycle is exemplified by Henry J. Raymond of the *New York Times.*

From early boyhood, Raymond showed promise as a thinker, and he was graduated from the University of Vermont in 1840 with the highest honors. "Like most of his honors," one of his biographers has said, "they cost more than they were worth." [13] His studies almost ruined his health, and the habit of overwork established in college may have contributed to his early death.

As a college student, Raymond contributed to Greeley's *New Yorker,* which the youth admired greatly. After a visit to the New York editor, Ray-

[12] H. L. Stoddard, *Horace Greeley* (New York: Putnam's, 1946), p. 322.
[13] *Dictionary of American Biography,* XV, p. 408.

mond became Greeley's chief assistant in 1841, the year the *Tribune* was founded. George Jones was a colleague in the business office of the *Tribune.* Together they planned to put out the "ideal daily." Neither had sufficient money, however, for already it was impossible to establish a New York paper with $500 and a few packing-box desks, as Bennett had.

Raymond and Greeley were naturally incompatible. The younger man could never appreciate the erratic mental behavior of his employer, and soon Raymond left to work for Colonel James Watson Webb on the *Courier and Enquirer.* During this interim he established a reputation as an orator and budding politician. He was elected to the State Assembly in 1849 and became speaker in 1851. At this point he broke with Webb on the Free Soil Party issue. He took a position as an editor of *Harper's New Monthly Magazine* (established in June 1850), where he remained until 1856 as a part-time editor.

It was in 1851 that Raymond and Jones realized their old ambition of publishing a New York newspaper of their own. The first issue of the *New York Daily Times* appeared September 18, 1851. It sold for one cent, and thus showed its intention of being a paper for the masses, but it eschewed the sensationalism of the *Sun* and *Herald,* and the whimsy of the *Tribune,* as described in the policy expressed the first day: ". . . we do not mean to write as if we were in a passion [a slap at Greeley, who was regularly the butt of Raymond's jibes]—unless that shall really be the case; and we shall make it a point to get into a passion as rarely as possible." [14] One of the *Times'* strong points was the interpreting of foreign news. Raymond sought to excel in reporting European events.

Raymond soon established a reputation as a reasonable and objective editor. Actually, compromise, rather than objectivity, was Raymond's chief characteristic. "The great temporizer," Maverick, one of his biographers, called the *Times* editor, adding that this quality ruined him as a politician and eventually as a leader.[15] He appealed to readers who liked the *Herald's* aggressiveness but resented its bad taste; who admired the *Tribune,* but suspected Greeley's fanaticism; or who had confidence in the solidness of the *Courier and Enquirer,* but were bored by its pompousness.

From the very beginning Raymond used every opportunity to plague his old mentor, Greeley. By 1852 Raymond was up to his neck in politics, despite the promise he had made to his partner after Jones warned that politics and editorships did not mix. At that time the prohibition of liquor was a big issue. It was one of Greeley's pet subjects, and he expected to be elected governor of New York because of his editorial stand on temperance. But Thurlow Weed, the Albany editor who controlled the state convention that year, needed an upstate man to hold the party together on the dry issue. That meant that the

[14] Willard G. Bleyer, *Main Currents in the History of American Journalism* (Boston: Houghton Mifflin, 1927), p. 240.

[15] Augustus Maverick, *Henry J. Raymond and the New York Press* (Hartford: A. S. Hale and Company, 1870), p. 170.

lieutenant governor had to be a big city "wet" in order to hold the party together on other issues. Weed selected Raymond, rather than his old teammate, Greeley. As Greeley once said of the episode: ". . . no other name could have been . . . so bitterly humbling to me."[16]

Indeed, from this time on, Raymond was as much a politician as he was an editor. As we shall see, the *Times* editor became a power in Republican circles. Greeley was to see his rival badly mauled in the postwar political arena, but in the 1850s Raymond rode the crest of the wave. Within two years after the founding of the *Times*, even Greeley admitted that it outsold the *Tribune* within the city limits. He left a reputation as one of the great journalists of the century.

Raymond's contribution was the development of reasonable decency in public reporting. There was a minimum of personal invective in the *Times*. It seldom presented issues in the black and white patterns favored by Greeley. It was invariably fair in tone, if not in content, and no rival equaled it in developing the technique of careful reporting. It substituted accuracy for wishful thinking, even when Raymond was deep in politics. Curiously, Raymond, who was addicted to politics, stood for a strangely objective nonpartisanship in his paper. It was as though the man had two completely different personalities.

THURLOW WEED, PARTY BOSS

Two other journalists of the period deserve passing mention. One was Thurlow Weed, better known as a political boss, and the other was Samuel Bowles III.

Thurlow Weed began a career of influence as an apprentice printer in upstate New York. For a time (1808–1817) he worked as a journeyman; became interested in politics as a follower of DeWitt Clinton; and worked on the *Rochester Telegraph*. By 1825 he had become a political power. He purchased the *Telegraph* that year and used it to promote his candidates. Weed had strong anti-Masonic principles in a day when Masonry was a burning political issue. The Anti-Masonic party raised funds to establish a paper at Albany, and Weed was made editor while he was still serving as a leader in the Assembly. The *Evening Journal* appeared in February, 1830, and under Weed it became virtually the official organ of the Whigs. Weed was given much of the credit for electing William H. Seward governor in 1838, and the two, plus Greeley, were instrumental in putting Harrison into the White House in 1840.

Weed was the typical party boss. It was said that Seward had the principles and Weed had the votes. Greeley was the sounding board for new

[16] Letter to Governor Seward, dated New York, November 11, 1854, in Thurlow Weed Barnes and Harriet Weed, eds., *Life of Thurlow Weed*, Vol. II (Boston: Houghton Mifflin, 1884), p. 280.

ideas. The big boss was Weed, however. He had the knack of making all acquaintances believe he was a special friend. The secret of his popularity was that he sincerely liked people—all kinds of people. During his heyday he was one of the important Americans of the period, and his paper was therefore influential.

Weed's power waned after Seward's defeat in 1842. He recouped his political fortunes somewhat when he backed General Zachary Taylor for president in 1848 and sent Seward to the Senate. The Whigs were doomed by 1850, however, and Weed went to Europe defeated and dejected. He accepted the new Republican party reluctantly, but was unsuccessful in promoting Seward within it. From then on, Weed's fortunes declined. He gave up the editorship of his paper in 1863. He tried to make a comeback as a journalist in 1867 by taking over the editorship of the *New York Commercial Advertiser*, but he had to give up the position because of poor health. He died in retirement in 1882.

BOWLES AND THE *SPRINGFIELD REPUBLICAN*

Another outstanding paper at this time was Massachusetts' *Springfield Republican*. Its founder was Samuel Bowles II, although his son, Samuel Bowles III, is more important to this history. The father was reared in Connecticut, where the family had been driven by depression. He was apprenticed to a printer at the age of 15, after the first Samuel Bowles, a grocer, died and bequeathed his entire worldly possessions to the boy—a Bible and a watch. Bowles grew up as a poor boy, but from an early age he was interested in cultural development, as evidenced by the literary club he established.

His first regular job was with the *New Haven Register*. In 1819 he joined with John Francis of Wethersfield as a partner in the *Hartford Times*, a weekly that soon failed under the adverse conditions of the time. He and his wife and family loaded their household possessions and the *Times* press on a flatboat and poled up the Connecticut River to Springfield, Massachusetts. There, a group of Anti-Federalists helped him re-establish as a publisher. First copies of the *Springfield Republican* appeared September 8, 1824. It was a weekly, and its 250 subscribers paid two dollars a year for it. Bowles ran the paper by himself; it grew slowly, but outlasted five rivals, and by 1840 Bowles had established a reputation as a reliable publisher. By that time Springfield was beginning to boom as a railroad center, and circulation was up to 1,200. The original publisher died in 1851, but by that time the paper was largely the product of the son.

Samuel Bowles III made the most of the excellent opportunities presented to him by his father, and it is the son who established the national reputation of the *Republican*. It was he who argued his father into "going daily" in March, 1844 (it was an evening paper then, but became morning a year later). Bowles made the paper successful by skillful organization of regional correspondence,

88 HARPER'S WEEKLY. [FEBRUARY 2, 1878.

SAMUEL BOWLES.

THE death of SAMUEL BOWLES, who breathed his last on the evening of January 16, has deprived American journalism of one of its most noteworthy representatives. The Springfield *Republican*, of which he was the editor, has for many years exercised a national influence in politics. Although published in a comparatively small New England town, half-way between New York and Boston, and overshadowed by the press of both cities, it has held its own for half a century, and is more prosperous and more widely quoted at this moment than ever it was before. It is altogether an exceptional journalistic outgrowth. Impersonal at least in the theory of his treatment of public affairs, it has derived a distinctive personality from its editor. Provincial in its professions and aims, seeking to represent the provincial life by which it is surrounded, it is regarded as a power in the land by the politicians of all parties.

An anomaly of this sort could be produced only in America, for the reason, perhaps, that we have no recognized centre of thought and action, no London or Paris, so that the newspapers of every section are enabled to display whatever is in them with the certainty of adequate consideration. Thus the *Republican*, in spite of its geographical situation, has built up a reputation as solid as that of any of its contemporaries which happen to be issued from cities of ten and twenty times the population of Springfield.

SAMUEL BOWLES, to whom the greater achievements of the *Republican* belong, was the son of the founder of the paper. SAMUEL BOWLES the elder was a Hartford printer, who went to Springfield in 1824, and began the publication of the *Weekly Republican*. SAMUEL BOWLES the second, or rather the third—for his grandfather bore the same name—was born in 1826. He grew up about his father's office. There is a tradition that he got the rudiments of a sound academic education in the schools of Springfield; but as he entered the service of the *Republican* before he was seventeen years of age, it is likely that he evolved the strong and simple writing which marked his editorial style out of an inner consciousness sharpened by contact with types, and purified by the free and early use of printers' ink. Certain it is that he was born, as he was raised, a journalist, owing his success, like so many eminent members of his profession, to the practical tuition of the composing-room.

In 1844 he prevailed upon his father to issue the *Daily Republican*, and from the outset had very much the charge of it. The years 1846–48 brought with them the Mexican war and the telegraph, and, of consequence, a revolution in journalistic practice. At this time "SAM" BOWLES, as his friends always called him, was just of age, full of ambition and ardor, with plenty of work in him; and here he laid the beginnings of the substantial fame and fortune he has enjoyed ever since. He did every thing—edited and made up the paper, helped work it off on an old ADAMS press, acted as mailing clerk, cashier, and reporter—eating, working, and sleeping in the office. The *Daily* became a passion with him. The *Republican* was SAM BOWLES, and SAM BOWLES was the *Republican*. It owed its character entirely to the features impressed upon it by its editor. Its rugged independence of the politicians, its tolerance and entertainment of new and original ideas, its shrewd every-day sense, its extraordinary compilation of news adapted to a certain peculiar audience, whose wants it studies and serves in the minutest way, its racy good nature, varied just enough by an occasional ugly streak or angry flash to give it the needful quantum of snap—all were characteristic of Mr. BOWLES.

In 1857 Mr. BOWLES was induced to go to Boston as editor of a paper made by the fusion of some half a dozen journals, under the title of *The Boston Daily Traveller*. It was an eight-page paper, modelled on the style of the New York daily journals. It did not take, however, and at the end of about six months Mr. BOWLES resumed the editorship of the Springfield *Republican*, of which he was still the owner. He gave a stanch and vigorous support to the Republican party until 1872, when he opposed the renomination of General GRANT, and in the Liberal Convention at Cincinnati pressed the name of CHARLES FRANCIS ADAMS as a candidate for the Presidency. Although deeply disappointed by his failure to carry the Convention, he supported Mr. GREELEY with great warmth and ability. At the same time he disclaimed all party allegiance, and proclaimed the political independence of the *Republican*.

Mr. BOWLES at one time incurred the enmity of the late JIM FISK by comments in the *Republican* on his career as a director of the Erie Railway, and FISK brought a libel suit against the editor for $50,000. One evening in December, 1868, while Mr. BOWLES was talking with some friends in the office of the Fifth Avenue Hotel, he was arrested on papers issued by Judge M'CUNN, and taken hastily to the jail, when the jailor denied him the privilege of writing a note to his wife or of receiving the friends who came to aid him. The numerous offers of bail were refused, as the sheriff declined to be annoyed with such matters after business hours. So Mr. BOWLES slept in Ludlow Street Jail. He was bailed out in the morning, and Mr. FISK's contemptible trick afterward formed the subject of a very spicy correspondence between Mr. BOWLES and FISK's lawyer, in which the editor had decidedly the best of the argument.

Mr. BOWLES was fond of travel in his own country and abroad. He visited California several times, and his book, *Across the Continent*, was the first really good picture of the Pacific slope which appeared. He was a singularly agreeable man, and was universally esteemed in society. In his family he was genial and hospitable, and some of the brightest men and women in the country were his warm friends and frequent guests. He was always a hard worker. When he supposed that he was about to die, he said, with a smile, to an old friend, "Nothing is the matter with me but thirty-five years of hard work;" and he added afterward, "I was never much of a boy; I had very little boyhood." The immediate cause of his death was paralysis of the brain. He had been ill with congestion of the lungs since the early part of October last, and that malady, combined with a disorder of the heart, caused him acute suffering. Toward the latter part of November he grew worse. On the 1st of December he thought the end had come, and bade his family and friends farewell. During the last two weeks of his life he gradually lost strength, though conscious all the time. He suffered little, was quiet in mind through the afternoon and evening of his last day on earth, and his death was like the peaceful closing of the eyes in sleep.

SAMUEL BOWLES.—[PHOTOGRAPHED BY SARONY.]

HEAD-QUARTERS OF MEHEMET ALI.

ON this page we give a picture of the quarters recently occupied by MEHEMET ALI at Kamarli, which is not far south of Orchanieh, on the road between Plevna and Sophia. The Russian advance from the captured stronghold of OSMAN PASHA compelled the abandonment of all the Turkish positions, and the soldiers of the Czar penetrated the passes almost without resistance where they had expected to fight their way step by step. The city of Sophia was hastily evacuated by the Turks, and immediately occupied by the Russians, who thus obtained a footing south of the Balkans, and an excellent base of operations against Adrianople.

The 1878 obituary picture and story for Samuel Bowles III in *Harper's Weekly*.

so that every little community in the upper Connecticut Valley had reason to take the paper. Young Bowles was educated for the role he was to take in journalism. He shared his room as a boy with his father's three apprentices. He grew up in the back shop. He delivered papers and knew personally all the local subscribers and their interests. At 18 he was ready to assume his place as a peer in the Fourth Estate. It was at this time that he persuaded his father to let him try a daily. It was hard going at first. He worked as much as 40 hours at a stretch without sleep. His health began to fail. The paper almost foundered financially. But in the end, Bowles produced one of the great newspapers of the nineteenth century.

Partly responsible for the success of the paper were William B. Calhoun, who wrote many of the editorials credited by readers to Bowles; Josiah Gilbert Holland, a fluent and articulate writer; and George Ashmun, friend of Abraham Lincoln and a noted politician. But the main emphasis of the *Republican* was news, and Bowles made that his special department.

He took over full control upon the death of his father in 1851 (Holland had an interest in the paper, but not enough to control it). Actually, it is not until the late 1850s and the 1860s that the *Republican* exerted its greatest influence, so that this discussion must be reserved for a later chapter. But the foundations of success were laid in the period covered in this section. Bowles was a sponsor of the new Republican party. By 1860 his weekly edition was a national institution, with a circulation of about 12,000, but with a reputation throughout the country exceeded only by that of the *Tribune*. The daily hovered around 6,000, but that, too, was good for a provincial paper. Bowles was the mainspring of this intricate mechanism. ". . . he knew everything, saw everything, dictated everything—and his dictation dictated every time," one of his biographers has said.[17]

He was his own slave driver, and expected others to keep up to him. There were no 40-hour weeks, daily hours, or regular holidays on the *Republican*. As Holland once described the routine,

> The sparkle, the vivacity, the drive, and the power of the *Republican* cost life. We did not know when we tasted it and found it so charged with zest that we were tasting heart's blood, but that was the priceless element that commended it to our appetites. A pale man, weary and nervous, crept home at three o'clock in the morning, and while all nature was fresh and the birds were singing and thousands of eyes were bending eagerly over the results of his night's labors, he was tossing and trying to sleep.[18]

Yet seldom was complaint heard about working hours in the *Republican* office. Its reporters and editors were craftsmen, proud of their product, and

[17] George S. Merriam, *Life and Times of Samuel Bowles*, Vol. I (New York: Appleton-Century-Crofts, 1885), p. 104.

[18] *Dictionary of American Biography*, II, p. 516.

absorbed in their work. Young men from all over the United States tried to get on the *Republican* staff. A tour with the Springfield paper was a kind of advanced degree in journalism. A "*Republican* man" was welcome on the biggest papers in the country.

Bowles was a charming and cultivated conversationalist, although he tended to be "often a gossip and never a safe confidant," according to Wendell Phillips Garrison,[19] who knew the editor well. He believed in what he called "the higher journalism"—a responsibility not to party, social group, or class, but to conscience alone. He was not always tactful. Because of a ruthless determination, he turned associates into enemies at times. This was apparent when a group of former *Republican* newsmen founded the rival *Union*. But Bowles' contributions to journalism were much more important than his few faults. He was the prophet of responsible provincial journalism, and the institution owes much to the standards he helped to establish.

Annotated Bibliography

Books

Barnes, Thurlow Weed, and Harriet Weed, eds., *Life of Thurlow Weed.* 2 vols. Boston: Houghton Mifflin, 1883–84. The first volume is the politician's autobiography, edited by his daughter, Harriet. The second volume comprises the memoirs, documents, and letters compiled by Weed's grandson.

Bigelow, John, *Retrospections of an Active Life,* IV. New York: The Baker and Taylor Company, 1909–13. The journalistic field of the period described by a well-known *Post* executive.

Brown, Francis, *Raymond of the Times.* New York: Norton, 1951. A first-rate biography of a great editor.

Carlson, Oliver, *The Man Who Made News.* New York: Duell, Sloan & Pearce, 1942. The best biography of James Gordon Bennett, Sr.

Crouthamel, James L., *James Watson Webb, A Biography.* Middletown, Conn.: Wesleyan University Press, 1969. Carefully documented study of a leader in news gathering.

Davis, Elmer, *History of the New York Times, 1851–1921.* New York: The New York Times Company, 1921. Valuable for the early period of the great newspaper.

Greeley, Horace, *Recollections of a Busy Life.* New York: J. B. Ford and Company, 1868. The editor's own version of his career.

Hale, William H., *Horace Greeley: Voice of the People.* New York: Harper & Row, 1950. A good modern biography.

Hooker, Richard, *The Story of an Independent Newspaper: One Hundred Years of the Springfield Republican, 1824–1924.* New York: Macmillan, 1924.

[19] *Ibid.,* p. 517.

Isely, Jeter Allen, *Horace Greeley and the Republican Party, 1853–1861.* Princeton: Princeton University Press, 1947. An examination of Greeley's writings for the eight years.

Maverick, Augustus, *Henry J. Raymond and the New York Press.* Hartford: A. S. Hale and Company, 1870. An outstanding authority, this book contains many valuable documents.

Merriam, George S., *Life and Times of Samuel Bowles.* New York: Appleton-Century-Crofts, 1885. More complete than the Hooker study, above, and full of interesting letters and documents.

O'Brien, Frank M., *The Story of The Sun.* New York: George H. Doran Company, 1918. Revised ed., New York: Appleton-Century-Crofts, 1928. The standard history of the first successful penny newspaper.

Parrington, Vernon L., *Main Currents in American Thought,* Vol. II. Greeley, Margaret Fuller, and Bryant are discussed.

Parton, James, *Life of Horace Greeley.* New York: Mason Brothers, 1855. The standard reference, written by a contemporary.

Stoddard, Henry L., *Horace Greeley: Printer, Editor, Crusader.* New York: Putnam's, 1946. Not as deep as some of the other biographies of the editor, but much more human, readable, and convincing than the earlier studies.

Van Deusen, Glyndon Garlock, *Horace Greeley: Nineteenth Century Crusader.* Philadelphia: University of Pennsylvania Press, 1953. This is the best, and most detailed, of the Greeley biographies of recent years, and was awarded the Albert J. Beveridge Memorial Prize of the American Historical Association. The same author is the biographer of Thurlow Weed and Henry Clay, who were so closely associated with Greeley.

Periodicals and Monographs

Abbott, Lyman, "Reminiscences," *Outlook,* CVI (April 25, 1914), 897. Sidelights on Raymond's brush with the courts on a contempt citation.

Borden, Morton, "Some Notes on Horace Greeley, Charles Dana and Karl Marx," *Journalism Quarterly,* XXXIV (Fall 1957), 457. It was Dana who kept Marx on the *Tribune*'s payroll. *See also* Summer 1959 issue for texts of five letters from Dana to Marx (p. 314).

Bradford, Gamaliel, "Samuel Bowles," *Atlantic Monthly,* CXVI (October 1915), 487. An excellent character study. Reprinted in Ford and Emery, *Highlights in the History of the American Press.*

Browne, Junius Henri, "Horace Greeley," *Harper's New Monthly Magazine,* XLVI (April 1873), 734. Describes Greeley's idiosyncrasies.

Coleman, Albert E., "New and Authentic History of the Herald of the Bennetts," *Editor & Publisher,* LVI–LVIII (March 29, 1924 to June 13, 1925).

Commons, John R., "Horace Greeley and the Working Class Origins of the Republican Party," *Political Science Quarterly,* XXIV (September 1909), 468. A significant article by a great authority and writer on American Labor.

Eberhard, Wallace B., "Mr. Bennett Covers a Murder Trial," *Journalism Quarterly,*

XLVII (Autumn 1970), 457. The 1830 trial of a sea captain, covered for the *Courier and Enquirer* in a style foreshadowing his *Herald* days.

Peebles, Paul, "James Gordon Bennett's Scintillations," *Galaxy,* XIV (August 1872), 258. A revealing and rewarding study of the editor. Reprinted in Ford and Emery, *Highlights in the History of the American Press.*

"Personal Reminiscences of Horace Greeley," *Bookman,* XIII (April 1901), 126. Sympathetic and readable anecdotes.

"Sketches of the Life and Labors of Horace Greeley," *National Quarterly Review,* XXVI (December 1872), 153. Strong posthumous defense of the editor's character.

"The *Herald*—Onward," *Democratic Review,* XXXI (November 1852), 409. A favorable appraisal of a maligned newspaper.

Turnbull, George, "Some Notes on the History of the Interview," *Journalism Quarterly,* XIII (September 1936), 272. An authority on journalism history holds that Greeley was the father of the modern interview.

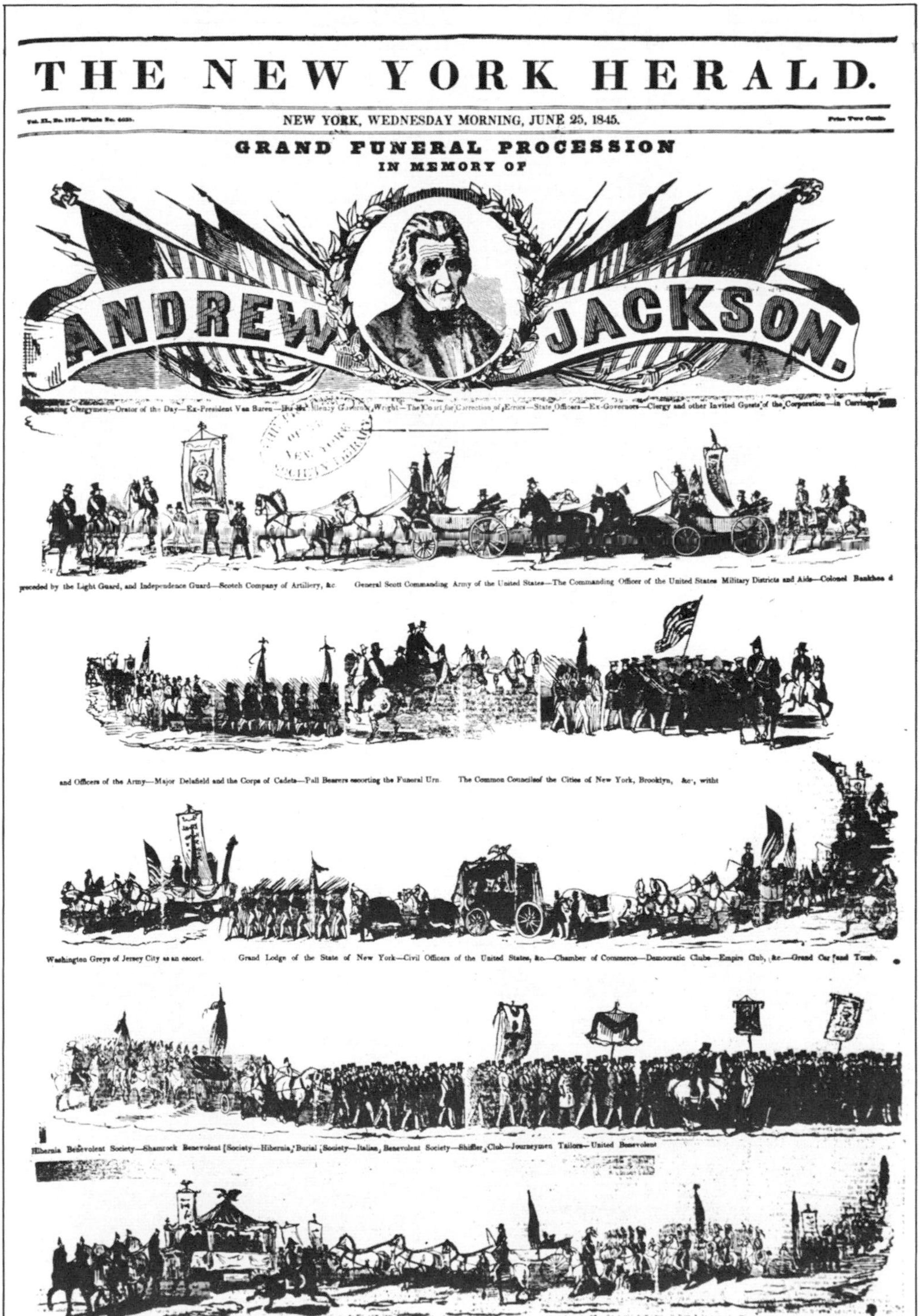

THE NEW YORK HERALD.

NEW YORK, WEDNESDAY MORNING, JUNE 25, 1845.

GRAND FUNERAL PROCESSION IN MEMORY OF

ANDREW JACKSON.

...ing Clergymen—Orator of the Day—Ex-President Van Buren—His Excellency Governor Wright—The Court for Correction of Errors—State Officers—Ex-Governors—Clergy and other Invited Guests of the Corporation—in Carriages

preceded by the Light Guard, and Independence Guard—Scotch Company of Artillery, &c. General Scott Commanding Army of the United States—The Commanding Officer of the United States Military Districts and Aids—Colonel Bankhead

and Officers of the Army—Major Delafield and the Corps of Cadets—Pall Bearers escorting the Funeral Urn. The Common Councils of the Cities of New York, Brooklyn, &c., with the

Washington Greys of Jersey City as an escort. Grand Lodge of the State of New York—Civil Officers of the United States, &c.—Chamber of Commerce—Democratic Clubs—Empire Club, &c.—Grand Car and Tomb.

Hibernia Benevolent Society—Shamrock Benevolent Society—Hibernia Burial Society—Italian Benevolent Society—Shiffler Club—Journeymen Tailors—United Benevolent

New York Herald (1845)

CALIFORNIAN.

SAN FRANCISCO, AUGUST 14, 1848.

☞ The "Californian" again appears before its patrons this morning, as it will continue to do occasionally in these "golden times," during the temporary suspension of business. As soon as a re-action takes place, and business resumes its wonted channels, and our thoroughfares again wear their usual business-like and bustling appearance, we will issue the paper regularly, as heretofore.

To Correspondents. — "Soldado" is inadmissible. Reason why—we do not wish to conflict in any manner with military proceedings, especially during the absence of the proprietors.

"One of the People" is crowded out to make room for the Peace intelligence.

Our Sonoma friend "O'C" we hope will continue his favors.

All correspondents should be aware when writing for this paper, that they are responsible, and if public or private character should, inadvertently on our part, get maliciously assailed in its columns, and it should become requisite, their names will be freely given; otherwise we preserve them as an inviolable secret.

For the matter which appears as editorial, during the absence of the legitimate editor, Benjamin Franklin Foster is solely responsible.

GLORIOUS NEWS.

RATIFICATION OF THE TREATY OF PEACE.

END OF THE WAR.

———ooo———

We have received by a Courier from Monterey, bringing dispatches for the military department here, the glorious intelligence of the ratification of the treaty of peace made between the United States and Mexico, as amended and ratified by the Senate of the United States.

There is now no longer a doubt about the treaty being concluded. We get the news officially. The mail left Col. Barton, at La Paz, on the 27th June, and reached Monterey on the 6th inst.

We have not the exact terms of the treaty, but the most important points are as follows: the boundary is to commence at the mouth of the Rio Grande, up that river to the parallel of latitude which will strike the head of the Gila, down that river to its junction with the Rio Colorado, and with that to the parallel which will strike the Pacific one league south of San Diago.

It is said that in consideration of this cession of territory by Mexico, that the United States pay their own expenses of the war, pay Mexico in cash fifteen millions of dollars, and assume the payment of the claims of the citizens of the United States against the Mexican government to the amount of three millions of dollars.

We have no disposition to speculate upon the terms of this treaty, as to its general bearing upon the two nations, nor have we the means of forming a proper judgment, but of one thing we feel satisfied; that the citizens of all the territory acquired by the United States, will be greatly benefited by the change, and so far as California is concerned, she will be elevated in the scale of human advencement beyond all possible calculation. Half a century has passed away since the first settlement of California, and although the mountains and the plains were covered with cattle and horses, yet the lands remained almost entirely uncultivated, the inexhaustible and unparalleled mineral wealth lay untouched in the bowels of the earth. The Indians made their houses literally of gold, without knowing that it was more valuable than other yellow dirt. The whole commerce was carried on by half a dozen ships called "hide drivers," and received in payment a few hides and some tallow. Our towns (for cities we had none.) consisted of a few adobie houses, built with very little regard to arrangement, regularity, elegance or convenience: with no other public improvement than the churches and missions. Not a road in the territory except such as nature in her exceeding bounty, had made for us. All the beautiful locations on the great bay of San Francisco left unoccupied, showing no other signs of life than the herds of cattle and wild game which occupy its shores.

But a change has already come over the land. Two years have elapsed since the "stars and stripes" have been unfurled in this highly favored portion of the globe, and the settlers, though protected only by a military occupancy, have built large commercial houses, towns and villages, in every direction, increased our commerce, discovered and are rapidly working the gold mines, at least five hundred per cent. richer than has ever been known in the world. Discovered mercury or quicksilver, silver, iron, lead and copper, all of which mines are extraordinary rich. They have located farms over a great portion of the territory, and were rapidly bringing the land into active cultivation. All these things have been done in two years of comparative peace, and the hope of being protected by the free institutions of the United States. What then are our hopes and prospects, under a permanent peace, equal rights, fair competition, and perfect protection in the right of property? The prospective view is grand, beyond all possible calculation. The immagination is lost in wonder, when we attempt to look forward and judge of the future by the past.

THE GOLD MINE.

A few months ago we were in the habit of speaking of the agricultural resources and the commercial qualities of California, as being the source of her greatest wealth, and although now they are not inferior to any portions of the world, the soil constitutes but a small part of her wealth, all interests having been absorbed in the working of the mines.

The present number of the "Californian" is intended for circulation abroad as well as at home, and will, by giving a minute and general view of the all absorbing topic, the gold mine, be found useful to persons to send to their distant friends. The information which we shall give, has been gathered from actual observation, and from persons who have been engaged at the mines, and from the most authentic sources, as it is desirable that the facts be correctly known through other countries, and especially through the United States.

Some time in the spring, Messrs. Marshall and Bennet, in opening a ditch for a tail race for a saw-mill, which had been built on the American Fork of the Sacramento, found some gold, which the current had collected in the bottom of the race, which, after being examined, was found to be very pure. It soon began to attract attention, and some persons discovered the gold in the river below and for some distance above, in large quantities, so much so that persons who only gave credit to one third of what was said about it left their homes and went to work in the mines. It was the work of but a few weeks, to bring almost the entire populotion of the territory together to pick up the precious metal. The result has been, that in less than four months, a total revolution has been effected in the prospects and the fate o Alta California. Then, the capital was in the hands of a few individuals engaged in trade and speculation, now labor has got the upper hands of capital, and the aboring men hold the great mass of the wealth of the country—the gold.

There are now about four thousand white persons, besides a number of Indians engaged at the mines, and from the fact, that no capital is required, they are working in companies on equal shares or alone with their basket. In one part of the mine called the "dry diggins," no other implements are necessary than an ordinary sheath knife, to pick the gold from the rocks. In other parts, where the gold is washed out, the machinery is very simple, being an ordinary trough made of plank, round on the bottom, about ten feet long and two feet wide at the top, with a riddle or seive at one end to catch the larger gravel, and three or four small bars across the bottom, about half an inch high to keep the gold from going out with the dirt and water at the lower end. This machine is set upon rockers, which gives a half rotary motion to the water and dirt inside. But far the largest number use nothing but a large tin pan or an Indian basket, into which they place the dirt and shake it until the gold gets to the bottom and the dirt is carried over the side in the shape of muddy water. It is necessary in some cases, to have a crowbar, pick and shovel, but a great deal is taken up with large horns, shapen spoon fashion at the large end.

From the fact that no capital is necessary, a fair competition in labor without the influence of capital, men who were only able to procure one month's provisions, have now thousands of dollars of the precious metal. The laboring class have now become the capitalists of the country.

As to the richness of the mine, were we to set down half the truth, it would be looked upon in other countries as a "Sinbad" story, or the history of "Alladin's Lamp," which required that its possessor should but wish, and his wishes should be accomplished. Many persons have collected in one day, of the finest grade gold, from three to eight hundred dollars, and for many days together averaged from 75 to \$150. Although this is not universal, yet the general average is so well settled, that when a man with his pan or basket does not easily gather 30 to 40 dollars in a day, he moves to another place, so that taking the general average, including the time spent in moving from place to place and in looking for better "diggins," we are of the opinion that we may safely set down an ounce of pure gold or \$16 per day to the man. Suppose there are 4000 persons at work, they will add to the aggregate wealth of the territory about 4000 ounces, or about 60,000 dollars a day.

The value of the gold, like all things else, is regulated by the demand. Four months ago, flour was sold in the market for four dollars per hundred, now sixteen; beef cattle six, now thirty; ready made clothing, grocer's and other good have not risen in the same proportion, but are at least double their original cost. If we make bread and meat the standard by which to determine the value of the gold, then it is only worth one fourth of what it is elsewhere. But if gold and silver be the standard, then the bread and meat is worth four times what it was. But the relative value of the grain gold, compared with gold and silver coin, can only be changed by the action of government, for, however abundant the gold may be, it must produce its relative value in coin, and while a five dollar gold piece will be received in the treasury as five dollars, so long must an ounce of gold be worth *sixteen dollars*.

As to the future hopes of California, her course is onward, with a rapidity which will astonish the world. Her unparalleled gold mines, silver mines, iron ore and lead, with the best climate in the world, and the richest soil, will make it the garden spot of creation.

We call the attention of our readers to the Proclamation of Gov. Mason, on first page.

Laws.—Governor Mason has had printed both in the English and Spanish languages, a code of laws for the better government of the territory of California—the preservation of order, and the protection of the rights of the inhabitants, during the military occupancy of the country by the U. S. forces.

Appointment.—His Excellency Governor Mason has appointed Charles V. Gillespie, to be Notary Public in and for the district of San Francisco.

We acknowledge, with pleasure, our indebtedness for news, to several citizen gentlemen and military officers, all of whom will please accept our humble thanks.

The second Alcalde of the district of San Francisco, Dr. Leavenworth, we understand, will remain for the present in the discharge of the duties of his office.

ILLUMINATION MEETING.

At a large and respectable meeting of the citizens of this town, held at the City Hotel on Thursday evening at 8 o'clock, for the purpose of making suitable arrangements to celebrate the glorious news of peace having been made between the United States and Mexico, the following gentlemen were elected officers, viz:

His Honor Judge Hyde was called upon to preside.

W. D. M. Howard, Esq., Lieut T. J. Roach, Capt. S. E. Woodworth, and E. H. Harrison, Esq, were then elected Vice Presidents, and Jas. G. Leighton, Esq, Secretary.

The Chairman briefly stated the object of the meeting, after which the following resolutions were proposed:

Resolved, That in consequence of the arrival of the glorious news of a permanent peace between the United States and Mexico, that the citizens of San Francisco give a general illumination on Friday evening, Aug. 11, at 8 o'clock.

Resolved, That all the citizens of the town be called upon to lend their hearty co-operation in throwing light upon this patriotic movement

Resolved, That the masters of the vessels in the harbor be requested to hoist their colors at sunrise and make every other demonstration of joy that may be possible to aid in making a suitable response to the same on shore.

Resolved, That a Committee of six be appointed to carry these resolutions into effect.

The following gentlemen were appointed as the Committee:

Robt Semple, Esq. of Benecia; Capt S Peny; Wm H Davis, Esq; Jas C Ward, Esq; C V Gillespie, Esq; Robt A Parker, Esq.

Wm M Smith, Esq. being called upon to address the meeting, stated that he was about leaving town to make an excursion to the "Gold Regions," and regretted that he would not be able to join with us in celebrating so glorious an event; still he would, he said, spread the news far and wide.

Dr Semple was then called upon to address the meeting, when he arose and said that he had not expected to be called upon for a speech, but upon an occasion like the present, he did not feel himself at liberty to decline. It was an event in which California was more interested and more benefited than any other portion of the United States or of Mexico. Whatever may be the terms of the treaty, it was enough for us to know that Upper California was left in the U. States. Give us equal privileges with citizens of that glorious Republic, and the industry, enterprise and intelligence of the "universal Yankee Nation" will soon develope the invaluable mineral wealth of this beautiful country to an extent hitherto unparallelled in the known world. Let us have peace with all Nations and ten years would make us one of the richest States in the Union. Every man here was directly interested in this question, and he asserted that the desire for peace on any terms which might be agreed on was unanimous in California. He thanked Providence that his feet were again finally in the U. States and that the "Star Spangled Banner" should continue to wave o'er this, his adopted land. Loud cheering.

Lt. Roach, of the New York Volunteers, was then called on for the patriotic song (by F Key,) of the "Star Spangled Banner"—which was sung by several gentlemen in chorus with great warmth of feeling.

Dr Leavenworth, Alcalde of San Francisco, was then called upon, and after making a few *peaceable* remarks, sat down amidst tremendous applause.

Ex-Gov Boggs of Sonoma was then called upon, and addressed the meeting in his usual happy style.

The meeting then adjourned,

Agreeably to the resolutions, on Friday the 11th, the ships in the harbor hoisted their flags and fired salutes, the merchants closed their doors, and citizens and soldiers one and all entered into the spirit of universal rejoicing. In the course of the day several gentlemen formed a cavalcade and passed through our principal streets in handsome order under the command of Lieut. Gilbert. In the evening, the Californian office, the hotels, and almost every dwelling house in town was brilliantly illuminated, some of them beautifully. Tar barrels were brought into requisition and bonfires blazed in every part of the town. A number of ladies and gentlemen promenaded the streets in social parties, while others followed the bent of their own inclinations, and the whole town presented one universal scene of rejoicing. Some were so much rejoiced with the news of peace that they first made war upon brandy, then upon each other, that they might have the pleasure of making a treaty of peace in which they alone were personally interested.

The Californian, first state paper, reports on the Gold Rush and the Mexican War.

12

The Race for News

Journalism is literature in a hurry. . . .
—Matthew Arnold

The pioneers of the penny press probably did not realize what a profound change they were to bring about in American journalism. As the historian-journalist, Gerald W. Johnson, once pointed out, editors like Day, Bennett, Greeley, and Abell lived in a period of great change—changes so profound that by comparison the modifications after the War of Independence were slight.[1] Many institutions were to be drastically altered after 1830, but none more than the press.

Three factors control the development of the newspaper. They are (1) the reading public, (2) the system of communications, and (3) improvements in production. In the second quarter of the nineteenth century, all three factors exerted great influence on the press. The public was more discerning as it acquired a greater literacy skill, and as more and more publications of various types were offered. The system of communications was developed beyond the wildest dreams of its promoters. The steam press, the beginning of automatic printing, and the perfection of paper-making also helped to change the character of the press. The pioneers of the penny press thus found themselves engaged in a game, all the rules of which had been cancelled, while the new regulations were still in the process of formulation. As Johnson says, "To survive, it was necessary to guess what the new rules would be, and to guess correctly most of the time. Conditions demanded alert and supple intelligence,

[1] Gerald W. Johnson, et al., *The Sunpapers of Baltimore* (New York: Knopf, 1937), p. 50.

backed by sturdy common sense; for policies whose necessity is as plain as day now were then wrapped in obscurity." [2]

Many Americans think of the period between 1830 and 1850 as a kind of historical doldrums. Few can recall the presidents of the period. Actually, this is one of the most interesting and productive periods prior to the twentieth century. There were interesting developments in literature, economics, and education. Most striking, however, was the technical progress of the age. This was the beginning of the railroad building era. The steamboat, the power loom, and the magnetic telegraph were to bring about profound changes in the American way of life. Industrialization was to modify society and create social strains that would eventually rend the country.

THE INCREASED SEARCH FOR NEWS

Successful publishers learned to adapt themselves and their papers to the new times. Most of them reacted intuitively. Arunah S. Abell, who was as articulate and shrewd as the greatest of his peers in the newspaper business, never did understand the forces around him. He believed the secret of his success was his policy of avoiding violent controversy, forgetting that some of the great papers of the day were continually so embroiled. The secret was in presenting news instead of the usual glut of opinion. The successful penny papers concentrated on presenting straight news, while rivals, once rich and powerful, died from circulation starvation on a diet of editorial comment. Bennett and Beach (successor to Day of the *Sun*) exceeded Greeley's *Tribune* in local circulation in just about the proportion that they offered news against Greeley's views. Greeley and Raymond, on the other hand, while famous for editorials, offered far more news than some of their rivals who were rapidly going to seed.

News of this period could be classified into five categories. One budget of information tied up interesting national and world events with community experience. Another classification included reports of crime, violence, and the activities of the famous or infamous—news that plays on the chord of universal passions. Local events, often presented in the form of a crusade, accounted for another news budget. A category that we now call "human interest" is also discernible—stories with appeal based on writing skill, rather than upon news value. Lastly, there was news of economic and political significance that could be made popular by emphasis upon speed of transmission and "exclusiveness."

The increased value of news meant that editors now were willing to invest heavily in means for obtaining and processing it. That was why the cost of newspapers went up so amazingly. Bennett started his paper on $500. Six years later, Greeley needed $3,000 to begin publication of a daily. Ten years later

[2] *Ibid.*, p. 51.

Raymond and his associates had to put up $100,000 to get the *Times* under way. Gathering the news and processing it quickly with complicated machinery accounted for most of this increased cost.

The colonial editor took his news as he found it. If someone came in with the report of an event it was inserted as news, but there was no systematic news gathering except in rare instances. No newspaper in the eighteenth century hired reporters of the type common in the nineteenth and twentieth centuries. The use of correspondents for the gathering of neighborhood gossip was common enough, but little of this material required investigation. Foreign and national news was largely gleaned from "exchanges," or newspapers traded back and forth. True, Sam Adams' "Committees of Correspondence" and the abortive cooperative news gathering agency on the eve of the Revolution were examples of organized reporting, but the effort was not destined to produce lasting results. During the early 1800s, newspapers began to seek ways of speeding up the arrival of news, particularly news from Washington and from Europe. But not until the penny press era did the idea of generating a newspaper's own news reports really take hold.

After 1833, newspapers began to go out after news. Editors still depended upon exchanges for outside sources of information, but more and more they began to work out organized systems of news gathering. One of the innovations of the first successful penny paper, as pointed out in the previous chapter, was the development of police news. This required a full-time reporter, who specialized in that type of news. Bennett assigned men to various "beats," such as Wall Street, the churches, society, and even sports. Thus the day of the specialist reporter was already at hand.

FIRST WASHINGTON REPORTERS

One of the first news sources to be tapped methodically was Congress—and the White House, of course. At the beginning of the century most metropolitan editors depended upon papers like the *National Intelligencer* to furnish such information. This continued to be the rule, but in a few cases special Washington reporters appeared. James Gordon Bennett was a pioneer Washington correspondent before he established the *Herald,* and he promoted this type of news in his successful penny paper. Bennett covered Congress for the *New York Enquirer* while the two houses were in session, and served as roving correspondent in the interim. When Colonel Webb bought the *Enquirer* in 1829 and merged it with the *Courier,* Bennett remained as Washington reporter. He wrote in a light, colorful style, and interspersed accounts of boarding-house life in his reports of legislative proceedings.

An authority on this subject has said that no one man can be singled out as the first Washington correspondent, but there was the beginning of such news coverage as early as 1808.[3] On January 4 of that year the *United States Gazette* announced that it had made arrangements to obtain earlier and "more full and correct information" about the government "than can be had from the Washington papers." [4] The *Gazette* used its own correspondent for the remaining weeks of the session, but reverted to the Washington *Federalist* and *Intelligencer* in November. In December, 1808, the *Freeman's Journal* of Philadelphia printed dispatches which it described as "From Our Correspondent at Washington." It began sending proof sheets of this material to the *New York Evening Post* in advance of the Philadelphia publication. The *Post* also credited the copy "From Our Correspondent," but gave credit to the Philadelphia source. Although the correspondent was not identified, he was actually James Elliott, a Vermont Congressman who concealed himself when necessary under the name "Ariel." After 1811, however, the *Post* and the *Freeman's Journal,* like the *Gazette* earlier, reverted to the old system.

The beginning of a permanent press corps in Washington can be traced to the establishment by Nathaniel Carter of a capital service for his paper, the *New York Statesman and Evening Advertiser,* as announced December 11, 1822. The first report was printed December 19. Carter was the first to use the phrase "Washington Correspondence" more or less regularly, but the service was discontinued in 1824 without explanation.

Eliab Kingman perfected the system. He was well known in the capital as a correspondent for out-of-town papers, and he actually prospered in this branch of journalism. He was one of the first accredited Washington correspondents. He came to the capital in 1822 or 1824, but none of his work has been identified before 1830. Kingman's significance is his permanent status as a stringer and correspondent, and as a pioneer in the development of the Washington press corps.

Bennett was a Washington correspondent in the full sense of the word. He knew the value of such news and promoted it to new standards of excellence after he founded the *Herald.* Soon the *Herald* had established a reputation for its Washington news coverage which made it widely read in Europe, especially in Great Britain, and it continued to lead in this branch of journalism.

THE SCRAMBLE FOR FOREIGN NEWS

Foreign news, taken from European papers, had always been presented in American newspapers. But not until after 1800 was there much concern shown in offering foreign news reports while they were still fresh. As such became more popular, editors vied with one another to offer it ahead of all rivals. The organized attempt to gather such intelligence can be traced back

[3] Frederick B. Marbut, "Early Washington Correspondents: Some Neglected Pioneers," *Journalism Quarterly,* XXV (December 1948), 370.

[4] *Ibid.,* p. 370.

to 1811. British naval vessels were then searching American ships at sea for British deserters. War was imminent, and every message from Europe told of new threats to American commerce. To satisfy the craving of his customers for such information, Samuel Gilbert had provided a reading room in his seven-story Exchange Coffee House, which dominated the Boston waterfront as the tallest building in America. The reading room was typical, in that it supplied available foreign newspapers, as was the custom of coffeehouses. Gilbert's special contribution was a Marine News Book, which offered much more current and local intelligence for the edification of his merchant and shipping office clientele. When the preparation of the news books began to take too much time, Gilbert hired an assistant to carry on this work. On November 20, 1811, he announced in the *Columbian Centinel* that young Samuel Topliff, Jr., would henceforth be in charge of the "Marine and General News Books."

Samuel Topliff was the son of a sea captain who had been murdered by a mutinous crew. He had planned to follow the sea, like his father, but had been forced to find a means to keep his widowed mother and her family together. That was the reason he had accepted Gilbert's offer of a position. Topliff began to meet incoming ships in his rowboat, so that he could return sooner with important news. It was the first systematic attempt in this country to gather foreign news. Later, Topliff hired correspondents in Europe to prepare the dispatches he received from incoming ship captains. The Topliff reports were so much more accurate and complete than the old haphazard accounts had been that other papers began to use them.

Other cities perfected similar services. The *Charleston Courier* was first in America with news of the peace with Great Britain in 1814, its ship-news reporter having learned of the event only seven weeks after its occurrence. By 1828 New York had taken the lead in such news gathering. The most enterprising news merchant in that fast-growing city was David Hale, manager of the *Journal of Commerce*, published by Arthur Tappan. The paper was the newest of the 10 dailies then being published in New York. Hale soon found that the older publications had combined to run him out of business. They had established a service for obtaining news from incoming ships, and they used rough tactics to keep Hale's boats from threatening the monopoly. In desperation, Hale purchased a fast sloop, which met the European packets as they were trimmed off Sandy Hook for the run up the bay to the city wharves. He was able to return with news hours before the merchantmen hove into view from Battery Place. When the New York combine set up a semaphore system from Sandy Hook to the Battery, Hale countered by establishing a pony express route across Staten Island, connecting his Sandy Hook sloop base with the Battery ferry. The rival semaphore was faster, but the news was hopelessly meager, and Hale had no difficulty in outperforming his competitors.

Not long after this Hale and his partner, Gerard Hallock, purchased the *Journal of Commerce* and made it into the most aggressive of the six-penny papers. Like the penny-press editors, the partners understood the value of news as a commodity. They sometimes put out extras when there were important stories to offer the public. They made the front page the show window, as in modern newspaper practice. But above all, they promoted any system that would speed the gathering and dissemination of news. It was Hale and Hallock who inaugurated the pony express service between Washington and New York. The *Courier and Enquirer* offered stiff competition, but until Bennett came along and outperformed the partners, Hale and Hallock led the New York pack in sniffing out the news.

PONIES, PIGEONS, TRAINS, STEAMBOATS

Bennett was of course not content with anything short of the best in news gathering. When Daniel Craig began using carrier pigeons to fly news reports from distant points, Bennett subscribed to the service, and even provided his own pigeons. When the steamship, the railroad, and the magnetic telegraph superseded sailing ships, ponies, and pigeons, Bennett was quick to use the new means of communication. But so were his competitors, and the intensified racing for news made its publishing increasingly expensive. Men like Hale began to see that while competition for the news was important, some degree of cooperation was necessary. There was a limit to what most newspapers could spend for news gathering, and gradually the competitors began to share the expenses. Eventually Hale, Bennett, and other New York publishers formed a cooperative association for the gathering of news—the forerunner of the modern press association. But before this logical development took place, the news enterprisers experimented further with the faster means of communication at their disposal.

The United States government had a hand in developing the rapid processing of news during this period. Following the lead of the newspapermen, Postmaster General Amos Kendall established regular pony express service between Philadelphia and New York, taking over a route from the *Courier and Enquirer* in 1835.[5] By 1836 this express service had been extended across the main routes, cutting the travel time between New York and New Orleans to less than seven days. Express riders did not carry the full newspapers, but rather proof sheets of important stories. These "slips," as they were called, preceded the regular papers by as much as a week on such long routes as the New Orleans system. The arrangement enabled newspapers around the country to work out cooperative exchange systems for beating rivals to big news.

In the 1830s and 1840s, railroads gradually began to replace the pony

[5] The *Courier and Enquirer* had found the cost of maintaining a pony route too great. But the *Journal of Commerce* continued its private express, extending it to Washington so as to gain a day over rival New York papers depending on the government's Philadelphia-New York express. Other papers were showing similar news enterprise, particularly those in Boston, the *Providence Journal,* and the *Charleston Courier.*

expresses. From 23 miles of track in 1830, construction went up to 9,000 miles by 1850. The railroad was a great boon to the newspapers. It not only provided fast distribution, but served also as a communications agency. In May, 1837, the *Baltimore Sun* rushed President Van Buren's message from Washington in less than two hours by way of the Baltimore & Ohio Railroad. Previously, Abell and his associates would have had to wait until the following morning to obtain such news from the Washington papers.

In 1841, Bennett, Swain *(Philadelphia Public Ledger)*, and Abell *(Baltimore Sun)* together hired a special locomotive to carry President Harrison's inaugural address from Washington to Baltimore, Philadelphia, and New York. The *Baltimore Sun* was able to put out an early afternoon extra covering the noonday speech. Proofs of the speech were mailed to the paper's exchanges, who thereby scored a 24-hour scoop over rivals.

The steamship also contributed to the development of fast news gathering. Travel across the Atlantic was reduced from weeks to days. In 1845, when the Oregon question brought a threat of war with England, leading papers cooperated in meeting fast ships at Halifax, the first port of call for the Atlantic steamers. Horses brought the news across the Nova Scotia peninsula to the Bay of Fundy, from where a fast steamer relayed the information to Portland, Maine. A railroad train brought the news to Washington less than 50 hours after it had been received in Halifax.

NEWS BY TELEGRAPH

But the biggest boost in speedy transmission of news was given by the telegraph. On May 25, 1844, Samuel F. B. Morse sat at a table in the old Supreme Court chamber in Washington and tapped out a message in code. His assistant in Baltimore decoded the sounds. The message: "What hath God wrought?" Later that same afternoon, Morse sent the first telegraphic message published in a newspaper, the *Baltimore Patriot:* "One o'clock—There has just been made a motion in the House to go into committee of the whole on the Oregon question. Rejected—ayes, 79; nays, 86." This was one of the significant reports of the century—not because of the intrinsic news value, but because it portended a whole new system of communication.

Swain, the Philadelphia publisher, was one of the incorporators of the Magnetic Telegraph Company, which promoted Morse's invention. Abell, in Baltimore, used the columns of his paper to demand help of Congress in subsidizing the inventor's work. He also helped finance the Washington-Baltimore test of the new device. But for some strange reason, the *Baltimore Sun* gave very little space to one of the big stories of the nineteenth century. The Monday paper relegated the first telegraphic news dispatch to the second page under local news headed "Magnetic Telegraph." Eleven lines had to tell the story of the experiment that was to do so much for communication throughout the world.

Newspapers were quick to make use of the new invention, however. In May, 1846, President Polk's message to Congress calling for war with Mexico was telegraphed to Baltimore for the exclusive use of the *Sun*. Bennett became famous for his use of the invention to help him outperform his rivals.

The telegraph also stimulated the growth of small-town dailies. It was high time; unchecked, the metropolitan papers might soon have dominated the field, as they did in Great Britain. In Illinois, where city dailies from St. Louis, Cincinnati, and other big publishing centers had absorbed more and more of the circulation, 30 daily newspapers were founded during the decade following the adoption of the telegraph to press service. The cost of this service made all of them likely customers for a cooperative news gathering agency. For example, when the wire from Albany reached Utica early in January, 1846, the *Daily Gazette* there received its first telegraphic bulletins. The news was so fresh, and the transmission so novel, that the editor devoted about a column to the dispatches. The telegraph line reached Buffalo in July and the Albany-New York leg opened in September. To share the costs, the publisher at Utica and others between Albany and Buffalo organized themselves and employed news agents in New York and Albany.

GENESIS OF THE ASSOCIATED PRESS

Development of a recognized agency to serve all these far-flung publications and to meet the needs of the big New York newspapers now seemed a logical step. Many persons had their eyes on the business, including Dr. Alexander Jones, a physician turned reporter, Daniel Craig, the pigeon expert, and various promoters of telegraph services. But the enterprising New York City dailies proved able to control the situation.

Frederic Hudson, the *Herald's* managing editor who later wrote a history of journalism, credits Hale of the *Journal of Commerce* with breaking the ice by calling on Bennett, whom he dispised, and suggesting that the rivals pool their news gathering resources for the reporting of the Mexican War in 1846.[6] Cooperation did result, although there was still continued rivalry in obtaining news from the Mexican front. Abell in Baltimore and Swain in Philadelphia were also invited into the alliance. The arrangements were satisfactory enough so that Hale decided to work out a more permanent organization.

Supposedly the publishers of the leading New York papers met in the *Sun* offices in May, 1848, and reached an agreement. No record was kept, but later accounts named as those present Bennett and Hudson of the *Herald;* Colonel

[6] Frederic Hudson, *Journalism in the United States* (New York: Harper & Row, 1873), pp. 366–67. Oliver Gramling, in his *AP: The Story of News* (New York: Farrar, Straus & Giroux, 1940), presents a dramatic account of the beginnings of the Associated Press, but the historical basis for the details he relates has never been established.

Webb and his assistant, Henry Raymond, of the *Courier and Enquirer;* Greeley of the *Tribune;* Beach of the *Sun;* Erastus and James Brooks of the *Express;* Hale and Hallock of the *Journal of Commerce.* On May 13, 1848, Raymond was writing to the telegraph agent in Boston, telling him those six papers wished "to procure foreign news by telegraph from Boston in common"—including both news arriving by steamships which docked in Boston before proceeding to New York and news relayed from Halifax. A week later Raymond was agreeing to a contract on behalf of the "Associated Press," providing for a payment of $100 for 3,000 words of telegraphic news and stating that the news would be forwarded also to newspapers in Philadelphia and Baltimore.[7]

There is no documentary evidence of a formal organization in 1848, however, and the best precise date for the legal founding of the predecessor organization which grew into the modern Associated Press is January 11, 1849. A copy of the agreement signed that day, forming the Harbor News Association among the six previously named New York dailies, was found in 1967 in the file of Henry J. Raymond papers in the manuscript division of the New York Public Library. Its previously unknown details provided the six partners would operate two boats to gather news in New York harbor from incoming ships, would share the costs, would sell news to papers outside New York City, and would set up membership rules.[8] In 1851, apparently because the selling of news by telegraph was becoming more important, the group signed a new agreement as the Telegraphic and General News Association.

The name "Associated Press" did not come into general use until the 1860s, but the New York City group was the forerunner of that modern-day press association. Dr. Alexander Jones became superintendent of the service, and was succeeded in 1851 by Daniel Craig. That year the *Times* became the seventh newspaper member of the combine. In 1856 the group tightened its organization by adopting what was called the "Regulations of the General News Association of the City of New York." [9] Soon called the New York Associated Press, the group established a firm grip on cooperative telegraphic news reporting, selling its service to outsiders.

THE MEXICAN WAR NEWS

The Mexican War provided the newspapers an excellent opportunity to demonstrate their enterprise. When war was declared in 1846 the telegraph lines reached only as far south as Richmond, Virginia. There was very little railroad development south of that city. Papers closer to the war events were

[7] Victor Rosewater, *History of Cooperative News-Gathering in the United States* (New York: Appleton-Century-Crofts, 1930), pp. 64–66.

[8] The document was uncovered by Richard A. Schwarzlose, a leading researcher in the history and operations of the press associations. See his "Harbor News Association: The Formal Origin of the AP," *Journalism Quarterly,* XLV (Summer 1968), 253, in which he reviews all the evidence concerning the genesis of the AP.

[9] Reprinted in Rosewater, *op. cit.,* pp. 381–88.

depended upon to furnish the news. For that reason the New Orleans dailies became nationally known during this period.[10] The South was particularly interested in the war because of its ultimate impact upon slavery and sectional balance. But the North was interested, too (a "criminal war," some editors called it). Bennett led the way, as usual, with a special pony express across the nation from New Orleans, although he soon joined forces with Abell and Swain in sharing the venture. The *Charleston Courier* and *New York Sun* ran another important service, to bring the news of the war from New Orleans, whither the correspondents sent their dispatches.

Star reporter of the Mexican War was the publisher of the *New Orleans Picayune,* George W. Kendall. He covered all the big battles from Monterey to Chapultepec, and gave accurate accounts of the military strategy involved. The biggest scoop of the war can be credited to the *Baltimore Sun.* In April, 1847, one of the pony expresses serving the paper brought the news that Vera Cruz had fallen. The capture of this fortress was a decisive victory for the invading forces. Abell was aware that his rider was at least a day ahead of the War Department courier, and so the Baltimore publisher sent a telegram to President Polk. It was the first news of the victory to reach the White House. The *Sun,* curiously enough, played its news beat on page two, in the column where editorials ordinarily appeared. But the single column head, topped with cuts of running ponies, bespoke the pride of a news enterprise paper. It had 11 decks, using 14 different type faces. The first six read: [11]

By Special Overland Expresses of
Nearly One Thousand Miles
Exclusively for The Baltimore Sun
Independent of All Telegraphic Communication!

Unparalleled Effort of
Newspaper Enterprise

Highly Important
From the South

Unparalleled Achievement
of the
American Arms!

The Greatest Military Exploit
of the
Present Century

[10] There were nine of them; the best known were the *Picayune, Delta, Crescent, Tropic,* and *Bee.* All had correspondents in Mexico to cover the war.

[11] As reprinted in Johnson, *The Sunpapers of Baltimore,* p. 80.

Fall, Surrender,
And Unconditional Capitulation of
The City of Vera Cruz
and
The Castle of San Juan D'Ulloa

It had taken 12 days for the news to reach Baltimore by runner, steamer, and pony express. This is typical of the energy and aggressiveness that went into news coverage during this period. Publishers and editors were providing more facts and accurate information than the public had ever had before.[12]

PRESSES FOR MASS CIRCULATION

This brings us to the final factor in developing the press. Mass circulation, and all the changes it brought about, could not have been accomplished unless papers could be produced cheaply, quickly, and in greater bulk. This problem had to be solved by the technical expert, especially the builder of printing presses.

The improvement in presses and the need for fast printing is indicated by the experience of the *Philadelphia Public Ledger*. It was founded in 1836 as a penny paper dependent upon circulation for success, but its printing equipment consisted of the usual hand press, seen in a majority of newspaper shops. In six months the paper acquired a circulation of nearly 8,000, and it was no longer possible to meet the demands of the public with the cumbersome Clymer press. Swain thereupon installed the finest equipment obtainable at the time—a Napier single-cylinder press powered by steam. A year later the publisher had to order another press, this time a double-cylinder machine. Bennett's progress was even more amazing. Ten years after he founded his paper without even a press of his own, he was using four double-cylinder presses with four men to each unit, in order to get out enough papers.

The first cylinder presses merely rolled back and forth over the flat type-bed—like some of the proof presses seen in printing shops today. Speed could be doubled by using two cylinders at a time. But even these presses were not fast enough to keep up to the circulations developed by the penny papers. The problem was solved for the time by Richard Hoe's type-revolving press,

[12] A study of papers from the Lower South, made as part of a larger study of U.S. newsgathering underway at the University of North Carolina, showed that the average time lag on publication of stories of news events dropped from 29 days in the 1820s to 10 days in the 1850s. The amount of news actively gathered by a reporter, editor, or correspondent of the sampled papers rose from 30 to 70 per cent in the same period. The study was reported by Professor Donald L. Shaw and Mary E. Junck in *Research Previews,* April, 1971.

first installed in the *Public Ledger* shop in 1846. Hoe substituted a horizontal cylinder for the flat bed. Countersunk in these cylinders were curved iron beds, one for each page in the paper. Type matter was locked in these beds by an ingenious system of wedge-shaped rules to keep the type from flying out as the cylinders revolved at high speed. In 1849 the *New York Herald* installed one of these "lightning" presses with six cylinders capable of printing 12,000 impressions an hour. Other New York papers had presses with up to ten such cylinders during the 1850s. By the outbreak of the Civil War it was possible for an enterprising publisher to print up to 20,000 impressions an hour.

This ingenious Hoe type-revolving press of 1855 printed 20,000 sheets an hour.

The type-revolving press speeded up the processing of news, but it also imposed limitations on the editor and publisher. On such a press it was difficult to print anything except one-column headlines. It was not practicable to hold type matter in place on the whirling cylinder when it was set in two- or three-column measure, because the wedges did not have enough purchase on the curved sides of the cylinder. Thus, as long as the type-revolving press was standard equipment, we find very few multiple-column headlines.

Another improvement in the technical process was the use of stereotype plates. James Dellagana, a London printer, produced curved, solid plates of type instead of the columns of loose type that presented such a hazard on the revolving cylinders. This was accomplished by making an impression of the type forms in a soft mold, curving this mold to fit the cylinder, and then pouring hot lead onto the mold or "matrix" to make a type plate. In 1854 Charles Craske, an American engineer, adapted this process to the presses of the *New York Herald*—another of that remarkable paper's "firsts." Stereotyping made it possible to make duplicates of pages so that several presses could run off an edition at the same time, thereby speeding the printing to a point limited only by the amount of equipment a publisher could afford. Bennett, for example, had five presses printing from duplicate stereotype cylinders at the same time, during the Civil War demand for papers. Stereotyping made possible bigger headlines, appropriate for war news. It also enabled advertisers to develop display devices.

NEWSPAPERS MOVE WEST

The small city newspapers changed much less radically than did their big city rivals, but even in the hinterland the press was experiencing the impact of the communications revolution. The telegraph lines reached Portland, Maine, by 1846, Charleston in the South the next year, as well as St. Louis in the Middle West, and were extended to Chicago and Milwaukee in 1848. Pony expresses continued to operate beyond the ends of the lines—notably the overland pony express from St. Joseph, Missouri, to Sacramento, California, which opened in 1860 and continued until the telegraph reached the Pacific in October, 1861. By that time there were more than 50,000 miles of wires.

Newspaper publishers in the interior did the best they could to publish creditable papers. They scrambled to get the Washington and foreign news from proof slips, exchange papers, and meager telegrams. Cincinnati and St. Louis, particularly, were major publishing centers and both had several daily newspapers by the 1850s. The leaders in Cincinnati were the *Gazette,* founded in 1815 as a weekly and transformed into a daily in 1827, and the *Commercial,* begun in 1843. St. Louis had as its top dailies the *Missouri Republican,* founded as the *Gazette* in 1808, and the *Missouri Democrat* of 1852. Secondhand presses, printing equipment, ink, and paper moved out from these centers to smaller towns as the newspaper followed the lines of settlement.

Population was booming in the Great Lakes area, where Chicago and Milwaukee became prominent. Chicago's first paper was the *Weekly Democrat,* begun in 1833 and made into a daily in 1840. The *Chicago Tribune* appeared in 1847, and after its purchase by Joseph Medill and his partners in 1855, it became the leading daily, absorbing the *Democrat* in 1861. Milwaukee's initial weekly was the *Advertiser,* which was founded in 1836 and which lived to become the *Wisconsin News.* The *Milwaukee Sentinel,* started in 1837, became the city's first daily in 1844. The transformation from weekly to daily publication was repeated elsewhere; the *Minnesota Pioneer* of 1849, the state's first paper, became a daily in 1854 and had several competitors in St. Paul. Even the smaller towns had competing papers in this era.

Establishment of rival papers as spokesmen for political groups accounted for some of the growth. Some of the western papers were founded as means of promoting settlement and sale of lands, like the *Oregon Spectator,* begun in Oregon City in 1846 as the first Pacific Coast publication. Others were missionary papers, like the first publications in Kansas and the Oklahoma region.

Army posts also contributed papers. The weeklies typically carried a good deal of literary material, in addition to local news. The dailies, too, attempted to satisfy the hunger for reading matter as well as news. The *Alta California*, which began in San Francisco in 1849 and which became that city's first daily in 1850, later achieved fame for publishing the writings of Bret Harte and Samuel Clemens, better known as Mark Twain. Nevada's *Territorial Enterprise*, founded in 1858, boasted Mark Twain as city editor in the early 1860s.

The push into the Far West and into the mining country produced other early newspapers: the *Oregonian* in Portland in 1850; the *Sacramento Union* (1851), *Los Angeles Star* (1851), and *San Francisco Bulletin* (1855) and *San Francisco Call* (1856); the Mormon Church's *Deseret News* in Salt Lake City in 1850; and the *Rocky Mountain News* in the Denver mining area in 1859. Easterners who flocked to the California gold fields and to the Nevada and Colorado mining towns wanted more news than the local papers offered, however. New York papers, particularly the *Herald* and the *Tribune*, issued California editions which were sent by steamer around the Horn, or by overland stage. Papers in other eastern cities soon followed suit. For wherever an American went in the expanding nation, he wanted the news which an aggressive press corps was providing.

Annotated Bibliography

Books

Copeland, Fayette, *Kendall of the Picayune*. Norman: University of Oklahoma Press, 1943. An interesting account of the life and times of a pioneer New Orleans editor and war correspondent.

Dabney, Thomas E., *One Hundred Great Years*. Baton Rouge: Louisiana State University Press, 1944. The centennial history of the *New Orleans Times-Picayune*.

Gramling, Oliver, *AP: The Story of News*. New York: Farrar, Straus & Giroux, 1940. A colorful account of the rise of the Associated Press. Its content cannot always be substantiated by document and evidence, however.

Greeley, Horace, *Overland Journey from New York to San Francisco in the Summer of 1859*, edited with notes by Charles T. Duncan. New York: Knopf, 1963. Valuable biographical material as well as Greeley's view of the West.

Hage, George S., *Newspapers on the Minnesota Frontier, 1849–1860*. St. Paul: Minnesota Historical Society, 1967. What frontier journalism was like, carefully researched and well written.

Harlow, Alvin F., *Old Wires and New Waves: The History of the Telegraph, Telephone, and Wireless*. New York: Appleton-Century-Crofts, 1936. First half of the book covers the pre-Civil War period.

Hoe, Robert, *Short History of the Printing Press*. New York: R. Hoe and Company, 1902. Obviously a promotional venture, but valuable in describing the various presses of the period.

Hudson, Frederic, *Journalism in the United States, 1690–1872*. New York: Harper & Row, 1873. One of the oldest journalism histories, but especially useful in the description of the mid-nineteenth century period because the author knew many of the persons he discusses.

Johnson, Gerald, et al., *The Sunpapers of Baltimore*. New York: Knopf, 1937. An excellent case history that reveals the significance of the penny press outside New York.

McMurtrie, Douglas C., and Albert H. Allen, *Early Printing in Colorado*. Denver: Hirschfeld Press, 1935. McMurtrie also wrote articles about the journalism of other western states, for *Journalism Quarterly* and other periodicals.

Marbut, Frederick B., *News from the Capital: The Story of Washington Reporting*. Carbondale: Southern Illinois University Press, 1971. History of reporting, both print and broadcast, by a longtime student of the Washington press corps.

Rosewater, Victor, *History of Cooperative News-Gathering in the United States*. New York: Appleton-Century-Crofts, 1930. Not as colorful as the Gramling book, but more factual. Describes services other than the Associated Press.

Periodicals and Monographs

Carter, John D., *The San Francisco Bulletin, 1855–1865*. Ph.D. thesis, University of California, 1941. A study in the beginnings of Pacific Coast journalism.

Firebaugh, Dorothy Gile, "The Sacramento Union: Voice of California, 1851–75," *Journalism Quarterly*, XXX (Summer 1953), 321. The story of a dominant early California paper.

Marbut, Frederick B., "Early Washington Correspondents: Some Neglected Pioneers," *Journalism Quarterly*, XXV (December 1948), 369.

———, "The United States Senate and the Press, 1838–41," *Journalism Quarterly*, XXVIII (Summer 1951), 342.

———, "Decline of the Official Press in Washington," *Journalism Quarterly*, XXXIII (Summer 1956), 335. Articles by an authority on Washington correspondence and the capital press corps.

Pickett, Calder M., "Technology and the New York Press in the 19th Century," *Journalism Quarterly*, XXXVII (Summer 1960), 398. Based on "Six New York Newspapers and Their Response to Technology in the 19th Century," Ph.D. thesis, University of Minnesota, 1959.

Schwarzlose, Richard A., "Harbor News Association: Formal Origin of the AP," *Journalism Quarterly*, XLV (Summer 1968), 253. Legal date of AP predecessor's founding is January 11, 1849, document discloses.

Weigle, Clifford F., "San Francisco Journalism, 1847–1851," *Journalism Quarterly*, XIV (June 1937), 151. The beginnings of a colorful journalistic tradition are recounted by a Stanford University journalism professor.

FREEDOM'S JOURNAL.

" *RIGHTEOUSNESS EXALTETH A NATION.*"

CORNISH & RUSSWURM, Editors & Proprietors. NEW-YORK, FRIDAY, MARCH 16, 1827. VOL. I. NO. 1.

TO OUR PATRONS.

IN presenting our first number to our Patrons, we feel all the diffidence of persons entering upon a new and untried line of business. But a moment's reflection upon the noble objects, which we have in view by the publication of this Journal; the expediency of its appearance at this time, when so many schemes are in action concerning our people—encourage us to come boldly before an enlightened publick. For we believe, that a paper devoted to the dissemination of useful knowledge among our brethren, and to their moral and religious improvement, must meet with the cordial approbation of every friend to humanity.

The peculiarities of this Journal, render it important that we should advertise to the world the motives by whic we are actuated, and the objects which we contemplate.

We wish to plead our own cause. Too long have others spoken for us. Too long has the publick been deceived by misrepresentations, in things which concern us dearly, though in the estimation of some mere trifles; for though there are many in society who exercise towards us benevolent feelings; still (with sorrow we confess it) there are others who make it their business to enlarge upon the least trifle, which tends to the discredit of any person of colour; and pronounce anathemas and denounce our whole body for the misconduct of this guilty one. We are aware that there many instances of vice among us, but we avow that it is because no one has taught its subjects to be virtuous: many instances of poverty, because no sufficient efforts accommodated to minds contracted by slavery, and deprived of early education have been made, to teach them how to husband their hard earnings, and to secure to themselves comforts.

Education being an object of the highest importance to the welfare of society, we shall endeavour to present just and adequate views of it, and to urge upon our brethren the necessity and expediency of training their children, while young, to habits of industry, and thus forming them for becoming useful members of society. It is surely time that we should awake from this lethargy of years, and make a concentrated effort for the education of our youth. We form a spoke in the human wheel, and it is necessary that we should understand our pendence on the different parts, and theirs on us, in order to perform our part with propriety.

Though not desirous of dictating, we shall feel it our incumbent duty to dwell occasionally upon the general principles and rules of economy. The world has grown too enlightened, to estimate any man's character by his personal appearance. Though all men acknowledge the excellency of Franklin's maxims, yet comparatively few practise upon them. We may deplore when it is too late, the neglect of these self-evident truths, but it avails little to mourn. Ours will be the task of admonishing our brethren on these points.

The civil rights of a people being of the greatest value, it shall ever be our duty to vindicate our brethren, when oppressed, and to lay the case before the publick. We shall also urge upon our brethren, (who are qualified by the laws of the different states,) the expediency of using their elective franchise; and of making an independent use of the same. We wish them not to become the tools of party.

And as much time is frequently lost, and wrong principles instilled, by the perusal of works of trivial importance, we shall consider it a part of our duty to recommend to our young readers, such authors as will not only enlarge their stock of useful knowledge, but such as will also serve to stimulate them to higher attainments in science.

We trust also, that through the columns of the FREEDOM'S JOURNAL, many practical pieces, having for their bases, the improvement of our brethren, will be presented to them, from the pens of many of our respected friends, who have kindly promised their assistance.

It is our earnest wish to make our Journal a medium of intercourse between our brethren in the different states of this great confederacy: that through its columns an expression of our sentiments, on many interesting subjects which concern us, may be offered to the publick: that plans which apparently are beneficial may be candidly discussed and properly weighed; if worthy, receive our cordial approbation; if not, our marked disapprobation.

Useful knowledge of every kind, and every thing that relates to Africa, shall find a ready admission into our columns; and as that vast continent becomes daily more known, we trust that many things will come to light, proving that the natives of it are neither so ignorant nor stupid as they have generally been supposed to be.

And while these important subjects shall occupy the columns of the FREEDOM'S JOURNAL, we would not be unmindful of our brethren who are still in the iron fetters of bondage. They are our kindred by all the ties of nature; and though but little can be effected by us, still let our sympathies be poured forth, and our prayers in their behalf, ascend to Him who is able to succour them.

From the press and the pulpit we have suffered much by being incorrectly represented. Men, whom we equally love and admire have not hesitated to represent us disadvantageously, without becoming personally acquainted with the true state of things, nor discerning between virtue and vice among us. The virtuous part of our people feel themselves sorely aggrieved under the existing state of things—they are not appreciated.

Our vices and our degradation are ever arrayed against us, but our virtues are passed by unnoticed. And what is still more lamentable, our friends, to whom we concede all the principles of humanity and religion, from these very causes seem to have fallen into the current of popular feeling and are imperceptibly floating on the stream—actually living in the practice of prejudice, while they abjure it in theory, and feel it not in their hearts. Is it not very desirable that such should know more of our actual condition, and of our efforts and feelings, that in forming or advocating plans for our amelioration, they may do it more understandingly? In the spirit of candor and humility we intend by a simple representation of facts to lay our case before the publick, with a view to arrest the progress of prejudice, and to shield ourselves against the consequent evils. We wish to conciliate all and to irritate none, yet we must be firm and unwavering in our principles, and persevering in our efforts.

If ignorance, poverty and degradation have hitherto been our unhappy lot; has the Eternal decree gone forth, that our race alone, are to remain in this state, while knowledge and civilization are shedding their enlivening rays over the rest of the human family? The recent travels of Denham and Clapperton in the interior of Africa, and the interesting narrative which they have published; the establishment of the republic of Hayti after years of sanguinary warfare; its subsequent progress in all the arts of civilization; and the advancement of liberal ideas in South America, where despotism has given place to free governments, and where many of our brethren now fill important civil and military stations, prove the contrary.

The interesting fact that there are FIVE HUNDRED THOUSAND free persons of colour, one half of whom might peruse, and the whole be benefitted by the publication of the Journal; that no publication, as yet, has been devoted exclusively to their improvement—that many selections from approved standard authors, which are within the reach of few, may occasionally be made—and more important still, that this large body of our citizens have no public channel—all serve to prove the real necessity, at present, for the appearance of the FREEDOM'S JURNAL.

It shall ever be our desire so to conduct the editorial department of our paper as to give offence to none of our patrons; as nothing is farther from us than to make it the advocate of any partial views, either in politics or religion. What few days we can number, have been devoted to the improvement of our brethren; and it is our earnest wish that the remainder may be spent in the same delightful service.

In conclusion, whatever concerns us as a people, will ever find a ready admission into the FREEDOM'S JOURNAL, interwoven with all the principal news of the day.

And while every thing in our power shall be performed to support the chracter of our Journal, we would respectfully invite our numerous friends to assist by their communications, and our coloured brethren to strengthen our hands by their subscriptions, as our labour is one of common cause, and worthy of their consideration and support. And we do most earnestly solicit the latter, that if at any time we should seem to be zealous, or too pointed in the inculcation of any important lesson, they will remember, that they are equally interested in the cause in which we are engaged, and attribute our zeal to the peculiarities of our situation, and our earnest engagedness in their well-being.

THE EDITORS.

From the Liverpool Mercury.

MEMOIRS OF CAPT. PAUL CUFFEE.

" On the first of the present month of August, 1811, a vessel arrived at Liverpool, with a cargo from Sierra Leone; the owner, master, mate, and whole crew of which are free blacks. The master, who is also owner, is the son of an American slave, and is said to be very well skilled both in trade and navigation, as well as to be of a very pious and moral character. It must have been a strange and an animating spectacle to see this free and enlightened African, entering as an independent trader with his black crew into that port, which was so lately the *nidus* of the slave trade.—*Edinburgh Review for August*, 1811.

We are happy in having an opportunity of confirming the above account, and at the same time of laying before our readers an authentic memoir of Capt. *Paul Cuffee*, the master and owner of the vessel above alluded to, who sailed from this port on the 20th ult. with a licence from the British Government, to prosecute his intended voyage to Sierra Leone.—The father of Paul Cuffee was a native of Africa,—whence he was brought as a slave into Massachusetts. He was there purchased by a person named Slocum, and remained in slavery a very considerable portion of his life. He was named Cuffee, but as it is usual in those parts, took the name of Slocum, as expressing to whom he belonged. Like many of his countrymen he possessed a mind far superior to his condition; although he was diligent in the business of his master, and faithful to his interest, yet by great industry and economy he was enabled to purchase his personal liberty. At the time the remains of several Indian tribes, who originally possessed the right of soil, resided in Massachusetts. Cuffee became acquainted with a woman descended from one of those tribes, named Ruth Moses, and married her. He continued in habits of industry and frugality, and soon afterwards purchased a farm of 100 acres at the point in Massachusetts.

Cuffee and Ruth had a family of ten children. The three eldest sons, David, Jonathan, and John, are farmers in the neighborhood of West Point; filling respectable situations in society, and endowed with good intellectual capacities. They are all married, and have families to whom they are giving good educations. Of six daughters four are respectably married, while two remain single. Paul was born on the Island of Cutterhumpker, one of the Elizabeth Islands, near New-Bedford, in the year 1759—when he was about fourteen years of age, his father died, leaving a considerable property in land, but which being at that time unproductive, afforded but little provision for his numerous family, and thus the care of supporting his mother and sisters devolved upon his brothers and himself. At this time Paul conceived that commerce furnished to industry more ample rewards than agriculture, and he was conscious that he possessed qualities which under proper culture, would enable him to pursue commercial employments with prospects of success—he therefore entered at the age of sixteen, as a common hand on board of a vessel destined to the bay of Mexico, on a whaling voyage. His second voyage was to the West Indies, but on his third he was captured by a British ship during the American war, about the year 1776—after three month detention as a prisoner, at New-York, he was permitted to return home to Westport, where owing to the unfortunate continuance of hostilities he spent about two years in his agricultural pursuits. During this interval Paul and his brother John Cuffee, were called on by the collector of the district, in which they resided, for the payment of a personal tax. It appeared to them, that by the laws and constitution of Massachusetts, taxation and the whole rights of citizenship were united. If the laws demanded of them the payment of the personal taxes, the same laws must necessarily and constitutionally invest them with the right of representing and being represented in the state legislature. But they had never been considered as entitled to the privilege of voting at elections, nor of being elected to places of trust and honor. Under these circumstances they refused payment of the demands. The collector resorted to the force of the laws, and after many delays and detentions, Paul and his brohter deemed it most prudent to silence them by paying the demands; but they resolved, if it were possible to obtain the rights which they believed to be connected with taxation. They presented a respectful petition to the state legislature. From some individuals it met with a warm, and almost indignant opposition. A considerable majority was, however, favorable to their object. They perceived the propriety and justice of the petition, and with an honorable magnanimity, in defiance of the prejudice of the times, they passed a law rendering all free persons of color liable to taxation, according to the established ratio, for white men, and granting them all the privileges, belonging to the other citizens. This was a day equally honorable to the petitioners and the legislature—a day which ought to be gratefully remembered by every person of color, within the boundaries of Massachusetts, and the names of John and Paul Cuffee, should always be united with its recollection.

To be Continued.

COMMON SCHOOLS IN NEW-YORK.—It appears from the report of the Superintendent of Common Schools in the state of New-York, presented last week to the House of Assembly, that of the 723 towns and wards in the State, 721 have made returns according to law: That in these towns there are 8114 school districts, and of course the same number of schools; from 7544 of which returns have been received: That 341 new school dis-

Vol. 1, No. 1 of the Black Press in America: "Too long have others spoken for us."

13

The Press and the Rise of Sectionalism

He who opposes the public liberty overthrows his own.
—William Lloyd Garrison

The Jacksonian era brought out clearly the increasing absorption in sectional differences. The beginning of the "irrepressible conflict," as one historian has called the War Between the States, can be traced back to colonial times.[1] The petitions to the King long before 1776; the arguments over the Constitution at the Philadelphia convention; the drafting of the Kentucky and Virginia Resolutions after the Alien and Sedition Acts were passed; and the debates over the tariff of 1828 are some of the evidences of the fault-line along which the country would one day split. By 1848, people were no longer voting by party, but by section.

Up to about 1820 there was no great southern unit with the regional cohesion that was apparent a decade later. The South actually was more torn apart by dissension than any other section up to 1820. The upland communities had fought against the tidewater elite in the Revolution, largely as a result of social strains. Large areas of the South had more in common with the West. And the Negro added another source of social friction.

[1] Arthur Charles Cole, *The Irrepressible Conflict* (New York: Macmillan, 1934). See also Avery Craven, *The Repressible Conflict* (Baton Rouge: Louisiana State University Press, 1939).

THE RISE OF SECTIONALISM

There is a tendency to think of the South as turning away from American traditions when it seceded in 1861. It was the North, meaning the industrial Northeast, not the South, that developed a different way of life after 1820. Generally speaking, the South was about the same in 1861 as it had been in 1761. On the eve of the War Between the States, the South retained the impress of the eighteenth century. It was still, in the middle of the nineteenth century, about what the founding fathers had apparently expected of the country when they wrote the fundamental document—a land dominated by the agrarian interests. Certainly Jefferson would have approved of the country developing as the South had developed, without the slave institution, of course. Curiously, the section where slavery flourished was also the region where some of the great national heroes of democracy emerged, including Washington, Jefferson, Madison, John C. Calhoun, and many others.

All this time the South provided more than its share of political leadership. The Speaker of the House of Representatives was likely to be a southerner. The section abounded in great orators, great statesmen, great humanitarians, and great literary spokesmen. This is in contrast to the virtual bankruptcy of southern leadership in the 75 years following the Civil War.[2] There was good reason for the South to lead politically. Life centered in the plantation, and so commercial cities did not assume the importance they had in the Northeast. Lacking such centers, the South had only a small middle class, and virtually no white proletariat. Southerners looked to foreign markets, and they usually negotiated directly with British cotton and tobacco buyers, who took a large share of the southern products. The southerner usually shipped from his own, or from a local, wharf, rather than from a great seaport. This was inefficient, perhaps, but it was pleasanter.

From this environment came a governing group with a high sense of honor and morals. Family and land counted for more than money in the South, because money was not so essential to the agrarian as it was to the northern capitalist and wage earner. Money was the sign of success in the North. Land was the criterion in the South. But land values declined in the South some time after 1800, as the staple crops exhausted the soil. Little was known of fertilization of soil then, and so immigrants moved to fresh land, thereby reducing the demand for, and consequently the value of, the older lands. Since there was no profit to be made in land speculation, trade, or industry, the capitalist tended to leave the agrarian in full control. Disbarred by circumstance from commerce, which was attracting some of the best young brains in the North, prom-

[2] There were of course important leaders in the South after the Civil War, but which of them approached the greatness of the prewar southern statesmen?

ising careerists in the South turned to politics as one of the outlets for their abilities.

Northern industrialists resented this southern political leadership. That is indicated by the growing friction over legislation. The struggle between capitalistic and agrarian ideologies was disclosed in the great Webster-Hayne debate of 1830. In this enunciation of principles the northern and southern spokesmen publicly presented the courses their respective sections would henceforth follow. And here it is evident that it was the North, not the South, that had changed.

The South had reason to fear for its future. The industrial North was growing much faster than the South. Population pressure would inevitably give the North political dominance. Already the "tariff of abominations" of 1828 had disclosed what the North would impose upon the South if given free rein. The tariff, which protected northern industry, might ruin an area dependent upon Europe for exchange of necessities. The North was willing to spend enormous amounts of tax money on the improvement of harbors and transportation systems, all very useful to an industrial economy but only a drain on southern financial resources.

Both sections turned to the West as an ally, when it became clear that the frontier region would determine the outcome of the conflict. The West was agrarian, like the South. It also suffered from high tariffs. Westerners had natural antipathies to the industrial North. They resented the northern sabotage of every legislative attempt to ease the debt of the farmer and to open up free lands. On the other hand, the westerner was not as dependent upon world markets as was the southerner. The westerner was interested in reaching local or regional markets. His problem was to get his produce to these markets cheaply and easily, and here he found an ally in the northern capitalist. Roads, canals, steamboat subsidies, and railroads were the prices paid by the North for the temporary allegiance of the West against the South.

The westerner also demanded the opening up of the frontier to homesteaders. Both the North and the South were opposed to this, in general. Some of the bitterest debates in Congress, from 1832 on, took place over this question. The West was certain it was being held back from its manifest destiny by the selfishness of the southern and northern blocs in Congress. Southerners feared the opening of new lands would lead to a preponderance of free states, which would add to the overwhelming weight against the South. Northerners, on the other hand, tended to block westward expansion because it depressed property values in their section and because free land kept wages higher than they would otherwise have been, or else reduced the reservoir of cheap labor in the industrial areas. The point here is that western victory on this issue was a kind of bribe paid by the North for the support of the West. One evidence of this is the Homestead Act, passed on the eve of the war after years of northern objection. Once the West had committed itself, the South had only two choices. It could admit defeat and modify its way of life to suit the North, or it could cast off from an alien system and go its own way—secede.

SLAVERY AS A WAR ISSUE

So far, nothing has been said about slavery as a main cause of the Civil War. If slavery had been such an important issue, time alone would have solved the problem. For slavery was already doomed. World opinion was against it. Already it had proved itself to be uneconomical in the upper tier of slave states. By 1860 these states were unloading surplus slave labor as fast as planters in the deep South could absorb it. The capitalist of the North had demonstrated that it was cheaper to pay a man only while he was useful than to support him as a slave throughout the unproductive years of his life.

Slavery was not a primary cause of the conflict, but it became important as the means for joining the battle, and here the journalist played his big role. There would probably have been sectional strife with or without slavery. But slavery, like the religious double talk of two centuries earlier, was the basket in which all the differences of peoples, regions, and ideologies could be carried. The slavery shibboleth was the rallying standard for all the various belligerents. It was the simplification of complex problems and summed up the attitudes of those who had to do the dying in battle.

It is unfortunate that slavery had to be the issue upon which the concept of the American union had to be tested. When the South seceded, it did so on the principle that the minority had the right to protect itself from the tyranny of a majority. Secession meant allegiance to states' rights, a principle that many honest men could uphold. That was more than could be said for the northern leaders who had suggested secession at the Hartford Convention in 1814, not on principle, but on expediency. At least the North had no right to attach stigma to the word "secession." When the South withdrew from the Union, it did so with profound regret. "The Union—next to our liberty, most dear," Calhoun, the spokesman of the South, once said.

Slavery lifted the doctrines and philosophies of North and South on to a plane that made them more discernible to the average man. Few would be willing to die for economic principles. But slavery could supply the hate transference that could make a John Brown, for example, die for such a cause at Harper's Ferry in 1859. To Ralph Waldo Emerson, "Old Ossawatomie" Brown had "made the gallows glorious like the cross." And Walt Whitman, poet and sometime journalist, wrote of Brown's execution:

> I would sing how an old man, with white hair, mounted the scaffold in Virginia,
> (I was at hand, silent I stood with teeth shut close, I watch'd,

> I stood very near you old man when cool and indifferent, but trembling with age and your unheal'd wounds, you mounted the scaffold . . .) [3]

This indicates what the slavery issue meant to men of lofty sentiment. It took some time to sweep the masses into the movement, but eventually the people of the North and South made slavery a fighting issue, and the press was effective in bringing this about. Advocates of the campaigns against slavery were known as "abolitionists." An outstanding abolitionist editor was William Lloyd Garrison. He makes an excellent case study of how the press became such an important factor in the struggle.

GARRISON AND THE *LIBERATOR*

Garrison was born in Newburyport, Massachusetts, of English and Irish stock. The father was a drunkard who abused his family, and the boy must have been influenced by these circumstances when he took up the temperance issue while still a youth. He was a jack-of-all-trades until he became a printer. That appeared to be his proper niche. Like Benjamin Russell and Isaiah Thomas, Garrison received most of his education at the type case. It was an education that made him literate rather than learned. As an editor, Garrison took an interest in politics, but he never appeared to master the political principles and traditions, and he had little knowledge of party backgrounds. He started out as a Federalist, more out of editorial imitation than of conviction, presumably. Day by day he became more dissatisfied with the way the world was run. Many men and women are radicals in youth and conservatives as they grow older. Garrison reversed this pattern. As he grew older, he became more rebellious. He was like some wines, which sour rather than mellow with age.

He was in his thirties when he met Benjamin Lundy, the gentle Quaker who had started out as a temperance missionary, but who had since carried this reforming zeal over into the antislavery movement. It is significant that Quakers had been important in the successful antislavery movement in Great Britain. At any rate, Garrison became one of Lundy's recruits. Soon Garrison had been satisfactorily persecuted—an essential step in the progress of any effective zealot. He had libeled one of his neighbors by calling him a "blackbirder," or importer of slaves. The complainant offered to drop the case if Garrison would print an apology. It was characteristic of the man that he preferred to suffer seven months in jail. He emerged a confirmed abolitionist, and with that supreme gift—a cause so absorbing that life itself is not too great a price for it. He moved to Boston, and on January 1, 1831, he issued there the first copy of the *Liberator*.

[3] Both quotations are reprinted in Louis L. Snyder and Richard B. Morris, eds., *A Treasury of Great Reporting* (New York: Simon & Schuster, 1949), pp. 124–25.

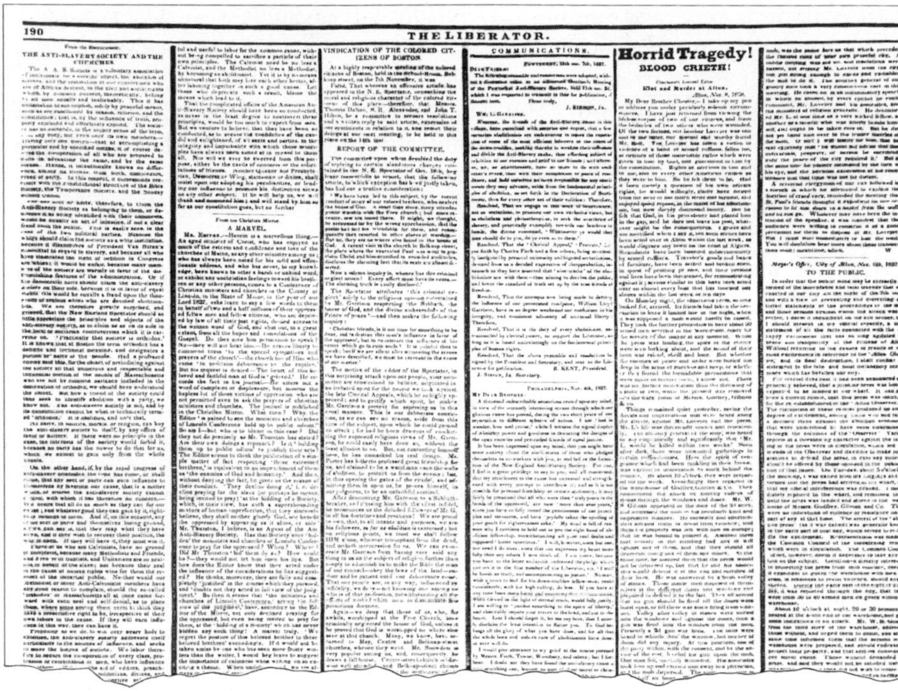

190 THE LIBERATOR.

THE ANTI-SLAVERY SOCIETY AND THE CHURCHES.

A MARVEL.

VINDICATION OF THE COLORED CITIZENS OF BOSTON

REPORT OF THE COMMITTEE.

COMMUNICATIONS.

Horrid Tragedy!

BLOOD CRIETH!

TO THE PUBLIC.

Garrison's *Liberator* reports the murder of abolitionist Elijah Lovejoy.

The paper was well edited and ordinarily consisted of four pages. It was a throwback to an earlier day, when views, rather than news, characterized the press. The *Liberator* was more like an abolitionist house organ. But there was also plenty of news pertaining to all aspects of the movement. Indeed, the paper is almost a complete textbook of the antislavery issue. All the gag rules imposed by irate politicians are recorded, for example. One can see how attitudes crystallized month by month, in reading the pages even at this late date.

It wasn't very impressive, this voice of the abolitionist. Garrison said in 1837 that his publication had never exceeded 3,000 subscribers. Much of the time it hovered around 1,500, and about one-fourth of the circulation was in Negro areas, where the readers were either disfranchised, or had little political influence. The editor was always losing entire blocks of readers because of his tactless scorn of men, institutions, or traditions sacred to certain publics. And yet this was part of the medium that was to rouse the North to battle.

His cause appeared to be hopeless at first. In 1831 he had 50 subscribers to his paper, and no following at all. He was so poor that he lived on little more than bread and water to conserve his meager resources for the *Liberator*. He was bitterly opposed—even more in the North than in the South, when the Whigs and others were putting all their faith in compromise as the solution to northern and southern differences. Garrison had one weapon, his press, but it was to make him invincible. Through this press he spread his creed far and wide, until the abolitionist movement began to work on the minds of the apathetic. He reached such persons with words like these:

> He who opposes the public liberty overthrows his own. . . .
> There is no safety where there is no strength; no strength without Union; no Union without justice; no justice where faith and truth are wanting. The right to be free is a truth planted in the hearts of men. . . .[4]

This describes Garrison, a man of courage and determination, imbued with righteousness, narrow and fanatical. These are the men who override all obstacles. They reach their goals when the broad-minded reformer has long since bogged down in the quicksand of his own objectivity. Men like Garrison are not easy to love or admire, but they cannot be ignored. He aroused the conscience of a people long lulled by politicians fearful of disturbing the false balance so artfully maintained. What he said was bad for business. Most of this time the country was prosperous. When people are comfortable, conscience is often half asleep. Garrison jerked consciences awake—always an unpopular move. Even the religious leaders resented the man, particularly his self-righteousness. One clergyman complained that abolitionists like Garrison did not do their work like "Christian gentlemen." To which Garrison replied:

> These are your men of "caution" and "prudence" and "judiciousness." Sir, I have learned to hate those words. Whenever we attempt to imitate our Great Exemplar, and press the truth of God in all its plainness upon the conscience, why, we are imprudent; because, forsooth, a great excitement will ensue. Sir, slavery will not be overthrown without excitement—a most tremendous excitement.[5]

Garrison caused the most violent public reaction since Tom Paine drew his red hot ploughshare through American history. Even the standard newspapers gave chase to the troublesome abolitionist. James Gordon Bennett, who had argued in defense of free expression during the moral war against the *Herald*, now saw nothing inconsistent in throttling the abolitionist editors. Amos Kendall, himself a great journalist, and a leader of Jacksonian democracy, believed that Garrison should be gagged. As postmaster general he allowed abolitionist papers to be rifled from the official mail sacks by southern

[4] Wendell Phillips Garrison and Francis Jackson Garrison, *William Lloyd Garrison: The Story of His Life Told By His Children*, Vol. I (New York: Appleton-Century-Crofts, 1885), p. 200.

[5] Vernon L. Parrington, *Main Currents in American Thought* (New York: Harcourt, Brace & Jovanovich, 1927), II, p. 356. Parrington's fascinating analysis of the abolitionist leader quotes many such statements of Garrison.

"committees" charged with that task.[6] The state of Massachusetts was ready to forbid the export of the *Liberator,* and in many states, distributors of the paper were intimidated without redress.

Such opposition only made Garrison the more rabid. It also made it impossible for him to compromise. Before long, he considered himself as not even an American. Every Fourth of July his paper printed a long editorial exposing the fallacies of American democracy. Long before the South proposed secession, Garrison called upon abolitionists to repudiate a government that could tolerate slavery. The right "ear," or upper corner, of his paper regularly attacked the very foundations of the state, a standard statement being: "The existing Constitution of the United States is a covenant with death and an agreement with hell." One of his favorite stunts on the lecture platform was to burn a copy of the Constitution to show his contempt for a national charter that sanctioned human bondage. He held that the law of conscience was superior to the law of the land.

MOBBING THE ABOLITIONISTS

James G. Birney, one of the more reasonable abolitionists, was mobbed when he began printing his paper, the *Philanthropist,* at Cincinnati. Note that this was a city in a northern, not a southern, state. From that day on, Birney began to devote his energy to fighting for a free press along with his fight for freeing slaves. The abolitionists saw very clearly that the slavery issue would sooner or later affect all the freedoms in both the North and the South. One of the most stirring messages on this subject, "Free Speech and Free Inquiry," appears in the April 2, 1847, issue of the *Liberator.*

At least one abolitionist died for this cause. He was Elijah Lovejoy, editor of the *St. Louis Observer,* a strident abolitionist weekly founded in 1835. A mass meeting of irate citizens resulted in a resolution informing Lovejoy that free expression as guaranteed in the Bill of Rights did not extend to editors such as Lovejoy who threatened the peace of the community. Lovejoy replied that public resolutions could not fetter an editor. As to the argument, in the choice between peace or principle, the righteous editor could only choose the latter. "The truth is, my fellow citizens," Lovejoy told his neighbors in answer to their arguments, "if you give ground a single inch, there is no stopping place."

[6] Kendall justified his action by holding that each issue of the *Liberator* reaching a southern state was a criminal libel; that is, a threat to public peace. He tried to explain the situation in his annual report for 1835, when he asked Congress for an official banning of "obnoxious" literature in southern states. This would have taken the responsibility out of the hands of the postmaster general, and indicates that Kendall knew his past actions had been arbitrary. It is interesting to see the South's great leader, John C. Calhoun, challenge the constitutionality of Kendall's request. Calhoun's alternative was a recommendation for states with appropriate laws to ban such literature at the source.

As an act of good faith, however, Lovejoy moved his press across the river to Alton, Illinois. His office was at once wrecked by a mob. He appealed nationally for support and received enough help to set up another press. This was also demolished. Again he appealed for assistance, and again there was a quick and positive response. The climax came in 1837 while he was setting up his third press in Alton. A group of citizens decided that the Lovejoy nuisance should be abated. They called a mass meeting to devise plans. Lovejoy refused to be intimidated and boldly attended the meeting to present his side. He promised to suspend publication if his readers requested him to, but he declared he would not be ruled by mob hysteria. He said he would return to his office and would defend his right to publish with his life, if need be. When the mob marched down the street after the meeting, it was motivated not by the desire just to destroy a press, but to destroy a man who refused to renounce his right to think and to express himself. Lovejoy was killed by the mob.

His murder served the abolitionist cause far better than his writings ever had. The abolitionists had a martyr. People who had never pondered the matter were horrified by the brutality. They began to wonder what the price of peace was to be. Slowly public opinion turned. Ministers began to see a moral relationship between slavery and sin. Respectable businessmen, once haters of abolitionists, saw that the movement could combine righteousness with an attack on southern economic obstructionism.

Sincere thinkers began to see the light. Fanatical abolitionists had glutted Congress with antislavery bills. Since Congress was still dominated by the South (thanks to the three-fifths rule that gave added representation for a part of the nonvoting slave population), the legislators passed the so-called Gag Law, which prevented any consideration of such measures. This was an attack on a fundamental right of popular sovereignty. Men who had no respect for fanaticism, but who recognized a growing threat, now became allies of the abolitionists. One such group was made up of responsible newspaper editors.

Curiously, many of the abolitionist papers first appeared in southern or border states. That was before 1831. In that year occurred the most frightening of the slave revolts under an educated Negro, Nat Turner. Turner was defeated, of course, but from then on, abolitionist literature was driven from the slave states, although there is no indication that such writing had instigated the revolt. By 1836 the southern press was completely muzzled on the slavery issue. There were laws against any "tendency to incite to insurrections" in most of the slave states; understandable, perhaps, when an entire population lived in fear. A Georgia code of 1835 made any such breach of the law punishable by death. By 1859 it was a prison offense in some states merely to subscribe to an abolitionist paper. Even southern editors winced at such control. Most southern editors had about the same views on slavery as their legislators, but it is noteworthy that a southern editor most seriously challenged the press laws. Samuel Janney, editor of the *Leesburg Washingtonian* in Virginia, had written an editorial refuting Biblical sanction of slavery in denial of the persuasive arguments for slavery presented by Thomas Dew, later president of William and Mary College. Janney was brought to trial under a Virginia law forbidding "agitation" through the printing of opinion detrimental to slavery. In a magnificent speech before a jury of slaveowners, the courageous editor called up the state's great traditions of freedom. He was acquitted.

By 1850 the South was driven to the defensive by the violent attacks of the abolitionists. Public opinion in the North began to demand overt action. Slaveholders were held up as beasts and sinners. Southerners had to devote more and more energy to defending themselves and their institutions. By 1850 world opinion was also forcing the southerner into a humiliating position. The irony was that he had to fight for a noble principle (states' rights) on terms made odious by his enemies. To maintain self-respect, the best brains of the South were devoted to a vindication of slavery. In the North, new ideas were in a ferment, and the tested ones were being used to increase standards of living. In the South, once a hotbed of radicalism, every new idea had to be filtered so as to separate any element that might corrode the institution of slavery. The slave appeared to be dominating his master.

THE SOUTHERN "FIRE-EATERS"

The southern counterpart of the abolitionist was the "fire-eater." Outstanding fire-eaters were William Lowndes Yancey, Edmund Ruffin, and Robert Barnwell Rhett. Yancey was one of the great orators of his era. It was Yancey who led the South from the Democratic convention of 1860. Ruffin was an agricultural writer, who introduced marl as a fertilizer to restore exhausted tobacco land. He was a tireless and indomitable southern patriot. When more timid souls hesitated to fire upon Fort Sumter in 1861, it was Ruffin who snatched the lanyard of the nearest cannon and sent the first ball screaming its message of war. And it was Ruffin who committed suicide rather than take the oath of allegiance after Appomattox. But of all the fire-eaters, Rhett was most effective.

Rhett, sometimes called the "father of secession," had close ties with the North, as did many a leading southerner. Calhoun, for example, was educated at Yale. Rhett went to Harvard. His real name was Smith, but he changed it to Rhett in 1837 when the lineage of an honored colonial forefather was about to die out. Rhett was a distant relative of John Quincy Adams, but he more nearly resembled Sam Adams, who was no kin.

Like Sam Adams, Rhett was a born revolutionist. He and Adams both hated the government under which they grew up. Each vowed to destroy it. Both were expert in the use of every trick that could arouse the public to rebellion. They understood the technique of agitation. Both used the newspaper as the primary medium for transmitting these ideas.

Robert Barnwell Rhett was born into modest circumstances, but he knew how to win friends and influence people. As a youth he "read law" for one of South Carolina's leading barristers. As a successful lawyer, and even more successful real estate operator, he acquired valuable property in Charleston. One such acquisition was the *Mercury,* which Rhett edited. He made it one of the leading papers in the deep south. Through the *Mercury* Rhett became so powerful that he eventually succeeded to the position of his rival, Calhoun, one of the great statesmen of the era.

Rhett emerged as the leading fire-eater of the South following the debate over the 1828 "tariff of abominations." He saw clearly where the North was heading. By 1832 he was declaring openly that the only safety for the South was for it to go its own way. Long before Calhoun had faced the facts, Rhett was arguing for nullification. Obviously, nullification carried to its logical conclusion could lead to disintegration of the Union. Rhett did not dodge the consequences of his arguments. South Carolina, he insisted, could exist by itself, although he hoped to find company for a new confederation.

No one paid much attention to Rhett at first. He was treated about as coldly in the South as Garrison had been in the North. He lost his seat in Congress because of his intemperate speeches on the issue. But as the North was whipped by the abolitionists into heaping more and more abuse upon the South, southerners began to heed Rhett's warnings. After such magnificent propaganda as *Uncle Tom's Cabin,* the South began to depend upon its Rhetts, Yanceys, and Ruffins for justification. By 1848, Rhett was once again powerful politically. In 1851 he succeeded to the Senate seat of the great Calhoun.

Ironically, Rhett had no intention of involving his section in a war. He had aroused the South to fighting pitch, but he had assumed all along that the North would not dare fight. On the day Sumter was fired upon, Rhett was still reassuring readers of the *Mercury* that the South would secede peaceably. He should have known better. Lincoln's refusal to evacuate the fort peacefully was proof that this time the North meant business.

The Rhetts and the Garrisons must take much of the blame for the hates engendered during this period. Writing to John Bigelow of the *New York Evening Post* in 1860, Rhett boasted that South Carolina would treat a Yankee reporter to the secession convention as a spy. But Rhett must not be dismissed as the villain of a tragedy. He was as much a contradiction as was his beloved South. A believer in constitutionalism, he did more than anyone else to wreck the National Charter. A champion of democracy, he fought to keep a class in bondage. He was accused of being overambitious, as indicated in his attacks on Confederate President Jefferson Davis, yet he gave up his cherished Senate seat after only a short incumbency, because of his belief in a principle.

Rhett's friends said that if the South had followed his leadership a decade earlier, it would have won its victory peacefully, as proposed by the editor. His bitterest opponents respected his integrity. J. L. Petigru and Benjamin

Franklin Perry, South Carolina Unionists, thought of the *Mercury* editor as a worthy foe.[7] But in the light of history, Rhett appears somewhat unstable—the forlorn leader of a lost cause. On his deathbed in 1876, he was still predicting that the South would one day be separate and free.

BLACK JOURNALISTS AS ABOLITIONISTS

Abolitionists like Garrison and fire-eaters like Rhett attracted both immediate and continuing attention because they represented the extremes of white America's reaction to Negro slavery, whose emotional clash eventually produced a civil war. Nothing the Negro could do or say for himself seemed important to a society that viewed him as an economic, political, and educational nonequal. In 1850 there were about a half-million free Negroes in the American population, half of them in the North and half in the South. But in the South, state laws prohibited Negroes from receiving any formal education, and chances to make decent incomes were few. In the North, state laws restricted Negro voting rights, and the uneven availability of public schools weighed quickly upon children of disenfranchised, poor, and illiterate blacks. There was a chance, however, to "get ahead," and some Negroes succeeded. A handful of freedmen won sufficient education to become writers, lawyers, physicians, businessmen in the era before the Civil War. To them, and to their friends in the white population, 40 struggling black newspapers were addressed between 1827 and 1865.[8]

These were virtually all dedicated contributions to the antislavery, abolitionist movement. And as such, they rank high in the regard of today's students of the black experience in America. It should not be startling to discover that there were blacks who spoke out for themselves; what is startling is that they could succeed as well as they did in the face of poverty and illiteracy among most of their audience, as well as in the face of almost total rejection by a white society that ignored their existence.

Slavery was not abolished everywhere north of the Mason-Dixon line until 1804, and early leadership among slaves seeking their freedom is found in Massachusetts and Pennsylvania before 1800. By 1830 there were some 50 Negro antislavery societies, with the most active located in New York, Philadelphia, Boston, and New Haven. Negro self-expression had long been centered in the folk songs and spirituals of the black slaves. Now a few freedmen

[7] Perry founded the *Southern Patriot* at Charleston in 1850 to express pro-Union sentiment in that most violently secessionist state. Petigru, once called "the greatest private citizen South Carolina has ever produced," opposed the state's course up to 1861. Despite their unpopular policies, both men were highly respected, and even loved, in their communities. It was typical of them to have accorded Rhett, their implacable adversary, the same respect they expected from him.

[8] Carter R. Bryan, "Negro Journalism in America Before Emancipation," *Journalism Monographs*, No. 12 (September 1969), 1, 30–33.

had become adept at oratory, at poetry, at autobiographical writing that had produced moving accounts in book form of what it meant to live as a slave. Some freedmen had seen their articles or letters published by white editors in the regular press; some had worked with Garrison and his *Liberator* group or with other white abolitionists. A particularly vicious attack upon these Negro leaders by Mordecai M. Noah, editor of the *New York Enquirer*, is credited with spurring the founding of the first black-published newspaper in the United States.[9]

Freedom's Journal was its name and in its first issue on March 16, 1827, it printed this simple explanation of the venture: "We wish to plead our own cause. Too long have others spoken for us." Its editors were John B. Russwurm, first Negro to graduate from a college in the United States (Bowdoin in 1826), and the Rev. Samuel Cornish, a Presbyterian who edited three different weeklies in New York City in this period. A four-page paper, 10 by 15 inches in size, *Freedom's Journal* agitated ruthlessly against the inhumanity of slavery, but also ran newsy items, sermons, poetry, and other literary fare. Russwurm left in 1828 to undertake a career as editor and government official in Liberia, and Cornish continued the paper under the name *Rights of All*. The known file ceases in October, 1829.[10]

It was in 1829 that David Walker issued his *Appeal* out of Boston, advocating violent measures to eliminate slavery, and George Moses Horton protested in Raleigh through the columns of his *Hope of Liberty*. During the racial turmoil in 1965 Walker's call for militant resistance was republished in paperback book form.

Another major effort at a black paper in New York City came in 1837 when Phillip A. Bell founded *The Weekly Advocate*. Renamed two months later as *The Colored American*, it appeared until 1842. Its first editor was the Rev. Samuel Cornish and the publisher was a Canadian, Robert Sears of Toronto. Cornish and Bell retired from the paper in May 1839 and Dr. Charles Bennet Ray became the guiding force of the spirited little paper. He made it not only an antislavery organ but also a "paper devoted primarily to the interests of the colored population, and . . . a first-rate family paper." Circulation reached 2,000 in an area from Maine to Michigan.[11]

When the regular dailies in Pittsburgh refused to run contributions by Negroes in 1843, Dr. Martin R. Delaney, first of his race to graduate from Harvard, founded *The Mystery*. William Wells Brown, the black writer and novelist of the period, described the physician as "decided and energetic in conversation, unadulterated in race, and proud of his complexion."[12] Delaney got

[9] I. Garland Penn, *The Afro-American Press and Its Editors* (Springfield, Mass.: Wiley Company, 1891), p. 28.

[10] Armistead S. Pride, *A Register and History of Negro Newspapers in the United States* (Ph.D. thesis, Northwestern University, 1950), p. 4.

[11] Bryan, *op. cit.*, pp. 11–14.

[12] As quoted in Bryan, *op. cit.*, p. 17.

in a libel suit but managed to keep his paper going until 1848 when it was purchased by the African Methodist Episcopal Church. Renamed the *Christion Herald,* then moved to Philadelphia in 1852 as the *Christian Recorder,* it was surviving in 1970 as oldest of the Negro religious weeklies.[13]

There were other notable efforts. One was the *Alienated American,* published from 1852 to 1856 in Cleveland by W. H. Day, a graduate of Oberlin College. Another was the *New Orleans Daily Creole,* an 1856 effort which was the first black-owned paper in the South and the first Negro daily. Bell, founder of the *Advocate* in New York, migrated to San Francisco and in 1865 began publishing *The Elevator,* which survived until 1889, an unusual feat for black papers.

But the most famous of the pre-Civil War black papers were edited by the dynamic leader of the freed slaves and inspiration of his race, Frederick Douglass.

FREDERICK DOUGLASS, EDITOR

By the 1970s, Frederick Douglass had become a symbol of black achievement and inspiration—his home in Washington had become a national shrine, his autobiographical writings enjoyed fresh printings, his face was on a postage stamp, young black males spelled their names with a double "s" if they were named Douglas. All of which was merited, for this son of a Negro slave woman and a white man ran away from a Maryland plantation to make himself a leader of those of the black race who needed his skill at writing and oratory to assert their cause.

Bettmann Archive

FREDERICK DOUGLASS

Born in 1817, he escaped slavery in 1838 and went to New England to work and gain additional education with the encouragement of William Lloyd Garrison, the abolitionist. He began to write for the newspapers, and to speak as an eyewitness to the

[13] Roland E. Wolseley, *The Black Press, U.S.A.* (Ames: Iowa State University Press, 1971), pp. 24–25.

tragedy of the slavery system. In 1845 he went to England where friends raised enough money to buy his freedom from his Maryland owner. Back in the United States, and known for the first of his autobiographical books (*Narrative of the Life of Frederick Douglass*), he was named an editor of *The Ram's Horn.* The paper was started in January, 1847 by Willis A. Hodges, as a black protest to such practices as that of the *New York Sun,* which had printed a letter from him and then sent him a bill for $15. Hodges' venture failed the next year but its columns carried this announcement in late 1847:

> PROSPECTUS for an anti-slavery paper; to be entitled *North Star.* Frederick Douglass proposes to publish in Rochester a weekly Anti-slavery paper, with the above title. The object of the *North Star* will be to Attack Slavery in all its forms and aspects: Advocate Universal Emancipation; exalt the standard of Public Morality; promote the Moral and Intellectual improvement of the COLORED PEOPLE; and hasten the day of FREEDOM to the Three Millions of our Enslaved Fellow Countrymen.[14]

Publication of *The North Star* began November 1, 1847. It quickly rose to a circulation of some 3,000 and both was read in and received contributions from Europe and the West Indies as well as much of the United States. In addition to articles about slavery and blacks, it carried a good cross section of national and world news. The masthead proclaimed: "Right is of no Sex—Truth is of no Color—God is the Father of us all, and we are all Brethren." Not everyone in Rochester thought so; just as the white abolitionists were terrorized, Douglass saw his house burned and his papers destroyed. But the spunky character of the paper and its literary quality were both so high that it survived financial difficulties and racial antagonism. Renamed *Frederick Douglass' Paper* in 1851 after a merger with a weaker sheet, the paper was symbolic of its editor's position as the recognized leader of the Negro population.

By mid-1860, with the issue of slavery clearly bringing the country to the verge of civil war, Douglass found the financial struggle too great and suspended his weekly. For the next three years he put out *Douglass' Monthly,* an abolitionist magazine aimed at a British audience, to aid the Northern war cause. In 1870 he became contributing editor of a Washington weekly, the *New Era,* which sought to aid the now-freed black people. The paper was no more popular than the cause; Douglass invested money in it, renamed it the *New National Era,* and became its fighting editor before admitting defeat (and a $10,000 loss) in 1875.[15] His second autobiographical effort, *My Bondage and My Freedom,* had appeared in 1855; now the final volume, *Life and Times of Frederick Douglass,* appeared in 1878. The remarkable ex-slave, skillful editor, polished orator, and inspirational fellow citizen died in 1895 at the age of 78.

[14] As quoted in Bryan, *op. cit.,* p. 19, from *The Ram's Horn,* November 5, 1847, p. 4.
[15] Wolseley, *op. cit.,* pp. 22–23.

He summed up his career in this paragraph which he wrote about his decision to become editor of *The North Star:*

> The grand thing to be done, therefore, was to change the estimation in which the colored people of the U.St. were held; to remove the prejudice which depreciated and depressed them; to prove them worthy of a higher consideration; to disprove their alleged inferiority, and demonstrate their capacity for a more exalted civilization than salary and prejudice had assigned to them. I further stated that, in my judgment, a tolerably well conducted press, by calling out the mental energies of the race itself; by making them acquainted with their own latent powers; by enkindling among them the hope that for them there is a future; by developing their moral power, by combining and reflecting their talents would prove a most powerful means of removing prejudice, and of awakening an interest in them. I further informed them—and at that time the statement was true—that there was not, in the United States, a single newspaper regularly published by the colored people; that many attempts had been made to establish such papers; but that, up to that time, they had all failed. These views I laid before my friends. The result was, nearly 2,500 dollars were speedily raised toward starting my paper.[16]

THE NORTHERN PRESS AND THE SLAVERY ISSUE

The important standard papers of the day picked up the slavery issue presented to them by the black editors, the abolitionists, and the fire-eaters. By 1852 Horace Greeley's weekly *Tribune* had a circulation of more than 200,000, much of it in the crucial West. Greeley's critics charge that he ignored Negro slavery until he was jolted from his complacency by the abolitionists. It is more likely that the editor understood that those who put slavery on a moral plane did not interpret the fundamental issue correctly. Greeley was opposed to all forms of slavery, including industrial exploitation of the defenseless, or what the South's William Grayson referred to as "northern slavery." But an editorial of November 7, 1842, refutes the critics who challenge Greeley's attitude on the South. His weekly editions of April 8 and 22, 1843, describe in detail plans for the freeing of slaves by public indemnity. A letter from a contributor in the latter edition applauds the editor for his stand. The fact is, Greeley was openly and strongly opposed to the slavery institution from the beginning of his editorship.

By 1850, the *Tribune* was the acknowledged leader of the standard dailies opposed to slavery. Greeley felt so strongly on the subject that he was willing

[16] Frederick Douglass, *My Bondage and My Freedom* (New York: Miller, Orton & Mulligan, 1885), pp. 389–90.

to cast off the lifetime allegiances of the Whig to help organize a new party originally called to stop the extension of slavery in new territories and states. Lincoln, still an obscure politician at the time, read the *Tribune* regularly, and was an admirer of "Uncle Horace." Greeley attended the convention of the new Republican party at Chicago in 1860 as the special delegate of Oregon, just admitted to the Union. There appears to be little doubt that he was influential in winning the nomination for Lincoln. Greeley's old partner, Seward, was the favored candidate. The *Tribune* editor had broken with Seward and Weed over the free soil issue, in the dying days of the Whig party, and in Chicago Greeley let it be known he preferred "any candidate but Seward."

On January 20, 1861, Greeley published the first of his "stand firm" editorials—accepted by readers, at least, as Lincoln's own commandments. In February he called for unity against the South by a slogan in large type at the head of the editorial column: "NO COMPROMISE/ NO CONCESSIONS TO TRAITORS/ THE CONSTITUTION AS IT IS." When the first shot of the war was fired April 12, 1861, Greeley wrote: "Sumter is temporarily lost, but Freedom is saved! It is hard to lose Sumter, but in losing it we have gained a united people. Long live the Republic." He asked for patience when critics, including Raymond, offered unreasonable suggestions, but by summer, he, too, was demanding action. On June 26 appeared the memorable editorial: "The Nation's War Cry: 'Forward to Richmond! The Rebel Congress must not be allowed to meet there on July 20. By that date the place must be held by the National Army.'" This was repeated in subsequent issues. After all this pressure, Greeley had a heavy conscience, following the horrible defeat of the Union Army at the first battle of Bull Run. It did not matter that Lincoln's cabinet had independently agreed on the advance; that General Winfield Scott was fully aware that his army was unfit for battle; or even that Greeley had nothing to do with the "Richmond" series of editorials.[17] Since everything in the *Tribune* was believed by most of its readers to be the work of Greeley, the editor had to bear the burden of public scorn. He suffered a serious collapse that kept him in bed for days.

All this time the "reasonableness" of Henry Raymond's *New York Times* had made the paper and its editor important journalistically and politically. When Greeley broke with Seward and Weed, Raymond largely succeeded as the mouthpiece of the old group. When the Whigs foundered on the free soil issue, Raymond threw in his lot with the new Republican party. He wrote the statement of principles at the Pittsburgh convention in 1856. It is noteworthy that he was lukewarm on abolitionism, however, until after Sumter. An early critic of Lincoln (possibly because his rival, Greeley, had helped nominate the

[17] The actual author of the editorials was Fitz-Henry Warren, the Washington correspondent for the paper. Greeley was not even around the *Tribune* while the articles were being printed. He had left his managing editor, Charles A. Dana, in full control of the paper while he made a speaking trip through the West. It was Dana who pounded out the war cry every day for a week. But because of his close identity with the *Tribune,* Greeley took the blame.

rail-splitter) Raymond quickly adjusted to circumstance, as usual. Once the fighting began, Raymond was a staunch defender of the President.

Samuel Bowles III, who took over the *Springfield Republican* in 1851 after the death of his father, was faithful to the obsolete Whig party up to the eve of its death. He attacked the abolitionists at every opportunity, on the presumption that they were more interested in causing trouble than in solving problems. His concern over the growing quarrel between the two sections was shown in his approval of the Fugitive Slave law. He did not approve of slavery certainly, but neither did he approve of the agitation over it that might wreck the nation. His conversion came after passage of the Kansas-Nebraska bill in 1854, which junked the old compromises and once more opened up the question of slavery in the West.

By the end of 1854 Bowles had repudiated the wishy-washy Whig leadership. He urged a new party, "able to win the great contest to be fought in '56 with the slave power of the country." Bowles tried to fuse various splinter groups together for this purpose, but he was confused by the apparently hopeless differences that had split the old Whigs. He exposed the so-called Know-Nothing, or Native American, party for the fraud that it was.[18] He believed that the Free Soilers, another alternative, lacked leadership. And so Bowles turned to the new party for rescue. The *Republican* was one of the first important newspapers to endorse the Republican party.

The *Republican* denounced the execution of John Brown, following the raid on the federal arsenal at Harper's Ferry. "John Brown still lives," the editorial of December 17, 1859, insisted. For Samuel Bowles saw that the disreputable fanatic symbolized a principle that could not be drowned by the logical reasoning of the politicians. Bowles supported Lincoln on most issues. He preferred less drastic measures for freeing the slaves than proposed by the President, mild as they appear to be today, and he offered some criticism of the wartime threats to civil liberties. But the paper supported the President's postwar program, and continued to support President Johnson's sorry efforts to carry them out.

The *New York Herald,* on the other hand, was mostly opposed to the abolitionist movement. It endorsed the Kansas-Nebraska Act, which the South looked upon as a victory for slavery. Bennett wrote on February 28, 1854: ". . . for twenty odd years, through good and evil report, the *New York Herald* has been the only Northern journal that has unfailingly vindicated the constitutional rights of the South." Naturally, the *Herald* was popular with southern leaders, who quoted it often. The *Herald* was the most popular American newspaper in Great Britain, and because the British were inclined to favor the South, through the close relationship of their textile industry and the cotton growers, it was widely reprinted. As a result, many British readers had a very false notion of the temper of the North on the eve of the war. Bennett gave

[18] And violated the confidence of a friend at the party convention in doing so.

grudging support to Lincoln, once the fighting began, but continued an annoyance.

The *New York Evening Post* under the guiding hand of William Cullen Bryant and his trusted assistants continued to offer the same enlightened editorial leadership to its readers as it had during the era in which the common man was emerging as a more important force. Bryant was especially eloquent in espousing freedom of the press when he believed it was being threatened during the persecution of abolitionist editors. It was Bryant who first put the more responsible elements of the standard press on the side of such men as James G. Birney, whose paper, the *Philanthropist,* was wrecked by anti-abolitionists at Cincinnati. Birney had asked if freedom of the press were possible when slavery had to be protected from its critics. If freedom of expression were to be repudiated permanently by such measures as the southern gag laws, could democracy continue to exist? he asked. Bryant picked up these arguments and made them respectable. The *Post* under Bryant became one of the most effective spokesmen for freedom in all its forms. When the Republican party was organized from the remnants of splinter groups who upheld such freedoms, Bryant offered reasonable leadership to men of good will.

In the West, Joseph Medill's *Chicago Tribune* was a thunderer against slavery. Founded in 1847, the paper made rapid progress after Medill and five partners took it over in 1855. Medill was one of the western leaders of the Republican party and was said to have suggested the name of the new political organization. The *Tribune* was an early supporter of Lincoln. Medill was largely responsible for the Lincoln boom. He enthusiastically followed the future president, reporting the speeches that are now history. Usually Medill followed his reports with a lively editorial on the subject. Lincoln often came to the *Tribune* office for conferences with the West's leading spokesman. Medill's intimacy with Lincoln is indicated by the crude familiarity with which he conversed with the rising politician. "Dammit, Abe, git yore feet off my desk," Medill is said to have told the lanky backwoodsman on one occasion.

By 1860, the newspaper press of the United States was highly developed. The typical daily was likely to be drab, by modern standards, but the makeup and readability had improved since the advent of the first penny papers. The standard paper was six columns wide. Eight pages usually sufficed, although Raymond's *Times* often ran to ten pages. There were few pictures or graphic illustrations. Many of the penny papers actually sold for twice that by the end of the period, and the *Times* was up to three. Headlines were mostly confined by the column rules to one-column labels, and the great development in display headlines was still waiting on the war. Advertising was increasing steadily. Three of the eight pages of the conservative-looking weekly edition of the *Springfield Republican* usually were devoted to classified notices, and this was common throughout the country.

As a whole, the press was strong and prosperous. It was well that the publishing industry was so healthy, for it was about to be tested as it never had been before. The test began on the day Edmund Ruffin sent the first shot of the Civil War toward Fort Sumter, April 12, 1861.

Annotated Bibliography

Books

Many of the references cited at the end of Chapter 11 will be found to be useful in a study of the period covered by this chapter, including the biographies of Greeley, Raymond, Bennett, and Weed, and the histories of the *New York Times* and *Springfield Republican.*

Cole, Arthur Charles, *The Irrepressible Conflict,* A History of American Life, Vol. VII. New York: Macmillan, 1934.

Craven, Avery, *The Repressible Conflict.* Baton Rouge: Louisiana State University Press, 1939.

Both of these books present the debatable issues leading up to the war in a frame of reference still being investigated by historians.

Dann, Martin E., ed., *The Black Press: 1827–1890.* New York: Putnam's, 1971. A collection of articles from black newspapers with theme of quest for national identity.

Detweiler, Frederick G., *The Negro Press in the United States.* Chicago: University of Chicago Press, 1922. Quotes extensively from the papers.

Dillon, Merton L., *Elijah P. Lovejoy, Abolitionist Editor.* Urbana: University of Illinois Press, 1961. Used primary sources.

Douglass, Frederick, *My Bondage and My Freedom.* Chicago: Johnson Publishing Company, 1970. Second of three autobiographical chronicles, originally published in 1855. Others: *Narrative of the Life of Frederick Douglass* (1845), *Life and Times of Frederick Douglass* (1878). Douglass lived from 1817 to 1895 as a slave, freeman, politician, reformer, editor, and orator.

———, *Narrative of the Life of Frederick Douglass.* Cambridge, Mass.: Harvard University Press, 1960. New York: New American Library, 1968.

Foner, Philip S., *Frederick Douglass.* New York: Citadel Press, 1963. By the author of the outstanding four-volume *Life and Writings of Frederick Douglass.*

Garrison, Wendell Phillips, and Francis J., *William Lloyd Garrison.* 4 vols. New York: Appleton-Century-Crofts, 1885–89. The life story of the famous abolitionist, told by his children.

Garrison, William Lloyd, *Selections.* Boston: R. F. Wallcut, 1852. Excerpts from speeches and writings of the famous abolitionist.

———, *The Spirit of the South Towards Northern Freemen, etc.* Boston: R. F. Wallcut, 1861. Extracts from southern newspapers and speeches bringing out the slavery issue as attacked by Garrison.

Genovese, Eugene D., *The Political Economy of Slavery.* New York: Pantheon, 1965. A New Left historian uses the comparative approach.

Gill, John, *Tide without Turning: Elijah P. Lovejoy and Freedom of the Press.* Boston: Beacon Press, 1958. A well-documented biography of the martyred abolitionist.

Isely, Jeter Allen, *Horace Greeley and the Republican Party, 1853–1861.* Princeton: Princeton University Press, 1947. Analysis of Greeley's writings in the *Tribune* about slavery.

Nevins, Allan, *The Evening Post: A Century of Journalism.* New York: Boni and Liveright, 1922. See especially chapters 4, 5, 6, and 7.

———, *Ordeal of the Union* (2 vols., 1847–57), *The Emergence of Lincoln* (2 vols., 1857–61), *The War for the Union* (4 vols., 1861–65). New York: Scribner's, 1947–71. The culminating work of a famous American historian.

Nye, Russel B., *Fettered Freedom: Civil Liberties and the Slavery Controversy, 1830–1860.* East Lansing: Michigan State College Press, 1963. How the abolitionists finally won popular support.

Parrington, Vernon L., *Main Currents in American Thought,* Vol. II. New York: Harcourt, Brace & Jovanovich, 1927. The sections on Garrison and Rhett are particularly revealing.

Penn, I. Garland, *The Afro-American Press and Its Editors.* Springfield, Mass.: Wiley Company, 1891. The source book for nineteenth-century black press history.

Quarles, Benjamin, ed., *Frederick Douglass.* Englewood Cliffs, N.J.: Prentice-Hall, 1968. Negro editor presented in own and peers' words.

Snyder, Louis L., and Richard B. Morris, eds., *A Treasury of Great Reporting.* New York: Simon & Schuster, 1962. Outstanding newspaper articles of the period.

Thomas, John L., *The Liberator: William Lloyd Garrison, a Biography.* Boston: Little, Brown, 1963. Excellent biography, but focuses on political activities rather than journalistic.

White, Laura A., *Robert Barnwell Rhett.* New York: Appleton-Century-Crofts, 1931. Describes the southern "fire-eater" and his part in the slavery issue.

Wolseley, Roland E., *The Black Press, U.S.A.* Ames: Iowa State University Press, 1971. Chapter 2 of this comprehensive study deals with nineteenth-century black papers.

Periodicals and Monographs

Bryan, Carter R., "Negro Journalism in America Before Emancipation," *Journalism Monographs,* No. 12 (September 1969). Careful study of early black press.

Cullen, Maurice R., Jr., "William Gilmore Simms, Southern Journalist," *Journalism Quarterly,* XXXVIII (Summer 1961), 298. A South Carolina editor first opposes secession, then defies the invading Union army.

Eaton, Clement, "The Freedom of the Press in the Upper South," *Mississippi Valley Historical Review,* XVIII (March 1932), 479. A study of the muzzling of press freedom prior to the Civil War.

Kennedy, Fronde, "Russell's Magazine," *South Atlantic Quarterly,* XVIII (April

1919), 125. Analysis of the periodical published at Charleston, which argued the pro-slavery viewpoint.

Martin, Asa Earl, "Pioneer Anti-Slavery Press," *Mississippi Valley Historical Review,* II (March 1916), 509. Describes the *Philanthropist,* an early abolitionist paper, and discusses other such publications of the early period.

Nye, Russel B., "Freedom of the Press and the Antislavery Controversy," *Journalism Quarterly,* XXII (March 1945), 1. Discusses one of the main considerations of this chapter.

Pride, Armistead S., "A Register and History of Negro Newspapers in the United States," Ph.D. thesis, Northwestern University, 1950. Most scholarly effort to identify black newspapers.

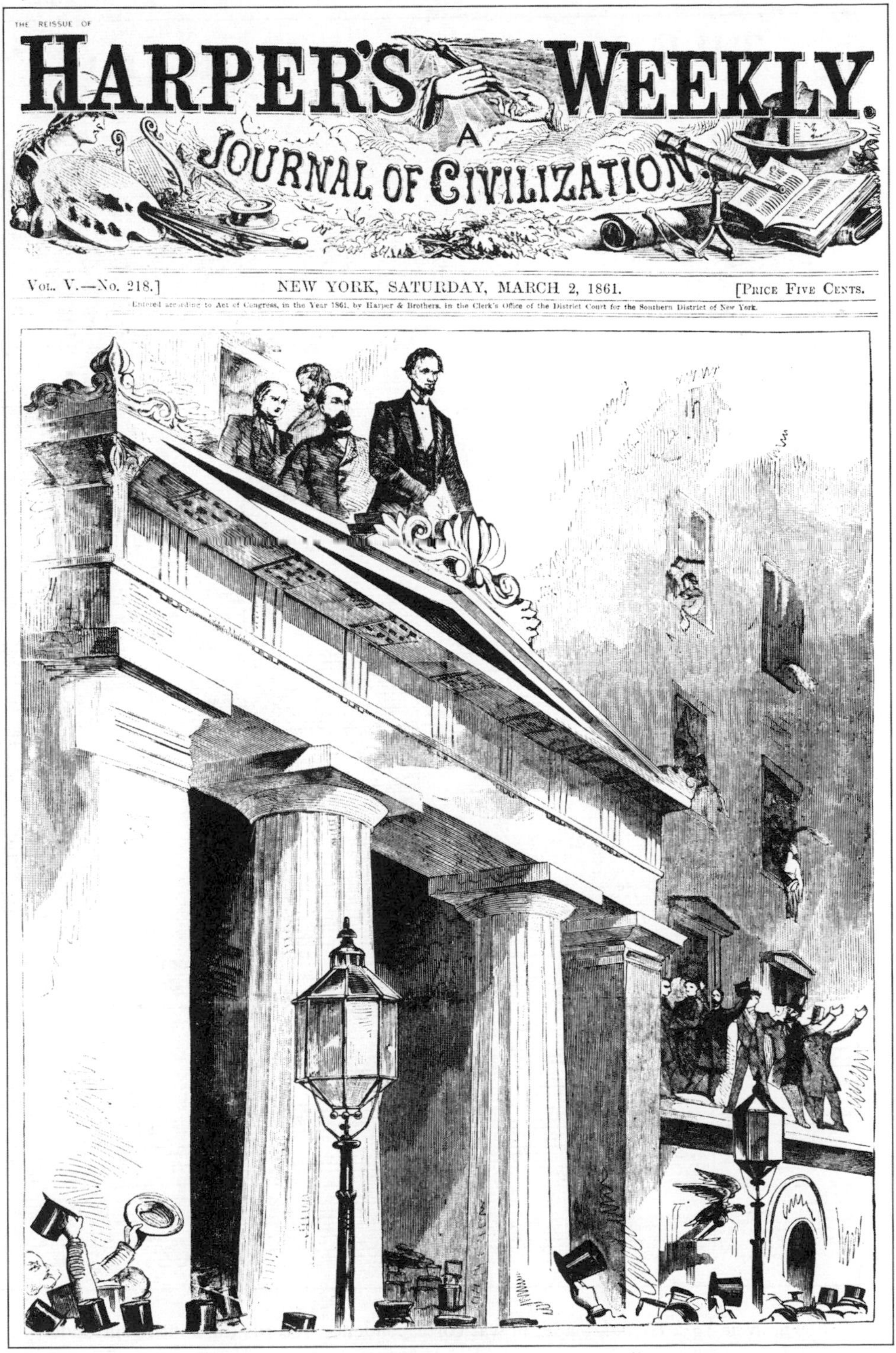

THE REISSUE OF

HARPER'S WEEKLY.

A JOURNAL OF CIVILIZATION.

Vol. V.—No. 218.] NEW YORK, SATURDAY, MARCH 2, 1861. [Price Five Cents.

Entered according to Act of Congress, in the Year 1861, by Harper & Brothers, in the Clerk's Office of the District Court for the Southern District of New York.

From *Harper's Weekly* (1861)

THE NEW YORK HERALD.

WHOLE NO. 10,451. NEW YORK, MONDAY, APRIL 10, 1865. PRICE FOUR CENTS.

THE END

SURRENDER OF LEE AND HIS WHOLE ARMY TO GRANT.

TERMS OF SURRENDER.

All Honor to Grant, Meade, Sheridan, Ord, Humphreys, Wright, Griffin, Parke, and their Brave Troops.

Highly Interesting Details of the Fighting Before the Surrender.

Ord Makes a Forced March of Thirty Miles a Day South of Lee's Line of Retreat.

Our Main Columns Follow Closely in the Enemy's Rear.

The Woods Filled with Rebel Stragglers and the Roads Strewn with Cannon, Caissons, Wagons, Ambulances, Muskets, Sabres, Knapsacks and Cartridge Boxes.

Announcement of the Capture of Richmond to the Troops.

INTENSE ENTHUSIASM.

Our Men Clamor to be Led Forward.

Stoneman, with a Force of Union Cavalry, Reported Destroying the Railroad Between Danville and Greensboro.

JEFF. DAVIS AT DANVILLE, &c., &c., &c.

THE SURRENDER.

Secretary Stanton to General Dix.

WAR DEPARTMENT, WASHINGTON, April 9—9 o'clock P. M.

To Major General DIX, New York:—

This department has received the official report of the surrender, this day, of General Lee and his army to Lieutenant General Grant on *the terms proposed by General Grant.*

EDWIN M. STANTON, Secretary of War.

General Grant to Secretary Stanton.

HEADQUARTERS, ARMIES OF THE UNITED STATES, April 9—4:30 P. M.

Hon. EDWIN M. STANTON, Secretary of War:—

General Lee surrendered the Army of Northern Virginia this afternoon, *upon the terms proposed by myself.* The accompanying additional correspondence will show the conditions fully.

U. S. GRANT, Lieutenant General.

The Preliminary Correspondence.

CLIFTON HOUSE, Va., April 9, 1865.

Hon. EDWIN M. STANTON, Secretary of War:—

The following correspondence has taken place between General Lee and myself. *There has been no relaxation in the pursuit during its pendency.*

U. S. GRANT, Lieutenant General.

GENERAL GRANT TO GENERAL LEE.

APRIL 7, 1865.

General R. E. LEE, Commanding Confederate States Army:—

GENERAL—The result of the last week must convince you of the hopelessness of further resistance on the part of the Army of Northern Virginia in this struggle. I feel that it is so, and regard it as my duty to shift from myself the responsibility of any further effusion of blood, by asking of you the surrender of that portion of the [illegible] known as the Army of [illegible]

[illegible] obedient servant,

U. S. GRANT, [illegible] General, Commanding Armies of the [United] States.

GENERAL LEE TO GENERAL GRANT.

APRIL 7, 1865.

GENERAL—I have received your note of this date.

Though not entirely of the opinion you express of the hopelessness of further resistance on the part of the Army of Northern Virginia, I reciprocate your desire to avoid useless effusion of blood, and therefore, before considering your proposition, ask the terms you will offer on condition of its surrender.

R. E. LEE, General.

To Lieutenant General U. S. GRANT, Commanding Armies of the United States.

GENERAL GRANT TO GENERAL LEE.

APRIL 8, 1865.

To General R. E. LEE, Commanding Confederate States Army:—

GENERAL—Your note of last evening, in reply to mine of same date, asking the conditions on which I will accept the surrender of the Army of Northern Virginia is just received.

In reply, I would say that, peace being my first desire, there is but one condition that I insist upon, viz:—

That the men surrendered shall be disqualified for taking up arms again against the government of the United States until properly exchanged.

I will meet you or designate officers to meet any officers you may name for the same purpose at any point agreeable to you, for the purpose of arranging definitely the terms upon which the surrender of the army of Northern Virginia will received.

Very respectfully, your obedient servant,

U. S. GRANT, Lieutenant General, Commanding Armies of the United States.

GENERAL LEE TO GENERAL GRANT.

APRIL 8, 1865.

GENERAL—I received at a late hour your note of to-day in answer to mine of yesterday.

I did not intend to propose the surrender of the Army of Northern Virginia, but to ask the terms of your proposition. To be frank, I do not think the emergency has arisen to call for the surrender.

But as the restoration of peace should be the sole object of all, I desire to know whether your proposals would tend to that end.

I cannot, therefore, meet you with a view to surrender the army of Northern Virginia; but as far as your proposition may affect the Confederate States forces under my command and tend to the restoration of peace, I should be pleased to meet you at ten A. M. to-morrow, on the old stage road to Richmond, between the picket lines of the two armies.

Very respectfully, your obedient servant,

R. E. LEE, General C. S. A.

To Lieutenant General GRANT, Commanding Armies of the United States.

GENERAL GRANT TO GENERAL LEE.

APRIL 9, 1865.

General R. E. LEE, Commanding Confederate States Army:—

GENERAL—Your note of yesterday is received. As I have no authority to treat on the subject of peace, the meeting proposed for ten A. M., to-day, could lead to no good. I will state, however, General, that I am equally anxious for peace with yourself; and the whole North entertain the same feeling. The terms upon which peace can be had are well understood. By the South laying down their arms they will hasten that most desirable event, save thousands of human lives and hundreds of millions of property not yet destroyed.

Sincerely hoping that all our difficulties may be settled without the loss of another life, I subscribe myself,

Very respectfully, your obedient servant,

U. S. GRANT, Lieutenant General, U. S. A.

THE TERMS.

GENERAL LEE TO GENERAL GRANT.

APRIL 9, 1865.

GENERAL—I received your note of this morning on the picket line, whither I had come to meet you and ascertain definitely what terms were embraced in your proposition of yesterday with reference to the surrender of this army.

I now request an interview in accordance with the offer contained in your letter of yesterday for that purpose.

Very respectfully, your obedient servant,

R. E. LEE, General.

To Lieutenant General GRANT, commanding United States Armies.

GENERAL GRANT TO GENERAL LEE.

APRIL 9, 1865.

General R. E. LEE, Commanding Confederate States Armies:—

Your note of this date is but this moment (fifty minutes past eleven A. M.) received.

In consequence of my having passed from the Richmond and Lynchburg road to the Farmville and Lynchburg road, I am, at this writing, about four miles west of Walter's Church, and will push forward to the front for the purpose of meeting you.

Notice sent to me on this road where you wish the interview to take place will meet me.

Very respectfully, your obedient servant,

U. S. GRANT, Lieutenant General.

GENERAL GRANT TO GENERAL LEE.

APPOMATTOX COURT HOUSE, April 9, 1865.

General R. E. LEE, Commanding Confederate States Army:—

In accordance with the substance of my letter to you of the 8th instant, I propose to receive the surrender of the Army of Northern Virginia on the following terms, to wit:—

Rolls of all the officers and men to be made in duplicate; one copy to be given to an officer designated by me, the other to be retained by such officers as you may designate.

The officers to give their individual paroles not to take arms against the government of the United States until properly exchanged, and each company or regimental commander sign a like parole for the men of his command.

The arms, artillery and public property to be parked and stacked and turned over to the officers appointed by me to receive them.

This will not embrace the side arms of the officers, nor their private horses or baggage.

This done, each officer and man will be allowed to return to their homes, not to be disturbed by United States authority so long as they observe their parole and the laws in force where they may reside.

Very respectfully,

U. S. GRANT, Lieutenant General.

GENERAL LEE TO GENERAL GRANT.

HEADQUARTERS, ARMY OF NORTHERN VIRGINIA, April 9, 1865.

Lieutenant General U. S. GRANT, Commanding United States Armies:—

GENERAL—I have received your letter of this date, containing the terms of surrender of the Army of Northern Virginia as proposed by you. As they are substantially the same as those expressed in your letter of the 8th inst., they are accepted. I will proceed to designate the proper officers to carry the stipulations into effect.

Very respectfully, your obedient servant,

R. E. LEE, General.

THANKS TO GRANT AND HIS ARMY.

WAR DEPARTMENT, WASHINGTON, D. C., April 9—9:30 P. M.

Lieutenant General GRANT:—

Thanks be to Almighty God for the great victory with which he has this day crowned you and the gallant armies under your command.

The thanks of this Department, and of the government, and of the people of the United States—their reverence and honor have been deserved—will be rendered to you and the brave and gallant officers and soldiers of your army for all time.

EDWIN M. STANTON, Secretary of War.

NATIONAL SALUTE.

WAR DEPARTMENT, WASHINGTON, D. C., April 9—10 P. M.

Ordered:—That a salute of two hundred guns be fired at the headquarters of every army and department, and at every post and arsenal in the United States, and at the Military Academy at West Point, on the day of the receipt of this order, in commemoration of the surrender of General R. E. Lee and the Army of Northern Virginia to Lieutenant General Grant and the army under his command; report of the receipt and execution of this order to be made to the Adjutant General, Washington.

EDWIN M. STANTON, Secretary of War.

THE PREVIOUS FIGHTING.

CITY POINT.

Mr. J. R. Trembly's Despatch.

CITY POINT, April 8—8 A. M.

THE LATEST FROM THE FRONT.

I have just arrived from General Grant's camp at Burkesville. As I left yesterday morning heavy firing of artillery was heard in the direction of High Bridge or Farmville, some fifteen miles north of Burkesville, and a little above the scene of the important captures of Friday evening. It was kept up vigorously for an hour, when it slackened off to a scattering fire, which was kept up with more or less frequency of reports until after twelve o'clock, when I passed out of hearing distance.

SUPPLIES GOING FORWARD.

Supplies were taken by rail yesterday as far as Sutherland station, ten miles from Petersburg. The different corps trains were all taking on loads last evening, and will reach the army to-morrow.

THE RAILROAD BEING RAPIDLY RECONSTRUCTED.

A large force is pushing the work on the track, and expect to reach Wellville to-day and Burkesville in two days more. A slight change of the gauge required retards the work; but all is going on finely, and everybody is happy.

THE PURSUIT.

Mr. S. Cadwallader's Despatches.

NEAR BLACK AND WHITES, April 5—10 A. M.

THE CORPS MOVEMENTS IN THE PURSUIT.

The Twenty-fourth corps encamped near Wilson's station last night, and moved this far this morning along the line of railroad to Burkesville Junction. Generals Grant and Ord are with this column. The Fifth corps and cavalry pushed on to Jettersville, on the Richmond and Danville Railroad, about ten miles north of Burkesville Junction, and arrived there without any fighting till last night. The Second, Sixth and Ninth corps are following closely in their rear on the roads between this and the Appomattox, and are already within supporting distance of Sheridan's advance. By to-night the latter corps will all undoubtedly be on the Danville road, and the Twenty-fourth corps very near, if not quite, to the junction.

LEE'S APPARENT FORCE.

Sheridan reports Lee to apparently not have more than twenty thousand men, and these nothing more than a disordered, disorganized mob. It is, probably, being daily swelled in numerical force by the arrival of stragglers and small organized detachments, but its morale will scarcely be improved by these, and no successful opposition can be offered us at any point for days or weeks.

PROSPECTS OF SPEEDILY FINISHING LEE AND JOHNSTON.

If our plans work as proposed Lee will be irretrievably separated from Johnston, and the two rebel armies speedily driven out of Virginia and North Carolina. By supreme efforts they may escape to the interior with armies the size of respectable body guards, and thence make their way westward to the Mississippi and Texas during the present season and cross into Mexico for an asylum. [illegible] may be considered a maxim in war that a retreating army can outmarch a pursuing one. This favors their escape. Lee's and Johnston's armies must henceforth be the objective points of ours and Sherman's operations. Where they retreat we must follow.

LEE'S PROBABLE EFFORTS TO JOIN JOHNSTON.

Lee will attempt to pass down towards Danville, through Scottsville, Cumberland Court House and Farmville, on the [illegible] road. The railroad trains loaded with subsistence for the rebel troops at Petersburg were ordered to the latter place when Petersburg was taken, and are reported to be there yet, awaiting the expected arrival of Lee's army. Jeff. Davis and Cabinet remained in Richmond until three o'clock A. M. on [illegible]

[illegible]

THE SECOND CORPS.

Mr. Wm. J. Starks' Despatch.

[illegible]

THE FIFTH CORPS.

Mr. L. A. Hendrick's Despatches.

[illegible]

(CONTINUED ON EIGHTH PAGE.)

The *New York Herald,* leader in war correspondence, records the South's surrender.

14

The Irrepressible Conflict

Come with a sword or musket in your hand, prepared to share with us our fate in sunshine and storm . . . and I will welcome you as a brother and associate; but come as you now do, expecting me to ally the reputation and honor of my country and my fellow soldiers with you, as the representative of the press, which you yourself say makes so slight a difference between truth and falsehood, and my answer is, NEVER.
—General Sherman to Knox, of the *Herald*

The War Between the States affected all aspects of journalism. Reporting, editing, circulation, printing, advertising, and illustration were all modified during the conflict. Relations between press and government also changed during this period. One of the serious problems of the war was how to keep the public properly informed without giving aid and comfort to the enemy. This was the world's first modern rehearsal of mass warfare—involving both armies and civilians. It was one of the costliest wars in terms of men and money ever fought up to that period. And because large elements of the populations opposed the bloody strife on both sides of the lines, there was continuous and outspoken criticism of both administrations. The most usual medium for this expression was the newspaper.

In contrast with World Wars I and II, reporters in the War Between the States were much more irresponsible. But it should be pointed out that the communications lessons of 1861–1865 were of invaluable assistance in working out later policies. For experience has shown that when a country with a free press tradition mobilizes, leaders must adjust themselves to a dilemma.

WAR RESTRICTS FREEDOM

War calls for strict discipline in the armed forces and drastic reorganization of civilian living. In both cases, peacetime liberties must be relinquished for the duration. But the American theory of free discussion assumes that it is good for the public to have an idea of what sacrifices to expect. The American believes he also retains the right of knowing how efficiently his leaders and representatives are working. But if the press maintains its right to criticise leaders and programs, does not that right jeopardize national security by creating confusion? On the other hand, if the press surrenders its peacetime rights, is there not danger that leaders will conceal their failures and attempts to hold power unjustifiably? The problem in wartime is to preserve this nice balance between national security and the right of the public to know.

The Civil War serves as a case history of this problem, which was aggravated by several factors never before considered in this country. One was the power that the press had won in the previous 20 years. Another was the development of new communications systems, including the railway post and the telegraph, capable of spreading dangerous information to distant areas in a relatively short time. Lastly, the military authorities in both the North and the South did not understand the true function of censorship. It took time to learn that unless some news service is provided by the government, means will always be found to get around censors.

It is also noteworthy that the war aroused hate and bigotry to a pitch that the country had never known before. That is a common phenomenon when countrymen fight each other. The attitudes during and after the war are in contrast to the tolerance and free inquiry that had amazed foreign observers before the war. Up to 1861 there was a willingness in America to experiment with new ideas promising a more abundant life for the ordinary citizen. The various utopian plans; the rise of aggressive religious and literary liberal movements as exemplified by the Unitarians and the Transcendentalists; the encouraging agitation for women's rights, temperance, public education, free soil, and universal suffrage—all these were manifestations of free inquiry reflected in the press of the second quarter of the nineteenth century. Most of these enthusiasms were early casualties of the war. By 1861, the idealistic resources of the nation were temporarily bankrupt. Journalism reflects this trend. For example, there was Charles A. Dana, once a power in the utopian movement, an avowed socialist after his newspaper experiences in the European revolutions of 1848, and one of Horace Greeley's most trusted lieutenants. But by 1870 Dana, as reflected in his editorials in the *New York Sun*, was a disillusioned and vindictive misanthrope—a man who knew the price of everything and the value of nothing. That is what war can do to a strong man.

GREELEY, RAYMOND, AND BENNETT IN WAR

A few voices still answered the roll call of the once-great legion of progress. Greeley did not change but he, too, was overwhelmed by the war. He lived to see all his illusions shattered on the rock of postwar public cynicism, but at least he stuck to his principles. His regard for mankind made Greeley abhor war. At one time he favored letting the South secede peacefully. But once the shooting began, Greeley concluded that the most humane course for the Unionists was to end the war quickly.

Lincoln liked the atmosphere of newspaper offices. He had made the *Sringfield Journal* in Illinois virtually the official voice of his party previous to the inauguration. The President met reporters easily and corresponded with some of them. Of all journalists, Greeley was his greatest concern. Lincoln was sometimes exasperated by the editor's temperamental outbursts, but he respected the man. By the close of 1861 the *Tribune* was engaged in a campaign to free slaves in conquered areas. The President had already discussed the issue with his cabinet, and he had definite plans for accomplishing emancipation. The climax of the *Tribune* crusade was Greeley's famous "Prayer of Twenty Millions" editorial of August 20, 1862, which was a call for action on the slavery issue. Lincoln replied by a personal letter to Greeley, which he also gave to the *National Intelligencer* for publication on August 23. The letter included the paragraph now so familiar to students of the period:

> My paramount object in this struggle *is* to save the Union, and is *not* either to save or destroy Slavery. If I could save the Union without freeing *any* slave, I would do it; and if I could save it by freeing *all* the slaves, I would do it; and if I could do it by freeing some and leaving others alone, I would also do that.

Greeley wrote another open letter to the President urging more concern with the issue. When Lincoln announced his preliminary Emancipation Proclamation a month later, to be effective January 1, 1863, many readers of the *Tribune* assumed that "Uncle Horace" had done it again. "It is the beginning of the new life of the nation," Greeley exulted in his September 23 issue. The President and his cabinet had worked out the details without any help from the editor, but surely a man so sensitive to public feelings as Lincoln must have been aware of the popular pressure.

By the time of the election of 1864, Lincoln and Greeley appear to have tired of each other. The war was increasingly unpopular in many sections. Greeley's criticism of the administration for failing to find some means of achieving a just peace had strained Lincoln's good nature. On the other hand, the editor had lost face by his unsuccessful attempts to work with southern peace factions. He tended to take out his frustration on the Chief Executive. "You complain of me—what have I done, or omitted to do, that has provoked the hostility of the *Tribune*?" asked the weary President.[1]

But eventually Greeley swung around behind his old friend again. Of the 17 New York daily newspapers, only five were solid supporters of the administration. They were the *Tribune, Times, Evening Post, Sun,* and *Commercial Advertiser.* Greeley did not hesitate to take unpopular stands, when wartime passions made such outspokenness highly dangerous. When Greeley supported the President in his call for more troops under the draft, the *Tribune* was stoned. That was in 1863. Next year another mob threatened bodily harm to the editor after his vain attempt to work out a peace agreement with unofficial representatives of the Confederacy. When Greeley went to Richmond in 1867 to serve as cosigner of Jefferson Davis' bail bond, there was some doubt as to whether the *Tribune* could survive the storm of public resentment, for by that time, the once-maligned Lincoln was "the martyred President," and Davis, the Confederate chief, was the focus of northern hate. These pressures had little effect upon Greeley. The founder of the *Tribune* had many weaknesses, but cowardice was not one of them.

War was the golden age for Henry J. Raymond, who had made the *New York Times* one of the outstanding dailies of its time. The paper offered reasonable, penetrating, and thorough reportage. The feeling for objectivity on the part of *Times* writers is indicated by the four open letters Raymond wrote to Yancey, the southern fire-eater. They were able and dispassionate antisecession arguments that showed an understanding of the southern viewpoint. On occasion the *Times* was highly critical of the administration. Raymond's enemies said he was jealous of the part Greeley had played in the selection of Lincoln over Seward at the Chicago convention. But on essential issues, the *Times* gave the President strong support.

Raymond was drafted after the war began, but he bought a substitute to take his place, which was a common procedure. This is no reflection upon his courage, for he was under fire as a correspondent for his paper at the first battle of Bull Run, and he acquitted himself well. He was an expert correspondent and writer, and his partner, George Jones, had wisely gotten him to confine his energy to journalism rather than politics. The temptation was too great, however. By the time the war was well under way, Raymond was devoting less time to his paper and more to politics. By 1863, he was chairman of the Republican National Committee, one of the key political positions in the nation. He managed the 1864 campaign, wrote the party platform, and was elected to the House of Representatives.

When Congress convened in 1865, Raymond seemed to be its most important member. It was assumed that he represented the administration and the party. That gave him great power in the councils of the House. He was so

[1] For relations of Lincoln and the press see James E. Pollard, *The Presidents and the Press* (New York: Macmillan, 1947), pp. 312–97.

HARPER'S WEEKLY.
A JOURNAL OF CIVILIZATION.

VOL. XIII.—No. 653.] NEW YORK, SATURDAY, JULY 3, 1869. [SINGLE COPIES, TEN CENTS. $4.00 PER YEAR IN ADVANCE.

HENRY J. RAYMOND.

ON Friday, June 18, we were startled by the sad intelligence of the death of HENRY JARVIS RAYMOND, the founder and editor of the New York *Times*. He had died suddenly that morning of apoplexy. Thus passed away in the prime of life—for he was only in his fiftieth year—one of the four most eminent journalists in this country, and also one of the most prominent politicians of this State.

HENRY JARVIS RAYMOND was born in the village of Lima, Livingston County, New York, January 24, 1820. His father, who died only a few months since, was a hard-working farmer of moderate means and of sound integrity. His mother—a woman of strong character—encouraged his early tendencies toward a life of study. After a short period of education in the district school during the winters of his boyhood years, he continued his studies at the village academy, and in 1833 commenced Latin and Algebra at the Genesee Wesleyan Seminary. He entered the University of Vermont in the summer of 1836, and there was graduated in 1840 with the highest honors of his class.

The youth of twenty then came to New York city, where he entered upon the study of law in the office of Mr. E. W. MARSH. But he had his living to earn, and the only prominent men of the city with whom he was at all acquainted were Mr. MANN, then a law-student in Wall Street, and HORACE GREELEY, then the proprietor of the *New Yorker*, a weekly newspaper, to which Mr. RAYMOND had contributed during his college course. He still wrote for that paper, and also earned $5 a week by daily news-letters to the Cincinnati *Chronicle*, then edited by E. D. MANSFIELD, since known as the "Veteran Observer." Meantime he received an offer of a school in North Carolina at $400 a year; but as Mr. GREELEY offered him the same for his services on the *New Yorker* he declined the first offer, and remained in New York.

In 1841 Mr. GREELEY established the *Tribune*, and retained Mr. RAYMOND's services as assistant editor. In this position he demonstrated his ability as a journalist. No one could make so rapid or so accurate a report of a speech; and he was also equally prepared to write a leading editorial. Whatever he did he did well. His report of WEBSTER's speech at Bunker Hill was a memorable event in those days when short-hand writing was unknown.

Mr. RAYMOND accepted an editorial position on the New York *Courier and Enquirer* in 1843. It was in this paper that his part of the celebrated controversy with Mr. GREELEY on the doctrine of Fourierism was published. It was during his connection with this journal that he became a reader in the publishing-house of HARPER & BROTHERS, a position which he held for ten years.

Mr. RAYMOND's political life began in 1849, when he was elected a member of the New York State Assembly by the Whigs. He was re-elected the next year, and was chosen speaker. In 1851 he started the *Times* newspaper. In 1852 he went to the Baltimore Convention to report the proceedings for his paper, but was given a seat as a delegate, and made an eloquent speech in exposition of Northern sentiment. In 1854 he was elected Lieutenant-Governor of this State, receiving 157,166 votes, a majority of 28,333 over LUDLOW, his principal opponent. As an organizer of the Republican party Mr. RAYMOND was an active worker. The "Address to the People," which was issued from Pittsburg in 1856, was from his pen. He was a supporter of FREMONT after the meeting of the first National Convention. In 1857 he refused to be a candidate for Governor of this State. The next four years were devoted to his profession. In 1858 he sided, apparently, with the supporters of Mr. DOUGLAS, but in the end resumed his relations with the Republican party. In 1860 he was a warm supporter of Mr. SEWARD for the Republican nomination, and he was peculiarly satisfied that Mr. SEWARD was placed in the Cabinet of Mr. LINCOLN.

In 1861 Mr. RAYMOND was again elected to the Assembly and was chosen Speaker. In 1864 he was elected to the United States House of Representatives from the Sixth District of this city. His career in that body, during a critical era of our political history, will be reviewed in another column.

His speech on the 29th of January, 1866, was his first elaborate effort in Congress. It was upon the Fourteenth Constitutional Amendment. In concluding this speech Mr. RAYMOND thus expressed his views as to what the Government ought to do:

"In the first place, I think we ought to accept the present *status* of the Southern States, and regard them as having resumed, under the President's guidance and action, their functions of self-government in the Union. In the second place, I think this House should decide on the admission of Representatives by districts, admitting none but loyal men who can take the oath we may prescribe, and holding all others as disqualified; the Senate acting, at its discretion, in the same way in regard to Representatives of States. I think, in the third place, we should provide by law for giving to the freedmen of the South all the rights of citizens in courts of law and elsewhere. In the fourth place, I would exclude from Federal office the leading actors in the conspiracy which led to the rebellion in every State. In the fifth place, I would make such amendments to the Constitution as may seem wise to Congress and the States, acting freely and without coercion. And, sixth, I would take such measures and precautions, by the disposition of military forces, as will preserve order and prevent the overthrow, by usurpation or otherwise, in any State, of its republican form of government......Above all, I beg this House to bear in mind, as the sentiment that should control and guide its action, that we of the North and they of the South are at war no longer. The gigantic contest is at an end. The courage and devotion on either side which made it so terrible and so long no longer owe a divided duty, but have become the common property of the American name, the priceless possession of the American Republic through all time to come. The dead of the contending hosts sleep beneath the soil of a common country and under one common flag. Their hostilities are hushed, and they are the dead of the nation for evermore. The victor may well exult in the victory he has achieved. Let it be our task, as it will be our highest glory, to make the vanquished, and their posterity to the latest generation, rejoice in their defeat."

On the expiration of his term Mr. RAYMOND, having declined the renomination that was pressed upon him by prominent men of both parties, withdrew almost wholly from public life, and devoted all his energies to the conduct of his paper. He was offered the Mission to Austria by President JOHNSON in 1867; but his name was sent to the Senate without his consent, and after he had notified the President that no considerations could induce him to accept the position. The last article written by Mr. RAYMOND for the *Times* was an editorial on Mr. SEWARD, which appeared on the morning of June 17.

"A remarkable instance of Mr. RAYMOND's working ability," says the New York *Tribune*, in an obituary sketch, "occurred on the occasion of the death of DANIEL WEBSTER, a statesman for whom he had the greatest admiration. The news of Mr. WEBSTER's death reached here on a Saturday afternoon. Mr. RAYMOND wrote an admirable biography, which appeared in Monday's paper, covering twenty-six columns of the *Times*, and in addition he wrote three columns of editorial on the same subject. Of this extraordinary biography Mr. RAYMOND wrote sixteen columns without stopping a moment for rest. As a feat of editorial labor we doubt its ever having been equaled."

Mr. RAYMOND passed the afternoon previous to his death in Greenwood, making arrangements for the interment of his son WALTER's remains, and called at the office of the *Times* about six o'clock in the evening. After a few minutes' conversation on matters pertaining to the business of the paper he returned home. After dinner he sat with his family and some friends who came in until between nine and ten o'clock, when he left them to attend a political consultation; and his family saw no more of him until he was discovered, about half past two next morning, lying in the hall-way unconscious and apparently dying. He had locked the outside door and shut the inner one, and was then apparently stricken with the malady that closed his life. The most eminent medical aid was at once summoned, and the utmost that science and skill could do were done,

THE LATE HON. HENRY J. RAYMOND.—[PHOTOGRAPHED BY BRADY, NEW YORK.]

The death of Henry J. Raymond is covered in drawing and story by *Harper's Weekly*.

obsessed with making friends with everyone and in preserving harmony, that the more ruthless rising leaders succeeded in using him. The editor who prided himself on his reasonable approach to issues offered no objection to Thaddeus Stevens' proposal for a joint committee to handle Reconstruction problems. Raymond was a shrewd and experienced politician, and he must have seen what the fanatical Stevens was striving to achieve. This was the beginning of the policy of punishment for the South. As an administration spokesman, Raymond should have had no part in the program. One will look in vain, however, for any objections from the *Times* or its editor as the Stevens "Directorate" prepared to submit the conquered states to the ravages of "Reconstruction," a term the South will never forget.

It was at this time that Raymond received the title, "The Trimmer," by voting for the Freedman's Bureau and then supporting President Johnson's veto of it. He opposed the Civil Rights bill, but approved its substance in the Fourteenth Amendment. Raymond was failing as a politician because of his indecisiveness. He knew he was beaten when he failed to sell his platform at the Philadelphia convention of 1866. The Stevens "Radicals" were now strong enough to have him rejected from the National Committee. Under the circumstances Raymond believed it less painful to decline his renomination to Congress. In the end, he bolted the party. That was the end of him politically. "Shocking Cruelty to a Fugitive Slave," Greeley headlined the account of the episode in the *Tribune*. Later, Raymond and the *Times* returned to solid ground with the Republicans, but the paper's founder died of a cerebral hemorrhage in 1869 while waging an editorial fight against the infamous Tweed ring of political corruptionists which was looting the city treasury.

Bennett and his *Herald* caused the Lincoln administration considerable annoyance. The paper was politically independent, but it was definitely "soft" toward the South, where it had great influence. Because of its extensive news coverage, particularly of business and commerce, the *Herald* was the most popular American newspaper in Europe. The British government at this time was making friendly overtures to the South, which provided British mills with cotton in normal times. The attitude of the widely-read *Herald* was therefore of concern to Lincoln and his cabinet, for it was important that European neutrals have a fair evaluation of the American issues.

After the first battle of Bull Run, Bennett gave his full, but somewhat grudging, support to the Lincoln administration and the war. Even so, it was necessary from time to time for the President to "sweeten up"—as Lincoln put it—the aggressive editor of the *Herald*. "I write this to assure you that the Administration will not discriminate against the *Herald*, especially while it sustains us so generously. . . ." Lincoln wrote to Bennett after personally interceding for a *Herald* reporter who had been refused a pass to go down the Potomac river with a military detachment.[2] As a former pro-southern news-

[2] Pollard, *The Presidents and the Press*, p. 360.

paper, the *Herald* continued to attack specific issues of the Republican party, but its intentions were not subversive.

In their zeal to satisfy the amazingly aggressive news policies of their employers, *Herald* reporters sometimes had to be rebuked by the higher authorities of the administration. There was the case of Henry Wikoff, known to some of his colleagues as "Chevalier." Wikoff was very attractive to the ladies, apparently. He was accused of using this charm to obtain information from Mrs. Lincoln. Parts of the President's first message to a regular session of Congress in December, 1861, appeared in the *Herald* the morning the document was presented to the legislators. Chairman John Hickman of the House Judiciary Committee turned aside from an investigation of telegraphic censorship to find out about this leak. It was traced to Wikoff, although the affair was hushed up before all the facts could be made public.[3]

There were other instances in which *Herald* reporters tangled with authorities. At times, the *Herald* retaliated, as in its editorial attacks on Hickman during the Wikoff case, but the government also held an ace card in this game—namely, the right to restrict *Herald* coverage of the war to the advantage of Bennett's rivals. Actually, the aggressiveness of the *Herald* could have caused it much more trouble, if military officials had exerted their authority. At any rate, the editorial tactics paid off, for the *Herald* climbed to a circulation of more than 100,000 soon after the beginning of the war. It was then the most popular newspaper in the United States.[4]

Few presidents suffered more from editorial abuse than Lincoln. Opposition editors and disappointed favor-seekers accused him in print of vicious deeds, which the patient President usually ignored. He was falsely accused of drawing his salary in gold bars, while his soldiers were paid in deflated greenbacks. He was charged with drunkenness while making crucial decisions, with granting pardons to secure votes, and with needless butchering of armies as a result of his lust for victories. Once he was accused of outright treason. Typical of his press detractors was the *La Crosse Democrat,* a Wisconsin weekly, which said of the draft: "Lincoln has called for 500,000 more victims."

Continuous and unlicensed criticism was voiced by political opponents. Democrats actually polled a larger vote than Republicans in 1860.[5] They were

[3] These and some other episodes of Civil War reporting are from a manuscript provided by Professor Frederick B. Marbut, Pennsylvania State University, now published as *News from the Capital: The Story of Washington Reporting* (Carbondale: Southern Illinois University Press, 1971).

[4] The *New York Times* climbed from 45,000 to about 75,000 in the same period. The daily *Tribune* trailed behind, but the weekly edition, largely responsible for Greeley's national reputation, reached more than 200,000. This was the largest circulation of any single American paper. The *New York Ledger* had almost twice that many subscribers, but it was not a newspaper, as its nameplate would indicate, but a weekly story periodical.

[5] Lincoln had only 40 per cent of the popular vote in 1860, and he won by only 400,000 votes in 1864, when none of the southern Democrats had any voice in the elections. This was a serious consideration for Republican leaders contemplating the postwar political problem.

so split by sectional differences, however, that they could not agree upon a candidate. The Republicans were aware that they had won by default. That was one reason Lincoln tried to be conciliatory where decisiveness was not absolutely essential.

THE OPPOSITION COPPERHEADS

Most northern Democrats were loyal during the war, although they tended to welcome almost any peace overtures from the South. But another group of northern Democrats served as a kind of fifth column for the South. Their sympathies for the Confederacy were of varying degrees, but often their overt actions smacked of treason. This faction of the Democratic party was known as Copperhead, after the dangerous reptile that gives no warning of its attack. One of the more fanatical Copperhead organizations was called "The Knights of the Golden Circle," later supplanted by the underground "Sons of Liberty." By 1863 they had been officially declared traitors, to be treated accordingly when captured.

This presented a nice problem to Lincoln. At what point did criticism of the government exceed the limits of free expression? A test case was that of Clement Laird Vallandigham, Ohio editor and politician. Vallandigham was hero or villain, depending upon the viewpoint. There was no doubt that he was courageous and sincere. He risked his life and all his property for what he believed to be his right of free expression. On the other hand, he gave great aid and comfort to the enemy in standing upon these principles.

Vallandigham was the youngest member of the Ohio legislature when he was elected to it in 1845. His skill as a politician in a region of master politicians is indicated by the fact that he maneuvered himself into the speakership at the age of 26. In 1847 he became co-owner of the *Dayton Empire,* soon the leading anti-abolitionist publication in the Middle West. The abolitionists brought about his defeat in the Congressional elections of 1852, but he gained his seat in 1858, and at once used his office as a forum from which to attack the Republican party for its stand on secession. As secretary of the Democratic National Committee in 1860, he tried to work out a compromise. His credo was "To maintain the Constitution as it is, and to restore the Union as it was." This was legitimate until the outbreak of war, but when he continued his activities after April, 1861, Vallandigham became a threat to the North. He was by this time leader of the aboveground Copperheads, or the "peace party," as he called it. In the spring of 1863, General Ambrose E. Burnside issued his General Order Number 38, warning the Copperheads that they would be arrested if they continued to make public statements harmful to the northern war effort. Vallandigham defied the order at Columbus, and again at Mount Vernon, Ohio.

He was arrested, tried in a military court, and sentenced to prison. Lincoln commuted the sentence to banishment behind the Confederate lines.[6]

WARTIME PRESS CENSORSHIP IN THE NORTH

The leniency and patience of Lincoln, often mistaken for weakness, kept the press reasonably free through the terrible war period. He made full use of the press as a sounding board of public opinion, and he respected the institution. After his election, he allowed Henry Villard, young *New York Herald* correspondent, to cover him "in depth" at his hometown in Illinois. The President had no official newspaper after he left Springfield, but Lincoln devised a much more effective way of communicating with the public. He began speaking openly with reporters, trusting he would receive a "good press" thereby, and that his cause would be presented fairly to the public. The New York Associated Press was particularly effective in this regard. Since it had to reach publishers of various political and social faiths, the AP confined its dispatches to straight reporting, minus the usual biased interpretations common to most news accounts of the time. If any part of the press served as Lincoln's organ, it was the AP. This policy caused the President much trouble, but apparently he believed the price he paid was warranted.[7]

No war had ever been so fully and freely reported before. New York newspapers usually devoted at least a third of their space to war news. But sooner or later the press had to work out an understanding with military authorities in the interests of public security. There is no record in War Department files of military censorship prior to the Civil War. There was no knowledge of the technique of censorship. A system therefore had to be developed by trial and error. As a result, both the press and the government made many mistakes in working out the problems, and criticism from all sides was often bitter. Yet many valuable lessons were learned in the Civil War about controls of communication agencies. This experience was put to good use in World Wars I and II.

The problem was aggravated by the fact that the American press had become so prosperous, aggressive, and independent in the years preceding the war that it was sensitive to any form of restriction. The telegraph and the railway posts were other factors to be considered. They made it possible to disseminate news much faster than before. The potential danger of information

[6] Later, Vallandigham returned openly to Ohio, by way of Bermuda and Canada. He even ran foı office while officially a fugitive from justice. Crowds cheered him when he appeared in Chicago. Lincoln ignored him at this time so as not to make a martyr for the Copperheads. After the war Vallandigham was accepted back in his community as a practicing lawyer. He accidentally killed himseif while demonstrating a pistol used in a murder case.

[7] See Robert S. Harper, *Lincoln and the Press* (New York: McGraw-Hill, 1951).

useful to the enemy was therefore all the greater. On the other hand, this was the first of the all-out wars, involving civilian populations, and since public morale was now a much more important factor in prosecuting the war, the channels of information had to be kept open.[8]

EARLY MILITARY CENSORSHIP

There were three stages in the development of Civil War military censorship. The first period of fumbling ended about 1862. It began with the denial by the Post Office of messages sent to enemy areas. Curiously, this was not until the war had been under way for several days. In this instance, the editors appear to have been more aware of the danger than the government, for there had been several newspaper warnings about the laxness of communication restrictions where the enemy was involved.

The high command in Washington began to realize that the enemy was obtaining valuable military intelligence through the free flow of information to the press and to persons in private life. The authorities began to do something about the situation when they were handed thousands of telegrams which had passed through the northern states in recent weeks. Federal officials in New York, Washington, and other large cities seized these telegrams on May 20, 1861. This is noteworthy as the first step toward an official censorship policy.[9] The telegrams revealed the names of traitors in the North and plans of the secessionists. One of those caught in the net was James E. Harvey, former *Tribune* reporter, friend of Lincoln, and recent appointee as minister to Portugal.

On July 8, 1861, General Winfield Scott, commander of the Union armies, issued an order, backed up by Secretary of War Simon Cameron, forbidding the telegraph companies from sending any information of a military nature. This was illegal, but it served the purpose until Congress gave the President such control in January, 1862.

The first drastic use of the telegraph censorship was after the first battle of Bull Run, July 21, 1861. Raymond, who had turned in a bulletin to the *Times* announcing a Union victory and was thereby put to shame by the reports of his rivals, maintained that his follow-up story had been blocked by the censors. The same thing happened to Lawrence A. Gobright of the New York Associated Press. But there was no doubt as to the need of censorship, and the legitimate correspondents themselves began to see the necessity for control. It would serve to protect them in the transmission of the type of news the public needed, but it would discourage the correspondent intent upon report-

[8] The outstanding study of this problem is Quintus Wilson, "A Study and Evaluation of the Military Censorship in the Civil War" (Master's thesis, University of Minnesota, 1945).

[9] *Ibid.*, p. 39.

ing fake news as a means of arousing interest at any price. Already it was clear that if the government had to restrict certain types of information, it was just as necessary to provide the news to which reporters were entitled.

McCLELLAN'S VOLUNTARY CENSORSHIP PLAN

Since honest journalists and military planners both recognized the problem, it was natural that they should try to work out some agreement. On August 2, 1861, General George B. McClellan, commanding the Army of the Potomac, called a historic press conference of Washington correspondents. He presented to them an unprecedented plan that was the forerunner of modern voluntary censorship. The meeting was held while editorial skepticism and military resentment were issues after the disastrous Union rout at Bull Run. Each of the delegates to the conference signed a document binding him to transmit no information of military value to the enemy. On the other hand, the general agreed to use all his considerable influence to facilitate the gathering of news that was of interest to the public. The men who left the meeting that day congratulated themselves on the wisdom of the plan.

Unfortunately, the program was unsuccessful, not because of any serious flaw in the agreement, but because of division of authority. The official censor was H. E. Thayer, who understood nothing about the problem. He was not under the supervision of the War Department, but was under the direction of the Secretary of State. The jealousy of the War and State Departments resulted in a complete breakdown of the voluntary censorship plan less than three months after it was proposed. For on October 22, Secretary of State Seward instructed Thayer to prohibit telegraphic dispatches from Washington which related to military *and civil* operations of the Government. Since this violated the very spirit of the McClellan agreement, the press reverted to its old system of getting news as best it could.[10]

The failure of a promising plan led to the first Congressional investigation of censorship. On December 5, 1861, a special House panel heard the complaints of the correspondents and turned a sympathetic ear to the demands for a revision of the State Department order. The committee was curious as to why the New York Associated Press should have been specifically exempt from the restrictions. This was explained by L. A. Gobright, chief of the AP's Washington bureau. Gobright said his association had achieved the status of what amounted to a semiofficial Gazette by confining reports to facts and by deleting political and military opinion. On March 20, 1862, the committee issued a report demanding an end to restrictions on reports of nonmilitary actions of the government.

[10] Wilson, "Military Censorship in the Civil War," p. 50.

STANTON'S FIELD CENSORSHIP

There was considerable improvement when the censor was taken from the State Department and was put under the direction of the Secretary of War. Lincoln had been hesitant to give Secretary of War Cameron any more powers. His appointment had been strictly a result of political expedience, and as soon as possible he was replaced by the tough but very able Edwin M. Stanton. He quickly brought order out of chaos, and one of his first steps was the revision of censorship. By an order of February 25, 1862, Stanton clarified the triple set of restrictions under which correspondents had been bound by voluntary, State Department, and War Department censorship. By the Stanton order, correspondents were to submit copy to provost marshals for approval before transmission, but it was understood that deletions would apply only to military matters. Now the reporters knew just about how far they could go in reporting battles, and the press was able to serve much more effectively.

In the meantime, the President had authorized the Commander of the Armies to suspend the writ of habeas corpus, an action which made it possible for the authorities to make arrests without presenting charges immediately. Such action was provided for in the Constitution under the emergency powers, but there was some doubt as to whether the President or Congress had the power of suspension. Since Congress was not in session, Lincoln resolved the doubt by taking the responsibility on himself. The President's action was challenged by Chief Justice Taney, and had to be considered by the Supreme Court, but by that time, the action of the President had accomplished what he intended.

THE GENERALS AND THE CORRESPONDENTS

The second period of censorship, which began after Stanton's order of February 25, 1862, showed a better understanding of the principles involved, but was marred by faulty administration. The Stanton directive was poorly enforced, and depended too much upon individual interpretation. Another serious fault was the abuse of prerogatives by ambitious military leaders. Many of these were political appointees. They were interested in favorable publicity. Through their power of censorship, they could exert pressure upon correspondents attached to them. General Grant discouraged this habit by removing from command one of the worst offenders, General John A. McClernand, during the siege of Vicksburg in July, 1863.

General Sherman contributed to the development of organized censorship. The general had been bedeviled by reporters, who were irked by his press relations. Sherman was certain much military failure could be blamed on information leaks. On several occasions he spoke his mind on this matter. The press retaliated by spreading the story that he was insane. The issue came to a showdown after Thomas E. Knox, a correspondent for the *Herald,* transmitted information that clearly violated military regulations of censorship. Sherman had the reporter arrested and held as a spy. He had no intention of shooting the man, as he had every right to do, but he was convinced that this was a good test case. In the end, the President intervened, Knox got out of his predicament, and Sherman got what he wanted—the understanding that all correspondents must be *accredited,* or recognized, journalists; and that they must be *acceptable* to commanders in the field. Thus was established a precedent followed ever since by military correspondents.

The controversial and colorful General Benjamin Butler also contributed to the lore of censorship during his occupation of New Orleans. His proclamation outlined censorship procedures that are still followed in conquered areas. It included instructions to local editors as to what they could or could not print. It prescribed the duties of censors in the interests of the best possible adjustment between the needs of the public and the necessities of the army in control.

From 1864 to the end of the war, censorship entered its third and successful phase. General Sherman marched all the way to the sea in hostile country without once having his plans disclosed by the press. On the whole, the press was cooperating by the end of the war. Curiously, as the North tightened its censorship, the South relaxed its controls, which had been so much more effective at the beginning of the conflict. The southern press will be discussed later in this chapter, but the point appears to be that censorship will not apply where the people will not consent to it. The South had an excellent press organization until defeat and the need for drastic action resulted in a breakdown of censorship.

SUSPENSIONS OF NORTHERN NEWSPAPERS

On the whole, the northern press enjoyed great freedom throughout the war. The great power of the President after his suspension of habeas corpus was used sparingly. Most of the punitive actions were taken by military commanders. In June, 1864, the *Chicago Times* was suspended for three days by order of General Ambrose Burnside, commanding the Department of Ohio, which included the military districts in Illinois. This was one of the so-called "Burnside Decrees," based on the right of a commander to silence public expression of ideas and information deemed harmful to the military effort. The general appears to have had plenty of provocation for his action. Wilbur F. Storey, publisher of the *Times,* lacked both conscience and principle. He used the most violent language in attacking Lincoln after the Emancipation Proclamation was issued. He repeatedly ignored military warnings to stop fomenting Copperhead dissatisfaction in the area. Pushed beyond endurance by the anti-Federal sentiments of the *Times,* General Burnside ordered the newspaper padlocked. Lincoln's reaction was typical. He wished to back up his own general, and he knew Burnside had much to complain about, but the President also had definite ideas about freedom of expression. After three days he rescinded the military order.

Other newspapers ran afoul of the censor. One was the *New York World,* established in 1860 as a penny paper with religious overtones. At first it was a supporter of the Lincoln administration. It lost money and continued to fail even after it absorbed the assets of the famous old *Courier and Enquirer.* Eventually it was taken over by Manton Marble, an able editor, who increased circulation by espousing the cause of the "Peace Democrats." After the Emancipation Proclamation, the *World* was openly hostile to the administration. It became the focus of Copperhead infection in an area where the war was already unpopular. In May, 1864, the military authorities had a chance to strike back.

The *World* and the *Journal of Commerce* published a forged presidential proclamation purporting to order another draft of 400,000 men. The document was actually the product of Joseph Howard, Jr., city editor of the *Brooklyn Eagle.* He had hoped to make a profit in the stock market by this hoax, although this was the least of his crimes. Such a story in the tense metropolis was almost certain to cause bloodshed and probably death by rioting. Other editors refused to carry the story, after checking the facts, but the *World* and *Journal of Commerce* appeared with the article prominently displayed. General John A. Dix promptly suppressed them. After a lapse of two days, during which the editors were severely reprimanded, they were allowed to resume publication.

It was not the first time the *Journal of Commerce* had brushed with the authorities. Gerard Hallock, who had contributed so much to journalism and cooperative news gathering, was publisher of the paper. Editorial policy was definitely pro-South. It was so critical of the Union that a grand jury was summoned to investigate the paper and four other publications in the area for indulging in "the frequent practice of encouraging the rebels now in arms against the Federal Government." The postmaster general then ordered the New York postal authorities not to accept these papers in the mail. At that point Hallock retired from the paper. His successor followed a less antagonistic policy, and the *Journal of Commerce* was allowed to use the postal services again.

One of the most celebrated suspension cases outside New York was that of Samuel Medary, editor of the *Crisis* and of the *Ohio Statesman* at Columbus. The *Crisis* was a special organ of the Copperheads, and it supported C. L. Vallandigham, the Copperhead candidate for governor. In 1864 Medary was indicted by a federal grand jury as the spokesman for a group then declared to be subversive. He was released from jail on bond furnished by the editor of the *Cincinnati Enquirer,* who wished to test the wartime freedom of the press. Medary died before the case was tried in court.

Much more effective repression was carried out by unofficial means. Many of the Copperhead papers, including the *Crisis,* mentioned above, were wrecked by mobs. So were pro-administration papers from time to time. The *New York Tribune* was seriously threatened on two occasions. Pro-southern editors sometimes had to flee from mob violence whipped up by returning veterans. In 1861 the pro-southern New York papers were warned by placards that national security was more important than their right to criticise. But three years later, the same type of mob actions forced editors to modify extreme opposition to northern peace feelers. A year later, other waves of public violence followed the assassination of Lincoln, and those who were known to have made it difficult for the President ran the risk of physical harm. But the fact remains that the press was relatively free throughout the war, and that considering the tensions, the responsible press emerged unscathed.

THE NORTH REPORTS THE WAR

Indeed, when it came to the reporting of military actions, Civil War correspondents, or "specials," as they were then called, enjoyed a freedom that would not be tolerated in modern times. Many of the battles were fought in remote areas, and the struggle to get back firsthand accounts often was heroic. Some of the best reporting in American journalism was offered the public by the hundreds of correspondents during this test of a nation.

Newsmen were everywhere. They roamed the South long after their detection might have resulted in their execution as spies. Some of them were famous already, including Raymond of the *Times,* who was at Bull Run, and William Howard Russell, the world-renowned British war correspondent fresh from his triumphs in the Crimea.

Some of the best war reporters earned their spurs after the conflict began, however. One of these was B. S. Osbon, a minister's son who had embarked on a life of seafaring and adventure. He was working for the *New York World* at nine dollars a week on that April morning in 1861, when the curtain went up on one of the great American tragedies. From the deck of a naval cutter, Osbon watched the bombardment of Fort Sumter. The lead of the story he sent back was a prototype of the news style developed during the war:

> CHARLESTON, APRIL 12–*The ball is opened. War is inaugurated.* The batteries of Sullivan's Island, Morris Island, and other points were opened on Fort Sumter at four o'clock this morning. Fort Sumter has returned the fire, and a brisk cannonading has been kept up.[11]

[11] Louis L. Snyder, and Richard B. Morris, eds., *A Treasury of Great Reporting* (New York: Simon & Schuster, 1949), p. 130.

Later Osbon shipped back on the U.S.S. "Baltic," carrying the exhausted Major Robert Anderson, commander of the fort's garrison. It was Osbon who disclosed in a published interview that a junior officer had raised the flag of surrender after Anderson had ordered the last round to be fired, and further resistance appeared to be hopeless.

Not long after, Bennett hired Osbon to report for the *Herald* at $25 a week. He was on the quarterdeck with Admiral Farragut at the siege of New Orleans. He seemed to be wherever a good story was about to break.

But there were other stars, too. Albert D. Richardson of the *Tribune* sent reports from the deep South through the line by transmitting his stories in cipher by way of the New York banks. He watched the great battle of Fort Henry from a treetop observation post. He saw Island Number Ten at the Vicksburg approaches reduced to rubble as he stood with Commodore Foote on the hurricane deck of a Union ironclad. He ran the blockade of Vicksburg; was knocked from the deck by the shock of a cannon ball that nearly struck him; and then was picked from the water and imprisoned by the Confederates. His escape through the lines was one of the exciting journalistic feats of the time.

George W. Smalley, later one of the pioneer foreign correspondents, first gained fame while covering the war for the *Tribune*. At the battle of Antietam, where he served as a dispatch rider for General Hooker, he lost two horses by gunfire. It was Smalley who first got the news of the battle to Washington, where Lincoln was anxiously waiting for some encouraging report before announcing his plans for emancipation.

Many of the correspondents wrote under a pen name. There was "Agate," for example, who was actually Whitelaw Reid, the successor to Greeley on the *Tribune* in the early 1870s. He was already famous for his report on the battle of Shiloh when he sent a dispatch one day from Gettysburg. His story, datelined "Field of Battle, Near Gettysburg, July 2," took up 14 of the 48 columns of the *Cincinnati Gazette*. It remains as a classic of Civil War reporting. Standing on Cemetery Hill, the point most exposed to rebel fire, Reid turned in an eyewitness account of the decisive battle, of which the following is an excerpt:

> . . . Hancock was wounded; Gibbon succeeded to command—approved soldier, and ready for the crisis. As the tempest of fire approached its height, he walked along the line, and renewed his orders to the men to reserve their fire. The rebels—three lines deep—came steadily up. They were in pointblank range.
>
> At last the order came! From thrice six thousand guns there came a sheet of smoky flame, a crash of leaden death. The line literally melted away; but there came a second, resistless still. It had been our supreme effort—on the instant we were not equal to another.
>
> Up to the rifle pits, across them, over the barricades—the momentum of their charge, the mere machine strength of their combined action swept them on. Our thin line could fight, but it had not weight enough to op-

> pose this momentum. It was pushed behind the guns. Right on came the rebels. They were upon the guns, were bayoneting the gunners, were waving their flags above our pieces.
>
> But they had penetrated to the fatal point. . . .[12]

In the Confederate camp near Hagerstown, Maryland, the reporter for the *Richmond Enquirer*, retreating with Lee's army, sent back this eloquent version of the same battle to soften the blow to the bereaved at home:

> . . . Though many a Virginia home will mourn the loss of some noble spirit, yet at the name of Pickett's division and the battle of Gettysburg, how the eye will glisten and the blood course quicker, and the heart beat warm, as among its noble dead is recalled the name of some cherished one. They bore themselves worthy of their lineage and their state. Who would recall them from their bed of glory? Each sleeps in a hero's grave. . . .[13]

The *New York Herald,* true to its tradition, exceeded its rivals in aggressive war coverage. It had more than 40 specials in the field at any given time. One of its foremost reporters was a young Bavarian immigrant, Henry Hilgard, who soon changed his name to Villard after his arrival in 1853. While learning the language, he edited the *Volksblatt,* a German paper published at Racine, Wisconsin. Later he covered the Lincoln-Douglas debates for the *Staats-Zeitung* of New York. His account of Lincoln's departure from Springfield for Washington, and of the long ride under increasing national tension, established Villard as one of the best correspondents of his day. He was only 25 when he began reporting the war for the *Herald.* He is best remembered for two great reporting "scoops." The first was his account of the first battle of Bull Run, the first accurate one to reach New York. The second exclusive account was his report of the battle of Fredericksburg.

ARTISTS AND PHOTOGRAPHERS: MATHEW BRADY

A small army of artists covered the war, describing the events in almost photolike drawings. These were printed only by a laborious process of engraving by hand on a wooden block. Such woodcuts were not new, but they were used in newspapers much more regularly after 1861 to depict battle scenes and the likenesses of leading wartime figures. In another development, some of the metropolitan papers printed large maps to illustrate campaigns, thereby

[12] Snyder and Morris, *A Treasury of Great Reporting,* p. 146.
[13] *Ibid.*, p. 149.

leading the way to new makeup no longer limited by column rules.[14] The *Herald* of September 12, 1863, is a good example of this technique. The paper was a little smaller than a modern standard daily and ran to eight pages, six columns wide. About a quarter of page one of this particular issue was devoted to a map accompanying a story on the Arkansas campaign. On page three a huge map of the Morris Island success in Charleston harbor filled all but two columns of the page from top to bottom.

Magazines also began to use illustrations more frequently. Because the publishers had more time to spend on engraving and printing, the magazines were able to offer excellent pictures. *Harper's Weekly* and *Frank Leslie's Illustrated Newspaper* were actually the forerunners of the picture magazines that were to flourish 75 years later.[15] Their artists' drawings were superb.

The most notable contribution to pictorial journalism in the 1860s was the photograph. Pioneer war photographer was a lovable Irishman, Mathew Brady. True, his photographs could not be used in newspapers of the time, since a practical method for transferring light and shade in the printing process was not perfected for another decade.[16] But Brady was famous for his war pictures, and his photographic record of the conflict comes down to us as one of the finest examples of reporting.

Brady was everywhere during the war, apparently. He recorded on his clumsy plates the scene at Fort Sumter. His photographic interpretations of famous battles and war leaders could not be matched in mood and accuracy by the printed word. It is surprising how many of the great men of the period posed for Brady.[17] And because he was so successful in using this new medium of reporting, he is worthy of recognition at this point.

Brady was born about 1823, either in Cork, Ireland, or more probably, in upper New York state. As a youth he worked for A. T. Stewart, the pioneer

[14] It was not impossible to print spread headlines and large maps on the earlier type-revolving presses, but it was hazardous and inconvenient, because the column rules had to be locked tight to keep the metal type from flying out as the presses revolved. It was accomplished now and then, however. Big maps were printed by the newspapers in the Mexican War period and after.

[15] An excellent study of this contribution has been made by Donald Christian Peterson in "Two Pioneer American Picture Magazines" (Master's thesis, University of Wisconsin, 1953).

[16] The pioneer in the photoengraving, which made possible the printing of various shades of black and white so as to give a photographic effect, was Frederic Eugene Ives. His "half-tone" process was first demonstrated at Cornell University in 1877 (see pp. 339–41).

[17] As must happen to all news photographers, Brady missed some great picture opportunities. He had his camera trained on President Lincoln at the time the immortal Gettysburg Address was delivered. Edward Everett, famous orator, and main speaker at the memorial, talked so long that Brady had to keep changing his plates, which had to be exposed while still wet with sensitizing solution. He was in the midst of removing a dried-out plate when the President arose to speak. The inspiring message was so short that Brady's assistant could not fetch a fresh plate from the portable dark room in time to photograph Lincoln before he bowed and retired. One of the great "news shots" of American history was thereby lost to posterity.

New York department store owner. Stewart took an interest in the bright lad. When Brady took up the study of photography, the wealthy merchant brought his protégé to the attention of Samuel F. B. Morse, famed as the inventor of the telegraph, but equally interested in the science of optics. Morse made Brady his understudy. Together they worked with Professor J. W. Draper of New York University, who was to make the first instantaneous photographic exposure in America.[18] In 1839, Morse took Brady to Europe, where they met Louis Jacque Mandé Daguerre, inventor of the "daguerreotype," a photograph on metal.

Brady returned to America and set up a daguerreotype shop at the corner of Broadway and Fulton Street, opposite Barnum's museum. That was about 1842. Soon he was famed as a photographer of the great and near-great.[19] Five years in a row he won the American Institute award for his contributions to photography. He was famous and prosperous.

But Brady was not satisfied with this success. The daguerreotype was too slow to be adaptable to anything but portrait work, and he sought a faster process. In 1855 he went to Scotland to learn about a new and faster "wet plate" developed by the scientist, Scott-Archer. Brady returned with Alexander Gardner, Scott-Archer's associate, and they set up offices in Washington as semiofficial government photographers. When the war loomed, Brady gave up this lucrative business.

He persuaded his friends, President Lincoln and Allan Pinkerton of the Secret Service, to let him make a photographic record of the war with Gardner. They were permitted to go anywhere, protected by the Secret Service. Soon Brady's little black wagon, which was his portable dark room, was a familiar sight on the active fronts. He had an uncanny knack of knowing where the fighting would start. Soldiers dreaded the sight of Brady arriving on the scene, for they knew that soon thereafter the shooting would begin. He was often under sniper fire as he set up his camera at exposed vantage points. By the end of the war he had collected about 3,500 photographs.[20]

These pictures give us an entirely different impression than the usual reports of people and events. Although Brady's equipment was inferior to the simplest box cameras of three generations later, he produced amazing pictures. Some of them were the equal of any produced in World War II, although he could not stop fast action, of course. Despite the limitations of his equipment, somehow he was able to capture through his lens the hysteria, horror, and occasional glory of war.[21]

[18] The word "instantaneous" had a much broader meaning then than now. It could mean anything up to several minutes.

[19] This period is well described in Robert Taft, *Photography and the American Scene: A Social History, 1839–1889* (New York: Macmillan, 1938).

[20] Some of the best of these are available in a single volume, Roy Meredith, *Mr. Lincoln's Camera Man, Mathew S. Brady* (New York: Scribner's, 1946).

[21] The sequel to this episode is not so happy. Neither Brady, nor Frederic Ives, who made the photoengraving such an essential part of the printed press, ever profited much from

THE SOUTH REPORTS THE WAR

Not much has been said about the southern press up to this point, although it played an important part in the fortunes of the Confederacy. In many ways editorial reactions were the same in the North and South. Southern editors were highly critical of military strategy, and journalists such as Rhett, for example, attacked the Confederate administration just as violently as Lincoln was being attacked in the North. War aims were not so much an issue as they were in the North, however, nor was there anything quite corresponding to the Copperhead press.

Most of the news of the battles was supplied to southern editors by the Press Association of the Confederate States of America, better known as "PA," which, appropriately enough, was just the reversed logotype of the biggest northern news agency, the AP.[22] When the war began, the South had no system for preparing or transmitting news of public interest to replace the severed connection with the New York AP. An Augusta editor began sending out a brief daily summary by telegraph to a few papers willing to pay for the service, but this was never widely used. In 1862, the combined newspapers of Richmond tried to establish a more effective organization. Publishers realized that to meet the enormous expense of covering a war, they would have to work together. They also saw that in order to place correspondents where they were needed, they would have to pool resources. It was soon evident that the Richmond papers could not achieve these results by themselves.

Following a series of conferences, Joseph Clisby of the *Macon Telegraph* summoned the editor of every daily in the South to attend a meeting at Augusta on February 4, 1862. The Association of the Richmond Press had just been organized, and the plan was to expand the idea by organizing the PA. A board of directors hired a superintendent, J. S. Thrasher, "at a salary not to exceed $3,000," and the organization was ready to function.

The value of the association was at once apparent in the signing of contracts with telegraph agencies and the abolishing of onerous postal regulations. On May 15, 1863, the directors passed a resolution defending Thrasher for his stand against unwarranted military censorship.

---

their contributions. Brady spent a hundred thousand dollars obtaining his pictures. Subsequent administrations were slow in turning over promised remuneration. He was finally offered $25,000 for the originals and for the duplicates he had made of every scene. By that time Brady, who had always been prosperous before, was in desperate financial straits. The panic of 1873 bankrupted him. His lucrative business had been taken over by creditors and rivals. By 1883 Brady did not even know where his pictures were stored. In 1895 he was injured in Washington by a runaway horse. He died the following year. Later, the magazine *Review of Reviews* published one of the sets after its accidental discovery in the vaults of the photographic supplier who had taken the pictures in debt.

[22] This subject is presented in detail by Quintus C. Wilson, "The Confederate Press Association: A Pioneer News Agency," *Journalism Quarterly*, XXVI (June 1949), 160–66.

On the whole, the PA served its clients well. When Gen. P. G. T. Beauregard began to hold up dispatches, Thrasher called on him personally and told the general that the aim of the press association was to obtain accurate reports for the good of the public, consistent with military security. The general was impressed. He told Thrasher that the PA reporters "should have every facility for early access to intelligence compatible with the public interests," and he wrote letters to high military authorities recommending similar cooperation. Thrasher won the confidence of other leaders. In return, he instructed PA correspondents to send no opinions or comments on events—the procedure that had so irritated northern commanders. They were warned to sift rumors and to offer no information that would aid the enemy. The objectivity of the PA stories has been regarded as constituting a "complete revolution" in journalistic writing.[23]

The superintendent, in return, was jealous of arrogant commanders who held up legitimate copy, and he used the power of his office to enforce cooperation from the military. Correspondents were ordered to send to the home office copies of dispatches unreasonably censored at the telegraph office. These reports were to include the name and rank of the responsible censor, and these documents were then used to pry greater concessions from those in higher authority.

The development of PA was a big step in the progress of southern journalism. The surviving 43 daily papers in the South were all members of the association. The editorial weight of this group was impressive. Dispatches were transmitted over the Military Telegraph Lines, the army system, at half rates. There was also a satisfactory arrangement with the private South-Western Telegraph Company. Newspapers that had seldom had access to regular wire news budgets were now able to keep readers up to date on the war. Short, but complete, reports supplanted the rambling, confused accounts of prewar days. Reporters with the armies were paid $25 a week, which was good for that time, and the writing was of good quality. On the whole PA gave a good account of itself until the crumbling Confederacy saw a collapse of restraints and organization. As in the northern armies, reporters were sometimes ejected for releasing information believed useful to the enemy. But Thrasher appears to have perfected a great news gathering agency. He offered relatively high objectivity. He kept the press as free as possible, considering the circumstances.

There were perhaps 800 newspapers being published in the 11 states of the Confederacy in 1861, of which about 10 per cent were dailies. Hand presses were in use in most of these newspaper offices and circulations were small. The *Richmond Dispatch*, with 18,000 subscribers when war broke out, was outranked only by the largest New Orleans dailies. And as important as the Richmond papers were in the journalism of the Confederacy, the *Dispatch* had more readers than the *Enquirer*, *Whig*, and *Democrat* combined. The

[23] Wilson, "The Confederate Press Association," p. 162.

Enquirer was the organ of the Jefferson Davis administration until 1863 when the *Sentinel* was established for that purpose. Richmond also spawned a *Southern Illustrated News* in 1862 to fill the void left by the disappearance of *Harper's Weekly;* it soon had 20,000 readers.[24]

Southern publishers were harassed by a shortage of print paper; they were reduced eventually to single sheets, to extras printed on galley proof slips, even to printing on the back of old wallpaper. They also ran out of ink, type, and men to man their shops. After 1863, when New Orleans fell, their cities were overrun by federal troops. About 20 of the dailies were still printing when Lee surrendered. But they had compiled a journalistic record of the Confederate arms, and had sent, all told, more than 100 correspondents to cover the Southern armies.

The historian of Civil War correspondents, J. Cutler Andrews, ranks two of these men as head and shoulders above the others.[25] One was Felix Gregory de Fontaine, who signed himself "Personne" in his dispatches to the *Charleston Courier.* The other was Peter W. Alexander, primarily identified with the *Savannah Republican,* but whose "P.W.A." signature was also found in the *Atlanta Confederacy,* the *Columbus Sun,* the *Mobile Advertiser,* the *Richmond Dispatch,* and the *Times* of London. Ranking behind them were such versatile war reporters as Samuel C. Reid, Jr., of the *New Orleans Picayune* and other papers; James B. Sener and William G. Shepardson of the *Richmond Dispatch;* Albert J. Street of the *Mobile Register;* John H. Linebaugh of the *Memphis Appeal;* and an unidentified "Shadow" who covered the Battle of Atlanta and who may have been Henry Watterson of future Louisville fame.

De Fontaine and Alexander crossed paths as "regulars" in the major campaigns; both were at Antietam in September 1862 when Lee was repulsed in his invasion of the North, escaping a vastly superior McClellan. De Fontaine wrote a seven-column story of more than 8,000 words about the campaign, in what Andrews calls his greatest story of the war. It appeared in the *Charleston Courier* first. At one point the young but war-weary correspondent described the scene in front of the Confederate center along a sunken road called "Bloody Lane":

> From twenty different standpoints great volumes of smoke were every instant leaping from the muzzles of angry guns. The air was filled with the white fantastic shapes that floated away from bursted shells. Men were leaping to and fro, loading, firing and handling the artillery, and now and then a hearty yell would reach the ear, amid the tumult, that spoke of death or disaster from some well aimed ball. Before us were the enemy. A regiment or two had crossed the river, and, running in squads from the woods along its banks, were trying to form a line. Suddenly a shell falls among them, and another and another, until thousands

[24] J. Cutler Andrews, *The South Reports the Civil War* (Princeton: Princeton University Press, 1970), pp. 26–33.
[25] Andrews, *op. cit.,* p. 50.

> scatter like a swarm of flies, and disappear in the woods. A second time the effort is made, and there is a second failure. Then there is a diversion. The batteries of the Federals open afresh; their infantry try another point, and finally they succeed in effecting a lodgement on this side. Our troops, under D. H. Hill, meet them, and a fierce battle ensues in the centre. Backwards, forwards, surging and swaying like a ship in a storm, the various columns are seen in motion. It is a hot place for us, but is hotter still for the enemy. They are directly under our guns, and we mow them down like grass. The raw levies, sustained by the veterans, come up to the work well, and fight for a short time with an excitement incident to their novel experiences of a battle; but soon a portion of their line gives way in confusion. Their reserves come up, and endeavor to retrieve the fortunes of the day. Our centre, however, stands firm as adamant, and they fall back.[26]

This was at noon; by two o'clock Hill was out of men to defend the center —but McClellan failed to mount a breakthrough and settled for less than an overwhelming victory. More soldiers died in a single day at Antietam than in any other battle in American history—23,000 in all.

Alexander was at Antietam also and composed his battle account for the *Mobile Advertiser* in the midst of the wounded and dying in an army hospital. "There is a smell of death in the air," he wrote, "and the laboring surgeons are literally covered from head to foot with the blood of the sufferers." It was Alexander who wrote the most penetrating Southern account of the Battle of Gettysburg, questioning Lee's wisdom in committing himself to full-scale assault the second day and wondering if Lee and his staff had not exhibited too much confidence in the ability of their troops to win against any odds. Most of the Southern press reprinted his story.[27]

WARTIME BRINGS TECHNICAL ADVANCES

War brought important technical changes to the press. Dependence upon the telegraph led to modification in news writing, as correspondents tried to save tolls by striving to be more concise. One way to compress stories was to omit opinion and coloration. By modern standards, Civil War reporting was rambling and colored, but compared with the journalism of an earlier day it was much more readable. Some of the copy, such as that transmitted out of Washington by the New York Associated Press, and out of Richmond by the Confederate Press Association, would not be much out of place in a modern newspaper.

The summary lead, which put the main feature of the story in the first

[26] *Charleston Daily Courier,* September 29, 1862.
[27] Andrews, *op. cit.,* pp. 316–17.

paragraph, was developed during the war by reporters in the field who feared that their complete dispatches might not get through. Bennett once said that the cable, rather than the telegraph, was responsible for this, but the cable was not in successful operation until 1866, and the summary lead was fairly common by that time. Here is the way the *New York Times* started off one of its important front page articles of April 16, 1865, for example:

> WASHINGTON, Saturday, April 15–12 A.M. Andrew Johnson was sworn into office as President of the United States by Chief Justice Chase today, at eleven o'clock. . . .

Because vital news streamed from the telegraph by the hour, metropolitan papers began to bulletin the highlights, and soon the smallest papers were imitating this procedure. These bulletins led to the modern newspaper headline, which summarizes the story in a few lines. The main story in the *New York Times* of May 10, 1864, is typical of this primitive headline system. It began:

VICTORY

"On To Richmond"

Lee's Defeat and Retreat
Confirmed

There followed *nineteen* crossline bulletins, which filled most of the column.

Most of the newspapers continued to use the eight-page, six-column makeup carried over from before the war. By modern standards they were likely to be drab, with their small type, lack of pictures, and the dreadful uniformity of one-column makeup limitations. But the use of huge maps was breaking down the confines of the column rule, and the experimentation with headlines indicates the contrast with the page dress of only a decade earlier.

Presses had to be fast to keep up with other developments in journalism. On the Sunday following the fall of Fort Sumter, the *Herald* printed 135,000 newspapers—a record press run up to that date. In 1863, William Bullock brought out the web perfecting press, which printed both sides of a continuous roll of paper on a rotary press. Although it was not until 1871 that R. Hoe and Company produced such presses as standard equipment, the stimulus of the war is nevertheless apparent.

Magazines also flourished in this period. A newcomer, *Harper's Monthly*, won a record 200,000 circulation within a few years after its founding in 1850, by featuring fiction and woodcut illustrations Another popular magazine deserves special mention. It was *Godey's Lady's Book,* founded in 1830. From a circulation of 25,000 in 1839, it jumped to 150,000 on the eve of the war. Louis A. Godey, the publisher, lavished money to make his magazine a beautiful product, and the investment paid off, for he was the first magazine publisher to leave an estate of more than a million dollars. The magazine indicated the growing recognition of women in the economic picture. It carried many hand-colored engravings, fiction and poetry, and department material designed especially for women.

It was indeed an exciting era that came to a close on the evening of April 14, 1865. Lawrence A. Gobright of the New York Associated Press was working late in his office. He had already sent out dispatches about President Lincoln's theater party, reporting that General Grant had declined an invitation to see the play, "Our American Cousin," in order to go to New Jersey with Mrs. Grant. The door burst open and an excited friend rushed in with news of the tragedy at Ford's Theater. Gobright quickly wrote out a bulletin before going to work on an extended account of the evening's development. No modern reporter could have broken the news more succinctly. The lead said:

> WASHINGTON, FRIDAY, APRIL 14, 1865—The President was shot in a theater tonight, and perhaps mortally wounded.

Annotated Bibliography

Books

Andrews, J. Cutler, *The North Reports the Civil War.* Pittsburgh: University of Pittsburgh Press, 1955. Most extensive (813 pages) of histories of Civil War reporting, and thoroughly documented. Lists several hundred northern reporters and their papers.

———, *The South Reports the Civil War.* Princeton: Princeton University Press, 1970. Like his *The North Reports the Civil War,* a prize-winning job of research and writing.

Catton, Bruce, *Mr. Lincoln's Army.* New York: Doubleday, 1951. Includes many instances of military-press relations.

Commager, Henry Steele, ed., *Documents of American History.* New York: Appleton-Century-Crofts, 1934. See especially Vol. I, p. 398, on the Merryman case and Vol. II, p. 22, on the Milligan case.

Crozier, Emmet, *Yankee Reporters, 1861–65.* New York: Oxford University Press, 1956. A readable account of correspondents' work.

Fahrney, Ralph Ray, *Horace Greeley and the Tribune in the Civil War.* Chicago: University of Chicago Press, 1929. Documented.

Gobright, Lawrence A., *Recollections of Men and Things at Washington during a*

Third of a Century. Philadelphia: Claxton, Remsen, and Haffelfinger, 1869. By the Associated Press correspondent.

Harper, Robert S., *Lincoln and the Press.* New York: McGraw-Hill, 1951. Readable and detailed account of Lincoln's press relations after 1858, written from newspaper sources.

Horan, James D., *Mathew Brady: Historian with a Camera.* New York: Crown, 1955. A good biography, with 453 pictures.

Klement, Frank L., *The Copperheads in the Middle West.* Chicago: University of Chicago Press, 1960. Wilbur Storey, C. L. Vallandigham, and Samuel Medary are among those covered.

Mathews, Joseph J., *Reporting the Wars.* Minneapolis: University of Minnesota Press, 1957. History of war news reporting since the mid-eighteenth century. See also F. L. Bullard, *Famous War Correspondents* (Boston: Little, Brown, 1914).

Meredith, Roy, *Mr. Lincoln's Camera Man, Mathew S. Brady.* New York: Scribner's, 1946. A colorful account of the pioneer war photographer, with some of the best of his reproductions.

Nicolay, John George, and John M. Hay, *Abraham Lincoln, A History.* New York: Appleton-Century-Crofts, 1890. 10 vols. Of all the histories of the Lincoln administration, this remains as one of the most comprehensive and readable. An account by the President's private secretaries.

Photographic History of the Civil War. New York: Review of Reviews Company, 1911. 10 vols. A very complete collection of Brady's pictures, with explanatory material in chronological order.

Pollard, James E., *The Presidents and the Press.* New York: Macmillan, 1947. The chapter on Lincoln and the press is very useful for those wishing to read a concise discussion of the problem.

Reynolds, Donald E., *Editors Make War: Southern Newspapers in the Secession Crisis.* Nashville, Tenn.: Vanderbilt University Press, 1970. Research in the files proved most Southern editors were in forefront of secession movement.

Salmon, Lucy B., *The Newspaper and Authority.* New York: Oxford University Press, 1923. The chapters on Civil War threats to a free press offer stimulating ideas on the subject.

Sandburg, Carl, *Abraham Lincoln: The War Years.* New York: Harcourt, Brace & Jovanovich, 1939. 4 vols. Contains excellent portraits of leading Civil War editors and newspapers.

Snyder, Louis L., and Richard B. Morris, eds., *A Treasury of Great Reporting*. New York: Simon & Schuster, 1962. Examples, with pertinent comment, of Civil War news stories are included.

Starr, Louis M., *Bohemian Brigade: Civil War Newsmen in Action.* New York: Knopf, 1954. One of the best studies; considers all aspects of the newspaper in wartime, including reporting, editing, censorship.

Weisberger, Bernard A., *Reporters for the Union.* Boston: Little, Brown, 1953. Mainly a study of correspondents' political biases and criticisms of the military; least useful of such books.

Periodicals and Monographs

Blackmon, Robert E., "Noah Brooks: Reporter in the White House," *Journalism Quarterly,* XXXII (Summer 1955), 301. Brooks was the Washington correspondent of the *Sacramento Union* in wartime.

Goldsmith, Adolph O., "Reporting the Civil War: Union Army Press Relations," *Journalism Quarterly,* XXXIII (Fall 1956), 478. A good summary of the problem.

Guback, Thomas H., "General Sherman's War on the Press," *Journalism Quarterly,* XXXVI (Spring 1959), 171. A well-done account, featuring Sherman's famous clash with the *Herald's* Knox.

Peterson, Donald Christian, "Two Pioneer American Picture Magazines." Master's thesis, University of Wisconsin, 1953. A detailed study of *Harper's Weekly* and *Frank Leslie's Illustrated Newspaper.*

Randall, James G., "The Newspaper Problem and Its Bearing Upon Military Secrecy During the Civil War," *American Historical Review,* XXIII (January 1918), 303. Long the main authority for a discussion of Civil War censorship, by a leading historian of the period. Criticises conduct of the press; admires skill of correspondents.

Reilly, Thomas W., "Henry Villard: Civil War Journalist." Master's thesis, University of Oregon, 1970. An excellent depth study.

Wilson, Quintus C., "A Study and Evaluation of the Military Censorship in the Civil War." Master's thesis, University of Minnesota, 1945. This is the most complete and best documented study of the subject, and largely supersedes Randall's monograph.

———, "The Confederate Press Association: A Pioneer News Agency," *Journalism Quarterly,* XXVI (June 1949), 160. A digest of a chapter in Wilson's censorship study.

Bettmann Archive

CHARLES A. DANA of the *New York Sun*

New York Post

E. L. GODKIN of the *Nation* and *Evening Post*

The Oregonian

HARVEY W. SCOTT of Portland's *Oregonian*

Louisville Courier-Journal

HENRY WATTERSON, *Louisville Courier-Journal*

15

The Press at a Watershed

. . . he was the last of those editors who wrote with the power of ownership.
—Arthur Krock, about Watterson

American history in many respects starts afresh at the close of the Civil War. This is not to deny the obvious fact that two and a half centuries of the American experience had produced fundamental guiding forces which would continue to influence the maturing of the nation's economy and the development of its political and social fabric. But great new forces were at work, and between 1865 and 1900 the United States was to pass through a revolution which affected every phase of the national scene. The forces were those of intensive industrialization, mechanization, and urbanization, bringing with them sweeping social, cultural, and political changes. At some point between the Civil War and the turn of the century, the slow maturing process of virtually every aspect of American life was given powerful new impetus or redirection.

So it was with the nation's journalism. The great development of communication and of journalistic techniques which had come in the Jacksonian period of American growth was continuing through the war period. There was a popular press which had appealed to the human interests of its readers, which had utilized the new communication facilities to develop news enterprise, and which had sometimes developed editorial force. But the patterns which had emerged, the techniques which had been created, were to be drastically affected by an intensive new effort born of the impact of the new environment.

No one man's actions, no single date, no crucial event may be selected as a dividing point in this story of the transformation of American life and of its journalistic expression. The account begins in this chapter and continues in three succeeding chapters with gathering intensity—the same gathering intensity which was felt by those who lived in that period of change and who finally pieced together many small impressions to form a new picture of their society.

A NEW GROUP OF EDITORS

Emphasizing this change is the passing from the scene of famous figures of the newspaper movement which had begun in the 1830s. Between 1869 and 1878, five leaders of the era of personal journalism died: Henry J. Raymond, founder of the *New York Times,* James Gordon Bennett, Sr., founder of the *New York Herald,* Horace Greeley, founder of the *New York Tribune,* Samuel Bowles III, most famous of his name to edit the *Springfield Republican,* and William Cullen Bryant, for half a century editor of the *New York Evening Post.*

The newspaper builders who followed them appeared not only in New York but from coast to coast as the nation rushed to complete its geographical expansion and began in earnest to consolidate its economy. The new leaders were maturing and refining the processes and practices of their predecessors. Soon, sensing the opportunities presented by the changing environment in which they worked, some were to create what came to be known as the "new journalism."

Among those who replaced the departing leaders of journalism were some editors who represent a middle group, bridging the gap between the old and new: Charles A. Dana of the *New York Sun,* Edwin Lawrence Godkin of the *Nation* and *New York Evening Post,* Henry Watterson of the *Louisville Courier-Journal,* and Harvey W. Scott of the *Oregonian* in Portland. But even while these men and others like them were making their contributions to journalistic advancement as the leaders of a transitional period, the representatives of the new order were appearing. For example, rising in the dozen years between 1876 and 1887 were Melville E. Stone and the *Chicago Daily News,* Edward Wyllis Scripps and the *Cleveland Press,* Joseph Pulitzer and the *St. Louis Post-Dispatch* and *New York World,* William Rockhill Nelson and the *Kansas City Star,* and William Randolph Hearst, at the *San Francisco Examiner.* These are among the most famous names of men and newspapers in American journalism, as we shall see later in detail, and their appearance with others of note in such a brief period testifies to the opportunity for journalistic advances which the revolution in American life afforded. By the time Hearst had invaded New York with his *Journal* to do battle with Pulitzer in the late 1890s —at a time when the careers of Dana and Godkin were closing—the transition from the older era to the new had been achieved. American journalism, like American history, is marked by what historian Henry Steele Commager calls "the watershed of the nineties," whose topography is as blurred as those watersheds, but whose grand outlines emerge clearly.[1]

CHARACTERISTICS OF A NEW JOURNALISM

There are several general characteristics of this new movement in journalism, including the ever-increasing concentration of effort on impartial gathering and reporting of the news as the basic function of the press; growing independence of editorial opinion from partisan pressures; active and planned crusading in the community interest; intensified popularization of content, through style of writing and choice of subject matter; utilization of new mechanical developments and format techniques to create a more interesting product; and a lessening of personal influence as the daily newspaper became a complex corporate institution. It is with the first two of these characteristics that we are most immediately concerned.

Recognition of the news function as the primary obligation of the press had been a gradual process, encouraged by access to rapid communication of news by telegraph and railroad in the two decades before the Civil War. Those newspapermen who took the lead in seeking out the news, and reporting it in the interest of the reader alone, found their ranks increasing during the war years and the following decade. They realized that while their subscribers wished to have editorial opinion presented, readers wanted to be certain that they could form their own opinions based upon a factual and comprehensive presentation of the news.

Similarly, the postwar political and social situation stimulated some editors to an examination of their roles in expressing opinion. Those who rebelled against giving uncritical partisan support to a single political camp, while still in the minority, found themselves at great advantage over editors who maintained traditional loyalty at the expense of editorial freedom. And by the end of the century the editor who felt himself to be a part of a political party or group, bound to give unswerving loyalty to its dictates, was a liability to his newspaper.

POSTWAR POLITICAL PROBLEMS

There was good reason for the development of new approaches to news reporting and editorial expression. The problems which the United States faced in the years after the Civil War were heavy ones. The political leadership which was at hand was not equal to the tasks, and for a generation the

[1] Henry Steele Commager, *The American Mind* (New Haven: Yale University Press, 1950), p. 41.

talent exhibited in public life was far less than that shown in industry and business. There was no really great president between 1865 and the turn of the century, although Grover Cleveland won considerable recognition, primarily for his honesty and courage. But whatever the shortcomings in presidential leadership, the remainder of the political scene was far more depressing. The effort at political reconstruction of the South degenerated into an ugly battle between a vengeful Congress and an inept president; carpetbaggers and scalawags put in power in the South through arbitrary reconstruction policies gave way in turn to southern home rule without participation by the Negro; scandals rocked the Grant administration and corruption permeated city governments; a "consistent rebellion" flared against economic maladjustments, money supply inequities, and life-squeezing transportation and interest rates assessed against the farmer. In such a setting an editor with notions of independent thinking and devotion to presentation of the news was definitely encouraged.

Before we consider what the editors did, we should examine in more detail the political and socioeconomic situation in which they worked. The long debate over the status of the Federal Union, which had preoccupied Americans and split their allegiances so sharply, had come to an end with the verdict of the war. And in the years which followed, the revolution in industry and communication insured the national character of American society and subordinated the importance of the individual states. This latter development could not be known to those who were living through the transition, however. Until the late 1870s there was widespread fear that the effort to destroy the Federal Union had not ended, and that the fruits of victory would be lost if the political rights of the South were restored. For another ten years, on into the 1880s, some political leaders found it useful to continue a pretended fear of a new challenge to the union.[2]

The Republican party, which had elected Abraham Lincoln as its first president in 1860, found it necessary to run a Union ticket in 1864, pairing Lincoln with a Tennessee Democrat, Andrew Johnson. Even then, Lincoln polled only 400,000 more votes than the Democratic candidate, General George B. McClellan, with the South excluded from voting. In light of this, many Republicans viewed the immediate return of the South to full voting privileges with real alarm. They feared the result of accepting Lincoln's theory that since the Union was indissoluble, southern states would automatically return to their former status when fighting ceased. Freed from this policy by Lincoln's death, Representative Thaddeus Stevens of Pennsylvania and Senator Charles Sumner of Massachusetts gave leadership to a group which maintained the South had committed "state suicide" and should be considered as conquered territory. They and their followers, who came to dominate the postwar Congresses, were named the "radical Republicans."

[2] Frederic L. Paxson, *Recent History of the United States* (New York: Houghton Mifflin, 1937), p. 2.

In Andrew Johnson, the radical Republicans found an opponent who was made vulnerable by personality weaknesses which obscured his other qualities. When southern states readmitted to the union by Johnson ignored Negro political rights, the radical Republicans moved to handle the South on their own terms. They passed a civil rights bill; they submitted the fourteenth amendment to the Constitution for ratification; they passed over Johnson's veto the reconstruction acts which forced all southern states to again seek re-entry into the Union on radical-Republican terms; and they instituted military rule in the South. Northern carpetbaggers and southern scalawags who took advantage of the unpreparedness of Negro voters for democratic responsibilities disrupted southern life, and home rule was not fully restored until 1877. The contest between the radical Republicans and the president was climaxed by the impeachment of Johnson, who was saved from removal from office by a single vote in the Senate. Thereupon the Republican party turned to General Ulysses S. Grant as its candidate in 1868, and won the election easily.

ECONOMIC AND FINANCIAL CRISES

Political reconstruction thus was a controversial problem, but financial reconstruction was even more so. Commodity prices in the North had doubled during the five years of war. Running of the printing presses to create legal tender paper money, dubbed "greenbacks," had driven coinage into hiding, intensifying the usual wartime inflationary trend. Congress in 1866 therefore voted to retire the greenbacks gradually over an 11-year period. The argument was advanced that retirement of the greenbacks, which constituted a part of the large federal debt, would deflate prices and increase the value of the dollar. Such action would be to the benefit of creditors, and of wage earners whose incomes had not kept pace with prices. But farmers, who generally were debtors, would find money dearer and prices for their products lower. Opposition to retirement of the greenbacks from circulation began to develop in the Middle West agricultural areas, and of course in the South, whose economy had been prostrated by the collapse of the Confederate currency and the ravages of war. The movement to keep the greenbacks, and even to issue more paper money as a means of easing the load of debts, became known as the "Ohio Idea." By 1868, pressure had mounted until Congress repealed the greenback redemption act. The debate continued, however, and the opponents of paper money forced final retirement of the greenbacks beginning in 1879, further intensifying the problem of an inadequate money supply for the rapidly-expanding American economy.

Currency supply was not the only complaint of the agricultural West and South. Farmers found interest rates on their borrowed money excessively high, and impossible to pay in years of poor crops or low prices. They found the railroads, which were extending their tracks across the country, were basing their rates on the axiom "charge all the traffic will bear." And they found grain elevators and other storage facilities usually were under the control of those who bought the crops. The system generally worked so that the farmer had to sell immediately after harvest to pay his debts, and could not hold his grain in storage for more advantageous prices. Transportation rates were inflexibly high, regardless of market conditions and the level of the nation's economy.[3]

By the early 1870s a depression was closing in on a country which had fought a costly and devastating war, which had plunged into a postwar expansion of capital investment at a faster rate than it was producing wealth, and which was still borrowing large amounts of money from European investors for its expansion. When the financial crash came in 1873, with declining prices for agricultural products, the farmers were certain that their lot was unbearable. A "consistent rebellion" began as the agricultural West and South sought economic redress. Currency reform, banking reform, regulation of railroad and grain elevator rates, and lowering of interest charges were the major political issues. The Greenback party flourished as a result, to be followed by the rise of the Populists. The Patrons of Husbandry formed their Grange organizations which forced passage of state laws in the Middle West fixing maximum railroad rates, and the United States Supreme Court in a famous decision (*Munn v. Illinois,* 1877) upheld the doctrine that the railroads were subject to regulation in the public interest.

GREELEY'S "MUGWUMP" PRESIDENTIAL RACE

In this troubled political and economic setting, the press found much significant news. And as the news principle gained ascendancy, the editorial columns showed definite signs of rebelling against unswerving loyalty to political parties and their beliefs. The way was eased by rebellion within the ranks of the political parties themselves, and particularly by the emergence of a "liberal Republican" faction opposing the radical Republicans and their President, General Grant. Independence of editorial expression meant primarily the freedom to criticise the leaders and policies of the party which the editor might normally support; but for some it also meant freedom to bolt the party and support a rival. Those who bolted were called "mugwumps" by their opponents.

The mugwumps of 1872 were led by a group of editors. The liberal Republicans, meeting in convention to find a suitable candidate to oppose Grant, included many newspapermen, the most important of whom were Samuel

[3] This is a brief summary of the farmers' problems, which are given full analysis in such studies as John D. Hicks' *The Populist Revolt* (Minneapolis: University of Minnesota Press, 1931), and Solon J. Buck's *The Granger Movement* (Cambridge, Mass.: Harvard University Press, 1913).

Bowles of the *Springfield Republican,* Horace White of the *Chicago Tribune,* Murat Halstead of the *Cincinnati Commercial,* and Carl Schurz of the St. Louis *Westliche Post.* The convention ended with the selection of a famous editor, Horace Greeley, as the candidate. Greeley also was nominated by the Democrats, and thus an important segment of the Republican-aligned press found itself allied with pro-Democratic papers. But Greeley's bid for the presidency was ill-starred. Many liberals could not find their way clear to support the aging editor, and others commented cruelly on his eccentricities. Thus such critics of the Grant administration as the *New York Evening Post* and *New York Sun,* and the influential magazines, *Harper's Weekly* and the *Nation,* shied away from the Greeley cause. And despite growing discontent with the radical Republicans' reconstruction policies, the administrative shortcomings of the Grant regime, and unsolved economic problems, Grant was reelected handily.

Even though the Greeley campaign had failed, the effect of the mugwump rebellion by such influential editors was a substantial gain in journalistic prestige. It added new proof that editors could shift their political positions and survive, and encouraged those newspapers which felt obliged to attack strong political groups. Previously, Henry J. Raymond of the *New York Times,* William Cullen Bryant of the *New York Evening Post,* and Charles A. Dana of the *New York Sun*—all supporters of the Republican party—had opposed the radical Republicans in their attempt to remove President Johnson from office in 1868. Now each successive episode strengthened the determination of some newspapers to put reporting of the news and maintenance of editorial independence ahead of partisan political considerations.

SCANDALS IN GOVERNMENT

Scandals in government offer a tempting target for any editor, and the political ineptness and moral laxity which characterized the postwar years further stimulated newspapers and magazines to action. The most notorious example of corruption at the city level was in the operations of the Tweed Ring in New York City. Tammany boss William M. Tweed and his Democratic party cohorts, who milked the city of an estimated million dollars, had grown so brazen by 1870 that they had listed a plasterer's pay at $50,000 a day for an entire month while constructing a courthouse. The Tweed Ring controlled some newspapers, and frightened others into silence, but it met its masters in the *New York Times* and *Harper's Weekly.* The *Times,* published by George Jones and edited by Louis J. Jennings after the death of Raymond in 1869, obtained documentary proof of the Tweed Ring's thefts in 1871 and broke the astounding story. *Harper's Weekly,* ably edited by George William Curtis, provided a gallery for Thomas Nast, the great political cartoonist who invented the donkey and elephant symbols for the two major parties. Nast used his pen

THE TAMMANY TIGER LOOSE.—"What are you going to do about it?"

Thomas Nast's famed Tammany Tiger cartoon in an 1871 *Harper's Weekly.*

and ink against Tweed in such devastating fashion that he was offered a bribe to halt his attacks. The answer was the driving of the Tweed Ring from power.[4]

The scandals which left the reputation of the Grant administration blackened were being hinted at before the 1872 presidential election, but it was not until the closing days of the campaign that the *New York Sun* publicized what became known as the Crédit Mobilier affair. When the evidence was developed fully after the election, it proved that promoters of the Union Pacific and Central Pacific railroads had developed a simple system for influencing legislators and others whose support was needed in the obtaining of federal land grants for railroad construction. The railroad builders, operating under the name Crédit Mobilier of America, had sold stock to many public men, lending them the money to pay for the stock and then declaring such huge profits that the loans could be repaid in a single year. Exposure of what amounted to gifts from those seeking legislative favor ruined some politicians, and cast suspicion

[4] Fuller details are given in Gustavus Myers, *The History of Tammany Hall* (New York: Boni and Liveright, 1917).

on many more, including the prominent Republican leader, James G. Blaine of Maine.

Other disclosures of weaknesses of the Grant administration came rapidly: the whiskey tax frauds in the Treasury Department, the bribing of the Secretary of War, W. W. Belknap, and the acceptance of improper gifts by Grant's private secretary. The dazed Grant was himself untouched by the scandals, but his party lost control of the House of Representatives to the Democrats in 1874, and politics became a seesaw affair. The country was entering a period of "dead center" government. For 16 of the next 22 years, control of the two houses of Congress and the presidency was split between the two major parties, so closely was the popular vote divided. Little political progress could be made in such a situation, and eventually the protective tariff became the principal issue of frustrated political aspirants who could not cope with the problems which were generating the "consistent rebellion" of the economically discontented West and South.

DANA AND THE *NEW YORK SUN*

Of the editors who worked in this turbulent postwar period, two in particular stand out as leaders. Their contributions are sharply different. Charles A. Dana in his years as editor of the *New York Sun* taught the journalist world new lessons in the art of news handling and writing. Edwin Lawrence Godkin in his years as editor of the *Nation* and of the *New York Evening Post* provided solid editorial page leadership. With the deaths of the older New York leaders —Bennett, Greeley, Raymond, and Bryant—Dana and Godkin became the strong men who influenced the maturing of the older press.

Dana and his *Sun* in many respects represent the bridge between the older press and the new journalism which was to develop before the end of the century. A New Englander who had been attracted to the Brook Farm socialist experiment in the 1840s along with other intellectuals seeking the answer to the problems created by the industrial revolution, Dana had met Horace Greeley there. He joined Greeley's staff and became managing editor of the *Tribune* in 1849—the first American to hold such a position. When the Dana-Greeley association was broken in the early days of the Civil War as the aftermath of the *Tribune's* mistaken military predictions, Dana entered government service, and emerged to struggle for a year as editor of a new Chicago paper, the *Daily Republican* (forerunner of the famous *Inter Ocean*). The newspaper venture was successful, but Dana wearied of Chicago. Returning to New York, he obtained sufficient backing to buy the *Sun*, the original penny newspaper. Its plant and 43,000 circulation were priced at $175,000 by Moses S. Beach, whose father had taken over Ben Day's paper. A career with Greeley on the *Tribune* already behind him, Dana in 1868 began a 29-year career as editor of the *Sun*.

Dana's audience consisted mainly of average New Yorkers, workers and small merchants. To them he addressed his first editorial in the *Sun,* which expressed his ideas on newspaper making. The *Sun,* he said, would present "a daily photograph of the whole world's doings in the most luminous and lively manner." Its staff would write simply and clearly as it tried to present that photograph of the life of the people of New York, as well as of the world's doings. The *Sun* would be low-priced and readable, yet it would use enterprise and money to be the best possible newspaper.

The journalist, Dana insisted, must be interested not only in politics, economics and government, but first of all in people. The average American, Dana knew, was hard at work, yet he loved sentiment and fun, and enjoyed stories reflecting a skillful touch of tenderness or wit. As one of the biographers of Dana and the *Sun* put it, Dana had "the indefinable newspaper instinct that knows when a tomcat on the steps of the City Hall is more important than a crisis in the Balkans." [5]

Writers who could make their stories come alive were prized on the *Sun,* and as a consequence reporters prized the *Sun* in turn. It became what the craft calls a "newspaperman's newspaper." Those who worked there were refining the sensationalized techniques of the penny press, as they wrote with increasing ability and discernment, seeking to report all manner of events, but looking especially for those happenings which make up "the poetry of life." The rule of the *Sun* was "be interesting," and its reporters obeyed whether they were writing about the doings of the Astors and the Vanderbilts, the commercial and financial life of the city, a murder, a political debate, or merely about a crying child on a curb, a neighborhood quarrel in one of New York's many sections, or the latest style in whiskers. Other newspapers were in quest of the same goal, of course, but the *Sun* under Dana's direction was more diligent and therefore more successful. Its readership doubled in the first two years of Dana's tenure and circulation reached 130,000 by 1876.

The office cat was one of the most celebrated members of the *Sun's* staff, and the subject of a famous editorial which reflected the paper's spirit. One night in the 1880s the *Sun's* copy of a message from President Cleveland to Congress blew out an open window. There was considerable concern, for the publishing of every presidential message was a must. One staff member, however, was unconcerned and suggested, "Oh, say the office cat ate it up." This Dana did, and soon the cat was a familiar trademark of Dana's *Sun.*[6]

Brilliant as the *Sun* was, however, it had serious weaknesses. Since Dana insisted on limiting its size to four pages, comprehensive coverage of significant news suffered. And the editorial page which could originate such ringing phrases as "No king, no clown, to rule this town!" to combat Tweed, and "Turn the rascals out!" to harass Grant, could also be so intellectually "smart"

[5] Frank M. O'Brien, *The Story of The Sun* (New York: George H. Doran Company, 1918), p. 231. New edition (Appleton-Century-Crofts, 1928), p. 151.

[6] *Ibid.,* pp. 287–89, carries the editorial in full.

as to approach cynicism. Dana's fondness for wit and levity made for entertaining reading, but his cynical and sometimes perverse comments on public issues greatly weakened the character of his newspaper.

In politics, Dana steered an erratic course. The *Sun* opposed the impeachment of Johnson by the radical Republicans in 1868, but supported their candidate, Grant, in the fall presidential election. By 1872 it had turned on Grant, but could not restrain itself from laughing at the candidacy of editor Greeley. Dana supported the Democratic presidential candidate, Samuel J. Tilden, in 1876 and was so enraged when the disputed electoral votes of three southern states were finally awarded to the Republicans that the *Sun* always referred to President Rutherford B. Hayes as a "fraud" and, in a drawing of him, printed that word across his forehead. In 1880 Dana refused to support any candidate, but devastatingly remarked that the Democrat, General Winfield S. Hancock, was "a good man, weighing 240 pounds." Perversity reached a climax in 1884 when Dana violently attacked the "tainted" candidacy of Republican James G. Blaine, then ignored Democrat Grover Cleveland and put the *Sun* behind the politically discredited candidate of a third party, Benjamin Butler. Butler's campaign failed dismally and the *Sun* lost a third of its readers. Dana then supported Cleveland in 1888, only to see him lose the presidency to Benjamin Harrison. When Cleveland ran again in 1892 and rewon the White House from Harrison, Dana was against him because it was Cleveland's third campaign. And in 1896, the year before he died, Dana bowed out opposing William Jennings Bryan.

In its discussions of issues, the *Sun* became increasingly conservative, in contrast to Dana's earlier beliefs. The paper detested labor unions. It poked fun at civil service reform advocates and others interested in good government, even though the *Sun* itself crusaded against misconduct in office. And it long advocated imperialistic schemes for the annexation of Canada, Cuba, and other neighboring areas.

GODKIN, THE *NATION*, AND THE *POST*

It remained for an English-born journalist to give the United States the vigorous and intelligent editorial leadership which it needed in the postwar period. He was Edwin Lawrence Godkin, the founder of the magazine, the *Nation*, and successor to William Cullen Bryant as the driving spirit of the *New York Evening Post*.

Of Godkin, historian Allan Nevins has written: "Godkin showed at once a distinctive style, a refreshing penetration, and a skill in ironic analysis never before equalled in American journalism." And because this was so, philosopher William James could write: "To my generation his was certainly the towering influence in all thought concerning public affairs, and indirectly his influence has assuredly been more pervasive than that of any other writer of the generation, for he influenced other writers who never quoted him, and determined the whole current of discussion."[7] President Charles W. Eliot of Harvard University, President Daniel Coit Gilman of Johns Hopkins, James Russell Lowell, James Bryce, Charles Eliot Norton—the intellectual leaders of Godkin's generation—all publicly acknowledged the debt they owed to the pages of the *Nation*. Not, of course, that they always agreed with its editor's viewpoints.

Godkin had been a reporter and editorial writer for English newspapers, and had written editorials for Henry J. Raymond's *New York Times,* before deciding that the United States needed a high-grade weekly journal of opinion and literary criticism, similar to those in England. In 1865 he found the financial backing for the *Nation,* and announced its aims.

The *Nation,* Godkin said, would discuss the political and economic questions of the day "with greater accuracy and moderation than are now to be found in the daily press." It would advocate "whatever in legislation or in manners seems likely to promote a more equal distribution of the fruits of progress and civilization." It would seek to better the conditions of the Negro. It would fix "public attention upon the political importance of education, and the dangers which a system like ours runs from the neglect of it in any portion of our territory." And it would print sound and impartial criticisms of books and works of art.[8]

Godkin was a mid-Victorian English liberal, of the John Stuart Mill school of economic thought. Therefore he believed that government should not intervene in economic matters. But unlike many of his time, he did believe that government should take action in social spheres. To a twentieth-century world which has used government as a regulatory force in both economic and social situations, Godkin thus appears at times to be reactionary and at other times liberal.

For example, Godkin fought the protective tariff which had been hiked to high levels by the Republicans during the Civil War, because tariffs represented government intervention in economic affairs. This placed him in the liberal camp. But he argued relentlessly against what he considered improper attempts by debtor groups to obtain legislation which would increase the money supply or regulate high interest rates. And he opposed any recognition of the right of labor unions to strike or to bargain collectively, although he admitted that an individual workman had little chance to bargain effectively. His use of cold, intellectual arguments against liberal groups with whom he at other times showed sympathy led his critics to call him cruel and snobbish.

But in many other areas, Godkin was in the forefront of progressive thought. He urged complete reconciliation with the South during the period of military rule; he was one of the earliest advocates of civil service reform to end the spoils system; he believed in women's suffrage when it was an unpopular

[7] As quoted in Allan Nevins, *American Press Opinion* (New York: Heath, 1928), p. 299.

[8] Godkin's full statement of purpose is found in Rollo Ogden, *Life and Letters of Edwin Lawrence Godkin,* I (New York: Macmillan, 1907), pp. 237–38.

idea; he was a strong supporter of public education and the new land-grant universities; and, as mentioned above, he wrote in behalf of the Negro. Above all, the *Nation* spoke out against corrupt and inefficient government, and ceaselessly badgered politicians who were interested more in personal gain than in progressive improvement of government. The magazine had other writers and well-known contributors. But it was Godkin's opinions, written usually in a measured and convincing style but pointed up with pungent phrases, which won it the enthusiastic attention of its 10,000 or so readers. And they in turn, as ministers, teachers, editors, writers, and other leaders of society, transmitted the *Nation's* arguments to millions of other Americans.

In 1881, Godkin moved onto a bigger but actually less influential journalistic stage. That year Henry Villard, a Civil War correspondent who later won a fortune building railroads, purchased the *New York Evening Post,* and obtained a trio of outstanding editors for the newspaper. One was Horace White, who had edited the *Chicago Tribune* from 1866 to 1874, taking that newspaper into the liberal Republican camp for a brief period as he advocated tariff reduction, civil service reform, and currency policies favorable to the farmers. A second was Carl Schurz, the former editor of the St. Louis *Westliche Post* who had become Secretary of the Interior in President Hayes' cabinet, and a leading American liberal. The third was Godkin, who sold the *Nation* to Villard but continued to edit it as the weekly edition of the *Evening Post.* Within two years, Schurz and Godkin quarreled over Godkin's antilabor union views, and Schurz resigned, leaving Godkin in control of the *Evening Post* with White as his assistant.

With Godkin, the *Evening Post* and the *Nation* rose to new fame in the presidential election year of 1884. The contest lay between James G. Blaine, the Republican congressional leader from Maine, and Grover Cleveland, Democratic governor of New York. Godkin, declaring that Blaine was unacceptable because of the post-Civil War scandals, fought his election with all his editorial skill. As the campaign progressed, charges of immoral conduct were made against Cleveland, and emotionalism ran high. Some stalwart Republican newspapers in leading cities found themselves opposing Blaine in company with the usual dissenters—the *Evening Post,* the *New York Times, Springfield Republican, Harper's Weekly,* and the *Nation.* Dana of the *Sun,* who would support neither major party candidate, fastened upon these papers the name "mugwump," indicating desertion of party regularity. It applied particularly to the *Evening Post,* which had been Republican since the founding of the party in 1856.

The *Evening Post's* particular contribution was Godkin's famous "deadly parallel" column, in which he matched Blaine's campaign statements and congressional record against his personal associations with railroad builders and financiers. The campaign became exceedingly bitter, and it was evident that the New York State vote would decide the election. When Cleveland carried New York by 23,000 votes and became the first Democrat to win the presidency since the Civil War, many explanations were advanced. A Blaine supporter who had described the Democrats as a party of "rum, Romanism, and rebellion" received heavy blame, as did the antilabor *New York Tribune,* whose advocacy of Blaine was judged to be a handicap in the wooing of working men's votes. But Godkin asserted, with some justice, that the victory was proof of the creation of a group of independent voters who would put the public welfare ahead of party loyalty, as had the mugwump newspapers and magazines.

Another great crusade against Tammany Hall in the 1890s found Godkin and the *Evening Post* in the forefront of a newspaper attack upon the revived political machine. Godkin called Tammany "an association for plunder" and began publishing before elections a "voter's directory" in which he exposed the police records and other shortcomings of Tammany men. Eventually the directory ran to 6,500 names, and anguished politicians filed as many as three suits for libel in one day against the *Evening Post's* editor, to no avail. By 1894 the voters of New York had elected another of the city's periodic reform administrations.

Godkin stood in the early 1880s as New York's leading editor primarily because of his great ability, but also because of the shortcomings of his contemporaries. The *Times,* after the death of Raymond, was slowly going downhill and exhibited spirit and influence only sporadically. Dana's *Sun* was erratic, and the Bennetts' *Herald* had little editorial force. Greeley's *Tribune,* after the founding editor's death in 1872, switched position and became the spokesman for the dominant conservative wing of the Republican party. The *Tribune's* new editor was a famous journalistic figure, Whitelaw Reid, but his editorial stand lacked the qualities of independence shown by an increasing number of editors. While Godkin was urging reconciliation with the South, the *Tribune* was waving the bloody shirt as late as 1880 to preserve Republican supremacy. Godkin was for tariff reform; the *Tribune,* for high tariffs and protection of the industrial interests of the expanding capitalism. Godkin long favored civil service reform, which found favor with the Republican leadership only after the assassination of President James A. Garfield. And the *Tribune* more than matched Godkin's opposition to labor unions, fighting a printers' strike against itself for 15 years.[9] Still, the *Tribune's* standards of news coverage and presentation were such that it was a formidable competitor for the readership of those whom the *Post* called the "gentlemen and scholars."

Unfortunately, Godkin was not a newspaperman despite his editorial genius. He cared little for the news policies of the *Evening Post,* beyond his specialized interests. He disliked sentiment and color in the news, and he would have liked to have kept all news of crime and violence out of the paper's columns. Whatever merit there was to his viewpoints, they put the *Evening*

[9] As previously noted, the *Tribune's* founder, Horace Greeley, had been the first president of New York City's Typographical Union No. 6, founded in 1850.

Post at a serious disadvantage in the competition for circulation, and the paper never attained the readership its editorial leadership deserved.

Godkin retired as editor of the *Evening Post* and the *Nation* in 1899. He died in 1902. When Henry Villard died in 1900, his son, Oswald Garrison Villard, became publisher and editorial leader of the two publications. They continued to be fighting liberal organs.[10]

HENRY WATTERSON AND THE *COURIER-JOURNAL*

Other strong editorial voices were raised outside New York during the period of Godkin's dominance. The most notable were those of Henry Watterson of the *Louisville Courier-Journal* and Harvey W. Scott of the *Oregonian* in Portland. Both enjoyed long careers which began at the close of the Civil War and continued until World War I, but both belong primarily in this transitional period of journalism history. Arthur Krock, an associate of Watterson on the *Courier-Journal* staff before becoming a *New York Times* fixture, offers one reason for setting Watterson apart from later editors: ". . . he was the last of those editors who wrote with the power of ownership."[11] The same was true of Scott. Other editors, like Godkin, exercised free rein because of their relationship to owners of their papers, and they have continued to do so since, but admittedly with increasing difficulty as the newspaper became a corporate institution.

Watterson was editor of the *Courier-Journal* for 50 years, and his personality did much to make the newspaper one of the foremost in the country. He was a colorful representative of the era of personal journalism who loved to engage in editorial-page duels with other editors. One of his first foes was Dana and he lived to banter with the editors of another journalistic generation in the twentieth century. He himself said that he belonged to the era of "the personal, one-man papers—rather blatant, but independent."[12]

Watterson had varied youthful ambitions: to be a great historian, a great dramatist, a great novelist, a great musician. He came no closer to those dreams than writing a rejected novel and serving as a music critic in New York, but his catholic interests served in time to make him a versatile and engaging writer of editorials. He was an editorial writer in Washington when the Civil War began, and he cast his lot with the South, editing a Tennessee newspaper named the *Rebel*. After stints on newspapers in Cincinnati, Atlanta, and Nashville, Watterson at the age of 28 found his lifetime work in Louisville.

[10] The younger Villard sold the *Evening Post* in 1918 but remained at the helm of the *Nation* until 1933.

[11] Arthur Krock, ed., *The Editorials of Henry Watterson* (Louisville: The Courier-Journal, 1923), p. 15.

[12] Tom Wallace, "There Were Giants in Those Days," *Saturday Evening Post*, August 6, 1938 (reprinted in John E. Drewry, ed., *Post Biographies of Famous Journalists*).

There Walter N. Haldeman, editor of the *Courier,* was in the process of consolidating the *Journal* and the *Democrat* with his newspaper, and the editorship and part ownership of the new *Courier-Journal* went to Watterson. The year was 1868. Watterson, who despite his work for the southern cause had believed secession to be wrong, raised his voice in behalf of reconciliation of the North and South, and gave advice freely to both sections. He told the North that military rule should be relaxed, and he was listened to because he also had sympathy for the Negro. He told the South that Lincoln was a great man, and that much of its misery had come about as a result of his assassination. And the South listened, because Watterson was a southerner of good family, not a reforming Yankee. Soon the *Courier-Journal* editorial columns, and particularly its weekly edition, won a position as a leading voice of the new South.

Watterson enhanced his position by exchanging fire with other leading editors, and by his picturesque and powerful comments, particularly in the field of politics. Although often verbose and sometimes florid, he was telling in his attacks upon those with whom he disagreed. The victims were legion; Watterson rarely was in harmony with those in authority, and he was a stalwart defender of the rights of the individual. When he used such phrases as "whack-whaddle," "pot-wholloper," and "bandy-shanked," or said of Theodore Roosevelt, "as sweet a gentleman as ever scuttled a ship or cut a throat," the reader was encouraged to continue perusing editorials which ran as long as three columns of type.

The combination of the Haldeman family and Watterson prospered. The editor looked and acted his part as a southern gentleman, equipped with shaggy eyebrows and mustache, and "Marse Henry" became a newspaper tradition. He lived in a country home graced with fine wines and fine cooking, and talked and wrote about politics, literature, music, and the arts. While the *Courier-Journal* advanced steadily and surely into the modern era of journalism, its "Marse Henry" contentedly remained in his role of personal journalist.

HARVEY SCOTT AND THE *OREGONIAN*

In the Far West, another voice was raised by an editor whose intellectual powers and forceful writing brought him attention as the leading spokesman of his area. He was Harvey W. Scott, who for 45 years edited the *Oregonian* in Portland. The *Oregonian,* founded in 1850 in a village near the junction of the Willamette and Columbia rivers, grew with the community. Scott gave up a law career to become its editor in 1865, and in 1877 he and Henry L. Pittock became the owners.[13]

[13] The Scott and Pittock family heirs retained control of the *Oregonian* until 1950, when the 100-year-old paper was sold to Samuel I. Newhouse. See the *Oregonian,* December 11, 1950.

Like Godkin, Scott was scholarly and forceful in his expression of opinion, but like Godkin, too, he lacked Watterson's human touch. There was one major reason why Scott's editorials were widely read and quoted: he had the ability to grapple with complex problems which many an editor shied away from, and to present new viewpoints originating in his own reasoning and analysis. His range of information seemed unlimited, and he used this resource as he thought an editor should, to guide public opinion in the public interest. The *Oregonian* was Republican by choice, but Scott wrote as an independent editor, taking his stand on the basis of his conception of the public good. An editor with Scott's abilities is rare in any period, and his fame spread from the home city in which he was a leading figure, as the *Oregonian* won statewide circulation and its editorial voice became nationally recognized.

Dana, Godkin, Watterson, and Scott—particularly the latter two—lived through the enormous changes which were occurring in American life as the industrial revolution hit full stride. They were aware of change, and accepted it, but their journalistic roles were more of the older order than of the new. There were other men among their contemporaries who might well be named but these were the leaders and the symbols of a transitional era. They and their fellow workers contributed new strengths to American journalism as it approached the "watershed of the nineties."

Annotated Bibliography

Books

Baehr, Harry W., Jr., *The New York Tribune Since the Civil War.* New York: Dodd, Mead, 1936. One of the better histories of newspapers.

Casual Essays of The Sun. New York: R. G. Cooke, 1905. A collection of *Sun* editorials including "Dear Virginia."

Fuess, Claude M., *Carl Schurz.* New York: Dodd, Mead, 1932. A biography of the famous liberal, whose own *Reminiscences* (1907) are rewarding reading.

Hicks, John D., *The American Nation.* Boston: Houghton Mifflin, 1964. A standard text for American history since 1865.

Josephson, Matthew, *The Robber Barons.* New York: Harcourt, Brace & Jovanovich, 1934. A scathing description of the low state of public morality after the Civil War, focusing particularly upon corruption in railroad building. *The Politicos* (1938) is a companion volume.

Keller, Morton, *The Art and Politics of Thomas Nast.* New York: Oxford University Press, 1968. A beautifully printed, illustrated, and researched story of the great cartoonist.

Krock, Arthur, ed., *The Editorials of Henry Watterson.* New York: George H. Doran Company, 1923. Excellent preface.

Nevins, Allan, *The Emergence of Modern America, 1865–1878,* A History of

American Life, Vol. VIII. New York: Macmillan, 1927. A rich social history, whose extensive documentation is accompanied by highly skillful writing.

———, *The Evening Post; A Century of Journalism.* New York: Boni and Liveright, 1922. The Godkin and other eras are presented against a general social and political background.

Nye, Russel B., *Midwestern Progressive Politics; a Historical Study of Its Origins and Development, 1870–1950.* East Lansing: Michigan State College Press, 1951. A comprehensive survey. For more specialized studies, see Solon J. Buck, *The Granger Movement* (Cambridge, Mass.: Harvard University Press, 1913), and John D. Hicks, *The Populist Revolt* (Minneapolis: University of Minnesota Press, 1931).

O'Brien, Frank M., *The Story of The Sun.* New York: George H. Doran Company, 1918. Revised. New York: Appleton-Century-Crofts, 1928. One of the most readable histories of newspapers.

Ogden, Rollo, *Life and Letters of Edwin Lawrence Godkin.* New York: Macmillan, 1907. The standard biography.

Paine, Albert Bigelow, *Th. Nast, His Period and His Pictures.* New York: Macmillan, 1904. Well-illustrated with Nast's famous cartoons.

Rhodes, James Ford, *A History of the United States Since the Compromise of 1850.* New York: Macmillan, 1892–1906. A nine-volume political history ending with the turn of the century, written with conspicuous success by a conservative businessman turned scholar.

Stampp, Kenneth M., *The Era of Reconstruction, 1865–1877.* New York: Knopf, 1965. New points of view admirably presented by consensus school revisionist.

Stone, Candace, *Dana and the Sun.* New York: Dodd, Mead, 1938. The top-ranking biography of Dana, critical in tone.

Wall, Joseph F., *Henry Watterson: Reconstructed Rebel.* New York: Oxford University Press, 1956. A well-documented study.

Watterson, Henry, *"Marse Henry"; An Autobiography.* New York: George H. Doran Company, 1919. The Louisville editor's own pungent story.

Wish, Harvey, *Society and Thought in Modern America.* New York: Longmans, Green & Company, 1962. The second volume in Wish's social and intellectual history, beginning with 1865.

Woodward, C. Vann, *Origins of the New South, 1877–1913.* Baton Rouge: Louisiana State University Press, 1951. Prize-winning study of the South's emergence from the Civil War.

Periodicals and Monographs

Downey, Matthew T., "Horace Greeley and the Politicians," *Journal of American History,* LIII (March 1967), 727. Liberal Republican convention of 1872.

Leiter, Kelly, "U.S. Grant and the *Chicago Tribune,*" *Journalism Quarterly,* XLVII (Spring 1970), 71. Based on his Ph.D. thesis, Southern Illinois University, 1969.

Mitchell, Edward P., "The Newspaperman's Newspaper," *Scribner's,* LXXVI (August 1924), 149. A vivid portrait of Dana and his *Sun* by a longtime *Sun* editor.

Nevins, Allan, "E. L. Godkin: Victorian Liberal," *Nation,* CLXXI (July 22, 1950), 76. An interpretive essay, followed by a study, written by Lewis Gannett, of Oswald Garrison Villard's editorship.

Plummer, L. Niel, "Henry Watterson's Editorial Style: An Interpretative Analysis," *Journalism Quarterly,* XXIII (March 1946), 58.

Pringle, Henry F., "Godkin of 'The Post,' " *Scribner's,* XCVI (December 1934), 327. A well-balanced article by a newspaperman turned biographer. Reprinted in Ford and Emery, *Highlights in the History of the American Press.*

———, "Kentucky Bourbon—Marse Henry Watterson," *Scribner's,* XCVII (January 1935), 10. Reprinted in Ford and Emery, *Highlights in the History of the American Press.*

Quarterly of the Oregon Historical Society, XIV, No. 2 (June 1913). An issue devoted to Harvey W. Scott, editor of the *Oregonian.*

Thorp, Robert K., " 'Marse Henry' and the Negro: A New Perspective," *Journalism Quarterly,* XLVI (Autumn 1969), 467. It was not as Marse Henry remembered it; he was scarcely their champion.

Turnbull, George, "The Schoolmaster of the Oregon Press," *Journalism Quarterly,* XV (December 1938), 350. A study of the influence of Harvey W. Scott by the author of the *History of Oregon Newspapers* (1939).

Wallace, Tom, "There Were Giants in Those Days," *Saturday Evening Post,* August 6, 1938. The color of the Marse Henry Watterson days is recaptured by another longtime Louisville editor. Reprinted in John E. Drewry, ed., *Post Biographies of Famous Journalists* (Athens: University of Georgia Press, 1942).

Wiley, Bonnie, "History of the Portland *Oregonian,*" Ph.D. thesis, Southern Illinois University, 1965. From Harvey Scott to Samuel Newhouse, 1850 to 1965.

FRANK LESLIE'S ILLUSTRATED NEWSPAPER

Entered according to Act of Congress in the year 1857, by Frank Leslie, in the Clerk's Office of the District Court for the Southern District of New York. (Copyrighted May 10, 1858.)

No. 128 —Vol. V.] NEW YORK, SATURDAY, MAY 15, 1858. [Price 6 Cents.

OUR EXPOSURE OF THE MILK TRADE OF NEW YORK AND BROOKLYN.

From a hundred sources we are receiving, day by day, thanks for our public spirit and fearless exposure of a nefarious and revolting trade, and good wishes and prayers for the ultimate and speedy success of our undertaking.

We feel sincerely gratified and deeply grateful for the outside encouragement we receive; it will move us to new exertions, for we feel that we have obtained the ear of the public; that its sympathies and hopes are with us, and armed with this assurance we feel our power equal to the emergency. That our blows have been dealt strongly and truly we have ample evidence. Our exposure has not only broken up all the milk routes we have published, but one whose name we were fortunately enabled to give, is selling off his swill milk cows. His stable is broken up, his swill trade gone, and mark the consequence—he has contracted with the country dairies for the milk he requires for his customers. Is not the good work begun? May we not hope for the future?

An early crusade: the 1858 "swill milk" campaign in *Leslie's Illustrated Newspaper*.

16

A Revolution in National Life

The newspaper has a history; but it has, likewise, a natural history. The press, as it exists, is not, as our moralists sometimes seem to assume, the wilful product of any little group of living men. On the contrary, it is the outcome of a historic process. . . .
—Robert E. Park

The journalism of Dana and Godkin was the product of an American society in transition; what was happening to the national life for the first dozen years after the close of the War Between the States could be called a transition. But then, the swelling tide of economic and social change brought not transition, but revolution.

In journalism, as in all other aspects of American life, the result was an emergence of new concepts and practices more akin to the twentieth century than to the immediate past. New leaders were to revolutionize the newspaper and the magazine by responding to the abruptly changed environment rather than by clinging to the older patterns. The contrast, by the 1890s, between Dana's cranky, change-resisting journalism and that of the dynamic symbol of the new order—Joseph Pulitzer—was glaring indeed. It was no more glaring, however, than the differences which had developed in literature, in science, in political and economic thought, in business and industry, in the way Americans lived and worked.

AN INDUSTRIAL ECONOMY

What was happening? Industrialization was happening on a major scale: mechanization of production processes, the rise of the city, vast expansion of communication facilities, the coming of the age of steel, the harnessing of electricity for light and power, and a host of inventions and new businesses.

This was the true nationalization of the United States, the achievement of economic and social interdependence.[1] National growth and increased wealth meant cultural progress in literature, science, and the social sciences. But the wealth was not equally distributed, and there was sharp questioning of the theory of individualism which permitted unrestrained exploitation, enormous concentrations of wealth and economic power, and the many injustices of a materialistic-minded age. Political unrest, the rise of labor unions, and demands for economic and social reform thus were added to the scene.

America was a rich continent for the aggressive and the ingenious to master. Between 1865 and 1880 the national wealth doubled, and by 1900 it had doubled again. The population doubled in those 35 years. The nation's iron ore, its oil, its lumber, and its western agricultural lands were sources of yet untapped wealth. Its people, who by and large admired the successful enterprisers, eagerly provided investment and speculative capital. Only when it became clear that the division of the spoils had been in favor of a few to the detriment of the many, did the protests take effect. In the meantime, the patterns had been set. The dynamic capitalism of an expanding America, seizing upon unparalleled natural resources and utilizing the new machines of the industrial revolution, had transformed the national economy.

Some of the figures which show what was happening to the United States are these:

Total manufacturing production increased sevenfold between the end of the Civil War and 1900: Using a base figure of 100 for the years 1909–1913, the index figure for 1865 was 8.5; in 1880 it was 27, and by 1900 it was 61.[2]

There were 140,000 industries of all types in 1860. By 1880 there were 250,000, and by 1900 the number was over 500,000. The number of persons employed in those industries doubled in each of the 20-year periods. The percentage of the labor force engaged in nonagricultural work was 41 per cent in 1860, 50 per cent in 1880, and 62 per cent in 1900.

Estimated national wealth in 1865 was 20 billion dollars. By 1880 it was 43 billions, and by 1900 the figure was 88 billions. Bank deposits tripled between 1865 and 1880, then quadrupled in the next 20 years.

A look at some production figures tells a similar story. The rate of increase was greatest in the twenty years from 1880 to 1900. Coal and pig iron production quadrupled; copper smelters scored a tenfold increase; steel and cement production increased eight times. Petroleum output more than doubled. While the production totals continued to climb steadily after 1900, the rate of increase declined, except in the case of petroleum.

[1] Documented in Allan Nevins, *The Emergence of Modern America, 1865–1878* (New York: Macmillan, 1927), and Ida M. Tarbell, *The Nationalizing of Business, 1878–1898* (New York: Macmillan, 1936).

[2] This and following statistical information is from U. S. Department of Commerce, *Historical Statistics of the United States, 1789–1945* (Washington: U. S. Government Printing Office, 1949).

CAPTAINS OF BIG BUSINESS

Familiar symbols of this new economic order are John D. Rockefeller and the oil monopoly, and Andrew Carnegie and the steel combine. But similar concentrations of wealth and business control developed throughout American industry and trade—Cornelius Vanderbilt, Jay Gould, and J. Pierpont Morgan in finance; Leland Stanford, Collis P. Huntington, James J. Hill, and George Pullman in railroading; C. C. Washburn and Charles A. Pillsbury in the milling industry which centered in Minneapolis as the great plains opened; Philip D. Armour and Gustavus F. Swift in the meat packing industry which grew in Chicago and Kansas City as cattle raising became big business; the makers of machine-sewed shoes, ready-made clothes, packaged foods, watches, cameras, farm machinery, and hardware; the lumbermen, the mining kings—all rose to dominate the American scene in the late nineteenth century.

The captains of industry and finance obtained power through a variety of means. Some gained control of large segments of natural resources. A few held patents on basic inventions. Others, of whom Rockefeller was the most noted, won supremacy in part through manipulation of transportation rates and ruthless competitive tactics. Some were lucky in the world of financial speculation. Most important, the Rockefellers and the Carnegies usually were successful because they had, or could hire, the brains necessary to create a new manufacturing or financial empire.

But, as usual, there was a flaw in the new order. As the machine revolutionized the American economy, it brought with it the threat of overproduction and disastrous competition among the new producers. The dislocation of labor which resulted, and the bankrupting of weaker businesses, also promoted economic instability. The captains of industry cast about for ways of avoiding the industrial and financial panics which threatened the strong as well as the weak.

One effort to overcome these dangers took the form of the pool agreement. Direct competitors sought by voluntary secret agreement to limit industrywide production, to allocate production quotas, and to stabilize prices. The trouble was that in times of distress the rule quickly became "every man for himself."

A more successful form of industry control was the trust, developed by the Standard Oil group around 1880. By this method the shareholders in the original companies assigned their capital stock to a board of trustees and received trust certificates in return. The trustees thus obtained legal control of the individual units. They could decide production quotas, set selling prices, and eliminate competition.

Hosts of other industries followed the lead of the oilmen before 1890. Sugar, salt, whiskey, rope, lead, tin plate, crackers, matches, newsprint, fence wire and many other products fell under near monopolistic control. The number of producing companies declined sharply in such fields as woolen goods, iron and steel, leather, and farm machinery. Congress passed the Sherman Anti-Trust Act of 1890 in an attempt to restore open competition, but the end result was hardly satisfactory to opponents of industrial monopoly. The sugar trust simply became an incorporated company under the laws of New Jersey, and the Standard Oil group developed the holding-company technique. The amalgamation of many businesses now took the form of a single great corporation, whether in manufacturing, in railroading, or in mining and cattle raising.

EFFECTS OF MASS PRODUCTION

The basic trend in this economic revolution was one which came to be intensified in twentieth-century America. It involved an increasing change from production of a small number of units at a comparatively large profit per unit to production of a large number of units at a smaller profit per unit. The familiar story of mass production by a decreasing number of producers was chronicled in many fields of business.

The American newspaper could not fail to be affected along with the rest of the national economy. Mass production methods meant that more and more businesses needed regional or national distribution of their goods. The result was the rise of new techniques in advertising and merchandising to popularize brand names. Newspapers thus received added advertising revenue, not only from this new source, but more important, from the retail stores of the expanding cities.

The blessings of the new order were mixed, however. Metropolitan papers, particularly, began to feel strong pressures for efficient operation which the increased mechanization of printing processes and pyramiding capitalizations entailed. It was costing more and more money to produce a competitive daily newspaper, and the publisher who wished his newspaper to grow—or even to survive—had to match the skills of his rivals. His increasing production costs had to be met by increased revenues from advertising and newspaper sales. This race for larger circulations, and expanded advertising volumes based upon readership, could only bring the eventual elimination of those competing newspapers which failed to match the pace, either in the quality of their product or in their business ability.

THE RISE OF THE CITY

The industrial concentration which was maturing between 1880 and 1900 was of vital significance, but it was only a part of the enormous change in American life. Mechanization, industrialization, and urbanization brought swift and extensive social, cultural, and political developments. People were being uprooted physically and mentally by the effects of the economic revolution, and in the new environment no social institution could remain static. Even a brief examination of the character of this new environment will indicate the basic causes of the tremendous changes which developed in the daily newspapers of American cities by the 1880s.

Arthur M. Schlesinger, Sr., chose the phrase "the rise of the city" to characterize the period from 1878 to 1898.[3] Census figures show that the number of American towns and cities of 8,000 or more population doubled between 1880 and 1900. The total population of those urban places more than doubled, jumping from some 11 million to 25 million. In 1880 there were 50 million Americans, of whom 22.7 per cent were living in towns and cities of more than 8,000. By 1900 that figure had risen to 32.9 per cent of a total population of 76 million.

The most rapid gain in urbanization occurred during the ten years between 1880 and 1890, which were the years of greatest ferment in the daily newspaper business. The rise of the city was particularly evident in the northeastern industrial states, where urban centers now predominated over declining rural areas, and in the older states of the Middle West. New York City jumped in population from a million to a million and a half during the decade. Chicago, the rail and trade center of inland America, doubled its size, passing the million mark in 1890 to become the nation's second city. Next in line were Philadelphia, at a million; Brooklyn, at 800,000; and Boston, Baltimore, and St. Louis, in the half-million class. Altogether there were 58 cities with more than 50,000 population in 1890. Eighty per cent of them were in the East and Middle West, and half of them were in the five states of New York, Pennsylvania, Massachusetts, New Jersey, and Ohio.

Into these cities was pouring an ever-rising tide of immigration, which brought new blood and new problems for American society. Again the decade of 1880–90 stands out, since in those ten years more than five million immigrants came to America, double the number for any preceding decade. All told, approximately nine million foreign-born were added to the population in the 20 years between 1880 and 1900, as many as had come during the 40 years preceding 1880. As a result, the newspapers of New York City in 1890 were serving a population that was 80 per cent foreign-born or of foreign parentage, and as might be expected, the character of some of the newspapers changed. Other American cities had from 25 to 40 per cent foreign-born residents. To the older Irish, British, and German streams of migration were added great numbers of Scandinavians, Poles, French-Canadians, Italians, Russians, and

[3] Schlesinger's *The Rise of the City, 1878–1898* (New York: Macmillan, 1932) is a classic study of the transformation of American life stemming from the economic revolution. See also Blake McKelvey, *The Urbanization of America, 1860–1915* (New Brunswick, N.J.: Rutgers University Press, 1969) and its companion volume, *The Emergence of Metropolitan America, 1915–1966* (1968).

Hungarians. Of these, the Germans and the Scandinavians particularly migrated to the Middle West, while the other groups tended to remain in the Atlantic states.

The rise of the city meant a quickening of material progress, reflected first in the life of the city dweller and transmitted gradually to the rest of the country. The new American cities hastened the installation of water and sewage systems in the years following the Civil War. They paved their streets with asphalt and bricks, and they bridged their rivers with steel structures patterned after the Roeblings' famed Brooklyn bridge of 1883. A ten-story Chicago building, constructed around a steel and iron skeleton in 1885, heralded the coming of the skyscraper. Horsecarts and cabs no longer could carry the throngs of city dwellers, nor could they serve adequately the suburbs which mushroomed about metropolitan centers. The first answers were New York's elevated trains and San Francisco's cable cars, adopted by other large cities in the 1870s. Then came the electric railway and streetcar, perfected in 1887, to meet the urban transportation problem. By 1895 some 850 electric lines were in operation.

Electricity was becoming a great new servant, both as a source of power for industry and transportation and as a source of light. American cities barely had begun to install arc lights in 1879 when Thomas A. Edison invented a practicable incandescent bulb. When the current flowed out from his Pearl Street generating station in 1882 to light the Stock Exchange and the offices of the *New York Times* and *New York Herald*, a new era in living had begun. By 1898 there were nearly 2,800 central electric power stations in the country, as businesses and homes were lighted, electric elevators were installed in the new tall buildings, and electric motors became widely used in industry.

THE COMMUNICATIONS NETWORK

America was being tied together by its industrial revolution, and its communications network kept pace with the sense of urgency which was characteristic of the new order. The telephone, invented by Alexander Graham Bell in the 1870s, already had one user for every thousand persons in 1880. By 1900 there was one telephone for each hundred. Intercity lines multiplied during the 1880s, until by 1900 the Bell System covered the country. Western Union quadrupled its telegraph lines between 1880 and 1900. The railroads, with 93,000 miles of track in 1880, reached a near-saturation point of 193,000 miles by 1900. The federal postal service, still the primary means of communication, greatly extended its free carrier service in cities during the two decades and instituted free rural delivery in 1897. Congress, by clearly defining second-class matter in the Postal Act of 1879, and by providing a one-cent-a-pound rate for newspapers and magazines in 1885, opened the way for cheap delivery of publications. In business offices the invention of the typewriter and adding machine speeded the work pace and simplified the handling of increased correspondence and records.

THE EXPANSION OF NEWSPAPERS

Each of these material advances and changes in the physical character of American society had its impact, large or small, upon the nation's journalism. The nationwide financial and industrial expansion which took the name of "big business" transformed the big city newspaper into a corporate enterprise rather than a personal venture. Increasing mechanization, spurred on by inventive genius, revolutionized the printing processes just as it had other industrial processes. The tremendous growth of the cities permitted larger newspaper circulations, which were in turn made necessary by larger investments and operating expenses. And a steady increase in the number of urban communities, as population expanded and the economic benefits of industrialization spread across the country offered a host of new publishing opportunities which were seized upon quickly.

The most striking evidence of what was happening to the newspaper is to be found in a bare statistical summary. Between 1870 and 1900, the United States doubled its population and tripled the number of its urban residents. During the same 30 years the number of its daily newspapers quadrupled and the number of copies sold each day increased almost sixfold. Both in numbers and in total circulation the daily newspaper was rising even more rapidly than the city which spawned it. The number of English-language, general-circulation dailies increased from 489 in 1870 to 1,967 in 1900. Circulation totals for all daily publications rose from 2.6 million copies in 1870 to 15 million in 1900.[4] A similar advance was being made by weekly newspapers, serving mainly the small towns and rural areas, but also the suburbs and sections of the cities. Between 1870 and 1900, the number of weekly publications tripled, increasing from approximately 4,000 to more than 12,000. The weeklies, however, still represented personal journalistic ventures, and the revolution in newspaper methods was taking place at the big city daily level.

There were many less tangible reasons why the newspaper was making such tremendous strides as an American social institution. The forces of social and economic interdependence, products of industrialization and urbanization, played a leading part in the creation of the lusty "new journalism." The peoples of the cities, being molded together as economic and cultural units, increasingly turned to the daily newspapers for the story of their urban life and their common interests. At the same time the country itself was being rapidly unified by the rush toward economic interdependence. Improved communications facilities were a manifestation of this nationalizing influence which per-

[4] The census figures for totals of all types of dailies were 574 in 1870 and 2,226 in 1900. The figures used above are more comparable to twentieth-century statistics.

vaded all American life. And again, the daily newspaper was the chronicler of the national scene, the interpreter of the new environment. The city reader, whether he was seated in new-found comfort on a streetcar or in his better-lighted home, was the eager customer of the publisher who met successfully the new challenge to journalism.

ADVANCES IN EDUCATION

As American social and economic life became more complex and as the national wealth accumulated, many cultural advances were possible which in turn promoted new interest in the newspaper. The cities, with their concentrated populations and earning capacities, naturally led in expansion of social and intellectual activity. But they also set the pace for a nationalized cultural development. The bookstores, libraries, art galleries, museums, theaters, opera houses, churches, retail stores, schools, and newspapers which brought higher standards in the cities stimulated the interests and the desires of all the country. Progress in education, the result of this general thirst for knowledge and a better life, was particularly important to the expansion of the mass media—newspapers, magazines, books. The percentage of children attending public schools in the United States rose from 57 to 72 per cent between 1870 and 1900, while illiteracy declined from 20 to 10.7 per cent of the population. The number of high schools jumped from approximately 100 in 1860 to 800 by 1880, and then skyrocketed to 6,000 by 1900.

At higher educational levels, growth of state universities and of private colleges financed by America's new men of wealth resulted in notable advances in the social sciences, as well as progress in the natural and physical sciences and the humanities. Federal land subsidies provided by the Morrill Act of 1862 encouraged the founding and expansion of state universities, particularly in the Middle West and West, where such state-supported universities as Wisconsin, California, Minnesota, and Illinois began to flourish. The private colleges and universities gained in numbers and influence with the founding of Cornell University in 1865 by Ezra Cornell, whose millions came from the electric telegraph; of Johns Hopkins University in 1876 by a Baltimore merchant; of Leland Stanford University in 1885 by a California railroad and business man; of the University of Chicago in 1892 by John D. Rockefeller's benefaction. Johns Hopkins, by emphasizing the role of research in higher education, and Harvard, by giving its students an elective choice of courses, set new patterns for the universities. And university presidents such as Charles W. Eliot of Harvard, Daniel Coit Gilman of Johns Hopkins, and Andrew D. White of Cornell gave effective leadership. No longer was it necessary for Americans interested in scholarly pursuits to go abroad; and the number of graduate students in the United States increased from 400 in 1880 to some 5,600 in 1900. Nor were women ignored in the new spread of education. The state universities became coeducational institutions; Smith College was founded in 1875, soon to be followed by Bryn Mawr and Radcliffe, as fruits of the woman suffrage movement.

NEW SOCIOECONOMIC PHILOSOPHIES

The scholars of the universities, and other men and women whose intellectual and cultural achievements were supported by the new wealth of the nation, made great advances in the years between 1880 and 1900. Most importantly, they challenged the socioeconomic philosophies which had developed in nineteenth-century society, and suggested new concepts better fitted to the revolutionized character of American life. They organized areas of knowledge which were needed if the country was to understand its problems and cope with them, and in doing so they laid the groundwork for the vast growth of research and interpretation in the twentieth century.[5]

A socioeconomic theory of individualism had been well developed by 1880 to bolster the argument that government should not interfere in economic affairs. The individual, this school of thought declared, supplies the enterprise which makes possible industrial progress, wealth, and national power. Therefore government should do nothing which would adversely affect individual economic enterprise. Government's function, ran the argument, is to provide an orderly society in which the individual is protected as he fulfills his destiny.

Powerful support for the theory of individualism was drawn from the work of the English scientist, Charles Darwin, who published his *Origin of Species* in 1859 and his *The Descent of Man* in 1871. Darwin's emphasis upon the struggle for individual existence in the process of evolution fitted nicely into the pattern. Another major influence on American thinking came from the writings of the English philosopher, Herbert Spencer. The Spencerian doctrine declared that man's ultimate achievement of a perfect society would be the result of a natural process—an inevitable development which men themselves should not attempt to hasten or to alter. In the United States, sociologist William Graham Sumner, historian John Fiske, and political scientist John W. Burgess shaped their teaching and writing to conform with Darwin's and Spencer's ideas of individualism. The influence of this socioeconomic doctrine became so strong, particularly in the rendering of Supreme Court decisions nullifying reform legislation, that Justice Oliver Wendell Holmes was led to protest that Spencer's *Social Statics* was not part of the Constitution.

Those who decried the negativism of this theory of individualism were being heard by the 1880s. They contended that man did have the ability to control his destiny, and to shape his economic and political actions as the gen-

[5] Well-discussed in Henry Steele Commager, *The American Mind* (New Haven: Yale University Press, 1950).

eral welfare of society might require. Unrestricted exercise of individual power by some only brings misery and poverty to others, and the outcome is not national strength, but national weakness, said this school of thought. True progress, they said, depends upon cooperation and the use of government's powers in the common good.

A sociologist, Lester Ward, who published the first volume of his *Dynamic Sociology* in 1883, provided logical arguments for the belief that government should be regarded as a positive force, and that it should actively seek ways of achieving social improvement. Economist Richard T. Ely attacked the pat theories of the laissez-faire advocates, theories which he and other economics professors pointed out as not conforming to the facts of industrial life. Ely's *Socialism, Its Nature, Strength and Weakness*, published in 1894, made definite proposals for reasonable reform legislation. Economist Thorstein Veblen compared the theories of economic individualists with the actual practices of industrial capitalism, and voiced his bitter protest in 1899 with his *Theory of the Leisure Class*. Henry George assailed the unearned increment of wealth through land ownership in his *Progress and Poverty* (1879), and Henry Demarest Lloyd denounced the oil monopoly in *Wealth against Commonwealth* (1894), an effective plea for sociocconomic cooperation.

Newspaper editors Dana, Godkin, and Reid, as we have observed, were supporters of the theory of individualism, and opposed government interference in economic spheres. One might expect, in light of what was happening, that other editors would appear who would support the principles of social cooperation and use of governmental power to regulate economic life. And indeed, one of the characteristics of the "new journalism" came to be the expression of editorial-page support for the "common man." What publishers and editors like Joseph Pulitzer and E. W. Scripps represented in the field of journalism was only an expression of a larger movement in American thought and life.

ADVANCES IN KNOWLEDGE

Those who thus argued directly with the supporters of individualism were aided by those whose contributions to knowledge widened the country's understanding of its history, its government, and human thought and action. The period of the 1880s and 1890s was one of intense activity in study and publication, and in every field there were major achievements which helped Americans to meet the challenge of economic and social change.

Historians broke new ground by studying and writing about social and economic history, as well as politics. John Bach McMaster pointed the way by using newspapers as source materials for his significantly-titled *History of the People of the United States*, begun in 1883. Henry Adams produced his brilliant history of the Jefferson and Madison administrations in 1889, and James

Ford Rhodes began publication of his *History of the United States* in 1892. Frederick Jackson Turner's famous essay on the "Significance of the Frontier in American History" appeared in 1893, to father a whole new school of historical interpretation. Colonial history was being rewritten by men with an understanding of economic and social conditions of the early American period.

The landmark for this period in the field of government and political science was James Bryce's *American Commonwealth,* in which the talented Englishman gave to the United States a description of its new environment. The same year, 1888, Frank W. Taussig wrote his *Tariff History of the United States.* Woodrow Wilson's *Congressional Government* appeared in 1885, and by 1903 Charles E. Merriam had completed his *History of American Political Theories.*

The list of men and books could be extended: anthropologist Lewis Henry Morgan's *Ancient Society* (1877); philosopher William James' *Principles of Psychology* (1890); philosopher Josiah Royce's *The Spirit of Modern Philosophy* (1892) and *The World and the Individual* (1900); historian Brooks Adams' *The Law of Civilization and Decay* (1895); educator John Dewey's *School and Society* (1899); Oliver Wendell Holmes' *The Common Law* (1881).

Literature offered Henry James' *Portrait of a Lady* (1881); Samuel Clemens' *Life on the Mississippi* (1883) and *Huckleberry Finn* (1885); and William Dean Howells' *The Rise of Silas Lapham* (1885), an early example of the rise of realism in American literature. In the 1890s, poets Emily Dickinson and Edwin Arlington Robinson and novelists Stephen Crane and Hamlin Garland were making major contributions, while such realistic writers as Theodore Dreiser and Frank Norris were on the verge of fame.

Nor was this great cultural stirring and extension of factual information limited to an intellectual class. Millions shared in the new knowledge through the chautauquas and public study courses which became of major importance toward the close of the century as means of adult education. The world fairs and expositions which caught America's fancy in this period were another means of mass education. At the Philadelphia Centennial of 1876 and Chicago's Columbian Exposition of 1893, millions of Americans viewed the material and artistic achievements of their generation. Free public libraries, spreading across the country after 1880, found their great benefactor in Andrew Carnegie. In these libraries were available the literary triumphs and the popular writings of American and British authors.

INFLUENCE OF MAGAZINES

Magazines came to have increasing influence upon American life. Earlier ventures like the *North American Review* (1815) and the *Knickerbocker,* a more popular magazine published from 1833 to 1865, had been eclipsed by *Harper's Monthly,* begun in 1850 by the New York book publishing firm. *Har-*

per's introduced extensive woodcut illustrations, published the writings of leading English and American authors, and ran up a world record circulation of 200,000 before the Civil War. Two women's magazines, *Godey's Lady's Book* and *Peterson's,* began their careers in 1830 and 1842, respectively, and offered hand-colored engravings of fashions and fiction stories to more than 150,000 readers each by the 1850s.

In 1881, the *Century* joined *Harper's* in the highly literary and artistic class of magazines. *Scribner's* made it a trio in 1886. Unillustrated, but of equal literary quality, was the *Atlantic Monthly,* begun in 1857 and specializing in publishing the writings of the New England authors. In the weekly field were two illustrated periodicals, *Frank Leslie's Illustrated Newspaper* (1855) and *Harper's Weekly* (1857). The latter exercised strong influence in public affairs, along with E. L. Godkin's weekly, the *Nation* (1865). In addition, the *Independent* (1848), the *North American Review,* and such newcomers as the *Forum* (1886), the *Arena* (1889), and the *Outlook* (1893) all discussed the new political and social environment. The *Literary Digest* began summarizing contemporary editorial opinion in 1890.

Coming into the field were publications which depended upon humor, cartoons, and political satire. *Puck* (1877) featured Joseph Keppler's dynamic color cartoons. The others were *Judge* (1881), and *Life* (1883), famed for its publication of the "Gibson girl" drawings of Charles Dana Gibson. In the children's magazine competition, *Youth's Companion* (1827) was joined by *St. Nicholas* (1873).

Helped by the cheap postage rates established by Congress under its 1879 act, some new leaders struck out in the 1880s for the mass readership which still awaited American magazine publishers. One was Cyrus H. K. Curtis, who founded the *Ladies' Home Journal* in 1883, and with Edward W. Bok as his editor, soon won a half-million circulation. Curtis bought the *Saturday Evening Post* in 1897 and with editor George Horace Lorimer quickly made it a leader in the low-cost weekly field, which *Collier's* entered in 1888. The older high quality monthlies found stiff competition from three low-priced popular magazines: *Munsey's,* begun in 1889 by Frank Munsey; *McClure's,* started in 1893 by S. S. McClure, and the *Cosmopolitan* (1886). It was these magazines, circulating more extensively than any of their predecessors, which were to open the minds of more readers to social and cultural trends.

THE SOCIETY'S SHORTCOMINGS AND DISCONTENTS

It must be noted, however, that the general level of cultural attainment was still low. Even by 1900 the average American had received only five years of schooling in his lifetime. If the public bought encyclopedias galore from the book publishers because it wanted to know more, it also bought dime novels by the millions. If the chautauqua was a booming institution, so were horse racing, prizefighting, and baseball. Cultural and business organizations were expanding in number, but growing even faster were fraternal and social groups. In the newspaper world Adolph Ochs would be able to find enough serious readers in the metropolis of New York to support the reborn *New York Times*, but the great mass of readers was attracted by the devices of a journalism which sought a popular level as it both entertained and informed.

It should be noted briefly, too, that not everybody was successful or contented in this new economic and social environment, despite the general blessings that industrialization had bestowed upon the country. Sharp divisions began to appear before those who had gained wealth in the process of national economic upheaval, and those who had gained only a crowded room in a city tenement, a poverty-stricken tenant farm in the South, or a precarious existence on the dry plains of the West. Falling farm prices in the 1880s spurred the political activities of the discontented in the South and West. There the Grangers, the Greenbackers, the Farmers' Alliance, and the Populists arose to demand economic equality for agriculture, and launched third party movements which showed real strength. Not until 1896 did one of the major political parties answer the call of the "consistent rebellion"; at that time, the merging of the forces of free silver coinage, paper money, and general political and economic reform under the Democratic banner of William Jennings Bryan provided America with the greatest political excitement of a generation. But despite the bitter experience of the depression of 1893, the advocates of William McKinley and political and economic conservatism won the decision.

In the cities the rise of the labor movement on a nationally organized scale provided a much sharper clash than that between business and agriculture. Some craft unions, such as those of the bricklayers, railroad engineers, and printers, had become established before the Civil War, and a National Labor Union of some stature was organized in 1866, only to disintegrate during the depression of 1873. The Knights of Labor, carrying on the "one big union" plan under the leadership of Terence V. Powderly, reached a peak membership of 700,000 during the two years of industrial turbulence which followed the panic of 1884. Powderly advocated moderate cooperative action by all working men to better their pay and working conditions, and the use of the strike weapon when necessary. Unfortunately for the Knights of Labor, their aggressive action was at its peak in 1886, when anarchists who advocated deeds of violence and terror touched off the Haymarket riot in Chicago. Public reaction coupled Powderly's legitimate labor movement with the troubles caused by the anarchists, and the Knights of Labor movement fell away. As a result the steadier American Federation of Labor, built in 1881 as a national organization of the various craft unions, became the principal voice of the labor movement. Its nationwide strikes in 1886 for a shortening of the ten-hour workday won a reduction to eight or nine hours for some 200,000 workers out of the 350,000 involved, and newly elected AFL president Samuel Gompers became the individual leader of labor. The reaction in many industries was the formation of employers' associations which raised defense funds to fight the carefully planned demands and strikes of the individual craft unions.

A NEW JOURNALISM EMERGING

In such a swiftly changing and exciting environment, then, the daily newspaper was coming of age. From 850 English-language, general-circulation dailies in 1880 to 1,967 in 1900; from 10 per cent of adults as subscribers to 26 per cent—these were the statistical evidences of its arrival as a major business. The enormous success of Joseph Pulitzer's *New York World*, which between 1883 and 1887 broke every publishing record in America, was evidence that a "new journalism" had been created which would change the character and the appearance of the daily newspaper and enormously increase its mass influence.

But before focusing attention on the *New York World*, whose triumphs caught the attention of even the most unobservant in the newspaper business, we should briefly examine the changes which were occurring in other cities. Certainly Henry W. Grady in Atlanta, Edward W. Scripps in Cleveland and Cincinnati, Melville E. Stone and Victor Lawson in Chicago, and William Rockhill Nelson in Kansas City also were engaged in the creation of the "new journalism" in the same years that Joseph Pulitzer was exhibiting his skill, first in St. Louis and then in New York. And in many another city, older newspapers were being challenged by bright-faced newcomers which, in some cases, were destined to take their places among America's best. The new papers were low-priced, aggressive, and easily read. They believed in the news function as the primary obligation of the press; they exhibited independence of editorial opinion; they crusaded actively in the community interest; they appealed to the mass audience through improved writing, better makeup, use of headlines and illustrations, and a popularization of their contents. These were the general characteristics of the "new journalism"; the individual newspapers, of course, exhibited them in varying degrees.

The rise of evening newspapers was a feature of this growth of the daily. The evening field claimed seven-eighths of the increase in numbers of daily newspapers between 1880 and 1900, and by 1890 two out of three papers were evening editions. The swing toward evening publication was due in part to the changed reading habits of the city populations, and it was strengthened by the discovery that the woman readers to whom retail store advertising was directed favored afternoon-delivered newspapers. Mechanical and news-gathering innovations permitted the evening papers to carry "today's news today," particularly in the Middle West and West, where time differentials aided inclusion of news from the East and from Europe on the same day events occurred. Some morning papers found an answer by publishing afternoon editions under the same nameplate, while others established separate evening papers.

JOURNALISM OF THE EAST

New York remained primarily a morning-paper city, with only the *Evening Post* achieving distinction as an afternoon paper before the Pulitzer invasion. Two additions to the field in 1867 were the *Evening Telegram,* begun by James Gordon Bennett as the afternoon edition of the *Herald,* and the *Evening Mail.* The *Mail* was merged with the older *Express* in 1882 to form the *Mail and Express.* The circulation winner of the period was the *Daily News,* a one-cent evening paper dating back to 1855 for its founding. The *Daily News,* cheap in content as well as in price, circulated in the tenement districts so widely that it challenged the *Sun* and *Herald* throughout the 1870s, and its success suggested to other publishers new ways of reaching the immigrant crowded tenement sections of the city.

In Philadelphia, two newcomers in the 1870s were the *Record* and the *Times.* The *Record,* begun in 1870, was taken over in 1877 by William M. Singerly, a millionaire railroad builder, who cut the paper's price to one cent, brightened its makeup and writing, and engaged in popular crusades against local abuses. By the early 1880s the *Record* was outselling its famous competitor in the morning field, the *Public Ledger,* which had been purchased from the Swain family in 1864 by the able George W. Childs. The *Times* (1875),[6] published by reform-conscious Alexander K. McClure, also pushed into the top circulation bracket, along with the *Evening Item* (1847), which hit its stride in the 1880s as a crusading penny paper, and the *Press* (1857). The *Evening Bulletin* (1847) and the *Inquirer* (1829), ultimately the two survivors in the Philadelphia field, trailed the *Public Ledger* in prestige and the other papers in circulation.

Boston's quiet journalism was upset by the appearance of the *Globe.* Founded in 1872, it had only 8,000 circulation when General Charles H. Taylor became publisher in 1877. Taylor established an evening edition, cut the price to two cents, ran big headlines, emphasized local news, and gave editorial support to the Democratic party. By 1890 the *Globe,* with combined morning and evening circulation of 150,000, ranked among the top ten papers in the country. The staid *Herald* (1846) and the sensationalized *Journal* (1833) kept pace by establishing evening editions. But the morning *Advertiser* (1813) and *Post* (1831), and evening *Transcript* (1830) and *Traveller* (1825), contented themselves with limited circulations. The *Advertiser* did establish an evening edition, the *Record,* in 1884.

The trend was similar in other eastern cities. Baltimore's new entry was

[6] Figures in parentheses indicate founding dates of newspapers.

the *Evening News* (1872), which in the 1890s under fighting editor Charles H. Grasty rose to challenge the famous *Sun*. The *Evening Penny Press* of Pittsburgh appeared in 1884 as the forerunner of the *Pittsburgh Press* and promptly undertook civic improvement campaigns. The Butler family's *Buffalo News* dates from 1880, and it immediately asserted leadership in the newspaper field as an aggressively-run evening paper. Another influential leader in the 1880s was the evening *Brooklyn Eagle,* begun in 1841. In Providence, the *Journal* (1829) saw the trend early and established the *Evening Bulletin* in 1863. The Noyes and Kauffmann families gave Washington a local evening paper in 1852, and by 1890 their *Evening Star* had as its only competitor the morning *Post* (1877).[7]

THE SOUTH: HENRY W. GRADY OF ATLANTA

In the South, Henry Watterson's well-established *Louisville Courier-Journal* started the *Times* as an evening edition in 1884 and soon saw it outsell the parent morning paper. New Orleans' morning leader, the *Picayune* (1837), found new competition from two evening papers, the *Item* (1877) and the *States* (1879). Two other New Orleans morning papers, the *Times* (1863) and the *Democrat* (1875), found the going more difficult and merged in 1881. A famous editor appeared in Raleigh, North Carolina, in 1885, when Josephus Daniels took over the *State Chronicle,* which he soon merged into the *News and Observer,* thereby establishing what became a great Daniels family newspaper.

Most brilliant of the southern newspaper-makers of the period was Henry W. Grady, who in his brief 39 years demonstrated the qualities of a great reporter and managing editor. Grady's talents were widely exhibited in the dozen years before he became managing editor of the *Atlanta Constitution* in 1880. Indeed, when Grady became editor and one-third owner of the *Atlanta Herald* in 1872, he nearly put the *Constitution,* founded four years before, out of business. But the *Herald,* for all its journalistic superiority, fell victim to the financial depression of 1873 after a four-year struggle. Grady then became a free-lance correspondent for such enterprising newspapers as the *Constitution,* the *New York Herald,* the *Louisville Courier-Journal,* the *Philadelphia Times,* and the *Detroit Free Press,* distinguishing himself for his coverage of politics and for his use of the interview technique in reporting and interpreting the news. He traveled widely and his grasp of events and his acquaintanceships increased accordingly.

[7] Crosby S. Noyes and Samuel H. Kauffmann were leading men in the early years of the *Star;* Noyes' sons, Frank and Theodore, became active before 1890 and guided the *Star* down to the 1940s.

HENRY W. GRADY

When the *Constitution*, published by Evan P. Howell after 1876, obtained Grady as a part owner and managing editor, things began to hum. A network of correspondents was built up, and Grady spent lavishly to get all the news coverage possible in every field from politics to baseball. Grady continued to report major news events and political affairs himself. His brilliant story of the Charleston earthquake of 1886 won him national attention as a newsman. The same year his address entitled "The New South," which advocated industrial advancement of the South as a means of reestablishing national solidarity, won him national fame as a spokesman for his area. As a consequence Grady devoted increased attention to the editorial page of the *Constitution* until his death in 1889, and his influence furthered the paper's position as sharing southern leadership with Henry Watterson's *Louisville Courier-Journal.*

Grady's biographer, however, points out his real function with these words:

> The success of the *Atlanta Constitution* was due, furthermore, to the fact that it had in its managing editor a great reporter and a master news executive. Just as in his public policies Grady belongs to the New South rather than to the Old, so in his journalistic methods he exemplifies not the personal journalism which the Civil War rendered obsolete, but the modern era, with its emphasis upon the gathering and interpreting of news. The South, certainly, has never seen his like as one who "perceived instantly the multitudinous interesting things of life" and who could picture even the most difficult of subjects in colorful strokes that caught the public fancy.[8]

With Grady's death, Clark Howell, Sr., son of the publisher, became managing editor of the *Constitution.* The other event of the 1880s in Atlanta jour-

[8] Raymond B. Nixon, "Henry W. Grady, Reporter: A Reinterpretation," *Journalism Quarterly*, XII (December 1935), p. 343. The full-length biography is Nixon's *Henry W. Grady, Spokesman of the New South* (New York: Knopf, 1943).

nalism was the founding in 1883 of the *Journal,* an evening paper which was destined to outmaneuver the Howells' *Constitution* by the 1950s.

NEW DAILIES IN THE WEST

To the West, the newspaper which is now the *Dallas News* was established in 1885, and its future publisher, George B. Dealey, appeared in Dallas that year. The *Los Angeles Times,* begun in 1881, saw Harrison Gray Otis assume its leadership in 1882. In San Francisco, the major event of the period was the sale of the *Examiner* (1865) to George Hearst in 1880, and the turning over of the paper to young William Randolph Hearst in 1887. San Francisco journalism had been lively before the Hearst entry, with the morning *Chronicle* (1865) leading in civic campaigns and political clean-up movements. Its publisher, Michel H. de Young, one of two brothers who founded the paper, remained in control of the *Chronicle* for 60 years.

A REVOLUTION IN THE MIDWEST: E. W. SCRIPPS

What has been described thus far would suffice to prove the point that things were happening to the nation's journalism everywhere. Singerly's *Philadelphia Record,* Taylor's *Boston Globe,* Grady's *Atlanta Herald* and *Constitution* exhibited the major characteristics of the "new journalism." The appearance of the Butler family in Buffalo, of the Noyes family in Washington, of Josephus Daniels in Raleigh, of the Howell family in Atlanta, of Harrison Gray Otis in Los Angeles meant in each case the beginning of the building of a noted American newspaper. But it was in the Midwest of the 1870s and 1880s that the biggest revolution in newspapering was brewing—Detroit, Cleveland, Cincinnati, Chicago, Kansas City, Milwaukee, St. Louis.

The name Scripps is written boldly into the story of midwestern newspaper-making in the 1870s and early 1880s. James E. Scripps, elder half-brother of the famed Edward Wyllis Scripps, started the family on its journalistic mission when, after working on newspapers in Chicago and Detroit, he founded the *Detroit Evening News* in 1873. By the end of 1880, the Scripps family had fostered newspapers in Cleveland, Cincinnati, St. Louis, and Buffalo. The story of the rise of the Scripps newspaper chain belongs later (Chapter 20), but the story of the early successes is a part of the general pattern of the rise of the "new journalism." Scripps newspapers were low-priced evening publications; small in size, but well written and tightly edited; hard-hitting in both news and editorial page coverage of the local scene. Above all, they were distinguished for their devotion to the interests of the working man.

When James Scripps needed help to keep his *Detroit News* afloat, he called upon his brother George and sister Ellen, and eventually upon young Edward, who was the thirteenth child of a thrice-married Englishman now settled on an Illinois farm. Edward helped to build circulation routes for the *News* and reported for it while the struggle to win advertising support was in progress. Detroit had well-established papers, such as the morning *Free Press* (1831), but by the 1880s the *News* emerged as a leading evening paper known for its business operation as well as for its qualities as a newspaper.

Scripps money went into four one-cent evening papers: the short-lived *Buffalo Evening Telegraph*, the ill-fated *St. Louis Chronicle*, and the famous *Cleveland Press* and *Cincinnati Post*. These two latter papers became the products of Edward Wyllis Scripps' own publishing genius, and the parent papers of his eventual chain.

Cleveland of 1878 had three going newspapers, the *Leader* (1854), the *Herald* (1835), and the *Plain Dealer* (1842). When the *Penny Press* appeared as a four-page, five-column evening paper, it looked no more permanent than the alley shack in which it was published. But the editor, Edward Wyllis Scripps, paid the top salary to his advertising solicitor, and put his own tremendous energy into the venture in a fashion which drove the circulation to 10,000 within a few months and foreshadowed the rise of the Scripps publishing empire.

What happened to Cleveland journalism as a result of the rapid growth of the *Press* can be briefly told. The *Plain Dealer* shifted its emphasis from the evening to the morning field in 1885 as one of the first acts of a new owner, L. E. Holden. Holden bought the plant and morning edition of the *Herald;* the evening editions of the *Leader* and the *Herald* were combined as the *News and Herald.* But the *Press* continued to harass its evening competitors, and in 1905 the other afternoon dailies were combined into a new paper, the *Cleveland News.*

The Scripps opposition in Cincinnati was more formidable. The evening *Times* (1840) and *Star* (1872) were merged in 1880 by Charles P. Taft (half-brother of the later president, William Howard Taft). The *Times-Star* was a two-cent, conservative Republican paper; the Scripps entry that year was one-cent and Democratic. But in the morning field were the *Enquirer* (1841), published by John R. McLean as a Democratic paper which was noted for its adoption of the techniques of sensationalism, and the *Commercial Gazette,* edited by the distinguished liberal Republican supporter, Murat Halstead.[9] The Scripps paper, which became the *Cincinnati Post* after Edward Wyllis Scripps took control in 1883, nevertheless soon gained circulation leadership as the *Press* was doing in Cleveland.

[9] The *Commercial Gazette* resulted from an 1883 merger of the *Gazette* (1815) and the *Commercial* (1843), which Halstead had edited since 1865. After Halstead left Cincinnati in 1890 to go to Brooklyn, the *Commercial Gazette* became the *Commercial Tribune* in 1896. It disappeared into the *Enquirer* in 1930.

STONE'S *CHICAGO DAILY NEWS*

Another star which was rising in the Midwest was that of the *Chicago Daily News*. Together with another newcomer, the *Herald*, the *Daily News* quickly won equal prominence with older Chicago papers. The *Tribune* (1847), with Joseph Medill as controlling owner and editor after 1874, was continuing its development as a substantially edited, alert newspaper leader. The *Inter Ocean* (successor to the *Republican* founded in 1865 with Charles A. Dana as first editor) became widely known for its enterprise in news-gathering and in adoption of new journalistic and printing techniques. But the circulation went to the newcomers, the *Daily News* and *Herald*.

Melville E. Stone, the founder of the *Daily News*, was a product both of Chicago journalism and of the new national newspaper environment. Stone became managing editor of the *Republican* in 1872, as an inexperienced young man of 24, and ended up as city editor when the paper became the *Inter Ocean* later that year. In the fall he went on tour for the paper, studying conditions in the South. He records in his autobiography an association with Henry W. Grady and his *Atlanta Herald* partners: "They spent almost every evening with me talking over the profession of journalism. In these discussions we all learned much." [10] On the same trip, Stone studied New Orleans and St. Louis papers, and in St. Louis met a talented young newsman, Eugene Field.

When Stone returned to Chicago he became managing editor of the *Post and Mail*, but almost immediately he left for Washington to serve as correspondent for his and other papers. And in his autobiography, Stone records another major influence; he was watching the successful one-cent *New York Daily News* and deciding that he would try the same price formula in Chicago. He experimented briefly in 1873, then returned to Washington for more seasoning as a correspondent, and laid his plans to leave the *Post and Mail*.

In January, 1876, the *Daily News* appeared as a four-page, five-column sheet with only a few thousand dollars in capital investment. Stone believed that his first responsibility was to print news; his second responsibility was to guide public opinion; and his third, to provide entertainment. The paper did not reject sensational techniques; Stone's personal favorite was the detection of criminals by the newspaper. Nor did the *Daily News* fail to entertain; Stone brought Eugene Field to Chicago in 1883 from his earlier St. Louis and Kansas City surroundings, and until his death in 1895 Field conducted the famous "Sharps and Flats" column, in which he commented upon politics and people in a witty and highly literary style. But the paper won its place by its style of news presentation, by its determination to remain free of political and outside financial pressures, and by its aggressive editorial page policies.

The going was difficult at first, however. There was a chronic shortage of pennies in circulation, so Stone had to import pennies for Chicago banks to

[10] Melville E. Stone, *Fifty Years a Journalist* (Garden City: Doubleday, 1921), p. 44.

Chicago Daily News

MELVILLE E. STONE

Kansas City Star

WILLIAM ROCKHILL NELSON

handle and promoted "99-cent sales" in stores in order to put a sufficient number of pennies in Chicagoans' pockets to sell his papers. In the first year a young Chicago financier, Victor F. Lawson, took over the business managership of the paper and two-thirds of the stock. But by 1878 the *Daily News* had bought out the *Post and Mail,* obtaining its Associated Press news rights. A morning edition, eventually named the *Record,* was begun in 1881, and by 1885 the combined circulation had passed the 100,000 mark. When Stone sold his interest to Lawson in 1888 for $350,000, only Pulitzer's *New York World* had a larger circulation among American newspapers than the *Daily News*' 200,000.

The editorial staff which Stone had built was a famous one: Eugene Field as a columnist, Slason Thompson as an editorial writer, George Harvey, George Ade, and Finley Peter Dunne (Mr. Dooley) as young reporters; literary figures, scientists, and professors such as Chicago's James Laurence Laughlin and Wisconsin's Richard T. Ely as special contributors. Lawson continued the same type of leadership until his death in 1925; Stone comes into the story again as the general manager and builder of the modern Associated Press.

Rivaling the *Daily News* as an exponent of the new order in journalism was the *Herald,* founded by James W. Scott in 1881 as a low-priced, liberal-independent morning paper. Scott had difficulties providing sufficient capitalization for his expanding paper, but it quickly won the runner-up position to the *Daily News* in circulation. The ambitious Scott followed William M. Singerly of the *Philadelphia Record* as the second president of the newly formed American Newspaper Publishers Association, serving from 1889 to 1895. With his business associates, he founded the *Evening Post* in 1890 and in 1895 he consolidated the older *Times* (1854) with the *Herald* as the *Times-Herald*.[11] At this moment of glory, Scott died and his papers passed into less talented hands.

NELSON'S *KANSAS CITY STAR*

Taking his place with Scripps and Stone as one of the great figures in this midwestern newspaper revolution was William Rockhill Nelson, founder of the *Kansas City Star*. Nelson had been a lawyer and a building contractor before buying into a Fort Wayne, Indiana, newspaper in 1879. But by the time he appeared in Kansas City in the fall of 1880 he was ready to follow the pattern of the times. He and his editors created a small, two-cent evening newspaper, well written and filled with entertaining material as well as news, and possessed of the crusading urge. Notably, however, the *Star* shunned sensational treatment of the news in use of headlines and illustrations.

One other difference stands out strongly. Unlike the other great figures of journalism before him, Nelson was not a writer. He believed that the reporter was the heart of the newspaper, and had seven of them on his initial staff, and he sought the best news editors and editorial writers. And he was constantly a part of the news, editorial, and business activities of the *Star*, but only as the publisher who guided the actions and writing of his staff. If he had something to say, as he usually did, he told it to others who put the ideas into the printed page. One of Nelson's biographers ascribes the reasons for the development of the *Star's* sparkling qualities in this fashion:

> Next to Nelson, but always through Nelson's triumphant spirit, it was the work of Nelson's editors and their staff of inspired reporters and editorial writers. Possibly Nelson's greatest genius lay in his ability to select editorial talent, to exploit it by giving it freedom, and to cherish its flowering, both by positive encouragement to expression and avoidance of negative rules of suppression. . . . By adhering to this policy, Nelson succeeded in exploiting the ablest men and gaining their loyalty despite a salary and wage scale which was niggardly.[12]

Nelson had great co-workers, such as managing editor Thomas W. Johnston and associate editor James B. Runnion (a former managing editor of the *Chicago Tribune*). The staff was blessed with a succession of young men will-

[11] The *Times,* under editor Wilbur F. Storey, had become known for its shocking sensationalism. Its most famous headline, over an 1875 story of the hanging of four repentent murderers, read "Jerked to Jesus."

[12] Charles E. Rogers, "William Rockhill Nelson and His Editors of the *Star,*" *Journalism Quarterly,* XXVI (March 1949), p. 15. The article is based upon *William Rockhill Nelson: Independent Editor and Crusading Liberal* (Ph.D. thesis, University of Minnesota, 1948).

ing to be "exploited" for the glory of being a *Kansas City Star* man: William Allen White, of *Emporia Gazette* fame; Frank L. Martin, who became dean of the University of Missouri School of Journalism; and in later years, editor Wesley Stout of the *Saturday Evening Post,* columnist Raymond Clapper, and writers Ernest Hemingway and Russel Crouse. But for all their contributions, the personality of the *Star* was that given it by Nelson. When he died in 1915, the institution which he had built continued without a quiver.

Kansas City was a rough, growing town of little beauty when Nelson came in 1880. It was the gateway to the plains, and the receiving point for western cattle. Half-built, cursed with the usual political corruption and vice of the utilitarian America of the 1880s, it offered a great chance for a strong editor. Nelson was that: a big man, with massive face and head, stubborn qualities of independence, and an air of dignity which gave him the title of colonel. William Allen White, writing about him the year he died, commented: "Not that he was ever a colonel of anything; he was just coloneliferous." [13]

Nelson gave Kansas City what he thought it needed, through his relentless crusades for big and little things. He fought for cheap and efficient public transportation, bringing cable cars to the city's hills. He battled against politicians and gamblers. He campaigned for years to establish Kansas City's famous parks and boulevards, then himself built model homes along the boulevards, and saw that those who lived in them planted trees and flowers. The *Star* helped to inaugurate the commission form of government in the city, and by its espousal of progressive reform in government, spread the doctrine throughout its circulation area in the Missouri Valley.

Kansas City and the state of Kansas were captured by 1890, and before Nelson's death the *Star's* circulation hit 170,000. The subscription price was ten cents a week at the start, but even after a Sunday edition had been added and the morning *Times* (1868) had sold out to Nelson in 1901, the price for morning, evening, and Sunday editions remained at a dime. A weekly edition, selling for 25 cents a year, climbed to 150,000 circulation. The price formula, plus the *Star's* intensive coverage of its area and its human interest and literary qualities, made the paper invulnerable to the attacks of competitors who tried to win by using the sensational techniques which Nelson shunned.[14]

Characterizations of Nelson are sometimes seemingly contradictory. To William Allen White he was both "coloneliferous" and "a big, laughing, fat, goodnatured, rollicking, haw-hawing person who loved a drink, a steak, a story, and a fight." He was niggardly in paying salaries, yet he spent large sums in courts of law to defend the victories won in his crusades, and practiced many private charities. He inspired his men to work and write as they had never

[13] William Allen White, "The Man Who Made the Star," *Collier's,* LV (June 26, 1915), p. 12.

[14] Two of the challengers were Scripps with his *Kansas City World* (1897) and the Denver team of Bonfils and Tammen, who operated the *Kansas City Post* from 1909 to 1922. Neither paper survived.

done before, yet one of his editors described him as a fighter, a hater, and a despot who loved power and used it arbitrarily. He did not write himself, but he would get up in the middle of the night to reread the columns of the *Star* and glory in its triumphs. In politics he supported Democrats and Republicans alternately—Grover Cleveland, Theodore Roosevelt, Woodrow Wilson. But this was no contradiction; the strong editor admired the strong men in political life, and his newspaper was following the main currents of American life.

OTHER MIDWESTERN CITIES

In other midwestern cities, changes in newspaper fortunes were in the air. Milwaukee's several dailies greeted a new competitor in 1882, Lucius W. Nieman and his *Milwaukee Journal,* which at once began to show some of the zeal which drove all its competitors, except the morning *Sentinel* (1837), to cover in the next 60 years. In Minneapolis another *Journal* began its career as a leading evening newspaper in 1878, while William J. Murphy gave the morning *Tribune* (1867) new life in the 1890s. St. Paul's *Pioneer Press* (1849), run by the distinguished team of editor Joseph A. Wheelock and manager Frederick Driscoll, found competition in the evening *Dispatch* (1868). Another aggressive evening newspaper was the *Indianapolis News* (1869).

But it was in St. Louis that the climax was reached. The river city long had been a newspaper center. The *Missouri Republican* (1808), which became the *St. Louis Republic* in 1888, the *Missouri Democrat* (1852), and Carl Schurz' German-language *Westliche Post* (1857) were leading papers. The first shock was the arrival of J. B. McCullagh from Chicago, and his consolidation of the newly-founded *Morning Globe* with the *Missouri Democrat* to start the *Globe-Democrat* on its way in 1875. The great event was the appearance of Joseph Pulitzer, a penniless immigrant who within ten years built the *St. Louis Post-Dispatch* and then turned to startle the publishing world with his *New York World.* All around him in America, a new daily newspaper was developing in keeping with the changed character of the national life, but Joseph Pulitzer by his spectacular genius became the recognized leader of the "new journalism." His story becomes the story of the emergence of the modern newspaper.

Annotated Bibliography

Books

Aaron, Daniel, *Men of Good Hope: A Story of American Progressives.* New York: Oxford University Press, 1951. Studies, among others, Henry George, Edward Bellamy, Henry Demarest Lloyd, Thorstein Veblen, William Dean Howells, and Theodore Roosevelt.

Adams, Henry, *The Education of Henry Adams*. Boston: Houghton Mifflin, 1918. A classic personal reaction to a changing society.

Beard, Charles A. and Mary R., *The Rise of American Civilization*. New York: Macmillan, 1930. The chapter in Vol. II, "The Second American Revolution," is the best interpretation of the rise of industry in the Civil War and postwar periods.

Brown, Dee, *Bury My Heart at Wounded Knee*. New York: Holt, Rinehart & Winston, 1971. The history of the West as finally written by the losers, the American Indians.

Clayton, Charles G., *Little Mack: Joseph B. McCullagh of the St. Louis Globe-Democrat*. Carbondale: Southern Illinois Press, 1969. Helps to illuminate a great figure in newspaper-making of the nineteenth century.

Commager, Henry Steele, *The American Mind*. New Haven: Yale University Press, 1950. A provocative and sweeping introduction to intellectual and social trends since the 1880s. It carries the reader past the uncompleted closing of Vernon L. Parrington's *Main Currents in American Thought*.

Dorfman, Joseph, *Thorstein Veblen and His America*. New York: Viking, 1934. A study of rebellion against the rugged individualists and their economic thinking.

Faulkner, Harold U., *American Economic History*. New York: Harper & Row, 1960. Standard one-volume college textbook.

Goldman, Eric F., *Rendezvous with Destiny: A History of Modern American Reform*. New York: Knopf, 1952. An interpretive synthesis which traces the tradition of dissent from post-Civil War years to the times of the Fair Deal.

Hart, Jim Allee, *A History of the St. Louis Globe-Democrat*. Columbia: University of Missouri Press, 1961. The story of founder J. B. McCullagh and of the paper, within a social framework.

Hartz, Louis, *The Liberal Tradition in America*. New York: Harcourt, Brace & Jovanovich, 1955. Major work of the consensus school of historians, based on theme U.S. was "born free" and had no opposition to liberalism in a land of plenty.

Hofstadter, Richard, *Social Darwinism in American Thought, 1860–1915*. Philadelphia: University of Pennsylvania Press, 1955. A harshly critical study.

Johnson, Icie F., *William Rockhill Nelson and the Kansas City Star*. Kansas City: Burton Publishing Company, 1935. The best published study of Nelson.

Karolevitz, Robert F., *Newspapering in the Old West*. Seattle: Superior Publishing Company, 1965. Pictorial history of "how it was" on the frontier.

McKelvey, Blake, *The Urbanization of America, 1860–1915*. New Brunswick, N.J.: Rutgers University Press, 1969.

———, *The Emergence of Metropolitan America, 1915–1966*. New Brunswick, N.J.: Rutgers University Press, 1968. Two new studies of the trend.

Mott, Frank Luther, *A History of American Magazines*. Vol. II, 1850–1865; Vol. III, 1865–1885; Vol. IV, 1885–1905. Cambridge, Mass.: Harvard University Press, 1938–57. The continuation of Professor Mott's authoritative study. Vol. V, 1905–1930 (1968) has a cumulative index.

Myers, John Myers, *Print in a Wild Land*. New York: Doubleday, 1967. Racy account of newspaperin' in the Old West.

Nixon, Raymond B., *Henry W. Grady: Spokesman of the New South*. New York: Knopf, 1943. The definitive biography of a leading southern editor, with emphasis upon his contributions as a newsman in stimulating the rise of the "new journalism."

North, Simeon N. D., *History and Present Condition of the Newspaper and Periodical Press of the United States.* Washington: Government Printing Office, 1884. Published as a part of the 1880 census; valuable particularly for its picture of the press in that year.

Paxson, Frederic L., *History of the American Frontier.* Boston: Houghton Mifflin, 1924. Records the passing of the frontier by 1893.

Potter, David M., *People of Plenty.* Chicago: University of Chicago Press, 1954. American progress has been shaped by the unifying character of economic abundance, not by efforts of radicals, advocates of change.

Schlesinger, Arthur M., *The Rise of the City, 1878–1898,* A History of American Life, Vol. X. New York: Macmillan, 1932. The best social history of a crucial period. See Ida M. Tarbell, below, for reference to companion volume.

Sharpe, Ernest, *G. B. Dealey of the Dallas News.* New York: Holt, Rinehart & Winston, 1955. A favorable biography; covers to 1946.

Stone, Melville E., *Fifty Years a Journalist.* Garden City: Doubleday, 1921. The first portion deals with Stone's Chicago newspaper career, the latter with the Associated Press.

Tarbell, Ida M., *The Nationalizing of Business, 1878–1898,* A History of American Life, Vol. IX. New York: Macmillan, 1936.

U. S. Department of Commerce, *Historical Statistics of the United States, 1789–1945.* Washington, D.C.: U. S. Government Printing Office, 1949.

Walsh, Justin E., *To Print the News and Raise Hell.* Chapel Hill: University of North Carolina Press, 1968. Biography of Wilbur F. Storey, controversial editor of the *Chicago Times* in Civil War period.

Ware, Norman J., *The Labor Movement in the United States, 1860–1895.* New York: Appleton-Century-Crofts, 1929. More compact than the massive history of labor by John R. Commons and associates, this book emphasizes the Knights of Labor. See also Lloyd Ulman, *The Rise of the National Trade Union* (Cambridge, Mass.: Harvard University Press, 1955), and autobiographies of Powderly and Gompers.

Wiebe, Robert H., *The Search for Order, 1877–1920.* New York: Hill & Wang, 1968. First general synthesis of an American historical period written from an institutional point of view.

Young, John P., *Journalism in California.* San Francisco: Chronicle Publishing Company, 1913. Principally a history of the *San Francisco Chronicle,* consistently one of the West's leading newspapers.

Periodicals and Monographs

"Fifty Years of Harper's Magazine," *Harper's,* C (May 1900), 947.

Hall, Mark W., "The *San Francisco Chronicle:* Its Fight for the 1879 Constitution," *Journalism Quarterly,* XLVI (Autumn 1969), 505. From M.A. thesis, University of Missouri, 1967.

Irwin, Will, "The Power of the Press," *Collier's*, XLVI (January 21, 1911), 15. The first article in Irwin's "The American Newspaper" series, discussing the birth of modern journalism and such publishers as William Rockhill Nelson of the *Kansas City Star* and Harrison Gray Otis of the *Los Angeles Times*.

Mott, Frank Luther, "Fifty Years of Life: The Story of a Satirical Weekly," *Journalism Quarterly*, XXV (September 1948), 224.

Nixon, Raymond B., "Henry W. Grady, Reporter: A Reinterpretation," *Journalism Quarterly*, XII (December 1935), 341. Reprinted in Ford and Emery, *Highlights in the History of the American Press*.

Peterson, Paul V., "The *Chicago Daily Herald:* Righting the Historical Record," *Journalism Quarterly*, XLVII (Winter 1970), 697. Melville Stone's early Chicago paper appeared in 1873.

Rogers, Charles E., "William Rockhill Nelson and His Editors of the Star," *Journalism Quarterly*, XXVI (March 1949), 15. Based upon the author's *William Rockhill Nelson: Independent Editor and Crusading Liberal* (Ph.D. thesis, University of Minnesota, 1948).

White, William Allen, "The Man Who Made the Star," *Collier's*, LV (June 26, 1915), 12. A portrait of William Rockhill Nelson by the editor of the *Emporia Gazette*. Reprinted in Ford and Emery, *Highlights in the History of the American Press*.

White, Z. L., "Western Journalism," *Harper's*, LXXVII (October 1888), 678. A contemporary picture of Ohio journalism, including the Scripps enterprises, and journalism farther west.

St. Louis Post-Dispatch

Joseph Pulitzer, from the portrait by John S. Sargent.

17

The New Journalism

. . . every issue of the paper presents an opportunity and a duty to say something courageous and true; to rise above the mediocre and conventional; to say something that will command the respect of the intelligent, the educated, the independent part of the community; to rise above fear of partisanship and fear of popular prejudice.
—Joseph Pulitzer

Joseph Pulitzer was one of those many immigrants who helped to build the new America of the post-Civil War period. In so doing, he both gave and received: the two great newpapers which he established won for him the honor of being named as the leading American editor of modern times,[1] and they also built for him a fortune appraised at his death at nearly 20 million dollars, one of the largest ever accumulated in the newspaper field.

The story of Joseph Pulitzer's journalistic success climaxes the story of the new national environment. Pulitzer made his own contributions to the creation of the "New Journalism," but more important, he achieved his leadership by being receptive to the ideas of others. His immense energy and his highly developed journalistic sense enabled him to adapt and to develop in his own way the publishing concepts and techniques of his time, and to satisfy his passionate desire to win unquestioned recognition as the builder of the brilliant staff and the complex mechanism of a great modern newspaper. This was a notable achievement, but it alone was not enough to win him his reputation as the most useful and worthy American editor in the estimate of his craft. His true greatness lay in his high-minded conception of a newspaper's role, particularly

[1] In a poll of American editors conducted by *Editor & Publisher* in 1934.

in exercising editorial leadership, and in the way in which he made that conception live in his newspapers.

JOSEPH PULITZER'S EARLY CAREER

Pulitzer was born in Hungary in 1847. His father was Magyar-Jewish, his mother Austro-German. At 17, after receiving a good private school education, he ran away from home to join an army. But he had weak eyesight and an unmilitary look which brought rejections from the Austrian army and the French Foreign Legion. Less particular, however, was an American agent who was seeking Europeans who would volunteer for the Union Army in that Civil War year of 1864. The agent enlisted Pulitzer, who became a member of the Lincoln cavalry.

Pulitzer's experiences with the army were all unfortunate. One of his biographers describes the youthful Pulitzer as clearly unfitted for soldierly life.[2] He was tall and thin, with long, thick black hair, a large head, and an oversized nose. His complexion was pink, his hands were those of an artist. Ungainly in appearance and awkward in movement, he seemed to be the ideal subject for the practical jokes of his fellow men. His only saving grace was that his eyes revealed a searching intelligence. He added to his troubles by continually asking questions, trying to find the reasons for army practices. These were admirable qualities for a newspaperman, but not for a recruit.

When the war ended, without his seeing real action, Pulitzer found himself in New York, virtually penniless, and handicapped by language difficulties in the competition for jobs. He tried to ship out on a whaler, but was turned down. He tried the newspapers on Park Row, but since he spoke only a little English along with his German and French, he was rejected. Eventually he decided that he would go to an inland city containing few immigrants, where he would by necessity improve his command of English. He asked his German acquaintances, and they played a final practical joke on him by sending him to St. Louis, a center of the German-speaking population.

In St. Louis he first fired a steamboat boiler, then became a hostler for 16 army mules. Most of his engagements were short; the mule-tending lasted two days. He became successively a river stevedore, a livery stable tender, and a waiter until he plopped a beefsteak upon a customer's head. Finally he won a position as assistant bookkeeper in a lumberyard, seemingly the measure of his ability.

But his restlessness, his tremendously inquisitive nature, and his unbounded energy led him upward. At the public library he was reading, learning, and studying for admission to the bar. In 1867 he became an American citizen. About the same time he became friendly with Carl Schurz, then the liberal editor of the leading German-language daily, the *Westliche Post*. When the

[2] Joseph W. Barrett, *Joseph Pulitzer and His World* (New York: Vanguard, 1941), pp. 3–4.

Post needed a new reporter in 1868, the city editor interviewed two candidates and chose Pulitzer because he thought the other candidate the more likely threat to the city editor's job security.

Now Pulitzer was at home in his work. Everything was his meat—beat reporting, politics, civic news, the important and the trivia, the obvious and the hidden news. He worked from 10 A.M. to 2 A.M. writing columns of copy each day. Other reporters laughed at his mannerisms, but after Pulitzer had surpassed them with his incredible reporting zeal, the laughter stopped.

One more practical joke helped to shape the Pulitzer career. He was nominated as the Republican candidate for the Missouri State Assembly in what was assumed to be a certain Democratic district. But Pulitzer made a house-to-house campaign and won the election. At the capitol, he became legislative correspondent for the *Westliche Post*.

Pulitzer's growing interest in public affairs led him to join with Schurz in the Liberal Republican movement of 1872, and he stumped the German-speaking areas of Missouri for the presidential candidate, Horace Greeley. When the Liberal Republican movement collapsed in defeat, Pulitzer became a Democrat. He also became a part owner of the *Westliche Post*, some of whose stockholders sold out cheaply because they thought the Greeley campaign had ruined the paper. But Pulitzer exhibited too much aggressiveness to suit Schurz and Dr. Emil Preetorius, the principal owners, and they soon paid him $30,000 to give up his stock.

The next year, 1874, Pulitzer again showed his financial ability by purchasing a mediocre St. Louis paper whose only virtue was an exclusive membership in the Associated Press of the time. Pulitzer foresaw that Joseph B. McCullagh, the highly qualified Chicago newspaperman who had entered the St. Louis morning field, would need the press association membership to help force a merger between his *Globe* and the rival *Democrat*. McCullagh did, and the price paid to Pulitzer was $20,000.

Again Pulitzer left St. Louis newspaper work. During the next few years he visited Europe four times, was married, and was admitted to the District of Columbia Bar. He took the stump for Samuel J. Tilden, the 1876 Democratic presidential nominee, and reported for Dana's *New York Sun* on the activities of the electoral commission which decided that disputed election in favor of Rutherford B. Hayes. His command of the English language was now excellent, and he had greatly increased his knowledge of his adopted country. Then, in 1878, he returned to St. Louis journalism.

FOUNDING OF THE *ST. LOUIS POST-DISPATCH*, 1878

Pulitzer's destiny now was to be fulfilled. The *Dispatch*, founded in 1864 and now bankrupt, was on the block at a sheriff's sale. Pulitzer won it with a $2,500 bid on December 9, 1878, again obtaining as his principal prize an

Associated Press membership. Within three days he had used the AP franchise to effect a combination with the *Post,* started by John A. Dillon in 1875 (Dillon lasted for a year as a partner but remained as a Pulitzer associate).

Thus was born the *Post-Dispatch,* a newspaper which was to become one of the country's greatest in the next 75 years. Almost immediately Pulitzer's newspaper sense began to produce a financial reward, and by 1881 the *Post-Dispatch* was the leading evening paper in St. Louis, netting $45,000 a year and rivaling the morning papers, the influential *Missouri Republican* and McCullagh's powerful *Globe-Democrat.*

Behind this achievement lay the talents of the editor-publisher. Pulitzer in his early thirties was a commanding figure: six feet two inches tall, thin and erect in stature, now wearing a short red beard. He was an ambitious and self-contained man, confident of his powers, in whom were combined intellectual capacity and a consuming energy. He had the artist's love for good music and good writing; he had the scholar's interest in economic, political, and social trends. But above all, he had a driving passion for accomplishment. His maturing facial features and his flashing eyes expressed the Pulitzer will; those who met him felt the full force of his nervous energy and his determination. He was not easily approachable and held even close associates at a distance, but in his own way he showed high appreciation for the work of men who measured up to his exacting standards for newspaper achievement.

Many capable newsmen were to serve under the Pulitzer banner in the years ahead, but the most influential was the right-hand man of these early years, John A. Cockerill. Cockerill came to the *Post-Dispatch* as managing editor in 1880, when the burden of supervising the expanding paper forced Pulitzer to find an able associate. Cockerill had none of Pulitzer's artistic qualities; he was a hard-fighting extrovert who carried the title of "Colonel." But he was a good news executive who had been trained in the journalism of Cincinnati, Washington, and Baltimore. He had served as a war correspondent during the Russo-Turkish War of 1877–78 and was editor of the *Baltimore Gazette* when Pulitzer discovered him. Upon the hard-working and pugnacious Cockerill fell much of the responsibility for carrying out Pulitzer's commands, and he responded ably. He also brought with him a keen sense of newspaper methods, which was to serve Pulitzer well for the next 12 critical years.[3]

But it was Pulitzer who imparted to the *Post-Dispatch* its distinctive spirit. His statement of policies for the new paper contains memorable words:

> The *Post and Dispatch* will serve no party but the people; be no organ of Republicanism, but the organ of truth; will follow no causes but its

[3] Cockerill's biographer contends that his experience as managing editor of the *Cincinnati Enquirer* in exploiting local news, and his subsequent exposures to national and international news in Washington and Baltimore and as a war correspondent, made Cockerill a definitely superior newsman to Pulitzer. Much of the imaginative handling of the news, and the sensational approach, is credited to Cockerill. See Homer W. King, *Pulitzer's Prize Editor: A Biography of John A. Cockerill, 1845–1896* (Durham, N.C.: Duke University Press, 1965).

> conclusions; will not support the "Administration," but criticise it; will oppose all frauds and shams wherever and whatever they are; will advocate principles and ideas rather than prejudices and partisanship. . . .[4]

Even more memorable are the words written by a more mature Pulitzer in 1907, near the end of his career, which have become the *Post-Dispatch* platform, printed on the editorial page:

> I know that my retirement will make no difference in its cardinal principles; that it will always fight for progress and reform, never tolerate injustice or corruption, always fight demagogues of all parties, never belong to any party, always oppose privileged classes and public plunderers, never lack sympathy with the poor, always remain devoted to the public welfare, never be satisfied with merely printing news, always be drastically independent, never be afraid to attack wrong, whether by predatory plutocracy or predatory poverty.

"Never be satisfied with merely printing news" was a cardinal Pulitzer policy. By that phrase was meant the kind of reporting Pulitzer himself had done, getting more than surface news or that which came by itself to the city room. It meant, too, the kind of crusading in the public interest which Pulitzer demanded when he wrote to an editor: "Never drop a big thing until you have gone to the bottom of it. Continuity! Continuity! Continuity until the subject is really finished."[5]

Crusading of this type, through both news and editorial columns, was a distinctive Pulitzer contribution to the "new journalism." For although crusading was a common characteristic of leading contemporary papers, the impact of the Pulitzer-inspired crusade was heightened both by the intensity of the effort and by the techniques employed in writing and in news display. In its first years the *Post-Dispatch* printed lists of wealthy tax-dodgers in the city; it fought the granting of an extortionate franchise to a public utility corporation; it warred constantly for three years to break up a police-protected gambling ring; and it poured editorial fire on crooked politicians.

At the same time the staff was taught to cover the news of the city incessantly, and to look for both the significant news and the "original, distinctive, dramatic, romantic, thrilling, unique, curious, quaint, humorous, odd, apt to be talked about" news. Pulitzer considered the day a loss if his newspaper did not have one distinctive feature—a crusade, public service, or big exclusive story.

Post-Dispatch men also came to know the famous Pulitzer dictum: "Accuracy! Accuracy!! Accuracy!!!" This meant not only avoiding simple errors, but also the half-truths and inadequate statements of sloppy reporting. Another

[4] As quoted in Don C. Seitz, *Joseph Pulitzer: His Life and Letters* (New York: Simon & Schuster, 1924), p. 101. The name of the paper was soon changed to the *Post-Dispatch*.

[5] As quoted in *The Story of the St. Louis Post-Dispatch* (St. Louis: Pulitzer Publishing Company, 1949), p. 3.

Pulitzer command which became familiar was: "Terseness! Intelligent, not stupid, condensation." As the years went by, Pulitzer news executives and newsmen received thousands of reminders from their publisher-editor on these subjects, and many proddings to do a full job of covering the news. An example of a Pulitzer memo on how to write a story is this one, sent to one of his New York editors in the last year of his life:

> Apropos of enclosed clipping from the London *Times* showing that there were 185 homicides in New York during 1910, this would make a good magazine feature article if properly worked up. Pick out the most interesting cases. What were these homicides? Who committed them? What was the motive? Give a table of motives, of social rank, of age, of nationality, etc. But print the facts more reliably, more strikingly than would the magazines. But don't print it from the standpoint of mere sensationalism, but rather from the moral point of view. It should be a thoughtful article with a great moral to it. Compare the figure with Paris, and with London, and with other great European cities. Allude also to the administration of justice and the methods of dealing with murder cases in the different countries, with statistics of indictments, convictions, executions and failure to punish or to solve murder mysteries.[6]

There is no record of how well the editor succeeded.

There were serious blemishes on the Pulitzer record during the early St. Louis years. Cockerill had brought with him a reputation for exploiting stories of murder, sin, and sex and for sensationalizing accounts of violence, lynchings, public hangings, and dramatic death. Pulitzer found many of these subjects fitting his "apt to be talked about" definition of news. They delighted in printing bits of gossipy scandal about the "best families" of the St. Louis oligarchy under such headlines as "St. Louis Swells," "An Adulterous Pair," "Loved the Cook," "Does Rev. Mr. Tudor Tipple?" Tales of sex and sin included "Duped and Deserted" and "A Denver Maiden Taken from a Disreputable House." On the day in 1882 when the assassin of President Garfield was executed, Cockerill, who advocated illustrations, ran a two-column drawing on page one of a condemned man "as he appeared today on the scaffold"—a technical impossibility. The James Boys, outlaws, gave the *Post-Dispatch* a big circulation lift the same year. In these and many other stories, exaggeration, half-truth, and humor at the expense of embarrassed citizens could be found.[7] This was also true, of course, of other papers of the times.

Editorially, Pulitzer's early *Post-Dispatch* hit hard at the wealthy families who monopolized control of the nation's fifth largest city. The crusades it developed, however, were focused not on the problems of the poor and work-

[6] As quoted in Seitz, *Joseph Pulitzer*, p. 423.

[7] Documented in the chapter, "A Sensational Newspaper," in Julian Rammelkamp, *Pulitzer's Post-Dispatch 1878–1883* (Princeton, N.J.: Princeton University Press, 1967), pp. 163–206. On the whole Rammelkamp endorses Pulitzer's record.

ing classes but on those of the middle class and the small businessmen with whom the publisher associated.[8] Everyone benefited, of course, from attacks on monopoly, from battles for cleaner living conditions, from crusades against vice. But the focus on the plight of the oppressed poor which was to be a Pulitzer trademark in New York was not yet present. The paper was also developing its coverage of middle class news interests, such as sports and women's news.

In every field of newspaper publishing, Pulitzer, Cockerill, and their associates on the *Post-Dispatch* were learning the lessons they were soon to apply in New York. There were many mistakes, many stories and editorials falling short of the Pulitzer goals. But there were successes, for as the *World* commented in 1890, "The foundation of the *New York World* was laid in St. Louis. . . . The battle of new ideas and new theories of journalism was fought there under the banner of the *Post-Dispatch*."[9] The *World* might have added that the editors of the *Post-Dispatch* were watching and learning from the other new midwestern papers: Nelson's *Kansas City Star*, Stone's *Chicago Daily News*, Scripps' *Cleveland Press*, McCullagh's rival *Globe-Democrat*—just as they in turn were watching Pulitzer.

By 1883 Pulitzer was a 36-year-old physical wreck. His poor eyesight was failing; his nerves were badly impaired by incessant work. Matters had not been helped when Cockerill shot and killed a prominent St. Louis attorney whom the *Post-Dispatch* had attacked in its columns. Cockerill successfully pleaded self-defense, but public indignation hurt the paper. Discouraged by this turn of events, Pulitzer was enroute to Europe for a long vacation in May, 1883, when he heard in New York that the *World* was for sale.

PURCHASE OF THE *NEW YORK WORLD*, 1883

Founded in 1860, the *World* had been well edited by Manton Marble as a Democratic morning newspaper, but had suffered financial reverses. Sale of the paper in 1879 to the unscrupulous financier, Jay Gould, had further damaged its prestige, and the *World* was losing $40,000 a year. Gould offered to sell for what he claimed he had in the paper—$346,000.

The situation looked unpromising. The *World* had but 15,000 circulation for its two-cent, eight-page paper. Its more powerful morning rivals were Bennett's *Herald*, printing from 12 to 16 pages at three cents a copy; Dana's *Sun*, still publishing but four pages for two cents; Whitelaw Reid's *Tribune* and George Jones' *Times*, both selling at four cents for eight pages. There was a

[8] Rammelkamp points out that Pulitzer "mobilized the middle class elements of St. Louis into a dynamic movement of reform" which finally bore fruit early in the twentieth century (*ibid.*, p. 303).

[9] As quoted in Willard G. Bleyer, *Main Currents in the History of American Journalism* (Boston: Houghton Mifflin, 1927), p. 325.

personal factor involved, however. Joseph Pulitzer's younger brother, Albert, also had come to the United States, and after working as a newspaperman had started the *Morning Journal* in New York in 1882 with $25,000 capital. It was catching on as a breezy, one-cent paper (he eventually sold it for a million dollars). The two brothers had little to do with each other, and Albert's successful gamble in New York journalism may have stimulated the ailing Joseph to make his own bid.

The deal with Gould was closed on May 9, 1883, and Pulitzer paid the first installment on the price of the *World* from *Post-Dispatch* profits. To Gould's surprise the remaining installments were paid from the profits of the *World*.

Pulitzer issued the first edition of the *World* under his editorship May 11. He fired some of the old editors; stole his brother's managing editor, a man who soon proved to be incompetent; wired St. Louis for two good *Post-Dispatch* men; changed the nameplate and the format; and sat down to edit the first issue.

His lead story was an account of a million-dollar storm in New Jersey. Other front page features were an interview with a condemned slayer, the story of a Wall Street plunger, a Pittsburgh hanging, a riot in Haiti, and the sad story of a wronged servant girl. Then Pulitzer ordered a press run of 22,000 copies and sold out by noon. Only the *Herald* had matched him in sensational coverage.

Next day the *World* blushingly admitted that it was the talk of the town. It took two columns to report the praises of New Yorkers, from the mayor to shop girls. In the upper corners of page one, alongside the short nameplate, what became known as "ears" appeared, expounding the virtues of the *World*. Here was exhibited another important factor in the Pulitzer formula—aggressive promotion of the newspaper's qualities. Within a week the *World* had found its first popular cause to promote: that the Brooklyn Bridge, just being opened as one of the new wonders of the world, should be a free bridge. It also ran an eye-catching drawing of the bridge.

But all was not sensation and promotion. The *World* was presenting good news coverage, and it was establishing its new editorial policies. In a signed statement in his first issue Pulitzer said:

> There is room in this great and growing city for a journal that is not only cheap but bright, not only bright but large, not only large but truly Democratic—dedicated to the cause of the people rather than that of the purse-potentates—devoted more to the news of the New than the Old World—that will expose all fraud and sham, fight all public evils and abuses—that will serve and battle for the people with earnest sincerity.[10]

A concise ten-point program soon appeared on the editorial page: tax luxuries; tax inheritances; tax large incomes; tax monopolies; tax the privileged

[10] *New York World*, May 11, 1883.

corporations; a tariff for revenue; reform the civil service; punish corrupt officeholders; punish vote-buying; punish employers who coerce their employees in elections.

To cap his fighting entry into New York, Pulitzer published a strongly worded editorial denouncing the aristocracy of Park Avenue, the aristocracy of the moneyed classes, and those who he said were aping foreign nobility. The *World,* he declared, believed in the aristocracy of labor, the aristocracy of brains and honor, the aristocracy of virtue. The editorial ended: "Money alone makes no aristocrats." To those who worshiped the successful dollar-chaser, this was unbelievable heresy. But it was delightful reading for many New Yorkers who resented the excesses of economic individualism and who, like Pulitzer, were believers in the necessity for economic and social reform.

If Pulitzer had not crusaded directly for the poor and helpless in St. Louis, he soon did in New York City. One could argue that this was opportunism, but the truth was that the mass audience was different, and immigrant Pulitzer was well aware of the change. His first two years at the *World* saw well-developed crusades in behalf of the immigrants, the poor, the laboring class. In July, 1883, a heat wave took a terrible toll in New York's teeming slums; the *World* found that of 716 reported deaths the previous week, 392 had been of children under five years of age. Its reporters went to the scenes of death; its headline writers produced "How Babies Are Baked" and "Lines of Little Hearses."[11] The injustices of the garment district's sweatshops for immigrant women, the lack of school opportunities in the tenements, the inequity of the tax burden, were all subjects for news stories and editorials.

Pulitzer's liberal political and social stands editorially were to pay handsome circulation dividends in 1884, when the *World* supported Grover Cleveland, Democratic governor of New York, for the presidency against the conservative Republican champion, James G. Blaine. Dana's *Sun,* which attacked both major party candidates and supported the discredited third party candidate, Benjamin Butler, lost a good share of its circulation to the hard-hitting *World,* which in both editorial spirit and news appeal was directing its attention to the mass of New York residents. Pulitzer himself was elected to Congress that year, but he soon abandoned this political career.

Much of the success of the news policy is credited to Cockerill, the *Post-Dispatch* managing editor who had now become managing editor of the *World.* Cockerill was adept in both playing up human interest stories and in maintaining a solid presentation of significant local, national, and international news; for despite the attention given to sensational material, the *World* tried to give its readers full coverage of the day's events. Cockerill gloried in a story that combined international importance and human drama; when news came of the death of Britain's General Gordon at Khartoum, the *World* filled five columns on one day in 1885 and followed with three more columns a week later giving

[11] George Juergens, *Joseph Pulitzer and the New York World* (Princeton, N.J.: Princeton University Press, 1966), p. 272.

The World

VOL. XXIII., NO. 7,947. NEW YORK, THURSDAY, MAY 24, 1883.

BUILDING THE BRIDGE.

INCEPTION AND BIRTH OF THE MAMMOTH ENTERPRISE.

To Whom the Honor is Due—The First Passenger—The Finishing Touches—All in Readiness to Wed the Cities.

Communication between Brooklyn and New York by a regular ferry service existed so long ago as 1642, and for more than a century Fulton street on the Brooklyn side and Peck slip on this side of the East River were the landings. The first steam ferry-boat began running in 1814, two years before the incorporation of the sister city as a village. Those who have read Stiles or Pierrepont know how formidable an undertaking the crossing of the East River was in the early days of the Republic. It was not so dangerous a passage as that to Paulus Hook.

In 1874 Mrs. Burr depicted the agony with which she heard that her husband had embarked on the North River ferry-boat, and the joy with which she received the announcement that it had reached Jersey City, and in 1780 the [illegible] of Mrs. Quincy so scared General Gates that he took off his overcoat and turned back from the ferry-house.

OLD TIME FERRIAGE.

The row-boat, the square-ended scow with a spritsail, and the two-masted periagua were the immediate predecessors of the steamboat, and with them should be mentioned the craft celebrated by the poet Banvard:

How well I remember the horseboat that paddled
Across the East River, ere the advent of steam;
Sometimes the old driver the horses would straddle
And sometimes ride round on the circling beam.

"It took just four coppers to cross o'er the tide." Commutation tickets were issued in 1814 at the rate of $10 a year or $6.67 for eight months. When the Nassau made her first trips in May of that year she performed very creditably, as the Long Island *Star* records: "her trips varied from five to twelve minutes, and carriages and wagons, however crowded, pass on and off the boat with the same facility as in passing a bridge," while the *Columbian* says that she took over at one trip 545 passengers, one wagon and a pair of horses, two horses and chaises, and one single horse. It is interesting to recall that, when, in 1817, the public clamored for the second steamer, the ferry company, composed of Fulton and Cutting, demurred on the ground of expense, further alleging that horse-boats were more easily navigated and much safer in winter than steamboats.

POPE'S PLAN.

The earliest plan for an East River bridge seems to have been that conceived by Pope in 1811. (Qy. 1819?) He showed in New York a model on the scale of three-eighths of an inch to the foot (?) of his proposed cantilever bridge with a span of 1,800 feet, describing the structure as follows:

Each semi-arc is built from off the top
Without the help of scaffold, pier or prop;
By [illegible] and cranes each part is lowered down,
And [illegible] the timber's end [illegible] so sound.
Sure all the bridges that we've ever built,
Repose their weight on centre, pier or stilt;
Not so the bridge the author has to boast,
His plan is sure to save such needless cost,
A ladder on each side is lowered down,
And shifted from the fulcrum to the crown.

In 1849 the building of a bridge across the East River was advocated in the daily press of New York, Mr. Thomas McKirath's paragraphs in the *Tribune* attracting the attention of Mr. Roebling, who assured the writer of the feasibility and desirability of the plan. On Christmas night of that year an ice-blockade, which lasted several hours, provoked a vigorous popular discussion of the project, and a similar blockade in 1852 directed the close attention of one of the sufferers, Mr. Roebling, to it, and evoked a letter from him, in [illegible] cost of a safe and permanent bridge was [illegible]

NEW YORK JOINS HANDS WITH BROOKLYN.

thousands of tons of granite and lowering the whole mass so steadily that the air-bubble in the spirit-level stood as if it had been a flaw in a block of solid glass, making the air drive out the water and the water imprison the air, a handful of pigmies dug their way down through the oozy bed of the East River, through boiling quicksands and jagged reefs, until far below the depths where the air could reach and rot the frail wood or the worm burrow it into tinder, the adamantine bedrock prepared from before the foundation of the world was laid bare, and thousands of tons of concrete were poured into the well-holes and working-spaces, welding the tower into the rock.

On the 2d of May, 1870, the Brooklyn caisson was towed into its berth; on the 10th of July the water was driven out and, notwithstanding a delay of some weeks caused by a fire in the caisson, on the 11th of March, 1871, it was anchored 45½ feet beneath the river with its charge of concrete.

In October, 1871, the New York caisson was placed in its berth; in May, 1872, it had found a resting-place 78 feet below high-water mark. In the Brooklyn caisson were 5,253 cubic yards of timber and iron and 5,669 cubic feet of concrete. The New York caisson weighed 7,000 tons, and its concrete filling 8,000. These anchored immovably, there was nothing to do but to pile up block upon block of granite until the roofing-course had been laid 275 feet up in the air.

THE GREAT TOWERS.

At high-water line the towers were 140 feet by 59 and at the roof course 136 by 53. The Brooklyn tower contained 38,214 cubic yards of masonry and weighed about 93,000 tons, the New York tower 46,945 cubic yards, with a weight of 120,000 tons. The material employed was blue limestone from Kingston, faced with granite. At an interval of [illegible]

the employees under the direction of Assistant Engineer McNulty. Four thousand chairs have been placed in the structure at Sands street, where the reception will be held, and the decorations, consisting of streamers, flags, banners and shields bearing the coats of arms of all the States, have been placed. Every available window within eyesight of the bridge has been reserved and seats on the roofs of the houses within spy-glass view of the structure have been taken and, in some instances, paid for at high rates.

Thousands of strangers could be seen on the streets yesterday, and the bridge office on Water street was besieged all day long by people who wanted to obtain tickets for seats inside the building. A bridge official said that ten thousand more tickets than the place could possibly accommodate had been issued.

All the United States men-of-war of the North Atlantic Squadron, under the command of Rear-Admiral Cooper, will anchor near the bridge in the early morning, and when President Arthur and suite arrive a salute will be fired in rotation by all the vessels, beginning with the Tennessee, the Rear Admiral's flagship. The ships will be decked with the flags of all nations, and the sailors will man the rigging.

The bridge authorities request that all boats except those used in local traffic be kept at least half a mile from the bridge, so that there may be no accidents.

PRECAUTIONS AGAINST FIRES.

The New York and the Brooklyn Fire Departments have been notified to and will each send an engine to guard against possible conflagrations. Lines of hose will be stretched the whole length of the footway, and before any of the fireworks are set off the [illegible] woodwork of the structure will be [illegible]

"NUMBER ONE" UNEARTHED

HE HOLDS A RECEPTION AT HIS HOUSE AND MAKES A STATEMENT.

Acknowledging He is the *Man Wanted*, He Declines to be Interviewed by Advice of Counsel.

"The discovery of Mr. Tynan's residence by THE WORLD," said General Pryor yesterday, "is a very clever piece of detective work. Now that his residence is known, further concealment on his part becomes impossible, and I think he will talk to you."

At No. 191 West Baltic street, Brooklyn, a very pleasant-featured middle-aged lady dressed in black silk received the reporter and said:

"I am Mrs. Tynan. My husband is not at home just at present, but he told me to say that if any reporter called he will be happy to see him at 4 o'clock."

Promptly to the minute the reporter was on hand and was ushered into the parlor, where he was received by Mr. Farrell, the gentleman who only a day before had so positively asserted that nobody of the name of Tynan was or had been living in the house.

SHALL BUTLER BE LL.D.?

The Harvard Overseers Get in a Wrangle Over the Question.

[SPECIAL TO THE WORLD.]

BOSTON, May 23.—The overseers of Harvard College held their regular meeting to-day and after acting on the list of nominations submitted by the President the question of awarding degrees at the Commencement was taken up.

Reporters were not admitted, but it is known that there was a stormy scene over the proposition not to conform to the time-honored custom of conferring the degree of LL. D. on the Governor of Massachusetts. Some of the members of this dignified body are said to have been extremely violent in denouncing Governor Butler and to have threatened dire disaster to the college should the degree be conferred.

After a protracted wrangle the board finally agreed to postpone action until the 31st inst.

Governor Butler's friends report that he is greatly amused by this affair.

The following nominations were confirmed: Clement L. Smith and James B. Greenough, Professors of Latin; George H. Palmer, Professor of Philosophy; James L. Laughlin, Assistant Professor of Political Economy for five years; Arthur Searle, Assistant Professor of Astronomy for five years.

A Raid on Philadelphia Gamblers.

[SPECIAL TO THE WORLD.]

PHILADELPHIA, May 23.—There was a [illegible]

NEW YORK, MONDAY, JULY 9, 1883.

LINES OF LITTLE HEARSES.

BURYING THE BABY VICTIMS OF THE HEATED TENEMENTS.

A Cool Wave Strikes the City and Brings Relief to All but the Sorrowing Families.

The expected cool wave struck this city yesterday morning, bringing with it an almost continuous shower of rain. Relief was immediately experienced by everybody, and was not received with more thankfulness by any persons than the poor in the crowded districts, where little children died by scores during the previous day from the effects of the extreme heat. At 3.30 o'clock in the afternoon yesterday, which is usually the hottest time of the day, the thermometer registered 62 degrees, showing a fall of 28 degrees in twenty-four hours. The hot weather had gone as it had come, and the poor people once more breathed cool if not pure air. Still, for all the cool weather, it was a day of sorrow, for when the people crossed the Brooklyn ferries they saw lines of little white hearses carrying the baby victims to their final resting places, where starvation and heat are no more. The little hearses sorrowfully wended their ways through the streets of Brooklyn and Long Island City to the various cemeteries in the suburbs. On one ferry-boat going to Hunter's Point there were three of the small white hearses and two with black plumes. So it was all day. Boats were run disregardless of schedule time, so as to accommodate the funeral processions.

RELIEF COMES TOO LATE.

Nor was the deadly work of the stifling atmosphere yet done. Many unfortunate persons who were prostrated when the temperature ranged up in the nineties lingered long enough to breathe the cool air and hear the refreshing rain patter down upon the scorching roofs of the hospital, only to die when that relief which they so vainly prayed for came—too late.

The funeral processions which crossed the Brooklyn ferries numbered as many as six to one boat; 80 per cent. of those were little children. Not since the Fourth street school disaster had so many little white hearses crossed on the boats at one time.

YESTERDAY'S DEATHS.

Despite the cool wave the death rate in this city did not decrease yesterday. It was even greater than on any of the preceding days. The number of deaths reported at the Bureau of Vital Statistics yesterday was 214, of which 123 were children under five years of age, an increase of 9 over the highest rate of the past week. All the deaths resulted from diseases caused by the extreme heat.

The cool wave was first felt about 9 o'clock in the morning. The people who had passed many sleepless nights hailed the approaching change with delight. At noon the thermometer marked 74, a fall of 16 degrees. From that time it began to fall steadily, until 9 o'clock last evening it reached the low figure of 62 degrees.

HAILING THE RAIN.

Shortly after 1 o'clock a refreshing rain began to fall. It continued throughout the day and evening, cooling the parched earth and bringing joy to the farmers. The storm came from the lake region and the Ohio valley. On Saturday evening it began its journey towards the suffering sections, sweeping across the northern part of New York State, sprinkling Montreal, Toronto and Quebec, causing a fall of 26 degrees in the temperature of the latter place. Yesterday morning it swept through Ohio and Pennsylvania, and on towards evening it visited Boston, cooling the atmosphere there 37 degrees, and New Haven, where it caused a fall of 28 degrees in the temperature. The storm reached as far South as Memphis, Tenn., lowering the temperature 4 degrees. The storm, which steadily advanced towards the Atlantic coast, will waste itself on the ocean.

THE DEATH RECORD.

The following cases of sudden deaths from the effect of the heat were reported at the Coroner's office yesterday:

Catharine Delahan, aged thirty-six, died a few minutes after being prostrated.

John Donlan, aged thirty-eight, of No. 211 East Thirty-ninth street.

Florence Solender, a Swiss, no home, died at No. 61 Pitt street.

Fritz Ryan, six months old, died at No. 138 Bleecker street.

Annie T[illegible]ner, aged six months, died at No. 344 West Thirty-ninth street.

Martha Griffin, aged three months, died at No. 48 East Fourth street.

OUT OF TOWN.

In Brooklyn two deaths were reported, those of Arthur Dempsey, who was overcome by the heat shortly before noon, and died a few hours later at his residence, No. 80 Union street.

Patrick Callahan, aged eighteen, a bar-tender, died from the effects of the heat in the Tenth Precinct Police Station.

Ex-Sheriff Daggett, who was prostrated by the heat on Friday, was said to be out of danger yesterday.

Joseph Duran died in St. Mary's Hospital, at Hoboken, yesterday from a sunstroke.

Henry McAvoy, of No. 7 Adams street, Hoboken, who was prostrated by the heat on Saturday, died at his residence.

Bridget Dalton, a widow, died at her residence, No. 113 Park avenue, Hoboken. She was overcome on Saturday, and leaves four small children.

DROWNED OUT AT CONEY ISLAND.

A summer resort, especially at the seaside, is the dullest of dull places in rainy weather. There is no promenading, no boating, no bathing. Everything is wet, dull and disagreeable. All the bright flags and banners which on a sunny Sunday afternoon flutter from hotels and booths at Coney Island wrapped themselves around their poles yesterday and absolutely refused to be lively as flags and streamers should always be. There was no business done except in the hotels, which have their quota of summer guests. The man who combs the mermaid's hair sat silently moping in his tent. The little donkeys that wander up and down the seashore were in their stables enjoying the cessation of fair weather, whacks and indigested bonbons, but pining for the sunlight.

A walk from one end of the beach to the other yesterday showed that no one was satisfied with such a Sunday. The fact that the rain had cooled the atmosphere was no consolation. Of what value is a philanthropic mixer of cooling drinks when one don't want to drink? The men fretted and fumed about the hotels, unable to amuse themselves. The consumption of cigars was enormous. The ladies alone seemed capable of killing time gracefully. At every window of the Oriental ladies could be seen, some dreamily finishing some piece of fancy work and others reading.

So the day dragged along and the night came. With it came the bands and they played, not in front of their sounding boards on the beach, but near the bars. There were not very many people at the island and yet it seemed as though there were more than on previous Sundays, for every one was crowded together.

The boats were not crowded going down, and yet they went back crowded, for many of the hotel guests got the impression that the rainy season had set in, and assuredly the city is more pleasant than the seaside on a wet day. All the trains, too, went back crowded. The Oriental Hotel was the only place that displayed any signs of life after nightfall. The cold east wind and the pouring rain had driven even the most venturesome indoors or to the city.

The hotels at the island are still very well filled, as the rush to the seaside on Saturday was unprecedentedly large. At the Manhattan over 200 guests arrived, and at the Oriental only three or four rooms were vacant. The managers of the Senator Kiernan dinner which is to be given to-day, were in a quandary and besieged the Coney Island prophets with questions about the weather. These oracles wisely remarked that if the wind would only change clearer weather might be looked for.

ROCKAWAY AND FORT LEE.

Rockaway Beach looked very dreary yesterday, although there were many persons there. As at Coney Island the hotels were uncomfortably crowded, as walking was not very desirable. One curious thing noticed was the number of umbrellas on the beach. No one seemed to come to the beach with umbrellas, yet every one going home was supplied.

The palace steamers Grand Republic and Columbia carried a large number of passengers yesterday morning. The low price of the trip and the good music discoursed by the military bands aboard the vessels doubtless drew large numbers to these vessels.

In fair weather there is no more pleasant place on a summer afternoon than the bluffs at Fort Lee on the Hudson. The steamers Pleasant Valley, Fort Lee and Harlem made trips every hour to the bluffs yesterday from Thirty-fourth street, starting from 9 A. M. The boats leave Fort Lee from 8 A. M. every hour until 10 P. M. Yesterday did not resemble the previous days of the season, when crowds are always to be found in the hotels and wandering on the heights. The hotels did a fair business yesterday, but not nearly as large as that of last Sunday.

Two examples of crusades from Joseph Pulitzer's *New York World* of the 1880s.

a description of Gordon's every move in the hours before he died.[12] The front page carried material that made it startling and eye-catching ("Ward M'Conkey Hanged, Shouting from Under the Black Cap that His Executioners Are Murderers") and featured stories that aroused public curiosity. The *World*, like the *Post-Dispatch*, had discovered women's and sports news, and Cockerill featured combinations of international, local, and sports stories on page one.

Typographically, the new *World* was using smaller and lighter type faces than its predecessor. But some of the headlines printed during the first month spoke for themselves: "Death Rides the Blast," "Love and Cold Poison," "All for a Woman's Love," "A Heroine or a Criminal?" "Screaming for Mercy," "A Bride but not a Wife," "The Wall Street Terror," "Terrible Times in Troy," "Little Lotta's Lovers," "Baptized in Blood."[13] Alliteration was frequent; so were sex, conflict, and crime.

Use of illustrations also contributed to the success of the *World*. Cockerill found that the use of woodcuts spurred circulation, and when they were omitted because Pulitzer disliked their crude appearance, circulation slumped. Back went the woodcuts along with line drawings, particularly as illustrations for feature articles in the *Sunday World*. Valerian Gribayédoff began to draw the likenesses of prominent New Yorkers in early 1884, and cartoonist Walt McDougall did a front page series of political drawings to further the presidential candidacy of Cleveland. The *Journalist*, newspaper trade publication, asserted in 1885: "It is the woodcuts that give the *World* its unparalleled circulation."[14]

And unparalleled circulation it was. The average daily circulation of the *World* doubled during the first three months of Pulitzer's editorship. Other New York papers cut their prices to meet the threat, and the *Herald* even resorted to advertising itself in the *World's* pages. But the *Herald*, in cutting its price, got into a war with newsstand dealers who were given smaller commissions, and thus further benefited the newcomer.

Daily circulation of the *World* at the end of a year was more than 60,000—a fourfold increase. Four months later the *Sunday World* hit the 100,000 mark, and Pulitzer's promotion men presented each employee with a tall silk hat and fired a hundred cannon shots in City Hall Park by way of celebration. When in 1887 the 250,000 figure was reached by the *World*, a silver medal was struck off in honor of America's largest newspaper circulation.

Most importantly, by the end of 1884 the *World* had passed the *Herald* as the leader in number of advertising columns printed, partly because of its low rate in relation to circulation figures and partly because of the city's interest in the new paper. The size of the newspaper jumped to 12 or 14 pages daily and 36 to 44 pages on Sunday. As expenses mounted, advertising rates were raised, but the sale price remained at two cents. Within three years the

[12] Juergens, *op. cit.*, p. 53.
[13] As quoted in Bleyer, *Main Currents in the History of American Journalism*, p. 328.
[14] *Journalist*, August 22, 1885.

World had become the talk, not only of New York, but of the country's newspaper fraternity. For Joseph Pulitzer's brash new paper had broken every publishing record in America and its annual profit was at the half-million-dollar mark.

REASONS FOR THE *WORLD'S* SUCCESS

What had Pulitzer done? First of all, he had recognized the characteristics of his potential audience. The population of New York City was increasing by 50 per cent during the 1880s, and Pulitzer worked to attract the attention of the newcomers to his newspaper. As an immigrant himself, he was alive to the fact that four out of five of the city's resident were either foreign-born or children of foreign-born parents. And as one who was aware of the social and economic trends of his time, he understood the desire of his readers for effective leadership reflecting progressive attitudes, as well as for entertainment.

Therefore he had enlivened the *World's* significant news coverage to satisfy one set of changing conditions, and he had achieved sensationalism both in news content and in newspaper appearance to satisfy another trend. He had combined great promotional skill with a popular editorial aggressiveness and crusading spirit to make the mass of readers feel that the *World* was their friend. He had plowed money into the building of a competent staff of newsmen and he had kept pace with mechanical innovations. He had given the readers their money's worth in size, in solid news and editorials, in entertaining human interest stories and illustrations. And he had never let his readers forget that the *World* was a dynamic newspaper of a dynamic era.

His critics said Pulitzer had done something else that did not reflect to his credit. He had revived, they said, the sensationalism which had marked the first mass newspapers of the penny-press period of the 1830s. Sensationalism was as old as the newspaper press, but no one had depended upon its devices so much in recent years as had Pulitzer. His success encouraged imitation, and this was viewed as a disastrous trend in journalism which made Pulitzer's constructive contributions seem not worth the price.

Pulitzer's answer was that human interest and sensational stories were needed to win a large circulation and that having won the circulation he would create sound public opinion through enticing readers into the editorial columns and news stories about public affairs. He admired the work of the talented Edwin Lawrence Godkin in the *Evening Post*, although he disagreed with Godkin's economic theories, but when he was chided about the contrast between the news policies of the *Post* and the *World* he made his famous retort: "I want to talk to a nation, not to a select committee." [15]

[15] James Creelman, "Joseph Pulitzer—Master Journalist," *Pearson's*, XXI (March 1909), p. 246.

Undoubtedly the critics were right in accusing Pulitzer of rationalizing when he presented this defense of the *World's* revival of coarse sensationalism. But they were not correct if they wrote Pulitzer off as a cynic. Pulitzer recognized the weakness of the sensational approach, and struggled much of the time to temper its uses. If he failed during conspicuous periods of his editorship, it was because of human frailty, whose consequences no editor has escaped.[16] The man who set an example for his profession in the creation of newspapers with a crusading spirit and an aggressive editorial leadership was basically high-minded in his conception of his responsibilities. This passage from a letter written by Pulitzer to one of his editors in later life reflects the spirit which won for him recognition as a courageous, worthy, and effective editor:

> . . . every issue of the paper presents an opportunity and a duty to say something courageous and true; to rise above the mediocre and conventional; to say something that will command the respect of the intelligent, the educated, the independent part of the community; to rise above fear of partisanship and fear of popular prejudice. I would rather have one article a day of this sort; and these ten or twenty lines might readily represent a whole day's hard work in the way of concentrated, intense thinking and revision, polish of style, weighing of words.[17]

Pulitzer's newspapers on many days fell short of attaining this high goal of journalism, but they approached it often enough to stimulate the efforts of other editors and to win their admiration.

The *World* did not rest upon the laurels it had won during the first three years of the Pulitzer regime. In every area of activity it continued to exploit its success. Sensational crusades were carried on against big corporations, bad tenement housing, white-slave traffic, city aldermen who accepted bribes. The paper inaugurated a series of public services—Christmas dinners for the poor, free ice for tenement dwellers in summer, a staff of 35 doctors to serve the needy, entertainments for thousands of children. Its most noted early success was a campaign to raise funds for the building of a pedestal in New York harbor on which was to be placed the Statue of Liberty. The *World* pointed out that the statue had been given to the people of the United States by the people of France, and it said that "the people's paper now appeals to the people to come forward and raise this money." Within five months news stories and editorials brought in the needed $100,000, mostly in nickels and dimes

[16] Indicative of that frailty was Pulitzer's admiration in particular of three publishers whose newspapers utilized sensational techniques, but did not measure up to the *World* in high-quality performance. They were William M. Singerly, *Philadelphia Record;* Charles H. Taylor, *Boston Globe,* and the British newspaper popularizer, Alfred Harmsworth, who later became Lord Northcliffe.

[17] As quoted in Seitz, *Joseph Pulitzer,* p. 286.

from 120,000 loyal *World* readers. Pulitzer later named his yacht the "Liberty" in honor of this campaign.

Stunts, as distinguished from useful crusades and promotions, were another *World* specialty. Most ambitious was the sending of Nellie Bly around the world in 1889 to see if she could beat the time suggested by Jules Verne in his fictional *Around the World in Eighty Days*. Nellie Bly was a byline name for Elizabeth Cochran, a girl reporter who had brightened the pages of the *World* by inviting the attention of mashers and then exposing them, and by feigning insanity in order to write about conditions in the New York asylum. As Nellie traveled around the world by ships, trains, horses, and sampans, the *World* ran a guessing contest which drew nearly a million estimates of her elapsed time. Nellie didn't fail her newspaper; a special train brought her from San Francisco to New York with banners flying as the country applauded her time of 72 days.[18]

Expanded size of the *World* permitted its editors to enliven its pages with stunts and features and still maintain coverage of serious and significant news. A large staff of ambitious reporters covered the city in the same manner Pulitzer had blanketed St. Louis. News editors sought equally hard to get national coverage and cabled news from abroad. Gradually the coarser sensationalism of the first few years of *World* publication under Pulitzer began to disappear, although there was no letup in the demand for well-written human interest stories and for reader-pulling illustrations.

The editorial page continued its political support of the Democratic party, backing Cleveland in 1888 and 1892. Yet at the same time it exhibited its independence by opposing the local Tammany Hall machine. Labor found the *World* a solid champion in 1892 when several strikers were killed by Pinkerton guards during the bitter Homestead steel strike in Pittsburgh. The *World* splashed the story on its front pages and denounced Andrew Carnegie's plant manager, Henry Clay Frick, on its editorial pages. The frailty which stems from the responsibilities of ownership was illustrated by the aftermath of this editorial stand, however. The *World's* editorial-page chief, William H. Merrill, had placed the paper on the side of the workers while Pulitzer was absent in Europe. The publisher, hearing of the uproar and conscious of the isolated position of the *World* as one of the few newspapers to take such an extreme stand, attempted to tone down Merrill's writing. In general, however, the "people's paper" took its stand on the side of fair play and progressive reform.

Pulitzer's publishing empire was expanded in 1887 with the establishing of the *Evening World*, on the heels of Dana's decision to publish an evening

[18] Three New York newspapers repeated the stunt in 1936. H. R. Ekins of the *World-Telegram* won with a time of 18½ days, defeating Dorothy ("Nellie Bly") Kilgallen of the *Journal* and Leo Kiernan of the *Times*.

edition of the *Sun*. The evening paper sold for one cent, and soon outdid the morning edition in popular appeal. It never attained the distinctive character of the morning edition, however, and to newspapermen the name *World* still meant the original paper.

A new $2,500,000 home for the three *Worlds* was the next order of business. It was an impressive building, among the tallest of its time, topped with a gilded dome and filled with the newest machines of the printing arts. But before the building was finished, tragedy struck. Pulitzer had become completely blind. His nerves were shattered as well, and he was under the care of European specialists. In October, 1890, he announced his retirement from active editorship of his newspapers, and the *Herald,* thinking that it was bidding him goodby, said "We droop our colors to him."

But Pulitzer was not gone. He was to live until 1911, and he was to continue to build his personality into the newspapers. His affliction left him incapable of bearing even the slightest noise, and he went to incredible lengths to isolate himself from tormenting sounds. His associates found him infuriatingly difficult, but they also found him keenly aware of the progress of the newspapers. No matter where the blinded and bearded Pulitzer was—aboard his yacht; at Bar Harbor, Maine; or on the Mediterranean coast—he was constantly in touch with the *World* staff. Copies of each issue were read to him by young male secretaries and streams of instructions and suggestions came to the offices in the *World's* gilded dome by cable, mail, and messenger.

There were important editors and managers there in the *World* offices. Some of them in the late eighties and early nineties included Cockerill, who became editor-in-charge; William H. Merrill, who had come from the *Boston Herald* to be chief editorial writer; Ballard Smith, former managing editor of both the *Louisville Courier-Journal* and the *New York Herald,* who served as managing editor; S. S. Carvalho, ex-*Sun* newsman who was city editor of the *Evening World* and later a Pulitzer executive; Colonel Charles H. Jones, a colorful southerner who served as publisher for Pulitzer in both New York and St. Louis; George Harvey, later to become an important political figure.

Conflicts between strong-willed rivals for authority and for Pulitzer's favor were inevitable under this policy of assembling many men of high talent under the *World's* dome. But no editor or manager became too powerful or long ignored the wishes of the absent owner. Cockerill lost his place in 1891 during one of the upheavals by which Pulitzer enforced his will upon the staff. Jones, who was given complete editorial control of the *Post-Dispatch* in 1895, was forced out two years later when he flouted Pulitzer's wishes. By a constant process of seeking loyal and able assistants from among the country's newsmen, Pulitzer was able to keep the *World* steadily progressing in the manner which he had conceived, as the leading exponent of what newspapermen were calling the New Journalism.

Annotated Bibliography

Books

Barrett, James W., *Joseph Pulitzer and His World.* New York: Vanguard, 1941. A colorful, rambling story of Pulitzer and the *New York World* by the last city editor of the *World.*

Ireland, Alleyne, *Joseph Pulitzer: Reminiscences of a Secretary.* New York: Mitchell Kennerley, 1914. Reprinted as *An Adventure with a Genius.* New York: Dutton, 1920. The eccentricities of the great publisher, and his struggles against physical handicaps.

Juergens, George, *Joseph Pulitzer and the New York World.* Princeton, N.J.: Princeton University Press, 1966. A detailed, enthusiastic account of Pulitzer's first four years at the World, 1883–87.

King, Homer W., *Pulitzer's Prize Editor: A Biography of John A. Cockerill, 1845–1896.* Durham, N.C.: Duke University Press, 1965. Only detailed study of the managing editor, whose biographer contends he overshadowed Pulitzer in handling news.

Rammelkamp, Julian S., *Pulitzer's Post-Dispatch, 1878–1883.* Princeton University Press, 1966. Documented study of evolving journalistic style of Pulitzer, Cockerill, others; restrained approval of Pulitzer's social contributions, criticism of his sensationalized news.

Seitz, Don C., *Joseph Pulitzer: His Life and Letters.* New York: Simon & Schuster, 1924. The first Pulitzer study; others draw upon it. Written by Pulitzer's onetime business manager.

Swanberg, W. A., *Pulitzer.* New York: Scribner's, 1967. Latest and best of the studies of the tempestuous editor-publisher.

Periodicals and Monographs

Brisbane, Arthur, "Joseph Pulitzer," *Cosmopolitan,* XXXIII (May 1902), 51. An intimate contemporary portrait by an editor who jumped from Pulitzer's *World* to Hearst's *Journal.*

Brod, Donald F., "John A. Cockerill's St. Louis Years," *Bulletin* of Missouri Historical Society, XXVI (April 1970), 227. Study of a political campaign and Cockerill's shooting of a politician to death.

Inglis, William, "An Intimate View of Joseph Pulitzer," *Harper's Weekly,* LV (November 11, 1911), 7. An article with considerable insight, published at time of Pulitzer's death.

Outlook, XCIX (November 11, 1911), 603 and 608, contains two estimates of Pulitzer and the *World.*

Saalberg, Harvey, "The *Westliche Post* of St. Louis: A Daily Newspaper for German-Americans, 1857–1938," Ph.D. thesis, University of Missouri, 1967. Pulitzer, Schurz, Preetorius figure in the story. See also his "The *Westliche Post* of St. Louis:

German Language Daily, 1857–1938," *Journalism Quarterly*, XLV (Autumn 1968), 452.

Seitz, Don C., "The Portrait of an Editor," *Atlantic Monthly*, CXXXIV (September 1924), 289. Reprinted in Ford and Emery, *Highlights in the History of the American Press.*

The Story of the St. Louis Post-Dispatch. St. Louis: Pulitzer Publishing Company, 1954. A booklet written by Charles G. Ross in 1928 and since revised, which recounts many of the paper's campaigns.

THE CHICAGO TIMES-HERALD, TUESDAY, JULY 12, 1898. 5

ON SCHOOL BOARD

Mayor Appoints Eight New Members and Renames Trude.

HARPER AND CUSACK ARE OUT

EIGHT NEW MEMBERS OF THE BOARD OF EDUCATION

HONORS FOR ILLINOIS.

STATE WINS EDUCATORS' FAVOR.

MISSIONS IN CHINA ATTACKED.

WINNIPEG EXHIBITION OPEN.

TRUSTEES TAKE THE PLANT.

MINISTER CONGER IS RECEIVED.

EXPLANATION BY MR. DE BACA.

LOW EXCURSION RATES

DR. CAMILLO VOLINI, WHO "DOWNED" LITTLE JOHNNIE POWERS

CARSON PIRIE SCOTT & CO.

Our After-Inventory Clearing Sale is now in progress—surplus stocks in all departments are being closed out at the smallest prices. The watchword all along the line is

"SUMMER GOODS MUST GO."

Imported Wash Goods. We have a department full to overflowing with those dainty, summery, comfortable and altogether faultless hot-weather fabrics, but a combination of circumstances left us with more of the goods than we ought to have this week of the year, therefore we have made the welcome reductions indicated below:

French Organdies—such makes as Koechlin, Baumgarten & Co., and Gros, Roman & Co.—light and dark grounds—all the latest novelties in printed Dresden and floral effects—45c, 50c and 60c qualities—the entire collection grouped together at one price to-day........ 25c

Real Sheer Printed and Dotted Swiss in a large variety of combinations of colors and designs—a stylish, cool fabric for evening and afternoon gowns—at, per yard........ 15c

Summer Silks. A peep at this department will gladden the heart of every thrifty buyer who knows the relation between value and price in dainty silken fabrics.

Extra Special—$1.00 Fancy Silks for 49c.

Printed China and Japanese Silk, high grades, best designs, positive reductions, values up to $1.00, for........ 29c 39c 50c

50 pieces genuine Japanese Habutai Silk, in white only, the greatest bargain ever offered........ 18c 25c 39c

Black Silks Special—50 pieces all silk Black Figured Louisine Silks, summer weight, new designs—positive bargains at........ 50c 65c 85c

10 pieces all-silk Black Satin Duchess and Peau de Soie, two superior qualities, for skirts and gowns—$1.25 values, at........ $1.00

Season's Greatest Sale Wash Shirt Waists. We have two great Shirt Waist departments—one on the 1st floor and one on the 3d, and the salespeople in both are kept busy as bees, supplying the needs of well-posted buyers. Here are bargains that will more than crowd the department this week.

Sale Manufacturer's Stock Shirt Waist Ginghams.

Women's Kid Boots, $3.50 Values, $2.15.

Cool, comfortable, dainty, Glove-Fitting Boots, that give comfort from the first day you wear them.

GREAT OXFORD SALE.

$1.15 and $1.65

MARSHALL FIELD & CO.

A prominent manufacturer's surplus stock of

Bureaus, Chiffoniers and Toilet Tables

in mahogany, bird's-eye maple and oak, has been placed on sale at a

Reduction of 25%

from regular prices—for two weeks only.

Women's Tan Kid Shoes $1.45.

Women's Oxfords $1.45.

Men's Shoes, $2.45.

Special Shirt Waists, 75c.

Two still-famous Chicago department stores advertise in an 1898 *Times-Herald*.

18

The Modern Newspaper Emerges

The magnitude of financial operations of the newspaper is turning journalism upside down.
—Lincoln Steffens (1897)

Much had happened to the nation's journalism during the first decade of Joseph Pulitzer's New York publishing career. He had bought the *World* in 1883 for $346,000. In the mid-nineties it was housed in a $2,500,000 building and its estimated worth was $10,000,000. Expenses for a year ran to some $2,000,000 and guesses at the annual profit hovered around $1,000,000. The number of full-time employees totaled 1,300.

This was big business. And what was happening to the *World* was happening to other metropolitan papers, and to a lesser degree to smaller dailies. Editorial staffs were growing in size and the quest for the world's news was sharpening. Circulation and advertising departments were becoming of major importance. Operating problems of these complex business institutions—mechanical innovations, labor contracts, newsprint supply—required constant attention. An examination of these changes in daily newspaper publishing will demonstrate the fact that the modern era was at hand.

THE EDITORIAL STAFF

The editorial staff of the metropolitan daily newspaper had taken recognizable modern form by 1890, in numbers and in departmentalized activities. Specialization of duties was necessary as the editing process became more complex, and as staffs grew in size. Looking back at the growth of the editorial staff after the founding of the popular press of the 1830s, we can see its evolution from a one-man status to the organization of scores of newsmen who constituted the staff of the *World.*

Regularly employed reporters were rare even after the penny press had become well established in the 1840s. Newspaper editors ran what local news they encountered or had time to cover, used their telegraph news, clipped their exchanges, and printed the contributions of correspondents, such as the group who covered Congress after the mid-1820s. Some owner-editors added chief assistants, notably Horace Greeley, who employed first Henry J. Raymond and then Charles A. Dana to help him handle the news on the *New York Tribune* in the early 1840s. The chief assistants soon became known as managing editors, two of the earliest to hold that title being Dana of the *Tribune* and Frederic Hudson of the *New York Herald.* In the 1850s chief reporters emerged, as forerunners of the city editors. The *Tribune* of 1854 had 14 reporters and 10 editors, and had introduced editorial writers, literary editors, and other specialists. But these editorial staff advances were found only on leading newspapers.

Intensified reporting of the Civil War by hundreds of correspondents in the field did much to stimulate the rise of news staffs. Some of the Civil War reporters who thus demonstrated their journalistic skill rose to become editors or owners of newspapers—Murat Halstead, Whitelaw Reid, Henry Villard. Others went on to cover wars in Europe, the Indian wars on the western American plains, and other major news events at home and abroad.

George W. Smalley was an example of the new type of newsman. A graduate of Yale and of the Harvard Law School, he covered the Civil War for the *Tribune,* then reported the Franco-Prussian War and remained in Europe as London correspondent for the paper. Henry M. Stanley of the *New York Herald* covered the Civil War and the Indian wars, went to Asia and Africa as a *Herald* correspondent, and climaxed his career with his expedition to Africa in 1871 to find the missing missionary, David Livingstone. Jerome B. Stillson, another *Herald* reporter, obtained an exclusive interview with the Indian chief Sitting Bull in 1877 that filled 14 columns of the paper. John A. Cockerill, Pulitzer's ace newsman and editor, had covered the Russo-Turkish War. Again, these are examples of a limited activity, but they foreshadow the intensified reportorial achievements of the 1890s.

Emphasis increasingly centered upon the reporter. Dana and Pulitzer, as editor-publishers, prized their reporters because they themselves had handled the news. Raymond put news coverage first in his *Times,* and himself covered the Austro-Italian War. Henry W. Grady, who served as a free-lance correspondent before becoming managing editor of the *Atlanta Constitution,* did as much as any man of his times to advance the status of the newsman. Grady's leadership in advancing the art of interviewing, as a means both of gathering and interpreting the news, made it more necessary for newspapers to have larger staffs.

By the 1870s the leading metropolitan dailies had a chief editor, a managing editor or night editor in charge of the news, a city editor who directed the work of as many as two dozen reporters and selected the stories which were to run, a telegraph editor who handled the increasing volume of wire and cable news, a financial editor, literary editor, drama critic, and editorial writers. The city editor, it should be noted, was becoming a key man on the large newspaper staff.

Further specialization of editorial staff duties came with the upsurge of competition in the 1880s. The coming of the telephone in newspaper offices meant that reporters could call in with news on fast-breaking stories. Increased numbers of editions also demanded more rapid handling of local news. Before the close of the century the legman on the beat and the rewrite man in the office began to appear as distinct personalities on the editorial staff, although special assignment men continued to write their own stories. The rewrite men learned to use typewriters, and they also began to favor the summary lead as a means of condensing stories. The literary stylists and the writers of rambling chronological stories were still numerous, however.

Deskmen who specialized in selecting and condensing news, and in writing headlines in the long and involved style of the day, became necessary assistants to the chief editors of newspapers whose volume of news was becoming greater each year. Growth of Sunday papers meant addition of special Sunday staffs for the major newspapers, along with cartoonists and artists.

Sports news, which had been covered since the 1830s in fairly good fashion, was a natural feature for a mass-circulated newspaper. One of Pulitzer's first acts on the *World* was to organize a separate sports department. Horse racing, prizefighting, international yacht racing, and baseball were attracting widespread popular interest, and specialized writers began to appear in each field.[1] Although regular sports pages did not appear until after the turn of the century, several columns of sports stories were run in big newspapers by 1890, and sports departments were on their way toward gaining their modern status. In the next few years bicycle racing was added to their coverage, and football became more important. And when the Corbett-Fitzsimmons heavyweight title fight was staged in Nevada in 1897, dozens of writers turned up from all parts of the country to herald the arrival of the sports "gigantic."

A rapid influx of women staff members was another development of the 1880s. Women were entering into the business offices of America as the industrial boom brought them new opportunities; they were working in the expanding retail stores; they were graduating from women's colleges and coeducational universities; they were winning some battles for recognition of women's rights. There had been women journalists of note before the Civil War—Margaret Fuller of the *New York Tribune*, for example, and Jane Grey Swisshelm as a Washington correspondent and newspaper editor—and the

[1] Henry Chadwick of the sports-conscious *New York Herald* became in 1862 the first of a long line of baseball writers.

New York Sun had employed Mrs. Emily Verdery Bettey as a general reporter as early as 1868. Now in the late 1880s several hundred women were in newspaper work and some of them became leading reporters and feature writers. Others by the 1890s became the first specialists in women's news, as newspapers began to run fashion articles, recipes, and other women's interest news in conjunction with society items.

Salaries for the editorial staff were generally low except for a few top men. The principal editors were paid from $25 to $60 a week in 1870; by 1890 managing editors of large papers received up to $125 a week, and city editors and star reporters made from $50 to $100 a week. These were very good salaries in 1890 dollars. But many of the staff stayed at the same $15 to $25 a week level which had existed for reporters after the Civil War, because there was no pressure on publishers to pay more. The "new journalism" attracted many hopeful cub reporters; if one man quit, another was waiting to try his luck, and there was no effective labor organization in the editorial offices as there was in the mechanical departments. Many beginners were paid only on space rates, and some volunteered their services free of charge. Willis J. Abbot, who ended his career as editor of the *Christian Science Monitor,* records that he worked 14 hours a day in 1886 for the *New York Tribune* and received only $2.85 a week in space rate payments.[2] He did it willingly, he said, because that was the only way to learn the newsman's skills.

Some newspapers became training centers for reporters who migrated to other cities and other staffs. They included older distinguished news gathering organizations, such as the *Sun, Herald, Tribune,* and *Times* in New York, and newcomers like Nelson's *Kansas City Star,* Stone's *Chicago Daily News,* and Pulitzer's *World.* Managing editors of the type of Cockerill of the *World,* John C. Reid of the *Times,* and Henry W. Grady of the *Atlanta Constitution* were able exponents of journalistic techniques. Perhaps the most famous were the leading editors of the *New York Sun:* Amos J. Cummings, managing editor and expert in the human interest story, John B. Bogart, city editor, and Chester S. Lord and Selah M. Clarke, managing editor and night city editor, respectively, after 1880. The *Sun* developed great reporters—Julian Ralph, Arthur Brisbane, S. S. Carvalho, Edward W. Townsend, Richard Harding Davis. It shared with the *Tribune* the reporting career of Jacob A. Riis, who wrote with discernment about conditions in the New York slums and the tragedies they bred.

There was competition for the services of reporters such as those developed on the *Sun.* Ralph, who once wrote an 11,000-word story in seven hours, and whose speed and writing style made him the foremost idol of the cub reporters, eventually became a prized Hearst correspondent. Brisbane, who joined the *Sun* in 1883 at the age of 19 and was sent to London two years later, became managing editor of the *Evening Sun* in 1888, joined the *World*

[2] Willis J. Abbot, *Watching the World Go By* (Boston: Little, Brown, 1933), p. 29.

in 1890 and then left to win a fortune with Hearst. Carvalho became the first city editor of the *Evening World*, rose to a managerial position and later was a Hearst executive. The dashing war correspondent, Davis, left the *Sun* to join Hearst, then achieved greatest fame as a *Herald* writer.

Some of the newspapermen of this period, like Henry Grady, were intelligent, perceptive men who were sensitive to the requirements of society and who helped to create a more comprehensive and interpretive journalism. Some, like Pulitzer, possessed a crusading spirit and outstanding editorial page ability. Some, like Ralph, were excellent reporters of news events. Some, like Cockerill and Cummings, were able exponents of the reader-attracting techniques of human interest writing.

But many others were less talented, more prone to seize upon the devices of sensationalism, or to substitute slovenly and dishonest work for the kind of journalism they should have produced. Many were unqualified for their work. Although more newsmen were products of colleges and universities, no one yet came into the field equipped with a professional education in journalistic techniques and responsibilities. The professional standards which were being set were those of the best qualified practitioners of newspaper work, and only a minority of newsmen worked on staffs which had able leadership. The quality of the editorial staff was improving, but in an uneven, spotty manner.

ADVANCES IN COOPERATIVE NEWS GATHERING

Pressure for speedier and more comprehensive coverage of the news, which stemmed both from increasing competition among the dailies and from the needs of the new social environment, brought advances in cooperative news gathering. The communications network was keeping pace with the needs of an America which was sensing the interdependency created by its industrial revolution, and which was imbued with the spirit of speed in tackling its new problems.

Newspapers had many new facilities which they could use in improving their coverage. The railroads and telegraph lines which had made possible the speedup of news coverage which began in the 1840s spurted ahead to cover the country. Between 1880 and 1900 the number of miles of railroad tracks doubled, while those of telegraph lines quadrupled. They were joined by the Bell System's telephone lines which in those 20 years spread from city to city. The federal postal service began free rural delivery in 1897, and improved its city carrier service. The Atlantic cable, which began operating in 1866, linked the United States to London, and to another cable stretching eastward to India and the Orient.

Still at the center of news gathering on a national and international scale for American dailies in the 1880s was the Associated Press of New York. It had been founded by the city's morning papers in 1848 so that they could share the cost of telegraphing news collected from European papers brought by ship to North Atlantic ports. Similarly, they pooled routine news coverage from Washington and other major eastern cities. The New York Associated Press group then had found it could sell its news to regional, state, and city newspaper groups which arose spontaneously as telegraph lines were extended inland. It obviously was both practical and financially necessary for papers along the lines to share the telegraphed news accounts from other points.

The New York papers which controlled this early version of the Associated Press adroitly maneuvered themselves into a monopolistic position. Their agreements with the Western Union telegraph company gave their press service preferred treatment and rates, and an exchange of favors between the New York Associated Press and Western Union served to build both into positions of dominance over their competitors. Opening of the Atlantic cable facilitated reciprocal exchange of news between the AP and the press agencies which had developed in Europe: Reuters in Britain (1851), Havas in France (1836), Wolff in Germany (1849), and Stefani in Italy (1854). World news reports of these agencies could be easily collected and transmitted exclusively by the AP.

The bait which the New York Associated Press group offered to other papers in the country was an extension of the news monopoly which the New York papers held. The regional and local groups which became clients of the Associated Press could restrict their membership, and prevent new competitors from obtaining the basic news coverage afforded by the AP. Thus the AP franchise became a valuable asset, usually obtainable only by sale in competitive newspaper cities. To discourage press service competitors, the New York AP forbade those receiving its service to buy the news of any other agency.

Papers outside New York had many complaints against the AP service, however. The seven charter member New York morning papers decided what news should be included in the report, and preferred to compete among themselves for many of the major news stories, leaving only the more prosaic news for the AP. They were mainly interested, obviously, in a news report for morning papers, and did not respond to the needs of the rapidly expanding evening dailies. Their rate charges to clients were arbitrarily assessed, and the outside papers felt they were paying too much of the cost and had too little say about the operations of the service.

As might be expected, the rapidly growing newspapers of the Middle West became the most powerful regional group among the AP clients. The Western Associated Press which they formed in 1862 soon began an agitation for reform which eventually led to the reorganization of the Associated Press into its modern cooperative form by the end of the century. The fact that the

Associated Press of 1880 served only half the morning dailies and a fourth of the evening papers made it inevitable that competing news services eventually would arise. Of those who tried before 1900, however, only the United Press (no relation to the present-day service of the same name) offered real competition to the AP, and it was quickly submerged in the battle between rival AP factions for control.[3]

In the meantime, however, cooperative news gathering was making forward steps. The first leased wire, reserved for the AP's use and carrying up to 20,000 words a day, was opened between New York and Washington in 1875. Chicago got this improved service in 1884. By 1890 the AP-leased wires had extended to New Orleans, Denver, and Minneapolis.

Smaller dailies were given inexpensive service by the making of thin stereotyped plates, which could be expressed rapidly and set directly into the news columns. The leading distributor of thin plates in the 1880s was the American Press Association, which used the news report of the Associated Press. It and other syndicates also offered feature stories, illustrations, and entertainment material in plate form.[4]

Older forms of obtaining the news still continued. Leading newspapers offered their exclusive stories to strings of clients, sending proof slips by express service or mail as they had done in the past, or sometimes using the telegraph. Editors clipped their exchange papers from other cities and subscribed to the *Congressional Record* for details on Washington news. City news services, which had taken definite form during the Civil War, continued to collect the routine news within metropolitan areas, and were formally organized in New York and Chicago in the early 1890s.

The largest papers found they needed to supplement the AP news report with stories from their own correspondents, if they were to keep pace with their rivals, and sometimes spent more money on their privately collected nonlocal news than on the AP service. The number of newspapers which had correspondents covering Congress rose from 45 at the outbreak of the Civil War to 130 by 1870. Improved AP service from Washington left the congressional press gallery at this level until the excitement of the Spanish-American war period. The Washington correspondents formed their famous Gridiron Club in 1885, and numbered some of the country's best newsmen.

Thus the new leaders in journalism were demonstrating that they were willing to spend more effort and more money on collecting the news. But the system was as yet unsatisfactory and inadequate, despite the advances made. The New York Associated Press depended heavily upon the news collected by member papers and by foreign press service. Regional AP groups expanded their own interexchange of news, but in many instances the AP depended upon

[3] The standard account of this subject is Victor Rosewater, *History of Cooperative News-Gathering in the United States* (New York: Appleton-Century-Crofts, 1930).

[4] Alfred M. Lee, *The Daily Newspaper in America* (New York: Macmillan, 1937), p. 511.

Western Union operators for coverage of spot news events. And papers outside the AP fold had to struggle along as best they could with unsatisfactory substitutes for the modern competitive news services which were to evolve with the opening of the twentieth century.

THE RISE OF BUSINESS MANAGERS

The expansion of the editorial staff and its news gathering activities, which thus was heralding the arrival of modern journalism, was made possible by tremendous developments in the business and mechanical departments of the metropolitan daily newspaper. But these developments in turn brought an overshadowing of the figure of the old-time editor and a relative lessening of his influence in the new era of corporate journalism.

This did not mean that editors and news executives were shunted aside, but they no longer could dominate the scene as in the days when an editor-owner stood in command of his less complex enterprise. The achieving of gains in editorial staff efficiency and in comprehensive coverage of the news was to be at the expense of the personal factor in newspaper editing.

Those larger dailies which had become complex business institutions—headed by the *New York World* with its 10-million-dollar valuation and its annual million-dollar profit in the mid-nineties—were harassed by a host of new problems. It was they who first reflected the corporate nature of the new journalism, although the pressure of the business problems they faced soon came to be felt by an increasing number of middle-sized dailies, and to some degree by any newspaper.

The scramble for advertising and circulation supremacy, widespread mechanical innovations and pyramiding capitalization costs, larger payrolls and more difficult labor relations problems, increasing concern over newsprint supply for skyrocketing circulations—these and other problems brought the rise of a managerial corps in newspaper publishing, just as managers were rising as a group in American business generally.

Thus, while men trained as reporters were assuming the leadership of the editorial staffs, men specializing in business problems were filling influential managerial posts and, increasingly, the publishers' chairs. News-trained men who also were publisher-owners found themselves forced to deal with business affairs much of the time, and to delegate their editorial responsibilities to others, who competed with the managers for the ear of the publisher. Only the strongest personalities on the editorial side could continue in such an atmosphere to exercise the kind of leadership the ablest editor-owners of the age of personal journalism could give. Where a combination of able management and effective editorial leadership existed, however, the change was all to the good, for it meant those newspapers had a firm financial basis for the expansion of their community services.

Symbolizing the ascendancy of business problems of the daily newspapers was the establishment of the American Newspaper Publishers Association in 1887 to serve as their trade association. The leaders in the association were representatives of aggressive new papers and of older papers which were alive to the problems of the new journalism. Most of the men taking part in association affairs held managerial posts on their newspapers, or were publishers who were primarily interested in business management.

Two of the early presidents were James W. Scott of the *Chicago Herald* and Charles W. Knapp of the *St. Louis Republic,* both news-trained publishers. But men like Colonel Charles H. Jones, S. S. Carvalho, John Norris, and Don C. Seitz—all of whom contended for managerial-side supremacy on Pulitzer's *World* in the 1890s—were more typical leaders of the ANPA. Seitz, who survived as manager of the *World,* and Norris, who became business manager of the *New York Times,* were particularly important leaders of the Publishers Association after the turn of the century. There they spoke for their absent publishers, Pulitzer and Adolph Ochs.

The ANPA was organized at the call of William H. Brearley, advertising manager of the *Detroit Evening News,* James E. Scripps' successful new paper. There were many state editorial associations—17 had been founded between 1853 and 1880—but most of their members published weeklies and small dailies. The National Editorial Association had been organized in 1885 by B. B. Herbert of the *Red Wing Daily Republican* of Minnesota, but it too showed little concern for the problems of the metropolitan press and became the national organization of the weeklies and smallest dailies.

What Brearley and his associates wanted primarily was a daily newspaper trade association which would help its members with the problem of obtaining national advertising. While the ANPA soon became deeply involved in problems of labor relations, newsprint supply, government mail rates, and mechanical developments, it centered much of its attention on the field of advertising and upon the advertising agencies.

DEVELOPMENTS IN ADVERTISING

The expansion of business upon a national scale, and the consequent necessity for increasing national advertising and merchandising efforts, had opened the way for a middleman between advertiser and newspaper. The first advertising agents had appeared in New York and other eastern cities in the early 1840s. Their business was a haphazard one, in which they bought space in newspapers and magazines with scanty knowledge of the worth of such space. They found that publishers would pay them discounts of from 15 to 30 per cent, and sometimes as high as 75 per cent, on stated advertising rates. The discount represented the agent's profit, since he did not then prepare copy for the advertiser or engage in research.

Larger metropolitan papers were able to deal fairly effectively with the agents, both in obtaining advertising and in limiting the agents' commissions to reasonable figures. But those newspapers which were published at distant points from manufacturing and business centers of the East, and smaller papers, were not as fortunate. The agents found they often were able to play one publisher against another and obtain handsome commissions for extending the favors they had to offer.

Not all advertising agents operated in this manner. The founding around 1870 of the businesslike and respected agencies of George P. Rowell, N. W. Ayer & Son, and Lord & Thomas helped to stabilize the situation. But there were still many sharp-dealing agents, particularly those representing patent medicine manufacturers, and there were newspapers which would deal with them.[5]

One of the problems was identifying the newspapers and magazines which were being founded in great numbers during the last decades of the century. Rowell began publication of his *American Newspaper Directory* in 1869, and N. W. Ayer & Son started its continuing annual publication in 1880. These directories listed the newspapers and periodicals and attempted, often unsuccessfully, to determine their true circulations. There was as yet no outside check on circulation statements, and to make matters worse, advertising rate cards varied widely even in relation to claimed circulations. Only after 1914, when newspaper and magazine publishers and advertisers succeeded in organizing the Audit Bureau of Circulations, was the problem solved.

For the publishers the problem was one of identifying the potential advertisers and the trustworthy advertising agents. The ANPA headquarters office in New York published regular bulletins notifying members of prospective accounts, and reporting on agents' activities. The association, after a dozen years of wrangling, agreed in 1899 to issue lists of recognized advertising agencies, and to blacklist those who engaged in unfair practices or who were bad financial risks. By common consent the discount payment to agencies became 15 per cent. In this work the publishers received the cooperation of the American Association of Advertising Agencies (the final name adopted in 1917 for a group which began to organize in the 1870s).

The amount of advertising revenue at stake was growing steadily. Advertising in newspapers and periodicals amounted to 39 million dollars in 1880; the census that year showed advertising in daily newspapers alone was worth 21 million dollars. No further breakdowns for daily newspapers are available in this period, but the spurt in advertising revenues was evident. In 1890 the advertising revenues of all newspapers and magazines totaled 71 million dollars; in 1900, 95 million dollars; in 1910, 200 million dollars. Of the 1910 figure, 148 millions is identified as advertising revenue of all newspapers, of which dailies received the greater bulk.

[5] The detailed story is told in Frank Presbrey, *The History and Development of Advertising* (New York: Doubleday, 1929).

The percentage of the revenue of the newspapers coming from advertising, as compared to circulation income, rose from half in 1880 to 64 per cent by 1910. Space given to advertising in most dailies rose from 25 per cent of the available columns to a 50-50 ratio with editorial material by World War I.

As the amount of advertising in daily newspapers increased after 1880, the variety and quality of the content of advertising columns improved. Retail store advertising gained steadily, with the impetus given it by three successful pioneer department store merchants, John Wanamaker of Philadelphia, Marshall Field of Chicago, and A. T. Stewart of New York. National advertising of soaps and foods—Ivory soap and Royal baking powder were two leaders—marked the 1880s, and was supplemented in the next decade by campaigns for Eastman Kodak, Wrigley's chewing gum, bicycles, phonographs, and various new products.

Slogans like "It Floats," "Do You Know Uneeda Biscuit?" and "His Master's Voice" became familiar to all Americans. Some of them made quick fortunes for their sponsors, too, and stimulated other concerns to use the various advertising media more energetically. The first copywriters appeared in the leading advertising agencies during the 1890s, followed by artists. As a result the layouts, type choices, and illustrations in the advertising columns improved.

Still, however, the leading advertising clients of newspapers and magazines were the patent medicine manufacturers. Their copy extolling the virtues of Castoria, Scott's Emulsion, Peruna, or Lydia Pinkham's Female Compound was the largest single type in the 1880s and continued to bulk large until World War I. These popular remedies, like Dr. Williams' Pink Pills for Pale People, didn't hurt anybody, but some of the cure-alls which were accepted as substitutes for medical attention in remote areas and in crowded tenements did. Some even contained poisons which brought death to incautious users. It is to the credit of a few publishers that they regulated this type of advertising themselves before patent medicines were regulated by Congress.

The major competitors for the advertising dollar were the newspapers and the magazines, with billboards and car-cards cutting in slightly. Growth of magazine circulation in the 1890s forced newspapers to view them with real concern as competitors both for reader attention and for advertising revenue, and caused publishers to join forces in better promoting the newspaper as an advertising medium.

NEW LEADERS FOR MAGAZINES

There were successful new leaders in magazine journalism, just as there were in newspaper making. One was Frank Munsey, a New Englander with a sober and industrious character, who struggled for a decade in the New York magazine publishing field before achieving success with his *Munsey's*, begun in 1889. Another was S. S. McClure, who after establishing a feature syndicate service for newspapers, brought out his *McClure's* in 1893. A third competitor was *Cosmopolitan,* founded in 1886 and sold to William Randolph Hearst in 1905.[6]

These well-edited, popularized monthly magazines had found the same answer to the problem of obtaining mass circulation that the daily newspapers had found in the past. The secret was the cutting of the price to first 15 cents, and then a dime, for magazines which competed with older 35 cent publications. The cheap one-cent-a-pound mail rate, in effect from 1885 until zone rates were established during World War I, helped to make this possible. By the turn of the century *Munsey's* had achieved 650,000 circulation to lead other general magazines by a wide margin, and *McClure's* and *Cosmopolitan* were runners-up. The formula for all three was popular fiction, general articles, and illustrations.

Cyrus H. K. Curtis provided new leadership in the women's magazine field with his *Ladies' Home Journal,* founded in 1883. With Edward W. Bok as editor after 1889, the magazine quickly rose to a half-million circulation at a one dollar annual subscription price. In the weekly five-cent magazine field the *Saturday Evening Post,* bought by Curtis in 1897, and *Collier's,* founded in 1888, pushed to even higher circulations than those of the monthlies.

These new popularly circulated magazines were the ones which made the biggest inroads on available advertising revenue, arising as they did to public notice at the moment when national advertising was expanding. But the general illustrated monthly magazines of high literary and artistic quality—*Harper's, Century,* and *Scribner's*—continued to have major influence, even though outstripped in circulation. Sharing in the competition for reader attention and revenue too were the illustrated weekly periodicals, *Harper's Weekly* and *Leslie's;* the weeklies depending upon humor and cartoons, *Puck, Life,* and *Judge;* and the children's magazines, *Youth's Companion* and *St. Nicholas,* as well as many specialized periodicals.

Newspapermen grumbled in the late 1890s that the magazines were getting too much of the advertising of the new products of American business. And the competition spurred them into doing better jobs of running their businesses and of selling their advertising space. Two new business associations were formed, the International Circulation Managers' Association in 1898 and the Newspaper Advertising Executives Association in 1900. Regional interests of the dailies were coming to be served by such organizations as the Inland Daily Press Association, the Southern Newspaper Publishers Association, the Northwest Daily Press Association, and the New England Daily Newspaper Association.

Testifying, too, to growing emphasis upon business problems and to the increased interest in what the other fellow was doing, was the growth of trade

[6] Hearst established *Hearst's Magazine* in 1901 and consolidated the two in 1925.

publications. The leaders were the *Journalist* (1884), the *Fourth Estate* (1894), and *Editor & Publisher* (1901), in the daily newspaper field; the *Publishers' Auxiliary* (1865), which became the Western Newspaper Union's newspaper for weekly publishers; and *Printers' Ink* (1888), in advertising.

Special advertising representatives, appointed to obtain national advertising for their client newspapers, began their work in the late 1870s. After 1900 they organized associations to promote the newspaper as an advertising medium. The Daily Newspaper Club, a group of larger newspapers, worked to the same ends after 1906. Its members persuaded the American Newspaper Publishers Association to sponsor the founding of the Bureau of Advertising in 1913. The Bureau, with a paid staff, did the most effective job yet in arguing the case of the newspapers with advertising agencies and national advertisers.

The result was that magazines, which were obtaining 60 per cent or more of national advertising revenue at the turn of the century, were forced to share the take with newspapers on an equal basis by the time of World War I. The number of national advertisers using newspapers or magazines rose from approximately 6,000 in 1900 to some 13,000 in 1914, and then leveled off, so that the 1914 figure remained a high until 1947.[7] The newspapers, of course, also had local advertising which gave them a wide lead over magazines in total advertising take, the newspapers receiving roughly 70 per cent of all advertising revenues in the early years of the twentieth century.

A REVOLUTION IN PRINTING

The growth of the modern newspaper thus far described—in editorial techniques, in circulation, and in advertising volume—went hand in hand with the development of new mechanical equipment. The practitioners of the new journalism demanded better printing techniques to increase the mass appeal of their product, and faster means of production to keep pace with their sense of speed. These demands helped to create a never-ending process of advancement in the printing arts and in editorial practices.

Mechanization of hand labor processes was one of the driving forces of the industrial revolution of the late nineteenth century—in factories, in manufacturing, in offices. Inventive genius, stimulated by the demands of a production-expanding society, brought new processes into being in many fields. In printing, the achievements were the typesetting machine, faster presses, stereotyping, color printing, dry mats and electrotyping, and photoengraving.

The first casting of a line of type for newspaper use was made in 1886 in the *New York Tribune* plant on Ottmar Mergenthaler's Linotype machine. Mergenthaler, a German immigrant whose work making patent models in-

[7] *Printers' Ink,* CXXV (October 29, 1948), 102.

terested him in the typesetting machine problem, successfully developed his machine after years of experimentation by himself and others. Some newspapers gave him financial backing; significantly the other principal backers along with the *Tribune* were two newspapers which were among the new leaders, the *Chicago Daily News* and the *Louisville Courier-Journal.*[8]

Mergenthaler's first Linotype was basically the same machine used today. It was operated by a keyboard, and cast a slug from a line of matrices, which were then redistributed automatically. It had at the start an output three times that of the traditional hand compositor, and it was quickly adopted by the larger papers, particularly by evening dailies which needed its timesaving performance in order to cover the day's news closer to press deadline time.

There were competitors, but the Linotype was improved in its performance and won dominance in the field. It was joined by other machines shortly after the turn of the century: the Monotype, used to cast type and rules in quantities; the Intertype, a slug-casting machine with easily changed magazines of matrices for setting copy requiring different kinds of type; and the Ludlow, which cast slugs from handset matrices for use in setting advertisements.

Some improvements in the type faces themselves were beginning to be made in the interests of legibility and reader appeal. The ugly Gothics which had dominated newspaper typographic style did not begin to disappear widely, however, until after 1900, when the newly-designed Cheltenham family, the graceful Bodoni, and other headline types began to come into favor. The *New York Tribune* was to win typographical fame by its early use of Bodoni upper and lower case headlines.

The pressrooms also were being affected by the new order. Larger circulations, and increased competition which pushed the deadline for closing the news pages closer and closer to the time for distribution of big dailies, brought demands for improved printing presses. Expanded size of editions, as the volume of advertising and news was upped, also meant larger presses were needed which could handle the large papers within the time limit of daily journalism.

American pressmakers, under the leadership of R. Hoe and Company, had converted the presses of the leading newspapers from hand to steam power and from flatbed to rotary printing before the Civil War. Ingenious pressmen figured out ways of fitting the type solidly enough between column rules so that it would stick on the revolving cylinder. These type-revolving presses were widely used. The next step was the adaptation of the stereotyped plate to the newspaper press. This permitted the breaking of column rules for illustrations, headlines, and advertising—a practice not practical for users of type-revolving presses.

More importantly, use of the solid stereotyped plate, produced from the

[8] The *Tribune* was interested because it was engaged in a long and bitter dispute with its printers.

type form and curved to fit the cylinder of the rotary press, permitted a speeding-up of the hourly rate of newspaper printing. The presses could run faster, and extra stereotypes of the same page could be produced for the running of two or more presses simultaneously.

Equally necessary to this speed-up was the development of presses which used a web, or continuous roll of newsprint, and which printed on both sides of the sheet in one operation. Larger papers were casting stereotyped plates and were using web presses from the 1860s on, but the type-revolving press held its place in many shops until the 1890s. By that time automatic folders operating at press speed also had been perfected. In 1890 the finest Hoe press could produce 48,000 12-page papers in an hour. Within the next 10 years that output was tripled as New York newspaper circulations skyrocketed, and banks of presses were installed in the effort to keep pace with potential circulation sales.

Color printing on rotary presses became another necessity for the larger metropolitan papers in the 1890s if they wanted to keep in the swim. Color inserts printed separately had been used earlier, but full-color presses modeled after those being used in Paris were first built for the *Chicago Inter Ocean* in 1892 by Walter Scott. Within a year Scott had installed a color press in the *New York World* plant. Soon feature sections of Sunday papers were carrying color printing—and the Sunday comic section was on its way to becoming a part of the American newspaper.

ILLUSTRATIONS AND PHOTOGRAPHS: PHOTOENGRAVING

Mechanical advances which made possible improvement of illustrations in newspapers were another major achievement of the 1880 to 1900 period. The leaders up to that time in providing pictures for readers had been the magazines. *Frank Leslie's Illustrated Newspaper* and *Harper's Weekly*, both founded in the 1850s, had competed during the Civil War in providing woodcut reproductions of drawings made on the battlefields by small armies of artists. They and other magazines continued to run illustrations of dramatic events, cartoons, and drawings. Monthly magazines like *Harper's, Century*, and *Scribner's* did highly artistic work with woodcuts, and women's magazines used engraved steel fashion plates. The magazines of comment and satire—*Puck, Life*, and *Judge*—which appeared about 1880 depended upon illustrations and cartoons for much of their appeal.

Newspapers had used some sort of illustrations upon occasion since colonial days, and had used small cuts in advertisements. But woodcut illustrations of news events were rare—the *New York Herald* stood out for its early work. Cuts which were symbolic of an event, or stock illustrations which could be used with any story of a general type, were the best most newspapers could do. The *Evening Telegram*, companion paper for the *Herald*, was the first to run a political cartoon regularly, in competition with the magazines, publishing a large drawing one day each week, beginning about 1870.

More than one newspaperman sensed that illustrations would be a big drawing card, but there were great difficulties involved in producing the cuts. One large woodcut might require several days' work by an engraver, after the artist had completed his drawing. A cheaper and faster process was found in the Civil War period, involving the use of plates covered with a chalk powder. The artist drew his picture on the chalk with ink, and the uncovered chalk was removed. Then the chalk drawing was hardened in an acid solution, a mold was made, and finally a stereotype. The printed reproduction was less satisfactory than that of the woodcuts, however, and the cost and time factors were still discouraging.

Zincographs, which were line cuts produced by etching on zinc plates with acid, were invented in Paris about 1860 and began to appear in American publications in the 1870s. Illustrators, meanwhile, had found that they could print photographs directly onto woodblocks or zinc plates, where they would form the guide for the artist or etcher who completed the cut.

Still in 1880 there was relatively little illustration work appearing in American newspapers. When Pulitzer and his managing editor, Cockerill, took over the *New York World* in 1883, their first successes with illustrations were woodcuts. They also could produce engravings of artists' drawings by what was called the "soft metal process," but 48 hours' time was required, and the uses of newspaper illustration seemed limited.

Then the *World* editors stumbled into a quite unexplored but perfectly obvious journalistic field—the running of sketches of prominent local citizens. The resulting furor pressed them into conducting new searches for better mechanical processes.

Valerian Gribayédoff, one of the leading artists of the period, described the rise of local illustrations, and of newspaper illustration generally, in a magazine article published in 1891.[9] The artist related that he prepared a series of caricatures of the "Wall Street Nobility," which appeared on the front page of the *Sunday World* in February, 1884. The response was overwhelming and on succeeding Sundays drawings of other New Yorkers were reproduced. Within a short time, the artist said, the *Albany Evening Journal, Detroit Journal, Chicago Tribune, Chicago Inter Ocean, Kansas City Times, Philadelphia Times,* and *St. Louis Post-Dispatch* were arranging for similar portraits of local celebrities. Vanity played its part, too; Gribayédoff said that many New Yorkers did everything they could to get their pictures in the paper.

Establishment of an engraving company in 1884 which could turn out zinc etchings in four hours' time further spurred the spread of illustration. The American Press Association began to use its facilities to distribute cuts widely

[9] *Cosmopolitan,* XI (August 1891).

to smaller papers. Illustrations became regular features of many papers, although they were still few in number.

Gribayédoff estimated in 1891 that there were a thousand artists at work in the country supplying illustrations for 5,000 newspapers and magazines. The vast majority of newspapers depended upon cut manufacturers, but an increasing number were employing their own artists and had installed their own engraving facilities. The *Boston Globe,* for example, was spending $30,000 a year on its engraving plant in 1893.

Photoengraving was to curtail quickly this boom for the artists, however. The halftone photoengraving process had been developed in England prior to 1860, but the results were unsatisfactory until Frederic E. Ives went to work on the problem of reproducing photographs in the printing process. Ives was made head of the photographic laboratory at Cornell University in 1876, when he was 20. The next year he produced a photoengraving of a pen drawing, which was published in the student paper at Cornell. In 1878 he made his first halftone. Ives saw that the way to break up masses of dark and light was to lay out a series of prominences on a plate which would transfer the ink to paper point by point. If the points were close together, the mass would be dark; and the more widely they were spaced, the lighter the mass would become. Ives moved to Baltimore, and then to Philadelphia, after 1879 and produced commercially-used halftones. He perfected his process in 1886, but unhappily he failed to obtain a patent and never realized financially on his invention.

There still remained, however, the problem of using the halftones on rotary presses. One of the heroes of the struggle to get pictures into the American newspaper was Stephen H. Horgan. Horgan was the art editor of an illustrated paper called the *New York Daily Graphic,* which began in 1873 and battled bravely until 1889 when it succumbed in the big city competition. It was Horgan who succeeded in publishing a newspaper halftone of good quality in 1880, a picture called "Shantytown." And it was Horgan who first had the idea of how to run halftones on rotary presses. He was rebuffed by doubting pressmen, however, and it was not until 1897 that he perfected the method for the *New York Tribune.*

Within a short time other large papers were running halftone reproductions of photographs. Pressure for quick printing of local pictures brought installation of photoengraving plants in larger shops; smaller papers got their cuts from centrally-located photoengraving companies.

The artists found the news photographers edging into their field in earnest, now that their photos could be reproduced directly. Both groups covered the Spanish-American War. Syndicates quickly added news and feature photographs to their stock in trade, and big city papers began to employ local photographers who carried their heavy, awkward equipment and their flashlight powder out on assignments. Pictorial journalism was on its way, although many a newspaperman scorned the new technique and lamented the waste of space.

THE PRINTING UNIONS

The sweep of mechanical improvements in the publishing business, bringing with it labor specialization and larger working forces, gave newspaper publishers some new labor relations problems. The printers, pressmen, and engravers were organized into unions which belonged to the American Federation of Labor, and the labor movement was pressing constantly for shorter working hours and higher pay in all industries.

Strikes and work stoppages were something most newspaper publishers wanted to avoid. In a highly competitive field, particularly in metropolitan areas, suspension of publication meant perhaps fatal loss of circulation and advertising. Suspension also could jeopardize the status of a newspaper which held a lucrative contract to publish legal advertising. Such arguments were more compelling at the turn of the century than later.

One factor favored the publishers in this situation. The International Typographical Union, which had been reorganized in 1852 and which had become one of the most powerful of the AFL craft unions, was splitting into four unions as specialization of labor increased in printing plants. The International Printing Pressmen and Assistants' Union broke away from the typographers in 1886, followed by the International Photo-Engravers' Union in 1900 and the International Stereotypers and Electrotypers' Union in 1901. Publishers thus were enabled to deal with the union groups separately, and the danger of plantwide strikes was reduced.

At first newspaper publishers organized city associations so they could bargain as a unit with the unions. Then these local publishers' associations began to sign arbitration contracts with their printers which would minimize the danger of labor disputes. In 1899 the final step was taken, when the American Newspaper Publishers Association decided to enter into nationwide arbitration agreements between its members and the unions.

These voluntary agreements called first for local conciliation and arbitration procedures in event of contract disputes. Appeal could be made to a national arbitration board, whose decision would be binding on both the newspaper and the union involved. Strikes and lockouts were banned.

The arbitration agreements were signed with all four unions and they were successful enough that they were continued through the World War I period, before disputes with the typographers over their union rules resulted in a breakdown of the major contract. Thus the efforts of the organized publishers and the labor unions brought comparative peace to the newspaper industry during a period of severe labor disturbances in other industries.

PRINT PAPER FROM WOOD PULP

All of these advances in newspaper publishing which have been traced thus far would have been impossible, however, without the appearance of the Fourdrinier papermaking machine. Newsprint is a prosaic subject, but the ability to make low-cost newsprint from wood pulp, by a process introduced into America from Germany in 1867, was the basic factor in the growth of the daily newspaper. The same process also permitted the making of higher-grade magazine and book paper in the quantities needed by a modern society.

Print paper made by hand from rag stock was the product of an expensive, limited industry. When newspapers had to pay as much as $440 a ton for paper during the Civil War, the time was ripe for the introduction of a new manufacturing process. This process used water power to grind spruce logs into wood pulp, which when combined with a small amount of rag stock could be made into a usable print paper. By the 1890s a chemically produced wood pulp, called sulphite pulp, replaced rag stock as the toughening element in newsprint.

These manufacturing advances, coupled with the increased productive efficiency of papermaking machines, brought the price of newsprint tumbling downward. Paper manufacturers, stimulated by the prospect of increased demands for newsprint and higher grade magazine and book paper, slashed into the forests of Maine, Michigan, Wisconsin, and Minnesota. Newsprint cost $246 a ton in 1870, $138 a ton in 1880, $76 a ton in 1890, and $42 a ton in 1899, the bottom price until 1933.[10]

In view of this rapid decline in newsprint prices, it would seem that American newspaper publishers should have been quite satisfied with the situation at the turn of the century. But in 1900 domestic newsprint consumption equaled domestic supply, both figures standing at 570,000 tons. What was worse, the domestic newsprint manufacturers had obtained a good-sized tariff on newsprint imported from abroad, and they had effected a virtual monopolistic control over domestic output and sales prices.

The American Newspaper Publishers Association therefore plunged into battle. It crusaded against the newsprint trust, and forced dissolution of the largest sales organization. And it campaigned steadily to win removal of the tariff on imported newsprint, so that the vast forest resources of Canada could be opened to the papermaking industry. The Canadians wisely had refused to ship logs or wood pulp to the United States for processing, knowing that eventually the entire industry would be theirs when American forests were gone.

[10] Lee, *The Daily Newspaper in America,* pp. 743–45.

Under the leadership of John Norris, business manager of the *New York Times,* and Herman Ridder, publisher of the German-language *New Yorker Staats-Zeitung* and president of the Publishers Association during much of the newsprint campaign, the battle went on. Newsprint prices rose to as high as $58 as supply tightened. But not until the Woodrow Wilson administration was elected in 1912 and a Democratic Congress carried out the party's pledge to lower tariffs, was the way cleared for full use of Canadian newsprint. By then the price was back at $42 a ton and a flood of Canadian-produced paper arrived on the American market. Even it was not enough to prevent a newsprint shortage and zooming prices after World War I.

It is evident, then, from this survey of the changing conditions in daily newspaper publishing that there was a "watershed of the nineties" for the American newspaper. The advance into the modern era had been accomplished, and for better or for worse, the older era of journalism was no more.

Annotated Bibliography

Books

Most valuable of the journalism histories for this period are still Frank Luther Mott's *American Journalism,* Willard G. Bleyer's *Main Currents in the History of American Journalism,* and Alfred McClung Lee's *The Daily Newspaper in America.* Lee's topical treatment of the problems covered in this chapter is particularly noteworthy. The *Union List of Newspapers,* beginning where Brigham's bibliography leaves off in 1820, is supplemented by directories: *Geo. P. Rowell & Co.'s American Newspaper Directory* (1869) and *N. W. Ayer & Son's American Newspaper Annual* (1880), later called the *Directory of Newspapers & Periodicals.* The *Editor & Publisher International Year Book* dates from 1921.

Abbot, Willis J., *Watching the World Go By.* Boston: Little, Brown, 1933. The experiences of a longtime newspaperman who eventually became editor of the *Christian Science Monitor.* Abbot gives a good picture of the 1890s.

Carnes, Cecil, *Jimmy Hare, News Photographer.* New York: Macmillan, 1940. The biography of one of the early leading press photographers.

Cone, Fairfax M., *With All Its Faults: A Candid Account of Forty Years in Advertising.* Boston: Little, Brown, 1969. By the head of famed Foote, Cone & Belding agency.

Downey, Fairfax D., *Richard Harding Davis: His Day.* New York: Scribner's, 1933. Biography of the glamor-boy of early modern journalism.

Ellis, L. Ethan, *Newsprint: Producers, Publishers, Political Pressures.* New Brunswick, N.J.: Rutgers University Press, 1960. The economics of print paper (includes his 1948 study, *Print Paper Pendulum*).

Emery, Edwin, *History of the American Newspaper Publishers Association.* Minneapolis: University of Minnesota Press, 1950. Covers the activities of the organized daily newspaper publishers in the fields of labor relations, newsprint, advertising, mailing privileges, mechanical research, and legislative lobbying, from 1887 on.

Gunther, John, *Taken at the Flood: The Story of Albert D. Lasker.* New York: Harper & Row, 1960. The career of a pioneer adman at the Lord & Thomas agency.

Hower, Ralph M., *The History of an Advertising Agency: N. W. Ayer & Son at Work, 1869–1949.* Cambridge, Mass.: Harvard University Press, 1949.

Irwin, Will, *The American Newspaper,* edited by Clifford F. Weigle and David G. Clark. Ames: Iowa State University Press, 1969. Reproductions of the original series in *Collier's* of 1911.

———, *The Making of a Reporter.* New York: Putnam's, 1942. Autobiography of a discerning newspaperman who ranked with the best.

Isaacs, George A., *The Story of the Newspaper Printing Press.* London: Cooperative Printing Society, 1931.

Jones, Edgar R., *Those Were the Good Old Days: A Happy Look at American Advertising, 1880–1930.* New York: Simon & Schuster, 1959. Illustrations of 50 years of advertising from magazines.

Knight, Oliver A., *Following the Indian Wars: The Story of the Newspaper Correspondents among the Indian Campaigners, 1866–1891.* Norman: University of Oklahoma Press, 1960. Well documented.

Loft, Jacob, *The Printing Trades.* New York: Holt, Rinehart & Winston, 1944. An inclusive account. See also Elizabeth F. Baker, *Printers and Technology: A History of the International Printing Pressmen and Assistants' Union* (New York: Columbia University Press, 1957).

Newhall, Beaumont, *The History of Photography from 1839 to the Present Day.* New York: Museum of Modern Art, 1964. The standard reference.

Ogilvy, David, *Confessions of an Advertising Man.* New York: Atheneum, 1963. Another bit of advertising history by a leading participant.

Presbrey, Frank, *The History and Development of Advertising.* New York: Doubleday, 1929. The standard history in its field.

Ralph, Julian, *The Making of a Journalist.* New York: Harper & Row, 1903. The autobiography of another top-ranking reporter of the period.

Rosewater, Victor, *History of Cooperative News-Gathering in the United States.* New York: Appleton-Century-Crofts, 1930. The recognized source for the early history of press associations.

Ross, Ishbel, *Ladies of the Press.* New York: Harper & Row, 1936. Valuable for stories of early women journalists.

Turner, E. S., *The Shocking History of Advertising.* Harmondsworth, England: Penguin Books, 1965. An updated revision of a good history.

Ware, Louise, *Jacob A. Riis.* New York: Appleton-Century-Crofts, 1938. Biography of a socially conscious reporter.

Watkins, Julian L., *The 100 Greatest Advertisements,* 2nd ed. New York: Moore Publishing Company, 1959. Who wrote them and what they did.

Wood, James Playsted, *The Story of Advertising.* New York: Ronald Press, 1958. Fairly detailed from the 1860s on.

Periodicals and Monographs

The trade journals become available in this period. The leaders were the *Journalist* (1884–1907), the *Fourth Estate* (1894–1927), and *Editor & Publisher* (1901) in the daily newspaper field; the *Publishers' Auxiliary* (1865) in the weekly newspaper field; and *Printers' Ink* (1888) in advertising. The fiftieth anniversary numbers of *Editor & Publisher* (July 21, 1934) and of *Printers' Ink* (July 28, 1938) are particularly valuable sources.

Hudson, Robert V., "Journeyman Journalist: An Analytical Biography of Will Irwin." Ph.D. thesis, University of Minnesota, 1970. Reportorial career researched in depth.

Irwin, Will, "The American Newspaper," *Collier's*, XLVI-XLVII (January 21–July 29, 1911). A series of 15 articles which constitutes a history of journalism after the Civil War. One article, "The Fourth Current," which traces the rise of yellow journalism, is reprinted in Ford and Emery, *Highlights in the History of the American Press.*

Jones, Douglas C., "Remington Reports from the Badlands: The Artist as War Correspondent," *Journalism Quarterly*, XLVII (Winter 1970), 702. His drawings were in *Harper's Weekly.*

Kahan, Robert S., "The Antecedents of American Photojournalism," Ph.D. thesis, University of Wisconsin, 1969. The artist vs. the camera.

Knight, Oliver A., "Reporting a Gold Rush," *Journalism Quarterly*, XXXVIII (Winter 1961), 43. The story of two young reporters from the *Inter Ocean* and *New York Herald* in the Black Hills of 1875.

Knights, Peter R., "The Press Association War of 1866–1867," *Journalism Monographs*, No. 6 (December 1967). An episode in the story of wire services.

Park, Robert E., "The Natural History of the Newspaper," a book chapter by a University of Chicago sociologist, originally published in *The City* in 1925 and reprinted in Mott and Casey, *Interpretations of Journalism.*

Schuneman, R. Smith, "The Photograph in Print: An Examination of New York Daily Newspapers, 1890–1937." Ph.D. thesis, University of Minnesota, 1966. The rise of photojournalism is developed by extensive research.

———, "Art or Photography: A Question for Newspaper Editors of the 1890s," *Journalism Quarterly*, XLII (Winter 1965), 43. Why the halftone waited until 1897 in big dailies.

Shaw, Donald L., "News Bias and the Telegraph: A Study of Historical Change," *Journalism Quarterly*, XLIV (Spring 1967), 3. News by telegraph sharply decreased bias in presidential election news. Based on Ph.D. thesis, University of Wisconsin, 1966, studying Wisconsin press of 1852–1916.

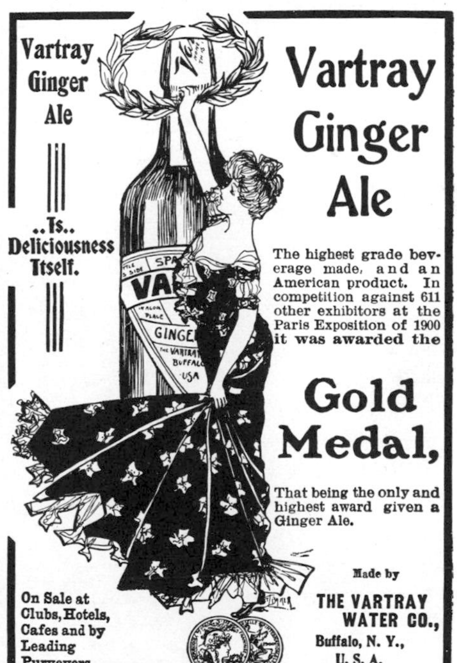

From *Harper's Monthly Magazine* (1901)

William Randolph Hearst takes a photo from his yacht during the Spanish-American War.

Wide World Photos

Hearst as he appeared at the peak of his career in the 1930s.

San Francisco Examiner

19

The Age of Yellow Journalism

The reason why such journals lie is that it pays to lie; or, in other words, this is the very reason for which they are silly and scandalous and indecent. They supply a want of a demoralized public.
—E. L. Godkin

The American newspaper was making great strides by the mid-nineties both as an instrument of society and as a business institution. Thanks to the publishing concepts and the techniques of the new journalism, many dailies had won larger circulations giving them greater public influence and support. Their increased advertising and subscription revenues provided the resources necessary for more intensive coverage of the news. And growing financial stability meant that conscientious publishers and editors could do a better job of telling the news honestly and fully, and of demonstrating their community leadership, because they were better able to resist outside pressures.

This, of course, was the brighter side of the growth of the modern newspaper. There could be shortcomings, as well. The financial bigness of metropolitan dailies brought a lessening of the personal element in editorial direction, and sometimes muffled the voice of the newspaper and dulled its social conscience. Mass circulation was achieved by a popularizing of the product, and sometimes the primary news function was overshadowed by efforts to entertain. It should be added, however, that corporate journalism did not need to speak in a timid voice. And popularization, while inevitable if mass readership was to be achieved, did not need to become mere sensationalism.

The tools which were now available—linotypes and faster presses, more striking typography and layout, color printing, cartoons and photographs, skillful writing by larger staffs of reporters and editors, better communications facilities—all could be used constructively to build better newspapers. Stories which were written in a more readable style, or which in their nature appealed to the human interests of readers, could increase popular acceptance of the newspaper without detracting from its social usefulness. Bigger headlines, pictures, blobs of color might give the newspaper a new face, and might cause some readers to grimace at the result and yearn for the bygone days; but effectively used, these devices too could be useful and desirable.

THE SENSATIONAL "YELLOW JOURNALISM"

By the same token, a modern daily newspaper could use the new techniques of editing and printing in another way. It could emphasize sensationalism at the expense of news; it could lavishly dress up its entertainment features; it could put success in snaring readers ahead of the primary obligations of journalism. Some newspaper editors proceeded in the mid-nineties to do these things, just as they had been done in earlier periods when newspapers reached out to attract new audiences. But now they had far better tools which made their sensationalism distinctive and seemingly new, and so their degrading kind of journalism became known as "yellow journalism."

Yellow journalism, at its worst, was the new journalism without a soul. True, the yellow journalists trumpeted their concern for "the people," and championed the rights of the common man; but at the same time they choked up the news channels upon which the common man depended, with a callous disregard for journalistic ethics and responsibility. Theirs was a shrieking, gaudy, sensation-loving, devil-may-care kind of journalism which lured the reader by any possible means. It seized upon the techniques of writing, illustrating, and printing which were the prides of the new journalism and turned them to perverted uses. It made the high drama of life a cheap melodrama, and it twisted the facts of each day into whatever form seemed best suited to produce sales for the howling newsboy. Worst of all, instead of giving its readers effective leadership, it offered a palliative of sin, sex, and violence.

Joseph Pulitzer had opened Pandora's box when he used the devices of sensationalism to help build the *World's* circulation during the early years of his editorship. Other papers, like the *Philadelphia Record* and the *Boston Globe,* were playing the same game, but it was Pulitzer's phenomenal success which had so strikingly demonstrated once again the appeal of this age-old technique of sensation. And now there were new devices, for super-sensationalizing the newspaper, available to those who eyed his progress and mistakenly attributed the *World's* circulation achievements to sensationalism alone. Those who became yellow journalists did not understand that Pulitzer had sought to achieve a balance between informing the reader and entertaining him, so that in the end the innovations of the new journalism would enhance the stature of his newspaper above the imitators. They saw the clever promotion and the lighter side of the *World,* but they did not see—or disregarded—the solid characteristics of its news coverage and the high qualities of its editorial page.

So the high priests of the yellow press set out to show Pulitzer how it really could be done. And their antics, which paid off handsomely in newspaper sales to the casual readers of the big cities, forced competing dailies to take on the yellow hue in varying degrees all across the country. Eventually most newspapers recovered from the disease, but modern journalism has exhibited some of the effects of the age of yellow journalism ever since.

WILLIAM RANDOLPH HEARST

The man who more than anyone else brought about the era of yellow journalism was watching with sharp interest while Pulitzer was setting New York journalism on its ear in the mid-eighties. He was William Randolph Hearst, who was to become the most controversial figure in modern journalism before his 64-year publishing career was ended. The youthful Hearst was a calculating witness to Pulitzer's climb to glory, and when eventually he invaded New York to challenge the supremacy of the *World,* he came prepared to dazzle the city with a sensationalized and self-promoted kind of journalism which would put Pulitzer to shame. The resulting struggle brought repercussions whose effects are still being felt.

Hearst was a Californian, born in 1863, the son of a successful pioneer who struck it rich in the silver mines of the Comstock Lode, and who later won more riches in Anaconda copper and western and Mexican ranch lands. The only child of George and Phoebe Hearst, he grew up in San Francisco under the guidance of a busy, ambitious father and a schoolteacher mother, who in later years became a noted philanthropist and able manager of the family fortune.

Having achieved wealth, George Hearst aspired to political power. In 1880 he acquired the *San Francisco Examiner,* a debt-ridden morning paper which lagged behind the *Chronicle,* and converted it into a Democratic party organ. Young Hearst showed an interest in the paper, but his father took a low view of the newspapermen who worked for him, and packed his heir off to Harvard in 1883.

The Hearst career at Harvard was sensational, if not successful. He was a free-spending westerner who drank too much beer, listened to too much band music, and who did his best job as business manager of the humor magazine, the *Lampoon.* He was suspended in his sophomore year for celebrating Grover Cleveland's election to the presidency with a noisy fireworks display, and was expelled a few months later for perpetrating a practical joke upon Harvard's professors. Distinguished faculty members like William James and Josiah Royce could see no humor, it seemed, in finding their likenesses decorating chamber pots.

But the eastern education had not been entirely wasted. Harvard may not have made its impression on Hearst's mind, but the *Boston Globe* and the *New York World* did. Hearst studied the somewhat sensational techniques of General Charles H. Taylor's successful *Globe* and visited its up-to-date mechanical plant. He was more interested in Pulitzer's *World,* however, and on one of his vacations he worked as a cub reporter for the newspaper he later was to battle. After bowing out at Harvard, Hearst again spent some time in New York studying the *World's* techniques and then returned to San Francisco.

HEARST'S *SAN FRANCISCO EXAMINER*

His father didn't want to see young Hearst take over the editorship of the *Examiner*—but that was what the strong-willed "Willie" intended to do. Furthermore, the confident son assured his doubting father, money could be made from newspapers as well as from mines and ranches. The *Examiner,* he said, would become "the *New York World* of the West." In 1887 George Hearst was named Senator from California, and as he left for Washington, 24-year-old William Randolph Hearst was given control of the *Examiner.*

The tall, blue-eyed, shy young editor, whose high-pitched voice contrasted with a commanding physical presence, immediately began to staff up his newspaper. For his managing editor he picked Sam S. Chamberlain, who had worked for both Bennett and Pulitzer, who had edited Bennett's Paris edition of the *Herald,* and who had founded the Paris newspaper *Le Matin* in 1884. Chamberlain's experience, and his grasp of news techniques, made him invaluable.

This was a typical Hearst move—to watch for a good man on another paper and then to buy him at his own figure. The salaries on the *Examiner* were good for men with ability, and word soon spread.

Coming onto the *Examiner* staff in the early years were many talented recruits. There was the brilliant Ambrose Bierce, who contributed his "Prattle" column to the paper, and who later became famous for his short stories. There were star reporters like Edward H. Hamilton, and up-and-coming newspapermen like Arthur McEwen, who became a key figure in developing Hearst-style journalism, and Charles Michelson, who some 40 years later achieved his greatest fame as publicity director of the Democratic party during the Hoover regime and the first eventful years of the New Deal. Homer Davenport began to draw his political cartoons, and artist James Swinnerton turned to the new field of comics. Giving the *Examiner* literary flavor of quite different degrees were Edwin Markham, whose poem "The Man With the Hoe" first appeared in the paper, and E. L. (Phinney) Thayer, whose contribution was "Casey at the Bat."

When Chamberlain one day decided to investigate the city hospital's management, he picked a young woman reporter and assigned her to the story.

She fainted conveniently on the street, was carried to the hospital, and turned out a story "with a sob for the unfortunate in every line." She was Winifred Black, who became known as "Annie Laurie" to future generations of Hearst readers. Her greatest early hit was an appeal to raise funds for the establishment of a "Little Jim ward" in the local children's hospital—a ward for incurables like little Jim, whose plight Annie Laurie described with such intensity that San Francisco women particularly were attracted to the *Examiner's* kind of human interest appeal. Hearst early saw the importance of the woman reader in the stimulation of retail advertising revenue.

Hearst was experimenting with crusades and stunts, and with devices for presenting the news in the most luring manner. As a stalwart Democrat, he relished attacking the Southern Pacific railroad company, bulwark of the Republican state machine. When a schooner went aground outside the Golden Gate, Hearst sent out a tugboat filled with reporters, who rescued survivors "courtesy of the *Examiner*." If the Del Monte hotel burned, or a murder took place near San Francisco, a special train carrying *Examiner* men and women reporters and artists went chugging to the scene. Hearst writers sought to play up a sensational, picturesque fact in their lead paragraphs—love, power, hate, or sympathy were the preferred themes. News which was important, but dull, took a back seat. Arthur McEwen summed up the Hearst approach when he said: "What we're after is the 'gee-whiz' emotion. We run our paper so that when the reader opens it he says: 'Gee-Whiz!' "[1]

Hearst's experiments on the mechanical side were important—and constructive—contributions to the new journalism. He worked with the typography of the *Examiner* to give it readable and attractive type faces. He tried many new patterns of makeup, arranging the heads in symmetrical patterns, introducing illustrations and large headlines, and eventually arriving at a distinctive Hearst formula which many another newspaper imitated. Hearst himself often worked over the page forms, but he also sought as eagerly for mechanical experts as he did for writers and artists. His greatest genius was George Pancoast, who joined Hearst on the *Examiner* in 1888, became superintendent of all Hearst mechanical plants and remained at this job for most of his 50-year career. Pancoast perfected the electric drive for presses, improved color printing processes, and designed 14 printing plants as the Hearst publishing empire expanded.

And Hearst was ready to expand his empire. His *Examiner*, which he proudly called "The Monarch of the Dailies," had doubled its circulation in the first year, reaching 30,000. By 1893 the figure was 72,000 and the *Examiner's* circulation had passed that of M. H. de Young's *Chronicle*, the recognized leading daily of the city. Senator Hearst, who died in 1891, lived to see his son make a handsome profit on the once money-losing paper, and the profit grew until it averaged between $350,000 and $500,000 a year.[2]

[1] Will Irwin, "The Fourth Current," *Collier's*, XLVI (February 18, 1911), 14.
[2] *Ibid.* Estimate by Will Irwin in 1911, for the period up to then.

HEARST INVADES NEW YORK

The profits from the *Examiner* now were available for an invasion of New York. But Hearst needed more capital, and eventually he persuaded his mother to sell the family holdings in the Anaconda copper mines for $7,500,000 and make the cash available for new publishing ventures.[3] Later, when a friend told Mrs. Hearst that she had heard the *New York Journal* was losing a million dollars a year, and expressed fear that the family fortune was being thrown away recklessly, Mrs. Hearst replied that, in such an event, her son could hold out for 30 years more.

Somewhat ironically, Hearst entered the New York field by buying the newspaper which Joseph Pulitzer's brother, Albert, had established in 1882. The *Morning Journal* had been a successful one-cent paper appealing to casual newspaper scanners. In 1894 its price was raised to two cents, and circulation fell off. Albert Pulitzer then sold the *Journal* for a million dollars to John R. McLean, ambitious publisher of the *Cincinnati Enquirer*. McLean was no stranger to sensational methods of publishing newspapers, but he was unable to break into the highly competitive New York field. In the fall of 1895, Hearst picked up the paper from the defeated McLean for $180,000.

PULITZER'S *SUNDAY WORLD*

Joseph Pulitzer had been busy during the 10 years since Hearst had left New York to launch his career in San Francisco. Particularly he had expanded the mechanical facilities available to his editors, and he had applied the new techniques to the development of the *Sunday World*.

It was Pulitzer who first demonstrated the full potentialities of the Sunday newspaper as a profitable news and entertainment medium. There had been weeklies issued as Sunday papers since 1796. The daily *Boston Globe* put out a Sunday edition briefly in 1833, but James Gordon Bennett's *Herald* was the first daily to print a Sunday edition steadily, starting in 1841. The demand for news during the Civil War stimulated Sunday publication, but even by the time Pulitzer invaded New York in 1883 only about 100 daily newspapers had Sunday editions. Most of them were appearing in eastern cities and a good share were printed in German and other foreign languages. Some carried a four-page supplement filled with entertaining features, fiction, and trivia.

[3] Ferdinand Lundberg, *Imperial Hearst: A Social Biography* (New York: Equinox Cooperative Press, 1936), p. 50. Lundberg presents much information about Hearst's finances, but paints the publisher in the blackest possible fashion. For the best balanced accounts see John Tebbel, *The Life and Good Times of William Randolph Hearst* (New York: Dutton, 1952), and W. A. Swanberg, *Citizen Hearst* (New York: Scribner's, 1961).

Pulitzer's new *Sunday World* added many more pages of entertainment to the regular news section. Feature material for women, for young readers, and for sports enthusiasts appeared. Humorous drawings and other illustrations were concentrated in the Sunday pages. The offerings of the literary syndicates, such as that developed by S. S. McClure, added to the Sunday paper's appeal. Circulation of the *Sunday World* passed the 250,000 mark in 1887 and by the early 1890s the paper had reached 40 to 48 pages in size, as retail advertisers realized the extent of its readership by families and by women. Other newspapers were quick to follow suit, and in 1890 there were 250 dailies with Sunday editions, crowding the metropolitan areas and driving the independent Sunday weeklies out of the picture.

Heading the *World's* Sunday staff was Morrill Goddard, a college graduate who as a young city editor had shown his ability to spot the feature possibilities of significant news events. Goddard was not content, however, to present interpretive stories reporting the advances being made by American scientists and scholars in the fields of medicine, psychology, archaeology, and the physical sciences, or by the inventive geniuses of the industrial age. He jazzed up his page spreads, exaggerating and popularizing the factual information. Scientists particularly were the victims of the Sunday newspaper's predilection for distortion and sensationalism, and the pseudoscientific stories of yellow journalism made the men of science shy away from newspaper coverage for the next 50 years.

This didn't bother Goddard, however; he knew that many of his readers enjoyed what they thought was an easy way to keep up with the world's new learning. One of his staff explained the operation this way:

> Suppose it's Halley's comet. Well, first you have a half-page of decoration showing the comet, with historical pictures of previous appearances thrown in. If you can work a pretty girl into the decoration, so much the better. If not, get some good nightmare idea like the inhabitants of Mars watching it pass. Then you want a quarter of a page of big-type heads—snappy. Then four inches of story, written right off the bat. Then a picture of Professor Halley down here and another of Professor Lowell up there, and a two-column boxed freak containing a scientific opinion, which nobody will understand, just to give it class.[4]

The Sunday staff had a similar approach to crime stories, to drama and literature, to the doings of prominent persons, and to advice to the lovelorn.

When the *World* installed its color presses in 1893, Goddard had a new medium to exploit. His illustrations, which had steadily expanded in size, now could appear in color, as could the bold-type headlines. As many as five colors could be used in the Sunday color supplement for illustrations ranging from wash drawings of cathedrals to comic drawings. It was the comic draw-

[4] Will Irwin, "The Fourth Current," *Collier's,* XLVI (February 18, 1911), 14.

The "Yellow Kid," in his nightshirt, was an 1896 smash hit in the *New York World.*

ings, Goddard knew, which were most effective in spurring circulation. The *World* began the first regular comic section in 1889, and it was the first newspaper to use color in these drawings (magazines had done so since the 1870s). These early comics were not the kind of continuous-action strips which are familiar to newspaper readers now, but they had the same kind of high reader appeal. Most successful of the artists was Richard F. Outcault, whose "Hogan's

Alley" depicted life in the tenements. The central figure in each drawing was a toothless, grinning kid attired in a ballooning dress. When the *World's* printers daubed a blob of yellow on the dress, he became the immortal "Yellow Kid."

HEARST STAFFS HIS *NEW YORK JOURNAL*

Thus, when William Randolph Hearst arrived on the New York scene, the *Sunday World* presented a variety of offerings to its readers: a good news section and editorial page: significant coverage of intellectual interests and society; lighter but high-class entertaining fare; and excursions into sensational presentations of pseudoscience, crime, and affairs of the heart. Hearst set out to buy the men who were doing the sensational jobs.

From an office which the *Examiner* had rented in the *World* building, Hearst conducted a series of raids on Pulitzer's staff. He offered Morrill Goddard a fabulous salary to come over to the *Journal,* and when Goddard explained that his staff of writers and artists did most of the work, Hearst bought them too. Pulitzer detailed S. S. Carvalho, publisher of the *World,* to woo Goddard back, but Hearst's typical unconcern for lavish spending made Pulitzer's counteroffers hopeless. Before long Carvalho himself was working at the *Journal* building along with the managing editor of the popularized *Evening World.*

Now the contest was on. Pulitzer turned to Arthur Brisbane, Socialist Albert Brisbane's brilliant young son who had broken into newspaper work on the *Sun* before joining the *World* staff, and made him Sunday editor. Brisbane, like Goddard, knew how to popularize scientific advances and scholarly thinking, and he drove the *World's* Sunday circulation to the 600,000 mark. Goddard had taken Outcault and his "Yellow Kid" with him to the *Journal,* but Brisbane had George B. Luks, later a well-known painter, continue the "Yellow Kid" in the *World.* Circulation men for both papers featured the happy-go-lucky kid in their posters, and his grinning but curiously vacant features became familiar to all New Yorkers. To opposition newspapermen, the "Yellow Kid" seemed symbolic of the kind of sensational journalism which was again developing, and the public agreed. The phrase "yellow journalism" soon became widely used. Hearst settled the matter of which paper was to have the most prominent personalities of yellow journalism on its staff in his usual manner, however; Brisbane became editor of the *Evening Journal* in 1897 and Luks took his version of the "Yellow Kid" over to the enemy. Outcault moaned:

> "When I die don't wear yellow crepe, don't let them put a Yellow Kid on my tombstone and don't let the Yellow Kid himself come to my funeral. Make him stay over on the east side, where he belongs." [5]

[5] *New York World,* May 1, 1898, p. 7 (supplement).

The *World* was not the only contributor to the *Journal's* staff. From San Francisco came the stars of the *Examiner:* managing editor Sam Chamberlain, editorial writer Arthur McEwen, cartoonist Homer Davenport, and sob-sister Winifred (Annie Laurie) Black. Dana's *Sun* lost its star reporters, Julian Ralph, Richard Harding Davis, and Edward W. Townsend, to the Hearst bankroll. Dorothy Dix joined the women's staff. Writers Stephen Crane, Alfred Henry Lewis, and Rudolph Block (Bruno Lessing) signed up, along with other leading newsmen, drama critics, and artists.

Two events helped Hearst build the *Journal* up as a formidable competitor for the *World* and other New York newspapers. In early 1896, when the *Journal* had won 150,000 circulation as a one-cent paper, Pulitzer cut the price of the *World* to a penny. Though the *World* gained circulation as a result, Pulitzer's action was interpreted as a recognition of Hearst's success, just as the *Herald's* price maneuver against Pulitzer in 1884 had been viewed. More importantly, the *World* deserted the Democratic party in the presidential election of 1896, leaving the *Journal* as the city's major supporter of William Jennings Bryan.

Bryan's candidacy in 1896 represented the flowering of the "consistent rebellion" by those who were dissatisfied with the theories of economic individualism which had dominated American political thinking since the Civil War. When Bryan cried, "You shall not press down upon the brow of labor this crown of thorns, you shall not crucify mankind upon a cross of gold," he not only won the Democratic nomination, but he expressed the desires of the labor movement, the populists and reformers of the Middle West, and the silver and paper money advocates who sought to break the hold of financial interests. Pulitzer, while sympathizing with many of the objectives of the movement Bryan led, refused to support his inflationary monetary program. Hearst as a silver mine owner had no great regard for the gold standard and ranged the *Journal* alongside "the people's choice," despite the conservative East's horror of Bryanism. He thus fared well among political partisans, just as Pulitzer had snatched circulation from the *Sun* in 1884 when Dana refused to support Grover Cleveland for the presidency.

THE "YELLOW JOURNALISM" WAR

But the most important reasons for the upward surge of the *Journal* were its frank adoption of the sins of yellow journalism, and its blatant promotion of what it called its journalistic achievements. The journalistic historian Willard G. Bleyer cited these headlines in issues of the *Journal* published during the fall of 1896, and undoubtedly was justified in linking them with a circulation jump of 125,000 in a single month: [6]

[6] Willard G. Bleyer, *Main Currents in the History of American Journalism* (Boston: Houghton Mifflin, 1927), pp. 357–64. This book documents the case against the *Journal's* rampant yellow journalism.

"Real American Monsters and Dragons"—over a story of the discovery of fossil remains by an archaeological expedition.

"A Marvellous New Way of Giving Medicine: Wonderful Results from Merely Holding Tubes of Drugs Near Entranced Patients"—a headline which horrified medical researchers.

"Henry James New Novel of Immorality and Crime; The Surprising Plunge of the Great Novelist in the Field of Sensational Fiction"—the *Journal's* way of announcing publication of *The Other House.*

Other headlines were more routinely sensational: "The Mysterious Murder of Bessie Little," "One Mad Blow Kills Child," "What Made Him a Burglar? A Story of Real Life in New York by Edgar Saltus," "Startling Confession of a Wholesale Murderer Who Begs to Be Hanged." Annie Laurie wrote about "Why Young Girls Kill Themselves" and "Strange Things Women Do for Love." When a *Journal* drama critic interviewed a famous actress the streamer headline read, "Mlle. Anna Held Receives Alan Dale, Attired in a 'Nightie' "—and a page-length sketch of the nightgown-clad actress accompanied the story.

The *Journal* was crusading, too, but it went beyond other New York newspapers in a manner which enabled it to shout, "While Others Talk the Journal Acts." The paper obtained a court injunction which balked the granting of a city franchise to a gas company, and pleased by its success, it took similar actions against alleged abuses in government. Hearst then solicited compliments from civic leaders across the country and printed them under such headings as, "Journalism that Acts; Men of Action in All Walks of Life Heartily Endorse the Journal's Fight in Behalf of the People," and "First Employed by the Journal, the Novel Conceit Seems Likely to Become an Accepted Part of the Function of the Newspapers of This Country." [7]

Before his first year in New York had ended, Hearst had installed bigger and better color presses at the *Journal* and had produced an eight-page Sunday colored comic section called the *American Humorist.* It was, the *Journal* said, "eight pages of iridescent polychromous effulgence that makes the rainbow look like a lead pipe." Most of the *Journal's* readers didn't catch the first few words, but they could understand the added explanation. Soon a 16-page color supplement was added under the name of the *Sunday American Magazine* (later, with Brisbane as editor, this was to become the famous *American Weekly*). Still another eight-page color supplement devoted itself to the interests of women. The result was that in late 1896, after a year of Hearst's editorship, the *Journal's* daily circulation was 437,000 and its Sunday circulation was 380,000. In another year's time, Sunday circulation reached the *World's* 600,000 figure. Circulation figures moved up and down according to the street sales appeal of the moment; on the day following the McKinley-Bryan election the *World* and the *Journal* each sold approximately 1,500,000 copies, to break all records.

[7] William Rockhill Nelson, editor of the *Kansas City Star,* also had used his own funds to fight court battles in behalf of the public interest, but not so sensationally.

The *Journal* and its New York competitors fought to obtain exclusive and dramatic coverage of major news events. The *Journal* sewed up the rights to statements by heavyweight fighters James J. Corbett and Bob Fitzsimmons when they met in Nevada in 1897. It sent Samuel Clemens to London to cover the sixtieth anniversary of Queen Victoria's coronation. When the Greco-Turkish War began in early 1897, King George of Greece cabled an exclusive message to the *Journal.* James Creelman, Julian Ralph, and two women were among seven *Journal* correspondents covering the conflict. And going along on the Klondike gold rush were two expeditions from Hearst's *Journal* and *Examiner.* The *World,* the *Herald,* and the *Sun,* among New York papers, and leading papers in other cities, were just as active in scrambling for the news.

THE SPANISH-AMERICAN WAR

It was in this kind of atmosphere, then, that American newspapers approached the events which led to an international crisis—and the Spanish-American War. For the yellow journalists, trouble in Cuba meant another chance for sensational stories, excitement, and adventure. For their competitors, the problem became one of maintaining caution and losing circulation, or matching the efforts of the yellow journalists in printing fact and fiction and thereby holding their readers. Only smaller papers, and those big city dailies which contented themselves with building a solid core of appreciative readers, could face the problem calmly.

Of all the wars the United States has fought, the Spanish-American War was the most painless. In fewer than four months the Spanish government was forced to request an armistice, at an extraordinarily small cost in American lives, and the American flag was floating over an empire stretching from Puerto Rico to the Philippines. Save perhaps for the Mexican War, it was also the most unwarranted war in American history.

Those who have sought to explain the causes of the war have often centered the blame on William Randolph Hearst in particular and the newspapers of the country in general. Carefully documented studies made by Marcus M. Wilkerson and Joseph E. Wisan in the early 1930s give ample evidence that Hearst's *Journal,* Pulitzer's *World,* the *Chicago Tribune,* the *Sun* and *Herald* in New York (and, as is usually ignored, many other American newspapers) so handled the news of events leading up to the crisis of the sinking of the "Maine" that a war psychosis was developed.[8] It must not be forgotten, however, that the newspapers were cultivating public opinion in a favorable atmosphere.

[8] Marcus M. Wilkerson, *Public Opinion and the Spanish-American War* (Baton Rouge: Louisiana State University Press, 1932); Joseph E. Wisan, *The Cuban Crisis as Reflected in the New York Press* (New York: Columbia University Press, 1934).

THE SPIRIT OF "MANIFEST DESTINY"

Throughout the nineteenth century the United States had pursued a policy of expansion. Its people in general subscribed to the belief in "manifest destiny" which spurred the westward movement. The War of 1812 was forced upon a reluctant New England by western expansionists who viewed the British in Canada as their mortal enemies. The Mexican War and cries of "54-40 or Fight" brought the completion of the continental United States. Americans liked to buy the territory they wanted, but they were also ready to take it by force if necessary.

As a new industrial America emerged after the Civil War, the country's interest in international affairs steadily grew. The Monroe Doctrine, which had proclaimed the freedom of the New World from the Old, became an instrument for the development of an American foreign policy which aimed at a domination of the Western hemisphere by the United States. The purchase of Alaska brought protection of one flank. James G. Blaine, in two terms as Secretary of State, began maneuvering to force the British out of any share in control of the interoceanic canal which would be built in Panama. Blaine also sought to build a Pan-American union in which the United States would play a leading role, but a controversy between the United States and Chile, marked by Yankee diplomatic ineptitude, reduced the effectiveness of Blaine's efforts.

At the same time the United States was increasingly interested in the Pacific area. Friendly relations were cultivated with Japan, and trade with China was increased to the point where John Hay was to enunciate the famous Open Door Policy in 1899 as a means of keeping China's trade open to all comers. Agitation for the annexation of Hawaii increased during the 1880s, and the United States successfully won a foothold in the Samoa Islands, in competition with Germany and Britain. Beginning in 1882 the United States had built a modern navy symbolic of the age of steel, and Captain Alfred Thayer Mahan was revolutionizing the theory of naval warfare with his writings on the influence of sea power on history. The United States, along with Britain, Germany, France, and Japan, was entering into a worldwide race for power.

Viewed in the long perspective, the Spanish-American War was but one incident in a series of events which marked this arrival of the United States as a world power. It was preceded by the Venezuelan crisis of 1895, in which President Grover Cleveland brought his country to the verge of war with Great Britain over a test of the Monroe Doctrine. It was followed by the annexation of Hawaii, the Philippines, Guam, and Puerto Rico, and the building of the Panama Canal. American interest in affairs on the Asiatic mainland brought about the Open Door Policy in China and the negotiation of the peace treaty ending the Russo-Japanese War in a little New Hampshire town. Pan-Americanism became open American intervention in the affairs of Central American countries and the building of a Caribbean defense for the United States and its new Panama Canal. President Theodore Roosevelt, who was the guiding force in the establishment of this new policy, took his country into European affairs by participating in the Algeciras conference which settled the Moroccan crisis of 1905 precipitated by German expansionism. The United States, as a powerful force in the modern era of industry and world commerce, henceforth was to be an important participant in international affairs.

IDEALISM VS. NATIONAL PRIDE

The desire for power was not the only driving force behind this American expansion of interest. There was pride felt by many Americans in the addition of new territories, and there was keen interest in the expansion of American trade and foreign investments as the domestic economy matured. But Americans also felt they had a role to play in promoting their idea of peace and justice in the world. There had been proposals for the annexation of Cuba throughout the nineteenth century, but there also had been widespread sympathy for the Cuban independence movement which had flared in ten revolts before the final crisis. Americans were disturbed by accounts of Turkish atrocities in Armenia, and many newspaper editors called Cuba "another Armenia." Americans also were following with keen interest the Greco-Turkish War of 1897, and were sympathizing with the Greeks in their struggle for independence. Some Americans wanted a Pan-American union in the full meaning of the phrase. Thus in the United States there were two major forces: a strong sympathy for another people whose freedom was being suppressed, and a growing sense of power in world affairs. Both forces came into play during the Spanish-American War period. If later the advocates of imperialism and "dollar diplomacy" gained the upper hand over the idealists, that was but one phase of America's coming of age in international affairs.

The newspapers which came to be blamed for precipitating the Spanish-American War played upon the American feeling of sympathy and social justice. They exaggerated the story of the Spanish-Cuban struggle and they presented it in a lurid manner, as will be shown. But if their stories and illustrations were sensationalized and sometimes untrue, they were nevertheless founded on a solid core of fact. Cubans were fighting for their independence against an inefficient and oppressive Spanish regime. There were atrocities committed during the insurrection. And disease and starvation were widespread. These established facts should not be overlooked, for other Americans than the newspapermen pointed them out in public discussion, and they formed the basis for acceptance of sensationalized reports and propaganda.

The newspapers involved also played upon American pride and sense of power. They openly discussed the nature of a war between Spain and the

United States, and pointed to the new American navy which awaited its first test in battle. They urged the United States to use force if need be to oust the Spanish from Cuba, so that the Cuban people would be freed from oppression. They suggested that the decadent Spanish military power would be an "easy mark." They were not thinking of the economic gains from such a war; the commercial interests of the country and those newspapers which reflected the thinking of America's new big business shrank away from a war which might upset the prosperity of the country, barely regained after the depression of 1893. The newspapers advocating intervention in Cuba were, in many cases, simply reflecting a desire to flex the nation's new muscles.

Nor were they alone in this desire. For 30 years the people of both North and South had lived in the aftermath of the Civil War, honoring its veterans and reliving its struggles in story and song. As the horror of war faded, older Americans began to wonder if their country's military prowess was still secure. Younger Americans were eager to match the valor of the honored men of Blue and Gray. For them war, 1898 style, still seemed to be an exciting personal adventure. John D. Hicks, an American historian of first rank who was not unaware of the role of the newspaper as an organ of public opinion, summed up his discussion of the causes of the Spanish-American War by saying:

> Years later, Theodore Roosevelt recaptured the spirit of 1898 when he mourned apologetically, "It wasn't much of a war, but it was the best war we had." America in the spring of 1898 was ripe for any war, and the country's mood was not to be denied.[9]

COVERING CUBAN NEWS, 1895–98

From March, 1895, when the Cuban insurrection began, until April, 1898, when Spain and the United States went to war, there were fewer than a score of days in which a story about Cuba did not appear in one of the New York newspapers.[10] This was due partly to the aggressive news policies of the big dailies, partly to the manufacturing of stories by some of the papers (notably the *Journal*), partly to increasing reader interest in a controversial story. It was also the result of the activities of the Cuban junta which fed information and propaganda to American newsmen in New York and at the Florida news bases nearest the island.

A considerable number of Cubans had emigrated to the United States, settling in New York, Philadelphia, Baltimore, Boston, and several Florida cities. The junta had its headquarters in New York, where a Cuban newspaper was published. Through the Cuban residents in the eastern cities, a program

[9] John D. Hicks, *A Short History of American Democracy* (Boston: Houghton Mifflin, 1943), p. 605.

[10] Wisan, *The Cuban Crisis,* p. 460.

of mass meetings was established. Money was raised, and several hundred volunteers were obtained in each city for service in running arms and taking part in filibustering expeditions. Cuban agents funneled information on the progress of the fighting on Cuba to the American newspapers. The work was well underway in 1895, and as the crisis intensified, the activities of the junta reached greater heights. Ministers, educators, civic leaders, and politicians were reached by the junta.

The Spanish decision in early 1896 to use strong repressive measures in Cuba brought the focus of attention upon what was happening to the native population. Captain-General Valeriano Weyler, a tough Spanish commander known as the "Butcher," was sent to the island to stamp out the insurrection, and quickly became the villain of the piece. Weyler ordered all loyal Cubans to congregate in small areas adjoining Spanish military bases. Those who did not obey were to be considered as enemies. This *reconcentrado* policy aroused quick resentment in the United States, for it meant in effect the creation of a military dictatorship. It was an unhappy decision for the Spanish in another way, too, since the Cubans who huddled in the towns and camps quickly became victims of epidemics, and many of them starved to death when food supplies became disrupted. Much of the newspaper copy centered about the effects of famine and pestilence, and estimates of Cuban deaths ran as high as 400,000. Wilkerson in his study sets the figure for all Cuban deaths during the three years of revolt at approximately 100,000,[11] and the discrepancy affords an illustration of the exaggeration by American newsmen of conditions in Cuba which were sufficiently serious in truth, but more striking when enlarged upon. The *reconcentrado* policy, and Spanish reprisals against revolutionary guerrilla bands, fitted Weyler's nickname of "Butcher" and he was compared in American newspaper stories to the "bloodthirsty Cortez and Pizarro" of the days of the conquistadors.

When Weyler's campaign began in February, 1896, there were correspondents in Cuba from the *World, Journal, Sun,* and *Herald,* of the New York newspapers. The *Washington Post,* the *New Orleans Times-Democrat,* and several Florida newspapers also were represented. The Associated Press had its own coverage, and also could use in its news report all the stories printed by its member papers.[12] In addition, the newspapers with correspondents on the scene sold their news services to other dailies across the country. In Chicago, for example, the *Tribune* bought both the *World* news service and the *Journal* syndicate, while the rival *Times-Herald* relied upon the *New York Herald* service. In San Francisco Hearst's *Examiner* had the *Journal's* coverage, while the opposition *Chronicle* tried to keep up in sensational news presentation by printing the offerings of both the *Herald* and *Sun.* Therefore, with the selling of the New York papers' stories to other dailies, the transmission

[11] *Public Opinion and the Spanish-American War,* p. 40.

[12] There was competition between the Associated Press and the old United Press until 1897. After that time, all the major New York papers except the *Sun* were AP members.

by the Associated Press of the "news beats" of the competing papers, and the growing attention in Congress to Cuban affairs, the Cuban story was broadcast widely across the country.

The *World's* first correspondent in Cuba, William S. Bowen, was fairly accurate in his reporting of conditions on the island. But two of his successors, James Creelman and Sylvester Scovel, gave the *World* thoroughly sensationalized coverage. Creelman saw sickening scenes in 1896, but he made certain that his reading audience was impressed by giving them such lines as, "Blood on the roadsides, blood in the fields, blood on the doorsteps, blood, blood, blood!" Scovel described in nauseating detail the mutilation of Cuban men, women, and children who had stayed in the countryside in defiance of Weyler's orders, and would drop in dubious reports—such as one that the Spanish were collecting the ears of their victims as trophies. Some of their stories were supposedly based on their eyewitness reporting; others admittedly were recountings of the stories of Cuban refugees.

HEARST'S CAMPAIGN FOR WAR

Hearst was not to be outdone in this competition. He persuaded Creelman to switch his allegiance from the *World* to the *Journal* in late 1896, and sent the famous team of Richard Harding Davis, the ex-*Sun* reporter, and Frederic Remington, the artist, to the island. They obliged with stories rivaling those of Scovel in exaggerated effect. The *Herald* correspondents kept to the same pace, while those of the *Sun* trailed in sensational coverage. Sketches were drawn in Cuba, or more frequently in the newspaper offices, to illustrate the stories, and many of them went beyond the facts. The impact of pictorial journalism was increased in 1897 when New York newspapers began to print photographs which sometimes were accurate portrayals of Cuban scenes and which sometimes were fakes. Enough of them seemed authentic, however, to give strong evidence to readers that what the reporters were writing was essentially true.

One of the episodes of this period did much to tag the *Journal's* owner with "Hearst's war." Creelman, in writing his reminiscences in 1901, said that Remington found his Cuban assignment an unhappy one. According to Creelman, the artist cabled Hearst that all was quiet in Cuba, that there would be no war, and that he was coming home. Whereupon Hearst was supposed to have replied: "Remington, Havana. Please remain. You furnish the pictures, and I'll furnish the war. W. R. Hearst." [13] There is no other evidence that Hearst sent this cable, so often quoted as conclusive evidence against him, but in a sense it reflected the situation. Of all the American newspapers, Hearst's *Journal* worked the hardest to create public sentiment for war.

[13] James Creelman, *On the Great Highway* (Boston: Lothrop Publishing Company, 1901), p. 178.

Open advocacy of war with Spain appeared in the *Journal* by the fall of 1896, and Hearst applied to this situation the paper's boast: "While Others Talk the Journal Acts." When Congress assembled in December the *Journal* polled senators on the question of open American intervention in Cuba, and it asked state governors how many volunteers they could raise in event of war. The *Chicago Tribune* and the *World* conducted similar polls, and the results gave further emphasis to the campaign for intervention, since many prominent political leaders gave pro-Cuban answers.

Still there was not sufficient fodder for the *Journal's* intervention policy, and Hearst looked about for incidents which could be exploited. His first notable discovery was the case of a Cuban dentist named Ricardo Ruiz who was found dead in a Havana cell. Ruiz had at one time taken out naturalization papers in the United States and the *Journal* played this angle to the hilt. The *Chicago Tribune*, the *New Orleans Times-Democrat*, the *New York Sun*, the *San Francisco Examiner*, and other interventionist papers picked up the chant.

Hearst's greatest exploit came in the summer of 1897 when he built up the story of Evangelina Cisneros. Miss Cisneros, a niece of the Cuban revolutionary president, had been accused of luring a Spanish officer to her home where insurrectionists tried to kill him. Nine months after she had been sentenced to a 20-year prison term for rebellious activity, the *Journal* took up her cause. It described her as the most beautiful girl in all Cuba and pictured her as living in indescribable quarters in a Havana prison while awaiting transportation to an African penal settlement. Cried the *Journal*: "The unspeakable fate to which Weyler has doomed an innocent girl whose only crime is that she has defended her honor against a beast in uniform has sent a shudder of horror through the American people." When the *World* printed Weyler's version of the incident, and proved that the *Journal's* account of her sufferings was greatly exaggerated, the *Journal's* editors accused Pulitzer of unpatriotic motives.

After a month during which the *Journal* solicited pleas for Miss Cisneros' safety from scores of prominent American women, the paper acted. With giant headlines in a Sunday edition, it announced that a *Journal* reporter, Karl Decker, had succeeded in rescuing the girl from her prison cell and had smuggled her aboard a New York-bound ship. Secretary of State John Sherman, the Bishop of London, Clara Barton, Henry George, and other notables congratulated the *Journal* on its achievement. Even President William McKinley, who was firmly opposed to a war with Spain, found himself greeting Miss Cisneros at the White House. Some idea of the *Journal's* exploitation of the Cisneros case may be found in a compilation of newspaper space given the story. It was big news which no newspaper could ignore, but the figures for New York newspapers were as follows: The *World*, 12½ columns; the *Times*, 10 columns; the *Tribune*, 3½ columns; the *Sun*, one column; the *Herald*, one column; the *Journal*, 375 columns.[14]

[14] Wisan, *The Cuban Crisis*, p. 331.

Despite the energies of the *Journal* and other pro-Cuban newspapers, and of Cuban sympathizers in the country, it did not seem probable in late 1897 that any warlike action would be taken. Indeed, the trend was the other way. A change in the Spanish government had brought a new prime minister and promises from the Spanish crown that Cuba would be granted autonomy. The concentration camp policy was to be ended, and Weyler was recalled. The *World* and some other newspapers abated their campaigns, and President McKinley announced that American diplomatic representations in Madrid had been properly answered by the Spanish. Polls of congressional sentiment made by the *Journal* and *Herald* in December, 1897, showed most Republicans backing up McKinley, and most Democrats favoring at least recognition of Cuban belligerency. The majority opposed any demand for Cuban independence, which would inevitably force the Spanish into a war with the United States.

At this point the *Journal* again acted, scoring its most significant "scoop." On February 9, 1898, the Hearst paper published a private letter written by Dupuy de Lome, the Spanish ambassador to the United States, to a Spanish newspaper editor visiting in Havana. The letter, stolen in Havana by a Cuban junta member, referred to President McKinley as "weak and catering to the rabble, and, besides, a low politician." At the same moment Theodore Roosevelt was commenting that his chief had the backbone of a chocolate eclair, but to have the Spanish ambassador say the same thing—even in a private letter—was a different matter. American indignation was universal, although not everyone called for immediate war as did the *Journal*. De Lome was recalled to Madrid, and American opinion of the Spanish government hit a new low. The significance of the de Lome letter episode lies in the fact that it preceded by just six days the sinking of the battleship "Maine" in Havana harbor, and the impact of the two events proved to be the turning point in the diplomatic crisis.

THE SINKING OF THE "MAINE"

No one has satisfactorily established the cause of the explosion which sank the "Maine" with the loss of 266 American lives. The ship had been sent to Havana because Cuban independence leaders were inciting riots in an effort to forestall public acceptance of the Spanish government's autonomy policy. Resentment among the revolutionists was strong against American acceptance of the Spanish plan for a measure of Cuban self-government under continued Spanish sovereignty. If the "Maine" was blown up by an outside agent, rather than by an internal explosion as seems probable, a Cuban sympathizer could have been responsible. Certainly the Spanish government itself had every reason to avoid such an aggressive act, and no one seriously believed that the plot was hatched in Madrid. But some American newspapers set about to make it appear that the Spanish were indirectly responsible for the sinking.

$50,000 REWARD.—WHO DESTROYED THE MAINE?—$50,000 REWARD.

EDITION FOR GREATER NEW YORK

The Journal will give $50,000 for information, furnished to it exclusively, that will convict the person or persons who sank the Maine.

NEW YORK JOURNAL

AND ADVERTISER.

The Journal will give $50,000 for information, furnished to it exclusively, that will convict the person or persons who sank the Maine.

NO. 5,572. Copyright, 1898, by W. R. Hearst.—NEW YORK, THURSDAY, FEBRUARY 17, 1898.—16 PAGES. PRICE ONE CENT in Greater New York and Jersey City. | Elsewhere, TWO CENTS.

DESTRUCTION OF THE WAR SHIP MAINE WAS THE WORK OF AN ENEMY.

$50,000!

$50,000 REWARD!

For the Detection of the Perpetrator of the Maine Outrage!

The New York Journal hereby offers a reward of $50,000 CASH for information, FURNISHED TO IT EXCLUSIVELY, which shall lead to the detection and conviction of the person, persons or government criminally responsible for the explosions which resulted in the destruction, at Havana, of the United States war ship Maine and the loss of 258 lives of American sailors.

The $50,000 CASH offered for the above information is on deposit with Wells, Fargo & Co.

No one is barred, be he the humble but misguided seaman eking out a few miserable dollars by acting as a spy, or the attache of a government secret service, plotting, by any devilish means, to revenge fancied insults or cripple menacing countries.

This offer has been cabled to Europe and will be made public in every capital of the Continent and in London this morning.

The Journal believes that any man who can be bought to commit murder can also be bought to betray his comrades. FOR THE PERPETRATOR OF THIS OUTRAGE HAD ACCOMPLICES.

W. R. HEARST.

Assistant Secretary Roosevelt Convinced the Explosion of the War Ship Was Not an Accident.

The Journal Offers $50,000 Reward for the Conviction of the Criminals Who Sent 258 American Sailors to Their Death. Naval Officers Unanimous That the Ship Was Destroyed on Purpose.

$50,000!

$50,000 REWARD!

For the Detection of the Perpetrator of the Maine Outrage!

The New York Journal hereby offers a reward of $50,000 CASH for information, FURNISHED TO IT EXCLUSIVELY, which shall lead to the detection and conviction of the person, persons or government criminally responsible for the explosions which resulted in the destruction, at Havana, of the United States war ship Maine and the loss of 258 lives of American sailors.

The $50,000 CASH offered for the above information is on deposit with Wells, Fargo & Co.

No one is barred, be he the humble but misguided seaman eking out a few miserable dollars by acting as a spy, or the attache of a government secret service, plotting, by any devilish means, to revenge fancied insults or cripple menacing countries.

This offer has been cabled to Europe and will be made public in every capital of the Continent and in London this morning.

The Journal believes that any man who can be bought to commit murder can also be bought to betray his comrades. FOR THE PERPETRATOR OF THIS OUTRAGE HAD ACCOMPLICES.

W. R. HEARST.

NAVAL OFFICERS THINK THE MAINE WAS DESTROYED BY A SPANISH MINE.

George Eugene Bryson, the Journal's special correspondent at Havana, cables that it is the secret opinion of many Spaniards in the Cuban capital that the Maine was destroyed and 258 of her men killed by means of a submarine mine, or fixed torpedo. This is the opinion of several American naval authorities. The Spaniards, it is believed, arranged to have the Maine anchored over one of the harbor mines. Wires connected the mine with a powder magazine, and it is thought the explosion was caused by sending an electric current through the wire. If this can be proven, the brutal nature of the Spaniards will be shown by the fact that they waited to spring the mine until after all the men had retired for the night. The Maltese cross in the picture shows where the mine may have been fired.

Hidden Mine or a Sunken Torpedo Believed to Have Been the Weapon Used Against the American Man-of-War---Officers and Men Tell Thrilling Stories of Being Blown Into the Air Amid a Mass of Shattered Steel and Exploding Shells---Survivors Brought to Key West Scout the Idea of Accident---Spanish Officials Protest Too Much---Our Cabinet Orders a Searching Inquiry---Journal Sends Divers to Havana to Report Upon the Condition of the Wreck. Was the Vessel Anchored Over a Mine?

BY CAPTAIN E. L. ZALINSKI, U. S. A.

(Captain Zalinski is the inventor of the famous dynamite gun, which would be the principal factor in our coast defence in case of war.)

Assistant Secretary of the Navy Theodore Roosevelt says he is convinced that the destruction of the Maine in Havana Harbor was not an accident.

The Journal offers a reward of $50,000 for exclusive evidence that will convict the person, persons or Government criminally responsible for the destruction of the American battle ship and the death of 258 of its crew.

The suspicion that the Maine was deliberately blown up grows stronger every hour. Not a single fact to the contrary has been produced.

Captain Sigsbee, of the Maine, and Consul-General Lee both urge that public opinion be suspended until they have completed their investigation. They are taking the course of tactful men who are convinced that there has been treachery.

Washington reports very late that Captain Sigsbee had feared some such event as a hidden mine. The English cipher code was used all day yesterday by the naval officers in cabling instead of the usual American code.

Hearst's *Journal* for February 17. The "Maine" sank the night of the 15th.

The *Journal* offered a $50,000 reward for information leading to the arrest and conviction of the criminals—a fairly safe offer—but tipped off amateur detectives with its first-day streamer: "DESTRUCTION OF THE WAR SHIP MAINE WAS THE WORK OF AN ENEMY." Both the *Journal* and *World* rushed ships to Havana harbor to conduct diving operations, and both were indignant when Spanish and American authorities preferred to conduct their own investigations. Both papers carried misleading reports on the outcome of the official inquiries, as did the Associated Press, primarily because all concerned were eager to have the news in advance of official release. Three days after the sinking the *Journal's* streamer read: "THE WHOLE COUNTRY THRILLS WITH WAR FEVER."

Other newspapers were reflecting the same attitude, however. The *St. Paul Pioneer Press,* for example, ran these successive headlines based on Associated Press reports during the first seven days after the sinking: "Cruiser Maine Lost"; "It Looks Suspicious"; "Americans Aspersed"; "Captain Warned" (of impending destruction of his vessel); "Done by Spaniards"; "More Than Suspicious"; and "A Hostile Nation: Spain May Be Declared Such at Any Hour." These front page headlines had more effect than the editorial urgings for calm judgment written by editor Joseph A. Wheelock, whose voice was important in his area. It was two months before the final break between the two countries but in many newspapers the ultimate verdict already had been made clear.

Large headlines and striking illustrations became common in big city papers like the *Journal* and *World* during the "Maine" crisis. The first three pages of the *World* were devoted daily to the war story; in the *Journal* it was the first eight. Leading the field in yellow journalism techniques was Arthur Brisbane, editor of the *Evening Journal.* Brisbane loved big headline types, and he experimented with giant artist-drawn types which virtually filled the front page with two or three words. Writing in a popular magazine at the close of the war, Brisbane had this to say about his activities:

> Before the type size reached its maximum, "War Sure" could be put in one line across a page, and it was put in one line and howled through the streets by patriotic newsboys many and many a time. As war was sure, it did no harm.[15]

If Brisbane wrote so frankly in 1898, clearly he thought the temper of the people was with him. And it was. During February and March the newspapers began to be filled with news of preparations for war, of the formation of volunteer troop units such as the Rough Riders, of the passage of a 50-million-dollar defense bill by Congress, of the marshaling of resources. President McKinley still stood against the war trend, but his Secretary of State, Sherman, who more than once made official statements based on news reports from the

[15] Arthur Brisbane, "The Modern Newspaper in War Time," *Cosmopolitan,* XXV (September, 1898), 541.

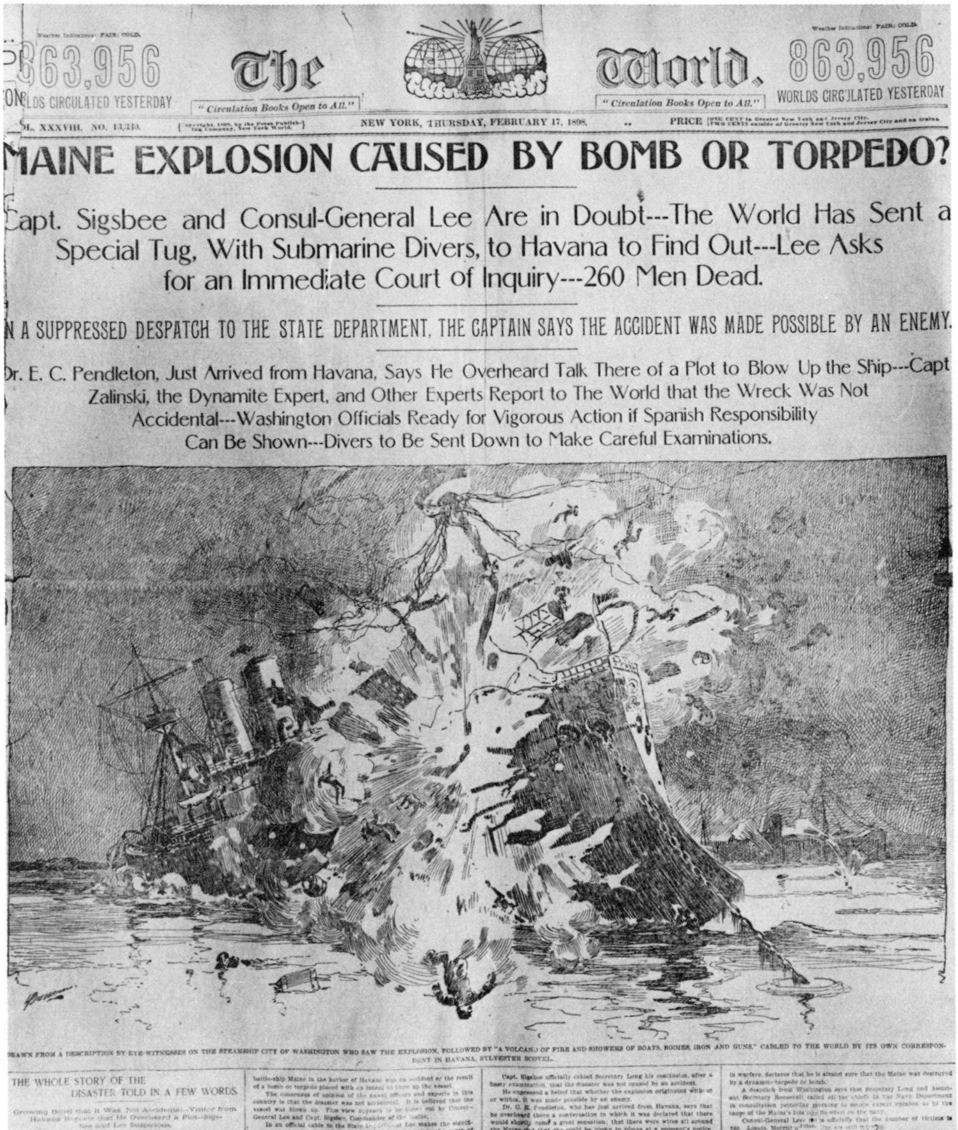

863,956 WORLDS CIRCULATED YESTERDAY

"Circulation Books Open to All."

The World.

"Circulation Books Open to All."

863,956 WORLDS CIRCULATED YESTERDAY

NEW YORK, THURSDAY, FEBRUARY 17, 1898.

MAINE EXPLOSION CAUSED BY BOMB OR TORPEDO?

Capt. Sigsbee and Consul-General Lee Are in Doubt---The World Has Sent a Special Tug, With Submarine Divers, to Havana to Find Out---Lee Asks for an Immediate Court of Inquiry---260 Men Dead.

IN A SUPPRESSED DESPATCH TO THE STATE DEPARTMENT, THE CAPTAIN SAYS THE ACCIDENT WAS MADE POSSIBLE BY AN ENEMY.

Dr. E. C. Pendleton, Just Arrived from Havana, Says He Overheard Talk There of a Plot to Blow Up the Ship---Capt Zalinski, the Dynamite Expert, and Other Experts Report to The World that the Wreck Was Not Accidental---Washington Officials Ready for Vigorous Action if Spanish Responsibility Can Be Shown---Divers to Be Sent Down to Make Careful Examinations.

DRAWN FROM A DESCRIPTION BY EYE-WITNESSES ON THE STEAMSHIP CITY OF WASHINGTON WHO SAW THE EXPLOSION, FOLLOWED BY "A VOLCANO OF FIRE AND SHOWERS OF BOATS, BODIES, IRON AND GUNS," CABLED TO THE WORLD BY ITS OWN CORRESPONDENT IN HAVANA, SYLVESTER SCOVEL.

THE WHOLE STORY OF THE DISASTER TOLD IN A FEW WORDS.

The *World's* February 17 front page, somewhat more cautious than that of the *Journal.*

Journal, swung back to his original pro-Cuban beliefs. The young Republicans, led by Theodore Roosevelt, were so outspoken that it became obvious to McKinley that a split was developing in his party. When in mid-March a leading Republican senator, Proctor of Vermont, made a speech based on his personal investigation of conditions in Cuba, which bore out much of what the newspapers had said for three years, the swing toward war was definitely underway. By the time diplomatic negotiations with Spain had produced a complete victory for the United States on issues which were at stake between the two countries, pro-war and anti-war newspapers alike were in a frame of mind to brush the Spanish offers aside as "untrustworthy and too late." Congress passed a resolution on April 18 looking toward United States intervention in Cuba, which Spain considered as a declaration of war.

The *World* at first had urged caution in handling the "Maine" question, in its editorial comment. But gradually it had swung around, until by April 10 Pulitzer had published a signed editorial calling for a "short and sharp" war. The *New York Sun,* which under Dana's cynical editorship had been extremely jingoistic, stood with the *Journal* and *World* in demanding intervention. The *New York Herald,* while keeping up in sensational news coverage, opposed intervention in its editorial stands—an incongruity also true of the *Chicago Times-Herald, Boston Herald, San Francisco Chronicle,* and *Milwaukee Sentinel.* Strongly interventionist were such papers as the *Chicago Tribune, New Orleans Times-Democrat, Atlanta Constitution,* and *Indianapolis Journal.* Keeping calm were such papers as the *New York Tribune, New York Times, Chicago Daily News, Boston Transcript,* and other papers that reflected the thinking of the business community in their editorial columns. Wilkerson, in his study of the newspapers for the period, ranks the *Journal* as the leader in excessive journalism, and the *Chicago Tribune* and the *World* next in order. Joseph Medill's *Tribune,* strongly nationalistic in its editorial columns, did not originate sensational news stories as did the *Journal* and *World,* but it ran the cream of those collected by both papers.

THE *WORLD'S* STAND ON NATIONALISM

It should be pointed out, too, that the *World* was not a jingo newspaper. It opposed annexation of foreign territory by the United States, in contrast with the *Sun* and *Journal,* which were willing to expand the country in any direction. Pulitzer fought the annexation of Hawaii, and when the Spanish-American War was over, sought to prevent the annexation of the Philippines. Most of the other interventionist papers approved of territorial expansion. The *World* based its call for war on the issue of human liberty, and in subsequent actions proved that it was not merely jingoistic. Pulitzer realized the part his paper played in preparing public opinion for the war, and later regretted it; in 1907, when Theodore Roosevelt ordered the American fleet to the Pacific to impress Japan, Pulitzer requested his editors to "show that Spain had granted to Cuba all that we demanded. . . . Give further details of jingoism causing Cuban War after Spain had virtually granted everything." [16]

[16] Don C. Seitz, *Joseph Pulitzer* (New York: Simon & Schuster, 1924), p. 312.

LAST EDITION The Evening Post. LAST EDITION

ESTABLISHED 1801.—VOL. 97. NEW YORK, WEDNESDAY, FEBRUARY 16, 1898. - - FOURTEEN PAGES. PRICE THREE CENTS.

BATTLE-SHIP MAINE BLOWN UP

LATEST DETAILS OF THE DISASTER AT HAVANA.

Two Hundred and Seventy-five Men Killed and Missing—Capt. Sigsbee and All Except Two Officers Saved—The War-Ship Destroyed—Aid from the Spanish Cruiser Alfonso XII.—Cause of the Explosion Not Yet Ascertained—Quiet in Havana.

ACTION IN WASHINGTON.

A SPECIAL CABINET MEETING HELD.

A Message of Information to Congress Prepared, but Withheld—Invitations Recalled by the President—A Despatch to Capt. Sigsbee.

THE ZOLA TRIAL.

ANOTHER DAY OF EXCITING TESTIMONY.

Strong Statements by Gen. Pellieux Regarding the Guilt of Dreyfus and the Experts who Testified in Support of the Charges Against Major Esterhazy.

SUNK IN THE DELAWARE.

A TUGBOAT SWAMPED.

TWO MEN DROWNED IN THE UPPER BAY.

Rescue of the Others by the Staten Island Ferry-boat Castleton—High Waves and the Wash of a Steamship the Cause of the Accident.

Godkin's *Post* played the "Maine" story in lead position, then column one, on February 16, saying simply: "BATTLE-SHIP MAINE BLOWN UP".

Indeed, only a little more than two years before the outbreak of the Spanish-American War, Joseph Pulitzer and the *World* had made a notable contribution to world peace by opposing President Cleveland's headstrong action in the Venezuelan crisis. The boundary line between Venezuela and British Guiana was in dispute, and Great Britain's demands upon the South American country violated the principle of the Monroe Doctrine, according to many Americans. Cleveland finally demanded that the British submit the dispute to arbitration, and warned that if necessary the United States would fight to uphold Venezuela's claims. The *World* immediately opposed the President, although most other New York papers rallied to his support.

Pulitzer's editorial column insisted that the spirit of the Monroe Doctrine was not being violated by the British (who, ironically enough, had helped Monroe make his statement stick in the 1820s). The *World* added that war between the two English-speaking countries would be a "colossal crime." Then Pulitzer sent cable messages to leading Englishmen, asking for their opinions. The Prince of Wales, the Duke of York, former prime minister Gladstone, and other men well known to Americans all replied that England did not want war. The *World* published their replies on Christmas eve, 1895, under a banner headline which read, "Messages of Peace, Common Sense and Humanity to the People of the United States." Secretary of State Olney and Senator Henry Cabot Lodge tried to prove that Pultizer had carried on diplomatic activities as a private citizen in violation of the law, but a reaction against war brought both a settlement of the international dispute and a resounding victory for Pulitzer.

In this instance, the *World* stood against popular sentiment in opposing war; in New York only Godkin's *Evening Post* put up the same kind of fight. But Godkin did not spare Pulitzer when he lashed out against the pro-war newspapers of 1898. Referring to Pulitzer and Hearst he said, "It is a crying shame that men should work such mischief simply in order to sell more papers." The *Evening Post* fought to the end against the decision to force Spain from Cuba, and bitterly attacked the sensational newspapers with such statements as this:

> A yellow journal office is probably the nearest approach, in atmosphere, to hell, existing in any Christian state. A better place in which to prepare a young man for eternal damnation than a yellow journal office does not exist.

Godkin was not guiltless on his side, however. When Senator Proctor made his crucial speech substantiating much of the evidence the correspondents had offered from Cuba, the *Evening Post* printed only a dozen lines in its news columns. Other newspapers carried extensive quotations from Proctor's speech, or printed the text in full. Godkin instead sought to minimize the impact of the speech by argument in his editorial column.[17]

All in all, while Godkin's criticism of Pulitzer was justified, the *World's* publisher did not deserve to be bracketed with Hearst, whose *Journal* gleefully asked in its front-page ears, "How do you like the Journal's war?"

THE CORRESPONDENTS GO TO WAR

The newspapers fought the war as determinedly as they had fostered it. Some 500 reporters, artists, and photographers flocked to Florida, where the American army was mobilizing, and to the Cuban and Puerto Rican fronts.[18] Small fleets of press boats accompanied the Navy into action. Correspondents sailed with Dewey to Manila and with Schley to Havana. They covered every battle and skirmish in Cuba and more than once took part in the fighting itself. A *Journal* correspondent lost a leg during one fighting charge. Richard Harding Davis, then reporting for the *New York Herald* and the *Times* of London, led another charge and won the praise of Rough Rider Roosevelt.

17 Wisan, *The Cuban Crisis,* p. 417.

18 Their story is told by Charles H. Brown in *The Correspondents' War* (New York: Scribner's, 1967).

Among the correspondents were famous writers, including Frank Norris, Stephen Crane, Julian Hawthorne, and of course Davis. Murat Halstead, James Creelman, Sylvester Scovel, and other leading correspondents took in this war as they had others. So did many less qualified journalists, even including the drama editor of the *Sun* and the humor editor of the *World*. As one newspaperman of the time put it, you didn't have any influence if you couldn't get to be a war correspondent.

Leading the *Journal's* contingent was the publisher himself, who exuded enthusiasm as he directed the work of his staff of 20 men and women reporters, artists, and photographers, including a motion picture man. Creelman, who was wounded in one battle, records a picture of Hearst—wearing a beribboned straw hat on his head and a revolver at his belt—taking the story from his bleeding reporter and then galloping away on horseback to get to a *Journal* press boat. Even more dramatic was Hearst's participation in the battle off Santiago when Admiral Cervera's hapless fleet was destroyed as it sought to escape along the Cuban shore. Hearst's flagship had to be warned off with a shot across the bow, so close did the eager *Journal* men get to the fighting. As the battle ended Hearst leaped from his yacht to capture a band of Spanish sailors huddled on the beach. He then sailed to the American flagship, delivered the prisoners, and hustled off to record the story for the *Journal's* readers.

American correspondents were learning how to use the cables to speed their messages to the news offices. Stories from Cuba had to be brought by boat to Key West for transmission to New York, with leading papers sending several thousand words a day. All this was expensive, but the race for news was an exciting one. The *World* scored the biggest single beat when Edward W. Harden, one of three correspondents to witness Dewey's amazing victory in Manila Bay, got his story off first by paying the "urgent" priority rate of $9.90 a word. Harden's beat arrived in New York too far into the dawn for the *World* to capitalize on it with a full-blown extra, but the *World's* news client, the *Chicago Tribune*, had time to revamp its final edition and carry the most dramatic story of the war.

Circulations leaped upward with the war news, but profits went down for the big dailies. The cost of the correspondents, press boats, and cable tolls ran high; the *Journal* spent half a million dollars to lead the pack in its coverage of the four-month war. Competition in extras was an expensive business, as well as a wearing one. The *Journal* put out as many as 40 extras in a single day, and Arthur Brisbane complained that it taxed the staff's ingenuity to make each new one look different from the last. Advertising volume declined during the war period, to make certain that there was no profit in the venture for Pulitzer and Hearst. Hearst said he did not care, so long as the *Journal* beat every paper in the world with its war coverage. But Pulitzer viewed the situation with dismay. He didn't like the many extras and big headlines; he liked even less the extravagant costs and the wiping out of the *World's* profits. When the war was over Pulitzer breathed a sigh of relief.

Yellow journalism did not come to an end at the same time, however. The competing newspapers turned to the familiar subjects of sensationalism: crime, sex, the doings of the famous and the infamous, disasters, and new wars. The devices of yellow journalism continued to be used: scare-heads and sensationalized makeup; lurid stories, many of them faked; attention to the unimportant but exciting news; the colored supplements of the Sunday paper; and lavish illustrations, with photographs ever more in demand. The yellow journalist did not care where he got his pictures; photos of European women would do nicely to illustrate wire stories from other cities. By 1900 about one-third of metropolitan dailies were following the yellow trend which the *Journal* had set in New York. It was another 10 years before the wave of sensationalism subsided, as it had before, and newspapermen concentrated on intelligent use of the devices which had marked its rise—headlines, pictures, and color printing.

The *World* withdrew from the competition in sensationalism at the turn of the century. A leading critic of the press, Oswald Garrison Villard, said of Pulitzer, "like many another he deliberately stooped for success, and then, having achieved it, slowly put on garments of righteousness." But Pulitzer foresaw what Hearst did not: the excesses of yellow journalism would undermine public confidence in the newspaper. Both Pulitzer and Hearst were champions of the common man—as was almost any yellow journal published, at least ostensibly—and in the first decade of the twentieth century both took strong stands in behalf of social justice and progress. But Hearst continued to exploit the news in a manner which seriously impeded the effectiveness of his role as a people's champion. It is to a period of the rise to prominence of the crusading liberal and the muckraker that we now turn.

Annotated Bibliography

Books

Beisner, Robert L., *Twelve Against Empire: The Anti-Imperialists, 1898–1900.* New York: McGraw-Hill, 1968. Two of the twelve were Godkin and Schurz.

Bleyer, Willard G., *Main Currents in the History of American Journalism.* Boston: Houghton Mifflin, 1927. The chapter on Hearst admirably documents charges of sensationalism.

Brown, Charles H., *The Correspondents' War.* New York: Scribner's, 1967. All the details of the press corps for the Spanish-American War.

Carlson, Oliver, *Brisbane: A Candid Biography.* New York: Stackpole Sons, 1937. A good critical analysis of the famous Hearst editor.

Carlson, Oliver, and Ernest Sutherland Bates, *Hearst, Lord of San Simeon.* New York: Viking, 1936. Better than other early biographies by John K. Winkler and Mrs. Fremont Older. Still useful for the early Hearst period, but supplanted by Tebbel and Swanberg (see below).

Davis, Richard Harding, *Notes of a War Correspondent.* New York: Scribner's, 1910. An American war correspondent in Cuba, Greece, South Africa, and Manchuria, covering four wars.

Lundberg, Ferdinand, *Imperial Hearst: A Social Biography.* New York: Equinox Cooperative Press, 1936. A bitter attack on the chain publisher; valuable particularly for financial data.

Merk, Frederick, *Manifest Destiny and Mission in American History: A Reinterpretation.* New York: Knopf, 1963. Newspapers document the story of the westward march.

Millis, Walter, *The Martial Spirit; a Study of Our War with Spain.* Boston: Houghton Mifflin, 1931. A readable, critical account.

Swanberg, W. A., *Citizen Hearst.* New York: Scribner's, 1961. A highly readable study, covering available printed sources in meticulous detail; has some new material.

Tebbel, John, *The Life and Good Times of William Randolph Hearst.* New York: Dutton, 1952. A well-balanced biography and the best documented study of the Hearst newspaper empire.

Wilkerson, Marcus M., *Public Opinion and the Spanish-American War.* Baton Rouge: Louisiana State University Press, 1932. A scholarly study of war propaganda and press influence.

Wisan, Joseph E., *The Cuban Crisis as Reflected in the New York Press.* New York: Columbia University Press, 1934. A good specialized study.

Periodicals and Monographs

Berg, Meredith and David, "The Rhetoric of War Preparation: The New York Press in 1898," *Journalism Quarterly,* XLV (Winter 1968), 653. Analysis of New York dailies after sinking of the "Maine."

Brisbane, Arthur, "The Modern Newspaper in War Time," *Cosmopolitan,* XXV (September 1898), 541. The *Journal* editor confesses his sins. See also his "Yellow Journalism," *Bookman,* XIX (June 1904), 400.

Brown, Charles H., "Press Censorship in the Spanish-American War," *Journalism Quarterly,* XLII (Autumn 1965), 581. It was more extensive and effective than believed.

Commander, Lydia K., "The Significance of Yellow Journalism," *Arena,* XXXIV (August 1905), 150. A contemporary analysis.

Donald, Robert, "Sunday Newspapers in the United States," *Universal Review,* VIII (September 1890), 79. A look at a then-new medium.

Hachten, William A., "The Metropolitan Sunday Newspaper in the United States: A Study of Trends in Content and Practices." Ph.D. thesis, University of Minnesota, 1960 (Ann Arbor: University Microfilms, 1960). The most complete study of the Sunday paper.

Irwin, Will, "The American Newspaper," *Collier's*, XLVI (February 18 and March 4, 1911). The sins of yellow journalism described.

Mott, Frank L., "The First Sunday Paper: A Footnote to History," *Journalism Quarterly*, XXXV (Fall 1958), 443. The *Boston Globe*.

Peters, Glen W., "The *American Weekly*," *Journalism Quarterly*, XLVIII (Autumn 1971), 466. A review of the Sunday supplements, especially Hearst's.

Steffens, Lincoln, "Hearst, the Man of Mystery," *American Magazine*, LXIII (November 1906), 3. Penetrating study based on interviews of Hearst, rarely obtained.

Vanderburg, Ray, "The Paradox That Was Arthur Brisbane," *Journalism Quarterly*, XLVII (Summer 1970), 281. Study of the great Hearst editor.

Zobrist, Benedict Karl, "How Victor Lawson's Newspapers Covered the Cuban War of 1898," *Journalism Quarterly*, XXXVIII (Summer 1961), 323. The non-sensational *Chicago Record* and *Daily News*.

Scripps-Howard

Edward Wyllis Scripps aboard his yacht near the close of his career.

20

The People's Champions

I have only one principle, and that is represented by an effort to make it harder for the rich to grow richer and easier for the poor to keep from growing poorer.
—Edward Wyllis Scripps

The opening of the twentieth century found the United States moving toward a consolidation of its position as an industrial nation. The framework had been completed by 1900: the economic expansion which had begun after the Civil War, the growth in population and the tying together of the country, the rapid development of rich natural resources, the inventive and productive genius, the political and cultural advances—all ensured the future of a new world power.

Vital contests still were in progress, however, which would affect the character of the new America. These contests assumed critical importance at a moment when the economic, political, and social trends of a new era were being shaped. How would the nation conduct itself in the world community? How democratic would it remain? Would there be a balance struck between the advocates of unrestricted economic individualism and the crusaders for social justice? Would the fruits of progress be shared by all the people, in the form of better living conditions, educational and cultural opportunities, higher health standards, and personal security? Would government be responsive to the general welfare? What was to be the role of the press in advancing or retarding necessary adjustments?

Men had struggled to obtain affirmative answers to these questions now confronting America since the industrial revolution changed the character of American society. The "consistent rebellion" in the agricultural areas against economic inequities represented one phase of the struggle; the rise of the labor unions in the cities another. The growth of strong political movements which sought to place more power in the hands of the people generally; the efforts of the social scientists to impart knowledge on which wise social and political decisions could be based; the appeals of reformers, agitators, political leaders, and writers for an arousing of the country's social conscience—all these had helped to shape the direction in which the country would turn.

But in the first years of the new century there were major divisions of thought and action which indicated the crucial importance of the struggle to shape public opinion, and to enforce the popular will. Nationalists and internationalists contended in the field of foreign affairs. Economic individualists and social reformers clashed in the domestic arena. The mass media of the times—newspapers, magazines, books—played a most important role in these national debates.

THE TRIUMPH OF "MANIFEST DESTINY"

America's movements on the world stage were contradictory, as might well be expected of the newcomer. Instinctive isolationism dominated the thinking of many Americans, while some advocated an aggressive nationalism. International "idealists," as they were called, had to contend with both oppositions, as they sought to put the weight of the United States behind actions which would lead to world peace and economic and social progress.

The supporters of nationalism and dollar diplomacy exercised considerable power in the years preceding World War I. The treaty which the United States wrote at the end of the Spanish-American War gave it an empire. The new American position in the Pacific was solidified by the crushing of a native revolution in the Philippines—with horrifying cruelties practiced on Filipino soldiers and massacres of civilians—and by Theodore Roosevelt's "showing of the fleet" as a warning to Japan. The Panama Canal was built in an annexed zone which Colombia complained had been torn from her by an American-backed revolution. This action, and the extension of American military and economic domination in the Central American and Caribbean areas, dissipated hopes for Pan-American understanding. Cuba and Panama virtually became American protectorates under the Platt amendment. The Dominican Republic, Haiti, and Nicaragua in turn were forced to accept United States intervention in their affairs under the Roosevelt corollary to the Monroe Doctrine, by which the United States undertook to preserve order in those countries and administer their financial affairs to prevent any possible intervention by European powers. The primary intent was to assure American security in a vital area, but American trade and financial interests followed the flag—and many persons complained that they sometimes preceded it.

At the same time, however, there were powerful forces in operation which sought to commit America to a quite different role in world affairs. Cultural and religious ties were made with China after the Boxer Rebellion. The Philippines were promised their eventual independence after a period of tutelage. Roosevelt himself acted as a mediator in helping to end the Russo-Japanese War and in smoothing relations among Germany, France, and Britain at the Algeciras conference. The United States accepted the idea of an international court of arbitration, advanced at The Hague Peace Conference of 1899, and negotiated several arbitration treaties. Americans played a leading part in the unsuccessful attempt to create an international court of justice during the second conference at The Hague in 1907. Out of these movements came American leadership in proposing the League of Nations and the World Court at the close of World War I—proposals which most of the other nations of the world adopted only to see the United States slump back into isolationism.

THE CRISIS OF ECONOMIC POWER

Important as was this contest over foreign policy, it was not the major concern of the American people in the years around the turn of the century. Their attention was centered largely upon domestic problems created by the industrial revolution: the growth of trusts and centralization of economic power in a few hands; the inadequate incomes of the workingman and farmer; corruption and inadequacies in political and business life. To many Americans it seemed that national wealth and strength, while reflecting basic progress for all the people, actually were mainly benefiting a plundering few who were usurping the freedoms of the many.[1]

Concentration of economic power, which had begun to develop rapidly in the 1880s, was greatly accentuated after 1900. A study made in 1904 listed 318 industrial trusts, three-fourths of which had been incorporated since 1898. These 318 trusts, capitalized at 7 billion dollars, represented the merging of 5,300 individuals plants. Seven big trusts—in steel, oil, copper, sugar, tobacco, and shipping—which had been organized in those six years were capitalized at 2½ billions. Census figures show that in 1914 one-eighth of American businesses employed more than three-fourths of the wage earners and produced four-fifths of the manufactured products.

The newspaper and magazine editors and the reporters and writers who joined in protesting this economic monopoly were even more concerned with the seemingly insatiable appetite of capitalists for power. Those who won

[1] One documented study of the period is Harold U. Faulkner, *The Quest for Social Justice, 1898–1914* (New York: Macmillan, 1931). A full and fascinating account by a journalistic historian is found in the first three volumes of Mark Sullivan, *Our Times* (New York: Scribner's, 1926 ff.). For a revisionist study with a New Left emphasis, see Gabriel Kolko, *The Triumph of Conservatism: A Reinterpretation of American History, 1900–1916* (Chicago: Quadrangle Books, 1967).

domination in one field promptly reached out into other spheres, until the country's financial power fell largely into the hands of two loosely-organized groups, the Morgan and the Rockefeller interests and their satellites. The famous Pujo committee investigation in 1913 reported that four allied financial institutions in New York held 341 directorships in banks, railroads, shipping lines, insurance companies, public utilities, and other businesses with total resources of 22 billion dollars.

Distribution of the wealth being created was heavily one-sided. Two-thirds of the male adult workers failed to earn $600 a year in wages, which was the figure set by sociologists as the minimum needed to maintain decent standards, at the current cost of living. There were many material and social advances being made—electricity, gas, and plumbing in homes; better schools and parks; the conveniences of city life; telephones, railroads, and highways. But they did not mean much to the millions in the New York tenements whose plight had been reported on by Jacob Riis.

Labor union membership increased between 1900 and 1910, jumping from 3.5 per cent of all workers to 7 per cent. The gains were being made by skilled workers: the railway brotherhoods, building trades, machinists, miners, printing trades, and garment workers groups. Unskilled workers, women workers, and immigrants remained victims of the economic order. Immigrants were a major factor in creating the social problem. The flood of immigrants of the period 1880 to 1900 was equaled in the single decade 1900 to 1910. The great bulk of the new immigration was from southern and eastern Europe, and a fourth of those arriving were illiterate. By 1910 one-seventh of the United States population was foreign-born, and in the industrial East more than half the population was foreign-born or of foreign-born parentage. These were the "poor and ill-informed" who were to be championed by such newspaper publishers as Edward Wyllis Scripps.

DEMANDS FOR POLITICAL AND ECONOMIC REFORM

Despite the fact that these conditions inevitably demanded reform, the "quest for social justice" was slow. Eugene V. Debs did see his Socialist party win nearly a million votes in the presidential election of 1912, and some 300 cities and towns elected Socialist officeholders. In the labor movement William D. Haywood and his Industrial Workers of the World sought a radical approach to the plight of the unskilled laborer. But political leadership remained in the hands of the two major political parties, and most labor followed the moderate program of Samuel Gompers and his American Federation of Labor.

The instruments for political action on the national level were Theodore Roosevelt's "Square Deal" and Woodrow Wilson's "New Freedom." But the decisions which these two administrations won in the fields of monetary reform, government regulation of business, welfare legislation, and tariff revision stemmed from the spirit of the times. This spirit was reflected in various forms by the agitation of the Populists, the great crusade headed by William Jennings Bryan in 1896, the governmental reforms being proposed by Robert La Follette and his individualistic Wisconsin progressives, the work of the labor union leaders, and the thinking and writing of the intellectuals.

In the Roosevelt years the winning of an antitrust suit against the Northern Securities Company, preventing a monopoly of railroad transportation west of the Mississippi, turned the tide against extreme concentration of economic power. The Hepburn Act brought effective government regulation of transportation rates. And Roosevelt's conservation policies saved a sizable residue of America's natural resources from ruthless exploitation. In the Wilson administration the creation of the Federal Reserve banking system brought a modern currency and credit system to the country for the first time; the Clayton Act struck at the abusive use of court injunctions and contempt citations against striking labor unions; the Federal Trade Commission was given power to regulate unfair business practices; and in other areas government extended its influence to a greater degree than ever before in American history.

But the progress which was being made, while substantial, was hampered and often balked by the supporters of big business. Senators like Nelson Aldrich of Rhode Island were frank spokesmen for the conservative cause and they had great influence. Congressmen like George Norris of Nebraska could clip the wings of House Speaker Joe Cannon, a powerful ally of the big-business forces, but they nevertheless lost many battles to their conservative opposition. William Howard Taft, succeeding Roosevelt as president, was unable to cope with the big-business elements of his Republican party, and an irate Roosevelt launched his third party Progressive movement in 1912. The Bull Moose crusade failed, but it split the Republican party so thoroughly that Woodrow Wilson entered the White House with a minority of the popular vote to inaugurate a Democratic administration.

Many of the gains were made at state and local levels. Popular election of United States senators, presidential primaries, and adoption of the referendum, initiative, and recall were manifestations of the new trend. State laws protecting working women and children, regulating hours of work, providing for workmen's compensation, and advancing social security generally ran the gauntlet of unfavorable court decisions. In the cities, reform movements led by such men as Samuel M. Jones in Toledo, Tom Johnson and Newton D. Baker in Cleveland, Seth Low in New York, and the advocates of commission government in Galveston did yeoman work in restoring governmental decency. Corruption in municipal councils and in state legislatures was a common mark of the times, and newspaper editors who wished to join with the reformers had almost unbelievable instances of bribe-taking and graft to expose.

"THE PEOPLE'S CHAMPIONS"

The crusading spirit is as old as journalism, but never in American history had there been more opportunity for "the people's champions" than in these years following 1900. Voices of protest were raised in colonial days by men like James Franklin and Samuel Adams, in the early years of the republic by Jeffersonian and Jacksonian editors, by the creators of the first mass press before the Civil War, by the leaders of the "new journalism" before the close of the century. The struggle between big business and workers and farmers was as old as the struggle between the Hamiltonians and Jeffersonians for control of the government. The battle for the rights of labor and for a more equitable distribution of wealth was a basic issue of similar standing. And warring upon corruption in city governments had been a job for conscientious newspapermen since the rise of urban life. In the ebb and flow of these contests, however, the years following 1900 became critical ones.

Some newspapers were conspicuous in their response to the challenge. So were some of the new popular magazines, which became important vehicles for those whom Teddy Roosevelt eventually termed the "muckrakers." And the school of realistic writers which flowered at the turn of the century added important books to the American literature which dealt with life and problems of the day. Joining hands with politicians and labor leaders, reformers and agitators, professors and ministers, social workers and philanthropists, the men of journalism and literature helped to shape the course of the great crusade.

PULITZER'S CRUSADES IN THE *WORLD*

Joseph Pulitzer and his *New York World* became increasingly effective as "people's champions" in the years which followed the Spanish-American War. In foreign affairs the *World* vigorously opposed the annexation of the Philippines and the imperialism of the Caribbean policy. It continued to support the internationalist movement and the policy of peaceful arbitration of the world's problems, which it had espoused during the Venezuelan crisis. In domestic politics, this stand of the *World* on foreign policy led it to support William Jennings Bryan for president in 1900 on an "anti-imperialism" platform, ignoring Bryan's radical monetary policies which Pulitzer disliked.

The independent qualities and the crusading spirit of the *World* reached new heights, both on local and national issues. This was not a sudden manifestation of interest in crusading, as in the case of some other newspapers of the period, but a flowering of the Pulitzer editorial-page philosophy. Pulitzer, while agreeing that the *World* was Democrat in political sympathy, argued that his newspaper was independent of party and supported only those elements in a political party whose objectives coincided with those of the *World.* In looking at the major political parties of his day, Pulitzer put little trust in a Republican party with strong elements representing the big-business interests of the country, although he admired and supported Republican insurgents who fought to break the power of Speaker Cannon, or Republican candidates of the caliber of Governor Charles Evans Hughes of New York. Pulitzer decided that the Democratic party best represented the political philosophy in which he believed, and was most likely to act as the defender of individual liberties, grass-roots government, and progressive democracy. The *World's* role, he believed, was to fight unceasingly for that kind of a Democratic party.

Thus the *World* fought bossism, whether that of Tammany Hall in New York City Democratic politics or that of Senator Thomas C. Platt in New York State Republican politics. The *World* lashed out against the conservatism of Mark Hanna, Nelson Aldrich, and other Republican defenders of big-business interests, and editorialized unceasingly against the "money power" of J. P. Morgan. But it also opposed what it called the "socialistic and paternalistic" policies of Bryan and what it called the "personal government" of Theodore Roosevelt, even though both men were in the liberal movement of their time. The *World* feared that centralization of governmental power would result in bureaucratic control of the business and individual life of the country—and it particularly feared that a centralized government of great power created by liberals would only fall under the domination of reactionary property and money interests. The *World,* like any other organ of opinion, was not always consistent in the application of its basic beliefs to specific events, however. While it feared Theodore Roosevelt's attempts to strengthen the powers of the federal government and the presidency, it favored Woodrow Wilson's extensive program of legislation enacted under Democratic auspices, from which came many of the results the *World* had feared in the Roosevelt period.

But the *World* did not follow blindly a political leader it admired nor did it oppose automatically one it disliked. It had first won national attention by supporting Grover Cleveland for the presidency in 1884, but it did not hesitate to oppose him on the Venezuelan issue. And while the *World* opposed Theodore Roosevelt personally, it applauded his mediation of the Russo-Japanese War, his prosecution of the Northern Securities case, and his efforts to intervene in business and industrial affairs as the champion of the public interest. When the lengthy coal miners' strike of 1902 became a paramount public issue, the *World,* unlike many conservative papers, agreed that Roosevelt was right in cooperating with John Mitchell, the coal miners' union leader, and forcing the mine operators to arbitrate the issues involved. This was a highly significant episode, for it not only involved recognition of the labor movement, but also the recognition by business management of the joint interests of owners, workers, and the public in the economic life of the country. The White House had intervened before in labor disputes of national import, but only to maintain order and to protect life and property. Henceforth the executive branch of the government, and the president, would take part in similar major crises as an interested party representing the public—a step which the *World* approved, even though its editors were fundamentally opposed to Roosevelt's "big stick" tactics.[2]

FRANK COBB EDITS THE *WORLD*

Part of the *World's* new strength in its editorial columns was the result of a revamping of its editorial-page staff. The ailing Pulitzer, tortured by the acute nervous disorders which made the last few years of his life a nightmare, found in 1904 a brilliant young editor who was destined to become the central force of the *World's* editorial page. His name was Frank I. Cobb.

Realizing that William H. Merrill, the effective editorial-page editor for 15 years, was nearing the end of his career, Pulitzer looked about for a successor. He had lost most of a talented staff of editorial writers, including George Cary Eggleston, David Graham Phillips, and John A. Dillon. So one of Pulitzer's personal secretaries was sent across the country, looking for an editorial writer who would disprove Pulitzer's epigram: "Every reporter is a hope; every editor is a disappointment."

The secretary found his man in Detroit. Cobb was then 35, a veteran of 15 years' newspaper experience who had been for four years the chief editorial writer for the *Detroit Free Press*. His somewhat limited formal education had been greatly supplemented by his scholarly interest and wide reading in the fields of history, government, and philosophy, and by his experiences as a newspaper reporter and as a political correspondent covering several Michigan legislative sessions and three national political conventions. Cobb early had demonstrated the maturity of his judgment and his great intellectual capacity; but he was also a man who understood human nature and who attracted others to him by his friendliness, his eagerness, and his enthusiasm for living.[3]

The secretary telegraphed to Pulitzer that the man had been found who could be entrusted with control of the *World's* editorial page while the editor-owner was absent, cruising on his yacht or sojourning in Europe in quest of the relaxation and quiet his health demanded. But Pulitzer's answer illustrates the extreme concern he had for the quality of the *World's* editorial columns and the heavy demands he made upon those who wrote for it:

> What has Cobb read in American history, Rhodes, McMaster, Trevelyan, Parkman? What works on the constitution and constitutional law?

[2] For Pulitzer's reactions to Theodore Roosevelt, see W. A. Swanberg, *Pulitzer* (New York: Scribner's, 1967), p. 308.

[3] For a sketch of Cobb and a collection of his important editorials, see John L. Heaton, *Cobb of "The World"* (New York: Dutton, 1924).

> Has he read Buckle's history of civilization? Where did he stand during the Bryan free silver campaigns? What about the state of his health? How tall is he? Is his voice harsh or agreeable? My ears are very sensitive. Take him to dinner and note his table manners. Is his disposition cheerful? Sound out his ambitions. . . . Describe minutely his appearance, color of eyes, shape of forehead, mannerisms, how he dresses. Search his brain for everything there is in it. JP [4]

Cobb passed the examination—particularly in his knowledge of American history—and joined the *World* staff. Pulitzer put him in competition with other editorial writers and subjected him to a rigorous, and to Cobb an infuriating, hazing on points of writing style, clarity of expression, and logical thinking. More than once Cobb was on the point of returning to Detroit. But within a year he had become the recognized chief editorial writer, who would succeed to the editorship upon Pulitzer's death.

Cobb now became an important force in conducting the *World's* editorial page. But Pulitzer remained the guiding spirit and mentor of his editorial writers. In an editorial published at the close of Pulitzer's life in 1911, Cobb himself described the continued influence of the tired and blinded editor to the moment of his death:

> His chief concern centered in the editorial page as the expression of the paper's conscience, courage and convictions. To that he devoted infinite care and attention. Sick or well, it was never wholly absent from his thoughts. When he was well he had it read to him every day and expressed his opinion about every editorial article, the style in which it was written, the manner in which the thought was expressed, whether the editorial was strong or weak, whether it served any useful public purpose, whether it said the thing that a great newspaper ought to have said.
>
> When ill-health made it impossible for him to have the editorial page read every day he would keep the files for weeks, and then when his condition permitted, he would go over them with painstaking care, always from the point of view of a detached critic, seeking only to determine whether the page was taking the fullest advantage of its opportunities for public service and whether it was measuring up to the high standards that he had set for it.
>
> Nothing was ever allowed to interfere with its independence and its freedom of expression. There were certain questions about which he became convinced that in spite of all his efforts he was possibly prejudiced. In these matters he exacted a pledge that no suggestions or instructions or even commands from him would ever be followed, but that the paper would always say what an independent, untrammelled newspaper

[4] As quoted in James W. Barrett, *Joseph Pulitzer and His World* (New York: Vanguard, 1941), p. 184.

> ought to say in performing its duties to the people. This pledge was never violated. . . .[5]

The most famous of all the *World's* crusades began in 1905, just as the new editorial-page staff—composed of Cobb, John L. Heaton, Samuel E. Moffett, Ralph Pulitzer, the publisher's son, and others—was proving its strength. A battle had developed for control of the management of the Equitable Life Assurance Society, one of the life insurance companies that had built up great financial resources as Americans took up the purchase of policies and benefits to provide for their personal and family security. Evidence was presented by two *World* reporters, David Ferguson and Louis Seibold, that officials of the company were using funds paid in by policyholders for their own private investments and thereby were building huge personal fortunes—gambling with the people's money, the *World* said. A series of editorials by William M. Speer on "Equitable Corruption" caught Pulitzer's attention and a full-fledged campaign was ordered under Cobb's direction. Other editors, like Ervin Wardman of the *New York Press,* joined in the battle and the spotlight was turned on the Mutual Life and New York Life companies as well.

Demand rose for an investigation by a legislative committee. As legal counsel for the committee, the newspapers suggested Charles Evans Hughes, a young and forceful attorney who had attracted attention by assisting in a campaign against the "gas trust" in New York City a few months before. Hughes documented the case against the insurance companies, proving that their vast assets were being used by those in control for investments of profit to themselves. He also substantiated the *World's* charges that the companies maintained a large fund of money to exert political influence and affect the progress of legislation in various states. The specter of the "money interests" dominating the life insurance companies and using their power to corrupt legislatures so aroused public opinion that strict regulatory legislation was enacted in New York State; Hughes rode into the governorship in 1906.

HEARST'S CRUSADING IN THE *JOURNAL*

While the *World* was thus rising to greatness, its chief competitor for mass circulation in New York was just as determinedly making a claim to leadership as "the people's champion." William Randolph Hearst, having seen the country start toward annexation of the Philippines and Hawaii, the development of military bases in the Caribbean, and the adoption of other nationalistic policies advocated by the *New York Journal,* turned his attention to domestic affairs. In early 1899 he set forth an editorial platform calling for public ownership of public franchises, the "destruction of criminal trusts," a graduated

[5] *New York World,* October 31, 1911.

income tax, election of United States senators by popular vote rather than by state legislatures, and national, state, and local improvement of the public school system. Soon Hearst was urging that the coal mines, railroads, and telegraph lines—the symbols of the new industrial era—all be nationalized. And he gave strong encouragement to the economic and political powers of labor unions.

Not only was this a more radical program than that of the *World* and other liberal newspapers of the day, but the impact of the Hearst editorial technique was bitter and extreme. In the presidential campaign of 1900, Homer Davenport's cartoons depicting President McKinley as the stooge of a Mark Hanna wearing a suit made of dollar signs were crude but effective. Hearst was supporting Bryan's domestic policies and ignoring his anti-imperialism, just as Pulitzer was doing the reverse, and the *Journal* was venomous in its attacks upon McKinley and his party. But the *Journal* did not subside when McKinley and his running mate, Theodore Roosevelt, won the election.

In April, 1901, the *Journal* declared editorially that "if bad institutions and bad men can be got rid of only by killing, then the killing must be done." Two months before, on February 4, Ambrose Bierce had written a quatrain for the *Journal* which read:

> The bullet that pierced Goebel's breast
> Can not be found in all the West;
> Good reason, it is speeding here
> To stretch McKinley on his bier.

Goebel was Governor Goebel of Kentucky, a victim of an assassin. When in September, 1901, President McKinley was fatally wounded by an anarchist, the offending lines in the *Journal* were recalled, along with the Hearst paper's continual assaults upon McKinley. Hearst found it advantageous to change the name of his morning New York paper to the *American*. But the incident was to haunt him for the rest of his life.

HEARST'S POLITICAL AMBITIONS

Hearst now sought to advance his political beliefs by seeking office himself. He served two terms in Congress from a Democratic district in New York City, from 1903 to 1907, but his eye was on the White House. His high point came in 1904 when 204 delegates cast votes for him in the Democratic national convention (Judge Alton B. Parker, the successful nominee, received 658). The next year Hearst ran as an independent candidate for mayor of New York and lost by some 3,500 votes as the result of Tammany's counting him out at the ballot boxes.

This was a notable achievement, and Hearst decided to make the race for the New York governorship in 1906, as a stepping-stone to the White House. He won the Democratic nomination in convention, but found himself up against Charles Evans Hughes in the November election. Theodore Roosevelt's close associate, Elihu Root, recalled the McKinley assassination episode in a public speech; the *World* and other New York newspapers turned against Hearst; and so did Tammany, which he had challenged the year before. Hughes won by 60,000 votes—the only Republican to be elected that year in the statewide balloting—and Hearst's political star had set. In 1908 he stage-managed a third party ticket for the presidency which polled few votes, and in 1909 Hearst himself was decisively beaten in another try for the New York mayoralty.

In his political races and in his newspapers, Hearst was making a heavy play for the support of the working man, the small businessman, and other ordinary people. His slashing attacks upon the "criminal trusts"—the ice trust, the coal trust, the gas trust—and crooked political bosses found favor with those who had grievances against the established order. His forthright support of the labor unions won him the backing of the American Federation of Labor. And the popularized content of his newspapers appealed to the mass of readers. Emphasis on sensational crime and vice stories, human interest features, pictures and cartoons, and readable typographical display helped draw crowds of new readers to Hearst papers.

New publishing ventures brought Hearst to the attention of three more large cities in the first few years of the twentieth century. To his *San Francisco Examiner*, *New York American*, and *New York Journal*, Hearst added four more papers which put him in the business of chain publishing. In Chicago, the evening *American* was begun in 1900 and the morning *Examiner* in 1902. Boston saw the birth of an evening *American* in 1904. Los Angeles was invaded in 1903 with the founding of the morning *Examiner*. The Los Angeles entry was welcomed with open arms by local labor unions, which had been engaged in a bitter fight with the antilabor *Los Angeles Times*. The *Times*, published by General Harrison Gray Otis, had become open shop in 1890 after a typographers union strike, and the labor unions cooperated with Hearst in establishing direct competition for the powerful Otis paper. Otis and his son-in-law, Harry Chandler, continued their fight against organized labor until the feud was climaxed in 1910 by the dynamiting of the *Times* building, a crime to which two radically-minded union men, the McNamara brothers, eventually confessed. Amid all this controversy in Los Angeles the Hearst *Examiner* established itself as one of the chain's strongest papers. In Chicago, against Medill's *Tribune*, and in Boston and New York the going was tougher.

In the first issue of the *Los Angeles Examiner*, the editors advertised their wares. They listed the Hearst writers: Ella Wheeler Wilcox, "world famous poet and essayist"; Mrs. John A. Logan, wife of a General and writer "on behalf of the American home and American womanhood"; Professor Garrett Serviss, noted astronomer; Dorothy Dix, whose name is the first one recognizable seven decades later; Ambrose Bierce, a truly great writer. The editorial page, the ad said, has "thought-stirring editorials which have done so much to mold public thought in this country." Editorial-page cartoonists listed were Opper, Powers, Davenport, and Howarth; comics included the Katzenjammer Kids and Childe Harold. And, said the editors, "There is nothing in the newspaper world like the magazine section of the Hearst newspapers." Within a month the *Examiner* claimed 32,500 readers, and it remained a strong paper for half a century.[6]

EVALUATIONS OF HEARST'S JOURNALISM

Despite the following that Hearst had attracted, there was widespread doubting of his journalistic and political motives. Admittedly Hearst journalism then was powerful; its master advocated progressive beliefs; his newspapers were widely read and were financially successful; and Hearst himself was a potent force in political life. But Hearst journalism was degrading in its use of techniques to snare the reader, his critics said, and above all, Hearst and his journalism lacked depth.

There were varying expressions of the criticism that Hearst journalism lacked depth: depth of intellectual appeal; depth of sincerity; depth of understanding of social issues; depth of responsible conception of public trust. In general the intellectual leaders of the time spoke out against both the degrading characteristics of Hearst's news techniques and the tone of his editorial opinions. His opponents viewed Hearst as the leader of a political movement which was tinged with fanaticism in its bitter criticism of the social and economic order. And they saw in Hearst's own political efforts a bid for personal power rather than a bid for public service.

Pulitzer, while applauding Hearst's fights against the Tammany machine in New York, viewed his rival as one who would destroy the existing Democratic party and substitute for it a party which would be semisocialistic in its nature. The Socialist party leader, Norman Thomas, said later that as a young man in 1905 he admired Hearst's crusading but quite distrusted the sincerity of his beliefs. The Republicans condemned Hearst unequivocally as a rabble-rouser. And indeed, the platform written for the third party he created in 1908 was a bitter, radical document which appealed to all the discontented.[7]

Will Irwin, writing about Hearst in 1911, said that his editorial policies

[6] *Los Angeles Examiner*, December 12, 1903, p. 4.

[7] W. A. Swanberg, in *Citizen Hearst* (New York: Scribner's, 1961), contends that the Hearst of 1904 presidential ambitions was not a demagogue, but sincerely believed he was the best-fitted Democrat to run. For his estimates of Hearst, see pages 208–19 for this period, and the summation, pages 523–27, in which he concludes Hearst was two men, "a Prospero and a Caliban." For further comments about the Hearst of this period see Oliver Carlson and Ernest Sutherland Bates, *Hearst, Lord of San Simeon* (New York: Viking, 1936), pp. 132–38.

might well represent a marriage of convenience and sincerity, but added that "those who knew Hearst best in this early era declare that under his cold exterior he kept a real sympathy for the submerged man and woman, a real feeling of his own mission to plead their cause." [8] If that were so, Hearst failed to convince intellectuals, whose support he needed, of the sincerity of his newspapers. They were alienated by his sensationalized treatment of the news; by his unblushing agitation for war in 1898; by Arthur Brisbane's frank explanation of how the *Journal* had capitalized on the war fever; and by the popularized editorial page.

The Hearst editorial page, following the "gee-whiz" approach, spoke in one-syllable words. It talked about human virtues, religion, science, and love more easily than it talked about significant current issues. And when it approached social and economic issues it often did it in this fashion, under an editorial page cartoon:

> Trusts and unions are both combinations, beyond question. But a pronounced difference distinguishes them, and we shall endeavor to make it clear.
>
> You see a horse after a hard day's work grazing in a swampy meadow. He has done his duty and is getting what he can in return.
>
> On the horse's flank you may see a leach sucking blood.
>
> The *leach* is the *trust*.
>
> The *horse* is the labor *union*.
>
> Possibly you have read "Sinbad the Sailor," with its story of the Old Man of the Sea. The Old Man of the Sea rode round on the sailor's back squeezing his neck with tightly twisted legs.
>
> The *old man* is the the *trust*.
>
> The *sailor* is the labor *union*.[9]

Hearst preferred the cartoonist and the man who could thus simplify an argument—Davenport and Brisbane, among others—to the editorial thinker. He had no men of the intellectual caliber of William H. Merrill and Frank Cobb of the *World* or Charles R. Miller of the *Times* in command of his editorial pages. As evidence of this, the testimony of Willis J. Abbot about life on the *New York Journal* in the late 1890s may be quoted. Abbot, who later became editor of the *Christian Science Monitor,* records the following in his autobiography about his introduction to Hearstian methods:

> Within an hour after meeting him (Hearst), I was engaged as "Editor-in-chief" of the *New York Journal.* The resonant title was most grateful to my still youthful and ingenuous mind. . . . It took months of cruel disillusionment to reveal to me the two facts that despite a liberal con-

[8] Will Irwin, "The Fourth Current," *Collier's,* XLVI (February 18, 1911), 14.

[9] As quoted in *Editorials from the Hearst Newspapers* (New York: Albertson Publishing Company, 1906), pp. 170–71.

ferring of titles, Mr. Hearst was the only editor-in-chief of any of his papers, and that of all his newspaper pages the editorial page of which I had charge was the one on which he looked with most tolerant contempt.[10]

Abbot continues by asserting that for three weeks he conducted the editorial page of the *Journal* without a single scrap of instructions from Hearst or any other editor. (Shades of Pulitzer and his rigorous training of Frank Cobb for his duties in heading the all-important *World* editorial page!) Abbot adds, however, that around 1910 Hearst himself took up in earnest the writing of editorials, and proved to be more effective than any of his editors. Thereafter he held the editorial page in slightly higher esteem, Abbot says.

Here, then, was an important reason for intellectual distrust of Hearst. The editorial page lacked depth of appeal, and to many this indicated lack of sincerity. In the New York morning field the combination of the sensationalism of the Hearst news policy and the popularized editorial page made the future of the *American* (the renamed *Journal*) increasingly insecure. Against the competition of the *World,* the *Times,* the *Tribune,* and the *Herald,* the Hearst entry gradually lost ground until in the newspaper world it was known as the "vanishing *American.*" This was not true of Hearst enterprises generally, however, for they remained as a continuing force in American journalism and will appear again in this story.

E. W. SCRIPPS AND HIS "PEOPLE'S PAPERS"

Another type of "people's paper" was emerging, meanwhile, under the direction of Edward Wyllis Scripps, the Ohio farm boy who had successfully started the first of his many Scripps newspapers by the time he was 24. Scripps got his start in the Middle West at the moment that Pulitzer was achieving his first success in St. Louis, and when Stone was succeeding in Chicago and Nelson in Kansas City. The *Detroit News,* on which Scripps had served his appenticeship under his brother James, had been one of the early practitioners of the "new journalism." His own first two papers, the *Cleveland Press* and the *Cincinnati Post,* were low-priced afternoon dailies appealing to the mass of readers.[11]

But unlike Pulitzer and Hearst, who sought giant circulations in big cities, Scripps set his sights upon the working people in the smaller but growing industrial cities of the country. For them he published brightly-written, easily-read newspapers, small in size but big in heart. Closely-edited news, human interest features, fearless news coverage and local crusades, and hard-fighting independent editorial opinion constituted the Scripps formula.

[10] Willis J. Abbot, *Watching the World Go By* (Boston: Little, Brown, 1933), pp. 134–35.

[11] See pages 296–97 for Scripps' early career.

What made Scripps a distinctive leader as a "people's champion" was his conception of his responsibility to the working man. "The first of my principles," Scripps said, "is that I have constituted myself the advocate of that large majority of people who are not so rich in worldly goods and native intelligence as to make them equal, man for man, in the struggle with individuals of the wealthier and more intellectual class."[12] Scripps viewed his newspapers as the only "schoolroom" the working man had. He believed that nearly all other newspapers were capitalistic and opposed to the working class or else too intellectual in appeal, and he said sadly that the educational system was a failure in its service to his "large majority." So he sought to drive home through his editorial columns the necessity for labor union organization and collective bargaining as the first prerequisite to a better life for the poor and ill-informed. To him the struggle was to keep the rich from getting richer and the poor from getting poorer, and his papers invariably lined up on the side of the have-nots.

Scripps was the first to admit that his papers did not always maintain the noble objectives he set for them, and that they sometimes made mistakes in "always opposing the rich, always supporting the working man." But Scripps believed that if he kept the focus on such a basic policy he would further the long-range pattern of society which he hoped would emerge in an industrialized America. And he exerted through his newspapers published in the growing industrial cities of the country a great influence on changing social and political attitudes. The Scripps papers struck closer to the hearts and the minds of working men than did Pulitzer's *World;* and they exhibited a more consistent liberal political and economic policy than that of Hearst, and won their readers without resorting to the extremes of sensationalism which marked the Hearst press.

Above all, the Scripps newspapers reflected a "spirit of protest" which was inherent in the character of their owner-editor. Scripps declared that he protested against everything; his motto was "Whatever is, is wrong." He protested against antiquated governmental systems, against undemocratic political actions, against usurpation of power and prestige by the rich and the intellectuals, against inequality of opportunity, against all sorts of authority in religion and law and politics save those exercised for the benefit of mankind, against corruption, against the power of business interests. His spirit of protest led him to ignore advertisers unless they came seeking the circulations which he had built, and to resist any kind of pressure they might seek to use to influence him. He pictured himself as a "damned old crank" who was in rebellion against society. But actually he was seeking to build a progressive democracy by raising the level of the working classes, and he was enough of a capitalist to

[12] As quoted in Oliver H. Knight, ed., *I Protest: The Selected Disquisitions of E. W. Scripps* (Madison: University of Wisconsin Press, 1966), p. 270. Knight edited from the Scripps papers a variety of his personal views which establish the publisher as a thinking observer of American affairs.

urge the worker to better himself by increasing his production and thereby adding to the wealth to be distributed.

THE SCRIPPS PUBLISHING EMPIRE

Scripps started his newspaper career with an investment of $600 in one share of stock in the *Detroit News*. With that collateral, and with the help of his brothers James and George, he started the *Cleveland Press* in 1878. In 1880 the Scripps family flirted with an ill-fated paper in Buffalo, the *Evening Telegraph*, and bought the *St. Louis Chronicle* (which faded out in 1905 in competition with the strong *Post-Dispatch* and *Globe-Democrat*). In 1883, with an income of $10,000 a year, Scripps turned to Cincinnati and took over management of a struggling penny paper which became the *Post*. A fourth paper, the *Kentucky Post*, was established in Covington in 1890 as an affiliate of the Cincinnati paper.

These were the formative years of the Scripps newspaper empire. In Cleveland Scripps found an editor, Robert F. Paine, who for more than 30 years was a leader in editorial policy-making. In Cincinnati Scripps found a business manager, Milton A. McRae, who was to become the managerial leader of the chain. Scripps and McRae formed a partnership in 1889, which in 1895 was expanded to include George Scripps. The organization took the name Scripps-McRae League of Newspapers. McRae was to be the speech-maker, the front man, the operations chief. Scripps was to set policy and live as he pleased on a California ranch. And in 1890, at age 36, Scripps did "retire" to a great ranch near San Diego, named Miramar, where he lived a burly life, wearing ranch clothes and cowhide boots, playing poker, drinking whisky, and smoking innumerable cigars.

Much has been made—particularly by Scripps himself—of his many affairs with women, of his intemperate drinking, and of his general violation of all of Horatio Alger's rules for success. Scripps claimed that he drank as much as a gallon of whisky a day for many years—undoubtedly a gross exaggeration—and he delighted in such proverbs as "Never do today what you can put off until tomorrow." But the rough-living and bearded Scripps also was a lover of poetry and music and the wife whom he took to Miramar was the daughter of a Presbyterian minister. At Miramar, too, he was still the director of the Scripps newspaper ventures, with which he kept in intimate touch through a mass of correspondence and through occasional conferences with his principal editors and managers. He also managed to live to the age of 71, and to build himself a fortune of some 50 million dollars.

The Scripps plan for expansion was simple. He and McRae looked for a growing industrial city, usually fairly small and with stodgy newspaper opposition. They put up a few thousand dollars and sent a young, ambitious editor and business manager off to start a paper. If the young journalists succeeded, they could obtain as much as 49 per cent of the stock; if they faltered, new faces replaced them. If the paper failed to make a profit within ten years, it was abandoned as a failure. Scripps papers, as a result of this policy, had a good many employee-stockholders, but they also paid the usual low journalistic salaries of the times to those who were not so blessed. In this respect, Scripps was typically capitalistic in his publishing behavior.

Since the papers were cheap afternoon dailies relying principally on circulation revenue they had to be edited carefully. Scripps saved newsprint costs by insisting upon small headlines and short, concisely-edited stories. Saving those extra words so that a Scripps newspaper would be packed with the most news possible became a fine art for Scripps newsmen. Word economy meant also that after the essential news had been told there would be plenty of space for editorial opinion and features—and, of course, space for the advertising which the Scripps newspapers sought for as avidly as any others, provided that their advertising space was bought on a strictly business basis.

Between 1897 and 1911 the Scripps-McRae League added 14 more papers to the original four. The first venture, the *Kansas City World* (1897) was a failure, for Nelson in Kansas City was as tough a competitor as were the St. Louis opposition papers. In Ohio, the new papers were the *Akron Press*, founded in 1899, the *Toledo News-Bee*, bought in 1903, and the *Columbus Citizen*, purchased in 1904. The League brought the *Des Moines News* into the fold in 1902. Then in 1906 eight new papers were started: the *Evansville Press* and *Terre Haute Post* in Indiana; the *Memphis Press* and *Nashville News* in Tennessee; the *Denver Express* and *Pueblo Sun* in Colorado; and the *Dallas Dispatch* and *Oklahoma City News*. The *Houston Press* followed in 1911. By the time of Scripps' death in 1926, 11 of these 18 first Scripps-McRae papers remained. Those which were abandoned or sold to competitors were the papers in St. Louis, Kansas City, Des Moines, Pueblo, Dallas, Nashville, and Terre Haute.

Scripps himself was building his own chain of West Coast newspapers, meanwhile. He started by buying the *San Diego Sun* in 1893, and in the next 15 years opened up shop in 10 other coast cities. Flying the Scripps banner were the *Los Angeles Record*, the *Seattle Star*, the *Spokane Press*, the *Tacoma Times*, the *Portland News*, the *San Francisco News*, the *Sacramento Star*, the *Fresno Tribune*, the *Berkeley Independent*, and the *Oakland Mail*.

Here in an only slightly industrialized West the Scripps record was extremely poor. The *San Francisco News* eventually emerged as a strong unit in the Scripps chain. But the Fresno, Berkeley, and Oakland papers in California all were unsuccessful; the *Sacramento Star* flickered out in 1926; and the *San Diego Sun* eventually died. The *Los Angeles Record* and the four Pacific Northwest papers seceded from the parent Scripps organization after a quarrel between Scripps and his son James in 1920, and formed the basis for the Scripps League. But all five of those papers succumbed in due time. While each paper lived, however, it breathed the Scripps fire so long as the founder and his policies remained a factor—and each city felt the "spirit of protest."

Scripps tried another experiment in 1911, when he established an adless tabloid in Chicago, named the *Day Book*. Negley D. Cochran was the editor, and poet Carl Sandburg was chief reporter. The little paper, which represented Scripps' fondest dream, reached a circulation of 25,000 and was within $500 a month of breaking even when the rising newsprint costs of the first war year, 1917, caused its suspension. A second adless paper, the *Philadelphia News-Post,* started in 1912 but also failed.

Through the years the Scripps papers continued to fight for the right of workers to organize. They crusaded for public ownership and against utility abuses. They attacked political bossism and corruption. They supported Theodore Roosevelt's reforms and his third party candidacy. And they backed Woodrow Wilson's "New Freedom" and his reelection campaign. In appearance and in content they were closer to being "labor papers" than any other general circulation newspapers, yet they also won the support of the intellectual liberals whom Scripps sometimes tried to avoid.

There is more to the Scripps story. Later chapters will describe the founding of the United Press Associations by Scripps and its growth under Scripps' eventual successor, Roy W. Howard. Scripps and his talented editor, Robert F. Paine, began the Newspaper Enterprise Association in 1902 as a general feature syndicate, and in 1921 Scripps sparked the formation of Science Service, a specialized news agency. Also in the Scripps fold were United Features, Acme Newspictures, and the surviving newspaper organization, Scripps-Howard. But what happened to the empire which Edward Wyllis Scripps built in his years as a "people's champion" is another episode in another era.

OTHER NEWSPAPER CRUSADERS

Pulitzer, Hearst, and Scripps were far from being the only champions of the common man among newspaper publishers and editors of the years around the turn of the century. Nor can all those who opposed the business trusts, who fought against one-sided public utilities franchises, who exposed political inadequacy and corruption, be listed. Some idea of the contributions made by newspapermen can be gained by a look across the country, however.[13]

One battle against a tightly-run political machine was that waged by Charles H. Grasty, editor of the *Baltimore Evening News,* and by the *Baltimore Sun.* Grasty, who came to Baltimore from the *Kansas City Star,* was a fighting editor in the Nelson tradition who had exposed the policy racket in Baltimore despite a criminal libel charge brought by his political opponents.

[13] One account, not confined to this period, is Silas Bent, *Newspaper Crusaders* (New York: Whittlesey House, 1939). Another is Jonathan Daniels, *They Will Be Heard: America's Crusading Newspaper Editors* (New York: McGraw-Hill, 1965).

When in 1895 the *Sun* broke with its Democratic party traditions and attacked Senator Arthur P. Gorman's state Democratic machine, Grasty pitched in to help oust the Gorman group. Maryland elected its first Republican administration since the Civil War and Gorman lost his senate seat for one term. Later, Grasty sold the *Evening News,* and after two years in St. Paul as part owner of the *Dispatch* and *Pioneer Press,* returned to Baltimore in 1910 as owner of the *Sun.* He supported Woodrow Wilson in the 1912 election before retiring from the *Sun* in 1914.

Across the country the spectacular but contradictory career of Fremont Older was being unfolded in San Francisco. Older, a typical roving newspaperman in his early years, settled down as managing editor of the *Bulletin* in 1895. He built the struggling evening sheet into a fairly substantial paper by his sensational methods, and then decided to join the solid civic leader, the *San Francisco Chronicle,* in its fights against city machine politics. The target was a Union-Labor party headed by Mayor Eugene E. Schmitz and a political boss, Abram Ruef. Older stepped out of his role as a newspaperman to become a civic reform leader, and his dominating personality made him the rallying point for the public-spirited of the city. Older printed sensational stories detailing charges of bribery of city officeholders by public utilities and the street transit company, and in one instance trapped city supervisors in a bribe-taking plot. The reform group brought Schmitz and Ruef to court on indictments for accepting payoffs from houses of prostitution, and saw Ruef sent to prison. Others involved escaped conviction, despite the work of prosecutors Francis J. Heney (who was shot and critically wounded in the courtroom) and Hiram W. Johnson. Older then confounded his admirers by insisting that Ruef was a victim of his environment, and that since he was the only one of his gang to be sent to prison, he should be released. His last great crusade was in behalf of Tom Mooney, who Older eventually decided had been unjustly convicted of the Preparedness Day bombing of 1916 in San Francisco. Breaking with the *Bulletin* management on the Mooney issue, Older joined Hearst's *Call* as editor in 1918, saw it become the *Call-Bulletin* in 1929, and died in 1935 before Mooney won his freedom.

Older had been kidnaped and nearly killed during the height of the San Francisco trials. In South Carolina, two editors were assassinated—Francis W. Dawson of the *Charleston News and Courier* in 1891 and N. G. Gonzales of the *Columbia State* in 1903. Gonzales was one of three brothers who battled against political boss Ben Tillman with their newspaper, founded in 1893. The paper continued to exert leadership, however, calling for compulsory public education and opposing child labor and "lynch law."

A less spectacular, but solid, champion of decency was Josephus Daniels, North Carolina's famous editor. Daniels fell in love with newspaper work as a school boy, went to work on a weekly at 18, and was running two weeklies and serving as president of the North Carolina Press Association at 22. He then studied law at the University of North Carolina and went to Raleigh to edit

Raleigh News and Observer

JOSEPHUS DANIELS

the *State Chronicle* in 1885. The paper was a weekly, started by Walter Hines Page two years before.

In his first few years in Raleigh, Daniels campaigned against the Southern Railway and its attempt to extend its control over other lines. He advocated a state public school fund as a means of equalizing educational opportunity, urged financial support of the state university, supported establishment of teacher training colleges, and argued for compulsory education as a means of overcoming illiteracy. When the American Tobacco Company was organized by the Duke family in 1890 he began his long campaign against the "tobacco trust."

The established daily in Raleigh was the *News and Observer*. Daniels made the *State Chronicle* a daily in 1891, but sold out in 1892 to a buyer who in turn sold out to the *News and Observer*. Daniels meanwhile established another weekly, the *North Carolinian*, and entered government service in Washington. Then in 1895 his chance to buy the *News and Observer* came and he returned to Raleigh to build one of the South's leading newspapers. Significantly, the Daniels paper in Raleigh was the first in the state to have Linotype machines and a perfecting press.

Daniels continued his fights against the railroads and the tobacco trust. He called for the establishment of a railroad commission, for reduced rates, and for abolition of passes granted to politicians and editors. He urged prosecution of the tobacco trust, and pointed out to farmers that the price of tobacco in the field had fallen 50 per cent since the smaller companies had been combined into one giant organization. The railroad and tobacco interests put another paper in the field against him, but it failed.

When a fusion party combining the support of Republicans, Populists, and Negroes won control of the state government, Daniels backed a "white supremacy" movement. But he was a strong opponent of lynching and he continually advocated equal educational opportunities for Negroes. For all working men he urged a three-point program: shorter hours, better wages, and abolition of child labor competition.

Daniels was a fervent supporter of the Democratic party, campaigning for Bryan in his three races for the presidency and supporting Woodrow Wilson with full enthusiasm. Wilson made him his Secretary of the Navy in 1913 and the Daniels political career was under way. In his autobiography Daniels says the greatest influence upon his early career as an editor was his admiration for Samuel Bowles III and his regular reading of the *Springfield Republican.*[14] Bowles, he said, taught him the principles of journalism and a conception of his public trust. And the newspaper which he established and continued to edit until the 1940s was evidence of lessons well learned and of the strength of his own personality.

In Chicago, the *Tribune* which Joseph Medill had built enjoyed a varied record. In the last years of Medill's editorship, before his death in 1899, the *Tribune* was strongly nationalistic in foreign policy and generally conservative in its outlook. It fought the liberal Illinois governor, John P. Altgeld, and bitterly attacked the Debs-led Chicago labor unions. But the *Tribune* vigorously crusaded against utility and street-railway franchise grabs, and used John T. McCutcheon's front-page cartoons with effectiveness after the artist transferred from the *Record* to the *Tribune* in 1903.

James Keeley, the *Tribune's* outstanding managing editor, helped develop one of the state's biggest exposés in 1910 when the paper published evidence that William Lorimer had won election to the U. S. Senate by bribing state legislators. Despite the evidence which Keeley had obtained, it took two years of campaigning by the *Tribune* and the *Record-Herald* before Lorimer was ousted from the Senate. Keeley also sponsored the *Tribune's* lengthy crusade for a "safe and sane" Fourth of July, in which carefully collected lists of victims of dangerous fireworks eventually led to restrictive legislation.

Chicago Tribune

JOSEPH MEDILL

Other newspapers kept the crusading spirit at full force. Nelson's *Kansas City Star* editorialized continually for civic improvements. In national politics Nelson became an admirer of Theodore Roosevelt and backed his Progressive party in 1912, calling for state laws establishing the initiative, referendum, and recall. Pulitzer's *St. Louis Post-Dispatch* con-

[14] Josephus Daniels, *Tar Heel Editor* (Chapel Hill: University of North Carolina Press, 1939), p. 92. The second volume of his autobiography, *Editor in Politics,* continues his story through this period.

ducted one of its outstanding campaigns from 1898 to 1902 when it charged that two-thirds of the municipal assembly had been bribed by the local traction company, and battled for four years before one of the culprits confessed and sent eight officials to the penitentiary. In New York, Ervin Wardman's *Press* accused city officials of bribery and joined in the fight against the insurance companies. And in Boston the *Traveler* centered fire upon the "bucket shops," which conducted a form of investment gambling and fleeced the unsuspecting.

Many a public service campaign was carried out by American newspapers. The *Chicago Daily News* sponsored a tuberculosis sanitarium. The *New York Herald* promoted an ice charity for sweltering tenement dwellers. Newspapers everywhere collected Thanksgiving and Christmas baskets for the poor, before the Community Chest movement came on the scene, and raised funds for the relief of disaster victims. Campaigns for better schools, for city parks, for recreation facilities, and against child labor were equally widespread. Few newspaper editors had as full an appreciation of the basic economic problems of the "poor and ill-informed" as did Scripps, but many of them caught some measure of the spirit of the times.

THE MAGAZINES: ERA OF MUCKRAKING

Highly important as "people's champions" were the magazines that, in the dozen years after 1900, developed a literature of exposure which Theodore Roosevelt dubbed the work of the "muckrakers." Roosevelt used the expression in a derogatory sense, comparing the more sensational writers to the Man with the Muckrake in *Pilgrim's Progress,* who did not look up to see the celestial crown but continued to rake the filth. The reformers, however, came to accept the designation as a badge of honor, and in the history of American magazines the period is known as "the era of the muckrakers." [15]

When in 1893 three new popular magazines—*McClure's, Cosmopolitan,* and *Munsey's*—cut their prices to a dime, their circulation figures started on an upward climb. After the turn of the century these magazines and such others as the *Ladies' Home Journal, Collier's, Everybody's,* and the *Saturday Evening Post* had circulations running into the hundreds of thousands. Most of them joined with great enthusiasm in the crusade against big business, against corruption, and for social justice. Their writers, who came largely from newspaper ranks, had national audiences for articles which were sometimes original but which also sometimes were drawn from the stories published by crusading newspapers in various cities. However the articles were obtained, the magazines performed the service of coordinating and interpreting information about

[15] The full story is told in C. C. Regier, *The Era of the Muckrakers* (Chapel Hill: University of North Carolina Press, 1932). Regier, however, ignores the contribution of newspapers in crusading and thus distorts the picture.

McClure's Magazine

VOL. XX *JANUARY, 1903* NO. 3

THE SHAME OF MINNEAPOLIS

The Rescue and Redemption of a City that was Sold Out

BY LINCOLN STEFFENS

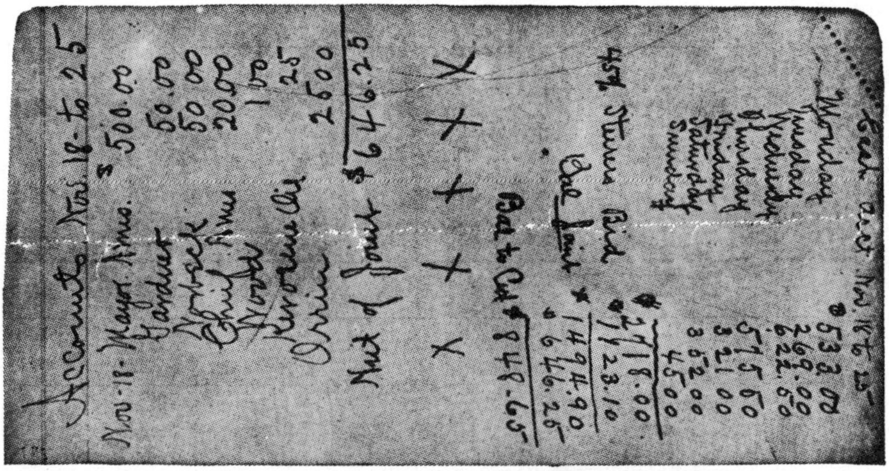

FAC-SIMILE OF THE FIRST PAGE OF "THE BIG MITT LEDGER"

An account kept by a swindler of the dealings of his "Joint" with City Officials, showing first payments made to Mayor Ames, his brother, the Chief of Police and Detectives. This book figured in trials and newspaper reports of the exposure, but was "lost"; and its whereabouts was the mystery of the proceedings. This is the first glimpse that any one, except "Cheerful Charlie' Howard, who kept it, and members of the grand jury, has had of the book

WHENEVER anything extraordinary is done in American municipal politics, whether for good or for evil, you can trace it almost invariably to one man. The people do not do it. Neither do the "gangs," "combines," or political parties. These are but instruments by which bosses (not leaders; we Americans are not led, but driven) rule the people, and commonly sell them out. But there are at least two forms of the autocracy which has supplanted the democracy here as it has everywhere it has been tried. One is that of the organized majority by which, as in Tammany Hall in New York and the Republican machine in Philadelphia, the boss has normal control of more than half the voters. The other is that of the adroitly managed minority. The "good people" are herded into parties and stupefied with convictions and a name, Republican or Democrat; while the "bad people" are so organized or interested by the boss that he can wield their votes to enforce terms with party managers and decide elections. St. Louis is a conspicuous example of this form. Minneapolis is another. Colonel Ed. Butler is the unscrupulous opportunist who handled the non-partisan minority which turned St. Louis into a "boodle town." In Minneapolis "Doc" Ames was the man.

One of the articles which made *McClure's* the leading muckraking magazine.

social, economic, and political problems for a nationwide audience, and thus had great impact.

Touching off the muckraking era was S. S. McClure,[16] whose magazine began three significant series of articles in late 1902. McClure, who had founded a newspaper feature syndicate in 1884 and attracted readers and writers to his service, invaded the magazine field in 1893 with a low-priced but unspectacular product filled with interesting and timely articles and literary material. He and his associate editor, John S. Phillips, had selected a staff of talented and responsible writers to handle the nonfiction section of *McClure's.* One was Ida M. Tarbell, whose specialties were biographies and research work. Another was Lincoln Steffens, former reporter for the *Evening Post* and city editor of the *Commercial Advertiser* in New York, who was to become one of the country's most famous crusading liberals. A third was Ray Stannard Baker, who came to *McClure's* from the *Chicago Record* in 1897 and who later was to achieve fame as Woodrow Wilson's biographer. Beginning in late 1902 Miss Tarbell exposed the business practices of John D. Rockefeller and the Standard Oil Company; Steffens opened his attack upon corruption in city and state governments; and Baker began discussing the problems of the working man. The circulation of *McClure's* mounted past the half-million mark and the muckraking trend in magazine editing was in full swing.

What McClure was doing was not entirely new to the magazine field. The older magazines of high quality—*Harper's, Scribner's,* the *Century,* and the *Atlantic Monthly*—had paid some attention to current affairs, although they were primarily literary in tone. There were several journals of opinion which had relatively small but influential audiences: Godkin's *Nation,* Albert Shaw's *Review of Reviews,* Lyman Abbott's *Outlook,* the *North American Review,* the *Forum,* and the *Independent.* In the same class but taking an early leadership in crusading for socioeconomic and political reform was Benjamin O. Flower's *Arena.* These magazines and others were giving attention to the rising business trusts, graft, and political machines, but it was *McClure's* which first made a frontal assault of real magnitude.

Miss Tarbell's "History of the Standard Oil Company" ran in *McClure's* until 1904, and her detailed, thoroughly-documented account of the unfair business practices used by the company to squeeze out competitors put Rockefeller on the defensive for many years to come. Steffens began his series on "The Shame of the Cities" by recounting the situation in St. Louis which had first been exposed by the *Post-Dispatch* and followed up with reports on corrupt government in Minneapolis, Pittsburgh, Philadelphia, Chicago, New York, and other cities. George Kibbe Turner, an alumnus of the *Springfield Republican,* continued the city series later in the decade. Baker dealt with labor problems, including child labor and the economic status of the Negro. Other contributors

[16] Revived interest in muckraking journalism brought two new biographies of McClure: Peter Lyon, *Success Story: The Life and Times of S. S. McClure* (New York: Scribner's, 1963), and Harold S. Wilson, *McClure's Magazine and the Muckrakers* (Princeton, N.J.: Princeton University Press, 1970).

to *McClure's* included Burton J. Hendrick, who wrote about the New York life insurance companies, and Kansas editor William Allen White. Newspaperman Will Irwin served as managing editor and editor for a year in 1906–07.

Cosmopolitan joined the muckrakers when the magazine passed from John Brisben Walker to Hearst, by running the series "The Treason of the Senate," which appeared in 1906. The author was David Graham Phillips, one of Pulitzer's editorial writers on the *World* staff, who retired from newspaper work to write a series of books examining problems of his time. Phillips denounced a score of conservative senators—both Republican and Democrat—as spokesmen of "the interests." Among other prominent muckrakers, Alfred Henry Lewis attacked the International Harvester Company in *Cosmopolitan* and followed up with a series examining the careers of America's leading millionaires. Charles Edward Russell, who had been managing editor of the *Minneapolis Journal* at 21 and who had worked for several New York and Chicago newspapers, surveyed the weaknesses of state governments in a 1910 series.

Active in the fray, too, was *Everybody's*, founded in 1899 and edited by John O'Hara Cosgrave. When in 1904 it persuaded a colorful Wall Street financier, Thomas W. Lawson, to write "Frenzied Finance," the public appetite for Lawson's inside information drove the magazine's circulation from 200,000 to 735,000 within a year. *Everybody's* also was a vehicle for Charles Edward Russell, who attacked the beef trust in its columns in 1905 and contributed a savage assault on Wall Street financiers in 1907. Less important, but influential, were *Pearson's*, *Hampton's* (which built a readership of 440,000 in the years 1907 to 1911), and *La Follette's Weekly*, the voice of the Wisconsin progressive movement.

Taking the lead from *McClure's* in muckraking after 1905 was *Collier's*. Published by Robert J. Collier and edited by Norman Hapgood, the magazine developed an effective editorial voice in national political affairs. Its articles ranged over many social and economic problems, but it caught popular attention for a series of articles by Samuel Hopkins Adams on the patent medicine trade, called "The Great American Fraud," published in 1905 and 1906. Adams exposed the false claims of many of the popular "cure-alls" and demonstrated that some of the patent medicines contained poisonous ingredients not identified on the labels. Newspaperman Mark Sullivan also contributed to the *Collier's* drug exposé, as well as covering Washington politics for the magazine.

Equally prominent in the attack on the patent medicine business was Edward W. Bok, editor of the *Ladies' Home Journal*. It was Bok who shocked his women readers by proving that Lydia E. Pinkham, to whom American women were supposed to write for advice, had been dead for 22 years. And he, too, crusaded for legislation which would force proper labeling of drugs and medicines, and prevent dishonest advertising of the products.

The attack on the patent medicines coincided with a drive against adulterated foods and unsanitary practices in packing plants. Under the leadership of Dr. Harvey H. Wiley, chief chemist of the Department of Agriculture, federal and state officials had proved widespread adulteration of food and addition of chemicals and artificial dyes by food manufacturers. But the lid was blown off when Upton Sinclair wrote *The Jungle* in 1906, a novel intended to portray the plight of immigrant workers in Chicago's packinghouses, but which was so terrifying in its charges of unsanitary and callous practices in meat handling that it caused a nationwide revulsion.

Passage of the Pure Food and Drugs Act of 1906 was the outcome. This regulated the activities of manufacturers, but the problem of "truth in advertising" remained. Some newspapers, like those of the Scripps-McRae League, had banned unethical advertising from their columns, as had the *Ladies' Home Journal.* But some state newspaper editorial associations, and the American Newspaper Publishers Association, had attempted to defend the patent-medicine business against regulation. Some newspapers had obtained testimonials from their readers, extolling the virtues of the medicines, and had run them in their news columns. This use of "readers," as they were called, also had been extended to cover publicity stories sent out by all manner of businesses and paid for by the column inch. As the campaign for "truth in advertising" grew, more newspapermen saw the need for reform. State laws making untruthful, deceptive or misleading advertising statements a misdemeanor were adopted after *Printers' Ink* drafted a model statute in 1911, and the federal Newspaper Publicity Law of 1912 required that all matter published for money should be marked "Advertisement."

Other magazines should be noted. One was the *American Magazine,* which was purchased in 1906 by a group of McClure's writers. A disagreement in policy led John S. Phillips, associate editor of *McClure's,* to leave its staff. He took with him Miss Tarbell, Steffens, Baker, William Allen White, and Finley Peter Dunne, America's "Mr. Dooley." These were the leaders of the muckrakers and for a few years they constituted a distinguished editorial board for the *American.* The high point of muckraking had been reached in 1906, but liberal insurgency continued, climaxed in 1912 by Theodore Roosevelt's third party candidacy and Woodrow Wilson's election as president. The *New Republic* began its career in 1914 under editor Herbert Croly, whose *The Promise of American Life* (1909) became a creed for Wilsonian liberals. Croly and staff member Walter Lippmann supported Wilson in wartime. Not so *The Masses,* edited by Max Eastman, and a brilliant voice of protest from 1911 to 1917 when its pacifist-socialist line led to wartime persecution and demise. Among its contributors were Lippmann, Carl Sandburg, Sherwood Anderson, and cartoonist Art Young.

THE AGE OF REALISM

Playing a role, too, in the quest for social justice were a group of America's writers. William Dean Howells and Henry James had pointed the way toward the realistic novel. Joining them in this movement were novelist Stephen Crane and short-story writers Ambrose Bierce and Hamlin Garland. Of the same school were poets Walt Whitman and Emily Dickinson. From this literary heritage, and from the pressure of the times, came a flowering of realism in literature after 1900.

Californian Frank Norris contributed two volumes of a planned trilogy on the "Epic of Wheat" before his career was cut short by death at 32. His *The Octopus,* appearing in 1901, told the story of the struggle of California farmers against the power of the Southern Pacific Railroad. His protest against Chicago wheat speculators, *The Pit,* made an equally deep impression. Another Californian, Jack London, captured in his stories of adventure and raw, brutal experience a full expression of the rising protest against the capitalistic system. London's *The Iron Heel,* published in 1907, and Upton Sinclair's *The Jungle* were high points in relentless realism. So were Theodore Dreiser's *Sister Carrie,* which was at first suppressed by a frightened publisher, and his later books, *The Financier* and *The Titan.*

More Americans, it is true, were reading historical novels, adventure stories, and popular favorites like *David Harum* and *Mrs. Wiggs of the Cabbage Patch* than were reading the works of Norris, Sinclair, London, and Dreiser. More Americans, too, were reading fiction in *Munsey's* and the *Saturday Evening Post* than were reading the exposés by Lincoln Steffens, Ida M. Tarbell, and Samuel Hopkins Adams. And among newspaper readers, relatively few were absorbing the editorial arguments of Edward Wyllis Scripps, Joseph Pulitzer, and their contemporaries of equal stature. Still, at a critical moment in American history, when an arousing of public opinion was needed to ensure economic and political progress and a more equitable social pattern, journalism and literature played their part and produced effective leaders.

The most common criticism of the muckrakers and the crusaders of this period has been that many of them offered nothing but protests against the injustices and inadequacies of American economic and political life. They aroused discontent, they exposed corruption and greed, they pointed to the inevitable growth of corporations and trusts, but they had few constructive solutions to offer, few alternatives to suggest. So the criticism runs, with some validity, although it should be tempered by the realization that the noisy, persistent radical often prods more cautious people into making needed reforms which keep society in balance. It should be remembered, too, that this criticism applies equally, when valid, to political leaders, labor organizers, ministers, teachers, reformers, and other persons as well as to newspaper and magazine editors and writers.

But it does not apply to those individuals who saw that the problem was one of making reasonable adjustments to changing conditions, rather than fighting blindly against the transition from one socioeconomic situation to another. There were leaders who so saw the problem, and they had many followers. There were La Follettes and Wilsons in politics who offered reasonable solutions; there were constructive leaders like Mitchell and Gompers in the labor movement; and there were journalists like Scripps and Pulitzer who rose to equal heights, as effective champions of progressive democracy. Together they helped to develop a new main current of American thought and action, in keeping with the requirements and the wishes of the majority.

Annotated Bibliography

For references to the literature about Pulitzer see the bibliography for Chapter 17; for the Hearst references see Chapter 19. Vol. IV of Mott's *History of American Magazines* covers this period (see Chapter 16).

Books

Baker, Ray Stannard, *An American Chronicle.* New York: Scribner's, 1945. The autobiography of one of the *McClure's* writers.

Bannister, Robert C., *Ray Stannard Baker: The Mind and Thought of a Progressive.* New Haven: Yale University Press, 1966. One of the reporters for *McClure's.*

Bok, Edward W., *The Americanization of Edward Bok.* New York: Scribner's, 1920. The famous autobiography of the editor of the *Ladies' Home Journal.*

Bowers, Claude G., *Beveridge and the Progressive Era.* Boston: Houghton Mifflin, 1932. A distinguished study of the Bull Moose progressives, of whom Senator Albert J. Beveridge was one.

Britt, Albert, *Ellen Browning Scripps: Journalist and Idealist.* London: Oxford University Press, 1961. Adds to the Scripps story in early years since Ellen was close to E. W.

Chalmers, David M., *The Social and Political Ideas of the Muckrakers.* New York: The Citadel Press, 1964. A brief analysis of thirteen muckrakers.

Cochran, Negley D., *E. W. Scripps.* New York: Harcourt, Brace & Jovanovich, 1933. A more factual biography than Gilson Gardner's *Lusty Scripps* (New York: Vanguard, 1932).

Daniels, Josephus, *Tar Heel Editor.* Chapel Hill: University of North Carolina Press, 1939. The first volume of the Daniels autobiography, it deals with his early newspaper career.

Editorials from the Hearst Newspapers. New York: Albertson Publishing Company, 1906. Selected reprints of the Hearst editorial-page offerings at the turn of the century.

Ellis, Elmer, *Mr. Dooley's America.* New York: Knopf, 1941. The life and times of Finley Peter Dunne, humorist and reformer.

Faulkner, Harold U., *The Quest for Social Justice, 1898–1914,* A History of American Life, Vol. XI. New York: Macmillan, 1931. This volume of the series measures up as a work of social history.

Filler, Louis, *Crusaders for American Liberalism.* New York: Harcourt, Brace &

Jovanovich, 1939. A study of the liberals and the muckrakers which is based on the political problems of the era.

Forcey, Charles, *The Crossroads of Liberalism.* New York: Oxford University Press, 1961. A case study of Herbert Croly, Walter Weyl, Walter Lippmann, and their *New Republic* of 1914.

Hapgood, Norman, *The Changing Years.* New York: Holt, Rinehart & Winston, 1930. Reflections of the editor of *Collier's.*

Heaton, John L., *Cobb of "The World."* New York: Dutton, 1924. Includes a sketch of Frank I. Cobb and a collection of his *New York World* editorials.

Knight, Oliver H., ed., *I Protest: Selected Disquisitions of E. W. Scripps.* Madison: University of Wisconsin Press, 1966. An admirable, condensed biography is followed by Scripps' private writings as a "thinker." Best book on Scripps.

Kolko, Gabriel, *The Triumph of Conservatism: A Reinterpretation of American History, 1900–1916.* Chicago: Quadrangle, 1967. A revisionist study by a leading New Left historian.

Lasch, Christopher, *The New Radicalism in America, 1889–1963.* New York: Knopf, 1965. A New Left historian examines social reform through essays about intellectual writers.

Link, Arthur S., *Woodrow Wilson and the Progressive Era, 1910–1917.* New York: Harper & Row, 1954. A volume in the New American Nation series by the biographer of Wilson.

Linn, James W., *James Keeley, Newspaperman.* Indianapolis: Bobbs-Merrill, 1937. The biography of the *Chicago Tribune's* crusading managing editor.

Lyon, Peter, *Success Story: The Life and Times of S. S. McClure.* New York: Scribner's, 1963. His muckraking magazine provides the climax of this prize-winning biography.

McClure, S. S., *My Autobiography.* New York: Frederick A. Stokes & Company, 1914. The story of the magazine publisher.

McRae, Milton A., *Forty Years in Newspaperdom.* New York: Brentano's, 1924. Autobiography of E. W. Scripps' partner and business manager.

Marcosson, Isaac F., *David Graham Phillips and His Times.* New York: Dodd, Mead, 1932. The biography of a muckraker.

Morrison, Joseph L., *Josephus Daniels Says.* Chapel Hill: University of North Carolina Press, 1962. Detailed biography of editor of Raleigh *News-Observer* 1894–1913; his crusading battles, his white supremacy. See also the political biography, *Josephus Daniels: The Small–d Democrat* (1966).

Mowry, George E., *Theodore Roosevelt and the Progressive Movement.* Madison: University of Wisconsin Press, 1946. Traces the relationship of Roosevelt to radicalism.

O'Connor, Richard, *Jack London.* Boston: Little, Brown, 1964. Best of the author's popular biographies of journalists.

Older, Fremont, *My Own Story.* New York: Macmillan, 1926. The fighting San Francisco editor tells his piece.

Phillips, David Graham, *The Treason of the Senate,* edited by George E. Mowry and Judson A. Grenier. Chicago: Quadrangle, 1964. Excellent discussion by the editors precedes texts of Phillips' famed articles in *Cosmopolitan*.

Pollard, James E., *The Presidents and the Press*. New York: Macmillan, 1947. Covers the newspaper relations of Theodore Roosevelt.

Pringle, Henry F., *Theodore Roosevelt*. New York: Harcourt, Brace & Jovanovich, 1931. A Pulitzer Prize biography of the key figure of the muckraking era by a former newspaperman.

Regier, C. C., *The Era of the Muckrakers*. Chapel Hill: University of North Carolina Press, 1932. An exhaustive study of the crusading magazines and their writers. Unhappily it ignores newspapers, thus implying that they lacked interest in muckraking.

Sedgwick, Ellery, *The Happy Profession*. Boston: Little, Brown, 1946. Includes a description of the hurly-burly times at *Leslie's*, the *American*, and *McClure's* before Sedgwick became owner and editor of the *Atlantic* in 1909.

Steffens, Lincoln, *The Autobiography of Lincoln Steffens*. New York: Harcourt, Brace & Jovanovich, 1931. One of the great journalistic autobiographies.

Sullivan, Mark, *Our Times*. New York: Scribner's, 1926 ff. Newspaperman Sullivan's six volumes are crowded with the color and the drama of the years 1900 to 1929, and in addition are historically sound. *Our Times* is a treasure house.

Tarbell, Ida M., *All in the Day's Work*. New York: Macmillan, 1939. The chief woman muckraker reviews her career.

Villard, Oswald Garrison, *Fighting Years*. New York: Harcourt, Brace & Jovanovich, 1939. The autobiography of the publisher of the *Nation* and *New York Evening Post*.

Weinberg, Arthur and Lila, eds., *The Muckrakers*. New York: Simon & Schuster, 1961. A compilation of some of the best magazine articles by the muckrakers, with comments by the editors.

Wilson, Harold S., *McClure's Magazine and the Muckrakers*. Princeton, N.J.: Princeton University Press, 1970. Solid contribution to the subject.

Periodicals and Monographs

Grenier, Judson A., "Muckraking and the Muckrakers: An Historical Definition," *Journalism Quarterly*, XXXVII (Autumn 1960), 552. A study of the movement and leading individuals from 1902–14.

Harrison, John M., "Finley Peter Dunne and the Progressive Movement," *Journalism Quarterly*, XLIV (Autumn 1967), 475. Mr. Dooley's creator was a philosophical anarchist.

Hudson, Robert V., "Will Irwin's Pioneering Criticism of the Press," *Journalism Quarterly*, XLVII (Summer 1970), 263. Based on his biography of Will Irwin, Ph.D. thesis, University of Minnesota, 1970. Authoritative biographical writing.

Knight, Oliver, "Scripps and His Adless Newspaper, *The Day Book*," *Journalism Quarterly*, XLI (Winter 1964), 51. Full story of the effort to create an adless daily.

Pringle, Henry F., "The Newspaper Man as an Artist," *Scribner's*, XCVII (February 1935), 101. The artist was Frank I. Cobb, editor of the *New York World*.

Starr, Louis M., "Joseph Pulitzer and His Most 'Indegoddampendent' Editor," *American Heritage,* XIX (June 1968), 18. The story of Frank Cobb, by a Pulitzer historian.

Stevens, George E., "A History of the Cincinnati *Post,*" Ph.D. thesis, University of Minnesota, 1968. Emphasizes local issues and political coverage of a mainstay Scripps daily. See his "Scripps' Cincinnati *Post:* Liberalism at Home," *Journalism Quarterly,* XLVIII (Summer 1971), 231.

Weigle, Clifford F., "The Young Scripps Editor: Keystone of E. W.'s 'System'," *Journalism Quarterly,* XLI (Summer 1964), 360. A case study of the founding of the *Houston Press.*

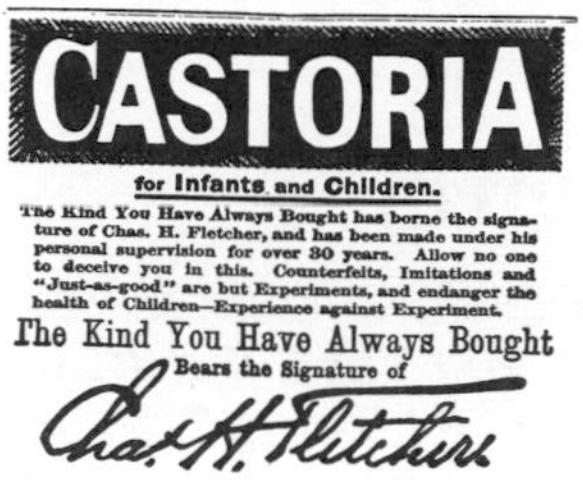

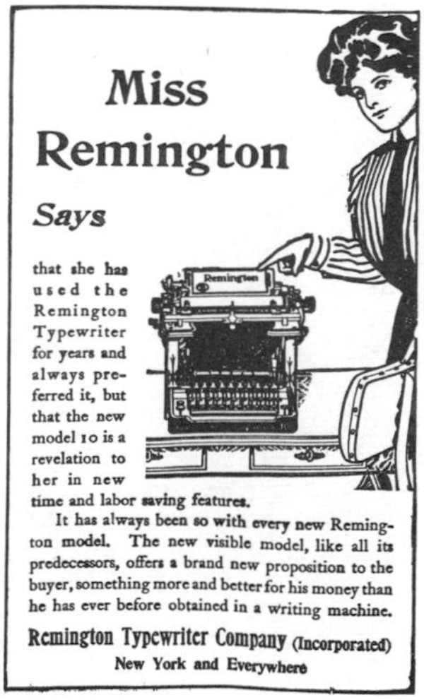

Copyrighted trademarks and brand advertising, 1900–1920

"All the News That's Fit to Print."

The New York Times.

THE WEATHER.

Unsettled Tuesday; Wednesday, fair, cooler; moderate southerly winds, becoming variable.

VOL. LXI...NO. 19,886. NEW YORK, TUESDAY, APRIL 16, 1912.—TWENTY-FOUR PAGES, ONE CENT

TITANIC SINKS FOUR HOURS AFTER HITTING ICEBERG; 866 RESCUED BY CARPATHIA, PROBABLY 1250 PERISH; ISMAY SAFE, MRS. ASTOR MAYBE, NOTED NAMES MISSING

Col. Astor and Bride, Isidor Straus and Wife, and Maj. Butt Aboard.

"RULE OF SEA" FOLLOWED

Women and Children Put Over in Lifeboats and Are Supposed to be Safe on Carpathia.

PICKED UP AFTER 8 HOURS

Vincent Astor Calls at White Star Office for News of His Father and Leaves Weeping.

FRANKLIN HOPEFUL ALL DAY

Manager of the Line Insisted Titanic Was Unsinkable Even After She Had Gone Down.

HEAD OF THE LINE ABOARD

J. Bruce Ismay Making First Trip on Gigantic Ship That Was to Surpass All Others.

The Lost Titanic Being Towed Out of Belfast Harbor.

CAPT. E. J. SMITH,
Commander of the Titanic.

PARTIAL LIST OF THE SAVED.

Includes Bruce Ismay, Mrs. Widener, Mrs. H. B. Harris, and an Incomplete name, suggesting Mrs. Astor's.

Special to The New York Times.

CAPE RACE, N. F., Tuesday, April 16.—Following is a partial list of survivors among the first-class passengers of the Titanic, received by the Marconi wireless station this morning from the Carpathia, via the steamship Olympic:

Biggest Liner Plunges to the Bottom at 2:20 A. M.

RESCUERS THERE TOO LATE

Except to Pick Up the Few Hundreds Who Took to the Lifeboats.

WOMEN AND CHILDREN FIRST

Cunarder Carpathia Rushing to New York with the Survivors.

SEA SEARCH FOR OTHERS

The California Stands By on Chance of Picking Up Other Boats or Rafts.

OLYMPIC SENDS THE NEWS

Only Ship to Flash Wireless Messages to Shore After the Disaster.

LATER REPORT SAVES 866.

BOSTON, April 15.—A wireless message picked up late to-night, relayed from the Olympic, says that the Carpathia is on her way to New York with 866 passengers from the steamer Titanic aboard. They are mostly women and children, the message said, and it concluded: "Grave fears are felt for the safety of the balance of the passengers and crew."

Special to The New York Times.

CAPE RACE, N. F., April 15.—The White Star liner Olympic reports by wireless this evening that the Cunarder Carpathia reached, at daybreak this morning, the position from which wireless calls for help were sent out last night by the Titanic after her collision with an iceberg. The Carpathia found only the lifeboats and the wreckage of what had been the biggest steamship afloat.

The Titanic had foundered at about 2:20 A. M., in latitude 41:46 north and longitude 50:14 west. This is about 30 minutes of latitude, or about 34 miles, due south of the position at which she struck the iceberg. All her boats are accounted for and about 655 souls have been saved of the crew and passengers, most of the latter presumably women and children.

There were about 2,100 persons aboard the Titanic.

The Leyland liner California is remaining and searching the position of the disaster, while the Carpathia is returning to New York with the survivors.

It can be positively stated that up to 11 o'clock to-night nothing whatever had been received at or heard by the Marconi station here to the effect that the Parisian, Virginian or any other ships had picked up any survivors, other than those picked up by the Carpathia.

First News of the Disaster.

The first news of the disaster to the Titanic was received by the Marconi wireless station here at 10:25 o'clock last night [as told in yesterday's New York Times.] The Titanic was first heard giving the distress signal "C. Q. D.," which was answered by a number of ships, including the Carpathia,

Continued on Page 2.

The *New York Times* handles one of the great news stories of the twentieth century.

21

The Great and the Colorful

It will be my earnest aim . . . to give the news impartially, without fear or favor. . . .
—Adolph S. Ochs

The several preceding chapters have been concerned with the historical development of patterns of press behavior. A segment of the press was involved successively in important general trends: the rise of the new journalism, the spread of yellow journalism, and service as "people's champions." But it is difficult to fit newspapers into such patterns, because each newspaper has an individuality born of its publishing environment. In some cases a newspaper's individuality is so pronounced that its story is best told apart from discussions of trends and patterns.

One conspicuous example is the *New York Times*. The *Times* was rescued from near-oblivion in 1896 and began a rise to greatness as a journalistic institution which eventually approached the status of a national newspaper. In the same years, fame also came to a unique and colorful Kansas editor, William Allen White, whose name was known to more persons than was that of the publisher of the *Times*, even though the *Emporia Gazette* was always a small-town paper. Across the country, other newspapers and newspapermen achieved distinctive notice within and without the craft, for varying reasons. Some are more colorful than great, but they are a part of journalistic lore. It is with their stories that this chapter is concerned.

ADOLPH OCHS AND THE *NEW YORK TIMES*

The story of the *New York Times* is the story of the man who rescued it from bankruptcy in 1896 and who guided it until he died in 1935. He was

Adolph S. Ochs, a onetime printer's devil from Tennessee, who salvaged the glories of the *Times* of Henry J. Raymond's day and set its course as America's leading newspaper. It was the men and women he selected to staff the *Times* who made it an institution.[1]

Ochs, like many another great publisher, struggled up from the ranks to win his place. His parents were Germans of Jewish faith, who emigrated to the United States before the Civil War. Adolph, born in 1858 in Cincinnati, was the oldest of six children. His father fought in the Civil War and at its close took his family to Tennessee in a covered wagon. The oldest son went to work, in the tradition of the times. Appropriately enough young Ochs became a carrier boy for the *Knoxville Chronicle* at 11, covering four square miles on foot beginning at 4 a.m. He worked in a grocery store, as a druggist's apprentice, and sandwiched in some schooling. When he was 14 he landed the job as the *Chronicle's* printer's devil.

For a few months in 1875 Ochs tried his hand at newspaper work in Louisville. He became assistant composing room foreman of the *Courier-Journal* and did some reporting for Henry Watterson. But he was a colorless and awkward writer; his genius lay in his business ability and in his capacity for developing ideas and exhibiting journalistic leadership.

Back in Knoxville in 1876 and setting type on the *Tribune,* young Ochs got his chance. The paper's business manager had $100, an impressive sum in the moneyless South of postwar days. The editor, a black-bearded Scotsman of 45 who had all the education Ochs lacked, wanted to start a newspaper in Chattanooga. The three joined forces to publish the *Chattanooga Dispatch.* Ochs was the advertising solicitor and put out a city directory on the side, but within a few months the venture had collapsed.

Chattanooga was an unlikely spot in which to seek success in journalism. It was a city of 12,000 but it was still in the frontier stage, with no sidewalks, muddy streets, and little interest in newspapers. The city had seen 16 newspapers come and go in 40 years and the only survivor was the *Times,* a paper with a decrepit printing shop and a circulation of 250. Ochs had the frontiersman's faith, however, and persuaded a businessman to endorse his note for a $300 bank loan. He got control of the *Times* for $250 and persuaded the old *Dispatch* staff to join him in his new venture. The Scottish editor, Colonel John E. MacGowan, agreed to work for $1.50 a day until times were better. A reporter was added, signing on with a publisher who had exactly $12.50 working capital.

It was July, 1878, and Ochs was not yet 21. But he and his editor promised Chattanooga big things. They would carry all the local news, the latest news

[1] Ochs' story is told in Gerald W. Johnson, *An Honorable Titan* (New York: Harper & Row, 1946). The *Times'* story was first told in Elmer Davis, *History of the New York Times, 1851–1921* (New York: The New York Times, 1921). The panorama of 100 years is presented in Meyer Berger, *The Story of the New York Times: 1851–1951* (New York: Simon & Schuster, 1951).

by telegraph, and particularly all the commercial news which was available. Chattanooga would become the capital of a commercial and agricultural area, Ochs said, and the *Times* would be its indispensable newspaper. He said flatly that he expected community support for "a paper primarily devoted to the material, educational and moral growth of our progressive city and its surrounding territory."

Ochs was a born gambler, and he gambled almost daily to save the *Times*. He borrowed money with one hand, and paid an old loan with the other. He paid his staff in orders on the town's merchants, and took whatever cash and goods he could from advertisers and subscribers. Business improved, but Ochs went deeper in debt in order to buy better presses and type. He built up a string of correspondents through the South to widen his news coverage. He started a weekly edition of the paper, as well as trade journal for southern industrialists, an agricultural journal, and a religious newspaper. His editorials in the *Times* called for a nonpartisan city government for improved river transportation, for sewers, parks, and schools, and for a Chattanooga University. When a fever of land speculation hit the town, the publisher was caught up in the enthusiasm.

Seemingly Ochs was a smashing success. His family moved to Chattanooga and his father and a brother, George, took positions on the newspaper. The *Times* by 1892 was clearing $25,000 a year and was regarded as one of the South's best newspaper properties. That year Ochs built a $150,000 gold-domed newspaper building which was the pride of Chattanooga. But in the meantime the real estate bubble had burst, and Ochs was in great financial trouble. To pay off his debts, he required more money than he could make with the *Chattanooga Times*. What he needed, Ochs decided, was another newspaper. He looked about the country for four years, and in March, 1896, he heard that there was a gambler's chance to buy the *New York Times*.

Ochs was properly impressed by this opportunity. He knew how respected the *Times* had been since its founding by Henry J. Raymond in 1851. After Raymond's death in 1869, the paper had come under the direction of its business manager, George Jones. Jones, editor Louis J. Jennings, and chief assistant John Foord had helped to smash Boss Tweed in the seventies. John C. Reid had served well as managing editor from 1872 to 1889 and the paper had maintained its place until the death of Jones in 1891. By then the impact of the "new journalism" was having its effect.

The new guiding spirit on the *Times* became Charles R. Miller, a graduate of Dartmouth and former staff member of the *Springfield Republican,* who assumed the editorship in 1883. With associate editor Edward Cary and other staff members, Miller negotiated purchase of the *Times* from the Jones family heirs in 1893 for approximately a million dollars. But the paper did not prosper. It had the smallest circulation of the city's eight morning dailies, a paltry 9,000 paid circulation concealed in a 21,000 press run. This was not far behind the

Tribune's 16,000 but far below the *Sun's* 70,000 morning circulation, the *Herald's* 140,000, and the *World's* 200,000 morning figure.

OCHS BUYS THE *TIMES*, 1896

Ochs did not have the money to save the *Times*, but he convinced Miller that he had the know-how and the vision which would be needed to put the paper in a sound competitive position. An elaborate refinancing plan was advanced which would give Ochs control of the paper within four years if he succeeded in revitalizing it. Ochs trudged through the Wall Street district for months persuading financiers, even including J. P. Morgan, to buy bonds in the new enterprise. Finally, in August, 1896, an agreement was completed, with Ochs putting up $75,000 of his own money and risking his Chattanooga paper on the outcome. The 38-year-old Tennessean, with 24 years of experience since his printer's devil days, now was competing with Pulitzer, Hearst, Dana, Reid, and Bennett in the New York field. Though he stood in awe of the journalistic greats, he felt confident that he would restore the *Times* to a position of leadership. After all, he told himself, he had sold J. P. Morgan on investing in a newspaper which currently was losing $2,000 a week.

The plan of attack which Ochs had devised to save the *New York Times* was simple. He would not attempt to match the sensationalism of Hearst and Pulitzer, nor would he popularize the paper's offerings in a halfway effort to keep up with the mass circulation leaders, as some other New York publishers were attempting to do. Instead he would publish a paper with solid news coverage and editorial opinion which would be designed for readers who did not like overemphasis of entertainment and features.

Ochs' declaration of principle contained these lines:

> It will be my earnest aim that the *New York Times* give the news, all the news, in concise and attractive form, in language that is parliamentary in good society, and give it as early, if not earlier, than it can be learned through any other reliable medium; to give the news impartially, without fear or favor, regardless of any party, sect or interest involved; to make the columns of the *New York Times* a forum for the consideration of all questions of public importance, and to that end to invite intelligent discussion from all shades of opinion.[2]

In the years which followed Ochs and his staff made good on these promises. The effort to give all the news with the greatest possible speed became the *Times'* working principle. "To give the news impartially, without fear or favor" became the *Times'* creed. And the promise to make the newspaper "a

[2] *New York Times*, August 19, 1896.

forum for the consideration of all questions of public importance" was carried out in both news and editorial columns.

Ochs' first steps were unspectacular, but effective. He used his printer's ability to revamp the paper's typographical appearance and to improve the mechanical department. With Henry Loewenthal, a veteran of 20 years of *Times* service whom Ochs named managing editor, he set out to develop news coverage which other papers were handling inadequately. The *Times* began to publish a guide listing the out-of-town buyers who were in the city. It reported daily real estate transactions. And it expanded its market reports, adding to the daily coverage a weekly financial review. The business and financial community began to find these *Times* features increasingly valuable. Lawyers similarly were attracted by another column listing court cases and records.

The class of readers to which Ochs was appealing also liked the emphasis placed upon reporting of news of government. It liked Ochs' Sunday magazine, which featured articles of current news significance rather than entertainment. It liked the *Times* book review section. It liked the expanded "letters to the editor" column which presented the comments and opinions of all contributors without regard to the paper's editorial policy. And it enjoyed an editorial-page feature begun in 1896 by Frederick C. Mortimer and continued by him for 30 years, consisting of paragraphs written in a lighter style and called "Topics of the Times."

On the business side Ochs found two valuable associates. One was Louis Wiley, who came from the *New York Sun* to become manager of the *Times*. Wiley soon established himself as Ochs' personal representative in civic and newspaper trade affairs, the relationship being similar to that between McRae and Scripps. As the "front man" and business manager, Wiley served ably until his death in 1935. Associated with him in the management was John Norris, from the *World* staff, an active leader in newspaper advertising and business affairs. Advertising linage passed that of the *Tribune* in the first year, and the *Times* used every device to increase its circulation, even becoming the first paper to solicit by telephone.

Still the *Times* was not prospering. Ochs determinedly set his face against the popular features of the new journalism, refusing to run "stunt" stories, banning comics from his columns, and giving pictures short shrift. He sniped at the yellow journalists, advertising the *Times* under the slogan "It Does Not Soil the Breakfast Cloth" before choosing the famous front-page ear, "All the News That's Fit to Print." But circulation in 1898 was still at the 25,000 mark. It was dwarfed by the huge circulations of the *World* and *Journal* during the Spanish-American War period, when the *Times* was hurt by its lack of resources to compete with its rivals for exclusive war stories.

Ochs decided in late 1898 to make one last gamble. The *Times* was selling for three cents, the *World* and *Journal* for two. Why not cut the price of the *Times* to a penny and thus win the circulation which was needed to ensure solid advertising support? His associates were skeptical. But Ochs insisted that the kind of readers who wanted to buy the *Times* could be found at all economic levels. Poor men and women, and those of limited incomes, would welcome the paper at a price they could afford, Ochs argued. They soon would discover that the *Times* was a different kind of penny paper from the usual venture at that price.

Once again the old formula of price adjustment was successful. The *Times* as a penny paper jumped to 75,000 circulation in 1899 and passed the 100,000 mark in 1901. Its advertising linage doubled within two years. The red ink turned to black and Ochs won majority control of the paper's stock under his purchasing agreement. He promptly went into debt again to build the Times Tower on Broadway, in what became Times Square, putting $2,500,000 into what was in 1904 one of New York's most spectacular buildings. The strategic location of the *Times* plant in what became the city's nighttime heart and the later development of its moving electric news bulletins helped to establish the paper as one of the city's institutions.

CARR VAN ANDA, MANAGING EDITOR

Far more important to the future of the *Times* was another event of 1904, however. That year Carr V. Van Anda, America's foremost managing editor, began his 25-year career as the guiding genius of the *Times* news staff. With Miller directing the editorial page, Wiley the business office, and Van Anda the news room, Ochs had completed the quartet which would build the *Times* to greatness by the 1920s. Of them all it was Van Anda who contributed most directly to the *Times'* reputation as a great news-gathering organization.

To single out Van Anda as America's foremost managing editor perhaps seems extraordinary, for comparisons of the accomplishments of men in different eras and different publishing situations are difficult to make. But it is generally agreed that the chief architect of the superior news department of the *New York Times* was Van Anda, a man who shunned personal publicity so completely that despite his incredible achievements he became almost a legendary figure even to his own craft.[3]

Alexander Woollcott once remarked that Van Anda "loved the editing of a newspaper more than anything in the world." Apparently he was born with this love, for as a boy of six in an Ohio village in 1870, he was pasting clippings on sheets of paper and selling them for 10 cents a copy. At 10 he made a press out of a wooden frame, an ink roller from a cloth-wrapped broom handle, and printed with type salvaged from the village paper. Next he acquired a small

[3] See Davis, *History of the New York Times,* p. 274, and Berger, *The Story of the New York Times,* p. 160, for two estimates of Van Anda's role in building the *Times.* Many tributes to Van Anda from leaders in his profession are found in a short biography: Barnett Fine, *A Giant of the Press* (New York: Editor & Publisher Library, 1933). Berger carries the story of Van Anda's achievements through several chapters.

New York Times

New York Times

Adolph S. Ochs (*above*) rescued the *New York Times* from bankruptcy in 1896 and made it one of the world's great newspapers before he died in 1935. His longtime managing editor, Carr Van Anda (*right*), achieved fame as the man most instrumental in developing the *Times'* superb news coverage. It was Ochs, however, whose leadership made the achievements of Van Anda and other staff members possible.

press and did job printing, using the profits to finance his study of chemistry and physics. When he entered Ohio University at 16 he specialized in mathematics and science and had not the lure of journalism been so strong he likely would have become a scholar in the realms of astronomy and physics. As it was, he became a layman who could keep step with the keen minds in those fields.

Van Anda left college at 18 to become foreman for his village paper. Next he set type and reported for the *Cleveland Herald* and other Cleveland papers. When he was 22 he applied for work on the *Baltimore Sun* and was selected for the important post of night editor. Two years later, in 1888, he moved to the *New York Sun,* where after five years he became night editor. Dana and his managing editor, Chester S. Lord, recognized the genius of the young night editor who had no thought other than to obtain all the news for the next morning's edition. Later, Van Anda described the work of a night editor in words which reflect his own ability:

> The man most to be envied is the night editor. The night editor's work, always of world-wide scope, is never dull. He is the appraiser of events. He is the keeper of a St. Peter's Ledger of the news of the day. To him the excellence of a newspaper is due. He can make or mar it. The night editor passes finally on every item. He is the retriever of errors and must always be on the lookout for shortcomings and neglected opportunities.
>
> He should be keen, alert, and well-informed. He must be sympathetic, imaginative, human. As he sits quietly reading proof slips, it is he who is framing the reflection of itself the world will see at the breakfast table. When you have achieved this post you have reached the highest place in your profession. It is true there are a few figures ahead of you, the managing editor and the editor-in-chief, but these are only offices to absorb the profit of other people's work.[4]

Van Anda set standards for the night editor which few other men could attain. He combined intellectual ability with a rare sense for news and news play. The qualities of imagination and integrity were both his to a high degree. And he had the physical stamina to edit the news thoroughly, accurately, and intelligently day in and day out, reading every story in copy or proof and yet standing ready to meet "shortcomings and neglected opportunities."

When Ochs decided in 1904 that his first managing editor, Henry Loewenthal, should devote full attention to business news, Van Anda's name was suggested to him. The association was to be an ideal one. Ochs was willing to spend money to get the news; Van Anda was more than willing to spend it for him. Both Ochs and Van Anda put every emphasis on getting all the news possible for the reader. The almost unlimited freedom which Van Anda found

[4] As quoted in Fine, *A Giant of the Press* (New York: Editor & Publisher Library, 1933), p. 29.

at the *Times* to utilize his skills was recognized by business manager Louis Wiley at a 1929 banquet celebrating the twenty-fifth anniversary of the Van Anda managing editorship, when he said, "It is well known that the *Times* prints only advertising for which Mr. Van Anda's news leaves room, in a paper of the size determined by him."[5] As the years went by there was an ever-increasing volume of both news and advertising, but the news came first.

Although he was now a managing editor, Van Anda never stopped serving as night editor. His routine at the *Times*, for 20 years, never varied. He appeared in the newsroom at 1 P.M., went home at 6 P.M. for dinner and a rest, and returned at 10 P.M. to stay until the last man departed at 5 A.M. Usually he was the last man. Twelve hours a day, seven days a week, Van Anda was riding the news, giving as much attention to the flow of stories as to the major news breaks. He loved to match his speed and wits against a deadline. He loved to exploit an important but undeveloped story and give it painstaking coverage and significant play. But he never lost sight of the importance of conscientious and intelligent handling of the bulk of the news, and he transmitted this spirit to his staff. He was not a colorful, dynamic leader; rather he was reserved and cold in appearance and his piercing gaze was called the "Van Anda death ray." But those who worked with him found him a modest, sympathetic chief who backed his men completely and who never flew into a rage. His secret was in doing his own job so well that the impress was made both upon the newspaper and upon its staff.

Some paragraphs from advice once given by Van Anda to journalism students indicate the qualities he sought in his staff:

> All who expect to become journalists must begin as reporters. The first requirement is a knowledge of the language. You must know your language as a musician knows his instrument. You must be able to detect the false word as readily as the musician does a false note. . . .
>
> When you go to work in a newspaper office, regard your particular task as the biggest thing in the world. Learn to distinguish what you know and what you think you know and write only what you are certain of. The vice of guessing is never eradicated. Don't use slang unless you have the faculty of seizing on those slang expressions of today that will be the idioms of tomorrow. You may not invent, but you may imagine. If you possess the gift of imagination to any degree, you'll be qualified to adorn your profession. . . .
>
> The first test of a good reporter is the collection of facts and impressions. He must be eager and curious about everything under the sun and beyond it. Next, he must have industry, and lastly, he must possess the ability to distinguish the true from the false, to differentiate the dull from the common-place. Here lies the opportunity to make journalism a profession, not a trade. . . .
>
> Let me commend the copyreader to you. His work is no less essential

[5] *Ibid.*, p. 103.

> to the paper than that of the reporter. A first rate copyreader can make a first rate newspaper out of third rate copy. On the other hand a poor copyreader can spoil the work of the best reporter. . . . He must possess keen literary appreciation. If he cannot write brilliantly he must write well enough to convert bad copy into good. He must be able to apply sandpaper to the bodily excrescences of an article, but not to its soul. His range of information must be wide and at instant command. He must know where to lay his hands on the facts he cannot draw from his memory. His chief joy is in the headlines. A two or three column story is told in a few words, luring the reader on if the subject interests him, warning him to pass on if it doesn't. In writing headlines . . . stick to honest nouns and verbs.[6]

VAN ANDA COVERS THE NEWS

There are many stories of Van Anda's almost legendary ability to practice what he preached. Soon after he became managing editor of the *Times,* word arrived that the decisive naval battle of the Russo-Japanese War might be at hand. Van Anda recognized the importance of the event and readied himself to handle the story. When the bulletin came, at 4:30 one morning, that the Japanese admiral, Togo, had smashed the Russian fleet, all of Van Anda's elaborate research and preparation went into play. Within 19 minutes the *Times* had put an extra to press with the bulletin and a half-page of war news on page one, running under headlines written by Van Anda as the page was being remade. Inside was more advance material which Van Anda long before had made ready for this moment. Forty thousand copies were run off and the managing editor rode about the city with a fleet of horse-drawn wagons at dawn seeing personally that his news play beat was prominently displayed on the newsstands.

It was Van Anda who took over when a big story broke at deadline time. He scanned the copy, and then sometimes ran to the composing room to set the headlines into type himself. He was "setting from the case," never stopping to write the heads—yet they always would fit. Van Anda's delight in beating an edition deadline in this manner often gave the *Times* a lead over its rivals in rushing the news to the readers.

More important than speed was Van Anda's ability to sense the news, to plan for expansion of a story, to calculate the true significance of an as-yet-undeveloped event. His classic achievement was his handling of the story of the sinking of the liner "Titanic" in 1912. Here, as in other situations, it was Van Anda's personal ability and the functioning of a well-trained staff of high caliber which combined to produce superior news coverage.

It was 1:20 A.M. Monday, April 15, 1912, when the first Associated Press

[6] As quoted in Fine, *A Giant of the Press,* pp. 81–83.

bulletin reached the *Times* newsroom reporting that the luxury liner "Titanic" had struck an iceberg on its maiden voyage from Britain to America. An SOS had been picked up by the Marconi wireless station in Newfoundland. The "Titanic" supposedly was unsinkable, but Van Anda's rapid calls to *Times* correspondents in Halifax and Montreal and to the offices of the White Star Line told him that the ship's wireless had fallen silent a half-hour after the first call for help, and convinced him that the ship must have gone down.

Before 3:30 A.M. Van Anda and his staff had organized the story. Among the more than 2,200 aboard were many famous persons. A background story was prepared on the passenger list, and a picture of the "Titanic" was prepared for page one. Two other vessels had reported close scrapes with icebergs in the North Atlantic area; this fitted the pattern of the news available about the "Titanic." The *Times* in several columns of type reported Monday morning that the ship had sunk, while other papers were handling the story in incomplete and inconclusive form.

Tuesday, Wednesday, and Thursday, the story commanded the world's attention, as the liner "Carpathia" sailed toward New York with survivors. Van Anda on Tuesday hired a floor in a hotel a block from the "Carpathia's" pier and installed four telephone lines directly connected to the *Times* city room. The entire staff was mobilized under the direction of Arthur Greaves, city editor, to cover the arrival of the rescue ship Thursday night. Van Anda persuaded Guglielmo Marconi, the wireless inventor, to board the ship to interview the wireless operator—and a *Times* reporter slipped through the police lines with the inventor. He got an exclusive story of the last messages from the "Titanic."

Within three hours after the arrival of the rescue ship the *Times'* first edition appeared, with 15 of its 24 pages devoted to the story of the loss of 1,500 lives in the "Titanic" disaster. In coverage and in organization of a great news story that edition of the *Times* remains a masterpiece.[7]

THE WIRELESS AND WORLDWIDE NEWS

Van Anda and Ochs both loved speed in the gathering of the news and this love had led the *Times* to leadership in the use of correspondents and communications facilities in such instances as the "Titanic" sinking. Both men had watched the work of Marconi, the Italian scientist who between the years 1895 and 1900 devised a practical system of sending telegraphic messages through space by means of electromagnetic waves. Marconi's "wireless" telegraphy was based upon the experiments of others, but it was he who obtained the basic patents and formed the first commercial wireless company in London in 1897.

[7] For the full story of the "Titanic" coverage see Berger, *The Story of the New York Times*, pp. 193–201. A contemporary account by Alexander McD. Stoddart appeared in the *Independent*, LXXII (May 2, 1912), 945.

Ship-to-shore communication and the use of the wireless by English newspapers and the *New York Herald* to cover sporting events soon followed. In December, 1901, Marconi successfully transmitted signals from England to Newfoundland. But it was not until 1907 that a headline in the *Times* reported:

"Wireless Joins Two Worlds. Marconi Trans-Atlantic Service Opened With A Dispatch To The *New York Times*." [8]

The front page carried the *Times'* promotional stories and congratulatory messages from notables in Britain. Wireless was faster and less expensive than the commercial cable, and as operating difficulties were overcome, the *Times* began to present two to three pages of wireless news from Europe each Sunday. During the first World War, correspondents in Germany used the wireless to reach the United States with their stories without intervention of British censorship, until American entry into the war. By 1920 the *Times*, as well as the *Chicago Tribune*, had built its own transatlantic wireless receiving station, and the activities of these and other newspapers led to the establishment of Press Wireless, Inc. The development of shortwave transmission after 1924 enabled the *Times* to complete its own radio facilities to receive press messages from any point in the world. Fred E. Meinholtz became the *Times* communications chief who kept his paper in the front rank technically so that the world's news could be received directly and exclusively.

The team of Van Anda and Ochs was spending money freely to establish a network of correspondents in the United States and abroad so that the *Times* would have its own men reporting the news. In 1919, when British astronomers decided to test the revolutionary mathematical formulae of the then-obscure Albert Einstein, Van Anda assigned his London bureau to the story. The result was a copyrighted piece reporting the confirmation of the Einstein theory. Later, according to *Times* legend, Van Anda edited a story containing extremely complicated material from an Einstein lecture and spotted an error which professional mathematicians had missed.

The field of archaeology provided Van Anda with one more triumph in 1922. An Associated Press story based on a dispatch to the *Times* of London reported in 250 words the discovery of the tomb of an Egyptian Pharaoh, Tutankh-Amen. Van Anda quickly obtained exclusive rights in the United States to the story of the man all America came to know as "King Tut." Van Anda, it turned out, had added a knowledge of Egyptology to his many accomplishments and astounded the staff by himself deciphering the hieroglyphics in a photograph late one night when a translator was not available. He also detected a 3,500-year-old forgery on the tomb and duly reported it.[9]

There also was space for the lighter side of the news in the *Times* of the Van Anda era. It paid handsomely in 1910 to have ex-prizefight champion John L. Sullivan cover the Jeffries-Johnson title bout in Reno. Van Anda preferred

[8] *New York Times*, October 18, 1907.

[9] According to Russell Owen, writing in the *New York Times Magazine*, December 21, 1947, p. 2.

non-sportswriters for his featured stories on the big fights, and had Irvin S. Cobb cover the Dempsey-Carpentier bout. Elmer Davis, a young reporter fresh from studies as a Rhodes Scholar, reported the Dempsey-Gibbons match. The *Times* also gave extensive coverage to major crime stories of the period. When Ochs was twitted about this departure from usual *Times* policy he replied, "The yellows see such stories only as opportunities for sensationalism. When the *Times* gives a great amount of space to such stories it turns out authentic sociological documents."[10] Ochs knew that even the audience to which the *Times* appealed was interested in this brand of sociology.

THE *TIMES* IN WORLD WAR I

Ranking above all else in bringing the *Times* to greatness, however, was its coverage of the events of the first World War. It was in this period that the paper began to publish the texts of documents and speeches, a policy which led to its becoming the leading reference newspaper for librarians, scholars, government officials, and other newspaper editors. The compilation of the *New York Times Index* further ensured the paper this position.

Six full pages in an August, 1914, issue of the *Times* presented the British White Paper to American readers. The *Times* had been the first American paper to obtain a copy of the British Foreign Office's correspondence with Germany and Austria, and printed it in full. Next day it published the text of the German version of events leading up to the war declaration, brought from Berlin by a *Times* correspondent, for another exclusive.

Van Anda meanwhile was giving his readers minute coverage of the military news, using press association accounts, the reports of his own correspondents with the various armies, and stories obtained from the *London Chronicle*. War pictures were carried in a rotogravure section, added by Ochs in 1914 after Van Anda had investigated rotogravure printing in Germany. Political and economic reporting from European capitals was given proper emphasis with the military news. On the editorial page, editor Charles R. Miller ably documented the Allied cause and placed the blame for the war upon the German and Austrian governments.

When the United States entered the war the *Times* expanded its coverage. Costs of cabled news reached $750,000 a year but Van Anda did not hesitate to order the most elaborate coverage, sent at costly "urgent" rates if necessary, in order to give the *Times* the lead on a significant story. As a result the paper piled up a record number of exclusive interpretive stories and news beats which gave it additional prestige. Among its own war correspondents or syndicated contributors were Walter Duranty, Philip Gibbs, and Wythe Williams, three of the leading foreign correspondents of their era; Charles Grasty, the onetime

[10] As quoted in Berger, *The Story of the New York Times,* p. 258.

Baltimore publisher; and a young *Times* staffman named Edwin L. James, who was destined to become the paper's managing editor. For its wartime coverage the *Times* was awarded one of the first Pulitzer Prizes in 1918.

The *Times* climaxed its wartime coverage with the only publication by a newspaper of the text of the Treaty of Versailles, a document which filled eight pages. Ochs and Miller wholeheartedly supported President Woodrow Wilson's fight for American entry into the League of Nations and the paper covered the lengthy peace negotiations and the postwar American political situation in detail, presenting official documents in increasing numbers even though advertising had to be curtailed to obtain the necessary space during a time of newsprint shortage. If there is a complaint to be registered against the *Times* of the Ochs and Van Anda period it centers upon its voluminous presentation of the news without sufficient interpretation for the average reader, who was lost in the columns of information presented in a "deadpan" objective fashion.

THE *TIMES* TO 1935

After 25 years of Ochs' ownership, the *Times* of 1921 had achieved major stature. There was one great reason for this success. The paper had taken in some $100,000,000 in those 25 years and had paid out but 4 per cent in dividends. Ochs had poured the millions into the *Times* for buildings and equipment, for staff, and for the tremendous news coverage which Van Anda had built. Circulation had reached 330,000 daily and more than 500,000 Sunday, while advertising linage had increased tenfold in the 25 years, passing the 23-million-mark. Ochs was a great builder and the *Times* was the symbol of his business success.

Politically the *Times* had been Democratic except during the Bryan campaigns. But it was essentially conservative in tone, particularly in its economic outlook. It was progressive in its social viewpoint but Ochs was not one of the crusaders of the "people's champions" variety. After going down to defeat on the League of Nations issue with the 1920 Democratic ticket of James M. Cox and Franklin D. Roosevelt, the *Times*' favorite Democrat of the early 1920s was John W. Davis, the New York lawyer who was defeated by Calvin Coolidge in the 1924 election. The *Times* supported Alfred E. Smith in 1928 and Franklin D. Roosevelt in 1932 in the final campaigns before Ochs' death.

The 1920s saw one era of *Times* history ending and another beginning. Editor Miller died in 1922 and was succeeded by Rollo Ogden, longtime *New York Post* editor. Van Anda went into semiretirement in 1925 although he continued to hold the title of managing editor until 1932. Frederick T. Birchall, his distinguished associate in the newsroom and also a leading foreign correspondent continued the Van Anda tradition. Appearing on the staff in the early twenties were such future *Times* luminaries as Mrs. Anne O'Hare McCormick, foreign correspondent; Lester Markel, Sunday editor; and Louis Stark, labor reporter. Following them were Waldemar Kaempffert and William L. Laurence in the field of science and Arthur Krock in the Washington bureau. David H. Joseph became city editor in 1927 for a 21-year term, and Edwin L. James became managing editor in 1932 after his European assignments.

While still active in management, Ochs groomed his son-in-law, Arthur Hays Sulzberger, and his nephew, Julius Ochs Adler, to succeed him. The deaths of Ochs and his business manager, Louis Wiley, in 1935 removed the last of the quartet which had been instrumental in building the *Times*. But the organization which they had created continued to carry the paper to new heights in the succeeding years. What the newspaper and its staff contributed to recent American journalism becomes a part of a later story.

WILLIAM ALLEN WHITE AND THE *EMPORIA GAZETTE*

While Ochs was guiding the destinies of the *Times* in his comparatively impersonal role as head of a journalistic institution, a small-town Kansas editor was making a highly personal impact upon American society. William Allen White was born in Emporia, Kansas, in 1868, and died there in 1944. But between those years he became a citizen of America and a spokesman for its small towns—of which Emporia became the symbol. The editor of the *Emporia Gazette* was anything but a typical representative of his kind of journalism, but nevertheless his newspaper editorship was the foundation for his larger activities.

Emporia Gazette

William Allen White

White declared in his *Autobiography* that never in his life did he want money for the necessities of life or for his few extravagances. He was in many respects a typical member of the American middle class, with an impulsive, sentimental streak that saved him from being as dull a small-town editor as he might have been expected to be, and a perceptiveness and understanding of changing American social and economic conditions which enabled him to be a thoughtful leader of his class. The historian Allan Nevins describes White admirably in this paragraph:

> White developed a burly, genial, neighborly personality which endeared him to a wide audience. Loving his profession of country editor, to him Emporia was a microcosm of the world. He liked the opportunity his editorial chair gave him of surveying human weaknesses and virtues, of being teacher and helper to the whole community, of expressing his own audacious opinion today upon some problem which affected a single family or block, and tomorrow upon some issue of world importance. His informality, the trait of a really great and transparently sincere personality, was captivating, and in combination with his spontaneous literary talent, enabled him to touch chords of humor and pathos, and to rise to occasional levels of literary beauty, which would have been quite impossible under the restraints of ordinary urban journalism. In his outlook upon national affairs, he began as a conservative, but rapidly worked around to a vigorous political and social insurgency, which in turn gave way to a philosophic tolerance of liberal stamp.[11]

White's father died before the son entered the University of Kansas and he decided he should earn his own way. So he worked as a printer and reporter for a weekly newspaper and as a college correspondent for several papers. After a year as a reporter and legislative correspondent for the *Kansas City Journal,* White went over to William Rockhill Nelson's *Star* in 1892 as an editorial writer. During his three years of exposure to the *Star's* journalistic atmosphere he wrote the first of his several books and married Sallie Lindsay, his lifelong helpmate. Then in 1895 he scraped together $3,000 and bought the *Emporia Gazette,* which had been started by the Populist party five years before. It had a poor reputation, a run-down shop, and fewer than 600 subscribers. But William Allen White, age 27, was home in Emporia.

Kansas had been captured during the 1893 depression by the Populists and the Democrats. White was an active Republican editor and politician—he loved politics all his life and remained a party worker and an intimate of politicians from the time of William McKinley and Theodore Roosevelt to that of Wendell Willkie and Franklin Roosevelt. On August 15, 1896, White exploded with anger at the Populists in an editorial which shot him into national fame. It was "What's the Matter with Kansas?" which White later referred to as representing "conservatism in its full and perfect flower." The editorial cited evidence that Kansas was declining in population and economic standing and placed the blame in fully unrestrained and effective style upon the "shabby, wild-eyed, rattle-brained fanatics" of the reform movement.[12] It was reprinted

[11] Allan Nevins, *American Press Opinion* (New York: D. C. Heath, 1928), pp. 455–56. Nevins reprints several of White's editorials.

[12] The editorial is reprinted in *The Autobiography of William Allen White* (New York: Macmillan, 1946), pp. 280–83. It also appears in Nevins, *American Press Opinion,* pp. 419–22.

in virtually every Republican newspaper in the country, as ammunition against the Democratic candidate for president, William Jennings Bryan. William McKinley's campaign manager, Mark Hanna, adopted the young editor. But Bryan and the Democrats won the election in Kansas.

WHITE ON THE NATIONAL STAGE

White now moved to the national stage. He became the friend of political leaders, and came to know the young New York Republican, Theodore Roosevelt, to whom he became deeply attached and who was his lifelong political hero. Publication of a volume of stories about life in Kansas had brought White to the attention, too, of literary and intellectual circles and he met William Dean Howells, Hamlin Garland, and other writers of the developing school of realism. More importantly, he met S. S. McClure and became a member of the circle which included Lincoln Steffens, Ray Stannard Baker, John Phillips, and Ida M. Tarbell. His articles and stories about Kansas and politics appeared in several magazines. White was now in tune with the times, hobnobbing with the muckrakers and becoming with his wife a frequent visitor at the Oyster Bay home of the Theodore Roosevelts. The *Emporia Gazette* began to demand reforms: conservation of natural resources, railroad rate control, working men's compensation, direct primaries, the initiative and referendum, abolition of child labor.

When Roosevelt split with William Howard Taft in 1912, and the Progressive party was formed, White was Kansas national committeeman for the new third party. He admired the liberal principles of Senator Robert M. La Follette of Wisconsin and of Governor Woodrow Wilson of New Jersey, but he followed Roosevelt and campaigned furiously for "the Colonel." He hoped that the Progressive party would supplant the Republican party in the national scene, but when the insurgent movement eventually collapsed, White re-entered Republican politics. He was a supporter of the League of Nations—an internationalist in isolationist territory—and when World War II came, he was a leader in the Committee to Defend America by Aiding the Allies. He admired the social gains of the New Deal, but he preferred the leadership of Theodore Roosevelt to that of Franklin Roosevelt.

In these later years White was forced to print a special weekly edition of the *Gazette* as a service to subscribers throughout the country. His most important book was *Puritan in Babylon,* a study of the America of the twenties as well as of Calvin Coolidge. But his most famous single piece of writing is the editorial, "Mary White," which appeared in 1921 when his teen-age daughter died in a horseback riding accident. In it is embodied the artistic soul of William Allen White.[13] His son, William L. White, became a newspaperman

[13] The editorial has appeared in many anthologies of literature and is reprinted in *The Autobiography of William Allen White,* pp. 606–09.

and writer in his own right and assumed the editorship of the *Gazette* when his father died in 1944. But although the *Gazette* continued to prosper, its peculiar qualities were no more.

ED HOWE AND THE *ATCHISON GLOBE*

Another of America's distinctive small-town editors also lived and worked in Kansas. He was Ed Howe, who in 1877 at the age of 22 founded the daily *Atchison Globe* with $200 capital. Howe was a superlative reporter. He knew people and how to report their little doings. However, he had none of White's expansiveness and sentimentality, but rather an amazing ability to make trouble for himself. He told the people of Kansas that religion was all bosh, and he asserted in a time of agitation for women's rights that a woman's place was strictly in the home. His terse, sardonic editorial paragraphs often reflected a keen understanding of human nature, however, and they were widely requoted in the country's newspapers as the work of the "Sage of Potato Hill." His excellent novel, *The Story of a Country Town,* added to his national fame.

THE LAST GREAT YEARS OF THE *NEW YORK WORLD*

Among the great and colorful editors of the years immediately preceding and following World War I were the aging editor of the *Louisville Courier-Journal,* Henry Watterson, and the dynamic editor of the *New York World,* Frank I. Cobb. Watterson, though reaching the close of a career which had started in Civil War days, was vigorously and colorfully attacking Theodore Roosevelt in his columns, expressing his distrust of "Professor" Woodrow Wilson, and delighting in an exchange of editorial argument with men like Cobb. Two months after World War I began, Watterson adopted the simple but effective battlecry: "To Hell with the Hohenzollerns and the Hapsburgs!" His more intellectual arguments for American entry into the war won for him the 1918 Pulitzer Prize for editorial writing—a fitting tribute to a great journalistic figure.

Cobb's editorial page represented the realization of Joseph Pulitzer's hopes for the full development of the *New York World.* The editor whom Pulitzer had carefully trained before his own death in 1911 was unexcelled in his forcible expression of logically developed opinions. The *World* commanded deep respect for its intelligent and fair-minded approaches to issues of public importance, for its progressive and hard-hitting crusades which combined the reporting abilities of its news staff and the support of the editorial writers, and for its brilliant, if sometimes erratic, news play. It became one of those favorites of the press world which are called "newspapermen's newspapers."

The *World* helped to "discover" Woodrow Wilson as a presidential candidate, and Cobb and Wilson became close friends. Cobb's often-expressed fear of centralization of authority was in part overcome by his association with Wilson, and the *World* vigorously supported the far-reaching New Freedom program of economic and social reform which gave the federal government vast new powers. Cobb was one of Wilson's advisers at the Versailles peace conference, giving expression to the hopes for international cooperation which the *World* had long held. His battles in the columns of the *World* for American participation in the League of Nations and the World Court were unavailing, but they further established the paper as the leading spokesman of the Democratic party.

Tragedy struck the *World* in 1923 when Cobb died at the height of his powers. For just eight years later the *World* itself succumbed, and many a sorrowing newspaperman muttered, "If only Cobb had lived. . . ." Probably there would have been no difference in the fate of the *World* but it was true that after Cobb's death the newspaper lacked the genius of leadership which it had enjoyed since its purchase by Pulitzer in 1883.

During the middle twenties the *World* seemed to be continuing its powerful position. Cobb had left behind a distinguished editorial-page staff, headed now by Walter Lippmann. Among the editorial writers were Maxwell Anderson and Laurence Stallings—more famous for their play, "What Price Glory"—and Charles Merz, later to become editor of the *New York Times.* Appearing on the *World's* "op. ed." page were Heywood Broun, the liberal-thinking columnist of "It Seems to Me" fame, Franklin P. Adams, conductor of the "Conning Tower," and Frank Sullivan, who like Anderson and Stallings moved to other creative fields. Rollin Kirby, the cartoonist, won three Pulitzer Prizes in this period for the *World.*

Despite this brilliance and the distinguished record of the paper, Joseph Pulitzer's creation was losing the battle in New York morning journalism. Pressing it on one side were Ochs' *Times* and the merger-created *Herald Tribune.* Soaking up circulation on the other side were the tabloids that appeared in the early twenties. The *World* failed to keep pace with its orthodox rivals in complete coverage of the news, even though it sometimes performed brilliantly, and it saw some of its subway-riding readers succumbing to the lure of the tabloids. Of the Pulitzer heirs, Joseph Pulitzer, Jr., had shown the most ability but he had assumed control of the *St. Louis Post-Dispatch.* His brothers, Ralph and Herbert, delegated much authority to Herbert Bayard Swope as executive editor, but Swope left the *World* staff in 1928. Already the newspaper was running a deficit, and in the depression of 1930 Pulitzer family losses on the morning, evening, and Sunday editions reached nearly two million dollars. Rumors of an impending sale began to be heard, and staff members made a desperate effort to raise enough cash to buy the *World* themselves. They argued, too, that the Pulitzer will forbade the sale of the paper, but in February, 1931, a New York court approved its purchase by Roy W. Howard for the Scripps-Howard interests. The evening *World* was merged with the *Telegram.* The morning *World*—symbol of Pulitzer's journalist genius—was dead, and there was scarcely a newspaperman who did not feel that something peculiarly precious and irreplaceable had been lost to the craft.[14]

There were other newspapers which, like the *World,* were regarded as "newspapermen's newspapers." Very few combined a conception of public responsibility and journalistic brilliance to the degree which made the *World* great. But wherever oldtime newsmen gathered in this period there likely would be mentioned the work of men who wrote for and edited the *New York Sun* and *New York Herald.* Quite likely, too, the name of the *Chicago Inter Ocean* would be mentioned. These papers, now dead, are a part of the colorful story of American journalism, and the alumni of their excellent training grounds were legion. They lagged behind in the journalistic advance into the modern era but they and the men who worked for them had proud traditions and moments of glory.

THE *NEW YORK SUN* GOES DOWN

The *New York Sun* of the days of editor Charles A. Dana and managing editor Amos J. Cummings had emphasized reporting skill, writing style, and human interest techniques to a degree worthy of the admiration of the practitioners of the "new journalism." It was a city editor of the *Sun,* John B. Bogart, who told a young reporter for the first time: "When a dog bites a man, that is not news; but when a man bites a dog, *that* is news." It was an editorial writer for the *Sun,* Francis P. Church, who in 1897 answered the "Is There a Santa Claus?" inquiry of a little girl named Virginia with an explanation which was reprinted widely for many years. It was a reporter for the *Sun,* Will Irwin, who in 1906 wrote the journalistic masterpiece, "The City That Was," in memory of San Francisco's destruction by earthquake and fire.[15]

Heading the *Sun* news staff from the eighties to the World War I period were managing editor Chester S. Lord and night city editor Selah M. Clarke, called "Boss" by his associates. They helped to train reporters like Irwin, Arthur Brisbane, Julian Ralph, Samuel Hopkins Adams, Richard Harding Davis, and Jacob Riis. From their night desk, too, Carr Van Anda went to his great career on the *Times.* Succeeding Dana as editor was the highly competent and graceful stylist, Edward P. Mitchell. The *Sun* was regarded as a "school of journal-

[14] The last city editor of the *World* told the story of its death in James W. Barrett, *The World, the Flesh, and Messrs. Pulitzer* (New York: Vanguard, 1931). See also Barrett's *Joseph Pulitzer and His World* (New York: Vanguard, 1941).

[15] Some of the color of the *Sun* is found in Frank M. O'Brien, *The Story of The Sun* (New York: George H. Doran Company, 1918). Church's "Is There a Santa Claus?" is reprinted on pp. 409–10.

ism" for young journalists and its graduates formed an alumni association. They were dismayed when control of the *Sun* passed in 1916 to Frank A. Munsey, a business-minded purchaser of newspapers who understood little of the journalistic traditions of the craft. The famous morning edition of the *Sun* disappeared in 1920 and the evening *Sun,* bearing little resemblance to the paper of old, trudged on toward eventual oblivion.

THE *NEW YORK HERALD,* LEADER IN NEWS

The *New York Herald,* under the guidance of founder James Gordon Bennett, had achieved leadership in news enterprise. When James Gordon Bennett, Jr., took control in 1872 the *Herald* ranked first in collecting and presenting the news. Its reporters and correspondents were the best and its insistence upon use of the fastest means of communication made it a hard-hitting rival for Pulitzer and Hearst when they invaded New York. Its traditions were still those of its adventurous correspondent of the early seventies, Henry M. Stanley, who spent two years searching in Africa on an assignment from the younger Bennett before he found the missing missionary and inquired, "Dr. Livingstone, I presume?" The *Herald* remained a news enterprise paper in the early twentieth century, contesting vigorously for complete and dramatic coverage of the world's events. It had Joseph L. Stickney with Dewey at Manila; Richard Harding Davis covering the Boer War; Oscar King Davis and W. H. Lewis giving it top coverage of the Russo-Japanese War; Dr. Frederick A. Cook reporting on his trip to the North Pole; and a network of political and war correspondents (supplied in part by the *Paris Herald*) that was the equal of any such group in World War I. Its use of art work and photographs embellished its crack coverage of such events as the sinking of the "General Slocum" and the "Titanic" disaster.[16]

In the struggle for survival in New York, however, the *Herald* was handicapped by the personality and practices of its owner, the younger Bennett. He was intelligent and alert, and his driving force dominated the paper. He established the *Evening Telegram* in New York and the Paris edition of the *Herald.* But in his 45 years as a publisher he proved to be a dictator who put his personal whims first. He lived in Paris most of his life, rarely visiting the *Herald* office, and his royal manner of living drained an estimated $30,000,000 from the profits of his papers.[17] No other publisher, save William Randolph Hearst, equaled Bennett in irresponsible personal control of a journalistic enterprise.

George Jean Nathan has described Bennett as he appeared in 1909, at the

[16] See, for example, *Herald* pages in Michael C. Emery, *et al., America's Front Page News, 1690–1970* (New York: Doubleday, 1970), pp. 83, 104, 109, 124.

[17] Don C. Seitz, *The James Gordon Bennetts* (Indianapolis: Bobbs-Merrill, 1928), p. 377.

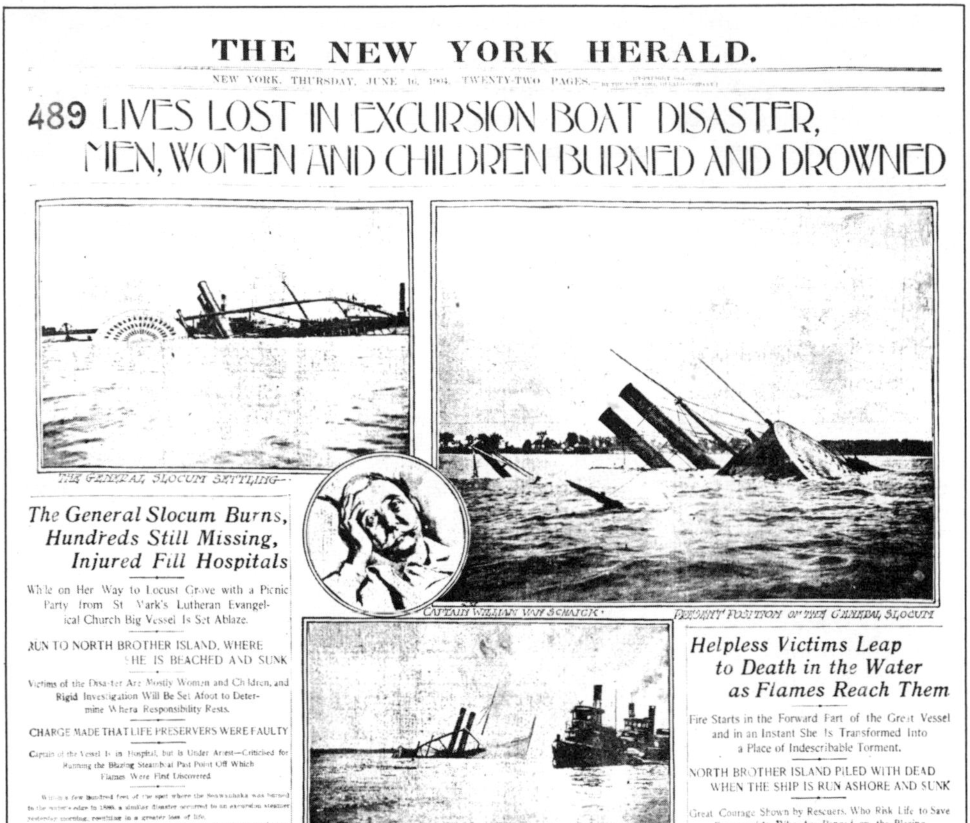

THE NEW YORK HERALD.

NEW YORK, THURSDAY, JUNE 16, 1904.—TWENTY-TWO PAGES.

489 LIVES LOST IN EXCURSION BOAT DISASTER, MEN, WOMEN AND CHILDREN BURNED AND DROWNED

THE GENERAL SLOCUM SETTLING

CAPTAIN WILLIAM VAN SCHAICK

PRESENT POSITION OF THE GENERAL SLOCUM

The General Slocum Burns, Hundreds Still Missing, Injured Fill Hospitals

While on Her Way to Locust Grove with a Picnic Party from St. Mark's Lutheran Evangelical Church Big Vessel Is Set Ablaze.

RUN TO NORTH BROTHER ISLAND, WHERE SHE IS BEACHED AND SUNK

Victims of the Disaster Are Mostly Women and Children, and Rigid Investigation Will Be Set Afoot to Determine Where Responsibility Rests.

CHARGE MADE THAT LIFE PRESERVERS WERE FAULTY

Captain of the Vessel Is in Hospital, but Is Under Arrest—Criticised for Running the Blazing Steamboat Past Point Off Which Flames Were First Discovered.

TUGS DRAWING AWAY AS THE GENERAL SLOCUM GOES DOWN

THE GENERAL SLOCUM

Helpless Victims Leap to Death in the Water as Flames Reach Them

Fire Starts in the Forward Part of the Great Vessel and in an Instant She Is Transformed Into a Place of Indescribable Torment.

NORTH BROTHER ISLAND PILED WITH DEAD WHEN THE SHIP IS RUN ASHORE AND SUNK

Great Courage Shown by Rescuers, Who Risk Life to Save Excursionists Who Are Penned on the Blazing Decks, Unable to Flee for Safety.

WOMEN AND CHILDREN CLING TO PADDLE WHEELS

Dead and Living Mingled in a Mass When the Great Flanges Cease to Revolve—Exhausted, Many Are Finally Forced to Fall and Are Instantly Drowned.

Life Preservers Rotten, Is the Accusation; "Passed" by the Inspectors Is the Answer

Life Preservers Rotten Is Charge

"We Did All That Inspectors Asked"

Test Not Complete Inspectors Admit

The *Herald* covers a 1904 ship disaster that had a final death toll of 1,000.

age of 67.[18] He was tall, slender, full of nervous energy, but bearing himself with a military erectness accented by steel-gray hair and moustache. Though he lived in Paris, his editors could neither hire nor fire a reporter without his consent. His editorial committee met at a table with an empty chair at the head—that was Bennett. At his place were set fresh copies of the paper each day, as though he might walk in at any moment.

Bennett's connection with the paper was far from being a psychological one, however. Cabled instructions arrived from Paris each day. Frequently department heads were called to Paris for conferences. Bennett kept close watch on the work of each employee, and practiced a policy of seeing to it that no individual achieved personal importance. While he had many good news instincts, he also forced the paper to observe many rules of conduct based upon his personal idiosyncrasies and ordered promotion of his personal beliefs. At Bennett's death in 1918, the *Herald* was sold to Frank Munsey, who could not make the leaderless paper profitable and let it disappear into the *Herald Tribune* in 1924. That paper maintained the Bennett news traditions.

CHICAGO'S FAMED *INTER OCEAN*

A newspaper in Chicago's past journalism history which for a time attracted a following of newspapermen was the *Inter Ocean.* It started its career in 1865 as the *Chicago Republican,* edited by Charles A. Dana for the first year. It became the *Inter Ocean* in 1872, a staunch Republican spokesman owned by William Penn Nixon. Through its reporting enterprise on the frontier, its religious news, and its agricultural news coverage it built up a midwestern circulation. It also led in introducing mechanical improvements, installing a color press in 1892 in advance of other American newspapers. During the nineties the paper lost money and was sold to Charles T. Yerkes, Chicago's traction line boss. Despite its record for conducting crusades in the public interest, the *Inter Ocean* suffered under Yerkes' ownership until he sold it in 1902 to George W. Hinman, who had come from the *New York Sun* to be the *Inter Ocean's* editor.

Under Hinman the *Inter Ocean* won notice as a training school for newspapermen. The paper had been one of those that had catered to the "tramp reporters" of the period and by so doing had obtained the services of many young men with journalistic futures. Belonging to the *Inter Ocean* alumni association were Marquis James, William Cuppy, and Ring Lardner, writers; Walter Howey, later a famous Hearst executive; Richard J. Finnegan, later editor of the *Chicago Times* and *Sun-Times;* and a score of other prominent

[18] In *Outing,* LIII (March 1909), 690.

newspapermen. In 1914, however, the *Inter Ocean* fell victim to Chicago's newspaper competition and was added to the list of newspapers which have become reminiscences.[19]

THE DENVER POST'S "BUCKET OF BLOOD" DAYS

No account of American journalism history is complete without a mention of the *Denver Post* of the days of Harry H. Tammen and Fred G. Bonfils. With its giant bannerlines printed in red ink, its startling and helter-skelter makeup, and its highly sensationalized news play, the *Post* won fame as a dynamic but irresponsible paper. Its owners won fame, too, as ruthless operators of a journalistic gold mine. Tammen, a onetime bartender, and Bonfils, who had come West to make money in real estate and the lottery business, joined forces in 1895 to buy the *Post.* Their yellow journalism tactics succeeded in the rough-and-tumble newspaper warfare of Denver and at the height of their fortunes in the 1920s the paper was making more than a million dollars a year.

The *Post* was filled with features and sensational stories, but it also engaged in stunts and crusades which spread its fame in the Rocky Mountain area, where it advertised itself as "Your Big Brother." The partners operated from an office with red-painted walls, which Denver promptly called "The Bucket of Blood." Victims of the *Post's* crusades and exposés filed libel suits against Tammen and Bonfils and accusations of blackmailing were leveled against the owners. No such charges were ever proved in court, however, and the *Post* continued in its proclaimed role as "the people's champion."

After Tammen's death in 1924, the *Post's* luck began to change. The conduct of the paper in withholding news of illegal oil leases at Teapot Dome, until Bonfils was in a position to force the lessees to make a contract by which the *Post* would profit by half a million dollars, led the committee on ethics of the American Society of Newspaper Editors to recommend that Bonfils be expelled from membership. Instead, however, he was allowed to resign. His reputation was further darkened just before his death in 1933 when he sued the rival *Rocky Mountain News* for libel and then lost interest when the *News* undertook to document many of the stories about the partners.

Still the *Post* roared on, while the stories about life on Denver newspapers multiplied.[20] Entry of the Scripps-Howard chain into intensified competition with the *Post* in 1926 through purchase of the morning *Rocky Mountain News,* and of the evening *Times* for merger with the Scripps-owned *Express,* brought about one of the country's greatest competitive struggles. No holds were barred by city desks and circulation departments for the next two years, and Denver

[19] The story of the *Inter Ocean* is told in Walter E. Ewert, "The History of the Chicago Inter Ocean, 1872–1914" (Master's thesis, Northwestern University, 1940).

[20] Many of the colorful stories are found in Gene Fowler, *Timber Line* (New York: Covici-Friede, Inc., 1933).

gorged itself on sensational news and free premium offers. In 1928 a truce was arranged by which the *Times* was killed, leaving the *Post* alone in the evening field, and the *News* in the morning. The journalistic habits of the days when anything went continued to haunt Denver, however, for another two decades, until a change in management at the *Post* brought new policies which pushed memories of the Tammen-Bonfils era into the background.

Annotated Bibliography

Books

Barrett, James W., *The World, the Flesh, and Messrs. Pulitzer*. New York: Vanguard, 1931. The best story of the sale of the *World*, by the paper's last city editor.

Berger, Meyer, *The Story of the New York Times, 1851–1951*. New York: Simon & Schuster, 1951. Mainly the story of the *Times* after Ochs bought it; other books are better for the pre-Ochs period. But reporter Berger gets many reporters into his story, too rare an event in newspaper history-telling, and thus has a lively and interesting book. The *Times* also issued *One Hundred Years of Famous Pages from The New York Times* in its centennial year.

Bond, F. Fraser, *Mr. Miller of "The Times."* New York: Scribner's, 1931. The biography of *New York Times* editor Charles R. Miller.

Davis, Elmer, *History of the New York Times, 1851–1921*. New York: The New York Times, 1921. Still good for its period.

Fine, Barnett, *A Giant of the Press*. New York: Editor & Publisher Library, 1933. A short biography of Carr Van Anda, the great managing editor of the *New York Times.*

Fowler, Gene, *Timber Line*. New York: Covici Friede, Inc., 1933. The colorful story of the Bonfils and Tammen era at the *Denver Post*. No tale was too tall for Denver newsmen.

Howe, E. W., *Plain People*. New York: Dodd, Mead, 1929. The story of an unusual small-town Kansas editor in the usual small town, and of the *Atchison Globe*.

Johnson, Gerald W., *An Honorable Titan*. New York: Harper & Row, 1946. A good, but comparatively uncritical, biographical study of Adolph S. Ochs.

Johnson, Walter, *William Allen White's America*. New York: Holt, Rinehart & Winston, 1947. Important not only as a biography of the *Emporia Gazette* editor, but as an interpretation of the swiftly changing half-century in which White was a national figure.

Mahin, Helen O., ed., *The Editor and His People*. New York: Macmillan, 1924. An excellent collection of William Allen White's editorials.

Mitchell, Edward P., *Memoirs of an Editor*. New York: Scribner's, 1924. By the distinguished editor of the *New York Sun*.

Nevins, Allan, *American Press Opinion*. New York: Heath, 1928. Nevins' brilliant interpretive essays and selected editorials continue through this period.

Perkin, Robert L., *The First Hundred Years: An Informal History of Denver and the Rocky Mountain News.* New York: Doubleday, 1959. By a staff member of Colorado's first paper.

Pickett, Calder M., *Ed Howe: Country Town Philosopher.* Lawrence: University Press of Kansas, 1969. Prize-winning biography of the editor of the *Atchison Globe.*

Seitz, Don C., *The James Gordon Bennetts.* Indianapolis: Bobbs-Merrill, 1928. The younger Bennett brings the *New York Herald* to its downfall.

White, William Allen, *The Autobiography of William Allen White.* New York: Macmillan, 1946. No one should miss this autobiography, and few do.

Periodicals and Monographs

Ewert, Walter E., "The History of the Chicago Inter Ocean, 1872–1914." Master's thesis, Northwestern University, 1940. An excellent account of a famous newspaper.

Fine, Barnett, "When 'Boss' Lord Ruled 'The Sun,'" *Editor & Publisher,* LXVI (April 22–July 15, 1933). A series of articles about Chester S. Lord, managing editor of the *New York Sun* during 33 of its best years.

Howe, Gene, "My Father Was the Most Wretchedly Unhappy Man I Ever Knew," *Saturday Evening Post,* October 25, 1941. A dramatic story about E. W. Howe, reprinted in Drewry, *Post Biographies.*

Irwin, Will, "The New York Sun," *American Magazine,* LXVII (January 1909), 301. The story of the *Sun's* school of journalism, by one of the pupils.

Nathan, George Jean, "James Gordon Bennett, the Monte Cristo of Modern Journalism," *Outing,* LIII (March 1909), 690. The drama critic criticises an erratic publisher.

Stolberg, Benjamin, "The Man Behind 'The Times,'" *Atlantic Monthly,* CXXXVIII (December 1926), 721. A discerning study of Adolph S. Ochs. Reprinted in Ford and Emery, *Highlights in the History of the American Press.*

White, W. L., "The Sage of Emporia," *Nieman Reports,* XXIII (March 1969), 23. Human interest piece by William Allen White's son.

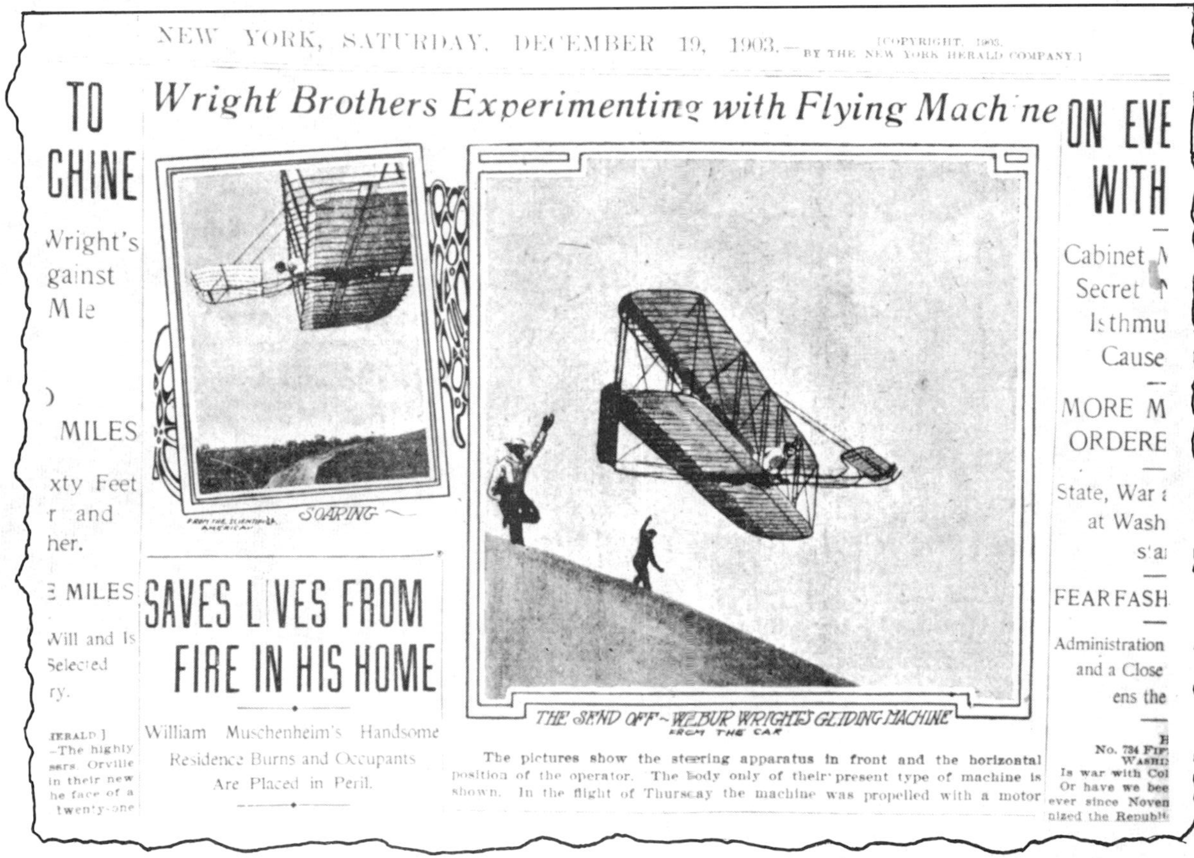

NEW YORK, SATURDAY, DECEMBER 19, 1903.—[COPYRIGHT, 1903, BY THE NEW YORK HERALD COMPANY.]

Wright Brothers Experimenting with Flying Mach'ne

SOARING

FROM THE SCIENTIFIC AMERICAN

THE SEND OFF ~ WILBUR WRIGHT'S GLIDING MACHINE FROM THE CAR

The pictures show the steering apparatus in front and the horizontal position of the operator. The body only of their present type of machine is shown. In the flight of Thursday the machine was propelled with a motor

SAVES LIVES FROM FIRE IN HIS HOME

William Muschenheim's Handsome Residence Burns and Occupants Are Placed in Peril.

TO
CHINE

Wright's
gainst
M le

MILES

xty Feet
r and
her.

MILES

Will and Is
Selected
ry.

HERALD.]
—The highly
sers. Orville
in their new
he face of a
twenty-one

ON EVE
WITH

Cabinet
Secret
Isthmu
Cause

MORE M
ORDERE

State, War
at Wash
s'a

FEAR FASH

Administration
and a Close
ens the

No. 734 Fif
Washi
Is war with Col
Or have we bee
ever since Noven
nized the Republ

New York Herald (1903)

Curtis Publishing Company

Wide World Photos

Cyrus H. K. Curtis (*above*) and Frank Munsey published both magazines and newspapers and took part in the ownership consolidations of the early twentieth century.

22

Media Consolidation Begins

There was nothing new about newspaper consolidations in these years except the large number of them.
—Frank Luther Mott

In the years of the rise of the "new journalism" it seemed that newspaper individuality was on a definite up-grade. As the daily newspapers took modern form and multiplied, a striving for innovations and for the individual appeal was the goal of an unusual number of publishers, editors, and newsmen. The Pulitzers, the Scrippses, the Gradys, and the Van Andas joined the Franklins, the Bennetts, and the Greeleys of the past who by achievement of new techniques and appeals enriched the total journalistic output. Their successes in creating newspapers with distinctively individualized appeals, combined with a doubling of the number of dailies between 1880 and 1900 (from 850 to 1,967), seemed to indicate that variety of competitive appeal was a permanent feature of American journalism.

But the forces which created the modern mass newspaper—industrialization, mechanization, and urbanization—made for less individuality and more standardization of the product as the twentieth century unfolded. The great and the colorful, representing individualistic deviation from the norm, survived in some instances, but variety of competitive appeal tended to decline in the cities and towns of a standardized civilization. Competition for the mass market in the urban centers, and other socioeconomic pressures stemming from technological change, led to an inevitable contraction of newspaper publishing. The story of newspaper consolidation, already suggested in the preceding chapter, now becomes a dominant theme.

NEWSPAPER CONSOLIDATIONS, 1910–30

The years 1910 to 1914 mark the high point in numbers of newspapers published in the United States. The census of 1910 reported 2,600 daily publications of all types, of which 2,200 were English-language newspapers of general circulation. General-circulation weekly newspapers numbered approximately 14,000. The totals hovered at these peaks until the economic pressures of the first World War were felt by American newspapers.

Wartime pressures, while of marked effect upon publishing, only accented trends which were developing as early as 1890. These trends were toward suspension of some competing newspapers, merger of others with their rivals, concentration of newspaper ownership in many cities and towns, and creation of newspaper chains or groups. Before 1930, each of these trends had been clearly developed, to set the pattern for twentieth-century American journalism.

Statistics often can be confusing, and this is true of those concerned with the number of American newspapers published over the years. For example, it might be assumed that if there were 2,200 English-language daily newspapers of general circulation in 1910, and but 1,942 in 1930, then 258 newspapers died in those two decades. Actually, 1,391 daily newspapers suspended publication or shifted to weekly status in those 20 years, and another 362 were merged with rival papers. In the same two decades, 1,495 dailies were being born.[1] The turnover among established dailies was less drastic than these figures might seem to indicate, however, since one-fourth of the newcomers died within the first year of publication, and another one-half eventually joined the suspension list. But some of the newcomers were healthy ventures in the growing small towns and cities of an increasingly urbanized country.

Between 1910 and 1930 the population of the United States increased by 30 million, from 92 to 122 million persons. Industrialization, steadily mounting in intensity after the great spurt prior to 1900, brought an increase in urban population of 25 millions. The number of towns and cities of 8,000 or more persons jumped from 768 to 1,208 between 1910 and 1930. Daily newspaper circulation increased at a faster pace, from 22½ million copies a day in 1910 to 40 million copies in 1930. Sunday newspaper circulation more than doubled in the two decades, moving from 13 million to 27 million copies. Total newspaper advertising revenue tripled in the years 1915 to 1929, increasing from an estimated 275 million dollars to 800 millions.[2]

[1] Royal H. Ray, *Concentration of Ownership and Control in the American Daily Newspaper Industry* (Columbia University Microfilms, 1951), pp. 401–8. A summary of this Ph.D. dissertation was published in *Journalism Quarterly*, XXIX (Winter 1952), 31.

[2] Census population figures and newspaper circulation totals are conveniently tabulated in the appendices of A. M. Lee's *The Daily Newspaper in America* (New York: Macmillan, 1937). Advertising revenue totals are from figures of the ANPA Bureau of Advertising.

Yet despite this great growth in advertising revenue, in numbers of readers, and in numbers of urban centers which could support daily newspaper publication, there was a net loss of 258 daily newspapers in the 20 years. Reduction of the number of competing dailies in larger cities, elimination of all but one newspaper in smaller towns, and suspension of daily newspaper publishing in some fading communities more than offset the number of new dailies started in growing towns and older publishing centers.

The figures given in Table 1 illustrate daily newspaper publishing trends from 1880 to 1930. Those for 1971 are included to indicate the full extent of the decline in number of dailies and of the rise in number of one-daily cities

TABLE 1 · Growth of One-Daily Cities

	1880	*1900*	*1910*	*1920*	*1930*	*1971*
Number of English-language general circulation dailies	850	1,967	2,200	2,042	1,942	1,748
Number of cities with dailies	389	915	1,207	1,295	1,402	1,511
Number of one-daily cities	149	353	509	716	1,002	1,312
Number of one-combination cities	1	3	9	27	112	162*
Number of cities with competing dailies	239	559	689	552	288	37
Percentage of daily cities with only one daily paper	38.3	38.6	42.2	55.3	71.5	86.3
Percentage of daily cities with competing dailies	61.4	61.1	57.1	42.6	20.6	2.4
Percentage of all dailies published in one-daily cities	17.5	17.9	23.1	35.1	51.6	73.4
Number of one-daily cities above 25,000 population	4	8	25	47	93	324
Number of one-daily cities above 100,000 population	0	1	1	5	6	15
Total daily circulation (millions)	3.1	15.1	22.4	27.8	39.6	62.1

* Includes 21 cities where two owners merged business and printing facilities.

Sources: For 1880: Data tabulated from S.N.D. North, *History and Present Condition of the Newspaper and Periodical Press of the United States* (Washington: Government Printing Office, 1884). For 1900–1920: W. Carl Masche, "Factors Involved in the Consolidation and Suspension of Daily and Sunday Newspapers in the United States Since 1900: A Statistical Study in Social Change," Master's thesis, University of Minnesota, 1932; and Morris Ernst, *The First Freedom* (New York: Macmillan, 1946), p. 284. For 1930: Alfred McClung Lee, "The Basic Newspaper Pattern," *The Annals of the American Academy of Political and Social Science,* CCXIX (January 1942), 46, except figures for one-daily cities of specified population, from Masche. For 1971: Based on analysis by Raymond B. Nixon of data in 1971 *Editor & Publisher International Year Book.* For most recent published study, see Raymond B. Nixon, "Trends in U. S. Newspaper Ownership: Concentration with Competition," *Gazette,* XIV (No. 3, 1968), 1.

For numbers of English-language general circulation dailies: 1880, tabulated from North; 1900, from Masche; 1910, from Royal H. Ray (see footnote 1); 1920–1971, *Editor & Publisher International Year Book* figures. The census counts of daily publications, which included foreign language, religious, trade, and technical dailies, were 971 dailies in 1880, 2,226 in 1900, 2,600 in 1910, and 2,441 in 1920. But those figures do not compare with the *Editor & Publisher International Year Book* figures available after 1920. Masche, Ernst, and Ray tabulated their data from Ayer directories; Lee and Nixon used *Editor & Publisher International Year Book* data, which Nixon adjusted through additional research.

and one-combination cities (one owner of two papers). The pattern was clearly set by 1930.

A study of country weeklies made for the decade years from 1900 to 1930 shows similar trends, as illustrated in Table 2. The figures are only for weekly

TABLE 2 · Growth of One-Weekly Towns

	1900	*1910*	*1920*	*1930*
Number of weeklies published in towns of 15,000 population or less	11,310	11,802	10,462	9,522
Number of towns of 15,000 population or less with weekly papers	7,827	9,260	8,798	8,295
Number with but one weekly	5,177	7,079	7,285	7,172
Percentage of country weekly towns with but one paper	66.1	76.4	82.8	86.5
Percentage of all weeklies studied published in one-weekly towns	45.8	60.0	69.7	75.3

Source: Malcolm M. Willey and William Weinfeld, "The Country Weekly and the Emergence of 'One-Newspaper Places,' " *Journalism Quarterly*, XI (September 1934), 250. The authors tabulated data from Ayer directories.

newspapers published in towns of 15,000 population or less, excluding publications in larger cities and some suburban weeklies. The percentages for one-weekly towns run higher than the percentages for one-daily cities given in Table 1. They show that by 1930 half the dailies and three-fourths of the country weeklies in the United States were published as the only newspapers in their respective communities. Seventy-one per cent of daily newspaper cities and 86 per cent of country weekly towns had but a single newspaper by 1930.

By 1960, with continued growth of both one-newspaper cities and one-combination cities, competition remained in only 4.2 per cent of daily cities and 5.2 per cent of country weekly towns.[3]

REASONS FOR CURTAILMENT OF COMPETITION

Many reasons can be listed for the decline in numbers of newspapers published, for the curtailment of competition in most communities, and for the increasing concentration of ownership. They fall under seven general headings: (1) economic pressures stemming from technological changes in the publishing pattern; (2) pressures resulting from competition for circulation and adver-

[3] For weeklies, see Wilbur Peterson, "Loss in Country Weekly Newspapers Heavy in 1950s," *Journalism Quarterly*, XXXVIII (Winter 1961), 15.

tising revenues; (3) standardization of the product, resulting in loss of individuality and reader appeal; (4) lack of economic or social need for some newspapers; (5) managerial faults; (6) effects of wartime inflation and general business depressions; (7) planned consolidation of newspapers for various reasons.[4]

TECHNOLOGICAL CHANGE

Technological change—the mechanical innovations of the 1880s and 1890s—brought increasing financial responsibility and risks for newspaper publishers, large and small. Typesetting machines, high-speed presses, engraving plants, and other expanded mechanical facilities meant not only constantly enlarged investments, but increased operating costs. The publisher who wished to keep abreast of technological developments had to increase his revenues from circulation and advertising; the larger number of pages to handle a greater volume of advertising and the printing of more copies in turn made necessary more elaborate mechanical departments. The new entrant in the business was faced with a greater financial problem as each decade passed. Melville E. Stone established the *Chicago Daily News* in 1876 with a few thousand dollars capital; Albert Pulitzer founded the *New York Morning Journal* in 1882 with $25,000 capital. Hearst paid $180,000 for the *Journal* in 1895; Ochs was able to take over the *New York Times* in 1896 with $100,000 working capital. But such opportunities were disappearing, as tremendous plant investments and other factors increasing the value of newspaper properties were putting metropolitan daily prices at million-dollar levels. Stone's *Chicago Daily News* sold for 13½ million dollars in 1925. The change was equally dramatic in smaller towns. In Spokane, Washington, the weekly *Review* founded in 1883 was printed on a Washington hand press by a printer-editor. After a decade of mechanical and editorial innovations William H. Cowles took control of the daily *Spokesman-Review* by assuming responsibility for an $80,000 mortgage and operating costs too heavy for numerous other competitors.[5]

CIRCULATION AND ADVERTISING COMPETITION

Competition for circulation, upon which advertising rates are based and upon which advertising volume largely depends, thus was heightened by eco-

[4] See bibliography at the close of this chapter for citations to the literature in this field.

[5] Ralph E. Dyar, *News for an Empire* (Caldwell, Ida.: The Caxton Printers, Ltd., 1952). Dyar's early chapters trace the economic changes in Spokane newspaper publishing as daily newspapers came to a frontier town at a moment when American newspapers were being revolutionized by the impact of the "new journalism." The *Spokesman-Review* and its evening affiliate, the *Chronicle,* are the only survivors of Spokane's score or more of weekly and daily newspaper ventures.

nomic necessity stemming from the changing business character of newspaper publishing. Weaker publications were eliminated in many localities as the newspaper fell into the general economic pattern of a mechanized and industrialized country, a pattern which favored those who produced for a mass market at the most efficient unit cost.

Advertisers deemed it more efficient to buy space in one metropolitan daily newspaper with substantial general circulation, than in several papers with overlapping or specialized circulations. In smaller cities and towns, advertiser preference for the larger in circulation of two papers often spelled disaster for the smaller. Advertiser preference for evening dailies, based particularly upon knowledge of readership habits of American women-shoppers, helped speed the decline of morning papers. In the field of national advertising, increased competition of other media—magazines, billboards, and by 1930, radio—complicated the problem of newspaper survival, although this factor did not become a critical one for newspaper owners until after 1930.

STANDARDIZATION OF THE PRESS

Standardization of the product, which was encouraged by economic pressures, also accounted for a reduction in the number of newspapers. Competition for the mass market discouraged individuality; the newspaper that appealed to a specialized group of readers by the distinctive nature of its news or editorial policy often found it had lost the race to a mass appeal newspaper whose circulation attracted an increasing volume of advertising revenue. Loss of individuality in turn discouraged readership of more than one newspaper by most persons. Contributing to standardization were the press associations, which supplied increasingly better news coverage, but also a uniform news content and standardized writing style; and the syndicates, with their mass distribution of the efforts of columnists, cartoonists, comic strip artists, and feature writers. Newspapers that came to rely too heavily upon such sources of content, at the expense of their own staff enterprise and local news initiative, jeopardized reader support.

LACK OF ECONOMIC OR SOCIAL NEED

It was not always desirable that all existing newspapers in a community should survive, however. The typical American town saw more newspaper publishing ventures attempted than its economy could support. Even after the initial weeding of newspaper ventures, steadily increasing costs of publishing required further adjustments of the number of newspapers which the community's business volume justified. Nor were all newspapers deserving of community support. Some were founded solely as voices for political parties or business groups. Such newspapers, inveterately partisan in their outlook and appeal, had little to recommend them to modern readers. Other newspapers were founded by men who were in the business to make money. They were attracted by the conspicuous successes of the "new journalism" and became publishers much as they might have become store owners or shoe manufacturers. If too many such hopefuls set up shop in one community, a contraction inevitably resulted, without much loss to journalism.

The newspapers of the frontier communities of the Middle West and West often were of a transient variety. Some were founded to promote the settlement of a town, or to lure easterners and immigrants to the farm lands for sale along the railroad rights-of-way. When they had served their purposes, they disappeared from the newspaper statistics which they had helped to bulk larger. Others were started as editorial spokesmen for the Republican, Democratic, and Populist parties, or even for factions of political parties. The 1880 census figures showed that 174 towns of less than 25,000 population had competing daily newspapers, as compared to 146 towns of similar size with only a single daily. By 1971 there were only 5 out of 1,187 daily newspaper towns of less than 25,000 population which had competing dailies. Publishing economics forced the elimination of the second, and sometimes third and fourth, dailies in these towns, as well as competing weeklies.

There were other changes in economic and social needs that affected newspaper publishing. Foreign-language papers which flourished during the peak years of immigration disappeared as the process of Americanization inevitably dried up their circulation potential. Movements of population in various sections of the country either decreased possibilities for publication or encouraged new starts. Improved transportation facilities, the advent of the automobile and paved roads, and better communications meant that newspapers in urban centers could expand their coverage on regional and statewide levels. Nearby dailies in smaller towns found sharper competition as a result. Among the weeklies, the county seat paper tended to squeeze papers in adjacent villages out of business. Movements of population from rural to urban areas further restricted opportunities for multiple publication, as communities with declining business activity or stagnant population saw their newspapers reduced to one or eliminated entirely.

MANAGERIAL INADEQUACIES

Managerial faults sometimes have contributed to the reduction in numbers of newspapers, and consolidation of ownership. Newspapers traditionally have lagged in setting advertising and circulation rates which realistically reflect current business conditions. Too often newspaper rates have been changed only after the business has gone into the red ink because of a sudden fluctuation in general economic conditions—or they have been set so low that in a period of inflation the publisher is unable to adjust rates to meet a new level of costs. Rigidity of newspaper rates is a complex problem, in part inherent in the business, but some managements have been more successful than others in providing adequate financial cushions for their papers in times of stress. And some managements have displayed conspicuous lack of ability as newspaper publishers. Continuity of efficient business direction and competent editorial leadership through stable ownership for long periods of time has been a key factor in the survival of many American newspapers. Loss of that leadership by death or sale has sometimes meant the sudden decline of a hitherto distinguished newspaper.[6]

INFLATION AND DEPRESSION

Periods of general business inflation or depression affect newspapers drastically. The economic pressures attending World War I reduced the number of dailies by 112 in four years, one of the sharpest contractions in American journalism history.[7] Weekly publications of all types slumped one-eighth in the same period, with nearly 1,800 disappearing. A newsprint shortage, and a tripling of the price between 1916 and 1921, spelled ruin for many a marginal paper. Wartime price fixing by the federal government, with the cooperation of the publishers, held the price of a ton of newsprint to a rise from $42 in 1916 to $80 in 1918. But a postwar runaway market after government controls ceased sent the figure soaring to $137 a ton at the 1921 peak. A gradual decline to $62 by 1929 brought newsprint prices into line with other price levels. Also affecting publishers was a wartime revenue measure which established zone rates for second-class mail, thereby increasing newspaper and magazine mailing costs. Other rising costs, including wages, forced increased circulation and advertising rates which weaker newspapers could not justify. Finally, when the "high cost of living" era was followed by a sharp postwar recession, sudden losses of advertising revenue by newspapers operating on a narrow margin of profit, and still paying inflated prices for materials and higher wages to workers, brought additional suspensions and mergers.

[6] Examples of the benefits of stable ownerships are the *New York Times, Chicago Tribune, Louisville Courier-Journal,* and *St. Louis Post-Dispatch,* among a score or more of similar leading papers with longtime continuous and effective direction. Examples of newspapers set adrift are the *New York World, Chicago Inter Ocean, New York Sun,* and *Chicago Record-Herald,* among others.

[7] Ray, *Concentration of Ownership and Control in the American Daily Newspaper Industry,* p. 6.

PLANNED CONSOLIDATIONS

Calculated planning sometimes has played a part in the consolidation of newspapers. Publication of both a morning and evening newspaper from the same mechanical plant is more efficient than operating separate newspapers in two plants, and by 1931 there were 152 cities with local combinations, including both those with and without other competition.[8] Before the news facilities of the Associated Press were opened more easily to non-AP newspapers in 1945 by a Supreme Court decision, the only practical way to obtain an AP membership was to buy the franchise of a member paper. Many a daily was bought and merged with another for this reason. In other cases, ambitious publishers, particularly those creating groups of newspapers, strengthened their positions by buying competitive papers.

Reduction of the number of American newspapers, and concentration of ownership of the remaining dailies, has caused a continuing debate over the social and political consequences of those trends. More will be said about that debate in a later chapter, but it is evident that the causes of newspaper consolidation were largely beyond the control of either the publishers or the reading public. In some cases newspapers have been sacrificed unnecessarily by inept management or by coldblooded elimination, but these examples are in the minority. Economic pressure has been the dominant cause for newspaper consolidation. In such circumstances, the survival of one financially stable newspaper in a community is preferable to the continued existence of two or three weak and mediocre ones—always provided that the "monopoly" newspaper strives to justify its community support and is edited by newspapermen who recognize their full responsibility to all segments of the community. Nevertheless, decline in variety of competitive appeal and loss of individuality in news presentation and editorial opinion have affected public opinion concerning newspapers. The trend toward one-owner newspaper operations in smaller communities ordinarily was recognized as inevitable, but the spread of one-owner control to good-sized cities, and the reduction of the number of competing dailies in even the largest cities, neither was anticipated nor readily accepted. It is important, then, that the historical development of these trends be understood.

NEW YORK: FRANK MUNSEY, BUTCHER

New York City boasted 15 general-circulation, English-language daily newspapers in 1890. Eight were morning papers and seven were afternoon

[8] Lee, *Daily Newspaper in America,* p. 222. Ray counted 31 local combinations formed between 1909 and 1919, and 142 formed between 1920 and 1929, the peak decade for such activity. The total between 1909 and 1948 was 302. Some did not survive, however.

papers. Twelve owners were represented. By 1932, when Joseph Pulitzer's famous *World* and Bernarr Macfadden's infamous tabloid *Graphic* had followed other New York dailies into oblivion, only three morning papers, four afternoon papers, and two tabloids remained. The nine papers represented seven ownerships. Since the list still retained seven papers in the early 1960s, it is evident that the story of the consolidation of New York's dailies is an old one.

The name of Frank A. Munsey plays a large part in that story. Munsey was a successful New Englander whose career had a Horatio Alger ring. He was a young telegraph operator in Augusta, Maine, with no assets but a fierce determination to break into the New York publishing business. When he reached the city in 1882, he had a stack of manuscripts for a juvenile magazine and $40 cash.

Several years of struggle and great promotional ability made his *Golden Argosy* a success; he then turned to the general magazine field with his *Munsey's*. As a ten-cent monthly, *Munsey's* hit 650,000 circulation by 1900 to lead its competitors by a wide margin. Its publisher had a million-dollar-a-year income by 1905 and was engaged in running a grocery chain, hotels, and banks in addition to his journalistic ventures.

Munsey apparently wanted even greater power and income, however. He dreamt of a great national chain of newspapers, directed from a central headquarters by the most brilliant of American editors and business managers. To Munsey, the successful business man, the newspaper business was a disorderly, if not chaotic, enterprise. In keeping with the trend of his times—toward concentration of control of segments of a business—he proposed to bring efficiency to the newspaper world, and thereby improve the product.

"There is no business that cries so loud for organization and combination as that of newspaper publishing," Munsey declared. "For one thing, the number of newspapers is at least 60 per cent greater than we need." And in another vein he added:

> Think of the possibilities involved in a chain of 500 newspapers under a single control! Such a faculty could be so maintained as no college could support; the greatest authors, artists, engineers, essayists, and statesmen could write with authority on every question of importance, each of the 500 papers getting the benefit of these great minds, while maintaining their individuality on purely local matters. There could be a $100,000 or $200,000 a year man at the head of the editorial force and another God-made genius in charge of the business end . . . and the combined genius of the men in control would be the most uplifting force the world has ever known.[9]

[9] Quoted from *Editor & Publisher*, LVIII (December 26, 1925), 8, in Willard G. Bleyer, *Main Currents in the History of American Journalism* (Boston: Houghton Mifflin, 1927), p. 413.

Munsey's first newspaper venture was buying the *New York Star* in 1891. It was a one-time political paper, which had been reinvigorated in the 1880s but which was losing out in the Pulitzer-era competitive struggle. Munsey, from his magazine experience, reasoned that a newspaper with pictures and human interest stories would sell, and he made the paper, renamed the *Continent*, a tabloid. His perfectly logical editorial formula failed to jell, however, and after losing $40,000 in four months he retired to his magazine business. The paper became the *Morning Advertiser* and was sold to William Randolph Hearst in 1897 for its AP membership rights.

By 1901 Munsey was ready to try again. He bought the old *New York Daily News* and the *Washington Times* that year as the nucleus of his chain. The *Boston Journal* was added in 1902, and in 1908 he invaded two more eastern cities, buying the *Baltimore Evening News* and founding the *Philadelphia Evening Times.*

The *Daily News,* founded in 1855, had prospered as a penny paper edited for the tenement districts of New York, until the Pulitzer-Hearst duel affected its circulation adversely. Munsey set about to improve the paper, installing color presses, featurizing its Sunday edition, and seeking to break into higher level readership groups. Again the public failed to respond, and the paper died in 1906 after Munsey had lost an estimated $750,000.

Munsey did no better with his other ventures. The Boston paper was sold at a loss in 1913; the Philadelphia paper was killed in 1914. Disappointed at the failure of his chain, Munsey sold his two successful papers in Baltimore and Washington before 1917. He, like Hearst, had been interested in politics, and he had been a solid champion of Theodore Roosevelt and the Bull Moose progressive movement, but his dream of attaining journalistic influence on a national scale was ended.

Not so his dream for bringing efficiency of operation to the newspaper business. There were too many small units operating in journalism, he said, and the only answer was orderly consolidation, similar to that taking place in manufacturing, railroading, oil, and retail selling.[10] He proposed to perform this service for New York City.

Munsey still owned one newspaper, the *New York Press,* which he had added to his chain in 1912. The *Press,* under the editorship of Ervin Wardman, had been effective in the newspaper crusades at the turn of the century, and it still had a comfortable circulation. But Munsey eyed the New York field for a newspaper which could be combined with it, and his choice was the *Sun.*

The *Sun,* founded in 1833 as the city's first penny paper, had slumped in circulation with the coming of Pulitzer and Hearst, but it was still a proud newspaper, edited after the death of Charles A. Dana in 1897 by Edward P. Mitchell. Munsey paid 2½ million dollars for the *Sun* and the *Evening Sun* in 1916, and merged the *Press* into the morning edition, making Wardman

[10] Munsey's philosophy and his career are detailed in George Britt, *Forty Years—Forty Millions; the Career of Frank A. Munsey* (New York: Holt, Rinehart & Winston, 1935).

publisher, Mitchell editor, and the *Press's* renowned Keats Speed, managing editor. The price was cut to a penny, and Munsey poured two million dollars more into the venture. But wartime publishing difficulties cost him the profit he hoped to make, and in 1920 he looked about for another prospect for consolidation. In the next five years, Munsey, who already had failed to resuscitate the old *Star* and *Daily News,* and who had killed the *Press,* was to remove four more newspapers from the publishing scene.

New York in 1920 still had 14 established general circulation newspapers. In the morning field were the *Times, World, Tribune, Herald, Sun, American,* and a new *Daily News,* first of the postwar tabloids and just founded by Robert R. McCormick and Joseph M. Patterson of the *Chicago Tribune* dynasty. In the evening field were the *Post, Evening Sun, Evening World, Telegram, Evening Journal, Mail,* and *Globe and Commercial Advertiser.* There were 10 ownerships, the *Telegram* being the evening edition of the *Herald,* and Hearst owning both the *American* and *Journal.*

Munsey's first move was to buy the *Herald,* the *Telegram,* and the Paris edition of the *Herald* for four million dollars. The younger Bennett had spent lavishly during his long lifetime, and when he died in 1918 his newspapers were in neither a financial nor competitive position to continue. Munsey merged the morning *Sun* into the *Herald* and gave the historical name *Sun* to the evening edition, which he continued to operate despite his ownership of the evening *Telegram.*

The next victim was the *Globe.* Started in 1904, it had been consolidated the next year with the *Commercial Advertiser,* founded in 1793 by Noah Webster as the *American Minerva.* The *Globe* was considered a healthy, liberal newspaper when Munsey bought it for two million dollars in 1923 for its evening AP membership and merged it in the *Sun.* The next year Munsey paid another two millions for the conservative *Mail,* merging it with the *Telegram.*[11] Both the *Sun* and *Telegram* gained circulation and advertising as a result of the mergers.

Munsey's morning paper, the *Herald,* was not faring as well. High operation costs in the postwar period and difficulties with advertising rates plagued the businessman-publisher. He turned his eyes toward the *Tribune,* lowest in circulation of the morning dailies and the only remaining morning newspaper supporter of the Republican party along with the *Herald.* Munsey argued that it was only logical that the two papers should merge. But the *Tribune's* owners, Ogden Mills Reid and his able wife, Helen Rogers Reid refused to sell the family paper and its modern publishing plant. Munsey, true to his belief that further consolidation was necessary, thereupon sold the *Herald* and its Paris edition to the Reids for five million dollars. Happily, the new *Herald Tribune* successfully added the bulk of the old *Herald's* subscribers to its list and saw its advertising volume expand under the business direction of Mrs.

[11] The *Evening Mail* dated from 1867. It had been consolidated in 1882 with the *Express* (1836), as the *Mail and Express.* Wartime charges that the paper had engaged in German propaganda efforts blighted its reputation.

Reid. Of all Munsey's newspaper maneuvering, his part in the creation of the *Herald Tribune* was the happiest, even though it meant the merger of the historic Bennett and Greeley papers.

Death claimed Munsey in 1925. His *Telegram* passed to the Scripps-Howard chain, which combined it with Pulitzer's *World* in 1931. The *Sun* became a staff-owned newspaper under the direction of William T. Dewart, and prospered for a while under editor Frank M. O'Brien and managing editor Keats Speed as a solid, conservative newspaper, but it too was to disappear into the Scripps-Howard *World-Telegram* in 1950. Undoubtedly the New York newspapers would have gone through a consolidation process whether Frank Munsey had lived or not, but undoubtedly, too, he had hastened the deaths of several of the city's dailies. Newspapermen generally were bitterly resentful of the cold and businesslike approach which Munsey had toward both them and their profession. William Allen White best expressed the rebels' sentiments in his famed terse obituary published in the *Emporia Gazette:*

> Frank A. Munsey contributed to the journalism of his day the talent of a meatpacker, the morals of a money-changer and the manners of an undertaker. He and his kind have about succeeded in transforming a once-noble profession into an eight per cent security. May he rest in trust!

PHILADELPHIA: CYRUS H. K. CURTIS, PUBLISHER

Another magazine publisher played a major role in the consolidation of Philadelphia's newspapers. He was Cyrus H. K. Curtis, who founded the *Ladies' Home Journal* in 1883, and drove it to leadership with Edward W. Bok as editor. His second major triumph had been the rejuvenation of the *Saturday Evening Post,* which as a nickel weekly led its field within 10 years after Curtis bought it in 1897.

Philadelphia had 13 general circulation dailies of importance in 1895, of which eight remained when Curtis entered the newspaper field in 1913. Coming to the top in circulation during this period was the *Evening Bulletin,* purchased by William L. McLean in 1895 and given a new home and a solid editorial character which solid Philadelphia admired. Within ten years the *Bulletin* rose from 6,000 to 220,000 in circulation, upsetting the city's newspaper balance. One of the losers in the circulation battle was the one-time crusading penny paper, the *Evening Item.* Another was Munsey's ill-fated *Evening Times.* Going downhill, but staying in business, was the *Record,* William M. Singerly's highly popular paper which passed to the control of Thomas B. Wanamaker in 1902.

Curtis entered the Philadelphia newspaper picture by buying the historic *Public Ledger,* founded by William M. Swain in 1836 in the first wave of penny papers. Ably edited by George W. Childs from 1864 until his death in

1894, the *Public Ledger* had gone up for sale in 1902. The purchaser was Adolph S. Ochs, who put his brother George in charge of the Philadelphia paper and himself remained interested solely in the *New York Times.* Ochs also bought the lively *Philadelphia Times* in 1902 and merged it with the *Public Ledger.* By 1913 Ochs was ready to sell to Curtis for two million dollars, $250,000 less than the purchase price.

Curtis' first move was to give Philadelphia another newspaper, the *Evening Public Ledger,* in 1914. But then, like Munsey, he moved in on the competition. The *Evening Telegraph,* dating back to 1864, was bought for its AP membership in 1918 and killed. The *Press,* founded in 1857, was purchased in 1920 for its newsprint contracts. Newspapermen mourned again in 1925 when the *North American,* on the scene since 1839 and with a reputation as a crusading force under editor E. A. Van Valkenberg, was killed.

Curtis poured money into his newspapers, building them a 15-million-dollar plant and developing a famous foreign news service which was widely syndicated. When Lee Ellmaker started the tabloid *Daily News* in Philadelphia in 1925 Curtis protected that flank by publishing the tabloid *Sun,* but it failed within three years. Meanwhile Curtis had bought the *New York Evening Post* in 1923, turning it from its traditional liberal course.

The expanded Curtis newspaper enterprises were financially unsound by depression time in 1930. In a final effort, Curtis bought the *Inquirer,* plunging an estimated 18 million dollars into the deal with the Elverson family owners which gave Curtis control of both the big Philadelphia morning dailies. When he died in 1933, leaving control of the newspapers to his business associate and son-in-law, John C. Martin, the empire crumbled. The *Public Ledger* was merged into the *Inquirer* and the property reverted to the Elverson family, to be sold in turn to Moses L. Annenberg in 1936. The *Evening Public Ledger* lived until 1942, competing with the *Bulletin* and the tabloid *Daily News.* The *Inquirer's* morning rival was the *Record,* rejuvenated after 1928 as a liberal, New Deal-supporting paper by J. David Stern. Stern also rescued the *New York Evening Post* from the Curtis regime.

Curtis' record in the newspaper business is an unhappy one. Of the seven Philadelphia newspapers he owned only one remains. He did succeed, however, in giving the *Public Ledger* additional glory, principally through an expansion of its foreign correspondence during World War I years and on through the 1920s.

CHICAGO: HERMAN KOHLSAAT, BAKER

Herman Kohlsaat was the chief figure in Chicago's newspaper consolidations. Enriched by a chain of bakeries and lunch counters, and enamored of the newspaper business, Kohlsaat bought into the *Inter Ocean* in 1891. Dissatisfied, however, by lack of complete control and dismayed by the activities of his less idealistic associates, he sold out and bought the *Times-Herald* and *Evening Post*. The *Times* and *Herald* had been consolidated by James W. Scott just before his death in 1895, with the *Mail*—evening edition of the *Times*—disappearing

Scott's successful morning paper had been a Democratic party supporter. Kohlsaat was a Republican, and he turned the *Times-Herald's* editorial course to parallel that of a competitor, Joseph Medill's redoubtable *Tribune*. By 1901 Kohlsaat was in trouble, which he hoped to solve by buying the *Record*, morning edition of Victor Lawson's *Daily News*. Kohlsaat's resources were not as extensive as those of Munsey and Curtis, however, and before the end of 1901 he had to dispose of his properties. The *Record-Herald*, as the paper was now called, went to Lawson. The *Evening Post* was sold to John C. Shaffer.

Chicago in 1902 thus had four morning papers: the *Tribune*, *Inter Ocean*, *Record-Herald*, and William Randolph Hearst's newly established *Examiner*. In the evening field were the *Daily News*, *Post*, *Journal*, and Hearst's *American*. The highly successful *Tribune* and *Daily News*, and the well-financed Hearst papers, were to squeeze out their competitors in the next 30 years.

One victim was the well-edited *Record-Herald*, which, when Lawson brought Frank B. Noyes from the *Washington Star* to run it from 1902 to 1910, ranked as one of the country's best. It boasted John T. McCutcheon's cartoons before the *Tribune* enticed the artist away, and was aggressive and distinctive in its news coverage. But the *Tribune's* competition was too much and Noyes resumed his Washington career in 1910. Kohlsaat returned as editor, and the *Record-Herald* had one more moment of glory when it joined the *Tribune* in a crusade which exposed the bribery accompanying the election of William Lorimer to the United States Senate. Lorimer lost his Senate seat, but Kohlsaat's brave campaign did not save the *Record-Herald*. In 1912 he turned again to the *Inter Ocean*, hoping to save that dying paper.

Failing this, too, Lawson and Kohlsaat had one constructive move left. If they could not defeat the *Tribune*, they could join the enemy, in effect, by selling out to one of the *Tribune's* most brilliant staff members, managing editor James Keeley. This they did in 1914, and the new paper arising from the ruins of the *Record-Herald* and the *Inter Ocean* became known simply as the *Herald*. But Keeley failed in his mission and sold out to Hearst in 1918. The new *Herald & Examiner*, sole competitor to the *Tribune* in the morning field, thus represented five journalistic ventures, the *Times*, *Herald*, *Record*, *Inter Ocean*, and *Examiner*.

In the evening field, the *Daily News* continued to excel. Lawson had started its distinguished foreign service and the paper was operating in full stride when its veteran publisher died in 1925. Control passed to a syndicate headed by Walter A. Strong, *Daily News* business manager, for 13½ million dollars, record price for a newspaper sale before Curtis' 18 million dollar investment in the *Philadelphia Inquirer*. Colonel Frank Knox obtained the controlling interest in 1931. The *Daily News* bought out two weak competitors in this reorganization period—the *Journal* in 1929 and the *Post* in 1932. Joining the *Daily News* and the *American* in the evening field, however, was the pro-New Deal, tabloid-style *Times*, founded in 1929 by Samuel E. Thomason, last owner of the *Journal*, and edited by Richard J. Finnegan.

DEATHS OF MORNING DAILIES

The sharp reduction in the number of morning dailies in New York, Philadelphia, and Chicago was part of a nationwide trend. Reader and advertiser preference for afternoon papers, and the time advantage these had in publishing European war news, helped to cut the number of morning papers from 500 in 1910 to 388 by 1930. Early in this period such morning papers as the *Atlanta Constitution, Indianapolis Star, Minneapolis Tribune,* and *St. Paul Pioneer Press* were alone in their fields. They were joined in 1915 by the *Detroit Free Press,* with the death of the old *Tribune*. Cleveland in 1917 saw the *Leader* disappear into the *Plain Dealer,* leaving the latter the only morning paper. Elimination of the *Free Press* in Milwaukee in 1919 left the *Sentinel* without morning competition. The same year the *St. Louis Globe-Democrat* bought its morning rival, the *Republic*. Merger in Buffalo in 1926 of the *Courier* (1831) and the *Express* (1846) ended that city's long morning rivalry. Pittsburgh's morning dailies were reduced to one in 1927, and Kansas City joined the trend in 1928. The *Cincinnati Enquirer* closed out its competition in 1930 by buying the *Commercial Tribune,* successor to Murat Halstead's old *Commercial Gazette*. By 1933 the journalistic historian Willard G. Bleyer could list 40 cities of more than 100,000 population which had only one morning daily.[12]

Morning paper mergers were the most spectacular in the first decades after 1900, but overall consolidation of metropolitan newspapers, and concentration of ownership, continued from coast to coast. Entry of the Hearst papers into Detroit through purchase of the *Times* in 1921 prompted the *News* (founded by James E. Scripps) to buy out the *Journal* in 1922. Thus Detroit, with more than a million population, was left with but three newspapers, the

[12] Willard G. Bleyer, "Freedom of the Press and the New Deal," *Journalism Quarterly,* XI (March 1934), 29. Those cities with but one morning daily but with two or more evening papers, in addition to the dozen listed above, were Baltimore, Providence, Rochester, Syracuse, Dayton, Columbus (Ohio), Louisville, Richmond, Memphis, Houston, Dallas, Fort Worth, Oklahoma City, Portland (Oregon), and Seattle. Those cities with but one morning and one evening paper were Hartford, New Haven, Tampa, Chattanooga, Knoxville, Grand Rapids, Tulsa, and Denver. One company owned all the dailies published in six cities: New Bedford and Springfield, Massachusetts, Duluth, Des Moines, Wilmington, Delaware, and Charleston, South Carolina. Springfield, however, had two morning and two evening dailies operating under a single ownership headed by Sherman H. Bowles of the historic *Republican* family.

morning *Free Press* and the evening *News* and *Times.* In New Orleans, the *Times-Democrat* and the *Picayune* were merged in 1914, leaving the new *Times-Picayune* alone in the morning field for 10 years. The *Times-Picayune,* owned by L. K. Nicholson, bought Colonel Robert Ewing's *States* in 1933 for an evening edition. The other evening paper, the *Item,* published a morning edition, the *Tribune,* from 1924 to 1941.

St. Louis afternoon journalism was dominated by Pulitzer's *Post-Dispatch.* The *Chronicle,* Scripps-McRae entry of 1880, merged with the *Evening Star* (1878) in 1905. The *Times* (1907) joined forces with the *Star* in 1932 as the *Star-Times,* leaving St. Louis with three ownerships. Kansas City rivals of Nelson's *Star* found the going equally difficult. Nelson bought the morning *Times* in 1901. The Scripps-McRae *World,* founded in 1897, faded from the picture. The evening *Post,* started in 1906 and bought by Bonfils and Tammen of *Denver Post* fame in 1909, was sold in 1922 to the owners of the morning *Journal* (1858), and the two papers became the *Journal-Post* in 1928. Kansas City thus dropped to two ownerships.

The team of publisher Gardner Cowles and editor Harvey Ingham captured the entire Des Moines newspaper field between 1903 and 1927, foreshadowing what was to happen in other cities after 1930. The *Leader* (1849) and the *Register* (1856) ended their long rivalry in a 1902 merger and Cowles assumed control the following year. In 1908 he bought the newly-founded *Tribune,* which became the evening associate of the morning *Register.* The evening *Daily News,* founded in 1886 and bought by Scripps in 1902, was eliminated in 1924. Cowles' last purchase was the evening *Capital,* dating from 1881, which surrendered in 1927 in the face of the effective Cowles promotional policies and editorial direction.

HEARST AND SCRIPPS-HOWARD CONSOLIDATIONS

Activities of the country's two biggest group ownerships—Hearst and Scripps-Howard—and of lesser chain aspirants caused newspaper consolidations in still other cities. The Hearst organization, in a buying splurge concentrated in the years 1918 to 1928, put 16 newspapers to death, as consolidations were carried out to bulwark the positions of Hearst-owned dailies. The Scripps-Howard group was responsible for the closing of 15 newspapers between 1923 and 1934.

Hearst's purchase of the *Chicago Herald* in 1918, to combine with his morning *Examiner,* already has been mentioned. He thus had the *Herald & Examiner* and the *American* in that city. In Boston, where the Hearst-owned evening *American* was founded in 1904, the publisher bought the century-old *Daily Advertiser* in 1917 and the *Record* in 1920. The two papers were juggled in an effort to bring tabloid publication to Boston, with the name *Record* surviving for the morning Hearst paper.[13] Meanwhile the *Boston Herald* was buying the *Traveler* in 1912 for an evening edition and was absorbing the Munsey-owned *Journal* in 1917. Thus Boston, which in 1900 had eleven major newspapers operated by seven ownerships, by 1930 had eight newspapers and five ownerships. The others were Edwin A. Grozier's highly successful morning *Post*, the Taylor family's morning and evening *Globes*, and the limping but traditional *Transcript*.

New York State extensions of the Hearst group were made in 1922, a year in which the publisher was seeking the governorship. The *Rochester Journal* was one addition, with the *Post-Express* being absorbed for its AP membership. In Syracuse the *Telegram*, bought in 1922, and the *Journal*, added in 1925, were merged as the *Journal Telegram*.

Washington was one of the few large cities to add newspapers during this period, but Hearst promptly consolidated the ownership of two newcomers. The morning *Post* and the Noyes family's evening *Star* were challenged by the founding of the *Times* in 1894 and the *Herald* in 1906. Munsey bought the *Times* in 1901 and killed its morning edition. When he retired from the Washington field in 1917 the *Times* passed to Arthur Brisbane, who sold it to Hearst two years later. The *Herald* was added to the Hearst group in 1922. Scripps-Howard gave Washington a fourth ownership when it established the tabloid *Daily News* in 1921.

Baltimore was less fortunate. The *Sun*, original penny paper of 1837, took over the *Evening World* in 1910 and made it the *Evening Sun*. The *Herald*, a morning penny paper, died in 1906. The *Evening News*, Grasty's crusading paper which fell into Munsey's control, was consolidated with the *Star* in 1921, and the paper was sold to Hearst in 1922. The *American*, dating from 1799, also passed from Munsey to Hearst and after 1928 was published only as a Sunday paper. A 1922 Scripps-Howard entry, the *Post*, was sold to Hearst in 1934. The Hearst *News-Post* thus survived as daily opposition for the *Sunpapers*.

Pittsburgh also saw its newspapers shuffled by the Hearst and Scripps-Howard organizations. The Scripps-Howard group bought the well-established *Press* in 1923 for six million dollars, under an agreement with the city's other newspaper owners that the *Dispatch* and *Leader* would be bought out and killed. Four years later Hearst and Paul Block, a Hearst associate and newspaper publisher and broker, bought the remaining four Pittsburgh dailies. The morning *Sun* and *Chronicle Telegraph* were transformed into the Hearst-owned *Sun-Telegraph;* the evening *Post* and *Gazette Times* into the Block-owned *Post-Gazette*.

Arthur Brisbane and Hearst teamed up in Milwaukee at the end of World War I, with the result that the *Evening Wisconsin*, the *News*, and the *Telegram* were rolled into the *Wisconsin News*, Hearst-owned after 1919. The morning

13 The name *Advertiser* was retained for the Hearst Sunday edition in Boston.

Sentinel joined the Hearst chain in 1924 to give the chain two footholds against the steadily increasing pressure of the *Milwaukee Journal*.[14] Also in the Midwest, the *Omaha News* and *Bee* were bought by Hearst in 1928 and merged as the *News-Bee,* a morning, evening, and Sunday publication.

On the West Coast Hearst created a strong evening companion for his *San Francisco Examiner* by combining three papers. He bought the *Call* (1855) in 1913 and combined the *Evening Post* with it to obtain an Associated Press membership. In 1929 the *Bulletin* (1856) was absorbed by Hearst to form the *Call-Bulletin.* The mergers left San Francisco with Hearst morning and evening papers, the locally-owned morning *Chronicle,* and the Scripps-Howard evening *News.* Across the bay in Oakland the *Post-Enquirer* was formed in a 1922 Hearst double purchase and merger as competition for the Knowland family's *Tribune.*

In Los Angeles, Hearst's morning *Examiner* was augmented in 1922 by purchase of the evening *Herald.* The *Express,* founded in 1871, was swallowed up by Hearst in 1931 to form the *Herald & Express.* The *Record,* established by Scripps in 1895, died in the 1920s but was replaced by the *Daily News,* a tabloid which Manchester Boddy developed into a pro-New Deal newspaper. Hearst's solid morning competition in Los Angeles still was Harry Chandler's conservative *Times.*

Hearst's other purchases, which did not involve consolidations, were the *Atlanta Georgian,* 1912; *Detroit Times,* 1921; *Seattle Post-Intelligencer,* 1922; *Fort Worth Record,* 1923 (soon sold to the *Star-Telegram*); *Albany Times-Union,* 1924; and *San Antonio Light,* 1924. The tabloid *Daily Mirror* was added to his New York City holdings, the *Journal* and the *American,* in 1924. At its peak in the early 1930s the Hearst organization totaled 26 dailies and 17 Sunday papers, published in 18 cities.

CHANGING PATTERNS FOR SCRIPPS-HOWARD

Changes after World War I in the direction of the group of newspapers started by E. W. Scripps brought newspaper consolidations to a dozen cities in the next 15 years. Scripps and his business associate, Milton A. McRae, parted company in 1914. A paralytic stroke suffered by Scripps in 1917 impelled him to put his sons, James and Robert, in charge of the chain. James withdrew from the organization after a family quarrel in 1920, taking five Pacific Coast papers with him. Two years later Roy W. Howard, head of the United Press, was given equal control with Robert Paine Scripps over what became the Scripps-Howard Newspapers.

Scripps and McRae had founded 27 papers and bought five more, between 1878 and 1917. Of the 32, only 13 remained at the time of Scripps' death in

[14] Paul Block leased the *Sentinel* from Hearst and operated it from 1929 to 1937.

1926. Robert Paine Scripps founded seven more papers in 1921 and 1922, but with the coming of Roy Howard the chain switched its tactics, thereafter only buying existing newspapers. In the next 14 years, 14 newspapers were acquired, 6 of them for merging with other Scripps-Howard papers. At the end of this burst of activity Scripps-Howard controlled 25 dailies, published in 24 cities, and 7 Sunday editions.

Strengthening of Scripps-Howard properties by elimination of competitors took place in several cities. Knoxville saw the *News-Sentinel* created by the merger of the *News*, started in 1921, and the *Sentinel*, bought in 1926. The *El Paso Post*, founded in 1922, became the *Herald-Post* with the acquisition of the *Herald* in 1931. The *Akron Press*, begun in 1899 by E. W. Scripps, received a badly needed transfusion in 1925 with the purchase of the *Times*, to form the *Times-Press*. The *Memphis Press*, founded in 1906, became the *Press-Scimitar* by absorbing the *News-Scimitar* in 1926; 10 years later Scripps-Howard added the morning *Memphis Commercial Appeal* to the chain. The *New York Telegram*, bought in 1927, became the *World-Telegram* in 1931 when Howard negotiated the purchase of the famous Pulitzer papers. The *Pittsburgh Press* was acquired in 1923 in a deal which saw the elimination of the *Dispatch* and *Leader*.

Denver's newspapers were reshaped by a cutthroat battle between Scripps-Howard and the *Denver Post*. The *Post's* evening opponents had dwindled over the years. The *Republican*, which had absorbed the *Tribune* in 1884, in turn was merged with the *Times* in 1913. The *Times* and the morning *Rocky Mountain News* came under the same ownership in 1902 and were sold in 1926 to Scripps-Howard. Thereupon the *Express*, in the Scripps fold since 1906, was merged into the *Times*. A truce arranged between the *Post* and the Scripps-Howard newspapers in 1928 brought the demise of the *Times* and left Denver with two newspapers.

On the loss side, Scripps-Howard sold the *Des Moines News*, *Sacramento Star*, and *Terre Haute Post* to competitors during the 1920s, and the *Baltimore Post* to Hearst in 1934. The *Washington Daily News*, *Fort Worth Press*, *Birmingham Post*, and *Norfolk Post* all were founded in 1921, but the Norfolk paper died almost immediately. Scripps-Howard purchased the *Indianapolis Times* and *Youngstown Telegram* in 1922 and the *New Mexico State Tribune* in Albuquerque in 1923, while the *Buffalo Times* was acquired in 1929. It should be noted that Scripps-Howard newspapers, generally speaking, were operated in smaller-sized cities than those invaded by Hearst.

THE GROWTH OF GROUP OWNERSHIPS

Rising to third place among group newspaper publishers in point of number of newspapers owned was Frank E. Gannett, New York publisher who began in earnest to build his chain during the 1920s. His activities brought newspaper mergers in Ithaca, Rochester, Utica, Elmira, Newburgh, and Beacon before 1930. The Gannett group, mainly in New York State, totaled 16 by 1935, and Gannett achieved some prominence and political influence.

Newspaper group ownership boomed during the 1920s, as already observed in the cases of Hearst, Scripps-Howard, and Gannett. There was both a sizable increase in the percentage of total daily newspaper circulation which was chain-owned, and in the number of the group operations, both daily and weekly. The "menace of the chains" became a topic for study and debate. A newspaper chain ownership was defined as ownership of two or more papers in two or more cities.

In 1900 there were 8 such groups of dailies, owning a total of 27 newspapers and controlling about 10 per cent of total daily circulation in the country.[15] A study of chain ownership for the year 1923 shows that there were by then 34 daily newspaper groups, owning 158 newspapers and controlling 31 per cent of total daily circulation. The same researcher found that by 1935 there were 63 daily newspaper chains, owning 328 newspapers and controlling 41 per cent of the country's daily circulation.[16] Group owners controlled 12 per cent of Sunday circulation in 1923 and 52 per cent in 1935. In 1932, their dailies represented 18 per cent of the total number of dailies, a peak figure for the period. Groups owned 27 per cent of Sunday papers the same year. As it turned out, the years of greatest influence of the big national chains were in the mid-1930s, when the numbers of their dailies and their percentages of total daily and Sunday circulations reach a zenith.

Hearst's always was the biggest chain. In 1923 his 22 dailies had 3,400,000 circulation, which represented 10.8 per cent of total daily circulation in the country. His Sunday circulation of 4,100,000 was 19.1 per cent of the total. By 1935 the 26 Hearst dailies had a total circulation of 5,100,000 representing 13.6 per cent of the country's daily circulation. The Sunday figure became 6,800,000, comprising 24.2 per cent of total Sunday circulation. This meant that in 1935 Hearst sold 13 out of every 100 daily newspaper copies issued in the country, and one-fourth of all the Sunday papers.

The McCormick-Patterson combine of the *Chicago Tribune* and *New York Daily News* ranked second in 1935 with 6.4 per cent of total daily circulation and 12.3 per cent on Sunday. Scripps-Howard was third, with 5.1 per cent daily and 2.1 per cent Sunday. No other group had as much as 2 per cent of daily circulation.

Among the many smaller groups which developed were some achieving numerical importance.[17] H. C. Ogden owned a group of 15 newspapers in 1935, comprising nearly half of West Virginia's dailies. The Lee Syndicate in Iowa, dating from 1903, had 12 dailies by 1935. The Scripps League on the

[15] Frank Luther Mott, *American Journalism* (New York: Macmillan, 1950), p. 648.

[16] William Weinfeld, "The Growth of Daily Newspaper Chains in the United States: 1923, 1926–1935," *Journalism Quarterly*, XIII (December 1936), 357.

[17] Weinfeld, *op. cit.*, carries tabulations of chain ownership in 1923 and 1935.

West Coast had 11. The Booth Newspapers group in Michigan, founded by George C. Booth of the *Detroit News* in 1893, totaled 8 in 1935. Newspaper publisher and broker Paul Block had a string of 7 dailies, as did the Ridder brothers of New York and Minnesota. Two other groups of long standing with 6 dailies each in 1935 were the Brush-Moore papers in Ohio, founded in 1901, and the Ira C. Copley group in Illinois and California, begun in 1905.

The two big national groups, Hearst and Scripps-Howard, had a steadily decreasing percentage of total newspaper circulation after the early 1930s. Fears that they and other groups would gobble up most of the country's papers proved unfounded. Instead, chain owners tended to concentrate on achieving local and regional dominance. Thus Gannett focused his attention on New York State, Ogden on West Virginia, Booth on Michigan. Another pattern which was to develop was the achieving of dominance in one city and then selection of another—as the Cowles family in Des Moines was to do by invading Minneapolis. These new patterns of group ownership had their effects upon newspaper consolidations and concentration of ownership, even more pronounced than the effects of the Hearst and Scripps-Howard ownerships.

Annotated Bibliography

Books

Bok, Edward W., *A Man from Maine*. New York: Scribner's, 1923. A life of Cyrus H. K. Curtis by his editor.

Britt, George, *Forty Years—Forty Millions; The Career of Frank A Munsey*. New York: Holt, Rinehart & Winston, 1935. A critical biography of the newspaper consolidator.

Dennis, Charles H., *Victor Lawson: His Time and His Work*. Chicago: University of Chicago Press, 1935. The authorized story of Lawson and the *Chicago Daily News*.

Ernst, Morris, *The First Freedom*. New York: Macmillan, 1946. Freedom-loving Mr. Ernst decries the trend toward newspaper consolidation.

Schramm, Wilbur, ed., *Mass Communications*. Urbana: University of Illinois Press, 1949; rev. 1960. Of these selected readings the recommended one on newspaper ownership is Raymond B. Nixon's "The Problem of Newspaper Monopoly."

Stewart, Kenneth, and John Tebbel, *Makers of Modern Journalism*. Englewood Cliffs, N.J.: Prentice-Hall, 1952. Chapter 21 tells the story of Philadelphia's recent journalism.

Villard, Oswald Garrison, *The Disappearing Daily*. New York: Knopf, 1944. Criticism of the trend toward consolidation and bigness.

———, *Some Newspapers and Newspaper-Men*. New York: Knopf, 1923. Like *The Disappearing Daily*, this book discusses newspapers in major cities as well as major publishers: New York, Boston, Philadelphia, Washington, among others.

Periodicals and Monographs

Bleyer, Willard G., "Freedom of the Press and the New Deal," *Journalism Quarterly,* XI (March 1934), 22. Report on trend toward newspaper combinations.

Duffus, Robert L., "Mr. Munsey," *American Mercury,* II (July 1924), 297. A gently critical rejection of Munsey as a newspaper owner. Reprinted in Ford and Emery, *Highlights in the History of the American Press.*

Evans, James P., "Clover Leaf: The Good Luck Chain, 1899–1933," *Journalism Quarterly,* XLVI (Autumn 1969), 482. The chain had a *Daily News* in Omaha, St. Paul, and Des Moines and a Kansas City *World.*

Gothberg, John A., "The Local Influence of J. R. Knowland's Oakland *Tribune,*" *Journalism Quarterly,* XLV (Autumn 1968), 487. Knowland's half-century as publisher evaluated.

Neurath, Paul, "One-Publisher Communities: Factors Influencing Trend," *Journalism Quarterly,* XXI (September 1944), 230.

Nixon, Raymond B., "Trends in U.S. Newspaper Ownership: Concentration with Competition," *Gazette,* XIV (No. 3, 1968), 181. A review with comprehensive data. See also Nixon, Raymond B., and Jean Ward, "Trends in Newspaper Ownership and Inter-Media Competition," *Journalism Quarterly,* XXXVIII (Winter 1961), 3. See also Nixon's "Trends in Daily Newspaper Ownership Since 1945," *Journalism Quarterly,* XXXI (Winter 1954), 3, and "Concentration and Absenteeism in Daily Newspaper Ownership," *Journalism Quarterly,* XXII (June 1945), 97.

Norris, Wendell W., "The Transient Frontier Weekly as a Stimulant to Homesteading," *Journalism Quarterly,* XXX (Winter 1953), 44. Based on "The Prairie Frontier Boom of the Weekly Press, 1865–1915." Master's thesis, University of Wisconsin, 1951.

Ray, Royal H., "Economic Forces as Factors in Daily Newspaper Concentration," *Journalism Quarterly,* XXIX (Winter, 1952), 31. An excellent summary of pressures for newspaper consolidation, taken from his *Concentration of Ownership and Control in the American Daily Newspaper Industry* (Columbia University Microfilms, 1951).

Robb, Arthur, "Chain Journalism in the Sixth Decade," *Editor & Publisher* golden jubilee number, July 21, 1934. A descriptive essay summarizing chain developments.

Weinfeld, William, "The Growth of Daily Newspaper Chains in the United States: 1923, 1926–1935," *Journalism Quarterly,* XIII (December 1936), 357. The first important study of the problem.

Rudolph Dirks' Katzenjammer Kids look down upon their successors: George McManus' Jiggs of 1926; Frank King's Gasoline Alley of 1923 with Walt adopting Skeezix; Harold Gray's Little Orphan Annie and Sandy, 1936; Chic Young's Blondie and Dagwood, 1936; Milton Caniff's Steve Canyon in 1939 "Terry and the Pirates"; Chester Gould's Dick Tracy as he began in 1931 and again in 1956; and Charlie Brown, Lucy, and Snoopy in a 1956 "Peanuts" strip by Charles M. Schulz (with © permissions for years indicated from United Feature, King Features, and Chicago Tribune-New York Daily News Syndicates).

23

The Common Denominators

. . . when one travels through the country on a Sunday on a fast train and buys . . . Sunday papers . . . one finds the same "comics," the same Sunday magazines, the same special "features" in almost all of them and, of course, in most of them precisely the same Associated Press news. . . The newspaper profession has turned out to be a business and as a result there was bound to be standardization . . .
—Oswald Garrison Villard (1930)

The rise of the American press associations—organizations dedicated to the rapid, thorough and impartial collection and dissemination of all the news—was an epochal development in the history of journalism. "The right of the people to know" was greatly advanced by the creation of news agencies which utilize journalistic skills and modern communications techniques to find the news, to report it impartially, and to speed it to every corner of the country and of the world. The development in the twentieth century of two strongly competitive press associations, the Associated Press and the United Press International, guaranteed newspaper editors and readers a better kind of national and international news coverage than the world had even known—despite acknowledged imperfections.

While the press associations have contributed mightily to the excellence of modern newspapers, nevertheless they have become one of the common denominators of a standardized journalism. The news they supply is a vital part of any daily, together with the paper's own local news. Only a few American dailies ever have been able to maintain staff correspondents in leading news centers of the country and world, and the press association logotypes

—AP, UPI—have become the symbols of trustworthy service from an outside source. At the same time the influence of the press associations upon the character of many daily newspapers has become pronounced. Their usual style of writing—summary lead, inverted pyramid story structure, jampacked facts—affected all newspaper writing, to the detriment of original, individualistic reporting. Their decisions on the relative importance of news events, indicated by the use of "bulletin" slugs and by transmission of news budget summaries to desk editors, became accepted by most papers. In too many newspaper offices the press associations' "flashes of life" and "today's chuckles" replaced local efforts, and entertaining stories of faraway crimes, violence, and romance became too readily available to uninspired and ineffectual news editors. The result was a standardization of content going beyond the beneficial and needed cooperative coverage of significant nonlocal news.

More strikingly emerging as common denominators of journalism were the syndicates and special services. Just as entertaining or exciting news attracts an audience anywhere, so do comic strips, cartoons, Sunday magazine sections, columns, and other features. Again, the syndicates have made available to newspapers of all sizes and localities the work of talented artists and writers whose services could not otherwise be obtained by the average paper. But in more than one city the race to corral the most successful comic strips, the best-read columnists, the most colorful features has at times overshadowed the more serious aspects of journalism. And sadly enough, ability to compete in newspaper publication has been affected by possession or lack of possession of popular syndicated material. Even more sadly, some newspapers ignored the fact that effectively produced local material outdraws most syndicated material in reader interest. Even when syndicated material was used wisely, it had an inevitable standardizing effect, which, combined with the similarity of news display, caused many a reader to refuse to buy more than one paper because "they're all alike." Oswald Garrison Villard, the famous editor of the *Nation* and thoughtful critic of the press whose quotation opens this chapter,[1] saw both the good and the bad in such standardization.

The United States has had three major press associations operating on nationwide and worldwide scales. One is the Associated Press, which arose out of nineteenth-century efforts at cooperative news-gathering. Its twentieth-century competitors were the United Press Associations, founded in 1907 by Edward Wyllis Scripps, and the International News Service, begun in 1909 by William Randolph Hearst. When these two services were merged in 1958 to form the United Press International, the new UPI became quite comparable in strength to the AP. Abroad, the UPI and AP of the 1970s sold their news and picture services to newspapers, radio and television stations in competition with two other worldwide services. These were Reuters of Great Britain, founded in 1851, and Agence France-Presse, which arose after World War II out of the ruins of the old French Havas agency (1836).

[1] Oswald Garrison Villard, "The Press Today," *Nation,* CXXX (June 1930), 646.

THE ASSOCIATED PRESS: GENESIS

The longest history among the American press associations is that of the Associated Press. The modern cooperative news-gathering association with that name took final form in 1900 after a bitter struggle for control of the press association facilities of the country. The agreement among New York City's leading newspapers in 1849 which brought about the establishment of the Associated Press of New York set the pattern for similar associations. Midwestern dailies formed the Western Associated Press in 1862, and before 1870 a New York state AP and the New England Associated Press were organized. Other subsidiary regional groups followed. But always the power of the Associated Press of New York was felt.[2]

The New York AP had been well-guided by its earliest general agents, Dr. Alexander Jones (1849–1851), news-gathering pioneer Daniel H. Craig (1851–1866), and former Washington correspondent and San Francisco newspaperman James W. Simonton (1866–1882). It had held its position as disseminator of foreign news obtained from European news agencies and it had maintained a monopolistic position through agreements with the Western Union for telegraph line use. By 1882, however, the non-New York dailies were ready to challenge the autocratic control of the founding papers.

One outcome that year was a partial recognition of the growing importance of the midwestern dailies. A joint executive committee was named to administer the AP organization, with three members from the New York group and two from the Western Associated Press. Serving on it were a consortium of four who dominated AP affairs: William Henry Smith, general agent of the Western AP since 1869, who was named general manager succeeding Simonton; Whitelaw Reid of the *New York Tribune;* Walter N. Haldeman of the *Louisville Courier-Journal* and Richard Smith of the *Cincinnati Gazette.*[3]

THE FIRST UNITED PRESS, 1882

More important was the creation in 1882 of a strong rival for the Associated Press groups. Newspapers outside the AP fold had attempted various organizations without much success. One of the promoters of a rival agency was Henry George, who 10 years before he wrote *Progress and Poverty* attempted to break an AP news monopoly in California. George and a friend,

[2] See pages 198–99 and 329–32 for earlier accounts.

[3] Victor Rosewater, *History of Cooperative News-Gathering in the United States* (New York: Appleton-Century-Crofts, 1930), p. 179.

John Hasson, began a news service in 1869 which two years later became the American Press Association. Western Union quickly raised its rates to discriminatory levels in order to protect the AP, but the independents were able to use the wires of rival telegraph companies. The association was reorganized in 1877 and again in 1882, when it took the name United Press (no relation to the present-day UPI).

Giving the United Press competent direction were its general manager, Walter Polk Phillips, a former Associated Press man; William M. Laffan, business manager of the *New York Sun;* and John R. Walsh, Chicago financier and partner with James W. Scott in the *Chicago Herald.* Such vigorous dailies as the *Boston Globe, Detroit News, Buffalo News, Philadelphia Ledger,* and *New York Daily News* were among the members. Phillips organized a first-rate foreign news service and within three years the United Press was challenging the AP.

The reaction of the ruling groups within the AP and UP was typical of the times. The AP executive committee entered into a secret agreement with the United Press' three strong men, providing for exchange of news between the two associations and a virtual end of competition. There were financial rewards for the insiders. When Western Associated Press members uncovered these arrangements in 1891, a new battle within the newspaper ranks was inevitable.[4]

Victor Lawson, publisher of the *Chicago Daily News,* took the lead for the westerners. Various attempts were made to consolidate the AP groups, which by then included a Southern Associated Press, with the United Press. Negotiations collapsed, however, and the *New York Sun* and *Tribune* bolted to the UP in 1892, to be followed the next year by the remaining members of the Associated Press of New York. Taking control of the AP organization was a new corporation, the Associated Press of Illinois, chartered in late 1892.

Melville E. Stone, who had sold his interest in the *Chicago Daily News* to Lawson in 1888, was drafted as general manager of the AP. One of his first steps was to obtain exclusive news exchange contracts with the leading European news agencies—Reuters in Britain, Havas in France, Wolff in Germany. Stone's contracts cut the United Press off from sources of foreign news long enjoyed by the New York dailies. Lawson and Stone then went to work on the eastern strongholds of the United Press, winning over to AP membership the *New York World* and the *Evening Post,* the *Washington Star,* most of the Philadelphia and Baltimore papers, and holding the southern papers in line. A four-year struggle, which cost the Associated Press members a million dollars in added expenses, finally ended in early 1897 when all the New York papers except Dana's *Sun* and Hearst's *Journal* were admitted to the AP. The United Press went into bankruptcy, but Laffan of the *Sun,* its stubborn leader, had organized the Laffan News Bureau and thus created a creditable

[4] See Rosewater, *History of Cooperative News-Gathering,* pp. 182–89.

news-gathering organization which operated until the sale of the *Sun* to Munsey in 1916.

Laffan indirectly was to cause the Associated Press more trouble before the association's course was finally set. The *Chicago Inter Ocean* went to court in 1898 to prevent the AP from discontinuing service to it as punishment for the *Inter Ocean's* use of Laffan News Bureau copy. An Illinois court decision, handed down in 1900, found that the incorporation papers of the AP were written so broadly as to make the press association a public utility, bound to provide its service to all newspapers wishing it. For the moment the Illinois ruling seemed to put an end to the exclusive membership character of the AP, but its leaders found a way out. The Associated Press of Illinois was dissolved, and a new Associated Press was formed as a nonprofit membership association under New York State law. Stone continued as general manager of the new AP, and Frank B. Noyes of the *Washington Star* succeeded Lawson as president, to serve until 1938.

THE NEW ASSOCIATED PRESS OF 1900

The most important fact about the new Associated Press of 1900 was that it was a cooperative. Its members were to supply each other with news originating in individual publication areas. They were to share the cost of this exchange of news, and the cost of maintaining a press association staff which would direct the flow of news and augment it with other coverage. The staff, headed by the general manager, was to be responsible only to the membership, through its officers and directors. The Associated Press thus would be an agency existing only for the benefit of its member newspapers.

There were some faults, however, in the AP organization. One was an association bylaw prohibiting members from using other news services. This was eliminated in 1915 after an advisory opinion of the U. S. Attorney General's office ruled such action monopolistic. Another complaint centered about extra voting privileges given the original members in 1900 by the issuing of low-denomination bonds carrying voting rights. The result was that the larger, older morning papers kept control of the board of directors despite the growth of evening papers and entry of many smaller dailies into the AP. Voting rights were spread more widely in 1928, and in 1937 the smaller dailies were given three directorships on a board of 18. Directors were limited to a maximum service of three terms beginning in 1942.

Protest rights, by which an AP member could prevent the entry of a direct competitor into the association, formed the basis for charges that the AP was monopolistic in character. These rights, at first restricted to the original membership, were extended to all members in 1928. If a member protested the election of a competing paper in the same city, a four-fifths vote of the entire membership was required to override the veto. In only a few cases was a member's protest thus overridden, and as a result, newspaper owners in larger cities usually could obtain AP service only by buying an existing membership.

This restriction of AP membership was challenged by the *Chicago Sun,* founded in 1941 by Marshall Field as a competitor in the morning field to the *Tribune.* Court action was begun in 1942, and in 1945 the U. S. Supreme Court held that the AP bylaws concerning protest rights constituted unfair restriction of competition. The AP thereupon amended its membership rules and elected several newspapers previously denied admission.

Another unhappy situation in which the Associated Press found itself stemmed from the news exchange contracts it made in 1893 with European news agencies. This meant that news of the United States which was collected by the Associated Press was distributed abroad by foreign news services. Many charges were made that Reuters and Havas mishandled American news. Foreign news given to the Associated Press by its associates likewise was suspect, since many of the foreign news services were under the control of their governments. Melville E. Stone, as AP general manager, did his best to open news channels in European countries [5] and the AP established some foreign bureaus before World War I to collect its own news. But lacking the right to sell its foreign news abroad, it could not build the kind of foreign service it eventually achieved. Not until 1934 was this restrictive arrangement finally broken down by the AP management.[6] An AP World Service was begun in 1946.

AP STAFF LEADERS: KENT COOPER

There were many notable names in the AP organization during its formative years under Stone's managership. Charles S. Diehl, a veteran of the Illinois AP regime, became an assistant general manager. So did Jackson S. Elliott, news chief during World War I. Frederick Roy Martin, successful editor of the *Providence Journal,* became assistant general manager in 1912 and succeeded Stone as manager in 1921. Among the noted bureau chiefs were Salvatore Cortesi in Rome, Seymour B. Conger in Berlin, and Edwin M. Hood in Washington. World War I correspondents included Charles T. Thompson, Frederick Palmer, and DeWitt Mackenzie, later an AP news analyst. Wilmer Stuart set up the Associated Press election coverage system on a state-by-state basis between 1904 and 1916, proving the completeness and accuracy of the coverage in the seesaw race between President Woodrow Wilson and Charles Evans Hughes in 1916. The AP correctly reported several hairline decisions in various

[5] For a description of Stone's activities see *"M.E.S."—His Book* (New York: Harper & Row, 1918).

[6] The whole story, from the AP's viewpoint, is told in Kent Cooper, *Barriers Down* (New York: Holt, Rinehart & Winston, 1942). Reuters became a cooperative, like the AP, in 1941, and invaded the American market with some success.

states, which gave Wilson the victory after it had once been generally conceded to Hughes.[7] Helping to organize that election coverage was the then young AP traffic chief, Kent Cooper.

The name of Kent Cooper was soon to dominate the history of the Associated Press. An Indianan, he had started reporting for his local paper at 14. His college education was interrupted by the death of his father, and he left school to join the *Indianapolis Press*. From there he went to the Scripps-McRae news service, becoming head of the Indianapolis bureau of what was to become the Associated Press' major rival. There Cooper got the idea that out-of-the-way papers could be better served by a system of telephoning the news report than by telegraphing it. In 1910 he went to General Manager Stone of the AP and so impressed Stone with his knowledge of news communications methods that he was made AP traffic chief. He became an assistant general manager in 1920 and succeeded Martin as general manager in 1925. Through his subsequent career Cooper demonstrated his strong administrative qualities, but he was never a "newspaperman's newspaperman."

Cooper had plans for improving the efficiency and quality of the Associated Press service, and many changes came with his rise to control. The number of bureaus was increased and staffs were expanded. The quality of writing was improved and some interpretation was introduced into factual AP stories which demanded explanatory background material. Human interest stories, long frowned upon by the AP, gained favor. The transition was marked by the AP's first Pulitzer Prize, won by Kirke L. Simpson in 1922 for a series on the burial of the Unknown Soldier in Arlington Cemetery. The changes in writing were not so much the result of Cooper's foresight as they were of the prodding the AP was receiving at the hands of rival press associations, as will be demonstrated later in this chapter.

Other changes indicated a modernizing of the AP. A mail feature service was begun in 1928. State services, permitting exchange of regional news on wires subsidiary to the main AP trunk wires, were expanded. A news photo service was established in 1927, and after a sharp clash between picture-minded publishers and their more conservative colleagues, the AP Wirephoto system was approved in 1935. The leased wire system of the Associated Press was tripled between 1920 and 1930 and the budget doubled, reaching 10 million dollars annually. Automatic news printers, called teletypes, were first used in 1913 and gradually replaced Morse operators.

The pressures of competition from other news services and of World War II coverage requirements brought further advances. A leased cable and radioteletype circuits across the North Atlantic, European leased land circuits, and an overseas radiophoto network were added to the service. The character of the news report was subjected to an increasingly intensive review by members of the Associated Press Managing Editors Association, a group formed in 1931.

7 This episode is described in Oliver Gramling, *AP: The Story of News* (New York: Holt, Rinehart & Winston, 1940), pp. 249–55.

The managing editors of member papers criticised the AP news coverage and writing style orally until 1947, when the reports of a Continuing Study Committee annually were put into printed form. State memberships began similar analyses of their wires. The AP management hired readability expert Rudolph Flesch to advise its staff, and correspondents like James Marlow of the Washington bureau did excellent work in pointing the way to better writing techniques. After a bitter battle, AP began to sell its news report to radio stations in 1940, five years later than the UP and INS. Radio stations were granted associate membership, without voting rights, in 1946. The Associated Press Radio-Television Association was formed in 1954.[8]

RECENT AP MANAGEMENT AND STAFF

New faces appeared in the AP management. Two of the men most respected by their colleagues for their capabilities as journalists were Byron Price and Paul Miller. Both served as chiefs of the Washington bureau. Price became the AP's first executive news editor in 1936 before retiring from the news service to become director of the Office of Censorship during World War II and later assistant Secretary General of the United Nations. Miller, after being named an assistant general manager, quit the AP to become an executive of the Gannett newspapers.

Their departures left Frank J. Starzel and Alan J. Gould as the leading AP executives under Cooper. Gould, sports editor since 1932, was executive editor from 1941 to 1963. Starzel, who was a newspaperman in Iowa and Illinois before joining the AP in 1929, became Cooper's chief assistant and succeeded him as general manager in 1948. More the traditional newsman than Cooper, he was regarded as a capable successor. Wes Gallagher, World War II correspondent, and Harry T. Montgomery became assistant general managers in 1954. Lloyd Stratton directed AP service abroad until Stanley Swinton was named director of the World Service in 1960.

Starzel's retirement at the close of 1962 brought Gallagher to the general manager's post, with Montgomery becoming his deputy. Louis Kramp was named assistant general manager for radio-television services. Daniel De Luce and Robert C. Eunson became assistant general managers in 1965. Gallagher, an aggressive spokesman for the AP, instituted "task force" reporting by a 10-man team based in Washington, opened AP reporting ranks to younger men and also to women, and presided over a massive modernization of the transmission wires.

On the publishers' side, Robert McLean of the *Philadelpha Bulletin* succeeded Noyes as AP president in 1938. His successors were Benjamin McKel-

[8] The radio news struggle is detailed in Chapter 26.

Associated Press

Associated Press

Kent Cooper (*left*) and Wes Gallagher, general managers of the Associated Press.

way of the *Washington Star* in 1957 and Paul Miller, the onetime AP executive who was now president of the Gannett newspapers, in 1963.

The names of AP staffmen should not be ignored. Serving in Washington were such newsmen as David Lawrence, who left the AP to become a columnist and news magazine publisher, and Stephen T. Early, who became President Franklin D. Roosevelt's press secretary. Pulitzer Prize winners of the 1930s were Francis A. Jamieson, who covered the Lindbergh baby kidnaping story, Howard W. Blakeslee, AP science editor, and Louis P. Lochner, Berlin bureau chief. Other noted byliners were Brian Bell, W. F. Caldwell, foreign correspondent James A. Mills, and Edward J. Neil, killed during the Spanish civil war.

World War II saw AP men distinguish themselves overseas. Hal Boyle, Larry Allen, and Daniel De Luce won Pulitzer Prizes as correspondents. Frank Noel, Frank Filan, and Joe Rosenthal were similarly honored as news photographers—Rosenthal for his famous picture of the Marines raising the flag on Iwo Jima's Mount Suribachi. Lloyd Lehrbas, Wes Gallagher, Don Whitehead, Edward Kennedy, Russell Brines, and C. Yates McDaniel were other leading war correspondents. In the Korean War, correspondents Relman Morin and Don Whitehead, and photographer Max Desfor won Pulitzer Prizes. Similar awards went to foreign correspondents Eddy Gilmore in 1947 and Lynn Heinzerling in 1961, and to diplomatic writer John Hightower in 1952. Whitehead and Morin repeated, with national reporting prizes, in 1953 and 1958, respectively. Morin won his covering the Little Rock school riots. Cited for Pulitzer Prizes for Vietnam War coverage were correspondents Malcolm W. Browne and Peter Arnett and photographers Horst Faas and Edward T. Adams. The latter photographed the execution of a Viet Cong by a pistol-wielding Saigon police chief. Steve Starr, 25, won in 1970 for his photo of a gun-carrying black Cornell student.

Other major figures included the general news editors, Paul Mickelson, Samuel G. Blackman, and Rene Cappon; foreign editor Ben Bassett; Washington bureau chiefs William L. Beale, Jr., and Marvin Arrowsmith; news analysts J. M. Roberts, Jr., and William L. Ryan; political writers Jack Bell, Douglas Cornell, Relman Morin, and Walter Mears; White House correspondents Arrowsmith, Ernest B. Vaccaro, and Frank Cormier; European correspondents Richard O'Regan, Henry Bradsher, and Richard K. O'Malley.

The many names of individuals mentioned illustrate the rising importance of the press associations, for all were well-known to readers or fellow newspapermen. But the men most often identified with the AP are its four general managers—Melville E. Stone, Kent Cooper, Frank J. Starzel, and, since 1962, Wes Gallagher.

SCRIPPS AND HEARST CHALLENGE THE AP

Rising alongside the Associated Press as aggressive competing press associations were the United Press Associations of Edward Wyllis Scripps and the International News Service of William Randolph Hearst. This new United Press and the INS were not cooperatives, as was the AP. They were regular business enterprises which sold their news services to clients on a contract basis. Both arose in answer to the Associated Press' closed-membership policy. The chain newspaper publishers who started UP and INS soon found the news they collected could be sold both at home and abroad to others who could not obtain, or did not wish to have, AP service. Serving a variety of clients, as both the UP and INS soon did, their identification with two strong-minded newspaper publishers became only incidental. Their operating staffs were as anxious to cover all the news thoroughly and impartially, for the benefit of their ultimate readers, as were AP men, or any other newsmen.

Edward Wyllis Scripps once said that he founded the United Press Associations because he was suspicious of his fellow publishers who controlled the Associated Press. He did not take his papers into the AP in 1897, when the old United Press folded up.

"I knew that at least 90 per cent of my fellows in American journalism were capitalistic and conservative," he explained, and went on:

> I knew that, at that time at least, unless I came into the field with a new service, it would be impossible for the people of the United States to get correct news through the medium of the Associated Press. . . . I have made it impossible for the men who control the Associated Press to suppress the truth, or successfully to disseminate falsehood.[9]

[9] As quoted in Rosewater, *History of Cooperative News-Gathering*, p. 354.

The rebellious Scripps undoubtedly was too critical of his fellow publishers, but his concept of competing press associations acting as checks on each other proved to be of inestimable value to American journalism.

Scripps had other reasons for establishing his own news service. The AP was most interested in the news report for its big morning paper members, and Scripps published evening papers. The closed-membership character of AP meant that Scripps would have trouble obtaining memberships for the new dailies he was establishing. If he ran his own news service, he could fashion its coverage and writing style to better serve the Scripps type of paper. And finally, he expected to make money running a press association.

THE SECOND UNITED PRESS, 1907, AND ROY HOWARD

After operating two regional news services for his own papers in the Middle West and West for 10 years, Scripps merged them in 1907 with the Publishers' Press Association (begun in 1898 by non-AP eastern papers) to form the United Press Associations. A young Scripps newspaperman named John Vandercook helped create the merger and became head of the United Press, but he died the following year. Succeeding him as general manager was 25-year-old Roy W. Howard, destined eventually to dominate the Scripps publishing empire. Howard had served on the *St. Louis Post-Dispatch* and the Scripps papers in Indianapolis and Cincinnati before getting his big chance with the UP.

Scripps described the Roy Howard of this period as "a striking individual, very small of stature, with a large head and speaking countenance, and eyes that appeared to be windows for a rather unusual intellect. His manner was forceful, and the reverse from modest. Gall was written all over his face. It was in every tone and every word he voiced. There was ambition, self-respect and forcefulness oozing out of every pore of his body." [10]

Both Scripps and Howard exhibited a certain amount of gall when they announced the new United Press to its 250 subscribing papers and to other prospective clients. Scripps underwrote a $300,000 preferred stock issue to start the business, but actually put no money into it. There were but a dozen staff members, a handful of bureaus, and almost no foreign news reports. Howard hustled abroad and established bureaus in the major European capitals. He made connections with leading foreign papers and with commercial news agencies not allied with the AP. Howard's biggest break came when the British cut off the cabling of German news service to belligerents and neutrals during World War I. Two leading Argentine newspapers, *La Prensa* and *La Nación*, rebelled against receiving only the one-sided reports of the French Havas

[10] As quoted in Charles R. McCabe, ed., *Damned Old Crank* (New York: Harper & Row, 1951), p. 219.

United Press International *United Press International*

Hugh Baillie (*left*), United Press president, and Roger Tatarian, UPI editor.

agency and requested Associated Press service. The AP, under its contract agreements, could not enter the South American area, and Howard rapidly rushed in to give the Argentine papers the type of war news coverage they wanted. Soon UP was on the way to building up an extensive string of clients in South America, and established its own bureaus there.

But Howard and the United Press came a cropper in November, 1918, just when the UP was winning attention. Howard was in American naval headquarters at Brest on November 7 when a message arrived from Paris saying the Armistice had been signed at 11 o'clock that morning. Howard flashed the news to the New York UP office, and by an incredible stroke of bad luck for his news service, the message passed the censors. The UP bulletin set off wild celebrations in the United States—until several hours later the AP broke the news that the UP had cabled a false report. Although Howard argued that he did what any newsman would have done when he saw the message at naval headquarters (he decided later that the message had originated with a German secret agent in Paris), some telegraph editors never again fully trusted the United Press. Even when in the 1930s the Associated Press flashed the wrong verdict on the outcome of the trial of Bruno Richard Hauptmann for the kidnaping and murder of the Lindbergh baby, and when in 1944 the AP flashed the news of the D-Day landing in France prematurely, oldtime newsmen still recalled how "Roy Howard ended the first World War four days early." [11]

[11] Howard gave his explanation in Webb Miller's *I Found No Peace* (New York: Simon & Schuster, 1936), p. 96. The Associated Press blunder on the Hauptmann verdict stemmed from the setting up of a signal system to get the news out of the courtroom. An overanxious AP man got the wrong signal and flashed news of a life sentence when the verdict was

The United Press survived the false Armistice Day report, however. When Howard left it in 1920 to become a partner in the Scripps newspaper chain, the UP had 780 clients and a fairly good news service. Scripps, who held 51 per cent of the controlling common stock, estimated he received $200,000 in dividends during the first 10 years. In the Scripps custom, the remaining 49 per cent of the stock went to key United Press men. The intangible "good will" assets were then valued at $2,500,000 by Howard.[12]

THE UP MAKES PROGRESS

There were good reasons why the United Press was making rapid progress. Its news report was dynamic, and, like the Scripps papers, conformed to the needs and interests of the mass of readers. The Associated Press in the early 1920s was still frowning upon human interest stories, and was so intent upon its strict rules of accuracy and objectivity that it served its members with only strait-laced and factual accounts. United Press staff men were backgrounding the news, personalizing it, and delving into kinds of coverage ignored by the AP. They also scuttled much of the routine commercial news which had long been the bulk of the AP report, and substituted byline stories, interviews, features, sports stories, and human interest bits.[13]

A common saying among young, low-paid UP men was, "They pay you with bylines." Early in its career, the UP began giving enthusiastic young staffers some glory and a chance to develop their own writing styles and news specialties. AP men covering World War I were largely anonymous newsgatherers. The UP turned loose young correspondents like Webb Miller, Fred S. Ferguson, William Philip Simms, William G. Shepherd, and Westbrook Pegler. Their vividly written and interpretative copy attracted attention, and helped to sell the UP service as a second wire for AP member papers.

Some of the UP's young men moved up rapidly. Among the war correspondents, Miller became European news manager and stayed in command until he was killed in a London blackout early in World War II. Ferguson became general news manager, then in 1926 was put in charge of the Scripps news feature service, Newspaper Enterprise Association. Simms became foreign editor for the Scripps-Howard newspapers. Pegler became a widely syndicated

---

death. The 1944 premature D-Day flash by AP was sent by a girl teletype operator who was "practicing," the AP said. The UP was similarly victimized by an employee who flashed the end of the Japanese war prematurely in 1945.

12 McCabe, *Damned Old Crank,* p. 204.

13 Estimates of the character of the UP service are found in Will Irwin, "United Press," *Harper's Weekly,* LVIII (April 25, 1914), 6, and in Rosewater, *History of Cooperative News-Gathering,* pp. 340–55. See Gramling, *AP: The Story of News,* pp. 175 and 313–18, for characterizations of AP service. The full UP story is told in Joe Alex Morris, *Deadline Every Minute* (Garden City: Doubleday, 1957).

columnist, as did three UP Washington staffers of the 1920s—Thomas L. Stokes, Paul Mallon, and Raymond Clapper.

The United Press jumped into several fields ahead of the AP, just as it did in developing its foreign news service. Acme Newspictures began operating in 1925, two years earlier than the AP picture service was established. The United Press pioneered in supplying news to radio stations, and, with INS, was first into the television news field in 1951. Acme became United Press Newspictures in 1952 and handled UP Telephoto, rival to AP Wirephoto. In 1954 both services began supplying pictures by facsimile, over the UP Unifax and AP Photofax networks. The teletypesetter, producing a tape which automatically runs a typesetting machine, arrived in 1951 and both UP and AP set up teletypesetter circuits for smaller papers, sports, and financial services.

UNITED PRESS MANAGEMENT AND STAFF

Howard's successors as president of the United Press all came up through the ranks. His assistant, William W. Hawkins, held the post from 1920 to 1923. Then a second strong man of the UP, Karl A. Bickel, moved into the top command. Bickel possessed abilities that made him a respected leader in journalistic circles. He had worked first for the Scripps papers and the United Press on the West Coast, then had won his spurs in the foreign service. As UP president, he became a leader in furthering freedom of international news coverage, and he did much to advance the UP's own position in worldwide service.

Hugh Baillie, who succeeded Bickel in 1935, also rose from the West Coast Scripps organization. At 19, after two years of college, he joined the *Record*, a Scripps paper in Los Angeles. Then he moved to the UP San Francisco office, where he was in charge of the "pony report." By 1918 the 28-year-old Baillie was chief of the Washington bureau. He then moved through executive posts to the presidency. Baillie loved nothing better than to whip his competitors with an exclusive story, preferably a vividly colorful one. He traveled extensively, impressing his own competitive drive for news upon his staff, and keeping his hand in by covering some big stories of the 1930s and World War II. When he moved up to board chairmanship in 1955, he was succeeded as president by Frank H. Bartholomew, also from the Pacific Coast and also a reporter. They presided over the 1958 merger of the UP and International News Service to form the United Press International. Among the major executives of the era were Earl J. Johnson, head of the news operation since 1935 and vice president and editor; Lyle Wilson, vice president and Washington manager; Thomas R. Curran, vice president and general European manager; and Harry R. Flory, director of communications.

Mims Thomason, who had been general business manager, succeeded Bartholomew as president in 1962. Roger Tatarian, an outstanding European news chief before becoming executive editor in 1962, succeeded Johnson as editor in 1965. Frank Tremaine became general manager for North America in 1969, Leroy Keller took charge of UPI international divisions, and Roderick W. Beaton was named UPI's general manager.

Serving as European news chiefs have been Webb Miller, Virgil Pinkley, A. L. Bradford, Harry Ferguson, Paul Allerup, and Daniel F. Gilmore. Foreign news editors have included Joe Alex Morris, Harrison Salisbury, Phil Newsome, Joseph W. Morgan, and John N. Fallon. Notable in the foreign service were W. R. Higginbotham, H. R. Ekins, Frederick Kuh, Norman Montellier, Henry Shapiro, Robert Musel, Jack V. Fox, Joseph W. Grigg, and K. C. Thaler. Shapiro in Moscow and Thaler as diplomatic correspondent became foremost European correspondents. Russell Jones won a 1957 Pulitzer Prize for covering the Budapest uprising.

Merriman Smith, the longtime dean of White House correspondents and winner of the Pulitzer Prize for his story of the assassination of President Kennedy, died in 1970 after 30 years covering six presidents. Major UPI Washington staffers included bureau manager Julius Fransden, diplomatic reporter Stewart Hensley, political writer Raymond Lahr, White House correspondents Helen Thomas and Eugene V. Risher, and Supreme Court reporter Charlotte Moulton.

Other Pulitzer Prize winners for UPI were Kyoichi Sawada and Toshio Sakai for Vietnam photos and Lucinda Franks and Thomas Powers for 1971 national reporting. Specialists were Alvin B. Webb, Jr., in space science; Bruce Munn, United Nations; Louis Cassels, religion; Joseph L. Myler, science; Robert Musel, H. D. Quigg, and David C. Smothers, senior editors with Cassels and Myler on depth reporting projects.

Byliners for the UP during World War II included Frederick C. Oeschner in Berlin, Ralph Heinzen in Paris, and war correspondents Webb Miller, M. S. Handler, Edward W. Beattie, Reynolds and Eleanor Packard, C. R. Cunningham, and Henry T. Gorrell in Europe. William F. Tyree, Frank Tremaine, and William B. Dickinson were leaders in the Pacific theater. Bert Brandt of Acme starred by getting the first pictures of the D-Day invasion.

THE INTERNATIONAL NEWS SERVICE, 1909–58

The third American press association competitor has been the International News Service. Smaller than its rivals, and later in establishing itself as a comprehensive news service, INS nevertheless won prominence for its competitive spirit.

INS was founded in 1909 as an outgrowth of earlier leased wire facilities of the Hearst newspapers. Richard A. Farrelly was its first manager. By 1918 INS was serving 400 clients and had a leased wire system approximately half as extensive as those of the AP and UP. In that year INS and a Hearst morning paper news agency, Universal Service, were put under the direction of Moses Koenigsberg, also head of Hearst's King Features Syndicate. INS developed full 24-hour operations by 1928, but Universal Service was killed in 1937. Executive control of INS passed to Joseph V. Connolly, and on his death in 1945 to Seymour Berkson. Berkson, former INS managing editor, now became general manager.

The sparkplug of the INS after 1916 was Barry Faris, editor-in-chief. He established fewer bureaus than the other services, concentrating INS resources on the major news centers. His most successful plan was to offer well-known bylines, and special coverage of major news events by talented writers. While only a few newspapers ever depended on INS as a single source of press association news, a substantial number subscribed to the service to obtain its well-written stories and occasional major news beats.

H. R. Knickerbocker, a Pulitzer Prize winner, and Floyd Gibbons were two longtime INS foreign correspondents. James L. Kilgallen began his roving coverage of major national stories in 1921. Later acquisitions as featured INS writers were Bob Considine and Inez Robb. Other glamor names on the INS wire were Quentin Reynolds, Frank Gervasi, Paul Callico, Damon Runyon, Arthur "Bugs" Baer, Louella Parsons, and Edwin C. Hill.

The INS foreign service developed stature by the 1930s. Among its leaders were J. C. Oestreicher, foreign editor, Pierre J. Huss, Berlin bureau chief, and J. Kingsbury Smith, who became European general manager. Top World War II correspondents were Howard Handleman, Kenneth Downs, Merrill Mueller, George Lait, Graham Hovey, Frank Conniff, and Kilgallen in Europe; and Richard Tregaskis, Lee Van Atta, and Clarke Lee (a former AP man) in the Pacific. Leading Washington bureau chiefs were George R. Holmes and William K. Hutchinson, while George E. Durno and Robert G. Nixon handled the White House assignment. Jack Lotto and Malcolm Johnson of the New York bureau won awards for general news coverage. Among the INS women correspondents, Rose McKee achieved prominence for political reporting. In a final burst of glory, the 1956 Pulitzer Prize for international reporting was won for INS and the Hearst newspapers by William Randolph Hearst, Jr., Kingsbury Smith, and Frank Conniff, who conducted interviews with Communist political leaders behind the Iron Curtain.

There were lumps in many throats when the hard-hitting INS staff of 450 saw their agency merged with the UP in May, 1958. William Randolph Hearst, Jr., and two of his associates took minority seats on the board of directors of the new United Press International, and some INS staffers joined UPI. A few of the brightest INS stars went to work for the newly formed Hearst Headline Service. Otherwise INS was no more. UPI also acquired International News Photos. The INS was serving 334 American newspapers and some 2,000 worldwide clients at the time of the merger.

UNITED PRESS INTERNATIONAL: RIVAL FOR AP

AP and UPI intensified their competition in the wake of the merger. The UPI opened a full double-trunk national wire circuit in 1959, giving it facilities comparable to those of the AP. As the 1970s opened, both associations leased more than 400,000 miles of telephone wires in the United States for transmission of news and pictures. Both were engaged in automating their transmission facilities, using computers and automatic news editing and retrieval systems. Both used globe-girdling radio teletype circuits and underwater cables to carry their news reports to Europe and Asia. Both had teletype circuits covering more than 20,000 miles in Europe, where their news reports were translated and fed into national wires. Both had European picture circuits and radio facilities for worldwide picture transmission. News reports could go around the world almost instantaneously.

Of 1,663 U. S. dailies listing press association service in the 1970 *Editor & Publisher International Yearbook,* 1,187 were receiving AP news and 872 UPI news (of these, 396 took both). Approximately 45 per cent of U. S. dailies received AP news only, 27 per cent UPI news only, 23 per cent both services, and almost 5 per cent, no listed service. The AP reported 1970 service to 3,221 U. S. radio and television stations; the UPI's last reported figure for U. S. stations was 3,209 in 1968 (3,598 broadcast stations worldwide in 1971). The UPI listed service to 114 countries and territories, the AP to 104. UPI listed 264 news or picture bureau locations, at about 30 more points worldwide than AP. At last survey in the mid-1960s, UPI had 291 staffers as foreign correspondents to the AP's 268. The figures seemed clear that the AP had a strong advantage in news service to U. S. dailies; the two were about even in service to U. S. broadcast stations (with UPI having an advantage in television newsfilm); and UPI still held the lead it built up abroad in 30 years prior to AP's 1946 World Service venture. For both it was big business; the AP budget had reached the $60,000,000 level by 1971 and UPI's was approximately $55,000,000. Both were up 50 per cent in a decade.

FOREIGN AND WASHINGTON STAFFS

The tradition of individual newspaper coverage of foreign and Washington news continued despite the rise of the press associations. Some of the more extensive newspaper services were syndicated to other papers, just as they had been since the race for news developed in the 1830s and 1840s.

Among newspapers that emphasized their own foreign news coverage in the early decades of the twentieth century were the *Herald, Tribune* (*Herald Tribune* after 1924), *World, Sun,* and *Times* in New York; the *Daily News, Tribune,* and *Record-Herald* in Chicago; the *Washington Post, Philadelphia Public Ledger,* and the *Baltimore Sun*. By the 1970s the leaders in foreign correspondence were the *New York Times, Los Angeles Times, Washington Post, Chicago Daily News, Christian Science Monitor,* and *Baltimore Sun.* Others with at least a European bureau included the *Chicago Tribune, Minneapolis Tribune, Cleveland Plain Dealer, Toledo Blade, New York Daily News, San Francisco Chronicle, Washington Star, Wall Street Journal,* and the Hearst newspapers.

Non-newspaper leaders in worldwide correspondents' staffs in the mid-1960s, after the UPI's 291 and AP's 268, were *Time-Life*, 63; McGraw-Hill World News, 28; NBC, 21; CBS, 19; *Newsweek*, 14; *U. S. News & World Report*, 13; Fairchild Publications, 12; and ABC 10. Altogether the U. S. mass media had about 1,500 correspondents gathering news for it abroad, half of them American citizens, according to studies made at Ohio University by John R. Wilhelm and Ralph E. Kliesch.

Washington's press corps increased steadily. The number of American daily newspapers with some sort of special representation in Washington was 110 in 1890, 180 in 1910, 300 in 1930, and 613 in 1971. About one-third had individual Washington correspondent representation; the others were served by correspondents writing for several different papers. There were also 118 foreign newspapers and press services represented, 141 U. S. broadcast stations and networks, 471 magazines and periodicals, and 194 newsletters. Nearly 2,000 correspondents and editors were registered.[14]

The elite of the Washington press corps have been the 50 members of the Gridiron Club, founded in 1885. The National Press Club was organized in 1908 and built the 14-story National Press Building in 1927. The White House Correspondents Association dates from 1914. Later on the scene were the Radio-Television Correspondents Association and the White House News Photographers Association.

Biggest of the Washington news bureaus in the early 1970s were, of course, those of the press associations. Associated Press bureau manpower was 100, that of the United Press International 80. The *New York Times* bulked large with 42 staff members in the capital. Other figures were Scripps-Howard newspapers, 31; McGraw-Hill News Service, 30; NBC 24; CBS, 24; Newhouse newspapers, 24; *Newsweek*, 24; Reuters, 22 (the British news agency was serving 41 U. S. dailies in 1970); ABC, 19; *Time*, 18; Fairchild Publications, 13; Knight newspapers, 11; Gannett newspapers, 10; Mutual radio, 9; Copley news service, 8; Hearst newspapers, 7; Ridder, Block, Booth, and Thomson papers, 3–4 each.

After that of the *New York Times*, the strongest Washington bureaus representing a single newspaper were those of the *Wall Street Journal*, 17; *Los*

[14] *Hudson's Washington News Media Directory* (Washington, D.C., 1971).

Angeles Times, 16; *New York Journal of Commerce*, 13; *New York Daily News*, 12; *Christian Science Monitor*, 12; *Chicago Tribune*, 11; *Baltimore Sun*, 11; *St. Louis Post-Dispatch*, 8; *Newsday*, 7; and *Chicago Daily News* and *Sun-Times*, 6 each. Maintaining staffs of 3 to 5 were the *Philadelphia Bulletin*, *Minneapolis Tribune*, *Cleveland Plain Dealer*, *Boston Globe*, *Boston Herald Traveler*, *Des Moines Register*, *Detroit News*, *Dallas News*, and *Buffalo News*. The three Washington dailies were strongly represented on capital news beats, particularly the *Post* and *Star*. The United Nations Correspondents Association in New York had 220 members.

NEWSPAPER SYNDICATES: WASHINGTON AND FOREIGN NEWS

Biggest of the newspaper syndicates was the *New York Times* News Service. Founded in 1917, it had 136 other U. S. dailies listed as subscribing to it in 1970 and was claiming 330 users worldwide in 1971. It was being transmitted in 1971 in combination with the service of the *Chicago Daily News* and *Sun-Times*, with some *Washington Star* material added, on a 24-hour U. S. teletype cycle. The *Times* listed 32 correspondents abroad at 23 bureaus in 1971, in addition to the 42 in Washington. *Times* foreign correspondents won 11 Pulitzer Prizes in the 40 years beginning in 1932, and 12 more Pulitzer awards went to other leading *Times* writers in the same period. Best known of the *Times* foreign correspondents winning the Pulitzer citations were Walter Duranty, 1932; Anne O'Hare McCormick, 1937; Otto D. Tolischus, 1940; and Hanson W. Baldwin, 1943. From the Washington bureau, Arthur Krock won prizes in both 1935 and 1938, and James B. Reston in 1945 and 1957. Their stories, and those of other leading *Times* reporters of each era, were available to newspapers subscribing to the syndicated news service.[15]

The *Chicago Daily News* Foreign Service grew out of the coverage begun in 1898 by Victor Lawson for the *Daily News* and *Record-Herald*. It won wide attention during World War I through the work of Edward Price Bell in London, Paul Scott Mowrer in Paris, and Raymond Gram Swing in Berlin. But it hit its most remarkable peak of performance in the 1930s and early 1940s under publisher Frank Knox and the foreign news director, Carroll Binder, himself a noted correspondent before he became head of the service in 1937.

[15] Other *Times* foreign correspondents winning Pulitzer Prizes were Frederick T. Birchall, 1934; Arnaldo Cortesi, 1946; Brooks Atkinson, 1947 (better known as a drama critic); Harrison E. Salisbury, 1955; the entire staff, 1958; A. M. Rosenthal, 1960; and David Halberstam, 1964. Winners for national reporting were Louis Stark, labor writer, 1942; C. P. Trussell, 1949; Anthony Leviero, 1952, and Anthony Lewis, 1963. Distinguished reporting awards went to Lauren D. Lyman, 1936; William L. Laurence, science writer, 1937 and 1946; and Meyer Berger, 1950. Other leading *Times* foreign correspondents during the World War II era were Raymond Daniell, C. L. Sulzberger, Herbert L. Matthews, and Drew Middleton.

Pulitzer Prizes were won by Paul Scott Mowrer in 1929 and by Edgar Ansel Mowrer in 1933. Ranking with the Mowrer brothers as among the best of American foreign correspondents of the day were John Gunther in London, William Stoneman in Moscow and London, Wallace Deuel in Rome and Berlin, Helen Kirkpatrick in Paris, and David Nichol in Berlin and Moscow. Other leading *Chicago Daily News* foreign correspondents of the World War II period were Leland Stowe, Robert J. Casey, William McGaffin, Paul Ghali, Ernie Hill, Nat A. Barrows, A. T. Steele, and George Weller, a Pulitzer Prize winner for distinguished reporting. Keyes Beech and Fred Sparks won Pulitzer awards for Korean War coverage. Paul Leach, Edwin A. Lahey, and Peter Lisagor were Washington bureau chiefs. As the 1970s began, Stoneman was chief European correspondent, Nichol was London bureau chief, and Lisagor and McGaffin were in Washington. William J. Eaton won the 1970 Pulitzer Prize for national reporting from the capital. The service had 90 U. S. daily users.

Newest on the scene was the *Los Angeles Times–Washington Post* News Service, begun in 1962 by publishers Otis Chandler and Philip L. Graham. By 1971 the *Times* had developed 18 overseas bureaus and 7 in the United States, adding to a dozen *Post* bureaus. The 1970 count of U. S. users was 75, and in mid-1971 the service was claiming 300 users worldwide. Its editors were given headquarters at the *Post,* where selections were made from the stories written for the two newspapers by their Washington, foreign, and local staffs. American continent users also received the news and features of two British papers, the *London Observer* and the *Guardian.* Among the *Post* staff whose work was thus made available were Karl Meyer and Alfred Friendly, London; Anatole Shub and Steven Rosenfeld, Moscow; Dan Kurzman and John Goshko, Latin America; Warren Unna and Stanley Karnow, Asia; Waverly Root, Paris; and Don Oberdorfer, the White House. *Los Angeles Times* foreign editor Robert Gibson had among his correspondents Jack Foisie, Vietnam; Robert S. Elegant and Don Shannon, Asia; Gene Sherman and Robert C. Toth, London; Don Cook, Paris; David Kraslow, Washington bureau chief, and Stuart Loory, the White House. Pulitzer Prizes for international reporting were won in 1968 by Alfred Friendly of the *Post* from Israel, in 1969 by William Tuohy of the *Times* from Vietnam, and in 1971 by Jimmy Lee Hoagland of the *Post* from Africa.

The *New York Herald Tribune* foreign service was built on that of the old *Tribune,* which had Frank H. Simonds and Richard Harding Davis as World War I writers. Leland Stowe won a 1930 Pulitzer Prize as a *Herald Tribune* correspondent and Homer Bigart was similarly honored for his World War II work. Other leading *Herald Tribune* correspondents of the war period were Joseph Barnes, Major George Fielding Eliot, Russell Hill, Joseph Driscoll, and John O'Reilly. A. T. Steele left the *Chicago Daily News* to join the *Herald Tribune.* Bert Andrews, while Washington bureau chief, won the 1948 Pulitzer Prize for national reporting. Jack Steele was a leading Washington staff member in the early 1950s before becoming Scripps-Howard's chief political writer.

Bigart and Marguerite Higgins won Pulitzer Prizes as Korean War correspondents; Bigart later joined the *New York Times*. Other Pulitzer Prizes for reporting were won by William H. Taylor in 1935 and by science writer John J. O'Neill in 1937. Columnist Walter Lippmann in 1962 won the paper's final Pulitzer Prize before its death in 1966.

The *Chicago Tribune* foreign service had as World War I stars Floyd Gibbons, Frazier Hunt, John T. McCutcheon, and Sigrid Schultz. Serving the *Tribune* overseas for varying periods were such well-known journalists as Vincent Sheean, William L. Shirer, George Seldes, Jay Allen, and Edmond Taylor. Wilfred C. Barber won the *Tribune* news service's only Pulitzer Prize in 1936. In the following years, the leading correspondents of other foreign and Washington services outshone the *Tribune* men.[16]

WALTER DURANTY AND THE MOWRER BROTHERS

Of all the foreign correspondents listed in the preceding paragraphs, special attention must be given Walter Duranty of the *New York Times* and the Mowrer brothers of the *Chicago Daily News*. Duranty was a resident correspondent in Russia between 1922–34 and until 1941 was a special traveling writer, spending an average of five months per year studying the land he loved. Even before he began the initial 19-year stint as the leading American reporter in Russia, Duranty had developed a strong philosophy about the rough character of Communist rule. At the outset he hated and feared the Bolsheviks, but as he told H. R. Knickerbocker of INS in 1935, he learned to appreciate the Russian position. "I don't see that I have been any less accurate about Russia because I failed to stress casualties so hard as some of my colleagues . . . I am a reporter, not a humanitarian." [17]

[16] Other Pulitzer Prize winners for international correspondence were three *Baltimore Sun* men, Mark S. Watson, 1945, Paul W. Ward 1948, and Price Day, 1949; Edmund Stevens, *Christian Science Monitor,* 1950; Austin Wehrwein, *Milwaukee Journal,* 1953; Joseph Martin and Philip Santora, *New York Daily News,* 1959; Hal Hendrix, *Miami News,* 1963; J. A. Livingston, *Philadelphia Bulletin,* 1965; R. John Hughes, *Christian Science Monitor,* 1967; and Seymour M. Hersh, Dispatch News Service, 1970 (for the My Lai massacre disclosure). Pulitzer awards for domestic correspondence went to three *St. Louis Post-Dispatch* men—Paul Y. Anderson, 1929, Charles G. Ross, 1932, and Edward A. Harris, 1946; to four members of the Cowles newspapers (*Minneapolis Star* and *Tribune, Des Moines Register* and *Tribune*) Washington bureau—Nat S. Finney, 1948, Richard L. Wilson, 1954, Clark R. Mollenhoff, 1958, and Nick Kotz, 1968; to four *Wall Street Journal* men—Edward R. Cony, 1961, Louis Kohlmeier, 1965, and Stanley Penn and Monroe Karmin, 1967; and to Dewey L. Fleming, *Baltimore Sun,* 1944; Edward T. Folliard, *Washington Post,* 1947; Edwin O. Guthman, *Seattle Times,* 1950; Anthony Lewis, *Washington Daily News,* 1955; Charles L. Bartlett, *Chattanooga Times,* 1956; Howard Van Smith, *Miami News,* 1959; Nathan Caldwell and Gene Graham, *Nashville Tennesseean,* 1962; Haynes Johnson, *Washington Star,* 1966; and Howard James, 1968, and Robert Cahn, 1969, both *Christian Science Monitor.*

[17] Walter Duranty, *I Write as I Please* (New York: Halcyon House, 1935), pp. 166–67.

New York Times

WALTER DURANTY

It was during the 1930s that Duranty received some bitter criticism for his open assessments of Stalin's ruthlessness and Soviet goals. Heywood Broun said he wrote "editorials disguised as news dispatches" and others claimed he was far too liberal. Stalin began his purge of the Kulaks, the wealthy peasant class, in 1928, and eventually an estimated 10 million persons were killed in the countryside. But on the other hand, Duranty had accepted one of the toughest individual reporting assignments of the twentieth century. His task was to report the unknown. Stalin consented to talk with Duranty only twice, in the fall of 1930 and at Christmas, 1933. Otherwise Duranty depended on his keen knowledge of Russian history and language to overcome physical handicaps. The politically risky business of collectivization was determining many careers within Russia, like that of Leon Trotsky. Duranty sent long interpretative dispatches to the *Times* but rarely did these efforts receive prominent display. America was involved with domestic and European problems. During the crucial winter of 1928–1929, for example, none of Duranty's nearly 100 stories made page one.[18]

Nevertheless, Duranty's contribution to the field of foreign correspondence was immense. His intellect and analytical ability made him invaluable to the growing *Times'* foreign staff, which at that moment included Wythe Williams in Vienna, Paul Miller in Berlin, Arnaldo Cortesi in Rome, and Allen Raymond in London. Duranty was a confident writer, hardened by scenes of death in World War I. He accepted the brutality of Russian life and wrote from that point. Stalin moved stealthily, the censor was a barrier, the Soviet press did not report internal arguments in any way, official names were rarely mentioned, and travel was restricted. Yet Duranty was able to give detailed and colorful reports of life in that tormented land.

William Henry Chamberlin lived in Russia from 1922–34, writing for the *Manchester Guardian* and then the *Christian Science Monitor* and *Atlantic*. Louis Fischer authored more than 40 articles, most of them for the *Nation*,

[18] Michael C. Emery, "The American Mass Media and the Coverage of Five Major Foreign Events, 1900–1950," Ph.D. thesis, University of Minnesota, 1968.

between 1925–32. And world traveler Maurice Hindus wrote a dozen articles and a best-selling book, *Red Bread.* Along with Duranty these men gave a few Americans their only real look at Russia; the bulk of U.S. newspapers, including those with prominent foreign staffs, carried only casual mention of Russian affairs. Duranty filed the only regularly-published newspaper accounts in the late 1920s, and his fair-minded and sometimes sympathetic portrayal of Bolshevik behavior helped restore the faith of some in the *Times,* which during the "Red Scare" period had been confused about Russian Communists and American Socialists. In fact, a special *New Republic* supplement of August, 1920, edited by Walter Lippmann and Charles Merz, had charged the usually reliable *Times* with irresponsible coverage. Duranty himself had said his paper's early attitude was caused by a fear of the "Red Bogey," which explains why he went to great lengths to provide balanced reports.

Paul Scott Mowrer began his long career in 1905, taking a job with the *Chicago Daily News.* Getting the Midwest out of his system proved to be a problem, as he later admitted.[19] While in Chicago he had shunned Stanley Washburn's dispatches from the Russo-Japanese front. He remembered riding in an elevator with Richard Henry Little, captured by the Japanese at Mukden. But Mowrer cared only for Minnesota, Michigan, and the bustling metropolis, which he considered the heart of journalism. In 1910 he arrived in London, joining men who worked for other papers such as Frederic William Wile, Wythe Williams, and a handful of others who knew Europe before war changed the politics and the boundaries. Writers like Will Irwin occasionally sailed to Europe to write for U.S. magazines, but the years were dull. Correspondents had flocked to the Boer War and Boxer Rebellion. The bitter subjugation of the Philippine rebels under Aguinaldo in the 1899–1901 period had attracted a host of reporters. That first U.S. experiment with colonialism and world power involved 50,000 American troops. The Russo-Japanese War of 1904–5, where Richard Harding Davis, Jack London, Frederick Palmer and another 100 American and British reporters had fought Japanese censorship, gained considerable attention in the U.S. press. But things were quiet in Europe, as Paul Scott Mowrer discovered when he showed up as a 22-year-old assistant to Edward Price Bell. At the outbreak of war nearly four years later he covered the assassination of French Socialist Jean Jaures and broke in his younger brother, Edgar Ansel Mowrer, who thus began his equally distinguished career. Edgar, who had been contributing to U.S. and British magazines and studying at the Sorbonne, snuck through enemy lines for an exclusive story. Then Edgar was allowed to accompany mining engineer Herbert Hoover to Holland, and finally in 1915 was given the job as Rome correspondent. Paul Scott Mowrer headed for the front and ended up reporting the horrors of Verdun.

Following the war, Paul Scott Mowrer was assigned to direct the *Daily*

[19] Paul Scott Mowrer, *The House of Europe* (Boston: Houghton Mifflin, 1945), p. 70. For his brother's personal account, see Edgar Ansel Mowrer, *Triumph and Tragedy* (New York: Weybright and Talley, 1968).

News' bureau at the Versailles conference. Based in Paris, he filed dispatches during the Moroccan campaign of 1924–25 and in 1934–35 became associate editor and chief editorial writer for his paper. The editorship itself was his between 1935 and 1944, until the last year of World War II saw him accept a position as European editor for the *New York Post.* Edgar Ansel Mowrer was bureau chief of the *Daily News* in Berlin and Paris during the "between wars" period. Connected with the Office of War Information after having been forced out of Germany at the start of World War II, he later was a columnist and broadcaster and with his brother contributed several books on foreign affairs. The Mowrer brothers teamed with many famous byliners, like Frederick T. Birchall of the *New York Times,* Reginald Wright Kauffman and Harold Scarborough of the *New York Herald Tribune,* Henry Wales of the *Chicago Tribune* and the others mentioned earlier to cover the League of Nations, rise of fascism, and coming of another war. They added color and depth to stories at a time when even familiar European situations were in heavy competition with American domestic concerns for space in newspapers.

SPECIAL NEWS SERVICES

Several special news and feature services were established for American newspapers after 1900. First was the Newspaper Enterprise Association, founded in 1902 by Robert F. Paine, E. W. Scripps' talented editor-in-chief. While NEA by the 1950s offered all types of features to newspaper clients, it also had foreign and Washington correspondence, highlighted by the work of prize-winning Peter Edson and of Fred Sparks, who transferred from the *Chicago Daily News.* A second Scripps contribution was Science Service, begun in 1921 and directed by Watson Davis as an authoritative science news agency. The Scripps-Howard Newspaper Alliance, developed for the chain's own papers, had its share of Pulitzer Prize winners—science editor David Dietz, Washington correspondents Thomas L. Stokes and Vance Trimble, columnist Ernie Pyle, and foreign correspondent Jim G. Lucas.

A major reorganization of the news syndicates took place in 1930 when the North American Newspaper Alliance was founded by a group of metropolitan newspapers under the managership of John N. Wheeler, head of the Bell Syndicate. NANA and Bell absorbed the Associated Newspaper, Consolidated Press, and McClure services and established NANA as the leading specialized news agency. Among its correspondents was military reporter and analyst Ira Wolfert, 1943 Pulitzer Prize winner.[20]

[20] Among other special news agencies were the Dow Jones News Service, with some 40 newspaper clients; the Jewish Telegraphic Agency, a world service headquartering in New York, and its Overseas News Agency; Associated Negro Press, largest for Negro papers; Religious News Service, serving 750 clients; and Copley News Service, specializing in Latin American news.

THE FEATURE SYNDICATES: ENTERTAINMENT

The impact of the syndicates upon newspaper content was heaviest in the non-news field. First to relieve newspaper editors of the necessity of clipping column material, fiction, poetry, and other entertainment features from newspaper and magazine exchanges was Ansel N. Kellogg, the Baraboo, Wisconsin, newsman who originated the ready-print service for small papers.[21] When Kellogg and another Wisconsin newspaperman, Andrew J. Aikens, founded feature services in Chicago after the Civil War the non-news syndicate idea began to flourish.

Kellogg's ready-print service—letters from New York, Washington, and foreign correspondents, serial stories, women's features, poetry and other material printed on one side of newsprint sheets supplied to small publishers who printed their local news and ads on the other side—expanded rapidly. Another idea was the supplying of stereotyped plates to publishers, begun about 1875 and developed by the American Press Association. Editors could cut the plate material to fit, a process which its critics dubbed "editing with a saw."

Destined to control the feature syndicate business for weeklies and small dailies was the Western Newspaper Union, a Des Moines enterprise dating from 1872. George A. Joslyn gained control of WNU in 1890 and set about to consolidate the businesses in his field, in keeping with the "big business" tendencies of the times. WNU bought the Kellogg company in 1906, added the Aikens enterprises in 1910, and snapped up other smaller services. Purchase of the American Press Association in 1917 gave WNU a virtual monopoly. WNU had by then become one of the "budget services," offering a wide variety of feature material to its customers rather than requiring purchase of a particular set of features. The ready-print service, which at its peak went to nearly 7,000 papers, gradually declined and was abandoned in 1952.[22]

While Western Newspaper Union was developing in the weekly field, dailies were being offered syndicated literary material by the feature services of Irving Bacheller (1883), S. S. McClure (1884), and Edward W. Bok (1886). McClure and Bok sensed the public demand for entertaining reading, which led to their own more famous careers as magazine publishers. Hearst joined the syndicate movement in 1895, and in 1914 began his King Features Syndicate. George Matthew Adams entered the field in 1907 and John N. Wheeler in 1913.

[21] Kellogg, short-handed at his weekly, got war news printed on one side of his news sheets at a bigger paper, then added his local news.

[22] The story of the Kellogg, Aikens, and other early syndicates is told in Elmo Scott Watson, *A History of Newspaper Syndicates in the United States 1865–1935* (Chicago: Publishers' Auxiliary, 1936).

COLUMNS WITH THE LIGHTER TOUCH

The early syndicates featured the writings of Robert Louis Stevenson, Rudyard Kipling, Mark Twain, Bret Harte, Henry James, Alfred Henry Lewis, Jack London, and other literary greats. They also could sample the work of a notable group of poetically-inclined columnists, and humorous writers, which appeared in newspapers throughout the country. Syndication spread the fame of "M. Quad" of the *Detroit Free Press* and *New York Herald;* Bill Nye of Laramie, Wyoming, and the *New York World;* David Ross Locke of the *Toledo Blade,* who created Petroleum V. Nasby; Opie Read of *Arkansaw Traveler* fame; Joel Chandler Harris of the *Atlanta Constitution;* and Finley Peter Dunne, the Chicago newspaperman whose "Mr. Dooley"—a saloon keeper who philosophized in a penetrating manner on current affairs—became a national institution. Also syndicated were the stories of George Ade of the *Chicago Record,* the verse of Edgar A. Guest of the *Detroit Free Press,* and the poems of Walt Mason.

To older newspapermen a column was "a little of everything"— wit, poetry, sentiment, and comment on personalities and events in the news. One such column conductor was Eugene Field, the St. Louis and Kansas City newsman whom Melville E. Stone brought to the *Chicago Daily News* to write his "Sharps and Flats" before 1900. Another was Bert Leston Taylor, who founded the *Chicago Tribune's* famed "A Line o' Type or Two" column in 1901. A third was Franklin P. Adams, who wrote for the *Chicago Journal* and *New York Mail* before beginning his "Conning Tower" in the *New York Tribune* in 1914. On the *New York Sun* it was Don Marquis with his "Sun Dial" column, inhabited by "archie," the noncapitalizing cockroach. There were other gracefully literate columns in individual papers, but the older columns came to be overwhelmed by new kinds of syndicated columns, and polished writing with the light touch tended to retreat to such publications as the *New Yorker* and *Saturday Review.*

Walter Winchell set the pace for one kind of syndicated column. A New Yorker who entered journalism with the racy tabloids of the 1920s, Winchell promoted the "gossip" column as the Broadway reporter of the tabloid *Graphic.* He shifted to the *Mirror* in 1929 and became a star of Hearst's King Features Syndicate. No other columnist ever approached Winchell's sensationalism and intimate coverage of private lives, but such Hollywood columnists as Louella Parsons and Hedda Hopper did their best. Leonard Lyons and Dorothy Kilgallen were other New York scene columnists of the personal type, while O. O. McIntyre and Mark Hellinger wrote about the metropolis in an older literary style.

THE POLITICAL COLUMNISTS

The political column began in the early 1920s with the writings of David Lawrence in his syndicated column and Washington publications, of Mark Sullivan in the *New York Herald Tribune*, and of Frank R. Kent in the *Baltimore Sun*. Walter Lippmann joined this trio as a *Herald Tribune* columnist when his editorship of the *World* ended in 1931. Their columns were concerned with current politics and issues of the day, as contrasted with Arthur Brisbane's philosophical commentary which began in 1917 and was front-paged by Hearst newspapers for nearly 20 years. But the coming of the New Deal in 1933 and a consequent revolution in Washington coverage brought a new version of the political column, to join the syndicated offerings of Lawrence, Sullivan, Kent, and Lippmann.

The four early leaders as political and current affairs columnists were identified as "pundits" who wrote in a sober style and with a serious-minded approach. Sullivan and Kent were masters of the practical political scene of the 1920s, but they were not responsive to the social and economic shifts which brought the widespread increase in governmental activity in the New Deal era. Sullivan, who had been an enthusiastic interpreter of Theodore Roosevelt's progressive program and an intimate of President Herbert Hoover, became far better known for his superb journalistic history of the 1900–1925 period, *Our Times,* than for his later columns. Lawrence continued to hold a place as a commentator on national affairs, as did Lippmann in the international field.

A new kind of political column after 1932 was the personalized or "gossip-type" column. The idea stemmed from the successful book, *Washington Merry-Go-Round,* published anonymously in 1931. The authors were soon identified as Drew Pearson of the *Baltimore Sun* and Robert S. Allen of the *Christian Science Monitor*. These two Washington correspondents quickly left their newspapers to co-author a behind-the-scenes column which Pearson eventually continued alone. Paul Mallon was in the personalized column competition from the start of the New Deal era; joining in as sympathetic commentators on the New Deal's activities were Ernest K. Lindley, Samuel Grafton, and Joseph and Stewart Alsop. Pearson continued to lead in the race to obtain inside stories and "predictions" until he died in 1969.

United Features offered a particularly strong and varied group of columnists and commentators in the 1930s. Raymond Clapper, before his death in a 1944 wartime plane crash, was recognized as perhaps the best-balanced interpreter of the Washington scene. His opinions on national and international problems were widely respected, largely because they were based upon report-

Thomas L. Stokes (*left*) and Marquis Childs, United Features political columnists.

Editor & Publisher

Washington Star

Walter Lippmann, longtime dean of commentators, and Mary McGrory, political expert.

Los Angeles Times

Joseph Kraft (*left*) and Art Buchwald became leading columnists during the 1960s.

ing ability and Clapper's long experience as a United Press newsman and political writer and as head of the UP Washington bureau and that of the *Washington Post.* Thomas L. Stokes, a hard-working reporter of the Washington scene for United Press and the Scripps-Howard newspapers, developed a large following for his vigorous and crusading columns. Stokes won a Pulitzer Prize for national reporting and a Clapper memorial award for his column before he died in 1958. Carrying on for United Features were Marquis Childs, distinguished Washington correspondent for the *St. Louis Post-Dispatch* who began his column after Clapper's death, and William S. White, from the *New York Times* Washington staff. Childs won a Pulitzer Prize for his column in 1970, the first given for commentary.

Also in the United Features group of columnists were some commentators of the personal variety. One was Westbrook Pegler, the caustic ex-sports writer and United Press and *Chicago Tribune* writer. Pegler had a distinctive, colorful style and won a 1941 Pulitzer Prize for his exposure-type crusading. Unhappily his work degenerated into monotonous and vicious attacks upon three small groups—labor unions, New Dealers, and members of the Franklin D. Roosevelt family—and Pegler switched from Scripps-Howard to Hearst sponsorship in the mid-1940s, becoming known as "the stuck whistle of journalism." Balancing Pegler was the witty, warm personality of Heywood Broun. Best described as "looking like an unmade bed," Broun was a deceptive writer who could switch from a gay and easy commentary to a hard-hitting defense of liberal traditions whenever his temper was aroused. His "It Seems to Me" ran first in the *New York Tribune,* then in the *World* during the 1920s, and finally in the Scripps-Howard papers. Broun's leading role in the American Newspaper Guild and his liberal line brought a break with Roy Howard and the column was headed for the *New York Post* when Broun died in 1939. Also writing columns for United Features were Mrs. Eleanor Roosevelt, first signed in 1935 in an unprecedented move for a president's wife, and the lovable Ernie Pyle, whose original cross-country tour columns about little people and things were followed by superb personal glimpses of American fighting men in World War II until Pyle was killed on a Pacific island in 1945.

Well to the right of the United Features columnists in political and social outlooks were the King Features group. Best known were Pegler and the conservative George Sokolsky, both of whom died in the 1960s. Later in the field for King were radio commentator Fulton Lewis, Jr., moral philosopher Bruce Barton, reporter Jim Bishop, and editor William F. Buckley, Jr., of the conservative *National Review.* Buckley was one of the intellectual conservatives who gained favor in the late 1960s and early 1970s. Two others were the former southern newspaper editor, James Jackson Kilpatrick of the *Washington Star* Syndicate, and the young writer for *Esquire* and the *National Review,* Garry Wills.

The Bell Syndicate offered the columns of two leading women journalists. One was Dorothy Thompson, a European correspondent for the *Philadelphia*

Public Ledger and *New York Post* before beginning a columnist career that closed in 1961. Her emotion-charged comments on international affairs were in contrast to the smooth political-type commentary of Doris Fleeson, who came to the columnist field from the *New York Daily News.* Miss Fleeson, a 1960s United Features star, became in 1954 the first woman to win the Raymond Clapper award for meritorious reporting. A third woman, Sylvia Porter, became the leading business columnist of the country for the Publishers-Hall Syndicate, which also offered Washington columnist Betty Beale. Marianne Means did similar commentary for King Features. Emerging in the early 1970s as a first-rate general political columnist in the tradition of Doris Fleeson was Mary McGrory of the *Washington Star.*

Joseph Kraft, a 1963 find for Publishers-Hall Syndicate, was one of a number of liberal-oriented columnists who emerged from the era of Kennedy politics. A speech writer for John Kennedy, he became a political commentator for *Harper's* in 1965 and was viewed as a possible successor to Walter Lippmann when the latter retired from column-writing in 1967. A 1968 liberal team launched by the *Los Angeles Times*–General Features combine was composed of Frank Mankiewicz, Robert Kennedy's press secretary, and California newspaper publisher Tom Braden. A hard-hitting team that gained increasing favor after its 1963 start by Publishers-Hall was that of Rowland Evans and Robert Novak, who had been Washington reporters for the *New York Herald Tribune* and *Wall Street Journal.* Their "Inside Report" became the top political exposure column of the 1970s. The country's leading Negro journalist, Carl T. Rowan, signed with the *Chicago Daily News* and Publishers-Hall after a government career.

The closing of the *New York Herald Tribune* in 1966 and its earlier difficulties sent its famed political columnists elsewhere—Lippmann to the *Washington Post,* David Lawrence to Publishers-Hall, and Joseph Alsop and Roscoe Drummond to the *Los Angeles Times* Syndicate. Both in presenting the old and the new columnists, these two new combines were taking the play away from the older United and King groups.

The *New York Times* contributed political columnists in the 1960s, its serious-minded James Reston and Tom Wicker, and its Washington "funny man," Russell Baker. Baker and Art Buchwald of the *Los Angeles Times* Syndicate used satire to make their political and social points during a period of national frustration that called for such relief.

THE EDITORIAL CARTOONISTS

Syndication also affected the profession of editorial cartooning. As in the field of columning, widespread readership offered fame and financial rewards to the talented. But easy access to their proved reader-drawing copy made it less likely that a newspaper would "bring up" its own cartoonist or columnist.

New York World-Telegram

Rollin Kirby's famous "Two chickens in every garage" barb at Hoover, 1932.

New York Herald Tribune

"Halloween 1936"—Jay (Ding) Darling jibed at Wallace, Farley, and FDR.

D. R. Fitzpatrick and St. Louis Post-Dispatch

"You gambled but I paid"—Daniel Fitzpatrick in a 1947 crusade.

Baltimore Sun

"The outstretched hand"—Edmund Duffy's 1939 Pulitzer Prize cartoon.

From the Herblock Book (© 1952 Beacon Press)

"Fire!"—Herbert L. Block defended freedom during the Joseph McCarthy era in the *Washington Post.*

© 1963 Chicago Sun-Times; courtesy Wil-Jo Associates and Bill Mauldin.

Bill Mauldin's famous drawing expressing a nation's grief at John Kennedy's death.

Local columnists always had their field, of course, but serious commentary on national and international affairs by a local staff member became scarcer. So did locally-drawn cartoons, although the "package" services could not touch subjects affecting the local scene in each community.

The period after the Civil War saw the development of the political cartoon as an editorial device. Until then, the cartoon was more likely to be seen in magazines because of newspaper production difficulties, but the introduction of stereotyping enabled dailies to use illustrations more readily. Thomas Nast, the cartoonist who so savagely attacked the Tweed political ring, drew for the *New York Times* after 1870, as well as for *Harper's Weekly*. In the magazines of the times, Joseph Keppler's work for *Puck* was outstanding. The presidential campaign cartoons of Homer Davenport, drawn for Hearst's *New York Journal* in 1896, scored a new high point, both in prominence and in the bluntness of their attack.

The first quarter of the twentieth century was a golden age for cartoonists. The issues were simple enough for easy pictorial interpretation, and they were elemental enough for clever satire. These are the ingredients of the political cartoon. One of the famous cartoonists was John T. McCutcheon, who began drawing for the *Chicago Tribune* in 1903 after serving on the *Chicago Record*, and who won a Pulitzer Prize before he retired in 1946. Clifford K. Berryman, who first appeared in the *Washington Post* as far back as 1889, was closely identified with the *Washington Star* after 1906. He and his son, James T. Berryman, were the only father and son combination to win Pulitzer Prizes for their work, after the younger Berryman succeeded his father in 1949. Reminiscent of the old school of flowery technique was Jay N. ("Ding") Darling, who began drawing for the *Des Moines Register* in 1906 and who was twice a Pulitzer Prize winner. His work was widely syndicated by the *New York Tribune* feature service through the 1940s.

Lesser known to the public, but influential among his colleagues, was Arthur Henry Young, who always signed his cartoons "Art Young." He suffered because of his devotion to left-wing causes, especially during the World War I period, but in his day, Young was the cartoonist's cartoonist. He was the first to produce a daily panel, for the *Chicago Inter Ocean*, but the best of his work appeared in *The Masses*, the militantly socialist magazine. Young, unlike earlier cartoonists, strove for simplicity. His technique was to focus attention on a main issue; for example, one of his cartoons showed a ragged child of the slums looking up at the night sky and saying: "Ooh, look at all the stars; they're thick as bedbugs." Actually, of course, Young was as much a social as a political cartoonist.

Two other great masters of the cartooning art were Rollin Kirby of the *New York World* and Edmund Duffy of the *Baltimore Sun*, both three-time Pulitzer Prize winners. Kirby was a fiercely liberal spirit who began cartooning in 1911 and hit his peak on the old *World* in the 1920s. His "Mr. Dry," a gaunt, black-frocked, blue-nosed caricature of the bigoted prohibitionists, became

Patrick Oliphant, © 1971 Denver Post

"Mightier Than the Sword"—Patrick Oliphant celebrated the defeat of Attorney General John Mitchell in the 1971 Pentagon Papers case.

Paul Conrad, © 1968 Los Angeles Times, with permission of The Register and Tribune Syndicate.

Paul Conrad selected this drawing as symbolic of his concern for civil rights and the economic plight of minorities.

Thomas F. Darcy, © 1970 Newsday

"Withdrawal"—Tom Darcy doubts the Nixon promise for Vietnam.

John Fischetti, © 1971 Chicago Daily News

"The Unknown Soldier"—John Fischetti pursued a relentless attack upon the Nixon "Vietnamization" policy and failure to achieve peace in Indochina.

famous. Duffy exhibited his mastery of satire and caricature for the *Baltimore Sun* for 25 years. In this era, too, was Nelson Harding of the *Brooklyn Eagle,* twice a Pulitzer award winner.

Beginning his work for the *St. Louis Post-Dispatch* in 1913 and continuing until 1958 was Daniel R. ("Fitz") Fitzpatrick, whose devastating cartoon attacks won for him two Pulitzer Prizes. He was succeeded by Bill Mauldin, of Willie and Joe fame in *Stars and Stripes,* who quickly won a second Pulitzer Prize in 1959—and then in 1962 became the syndicated cartoonist of the *Chicago Sun-Times,* which also had the liberal Jacob Burck as a Pulitzer award-winning cartoonist for its editorial page.

The signature "Herblock" became famed in the 1950s and continued to be a solid favorite in the early 1970s. Herbert L. Block of the *Washington Post* was widely known through syndication for his distinctive style and extremely effective liberal comment. He was challenged by several other Pulitzer Prize winners who attracted attention for their incisive liberal-based commentary beginning in the 1960s. Becoming almost equally popular in the syndicate race was Paul Conrad, 1964 and 1971 award winner, who started at the *Denver Post* and became the *Los Angeles Times* editorial-page cartoonist in 1964. His successor at the *Denver Post,* the Australian-born satirist Patrick Oliphant, was 1967 winner. John Fischetti, 1969 Pulitzer Prize artist who drew for the *New York Herald Tribune* and the *Chicago Daily News,* offered a popular new style, as did young Thomas F. Darcy, 1970 winner from *Newsday.*

Other award-winning cartoonists of more conventional outlook who won syndication were Vaughan Shoemaker of the *Chicago Daily News,* Frank Miller of the *Des Moines Register,* Reg Manning of the *Arizona Republic,* and the hard-nosed C. D. Batchelor of the *New York Daily News.*

THE WORLD OF COMICS

Highly lucrative for the syndicates was the distribution of the drawings of a different set of artists—the comic strip and humorous panel originators. The battle between Pulitzer and Hearst for possession of Richard F. Outcault's "Yellow Kid" in 1896 set off a fierce competition in Sunday color comic sections and gave the name to yellow journalism. Early favorites like "Foxy Grandpa," "Buster Brown," and "Little Nemo" tickled newspaper readers with portrayals of humorous episodes centering about the same set of characters, but not relating a continuing story. Charles E. Schultze's gay grandpa who played tricks on boys and Winsor McKay's childish wonderland of Little Nemo both appeared in the *New York Herald* at the turn of the century. But Schultze soon deserted to Hearst's *American.* There "Foxy Grandpa" joined Outcault's "Buster Brown" and other Hearst comics in the same vein.

One was Rudolph Dirks' "Katzenjammer Kids," longest-lived of all American comics. Dirks began drawing Hans, Fritz, Mama, and the Captain in an 1897 color comic. When he transferred to the *World* in 1912, Hearst successfully sued to retain rights to the title and King Features continued the strip into the 1970s. So did Dirks and his son, for United Features, using the name "The Captain and the Kids."

Other Hearst comic successes before 1910 were James Swinnerton's "Little Jimmy," Frederick Burr Opper's "Alphonse and Gaston" and "Happy Hooligan," and George Herriman's "Krazy Kat." In the *World* were "The Newlyweds," drawn by George McManus of later Jiggs and Maggie fame. The doings of the "Toonerville Folks" were first portrayed by Fontaine Fox in the *Chicago Post* of 1908. H. C. (Bud) Fisher's "Mutt and Jeff" was the first regular daily cartoon strip, appearing in the *San Francisco Chronicle* in 1907. When John N. Wheeler organized the Bell Syndicate he obtained Fox and Fisher as two of his major drawing cards.

Arising as major competitors in the comic strip business by the end of World War I were the Hearst-owned King Features Syndicate and the *Chicago Tribune–New York Daily News* combine, whose comics were masterminded by Captain Joseph M. Patterson and Colonel Robert R. McCormick. Some of the longtime Hearst favorites, distributed in *Puck* as a Sunday comic section to millions of Hearst readers and also sold separately, were George McManus' "Bringing Up Father," dating from 1912; Cliff Sterrett's "Polly and Her Pals," 1912; James E. Murphy's "Toots and Casper," 1918; Billy De Beck's "Barney Google," 1919; Elzie C. Segar's "Thimble Theatre" featuring Olive Oyl and Popeye, 1919; Russ Westover's "Tillie the Toiler," 1921; Rube Goldberg's "Boob McNutt," 1924; and the most popular of all American comics, Chic Young's "Blondie," 1930. Winning millions of readers, too, for the *Chicago Tribune-New York Daily News* group have been Sidney Smith's "Andy Gump," 1917 (drawn after Smith's death in 1935 by Gus Edson); Frank King's "Gasoline Alley," 1919; Carl Ed's "Harold Teen," 1919; Martin Branner's "Winnie Winkle," 1920; Frank Willard's "Moon Mullins," 1923; and Harold Gray's "Little Orphan Annie," 1924.

People still called them "the funny papers" in this period. But two developments were under way which would change the character of the comics. One was the continuing story strip originating with "Andy Gump" in 1917. Many adults of the 1970s remember how baby Skeezix was abandoned on Uncle Walt's doorstep in the "Gasoline Alley" of 1921 to begin a chronicle of family life now in a third generation. Far less satisfying was the continuity of "Little Orphan Annie," whose waif has been lost from Daddy Warbucks every little while and has never finished school. King died in 1969 and Gray in 1968 but Skeezix and Annie lived on.

The other development was the action story, entering the comic pages with United Features' "Tarzan" in 1929 and soon extending through countless strips involving detectives, cowboys, adventurers, gangsters, and finally, supermen. The greatest detective of the comic strip world has been operating in

Chester Gould's "Dick Tracy" strip for the McCormick-Patterson syndicate since 1931. His principal competitors have been Alex Raymond's "Rip Kirby," begun in 1945 for King Features, and Alfred Andriola's "Kerry Drake," a 1943 discovery. Swashbuckling adventure has been most cleverly portrayed by Milton Caniff whose "Terry and the Pirates" was a 1934 McCormick-Patterson gold mine. When Caniff left the *Chicago Tribune* in 1947 to start "Steve Canyon" for the *Chicago Sun-Times,* George Wunder continued involving Terry and his friends in "real life" adventures. The McCormick-Patterson syndicate also featured Zack Mosley's "Smilin' Jack" strip and a comics heroine, "Brenda Starr," drawn by Dale Messick, only woman creating a successful comic. Ham Fisher's "Joe Palooka" began fighting in 1931. The first of the superhumans was Buck Rogers, whose twenty-fifth-century era began in 1929. Superman himself, drawn by Jerry Siegel and Joe Schuster, caught on in 1939.

There still was some humor left in the comic pages, despite the invasion of crime, tragedy, death, and lurid action in the 1930s. Harry J. Tuthill's "The Bungle Family," begun in the *New York Evening Mail* in 1918, and Sol Hess' "The Nebbs," dating from 1923, were family favorites. So were Cal Alley's 'The Ryatts," Carl Grubert's "The Berrys," and "Hi and Lois," a 1954 entry by Mort Walker and Dik Browne. New heroines were "Ella Cinders," drawn by Charlie Plumb and Bill Conselman since 1925, and "Dixie Dugan," created by J. P. McEvoy and John H. Striebel in 1929. Children and their antics were not ignored; some of the favorites were Edwina Dumm's "Cap Stubbs and Tippie," Ernie Bushmiller's "Fritzi Ritz and Nancy," Robert Brinkerhoff's "Little Mary Mixup," Harry Haenigsen's "Penny," and four King Features offerings—Carl Anderson's "Henry," Percy Crosby's "Skippy," Charles H. Kuhn's "Grandma," and Jimmy Hatlo's "Little Iodine." Sweeping to fame in this field in the 1950s was Hank Ketcham's "Dennis the Menace." Right behind were Charlie Brown, Lucy, Linus, and Snoopy of the "Peanuts" strip by Charles M. Schulz, for United Features. The little folks of the Schulz drawing board were more popular than ever in the 1970s and made Schulz the wealthiest cartoonist.

Of all the comic characters, none became better known than Al Capp's "Li'l Abner." Capp began his work for United Features in 1935, and by the time Li'l Abner finally married Daisy Mae in 1952 the event was featured as a news item in many papers. Capp's strip sometimes had a social message for its readers going beyond the doings in Dogpatch. Considerably more subtle in its satire was Walt Kelly's "Pogo" sequence dealing with animal characters, a 1950s offering appealing to the intellectuals among the comic page readers. "Andy Capp," the little guy who is some part of all men, drawn by British artist Reggie Smythe, was in 500 newspapers by the 1970s.

The best humor has been that of the panel artists. Stars of the 1920s were Clare Briggs of the *New York Tribune,* T. A. (Tad) Dorgan of the *American* and *Journal,* and H. T. Webster of the *World* and *Herald Tribune*. Briggs originated "Mr. and Mrs.," a favorite *Herald Tribune* feature. Dorgan's panels were "For Better or Worse" and "Indoor Sports." The master performer was

Webster, who invented Caspar Milquetoast for "The Timid Soul" and who drew "The Thrill That Comes Once in a Lifetime," "Life's Darkest Moment," "How to Torture Your Wife," and a humorous series on bridge addicts. Webster's "The Unseen Audience" effectively criticised radio and television until his death in 1952. In a similar tradition were J. R. Williams' "Out Our Way" and "Born Thirty Years Too Soon," Otto Soglow's "Little King," and Clifford McBride's "Napoleon."

The impact of the comics is enormous. Chic Young's "Blondie," consistently first in reader preference surveys, runs in 1,200 papers. It and other strips claim from 40 to 80 million readers in up to 50 countries. Mort Walker's "Beetle Bailey" caricature of Army life swept into 800 papers in a few years. Today a capable editor must watch the pulling power of his comics, his cartoonists and columnists, and his features (use "Dear Abby" or Ann Landers, or stick to Mary Haworth?). And he must choose between running them or news when space is limited. The choices are hard ones, for the common denominators of journalism have proved their effectiveness.

Annotated Bibliography

Books

Alsop, Joseph and Stewart, *The Reporter's Trade*. New York: Reynal & Company, 1958. A discussion of Washington reporting and compilation of the Alsop brothers' columns, 1946–58.

Baillie, Hugh, *High Tension*. New York: Harper & Row, 1959. Readable autobiography of the former United Press president.

Becker, Stephen, *Comic Art in America*. New York: Simon & Schuster, 1959. Surveys comics, political cartoons, magazine humor.

Block, Herbert L., *The Herblock Gallery*. New York: Simon & Schuster, 1968. One of several collections of the great cartoonist's work.

Cater, Douglass, *The Fourth Branch of Government*. Boston: Houghton Mifflin, 1959. Surveys the Washington press corps.

Childs, Marquis, and James B. Reston, eds., *Walter Lippmann and His Times*. New York: Harcourt, Brace & Jovanovich, 1959. Twelve essays by admirers of the columnist.

Clapper, Raymond, *Watching the World*. New York: Whittlesey House, 1944. A collection of the writings of a great Washington correspondent and columnist, edited by his wife.

Considine, Bob, *It's All News to Me*. New York: Meredith, 1967. Autobiography of a great press association reporter, for INS, and Hearst star.

Cooper, Kent, *Kent Cooper and the Associated Press*. New York: Random House, 1959. Autobiography of the former general manager. For the story of the AP's restrictive news exchange agreements, see his *Barriers Down* (New York: Holt, Rinehart & Winston, 1942).

Couperie, Pierre, and Maurice C. Horn, *A History of the Comic Strip.* New York: Crown, 1968. Covers the comic strip worldwide with emphasis upon American.

Darling, Jay N., *Ding's Half Century,* edited by John M. Henry. New York: Duell, Sloan and Pearce, 1962. Ding's best cartoons for *New York Tribune* and *Des Moines Register.*

Dennis, Charles H., *Victor Lawson: His Time and His Work.* Chicago: University of Chicago Press, 1935. Contains information about the building up of *Chicago Daily News* foreign service.

Desmond, Robert W., *The Press and World Affairs.* New York: Appleton-Century-Crofts, 1937. Traces press association developments.

Drewry, John E., ed., *Post Biographies of Famous Journalists.* Athens: University of Georgia Press, 1942. *More Post Biographies.* Athens: University of Georgia Press, 1947. Dated profiles of then-current famous.

Ellis, Elmer, ed., *Mr. Dooley at His Best.* New York: Scribner's, 1938. Writings of Finley Peter Dunne.

Fisher, Charles, *The Columnists.* New York: Howell, Soskin, Publishers, Inc., 1944. A lively study, outdated but still valuable.

Gramling, Oliver, *AP: The Story of News.* New York: Holt, Rinehart & Winston, 1940. Unreliable in its survey of early period of AP history, on which Rosewater is the authority, the book contains valuable details for the modern era. The author was an Associated Press executive.

Harrison, John M., *The Man Who Made Nasby, David Ross Locke.* Chapel Hill: University of North Carolina Press, 1969. An excellent biography of the editor of the *Toledo Blade,* who was creator of Petroleum V. Nasby.

Hess, Stephen, and Milton Kaplan, *The Ungentlemanly Art: A History of American Political Cartoons.* New York: Macmillan, 1968. A well-done survey from Franklin to Herblock.

Hiebert, Ray Eldon, ed., *The Press in Washington.* New York: Dodd, Mead, 1966. Talks by 16 capital newsmen at American University.

Hohenberg, John, *Foreign Correspondence: The Great Reporters and Their Times.* New York: Columbia University Press, 1964. Foreign correspondence since the French Revolution; best survey of the reporters and the trends.

Johnson, Gerald W., *The Lines Are Drawn.* Philadelphia: Lippincott, 1958. A study of Pulitzer Prize cartoons.

Kramer, Dale, *Heywood Broun.* New York: A. A. Wyn, Inc., 1949. Biography of a liberal columnist.

Krock, Arthur, *Memoirs: Sixty Years on the Firing Line.* New York: Funk & Wagnalls, 1968. By the longtime Washington chief of the *New York Times.*

McCabe, Charles R., ed., *Damned Old Crank.* New York: Harper & Row, 1951. Contains a chapter in which E. W. Scripps explains why he started the United Press, and gives some financial details.

Mauldin, Bill, *I've Decided I Want My Seat Back.* New York: Harper & Row, 1965. Cartoons of 1961–65 period.

"M.E.S." His Book. New York: Harper & Row, 1918. A book commemorating Melville E. Stone's first 25 years as Associated Press general manager. Much of Stone's

own writing and his major speeches are included, along with other historical materials. See also Stone's autobiography, *Fifty Years a Journalist.*

Morris, Joe Alex, *Deadline Every Minute: The Story of the United Press.* New York: Doubleday, 1957. By a UP staff member, observing the press association's fiftieth anniversary. Highly readable; much information about both UP executives and its newsmen.

Mowrer, Edgar Ansel, *Triumph and Turmoil: A Personal History of Our Times.* New York: Weybright and Talley, 1968. Autobiography of one of greatest foreign correspondents, World War I to cold war.

Murrell, William, *A History of American Graphic Humor, 1865–1938.* New York: Macmillan, 1938. The second volume of a work which reproduces many newspaper cartoons.

Nevins, Allan, and George Weitenkampf, *A Century of Political Cartoons.* New York: Scribner's, 1944. The cartoons are presented in historical setting.

Perry, George, and Alan Aldridge, *The Penguin Book of Comics.* Harmondsworth, England: Penguin, 1967. History of comics with copious examples.

Phillips, Cabell, et al., eds., *Dateline: Washington.* Garden City: Doubleday, 1949. The Washington correspondents write about their work and about the National Press Club.

Rivers, William L., *The Opinionmakers.* Boston: Beacon Press, 1965. A top-flight study of Washington journalists. See also *The Adversaries* (1970).

Rosewater, Victor, *History of Cooperative News-Gathering in the United States.* New York: Appleton-Century-Crofts, 1930. The authoritative source for the rise of the press associations.

Salisbury, Harrison, *Moscow Journal.* Chicago: University of Chicago Press, 1961. Problems of reporting Soviet news, 1949–53.

Spencer, Dick, III, *Pulitzer Prize Cartoons.* Ames: Iowa State College Press, 1953. A history of the winning cartoons since 1922.

Stokes, Thomas L., *Chip Off My Shoulder.* Princeton: Princeton University Press, 1940. An autobiography which explains the background of a distinguished reporter-columnist.

Sullivan, Mark, *The Education of an American.* New York: Doubleday, 1938. The autobiography of one of the first political columnists.

Sulzberger, C. L., *A Long Row of Candles.* New York: Macmillan, 1969. Memoirs and diaries of the chief *New York Times* foreign correspondent, 1934–54. His *The Last of the Giants* (1970) carried the story through 1963.

UNESCO, *News Agencies: Their Structure and Operations.* New York: Columbia University Press, 1953. Includes discussions of AP, UP, and INS and examines their roles in worldwide news distribution. Later information is found in John C. Merrill, Carter R. Bryan, and Marvin Alisky, *The Foreign Press: A Survey of the World's Journalism* (Baton Rouge: Louisiana State University Press, 1970).

Watson, Elmo Scott, *A History of Newspaper Syndicates in the United States, 1865–1935.* Chicago: Publishers' Auxiliary, 1936. Source for the story of Western Newspaper Union and for rise of other early syndicates.

Waugh, Coulton, *The Comics.* New York: Macmillan, 1947. A first-rate history of the comic pages; detailed but well-written and well-illustrated.

Webster, H. T., *The Best of H. T. Webster.* New York: Simon & Schuster, 1953. One of the best collections of newspaper humorous drawings.

Weingast, David E., *Walter Lippmann.* New Brunswick: Rutgers University Press, 1949. An impartial study of the political, social, and economic views of an essentially conservative columnist.

Periodicals and Monographs

Abbot, Willis J., "Melville E. Stone's Own Story," *Collier's,* LXV (February 7, 1920), 51. A well-written portrait of the AP general manager.

Alsop, Joseph and Stewart, "Our Own Inside Story," *Saturday Evening Post,* CCXXXI (November 8–15, 1958). How the columnists operated, 1946–58.

Barcus, Francis E., "A Content Analysis of Trends in Sunday Comics, 1900–1959," *Journalism Quarterly,* XXXVIII (Spring 1961), 171. The first report from a major study of comics at Boston University.

Benét, Stephen Vincent, "The United Press," *Fortune,* VII (May 1933), 67. A compact treatment of UP history and its 1933 status.

Dam, Hari N., "Walter Lippmann: A Study of His Changing Views," Ph.D. thesis, University of Minnesota, 1968. Lippmann's public philosophy, 1910–60, analyzed interestingly and competently.

Emery, Michael C., "The American Mass Media and the Coverage of Five Major Foreign Events, 1900–1950: the Russo-Japanese War, Outbreak of World War I, Rise of Stalin, Munich Crisis, Invasion of South Korea," Ph.D. thesis, University of Minnesota, 1968. The press corps and how the media used their coverage.

Harrison, Richard Edes, "AP," *Fortune,* XV (February 1937), 89. The rise of the AP and a contemporary picture of its operations.

Irwin, Will, "United Press," *Harper's Weekly,* LVIII (April 25, 1914), 6. An estimate by a top-flight newsman of early UP progress.

Kliesch, Ralph E., "History and Operations of the McGraw-Hill World News Service," Ph.D. thesis, University of Minnesota, 1968. Describes McGraw-Hill news gathering since 1880s, and the World News Service, 1945–68.

Marbut, Frederick B., "Congress and the Standing Committee of Correspondents," *Journalism Quarterly,* XXXVIII (Winter 1961), 52. The history of the press gallery rules is traced from 1879.

Miller, Merle, "Washington, the World, and Joseph Alsop," *Harper's,* CCXXXVI (June 1968), 43. The imperious columnist examined.

Odendahl, Eric M., "The Story and Stories of the Copley News Service," Ph.D. thesis, University of Missouri, 1966. History of the service and analysis of its content.

Pearson, Drew, "Confessions of 'an S.O.B.'," *Saturday Evening Post,* CCXXIX (November 3–24, 1956). Story of an "inside" columnist.

Schwarzlose, Richard A., "The American Wire Services: A Study of Their Development as a Social Institution," Ph.D. thesis, University of Illinois, 1965. By a leading student of the press associations.

———, "Trends in U.S. Newspapers' Wire Service Resources, 1934–66," *Journalism Quarterly,* XLIII (Winter 1966), 627. A lessening of competitive service appears in these detailed figures.

Smith, Henry Ladd, 'The Rise and Fall of the Political Cartoon," *Saturday Review,* XXXVII (May 29, 1954), 7. A well-illustrated essay.

Strout, Richard L., "Tom Stokes: What He Was Like," *Nieman Reports,* XIII (July 1959), 9. A portrait of a great Washington reporter.

"The Funny Papers," *Fortune,* VII (April 1933), 45. An excellent major study, well-illustrated.

Witcover, Jules, "Washington: The News Explosion," *Columbia Journalism Review,* VIII (Spring 1969), 23. A survey of new trends and people in Washington reporting.

On Today's Editorial Page
Attacking Adversity By Incantation: Editorial
A Real Conservative: Editorial

ST. LOUIS POST-DISPATCH

FINAL

VOL. 92 NO. 120 FRIDAY, MAY 1, 1970 52 PAGES 10c

Nixon Orders U.S. Troops Into Cambodia To Hit Reds

Text on Page 5A
By JAMES DEAKIN
A Washington Correspondent of the Post-Dispatch

WASHINGTON, May 1—In a sharp change in policy, President Richard M. Nixon has expanded the Vietnam war by sending United States troops into Cambodia to clean out Communist sanctuaries.

The decision, announced last night by Mr. Nixon in a 20-minute televised speech to the nation, was considered almost certain to reopen an intense national debate over the course of U.S. policy in Southeast Asia.

The President defended his action as essential to protect the lives of American soldiers in South Vietnam, to make it possible to continue the withdrawal of U.S. troops from the war zone, and to achieve "the just peace we all desire."

Transcend Politics

"I would rather be a one-term President and do what I believe is right than to be a two-term President at the cost of seeing America become a second-rate power and see this nation accept the first defeat in its proud 190-year history," Mr. Nixon said.

Thousands of Troops

CARRYING A HIGH PRESSURE tear gas dispenser, a marine deplanes today at Quonset Point Naval Station, R.I., for possible deployment to New Haven, Conn., about 100 miles away. (UPI Telephoto)

AMERICAN SOLDIERS MOVING BLINDFOLDED Prisoners, including a woman, to a collection point in Cambodia today. The prisoners were captured in initial thrusts to secure helicopter landing zones. (AP Radiophoto)

Nixon Assails 'Campus Bums'

Hard Rains Flood Area Highways

Troops Alert In Rally Area

Clearing, Cooler

Senators Seek Nixon Parley

8000-Man U.S. Force Moves Into Cambodia

Mayor Calls Meeting Of Teamsters, Carriers

Mafia Figure Pickets FBI

ALLIED COMBAT OPERATIONS are under way in the shaded areas of Cambodia. (AP Wirephoto)

TURN TO PAGE 16, COL. 1

News Index

The *St. Louis Post-Dispatch* records the widening of the Indochina war in 1970.

24

The Press in Modern War

This is a people's war, and to win it the people should know as much about it as they can.
—Elmer Davis

The great war which began in Europe in August, 1914, completely altered the pattern of civilization which a comparatively peaceful nineteenth century had produced. By 1917 it had become a World War, with the embarking of the United States upon a "great crusade" to make the world safe for democracy. But men found at war's end that they neither could restore the old order nor build a peaceful new one. Political and social disillusionment, economic depression, and the rise of modern dictatorships brought a second great war in 1939, and the designations World War I and II came into the language. After 1950, when the United States found itself leading a United Nations army into Korea to fight the forces of Communist aggression and ended up in the quagmire of Vietnam, war seemed an unending morass. What happened to the American press in these periods of international war, interrupted by what proved to be only brief interludes of fitful peace, thus becomes a continuing story; equally important is the account of the role played by communication agencies during the periods of conflict.

AMERICAN REACTION TO EUROPE'S 1914 WAR

No one could foresee in 1914 the ultimate consequences of Germany's transformation of a "Balkan incident" into a general European war. Even though the United States had entered into the world diplomatic arena after the war with Spain, most Americans probably felt secure behind two oceans and were interested only in preserving peace as far as this country was concerned. No doubt the jesting comment of the *Chicago Herald* summarized this attitude: "Peace-loving citizens of this country will now rise up and tender a hearty vote of thanks to Columbus for having discovered America." [1]

Yet underneath this denial of concern by Americans for what was happening in the Old World lay the first instinctive reactions to the shattering of peace, reactions which were to lead to the declaration of war in 1917. The war was real to Americans only insofar as newspaper stories and pictures were able to make it so. But the newspapers of Maine reflected a spontaneous anti-German reaction immediately upon the news of the German declaration of war and invasion of Belgium.[2] As Americans read the vivid account by Richard Harding Davis of the entry of the German army into Brussels—"one unbroken steel-gray column . . . twenty-four hours later is still coming . . . not men marching, but a force of nature like a tidal wave, an avalanche"—and as they looked almost unbelievingly at pictures of the sacked city of Louvain, they became increasingly uncomfortable.

It is important to record these first American reactions, since in the depths of later disillusionment, when it was evident that our participation in war had failed to bring a lasting peace, a literature appeared which told a different story. British propagandists, American munitions makers, and cynical politicians had led gullible Americans to an unnecessary slaughter, the theme ran, carrying with it the implication that American newspapers were duped by foreign propagandists and by war-mongering capitalists, and thereby misled their readers. A quite convincing case was built upon partial evidence for such a thesis—ignoring or overriding such important factors as these:

The impact upon American public opinion of crisis events, such as the sinking of the "Lusitania," which were predominantly unfavorable to the German side;

The effects of Allied censorships and control of overseas communications in shaping the available news (as distinct from overt propaganda efforts);

The effects of socially-important pressure groups in shaping American thought;

The natural ties between English-speaking peoples, and the distaste of Americans for German "Kultur";

The legitimate pro-Allied decisions of American officials and diplomats based upon German-caused events;

[1] As quoted in Mark Sullivan, *Our Times*, Vol. V (New York: Scribner's, 1933), p. 32. Sullivan's six-volume journalistic coverage of the years 1900–1925 reflects both the life and history of America in an engrossing manner.

[2] Edwin Costrell, "Newspaper Attitudes Toward War in Maine, 1914–17," *Journalism Quarterly*, XVI (December, 1939), 334. This measurement of an immediate anti-German reaction, before the introduction of concerted propaganda by the belligerents and before the cutting of cable communications with Germany, is significant.

The feeling that a strong British navy was less hazardous to American interests than a strong German navy;

And, most importantly, the basic United States objection to one-nation domination of Europe—an objection which led to two wars with German militarism in defense of the American national interest.[3]

The American press quite definitely was handicapped in its presentation of the war news by the existence of wartime censorships and by Allied control of cable facilities. All of the belligerents exercised close control over correspondents in the fighting areas. News of military actions was delayed by both sides, and official communiques often attempted to conceal news of reversals. Some correspondents managed to obtain beats on news of important battles, but largely as a matter of luck. Front area reporters more often won recognition for their feature stories than for their straight factual accounts, while military analysts in the various European capitals provided the continuing story of the fighting along the sprawling western and eastern fronts. This news, after clearing the military censorships, still had to funnel through the London communications center. This was the result of the British action in cutting the German Atlantic cable on August 5, 1914. Stories written in Berlin, Vienna, and in neutral capitals thereafter had to travel through London to reach the United States.[4]

AMERICA MOVES TOWARD WAR

The course of events was rapidly bolstering pro-Allied sentiment in the United States. The *New York Times* printed the various "white papers" giving each belligerent power's version of the events leading up to the war, but Germany's obvious preparation for war and smashing early victories added reason to believe the Allied versions, imperfectly as they were presented. Natural ties of many Americans to the English traditions, which were particularly strong among social and intellectual leaders, made it fashionable to be pro-British. Yet large segments of the population opposed America's going to war up to the last, for various reasons. The Middle West was more isolationist than the seaboard sections and was suspicious of the pro-Allied easterners. The Irish, a strong minority, were naturally anti-British because of the Irish civil war,

[3] Among the more responsible books of the era of disillusionment were C. Hartley Grattan's *Why We Fought* (1929), Walter Millis' *Road to War* (1935), and H. C. Peterson's *Propaganda for War* (1939). For criticism of Peterson's attitude toward newspapers, see Ralph D. Casey, "The Press, Propaganda, and Pressure Groups," *The Annals of the American Academy of Political and Social Science*, CCXIX (January 1942), 68.

[4] The best-balanced picture of American press difficulties in covering the war is found in Ralph O. Nafziger's *The American Press and Public Opinion During the World War, 1914 to April, 1917* (Ph.D. thesis, University of Wisconsin, 1936). Nafziger ranks overt propaganda efforts as having less effect upon American news presentation than (1) rigid war censorships and (2) limited and controlled communications facilities.

although this did not necessarily make them pro-German, it should be pointed out. The large groups of German-Americans who were, on the whole, loyal to the United States, were at the same time naturally sympathetic with the aims of the Fatherland. They regarded Germany's ambitions as being no more dangerous or imperialistic than the aims of Britain, France, and Russia.

One decisive event was the torpedoing of English Cunard line ship "Lusitania," then the queen of the Atlantic run. When the "Lusitania" went down off the Irish coast on May 7, 1915, with the loss of 1,198 of the 1,924 persons aboard—including 114 of 188 American passengers—Germany celebrated the accomplishment of her U-boat captain. But resentment ran high in the United States, particularly when it was remembered that an Imperial German Embassy advertisement warning travelers on Allied ships that they did so "at their own risk" had appeared in New York newspapers the morning the "Lusitania" left port. President Wilson held to his decision to remain neutral, uttering his famous phrase, "There is such a thing as a man being too proud to fight." Public opinion calmed somewhat, but many newspapers, civic leaders, and groups which theretofore had professed neutrality now swung to the Allied camp.

Even though Germany relaxed its submarine warfare after months of diplomatic note-writing by President Wilson, the summer of 1916 was dominated by pro-Allied arguments and by talk of preparedness. Former President Theodore Roosevelt and General Leonard Wood opened a volunteer training camp at Plattsburg. President Wilson adopted the preparedness issue during his successful reelection campaign, even though his most effective slogan was "He kept us out of war."

In December, 1916, Wilson suggested that a "peace without victory" be arranged through the auspices of the United States. The peace would be kept in the future by a League to Enforce Peace, which for years had been advocated by former President William Howard Taft and other leading American internationalists. But Wilson's hopes of the United States serving as a neutral arbiter were dashed by two final German actions.

One was resumption of unrestricted submarine warfare by the Germans in February, 1917. This brought a break in diplomatic relations. Clinching the American decision was the Allied interception of German Foreign Minister Zimmermann's note to the Mexican government, offering Mexico the return of Texas, New Mexico, and Arizona after an American defeat, if Mexico would ally itself with Germany. The text of the note, given to the Associated Press unofficially, created a sensation. The sinking of three American ships by U-boats in March brought Wilson's war call on April 2—"The world must be made safe for democracy"—and the declaration of war on April 6. Wilson's masterful phrases played no small part in the determination of the issue. His denunciation of a group of 11 senators, led by Robert La Follette of Wisconsin, as "a little group of willful men" for filibustering against arming of American merchant ships in early March did much to discredit the bitter-end opponents of war.

Some periodicals had been pro-Ally almost from the start. Among the most outspoken were the old *Life* magazine, Henry Watterson's *Louisville Courier-Journal,* and the *New York Herald.* The *New York Times* was solidly pro-Ally, along with the *World* and most other New York newspapers. After the sinking of the "Lusitania" the number of anti-interventionist newspapers dwindled. William Randolph Hearst's chain of papers stood out as bitterly anti-British and was tarred as pro-German because Hearst made special efforts to obtain German-originated news to balance Allied-originated stories. Other holdouts against war were the *New York Evening Mail* (which had been bought secretly by German agents), *Chicago Tribune, Cincinnati Enquirer, Cleveland Plain Dealer, Washington Post, Milwaukee Sentinel, Los Angeles Times, San Francisco Chronicle,* and *San Francisco Call.*[5] All, of course, supported the war once it was declared. William Jennings Bryan's *Commoner, La Follette's Magazine,* and Oswald Garrison Villard's *Nation* and *New York Evening Post* were pacifist. And the German-language press was in the main pro-German.

GEORGE CREEL'S COMMITTEE ON PUBLIC INFORMATION

Now that America was in the war, President Wilson turned to the problem of stimulating the country's morale and of educating the people to the task ahead. Himself a master of the art of creating public opinion, he knew the value of using the agencies of communication. And although he wanted those agencies to remain as free as possible, he knew that some control was necessary.

Only a week after the declaration of war, Wilson appointed a Committee on Public Information. Its job primarily was one of disseminating facts about the war. It also was to coordinate government propaganda efforts, and to serve as the government's liaison with newspapers. It drew up a voluntary censorship code under which editors would agree to refrain from printing material which might aid the enemy. Before it was through, the committee found itself "mobilizing the mind of the world," and Mark Sullivan characterized it as an American contribution to the science of war. George Creel, the newspaperman who was named by Wilson to direct the committee's work, explained that "it was a plain publicity proposition, a vast enterprise in salesmanship, the world's greatest adventure in advertising." [6]

[5] Frank Luther Mott, *American Journalism* (New York: Macmillan, 1950), p. 616.
[6] George Creel, *How We Advertised America* (New York: Harper & Row, 1920), p. 4.

Why the United States, entering the war so late, should be credited with taking a foremost part in informational and propaganda activities, might not seem clear. The work of Wellington House, a British propaganda agency, in mobilizing neutral opinion on the side of the Allies was a notable achievement. But the British did not unify the work being carried on in their various regular governmental agencies until January, 1917, when a Department of Information was created. It was February, 1918, before two British press lords were named to coordinate posts: Lord Beaverbrook becoming Minister of Information and Lord Northcliffe assuming the title of Director of Propaganda in Enemy Countries. This organization was popularly known as Crewe House. The Germans used a loosely-organized Press Conference to coordinate the informational and propaganda activities of their various bureaus while the French operated only through the Maison de la Presse and their regular governmental agencies.[7]

The opportunity which Wilson gave to Creel was a greater one than any other person had enjoyed in the propaganda arena. Creel was a liberal-minded and vigorously competent product of New York, Kansas City, and Denver journalism. He was intensely anxious to achieve every possible task which his committee might embrace, and he eventually mobilized 150,000 Americans to carry out its varied and far-flung missions.

Creel's first job was to open up government news channels to the Washington correspondents. Officials were so fearful that any slip might give information to a German spy that they were treating much routine news as vital military secrets. Creel insisted that only news of troop movements, ship sailings, and other events of strictly military character should be withheld. He issued a brief explanatory code calling upon the newspapers to censor such news themselves, voluntarily. Throughout the war newspaper editors generally went beyond Creel's minimum requests in their desire to aid the war effort.

Creel soon found that the Washington correspondents needed help in covering the home front activities. His staff compiled information and served as an agency for the release of special war stories. In May, 1917, the CPI began publishing an *Official Bulletin* in which releases were reprinted in newspaper form. Before the war was over this publication reached a daily circulation of 118,000. A weekly newpaperman prepared a digest of the news for rural papers. Still photographs, plates, and mats also were utilized.

A historian who studied the accuracy of CPI news releases years later came to this conclusion: "One of the most remarkable things about the charges against the CPI is that, of the more than 6,000 news stories it issued, so few were called into question at all. It may be doubted that the CPI's record for honesty will ever be equalled in the official war news of a major power."[8]

[7] Harold D. Lasswell, *Propaganda Technique in the World War* (New York: Peter Smith, 1927), p. 20.

[8] Walton E. Bean, "The Accuracy of Creel Committee News, 1917–1919: An Examination of Cases," *Journalism Quarterly*, XVIII (September 1941), 272. The major study of the CPI is James R. Mock and Cedric Larson, *Words That Won the War* (Princeton: Princeton University Press, 1939).

The same high opinion of Creel's honesty and diligence in keeping news flowing was expressed by other students of CPI activities.

CREEL SELLS THE WAR

Creel's imaginative conception of his job was fully expressed in the work of the CPI in other areas than the dissemination of news. It was in the use of several media and techniques that his publicity, advertising, and salesmanship talents came into full play. Creel rallied advertising men, painters, sculptors, illustrators, cartoonists, photographers, public speakers, writers, movie stars, singers—even college professors—to the colors. They used their skills to stimulate military enlistments, to obtain cooperation for Bernard Baruch's industrial mobilization, and for Herbert Hoover's food conservation program.

Creel asked major advertisers and the publications themselves to donate space for various government campaigns, for the Red Cross, and other war-related activities. The advertising agencies were organized, and their copy men and artists were used to create newspaper and magazine advertising, streetcar placards, and outdoor posters. The artists in the CPI's division of pictorial publicity, headed by Charles Dana Gibson, contributed stirring posters. The infant motion picture industry produced films of both patriotic and instructive nature. Its stars, including Douglas Fairbanks and Mary Pickford, sparked Liberty bond sales. The college professors served in a division of pamphleteering. It produced a *War Cyclopedia* and 75 million pieces of printed matter. Historian Guy Stanton Ford of the University of Minnesota headed the division, which numbered among its scholars such noted historians as Carl Becker of Cornell University, Evarts B. Greene of the University of Illinois, and Frederic L. Paxson of the University of Wisconsin.[9]

The publications of the college professors became a part of Creel's campaign abroad. Creel distributed materials directly in Allied countries, in neutral areas, and inside the enemy countries themselves. His principal weapons were the ringing phrases of Woodrow Wilson, who was offering freedom to submerged nationalities, a just settlement of political boundaries, open covenants of peace, protection for the vanquished enemy peoples once their rulers had been overthrown, and an association of nations which would preserve the peace. It was one of Creel's newsmen assistants, Edgar G. Sisson, who suggested that Wilson's speeches be condensed into a journalistic summary for distribution abroad, and thus prompted Wilson to produce his famed "Fourteen Points." The result was that when Wilson journeyed to Europe for the

[9] Paxson eventually wrote a three-volume series titled *American Democracy and the World War*. The war itself is covered in detail in the second volume, *America at War, 1917–1918* (Boston: Houghton Mifflin, 1939).

"All the News That's Fit to Print."

The New York Times.

THE WEATHER

VOL. LXVIII...NO. 22,206. NEW YORK, MONDAY, NOVEMBER 11, 1918. TWENTY-FOUR PAGES. TWO CENTS

ARMISTICE SIGNED, END OF THE WAR! BERLIN SEIZED BY REVOLUTIONISTS; NEW CHANCELLOR BEGS FOR ORDER; OUSTED KAISER FLEES TO HOLLAND

SON FLEES WITH EX-KAISER

Hindenburg Also Believed to be Among Those in His Party.

ALL ARE HEAVILY ARMED

Automobiles Bristle with Rifles as Fugitives Arrive at Dutch Frontier.

ON THEIR WAY TO DE STEEG

Belgians Yell to Them, "Are You On Your Way to Paris?"

LONDON, Nov. 10.—Both the former German Emperor and his eldest son, Frederick William, crossed the Dutch frontier Sunday morning, according to advices from The Hague. His reported destination is De Steeg, near Utrecht.

The former German Emperor's party, which is believed to include Field Marshal von Hindenburg, arrived at Eysden, [midway between Liége and Maastricht,] on the Dutch frontier, at 7:30 o'clock Sunday morning, according to Daily Mail advices.

Practically the whole German General Staff accompanied the former Emperor, and ten automobiles carried the party. The automobiles were bristling with rifles, and all the fugitives were armed.

The ex-Kaiser was in uniform. He alighted at the Eysden station and paced the platform, smoking a cigarette.

Many photographs were taken by [of?] the members of the Imperial party. On the whole the people were very quiet, but Belgians among them yelled out "En voyage a Paris." (Are you on your way to Paris?)

Chatting with the members of the staff, the former Emperor, the correspondent says, did not look in the least distressed. A few minutes later an imperial train, including restaurant and sleeping cars, ran into the station. Only servants were aboard.

The engine returned to Visé, Belgium, and brought back a second train, in which were a large number of staff officers and others, and also stores of food.

The preparations began for the departure at 10 o'clock this morning, but at 10:40 o'clock the train was still at Eysden. The blinds of the train were all drawn.

The Daily Mail remarks that, if the party arrived in Holland armed, all of them must be interned.

While other dispatches con-

Continued on Page Three.

Kaiser Fought Hindenburg's Call for Abdication; Failed to Get Army's Support in Keeping Throne

By GEORGE RENWICK.

Copyright, 1918, by The New York Times. Special Cable to The New York Times.

AMSTERDAM, Nov. 10.—I learn on very good authority that the Kaiser made a determined effort to stave off abdication. He went to headquarters with the deliberate intention of bringing the army around to his side. In this he failed miserably.

His main support consisted of a number of officers, nearly all of Prussian regiments, who formed themselves into two regiments and placed themselves at his Majesty's disposal. To do anything with such support was seen, of course, to be Gilbertian.

During the night the Kaiser called the Crown Prince, Hindenburg, and General Gröner to him, and the consultation lasted a couple of hours. Both officers strongly pressed the Kaiser to bow to the inevitable, and Hindenburg informed him that any more delay in coming to a decision to abdicate would certainly have the most terrible consequences and lead to serious events in the army. For those consequences Hindenburg said he must refuse responsibility.

The Crown Prince, it is said, was the first to give way. General Gröner fully supported Hindenburg's view, but when the conference broke up the Kaiser remained unconvinced of the advisability of abdication. He is said to have come to his final decision an hour or so later, after several communications had reached him from Berlin and after another short and stormy talk with Hindenburg.

Meanwhile, his son-in-law, the Duke of Brunswick, for himself and his heir, had abdicated. "Brunswick's Fated Chieftain" was forced without fighting to abdicate. Reports have it that the republican movement in Brunswick, which long before the war was chafing under autocratic conditions, began to be noticed even before it was set in motion at Kiel.

Kaiser Shivered as He Signed Abdication

LONDON, Nov. 10.—Emperor William signed his letter of abdication on Saturday morning at the German Grand Headquarters in the presence of Crown Prince Frederick William and Field Marshal Hindenburg, according to a dispatch from Amsterdam to the Exchange Telegraph Company.

The Crown Prince signed his renunciation of the throne shortly afterward.

Before placing his signature to the document, an urgent message from Philipp Scheidemann, who was a Socialist member without portfolio in the Imperial Cabinet, was handed to the Emperor. He read it with a shiver. Then he signed the paper, saying:

"It may be for the good of Germany."

The Emperor was deeply moved. He consented to sign the document only when he got the news of the latest events in the empire.

The ex-Kaiser and former Crown Prince were expected to take leave of their troops on Saturday, but nothing had then been settled regarding their future movements.

GERMAN DYNASTIES BEING WIPED OUT

King of Wuerttemberg Abdicates — Sovereign of Saxony to Follow Suit.

PRINCES MAY BE EXILED

Socialists Are Demanding That Every Sovereign in the Empire Shall be Dethroned.

LONDON, Nov. 10.—A Havas dispatch from Basle says:

"Wilhelm II., the reigning King of the monarchy of Württemberg, abdicated on Friday night."

A Wolff Bureau dispatch from Stuttgart, by way of Amsterdam, says that the King has issued a proclamation saying that his person would never serve to hinder the development of the wishes of the people.

According to a report received from Berne, the German Socialists are demanding that every dynasty in Germany be suppressed and all the Princes exiled. It is reported that the Kings of Bavaria and Saxony intend to abdicate soon.

Continued on Page Two.

MORE WARSHIPS JOIN THE REDS

Four Dreadnoughts in Kiel Harbor for Espouse the Revolutionary Cause.

GUARDSHIPS ALSO GO OVER

Those Protecting Mines in the Great Belt and the Baltic Abandon Their Posts.

Continued on Page Three.

BERLIN TROOPS JOIN REVOLT

Reds Shell Building in Which Officers Vainly Resist.

THRONGS DEMAND REPUBLIC

Revolutionary Flag on Royal Palace — Crown Prince's Palace Also Seized.

GENERAL STRIKE IS BEGUN

Burgomaster and Police Submit—War Office Now Under Socialist Control.

LONDON, Nov. 10.—The greater part of Berlin is in control of revolutionists, the former Kaiser has fled to Holland, and Friedrich Ebert, the new Socialist Chancellor, has taken command of the situation. The revolt is spreading throughout Germany with great rapidity.

Dispatches received in London today announce these startling developments. The Workmen's and Soldiers' Council is now administering the municipal government of the German capital.

The War Ministry has submitted, and its acts are valid only when countersigned by a Socialist representative. The official Wolff telegraphic agency has been taken over by the Reds.

The red flag has been hoisted over the royal palace and the Brandenburg Gate. The former Crown Prince's palace is also in possession of the revolutionists.

There was severe fighting in Berlin between 8 and 10 o'clock last night and a violent cannonade was heard from the heart of the city.

Burgomaster and Police Join.

A Copenhagen dispatch states that Dr. Liebknecht, the famous Socialist, who spent many months in prison for antagonizing the German Imperial Government and who was recently released, has issued the following announcement in Berlin in behalf of the Workmen's and Soldiers' Council:

"The Presidency of the police, as well as the Chief Command, is in our hands. Our comrades will be released."

A dispatch from Berne states that the Burgomaster of Berlin has placed himself and his staff at the disposal of the new Government.

Some German newspapers describe the movement as Bolshevism. The people are shouting "Long live the Republic!" and singing the "Marseillaise."

Officers Shelled by Reds.

When revolutionary soldiers attempted to enter a building in Berlin in which they supposed that a number of offi-

cers were concealed shots were fired from the windows. The Reds then began shelling the building. Many persons were killed and wounded before the officers surrendered.

When the cannonade began the people thought the Reichsbank was being bombarded, and thousands rushed to the square in front of the Crown Prince's palace. It was later determined that other buildings were under fire. Among those killed in the fighting at the "Cockchafer" Barracks was one of the workmen's leaders known as "Comrade" Habersroth.

Socialist Chancellor Appeals to All Germans To Help Him Save Fatherland from Anarchy

BERNE, Nov. 10, (Associated Press.)—In an address to the people, the new German Chancellor, Friedrich Ebert, says:

Citizens: The ex-Chancellor, Prince Max of Baden, in agreement with all the Secretaries of State, has handed over to me the task of liquidating his affairs as Chancellor. I am on the point of forming a new Government in accord with the various parties, and will keep public opinion freely informed of the course of events.

The new Government will be a Government of the people. It must make every effort to secure in the quickest possible time peace for the German people and consolidate the liberty which they have won.

I know it will be difficult for some to work with the new men who have taken charge of the empire, but I appeal to their love of the people. Lack of organization would in this heavy time mean anarchy in Germany and the surrender of the country to tremendous misery. Therefore, help your native country with fearless, indefatigable work for the future, every one at his post.

I demand every one's support in the hard task awaiting us. Food shortage signifies pillage and robbery, with great misery.

I ask you immediately to leave the streets and remain orderly and calm.

COPENHAGEN, Nov. 10.—The new Berlin Government, according to a Wolff Bureau dispatch, has issued the following proclamation:

Fellow-Citizens: This day the people's deliverance has been fulfilled. The Social Democratic Party has undertaken to form a Government. It has invited the Independent Socialist Party to enter the Government with equal rights.

Continued on Page Four.

WAR ENDS AT 6 O'CLOCK THIS MORNING

The State Department in Washington Made the Announcement at 2:45 o'Clock.

ARMISTICE WAS SIGNED IN FRANCE AT MIDNIGHT

Terms Include Withdrawal from Alsace-Lorraine. Disarming and Demobilization of Army and Navy, and Occupation of Strategic Naval and Military Points.

By The Associated Press.

WASHINGTON, Monday, Nov. 11, 2:48 A. M.—The armistice between Germany, on the one hand, and the allied Governments and the United States, on the other, has been signed.

The State Department announced at 2:45 o'clock this morning that Germany had signed.

The department's announcement simply said: "The armistice has been signed."

The world war will end this morning at 6 o'clock, Washington time, 11 o'clock Paris time.

The armistice was signed by the German representatives at midnight.

This announcement was made by the State Department at 2:50 o'clock this morning.

The announcement was made verbally by an officila of the State Department in this form:

"The armistice has been signed. It was signed at 5 o'clock A. M., Paris time, [midnight, New York time,] and hostilities will cease at 11 o'clock this morning, Paris time. [6 o'clock, New York time.]

The terms of the armistice, it was announced, will not be made public until later. Military men here, however, regard it as certain that they include:

Immediate retirement of the German military forces from France, Belgium, and Alsace-Lorraine.

Disarming and demobilization of the German armies.

Occupation by the allied and American forces of such strategic points in Germany as will make impossible a renewal of hostilities.

Delivery of part of the German High Seas Fleet and a certain number of submarines to the allied and American naval forces.

Disarmament of all other German warships

The famous 1918 Armistice Day edition of the *New York Times*.

peace conference he was the object of mass worship. His political opponents in the United States, who feared Wilson's motives and his prestige, bitterly attacked Creel as Wilson's personal publicity man in this phase of CPI activity.

CENSORSHIP OF GERMAN AND SOCIALIST PAPERS

The Espionage Act of June 15, 1917, provided the opening wedge for suppression of those who were considered to be disloyal to the American and Allied war cause. Among the crimes, punishable by heavy fines and imprisonment, which the Act defined were the willful making of false reports or false statements with the intent to interfere with the successful operation of the military or naval forces, and willful attempts to promote disloyalty in the armed forces or to obstruct recruitments. A section on use of the mails empowered the Postmaster General to declare unmailable all letters, circulars, newspapers, pamphlets, books, and other materials violating provisions of the act. Taken alone, the section provided only for the barring of specific material, a screening process that required an enormous expenditure of effort. In the case of a newspaper or magazine, the postal authorities employed a far more efficient method by ruling that a periodical which had had a particular issue declared unmailable no longer met the requirements to qualify for the low second-class postal rates, namely, that it was not "regularly issued." Given the power to prevent future issues from going out at second-class rates, Postmaster General Albert S. Burleson enjoyed life-or-death authority over publications using the mails for distribution. Recourse to the courts was a slow and unrewarding process since the courts generally refused to tamper with postal decisions unless they were "clearly wrong."

The axe fell most heavily upon Socialist organs and German-American newspapers, with a few other pacifist or anti-Ally publications losing their mail privileges. The *American Socialist* was banned from the mails immediately, and was soon followed by *Solidarity*, journal of the left-wing International Workers of the World—the much-feared anticapitalistic IWW. A vociferous advocate of the Irish independence movement, Jeremiah A. O'Leary, lost mailing privileges for his publication, *Bull*, in July, 1917, for opposing wartime cooperation with the British. The magazine *The Masses*, brilliantly edited by Max Eastman, felt the ban in August for publishing an issue containing four antiwar cartoons and a poem defending radical leaders Emma Goldman and Alexander Berkman. An indictment against the editors under the Espionage Act was dismissed in 1919.

Altogether some 75 papers either lost their mailing privileges during the first year of the Espionage Act, or retained them only by agreeing to print nothing more concerning the war. The best known were two Socialist dailies, the *New York Call* and Victor Berger's *Milwaukee Leader*. The Austrian-born

Berger, in 1910 the first Socialist elected to Congress, was convicted on charges of conspiracy to violate the Espionage Act and sentenced to 20 years imprisonment. The U. S. Supreme Court later overturned the decision due to the prejudicial actions of the presiding judge. Twice the House of Representatives denied him the seat to which he had been reelected. For a time during and after the war, all incoming mail was prevented from reaching the *Leader*. The Supreme Court upheld the Post Office ban on the *Leader* in a 1921 decision, and it was not until June, 1921, when Postmaster General Will Hays restored their second-class mailing privileges, that the *Leader* and the *Call* were once again able to reach their numerous out-of-town subscribers. The German-language press likewise was hard hit by mail bans and prosecutions and declined one-half in numbers and in circulation during the war.

Other papers felt the weight of public opinion against those who did not wholeheartedly support the war. The Hearst newspapers, which had bitterly opposed American entry into the war and which continued to be clearly anti-Ally even though they supported the American war effort itself, were widely attacked. Hearst was hanged in effigy, his papers were boycotted in some places, and he himself was denounced as disloyal. The *New York Tribune,* itself a strong critic of the way in which the Wilson administration was conducting the war, ran a famous cartoon showing a snake coiled in the flag, with the snake's body spelling the legend "Hears--ss-ss-t." Oswald Garrison Villard's pacifist views and defenses of civil liberties brought such a decline in the fortunes of the *New York Evening Post* that he was forced to sell it in 1918, and one issue of the *Nation* was held up in the New York Post Office because it carried an editorial titled "Civil Liberty Dead."

THE SEDITION ACT OF 1918

The powers of the government to control expression of opinion were strengthened by the passage of two other laws. The Trading-with-the-Enemy Act of October, 1917, authorized censorship of all communications moving in or out of the United States and provided that translations of newspaper or magazine articles published in a foreign language could be demanded by the Post Office—a move to keep the German-language papers in line. The Sedition Act of May, 1918, amended and broadened the Espionage Act by making it a crime to write or publish "any disloyal, profane, scurrilous or abusive language about the form of government of the United States or the Constitution, military or naval forces, flag, or the uniform" or to use language intended to bring these ideas and institutions "into contempt, scorn, contumely, or disrepute." The application of these broad provisions by the Post Office in banning publications from the mails gave the Postmaster General immense powers which he hesitated to use. The memory of the blundering Sedition Act of 1798 kept him from using his authority to harass orthodox Republican opponents of the administration, and the brunt of persecution continued to fall upon the unpopular radical and pro-German minorities.

Former President Theodore Rooevelt was asking heatedly why the Hearst newspapers had not been denied mail privileges (some Republicans said Hearst escaped because he was a Democrat). Roosevelt also was writing editorials for the *Kansas City Star* criticising the administration, and was speaking strongly against what he called its incompetence and softness in dealing with the enemy. Senator Robert La Follette of Wisconsin, who was politically crucified by an error which the Associated Press made in reporting one of his speeches,[10] likewise was a possible candidate for prosecution.

The Department of Justice, however, moved against lesser-known persons like the IWW leaders, who were arrested and imprisoned, and like Mrs. Rose Pastor Stokes, who got a ten-year sentence for writing a letter to the *Kansas City Star* saying "No government which is for the profiteers can also be for the people, and I am for the people, while the government is for the profiteers." The verdict against Mrs. Stokes was reversed in 1920. But not so fortunate was the four-time Socialist party presidential candidate, Eugene V. Debs. When he told a Socialist convention in June, 1918, that the Allies were "out for plunder" and defended the Bolshevists in Russia, he was jailed. Debs' conviction for violation of the Espionage and Sedition Acts was upheld unanimously by the Supreme Court. He received the record Socialist party presidential vote total of 920,000 while campaigning in 1920 from a federal prison, however, and was pardoned by President Harding in December, 1921.

The wartime atmosphere was favorable to restriction of civil liberties. State laws were adopted generally which contained antipacifist, anti-Red, and criminal syndicalism clauses designed to protect business and industry against radical-inspired strikes and violence. Mobs and citizens' committees took care of unpopular persons, including Americans of German ancestry. Many an American was persuaded by community pressure to buy more Liberty bonds than he desired to own. Prosecutors, juries, and judges went beyond the words of the Espionage and Sedition Acts, often because of public pressure. Zechariah Chafee, Jr., the distinguished Harvard law professor, documented the damage done to the spirit of the Constitutional guarantee of free speech in his 1920 work, *Freedom of Speech*.[11] In such circumstances the great bulk of the American press was fortunate to escape not only direct and violent censorship, but also the harassments visited upon its Socialist and German-language fringe.

[10] The AP committed a familiar journalistic blunder by adding a "no" to a La Follette statement concerning the American declaration of war, making it read "we had no grievance." An unsuccessful move to oust La Follette from the Senate resulted.

[11] Enlarged and brought up to date in his *Free Speech in the United States* (Cambridge, Mass.: Harvard University Press, 1941).

MILITARY CENSORSHIP

Censorship of foreign communications sent by cable, telephone, or telegraph, as provided in the Trading-with-the-Enemy Act, was carried out by a Censorship Board, which Wilson established in October, 1917, to coordinate control of communications facilities. The board was mainly concerned with outgoing messages and news dispatches. Its principal operations involved communications with Spain, Latin America, and the Orient. Censorship stations were established at control points along the southern borders. News filed to Europe also was checked. In some cases the censors intervened because news stories did not correctly represent the United States to the world. In a few other cases, news of labor disturbances in the United States was suppressed as detrimental to Allied morale. There were few causes for complaint against the Censorship Board, however, and it received a "job well done" commendation.[12]

American war correspondents in France found themselves freer to observe military actions of the American Expeditionary Force than those of the other Allied armies. In General Pershing's area correspondents could go into the front lines without military escorts, they could follow the fighting advances, and they could roam the rear areas, living where they chose. This had not been the case for correspondents with the British, French, and German forces in the early years of the war. But everything the correspondents wrote went through the censorship of the press section of the Military Intelligence Service, headed by Major Frederick Palmer, formerly of the Associated Press. News of general engagements, of casualties suffered, and of troop identifications was releasable only if it had been mentioned in official communiques. Press officers also were attached to the training camps and cantonments at home.

LEADING WAR CORRESPONDENTS

Notable among the early war reporting of Americans was Richard Harding Davis' story of the entry of the German army into Brussels, written for the *New York Tribune* and its syndicate, and Will Irwin's beats on the battle of Ypres and the first German use of poison gas, also printed in the *Tribune*. Irwin was one of several correspondents who represented American magazines in Europe, first writing for *Collier's* and then the *Saturday Evening Post*. However, the brunt of the news coverage responsibility fell upon the men in the European capital bureaus and those who served as military analysts. Some of the leaders were Karl H. von Wiegand of the United Press, Sigrid Schultz of

[12] James R. Mock, *Censorship 1917* (Princeton: Princeton Univrsity Press, 1941), pp. 81, 93.

the *Chicago Tribune,* and Cyril Brown of the *New York Times* in Berlin, Paul Scott Mowrer of the *Chicago Daily News* and Wythe Williams of the *New York Times* in Paris, and Edward Price Bell of the *Chicago Daily News* in London. Frank H. Simonds of the *New York Tribune* did distinguished work as a military critic.

There were some 500 American correspondents for newspapers, magazines, press associations, and syndicates in Europe by 1915 and the number was augmented when American troops joined the fighting. About 40 actually covered the actions of the AEF. Among the best-known byliners was Fred S. Ferguson of the United Press, who beat his competitors in reporting the battle of Saint-Mihiel by writing an advance story, based on the American battle plan, and having it filed section by section as the battle proceeded. Webb Miller of the United Press and Henry Wales of INS also won prominence, along with Edwin L. James of the *New York Times,* Martin Green of the *New York World,* and Junius Wood of the *Chicago Daily News.* Floyd Gibbons of the *Chicago Tribune* was hit by German machine-gun fire and lost an eye.

A soldiers' journalism also sprouted during wartime, the best-known example being the *Stars and Stripes.* The eight-page paper was established in Paris in February, 1918, and quickly became the favorite reading matter of the AEF. Its editors were given freedom of action and comment unheard of in ordinary Army circles and they filled their pages with news, editorials, features, cartoons, and advertising. Harold Ross, later editor of the *New Yorker,* became the chief editor, assisted by such well-known newspapermen as Grantland Rice and Alexander Woollcott. Other overseas units had their publications, as did all of the camps in the United States.

BETWEEN THE WARS: RED SCARE AND ISOLATIONISM

With the coming of the Armistice, coverage in Europe turned to the routine of the Army of Occupation in Germany, and to the postwar political and economic news, centering about the Versailles peace conference. In the United States a reaction set in against President Wilson's proposed League of Nations. Wilson's physical breakdown while on a nationwide speaking tour in defense of the League left the internationalist leaderless, and the assaults of the Republican Senate leader, Henry Cabot Lodge of Massachusetts, and of the tireless senatorial orators, Hiram W. Johnson of California and William E. Borah of Idaho, had their effect. The peace treaty was loaded with reservations affecting American participation in the League of Nations and the World Court to the point where the ailing Wilson refused to accept a compromise. The United States Senate failed to ratify the treaty, thereby backing out of the international association which Wilson had sponsored. As far as the newspapers and magazines were concerned, the League enjoyed a good press on the whole, right up to the end. Republican politics and Wilson's mistakes killed it.

The other major postwar reaction was a gigantic "Red scare," stimulated in part by the events of the Russian Revolution and also by the threat of the IWW movement. Attorney General A. Mitchell Palmer hustled groups of "Reds" to Ellis Island for deportation; the display of red flags was forbidden in New York and other states; the offices of the *New York Call* were raided and wrecked; Socialists were ousted from the New York state legislature and the U. S. Congress; bombings and a dynamite explosion in Wall Street added to the confusion. Many states passed "anti-Red" and criminal syndicalism laws. The conviction of Benjamin Gitlow, an obscure radical, in New York for his writings in the *Left Wing Manifesto* and *Revolutionary Age* was upheld by the Supreme Court despite the arguments of Justices Holmes and Brandeis that Gitlow offered no serious threat to the government. In general, the newspapers failed dismally to defend the civil liberties of those being questionably attacked. One of the worst records on this score was compiled by the usually stable *New York Times*. Civil liberties were best defended by the liberal magazines, led by the *New Republic* and the *Nation*, and by a few newspapers, including the *St. Louis Post-Dispatch*, *New York Globe*, and *New York World*.

Eventually the turbulence of the wartime period faded into the relatively complacent years of the 1920s. Each president after Wilson attempted to obtain American adherence to the World Court, but the Senate failed to go even that far in international cooperation. The American government did sponsor the naval limitation treaty at the Washington Conference of 1922 and cooperated in a scaling down of the German war reparations and Allied war debts. In the happy year of 1928 Secretary of State Frank B. Kellogg and French Premier Aristide Briand won solemn promises from other nations that they would outlaw war as an instrument of national policy. But then the economic and political storm which had been brewing since the end of the war broke across the world.

Soberly the American people watched the steady march of new aggressive forces, beginning with the Japanese invasion of Manchuria in 1931. Working outside the League of Nations, the American government attempted to rally world opinion against the Japanese militarists, but there was no unity of diplomatic action. Mussolini's use of his war machine in Ethiopia, Hitler's defiance of the Versailles Treaty by occupying the Rhineland and later seizing Austria, the lining up of fascist and antifascist forces in the Spanish Civil War —each episode brought disturbing headlines and debate in the United States. The disillusionment which had produced the antiwar literature of the 1930s and set the stage for neutrality legislation was slowly passing. A nation which had found new social and economic strength during the years of the New Deal stood ready once again to play its part in the new world crisis.

Isolationism died hard, however. A Senate committee headed by Gerald P. Nye of North Dakota had advanced the thesis in 1935 that American munitions makers and bankers were almost solely responsible for the country's entrance into the first World War. The neutrality legislation which followed was designed to prevent American loans or sale of war materials to belligerents, on the theory that such a ban would prevent American involvement in "foreign" wars. Even after the Munich crisis of September, 1938, and Hitler's occupation of the remainder of unhappy Czechoslovakia in March, 1939, the isolationists held the upper hand.[13]

WORLD WAR II BEGINS

The diplomatic bombshell which signaled the opening of World War II was the signing of the German-Russian neutrality pact on August 23, 1939. A week later Hitler marched on Poland and the British and French answered with declarations of war. In November, President Roosevelt obtained a revision of the Neutrality Act as the first step in a reversal of the isolationist trend. Congress repealed the embargo on sale of arms and authorized a cash-and-carry trade with the Allies.

The full nature of Hitler's aggressive designs was revealed in the spring of 1940, when Nazi armies first invaded Denmark and Norway, and then on May 10 launched a gigantic offensive against Holland, Belgium, and France. The shock of Dunkerque, the fall of France, and the opening of the Nazi air blitz against Britain in August produced strong pro-Allied sentiment in the United States. In September the Selective Service Act was passed and President Roosevelt announced the trade of 50 destroyers to Britain in return for leases on air-sea bases in the Western Hemisphere. Many American newspapers supported both actions. So did the Republican presidential candidate, Wendell Willkie, who was unsuccessful in stopping Roosevelt's third-term bid.

By now the lines had formed between isolationists and interventionists. On one side was the America First Committee, headed by General Robert E. Wood and championed by Colonel Charles A. Lindbergh, the hero of the first New York-to-Paris flight in 1927. Senators Nye and Burton K. Wheeler were on the America First side. Unfortunately for their cause, so were such assorted rabble-rousers as Father Charles E. Coughlin, Gerald L. K. Smith, William Dudley Pelley of the Silver Shirts, Fritz Kuhn of the German-American Bund, and Communists William Z. Foster and Earl Browder. On the other side was the Committee to Defend America by Aiding the Allies, led by Kansas editor William Allen White. The White group attracted many influential newspaper editors, and carried out a newspaper advertisement campaign which brought the formation of hundreds of local committees. Among the journalistic leaders

[13] One of the isolationists was historian Charles A. Beard, whose later writings attacking Roosevelt's foreign policy were ably answered in Basil Rauch, *Roosevelt from Munich to Pearl Harbor* (New York: Creative Age Press, Inc., 1950).

were columnist Joseph Alsop, radio commentator Elmer Davis, and playwright Robert E. Sherwood.

The Lend-Lease Act of March, 1941, which empowered the President to provide goods and services to those nations whose defense he deemed vital to the defense of the United States, represented a victory for the pro-Allied group. It also served to make America a nonbelligerent ally of the British. In May, 1941, President Roosevelt proclaimed an unlimited state of national emergency to facilitate the American mobilization program. In August Roosevelt met Prime Minister Winston Churchill on the high seas and the two announced their peace aims in the Atlantic Charter. The isolationists were far from beaten, however; that same month the House of Representatives continued the military draft by the narrow margin of one vote. Not until December 7, 1941, when Japanese bombs fell on Pearl Harbor, was unity for war achieved. The isolationist minority of the American press, led by the McCormick-Patterson *Chicago Tribune* and *New York Daily News* and the Hearst chain, abruptly subsided in the face of this direct enemy attack.

WARTIME CENSORSHIP AGAIN

With organization of the country for war, newspapermen recalled that the Espionage Act and Trading-with-the-Enemy Act of 1917 were still on the statute books. The more sweeping generalities of the Sedition Act had been repealed in 1921, however. Use of these acts to bar publications from the mails and to suppress free speech was more sharply limited than during World War I. Father Coughlin's *Social Justice* was discontinued after a warning from the Postmaster General. A Philadelphia German-language paper, the *Herold,* was barred from the mails. The editors of the magazine *Scribner's Commentator,* of the Rev. Gerald B. Winrod's *Defender,* and of the *New York Enquirer,* a Sunday paper, were indicted by a federal grand jury, along with publishers of a score of pro-Fascist and subversive propaganda sheets. The greatest invasion of civil liberties took place when Japanese living in the United States, including many American citizens of Japanese ancestry, were rounded up and kept in what amounted to protective custody in isolated camps during the early years of the war.

Military censorship by Navy and Army intelligence officers began on Pearl Harbor day. Within two weeks Congress passed the First War Powers Act giving the President power to establish censorship over all communications between the United States and foreign countries—by mail, cable, telegraph, telephone, wireless, and radio-telegraph and telephone. President Roosevelt immediately created the Office of Censorship to handle this assignment. He also requested its director, in a letter based upon no legislative authority, to coordinate the efforts of the American press and radio in voluntarily withhold-

EXTRA!

THIS WORLD TODAY

By ROYCE BRIER

San Francisco Chronicle

THE CITY'S ONLY HOME-OWNED NEWSPAPER

COMPARATIVE TEMPERATURES

Local Forecast: Fair

FOUNDED 1865—VOL. CLIII, NO. 146 CCCC** SAN FRANCISCO, MONDAY, DECEMBER 8, 1941 DAILY 5 CENTS, SUNDAY 10 CENTS

U.S. AT WAR!

Japan Bombs Hawaii, Manila, Invades Thailand, Malaya; 2 U.S. Battleships Claimed Sunk; FDR Talks to Congress Today!

25 YEARS AGO TODAY IN S. F. HEADLINES

LLOYD GEORGE ACCEPTS BRITISH PREMIERSHIP . . . CONVICT WALKS OUT AT SAN QUENTIN . . . SEA-TO-SEA STEAMER LINE FINANCED TO CURB RATES . . . STREET CARS HERE CARRY MORE PASSENGERS THAN IN L. A.

America at War!

EDITORIAL

By the act of Japan, America is at war. The time for debate has passed and the time for action has come. That action must be united and unanimous. "Politics is adjourned," whether between parties, factions or economic groups. From now on America is an army with every man, woman and child a soldier in it, all joined to the one end of victory.

If war had to come, it is perhaps well that it came this way, wanton, unwarned, in fraud and bad faith, virtually under a flag of truce. For in war there can be only one side in action, and now there is only one side in thought or feeling. Its slogan is, "Americans unite, for victory and freedom."

We can not know how long this war will last, how wide it will range, nor what it will cost us, in toil, in sacrifice and in treasure. We do know that whatever the cost, we will pay it, and that our reward will be to hand down to our children the free America which our fathers bequeathed to us.

Americans, unite!

U. S. Faces War: Losses May Be Heavy, Nation Warned

Without Warning, Bombs Break the Peace

350 Slain--Then Tokyo Declares War on U. S., Britain

Pacific Coast, Electrified, Springs to Wartime Alert

Air Raid Precautions Taken; Military Leaves Cancelled; Coastal Guns Manned

FDR on Air

Raids Took a Heavy Toll, Hawaii Says

INSIDE

You'll find full war coverage—news, background and pictures: See Pages A, B, C, D, E, F, G, H, 4, 5 and 6.

Chronicle News Conference Off Air for Duration

Hoover: Our Decision's Clear

Canada, Dutch Indies, Costa Rica Declare War on Japan; Wake Is Reported Taken

By the Associatd Press

Japan assaulted every main United States and British possession in the central and western Pacific and invaded Thailand today (Monday) in a hasty but evidently shrewdly-planned prosecution of a war she began Sunday without warning.

Her formal declaration of war against both the United States and Britain came two hours and 55 minutes after Japanese planes spread death and terrific destruction in Honolulu and Pearl Harbor at 7:35 a. m., Hawaiian time (10:05 a. m., San Francisco) Sunday.

FDR Talks to Nation

Today at 9:30 a. m. San Francisco time, President Roosevelt will address a joint session of Congress and a declaration of war by the United States against Japan is expected. The speech will be carried on all major radio networks.

The claimed successes for this fell swoop include sinking of the U. S. battleship West Virginia and setting afire of the battleship Oklahoma.

From that moment, each tense tick of the clock brought new and flaming accounts of Japanese aggression in her secretly launched war of conquest or death for the land of the rising sun.

Japanese Surprise Attacks

As compiled from official and unofficial accounts from all affected countries, the record ran like this.

Big type announced the coming of World War II to America at Pearl Harbor.

ing from publication military and other information of value to the enemy. Thus the patterns of censorship which were developed in World War I were reinstated for World War II.

BYRON PRICE'S OFFICE OF CENSORSHIP

Byron Price, executive news editor of the Associated Press and long a Washington newsman, was named director of the Office of Censorship. Probably no other man could have held the respect and confidence of newspapermen everywhere better than Price, who was temperamentally and intellectually equipped to handle the most difficult part of his job—the direction of the voluntary press censorship. He brought into his organization a score of seasoned newspapermen to handle press relationships, headed by John H. Sorrells, executive editor of the Scripps-Howard newspapers, and Nat R. Howard, editor of the *Cleveland News*.[14]

A *Code of Wartime Practices for the American Press* was issued on January 15, 1942. It carefully outlined to those who published newspapers, magazines, books, and other printed materials what would constitute improper handling of news having to do with troops, planes, ships, war production, armaments, military installations, and weather. Similar instructions were given radio stations. The code became a Bible for American newsmen, who usually erred in the direction of oversuppression of news possibly harmful to the war effort.

Several outstanding successes were chalked up to the credit of newspaper and radio men and the Office of Censorship. No hint of the successful development of the atomic bomb was published or broadcast despite the enormous activities preceding the trial explosion in New Mexico and its first use at Hiroshima. The secrets of radar and the proximity fuse likewise were protected. Details of the massing of troops in Britain for the D-Day invasion were kept from the Germans. Editors and broadcasters loyally refrained from mentioning cross-country trips by President Roosevelt even though thousands of their readers and listeners were aware that the President had been in their locality.

Throughout the war, Price rarely had to do more than softly remind violators of the voluntary press and radio censorships that they were being forgetful of their own best interests and those of the country to win renewed efforts to comply. He in turn was awarded a special Pulitzer Prize citation for his work and received genuine congratulations from the country's newsmen when he closed down the Office of Censorship at the end of the war, and became an official of the United Nations Secretariat.

[14] The activities of the Office of Censorship and the work of other individuals are described by Theodore F. Koop, an Associated Press man and assistant to Price, in *Weapon of Silence* (Chicago: University of Chicago Press, 1946). Sorrells, Howard, managing editor Jack Lockhart of the *Memphis Commercial Appeal,* and Koop were successive heads of the voluntary press censorship division. J. Howard Ryan directed the radio division.

Most of the 14,462 persons in the Office of Censorship were engaged in the mandatory censorship of mail, cables, and radio communications between the United States and other countries. Price's Office of Censorship in World War II thus combined the World War I operations of the Censorship Board and the voluntary press censorship portion of George Creel's work. Price, however, had nothing to do with the originating of news or with the government's propaganda effort. Those aspects of the work of the World War I Committee on Public Information were handled during World War II by a separate agency.

ELMER DAVIS AND THE OFFICE OF WAR INFORMATION

This was the Office of War Information, established by an executive order of the President in June, 1942, to supersede four earlier government agencies. One of the original agencies had been the Office of Government Reports, headed by Lowell Mellett, which operated a clipping service, handled queries from the public concerning governmental activities, and coordinated the making of films by the government. Another was the Office of Facts and Figures, charged with correlating information about defense and foreign policies, and directed by poet Archibald MacLeish, Librarian of Congress. The third was the Division of Information in the Office of Emergency Management, headed by Robert Horton, which handled news of the war agencies. The fourth was the Office of the Coordinator of Information, established to collect and analyze all information bearing upon national security. Its foreign information section, which became a part of the OWI, was headed by Robert E. Sherwood. The remainder of the OCI, headed by William J. Donovan, became the Office of Strategic Services.

The Office of Government Reports was established in 1939, and the other three agencies in 1941, prior to American entry into the war. Work of the four agencies overlapped and there was dissatisfaction on the part of the press with some of the performances of the agencies. This led President Roosevelt to create the OWI. The President made a wise choice in the person of Elmer Davis as director.

Davis, like Price, was a veteran newsman. He had served on the *New York Times* staff for 10 years and had been a news analyst and commentator for the Columbia Broadcasting System prior to his appointment. For his work with CBS, and after the war with the American Broadcasting Company, he three times won radio's Peabody award for radio news reporting and interpretation. A highly capable and conscientious newsman, Davis declared that the OWI would do its best to tell the truth and nothing but the truth, both at home and abroad.

"It is the job of OWI," Davis said, "not only to tell the American people how the war is going, but where it is going and where it came from—its nature and origins, how our government is conducting it, and what (besides national survival) our government hopes to get out of victory."[15] This concept of the total function of OWI also was applied to its work abroad.

One function of the OWI was to act as a city desk for the nation's war news. Government departments and war agencies continued to handle approximately 40 per cent of government publicity stories without reference to OWI. But those news releases relating significantly to the war effort or dealing with activities affecting more than one government agency had to pass through the OWI News Bureau. OWI thus was enabled to keep news flowing from the government agencies, to represent the interests of the press and of its readers in disputes with officials over what should or should not be said, to discourage official inclination to hide bad news and overplay good news, and to coordinate information given it by different agencies and put the news into proper perspective. OWI did not always win in its struggles with bureaucracy, but it succeeded in untangling poor news coverage situations far more often than it lost. The OWI also cooperated with the War and Navy Departments in handling military news, and the Army and Navy were required to consult with Davis about withholding of specific military information. The services, however, retained final authority over such withholding of news and Davis did not often win arguments with them. As a result, Davis took a steady drumming of criticism from those suspicious of any information agency.

Davis had as his associate director Milton Eisenhower, brother of the general and a trained public official. Gardner Cowles, Jr., publisher of the *Des Moines Register* and *Tribune* and *Look* magazine, became director of domestic operations, being succeeded by Palmer Hoyt, publisher of the Portland *Oregonian.* George H. Lyon, former editor of the *Buffalo Times* and managing editor of *PM,* headed the News Bureau, most important subdivision of the domestic section.

The News Bureau operated on a million-dollar annual budget, with 250 regular employes. Three hundred reporters and correspondents used its facilities, including some 50 reporters working full time in the OWI pressroom. Copy flowed from the general news desk, where policy decisions were made, to the domestic and foreign news desks, the radio news desk, the picture desk, and the feature desk. Cartoons, pictures, features, weekly digests, and fillers became a part of the OWI offering. Background information concerning desired propaganda and informational objectives of the government was given to editorial writers, cartoonists, and columnists.

[15] Elmer Davis, "OWI Has a Job," *Public Opinion Quarterly,* VII (Spring 1943), 8. For Davis' account of his stewardship, see *Report to the President* (*Journalism Monographs,* No. 7, August 1968), edited by Ronald T. Farrar. Also see Robert L. Bishop and LaMar S. Mackay, *Government Information in World War II* (*Journalism Monographs,* No. 19, May 1971).

The OWI domestic section had several other bureaus. One handled the preparation of copy for use by radio stations, and worked with radio commentators and analysts. Another supervised the making of motion pictures by the government. There was a bureau of publications and graphics, although domestic use of pamphlets was restricted. A bureau of intelligence engaged in audience research, analyzed basic public attitudes, and surveyed the contents of communications media. The division of campaigns directed appeals in behalf of war bond sales, salvage drives, fuel conservation, and victory gardens. In this work the OWI had the cooperation of the War Advertising Council and the nation's publishers. The government paid for recruiting advertising, but all other war-related newspaper, magazine, radio, and billboard advertising space was donated by the media or by national and local advertisers.

THE OWI OVERSEAS

Overseas operations of the OWI were directed by Robert E. Sherwood, with Joseph Barnes, foreign editor of the *New York Herald Tribune,* being deputy director for the important Atlantic area. The overseas news and propaganda programs of the OWI were far more extensive than Creel's work in World War I, particularly because of the availability of radio communication for what became known as the Voice of America. OWI cooperation with the military in the development of psychological warfare techniques also was an advance over World War I methods.

The overseas section received up to 30,000 words a day of teletyped news from the OWI domestic News Bureau. The overseas offices in New York and San Francisco also used the news reports of the press associations, radio networks, and OWI's own regional offices. At its height of activity in 1943, the overseas news and features bureau, headed by Edward Barrett, cabled 65,000 words daily to all parts of the world, mailed hundreds of thousands of words of feature material, and airmailed or radioed 2,500 pictures.[16]

OWI was given a 36-million-dollar budget in 1943, of which 27 million dollars was allotted for overseas operations. Two-thirds of that sum went for radio operations, mainly the Voice of America, but it also covered programs for military and civilian personnel overseas. When the war began, the United States was making one radio broadcast a day, over the British Broadcasting Corporation's facilities. At the end of 1942 there were 21 American-run short-wave transmitters, beaming 2,700 programs a week to Europe and Africa alone in 24 different languages. The number of transmitters was increased to 39 before the end of the war and the Voice of America was beamed increasingly into Asia.

[16] OWI operated everywhere abroad except in Latin America, where Nelson Rockefeller's Office of the Coordinator of Inter-American Affairs held jurisdiction.

MILITARY CENSORSHIP

Military censorship for World War II picked up where it had left off at the end of World War I, with the added problem of controlling radio broadcasts. In the early months of the war British censorship was blundering and severe, and it remained tight even after the Ministry of Information became better organized. Nazi Germany was not so badly handicapped by Allied control of cables during World War II, since wireless and radio facilities were available. The Nazis did not censor foreign correspondents before publication, but if they sent stories which Dr. Joseph Goebbels' Ministry of Propaganda did not like, they were subject to expulsion from Germany. Two victims of this policy in the first few months of World War II were Beach Conger of the *New York Herald Tribune* and Otto D. Tolischus of the *New York Times.* Edgar Ansel Mowrer of the *Chicago Daily News* was compelled to leave by reason of threats against his person.

As the war developed newsmen found the British Admiralty and the U. S. Navy Department most prone to suppressing news of war actions. The American Navy withheld details of the Pearl Harbor disaster, and of the sinkings of ships in the Pacific, for long periods of time on the plea that the Japanese should not be given vital information on a confirmed basis. Newsmen grumbled, however, that evidence of inefficient naval operations also was being kept back. The British censorship in Egypt, conflicting British and American censorships in the India-Burma theater, the Chinese censorship in Chungking, and General Douglas MacArthur's censorship in the Pacific also drew heavy fire from correspondents and editors. Many newsmen said MacArthur's information officers insisted unduly upon personal glorification of the commander. Techniques used by General Dwight D. Eisenhower in Europe were, on the other hand, considered generally satisfactory.

PRESS AND RADIO COVER THE WAR

Coverage of World War II by the American press and radio was considered by most observers to be the best and fullest the world had ever seen. A great share of the credit for this achievement went to the overseas and war front correspondents for press associations, newspapers, magazines, and radio. As many as 500 full-time American correspondents were abroad at one time. Altogether the U. S. armed forces accredited 1,646 different persons. The biggest staffs were those of the press associations and radio networks; the *Times* and *Herald Tribune* in New York; the *Daily News, Tribune,* and *Sun* in Chicago; the *Christian Science Monitor, Baltimore Sun,* and *Time, Life,* and *Newsweek.*

Of the 37 American newsmen who lost their lives during the war, 11 were press association correspondents, 10 were representing individual newspapers, nine were magazine correspondents, four were photographers, two were syndicated writers, and one was a radio correspondent.

One of the early standouts among American correspondents was the veteran Leland Stowe of the *Chicago Daily News*, who reported the Russo-Finnish War and the Nazi invasion of Norway, and who was the first American to reach the Nazi-Soviet front lines after Hitler's invasion of Russia. Webb Miller of the United States covered his eleventh war in Finland, then returned to London to be killed in a blackout accident. Frazier Hunt of International News Service and Marcel W. Fodor of the *Chicago Daily News* filed notable accounts of the French retreat in 1940. On the other side, with Hitler's triumphant army, were Louis P. Lochner of the AP, Pierre J. Huss of INS, and Frederick C. Oechsner of UP.

There were many distinguished examples of war correspondence, and many personal stories of performance in the face of danger by newsmen. Pulitzer Prizes went to Larry Allen of the AP for his exploits with the British Mediterranean fleet; to Hal Boyle and Daniel De Luce of the AP European staff; to military analyst Hanson W. Baldwin of the *New York Times* and Ira Wolfert of the North American Newspaper Alliance; to Mark S. Watson of the *Baltimore Sun* and Homer Bigart of the *New York Herald Tribune;* to AP war photographers Frank Noel, Frank Filan, and Joe Rosenthal; and to Ernie Pyle of the Scripps-Howard Newspaper Alliance. Clark Lee of the Associated Press and Melville Jacoby of *Time* were among the newsmen who shared the dangers of the Bataan evacuation; Jacoby died later in a plane crash but Lee survived to become an INS byline writer. Among other leading war reporters were Vern Haugland and Wes Gallagher of the AP, Quentin Reynolds of *Collier's*, Edward W. Beattie and Henry T. Gorrell of the UP, James Kilgallen and Richard Tregaskis of INS, Drew Middleton of the *New York Times*, and Russell Hill of the *Herald Tribune*.

World War II had its women correspondents. The INS sent its featured writer, Inez Robb, to North Africa and Europe. Three other INS women war correspondents were Lee Carson, with the U. S. First Army, Dixie Tighe with the British, and Rita Hume in Italy. Among the United Press women correspondents were Eleanor Packard and Dudley Anne Harmon, while the AP had Ruth Cowan and Bonnie Wiley in the field. Other correspondents were Helen Kirkpatrick, *Chicago Daily News;* Peggy Hull (Mrs. Harvey Deuel) of the *Cleveland Plain Dealer*, who served in World War I; Margaret Bourke-White, photographer for *Time* and *Life;* Iris Carpenter, *Boston Globe;* and Leah Burdette of *PM*, who lost her life in Iran.

Such radio voices as those of William L. Shirer from Berlin and Edward R. Murrow from London for the Columbia Broadcasting System, and that of the National Broadcasting Company's H. V. Kaltenborn, brought the war close to

American homes. Bill Henry of CBS and Arthur Mann of Mutual became the first front-line radio reporters in the fall of 1939. Development of mobile units and use of tape recordings soon brought greatly increased radio coverage. Direct reports came from battlefields, from bombers flying over Berlin and Tokyo, and other centers of action. Radiomen covered D-Day brilliantly, with George Hicks of the American Broadcasting Company doing an outstanding broadcast from a landing barge under German fire. Wright Bryan of the *Atlanta Journal* gave NBC and CBS the first eyewitness account from the cross-channel front by flying over with a planeload of paratroopers.

Usually acclaimed as the greatest reporter of the second World War was the columnist friend of the G.I., Ernest Taylor Pyle. Pyle had won attention before the war for his personal notes on life in the United States, as observed in his wanderings across the country. In 1940 he told his readers what the people of Britain felt as they resisted the Nazi air blitz. Then he attached himself to the American army, writing in a home-town style of the intimate daily life of the G.I. in Ireland, North Africa, Sicily, Italy, and France. His column for Scripps-Howard and his *Here Is Your War* and *Brave Men* won him a national reputation and a Pulitzer Prize. Pyle left Europe in 1944, but after a rest he flew out to cover the final stages of the Pacific war. When a Japanese sniper killed Ernie Pyle on Ie Shima during the Okinawa campaign of April, 1945, the saga of a great American war correspondent came to a close.

Editor & Publisher

ERNIE PYLE

There was a soldiers' journalism again in World War II. The *Stars and Stripes* reappeared as the leading G.I. newspaper in 1942 and eventually had European and Pacific editions. *Yank*, a magazine with 22 editions, gained a circulation of 2½ millions. The resentments of the enlisted man were portrayed in the *Stars and Stripes* by cartoonist Bill Mauldin, while Sgt. George Baker's "Sad Sack" and Milton Caniff's sexy "Male Call" ran in both publications. Almost every major unit and camp had its own publication. And unlike World War I, the services developed extensive public relations units, of which combat correspondents of the Marine Corps were most effective. Sergeant Jim G. Lucas of the Marines, formerly of the *Tulsa Tribune* staff, wrote one of the outstanding eyewitness stories of the war for American newspapers from the beach at Tarawa.

Coverage of World War II ended in Europe with the confusion of the Edward Kennedy case. Kennedy, Associated Press chief on the western front, was one of 16 Allied newsmen taken to the military headquarters in Reims to witness the German surrender. All were pledged not to release their stories until an officially prescribed time. Kennedy, angered by the news that the German radio was announcing the surrender in advance of the time set by American, British, and Russian political leaders, made an unauthorized telephone call to London and dictated part of his story for transmission. The AP thus had the official story of the German surrender a day in advance of V-E day. But Kennedy's 54 colleagues in Paris charged him with committing "the most disgraceful, deliberate, and unethical double cross in the history of journalism." Kennedy defended his action as necessary to counteract a needless political censorship, and eventually won reinstatement as a war correspondent a year after his suspension. But the AP disassociated itself from its stormy petrel, and he left its service in 1946.

POST-WAR: USIA AND THE VOICE OF AMERICA

The year 1945 brought hope to the world, with the defeat of the German and Japanese war machines, and the founding of the United Nations. But the failure of the Soviet Union and the United States to adjust to each other in the postwar era quickly renewed the feeling of tension and uncertainty which the world had endured since the early 1930s. Newsmen found barriers to the collection of news being erected higher than ever before, and the phrase "Iron Curtain" became a familiar one.

Realizing it had to work actively to tell the story of the free democracies to the world, the United States government continued to conduct international propaganda on a worldwide scale as initiated by the Office of War Information in 1942. The first such peacetime operation was the Office of International Information and Cultural Affairs, established within the State Department in 1945 with William Benton as head. In 1948, under the Smith-Mundt Act, the functions were split into an Office of International Information, headed by George V. Allen (later by Edward W. Barrett), and an Office of Cultural Exchange to handle exchange of scholars and students. But the annual budget was a third of OWI's, a mere 12 million dollars.

As the Soviet Union consolidated its grip on the satellite states of eastern Europe and attempted the 1948 Berlin blockade, and with the opening of the Korean War in 1950, Congressional appropriations rose swiftly. By 1952 the revamped International Information Administration, headed by Wilson Compton, had 87 million dollars, 25 per cent for the Voice of America.

Creation of an autonomous United States Information Agency in 1953 gave stability to the program. Its annual budget was stabilized at well over 100 million dollars. The Voice of America in 1970 was heard in 40 languages over 92 transmitters by an estimated audience of 43 million. The overseas United States Information Service was operating information libraries and reading rooms in 70 countries, and was distributing news services, motion pictures, magazines, and pamphlets. The policy and planning and the research and assessment sections were involved in the country's foreign policy making, but not enough to satisfy many of the staff. During the 1950s and 1960s there was a running duel between the professionals who viewed USIA and the Voice as agencies for "tell it like it is" journalism, properly interpreting U. S. involvement in news events, and officials who wished the agencies to reflect their image of how the world should respond to current U. S. policy, and who wished to minimize news in conflict with such an image. Increasing White House concern with the war in Indochina polarized the debate after 1965.

USIA heads during the Eisenhower administration were Arthur Larson and George V. Allen. Appointment by President Kennedy of broadcaster Edward R. Murrow in 1961 brought support for professionalism in the Voice of America program, which had been badly damaged by inept propaganda during the abortive 1956 uprising in Budapest. Educational and cultural activities were also added to USIA in 1961. Murrow's ill health brought his resignation in January, 1964, and appointment by President Johnson of Carl T. Rowan, Negro newspaperman, as director. When Rowan resigned in mid-1965, his successor was Texas lawyer Leonard H. Marks. John Chancellor and John Charles Daly gave the Voice of America professional leadership from 1965 to 1968, but Daly resigned in 1968 after a battle with Marks over the Voice's integrity. Their successors were Frank Shakespeare as USIA director and Kenneth R. Giddens as head of the Voice of America.[17]

THE WAR IN KOREA, 1950–53

The news of the Communist North Korean attack upon the Republic of South Korea on June 25, 1950, was first flashed to the world by Jack James of the United Press. Headed for a Sunday morning picnic, he stumbled onto

[17] For an account of USIA from 1948 to 1960 see Wilson P. Dizard, *The Strategy of Truth* (Washington: Public Affairs Press, 1960). Analysis of ups-and-downs is given in Ronald I. Rubin, *The Objectives of the U. S. Information Agency: Controversies and Analysis* (New York: Praeger, 1968).

the invasion story at the U.S. embassy in Seoul and after confirming it got off his bulletin, which beat the ambassador's cable to Washington by 20 minutes.

Korea had been divided at the 38th parallel for occupation purposes in 1945. Russian troops left North Korea after establishment of a government there in 1948 and Americans left South Korea, save for a small advisory force, early in 1949. No one expected an attack in Korea; State Department representative John Foster Dulles had been in Seoul a week before and had left reassured of the area's stability. The bad news which James and others sent by wireless brought a decision by Secretary of State Dean Acheson and President Truman to seek a United Nations armed intervention, which was voted by the Security Council June 28 after Truman had ordered General Douglas MacArthur to force the North Koreans back.

Walter Simmons of the *Chicago Tribune,* who had traveled to Seoul with Dulles, had stayed on and filed the first action story by a newspaper correspondent. The press associations rushed in Peter Kalischer and Rutherford Poats, UPI; O.H.P. King and photographer Charles P. Gorry, AP; and Ray Richards, INS. Richards was first to fly over the battle area; caught with a lost battalion at Chonan, he was killed 10 days after his arrival. Six American newsmen were killed in the first confused month of fighting and four more before the war was over, among a total of 17 from all nations.[18]

Two of the toughest and most outspoken stars of the Korean news brigade flew to Seoul June 17 from Tokyo under fighter escort. They were Marguerite Higgins of the *New York Herald Tribune* and Keyes Beech of the *Chicago Daily News.*[19] Landing with them at Kimpo airfield were Burton Crane of the *New York Times* and Frank Gibney of *Time.* They were routed from the city during the night as Seoul fell; the men missed death by 25 yards at the River Han and Higgins (she used no "miss") flew back to Tokyo to file her story. She returned June 29 with General MacArthur on his first visit to the front and got an exclusive interview on the return trip. Next day she, Beech, Tom Lambert of the AP, and Gordon Walker of the *Christian Science Monitor* were at the fall of Suwon airfield. With Carl Mydans of *Life* and the bureau chief of Reuters, Ray McCartney, Higgins saw the first U.S. soldier killed in action July 5. David Douglas Duncan of *Life* was taking the first of his great Korean war photographs and *Life's* July 10 issue brought home the war to a country not yet linked by television.

[18] Four of the dead were INS—Richards and Frank Emery, correspondents, and Charles D. Rosecrans, Jr., Ken Inouye, photographers. Eight of the total of 17 died in front-line fighting, nine in air crashes. Among them were Wilson Fielder, *Time-Life;* Charles O. Supple, *Chicago Sun-Times;* and Albert Hinton, *Norfolk Journal and Guide,* first black correspondent to lose his life covering a U.S. war.

[19] For an evaluation and account of the early weeks of the war coverage see Michael C. Emery, "The American Mass Media and the Coverage of Five Major Foreign Events, 1900–1950," Ph.D. thesis, University of Minnesota, 1968, pp. 316–72.

NEW YORK
Herald Tribune
A European Edition Is Published Daily in Paris
Late City Edition
MONDAY, JULY 3, 1950
FIVE CENTS

U. S. Troops Face Battle in Korea Today; 4 Red Columns Breach Han River Line

Ships Collide At Night; 35 Saved in Bay
11,000-Ton Collier Rams Sand Dredge
Latter Goes Down in 10 Minutes; Crew Rescued in Spite of Heavy Tide

A Spinster's Counsel to Wives: Get a Job, Help Support Family
Dr. Scott Says Husbands Die Early by Overwork for Economic Parasites

U.S. Warships Sink Korean Navy Vessels
British Help to Bag Five Torpedo Boats
U.S. Troops Deploying to Front; MacArthur Puts Gen. Dean in Command

First American Infantry in Korea

Felled Plane Has Russian Red Insigne
4 Others in Battle Carry Soviets' Star
Red Tank Columns Sweep Past Suwon; Situation Is 'Seriously Worsened'

'Free Europe' To Broadcast to Red Satellites
Radio at Undisclosed Spot to Supplement Messages of the Voice of America

Moscow Protest On Potato Bugs Alarms Berlin

Union Rejects U.S. War Plea to End Rail Strike

First American Casualty List

His 1897 Baseball At Hand, Man Dies

First Partial Mobilization Step In U.S. May Be Taken This Week
Move Envisaged as Preparation for Any Soviet Action; Call for Volunteer Reserves Possible

In and Out of the City on the Holiday Week End

Troop Planes Circle 6 Hours Over Korea

The Korean War opens for U.S. troops; Marguerite Higgins and Homer Bigart report.

The South Koreans and their American reinforcements were being forced back upon the beachhead port of Pusan. Its outer defense, Taejon, fell in late July and General William P. Dean was captured. By now many more newsmen were risking their lives in the foxholes, rice paddies, and back roads. The *Herald Tribune* sent Homer Bigart to relieve Higgins but she refused to leave Korea and engaged in a give-and-take duel with Bigart for front-page play. The Associated Press sent Relman Morin, Don Whitehead, and Hal Boyle, all veteran war reporters. Fred Sparks came to work with Keyes Beech for the *Chicago Daily News*. When the Pulitzer Prize committee met the following April they honored the *Herald Tribune*, the *Daily News*, and the AP by giving six awards to Bigart and Higgins, Beech and Sparks, Morin and Whitehead. (At that point in time, no one from UP or INS had ever won a Pulitzer Prize.)

Editor & Publisher

MARGUERITE HIGGINS

Behind the correspondents at the front were the bureau chiefs in Tokyo, Earnest Hoberecht of UP, Russell Brines of AP, Howard Handleman of INS, and William H. Lawrence coordinating for the *New York Times.* Edward R. Murrow came to tie CBS coverage together; broadcast coverage essentially was by radio, with film being shot for television and news reels.

Instead of being driven off the Korean beachhead, MacArthur mounted a brilliant amphibious landing with troops from Japan at Inchon September 15 and recaptured Seoul September 26, cutting off the North Koreans to the south. One of the correspondents present was Jim G. Lucas, the chronicler of Tarawa, now reporting for Scripps-Howard. Lucas was to win a 1954 Pulitzer Prize for his stories of "Porkchop Hill" during the long stalemate. Another Pulitzer award went to Max Desfor, AP photographer.

General MacArthur, as United Nations commander in Korea, at first left correspondents to their own devices, refusing to institute the field censorship which had prevailed during both World War I and II. In the confused situation of the first months of the fighting, the press and radio men found themselves on their own in the thick of battle. They also found themselves subject to criticism for the stories they filed without benefit of adequate military supervision and censorship. Lambert of AP and Kalischer of UP temporarily lost their accreditations on charges of giving aid and comfort to the enemy. Relations between Colonel Marion P. Echols, MacArthur's press officer, and the newsmen became even more strained than they had been during the years of the occupation of Japan, when dissenting reporters had found their accreditations endangered.

The September, 1950, victories following MacArthur's Inchon landing brought an easing of the correspondents' problems. Their interviews with critical and despondent soldiers, which had aroused MacArthur's ire earlier in the summer, were at an end. Nearly 300 correspondents from 19 countries were reporting the advance of United Nations troops to the Yalu. Then came the entry of the Chinese Communist army into the war and a disastrous retreat of the UN's units, best pictured by *Life's* Duncan, with the Marines at Chosin reservoir. Seoul fell to the Chinese in January but was regained two months later as the UN forces stabilized a line near the 38th parallel. Keyes Beech had reported that at the height of the retreat panic MacArthur had recommended withdrawal from Korea, and other correspondents had criticised MacArthur's tactics in splitting the commands of his forces in northern Korea. The general's answer was the institution of a full and formal censorship, which he claimed had been recommended by the country's top newspaper executives.[20]

Stringent regulations imposed in January, 1951, went further, however, than any newsman would have desired.[21] They covered not only censorship of military information but of all statements which would injure the morale of UN forces or which would embarrass the United States, its allies, or neutral countries. Correspondents complained that use of the word "retreat" was interpreted by the censors as being embarrassing, and they contended that MacArthur had brought about a political and psychological censorship, as well as a military one. The most dangerous provision of the new censorship was one making correspondents subject to trial by court-martial for serious violations of the rules.

The removal of MacArthur from the Korean command in April for insubordination by President Truman brought another easing of the censorship situation, although his chief intelligence officer, Major General C. A. Willoughby, continued to attack such respected reporters as Hal Boyle, Hanson W. Baldwin, Homer Bigart, and Joseph Alsop as 'inaccurate, biased, and petulant." When truce negotiations began in Korea in July, 1951, the United Nations Command insisted that newsmen be permitted to cover the truce site. Reporting of the war during the prolonged negotiations became a routine affair, punctuated by excitement over the status of prisoners of war. The Defense Department issued new field censorship instructions in December, 1952, which transferred censorship duties from intelligence officers to public relations officers, and put the Army, Navy, and Air Force under a uniform plan. Censorship for reasons other than those involving security was forbidden, but as usual the differing between newsmen and censors about a definition of "security" continued to the end.

Signing of a truce at Panmunjom in July, 1953, brought an end to the fighting phase of the Korean War. The repatriated prisoners, whose fate had been such an issue, reappeared at the "Bridge of No Return." In the early 1970s the UN Command, through U.S. troops, still stood guard at Panmunjom. No peace had yet been signed. The war had cost 33,629 U.S. dead, 1,263 other UN allied dead, some 2 million Korean casualties, and several hundred thousand Chinese losses. The principle involved, that the will of the United Nations could not be openly flaunted, had been defended. But one view held it had been de-

[20] In a letter to *Editor & Publisher,* LXXXIV (January 20, 1951), 7.

[21] Text of the censorship code was carried in *Editor & Publisher,* LXXXIV (January 13, 1951), 8.

fended by the first recapture of Seoul and that MacArthur's advance to the Yalu River boundary of Communist China had changed the character of the war and had polarized Chinese-American relations for decades to come. Whatever the reason, U.S. newsmen did not again see Peking until 1971.

A DECADE OF ALARMS

Disillusionment ran deep in the United States of the early 1950s. A Cold War, rather than eternal peace, had followed World War II and Joseph Stalin had proved to be a treacherous ally by his actions in Hungary, in Czechoslovakia, and in blockading Berlin. The American monopoly of the atom bomb secret had been short-lived, and most Americans believed the Soviets would not have developed atomic capability without the aid of treacherous Americans and Soviet spies (the Rosenbergs were executed on this premise); the astounding proof of Soviet scientific capability, by being first in space, was not to come until their 1957 Sputnik launching. The Korean War had been a frustrating draw, and many viewed it as a defeat. Senator Joseph McCarthy of Wisconsin had been charging treason against various officials since 1950 with unbroken success.

President Eisenhower's election, and his ability to get a truce in Korea within six months, brought some relaxation. Stalin's death in 1953 brought more. The long French effort in Indochina came to an end at Dienbienphu in 1954 and a Geneva conference made arrangements for peace in Vietnam and Laos. Senator McCarthy overstepped himself by charging the Army with treason and was censured by his colleagues by a vote of 67–22. The Big Four met once again at Geneva in 1955 and Eisenhower and the Russians talked cordially.

But the brief thaw, highlighted by Nikita Khrushchev's "secret" anti-Stalin speech in February, 1956, came to an end later that year when Poland and Hungary became restive. Soviet tanks crushed a revolt in Budapest that had won the sympathy of the world but not its active support. Of the newsmen there, Russell Jones won UP's first Pulitzer Prize for his reporting. A team of INS-Hearst stars led by William Randolph Hearst, Jr., had won their first a year earlier for interviews behind the Iron Curtain.

War correspondents rushed to the Middle East in 1956 when Israel, threatened since it became an independent state in 1948, attacked Egypt by land while Britain and France sought to occupy the Suez Canal. Eisenhower and State Secretary Dulles refused to support their allies and forced a UN peacekeeping arrangement. The debacle brought down the government of Anthony Eden and hastened the crisis in France over Algerian independence, and the rise of General De Gaulle to power in 1958. The standoff between Israel and Egypt resulted in the six-day war of 1967, won by Israeli planes and tanks before correspondents could catch their breaths. Ted Yates, an NBC producer, and Paul Schutzer, *Life* photographer, were U.S. casualties in the blitz war.

War broke out in the Congo in 1960 and was covered by a small band of newsmen. Two, Henry N. Taylor of Scripps-Howard and George Clay of NBC, were shot and killed; Sanche de Gramont of the *New York Herald Tribune* was injured. Lynn Heinzerling of the Associated Press won a Pulitzer Prize for his reporting. Ray Wilson of NBC had to eat his UN press pass to appease some Congolese soldiers.

The visit of Premier Khrushchev to the United States in 1959 seemed to follow in the "thaw" pattern, but major confrontations now arose between the U.S. and the Soviets. The U-2 spy plane incident undermined Khrushchev at home and forced him to break up the Summit Conference held in Paris in May, 1960, with more than 3,000 newsmen present for the never-held sessions between Eisenhower, De Gaulle, Macmillan, and Khrushchev. The abortive effort to overthrow the Castro government in Cuba, resulting in the 1961 "Bay of Pigs," put President Kennedy's administration on the defensive. The Berlin Wall crisis later in the year brought a small-scale U.S. mobilization. The air was cleared by the Cuban missile crisis of mid-October 1962, which brought the world to the verge of nuclear war before Khrushchev withdrew Soviet missiles from Cuba upon receiving Kennedy's pledge the United States would not again attempt to overthrow the Castro government. In 1963 the nuclear test ban treaty gave the Kennedy administration its first major triumph in forwarding U.S.-Soviet agreements. At that point, President Kennedy was assassinated and Khrushchev was shortly ousted from power.

And at that moment the focus of American attention became Indochina. There a small American press corps was already vainly warning that U.S. policy was leading to war, not peace. But the relentless grinding of the glacier called the Cold War could not be stopped.

THE QUAGMIRE IN VIETNAM

Robert Capa, the Hungarian-born photographer who was world-renowned for his graphic pictures of the Spanish Civil War and the Normandy invasion beaches, was the first American journalist to die in Vietnam. He stepped on a land mine while photographing for Magnum in 1954, the year the French extricated themselves from the Indochina quagmire by surrendering at Dienbienphu. They watched as the Americans then took their places in the quagmire that swallowed up one President and threatened another.[22]

The American phase of the 25-year struggle in Indochina—in Vietnam, in Cambodia, in Laos—became perhaps the most thoroughly covered war in

[22] *The Making of a Quagmire,* by David Halberstam (New York: Random House, 1965), sets this tone. Halberstam was the Pulitzer Prize-winning correspondent of the *New York Times* in Vietnam who forecast the tragedy.

history. Certainly it caused more moral searching than ever before, and by 1971 it seemed possible that it represented the final gasp of the Cold War mentality and an ebbing of the spirit of manifest destiny. Much credit should accrue to the print and broadcast correspondents and photographers covering the war, including the 51 more who were to die by 1971, as well as to those who clarified the issues through their dissent at home.

Vietnam's national hero, Ho Chi Minh, proclaimed a Democratic Republic of Vietnam at Hanoi in 1945, in the wake of the Japanese surrender. But by 1946 the French who had returned to Saigon were engaged in hostilities with Ho's Viet Minh. Ex-emperor Bao Dai was installed in 1948 as chief of state in Saigon by the French, who then obtained financial aid from the United States in 1950 at the time of the Korean crisis. But they later were denied military aid by President Eisenhower, despite the imminence of Dienbienphu. The Geneva agreements of 1954 ending hostilities provided for a partitioning of Vietnam at the 17th parallel and reunification through national elections in 1956. The Bao Dai government did not sign the agreement or honor it; the United States created the SEATO alliance and included South Vietnam in the protected areas. Premier Ngo Dinh Diem ousted Bao Dai, refused to allow the elections, and obtained the help of the U.S. Military Assistance Advisory Group to train his army beginning in 1955. His opposition in South Vietnam formed the National Liberation Front and its guerrilla force, the Viet Cong.

By 1960 there were 686 U.S. military advisers, a figure raised to 3,200 at the close of President Kennedy's first year in office (1961) as insurgency grew. Diem, his sister-in-law Mme. Nhu, and the ruling Catholic party became increasingly oppressive. The Buddhist uprisings of 1963 in Saigon and Hue, and countryside insurgency, brought a November coup and the death of Diem. The American supporters, now transformed into a U.S. Military Assistance Command with 16,300 men, took over military affairs as 10 Saigon governments came and went in the next 18 months. A new President also was entering the White House three weeks after the Saigon coup.

THE SAIGON PRESS CORPS FORMS

The Saigon press corps already had distinguished itself by the time of Diem's downfall. Three who became the leaders in pointing out the quagmire's dangers were Malcolm Browne, who came to Vietnam in November, 1961, for the Associated Press; Neil Sheehan, who came in April, 1962, for the United Press International; and David Halberstam, who joined them in May for the *New York Times.* François Sully, the Frenchman who had covered Dienbienphu and who stayed on to interpret the war for *Newsweek* and others until he died in Cambodia in 1971, was expelled by Diem in 1962 and could not return until his overthrow. Among others who appeared in 1962 were Horst Faas, photographer, and Peter Arnett, correspondent, for the AP; Homer Bigart, now with the *New York Times;* Peter Kalischer, now with CBS; Charles Mohr, *Time;* and Beverly Deepe, *Newsweek,* a freelancer who took Sully's place and who later joined the *Christian Science Monitor.*

These and other correspondents had bad news to report about the progress of the war, about the weaknesses of the Diem government, about the very ability of anyone to achieve what the United States government had set out to do in Vietnam. But the spirit of the military command and of the civilians in the embassy and aid missions was most often one of "we have a policy and it has to work if we just try hard enough." Anyone reporting facts that pointed in a contradictory direction was labeled noncooperative. When Sheehan and Halberstam viewed a military debacle at Ap Bac in January, 1963, which proved that the U.S. military advisers had a long way to go to infuse a winning spirit in their allies, they reported the failure of South Vietnamese arms. The U.S. command described it as a victory, and the undermining of the journalistic reputations of the Saigon press corps had begun.[23]

THE SAIGON PRESS CORPS UNDER ATTACK

As Buddhists set themselves afire, and the pressures against the Diem dictatorship increased, the Saigon press corps also found conflict within its own ranks. Coming to Saigon for varying amounts of time were Joseph Alsop, the columnist; Marguerite Higgins of the *New York Herald Tribune* and Keyes Beech of the *Chicago Daily News,* veterans of World War II and Korean press corps; and Jim Lucas, Scripps-Howard, who was to win the 1964 Ernie Pyle award for his coverage in Vietnam. These correspondents were typified by Lucas: hard-nosed, ready to fight any attempt at censorship, but more or less ready to accept war as a necessary fact of life and not activists in probing into the humaneness of the military tactics. Indeed, correspondent Higgins was an avowed "hawk" who advocated the use of the atomic bomb if needed to repel the Communists wherever they were; tragically, she was to fall victim to an Asiatic infection on a 1965 trip and die a lingering death in 1966. The criticism by Alsop, Higgins, Beech, and Lucas of the reporting and interpretation given by Browne, Sheehan, Halberstam, and Kalischer left the established Saigon press corps vulnerable to attack by outsiders.

Those attacks mounted in 1963. The correspondents had fought off a State Department "press guidance" issued in 1962 by Carl T. Rowan saying "newsmen should be advised that trifling or thoughtless criticism of the Diem gov-

[23] Dale Minor, *The Information War* (New York: Hawthorn Books and Tower Publications, 1970), pp. 29–34. Minor, who finds both heroes and villains in the Saigon press corps, dismisses the war correspondents of earlier wars as "team players" who accepted the official "line" and the necessity of the war itself. His analysis of the conflict between press and government in Vietnam, and between moral philosophies and concerns for humanity, is perceptive.

ernment would make it difficult to maintain proper cooperation between the United States and Diem," only to find in 1963 that Diem's police would beat them over the head and smash their cameras.[24] The pot boiled over in September, 1963, when *Time* attacked the Saigon press corps as propagandists plotting to overthrow the Diem government and, through distorted reporting, "helping to compound the very confusion that it should be untangling for its readers at home."[25] *Time* correspondents Charles Mohr and Mert Perry resigned in outraged protest; Mohr joined the *New York Times* and Perry *Newsweek* to stay in Saigon. Mme. Nhu castigated the AP, UPI, *New York Times, Washington Post,* and *Newsweek* as enemies of her brother-in-law, Diem. *Time,* unrepentant, continued to doubt the analyses of the Saigon correspondents until long after their definition of a quagmire had been accepted by all disinterested observers of the Vietnam War.

The attacks on the integrity of the press corps led Halberstam, Sheehan, Browne, and later others to undertake activist roles in writing books and lecturing at home about the nature of the Vietnamese conflict and the danger to the U.S. national interest of a "win at any cost" policy there. Halberstam and Browne shared the 1964 Pulitzer Prize for international reporting. Sheehan joined the *New York Times* staff in 1964 and in 1971 was instrumental in the publishing by the *Times* of the "Pentagon Papers," taken from a secret analysis by Pentagon researchers and validating the 1961–65 reporting of the Saigon press corps. The furor over this, and the problem of the "credibility gap," which came to affect the mass media as well as Presidents Johnson and Nixon, will be discussed in more detail in Chapter 31, as a polarizing problem affecting all aspects of American life.

In Vietnam the central problem was not that the military consistently and deliberately falsified information, but rather that it more often withheld information detrimental to continued belief in the eventual success of U.S. policies, and it established elaborate statistical counts to justify the policies of the White House and the Pentagon. General William Westmoreland became the American commander in Saigon in 1964 and remained until military action was curtailed in 1968; it was through him that the twin "search and destroy" and "bomb the North" policies were instituted. The first employed the famed "body count" statistics used by Defense Secretary Robert McNamara to prove the enemy was being exhausted. The second utilized minute reports of "precision bombing" of enemy convoys, roads, factories, and troop concentrations at an unprecedented saturation level. At the daily briefing in Saigon, dubbed "The Five O'Clock Follies" by the correspondents, communiques on the previous day's action were read; it was folly to attend, the press corps said, because the briefing officer only knew what was in his communique. Critics of the press contended that the correspondents nevertheless filed stories filled with body

[24] *Newsweek,* October 7, 1963, pp. 98–99; Malcolm W. Browne, "Viet Nam Reporting: Three Years of Crisis," *Columbia Journalism Review,* III (Fall 1964), p. 4.

[25] *Time,* September 20, 1963, p. 62, and October 11, 1963, p. 55.

count reports they doubted, as major news events, and created an illusion of conventional battle warfare when none really existed except in calculated situations.

THE WAR ESCALATES, 1964–68

The decision to make the war in Indochina a major U.S. war came in August, 1964, when the administration asserted that two American destroyers on patrol in the Gulf of Tonkin had been attacked by North Vietnamese PT boats. Although it developed later there was common doubt about the incident, President Johnson requested, and Congress quickly approved, a resolution giving him power to repel attacks and to prevent further aggression. It was the contention of Secretary of State Dean Rusk that an aggression from the North was in progress; others contended that the war in Vietnam was a civil war, particularly the actions involving the Viet Cong, guerrilla arm of the South Vietnamese National Liberation Front. The incident in the Gulf of Tonkin seemed to foreclose the issue. Bombings of North Vietnam, secretly planned since the previous August, began in earnest in February, 1965, and U.S. advisers went into combat in June, 23,000 strong. By the end of 1965 there were 160,000 more U.S. men in Vietnam. Intensified bombing of the Hanoi-Haiphong area was carried out during 1966. U.S. troops carried out search-and-destroy missions and supported the pacification program aimed at regaining control of the villages.

Two major controversies developed in this period, not between the correspondents and the military, but between the correspondents and the public. In August, 1965, Morley Safer of CBS News and two Vietnamese cameramen shot "The Burning of the Village of Cam Ne." U.S. Marines had been fired upon in the village area, and in retaliation (after the Viet Cong had slipped away) leveled the 150-home village. "This is what the war in Viet Nam is all about," Safer narrated as he stood in front of the burning huts with bullets whizzing about him and his crew. "The Viet Cong were long gone . . . the action wounded three women, killed one baby, wounded one Marine and netted four old men as prisoners."[26] Walter Cronkite used the film; a storm broke. The film was too realistic, its critics contended; U.S. soldiers should not be criticised; the presentation was one-sided and negative. Safer, who had thought to show the inhumanity of war, nearly lost his job.

But a greater sensation came in December, 1966, when the respected Harrison Salisbury, a senior editor-correspondent of the *New York Times,* began filing stories from Hanoi. He had been granted a visa since North Vietnam did not consider itself at war with the United States. Salisbury's series of stories, filled with detailed observations, directly contradicted much of the claimed

[26] *Time,* October 14, 1966, p. 58.

Warmer

Tonight — Clear, low in 30s. **Thursday** — Sunny, high upper 60s. **Friday** — Sunny, mild. **Chances of rain:** Less than 10 per cent.

Map and chart on Page 41.

CHICAGO DAILY NEWS

©1966 by Field Enterprises Inc.

91st Year, Number 252 8 Sections Wednesday, October 26, 1966 10 Cents Phone 321-2000

Final Markets
RED STREAK
Stocks Up

Secret 2½-Hour Visit

LBJ Goes to Viet Nam

"I came here today for one good reason: simply because I could not come to this part of the world and not come to see you. "I came here today for one good purpose, to tell you and through you to tell every soldier, sailor, airman and marine in Viet Nam how proud we are of what you are doing and how proud we are of the way you are doing it. "I came here today with only one regret: that I could not begin to personally thank every man in Viet Nam for what he is doing."

43 Yanks Die in Fire On Carrier

Daily News Wire Services

SAIGON — A soaring fire touched off by an explosion of photo flares raged through five decks of the U.S. Aircraft Carrier Oriskany off the coast of North Viet Nam. The blaze killed 43 men and injured 16.

Some men were trapped below decks and died in their bunks. It was the worst naval tragedy of the Viet Nam war.

Firemen, damage control and demolition experts darted into thick, choking smoke and flames so hot it melted steel girders to drag out bombs, rockets and planes.

Other sailors wheeled fighter-bombers out of danger and still other dived into a nearby officers' quarters and dragged out pilots overcome by heat and smoke.

They were too late for some of the other fliers who had flown through enemy fire over North Viet Nam just a few hours before and died in bed.

THE FIRE broke out shortly after dawn in a locker containing flares on the hangar deck, just below the flight deck, and then spread rapidly to envelop five decks, the Navy said.

Two helicopters were destroyed by the blaze and an undisclosed number of A-4E

Turn to Page 2, Column 1

Closeup Look

President Johnson leans from a jeep to shake hands with servicemen at the U.S. base at Cam Ranh Bay, South Viet Nam. Gen. William Westmoreland, U.S. commander in South Viet Nam, is at his side. (AP)

President Visits GIs At Big Base

By Peter Lisagor
Our Washington Bureau Chief

CAM RANH BAY, South Viet Nam—President Johnson flew to Viet Nam Wednesday for a dramatic 2½-hour visit with American troops and told U.S. commanders to "come home with that coonskin on the wall."

Dressed in light suntan jacket and trousers, with a Presidential seal on the right

Text of President's talk to troops is on Page 2.

Full page of pictures on Back Page.

breast of his jacket, Mr. Johnson stood on a hastily built platform on the airstrip and declared to several hundred troops:

"I give you my pledge: We shall never let you down, nor your fighting comrades, nor the 15,000,000 Vietnamese, nor the hundreds of millions of Asians who are counting on us to show here in Viet Nam that aggression doesn't pay and that aggression cannot succeed."

THE PRESIDENT toured the vast base in a jeep with Gen. William C. Westmoreland, com[illegible] of U.S. troops in [illegible] visited

A confident President exhorted, "Come home with that coonskin on the wall."

success of the U.S. bombing program. The bombing had not been pinpointed on military targets; many smaller towns had been reduced to ghostly ruins; bombs had been dumped indiscriminately by fliers who needed to lose their payloads; and, worst of all, the unprecedented bombing attack had scarcely made a dent in the transportation and war supplies capability of the North Vienamese. Angry attacks were made on Salisbury and the *Times;* he was denied a Pulitzer Prize voted him by a judging committee for what most newsmen conceded was the outstanding news beat of 1966. In some sectors of the American public, the credibility of the press suffered (it should not run material favoring the enemy and derogatory to the armed forces); but in more sectors the c[illegible] blow. For there were als[illegible]

[illegible] th

could see "a light at the end of the tunnel," a phrase which became a bitter joke for cartoonists. President Johnson, visiting Camranh Bay in late 1966, had urged his soldiers to "come home with that coonskin on the wall," [27] and his commanders were trying to oblige. Some journalists, including columnists Joseph Alsop and Hanson W. Baldwin, were assessing the North Vietnamese as badly hurt and incapable of winning. But more were foreboding. Peter Arnett of the AP, whose tireless reporting had won him the 1966 Pulitzer Prize, said Westmoreland was "in a critical position." Ward Just, *Washington Post* correspondent, said all the statistics reported by the government gave a false picture of conditions; the country was not pacified when you could not travel on the roads. R. W. Apple, Jr., of the *New York Times* said: "Victory is not close at hand. It may be beyond reach." Robert Shaplen, the *New Yorker* magazine's talented correspondent, and Denis Warner of the *Reporter* magazine added their realistic estimates of a stalled effort in Vietnam.[28]

Those who read and believed these leading members of the Saigon press corps were not as badly surprised as most of the public, the U.S. Command in Saigon, and official Washington by the fury of the Tet offensive of late January, 1968. The National Liberation Front forces assaulted Saigon and put the U.S. embassy under siege, held Hue for 25 days, and wiped out most of the pacification program in the countryside. General Westmoreland asked President Johnson for another 206,000 men. The answer was a topping off at a total of 538,900 and a reassessment of the Vietnam war policy.

On March 31, the President stunned a vast television audience by withdrawing from the 1968 presidential race, sharply limiting the bombing of North Vietnam, and initiating plans for preliminary peace talks in Paris which got underway in May. General Creighton Abrams replaced General Westmoreland, who came home to be chief of staff. Final details of the bombing halt in the North were not worked out until a few days prior to the election, too late to benefit the Democratic candidate who had inherited much of the Johnson war mantle. The new president, Richard Nixon, announced a "Vietnamization" policy in November, 1969, under which defense of South Vietnam would be turned over to South Vietnamese troops. As U.S. troops were gradually withdrawn, the command ceased placing troops in exposed positions, as had occurred at Con Thien in 1967 and at Khesanh in 1968, in order to draw the enemy out to fight. The country was shocked in 1970 by a U.S.-supported invasion of Cambodia, defended as necessary to distract the enemy from attacking remaining U.S. troops in South Vietnam [illegible] vasion of Laos along the Ho Chi [illegible] talks had run [illegible]

New York Times

Associated Press

Saigon press corps leaders: Neil Sheehan (*left*), UPI, and Malcolm Browne, AP.

New York Times

New York Times

New York Times Vietnam correspondents: David Halberstam (*left*), and Harrison Salisbury.

THE PRESS CORPS: CHANGES AND CASUALTIES

There were changes in the Saigon press corps through the years. Browne shifted to ABC News in 1965 and then became a freelancer; his successor at the AP was Edwin Q. White.[29] Bryce Miller, Alvin Webb, and Dan Southerland

[29] Of the three early leaders of the Saigon press corps, both Browne and Sheehan were *New York Times* correspondents in 1971, Browne in Moscow and Sheehan at the Pentagon. David Halberstam resigned early in 1971 as a contributing editor for *Harper's*.

were principal UPI men. William Tuohy won the 1968 Pultizer Prize for his reporting for the *Los Angeles Times*. Peter Braestrup divided four years between the *New York Times* and *Washington Post*. Richard Critchfield won distinction for the *Washington Star*. CBS had, among others, [redacted] John Laurence, Don Webster, and Murray Fromson; NBC, Ron Nessen, Kenley Jones, and Howard Tuckner; ABC, Don North and Roger Peterson. In Cambodia were Laurence Stern, *Washington Post;* Henry Kamm, *New York Times;* Raymond Coffey, *Chicago Daily News;* the indefatigable Arnett of AP; and three who were captured and released: Richard Dudman, *St. Louis Post-Dispatch,* Elizabeth Pond, *Christian Science Monitor,* and Kate Webb, UPI. There were other women correspondents, including Betsy Halstead of UPI and Michele Ray, a French freelancer who also was captured by the Viet Cong and released.

Four photographers won Pulitzer Prizes for their work in Vietnam. First was the German-born Horst Faas, 1965 winner, who sparked the Associated Press coverage from the beginning, was wounded in 1967 and met the Tet crisis while still convalescing. Kyoichi Sawada of UPI was the 1966 Pulitzer winner for a picture of a Vietnamese family swimming together in a river current, children's heads bobbing. Sawada won many other prizes, then was killed in 1970 in Cambodia. Toshio Sakai repeated for UPI in 1968. Edward T. Adams of AP swept all 1969 competition with his photo of the Saigon police chief executing a Viet Cong during the Tet offensive. David Douglas Duncan of *Life* won the 1967 Robert Capa Award and Catherine Leroy, a freelancer for AP, an Overseas Press Club award.

Death struck heavily in the ranks of photographers. Besides Sawada, two other major prize winners died: Larry Burrows of *Life,* in Vietnam since 1962 and twice a Capa award winner, and Henri Huet, who had worked for both UPI and AP and won a Capa award. They died together covering the 1971 Laos invasion. UPI lost three other staff men: Hiromichi Mine, Kent Potter, and Charles Eggleston. Bernard J. Kolenberg of AP and Dickey Chapelle of the *National Observer* died in 1965. Robert J. Ellison of Empire/Black Star was killed at Khesanh. Paul Schutzer of *Life* won a 1965 Capa award in Vietnam, then died in the 1967 Israeli war.

Bernard Fall, the distinguished historian of the Indochina war, was a 1967 casualty. *Look* editor Sam Castan was killed in 1966. Among the dead and missing in the Cambodian invasion were Frank Frosch of UPI, George Syvertsen and Gerald Miller of CBS, and Welles Hangen of NBC.

MILITARY CENSORSHIP IN VIETNAM

To the credit of the U.S. military command in Saigon, only a minimum of censorship was imposed on the Saigon press corps; its principal troubles were with the South Vietnamese government and critics at home. When bombings of North Vietnam were stepped up in 1965, and troop ships flooded in, some correspondents among the 150 Americans and 400 or more other newsmen ran afoul of military police. As casualties mounted, exact numbers were discontinued in daily briefings in favor of weekly totals, another minor complaint. After Tet, and the limiting of U.S. military actions, a simple field censorship was imposed which correspondents readily accepted. Major complaints were heard during news blackouts preceding the Cambodian and Laos invasions of 1970 and 1971. In the latter, restrictions on the use of U.S. helicopters by photographers cost the lives of four in the crash of a Vietnamese substitute craft. Among correspondents, François Sully had been an early victim of expulsion by the Vietnamese; Homer Bigart narrowly missed the same fate, as did Everett Martin of *Newsweek*. Jack Foisie of the *Los Angeles Times* and John Carroll of the *Baltimore Sun* had credentials temporarily suspended by the U.S. Command for reporting military actions prematurely.

Major censorship in Vietnam affected the newspaper of the GI, the *Stars and Stripes,* and the Armed Forces Vietnam Network, supplying radio programs and news to the troops. The Armed Forces Network, particularly, fell under the heavy hand of the U.S. Command's Office of Information, which endeavored to eliminate stories that would embarrass the South Vietnamese government or adversely affect morale. The result was a rebellion of staff newsmen, amid charges that the Saigon Command was violating Defense Department regulations and policy. The controversy simmered down with the censors still in control. *Stars and Stripes* weathered charges it was undermining morale by reporting life in Vietnam "like it is." The most sharply-censored press in Vietnam was, of course, the local one in Saigon, whose ranks were thinned periodically of political dissenters, by charges of aid to the enemy.

One of the biggest stories of the war in Vietnam escaped the Saigon press corps. This was the story of the massacre at My Lai of civilians by U.S. troops, for which Lt. William Calley was convicted of murder in 1971. Despite the taking of military pictures at the massacre scene, and floating stories of the "Pinkville" affair, the story did not break until October, 1969, when a freelance writer in Washington was tipped to Calley's interrogation. The writer, former AP Pentagon reporter Seymour M. Hersh, won the 1970 Pulitzer Prize for international reporting for a story he had to market through the unknown Dispatch News Service. My Lai was a story Americans did not want to read, just as they had not wanted to hear Morley Safer's anguished broadcast in 1965.

U.S. CORRESPONDENTS IN PEKING

The bamboo curtain parted in April, 1971, when an American ping pong team was invited to play in Peking. China watcher correspondents routinely asked to accompany them, and were astounded to be admitted in some cases. John Roderick of the Associated Press returned after 23 years. So did veterans

John Rich of NBC and Tillman Durdin of the *New York Times*. Others soon followed. And for the first time since Mao's forces swept Chiang Kai-shek off the mainland in 1949, there was hope for a return to normal press exchange between mainland China and the United States. If so, a new opportunity was in prospect for an Asiatic press corps, which also looked forward to President Nixon's announced visit to Peking.

Annotated Bibliography

Books

The literature concerning the journalistic aspects of the two World Wars, Korea, and Vietnam is voluminous. Listed here are the major works in the fields of wartime censorship, propaganda, and informational activity; the most important historical accounts; and a few of the dozens of excellent books by war correspondents.

Browne, Malcolm W., *The New Face of War.* Indianapolis: Bobbs-Merrill, 1968. By AP's Pulitzer Prize winner in Vietnam.

Capa, Robert, *Images of War.* New York: Grossman Publishers, Inc., 1964. Capa's World War II photographs, with text, published after he lost his life in Indochina.

Carroll, Wallace, *Persuade or Perish.* Boston: Houghton Mifflin, 1948. An excellent account of the World War II propaganda effort.

Chafee, Zechariah, Jr., *Free Speech in the United States.* Cambridge, Mass.: Harvard University Press, 1941. The major study of the problem, by a Harvard law professor.

Cooper, Chester L., *The Lost Crusade: America in Vietnam.* New York: Dodd, Mead, 1970. A dispassionate historical reconstruction of the intervention in Indochina.

Creel, George, *How We Advertised America.* New York: Harper & Row, 1920. The chairman of the World War I Committee on Public Information makes his report to the public. See also Creel's autobiography, *Rebel at Large* (New York: Putnam's, 1947).

Crozier, Emmet, *American Reporters on the Western Front, 1914–1918.* New York: Oxford University Press, 1959. Much detail about both star reporters and "specials."

Fall, Bernard B., *The Two Viet-Nams: A Political and Military Analysis,* 2nd rev. ed. New York: Praeger, 1967. The most important study of the historical background and changing nature of the Vietnam War.

Feis, Herbert, *From Trust to Terror: The Onset of the Cold War, 1945–1950.* New York: Norton, 1970. A scholarly examination of six fateful years.

Halberstam, David, *The Making of a Quagmire.* New York: Random House, 1965. By the *New York Times'* Pulitzer Prize winner in Vietnam.

Koop, Theodore F., *Weapon of Silence.* Chicago: University of Chicago Press, 1946. The story of the World War II Office of Censorship by one of its principal executives.

Langer, William L., and S. Everett Gleason, *The Challenge to Isolation, 1937–1940;* and *The Undeclared War, 1940–1941.* New York: Harper & Row, 1952–53. An exhaustive, well-documented analysis in two volumes, published for The Council on Foreign Relations under the joint title, "World Crisis and American Foreign Policy." It fairly and objectively traces the story of American entrance into World War II.

Lasswell, Harold D., *Propaganda Technique in the World War.* New York: Peter Smith, 1927. A standard source for World War I propaganda efforts in the major belligerent countries.

Lerner, Daniel, ed., *Propaganda in War and Crisis.* New York: George W. Stewart, Inc., 1951. A collection of writings in the field of psychological warfare, giving the background of twentieth-century war propaganda efforts.

Meyer, Robert, Jr., *The "Stars and Stripes" Story of World War II.* New York: McKay, 1960. Anthology of stories, with background.

Miller, Lee G., *The Story of Ernie Pyle.* New York: Viking, 1950. Biography of the famed World War II columnist.

Miller, Webb, *I Found No Peace.* New York: Simon & Schuster, 1936. One of the best of the foreign correspondents' books, by a longtime United Pressman.

Minor, Dale, *The Information War.* New York: Hawthorn, 1970. Perceptive analysis of press-government conflict in Vietnam.

Mock, James R., *Censorship 1917.* Princeton: Princeton University Press, 1941. The major work on World War I censorship activities.

Mock, James R., and Cedric Larson, *Words That Won the War.* Princeton: Princeton University Press, 1939. Best account of the work of the Committee on Public Information during World War I.

Murray, Robert K., *Red Scare: A Study in National Hysteria, 1919–1920.* Minneapolis: University of Minnesota Press, 1955. A well-documented study of a period of violation of civil liberties. Lacks a summary evaluation of newspaper performance.

O'Connor, Richard, *Pacific Destiny: An Informal History of the U. S. in the Far East.* Boston: Little, Brown, 1969. Thesis is that America moved from Atlantic to Pacific role through deep desires and motives of political, military, and religious leaders at pivotal moments, from Commodore Perry's time to Vietnam.

Palmer, Frederick, *With My Own Eyes.* Indianapolis: Bobbs-Merrill, 1933. Biographical account by a leading World War I correspondent who became military field censor.

Paxson, Frederic L., *American Democracy and the World War.* Boston: Houghton Mifflin, 1938 ff. A three-volume study of the 10 years, 1913 to 1923, that ranks at the top for its completeness, balance, and perceptiveness. The volume titles are: *Pre-War Years, 1913–1917, America at War, 1917–1918,* and *Post-War Years: Normalcy, 1918–1923.*

Pyle, Ernest Taylor, *Here Is Your War.* New York: Holt, Rinehart & Winston, 1943. A compilation of Pyle's columns.

Rauch, Basil, *Roosevelt from Munich to Pearl Harbor.* New York: Creative Age Press, Inc., 1950. An able and spirited answer to the isolationist argument.

Salisbury, Harrison, *Behind the Lines.* New York: Harper & Row, 1967. *New York Times* editor's trip to Hanoi opened many eyes to conduct of Vietnamese war, almost won him a Pulitzer Prize.

Schreiner, George A., *Cables and Wireless.* Boston: Stratford, 1924. Analyzes effect of World War I on communications.

Sherwood, Robert E., *Roosevelt and Hopkins.* New York: Harper & Row, 1948. An intimate history of the wartime partnership by the writer-confidant of F.D.R.

Shirer, William L., *Berlin Diary.* New York: Knopf, 1941. The years 1934 to 1940 in diary form, by the CBS radio correspondent who covered Hitler's rise to power.

Slosson, Preston W., *The Great Crusade and After, 1914–1928,* A History of American Life, Vol. XII. New York: Macmillan, 1930. An excellent social history.

Snyder, Louis L., ed., *Masterpieces of War Reporting.* New York: Julian Messner, 1962. Great moments of World War II.

Sorensen, Thomas C., *The Word War: The Story of American Propaganda.* New York: Harper & Row, 1968. Focuses on USIA in postwar crises.

Stein, M. L., *Under Fire: The Story of American War Correspondents.* New York: Julian Messner, 1968. Good popularly-written history.

Sullivan, Mark, *Our Times.* New York: Scribner's, 1926–35. Volume 5, *Over Here, 1914–1918,* and volume 6, *The Twenties,* are invaluable references for the period.

Thomson, Charles A. H., *Overseas Information Service of the United States Government.* Washington: Brookings Institution, 1948. Authoritative account.

Toland, John, *The Rising Sun: The Decline and Fall of the Japanese Empire, 1936–1945,* 2 vols. New York: Random House, 1970. A comprehensive account of war in the Pacific.

Williams, William A., *The Contours of American History.* Chicago: Quadrangle, 1966. *The Roots of the Modern American Empire.* New York: Random House, 1969. Dissent from U.S. foreign policy since the 1890s by a leader of the New Left historians.

Williams, Wythe, *Passed by the Censor.* New York: Dutton, 1916. A World War I correspondent's story. Twenty years later his *Dusk of Empire* pictured the decline of Europe into another war.

Wittke, Carl F., *The German-Language Press in America.* Lexington: University of Kentucky Press, 1957. A history from 1732 to 1956; three chapters devoted to World War I period.

Periodicals and Monographs

The files of the *Journalism Quarterly* and *Public Opinion Quarterly* contain many important articles published about World War II censorship and propaganda activities. See particularly the Spring, 1943, issue of *Public Opinion Quarterly* and *Journalism Quarterly* from 1942 to 1944. Other important articles include the following:

Bean, Walton E., "The Accuracy of Creel Committee News, 1917–1919: An Examination of Cases," *Journalism Quarterly,* XVIII (September 1941), 263.

Beck, Elmer A., *Autopsy of a Labor Daily: The Milwaukee Leader. Journalism Monographs,* No. 16, August 1970.

Bishop, Robert L., and LaMar S. Mackay, *Mysterious Silence, Lyrical Scream: Government Information in World War II. Journalism Monographs,* No. 19, May 1971. The OWI and other efforts analyed.

Braestrup, Peter, "Covering the Vietnam War," *Nieman Reports,* XXIII (December 1969), 8. By a Vietnam correspondent for the *New York Times* and *Washington Post.*

Browne, Malcolm W., "Viet Nam Reporting: Three Years of Crisis," *Columbia Journalism Review,* III (Fall 1964), 4. By the AP senior correspondent in Saigon.

Casey, Ralph D., "Propaganda and Public Opinion," a chapter in Willard Waller, *War in the Modern World* (New York: Random House, 1940).

Davis, Elmer, *Report to the President,* edited by Ronald T. Farrar. *Journalism Monographs,* No. 7, August 1968. On his OWI stewardship.

Fitzpatrick, Dick, "America's Campaign of Truth Throughout the World," *Journalism Quarterly,* XXVIII (Winter 1951), 3.

Fought, John P., "News and Editorial Treatment of Alleged Reds and Radicals by Selected Newspapers and Periodicals During 1918–21," Ph.D. thesis, Southern Illinois University, 1970.

Larson, Cedric, "Censorship of Army News During the World War, 1917–1918," *Journalism Quarterly,* XVII (December 1940), 313.

———, "OWI's Domestic News Bureau: An Account and Appraisal," *Journalism Quarterly,* XXVI (March 1949), 3.

Miller, Robert C., "Censorship in Korea," *Nieman Reports,* VI (July 1952), 3.

Nafziger, Ralph O., "World War Correspondents and Censorship of the Belligerents," *Journalism Quarterly,* XIV (September 1937), 226. By the author of *The American Press and Public Opinion During the World War, 1914 to April, 1917* (Ph.D. dissertation, University of Wisconsin, 1936).

Pickett, Calder M., "A Paper for the Doughboys: *Stars and Stripes* in World War I," *Journalism Quarterly,* XLII (Winter 1965), 60. The flavor of the soldier's paper is captured here.

Stevens, John D., "Press and Community Toleration: Wisconsin in World War I," *Journalism Quarterly,* XLVI (Summer 1969), 255. Based on Ph.D. thesis, University of Wisconsin, 1967.

"Vietnam: What Lessons?" A symposium by Jules Witcover, Fred W. Friendly, Robert Shaplen, James McCartney, Edwin Diamond, Don Stillman, and Nathan Blumberg, in *Columbia Journalism Review,* IX (Winter 1970–71). Media plusses and minuses.

Average net paid circulation of THE NEWS, Dec., 1927:
Sunday, 1,357,556
Daily, 1,193,297

DAILY NEWS

NEW YORK'S PICTURE NEWSPAPER

FINAL EDITION

Entered as 2nd class matter Post Office, New York, N. Y.

Vol. 9. No. 174 28 Pages New York, Saturday, January 14, 1928 2 Cents IN CITY LIMITS | 3 CENTS Elsewhere

FUNERALS HELD For Gray, Mrs. Snyder

Story on Page 3

(© 1928 by Pacific & Atlantic Photos)

WHEN RUTH PAID HER DEBT TO THE STATE!—The only unofficial photo ever taken within the death chamber, this most remarkable, exclusive picture shows closeup of Ruth Snyder in death chair at Sing Sing as lethal current surged through her body at 11:06 Thursday night. Its first publication in yesterday's EXTRA edition of THE NEWS was the most talked-of feat in history of journalism. Ruth's body is seen straightened within its confining gyves, her helmeted head, face masked, hands clutching, and electrode strapped to her right leg with stocking down. Autopsy table on which body was removed is beside chair.

—*Story and another electrocution picture …*

This 1928 front page represented the extreme in New York tabloid sensationalism.

25

From Jazz Journalism to Interpretative Reporting

It is much easier to report a battle or a bombing than it is to do an honest and intelligible job on the Marshall Plan, the Taft-Hartley Law or the Atlantic Pact.
—Edward R. Murrow

A new cycle of sensationalism in journalism began with the close of World War I. Just as in 1833, when the penny press appeared, and in 1897, when the Pulitzer-Hearst duel climaxed the introduction of the new journalism, the times were right for a sensationalized appeal to the people. And there was an untapped audience awaiting such an appeal, just as there had been in 1833 and 1897. In the seven years between 1919 and 1926 three new papers in New York City found more than a million and a half readers without unduly disturbing the circulation balance of the existing dailies. Their sensationalism was accompanied by the use of two techniques which identify the period: the tabloid-style format and the extensive use of photography. As in earlier periods, the wave of sensationalism had its effect upon all of the press before it subsided; and, as before, a more substantial journalism followed the era of sensationalized appeal. The 1920s are known as the decade of "jazz journalism,"[1] while the years which followed were marked by a rapid rise in emphasis upon the techniques of interpretative reporting, not only in the newspaper field, but in magazine publishing and broadcasting as well.

[1] The title of a history of the tabloids: Simon M. Bessie, *Jazz Journalism* (New York: Dutton, 1938).

THE TABLOIDS' ENGLISH STYLE

The tabloid format introduced so successfully in New York after 1919 was not a stranger to journalism. Before newsprint became relatively plentiful in the middle of the nineteenth century, small-sized pages were common. The *Daily Graphic* which was published in New York between 1873 and 1889, and which carried Stephen H. Horgan's early experimental halftone engravings, had a tabloid format. So did Frank A. Munsey's ill-fated *Daily Continent* of 1891, which like the *Daily Graphic* was heavily illustrated but no more sensationalized than other newspapers. It was not these American efforts which stimulated the tabloid era of the 1920s, however. For better or for worse, America owes its tabloids to the cradle of English-language journalism, Great Britain.

Even though English journalistic preoccupation with crime news and court stories played its part in suggesting the advantages of sensationalism to the first American penny press newsmen in 1833, newspapers for the masses lagged in Great Britain because of stamp tax regulations which did not disappear until 1855. The *Daily Telegraph* then became the first penny paper in England, but its appeal was to the middle classes. Not until after the introduction of compulsory education in England in 1870 was there a market for a truly popularized newspaper. Into that market stepped a discerning young man named Alfred C. Harmsworth, who as Lord Northcliffe was to become one of Britain's great press lords. His first project, in 1883, was a human interest weekly magazine named *Answers,* which was modeled after George Newnes' *Titbits* of 1881. Both publications used the contest idea as a means of enticing working class readers, and Harmsworth had 250,000 of them within 10 years.

Meanwhile Harmsworth was watching the progress of Joseph Pulitzer's *New York World* and of James Gordon Bennett, Jr.'s *Paris Herald* with its short-lived London edition. He first adapted the new American techniques to the *London Evening News,* which he bought in 1894, and then to his far more famous *Daily Mail,* founded in 1896. Soon Pulitzer was taking lessons from Harmsworth, whom the *World's* publisher admired so greatly that he permitted the Englishman, as guest publisher, to turn the January 1, 1901, issue of the *World* into a tabloid representing "the newspaper of the twentieth century." New York was unimpressed however, and it remained for Harmsworth to do the job in England.

The first widely circulated tabloid was the *Daily Mirror,* which Harmsworth began in London in 1903 as a newspaper for women but soon converted into a "half-penny illustrated," small, sensational, and amusing. By 1909, its circulation had reached a million copies, and the *Daily Sketch* and *Daily Graphic* jumped into the tabloid field. Harmsworth had become Lord Northcliffe and a leading figure in English journalism by the time of World War I. He still felt that someone should be publishing a tabloid like his *Daily Mirror* in New York, and when he met an American army officer who was overseas from his newspaper desk, Northcliffe told him how lucrative the tabloid could be.

FOUNDING OF THE *NEW YORK DAILY NEWS*

The army officer was Captain Joseph Medill Patterson, partner with Colonel Robert R. McCormick in the publishing of the *Chicago Tribune* since 1914. The two grandsons of Joseph Medill met later in France, and agreed to a plan to start a New York tabloid to be called the *Daily News*. The cousins had other reasons than the arguments which Northcliffe had advanced for undertaking the New York venture. Colonel McCormick, as will be shown in detail in a later chapter, was a king-sized chip off the conservative Medill block. Captain Patterson was unconventional enough to have written two novels (*A Little Brother of the Rich* and *Rebellion*) which constituted protests against social injustice and economic oppression, and was considered socialistic in his thinking by others of his wealthy class. The plan for Patterson to start a tabloid in New York would thus give him an opportunity to reach the many immigrants and least literate native-born, as he wished to do, and at the same time would rid Colonel McCormick of an embarrassing co-publisher arrangement in Chicago.

So the *Illustrated Daily News,* as the paper was called the first few months, made its bow in New York on June 26, 1919. Its half-size front page was covered with a picture of the Prince of Wales (later King Edward VIII and Duke of Windsor), whose forthcoming visit to America already had stirred anticipatory feminine heartthrobs. Its promotion gimmick was the sponsoring of its own beauty contest, which was announced to startled readers of the *New York Times* in a full page ad that read: SEE NEW YORK'S MOST BEAUTIFUL GIRLS EVERY MORNING IN THE ILLUSTRATED DAILY NEWS. New York newsmen of 1919, like those of 1833 who had sniffed at Benjamin Day's newly-founded *Sun,* dismissed the tabloid venture without much concern. But one of them, at least, foresaw the effect its sensationalism, its entertainment emphasis, and its reliance upon photography would have. He was Carr Van Anda, the astute managing editor of the *Times,* who while hardly in the sensationalized picture paper field himself, realized that the *Daily News* would satisfy a widespread postwar public craving and reach a new reading audience. "This paper," he said, "should reach a circulation of 2,000,000." [2] Patterson and his editors did not disappoint Van Anda. In 1924 the *Daily News* circulation of 750,000 was the largest in the country. By 1929 the figure was 1,320,000—gained while the combined circulation of the other New York morning papers stood still. And before World War II it had hit the two million mark.

[2] As quoted in Bessie, *Jazz Journalism,* p. 82.

THE ATMOSPHERE OF THE 1920s

The 1920s were made to order for the extreme sensationalism of the tabloid and for a spreading of its degrading journalistic features to the rest of the press. The great crusade of 1917 was over, and Woodrow Wilson's hopes for American leadership in world affairs were dissolving into a "Red scare" at home and a nationalistic-isolationist outlook toward events abroad. The country's cry was "back to normalcy" insofar as politics was concerned. This did not mean that America wanted to stand still; rather it wanted to forget the troubles of the war years and concentrate on "living." There were exciting new wonders to explore. The radio, airplane, and movie were just beginning to become familiar. A federal network of roads, started in 1920, opened the highways to every man and his "tin lizzie." Manufacturing and service industries built about the auto, radio, movie, and home appliances spurred industrialization and urbanization, and for a time buttressed the economy against the adverse effects of the disastrous postwar depression in agriculture. Mass production was the talisman which supposedly would make the nation rich, and solid economic accomplishment soon disappeared under a wave of overproduction and speculation.

Political conservatism and laissez-faire policies thus prevailed over rebellious but outvoted progressivism. Occupying the White House were three Republicans, the sincere but scandal-plagued Marion, Ohio, newspaper publisher, Warren G. Harding; the close-mouthed Yankee believer in the status quo, Calvin Coolidge; and the efficient but depression-plagued Quaker, Herbert Hoover. Harding beat back the 1920 challenge of another Ohio newspaper publisher, James M. Cox, and his youthful running mate, Franklin D. Roosevelt, who vainly supported the League of Nations. Coolidge won over the colorless Democratic compromise candidate of 1924, John W. Davis, but he also shunted aside the colorful Progressive candidate, Senator Robert M. La Follette of Wisconsin. Hoover rode a high tide of prosperity, and benefited from vicious word-of-mouth attacks upon his 1928 opponent as he swamped the liberal Democratic candidate, Governor Alfred E. Smith of New York. America was a relatively complacent land, and business prosperity and the doings of Wall Street outweighed interest in political and social reform.

The press, preoccupied in many instances with sex, crime, and entertainment, reflected the spirit of the times. The majority of newspapers went with the tide, rather than attempting to give the country leadership either by determined display of significant news or through interpretation. There was good copy in the evidences of political laxity which emerge in all postwar periods, however, and even the tabloids played up the Teapot Dome oil lease scandal and others which issued from the unhappy Harding administration. Dapper Mayor Jimmy Walker's casual handling of New York City affairs was both entertaining and productive of graft exposés. The hue and cry against corruption were valuable, but sober examination of the country's own economic trend and of the world situation went begging in many papers.

And after all, the atmosphere of the 1920s made this inevitable. The national experiment called Prohibition brought rumrunners, speakeasy operators, and gangsters into the spotlight, and they were interesting people. Al Capone, Dutch Schultz, Waxey Gordon, Legs Diamond, and their rivals were sensational copy. Socialites caught in a speakeasy raid made good picture subjects. And the little man nabbed by the prohibition agents while making his own home brew or gin won the sympathy always extended to a rebel against a debatable law. Prohibition was a Godsend to the tabloid editors, but it was only a small part of the picture in the wacky 1920s.

Tabloid editors feasted, too, on stories about glamorous and sexy Hollywood and its stars—Rudolph Valentino, Fatty Arbuckle, Clara Bow. They gloried in the love affairs of the great and not-so-great—Daddy Browning and his Peaches, Kip Rhinelander, the Prince of Wales. They built sordid murder cases into national sensations—Hall-Mills, Ruth Snyder. They glorified celebrities—Charles A. Lindbergh, Queen Marie of Rumania, Channel swimmer Gertrude Ederle. They promoted the country's sports stars—prizefighter Jack Dempsey, golfer Bobby Jones, tennis champion Bill Tilden, football coach Knute Rockne, and homerun hitter Babe Ruth.

Joe College in his raccoon coat and Betty Coed in her tight short skirt were on the college campuses; the flapper was being emancipated, and according to the tabloids, every other flat was a Love Nest. The country was doing the Charleston and singing an inane song called, "Yes, We Have No Bananas." It tolerated H. L. Mencken but it listened to Elinor Glyn. John Held, Jr.'s flapper-days cartoons and the writings of F. Scott Fitzgerald best reflected the jazz age, which to the tabloid reader was a sensational mixture of sex, crime, conflict, and rags-to-riches stories. An imperfect picture of the real 1920s, yes; but nevertheless one which reflected the social mood.

The only complaint which a tabloid editor might have had was that the regular-sized dailies were panting nearly as avidly for the same stories. Big headlines, born of the wartime excitement, and pictures were not limited to the tabloids, nor were sensationalism and entertainment. By and large the tabloids were not much different from other dailies except in two important respects: the true tabloid of the early 1920s paid scant attention to the legitimate news of the day which other papers carried, and it went beyond the remainder of the press in raucous coverage of the most sensational material.

The *Daily News* did badly at first. Its initial circulation of 200,000 dropped to 26,000 the second month, and two of its four reporters were fired. But Captain Patterson was discovering that his circulation potential was not among readers of the *Times,* but among the immigrant and poorly educated American-born population of New York. The *News* was put on stands where only foreign-language papers had sold before, and its pictures sold the paper. Patterson went on what he called snooping expeditions to find out what people read. He watched his readers scan the pictures, stop at the new comic strips which the *Daily News* and *Tribune* were developing, and favor crime news, sports stories, and other features. He was pleased to see that subway riders chose the *News* because it was easy to handle in the crowded cars. After a year he was more pleased to see that the *News* was selling to all types of readers. By 1921 it was second in circulation to Hearst's *Evening Journal.* Hearst's morning *American* tried to capture some of the readership going to the *News* by filling its columns with pictures and features but the tabloid won the verdict. The sharp battle between Hearst and McCormick circulation men in Chicago was transferred to New York, with lotteries, coupon prizes, and other inducements for readers. Patterson was the victor again with a limerick contest keyed to the popular taste.

THE *MIRROR* AND THE *GRAPHIC*

Direct competition arrived for the *News* in 1924, the year it became America's most widely circulated newspaper. Hearst had experimented unsuccessfully with the tabloid format in Boston—always a poor town for journalistic innovations—but in despair of the *American's* ever whipping the *News,* he began his tabloid *Daily Mirror.* Close behind him was Bernarr Macfadden, publisher of *Physical Culture* and *True Story* magazines, and a millionaire with a yen to influence the public and hold high office. But as in his successful *True Story* venture, his newspaper aims were unconventional. He wanted a paper, he said, that "will shatter precedent to smithereens." [3] Macfadden selected Emile Gauvreau, up to that time the managing editor of the respectable *Hartford Courant,* as his chief editor, and the two brought out the *Daily Graphic.* The *Mirror* began to challenge the *News* on more or less straight journalistic terms, but the *Graphic* set out to see just how sensational and lurid it could be. The result was the battle of what Oswald Garrison Villard called "gutter journalism."

The *Graphic* quickly became the most notorious of the tabloids. Indeed, Macfadden had no intention of running a newspaper. He did not bother with subscribing to a press association service, and played only the "gigantic" general news. He was trying to build a million-reader audience on newsstand sales of a daily which was to be the *True Confessions* of the newspaper world. Reporters wrote first-person stories to be signed by persons in the news, and editors headlined them "I Know Who Killed My Brother," "He Beat Me—I Love Him," and "For 36 Hours I Lived Another Woman's Love Life." Love was a good headline word and it was paired in many ways: love pact, love thief, love slayer, love nest, love child, love cheat, love coward. A metropolitan area always has its grist of crime and sex news, murders, and court trials—but never before did one have tabloids making the most of each incident, big or grubby. Sensationalism in

[3] William H. Taft, "Bernarr Macfadden: One of a Kind," *Journalism Quarterly,* XLV (Winter 1968), 631.

handling crime news aroused the ire of all responsible citizens, who were revolted by such banks of headlines as these: "Boys foil death chair. Mothers weep as governor halts execution. Would have kicked off with grin." Gauvreau's retort was that the public wanted "hot news," [4] and the evidence seemed to be on his side, as newsstand sales of the *Graphic* mounted.

Climax year of the war of the tabloids was 1926. First the Broadway producer, Earl Carroll, gave a party at which a nude dancing girl sat in a bathtub full of champagne. Before the furor had died down, the tabloids discovered a wealthy real estate man, Edward Browning, and his 15-year-old shopgirl bride. This was "hot" romance indeed and the pair became Daddy and Peaches to all of America. The *Graphic* portrayed them frolicking on a bed with Daddy saying "Woof! Woof! I'm a Goof!" Gauvreau decided to thrill his shopgirl audience with the details of Peaches' intimate diary, but at that point the law stepped in.

Next into the spotlight stepped wealthy socialite Kip Rhinelander, who charged in court that his bride of a few months had Negro blood, a fact he had not known at the time of the marriage. The sensation-hungry reporters were balked at the climax of the trial, when the judge ousted them before the attractive Mrs. Rhinelander was partially disrobed to prove a point for the defense. But Gauvreau hastily posed a bare-backed chorus girl among some of his reporters, pasted likenesses of court participants in place of the reporters' faces, and hit the street with a sell-out edition. The *Graphic* said in small type that its sensational picture was a "composograph" but most of its readers assumed that it was the real thing.

Meanwhile the desperate editors of the *Mirror* had dug up a four-year-old murder story in New Jersey. In 1922 a New Brunswick, New Jersey, minister named Edward Hall and his choir-singer sweetheart, Eleanor Mills, were found dead, apparently suicides. The *Mirror* succeeded in having the minister's widow brought to trial and for months the New Jersey town became one of the most important filing points for press associations and big newspapers in America. One witness became "the pig woman" to the 200 reporters at the trial. Unfortunately for the *Mirror,* Mrs. Hall was acquitted and sued the paper for libel.

While the Hall-Mills story was running Gertrude Ederle swam the English Channel to become America's heroine for a day. In late August of 1926 former President Charles Eliot of Harvard, and "the Sheik" of motion pictures, Rudolph Valentino, died. The *Daily News* gave Valentino six pages of space and Eliot one paragraph, thereby setting off more irate complaints from serious-minded folk. But "Valentino Dies With Smile as Lips Touch Priest's Crucifix" and "Rudy Leaped from Rags to World Hero" were tabloid copy, and the death of an educator was not. In most of the press, too, Valentino rated more attention.

A second sensational murder trial was drummed up in the spring of 1927. A corset salesman named Judd Gray and his sweetheart, Mrs. Ruth Snyder, had collaborated in disposing of the unwanted Mr. Snyder. When it came time for

[4] Gauvreau used this phrase as the title for a thinly fictionalized account of his editorship of the *Graphic:* Emile Gauvreau, *Hot News* (New York: Macaulay Company, 1931).

Mrs. Snyder's execution in the electric chair at Sing Sing the *Graphic* blared to its readers:

> Don't fail to read tomorrow's *Graphic*. An installment that thrills and stuns! A story that fairly pierces the heart and reveals Ruth Snyder's last thoughts on earth; that pulses the blood as it discloses her final letters. Think of it! A woman's final thoughts just before she is clutched in the deadly snare that sears and burns and FRIES AND KILLS! Her very last words! Exclusively in tomorrow's *Graphic*.[5]

It was the photography-minded *News* which had the last word, however. The *Graphic* might have its "confession" but the *News* proposed to take its readers inside the execution chamber. Pictures were forbidden, but a photographer, Tom Howard, strapped a tiny camera to his ankle and took his picture just after the current was turned on. The *News* put a touched-up shot on its front page, sold 250,000 extra copies, and then had to run off 750,000 additional pages later.

PATTERSON'S NEWS VALUES CHANGE

Patterson's news and photo enterprise went beyond shocking people. When the steamer "Vestris" sank off the Atlantic coast with the loss of several hundred lives, Patterson sent all his staffers to interview the survivors on the chance that one of them had taken a picture. One had, and for $1,200 the *News* bought one of the greatest action news pictures ever taken, showing the tilted ship's deck and recording the expressions of the victims as they prepared to jump into the water, or go down with the ship. Patterson put $750,000 into Associated Press Wirephoto in the early 1930s, when other publishers were balking, and for a while had exclusive New York use of Wirephoto. The *News* developed its own staff of crack photographers and in addition welcomed shots taken by freelancers in the vast New York area. The payoff was consistent.

With 1929 came the Wall Street crash, depression, and deepening years of unemployment; Herbert Hoover's promise of two chickens in every pot and a car in every garage gave way to soup lines and apple stands despite the president's conscientious efforts. Patterson, with his finger on the pulse of the people, told his editors and reporters that the depression and its effects upon the lives of all Americans was now the big story. What caused the bust, and what was going to be done for its victims, were more vital news subjects than the entertainment of the twenties. Not that the *News* and other papers stopped playing crime and sex news and features. But they also gave great space to the serious news of a people in trouble. America had stopped singing "My God, How the

[5] As quoted in Helen M. Hughes, *News and the Human Interest Story* (Chicago: University of Chicago Press, 1940), p. 235.

Money Rolls In," and it hoped desperately that the Franklin D. Roosevelt campaign song, "Happy Days Are Here Again," bore promise of a real New Deal in establishing genuine economic security for all classes of Americans. Patterson's *Daily News* became a firm supporter of Roosevelt's New Deal through the 1930s, to the disgust of the fiercely anti-New Deal Colonel McCormick in the *Chicago Tribune* tower.

The *Daily News* still wisecracked in its editorial columns, and still produced its headlines with a twist that caught any reader's eye. But after 1939 it had no gay greetings for the man in the White House. It broke with Roosevelt over involvement in World War II and became bitterly isolationist. Patterson's distrust of the President's foreign policy then led him to fight the administration all down the line. After his death in 1946, the *News* was under the control of Colonel McCormick, although its operations were directed by Patterson's former executives. Despite this political break with the Democratic party the *News* remained a "people's paper," climbing to peak circulations of 2,400,000 daily and 4,500,000 Sunday in 1947, before it felt the effects of a general slackening of metropolitan newspaper circulations that cut its figures to 2,130,000 daily and 2,950,000 Sunday by 1970.[6]

THE END OF THE TABLOID ERA

Things did not go so well with the *Mirror* and *Graphic*. Hearst sold the *Mirror* in 1928, had to take it back in 1930, and then bolstered it by stealing columnist Walter Winchell from the *Graphic* and sending Arthur Brisbane in as editor. But the *Mirror* never became a profitable Hearst property and was closed in 1963. The *Graphic* never won any advertising support and died unmourned in 1932.

Two points should be made clear: very few of the other newspapers which adopted the tabloid format were of the racy character of the New York tabs; and the quest for sensational news did not die with the passing of the *Graphic* and the semi-transformation of the *Daily News*. One hopeful tabloid publisher was Cornelius Vanderbilt, Jr., who started crusading, nonsalacious picture papers in Los Angeles, San Francisco, and Miami in the early 1920s. Vanderbilt won good-sized circulations for his papers, but failed to build up advertiser support, and the chain soon withered. The *Los Angeles Daily News* passed to liberal-minded Manchester Boddy, who built it into a pro-New Deal paper much like orthodox dailies except for a freewheeling style of writing. The *Chicago Times,* founded in 1929, was likewise a liberal, tersely-written paper, and less sensational than the Hearst Chicago papers, although still lively. When

[6] See Walter E. Schneider, "Fabulous Rise of N. Y. Daily News," *Editor & Publisher,* LXXII (June 24, 1939), 5, for an extensive account of 20 years of the paper's history. Patterson's obituaries appeared in *Editor & Publisher,* LXXIX (June 1, 1946), 9, and in *Time,* XLVII (June 3, 1946), 87.

Marshall Field combined his *Chicago Sun* with the *Times* in 1947 he kept the tabloid format. The *Daily News* and *Post* in New York and *Newsday* on Long Island were 1970 tabloid leaders. The Scripps-Howard *Washington Daily News* and Denver *Rocky Mountain News* were other tabloids of note, outside New York. No more than 60 dailies had adopted the tabloid format by the 1970s, however, and it was more popular with the small town and collegiate press, and for supplements to regular-sized dailies.

Although the newspapers of the 1930s devoted far more space to stories about political and economic events and foreign affairs than those of the 1920s, they did not lose the "big story" complex which characterized postwar journalism. The trial of Bruno Hauptmann in 1934 for the kidnaping and murder of the Lindbergh baby drew more than 300 reporters, who wired more than 11 million words in 28 days. The publicity-seeking judge turned the trial into a newsman's paradise and there was much criticism of "trial by newspaper." Lindbergh later accused the press of hounding him out of the country by relentless coverage of his private life. The Dionne quintuplets, major prizefights, the FBI's pursuit of John Dillinger, the "wrong way" flight of Douglas Corrigan to Ireland and other diverting stories were given concentrated news treatment. After World War II a fresh stream of murders and other sensational or entertaining stories hit the news wires, and in big cities competition in that field increased in intensity.

THE RISE OF INTERPRETATIVE REPORTING

The rise of interpretative reporting was the most important development of the 1930s and 1940s, however. Proper backgrounding of news events, and covering of major areas of human activity by specialists, were not unknown before that time, just as uncritical and sensationalized treatment of news continued in the press after that time. But the impact of the political-social-economic revolution of the New Deal years, the rise of modern scientific technology, the increasing interdependence of economic groups at home, and the shrinking of the world into one vast arena for power politics forced a new approach to the handling of news. "Why" became important, along with the traditional "who did what," because the reader, more than ever, wanted and needed to know the meaning of the news. Coverage of politics, economics and business, foreign affairs, science, labor, agriculture, and social work was improved by reporter-specialists. Editorial pages also became more interpretative. The news magazines and some specialized newspapers and magazines joined in the movement, together with radio commentators. Old-style objectivity, which consisted in sticking to a factual account of what had been said or done, was challenged by a new concept of objectivity which was based upon the belief that the reader needed to have a given event placed in its proper context if truth really was to be served. Old beliefs that difficult subjects like science and economics could not be made interesting to readers likewise were discarded, out of sheer necessity.

Washington reporters found that a mere knowledge of political leaders and their ups-and-downs no longer sufficed with the coming of the New Deal. The banking crisis; the creation of the NRA, WPA, AAA, and many other new government agencies with vast socioeconomic power; a rapid growth of labor unions under the NRA and Wagner Act collective bargaining guarantees; extensive government intervention in the affairs of business and agriculture; regulation of the security exchanges, and other events of the New Deal era presented one challenge after another to reporters and the desk men who handled their copy. And as international tensions built up before World War II, and as America assumed world leadership during that war and after, proper interpretation of international news became vital.

The Washington and foreign correspondents responded with increasing success to the demands thus made upon them by the pressure of the news. As the 1970s opened, there were talented Washington bureau chiefs like David Kraslow of the *Los Angeles Times,* Richard Dudman of the *St. Louis Post-Dispatch,* Peter Lisagor of the *Chicago Daily News,* Philip Potter of the *Baltimore Sun,* Charles W. Bailey of the *Minneapolis Tribune,* Jack Steele of Scripps-Howard, and Hugh Sidey of *Time.* There were capable Washington reporters like Stewart Hensley of UPI and John Hightower of AP, Don Oberdorfer and Chalmers Roberts of the *Washington Post,* Edwin L. Dale, Jr., of the *New York Times,* Richard L. Strout of the *Christian Science Monitor,* Mary McGrory of the *Washington Star,* Philip Meyer of the Knight newspapers, and Charles W. Roberts of *Newsweek.* There were interpretative writers like James Marlow of AP and Louis Cassels of UPI in Washington and foreign news analysts like K. C. Thaler of UPI and William L. Ryan of AP. Abroad there were interpretative reporters like David M. Nichol of the *Chicago Daily News* and Lynn Heinzerling of AP in London, Henry Shapiro of UPI and Malcolm Browne of the *New York Times* in Moscow, Don Cook of the *Los Angeles Times* in Paris, and Stanley Karnow of the *Washington Post* in Tokyo. Many more could be named.

LABOR NEWS SPECIALISTS

Specialists were required, however, both in Washington and in newspaper offices across the country. The rise of "big labor" to challenge "big business" under the collective bargaining guarantees of the New Deal brought the labor beat into full prominence. Louis Stark of the *New York Times,* the paper's labor reporter and, with John Leary of the *New York World,* one of the first men in the field, transferred his base of operations to Washington in 1933. There Stark became the acknowledged dean of American labor reporters, as newsmen covered national labor-management bargaining in the steel and coal industries, the activities of the National Labor Relations Board, and legislative contests which culminated in the replacement of the Wagner Act by the Taft-Hartley Law. Coverage of strikes always had been a part of the nation's news report, but fuller interpretation of the problems of labor-management relations now became the good reporter's goal. He also sought to increase direct coverage of organized labor's activities and attitudes. Both Washington and local reporting were improved by numerous labor specialists.

The story of Louis Stark is an example of the manner in which some older newsmen met the challenge of specialized reporting. Stark grew up on New York's East Side and became a City News Association reporter. He joined the *Times* staff in 1917 and became a labor reporter in 1923. For the next ten years he made it his business to get acquainted with both leaders and followers in the labor movement, and studied the problems of labor and business. He covered the Sacco-Vanzetti case, the bloody coal riots in Harlan County, and other major news breaks.[7] When he went to Washington, Stark's intimate knowledge of persons and facts paid off with numerous beats and consistent leadership in labor news coverage. In 1951 he left Washington to become a *Times* editorial writer, taking with him a Pulitzer Prize and the plaudits of his newsmen associates. He told colleagues at a farewell dinner that newcomers to the labor reporting field had to be better prepared educationally than he had been since they could not grow up with their subject as he had.[8] Stark thought there should be more full-time labor reporters, but he noted with satisfaction that the list had grown considerably in 30 years. It included such men as Edwin A. Lahey of the *Chicago Daily News*, Fred Carr of the *Christian Science Monitor*, John Turcott of the *New York Daily News*, John F. Burns of the *Providence Journal*, A. H. Raskin of the *New York Times*, and a score or more of equally competent associates.

SCIENCE AND AGRICULTURE

The worlds of science and medicine were better covered, too, by men who repaired the damage done by the sensationalized science stories of the days of yellow journalism. Science Service, directed by Watson Davis, did much to improve the science coverage of its subscribers after 1921. The *New York Times* again was early in the field. Waldemar Kaempffert, an engineer, joined the paper as a science specialist in 1927, joined by William L. Laurence in 1930. Pulitzer Prizes were given in 1937 to a group of pioneer science writers, including Laurence, David Dietz of the Scripps-Howard newspapers, Howard W. Blakeslee of the Associated Press, John J. O'Neill of the *New York Herald Tribune*, and Gobind Behari Lal of Hearst's Universal Service. The National

[7] Stark's story of the execution of Sacco and Vanzetti is one of the most moving pieces of reporting of that period. Reprinted in Snyder and Morris, *A Treasury of Great Reporting*, pp. 454–60.

[8] "Louis Stark's Own Story," *Nieman Reports*, VI (January, 1952), 3.

Association of Science Writers, formed in 1934, had 867 members by 1970. Top writers included Laurence and Dietz, Arthur J. Snider of the *Chicago Daily News,* Victor Cohn of the *Washington Post,* David Perlman of the *San Francisco Chronicle,* Josephine Robertson of the *Cleveland Plain Dealer,* Harry Nelson of the *Los Angeles Times,* Delos Smith of UPI, and Alton Blakeslee, Frank J. Carey, and John Barbour of AP.

Federal action to stabilize agricultural prices, to provide economic security for farmers, and to conserve soil resources became major news with the advent of the Agricultural Adjustment Administration. But the agricultural story had been an important one even before the concerted actions of the New Deal. Alfred D. Stedman of the *St. Paul Pioneer Press* and *Dispatch,* and Theodore C. Alford of the *Kansas City Star* arrived in Washington in 1929 as the first specialists in agricultural news correspondence. The press associations then did not sense the significance of many stories involving agriculture and even left some major stories uncovered or undeveloped. Early in the 1930s, however, the Associated Press selected an agricultural expert, Roy F. Hendrickson, and coverage from Washington by the AP and its competitors sharply improved. As in other specialized fields, however, lack of qualified manpower in bureaus around the country kept coverage from regional areas at a lower level than that developed in the capital. Farm editors like the veteran J. S. Russell of the *Des Moines Register* and *Tribune* and Stedman, returned to St. Paul from a long Washington career, kept their own regional coverage at a high pitch through their intimate knowledge of agricultural problems and trends.

URBAN AND ENVIRONMENT WRITERS

An Urban Writers' Society was formed in 1968, reflecting the concern of Americans about urban society and the environment. Outstanding among the urban specialists were Ada Louise Huxtablė, architecture critic of the *New York Times* since 1963 and winner of the 1970 Pulitzer Prize for criticism; Wolf Von Eckardt, urban and architecture specialist for the *Washington Post* since 1964; George McCue, art and urban-design critic for the *St. Louis Post-Dispatch* since 1956; and Allan Temko, the *San Francisco Chronicle's* urban columnist since 1961. When *Editor & Publisher* in 1970 asked the nation's dailies to send in names of their writers specializing in environmental news coverage on the ecology beat, 100 did.[9]

THE SPREAD OF INTERPRETATION

Education writers became specialists, too, like Marjorie Schuster of the *Cleveland Press,* Patricia Doyle of the *Kansas City Star,* and Fred M. Hechinger

[9] *Editor & Publisher,* August 8, 1970, p. 45.

of the *New York Times.* Civic and business news editors, reporters on social work and public health activities, food editors, religious editors who were more than church news rewrite men, automotive and aviation editors, and other new specialists joined the older established financial, book, music, fashion, travel, garden, theatrical, and sports editors. Coverage of crime news became a sociological problem for some newspapers, an advance over the usual sensationalized treatment.

Some larger dailies developed editorial-page staffs of a size and quality in keeping with the trend toward specialized news coverage and interpretation. Papers like the *New York Times,* the *Milwaukee Journal,* and the *St. Louis Post-Dispatch* had the resources and the inclination to keep their editorial pages staffed in this superior manner. Others, like the *Washington Post* and *Minneapolis Star* and *Tribune,* put emphasis upon editorial writers traveling or going directly to news sources as part of their work. No editor or editorial writer worth his salt could ignore the increasing number of specialized news fields and the pressure upon editorial page men became greater each decade. Fortunately an ever-growing amount of explanatory interpretation was being done by the reporters and specialized writers themselves, and the editorial-page role became more one of putting events into perspective and stating of opinion.

The newspaper thus became more interpretative in its style of writing and in its content. During the 1930s books appeared which urged backgrounding of the news, adequate preparation of reporters and editors for their specialized tasks, and a breaking away from old traditions.[10] Some newspapers attempted to departmentalize the news as a means of calling reader attention to various areas of significant news, but the idea did not catch on. Others used typographical devices to indicate insertions of background information and interpretation into news stories, but most papers preferred simply to give their writers greater latitude in adequately reporting their stories.

The extreme in interpretation was reached by the New York tabloid, *PM,* founded in 1940 and financed by Marshall Field. *PM,* under the editorship of Ralph Ingersoll, made it a policy to express its liberal point of view in its news columns, to the point where it became a daily journal of opinion. The paper had a notable staff and contributed a fighting spirit to New York journalism. But its hopes that it could exist on the basis of its intelligent writing, excellent pictures, and interpretative appeal—without solicitation of advertising—had faded by 1946. Even when it accepted advertising, *PM* languished financially. Field sold out in 1948, the paper became the *New York Star,* and fought for life under the editorship of Joseph Barnes. It backed President Harry S. Truman for reelection before suspending publication in 1949.

[10] Two of them were Herbert Brucker's *The Changing American Newspaper* (New York: Columbia University Press, 1937), and Sidney Kobre's *Backgrounding the News* (Baltimore: Twentieth Century Press, 1939).

THE CHRISTIAN SCIENCE MONITOR

The Christian Science Monitor and the *Wall Street Journal* became nationally read as specialized newspapers of interpretation. The *Monitor* in 1971 was approaching 275,000 circulation, and was printing offset from photo negatives flown to New Jersey, Chicago, Los Angeles, and London from its Boston offices. It had 12,000 British readers. The *Wall Street Journal,* however, was printing 1,215,000 copies of four regional editions in eight nationwide plants. The *New York Times* led other regular dailies in national circulation with 150,000 daily and a half-million Sunday, all printed in New York and sent by air.

The *Monitor* was begun in 1908 by Mrs. Mary Baker Eddy, founder of the Church of Christ, Scientist, in protest against the sensationalism of other dailies and their emphasis upon news of crimes and disasters. It was not intended to be, and did not become, a religious propaganda organ, but rather a serious-minded afternoon daily. Since by Christian Science tenets it avoided or minimized stories involving disasters, crime, or death, it had space in which to develop Washington and foreign correspondence, significant regional stories from around the country, and features dealing with literature, music, and art. Eventually it became noted for its ability to sit back periodically and take a long-view look at major news developments, thereby contributing interpretative analyses of problems and trends in government, world affairs, economics, and social development.

In its first ten years the *Monitor* gained 120,000 readers under the editorship of Frederick Dixon, then was temporarily disrupted by a dispute over its management. Editor Willis J. Abbot helped to restore its prestige in the 1920s. But the *Monitor's* outstanding editor has been Erwin D. Canham, who joined the staff in 1925 and served as a Washington and foreign correspondent before becoming managing editor in 1940 and editor in 1945. Canham's voice was often raised in discussions of journalistic problems and his professional associates soon came to regard him as an influential editor of a great newspaper. Paul S. Deland and Saville R. Davis followed Canham as managing editors. In 1964 Canham was named editor-in-chief and DeWitt John, a former *Monitor* foreign correspondent, was named editor to help reverse a circulation slump that had touched 185,000. The *Monitor* adopted a five-column front-page makeup, larger type, splashy art work, and more sparkling writing. Before 1970 the staff had won two national reporting Pulitzer Prizes, by Howard James and Robert Cahn, and the international award, by R. John Hughes in Tokyo. In 1970 Hughes succeeded John as editor, and Earl W. Froell became managing editor. Among the top staff members were Richard L. Strout and Godfrey Sperling in Washington politics, Saville R. Davis as chief Washington correspondent, Lucia Mouat in education, and Edmund Stevens, Pulitzer Prize winning Moscow correspondent. Joseph G. Harrison and William H. Stringer wrote for the noncrusading but thoughtful editorial page, long conducted by Donovan Richardson. Under Hughes' editorship the circulation jumped 20 per cent to reach 260,000 by mid-1971.

THE WALL STREET JOURNAL

The *Wall Street Journal* was a solidly-edited financial daily like its New York competitor, the *Journal of Commerce*, until Bernard Kilgore became its managing editor in 1940. It had been founded in 1889 by Charles H. Dow as the voice of the Dow Jones and Company financial news service. Clarence W. Barron became owner in 1902. Circulation was at a post-depression level of 30,000 daily when Kilgore took charge. He broadened the paper's coverage to include lucidly written summaries of important national and world news and comprehensive stories interpreting trends in industry. Circulation jumped to 65,000 in 1950, hit 360,000 in 1955, then leaped past 700,000 by 1960 as the *Journal* expanded to eight printing plants across the country, connected to the New York office by electric typesetting devices. In 1970 the circulation was 1,215,000, exceeded only by that of the *New York Daily News*.

Harris & Ewing

Wall Street Journal

National newspapers were edited by Erwin D. Canham (*left*) and Bernard Kilgore.

When Kilgore died in late 1967 he was company president, with a group of former managing editors of the paper serving in key positions. One, William F. Kerby, succeeded Kilgore as president of Dow Jones and Company. Buren H. McCormack became executive vice president, and Warren H. Phillips the editorial director of the company's publications. Edward R. Cony, a 1961

Pulitzer Prize winner, became executive editor in 1970, Sterling Soderlind progressed to managing editor, and Joseph E. Evans became editor of the editorial page. Editors William H. Grimes and Vermont Connecticut Royster both won Pulitzer awards for editorial writing; Royster, editor since 1958, retired in 1971. Louis Kohlmeier, Stanley Penn, and Monroe Karmin all won Pulitzer Prizes for national reporting during the 1960s. The paper had 20 U.S. news bureaus in 1971, with some 200 reporters and editors, plus bureaus in London, Paris, and Hong Kong, and 60 to 80 special correspondents at other business points. Dow Jones launched a weekly newspaper of general appeal, the *National Observer,* in 1962 which won more than a half-million circulation after uneasy early years. William Giles, Don Carter, and Henry Gemmill were principal editors the first decade. The company also still had its Dow Jones news service and *Barron's,* a business and financial weekly.

MAGAZINES OF OPINION AND INTERPRETATION

Some of the country's magazines became important factors in the trend toward interpretation and news specialization. There was a new element injected into the magazine world, however. The news magazines, as well as the magazines of opinion and general magazines, became important in magazine journalism's contribution to coverage of public affairs.

In the muckraking era, such general magazines as *Collier's, McClure's, Everybody's,* the *American,* and *Cosmopolitan* served both as entertainment media and as "people's champions," exposing industrial monopolies and political corruption and crusading for a broadening of political and economic democracy. But that phase ended by World War I and the old champions withered. *McClure's* went downhill before 1920 and flickered out in 1933; *Everybody's* died in 1930, and *Collier's* and the *American* in 1956. The *Saturday Evening Post* joined them in 1969, and *Look* in 1971. *Cosmopolitan* remained in the 1970s general magazine field, along with *Reader's Digest, Life,* and *Ebony.* These continued to carry significant articles on public affairs. The women's magazines—*Ladies' Home Journal, McCall's,* and *Good Housekeeping*—made some contribution to current affairs coverage. But the influence of the general magazines was far less than at the turn of the century.[11]

Most of the serious magazines which were important as sources of information and as vehicles of opinion before World War I fell by the wayside in the 1920s and 1930s. The *Century* was merged with the *Forum* and then both disappeared into *Current History. World's Work,* one of the best, had to com-

[11] For the modern era, see Theodore Peterson, *Magazines in the Twentieth Century* (Urbana: University of Illinois Press, 1964). Economics of magazine publishing and current magazine empires will be covered in Chapter 27 of this book.

bine with *Review of Reviews,* which in turn was sold to the *Literary Digest.* The *Digest,* founded in 1890 and long a highly popular reporter on American newspaper opinion and current affairs, slumped away before the onslaught of newer-type news magazines and abruptly ended its career by publishing the results of a postcard poll which predicted that Alfred M. Landon would defeat Franklin Roosevelt for the presidency in 1936 (Landon carried two states). Of the distinguished literary magazines, *Scribner's* collapsed in 1939.

HARPER'S, ATLANTIC, SATURDAY REVIEW

Harper's, once a leading literary journal, became primarily a public affairs magazine after the mid-twenties and reached its hundredth anniversary in 1950 under the editorship of contemporary historian Frederick Lewis Allen. John Fischer succeeded Allen as editor in 1953 and furthered *Harper's* position among high-grade magazines. His reading audience, he once said, was 85 per cent college graduates; more than half had taken some graduate work and had traveled abroad within the calendar year surveyed. But only 6 per cent read the more literary-based *Atlantic.* It was this audience which in 1965 attracted John Cowles, Jr., president of the Minneapolis Star and Tribune Company and Harvard graduate, to buy a half-interest from Harper & Row, successor to the House of Harper dating from 1817. Soon Cowles controlled all the stock. He served as company chairman, with Cass Canfield as vice chairman and advertising man William S. Blair as publisher.

Willie Morris, liberal young writer who had achieved notice for his muckraking articles for the *Texas Observer,* joined the *Harper's* staff in 1963, and was Cowles' choice at the age of 32 to succeed Fischer in 1967 as *Harper's* eighth editor in 117 years. Morris built a freewheeling staff of Midge Decter, executive editor; Robert Kotlowitz, managing editor; contributing editors David Halberstam, Larry L. King, John Corry, and Marshall Frady. The magazine became unpredictable, imaginative, and a vehicle for personal journalism of social and political concern. Morris ran huge excerpts of William Styron's *The Confessions of Nat Turner* and Norman Mailer's *The Armies of the Night,* the latter reporting the protesters' march on the Pentagon. But not all of Fischer's college-bred audience appreciated the change. Circulation slumped despite purchase of the *Reporter* magazine's circulation list in 1968. The widespread recession in advertising also hit *Harper's* despite the attention it had received in publishing circles and Morris' own success with his books, *North Toward Home* and *Yazoo.* A storm broke at *Harper's* in March, 1971, in the wake of publication of an issue devoted mainly to Norman Mailer's earthy essay on the women's liberation movement, "The Prisoner of Sex." When the smoke had cleared Cowles and Blair were looking for *Harper's* ninth editor in 121 years. John Fischer was acting editor and Kotlowitz acting managing editor. The rest of the staff had resigned, along with author Mailer.[12] In July, Robert Shnayerson, senior editor at *Time,* took the now uneasy chair at *Harper's.* Lewis H. Lapham became managing editor.

Things were quieter in 1971 at the 114-year-old *Atlantic.* It had shifted toward public affairs articles, but to a lesser degree, after Edward A. Weeks replaced longtime editor Ellery Sedgwick in 1938. But the pages which once carried the contributions of Emerson, Thoreau, and Longfellow continued to present the literary great: Ernest Hemingway, Edwin O'Connor, Saul Bellow, Lillian Hellman. Public affairs articles gained ground with the appointment in 1964 as executive editor of Robert Manning, an experienced newspaperman and Assistant Secretary of State for Public Affairs in the Kennedy and Johnson administrations. Manning became the *Atlantic's* tenth editor in 1966, with Michael Janeway as managing editor. Elizabeth Drew wrote the Washington commentary. In 1970 the *Atlantic* had 325,000 circulation to *Harper's* 380,000.

H. L. Mencken's *American Mercury* was a bright new star of the magazine world in 1924, challenging American complacency, shocking solid citizens, and delighting the young rebels who already had enjoyed the work of Mencken and George Jean Nathan in *Smart Set* since 1914. But *American Mercury* declined after Mencken and his associates let it pass into other hands in 1933.

Another newcomer of 1924 was the *Saturday Review of Literature,* founded by Henry Seidel Canby (who also was first editor-in-chief of the Book-of-the-Month Club). After Norman Cousins became editor in 1942, the *Saturday Review* (its title was shortened in 1952) expanded its interests beyond literature to include music, science, education, communications, and travel. With circulation mounting to 265,000, the magazine put its business affairs in the hands of the *McCall's* publishing corporation in 1961. Cousins advocated restraint in circulation seeking, yet *SR* had 615,000 by 1970. Ownership changed in 1971, to Nicolas H. Charney and John J. Veronis. Ronald P. Kriss was executive editor. Departmental editors included Richard L. Tobin, communications; John Lear, science; James Cass, education; David Butwin, travel; Rochelle Girson, books; John Ciardi, poetry; and Katharine Kuh, art.

THE LIBERAL LEFT AND RELIGION

Among the struggling magazines of opinion operating at the liberal left, the *Nation* (founded in 1865) and the *New Republic* (founded in 1914) survived into the 1970s. Godkin's *Nation* was owned by the Villard family from 1881 to 1934 and followed Oswald Garrison Villard's liberal, pacifist course. Freda Kirchwey became editor in 1937 and Carey McWilliams in 1955 as the magazine passed through financial crises and intrastaff dissensions over policy toward the Soviet Union. A vigorous liberalism prevailed and by the mid-

[12] Stuart Little, "What Happened at Harper's," *Saturday Review,* LIV (April 10, 1971), 43.

1960s the *Nation* made perhaps the most passionate attacks upon the intensified war in Vietnam. McWilliams and Washington correspondent Robert Sherrill were writers of columns of incisive, fact-supported editorials which accompanied the magazine's articles and sections on books and the arts. Advertising was meager and the unreported circulation was scant, perhaps 25,000.

The *New Republic,* founded with money from the Willard D. Straight family in 1914, exerted influence during the Wilsonian era with the writings of editor Herbert Croly and Walter Lippmann. It again had force in the 1930s under editor Bruce Bliven. When Michael Straight took over its direction in 1946 he appointed Henry A. Wallace editor. Circulation touched 100,000, but Wallace's involvement in the ultra-liberal Progressive Party as its 1948 presidential candidate brought his resignation. Sales slumped, but were restored after 1956 by editor Gilbert A. Harrison. One bright feature was a column of hard-hitting comment from Washington signed merely "TRB" which eventually was identified as the moonlighting activity of Richard L. Strout, mild-mannered *Christian Science Monitor* staff writer. Begun in 1943, the "TRB" column still appeared in 1971 although Strout was in his seventies. Circulation of the *New Republic* had surged to 140,000.

Not as fortunate was the *Reporter,* launched in 1949 by Max Ascoli as a fortnightly. It won widespread praise from its liberal and academic audience for its high-grade research articles and sharply pointed opinion pieces, but audience enthusiasm waned when Ascoli supported the escalated war in Vietnam. Despite 200,000 circulation, the disappointed Ascoli sold out in 1968 to *Harper's,* which discontinued it. Douglass Cater had been its star Washington correspondent.

Other opinion magazines with smaller circulations were publishing in the 1960s and early 1970s. The *Progressive,* founded in 1909 by the La Follette family in Wisconsin, continued its excellent work under the editorship of Morris H. Rubin. The *New Leader,* socialist but strongly anticommunist in its origins, appeared in 1924 as a tabloid and adopted magazine format in 1950. Samuel M. (Sol) Levitas made it a stronghold of intellectual thought and writing from 1930 until his death in 1961. The *Commonweal,* founded in 1924 by a group of Catholics but not connected with the church, won wide respect under the editorship of Edward Skillin. Another leading religious spokesman was the *Christian Century,* a nondenominational Protestant organ dating from 1884 which was given stature by editor Charles Clayton Morrison between 1908 and 1947. His successors were Dr. Paul Hutchison and Harold E. Fey. A rebellious weekly newspaper owned and edited by Catholic laymen made its appearance in Kansas City in 1964; edited by Robert Hoyt until he was forced out in 1971, the *National Catholic Reporter* brought strong support to reform elements within the church. There were other religious publications, such as *Christianity in Crisis* and *Christianity Today,* which appeared as public interest in religion grew steadily during the 1960s, but unfortunately they received little subscriber support and were imperiled by spiraling printing costs of inflation years. Pursuing an unsteady course was a muckraking San Francisco monthly, *Ramparts,* which achieved distinction by exposing CIA incursions into educational and international enterprises. Founded in 1962 as a Catholic journal by wealthy Edward Keating, *Ramparts* nearly died in 1967 when editor Warren Hinckle and his staff supporters ousted publisher Keating and plunged the magazine into bankruptcy. Robert Scheer of the New Left movement replaced Hinckle in 1969 and revived the 250,000-circulation journal. Hinckle went to New York and helped found the scandal-seeking *Scanlan's Monthly* in 1970. Given a better chance to prosper was the *Washington Monthly,* a well-edited muckraking entry of 1969 edited by Charles Peters, who won a national award for uncovering Army intelligence units' surveillance of U.S. civilians.

BUCKLEY'S *NATIONAL REVIEW*

The strongest and most intelligent voice of the far right in American political opinion was that of the *National Review.* Founded in 1955 by William F. Buckley, Jr., it had 32,000 readers and an $860,000 deficit by 1960. Buckley and the leaders of political conservatism persisted and by 1970 circulation was 111,000. But in 1969 Buckley was still passing the hat for large contributions among his readers to cover a $250,000 shortage, while complaining about a shortage of advertising. Election of his brother James, Conservative party candidate, to a United States Senate seat for New York in 1970 stimulated the Buckley family and its publishing enterprise. The editor's wife, Priscilla, was managing editor. Other key staff editors included James Burnham and Russell Kirk. James Jackson Kilpatrick and Ralph de Toledano were contributing editors. Listed as contributing writers in the masthead in 1971 were, among other leaders of U.S. conservatism, John Chamberlain, Joan Didion, Henry Hazlitt, and Suzanne La Follette.

CITY MAGAZINES: *NEW YORK*

The most spectacular magazine success of the 1960s was that of *New York.* More than a typical city magazine such as those which appeared in other metropolitan centers, *New York* was a continuation of the magazine supplement of the *Herald Tribune.* Editor Clay Felker had developed a style there, printing such "new journalism" muckrakers as Tom Wolfe, Jimmy Breslin, and Peter Maas. In 1967 Felker obtained the right to the name and recruited enough support to launch the magazine in April, 1968. He aimed it at the young city dwellers and was rewarded with some 150,000 readers within a year, including a 25,000 newsstand sale that exceeded that of the proud *New Yorker.* His business associate was publisher George Hirsch. Wolfe, Breslin, and Maas continued as contributing editors, along with Judith Crist and George J. W. Goodman ("Adam Smith"). Star writer was Gloria Steinem, whose articles had appeared in other magazines. *New York* did some muckraking, more often carried articles, departments, and tips to better living that served its city audience. But it also interested out-of-towners, who subscribed in growing numbers as the 1970 total reached 220,000. There were other city magazines appearing in the 1960s with varying success; attracting attention were *Philadelphia* and *Seattle,* as critics of urban decay, *Los Angeles, Atlanta,* and *Boston.*

ROSS AND THE *NEW YORKER*

Possibly the most distinctive of American magazines arrived in 1925, when Harold Ross began publication of his *New Yorker.* Ross was editor of the *Stars and Stripes* in World War I days and met Franklin P. Adams and Alexander Woollcott on that distinguished staff. In New York in 1925 they helped him to get his magazine venture under way, with the financial backing of Raoul Fleischmann. The magazine, Ross said, would be a humorous one, reflecting metropolitan life and keeping up with the affairs of the day, with a gay and satirical vein which would mark it as not "for the old lady in Dubuque." Ross was a demanding, irascible editor who hired and fired about 100 staff members in the first struggling year and a half before he began to find his stars: E. B. White, conductor of "Talk of the Town"; Rea Irvin, art editor who drew Eustace Tilley, the supercilious dandy who is the *New Yorker's* trade mark; writers James Thurber, Ogden Nash, Wolcott Gibbs, S. J. Perelman, A. J. Liebling, Frank Sullivan; artists Peter Arno, Helen Hokinson, Otto Soglow, Charles Addams, and a host of others who contributed the famous *New Yorker* cartoons. But the *New Yorker* was more than cartoons, whimsy, and curiously plotless fiction; it had its penetrating "Profiles," its "Reporter at Large," and other incisive commentaries on public affairs. When Ross died in 1951, his magazine was a solid success, both in circulation and in advertising, and under a new editor, William Shawn, it continued its career. There was some criticism as bylines inevitably changed (*Time* reported in 1960 that Shawn's *New Yorker* had 97 subscribers in Dubuque, including several old ladies). But there were 450,000 subscribers and substantial advertising profits, as well as such newer talent as Washington correspondent Richard Rovere, writer John Updike, public affairs reporters Calvin Trillin and Jonathan Schell, and critic Penelope Gilliatt.

DEATH COMES TO THE *POST*

Editing his magazine for the old lady in Dubuque, on the other hand, was George Horace Lorimer of the *Saturday Evening Post.* The solid success of that Cyrus H. K. Curtis enterprise enabled Lorimer to publish the fiction of the leading American writers of the first third of the twentieth century. With the fiction went inspirational biographies, articles stressing the material success of American business, and factual reporting pieces on a variety of current events. The *Post* became the reflection of a middle-of-the-road America, and its influence was spread to all corners of the country. After Lorimer's retirement in 1937 the *Post* had a shakedown, and under the editorship of Ben Hibbs its appearance and contents were modernized and strengthened. By 1961, when Hibbs passed the editorship to Robert Fuoss, the *Post* had 6½ million circulation. But it was caught in the same downswing of advertising that had caused the deaths of *Collier's* and other general magazines in the era of television, and Fuoss instituted makeup and content changes that would have left Lorimer speechless. Fuoss was replaced by his assistant, Robert Sherrod, when the *Post's* 1961 4-million-dollar loss escalated into a 19-million-dollar loss by 1962. The *Post* moved to New York late in the year and Clay Blair became editor. Muckraking tactics and careless editing lost a major libel suit and Blair was dismissed in late 1964 as the two-year loss totaled 17½ million. William Emerson was named editor and Otto Friedrich managing editor. With the Curtis Publishing Company's business affairs incredibly mishandled by opportunistic businessmen, and 25 million dollars in losses over four years, the *Post* became a biweekly and then ceased publishing in January, 1969. It was the last of its kind.[13]

ESQUIRE: QUALITY WRITING

Filling a void in both the literary and essay-article areas was *Esquire*, still published in 1971 by its founder of 1933, Arnold Gingrich. Once overburdened with sexy material, *Esquire* began to run the top bylines of American writing: Wolfe, Hemingway, Faulkner, Steinbeck, Capote, Mailer, Talese. It also afforded an opportunity for new writers, both fiction and nonfiction, in a rapidly foreclosed magazine world. Key editors have been Harold T. P. Hayes, chief architect of slambang illustrations and articles of the 1960s, and managing editor Don Erickson. Garry Wills, Gay Talese, and Robert Sherrill were among a distinguished group of contributing editors. By 1970 *Esquire* had adopted a "shock" technique with somewhat outrageous covers and story lines but inside it was still catering to the fashionably dressed young man and offering top-grade writing. Circulation was 1,175,000 and advertising was solid.

WALLACE'S *READER'S DIGEST*

Very likely contributing to the demise of the quality magazines was the spectacular success of the *Reader's Digest*, which began in 1922 to print condensed versions of articles of current interest and entertainment value which

[13] Otto Friedrich, the *Post's* last managing editor, tells its sad story best in *Decline and Fall* (New York: Harper & Row, 1970). An attempted revival of the *Post* as a quarterly, using its old-time flavor and material, appeared on newsstands in 1971.

had appeared in other magazines. The brainchild of DeWitt Wallace and his wife, Lila Acheson Wallace, the *Reader's Digest* slowly won readers during the 1920s, and then mushroomed to a one-million circulation by 1935. The pocket-size style of the magazine, its staff's keen judgment of popular tastes, and skillful editing for condensation continued to make it a national best seller as circulation reached 3 million in 1938, 5 million in 1942 and 9 million in 1946. Wallace now began to develop his own articles, partly because some magazines began to refuse him reprint rights, and partly to support his personal outlook on life. Gradually during the 1940s, the magazine, which supposedly was an impartial digest of material in other publications, began to acquire a noticeable and conservative point of view of its own. Critics complained that its "inspirational" tone was unrealistic, if not Pollyanna-like, and offered little help in meeting major national and world problems. Nevertheless the *Reader's Digest* grew in size and influence. In 1970 it had nearly 18 million circulation in the United States and an additional 10 or more million for foreign language editions in 60 countries. Wallace reversed an old ban and accepted advertising, beginning in 1955, further adding to the *Digest's* profits and to the woes of other publishers.

HENRY LUCE, *TIME*, AND *LIFE*

The other big new name in magazine journalism was that of Henry R. Luce. He, like Wallace, became extraordinarily successful and therefore a controversial figure. His weekly newsmagazine, *Time*, became dominant in its field, while his picture magazine, *Life*, became a runaway success in circulation and advertising.

The story of Time Inc. began in March, 1923. Luce and a fellow Yale man, Briton Hadden, brought out the first issue of *Time* that month. Both had been editors of the *Yale Daily News* and had worked briefly for New York newspapers—Hadden for the *World* and Luce for the *Daily News*. The young men in their twenties looked about them in the era of the 1920s and announced in their prospectus:

> Although daily journalism has been more highly developed in the United States than in any other country in the world—
>
> Although foreigners marvel at the excellence of our periodicals, *World's Work, Century, Literary Digest, Outlook,* and the rest—
>
> People in America are, for the most part, poorly informed.
>
> This is not the fault of the daily newspapers; they print all the news.
>
> It is not the fault of the weekly "reviews"; they adequately develop and comment on the news.
>
> To say with the facile cynic that it is the fault of the people themselves is to beg the question.
>
> People are uninformed because no publication has adapted itself to the time which busy men are able to spend on simply keeping informed.

Time Inc. Halsman

Fabian Bachrach

Magazine founders: Henry R. Luce (*left*) of *Time* and Harold Ross, the *New Yorker.*

Time, its editors promised, would organize and departmentalize the news of the week. Its slogan became: "*Time* is written as if by one man for one man." Its coverage of national affairs, foreign news, science, religion, business, education, and other areas was to be written not for people who had expert knowledge of each of the fields, but for *Time's* "busy man." The editors developed the use of the narrative story in telling the news and injected strong elements of human interest. To accumulate myriads of facts which could be woven into each story, *Time* developed an extensive research and library staff as well as a good-sized news-gathering organization of its own to supplement press association services.

Hadden died in 1929, after seeing *Time* reach a circulation of 200,000, and Luce went on alone. A "March of Time" radio program was begun in 1931 and its motion picture version in 1935. *Fortune,* Luce's lavish magazine for businessmen selling at a dollar a copy, was successful even in the first depression year of 1930. *Life,* hitting the newsstands in 1936, caught the interest of a photography-conscious people and had customers fighting for copies. *Sports Illustrated,* less of a success, was added in 1954. Time Inc. moved to Rockefeller Center in 1938, opened its own 48-story Time & Life building there in 1960, and counted a record-breaking 270 million dollars annual gross. *Time* claimed 3 million circulation for its domestic, Canadian, and three overseas editions. *Life* reached 7 million at the start of 1962. Luce retired as editor-in-chief in 1964 in favor of Hedley W. Donovan, and died in 1967. By 1970 a severe curtailment in *Life's* advertising revenues made Time Inc. hustle to maintain its stability; the annual gross had passed 600 million dollars but net income had dropped to 20 millions. Circulations had stayed high: *Time* well above 4 million,

Life 8½ million, *Sports Illustrated* 2 million. In 1971 there were 10 U.S. bureaus and 23 abroad for *Time* and a total of 7 for *Life*. *Time's* publisher was Henry Luce III and its managing editor Henry Grunwald.

Life was the pioneer of magazine photojournalism in the United States. Its first star photographers in 1936 were Margaret Bourke-White, Alfred Eisenstaedt, Peter Stackpole, and Thomas McAvoy. Wilson Hicks came from the Associated Press within three months to be picture editor, then executive editor. He built a staff of 40 within three years and directed it until 1950. Some of *Life's* noted photojournalists have been Gjon Mili, W. Eugene Smith, Robert Capa, Carl Mydans, David Douglas Duncan, and Gordon Parks. *Life's* managing editors were John Shaw Billings, Edward K. Thompson, George Hunt, and Ralph Graves, holder of the title in 1971. Thomas Griffith was editor.

There were many things about *Time* which aroused criticism. Luce and his editors made no pretense of sticking to the usual concepts of journalistic objectivity, which they considered mythical. Nor did *Time* want to be called impartial, it said; rather, "fairness" was *Time's* goal. In a historical essay published on its twenty-fifth anniversary *Time* said: "What's the difference between impartiality and fairness? The responsible journalist is 'partial' to that interpretation of the facts which seems to him to fit things as they are. He is fair in not twisting the facts to support his view, in not suppressing the facts that support a different view." [14]

Some critics felt, however, that *Time* sometimes was not fair to its readers since it presented opinion and editorial hypothesis intermingled with the straight news. The editors thus were doing the thinking for the "busy man" reader. *Time's* editorial biases were accented by its use of the narrative and human interest techniques, and in its earlier years by its overuse of adjectives and its development of that journalistic "horror" called *Time*style (reverse word order, inverted sentences, and telescoped words). Still, *Time* had widespread influence and it served many readers by summarizing day-by-day news in its weekly digests. Particularly, its specialized departments brought news of science, medicine, religion, business, education, art, radio, the press, and other areas to many who never before had followed happenings in such diverse fields of interest. Its "Essays," begun in the mid-1960s, further enhanced the magazine's appeal for serious readers.

OTHER NEWS MAGAZINES: *NEWSWEEK, LOOK*

After *Time* bought the remains of the *Literary Digest* in 1938 its only direct competitor was *Newsweek*, founded in 1933. *Newsweek's* format was almost identical to that of *Time*, but its editors injected less opinion into its

[14] *Time*, LI (March 8, 1948), 66.

columns. Financed by the wealth of the Astor and Harriman families and directed by Malcolm Muir after 1937, *Newsweek* grew steadily in influence. By 1961 it had 1½ million circulation, its own New York headquarters building, two overseas editions, and a network of domestic and foreign news bureaus. That year it was sold to the *Washington Post's* publisher, Philip L. Graham, for 9 million dollars. Graham took control of *Newsweek* as chairman of the board but died in 1963 before his plans for the magazine could be fully developed. Katharine Meyer Graham succeeded her husband as head of the *Post* and *Newsweek.* Osborn Elliott became editor-in-chief of *Newsweek,* which by 1970 had 2,600,000 circulation and a network of 10 U. S. and 12 foreign bureaus.

Devoting itself exclusively to news of national and international importance was *U. S. News & World Report,* a combination of David Lawrence's publishing ventures. Lawrence ran the *United States Daily* in Washington from 1926 to 1933, then changed it to a weekly. In 1946 he launched *World Report,* which he combined with his older journal in 1948. By 1970 the magazine had 1,875,000 readers, a large Washington bureau, and several overseas bureaus. Specializing in news of business and industry was *Business Week,* founded in 1929 by the McGraw-Hill Publishing Company. It and 34 other McGraw-Hill publications were served by the McGraw-Hill World News Service, which had seven domestic bureaus and 10 more overseas. *Business Week's* circulation was 670,000.

The longtime competitor to *Life* was *Look,* begun by Gardner Cowles in 1937. It at first adopted the rotogravure techniques of the Cowles family newspapers in Des Moines and Minneapolis, but gradually developed major articles on public affairs. A fortnightly, it reached 2 million circulation in 1945, passed 4 million in 1955, and had touched 8 million when it was suspended in 1971, a victim of inflated costs and deflated advertising revenues. Daniel D. Mich was *Look's* longtime editor, succeeded by William B. Arthur. Arthur Rothstein came from the Farm Security Administration photojournalism group to be director of photography. Achieving distinction with their cameras were John Vachon, Phillip Harrington, and Paul Fusco. The magazine was a national leader in art direction under art directors Allen Hurlburt and William Hopkins.

The success of *Time* prompted some newspapers to start Sunday news-in-review sections. The *Cincinnati Enquirer* began such a feature in 1930, followed by the *New York Sun* in 1933. A "News of the Week in Review" section of the *New York Times* appeared in 1935 under the direction of the Sunday editor, Lester Markel. Its two pages summarizing the week's leading news developments, and its several pages of special articles by Washington and foreign correspondents, made the section a Pulitzer special citation winner. Another excellent summary was the *New York Herald Tribune's* "History in the Making." The *San Francisco Chronicle's* "This World" tabloid-style section followed the news magazine technique closely. Other extensive news-in-review sections were to be found in the *St. Louis Post-Dispatch* and *Washington Star.*

No one in newspaper or magazine work had the mass audiences which radio and television provided for their news analysts and commentators—a subject to be developed in the following chapter. For all, the job of trying to put the jumble of the news into true focus was an incredibly difficult one, considering the space and time limitations of print and electronic journalism, and some of their time-honored but hampering practices. The challenge remained the same: more qualified men and women with more time to do real jobs of interpretative reporting in increasingly complex news situations.

Annotated Bibliography

Books, Background History

Aaron, Daniel, *Writers on the Left: Episodes in American Literary Communism.* New York: Harcourt, Brace & Jovanovich, 1961. Left-wing writers from 1912 to 1940s in *The Masses, Liberator, New Masses, Daily Worker, Partisan Review.*

Allen, Frederick Lewis, *The Big Change.* New York: Harper & Row, 1952. Life in the first half of the twentieth century, as interpreted by the former editor of *Harper's* who also covered the 1920s in *Only Yesterday* (1931) and the 1930s in *Since Yesterday* (1940).

Barck, Oscar T., and Nelson M. Blake, *Since 1900.* New York: Macmillan, 1965. A general history of America starting at the turn of the century.

Beard, Charles A. and Mary R., *America in Midpassage.* New York: Macmillan, 1939. Vol. III of the *Rise of American Civilization,* surveying life and thought in the 1920s and 1930s.

Goldman, Eric F., *The Crucial Decade: America, 1945–1955.* New York: Knopf, 1956. A sequel to *Rendezvous with Destiny.*

Hofstadter, Richard, *The Age of Reform.* New York: Knopf, 1955. A study of reform leaders from Bryan to F.D.R. which won a Pulitzer Prize.

Link, Arthur S., and William B. Catton, *American Epoch.* New York: Knopf, 1963. A history of the United States since the 1890s.

Morris, Lloyd, *Postscript to Yesterday.* New York: Random House, 1947. An unconventional but valuable social history which surveys the American scene of the past 50 years. Included is a section on the newspapers and magazines.

Murray, Robert K., *The Harding Era.* Minneapolis: University of Minnesota Press, 1969. A detailed study of the ill-fated Harding administration.

Phillips, Cabell, *From the Crash to the Blitz, 1929–1939, New York Times* Chronicle of American Life Series. New York: Macmillan, 1969. A continuation in spirit of Mark Sullivan's *Our Times* series for 1900–1929, newspaper-based.

Schlesinger, Arthur M., Jr., *The Age of Roosevelt.* Boston: Houghton Mifflin, 1957 ff. A multi-volume history of the New Deal years, ranking at the top.

Sullivan, Mark, *The Twenties* (*Our Times,* Vol. VI). New York: Scribner's, 1935. This volume provides the political and social background for the era of jazz journalism in a delightful manner.

Wecter, Dixon, *The Age of the Great Depression, 1929–1941*, A History of American Life, Vol. XIII. New York: Macmillan, 1948. Excellent social history.

Wish, Harvey, *Contemporary America: The National Scene Since 1900*. New York: Harper & Row, 1966. Excellent social history.

Books, Newspapers

Andrews, Sir Linton, and H. A. Taylor, *Lords and Laborers of the Press*. Carbondale: Southern Illinois University Press, 1970. Presents major figures in British journalism of late 19th and 20th centuries.

Becker, Stephen, *Marshall Field III: A Biography*. New York: Simon & Schuster, 1964. Good portrait of the founder of *PM* and the *Chicago Sun*.

Bessie, Simon M., *Jazz Journalism*. New York: Dutton, 1938. The best story of the tabloids, prefaced with a readable account of the rise of sensationalism.

Canham, Erwin D., *Commitment to Freedom: The Story of the Christian Science Monitor*. Boston: Houghton Mifflin, 1958. By the editor of the *Monitor*, tracing 50 years of service.

Chapman, John, *Tell It to Sweeney: The Informal History of the New York Daily News*. New York: Doubleday, 1961. Light touch account.

Hughes, Helen M., *News and the Human Interest Story*. Chicago: University of Chicago Press, 1940. A sociological study of the feature story and sensationalism, with some discussion of the tabloid era.

Krieghbaum, Hillier, *Science and the Mass Media*. New York: New York University Press, 1967. Impact of science and science reporters since Sputnik.

Marty, Martin E., John G. Deedy, Jr., and David W. Silberman, *The Religious Press in America*. New York: Holt, Rinehart & Winston, 1963. Protestant, Catholic, and Jewish editors combine to analyze their subject.

Mott, Frank Luther, *The News in America*. Cambridge, Mass.: Harvard University Press, 1952. Chapters 6, 7, and 8 of this study of news cover problems discussed in this chapter.

Pound, Reginald, and Geoffrey Harmsworth, *Northcliffe*. London: Cassell, 1959. Based on family papers, most definitive of 15 biographies.

Preston, Charles, ed., *Main Street and Beyond: The World of the Wall Street Journal*. New York: Simon & Schuster, 1959. A compilation of reprints, with a brief history of the paper.

Rucker, Bryce W., ed., *Twentieth Century Reporting at Its Best*. Ames: Iowa State University Press, 1964. Good collection.

Stewart, Kenneth, and John Tebbel, *Makers of Modern Journalism*. Englewood Cliffs, N.J.: Prentice-Hall, 1952. Includes discussions of Joseph M. Patterson, Henry Luce, DeWitt Wallace, Erwin D. Canham, and the *PM* experiment.

Tebbel, John, *An American Dynasty*. Garden City: Doubleday, 1947. The story of the McCormick and Patterson newspapers, including the *New York Daily News*.

Willey, Malcolm M., and Ralph D. Casey, eds., *The Press in the Contemporary Scene*, Annals of the American Academy of Political and Social Science, CCXIX (January 1942). Contains several articles on interpretative reporting trends of historical value.

Books, Magazines

Bainbridge, John, *Little Wonder*. New York: Reynal & Hitchcock, 1946. A critical study of the *Reader's Digest,* which originally appeared as a *New Yorker* profile.

Baker, Carlos, *Ernest Hemingway: A Life Story*. New York: Scribner's, 1969. By far the best biography of Hemingway.

Bode, Carl, *Mencken*. Carbondale: Southern Illinois University Press, 1969. Catches the flavor of Mencken; best documented of Mencken biographies.

Busch, Noel F., *Briton Hadden*. New York: Farrar, Straus & Giroux, 1949. The biography of the co-founder of *Time,* covering the magazine's early years.

Christman, Henry M., ed., *One Hundred Years of the "Nation."* New York: Macmillan, 1965. An anthology.

Cousins, Norman, *Present Tense: An American Editor's Odyssey*. New York: McGraw-Hill, 1967. The history of the *Saturday Review* at age 25 by its editor.

Elson, Robert T., *Time Inc.: The Intimate History of a Publishing Enterprise, 1923–1941*. New York: Atheneum, 1968. Successfully done first volume of a two-volume project under company auspices.

Forcey, Charles, *The Crossroads of Liberalism*. New York: Oxford University Press, 1961. A study of three men who founded the *New Republic*—Croly, Weyl, and Lippmann.

Ford, James L. C., *Magazines for Millions*. Carbondale: Southern Illinois University Press, 1969. An account of specialized publications in such areas as industry, farm, religion, business, shelter, leisure.

Friedrich, Otto, *Decline and Fall*. New York: Harper & Row, 1970. Best of the books about the crumbling of the Curtis Publishing Company and death of the *Saturday Evening Post*.

Goulden, Joseph C., *The Curtis Caper*. New York: Putnam's, 1965. Fun before the curtain fell on the magazine empire.

Hemingway, Ernest, *ByLine: Ernest Hemingway,* edited by William White. New York: Scribner's, 1967. His stories in papers and magazines over four decades.

Kramer, Dale, *Ross and the New Yorker*. Garden City: Doubleday, 1951. A biography of Harold Ross, editor of the *New Yorker,* which appeared just before Ross died. Ross didn't like the book. See also *The New Yorker Twenty-fifth Anniversary Album: 1925–1950* (1951), for the magazine's delightful cartoons.

Manchester, William, *Disturber of the Peace*. New York: Harper & Row, 1950. Best of the biographies of H. L. Mencken, whose autobiography is titled *The Days of H. L. Mencken* (New York: Knopf, 1947).

Morris, Willie, *North Toward Home*. Boston: Houghton Mifflin, 1967. Autobiography of 33-year-old who moved from editorship of *Texas Observer* to editorship of *Harper's,* where his chair proved uneasy.

Mott, Frank Luther, *A History of American Magazines*. Vol. 5, *Sketches of 21 Magazines, 1905–1930*. Cambridge, Mass.: Harvard University Press, 1968. Contains index for all five volumes.

Peterson, Theodore, *Magazines in the Twentieth Century*. Urbana: University of

Illinois Press, 1964. A gold mine of interpretation and factual detail about the magazine industry and hundreds of publications.

Singleton, M. K., *H. L. Mencken and the American Mercury Adventure*. Durham, N.C.: Duke University Press, 1962. Mencken at both *Smart Set* and *American Mercury*.

Tebbel, John W., *The American Magazine: A Compact History*. New York: Hawthorn, 1969. Main threads of magazine in U. S. social history.

———, *George Horace Lorimer and The Saturday Evening Post*. Garden City: Doubleday, 1948. Both a biography of Lorimer and a history of the *Post,* which he edited from 1899 to 1937.

Thurber, James, *The Years with Ross*. Boston: Little, Brown, 1957. A first-rate biography by a *New Yorker* writer. Ross might have liked it.

Wood, James Playsted, *Magazines in the United States*. New York: Ronald Press, 1956. Social background is provided.

———, *Of Lasting Interest: The Story of the Reader's Digest*. Garden City: Doubleday, 1958. Friendly tone.

Books, Photojournalism

Bourke-White, Margaret, *Portrait of Myself*. New York: Simon & Schuster, 1963. Illustrated autobiography of *Life's* great photojournalist.

Duncan, David Douglas, *Yankee Nomad*. New York: Holt, Rinehart & Winston, 1966. A photographic autobiography by a great photojournalist who won his spurs with *Life*. See also *I Protest!,* his 1968 collection from Vietnam.

Eisenstaedt, Alfred, *Witness to Our Time*. New York: Viking, 1966. Photographs over 40 years by one of *Life's* best.

Faber, John, *Great Moments in News Photography*. New York: Nelson, 1960. From Mathew Brady to Robert Capa in 57 photographs.

Periodicals and Monographs

Alexander, Jack, "Vox Populi," *New Yorker,* XIV (August 6–20, 1938). A profile of Captain Patterson.

Bennion, Sherilyn Cox, "*Saturday Review:* From Literature to Life," Ph.D. thesis, Syracuse University, 1968. Reviews *SR's* 43-year history, traces editorial change.

Erwin, Ray, "Wall Street Journal Grows into a National Newspaper," *Editor & Publisher,* XCIV (August 19, 1961), 12. An extensive article with historical background.

Gibbs, Wolcott, "Time—Fortune—Life—Luce," *New Yorker,* XII (November 28, 1936), 20. A dissection of the Luce empire.

Goebbel, Alfred R., "*The Christian Century:* Its Editorial Policy and Positions, 1908–1966," Ph.D. thesis, University of Illinois, 1967. Descriptive study.

Krieghbaum, Hillier, ed., "Reporting Science Information in the Mass Media," a special section of seven articles in *Journalism Quarterly,* XL (Summer 1963), 291.

Lasch, Robert, "PM Post-Mortem," *Atlantic Monthly,* CLXXXII (July 1948), 44. An excellent analysis of the *PM* experiment and of the reasons for the newspaper's failure.

Leaming, Deryl Ray, "A Biography of Ben Hibbs," Ph.D. thesis, Syracuse University, 1969. The editor of the *Saturday Evening Post.*

Lear, John, "The Trouble with Science Writing," *Columbia Journalism Review,* IX (Summer 1970), 30. By the science editor of *Saturday Review.*

Little, Stuart, "What Happened at *Harper's,*" *Saturday Review,* LIV (April 10, 1971), 43. The dismissal of Willie Morris as editor.

McWilliams, Carey, "One Hundred Years of *The Nation,*" *Journalism Quarterly,* XLII (Spring 1965), 189. By the then-current editor.

Manago, B. R., "The *Saturday Evening Post* Under Ben Hibbs, 1942–1961," Ph.D. thesis, Northwestern University, 1968. Decline began in 1950s through mismanagement.

Moon, Ben L., "City Magazines, Past and Present," *Journalism Quarterly,* XLVII (Winter 1970), 711. A survey of city-based periodicals.

Pollack, Richard, "*Time:* After Luce," *Harper's,* CCXXXIX (July 1969), 42. No real passion, a polite member of the club.

Taft, William H., "Bernarr Macfadden: One of a Kind," *Journalism Quarterly,* XLV (Winter 1968), 627. Based on extensive research about the publisher of *Physical Culture* and *New York Graphic.*

"The Story of an Experiment," *Time,* LI (March 8, 1948), 55. *Time* evaluates itself after 25 years.

Trayes, Edward J., "The *National Observer:* History and Development," Ph.D. thesis, University of Iowa, 1967. Also includes content analysis.

Whalen, James W., "*The Catholic Digest:* Experiment in Courage," *Journalism Quarterly,* XLI (Summer 1964), 343. Story of the growth of the largest of religious periodicals, 1936–64, taken from primary sources.

"What's Happened to Magazines?," a special issue of *The Antioch Review,* XXIX (Spring 1969). Articles by Clay Felker, Benjamin DeMott, Robert Sherrill, Beverly Gross, others.

26

Radio and Television: Revolution in Communication

Radio broadcasting is an essential part of the modern press. It shares the same functions and encounters the same problems as the older agencies of mass communication. On the other hand, radio exhibits significant differences. Its ability to draw millions of citizens into close and simultaneous contact with leaders and with events of the moment gives it a reach and an influence of peculiar importance in the management of public affairs.
—Commission on Freedom of the Press

The first American radio stations to seek regular public listenership made their bows in 1920. Fifty years later, there were four to five times as many radio and television stations in the United States as there were daily newspapers. In the interval the scratchy-sounding crystal sets of radio's headphone days had been transformed into big-screen television whose picture tubes could give home viewers on-the-spot journalistic coverage of history in the making. The reader of the printed page thus also had become a listener and a viewer for new communications media competing with newspapers, magazines, and books.

Competition among the media for the attention of the mass audience involved competition to inform as well as to entertain, for radio almost from the first sought to capitalize on the intrinsic drama of news events. And inevitably the growth of broadcasting led to a sharp battle with the print media for advertising revenue. This chapter, and the one which follows, will trace the varying fortunes of the mass media in the years of vast economic and social change which followed the advent of radio.

EARLY BROADCASTING EXPERIMENTS

The name De Forest has the same relationship to the history of radio broadcasting as that of Marconi to wireless telegraphy.[1] While the Italian scientist was perfecting wireless transmission of messages, other inventors were seeking a way to transmit the sounds of the human voice. Radio was the product of many individual efforts, but the improvement made by Dr. Lee De Forest in 1906 in the vacuum tube was essential to the development of voice broadcasting. Within the year both De Forest and Reginald A. Fessenden achieved successful voice transmissions. Public attention was attracted in 1910, when De Forest broadcast Enrico Caruso's tenor voice from the stage of the Metropolitan Opera in New York. It was De Forest, too, who did the first newscasting in the United States when he broadcast the 1916 Wilson-Hughes presidential election returns from his Highbridge, New York, experimental station, using bulletins furnished by the *New York American*.

Despite these successes in voice broadcasting, there was no immediate attention paid to the possibilities of mass radio listening. Marconi and other wireless telegraphy pioneers had been interested primarily in point-to-point message communication. The government, too, had an interest in using the new process. The U. S. Navy had 20 wireless stations in operation by 1904, sending code messages, and it was interested in De Forest's success in voice transmission. The Navy quickly had become a rival of the American Marconi Company in developing what the Navy dubbed "radiotelegraph."

Primarily to prevent interference with government broadcasting, Congress enacted in 1912 a law which provided that the Department of Commerce should issue licenses to private broadcasters and assign a wave length for commercial operators which would not conflict with government wave lengths. During World War I all use of wireless was placed under government control and experimentation was concentrated upon military uses. But by March 1, 1920, private operation of broadcasting facilities was fully restored.

THE FIRST RADIO STATIONS

The radio experimenters now found that they had an audience of some size. It was composed of amateur enthusiasts who had built their own receivers and transmitters to become wireless "hams," and of crystal set owners who could pick up broadcasts on their headphones. When Dr. Frank Conrad, a Westinghouse engineer who operated experimental station 8XK, used music rather than spoken signals to test reception of his 1919 broadcasts in Pittsburgh, he got fan mail from hundreds of radio amateurs. A local department store began advertising Westinghouse crystal sets for sale to hear "Dr. Conrad's popu-

[1] See page 423 for the story of Marconi's development of wireless.

lar broadcasts." Westinghouse decided that there was a new sales market awaiting it and applied for the first full commercial license for standard broadcasting. Its station, KDKA, began operating November 2, 1920, with a broadcast of returns from the Harding-Cox presidential election.

KDKA was not the first station on the air with news, despite claims it was. Regular daily programs first began in Detroit, where a De Forest sales organization had obtained a license for experimental station 8MK. On August 20, 1920, that station began daily operations from the *Detroit News* building, under the newspaper's sponsorship. August 31 it broadcast the results of a Michigan primary election and from that time on it carried music, talks, and news for a part of each day. The *News* obtained its full commercial license for what became station WWJ in October, 1921.[2]

Radio broadcasting thus began as a means of promoting another enterprise. The *Detroit News* looked upon WWJ as a service to the public which would gain goodwill and sell papers. Other newspapers soon followed in establishing stations, among them the *Kansas City Star, Milwaukee Journal, Chicago Tribune, Los Angeles Times, Louisville Courier-Journal, Atlanta Journal, Dallas News,* and *Chicago Daily News.* Department stores also built stations which would promote their names and wares.

AT&T, WESTINGHOUSE, AND GE

But the most important elements in the growth of national radio broadcasting were the big companies of the communications and electric manufacturing industries: American Telephone & Telegraph, Westinghouse, and General Electric. Radio's growth would mean expansion of outlets for their products and services.

The pioneer Westinghouse station, KDKA, scored many radio firsts as it pointed the way toward achieving public interest in buying radio sets. During 1921 it broadcast a series of public speeches by national figures, an on-the-spot report of a prizefight, and major league baseball games. Westinghouse also opened stations in New York, Chicago, Philadelphia, and Boston. General Electric built WGY, its powerful Schenectady, New York, station, and American Telephone & Telegraph built WEAF (now WNBC) in New York City.

THE RADIO CORPORATION OF AMERICA

More importantly, the three companies had gone together in 1919 to form the Radio Corporation of America. At government urging, stimulated by U. S.

[2] The best account of the development of radio newscasting is in Mitchell V. Charnley, *News by Radio* (New York: Macmillan, 1948). For the history of radio to 1933, see Erik Barnouw, *A Tower in Babel* (New York: The Oxford Press, 1966).

Navy officers interested in the new medium, the companies had bought up British-owned Marconi patents on radio equipment, which they pooled with their own patent rights in the new RCA. They thus brought into being the future giant of the radio industry, although at first RCA devoted itself to wireless message service.[3]

In 1922 the big companies began a competitive struggle for control of radio. American Telephone & Telegraph held two trump cards. Under the patent-pooling agreements with its competitors AT&T held considerable power over many stations' rights to charge fees for broadcasting. And the telephone company observed that KDKA had been successful in using telephone lines to bring church and theater programs into the studio for broadcasting.

So when WEAF went on the air in August, 1922, American Telephone & Telegraph announced that it would be an advertising-supported station. Within seven months it had some two dozen sponsors using air time, and the era of commercialization of radio had dawned.[4] At the same time WEAF was experimenting with use of telephone lines to air intercity broadcasts—telephone lines which AT&T now withheld from its competitors.

DAVID SARNOFF, RCA, AND NBC

But despite AT&T's advantage, and its withdrawal from the RCA consortium, its rivals were not discouraged. Coming to power in RCA was David Sarnoff, son of a Russian immigrant family who had got his start as a Marconi wireless operator. Sarnoff had been an advocate of mass radio broadcasting since 1916 and he saw promise long before 1923 that radio could become a major industry.

And indeed it was clear that radio could become a paying proposition for many. The number of stations in the country had increased from 30 in January, 1922, to 556 in March, 1923. The number of receiving sets jumped from some 50,000 in 1921 to more than 600,000 in 1922. Newspapers found the story of radio's growth one of continuing interest—in June, 1922, the *New York Times* was averaging 40 column inches of radio information daily.[5] The public was demonstrating avid interest in radio's newly-developing stars—announcers Graham MacNamee and Milton Cross, the vocal duet of Billy Jones and Ernie Hare, and the performers on the Eveready Hour, sponsored by a radio battery company. There were objections to radio's introduction of direct advertising to pay

[3] The full story of RCA's rise and of other concentration of radio control is told in Llewellyn White, *The American Radio* (Chicago: University of Chicago Press, 1947).

[4] The *Kansas City Star* offered a combination newspaper-radio rate for advertising users of the *Star* and its station WDAF in 1921 but there were few immediate takers.

[5] From testimony by Ralph D. Casey, director of the University of Minnesota School of Journalism, before the Federal Communications Commission, reprinted in part by the Newspaper-Radio Committee in *Freedom of the Press* (booklet, 1942), pp. 5–21.

the costs of programming, but they were to prove unavailing in the onward rush of the new medium.

Sarnoff's problem was to break the hold AT&T had won on big-time radio. The outlook appeared grim so long as RCA was hampered in accepting advertising fees or in using telephone lines for intercity programming. WEAF, after broadcasting the 1922 Chicago-Princeton football game from Stagg Field, expanded its experimental circuit to Boston, Washington, Providence, and other cities. In early 1924 the Eveready Hour bought time over a dozen stations—the first use of national radio advertising. A year later the chain headed by WEAF had 26 outlets, reaching as far west as Kansas City. RCA and General Electric set up a competitive network, headed by WJZ, RCA's New York station, and WGY, Schenectady, but it had to use telegraph wires which proved to be inferior in transmitting voices and music. And only by straining the agreement concerning advertising could RCA accept payment of program costs by sponsors.

Then, at the moment Sarnoff was planning to create an RCA broadcasting subsidiary which could accept unrestricted advertising, the telephone company offered to withdraw from the broadcasting business. WEAF was sold to RCA in 1926. Immediately RCA, General Electric, and Westinghouse incorporated the National Broadcasting Company as an RCA subsidiary, with Merlin H. Aylesworth as president. Networks were extended coast-to-coast in 1927 as the WEAF-led chain became the Red network of NBC and the WJZ-led chain the Blue network. In 1930 a federal antitrust action forced General Electric and Westinghouse to dispose of their holdings in RCA and the management headed by Sarnoff became supreme. RCA had acquired the Victor phonograph interests and had established the RCA-Victor manufacturing unit to produce phonographs, radio sets, and tubes. RCA Communications, Inc., operated a worldwide radiotelegraph system. And two big coast-to-coast NBC networks were under RCA control.[6]

CBS AND MUTUAL NETWORKS

NBC's first competition came in 1927 when rival radiomen and the Columbia Phonograph Company formed the Columbia Broadcasting System. William S. Paley, a CBS advertiser, was so delighted with radio's ability to increase sales of his company's cigars that he bought control of CBS in 1928 and began giving it the vigor and enterprise that were to bring it to equal stature with NBC. By 1934, CBS had 97 affiliated stations, to 127 for the two NBC networks. That year four independent stations, headed by WOR, New York, and WGN, the *Chicago Tribune* station, organized the Mutual Broadcasting System, which primarily served to affiliate smaller stations. Chains of a regional nature devel-

[6] Pressure by the Federal Communications Commission brought the sale of the Blue network in 1943 to Edward J. Noble, who renamed it the American Broadcasting Company in 1945.

oped, such as the Yankee network in New England, the Texas and Michigan networks, and the Don Lee network on the West Coast. Networks, radio found, could produce more costly and successful programs because they could draw upon the support of national advertising, and their growth made radio a more formidable competitor each year for the advertising dollar.

FEDERAL REGULATION: THE FCC

None of this development of radio would have been possible, however, had not the federal government's power been used to avert chaos on the airwaves. Secretary of Commerce Herbert Hoover had endeavored to regulate the growing number of stations, but he lacked sufficient authority under the 1912 law to prevent one station from interfering with the broadcasts of another. By early 1927, when the number of stations had increased to 733, listeners found stations jumping about on the broadcast band to avoid interference, which in metropolitan areas particularly had reached the point of curtailing sales of radio sets.

National radio conferences held in Washington each year after 1922 urged additional federal regulation of use of the limited number of available broadcast channels, which by common consent were recognized as being in the public domain. Radio manufacturers wanted the government to unscramble the situation. So did the National Association of Broadcasters, which had been formed in 1923. So did the listening public. The American Newspaper Publishers Association, a substantial number of whose members owned stations, also wanted the government to resolve the problem. Walter A. Strong of the *Chicago Daily News* served as chairman of a coordinating committee which sought passage of a new federal radio act. The bill was approved by Congress in February, 1927.

The Radio Act of 1927 established a five-man Federal Radio Commission which was empowered to regulate all forms of radio communication. The federal government maintained control over all channels, with the Commission granting licenses for the use of specific channels for three-year periods. Licenses were to be granted "in the public interest, convenience, or necessity" to provide "fair, efficient, and equitable service" throughout the country.

Under this authority the Federal Radio Commission set about eliminating confusion on the broadcast band. The number of stations fell by approximately 150, and the total remained just above the 600 mark for the next ten years. The commission established a group of "clear channels" on which only one station could operate at night. Of the 57 clear channel stations in 1947, designed to give rural areas unimpeded reception of a powerful metropolitan station's programs, 55 were owned by, or affiliated with, the networks. They were the lucrative prizes of radio.[7]

Federal authority was broadened by passage of the Communications Act

[7] White, *The American Radio,* pp. 144–47.

of 1934, which established the seven-man Federal Communications Commission. It took over not only authority to regulate radio broadcasting, but also jurisdiction over all telecommunications. The responsibility of the license holder to operate his radio station in the public interest was more clearly spelled out, with the commission having the power to refuse renewal of a license in cases of flagrant disregard of broadcasting responsibility. The law forbade, however, any attempt at censorship by the commission; no station can be directed to put a particular program on or off the air. The FCC rarely used its power to cancel the licenses of broadcasters; rather it resorted only to indirect pressure in carrying out its supervision of station operations. However that pressure was to become substantial in later years.

THE CLASH OVER RADIO NEWS

With the development of widespread network broadcasting, and the unscrambling of the airwaves by exercise of federal authority, radio had come of age. But radio's development ran head-on into the interests of other media, particularly incurring the wrath of the newspaper publishers. The major conflict involved radio's growing income taken from the nation's advertising budget. A second involved radio's broadcasting of the news.

Newspaper reaction to radio in the early days of broadcasting was mixed. Newspapers carried the radio log as a reader service and publicized radio's progress and stars. A report by the American Newspaper Publishers Association's radio committee in 1927 showed that 48 newspapers were owners of stations, that 69 sponsored programs on unowned stations, and that 97 gave news programs over the air. More than half the high-grade stations had some newspaper affiliation. The ANPA's radio committee took the position that radio reporting of news events stimulated newspaper sales—a belief borne out fully by later experience.[8]

But others took a different view. The Associated Press tried to retain its 1924 presidential election returns for newspaper publication only, and fined the Portland *Oregonian* $100 for broadcasting them, but some 10 million Americans listened in on 3 million radio sets to hear of Calvin Coolidge's victory. By 1928, the NBC and CBS networks could reach many of the nation's 8 million receiving sets. Both Republican Herbert Hoover and Democrat Alfred E. Smith took to the air, spending a million dollars on campaign talks. That year the press associations—AP, UP, and INS—supplied complete election returns to radio stations.

Stimulated by public interest in radio's coverage of the election, a few stations began to expand their news operations. In December, 1928, KFAB in

[8] The story of the newspaper-radio struggle and ANPA's part in it is told in Edwin Emery, *History of the American Newspaper Publishers Association* (Minneapolis: University of Minnesota Press, 1950), chap. 13.

Lincoln, Nebraska, employed the city editor of the *Lincoln Star* to run its newscasts. Stations followed suit in other cities. The most elaborate early news effort was made by KMPC in Beverly Hills, California, which put 10 reporters onto Los Angeles news runs in 1930.[9] Some newspaper publishers complained, justifiably, that radio was using public interest in newscasts as one selling point in attracting advertising.

ADVERTISING: NEWSPAPERS VS. RADIO

In 1929 newspaper fear of radio seemed unjustified. It was true that radio had advanced spectacularly in advertising revenue, from 4 million dollars in 1927 to 40 million in 1929. But that year newspapers carried a record 800 million dollars' worth of advertising, according to the U. S. Census of Manufactures.

Then came the depression, whose opening phase was recorded with the simplicity that has made *Variety* famous for its headlines: WALL ST. LAYS AN EGG. The financial collapse of October, 1929, brought industrial slowdown, decreasing retail sales, growing unemployment, and, by 1933, a virtual paralysis of business and banking and 10 million unemployed. Newspaper advertising revenue fell 45 per cent from the 1929 peak by 1933, while that for magazines was cut in half. But radio advertising revenue doubled in those depression years. It seemed logical for newspaper publishers to eye radio as a source of trouble.

Actually, however, radio was not taking much advertising away from newspapers in those early depression years. Newspapers' loudest complaints were that national advertising was being lost to radio. But out of the total amount spent by national advertisers each year in just the three major media—newspapers, magazines, radio—how much did each of the media receive? According to ANPA Bureau of Advertising estimates, newspapers got 54 per cent in 1929, still received 50 per cent in 1935. Magazines lost some ground, from 42 per cent in 1929 to 35.5 per cent in 1935. Radio increased from 4 per cent to 14.5 per cent. By 1939, however, the figures for this three-way split of national advertising showed a different picture: newspapers, 38 per cent; magazines, 35 per cent; radio, 27 per cent. The publishers' fears had been justified.

Another set of figures—estimates of total expenditures for all forms of advertising by both national and local advertisers—is available for the years after 1935. These estimates, made by McCann-Erickson, Inc., advertising agency, include all types of advertising-connected expense in addition to the direct revenues of the media. Besides the major media, they include direct mail, business papers, farm papers, outdoor, and a large miscellaneous category. Table 1 shows the varying fortunes of newspapers, magazines, radio, and, beginning in 1950, television.

[9] Charnley, *News by Radio,* p. 9.

TABLE 1 · Advertising in the Mass Media as a Percentage of Total Advertising Expenditures

Year	*Newspapers*	*Magazines*	*Radio*	*Television*	*All Other*
1935	45.2	8.3	6.5		40.0
1940	39.2	9.6	10.5		40.7
1945	32.0	12.5	14.6		40.9
1950	36.5	9.0	10.7	3.0	40.8
1955	34.0	8.0	6.1	11.2	40.7
1960	31.0	7.9	5.8	13.3	42.0
1965	29.4	7.9	5.9	16.5	41.3
1970	29.7	6.7	6.5	18.6	38.5

Source: McCann-Erickson, Inc., estimates. Current estimates appear in *Marketing/Communications* (formerly *Printers' Ink*) in February, with revisions in August. Original estimates for years prior to 1945 were later substantially revised.

Again, what hurt most in the 1930s was that among the mass media only radio was taking in more dollars; newspapers and magazines suffered heavy cuts in actual cash revenue because of declining dollar advertising volume. Some could stand the cuts; some could not. As the depression deepened, newspaper publishers took out after the well-heeled culprit, radio, with new vengeance.

THE RISE OF NETWORK NEWS

The furnishing of 1932 presidential election returns to the radio networks by the Associated Press, to forestall sale of election coverage by the United Press, precipitated action by the ANPA board of directors in December, 1932. The board recommended that press associations should neither sell nor give away news in advance of its publication in the newspapers. Broadcasting of news should be confined to brief bulletins which would encourage newspaper readership. And radio logs should be treated as paid advertising. There were many qualified observers who felt radio was too well established as a news medium to be hobbled in this way.[10] But the ANPA recommendations led to a futile two-year effort to eliminate radio news competition. After a spirited fight, the 1933 AP membership meeting voted not to furnish news to the radio networks and to limit broadcasting of news by AP members to occasional 35-word bulletins. The UP and INS bowed to their newspaper clients' desires and stopped their sale of news to radio stations. The answer of the radio industry was to undertake the job of gathering news itself.

Columbia Broadcasting System set up the leading network news service

[10] Including *Editor & Publisher,* which expressed skepticism in its issue of December 10, 1932, p. 5.

under the direction of Paul White, former UP newsman. White staffed bureaus in New York, Washington, Chicago, Los Angeles, and London with other newspapermen, built up an extensive system of correspondents, and imported the British Exchange Telegraph agency's news report. By the fall of 1933 commentators H. V. Kaltenborn and Boake Carter were doing daily CBS newscasts. NBC organized a less extensive news service. Local stations continued to broadcast news regularly, all the while, by the simple expedient of using early editions of newspapers.[11]

THE PRESS-RADIO BUREAU

The networks found the collection of news expensive, while the publishers disliked the new competition. So in December, 1933, a new solution was proposed. This was the Press-Radio Bureau, which would present two five-minute unsponsored news broadcasts daily on the networks from news supplied by the press associations. Bulletin coverage of extraordinary events also would be provided. In return, the networks would stop gathering news.

The Press-Radio Bureau began operating in March, 1934, and after a year had 245 subscribers. But it was doomed from the start. Not only was it unrealistic, but it left the door open for the founding of new news-gathering agencies not bound by the agreement. Five news services jumped into the field, led by Herbert Moore's Transradio Press Service, which at its peak in 1937 served 230 radio clients and even signed up several newspapers.

Collapse of the effort to curtail news broadcasting came in 1935. The United Press and International News Service obtained releases from the Press-Radio Bureau agreement, so that they could meet Transradio's competition by selling full news reports to stations. UP began a wire report especially written for broadcasting, which AP matched after it joined the race for radio clients in 1940. The Press-Radio Bureau suspended in 1940; Transradio slumped away, and died in 1951. The United Press International and the Associated Press, which were serving some 3,200 American radio and television stations each by 1970, became dominant in both the newspaper and broadcast news fields.

RADIO NEWS COMES OF AGE

The networks continued to develop their own news staffs and news analysts and commentators. Hans Von Kaltenborn was the first of a long line of radio commentators. A foreign correspondent, managing editor, and associ-

11 The AP won suits against KSOO, Sioux Falls, South Dakota, and KVOS, Bellingham, Washington, to stop this practice. Eventually the period of time during which there is a protectible property right in news came to be recognized as a minimum of four to six hours after publication.

ate editor of the *Brooklyn Eagle* in his first journalistic assignments, Kaltenborn started broadcasting in 1922, two years after the first stations went on the air. He became a CBS commentator in 1930, leaving to join NBC in 1940. Radio was building audiences in many ways, but coverage of major news events of the 1930s helped: President Roosevelt's "fireside chats," the presidential nominating conventions and campaigns, King Edward VIII's abdication talk delivered for worldwide shortwave broadcast. The voices of Kaltenborn, Boake Carter, Gabriel Heatter, Lowell Thomas, and other pioneers became familiar to millions of Americans. So did those of many regional and local radio newsmen.

The Munich crisis of 1938 and the outbreak of war in 1939 gave radio newsmen an opportunity which they fully accepted. Beginning with a patched-together but impact-laden coverage of the Munich crisis, the networks expanded their news reporting and technical facilities tremendously during World War II. At the station level, newscasts won a place of prime importance.

In 1937 CBS sent a then-unknown Edward R. Murrow to London as European news chief. He hired as an assistant William L. Shirer, out of a job after the closing of Hearst's Universal Service. The pattern was to do cultural programs and human-interest stories for shortwave broadcasts which were rebroadcast by U.S. stations. Then came Hitler's invasion of Austria. Murrow hustled to Vienna, and on March 12, 1938, improvised the first multiple news broadcast pickup in history. Shirer spoke from London, Murrow from Vienna, and three newspapermen CBS had hired gave their impressions from Berlin, Paris, and Rome. The pattern was thus set for radio coverage of the 20 days of crisis in September, beginning with Hitler's demand that the Czechs give him the Sudetenland and ending with the signing of the Munich Pact.

American radio listeners heard live broadcasts from 14 European cities during the 20-day Munich crisis period. The voices of Adolf Hitler, President Benes of Czechoslovakia, Chamberlain, Goebbels, Litvinoff, Mussolini, and Pope Paul XI came in firsthand. In his "Studio Nine" in New York City, Kaltenborn spent the three weeks backstopping the CBS European correspondents, analyzing the news reports and giving hours of analysis and commentary. It was Kaltenborn who translated Hitler's fiery oratory for American listeners, and who predicted the diplomatic steps that would follow given events. He was heard 85 times during the three weeks, catnapping between his stints on a cot. CBS devoted 471 broadcasts to the crisis, nearly 48 hours of air time; of these 135 were bulletin interruptions, including 98 from European staffers. NBC's two networks logged 443 programs during 59 days of air time.[12]

NBC's Max Jordan was a worthy competitor for Murrow and Shirer. He had a 46-minute beat on the actual text of the Munich Pact, which he broadcast from Hitler's own radio station. Like CBS, he had a backup crew of top-flight newspaper and press association correspondents to draw upon. Mutual had John Steele in London and Louis Huot in Paris. Of the radio men involved in

[12] Michael C. Emery, "The Munich Crisis Broadcasts: Radio News Comes of Age," *Journalism Quarterly*, XLII (Autumn 1965), 576.

the Munich crisis coverage, CBS had the most colorful: Kaltenborn went on analyzing the news in his clipped, high-pitched, precisely accentuated tones for another 20 years as NBC's acknowledged dean of political commentators; Murrow became television's best-known and effective commentator and director of the United States Information Agency; Shirer achieved fame as the author of *Berlin Diary* and *The Rise and Fall of the Third Reich.*

Eric Sevareid, a young journalism graduate from Minnesota, was added to Murrow's staff in the summer of 1939; he was to become a leading television commentator for CBS. When the German-Soviet pact signaled the destruction of Poland, Americans tuned in their radios to hear the sad voice of Prime

RCA

NBC

David Sarnoff (*left*), RCA's head; H. V. Kaltenborn, pioneer radio news commentator.

ABC

CBS

Two great commentators: Elmer Davis (*left*), ABC, and Edward R. Murrow, CBS.

Minister Chamberlain announcing Great Britain was at war. Bill Henry of CBS and Arthur Mann of Mutual gave the first front-line broadcasts; James Bowen of NBC described the scuttling of the "Graf Spee"; Shirer and William C. Kerker of NBC watched the strutting Hitler at the railroad car at Compiègne. Dunkirk, the fall of Paris, and Churchill's stirring oratory followed. But the greatest impact was made on American minds by the "This Is London" broadcasts given by Murrow beginning in August, 1940. His graphic reporting in a quiet but compelling voice of the Battle of Britain, and his images of a bomb-torn and burning London, did much to awaken a still neutral United States to the nature of the war.

The Sunday quiet of December 7, 1941, was shattered for most Americans by radio bulletins announcing the bombing of Pearl Harbor. A record audience heard President Roosevelt's "day of infamy" address to the Congress next day. Radio newsmen used mobile units and wire recorders to report the action: Cecil Brown of CBS describing the fall of Singapore; Murrow riding a plane in the great 1943 air raid on Berlin and living to broadcast about it; George Hicks of ABC winning D-Day honors by broadcasting from a landing barge under German fire. As the war neared its end, radio brought the American people the shocking news of their President's death and solemn music reflecting the sadness of millions of mourners. The figures tell how fully radio news had come of age: In 1937, NBC had devoted 2.8 per cent of its total program hours to news, in 1944 26.4 per cent.

Taking Kaltenborn's place at home on CBS was former *New York Times* staff member Elmer Davis. Davis, in his three years with CBS before becoming OWI director, and in his work with ABC after the war, won high praise for his clear-eyed reporting, his dry humor and telling barbs, and his ability to cut through conflicting news reports and statements to find the truth. He and Murrow came to represent the best in interpretative broadcasting in the 1940s. Coming to the top, too, was Eric Sevareid, whose analyses from Washington won top professional awards.

RADIO ADJUSTS TO TELEVISION

Radio was now reaching its maturity. As Table 2 shows, the number of stations on the air more than doubled between 1940 and 1950. Program quality improved, despite increasing emphasis upon advertising messages and despite radio's tendency to permit advertising agencies to control the content of their sponsors' entertainment shows.[13] Then came television as the 1950s opened.

Television had written radio's obituary, many observers said. But time proved there was room for both. Network radio withered, as its established

[13] A policy thoroughly criticised in White, *The American Radio,* and in Charles A. Siepmann, *Radio's Second Chance* (New York: Holt, Rinehart & Winston, 1946).

TABLE 2 · Numbers of Radio and Television Stations and Sets in Use

Year	AM Stations (on the air)	FM Stations (on the air)	TV Stations	Radio Sets (millions)	TV Sets (millions)
1930	612			13	
1935	605			30	
1940	814			51	
1945	943	53	9	60	(8,000)
1950	2,086	733	97	80	6
1955	2,669	552	439	115	33
1960	3,398	688	573	156	55
1965	4,009	1,270	586	228	61
1970	4,269	2,476	872	303	84
1971	4,323	2,636	892	315	90

Source: Broadcasting Yearbooks. Radios were in 96 per cent of all U. S. households in 1950, 98.6 per cent in 1970. Television household figures were 13 per cent in 1950, 68 per cent in 1955, 97 per cent in 1970. Of the 1970 radio sets, 218 million were in homes, 75 million in cars, 10 million in public places. Radio sets were selling at a rate of 50 million a year, television sets at 13 million.

stars moved (with the advertising budgets) to network television. The value of time sales for national radio networks was 40 million dollars in 1935, rose to a high of 133 million in 1948, then dropped back to 35 million in 1960, and stood at 50 million by 1970. But the time sales for all of radio increased virtually every year. The "music, news, and sports" pattern proved successful for the spreading number of smaller stations. Incessant newscasts, rather than longer and more meaningful ones, proved annoying, but radio still produced many excellent network and local news and public affairs broadcasts.

The networks, with the exception of the loosely-organized Mutual, moved into television, but they also stayed in radio. American Broadcasting Company (the NBC Blue network until 1943) merged with Paramount Theatres in 1953 in a mutual defense pact against television. ABC had 1,233 radio station affiliates in 1970 in four sub-networks; CBS had 251, and NBC had 221. Mutual, serving 560 stations, went into bankruptcy in 1959 but was reorganized successfully. The number of regional radio networks increased to 81 by 1961, dropped to 53 by 1971.

THE BOOM IN FM RADIO

FM (frequency modulation) radio made a bid against the normal AM (amplitude modulation) radio in the 1940s, as Table 2 shows. FM radio was looked upon as the means of providing smaller towns with thousands of radio stations, since FM covers a smaller area with better reception. But only a few hundred FM stations survived in the 1950s, primarily as "better listening" stations, because transistor radio sets produced by mass methods did not tune in FM channels until the mid–1960s. But as the 1970s began, FM had become one of the fastest growing elements in American broadcasting. At the decade year of 1960 there were 688 FM stations; in 1965 there were 1,270; in 1971, the total was 2,636 including 2,200 commercial stations. There were several reasons for this mushrooming of FM broadcasting: 1) investors had a better chance for success than in the network-dominated television area and the badly-overcrowded AM station field; 2) an increased interest in cultural affairs and classical music; 3) the arrival of stereo and the high-fidelity industry, coinciding with this interest in better music; 4) various FCC decisions which helped give FM a separate identity from AM, its longtime subsidizer; 5) driving away by television and radio of some of the audience by poor programming; 6) increasing use of FM by advertisers as the quality and quantity of audience became known; 7) mushrooming sales of FM sets, from 2 million a year in 1960 to 21 million in 1968.[14]

Appearing on the scene with FM was facsimile broadcasting, also limited in scope of reception. Facsimile broadcasting, begun on a daily basis by KSD, St. Louis, in 1938, was viewed as a possible way of delivering printed newspapers into the home. But the innovation failed to reach mass-production use.

THE RISE OF TELEVISION

Television became the successful competitor, combining the appeals and techniques of film and radio. As early as the 1860s there were efforts to achieve the illusions of depth and movement by projecting pictures on screens. Thomas A. Edison used some of George Eastman's early Kodak film in inventing the Kinetoscope in 1889, and one of his assistants projected *The Great Train Robbery* in 1903, the first motion picture to tell a story. Sound motion pictures were developed by Warner Brothers in 1926; color arrived in 1935. Newsreels had been popular since 1897; in the 1930s documentaries, focusing on a social problem or economic issue, were filmed. By the time of the arrival of commercial television the technological processes and artistic techniques of film making were well established.

Experimental television broadcasting began in the 1920s in the United States. A picture was televised between New York and Philadelphia in 1923, and WGY, the General Electric station in Schenectady, was televising regularly in 1928. By 1937 there were 17 experimental stations on the air. Commercial

[14] Christopher H. Sterling, "Decade of Development: FM Radio in the 1960s," *Journalism Quarterly,* XLVIII (Summer 1971), 222.

broadcasting began in 1941, but World War II put a halt to production of sets and equipment. Stimulated by the development of the coaxial cable and the microwave relay, which made possible network television, 108 stations were broadcasting by 1949. Some soon failed.[15]

That year the Federal Communications Commission ordered a "freeze" in channel allocations. For three years the FCC replanned and reallocated channels, to permit more than 2,000 channel assignments to nearly 1,300 communities, including 242 channels for noncommercial educational stations. To do this, the FCC extended television broadcasting from the established VHF (very-high-frequency) channels (numbered 2 through 13) to 70 more channels called UHF (ultra-high-frequency). There were more than twice as many UHF as VHF assignments. But different equipment was needed to tune a set to the UHF and VHF stations, and the established patterns of set-making and broadcasting were VHF. By 1971 there were 511 commercial VHF stations, only 185 commercial UHF stations. And there were only 85 VHF and 111 UHF educational stations.

THE DOMINANT TV NETWORKS

Even if the mechanical problems had been overcome, the FCC's hopes for thousands of television stations probably could not have been realized. For the profits were made by big-time network stations. During the freeze period, the transcontinental relay was completed, and the nation's television viewers saw the Japanese peace treaty conference in San Francisco during September, 1951, as their first cross-country program. The networks grew, with stations served numbering 221 for NBC, 192 for CBS, and 159 for ABC in 1971. There were 11 regional chains. The national television networks had just 2½ million dollars in time sales in 1948; by 1960 the figure was 470 million dollars, and and by 1970 it had skyrocketed to more than 1½ billions.

The FCC reported that in 1969 the three major networks made profits of 5.7 per cent before taxes. Their 15 owned-and-operated television stations earned 34.6 per cent before taxes, and some other big-city network affiliates did nearly as well. The typical television station earned 21 per cent before taxes. But 17 per cent of VHF stations and 65 per cent of UHF stations were losers. Among independent stations a third of VHF and 96 per cent of UHF lost money. In television, production costs were so heavy that high-grade programming could be achieved only by the networks and largest stations—a factor not true in radio.

[15] For the use of television and radio's adjustment to it, 1933–53, see Erik Barnouw, *The Golden Web* (New York: The Oxford Press, 1968). His *The Image Empire* (1970) continues the story.

COLOR, CATV, AND SATELLITES

Color television was authorized by the FCC in 1953 after a false start in 1950 when the CBS noncompatible color system was given preference over the eventually adopted RCA compatible system—i.e., a system which enables either color or black-and-white sets to receive the same broadcast. The networks expanded telecasting in color, but high prices of color-receiving sets kept their use at only 600,000 in 1961. Ten years later, with price declines and quality improvement, there were 25 million color TV homes, 42 per cent of the 60 million total.

The "hottest" mass communications industry in the United States as the 1970s opened was cable television, called CATV for Community Antenna Television system. Cable television started as a means of bringing commercial television signals into isolated communities whose residents could not receive good pictures through their own antennas. It developed rapidly when it became apparent the coaxial cable could be used to bring a variety of programming to smaller communities—including the shows of all three major U.S. networks. It also became apparent that CATV has the capability of using large numbers of channels (20 to 40 in some U.S. systems by 1970) for varying purposes in metropolitan areas. In 1960 there were 640 CATV systems serving 650,000 homes, 1.4 per cent of all TV homes. In 1971 there were 2,550 CATV systems serving 5½ million homes, 9.2 per cent of all TV homes. There were another 1,500 systems under construction and thousands of applications pending. The systems took in an estimated 300 million dollars annually from installation fees of $10 to $20 and service charges of about $5 monthly.

Many CATV proposals and ideas were still at issue in the early 1970s. CATV operators thought they would win the right to serve major markets (color images delivered over coaxial cable are superior to those taken out of the air) and developed widespread networks. Others expected the cables to carry the kind of local programming originally expected from UHF and FM—local public affairs, "town meetings," and the like—on extra cable channels. Other projected uses were foreseen if costs could be low enough: delivery of news in printed form, information retrieval hookups with libraries, connections to banks, stores, and other institutions for business purposes. In some localities the development of local news and "town meeting" programs had occurred.

But the conflict over jurisdictions between CATV and older broadcast forms slowed the process. The FCC, in a 1970 "Public Dividend Plan" for CATV, banned cross-ownership of CATV and television stations in a market, ordered networks out of the business, and invited comment on whether radio stations and newspapers should own cable systems. The plan also required cable systems to help subsidize noncommercial television, to pay copyright owners for use of their material (a setback for CATV), and ordered larger operators to start originating programs of their own.

Further detailing of the FCC position on CATV came in August 1971 when the commission issued a "letter of intent" to the Congress, outlining rules FCC expected to adopt and put into effect by March 1972 unless Congress intervened. These rules would permit cable operators to import two distant signals into each of the top 100 markets (one to be a UHF station within 200 miles if available). Minimum service standards would be three full network stations in all markets, plus three independent stations in markets 1–50, two in markets 51–100, and one in lesser markets. As the plan worked out, cable operators in the smaller markets would carry at least five stations, those in the giant Los Angeles area as many as 13.

In return for this concession, the FCC would require of cable operators in the top 100 markets: 1) an actual or potential capacity of at least 20 channels; 2) for each broadcast signal carried, an equivalent amount of nonbroadcast bandwidth; 3) a free, noncommercial public-access channel, a channel for educational use, and a channel for state and local government use; 4) provision for additional channels if some became overcrowded; 5) two-way communication capability for nonbroadcast uses. Cable operators would be free to carry educational stations' signals if the latter did not object. And they could sell advertising if they originated programming.

News by satellites became television's most sensational achievement of the 1960s. The successful launching of AT&T's Telstar on July 10, 1962, permitted the first live transmissions of pictures between the United States and Europe. These were staged shows lasting for the few minutes the signal could be bounced off the moving satellite. RCA's Relay carried pictures to 23 nations at the time of President Kennedy's assassination. The effort to develop continuous service by launching a satellite that would achieve a fully synchronous orbit (an orbit and speed that keep the craft directly over one spot on earth) met success when Howard Hughes launched Syncom III in 1964. Four such satellites, equally spaced around the world, could provide television coverage to all inhabited portions of the planet.

The Communications Satellite Corporation (called Comsat), formed by Congress in 1962 to unify the U.S. effort and to provide international leadership, carried out technical progress well. Early Bird went into synchronous orbit in 1965, followed by the Intelsat II series in 1966 and 1967 and the larger Intelsat III series in 1968 and 1969. By the time Intelsat IV satellites followed in 1971–73, no fewer than 78 ground facilities in 53 countries would be connected to a greatly expanded television facility whose sociopolitical use remained to be determined. In May, 1971, a 79-nation Intelsat conference wound up two years of work to develop revised rules for the International Telecommunications Satellite Consortium. Comsat had held control of the group's policies and technical operations; it agreed to drop U.S. voting power to 40 per cent and to give up managerial duties within the decade. Domestically, the FCC invited appli-

THE CHRISTIAN SCIENCE MONITOR

Registered in U. S. Patent Office

AN INTERNATIONAL DAILY NEWSPAPER

VOLUME 52 NO. 257 | © 1960, THE CHRISTIAN SCIENCE PUBLISHING SOCIETY All Rights Reserved | BOSTON, TUESDAY, SEPTEMBER 27, 1960 | • ATLANTIC EDITION | TWO SECTIONS | BEYOND 15 MILES TEN CENTS | SEVEN CENTS

Threat to UN Eases; Peking Casts Shadow

By the Associated Press

New York

President Eisenhower and British Prime Minister Harold Macmillan agreed Sept. 27 to give "full support" to United Nations Secretary-General Dag Hammarskjold in his tasks. Mr. Hammarskjold has been a target of Soviet Premier Nikita S. Khrushchev.

By Joseph C. Harsch

Special Correspondent of The Christian Science Monitor

United Nations, N.Y.

The delicate composure of Indian Prime Minister Jawaharlal Nehru and the phlegmatic urbanity of British Prime Minister Harold Macmillan flowed over the United Nations scene as its General Assembly went into the second week of its extraordinary session here in New York.

The effect was steadying on all—with, of course, the exception of Premier Fidel Castro of Cuba, who embarrassed his supposed friends and bored the rest of his audience with his inability to distinguish interminable rhetoric from logic.

The importance of Soviet Premier Nikita S. Khrushchev's role has visibly diminished as the awareness spreads that he has neither wrecked the UN nor possesses the capacity to do so. Dag Hammarskjold is still Secretary-General and will continue to be so.

A count of hands shows that Mr. Khrushchev could barely get 15 votes for his proposals which sounded so ominous a few days before, and the conviction grew that he had launched his assault on the UN—not for an instant expecting to get anywhere with it, but primarily as a talking point for his running argument with the Chinese Communists, with some incidental possible bargaining value here.

It is conceivable that he might at some point withdraw his threats against the UN in return for some benefit in future negotiations with the West, but his real purpose, it was agreed among Western diplomats, had been to forge a weapon he could use in the murky waters of Communist-bloc politics.

Mr. Nehru and Mr. Macmillan arrived on the scene not overexcited by the superficial discussions on disarmament which reflected the theoretical purpose of this gathering; and not unduly disturbed by the flurry over the future of the UN which struck both of the new arrivals as equally unrealistic. Mr. Khrushchev had produced massive sound and fury which on examination proved to be nothing but froth.

Nehru's Concern

What concerned Mr. Nehru the most was not Dr. Castro's display of vulgar histrionics, but the flexing muscles of the Chinese giant across his northern frontier. And what was reportedly uppermost in Mr. Macmillan's thinking was the long-term implication of the Soviet-managed operation of recent weeks in the Congo.

The real dangers, as these men see them, and as their Washington colleagues agreed, are not immediate nor here in the UN, but in the fact that Moscow was able to deploy hundreds of "technicians" in the Congo on the first visible sign of an opportunity to make a new conquest for communism there, and of the even more disturbing implication that this abrupt action reflected a level of willingness in Moscow to take long and dangerous risks with the peace under the steady jabs of Peking incitement to violence which is the brand of Communist bloc behavior this year.

Key Question Cited

The visitors from London have been sobered by the Congo operation and while Mr. Macmillan himself can still see much theo- [illegible] Khrushchev, he and his associates have faced the fact that Moscow proved in the Congo both its possession of a highly trained apparatus for suddenly exploiting an opportunity for conquest far beyond its frontiers and the cynical willingness to use it.

The visitors from India have been sobered by their own experiences under the shadow of Chinese expansionism and the many current indications that the dragon is still hungry and is still pushing with increasing insistence against the walls around it.

The real question which the Western statesmen talked about off the UN stage in the hotel rooms was the long-term problem of how to persuade, some would say help, Mr. Khrushchev to resist the arguments which have for months been beating upon him from Peking to resort to ever greater violence and revolution in a major Communist attack.

Soviet Tack?

The most significant event at this session may well prove to be the meeting between Mr. Nehru and Mr. Khrushchev, although it will certainly be years, if ever, before the real essence of this encounter will be spread on the public record.

It is perfectly obvious that Mr. Nehru called on Mr. Khrushchev to discover as best he could whether Mr. Khrushchev either willingly or under pressures which he thinks he can no longer resist is committed to the Chinese dictated course. Mr. Nehru is far too responsible a statesman to disclose what, if anything, he learned.

The dominant fact overshadowing this meeting is that Mr. Khrushchev, while clinging to his theories of the noninevitability of war and "peaceful coexistence," has done in the Congo precisely the sort of thing which Peking has been urging.

Is he committed permanently down this line, or is he treading it to build strength within the Communist bloc for a showdown with Peking which some Western experts increasingly suspect may be the greatest struggle looming on the world's horizon today?

Meeting Unlikely

Communist bloc leadership is bidden to assemble in Moscow in early November. Every Communist move here is quite probably shaped to that gathering of the clan where the issues outstanding between Moscow and Peking must be handled one way or another whether China is represented or stays away.

Under these circumstances it may now be assumed that the idea of any major effort to bring Mr. Eisenhower and Mr. Khrushchev together has been all but eliminated. Conceivably Mr. Khrushchev might change his tone and strategy before he leaves here sufficiently to permit a personal reconciliation. The likelihood is negligible.

If, as is now widely believed, he came here not to seek reconciliation but to build a record for use in his impending great struggle with Communist China, then there is no possibility of any news here of a surprise meeting between the two men who estranged each other in Paris last May.

The most alarming possibility is that the failure of the Congo venture and the impending failure here to stampede the new African countries into the Communist fold can goad Mr. Khrushchev not toward moderation but toward even more dangerous ventures.

In the meantime, though, the excitement is diminishing here and the British intend to express their views on all this by sending both their Prime Minister and their Foreign Minister back to London come next weekend.

Associated Press Wirephoto

U.S. and U.A.R. Presidents Meet

President Eisenhower (left) and United Arab Republic President Nasser had a show of hands as they met at President Eisenhower's hotel suite in New York Sept. 26. Mr. Eisenhower arrived from Washington earlier and held talks with various foreign dignitaries in New York for the 15th UN General Assembly. President Nasser is reported to have invited Mr. Eisenhower to pay a visit to the U.A.R. as Mr. Nasser's guest of honor.

Eisenhower's busy New York day: Page 3

MDC Probe Hears Political Echoes

By Albert D. Hughes

Staff Writer of The Christian Science Monitor

Political overtones today were injected into the special Massachusetts Senate committee investigation of the Metropolitan District Commission.

Senator John E. Powers (D) of Boston implied that the administration of Gov. Christian A. Herter and MDC commissioner Charles W. Greenough called off the Pleasure Bay project in South Boston for political reasons. The project was an enclosed area along a Boston harbor which would be free of tides and available throughout most of the day as a bathing beach.

Associate Commissioner Greenough, who was on the witness stand, suggested that the project was large and had been politically controversial. He furthermore asserted "I was not ordered to call it off."

Start Recalled

The associate commissioned testified that the Pleasure Bay project originated in a telephone call between himself and Senator Powers while he was on a vacation in Maine. Upon his return the then Commissioner said he sat down with Senator Powers and talked over the project.

Mr. Greenough further asserted that the Herter administration had expressed itself as strongly opposed to the project. Earlier in his testimony Senator Powers interupted Mr. Greenough to ask him what steps he had taken to reorganize the MDC after he became Commissioner.

Mr. Grennough displayed copies of bills which he had placed in the Legislature to put the executive and administration of the MDC under the Commissioner rather than the Board of Commissioners.

Bill Quoted

Senator Powers took a copy of the bill and stated that nowhere in it was there any indication that an MDC official was interested in the legislation, even though it concerned the MDC.

Resentment of key career employees over politics and waste in the operations of the Metropolitan District Commission was illustrated in testimony of Benjamin W. Fink, of Newton, chief engineer in the MDC Parks Division, before the special Senate committee investiing the MDC yesterday.

A career employee with the MDC for 36 years and for 12 years head of its Parks Division, Mr. Fink charged that the MDC is wasting half of the millions it spends on consultants' fees.

The special inquiry is expected to conclude today with testimony from MDC Commissioner John E. Maloney and Associate Commissioners Charles W. Greenough and John Hill.

Already, disclosures at the hearings have promoted one reform and other changes are in stores for the MDC. At its regular meeting last week on Tues- voted to review all new under-$1,000 contracts.

On the subject of these contracts, which it is charged were split to evade requirements for public bidding, Mr. Fink said political overtones were responsible for "poor supervision" of such contracts.

Mr. Fink testified he was forced to rely on subordinates for checking the under-$1,000 contracts and stated that it was a "physical impossibility" for him to oversee this work personally, though it carried his approving signature.

The MDC engineer also testified that members of his staff asked him to relay their complaints over the under-$1,000 "political contracts" to the hearings.

The Newton engineer also said that he has stopped all payment of under-$1,000 contracts, since the investigations began, except for emergency work.

Resignations Sought

Mr. Fink also testified to proposing that qualified steel inspectors be engaged when the Longfellow Bridge contract was begun and of being turned down by the commission. He said the MDC had five inspectors on the Longfellow Bridge job but none of them were qualified steel inspectors.

The disclosures brought from George A. McLaughlin, chief counsel, a statement that "we are going to ask, in our final report, that the Legislature establish one construction division to build all state roads, bridges, buildings, both for the state and the MDC, and that it be properly staffed with a central engineering division, and that it pay these engineers the going rates."

Senator Francis X. McCann (D), of Cambridge, committee member, also remarked "I think resignations are in order."

The Cambridge legislator made this statement after listening to testimony of William A. Meagher, of Wakefield, administrative assistant to Commissioner Maloney.

Pictures: Page 2

Associated Press Wirephoto

John F. Kennedy

Resolved . . .

Associated Press Wirephoto

Richard M. Nixon

Resolved . . .

Debate Winner? Voters of Nation

By Godfrey Sperling, Jr.

Chief of the Central News Bureau of The Christian Science Monitor

Chicago

The focal point of some 130,000,000 eyes, the presidential candidates squared off in the first of four unprecedented joint appearances before a vast TV audience.

The winner? The American public was the winner.

The silent Chicago streets, the cavernous ball park, the almost empty theaters. All this attested to the public's intense interest in the two candidates and a clash that centered on the farm, the aged, the schools, the economic growth rate, the lowering of the national debt, the relative maturity and experience of the two men. But the impact naturally spilled over into America's posture in the world today, and who was best qualified to provide leadership for the next four or eight years.

For reporters who have been following the candidates around the United States, there was little that was new in what the two men said. Senator John F. Kennedy, again, was saying that America's performance, vis-à-vis the Soviet Union, was not good enough. Vice-President Richard M. Nixon was saying it had, indeed, been good enough. And both were agreeing that there must be a step up for the future—militarily, scientifically, educationally, economically.

In the main, the verbal exchanges here showed that the objectives of the two candidates are quite similar. The difference lies in the means—and the cost of the means.

Mr. Nixon said, as he has said before, that he has tabulated the Democratic program and thinks it will cost $13,200,000,000 to perhaps $18,000,000,000 while, he said, his own program would cost some $4,000,000,000 to $4,900,000,000.

First, the Costs

Senator Kennedy later countered by asserting that the revenue for his program would come readily from the expanded growth that would accompany this program.

Even this was not a narrowing or sharpening of issues. It had all been said before as the presidential campaign jets moved back and forth across the country.

But here, for the first time, all these little speeches on all these [illegible] understood package. And the pulling together of all this information was of inestimable value to a public intent on learning more about the candidates and getting a better grasp of the issues.

The men as TV performers? Both were superb. But was this a display of outstanding mental capacity or was this, at least in part, the expression of countless little memorized speeches? The limitations of TV could not answer this with a certainty, although the viewers—and particularly those who had already chosen up sides—probably resolved this question to their own satisfaction.

Actually, the question-from-panel format is not one that brings about a true clash of the "debaters." There was really little opportunity for either of the candidates to probe the other's mind—or to pressure the other with an incisive query.

Production Figures

It was Mr. Nixon, the man of experience under fire, the man of the kitchen debates with Soviet Premier Nikita S. Khrushchev, who looked strained in the early minutes of the discussion. He rallied well, but Kennedy had probably made a point. His consistent poise no doubt helped to put the immaturity charge to rest—for the evening, and, perhaps, for the entire campaign.

In the exchange of figures on economic growth, Mr. Nixon finally said that the Soviet production was 44 per cent that of the United States—the same that it was 20 years ago.

Senator Kennedy seemed to accept this figure but said it was important that the Soviets' production did not rise to 60 or 90 per cent in the next few years.

Earlier, Mr. Nixon had said that the Soviet's economic growth rate had been good in late years only because it was measured against a very low base.

Had Mr. Nixon nailed Senator Kennedy on this acceptance of a production figure, an acceptance that current production was not as bad as he had pictured? Perhaps so, but then, again, maybe only in the minds of Mr. Nixon's partisans.

Public the Critic

Actually, this was a strange occasion, where the press was not reporting anything that the public was not, itself, seeing—and analyzing for itself. And even a reportorial critique seems inconsequential. For the viewers are the critics.

Was Senator Kennedy or Mr. Nixon more persuasive than the other? How many votes were changed or won? The real critiques will be coming in on Nov. 8, in terms of votes for the new President of the United States.

Text of Statements In TV Debate: Page 16

Not One Slip On Banana Peel!

By Richard L. Strout

Staff Correspondent of The Christian Science Monitor

Washington

The first reception of the unprecedented Nixon-Knnedey debate in millions of homes was a gasp of surprise. For all that had been written about it in advance, most viewers were not prepared for the bare, bleak, brutal stage, utterly devoid of [illegible] flying in space for 65 million to watch.

As the ordeal continued, many viewers must have had a sense of sympathy for either candidate, whatever their political affiliation, at the terrible strain to which they were subjected. Any slip might have spelled ruin for either candidate and his party's hopes. The bare stage was actually strewn with invisible banana peels, and it was hard for the viewer not to feel a sense of admiration for the sure-footed young men, each of whom, in the opinion of many, displayed a quite astonishing grasp of detail and facility for quick mobilization of ideas.

Rise to Challenge

The cameras showed close-ups of the listening candidate's face while the other talked—Senator John F. Kennedy, his chin raised in a Roosevelt tilt with clean profile and lips slightly moving; Vice-President Richard M. Nixon, in turn, looking to many weary from endless campaigning, with chin perspiring under the hot TV lamps. Both men moistened their lips in the tropical glare. No other candidates in American presidential history went through such an ordeal, which seemed at times almost cruel in its revealing details.

The candidates rose to the challenge, however, and after a preliminary period of rigidity seemed to relax in the hour-long interrogation and reply which is the first of four such performances.

By the toss of a coin Mr. Kennedy not merely spoke first but had the last word, an advantage which Mr. Nixon will have at later meetings. Some observers felt that Senator Kennedy was strongest in his opening statement, which was composed of fragments of campaign speeches which he has by heart. In turn, Mr. Nixon seemed to gather strength as the proceedings continued as he threw constantly increasing objections in the path of Mr. Kennedy's sweeping proposals.

To some Senator Kennedy seemed to have a second preliminary advantage in that he was making the attack on the Eisenhower-Republican policies, while Mr. Nixon, at first, was in the position of a defender. As interrogations continued, however, Mr. Nixon in turn took the offensive when he charged that the cost of the Kennedy legislative proposals would be "13.2 to 18 billion dollars" compared with the "4 to 4.9 billion dollar" price tag which he placed on the Republican program.

This confrontation was no exception to the rule that when candidates meet, there is a degree of politeness that hardly obtains when they speak apart. It was evident that neither man dared risk the danger of a breach of decorum with the vast unseen audience. The adept Mr. Nixon managed one ad hominem argument when he obliquely pointed up Mr. Kennedy's wealthy background by saying he was sure of the latter's sincerity and adding for himself, "I know what it means to be poor. . . . I know Senator Kennedy feels as deeply about these problems as I do. . . ."

Both men cited statistics of national "growth" which must have thoroughly confused unseen viewers because they were based on different and irreconcilable years of comparison. Senator Kennedy cited his familiar charges of a low growth rate under President Eisenhower; Mr. Nixon replied by taking Truman versus Eisenhower years.

Public Gains Insight

Millions of American families snapped off the TV to debate, "who won?"

One answer was that everybody won.

Beyond question the uniquely dramatic personal confrontation quickened political interest over the country six weeks before election. For the first time, many people became aware of the rival approaches to minimum wage, school aid, health aid for the aged, and the like, as well as of the contrasting personalities of the two men.

An argument could be made that either candidate benefited.

Senator Kennedy gained, in the opinion of many, because he had the more to win by making his personality known. He is the less familiar figure and has a certain amount of lag to make up by appearing on terms of equality with the Vice-President—a national celebrity for eight years.

Vice-President Nixon benefited for different reasons, it is argued. What the Republicans needed was a stir of excitement to get their supporters to register, to overcome the advantage Democrats are felt to have by their affiliation with nationally organized trade unions. This the Nixon-Kennedy clash has done.

State of the Nations

Who Pays for Reform?

By William H. Stringer

Chief, Washington News Bureau, The Christian Science Monitor

Washington

The first Nixon-Kennedy televised debate points up a consideration which the voters will have to resolve for themselves, and it is this:

Quite evidently, Senator John F. Kennedy would proceed more vigorously—or drastically—using more costly [illegible] in his efforts to handle the problems of aid to education, minimum wage, federal power, medical care for the elderly, perhaps defense. The question then is not merely that raised by Mr. Nixon, which is whether Congress would approve the 96 days of vigorous legislation which a President Kennedy in the White House would launch.

The question is also whether the business and industrial community of the United States would take this added burden, which almost certainly would mean an additional tax burden, in stride. Or would such a program disturb and unsettle the free enterprise system which lays the "golden eggs" of national wealth so that business would not respond, would not boost "national growth" levels, and we would be again in the doldrums of the 1930's.

* * *

Not until World War II came along was President Roosevelt able really to terminate the nation's business slump and get full production rolling after the great depression. Necessary reforms, pump priming for business, exhortations and denunciations had little effect. A climate of business opportunity had not been created by Washington, and so business did not boom. Would a President Kennedy encounter a like resistance, a similar failure to go forward?

The answer is partly psychological. If a new administration comes in on a big national tide of endorsement—if the nation has concluded that only vigorous measures will suffice to build educational standards higher, clear out the slums and big-city rot, take care of the elderly and raise the minimum wage—then a national climate will have been created to which the business community will perforce accommodate itself.

If this means added taxation—and there are indications that it must somewhere along the line—then industry will buckle too, and pay the taxes, in response to patriotic purpose. But if there is no evident national resolve that heroic measures are vital now, then a drastic Kennedy program could meet serious resistance and discourage good behavior in the business community.

* * *

The Kennedy brain trusters say that the whole round of additional government enterprise, defense spending, and management of debt and in- [illegible] geoning economy with high economic growth and that this would develop sufficient taxable wealth so that deficit financing and seriously unbalanced budgets could be avoided.

This may be so, but it would require a ratification by the business world of the proposition that the Kennedy program was either unavoidably crucial or designed to create a favorable business climate, to cause all this to work together for prosperity.

Per Jacobsson, the able and well-traveled Swede who heads the International Monetary Fund, observed last week that one main reason for today's rolling readjustment or lack of boom in business is that the American economy is getting used to moving along without inflation. This is a novel atmosphere; creeping inflation has been here for years, but now it seems to have been halted.

Mr. Jacobsson further reports that as Europeans survey the American economy and consider the possibility of a Kennedy victory, they wonder if this is going to touch off a new round of inflation. They note hopefully that Democrats talk of a national sales tax that could produce perhaps $8,000,000,000 to pay for all of Senator Kennedy's "new frontier" legislation.

If Senator Kennedy should be elected, would Congress pass such a tax? Would the United States's businessmen glance at the Soviet Union's strides and say, "We must sustain whatever burden is necessary to boost production and advance our social progress"? Or would the proposals be deemed too zealous, too drastic, and would business, disturbed or apprehensive, simply not undertake the sufficient investment in new plant, equipment, and enterprise necessary for really massive national growth?

* * *

Certainly Senator Kennedy must make an effective case for the urgencies of larger-scale government intervention, if such a program as he proposes were to be financed without slump, inflation, or seriously unbalanced budgets.

Goldfine Case To Open in Boston

The World's Day

Reg. U.S. Pat. Off.

New England: Tax-Evasion Trial Set for Oct. 3

The $800,000 tax-evasion case of industrialist Bernard Goldfine will open Monday, Oct. 3, in United States District Court, Boston. Mr. Goldfine, currently in the Federal Correctional Institution in Danbury, Conn., on a contempt-of-court sentence ending Monday, will be brought to Charles Street Jail this weekend. United States Attorney Elliot L. Richardson will prosecute the case.

National: Candidates Back on Campaign Trail

Following the "great debate" Vice-President Richard M. Nixon headed south for campaign activities in Tennessee and Arkansas. Senator John F. Kennedy flew to Ohio for a one-day political swing.

The father of U-2 pilot Francis Gary Powers, who failed in attempts to see Soviet Premier Nikita S. Khrushchev on behalf of his son, appealed to the Kremlin leader through the Dave Garroway "Today" show on NBC television.

Asia: South Korea Plans to Grant Pardons

Premier John M. Chang's South Korean Government decided to grant pardons or reduction of sentences to nearly 15,000 prisoners Oct. 1 in celebration of the founding of the Second Republic. Meanwhile, the government prosecution demanded capital punishment for four top-ranking police officials charged with rigging national elections last March.

Weather: Cloudy Tonight and Wednesday [Page 2]

Arts. Music. Theater: Page 7. Radio. TV. FM: Page 6

Inside Reading

Facts and fireworks over school center managers. Page 2

Lynn residents take strike threat in stride. Page 2

Congo: Ghana keeps up pressure. Page 10

Glitter gone from golden Prague. Page 12

Research by NASA discloses goals for moon probing. Page 13

Southern Democrats take stand on foreign policy. Page 14

Associated Press Wirephoto

Just Before the Opening Gavel

Presidential candidates Nixon and Kennedy trade grins

The crucial first "Great Debate" on TV decided the 1960 presidential race.

cations in 1970–71 from all groups interested in providing satellite transmission of television, telephone, news, and data services. There was indication that President Nixon's administration favored open competition in the field, as against a Comsat monopoly favoring existing communications companies that control it.

Television had recorded massive audiences for news events since the 1950s. Some 60 million Americans saw President Eisenhower inaugurated in 1953. At least 85 million saw one of the "Great Debates" between John F. Kennedy and Richard M. Nixon in 1960. John Glenn's first manned orbital flight by an American drew 135 million to the edges of their chairs in 1962. When news of President Kennedy's assassination in 1963 became known, the New York City television audience jumped from 25 per cent to 70 per cent, and rose to 93 per cent for the funeral service. When men first walked on the moon in 1969, and live television pictures were directly transmitted to earth, some 125 million Americans saw the climactic nighttime broadcast, and a satellite network carried the pictures to an eventual world audience estimated at 500 million. But Intelsat broke all records in 1970 when in the most elaborate of all satellite coverage attempts, an estimated 900 million soccer fans viewed live coverage of the World Cup matches in Mexico City. Not only the country, but the world, could sit in at a town meeting.

CBS NEWS, NBC NEWS, ABC NEWS

Radio's pioneers were still active in the early 1970s. David Sarnoff, the Russian-born genius of the world of wireless and television, retired in 1970 to the honorary chairmanship of the Radio Corporation of America, which he had built. RCA was a 2-billion-dollar business and the largest communications organization in the world. His son Robert became both president and board chairman of RCA, and father and son sat on the NBC board. Dr. Frank Stanton, the researcher with doctorate who rose to the presidency of CBS, continued as an intelligent spokesman for broadcasting. William S. Paley, CBS founder, was board chairman. Each network had a separately organized division for news and public affairs. Their presidents in 1971 were Richard S. Salant, CBS News, Reuven Frank, NBC News, and Elmer W. Lower, ABC News.

Covering the news was a 120-million-dollar operation for the three networks in 1970, according to FCC reports, but much of the expenditure was reclaimed by advertising sales. CBS and NBC each had some 40 correspondents and as many staff cameramen in the United States, a dozen key overseas bureaus, and hundreds of stringers. Transmission advances enabled the networks to show live film via satellite of faraway events and to use videotape for later reshowings. Radio could call in correspondents at will, around the world.

Edward R. Murrow's "Hear It Now" became "See It Now" in 1951 for CBS News and ran until 1958. His documentaries became centers of contro-

ard K. Smith, Quincy Howe, and Frank Reynolds. ABC teamed Smith with Harry Reasoner, number two man at CBS, in 1970 and improved the network's rating in the nightime news derby. James C. Hagerty, President Eisenhower's press secretary, built up the staff in the 1960s before giving way to Elmer Lower as news chief. Leading correspondents were Edward P. Morgan, William H. Lawrence, John Scali, Robert Clark, Peter Jennings, Peter Clapper, and, until her death, Lisa Howard. "ABC Close-Ups" and "ABC News Reports" were the major documentary efforts of the network, which scored with such programs as "The Making of the President" and "The Soviet Woman." John Daly long conducted the network's top television news show. For Mutual, Stephen J. McCormick headed news and Washington operations.

THE FCC AND THE BROADCASTERS: LICENSING

Radio and television were still under public regulation, through the Federal Communications Commission. The FCC held license control over stations and limited holding of multiple licenses. No person or group could own more than seven TV stations (only five of them VHF) plus seven FM and seven AM stations. No one could own more than one radio and one television station in the same city.

The FCC also looked askance at ownership of broadcast stations by newspaper publishers, whether or not in the same city. Extensive hearings were held on the subject in 1941, which showed newspapers owned 30 per cent of AM stations, were heavily interested in FM stations, and had applied for 28 of the first 60 television licenses. The argument was to distribute the ownership of the mass media as widely as possible, by using the FCC licensing power to minimize cross-media ownership involving broadcasting (there being no power to limit multiple ownership of newspapers, magazines, and publishing houses). A federal court ruling in 1942 held FCC could inquire into the issue but could not use the fact of newspaper ownership alone to deny a license. The FCC closed the issue in 1944, commenting that licenses would be granted on the merits of individual applications, under the guiding rule of as much diversification as possible. In general, newspapers won licenses without undue difficulty.

Denial of a license renewal for Boston television station WHDH in 1969 to the owners of the *Boston Herald Traveler* touched off speculation and a flurry of attempts to up-end other license holders as they applied for the required periodic renewals. It was clear that the primary reason for the license change in Boston was unrelated to the newspaper ownership issue, but rather stemmed from a tangle of conflict between the station and the FCC. But the FCC made it clear in 1970 it was not resting the matter.

First it voted to prohibit future acquisitions of both a VHF television station and a radio station in the same market. This was implementation of a proposal made by the FCC in 1968 after prodding by the Department of Justice's antitrust division.

Then the FCC proposed a sweeping rule to undo existing television-radio combinations and newspaper-broadcast cross-ownerships in the same market, as argued by the Justice Department. This would mean, if the FCC adopted its proposal after hearings, that within five years those persons who owned both a newspaper and a station in a single city would have to dispose of one. The proposal came at the same time the FCC was barring television stations from CATV ownership and proposing the barring of radio stations and newspapers. The FCC was promptly challenged by media owners and any final verdict would be by the Supreme Court.[16] Existing owners were further disturbed by a U.S. Court of Appeals ruling in mid-1971 that the FCC was still giving too much preference to license holders in renewal hearings required every three years. The court sought to open the door for serious consideration of license challenges by minority groups, and for the shifting of licenses upon FCC findings of inferior performance by stations. Such challenges were in progress in various metropolitan areas, so far unsuccessfully.

Television found itself subjected to other regulation in 1970. Congress passed legislation banning cigarette advertising from the screens beginning in 1971, for health reasons (magazine cigarette advertising promptly doubled and that in newspapers increased). The immediate loss to the broadcast industry was 225 million dollars in advertising revenues, unless the time were sold to other advertisers. And the FCC voted to limit network-TV affiliate stations in the top 50 markets to three hours of network programming in prime time (forcing the stations to scramble around for 30 minutes of fill-in each evening).

THE FCC FAIRNESS DOCTRINE

The problems of editorializing on the air and fairness in presenting all sides of public issues were others involving the stations and the FCC over many decades. In a 1941 ruling, called the "Mayflower decision" because it involved renewal of a Boston station license held by the Mayflower Broadcasting Corporation, the FCC said, "The broadcaster cannot be an advocate." Radiomen presented arguments against this policy, and in 1949 the FCC decided broadcasters could—and should—"editorialize with fairness." Station owners were cautious in taking up the invitation, but by 1967 a survey showed 57 per cent of radio and television stations were presenting editorial opinion, one-third of them either daily or weekly, the rest occasionally. Some problems of covering politics were removed in 1959 when bona fide newscasts and news programs were exempted from the FCC's "equal-time" rule, but the basic prob-

[16] "FCC Makes Major Moves to Rip Up Broadcasting," *Broadcasting*, LXXVIII (March 30, 1970), 27.

lem of obtaining "fairness" in access to the air and in presenting all sides of controversial issues remained.

The requirement to be "fair" was based on two arguments: the airwaves are public property, by act of Congress, and the FCC was given power to license broadcasters in the "public interest, convenience, and necessity." The public interest is served, FCC held, if the airwaves are made accessible to many differing viewpoints.

Broadcasters said it was hard to define the "public interest" legally. They also said such extreme efforts to balance editorial comment and interpretative documentaries mitigated against broadcasters covering important social issues. If, as the FCC implied, a station had to go out and look for at least one other side to any issue it discussed, in order to be fair, it would not go out at all (CBS looking for the other side to the migrant labor problem, or the other side of military propaganda, for example). And if the "other side" came in with program demands by any number of offended or interested groups (as in the case of the Vietnam war and activist resistance to war), the station's time would be filled with programming of little interest to the majority of viewers (any newspaper editor knows a large percentage of citizens is not interested in a given social or political issue, a fact confirmed by opinion polls). To all this, the Supreme Court in a 1969 decision did not agree.

Specifically the court upheld FCC rules requiring notice be given to any person subjected to "personal attack" in an editorial or program, or to candidates for office opposing one endorsed, with right of similar reply. But the decision ranged more widely in the "fairness doctrine" issue, noting "it is the right of the viewers and listeners, not the right of the broadcasters, which is paramount." If broadcasters were not willing to present representative community views on controversial issues, Justice Byron White wrote, the granting or renewal of a license might be challenged within the spirit of the U.S. constitution.[17] Promptly dubbed the *Red Lion* doctrine, this decision created excitement. But when in 1970 Dr. Frank Stanton of CBS decided to afford the Democratic party time to answer President Nixon's unprecedented number of prime time requisitionings to give arguments concerning his foreign policy and the Vietnam war, the FCC emasculated its new power. Yes, it said, CBS was correct in giving the right of reply, but it also had to let the Republican party answer the Democrats, and, presumably, so on and on in an endless circle. CBS cancelled the public discussion it wanted to have and appealed to the courts for relief. The incident served to prove that it is very difficult to legislate "fairness."

Radio stations were stimulated to increase their use of local live programs —including news and public affairs—by publication of the 1946 FCC "Blue Book," called "Public Service Responsibility of Broadcasting Licensees." The Radio-Television News Directors Association and the National Association of

[17] *Red Lion Broadcasting Co., Inc. v. Federal Communications Commission*, 394 U.S. (1969).

The Weather

The Washington Post

Times Herald

92d Year ... No. 228 — MONDAY, JULY 21, 1969 — 10¢

'The Eagle Has Landed'— Two Men Walk on the Moon

Neil Armstrong and Edwin Aldrin plant the American flag on the surface of the moon. The flag is kept "flying" on the airless moon by a spring device.

'One Small Step For Man . . . Giant Leap for Mankind'

By Thomas O'Toole
Washington Post Staff Writer

HOUSTON, July 20—Man stepped out onto the moon tonight for the first time in his two-million-year history.

"That's one small step for man," declared pioneer astronaut Neil Armstrong at 10:56 p.m. EDT, "one giant leap for mankind."

Just after that historic moment in man's quest for his origins, Armstrong walked on the dead satellite and found the surface very powdery, littered with fine grains of black dust.

A few minutes later, Edwin (Buzz) Aldrin joined Armstrong on the lunar surface and in less than an hour they put on a show that will long be remembered by the worldwide television audience.

American Flag Planted

The two men walked easily, talked easily, even ran and jumped happily so it seemed. They picked up rocks, talked at length of what they saw, planted an American flag, saluted it, and talked by radiophone with the President in the White House, and then faced the camera and saluted Mr. Nixon.

"For every American, this has to be the proudest day of our lives," the President told the astronauts. "For one priceless moment in the whole history of man, all the people on this earth are truly one."

At 1:10 a.m.—2 hours and 14 minutes after Armstrong first stepped upon the lunar surface—the astronauts were back in their moon craft and the hatch was closed.

In describing the moon, Armstrong told Houston that it was "fine and powdery. I can kick it up loosely with my toe.

"It adheres like powdered charcoal to the boot," he went on, "but I only go in a small fraction of an inch. I can see my footprint in the moon like fine grainy particles."

Armstrong found he had such little trouble walking on the moon that he began talking almost as if he didn't want to leave it.

"It has a stark beauty all its own," Armstrong said. "It's like the desert in the Southwestern United States. "It's very pretty out here."

Amazingly Clear Picture

Armstrong shared his first incredible moments on the moon with the whole world, as a television camera on the outside of the wingless Eagle landing craft sent back an amazingly clear picture of his first steps on the moon.

Armstrong seemed like he was swimming along, taking big and easy steps on the airless moon despite the cumbersome white pressure-suit he wore.

"There seems to be no difficulty walking around," he said. "As we suspected, it's even easier than the one-sixth G that we did in simulations on the ground."

One of the first things he did was to scoop up a small sample of the moon with a long-handled spoon with a bag on its end like a small butterfly net.

"Looks like it's easy," Aldrin said, looking down from the Lem.

"It is," Armstrong told him. "I'm sure I could push it in farther but I can't bend down that far."

Guides Aldrin Down Ladder

At 11:11 p.m., Aldrin started down the landing craft's ten-foot ladder to join Armstrong.

Backing down the nine-step ladder, Aldrin was guided the entire way by Armstrong, who stood at the foot of the ladder looking up at him.

"Okay," Armstrong said, "watch your 'pliss' (PLSS, for portable life support system) from underneath. Drop your pliss down. You're clear. About an inch clear on your pliss."

"Okay," Aldrin said. "You need a little arching of the back to come down."

When he stepped onto the first rung of the ladder, Aldrin went back up to the Lem's "front porch" to partially close the Lem's hatch.

"Making sure not to lock it on my way out," he said in comic fashion. "That's our home for the next couple of hours and I want to make sure we can get back in."

Aldrin reported it was a "very simple matter to hop down from one step to the next." To make the last and longest step, he said he put both hands on the fourth rung up and leaned back with his left foot first.

"Beautiful," said Aldrin when he met Armstrong on the lunar surface.

"Isn't that something," said Armstrong. "It's a magnificent sight out here."

See APOLLO, A9, Col. 1

Moon Walk Yields Data for Science

By Victor Cohn

See SCIENCE, A10, Col. 4

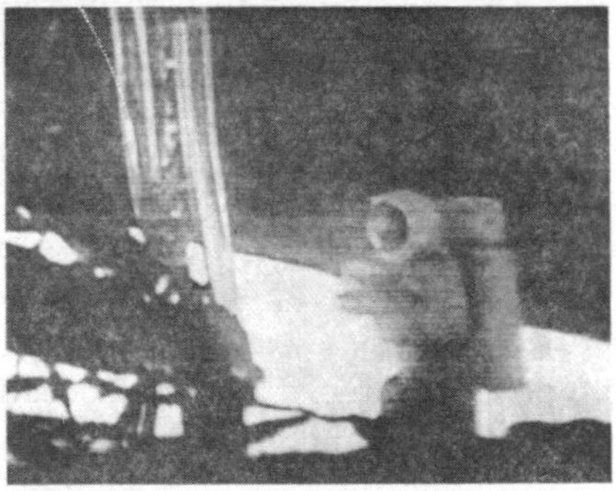

Armstrong takes his first steps on the moon. At left is the Eagle, the lunar landing craft.

'Squared Away and in Good Shape . . .'

See TRANSCRIPT, A11, Col. 1

Apollo Liftoff Schedule

Millions Follow Moon Landing Around the World, Except in China

By Robert C. Jensen

See REACT, A8, Col. 4

Newspapers reproduced television's historic news beats on their front pages.

Broadcasters also upheld the importance of high-level news and comment. Broadcast newsmen won their way into public events previously covered by newspapermen, beginning with the successful fight by Fulton Lewis, Jr., of Mutual to get radiomen into the Congressional press galleries in 1939. Beginning in 1961, Presidential press conferences were televised live—full recognition of the importance of radio and television as news and opinion-making media.

Annotated Bibliography

Books

Barnouw, Erik, *A History of Broadcasting in the United States.* Vol. 1, *A Tower in Babel* (to 1933); Vol. 2, *The Golden Web* (1933–53); Vol. 3, *The Image Empire* (from 1953). New York: The Oxford Press, 1966, 1968, 1970. Best account of radio and television; third volume necessarily becomes less historical in tone.

Barrett, Marvin, ed., *Survey of Broadcast Journalism, 1969–1970.* New York: Grosset & Dunlap, 1970. Like its predecessor, a paperback review of major events sponsored by Alfred I. duPont-Columbia University Awards.

Bluem, A. William, *The Documentary in American Television.* New York: Hastings House, 1965. Includes historical development and 100 pages of photographs.

Bulman, David, ed., *Molders of Opinion.* Milwaukee: Bruce Publishing Company, 1945. Includes chapters on H. V. Kaltenborn, Gabriel Heatter, Fulton Lewis, Jr., and Raymond Gram Swing.

Burlingame, Roger, *Don't Let Them Scare You: The Life and Times of Elmer Davis.* Philadelphia: Lippincott, 1961. A good biography of a top-flight news analyst.

Charnley, Mitchell V., *News by Radio.* New York: Macmillan, 1948. The best source for the growth of radio news.

Chase, Francis, Jr., *Sound and Fury.* New York: Harper & Row, 1942. An informal history of radio with much information, but sometimes inaccurate in precise details.

De Forest, Lee, *Father of Radio: The Autobiography of Lee De Forest.* Chicago: Wilcox & Follett, 1950. The early years.

Emery, Walter B., *Broadcasting and Government.* East Lansing: Michigan State University Press, rev. ed., 1971. An encyclopaedic survey of all aspects of government interest in, and regulation of, U.S. broadcasting.

Friendly, Fred W., *Due to Circumstances Beyond Our Control . . .* New York: Random House, 1967. The story of life with Edward R. Murrow, of their controversial CBS documentaries, and of Friendly's break with CBS.

Head, Sydney W., *Broadcasting in America: A Survey of Television and Radio.* Boston: Houghton Mifflin, 1972. Covers the physical bases of broadcasting, its history, economics, and problems of social control.

Kahn, Frank J., ed., *Documents of American Broadcasting.* New York: Appleton-Century-Crofts, 1968. The pertinent documents, cases to mid-1960s.

Kaltenborn, H. V., *Fifty Fabulous Years, 1900–1950: A Personal Review*. New York: Putnam's, 1950. Autobiography of a commentator who began on the air in 1922.

Kendrick, Alexander, *Prime Time: The Life of Edward R. Murrow*. Boston: Little, Brown, 1969. Biography of the great commentator; thorough but misses catching drama of the great events in which Murrow participated.

Levin, Harvey J., *Broadcast Regulation and Joint Ownership of Media*. New York: New York University Press, 1960. A study of radio and television economics and public regulation.

Lyon, Eugene, *David Sarnoff*. New York: Harper & Row, 1966. Wireless and broadcasting developments at RCA in a favorable biography.

Murrow, Edward R., *In Search of Light: The Broadcasts of Edward R. Murrow, 1938–1961*. New York: Knopf, 1967. Broadcast history through memorable scripts.

Pierce, John R., *Science, Art and Communication*. New York: Clarkson N. Potter, 1968. A readable history of developments in communications, satellites, science, and relation to the arts.

Sarnoff, David, *Looking Ahead: The Papers of David Sarnoff*. New York: McGraw-Hill, 1968. Papers of the broadcasting pioneer.

Sevareid, Eric, *This Is Eric Sevareid*. New York: McGraw-Hill, 1964. The CBS commentator's thoughts between 1955 and 1964.

Siepmann, Charles A., *Radio, Television, and Society*. New York: Oxford University Press, 1950. Social criticism of the media, by the author of *Radio's Second Chance* (1946).

Skornia, Harry J., and Jack W. Kitson, eds., *Problems and Controversies in Television and Radio*. Palo Alto, Calif.: Pacific Books, 1968. Broadcasting leaders discuss problems of the 1960s.

Tebbel, John W., *David Sarnoff: Putting Electrons to Work*. Chicago: Encyclopaedia Britannica, 1964. A biography of the RCA chairman.

White, Llewellyn, *The American Radio*. Chicago: University of Chicago Press, 1947. A publication of the Commission on Freedom of the Press. Best single discussion of radio's growth.

Periodicals and Monographs

Principal sources are the trade journal *Broadcasting* and *Broadcasting Yearbook*. The Summer, 1957, issue of the *Journalism Quarterly* was devoted to articles about radio and television, and an extensive bibliography.

"Broadcasting at 50," *Broadcasting*, LXXIX (November 2, 1970). A special issue, including a year-by-year review of major events, 1931–70.

Cranston, Pat, "Political Convention Broadcasts: Their History and Influence," *Journalism Quarterly*, XXXVII (Spring 1960), 186. A survey from 1924 to 1956.

Clark, David G., "The Dean of Commentators: A Biography of H. V. Kaltenborn," Ph.D. thesis, University of Wisconsin, 1965. Written from the Kaltenborn papers.

———, "H. V. Kaltenborn's First Year on the Air," *Journalism Quarterly*, XLII (Summer 1965), 373. The *Brooklyn Eagle* editor takes to the air in 1923 on WEAF for a stormy year.

Emery, Michael C., "The Munich Crisis Broadcasts: Radio News Comes of Age," *Journalism Quarterly,* XLII (Autumn 1965), 576. Kaltenborn, Murrow, and Shirer penetrate American minds.

Emery, Walter B., "Nervous Tremors in the Broadcast Industry," *Educational Broadcasting Review,* III (June 1969), 43. A review of FCC rulings and actions affecting license holders.

Federal Communications Commission, *Annual Report for Fiscal Year 1964.* Washington: Government Printing Office, 1964. Summarizes, as 30th anniversary issue, communication developments since 1934.

Ferretti, Fred, "The White Captivity of Black Radio," *Columbia Journalism Review,* IX (Summer 1970), 35. Of 310 radio stations serving blacks at least in part, only 16 are owned by blacks—and no TV licenses.

"How They Do It," *Newsweek,* LXXIII (December 1, 1969), 56. Story of the Huntley-Brinkley broadcast. See also "First Team," *Newsweek,* LVII (March 13, 1961), 53.

"The 'Red Lion' Decision," *Journal of Broadcasting,* XIII (Fall 1969), 145. Text of Supreme Court decision on application of the fairness doctrine.

Shaplen, Robert, "A Farewell to Personal History," *Saturday Review,* XLIII (December 10, 1960), 46. Summarizes radio and television network coverage abroad in the 1950s.

Smith, Ralph Lee, "The Wired Nation," *Nation,* CCX (May 18, 1970). A pioneering report on CATV in a special issue.

Sterling, Christopher H., "Newspaper Ownership of Broadcast Stations, 1920–68," *Journalism Quarterly,* XLVI (Summer 1969), 227. Data and discussion of issues.

———, "Decade of Development: FM Radio in the 1960s," *Journalism Quarterly,* XLVIII (Summer 1971), 222. Analysis of reasons for rapid growth.

Wertenbaker, Charles, "Profiles," *New Yorker,* XXIX (December 26, 1953), 28. An excellent profile of Edward R. Murrow.

CBS

Thomson Newspapers

Media leaders: William S. Paley (*left*), broadcasting; Lord Thomson, newspapers.

Ebony

Time

Magazine group owners: John H. Johnson (*left*), *Ebony;* Henry Luce III, Time Inc.

27

Economic Pressures Shape the Mass Media

It is often made a matter of boasting, that the United States contain so many public journals. It were wiser to make it a cause of mourning, since the quality, in this instance, diminishes in an inverse ratio to the quantity.
—James Fenimore Cooper (1838)

Competition among the media, in the years after the rise of radio and television, was intense, both for advertising revenues and for attention from the reader, listener, or viewer. But the effects of intermedia competition upon the fortunes of any one were less important than were the effects of general changes in the country's economy, fashioned in turn by a great depression, a world war, and a postwar boom. Deflation, inflation, and war accentuated the already well-developed trend toward newspaper suspensions and mergers which was discussed in Chapter 22, and likewise adversely affected magazine publishing. On the other hand, a tremendous expansion of the gross national product and a population explosion beginning in the 1940s served to bulwark the publishing industry's position by providing a wider base for the support of both the old and new media.

At the same time the socioeconomic pressures inherent in modern American society, which had brought about concentration of newspaper ownership throughout the twentieth century, continued to have their effects, both on newspapers and other media. Competition for the mass market encouraged further standardization at the expense of individuality—common denominators for mass readership, listenership, or viewership to win mass advertising. Failure of individual enterprises to keep pace with the requirements of a modern socioeconomic situation also continued to play a part. And increasingly heavy investment costs in both publishing and broadcasting lessened ability to compete. Small radio stations, like small daily and weekly newspapers, could and did spread across the country as community enterprises. But big-time radio and television, like big-time newspaper and magazine publishing, was conducive to concentration of ownership—and radio and television proved to be easily adapted to chain operation. Finally, the natural tendency of publishers to become interested in new communications agencies, and their desire to spread their investments into radio and television, led to extensive interlocking ownership among the media.

INTERMEDIA ADVERTISING COMPETITION

As explained in Chapter 26, only radio made gains in advertising revenue during the 1930s.[1] During that decade of depression, recovery, and recession, expenditures on radio advertising rose from 40 million dollars in 1929 to 225 million dollars in 1941, last peacetime year. Newspaper advertising revenue, peaking at 800 million dollars in 1929, fell 45 per cent by 1933 and was still down 20 per cent in 1941, at 650 million. Magazine advertising revenue followed a similar pattern, being cut in half by 1933 from its 240 million 1929 high and recovering to 210 million by 1941. Then came the general advances in the economy of the war years, and corresponding gains in advertising revenues.

The story of competition for advertising among the media after 1945—and of the rise of television—can be told in two statistical tables. Table 1 shows the

TABLE 1 • Dollar Volumes (in Millions) and Percentages of Total Advertising Expenditures Obtained by the Mass Media

	Newspapers		*Magazines*		*Radio*		*Television*	
Year	*Dollars*	*%*	*Dollars*	*%*	*Dollars*	*%*	*Dollars*	*%*
1945	920	32.0	360	12.5	420	14.6		
1950	2,080	36.5	510	9.0	610	10.7	170	3.0
1955	3,070	34.0	720	8.0	550	6.1	1,010	11.2
1960	3,700	31.0	940	7.9	690	5.8	1,590	13.3
1965	4,435	29.4	1,200	7.9	890	5.9	2,500	16.5
1970	5,850	29.7	1,320	6.7	1,280	6.5	3,660	18.6

Source: McCann-Erickson, Inc., estimates. The percentage for all other advertising expenditures was approximately 40 per cent for each period.

total dollar costs of all advertising expenditures by both national and local advertisers, including advertising-related costs. The percentage figures make it clear that television's inroads were made most heavily against radio, with magazines taking the next heaviest percentage drop. Radio's rather steady dollar

[1] See pages 594–95.

volume in the 1950s, in contrast to the gains of other media, was due to its substantial cutting of advertising time rates (and parallel cutting of operating costs), and declines in national advertising.

Total advertising expenditures increased from 2 billion, 870 million dollars in 1945 to 19 billion, 715 million dollars in 1970, according to McCann-Erickson, Inc., estimates. But total disposable income in the country was also increasing greatly, and the amount of advertising expenditures stayed at a range between 2 and 3 per cent of disposable income. Thus the sizable dollar gains kept the mass media only roughly even in their financial race. Another measure of the support of the mass media was found in a study of average expenditures per household by advertisers, made by Scripps-Howard's research organization. It showed that, keeping dollar purchasing power constant, advertisers spent 10 per cent more per household in 1957 than they did in 1929,[2] with two new media present.

Table 2 shows the division among the major mass media of the national and local advertising revenues spent on them alone. In other words, the four major media together were allotted varying amounts of advertising expenditures each year by national and local advertisers. How were these total sums split among the contestants? Table 2 shows that television made its gains in this

TABLE 2 · Division of Advertising Expenditures Allotted Only to the Mass Media (Percentages)

	National Advertising in				*Local Advertising in*		
Year	*Newspapers*	*Magazines*	*Radio*	*Television*	*Newspapers*	*Radio*	*Television*
1948	33.5	37.0	29.5		84.1	15.9	
1950	33.6	32.4	24.8	9.2	82.4	14.6	3.0
1952	28.8	31.5	18.9	20.8	80.6	13.6	5.8
1956	28.6	28.8	8.0	34.6	80.3	11.3	8.4
1960	25.0	28.0	7.9	39.1	80.2	12.0	7.8
1965	19.3	26.7	7.1	46.9	78.4	12.6	9.0
1970	18.1	23.0	7.2	51.7	75.6	13.6	10.8

Source: McCann-Erickson, Inc., estimates.

division of national advertising mostly at the expense of radio, but also trimmed the percentages of newspapers and magazines (particular victims among the magazines were large general magazines appealing to mass audiences, rather than specialized ones).

The changes in divisions of local advertising were small, with television taking relatively small amounts from radio and newspapers, percentagewise. The percentage of total newspaper advertising revenue coming from local adver-

[2] "Economic Support of Mass Communications Media, 1929–1957," Scripps-Howard Research, New York, 1959.

tisers increased from 70 to 82 per cent between 1950 and 1970; the percentage of total radio advertising revenue coming from local sources jumped from 41 to 68 per cent. Television decreased in percentage of local advertising during the same 20 years, from 27 to 19 per cent, as its volume of national advertising revenue increased so dramatically. Radio thus joined newspapers as primarily a local advertising medium. Magazines have no advertising categorized as local, although by the 1970s they offered split-runs so that advertisers could buy space in copies being distributed in restricted areas, with perhaps 15 per cent of advertising revenue regional in origin.

STABILIZING THE NUMBERS OF DAILIES

What were the effects upon newspapers of this intermedia competition, and of the ups and downs in the economy from 1930 to 1970? In broad strokes, the number of dailies decreased, then stabilized near the 1,750 figure; ownership concentration increased as the number of competitive dailies declined; circulation steadily increased; and while financial problems were many, newspaper publishing economy tended to stabilize comfortably.

The sharp drop in advertising revenue in the early 1930s wiped out many newspaper profit margins despite cutbacks in salaries, production costs, and newsprint prices, which fell as low as $40 a ton. There were 145 suspensions of dailies during 1931–33, and 77 more in the recovery years of 1934–36. Then came the business recession of 1937, dropping advertising revenues at a time when labor and production costs had mounted to substantially higher post-depression levels. Some newspaper managements, hit by these new disasters after surviving the great depression, were too tired to struggle any longer. Daily newspaper suspensions and mergers accelerated, totaling 165 in the years 1937 to 1939. These were in many respects the blackest years in the history of American newspapers, with one-third of salaried employees in the newspaper industry losing their jobs, according to census statistics. The war years of 1940 to 1944 brought another 197 newspaper deaths, most of them small dailies pinched by production problems. With 584 suspensions and 386 new starts of dailies since 1931, the number of English language general-circulation daily newspapers dropped from 1,942 in 1930 to a twentieth-century low of 1,744 in 1945.

Postwar expansion brought an excess of new starts over suspensions in the daily field. The mid-1940s and mid-1950s were profitable years for newspapers in general. Despite the loss of 350 dailies between 1945 and 1960, their number rose to 1,786 in 1952, then settled back to 1,763 in 1961. Inflation and recession then took a slight toll, to 1,748 in 1971.

Circulation of dailies was approximately 40 million copies in 1930 for a population of 122 million; by 1970 it was 62 million for a population of 200 million. Newspaper circulation stayed even with population expansion to 1960, thanks to a heavy increase in circulation in the 1940s which counterbalanced the population explosion of the 1950s. The number of papers for each household decreased slightly, however, from 1.32 to 1.16 in the period.[3] But the number of papers per household dropped to an even 1.0 by 1970, and circulation trailed the population expansion with its young bulge.

DECLINE OF NEWSPAPER COMPETITION

Table 3 shows the extent of the decline in competition in cities having daily newspapers, since 1930.[4] The number of one-daily cities steadily increased, and there were more one-combination cities (one owner of two papers) until the 1960s. Joint-printing cities are those in which two owners have merged their printing and business operations, and thus are not fully competitive.

TABLE 3 · Competition in Daily Newspaper Cities

	1930	*1940*	*1945*	*1954*	*1961*	*1971*
Number of English language general circulation dailies	1,942	1,878	1,744	1,785	1,763	1,748
Number of cities with dailies	1,402	1,426	1,396	1,448	1,461	1,511
Number of one-daily cities	1,002	1,092	1,107	1,188	1,222	1,312
Number of one-combination cities	112	149	161	154	160	141
Number of joint-printing cities		4	11	19	18	21
Number of cities with competing dailies	288	181	117	87	61	37
Percentage of daily cities with competing dailies	20.6	12.7	8.4	6.0	4.2	2.4
Total daily circulation (millions)	39.6	41.1	45.9	54.5	58.9	62.1

Sources: For number of dailies and circulation, *Editor & Publisher International Year Books.* For other data, Raymond B. Nixon and Jean Ward, "Trends in Newspaper Ownership and Inter-Media Competition," *Journalism Quarterly,* XXXVIII (Winter 1961), 3. For 1971, compiled from 1971 *Yearbook* data by Nixon; circulation figures as of September 30, 1970, and numbers of papers as of January 1, 1971. See table in *Editor & Publisher,* July 17, 1971, p. 7.

Of the 1,500 cities with dailies at the start of 1968, there were competitive dailies in only 18 of 1,373 cities with 100,000 population or less, and competitors in only 12 of the 100 cities with populations between 100,000 and 500,000. The 21 cities of a half-million to a million had competition in only 9 cases. There were, however, competing papers in all six cities of more than a million. The prevailing pattern was one daily for cities under 100,000 in population,

[3] Wilbur Peterson, "Is Daily Circulation Keeping Pace with the Nation's Growth?," *Journalism Quarterly,* XXXVI (Winter 1959), 12.
[4] See page 443 for similar data from 1880–1930.

and single ownership or joint-printing of a morning-evening combination in cities from 100,000 to 500,000.[5] But if there were only 123 competing voices of daily newspapers in 45 competitive cities in 1968, radio and television added other voices. With the addition of the independently owned radio and television stations to the 1,749 dailies in the 1,500 daily cities, the total of media voices rose to 5,079. Now there were 4,879 competing voices in 1,298 cities. And the number of single voice cities was only 202, as compared to 1,284 single daily cities. In all but those 202 cities, there was at least competition between a newspaper and a broadcast station. And many of those 202 were large suburban cities close to a central city.[6]

THE METROPOLITAN DAILIES

Still, there was little direct newspaper competition remaining by 1971. Only three cities had three daily newspaper owners: Boston, with three owners of four dailies, and New York and Washington, with three dailies each. Only six other cities supported more than two dailies (all had just two ownerships): Chicago, with four dailies, and Philadelphia, Baltimore, San Antonio, Fort Worth, and Oklahoma City with three each. Eleven of the largest 25 cities had two separately owned dailies: Los Angeles, Detroit, Houston, Dallas, Cleveland, San Francisco, St. Louis, Columbus (Ohio), Seattle, Pittsburgh, and Denver. Seven of the largest 25 cities had just one owner of their two dailies: Indianapolis, Milwaukee, San Diego, Memphis, New Orleans, Phoenix, and Jacksonville. Oakland, California, thirty-eighth in size, was the largest one-daily city.

Newspaper managements could cite several reasons for these contractions and for continued concern over newspaper financial stability: a steady increase in the price of newsprint, which after leveling off at $135 a ton in 1957 to 1966, jumped to $162 a ton in 1970; increasing supply costs; rising wages and salaries; losses of national advertising to television. Their critics, however, generally agreed that a major difficulty was one of rigidity of advertising rates, which had not been advanced sufficiently in light of circulation increases and rising production costs. Many dailies, however, advanced sale prices to

[5] The *Jackson State Times* of Mississippi, founded in 1955 to compete with a morning-evening combination, was the only new daily begun in a city of more than 100,000 in the 1950s. It suspended in 1962. The *Atlanta Times*, founded in 1964 by conservatives, died in 1965. The *Arizona Journal*, liberal Phoenix offset paper, published 1962–64. The *Portland Reporter*, born of a Guild strike in 1960 to become a regular daily, suspended in 1964. But the *Oklahoma Journal* of Oklahoma City, founded as an offset morning daily in 1964, had a 51,000 circulation in 1971 (as against 180,000 for the *Oklahoman*).

[6] Raymond B. Nixon, "Trends in U.S. Newspaper Ownership: Concentration with Competition," *Gazette*, XIV (No. 3, 1968), 1–13.

10- or 15-cent levels. Annual *Editor & Publisher* surveys of newspaper profits showed expenses increasing slightly more than revenues in most years. Nevertheless, informed estimates of newspaper profits, as the 1970s opened, put them at 6 to 10 per cent of gross income as a general picture. Smaller dailies, and noncompetitive larger ones, were likely to be making greater profits than highly competitive big-city dailies. Twenty-one major metropolitan dailies were suspended between 1950 and 1970, and six others were sold to competitors. Some were losing a million dollars a year at the end.

Circulation gains were going to moderate and smaller-sized dailies, especially in the suburbs. Metropolitan papers were hardpressesd to stay even. Of the 10 largest dailies in 1960, two were no longer publishing in 1970, two had dropped off the list, and four more had lost circulation. The largest daily, the tabloid *New York Daily News*, still had 2,130,000 daily circulation and 2,950,-000 on Sunday. But it had lost 1,175,000 Sunday circulation and 132,000 daily in the two decades since 1950. The *Chicago Tribune* had lost 163,000 daily and 472,000 Sunday over the same period. Papers depending heavily on entertainment appeal were the largest losers; the *Mirror* and *Journal American* in New York disappeared altogether. All dailies in Chicago and Philadelphia lost circulation between 1950 and 1970 in amounts ranging from 77,000 to 215,000. Those in New York, Los Angeles, and Detroit gained, primarily because their numbers were thinned. The biggest gainer was the country's second-largest daily in 1970, the *Wall Street Journal*, whose four nationwide editions had 1,215,000 circulation as against 153,000 in 1950. Other major gains since 1950 were by the *Los Angeles Times*, 573,000; *New York Times*, 341,000; and *New York Post*, 312,000.[7]

The suburbs offered opportunity for new papers, both daily and weekly. By 1971 there were some 2,000 suburban papers, including 300 dailies, and as many more big-city neighborhood sheets. Major centers for this growing journalism included Los Angeles, Chicago, New York, Philadelphia, and Detroit. Suburban dailies were growing particularly rapidly in the Los Angeles and New York areas. One conspicuous success was *Newsday*, founded in 1940 on Long Island by Alicia Patterson. Its excellence in publishing both local and world news gave it a circulation above 450,000 by 1971 and a standing as one of the top half-dozen evening newspapers in the country. Other new ventures attracting attention were the Gannett group's *Today*, in the Cape Kennedy area of Florida, and the *Los Angeles Times*' satellite paper, the *Orange Coast*

[7] The 10 largest daily circulations in 1970 were *New York Daily News*, 2,130,000; *Wall Street Journal*, 1,215,000; *Los Angeles Times*, 966,000; *New York Times*, 846,000; *Chicago Tribune*, 767,000; *Detroit News*, 639,000; *Philadelphia Bulletin*, 634,000; *New York Post*, 623,000; *Detroit Free Press*, 593,000; *Chicago Sun-Times*, 536,000. Top Sunday circulations were *New York Daily News*, 2,950,000; *New York Times*, 1,400,000; *Los Angeles Times*, 1,250,000; *Chicago Tribune*, 1,000,000. The six leading papers in advertising linage were the *Los Angeles Times, Miami Herald, New York Times, Chicago Tribune, Washington Post,* and *Houston Chronicle.*

Daily Pilot. The existence of growing suburban dailies was a factor in big city journalism's decline.

CHANGES IN MAJOR CITIES

New York City suffered the most severe losses of any U.S. metropolis, dropping from six owners and seven dailies in 1960 to three owners and their three dailies in 1967. The attrition had been steady. Hearst's *American* (his pride and joy as the old morning *Journal* of the 1890s) went in 1937. The evening *Sun* was sold to Scripps-Howard in 1950 for merger with the *World-Telegram.* Hearst's tabloid *Mirror* was next to go in 1963. A 114-day strike in 1963 crippled all the dailies and a second strike in 1965 and management ineptness intensified the crisis. In April, 1966, John Hay Whitney of the *Herald Tribune,* the Scripps-Howard interests of the *World-Telegram and Sun,* and the Hearst interests of the *Journal-American* announced plans to publish jointly morning, evening, and Sunday. But strikes again disrupted New York newspapers, and the *Herald Tribune* ceased publication. The new daily, named the *World Journal Tribune,* appeared but died in 1967. With it went the shades of Pulitzer, Greeley, Bennett, Dana, Scripps, Howard, Hearst, and a dash of Munsey. Left to publish were the *Times,* the *Daily News,* and the *Post.* Brooklyn lost its *Citizen* in 1947 and its 114-year-old *Eagle* in 1955.

Boston saw two suspensions: the 111-year-old staid *Transcript* in 1941 and the 125-year-old *Post* in 1956. Two Hearst tabloids were combined as the *Record American* in 1961. Other survivors were the two *Globes* and the 1967-merged *Herald Traveler.* In Washington, Mrs. Eleanor Patterson bought the *Times* and *Herald* from Hearst and merged them in 1939. Ownership passed to her cousin, Robert R. McCormick, in 1949; he in turn sold the *Times-Herald* in 1954 for merger with its morning rival, the *Post.* Evening competitors were the *Star* and the Scripps-Howard *News.*

Chicago was cut to two morning-evening combinations owned by the McCormick and Marshall Field interests. After Hearst killed his *Herald & Examiner* in 1939 in the wake of a Newspaper Guild strike, Field launched the *Sun* in 1941 to do battle with McCormick's *Tribune* in the morning field. Finding the going rough, he bought the *Times* in 1947 and made the merged *Sun-Times* a tabloid. The *Tribune* purchased Hearst's *American* as an evening affiliate in 1956 and later renamed it *Chicago Today,* turning it into a tabloid. The *Sun-Times* countered by buying the *Daily News* from John S. Knight in a record 24 million dollar 1959 transaction. The futures of the two afternoon papers appeared to be in doubt, however, with 1971 estimated reported annual losses of 5 million dollars for the *Daily News* and 7 million for *Chicago Today* being absorbed by their wealthy corporate owners.

Five other cities had two ownerships but retained three dailies. In Philadelphia, Walter H. Annenberg's *Inquirer* bought the tabloid *Daily News* in 1957, to step up competition with the McLeans' *Bulletin*. The Annenberg papers were then sold to the Knight group in 1969. The liberal *Record* died in 1947 after a Guild Strike. Baltimore's survivors were the two *Suns* and the Hearst *News-Post*. San Antonio's trio were the jointly-owned *Express* and *News* and Hearst's *Light*. Fort Worth had Amon Carter, Jr.'s two *Star-Telegrams* and the Scripps-Howard *Press*. Oklahoma City saw the *Oklahoma Journal* started to compete with the *Oklahoman* and *Times* in 1964.

Los Angeles, the third largest city, dropped to two dailies, joining 10 others of the largest 25 cities in that class. The Chandler family's *Times* began the tabloid *Mirror* in 1948 to give it a breezier afternoon entry against two Hearst papers, the morning *Examiner* and evening *Herald-Express*. The competition was fatal for a fifth paper, the liberal tabloid *Daily News*, which suspended in 1954. The *Mirror*, edited drably after a 1957 management shakeup, faltered and was suspended in January 1962. The Hearst group at the same time elected to kill the *Examiner*, naming their evening paper the *Herald-Examiner*.

Two Scripps-Howard papers disappeared in Houston and San Francisco in the 1960s. The *Houston Press*, one of the group's liveliest, gave up the struggle against the *Chronicle* and the *Post* in 1964. In San Francisco, the Hearst and Scripps-Howard evening papers had been combined into the jointly-owned *News-Call Bulletin* in 1959; Scripps-Howard bowed out in 1962 and the paper succumbed in 1965 as Hearst's morning *Examiner* moved to the evening field in a joint-business arrangement with the *Chronicle* that saw the two rivals sharing a Sunday edition.

Detroit lost Hearst's *Times* in 1960, victim of a battle with the *News* and *Free Press*. In Cleveland, the *Plain Dealer* disposed of its evening paper, the *News*, to the Scripps-Howard *Press* in 1960. The *St. Louis Star-Times*, published by Elzey Roberts and ably edited by Norman Isaacs, fell before the *Post-Dispatch* and *Globe-Democrat* in 1951. Pittsburgh saw Hearst's *Sun-Telegraph* merged with the Block family's *Post-Gazette* in 1960, with the Scripps-Howard *Press* the remaining rival. Seattle's *Star* blinked out in 1947, leaving the *Times* and Hearst's *Post-Intelligencer*. Columbus had its *Citizen-Journal* and *Dispatch;* Dallas its *News* and *Times Herald;* Denver its *Post* and Scripps-Howard *Rocky Mountain News*.

Seven of the 25 largest cities of 1970 had two papers but only one ownership. Memphis fell to this status in 1936 when Scripps-Howard bought the *Commercial Appeal* to complement its *Press Scimitar*. In San Diego, James S. Copley's *Union* and *Tribune* eliminated the *Journal* in 1948. The *New Orleans Item* was merged with the *States* in 1958, under the ownership of the *Times-Picayune*. In Milwaukee, Hearst's old *Sentinel* was sold to the *Journal* in 1962. After 78 years, Scripps-Howard's *Indianapolis Times* left the field to Eugene C. Pulliam's *Star* and *News* in 1965. Pulliam also had the field to himself in

Phoenix with his *Republic* and *Gazette.* In Jacksonville, the *Florida Times-Union* and the *Journal* came under common ownership in 1959.[8]

CHANGES IN THE NEWSPAPER GROUPS

Among the group ownerships, Scripps-Howard dropped from 25 dailies in 1935 to 17 in 1971, with 6 Sunday editions. In the late 1930s papers were disposed of in Akron, Toledo, Youngstown, Oklahoma City, San Diego, and Buffalo. In addition to later changes already described, Scripps-Howard in 1950 merged its *Birmingham Post* with the *Age-Herald* to form the *Post-Herald,* and in 1959 merged its *Columbus Citizen* with the *Ohio State Journal* to form the *Citizen-Journal.* In these and five other cities the chain had common printing and business operations with rivals. Scripps-Howard bought the *San Juan Star* in 1970.

The Hearst chain's 26 dailies of 1935 were cut to 8 by 1971, with 7 Sunday editions. Sold or killed between 1937–40 were nine dailies: the *Rochester Journal, Syracuse Journal, Omaha News-Bee, Wisconsin News, Washington Times* and *Herald, Chicago Herald & Examiner, Atlanta Georgian,* and *Pittsburgh Post-Gazette.* The *Oakland Post-Enquirer* died in 1950. Then came the 1956–66 withdrawals from Chicago, Pittsburgh, Detroit, Milwaukee, and New York, and contractions in Boston, Los Angeles, and San Francisco. On the plus side, the *Albany Knickerbocker News* was added in 1960 as a companion to the *Times-Union.*

Rising rapidly among the group owners was Samuel I. Newhouse. He bought the *Portland Oregonian* in 1950 for 5 million dollars; the *St. Louis Globe-Democrat* in 1955 for 6 million; the *Birmingham News* in 1955 for 18 million; the *Oregon Journal* in Portland in 1961 for 6 million; the *New Orleans Times-Picayune and States-Item* in 1962 for 40 million; and the *Cleveland Plain Dealer* in 1967 for 50 million. That gave him 22 dailies with 14 Sunday editions. His other major holdings included the *Jersey Journal, Long Island Press, Newark Star-Ledger,* and the dailies in Syracuse and Harrisburg. Newhouse's reputation was primarily that of a successful businessman who watched the profits of his papers closely but permitted local autonomy in opinion.

John S. Knight, starting with the *Akron Beacon-Journal,* bought the *Miami Herald* in 1937, the *Detroit Free Press* in 1940, and the *Chicago Daily News*

[8] Among other cities which dropped to one-owner status were Akron and Toledo, through Scripps-Howard withdrawals of the late 1930s, and Omaha (one paper status) and Rochester by 1937 Hearst sales. Other dates for elimination of competition included Louisville, 1936; Providence, 1938; Richmond, 1940; Minneapolis, 1941; Kansas City, 1942; Syracuse, 1943; Harrisburg, 1948; Dayton and Tacoma (one paper), 1949; Oakland (one paper), and Atlanta, 1950; Raleigh, 1955; Tampa and Grand Rapids (one paper), 1958; Charlotte, 1959; Wichita and Albany, 1960; St. Petersburg, 1962. Among well-known dailies disappearing not mentioned in the text above were the *Louisville Herald-Post, Providence Tribune,* and *Kansas City Journal-Post.*

in 1944. He sold the latter in 1959, but added the *Charlotte Observer* in 1954 and *Charlotte News* in 1959. Ten years later he bought the *Philadelphia Inquirer* and *News* to bring the group to 11 dailies and 8 Sunday papers. The importance of Knight's papers and his signed personal opinion column made him a major figure.

The Times Mirror Company, parent company for the burgeoning *Los Angeles Times,* vaulted into the top half-dozen of daily newspaper group owners during the 1960s, measured by total group circulation. The bigger share of that circulation was the *Times'* own, as third ranking U. S. daily. Balked from purchasing the San Bernardino papers by an antitrust action, Otis Chandler developed a small Orange County daily into a satellite venture called the *Orange Coast Daily Pilot.* During most of the 1960s he was expanding the news syndicate he developed with the *Washington Post.* But in 1970 the Times Mirror interests bought the *Dallas Times Herald* and its television station, KRLD, in a 90-million-dollar stock transaction. The same year Chandler bought Captain Harry Guggenheim's 51 per cent interest in *Newsday* in a 33-million-dollar transaction. Thus two exciting U. S. newspapers were joined in coast-to-coast ownership.

John Cowles, whose family owned the *Des Moines Register* and *Tribune,* invaded Minneapolis in 1935 by purchasing the evening *Star,* into which he merged the rival *Journal* in 1939. Two years later the heirs to William J. Murphy's morning *Tribune* sold out to Cowles. The *Tribune's* evening edition, the *Times,* was killed in 1948. Cowles bought the *Valley Times Today* in San Fernando, California, in 1960 but sold it during the 1960s while purchasing through his Minneapolis Star and Tribune Company the *Rapid City Journal* in South Dakota and *Great Falls Tribune* in Montana. His brother, Gardner Cowles, head of the Des Moines papers, invaded Long Island in 1967 to start the *Suffolk Sun* but suffered heavy losses and was forced to suspend the daily in 1969. Next year he sold the *San Juan Star* to Scripps-Howard and various Cowles Communications properties to the *New York Times.*

Another growing multi-newspaper ownership was that of the Ridder family. The founder was Herman Ridder, publisher of the *Staats-Zeitung* in New York City. His three sons—Bernard H., Joseph E., and Victor F. Ridder[9]—bought control of the *Journal of Commerce* in New York in 1926. The next year they acquired the *St. Paul Pioneer Press* and *Dispatch,* eliminating the rival *Daily News* by 1938. Added to the chain were the *Duluth News-Tribune* and *Herald,* two papers in the Dakotas, and a 49 per cent interest in the *Seattle Times.* Then, in 1952, the Ridders invaded California by buying the *San Jose Mercury*

[9] Bernard H. Ridder headed the family's newspaper expansions from St. Paul. His son, Bernard H., Jr., became publisher in St. Paul and Duluth. His other three sons became publishers in California—Joseph B. in San Jose and Herman H. and Daniel as co-publishers in Long Beach. Joseph E. Ridder centered his attention on the *Journal of Commerce,* of which one of his sons, Eric, became publisher. The other, Bernard J., published the Pasadena newspapers. Victor F. Ridder's son Walter headed the Ridders' Washington bureau, son Robert the family's radio-TV interests.

Newhouse Newspapers

Gannett Newspapers

Group owners: Samuel I. Newhouse (*left*); Paul Miller, head of Gannett Newspapers.

Jean Raeburn

Chicago Defender

John S. Knight (*left*); John H. Sengstacke, head of the *Defender* newspaper group.

Minneapolis Tribune

Grinsted Studio

John Cowles, Jr. (*left*), Minneapolis-based; Marshall Field V, of Field Enterprises.

and *News,* and the previously competing *Long Beach Press-Telegram* and *Independent.* The *Pasadena Star-News* and *Independent* were added in 1956 and the *Boulder Camera* in Colorado and the *Gary Post-Tribune* in Indiana during the 1960s to make a total of 16.

James M. Cox built a sizable empire by acquiring the *Miami News* and *Atlanta Journal* in the 1930s and the *Atlanta Constitution* in 1950. Other Cox holdings were four Ohio papers in Dayton and Springfield and four in the Palm Beach area in Florida.

Largest of the newspaper groups in terms of numbers of dailies in 1971 was the Gannett Company, with 50 dailies and 20 Sunday editions. Long an established New York state group, the Rochester-based company expanded by buying other groups: the Westchester Rockland group in New York state in 1964; the Federated group of Michigan, Indiana, Idaho, and Washington in 1971; and the *Honolulu Star-Bulletin* and its satellites in 1971. Gannett had dailies in 11 states, including such leaders as the *Democrat & Chronicle* and *Times-Union* in Rochester; *Hartford Times* in Connecticut; *San Bernardino Sun* and *Telegram* in California; and *Today* in Cocoa, Florida. Runnerup in total number of dailies was the Thomson Newspapers group, part of Lord Thomson's worldwide enterprises, with 43 U. S. dailies and 16 Sunday editions. But these were predominantly small papers, averaging 20,000 circulation.

The national newspaper groups were no particular menace, however, despite their seeming bulk. The 63 chains of 1935 controlled 328 newspapers with 41 per cent of daily circulation and 52 per cent of Sunday sales.[10] More exhaustive studies by Raymond B. Nixon uncovered the existence of more of the smaller chains, and new groups were formed. By 1960 there were 109 groups controlling 560 dailies. The number of groups increased until 1965, then leveled off until 1971. That year there were 157 groups controlling 879 dailies, or 50 per cent of all dailies, with 63 per cent of total daily circulation and 65 per cent of Sunday. But the average number of dailies for each group was 5.6. And no group held more than a small percentage of total circulation.

Most powerful in 1971 in terms of weekday circulation was the group owned by the Chicago Tribune Company, including the *Tribune,* the *New York Daily News,* and a 1965 purchase, the *Orlando Sentinel* and *Star* in Florida. They had 5.8 per cent of daily circulation and 9.5 per cent of Sunday sales. In contrast, the once-dominant Hearst chain in 1935 had boasted 13.6 per cent of the country's daily circulation and 24.2 per cent on Sunday (by 1971, it was reduced to 3.3 daily, 4.8 Sunday). In terms of circulation, the Chicago Tribune Company group was at 3.6 million and Newhouse at 3 million. Scripps-Howard, Knight, Gannett, and Hearst were above the 2 million level. Others above a million were the Times Mirror group, the Dow Jones and Ottawa group, Ridder, and Cox. Cowles was at 940,000 and Thomson at 840,000. Among leading smaller-circulation groups were the 7 Central Newspapers owned by Eugene Pulliam; the Scripps League with 31 dailies, in

[10] See pages 460–62 for development of chains prior to 1935.

western states; the James S. Copley group in California and Illinois, with 14; the Stauffer publications in Kansas, 15; Harte-Hanks, in Texas, 15; Lee, in the midwest, 15; and Speidel, in California, 11. Leaning to the right were the Freedom Newspapers of California and Texas, in 22 cities.[11]

WEEKLIES AND SPECIALIZED DAILIES

Weekly newspapers followed the same general trends. In 1930 only 13.5 per cent of country weekly towns had competing papers; by 1960 the figure was 5.2 per cent. The number of weeklies of all types stood at 10,000 in 1940, at 9,800 in 1950, and at 9,400 in 1970. Most of the decrease was in the smallest towns. True country weeklies numbered some 5,800; a typical one had a circulation of 1,500 copies in a small town and agricultural countryside, and a net income of $9,500. Larger county seat weeklies and the fast-growing suburban weeklies were more profitable—some of the suburban press chains were major businesses.[12]

Those who found the country's newspapers too closely conforming in socioeconomic opinion—whether published in one-owner or competitive cities—attempted to publish their own papers, with mediocre success. The Socialist labor press was led by the *New York Evening Call* (1908–23) and the *Milwaukee Leader* (1911–42), both of which achieved substantial circulations before succumbing. However, the Jewish language Socialist paper *Vorwärts* (*Jewish Daily Forward*), published in New York with editions in other cities, attained more than 100,000 circulation under editor Abraham Cahan. The Communist *Daily Worker,* founded in 1924, had 100,000 circulation in the late 1930s, but only 5,600 when it dropped to weekly status in 1958. In the Middle West, farmer-labor groups founded the *Minnesota Daily Star* and the *Oklahoma Leader* in 1920, but the *Leader* ceased daily publication in 1922 and the *Star* went into receivership in 1924.

In other specialized newspaper publishing fields, the foreign-language press steadily declined during the twentieth century. In 1914, peak year for foreign language newspapers, there were approximately 1,000 papers, of which 140 were dailies. By 1961 there were fewer than 70 dailies and perhaps 600 other papers. German-language dailies, dominant in 1914, declined 90 per cent. *Editor & Publisher* listings show dailies in 21 languages, with Chinese,

[11] The groups are listed annually in *Editor & Publisher International Yearbook.* For 1971 data see Raymond B. Nixon, "Half of Nation's Dailies Now in Group Ownerships," *Editor & Publisher,* July 17, 1971, p. 7.

[12] See Wilbur Peterson, "Loss in Country Weekly Newspapers Heavy in 1950s," *Journalism Quarterly,* XXXVIII (Winter 1961), 15, and John Cameron Sim, "Weekly Newspapers Again Facing Challenge to Move," *Journalism Quarterly,* XXXV (Spring 1958), 195. The suburban papers are analyzed in Sim's *The Grass Roots Press: America's Community Newspapers* (Ames: Iowa State University Press, 1969).

Spanish, Polish, Japanese, Russian, Italian, Yiddish, German, and Lithuanian the most numerous. New York, Chicago, San Francisco, and Cleveland were major publishing centers.

THE MAGAZINE OWNERSHIPS

Variety of reader appeal and diversity of opinion were more possible in the magazine field, where periodicals of every shade of interest could find countrywide audiences. By 1971 there were 8,400 periodicals of all types. Of these, however, no more than 600 were magazines of general interest (a figure which nevertheless was more than double that for 1900). Approximately 50 had circulations of more than a million. The larger of these mass circulation magazines exhibited the same characteristics of bigness and ownership concentration as other media.

The major groups and their leading magazines were: Time Inc. (six, including *Time, Life, Fortune, Sports Illustrated*); McGraw-Hill (*Business Week* and 37 trade publications); McCall Corporation (*McCall's, Redbook*); Hearst Magazines (14, including *Good Housekeeping, Cosmopolitan, Popular Mechanics, Sports Afield, Harper's Bazaar*); Samuel Newhouse (11 Condé Nast and Street & Smith magazines purchased in 1959, including *Vogue* and *Mademoiselle*); Meredith Publishing Company (*Better Homes and Gardens, Successful Farming*); and Walter H. Annenberg's Triangle Publications (three, including *TV Guide* and *Seventeen*).[13]

Of eight major general interest magazines remaining in 1971, all but *Reader's Digest* were group-owned. The others were *Life* (weekly) and *Ebony* (monthly), picture magazines; *Redbook* and *Cosmopolitan* (general monthlies), and *McCall's, Ladies' Home Journal,* and *Good Housekeeping* (women's monthlies).

Gone were the famous Crowell-Collier magazines—*Collier's,* the *American,* and *Woman's Home Companion*—which dated from the 1870s and 1880s. They suspended in 1956 due to mismanagement, top-heavy costs, and loss of advertising to television. *Collier's* had almost 2 million circulation, the other two more than 4 million each. *Coronet,* running mate of *Esquire,* was a 1961 casualty, despite a 3 million circulation. As described in Chapter 25, the once-dominant Curtis Publishing Company began to show great deficits in 1961 and came crashing down by 1969 with the casualty being the *Saturday Evening Post.* The other Curtis-owned magazines continued to appear, but *Holiday* only in an abbreviated form after 1971, and *Ladies' Home Journal* for a million

[13] Leading circulations in 1971, in round numbers, were *Reader's Digest,* 18 million; *TV Guide,* 15 million; *Life* and *McCall's,* 8½ million; *Better Homes and Gardens,* 8 million; *Ladies' Home Journal, Family Circle,* and *Woman's Day,* 7 million; *National Geographic, Good Housekeeping,* and *Playboy,* 5 to 6 million; *Redbook* and *Time,* 4 to 4½ million; *American Home,* 3½ million. *Life* cut to 5½ million in 1972 to reduce ad rates.

fewer subscribers. The Cowles magazines (the picture magazine *Look* and travel magazine *Venture*) vanished in 1971's cost inflation.

Gone, too, was Hearst's 65-year-old Sunday newspaper supplement, the *American Weekly*, which was withdrawn from all but the Hearst papers early in 1962 and killed in 1963. *This Week* ceased publication in 1969. Remaining were *Parade*, with 17 million, and *Family Weekly*, with 8 million circulation.

GROUP OWNERSHIP IN BROADCASTING

Those who complained about a sameness in their newspapers and their mass-circulated magazines fared little better when they turned to television and radio. The major radio networks grew steadily, having 228 station affiliates in 1934, 702 in 1944, and 1,324 (55 per cent of all stations) in 1953. The decline in network broadcasting and expansion in number of stations changed the figures to 2,265 affiliates (52 per cent of all stations) in 1971. The 696 television stations of 1971 had 668 network affiliations (two or three for some stations).

Group, or chain, ownership became strong in radio, and stronger in television than in daily newspaper publishing. A 1949 study arrived at this picture: group ownerships controlled 281 AM radio stations, or 13.2 per cent of the total; 24 television stations, or 40 percent of the total; and 386 dailies, or 21.6 per cent of the total.[14] Ten years later the figures for group ownership were 776 AM radio stations, or 23.5 per cent of the total; 278 television stations, or 53.3 per cent of the total; and 560 dailies, or 32.2 per cent of the total.[15] More than half the groups were involved in more than one medium.

CROSS-CHANNEL OWNERSHIP

A final threat to diversity of communications ownership thus became such cross-channel ownership of the mass media. The Hearst organization led in 1971 with 8 dailies, 14 magazines, four AM stations, three FM stations, three TV stations, a news service, a photo service, a feature syndicate, and the Avon paperback book firm. Samuel Newhouse was not far behind, with 22 dailies, 11 magazines, four AM stations, three FM stations, and five TV stations. Scripps-Howard controlled 17 dailies, one AM station, one FM station, four TV stations, a press association, a photo service, and a feature syndicate.

There were many other cross-channel combinations. Two magazine groups were in broadcasting, Meredith Publishing Company with 10 stations (four

[14] Warren K. Agee, "Cross-Channel Ownership of Communication Media," *Journalism Quarterly*, XXVI (Fall 1949), 410.

[15] Harvey J. Levin, *Broadcast Regulation and Joint Ownership of Media* (New York: New York University Press, 1960), p. 41; and Nixon and Ward, *op. cit.*

TV) and Time, Inc. with 10 stations (four TV). The Chandler family had four dailies, two TV stations, and the Signet and Mentor paperback book companies. Katharine Graham owned the *Washington Post*, *Newsweek*, and four stations (three TV). The Cowles family still owned six dailies, six stations (three TV), *Harper's*, and the *Insider's Newsletter*. The *New York Times* Company, after obtaining various new holdings from Gardner Cowles, owned such diverse enterprises as *Family Circle*, Quadrangle Books, *Golf Digest*, the Microfilming Corporation of America, the Arno Press reprint house, three Florida dailies, Modern Medicine Publications, and the Interstate Broadcasting Company (WQXR).

As the numbers of stations increased, the percentages of those affiliated with newspapers and magazines declined. In 1971 they stood at 9.3 for AM stations, 11.2 for FM stations, and 27.4 for TV stations. In 1961 the percentages were 11.4 for AM stations, 15.8 for FM stations, and 29.3 for TV stations. In 76 cities there was single ownership of all daily newspaper and broadcasting facilities, while in 29 towns the weekly owned the only radio station. This meant that only 4.2 per cent of the 2,475 cities or towns with radio or television stations had a newspaper-broadcasting monopoly.[16] Few Americans did not have access to a variety of news or opinion, if they wished, despite the economic pressures affecting the mass media.

THE BLACK PRESS SURVIVES

One group of Americans who found little to represent their aspirations and interests in the mass media was the Negro population. Not until the 1950s did the average U.S. newspaper or magazine exhibit an understanding interest in the black 10 per cent of citizens, and even then few were sensitive to them as readers. There was a clear need for a black press, but little economic support for it from a black community with few socioeconomic resources. Nevertheless, the black press which began in 1827 survived and gained in stature.[17]

More than 3,000 Negro newspapers—owned and edited by blacks for black readers—have appeared since *Freedom's Journal* made its 1827 bow. The best historical statistics were gathered by Professor Armistead Scott Pride of Lincoln University for his 1951 doctoral dissertation. His figures showed that 1,187 black papers were added during the years 1865–1900 to the 40 founded before 1865. Another 1,500 had been added by 1951, but the survivors numbered only 175. The average life span of a Negro newspaper, Pride found, was nine years.[18]

A 1971 survey of black newspapers, verified by telephone calls to all listed

[16] Nixon and Ward, *op. cit.*

[17] See Chapter 13, pp. 218–22, for the story of the founding of the black press.

[18] Armistead Scott Pride, "Negro Newspapers: Yesterday, Today and Tomorrow," *Journalism Quarterly*, XXVIII (Spring 1951), 179.

offices and personal interviews with a third of the editors, found a total of 196, including 2 dailies, 4 semiweeklies, 179 weeklies, and 11 biweeklies or monthlies. Their circulation total (free and paid) was 3,584,000. More than half the papers had been founded since 1950, a third during the 1960s. Of the 196, nearly half (93) had a circulation under 10,000; a quarter (51) exceeded 20,000; only 12 topped 40,000 and the largest audited circulation was 80,000 for the *Amsterdam News* in New York City. One giant, *Muhammad Speaks* of the Nation of Islam, claimed 600,000. There was tremendous turnover among the papers. The researcher, Henry G. La Brie III of the University of Iowa, learned through telephone calls that 41 black weeklies listed in current reference works were defunct; 13 of the 196 he recorded were started in 1970 or 1971.[19] Professor Roland E. Wolseley of Syracuse University, author of a 1971 book on the black press, said he had records of 199 black newspapers for 1970 and 225 for 1971.[20] Statistics kept by Professor Pride gave totals of 155 in 1939, 172 in 1958, 133 in 1962, and 172 again in 1966.

Just as the standard daily press grew in numbers, circulation, and stature during the New Journalism era between 1880 and World War I, so did the black press. Among today's leaders which have founding dates in that period are the *Philadelphia Tribune* (1884), Baltimore's *Afro-American* (1892), the *Chicago Defender* (1905), New York's *Amsterdam News* (1909), Norfolk's *Journal and Guide* (1909), and the *Pittsburgh Courier* (1910). Historically important from that period are the *New York Age* (1890), *Boston Guardian* (1901), and *The Crisis* (1910). Founded later, among 1970's leaders, were the *Atlanta World* (1928), *Los Angeles Sentinel* (1934), Detroit's *Michigan Chronicle* (1936), Chicago's *Muhammad Speaks* (1961), and Berkeley's *The Black Panther* (1966), voice of the Black Panther party.

Pride gives several reasons for the increase in black papers beginning in the mid-1880s: increased educational opportunities for Negroes, support of black papers by religious and welfare groups working in the South, establishment of political sheets for enfranchised Negroes, and growth of urban black communities which could support papers. The impact of two world wars and heavy Negro migration to northern industrial cities brought a peak of circulation influence to the leading papers; between 1940 and 1947 the circulations of the *Amsterdam News* rose from 35,000 to 111,000, the *Pittsburgh Courier* from 126,000 to 286,000, and the *Chicago Defender* from 82,000 to 161,000.[21] Black paper circulations then declined, nationally circulating papers lost ground to community-based ones, and smaller but more stable enterprises survived in 1971.

[19] La Brie supplied revised figures in September 1971 for the data in his *The Black Newspaper in America: A Guide* (Iowa City: University of Iowa Institute for Communication Studies, 1970).

[20] Roland E. Wolseley, *The Black Press, U.S.A.* (Ames, Iowa: Iowa State University Press, 1971), p. 11.

[21] Wolseley, *op. cit.*, p. 56.

THE FOUNDING PUBLISHERS

Ranking in fame with Frederick Douglass and his *North Star* of 1847 are W. E. B. Du Bois and his *The Crisis* of 1910. Other major figures in Negro publishers' ranks to 1910 included John H. Murphy, Sr., of the *Afro-American* papers, T. Thomas Fortune of the *New York Age,* William Monroe Trotter of the *Boston Guardian,* Robert S. Abbott of the *Chicago Defender,* and Robert L. Vann of the *Pittsburgh Courier.* Their stories, and those of other major black papers, follow.

The semiweekly *Philadelphia Tribune,* which celebrated its eighty-fifth anniversary in 1969, is the oldest continuously published black newspaper in the United States. Founded in 1884 by Chris J. Perry, Sr., it became one of the most substantial and best-edited Negro weeklies. Perry's widow and two daughters continued the *Tribune* after his death in 1921. A son-in-law, E. Washington Rhodes, was publisher and editor until he died in 1970. Rhodes took a moderate view, concentrated on improving the lot of Philadelphia's black citizens. Criticising the more affluent Negroes for not doing enough to help the poor, the *Tribune* organized charities and scholarship programs as a part of its community responsibility.[22]

John H. Murphy, Sr., is regarded as the founder of the *Afro-American* editions, four regional and one national, centered in Baltimore. Murphy, who did whitewashing for a living, was superintendent of an African Methodist church Sunday school. He began publishing a small paper for it in his basement. When a Baptist minister, the Rev. William M. Alexander, began another religious paper, the *Afro-American,* in 1892, Murphy gained control of it; in 1907 he merged it with the *Ledger,* a third religious paper edited by an Episcopal pastor, the Rev. George F. Bragg. The paper gained a national reputation before 1920. Murphy wrote a credo that year calling for the *Afro-American* to keep faith with the common people, to fight to get rid of slums and to provide jobs for all, and to "stay out of politics except to expose corruption and condemn injustice, race prejudice and the cowardice of compromise." The credo still appears in his newspapers, which were continued after his death in 1922 by his son, Dr. Carl J. Murphy.

T. Thomas Fortune was one of the best-known Negro editors at the turn of the century, and his *New York Age* won national attention. Born to slave parents, Fortune ran errands for a southern newspaper, learned to set type, and entered New York journalism through the back shops. In 1879 a Negro tabloid named *Rumor* was changed to standard size by George Parker and renamed the *New York Globe;* Fortune and W. Walter Sampson were the printing crew and became Parker's partners. Within a decade Fortune was the

[22] Substantial accounts of leading black papers can be found in Wolseley, *The Black Press, U.S.A.* See its bibliography for additional references.

Mayor Of Small Arkansas Town Wins Respect From Whites

(Continued on Page 2)

SCLC SEEKING POLITICAL ROLE (SEE STORY PAGE 6

The Afro-American

TYPICAL NON-WHITE FAMILY DEPICTED (SEE STORY PAGE 22)

80th Year No. 1 — Contents of Newspaper Copyright 1971 by the AFRO-AMERICAN Co. — BALTIMORE, MD., AUGUST 21, 1971 — NATIONAL—CAROLINA NEW ENGLAND EDITION — 26 PAGES 25 CENTS

Prophet Jones, 64, Dies In Detroit

Nixon Bans Busing Of Students

Wallace gives helping hand in implementation of order

(Continued on Page 2) (Continued on Page 2)

Has heart attack at home of friend

PROPHET JONES

(Continued on Page 2)

EPILEPSY POSTER CHILD, SEN. TAFT, CALL ON PRESIDENT — Zachery Williams, 6-year-old Jackson, Miss. lad who is the national poster child of the Epilepsy Foundation of American (EFA), visited the White House, receiving a warm greeting from President Nixon. With Zachery, who has had epilepsy for four years, was Sen. Robert Taft, Jr., of Ohio, a longtime friend of the epilepsy movement. Zachery took the foundation's message of understanding to the president, symbolizing the fact that the beacon of hope for the more than 4 million Americans who suffer convulsive disorders has reached the highest office in the land. Zachery, through use of modern medication, leads an active normal life.

Four men found slain near Detroit in gangland-style execution

(Continued on Page 2)

What President's message means to you

Rent, food prices will freeze while autos may be cheaper

Nixon orders wage, price controls

(Continued on Page 2)

A typical front page of a leading black paper, the *Afro-American*, in 1971.

principal figure and the paper had become the *Age*. As its editorial writer, Fortune was quoted by the nation's press and was read by political leaders, including Theodore Roosevelt. Booker T. Washington selected the *Age* as national spokesman for the Negro and began to subsidize it. This won the disapproval of W. E. B. Du Bois and other militant black leaders who said Washington was accepting segregation and subservience to whites. Fortune sold his share of the *Age* in 1907 and in 1920's supported the back-to-Africa movement of Marcus Garvey, writing for Garvey's widely circulating magazine, *Negro World*. The *Age*, under the editorship of Fred R. Moore, remained a major New York black newspaper until it was sold to the expanding *Defender* group of Chicago in 1952.

William Monroe Trotter, another great black leader at the turn of the century, had a background opposite from Fortune's. His father, a Union army officer, became interested in racial equality and married a black slave. He then became a merchant in Boston, where the mulatto son won election to Phi Beta Kappa at Harvard and a master's degree. With George Forbes, an Amherst graduate, Trotter founded the *Boston Guardian* in 1901. It was provocative and militant enough to win the praise of Du Bois. When Booker T. Washington spoke in Boston in 1905 the *Guardian* challenged his conservative leadership, particularly on black education and voting. Trotter later led a protest delegation to the national capital to meet with President Woodrow Wilson and plead the cause of blacks. But in the 1920s his paper languished; Trotter and his wife lost their home and Trotter died in 1934. His sister continued the *Guardian* until her death in 1957.

Robert S. Abbott's *Chicago Defender*, founded in 1905, fared better in the quest for public support than did Trotter's *Guardian*. By 1915 it reached a circulation of 230,000. The figure declined two-thirds by the depression year of 1935, but rose again to 160,000 in post-war 1947. The Chicago paper, with its national edition, then became the cornerstone of the largest U.S. black newspaper group. Abbott was born in 1868 of black parents in Georgia. When his father died, his mother married John H. H. Sengstacke, son of a German merchant who had married a slave girl. Abbott learned printing at Hampton Institute, worked on his stepfather's small paper, studied law, and in 1905 founded the *Defender* among Chicago's 40,000 black population. It was run on a shoestring from his landlady's house until Abbott developed a familiar black newspaper formula: muckraking on behalf of his race, sensationalizing through "race-angling" of headlines and stories, use of crime and scandal stories, and resolute challenges to the Ku Klux Klan, racial rioting, lynchings, and other threats to black Americans' security. By the 1930s Abbott had moderated the *Defender's* tone and had added much more personal, social, cultural, and fashion news. When he died in 1940 his successor was John H. Sengstacke, a nephew.

Robert L. Vann's *Pittsburgh Courier*, founded in 1910, became the largest in circulation of all black newspapers, approaching 300,000 in the late 1940s.

Vann was a lawyer who took over a church-sponsored publishing venture and who struck out to fight against racial discrimination and the Jim Crow tradition. The *Courier* backed black athletes, helping Jackie Robinson to break the color barrier. Vann developed a circulation in the South, and used his national influence to attract capable black journalists to his staff.

P. Bernard Young was another black publisher who developed a national newspaper, taking over the *Journal and Guide* in Norfolk in 1910 and running it as a moderate, nonsensational weekly until his death in 1962. By contrast, the various publishers of New York's *Amsterdam News* have concentrated on local circulation since its founding by James H. Anderson in 1909, gradually winning their way to dominance in the competitive Harlem scene.

W. E. B. DU BOIS AND *THE CRISIS*

W. E. B. Du Bois, the militant apostle of protest in the opening decades of the century, became one of the major folk heroes of the black equality movement of the 1960s. His appeal was strong for the radical left of that movement because late in life he became a member of the Communist party and went to live in the new African nation of Ghana, where he died in 1963, aged ninety-five.

Du Bois was not a newspaperman, although he was a correspondent or columnist for several. He was primarily a writer and a teacher, with a cause to promote—that of rescuing the black race from a crisis that threatened to crush its capability. He is best known for his work between 1910 and 1934 as an executive of the National Association for the Advancement of Colored People and for the founding and editing of its magazine, *The Crisis*. That journal served so well as a combination of a news magazine reporting items of concern to Negroes, a journal of editorial opinion, a review of opinion and literature, and a literary magazine that its entire file for the first 50 years has been reproduced as "A Record of the Darker Races."

Born in New England in 1868, Du Bois was raised by his mother in a white society relatively free of discrimination. He himself was of mixed blood. He edited a high school paper and was correspondent for the *Springfield Republican* and the *New York Age*. At Fisk University he edited the student paper. He studied sociology at Harvard and in Germany and contributed articles to the *Atlantic* and *World's Work*. After attempting two other Negro journals, he succeeded with *The Crisis*. In it he set out to challenge the whole concept of white supremacy then nationally accepted, and its counterpart of black inferiority. He said his object was to "set forth those facts and arguments which show the danger of race prejudice, particularly as manifested today toward colored people. It takes its name from the fact that the editors believe that this is a critical time in the history of the advancement of men."

"Mentally the negro is inferior to the white," said the 1911 *Britannica.* It was this belief which Du Bois set out to destroy. His editorials also attacked immediate ills: wartime discrimination against black soldiers, the widespread race riots and lynchings following World War I, the climax of Ku Klux Klan terrorism, continued white refusal to consider Negro rights in the fields of voting, education, and housing. Circulation of *The Crisis* passed 100,000 in 1918. But dissention within the NAACP and other factors reduced it to fewer than 10,000 when Du Bois retired as editor in 1934, aged sixty-five. Under editor Roy Wilkins until 1949 and then Henry Lee Moon, circulation revived to well above 100,000.

Du Bois became sociology department head at Atlanta University, founded a scholarly journal on world race problems named *Phylon,* and wrote books and countless articles for major publications. Like Frederick Douglass, his writings were being edited and published in the 1970s as a symbol of achievement by a distinguished member of the black race—and, of course, the human race.

CURRENT BLACK PRESS LEADERS

In 1970 John H. Sengstacke, editor and publisher of the *Chicago Daily Defender* and head of the Sengstacke Newspapers group, was elected to a three-year term on the board of directors of the American Society of Newspaper Editors. He was the first black editor to be so honored. This personal recognition also reflected the status of the *Defender* group as the largest in black newspaper publishing, with community and national circulation claims totaling more than 200,000. The *Afro-American* group was credited with an overall circulation of some 135,000. The largest audited circulation in 1971 for a publication of either group was 30,000 for the Saturday Baltimore edition of the *Afro-American.* Major units in the Sengstacke group were the *Michigan Chronicle,* founded in 1936 in Detroit, and the *New Pittsburgh Courier,* purchased in 1966 by Sengstacke along with the *Courier* group. These claimed circulations of 50,000 and 36,000, respectively. Biggest *Afro-American* properties were semiweeklies in Baltimore and Washington and a weekly in Richmond. Head of the *Afro-American* enterprise was John H. Murphy III, with Mrs. Elizabeth Murphy Moss vice-president and treasurer. In 1969 the *Afro-American* received the first award made to a black newspaper by the American Society of Journalism School Administrators. Mrs. Moss of the *Afro-American* became a leading reporter and war correspondent; so did Ethel L. Payne, Washington correspondent of the Sengstacke newspapers and only black newswoman to cover the Vietnam war.

The *Amsterdam News,* largest circulating of standard black community papers, was purchased by Dr. C. B. Powell in 1936 and controlled by him until 1971 when ownership passed to Clarence B. Jones. It concentrated on local items and sensationalized crime and sex news to combat its competition in Harlem from Congressman Adam Clayton Powell's *People's Voice* and the old *New York Age*. Like the *Afro-American* and *Defender* papers, it became moderate in tone, heavily local in news coverage, strong in sports and women's news, and occasionally crusading.

Out of 45 efforts to publish black dailies in the United States, as reported by Pride, only two prevailed. One was the *Chicago Daily Defender*, with daily status since 1956. The other was the *Atlanta Daily World*, founded as a weekly in 1928 and a daily since 1932. Its founder, William A. Scott, was assassinated in 1934; his successor, Cornelius A. Scott, edited a consistently conservative paper in news content, typographical appearance, and editorial direction. World news coverage was good. It supported the Republican party politically and opposed such militant black action as economic boycotts of white merchants who discriminated in hiring blacks. Its 1971 circulation was about 25,000.

Second largest in audited 1971 circulation among black papers was the *Los Angeles Sentinel*, founded in 1934 and owned by Leon H. Washington. Its 45,000 paid circulation made it the most important black publication in Los Angeles, where it displayed a mildly sensational front page and liberal-moderate editorial page. The *Philadelphia Tribune* had 40,000 audited circulation to rank third. Other noteworthy black papers were the *Cleveland Call and Post*, 25,000; Norfolk's *Journal and Guide*, 20,000; the semiweekly *Tampa Sentinel-Bulletin*, 20,000; the *Kansas City Call*, founded in 1919, 15,000; and the *Louisiana Weekly*, 15,000. There were large free circulation shopping papers, like the Wave Publications in Los Angeles with a distribution of 230,000 and the Berkeley Post Group claiming 70,000.

La Brie found in his 1970 survey that 80 per cent of the black newspapers were printed by the offset method, usually on presses not owned by the publishers. The others owned letterpress equipment. Like the regular weeklies, the black weeklies usually appeared on Thursdays. The reported labor force for 175 papers was 2,500, of whom 200 were white. Advertising occupies about one-third of total space, with two-thirds or more local in origin but national advertising increasing in larger black papers beginning in the 1960s.

Most of the national black papers and largest weeklies subscribe to the United Press International for their state, regional, national, and international news. Best known of specialized press services was the Associated Negro Press, founded in 1919 by Claude A. Barnett. At its peak, in 1945, it had 112 U.S. subscribers. Barnett made many trips to Africa after World War II and added 100 subscribers there as well as developing African news. But by 1966 ANP had so much competition in coverage of blacks news events that it went out of business.[23] The National Negro Press Association, with Louis Lautier as Washington correspondent, operated between 1947 and 1960 with the sup-

[23] Richard L. Beard and Cyril E. Zoerner II, "Associated Negro Press: Its Founding, Ascendency and Demise," *Journalism Quarterly*, XLVI (Spring 1969), 47.

port of the larger black papers. With the disappearance of these two news services, no major black news service existed. Liberation News Service, founded in 1967 for underground and college papers and militant magazines, had few black subscribers.

Noteworthy was the Community News Service, financed with a 1968 Ford Foundation grant in response to Kerner Report criticism of minority news coverage. In 1970 it began covering the Negro and Puerto Rican neighborhoods of New York City, selling its news to newspapers, broadcasting stations, and others who wish to know about life in the ethnic neighborhoods. Philip Horton, former editor of *Reporter* magazine, directed the staff of experienced and apprentice nonwhite reporters and editors. It could serve as a model for other cities.

THE BLACK MAGAZINES

John H. Johnson is the publisher of one of the country's leading magazines, *Ebony,* and his Johnson Publishing Company in Chicago produces three other important black magazines—*Jet, Tan,* and *Black World.* The Johnson story is one of imitation: *Ebony* is a companion magazine to *Life; Jet,* a news magazine, succeeded with the format of the ill-fated *Quick* of the Cowles magazines; *Tan* is a true confessions book; and *Black World* was called *Negro Digest* until 1970 in honor of its model.

Johnson grew up in Chicago, was befriended by a white businessman, attended University of Chicago, and eventually borrowed $500 from his widowed mother to found *Negro Digest* in 1942. Its newsstand success enabled him to launch *Ebony* in 1945, as a monthly version of *Life.* Finding sensationalism did not pay, Johnson built a magazine for middle-class Negroes in the 1950s that reached a level of 70 per cent home-delivered circulation by 1971 on 1,250,000 copies. As black militancy grew in the 1960s, *Ebony* became more concerned with black problems, and ran extensive articles in addition to pictures and cartoons. *Jet,* a small-sized news weekly, had 400,000 circulation to rank second among black magazines, while *Tan* numbered 117,000 readers. *Black World,* published by Johnson as an outlet for black authors, was relatively unsuccessful. Johnson's only publishing company rival was the Good group of Forth Worth, with *Sepia,* a competitor to *Ebony,* and sexy *Jive* and *Bronze Thrills.* All had 55,000 to 60,000 circulations.

Tuesday, a magazine supplement edited by blacks but appearing in conventional big dailies, was started in 1965 by W. Leonard Evans, Jr., to reach white readership with a "black leveler," he explained. It won 2,400,000 circulation in five years, with an estimated 20 per cent white readership. Among other noteworthy black magazines were *The Crisis,* the literary-styled *Freedomways,* and such scholarly journals as *Negro History Bulletin, Journal of Negro History,* and *Journal of Negro Education.*

BLACK BROADCASTING

No U.S. television station license was held in 1971 by anyone in the 10 per cent of the population called black. Even so, viewership studies show blacks spent more time watching television than any other identified group. There were 16 radio stations owned by blacks in 1970. Of 13 AM stations, five were in northern cities, three in border cities, and five in the south. Three were college-owned FM stations.

About 180 radio stations devoted 10 hours or more of time each week to the black listening audience; of these, 65 were all-black in programming, according to *Broadcasting Yearbook.* Listenership studies showed nearly all blacks tuned in black-oriented radio and 60 per cent preferred it to regular stations. In ghetto areas, black radio was the common denominator of communication, followed by television, with print media trailing. Yet a 1970 study of black-oriented radio stations found them so predominantly "rhythm-and-blues"-oriented that little time remained for news, public affairs, even sports. News rarely ran beyond five minutes, was usually headlines; public affairs programs fell far short of the potential if operators were interested in serving the black community.[24]

In broadcasting, it seemed, the economic pressure minimized black-ownership participation even more than in the print media. This was especially true of television. Even in a city as predominantly black as Washington, D.C., blacks did not own a station until the *Washington Post* gave them WTOP-FM.

MUSLIM AND PANTHER PAPERS

A strong voice of protest, *Muhammad Speaks,* ranked second to *Ebony* in 1971 in ability to reach the black U.S. audience. With a 600,000 copy press run, the tabloid weekly of the Nation of Islam ranked far ahead of other black papers. Next in line, with an estimated 100,000 circulation, was the *Black Panther,* voice of that militant movement.

Malcolm X, later assassinated, was an early editor and writer for Elijah Muhammad's Nation of Islam, founding the magazine *Messenger* in 1960 and a Harlem newspaper. Out of it in 1961 came the Chicago-based operation, *Muhammad Speaks.* Each Friday by 1971 600,000 smartly printed copies poured out of a lavishly equipped offset printing plant. In a forced-sale operation, distributors purchased nonreturnable papers for sale in black communities throughout the country. John N. Woodford, the Harvard-educated

[24] Anthony J. Meyer, S.J., *Black Voices and Format Regulations: A Study in Black-Oriented Radio* (Stanford, Calif.: Institute for Communication Research, Stanford University, 1971).

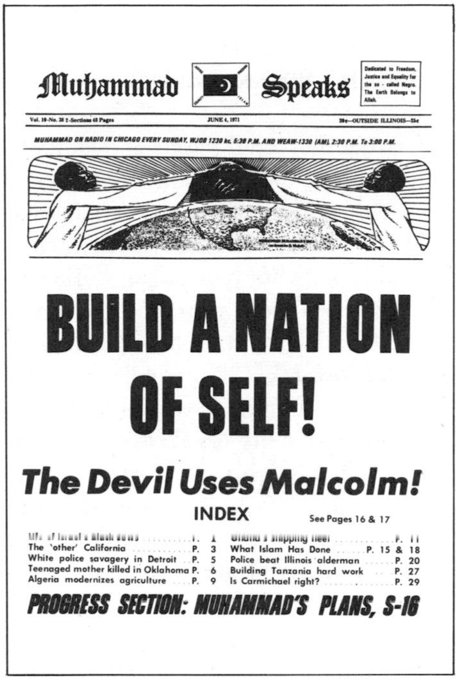

Muhammad Speaks

Dedicated to Freedom, Justice and Equality for the so - called Negro. The Earth Belongs to Allah.

Vol. 10-No. 38 2-Sections 48 Pages | JUNE 4, 1971 | 20¢—OUTSIDE ILLINOIS—25¢

MUHAMMAD ON RADIO IN CHICAGO EVERY SUNDAY, WJOB 1230 kc, 5:30 P.M. AND WEAW-1330 (AM), 2:30 P.M. To 3:00 P.M.

BUILD A NATION OF SELF!

The Devil Uses Malcolm!

INDEX

See Pages 16 & 17

The 'other' California ... P. 3
White police savagery in Detroit ... P. 5
Teenaged mother killed in Oklahoma P. 6
Algeria modernizes agriculture ... P. 9
What Islam Has Done ... P. 15 & 18
Police beat Illinois alderman ... P. 20
Building Tanzania hard work ... P. 27
Is Carmichael right? ... P. 29

PROGRESS SECTION: MUHAMMAD'S PLANS, S-16

LA RAZA

EL BARRIO COMMUNICATIONS PROJECT
P.O. BOX 31004
LOS ANGELES, CALIF. 90031
261-0128

CHICANO PRESS ASSOCIATION SPECIAL

RUBEN SALAZAR MURDERED

Left, a 1971 *Muhammad Speaks; right, La Raza* protests the death of a Chicano newsman.

editor, described the circulation and operation to La Brie, setting the number of employes at 75 to 100. Well illustrated and designed, *Muhammad Speaks* carries considerable news and opinion. It supports the Muslim goals, including achievement of black industrial and agricultural self-sufficiency. It interprets the African national movement, is pro-Arab, pro-Cuban, shows sympathy for the Viet Cong, and opposes U.S. war policies.

The *Black Panther,* begun in 1966 by the Black Panther party, is far more militant. Begun as a mimeographed paper in San Francisco, it became a weekly tabloid in 1969, produced by its Panther party staff in Berkeley. In 1970 its slogan of "All Power to the People" was changed to "Death to the Pigs" and the paper's artist put guns in the hands of all people illustrated—"to show the readers what to do." [25] The paper seeks to win black support for the Panther party; it also crusades for community improvement. It is anti-police, antiwar, and revolutionary. The press run was reported as 200,000 in 1970 with perhaps 100,000 sales.

[25] Su Debroske, "The Black Revolution in Print," *New York University News Workshop* (December 1970), p. 4.

CHICANO AND AMERICAN INDIAN PAPERS

The 1960s saw strong new sparking of two other civil rights movements, in behalf of the Mexican-American and the American Indian. A semiformal Chicano Press Association developed among the perhaps 50 newspapers that sprang up from California to Chicago.[26] These activist sheets were distinct from the older Spanish language press and radio, with its half-dozen dailies in New York, Miami, Los Angeles, and Texas. Different, too, were the 75 American Indian papers reported by the National Council on Indian Opportunity for the 1971 *Editor & Publisher International Yearbook.*

The Chicano movement and the Chicano press emerged from the grapeworkers strike in California's San Joaquin Valley under the leadership of Cesar Chavez. *El Malcriado* became the voice of the United Farm Workers union in 1964, published from a shack in Delano. More substantial was the Los Angeles Chicano paper founded in 1967, *La Raza,* which circulated among the huge Mexican-American population of that area, numbering more than one million. Other California sheets appeared in San Francisco, San Jose, San Bernardino, and San Diego. *El Rebozo,* published by women, appeared in San Antonio among five Texas Chicano papers. Other Chicano efforts were *El Gallo* in Denver, *Adelante* in Kansas City, *La Guardia* in Milwaukee, and *Lado* in Chicago.

Chicano papers printed their news and opinion in both Spanish and English, used large numbers of pictures, and reflected the cultural stirrings of the Chicano movement in poetry, essays, and interpretative writing. Their aim was to organize Mexican-Americans as sensitive, progressive communities. Much of their support and reportorial skill came from Chicano college students.

THE UNDERGROUND PRESS REVOLUTION

The roots of the "underground press" movement that swelled to prominence in the mid-1960s can be found in the words of all the radicals of American journalism, starting with James Franklin and including more recently the radical *Guardian* founded in New York City in 1948 and *I. F. Stone's Weekly,* which began its steady drumfire of criticism from Washington in 1953. The inspiration for the movement came from men like Allan Ginsberg, Bob Dylan, Jack Kerouac, Lenny Bruce, and Norman Mailer. The immediate stimuli were the four-letter word movement, the sex revolution, the generation and credi-

[26] Frank del Olmo, "Chicano Journalism: New Medium for New Consciousness," in Michael C. Emery and Ted C. Smythe, *Readings in Mass Communication: Concepts and Issues in the Mass Media* (Dubuque, Iowa: Wm. C. Brown, 1972).

bility gaps that created the anti-Establishment era, and, above all, the bitter antiwar protest typified by the March on the Pentagon.

Underground papers were printed cheaply by offset, free-swinging in style and content, uninhibited in graphic design, unrestricted in viewpoint, and in many cases, also unprofitable. They reflected a rebellion not only against the national Establishment but also against its conventional mass media. The best of the underground papers did a capable job of criticising both, and of breathing new life into the dead-center American social and political scene of the 1960s.

One historian of the underground papers, Robert Glessing, listed 457 titles of papers in his 1970 book[27] and comments that they were coming and going almost too rapidly to list. Included in his total were 55 military papers and campus, black, and Chicano publications. He estimated there were 3,000 underground high school papers.

First of the underground papers was *Village Voice*, a sensational weekly when it was founded in Greenwich Village in 1955. Its creators were Daniel Wolf, a freelance writer who became editor; Edward Fancher, a psychologist who became publisher; and novelist Norman Mailer. Its political line was anti-Establishment Democrat, it exhibited the Village interest in books and the arts, and its great coup was to break the four-letter word barrier. It started cartoonist Jules Feiffer on his way, helped Jack Newfield upward, and ran contributions from most of the writers who also appeared in the "new journalism" columns of *Esquire, New York,* and *Harper's*. By 1970 it was a fat 48 pages, with top "underground" circulation of 130,000.

Most successful of the really radical underground publishers of the 1960s was former machinist Art Kunkin, who used $15 to start his *Los Angeles Free Press* in 1964. By 1970 his estimated circulation was 95,000 and Kunkin had not missed a week with his antipolice cartoons, his swinging classified ads, and his put-downs of politicians and society leaders. His paper gained additional attention through serious comment on both national and local issues, however startling the language. A four-year battle between Kunkin and the Los Angeles police over his right to a press pass ended in March 1971 when the U.S. Supreme Court refused to hear the *Free Press's* appeal of an appellate court decision holding that the weekly paper did not automatically qualify for a press pass under the First Amendment. In New York a media council granted press passes to underground papers, but Los Angeles police were adamant about Kunkin, who had published a list of names of narcotics undercover agents in one defiant episode. He sold the paper late in 1971.

Best known and most successful of campus-related papers was the *Berkeley Barb*, born in the summer of 1965 out of passionate dislike for the University of California administration and the excitement of the Berkeley "free speech" movement. Its founder, Max Scherr, was in his fifties but still in

[27] *The Underground Press in America* (Bloomington, Ind.: Indiana University Press, 1970).

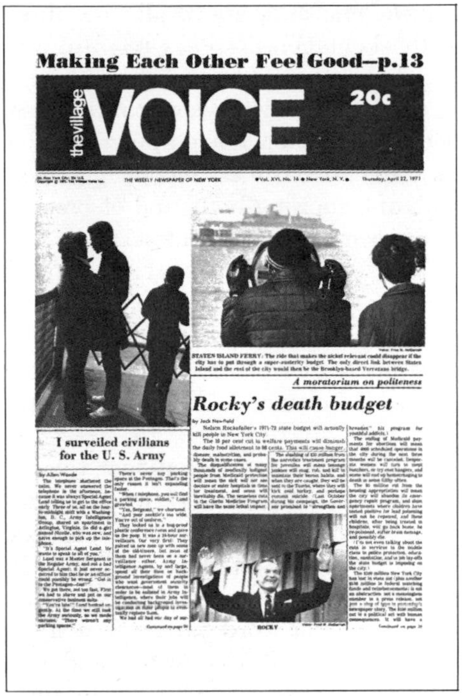

Making Each Other Feel Good—p.13

the village VOICE 20¢

THE WEEKLY NEWSPAPER OF NEW YORK

A moratorium on politeness

Rocky's death budget

I surveiled civilians for the U. S. Army

ROCKY

News in Brief

Fraternity to aid Freep

To free Tijerina

Confessions of a Vietnamese Conscript

LOS ANGELES FREE PRESS
7813 Beverly Boulevard
Los Angeles, California 90036

Left, a 1971 *Village Voice; right,* page 2 of the *Los Angeles Free Press.*

touch with the alienated people of the streets. The *Barb* produced major Bay area exposés, led the disruptive student protests that split the campus apart, advanced to the sex revolution's frontiers, and grew fat on profits from suggestive classified ads and circulation. In 1969 Scherr and some of his staff split, with the dissidents producing the *Tribe.* The resulting controversies diminished the influence of the *Barb,* but it had 85,000 circulation.

There were other important underground papers of the mid-1960s: Detroit's *Fifth Estate* of 1965, the *Washington Free Press* of 1966, and three products of the climactic year of 1967, *Seed* in Chicago, *Kaleidoscope* in Milwaukee, and *Distant Drummer* in Philadelphia. Praised for their graphic effects were Boston's *Avatar* of 1967 and the *San Francisco Oracle,* a 1966 sensation for its psychedelic effect. Closely connected to rock music were John Bryan's *Open City* of 1967–69 in Los Angeles and San Francisco's later *Rolling Stone.* Breaking down the barriers the *Village Voice* had not tested in New York City were Paul Krassner's *Realist,* founded in 1958, and *East Village Other,* a 1965 protest journal with innovative art forms.

New York's radical political paper, the *Guardian,* became underground in outlook by 1970. The dismal wind-down of the Vietnam War proved I. F.

Stone and his *Weekly* to have been right as well as cantankerous. Joining them as journals of tough-minded criticism in the 1960s were the *San Francisco Bay Guardian* and the *Texas Observer*. Each took out after the established press in its area, as well as the political and social establishments, in the best tradition of crusading journalism. The *Bay Guardian's* editor, Bruce Brugmann, ended up suing the San Francisco dailies for abridging freedom of the press through their joint publishing agreement.

Behind the underground press revolution were its press associations. One, the Liberation News Service, was founded in 1967 during the march on Washington by two graduate students who had been editors of their college papers, Ray Mungo and Marshall Bloom. Bloom became involved in supporting Students for a Democratic Society and left LNS. LNS scored with the only "inside" story of the 1968 Columbia University riots. That year a teletype service was introduced by the Underground News Service. The Underground Press Syndicate, organized in 1966 and developed by Tom Forcade, became a trade association clearing house, and advertising representative for the papers which invariably, as they prospered, joined the aboveground press in Establishment practices.

Annotated Bibliography

Books

Braddon, Russell, *Roy Thomson of Fleet Street*. London: Collins, 1965. A detailed and favorable portrait of a world press lord.

Brooks, Maxwell R., *The Negro Press Re-examined*. Boston: Christopher, 1959. A study of content with extensive tables and evaluations.

Clarke, John H., et al., *Black Titan W. E. B. Du Bois: An Anthology by the Editors of Freedomways*. Boston: Beacon Press, 1970. Writings about Du Bois, first editor of *The Crisis* and legendary black leader.

Detweiler, Frederick G., *The Negro Press in the United States*. Chicago: University of Chicago Press, 1922. Basic historical study together with Vishnu V. Oak, *The Negro Press* (Yellow Springs, Ohio: Antioch Press, 1948).

Du Bois, W. E. B., *The Autobiography of W. E. Burghardt Du Bois*. New York: International Publishers, 1968. Written at age 90 by the editor of *The Crisis* as volume three of his autobiography.

Ellis, L. Ethan, *Newsprint: Producers, Publishers and Political Pressures*. New Brunswick: Rutgers University Press, 1960. Study of costs, 1940–60; includes his earlier *Print Paper Pendulum*.

Ernst, Morris, *The First Freedom*. New York: Macmillan, 1946. Discusses press and radio ownership concentration problems.

Glessing, Robert J., *The Underground Press in America*. Bloomington: Indiana University Press, 1970. Good survey with some documentary detail.

Johnson, Michael L., *The New Journalism.* Lawrence: University Press of Kansas, 1971. Covers underground press, "new journalism" writers Capote, Mailer, Tom Wolfe, others. See also Everette E. Dennis, *The Magic Writing Machine* (Eugene: University of Oregon School of Journalism, 1971), for analyses of "new journalism" magazines and reporters.

La Brie, Henry G., III, *The Black Press in America: A Guide.* Iowa City: Institute for Communication Studies, University of Iowa, 1970. A list of black newspapers with basic data. See also *Black List* (New York: Panther House, Ltd., 1971), a reference guide to publications and broadcast media.

Levin, Harvey J., *Broadcast Regulation and Joint Ownership of Media.* New York: New York University Press, 1960. Contains a wealth of statistical information on the problem.

Peterson, Theodore, *Magazines in the Twentieth Century.* Urbana: University of Illinois Press, rev. ed. 1964. The most comprehensive discussion of magazine industry economics.

Rucker, Bryce W., *The First Freedom.* Carbondale: Southern Illinois University Press, 1968. Prize-winning analysis of position of mass media, designed as updating of Morris Ernst's *The First Freedom.*

Sage, Joseph, *Three to Zero: The Story of the Birth and Death of the World Journal Tribune.* New York: American Newspaper Publishers Association, 1967. A brief analysis placing most blame for the fiasco on labor unions.

Schramm, Wilbur, ed., *Mass Communications.* Urbana: University of Illinois Press, 1949, rev. 1960. Selected readings, including sizable portions of Llewellyn White's *The American Radio* and Neil Borden's *The Economic Effects of Advertising,* and articles on communications ownership and income problems.

Sim, John Cameron, *The Grass Roots Press: America's Community Newspapers.* Ames: Iowa State University Press, 1969. The most recent and penetrating study of weeklies, rural and suburban, and their community roles.

Stewart, Kenneth, and John Tebbel, *Makers of Modern Journalism.* Englewood Cliffs, N.J.: Prentice-Hall, 1952. Contains chapters on the Knight, Cox, Cowles, Gannett, Luce, Field, and other major ownerships.

Wolseley, Roland E., *The Black Press, U.S.A.* Ames: Iowa State University Press, 1971. A comprehensive survey, with substantial historical material for black newspapers, magazines, and broadcasting.

Periodicals and Monographs

Agee, Warren K., "Cross-Channel Ownership of Communication Media," *Journalism Quarterly,* XXVI (Fall 1949), 410. Summary of Master's thesis, 1949, University of Minnesota.

Akers, Milburn P., "Chicago's Newspaper Concentration," *Nieman Reports,* XIII (July 1959), 20. Factual reasons for Chicago's two-ownership situation, by *Sun-Times* editor.

Bogart, Leo, "Magazines Since the Rise of Television," *Journalism Quarterly,* XXXIII (Spring 1956), 153. A study of magazine readership and economics from 1946–55.

"The Cowles World," *Time,* LXXII (December 8, 1958), 55. An extensive press section report on the Cowles family enterprises.

Furlong, William B., "The Midwest's Nice Monopolists, John and Mike Cowles," *Harper's,* CCXXVI (June 1963), 64. A sketch of responsible monopoly publishers in Minneapolis and Des Moines.

Grotta, Gerald L., "Changes in the Ownership Structure of Daily Newspapers and Selected Performance Characteristics, 1950–1968," Ph.D. thesis, Southern Illinois University, 1970.

Guimary, Donald, "The Decline and Death of Portland's *Daily Reporter," Journalism Quarterly,* XLV (Spring 1968), 91. A strike-born daily lived on a shoestring, 1961–64.

Hensher, Alan, "No News Today: How Los Angeles Lost a Daily," *Journalism Quarterly,* XLVII (Winter 1970), 684. Death of the *Daily News* in 1954.

Hirsch, Paul M., "An Analysis of *Ebony:* The Magazine and Its Readers," *Journalism Quarterly,* XLV (Summer 1968), 261. Covers 1945–66.

"Knight of the Press," *Newsweek,* XLV (April 25, 1955), 97. A special report on John S. Knight and his newspaper group.

La Brie, Henry G., III, and William J. Zima, "Directional Quandaries of the Black Press in the United States," *Journalism Quarterly,* XLVIII (Winter 1971), 640. Black editors re-examine function of their press in depth survey.

McHam, David, "The Authentic New Journalists," *Quill,* LIX (September 1971), 9. A report on the writers at *Esquire, Harper's, New York* magazines.

Nelson, Harold L., "The Political Reform Press: A Case Study," *Journalism Quarterly,* XXIX (Summer 1952), 294. An analysis of an almost successful farmer-labor newspaper, the *Minnesota Daily Star* (1920–24). Summary of Master's thesis, 1950, University of Minnesota.

Nixon, Raymond B., "Trends in U.S. Newspaper Ownership: Concentration with Competition," *Gazette,* XIV (No. 3, 1968). Most recent study of competition and groups. See also *Editor & Publisher,* July 17, 1971, p. 7.

Nixon, Raymond B., and Jean Ward, "Trends in Newspaper Ownership and Inter-Media Competition," *Journalism Quarterly,* XXXVIII (Winter 1961), 3. The most comprehensive study of the subject. See bibliography for Chapter 22 for Nixon's 1945 and 1954 studies.

Palmer, L. F., Jr., "The Black Press in Transition," *Columbia Journalism Review,* IX (Spring 1970), 31. A survey, 1945–70.

Peterson, Paul V., "The Omaha *Daily World* and *World-Herald,* 1885–1964," Ph.D. thesis, University of Minnesota, 1965. Story of a major midwest daily.

Peterson, Wilbur, "Is Daily Circulation Keeping Pace with the Nation's Growth?," *Journalism Quarterly,* XXXVI (Winter 1959), 12. Covers the period 1929–57 with extensive statistical analysis.

———, "Loss in Country Weekly Newspapers Heavy in 1950s," *Journalism Quarterly,* XXXVIII (Winter 1961), 15. An evaluation of the community weekly's situation, with full data.

Pride, Armistead, *The Black Press: A Bibliography.* Jefferson City, Mo.: Lincoln University Department of Journalism, 1968. Sponsored by AEJ.

Raskin, A. H., "The New York Newspaper Strike," *Columbia Journalism Review,* II (Spring 1963), 13. Text of the *New York Times'* labor reporter's story in the *Times.*

Reichley, A. James, "How John Johnson Made It," *Fortune,* LXXVIII (January 1968), 152. Profile of Negro publisher.

Shapiro, Fred C., "The Life and Death of a Great Newspaper," *American Heritage,* XVIII (October 1967), 97. Extensive portrait of the *New York Tribune* and *Herald Tribune.*

Shaplen, Robert, "The Newhouse Phenomenon," *Saturday Review,* XLIII (October 8, 1960), 55. Analysis of the rise of Samuel Newhouse, group owner of newspapers, magazines, and broadcasting stations.

Small, Collie, "Little Publisher, Big Empire," *Collier's,* CXXVIII (August 4, 1951), 31. An earlier article on Samuel Newhouse.

Smythe, Ted C., "A History of the *Minneapolis Journal,* 1878–1939," Ph.D. thesis, University of Minnesota, 1967. Leading Minneapolis afternoon daily until blitzed by John Cowles.

Thornbrough, Emma Lou, "American Negro Newspapers, 1880–1914," *Business History Review,* XL (Winter 1966), 467. Of hundreds of papers, only a few subsidized ones survived any length of time.

Udell, Jon G., "Economic Trends in the Daily Newspaper Business 1946 to 1970." A research report of the Bureau of Business Research and Service, University of Wisconsin, Madison, 1970. Data-laden; sponsored by ANPA.

Wertheimer, Jerrold L., "The Community Press of Suburbia." Ph.D. dissertation, Northwestern University, 1960. Chicago case study.

Witcover, Jules, "Washington's White Press Corps," *Columbia Journalism Review,* VIII (Winter 1969–70), 42. Scarcity of capable black reporters reviewed.

Wilson, Noel Avon, "The *Kansas City Call:* An Inside View of the Negro Market," Ph.D. thesis, University of Illinois, 1968. History and influence of the *Call* on Negro community.

The Vatican

The Power and the Glory are passing

Jailed or married priests, and bishops who gave up hope, are only signs of the crisis in Roman Catholicism. At its center is the question of the infallibility of the Pope.

BY JOSEPH RODDY
LOOK SENIOR EDITOR

It seemed a good place for a miracle—Saint Peter's Basilica in Rome, and in the winter of 1965 after Vatican Council II closed there were many Roman Catholics who thought a miracle of sorts had happened in the vaulting central shrine of their faith. Twenty-four hundred bishops who had gathered there from all over the world, men whose skill at business administration was certain but whose ardor for theological change was faint, had somehow moved an ancient church with medieval ways into the modern world. Not all of them had helped, of course. There were resisters and obstructors, bishops who smelled heresy in the house and cardinals who felt God-summoned to save their Church from its popes. Still, as the bishops went back to their chanceries after the Council, a Catholic looking about could not help but be astonished at what God—or was it the bishops?—or was it a small band of willful men behind the scenes?—had wrought.

Even those outside Rome's fold were impressed. One was Ignazio Silone, the rugged old Italian who had been a devout Catholic, then a devout Communist, and is now a devout Christian without a church. "In the effort made to bring herself up to date and to overcome internal resistance," he wrote, "the Church has shown a spiritual vitality of which many believed her incapable. How can one fail to rejoice?" So a creed that had claimed its ways timeless had found the time right to change its ways. It would be a true *aggiornamento*, a renewal, an opening out. From then on it would worship in vernaculars and forgo a dead Latin. It would retire cultic pietisms and accent the dignity of prayer. It would look to the rights of other faiths in officially Catholic states. In no state would it countenance oppression in this life with allusions to a good life after death. It would search for ecumenical reunion with all sects calling themselves Christian. It would lift the charge of deicide from the Jews, and even foresee divine mercy for those who deny divine order. And it would do an amazing thing to its governing structure: Its popes, instead of carrying on as absolute monarchs long after the age of kings had passed, would share their power with the universal college of bishops, the same twenty-four hundred very mortal men with their vanities and virtues about them in Saint Peter's. The bishops' new power was called "collegiality," and those who inquired about it were told to regard collegiality as the needed counterbalance to the primacy and infallibility of the pope, attributes of his office that few bishops had even thought to contest.

In prospect, collegiality was the Vatican Council's greatest accomplishment. In practice, it was to evaporate without a trace the first chance it had to work. That was only a few months after the Council. At an audience with Italian gynecologists, Pope Paul VI re-proclaimed his faith's old stand against contraception. The theological, medical and population experts whose advice he sought advised him not to do it, and the laity had plainly been disregarding it. Long before the bishops defined their collegial function with him, Paul had said he would hear all the advice but decide the birth-control issue himself. That he still decided it himself after collegiality became Church law was only a maladroit reminder of papal power. Had he accepted the counsel of his advisers to change birth-control teaching, and then invited the bishops to join with him in changing it, the Pope would have set collegiality off to a good start. But to reject the counsel and then bypass the bishops was an act of desperation. The Roman Catholic Church has been in disorder ever since.

The prospect now is that the Vatican Council the Catholics were so proud of may have accomplished little more than the trivialization of their beliefs. The liturgy of the Mass, shorn of its Latin, has degenerated in places into speech and song at its most primitive, crying out for the noble cadence of a *Dominus vobiscum*. In no country has the religious liberty of other creeds improved through the efforts of the Catholics. No non-Communist government has had its moves called immoral even when they were at the edge of, or into, genocide. The momentum has gone, and with it the heart, from the ecumenical movement toward Christian unity. Jews the world over felt Rome turn remote at the start of the Six Day War. And the unbelieving who looked for a few years with some interest at the faith because it gave the world such a good and true man as Pope John, have mostly turned from it now as just one more light that failed. Apart from their obliterating effect on collegiality, the Pope's long-awaited words on contraception included the stunning claim that his Church's teaching on birth control had at no time been in any question. But if it had never been in any question, then why had the Pope gathered around him banks of experts to draft the cases for and against changing it? That question drove Father Charles Davis, the leading young Catholic theologian in England, to answer that the Pope lied, and that under Paul, the Church was hopelessly irreformable. Davis then made his own exit from Roman Catholicism with regrets. There has been a steady flood of defections from the clergy since then, including two U.S. bishops, at least 11,000 priests by the Vatican's count, and an incalculable number of laymen and laywomen who may never be counted among those who have given up their faith—for, in fact, most haven't given it up at all. What they have given up is their allegiance to a besieged institution—that once-august, ecclesiastic principality whose temporal strength was reckoned at all the parliaments of great power "A noble, a venerable superstructure," Silone wrote. "But what happens to poor Christ in such a superstructure?"

There are now two irreconcilable Roman Catholic churches and an array of others between them, sharing one ancient foundation. There is the Pope's fortress church behind the Vatican walls, with outposts in most dioceses where bishops minister to comfortable flocks unaffected by the suffering about them. And there is the servant church of the Christ-ridden, some of them baptized Catholics, some not, but all ill at ease in their skins because they care deeply about the suffering they combat. Ignored by the servant church with no center, the Pope's fortress church is what remains of a once-solid structure now cracked in many places, its foundation not yet fragmented perhaps, but not very far from it either. There are Roman Catholics uncertain that God exists, who believe the Word just became semantics. Once a Mass was the same, sound for sound, sign for sign, whether in the center of Brazil or the hamlets of the Great Plains. Now there may well be drumbeaters at one, folk-rock singing at the other, and at neither can a worshiper be sure that the priest isn't planning to marry—if he doesn't already have a wife.

continued

From final issue of *Look*, 1971

WEATHER

Today: Sunny and cool.
Tomorrow: Cloudy, milder.

Reports and Maps—Page 16

NEW YORK

Herald Tribune

THE CITY

Established 123 Years Ago, A European Edition Is Published Daily in Paris

Vol. CXXIII No. 42,613 — MONDAY, NOVEMBER 25, 1963 — TEN CENTS

A Nation Appalled

IN THE NEWS THIS MORNING

BULLET STRIKES VITALS of accused assassin Lee Oswald as night club owner Jack Ruby pulls the trigger, detective recoils, in crowded corridor of city hall basement.

Nightclub Owner Silences Assassin

By Maurice C. Carroll
Of The Herald Tribune Staff

DALLAS.

Lee Harvey Oswald met an assassin's death yesterday just 48 hours and seven minutes after the bullets he was accused of firing killed the President of the United States. With much of the nation watching on television, Oswald was shot down amid a crowd of reporters, photographers and policemen...

MOURNING IN CAPITAL

By David Wise
Washington Bureau Chief

WASHINGTON.

Under an American flag and a bright autumn sun, to the roll of muffled drums, the body of John F. Kennedy, 35th President of the United States, was...

ON THE WHITE HOUSE STEPS, the woman the slain assassin widowed, Jacqueline Kennedy, appears with her children, John jr. and Caroline, to escort the President's body to the Capitol where it lay in state in the Rotunda.

The great *New York Herald Tribune* records history with superb journalistic skill.

28

The Surviving Newspaper Press

. . . it is as difficult to apply objective standards to newspapers as it is to people, and the greatest newspaper is as difficult to identify as the greatest man. It all depends upon what you require.
—Gerald W. Johnson

The obligations of any newspaper to its community are to strive for honest and comprehensive coverage of the news, and for courageous expression of editorial opinion in support of basic principles of human liberty and social progress. Those newspapers which have been most consistent in fulfilling these obligations have been rewarded with public and professional acclaim. Other factors which have operated to give some newspapers greater professional recognition are brilliance of individual leadership on the staff, and the maintenance of a steady and sound publishing tradition. No one, however, can with any certainty rank America's leading papers in numerical order. But the results of three opinion polls on the subject, taken in 1960 and 1961, offer some at least interesting results. One was of 335 editors, one of 311 publishers, and the third of 125 journalism professors.

The *News York Times, Christian Science Monitor, St. Louis Post-Dispatch, Washington Post,* and *Milwaukee Journal* were rated among the top six dailies in all three polls. The *Louisville Courier-Journal* was in the first eight of all three polls. The *Chicago Daily News, Wall Street Journal, New York Herald Tribune,* and *Chicago Tribune* were in the first ten of two of the polls. Included in the top 15 dailies by one or more polls were the *Baltimore Sun, Atlanta*

Constitution, Minneapolis Tribune, Kansas City Star, Los Angeles Times, Miami Herald, Detroit Free Press, and *Des Moines Register.*[1]

A mail poll taken in 1970 by veteran public opinion expert Edward L. Bernays showed 130 publishers confirming most of the selections of the previous decade. The *New York Times* again ranked a clear first, with 60 per cent of the ballots listing it. A clear second was the *Los Angeles Times,* with a 50 per cent rating, up sharply during the 1960s. Clustered at 40 per cent were three dailies with distinguished editorial pages—the *Louisville Courier-Journal, St. Louis Post-Dispatch,* and *Washington Post.* At the 30 per cent level were the *Christian Science Monitor, Milwaukee Journal,* and moving upward, the *Miami Herald.* Ninth and tenth, at the 20 per cent level, were the *Chicago Tribune* and *Wall Street Journal.* Of the top ten of 1960, the *New York Herald Tribune* had ceased publishing in 1966 and the *Chicago Daily News* had moved down into such still distinguished company as the *Atlanta Constitution, Kansas City Star, Detroit Free Press,* and *Washington Star.* Threads of journalistic achievement can be woven together by examining the current status of these and some other representative daily newspapers whose accounts were not completed in earlier chapters of this volume.[2]

THE *NEW YORK TIMES*

The *New York Times* ranked first in all four polls, continuing to hold its place in the forefront of American journalism by maintaining the tradition of telling the news with completeness and integrity. Arthur Hays Sulzberger, who became publisher when his father-in-law, Adolph S. Ochs, died in 1935, lived up to his responsibilities as the head of the country's "newspaper of record." Throughout the 1930s and 1940s, the news staff was led by the team of Edwin L. James, managing editor, and David H. Joseph, city editor. Responsibility for the editorial page, which rested briefly with John H. Finley after the death of Rollo Ogden in 1937, passed in 1938 to Charles Merz. Merz had been managing editor of *Harper's Weekly* and an associate editor of the *New York World.*

Turner Catledge, well-tested as a Washington correspondent, became managing editor in 1951, the *Times'* centennial year. Catledge named two *Times* veterans, Theodore Bernstein and Robert E. Garst, as assistant managing editors with responsibility for enlivening the paper's writing and news presentation. Frank S. Adams became city editor, presiding over a block-long city room in the 18-million-dollar Times building down 43rd Street from the old Times Square location (the Times Tower was sold in 1961). Major changes came in

[1] For the poll of editors, see *Editor & Publisher,* XCIII (April 2, 1960), 12. For the poll of publishers, see *Editor & Publisher,* XCIII (April 9, 1960), 66. For the poll of journalism professors, see John Tebbel, "Rating the American Newspaper," *Saturday Review,* XLIV (May 13 and June 10, 1961).

[2] The stories of the *Christian Science Monitor* and *Wall Street Journal* are told on pages 567–69 of Chapter 25, and that of the *Chicago Tribune* on pages 706–11 of Chapter 30.

1961 when Sulzberger turned over the publisher's chair to his son-in-law, Orvil E. Dryfoos, and Merz retired as editorial page chief in favor of John B. Oakes (a nephew of Adolph Ochs), who had won distinction as an editorial writer. Lester Markel remained as editor of the Sunday edition, a post he had held for 40 years. In 1962 the *Times* began a Western edition printed in Los Angeles but lost heavily and killed it in 1964.

The management struggle described by Gay Talese in *The Kingdom and the Power* began with the sudden death of Dryfoos in June, 1963. The family turned to Arthur Ochs (Punch) Sulzberger, 37, as publisher. Strong man Amory Bradford, chief negotiator for the publishers in the disastrous 1963 New York strike, quit as business manager. In September young Sulzberger named Turner Catledge executive editor for both daily and Sunday editions, relegating Markel to retirement. Clifton Daniel was named managing editor and Tom Wicker replaced columnist James B. Reston as head of the Washington bureau.

A crisis arose over control of the Washington bureau early in 1968 when a non-*Times* man, James L. Greenfield, was nominated to head it. Wicker and Reston reversed the decision and the struggle undermined Catledge, who was soon moved up to a vice-presidency in favor of Reston as executive editor. The elder Sulzberger died at the close of 1968 and his son then took full command. Reston was made a vice president in August 1969 and returned to column writing in Washington, where Wicker was also a columnist and Max Frankel the bureau chief. Clifton Daniel was shunted to control of the New York Times Service and Abe Rosenthal, a loser in the 1968 crisis, became Sulzberger's managing editor. He brought Greenfield to the staff as foreign editor. The *Times* modernized more of its appearance and style and held its position as the center of journalistic power.

Editorially the *Times* was staunchly internationalist in world outlook, progressive-conservative in domestic affairs. It supported Democrat Franklin D. Roosevelt in 1936 and 1944 and backed Republicans Wendell Willkie in 1940, Thomas E. Dewey in 1948, and Dwight D. Eisenhower in 1952 and 1956. During the 1960s it supported Democrats John F. Kennedy, Lyndon B. Johnson, and Hubert H. Humphrey. Like other responsible newspapers it vigorously defended individual freedoms against reactionary attacks which characterized the years of stress following World War II. By 1971 the *Times* and its staff had won a record number of 38 Pulitzer Prizes, including two for meritorious public service in 1918 and 1944.

THE *INTERNATIONAL HERALD TRIBUNE*

After 1966 the legend "*Herald Tribune*" could be found only on a paper circulating throughout Western Europe: "The *International Herald Tribune*. Published with the New York Times and the Washington Post." For reasons of both quality and tradition, the paper should be included among the surviving greats.

The *New York Herald Tribune* was for 42 years a distinguished morning rival of the *Times*. Ogden M. Reid and his wife, Helen Rogers Reid, succeeded to control of the *Tribune* when editor Whitelaw Reid died in 1912. With the purchase of the *Herald* from Frank Munsey in 1924, and the creation of the *Herald Tribune*, a distinctive newspaper emerged. Ogden Reid was content to have his wife assume the major responsibilities of the publisher's office.

Like the *Times*, the *Herald Tribune* became known for its foreign and Washington correspondence, and for its coverage of cultural news. Its syndicated columnists included Mark Sullivan, Walter Lippmann, Joseph Alsop, and Roscoe Drummond. Geoffrey Parsons, a Pulitzer Prize winner, served as chief editorial writer from 1924 to 1952. Stanley Walker became one of New York's best known city editors, and assistant editor Wilbur Forrest was an important journalistic figure. When Ogden Reid died in 1947 his sons, another Whitelaw Reid and Ogden R. Reid, joined their mother in directing the paper's affairs. But difficulties piled up, and in 1958 the Reids reluctantly sold the *Herald Tribune*.

John Hay Whitney, millionaire new owner of the paper, first selected Robert M. White II, co-owner of the *Mexico Ledger* in Missouri, as *Herald Tribune* president and editor. But Whitney assumed direct control of the paper in 1960 as publisher and editor-in-chief, and chose John Denson, former editor of *Newsweek*, to replace White as editor. Denson revamped the *Herald Tribune's* makeup, adopting a magazine-style format. Dwight E. Sargent became editor of the editorial pages but left in 1964 to become curator of the Nieman Foundation at Harvard.

Lippmann won what proved to be the paper's final Pulitzer Prize in 1962. Denson resigned after a struggle with other executives and James G. Bellows took command. Crippled by the 114-day 1963 strike, the *Herald Tribune* still presented some of the best designed front pages and the most literate writing in U.S. journalism. But most New York newspapers were losing money and in early 1966 Whitney, the Hearst group, and Scripps-Howard planned a merger in which the *Herald Tribune* would become the morning edition of a World Journal Tribune Company. The final edition of the *Herald Tribune* appeared April 24; agreement could not be reached with the printing unions and Whitney announced its death August 15. A *World Journal Tribune* appeared evenings and Sundays from September, 1966, to May, 1967. Mrs. Helen Rogers Reid died in 1970 and an era was no more.

Left from the wreckage was the *International Herald Tribune*, successor to the Bennetts' old *Paris Herald*. In 1967 the *New York Times* gave up its European edition and Whitney, Katharine Graham of the *Washington Post*, and Sulzberger became joint owners of the Paris-based "Trib." It ran editorials from all three ownership sources.

Consistently conservative in its outlook, the old *Herald Tribune* won wide respect for fairness and for high quality interpretative writing. It supported the internationalist wing of the Republican party and early promoted the presidential bids of Willkie and Eisenhower, as against that of Senator Robert A. Taft. In its final campaign in New York the *Herald Tribune* rejected Goldwater for Lyndon Johnson.

THE *LOS ANGELES TIMES*

Bursting out almost as dramatically as California's population in the 1960s, the *Los Angeles Times* became a major force in national and international journalism by 1970. It had led all the nation's dailies in total advertising linage by a wide margin, and also led in space allotted to editorial material. Now it reached the million mark in circulation and became something more than the fat, dullish paper which the *New York Times* had thought could be challenged on its home grounds.

The heritage of the *Los Angeles Times* was strictly conservative. Harrison Gray Otis assumed control in 1882 and became a civic booster and Republican stalwart. When his plant was dynamited in 1910 by union radicals, his support of anti-union forces in the city was intensified. His son-in-law, Harry Chandler, was an equally conservative publisher engaged in a circulation struggle with the Hearst papers in Los Angeles. The *Times'* political editor, Kyle Palmer, so slanted his news stories that the Washington correspondents in 1937 voted the paper next to Hearst and McCormick papers as "least fair and reliable." Norman Chandler, publisher from 1944 to 1960, was more middle-of-the-road, but the paper lacked drive. It did win Pulitzer Prizes for public service in 1942, for fighting a contempt of court charge to the Supreme Court, and in 1960 for an exposure of narcotics traffic.

Changes in the *Times* were being planned even before Norman Chandler's death in 1960. His wife, Dorothy, and son, Otis, were working with Nick B. Williams, appointed editor in 1958, to revitalize the paper. Otis Chandler, 32 when he became publisher, proved to be one of the most effective U.S. publishers of the 1960s. Two new Sunday sections were created, "Opinion" and "Outlook," and two Sunday magazines named *West* and "Calendar." Acres of local and regional news releases were replaced with significant national and foreign news. Otis Chandler struck a bargain with youthful Philip L. Graham of the *Washington Post* to form the Los Angeles Times-Washington Post News Service. Within a decade it was one of the most important interpretative news services in the world and the *Times* had 7 domestic bureaus and 18 foreign bureaus of its own as well as the resources of the *Post*.

Williams retired to a consultant's post in 1971, and Chandler named as the new editor William F. Thomas, formerly metropolitan editor. Robert J. Donovan, *New York Herald Tribune* bureau chief in Washington, was lured to a similar position with the *Los Angeles Times* in 1963, becoming an associate editor and Washington columnist after 1970. James G. Bellows, last editor of the *Herald Tribune*, joined the *Times* in 1966 and became an associate editor, as did James Bassett. Anthony Day became editor of the liberally-tough editorial pages and Frank P. Haven managing editor. David Kraslow was head of a Washington bureau of 16.

Richard Nixon noted the *Times'* changing outlook during his ill-fated gubernatorial campaign in 1962, attacking the paper among others in his post-election "blow-up." In 1964 the *Times* backed Nelson Rockefeller for the Republican nomination but, failing, endorsed Goldwater for election. That year Paul Conrad joined the paper as editorial cartoonist and his liberal-line drawings won Pulitzer Prizes in 1964 and 1971. The paper also won the 1966 local coverage award for reporting the Watts riot, and the 1969 international reporting and public service awards, the latter for an exposure in city government. The *Times* bitterly fought Mayor Sam Yorty and joined a coalition unsuccessfully supporting his black opponent in the 1969 election. Early in 1971 it called upon President Nixon for an immediate withdrawal of troops from Indochina. Within a decade the *Times* had moved to an independent-minded editorial position which matched the news-gathering skill of its 516 staff members, a number which had doubled in ten years under editor Williams' direction. Chandler moved further onto the national stage by purchasing control of both *Newsday* and the *Dallas Times Herald* in 1970.

THE *WASHINGTON POST*

Other than the *Los Angeles Times,* no American newspaper rose more rapidly in esteem in recent decades than did the *Washington Post* after Eugene Meyer, a civic-minded financier, rescued it from a receivership in 1933. Meyer's object in buying the *Post* from the McLean family heirs was to give Washington a newspaper with a sound and intelligent editorial page. This he achieved with two editors who won Pulitzer Prizes for editorial writing: Felix Morley, editor until 1940, and Herbert Elliston, who served until 1953. Robert H. Estabrook then became editor of the editorial page. Giving the page added distinction were the cartoons of Herbert L. Block, better known as Herblock. Through its editorial page and its interpretative coverage of national news, the *Post* won recognition as the most independent paper in the capital. It also carried a large volume of foreign news.

When Meyer became president of the International Bank in 1946, he named Philip L. Graham, his son-in-law, as publisher, but he and his wife, Mrs. Agnes E. Meyer, remained influential in the newspaper's continued progress. Purchase of the *Post's* morning competition, the *Times-Herald,* in 1954, ensured the *Post's* economic stability. With James Russell Wiggins as editor and Alfred Friendly as managing editor, the paper had effective news-side leaders. They joined Graham in raising voices in behalf of improved journalistic practices and in defense of fundamental press freedoms. Editorially the *Post* avoided direct endorsements, but it favored the Dewey, Eisenhower, and Ken-

New York Times

Don Rice

Arthur Hays Sulzberger, *New York Times;* Mrs. Helen Rogers Reid, the *Herald Tribune.*

Washington Post

Los Angeles Times

Katharine Graham, *Washington Post;* Otis Chandler, *Los Angeles Times* and *Newsday.*

Louisville Courier-Journal

St. Louis Post-Dispatch

Barry Bingham, *Louisville Courier-Journal;* Joseph Pulitzer III, the *Post-Dispatch.*

nedy candidacies. It was strongly internationalist in outlook, and became known for its outspoken and early criticism of Wisconsin Senator Joseph R. McCarthy's political movement of the early 1950s which became known as "McCarthyism." Herblock, who had won a 1942 Pulitzer Prize, repeated in 1954 with his dramatically liberal cartoons, which had McCarthy as a particular target. Another was Vice President Nixon, whom the *Post* continued to oppose in future years.

Graham's tragic suicide in 1963 brought his wife Katharine to control of the Washington Post Company, including its television stations and *Newsweek*, purchased in 1961. Mrs. Graham was a friend of both President Kennedy and Johnson and a firm supporter of their reform policies. In 1965 she moved Benjamin C. Bradlee to the *Post* from *Newsweek* and made him managing editor in 1966. Friendly became a roving reporter and won the Pulitzer Prize for covering the war in Israel. Wiggins retired to become UN ambassador in 1968. Bradlee, then 47, became executive editor and Howard Simons managing editor.

The *Post* vigorously favored Hubert Humphrey in 1968, sympathized with dissent movements, and supported the black population of its area, employing more blacks than any other U.S. paper. When activist-philanthropist Agnes Meyer died in 1970, she had seen her daughter's paper pass the half-million mark in circulation and take a position as the most influential of the country's liberal-intellectual newspapers. Editorial page editor Philip L. Geyelin won the 1970 Pulitzer Prize in the spirit of Eugene Meyer.

THE *ST. LOUIS POST-DISPATCH*

The revolution of the 1870s and 1880s known as the "new journalism" gave the Middle West nationally known newspapers which continued to demonstrate their leadership in the 1960s. None was more consistently in the foremost rank of American newspapers than the *St. Louis Post-Dispatch,* founded in 1878 by the first Joseph Pulitzer, edited from 1911 to 1955 by the second Joseph Pulitzer, and since then by the third of the line, Joseph Pulitzer III, who began assuming authority in the late 1940s.

Continuity, both of Pulitzer family ownership and of the *Post-Dispatch* editorial policies, proved to be the key to greatness. Hammering away consistently to make the editorial page an independent, liberal voice have been six editorial page editors: George S. Johns, who served from 1897 to 1928, Clark McAdams, Charles G. Ross, Ralph Coghlan, Irving Dilliard, and Robert Lasch. Daniel R. Fitzpatrick's incisive cartoons dramatized *Post-Dispatch* crusades from 1913 until 1958.

O. K. Bovard, one of America's great newsmen, provided the necessary complement of leadership during his 30 years as *Post-Dispatch* managing editor, from 1908 to 1938. Under his tutelage, such brilliant reporters as Paul Y. Anderson, Charles G. Ross, Marquis Childs, and Raymond P. Brandt advanced from

St. Louis to the Washington scene to help win a national reputation for the paper. Anderson proved to be the mainspring of Bovard's effort after World War I to expand *Post-Dispatch* coverage of the national scene. Through his efforts the paper successfully led a campaign in 1923 to obtain the release of 52 Americans still imprisoned five years after the war's end for expression of radical antiwar opinion. Anderson and his paper were the first to realize the significance of the Teapot Dome scandal. And as a Washington correspondent, Anderson aided in the impeachment, for improper conduct, of federal judge George W. English of East St. Louis in 1926. English resigned before his impeachment trial.

What *Post-Dispatch* men called the "dignity page"—the opening page of the editorial section—was developed by Bovard to carry special articles on political, economic, scientific, and cultural subjects. When Bovard resigned in 1938 after differences with his publisher, Benjamin H. Reese became managing editor. Raymond L. Crowley succeeded Reese in 1951.

During the 15 years beginning in 1937 the *Post-Dispatch* won five Pulitzer Prize gold medals for meritorious public service, two more than the number won by the *New York World*, second-ranking in this awards category.[3] In its campaigns, the paper obtained abatement of the city's smoke nuisance and exposed two political scandals in St. Louis and two in nearby Illinois. Politically, *Post-Dispatch* support has usually been given to Democratic presidential candidates —but not to some Missouri party leaders. Franklin D. Roosevelt incurred the paper's wrath in 1936, although it endorsed him three other times, and it opposed Harry S Truman in 1948. Its devotion to liberal principles led also to unrelenting attacks upon McCarthyism and other right-wing movements. It found no favor with Richard Nixon or Barry Goldwater, opposing their candidacies of the 1960s.

Crowley's retirement in 1962 brought Arthur R. Bertelson to the managing editorship; when he advanced to executive editor, Evarts A. Graham, Jr.. succeeded him. Raymond P. Brandt retired in 1967 after 44 years in the Washington bureau; Marquis Childs, his successor as bureau chief, won the 1970 Pulitzer Prize for his commentary. Editor Lasch won a Pulitzer award in 1966.

[3] A series of articles on the Pulitzer Prize public service awards, by Ray Erwin, began in *Editor & Publisher*, XC (December 7, 1957), 13. Large daily winners not mentioned in the text of this chapter were the *Boston Post*, 1921; *Memphis Commercial Appeal*, 1923; *Indianapolis Times*, 1928; *Indianapolis News*, 1932; *New York World-Telegram*, 1933; *Miami Daily News*, 1939; *Omaha World-Herald*, 1943; *Brooklyn Eagle*, 1951; and the *Boston Globe*, 1966. Smaller dailies won, too: the *Columbus* (Ga.) *Enquirer-Sun*, 1926; the murdered Don R. Mellett's *Canton* (Ohio) *Daily News*, 1927; *Medford* (Ore.) *Mail Tribune*, 1934; *Cedar Rapids* (Iowa) *Gazette*, 1936; *Bismarck* (N. D.) *Tribune*, 1938; *Waterbury* (Conn.) *Republican* and *American*, 1940; *Scranton* (Pa.) *Times*, 1946; Lincoln *Nebraska State Journal*, 1949; *Whiteville* (N. C.) *News Reporter* and *Tabor City* (N. C.) *Tribune* (weeklies), 1953; *Columbus* (Ga.) *Ledger* and *Sunday Ledger-Enquirer*, 1955; *Watsonville* (Calif.) *Register-Pajaronian*, 1956; *Utica* (N. Y.) *Observer-Dispatch* and *Daily Press*, 1959; *Amarillo* (Tex.) *Globe-Times*, 1961; *Panama City* (Fla.) *News-Herald*, 1962; *Hutchinson* (Kan.) *News*, 1965; *Riverside* (Calif.) *Press-Enterprise*, 1968.

THE *MILWAUKEE JOURNAL*

The *Milwaukee Journal* stood in the uppermost level of the country's newspapers in the 1970s as a conscientiously edited, well-written, community-conscious daily blessed with one of the nation's largest volumes of advertising and space for comprehensive news coverage. Its editorial page ranked in stature with those of the *St. Louis Post-Dispatch* and *Washington Post*.

The *Journal*, founded in 1882, faced strong competition through all its early years. Publisher Lucius W. Nieman set the trend for its community leadership and first attracted national attention when he courageously exposed disloyal elements among Milwaukee's large German-American population during World War I. For this the *Journal* won the Pulitzer Prize for public service.

Under Nieman's guidance the *Journal* developed an international outlook, supporting the League of Nations and the United Nations. The paper clashed with the isolationist-minded La Follette family and Milwaukee's Socialist leader, Victor Berger, on foreign policy. But as a middle-of-the-road, independent paper it tended to support progressive-minded politicians of whatever party. Nationally, it supported Roosevelt in 1932, 1936, and mildly in 1944; Willkie in 1940, Dewey in 1948, and then the Stevenson candidacies. Its fiercest battle was with Senator Joseph R. McCarthy on his home ground; when McCarthy won reelection in 1952 he failed to carry Milwaukee. It refused to support either Nixon or Goldwater in the 1960s, endorsing Kennedy, Johnson, and Humphrey.

A dominant personality appeared on the *Journal* staff in 1916 when Harry J. Grant became business manager. Grant acquired 20 per cent of the stock and the title of publisher in 1919. He imported Marvin H. Creager from the *Kansas City Star* and Creager, as managing editor and later as editor and company president, reinforced the *Journal's* local coverage and writing qualities with an insistence born of his *Star* experience. The Kansas City paper, indeed, long had an important influence on *Journal* policies. In the years which followed, the *Journal* became a paper which made its influence felt in every Milwaukee activity, big or little.

Nieman died in 1935 and his wife in 1936. Part of the Nieman fortune was left to Harvard University, which used it to establish the Nieman Fellowships for newspapermen. The Nieman stock holdings in the paper were up for sale, but Grant saved the situation by organizing an employee-ownership plan similar to that of the *Star* in Kansas City. Grant, as board chairman and a substantial stockholder, remained in firm control. J. Donald Ferguson succeeded Creager as president and editor in 1943. In 1961, publisher Irwin Maier became president and Lindsay Hoben editor. Wallace Lomoe was named executive editor and Arville Schaleben managing editor in 1959. All had long careers with the paper.

Richard H. Leonard became managing editor when Lomoe retired in 1962 and Schaleben became associate editor. Leonard moved up to editor in 1967 upon the death of Hoben. The *Journal* won the Pulitzer Prize for public service that year. Its employes by then owned 80 per cent of the stock in the Journal Company, which also owned the *Milwaukee Sentinel* and the city's major television station.

THE *LOUISVILLE COURIER-JOURNAL*

The South, with a more slowly developing industrial economy, smaller population, and fewer major cities, did not match the East and Middle West in producing newspapers which could win the highest possible rankings in the estimate of the craft. But as early as the 1950s at least one—the *Louisville Courier-Journal* from the border state of Kentucky—became a newspaper which ranked among the nation's best.[4]

The retirement in 1919 of Henry Watterson, editor of the *Courier-Journal* since 1868, brought the Bingham family to the fore. Judge Robert Worth Bingham bought the *Courier-Journal* and the afternoon *Times* in 1917. Before he died in 1937 he saw his son, Barry Bingham, well established as directing owner of the newspapers. At his right hand was Mark Ethridge, former associate editor of the *Washington Post* and publisher of the *Richmond Times-Dispatch*, who came to Louisville as general manager in 1936 and became publisher in 1942. Bingham took the title, and writing responsibilities, of editor of the *Courier-Journal*.

Events moved rapidly at Louisville under the Bingham-Ethridge regime. James S. Pope became executive editor of the two papers. Norman E. Isaacs, managing editor of the *St. Louis Star-Times* when it closed down in 1951, came to Louisville as managing editor of the *Times*. Bingham, Ethridge, Pope, and Isaacs all were recognized as vocal, intelligent leaders in the journalistic profession. Russell Briney became editor of the *Courier-Journal* editorial pages and George Burt editor of those for the *Times*.

Steadily Democratic in its political preferences, the *Courier-Journal* exerted a strong influence as a progressive, fair-minded newspaper dedicated to defending basic democratic principles. In news play, it excelled in international and national coverage, but it also paid close attention to Louisville, where it did effective work in behalf of the Negro, union labor, education, music, and art.

The deaths of two of Bingham's sons in accidents left Barry Bingham, Jr., who had enjoyed work with CBS and NBC News and the paper's station, WHAS. His brother Worth was an influential executive when he died in 1966. Barry, Jr., then entered the news and business operations and became editor and publisher in 1971, with his father remaining as board chairman. Ethridge and Pope had retired; Isaacs left the executive editorship in 1970 to teach at Columbia University. Robert P. Clark succeeded him. Ben F. Reeves was managing editor of the *Courier-Journal*. Molly Clowes succeeded Briney as head of the editorial pages in 1966, giving way in 1970 to Robert T. Barnard. The

[4] It is interesting to note that Baltimore, Washington, Louisville, St. Louis, and Kansas City, all border state cities, developed outstanding newspapers.

Courier-Journal won the 1967 Pulitzer Prize for public service, the judges citing a successful campaign to control the Kentucky strip mining industry and thus preserve the environment.

THE *MIAMI HERALD*

The most progressive newspaper in the South, winning its way to a top place nationally by 1970, was the *Miami Herald,* a member of the Knight newspaper group. It was the twelfth largest morning daily in circulation and second largest daily in advertising volume, despite Miami's rank in city size—42 by population, 26 by market area.

John S. Knight began his career in the 1920s on the family's *Akron Beacon-Journal.* Their first expansion outside Ohio was to the *Miami Herald* in 1937. Purchase of the *Detroit Free Press* in 1940 gave the Knights a major group, to which they added the Charlotte and Macon newspapers and the *Philadelphia Inquirer* and *Daily News.* James L. Knight, a brother, concentrated his interest on the Miami and Charlotte operations, while John Knight focused on Detroit. But the management was integrated.

Lee Hills joined the *Herald* in 1942, coming from the Scripps-Howard papers. As managing editor, he built up the Latin American coverage of the *Herald* and began an international air express edition. In 1951 the *Herald* won a Pulitzer public service award for a drive on organized crime. The same year Hills was named executive editor of the *Detroit Free Press,* where he won a 1955 Pulitzer Prize for spot news. He became executive editor of all Knight newspapers in 1959. Directing the *Herald's* news operations in 1971 was George Beebe, also a specialist on Latin America.

John S. Knight had written his famed column, "The Editor's Notebook," for 32 years before he won the Pulitzer Prize for editorial writing in 1968. Both he and Hills served as president of the American Society of Newspaper Editors, Knight twice. Knight helped found and was president of the Inter American Press Association, which Hills later headed. Among U.S. publishers of the 1970s, Knight was one of the most outspoken. Against participation in the Indochina war since 1954, he had a loud and clear position on that issue. Knight and his group of papers generally supported Republicans for the presidency, but deserted Senator Goldwater in 1964.

OTHER EASTERN LEADERS

Vying with the *Washington Post,* the *New York Times,* and the *Herald Tribune* for position on important Washington breakfast tables was the *Baltimore Sun.* The *Sun,* giving special attention to Washington coverage since its founding in 1837, had developed one of the strongest capital bureaus as well

St. Louis Post-Dispatch

Milwaukee Journal

Editors: O.K. Bovard, *St. Louis Post-Dispatch;* Harry J. Grant, *Milwaukee Journal.*

New York Times

Los Angeles Times

James B. Reston, *New York Times;* Nick B. Williams, *Los Angeles Times.*

Washington Post

Knight Newspapers

Benjamin C. Bradlee, *Washington Post;* Lee Hills, the Knight Newspapers.

as a notable foreign service. Rejuvenated in the decade preceding World War I by Charles H. Grasty and Van-Lear Black, the *Sun* prospered under the effective leadership of Paul C. Patterson, publisher from 1918 to 1950. Hamilton Owens directed an aggressive editorial page. Washington columnist Frank R. Kent, H. L. Mencken, and Gerald W. Johnson were well-known staff members, followed by four Pulitzer Prize winners of the 1940s—Dewey L. Fleming, Paul W. Ward, Mark S. Watson, and Price Day. Day became editor-in-chief in 1960, succeeding J. Hamilton Owens. Philip Potter, longtime foreign and Washington correspondent, took over the capital bureau in 1964. The *Sun* won the Pulitzer Prize for meritorious public service in 1947.

Among other leading newspapers of the East was the *New York Post*, which completed 170 years of continuous daily publication in 1971, a record for currently-published American dailies. The *Post* entered a new phase when Dorothy Schiff bought it in 1939. With editor Ted O. Thackrey, she made the paper a streamlined tabloid, departmentalized the news, and added feature content. Its columnists, led by Max Lerner, were prominently displayed. James A. Wechsler, from the staff of *PM*, became editor in 1949. The *Post* was the only New York City daily supporting Democratic candidate Adlai Stevenson in 1952 and 1956, and backed Kennedy, Johnson, and Humphrey. When metropolitan New York journalism collapsed in the mid-1960s, the *Post* emerged as the only afternoon daily and increased its circulation by two-thirds. It picked up from defunct rivals Lippmann, Buchwald, Buckley, Ann Landers, and the Los Angeles Times-Washington Post News Service. Executive editor Paul Sann, publisher Schiff, and editor Wechsler moved with some financial assurance into the 1970s.

Long Island's *Newsday*, founded by Alicia Patterson in 1940 and controlled by her until she died in 1963, won its spurs as one of the top evening papers by combining local area coverage with substantial national and world news. It won the Pulitzer Prize for public service in 1954 and again in 1970 for uncovering Long Island governmental scandals. Tom Darcy won the 1970 Pulitzer award for cartooning. Alicia Patterson and her husband, Harry F. Guggenheim, differed on politics, he being the more conservative. In presidential races the paper supported Democrats in 1956, 1960, and 1964 and Republicans in 1952 and 1968. The switch to Nixon in 1968 came after Guggenheim took control in 1963. His editors were Mark Ethridge, from Louisville, followed by Bill D. Moyers, President Johnson's press secretary, in 1966. Guggenheim apparently intended to put Moyers in control of *Newsday* but became fearful of his policies and sold his 51 per cent stock interest to Otis Chandler of the *Los Angeles Times* in 1970. Moyers resigned and William Attwood came from the Cowles magazines to head *Newsday*. Guggenheim died in 1971.

The *Washington Star*, solid if unspectacular, celebrated its centennial in 1952, still in the possession of the Noyes and Kauffmann families which took control of it in 1867. Its editors have been Crosby Noyes, 1867 to 1908; Theodore Noyes, to 1946; an outsider, Benjamin McKelway, to 1963; and then Newbold Noyes. Frank B. Noyes, longtime AP president, was president of the *Star* from 1909 to 1948. Samuel H. Kauffmann followed him to 1963 and was succeeded by his son, John. Trailing the *Post* by the 1960s, the *Star* attracted attention with such staff members as Pulitzer Prize-winning national reporter Haynes Johnson and columnist Mary McGrory.

Equally as civic-minded as the *Star* was the *Philadelphia Bulletin*, purchased in 1895 by William L. McLean and later published by his son, Robert McLean, with William B. Dickinson as executive editor. The Butler family's *Buffalo Evening News*, long edited by Alfred H. Kirchhofer, also excelled in news coverage.

Achieving distinction for editorial page leadership and substantial news presentation were the *Providence Journal* and *Bulletin* and the *Hartford Courant*. Sevellon Brown, an executive of the Providence papers from 1921 to 1957, made them "the conscience of Rhode Island." Their excellence continued under executive editor Michael J. Ogden. The *Hartford Courant*, begun as the weekly *Connecticut Courant* in 1764 and claimant to the longest publishing record in America, was kept at a high level by publisher John R. Reitemeyer and editor Herbert Brucker. Bob Eddy succeeded to both posts by 1968.

In Ohio, publisher Paul Block, Jr.'s *Toledo Blade* advanced rapidly in the 1950s in comprehensive news coverage, community leadership, and independence of opinion. With its morning edition, the *Times*, it was allied in ownership with the *Pittsburgh Post-Gazette*, published by William Block. The *Blade* also was one of the few American dailies to have a European correspondent. The *Cleveland Press*, long edited by Louis B. Seltzer, remained the best of the Scripps-Howard group, and a strong civic leader. John S. Knight's *Detroit Free Press*, survivor with the *News* in that city's circulation battle, won the Pulitzer Prize for public service in 1945, and editor Royce Howes won for editorial writing in 1955. The prize for local reporting followed in 1968. But the *Free Press* and rival *News* were crippled by long strikes and major racial disturbances in the 1960s. The *Free Press* in 1971 was led by publisher Lee Hills, editor Mark Ethridge, Jr., executive editor Derick Daniels, and managing editor Frank Angelo.

MIDWEST JOURNALISTIC LEADERS

The *Chicago Daily News* retained a high place among newspaper leaders despite a series of ownership changes after the deaths of owners Victor F. Lawson in 1925 and Walter A. Strong in 1931. Colonel Frank Knox, former general manager of the Hearst newspapers and a leading Republican political figure, then became publisher. Knox kept the *Daily News* operating in its old traditions until his death in 1944. Its famous foreign and Washington news service reached brilliant heights. Henry Justin Smith, a news executive from 1901 to 1936, ran a "school for reporters."

Sale of the *Daily News* to John S. Knight in 1944 brought in Basil L. Walters as executive editor. Walters introduced new typographical and readership techniques he had learned while with the Cowles newspapers in Des Moines and Minneapolis. The paper emphasized local news and developed crusades on local issues. As a result, the *Daily News* printed the stories of its own foreign staff in less depth, although the service remained a strong one. The paper won two Pulitzer Prizes for public service, in 1950 and 1957, and gained in circulation and financial position.

Chicago newspaper ownership was streamlined in 1959, when Knight sold the *Daily News* to Marshall Field IV, owner of the morning *Sun-Times*. Field's father, founder of the *Sun* in 1941, had died in 1956. The *Daily News* became the evening affiliate of the *Sun-Times* in Chicago's circulation battle, and Field named himself its editor when Walters retired in 1961. His death at 49 in 1965 left control to the Field Enterprises executives until Marshall Field V was ready to assume command in 1969 at age 28. Larry S. Fanning gave way as *Daily News* editor to Roy M. Fisher in 1966; when Fisher resigned in 1971 to become dean of the Missouri School of Journalism, Daryle Feldmeir was chosen editor. James F. Hoge, Jr., was editor of the *Sun-Times*.

The *Daily News* won a Pulitzer Prize for public service once again in 1963. Reporter William J. Eaton received the 1970 national reporting prize for exposing the inadequacies of Supreme Court nominee Clement Haynsworth after his paper had endorsed President Nixon's selection. Cartoonist John Fischetti won a Pulitzer Prize in 1969. Another staff star was local columnist Mike Royko. Both Field papers favored Republican presidential candidates, but backed those from either major party in seamy Chicago and Illinois politics. Both were internationalist in outlook.

When journalism educators were asked in a 1961 poll to select the best combinations of morning and evening newspapers published by the same organization, they placed the Cowles-owned *Minneapolis Star* and *Tribune* and *Des Moines Register* and *Tribune* second and third, close behind the *Louisville Courier-Journal* and *Times*. Of the four papers owned by John and Gardner Cowles, the *Minneapolis Tribune* ranked highest as an individual daily.

Under publisher John Cowles the morning *Tribune* and evening *Star* developed wide upper Midwest circulations from their Minneapolis base. Gideon Seymour, after a successful career with the Associated Press, joined the papers in 1939 and was named executive editor in 1944. Carroll Binder, *Chicago Daily News* foreign editor, became editorial page editor of the *Tribune* in 1945.

Cowles, Seymour, and Binder teamed together to give the papers broadened news coverage, strong interpretative qualities, and independent-minded editorial pages strongly internationalist in outlook. Seymour died in 1954 and Binder in 1956. William P. Steven became executive editor and Wilbur E. Elston editorial pages editor. Both left when John Cowles, Jr., took direct control of the news and editorial pages after 1960. The Minneapolis papers placed staff correspondents in the European and Far Eastern areas. Republican in national politics through 1960, they endorsed Democrats Johnson and Humphrey and vigorously opposed the Vietnam war. By the 1970s they had won a reputation for independent editorial endorsements from both parties for local and state offices, and for a crusading opposition to right-wing movements.

In Des Moines, editorial editors W. W. Waymack, Forrest W. Seymour, and Lauren K. Soth all won Pulitzer Prizes for editorial writing. The Cowles Washington bureau won four Pulitzer awards for national reporting, and the four papers won the 1957 Sigma Delta Chi award for public service. Kenneth MacDonald became chief operating officer for Gardner Cowles in Des Moines.

While other leading dailies were expanding staff reporting of national news, the *Kansas City Star* was sticking principally to the local and regional area coverage which William Rockhill Nelson had emphasized from the time he founded the *Star* in 1880 until his death in 1915. Fine writing of news and features, and vigorous crusading in the community interest, were special ingredients which kept the *Star* high in newspaper ratings. Continuity was ensured for the paper when the staff bought stock control in 1926, with some 90 employes raising 2½ million dollars in cash and assuming an 8½ million dollar mortgage which was paid off by 1939.

Two men became particularly prominent in *Star* affairs. One was Henry J. Haskell, named editorial page director in 1910 and editor from 1928 to 1952. The *Star* won two Pulitzer Prizes for editorial writing during his tenure. Overshadowing him, however, was the bulky, jovial Roy A. Roberts, who came to be Kansas City's leading citizen. Roberts joined the staff in 1908, served as the paper's Washington correspondent 15 years, and then became managing editor in 1928. He was elected president and general manager of the *Star* and its morning edition, the *Times,* in 1947. Roberts loved politics as well as newspapering and he became an important, if unofficial, figure in Republican party affairs, maintaining the paper on that political course into the 1960s. Roberts retired in 1965 and left a million-dollar estate based on his holdings in the employee-owned newspaper company's stock when he died in 1967. William W. Baker became editor.

The morning *St. Louis Globe-Democrat* was the *Post-Dispatch's* only rival after closing of the *Star-Times* in 1951. The *Globe-Democrat,* built to prominence by Joseph B. McCullagh before 1900, also worked vigorously for civic progress, although less dramatically and in a conservative political atmosphere. E. Lansing Ray was publisher from 1925 to 1955, when the paper was sold to Samuel I. Newhouse. Editorial editor Louis LaCoss won the Pulitzer Prize for editorial writing in 1952, the paper's centennial year.

OTHER TOP PAPERS OF THE SOUTH

Affiliated with the *Miami Herald* through the Knight newspapers group, the *Charlotte Observer* rose to prominence during the 1960s in southern journalism. Purchased by the Knight family in 1954, it was given the personal attention of James L. Knight, who became publisher. Named editor in 1955 was C. A. (Pete) McKnight, who had been editor of the small evening *News* (later bought by Knight). McKnight had just served as editor of the *Southern School News,* an objective reporter of school desegregation developments, and took the *Observer* along a conciliatory road on civil rights. Cartoonist Eugene Payne won a 1968 Pulitzer Prize. Other rising North Carolina papers were the *Winston-Salem Journal* and *Twin City Sentinel,* edited by Wallace Carroll, winners of the 1971 Pulitzer Prize for public service for blocking a strip mining operation that would have defaced the Carolina hill country.

Long known for its liberalism and stubborn fight against the conservative *Nashville Banner,* the paper developed by Silliman Evans, the *Nashville Tennessean,* also won respect for its civil rights attitudes. The paper's fortunes declined after Evans' death in 1955, but they rose again when his younger son Amon Carter Evans became publisher at age 29 in 1962. With liberal John Seigenthaler as editor, the *Tennessean* supported the Kennedy-Johnson-Humphrey program for domestic reform. It also resumed the local crusading for which the elder Evans was famous.

Nelson Poynter's *St. Petersburg Times* won the 1964 Pulitzer Prize for public service for uncovering frauds in the state turnpike authority. The paper won a reputation for good reporting and news display based in part on Poynter's national journalistic reputation. In Memphis, the Scripps-Howard group had one of its best representatives in the *Commercial Appeal,* which developed its coverage and influence across state lines.

Atlanta gave the South two strong newspapers, the *Constitution* and the *Journal.* Clark Howell, Sr., who succeeded Henry Grady at the *Constitution* in 1889, became the paper's owner and served as editor until 1936. His son, Clark Howell, Jr., named Ralph McGill as editor in 1938. McGill opposed the Ku Klux Klan and the Talmadge political machine in Georgia, and won a Pulitzer Prize for editorial writing in 1959. James M. Cox, owner of the *Journal,* obtained control of the *Constitution* in 1950, but the papers continued to have separate editorial policies. The *Constitution* won a Pulitzer Prize for public service in 1931, and both papers won Sigma Delta Chi awards for public service in the 1950s. When McGill became a syndicated columnist and publisher of the *Constitution* in 1960, Eugene C. Patterson was named editor. He won the Pulitzer Prize in 1967 for his daily column and editorials attacking racism and political demagoguery. Then, declaring he lacked support by his management, he left in 1968 to become managing editor of the *Washington Post* and then a college professor. McGill died in 1969.

There were other famous names in southern journalism. Josephus Daniels continued his interest in the *Raleigh News and Observer* until his death in 1948, and passed on his editorship to his son, Jonathan, who also exerted influence in community and political affairs. Editor Virginius Dabney of the *Richmond Times-Dispatch* eyed traditional attitudes skeptically and jarred complacent conservatives with his editorials from 1928 into the 1960s. He won a Pulitzer Prize in 1948. Dr. Douglas Southall Freeman, editor of the *Richmond News Leader* from 1915 to 1949, won Pulitzer Prizes for his biographies of Robert E. Lee and George Washington. In Little Rock, J. N. Heiskell completed 60 years as editor of the respected *Arkansas Gazette* in 1961. His paper won the Pulitzer Prize for public service, and executive editor Harry S. Ashmore the award for editorial writing, for leadership during the 1957 school desegregation crisis in Little Rock. The stand cost the paper some of its public support and Ashmore left to join the Ford Foundation.

Rapidly growing Texas fostered a journalism which was in keeping with the state's free enterprise economic atmosphere. Vigorous competition existed in many cities, but among dailies essentially conservative in their editorial outlooks. The *Dallas News,* inherited by E. M. (Ted) Dealey in 1946 from his father George, became an arch-conservative voice in Republican-voting Dallas. Houston's two largest papers, the morning *Post* and evening *Chronicle,* were carefully conservative. The *Post* was built into prominence by William P. Hobby and his editor-wife, Oveta Culp Hobby. The *Chronicle,* owned by financier Jesse Jones until his death in 1956, obtained William P. Steven as editor in 1960 but discharged him in 1965 for moving too rapidly. Another financier, Amon G. Carter, firmly established the *Fort Worth Star-Telegram* as a leading Texas daily. Noteworthy for taking a strong liberal stand on the integration issue were the *San Antonio Express* and *News.* Among Texas editors who achieved national prominence professionally were Felix R. McKnight of the *Dallas Times Herald* and Walter R. Humphrey of the Scripps-Howard *Fort Worth Press.* A vigorous smaller daily was published in Corpus Christi by the Harte-Hanks group with Robert M. Jackson as editor. The morning *Caller* and the evening *Times,* joined on Sunday as the *Caller-Times,* typified the excellence of growing small dailies in various parts of the country.

VOICES OF THE WEST

Palmer Hoyt's entry into Denver journalism as publisher of the *Post* signaled a definite end of the Tammen-Bonfils type of newspapering. Hoyt gradually modified the *Post's* gaudy makeup, increased its interpretative news coverage, and gave the paper a better editoral balance. The *Post* developed a strong internationalist point of view and an independent editorial page which swung the usually Republican paper to the Kennedy camp in 1960. It continued to support Democratic presidential candidates in 1964 and 1968. Some of the paper's energy was expended in fighting lengthy court battles over attempts by the S. I. Newhouse group to add enough stock to their minority interest to control the *Post.* Hoyt retired in 1970 and was succeeded as editor and publisher by the *Post's* general manager, Charles R. Buxton. The paper ranked after the *Los Angeles Times* among western dailies of national reputation.

The *San Francisco Chronicle* was famed under publisher George T. Cameron, editor Chester Rowell, and general manager Paul C. Smith in the 1930s and 1940s for its comprehensive national and foreign news coverage. But in the 1950s, under new direction, the *Chronicle* turned heavily toward features, columnists, and circulation-getting news. It passed the Hearst-owned *Examiner* in readers, but saw the *Examiner* surpass it in solid news. The *Chronicle* was always an interesting paper, however, under the editorship of Scott Newhall, who resigned in 1971 to protest what he felt was an increasing managerial conservatism in sociopolitical outlook.

In Portland, the long respected *Oregonian* ran into difficulties. Its famous editor, Harvey W. Scott, died in 1910, and manager Henry L. Pittock in 1919. Their heirs found a strong editor in Palmer Hoyt, from 1933 until he left to become publisher of the *Denver Post* in 1946. Control of the *Oregonian* passed to Samuel Newhouse in 1950, as did ownership of the rival *Oregon Journal* in 1961. The papers were badly hurt by a prolonged strike beginning in 1959 which sharply reduced their staff morale. Robert C. Notson, a longtime *Oregonian* editor, was named publisher in 1967.

The McClatchy-owned *Bee* newspapers in California, published in Sacramento, Fresno, and Modesto, won a reputation as fiercely independent dailies. The *Sacramento Bee,* founded in 1857, became well known under its publisher-editor, C. K. McClatchy, who served from 1883 to 1936. The *Bee* crusaded for public power, spoke out for individual liberties, and won a Pulitzer Prize for public service in 1935 for exposing political corruption. Eleanor McClatchy succeeded her father as publisher and kept to his usually pro-Democratic political beliefs.

Two new prospects arose among western newspapers in the 1960s. National attention was focused on the *Santa Barbara News-Press* in 1962 when its publisher, Thomas M. Storke, won the Pulitzer Prize for editorials written in early 1961 revealing the character of the secret John Birch Society. Purchase of the paper by Robert McLean of the *Philadelphia Bulletin* gave it additional attention. Executive editor was Paul Veblen. The other prospect came from a government antitrust suit which forced the *Tucson Daily Citizen* to divest itself of the morning *Arizona Daily Star.* In the subsequent 1971 sale, Tucson got a grandson of Joseph Pulitzer as the *Star's* new owner, Michael E. Pulitzer, who had been assistant managing editor of the *St. Louis Post-Dispatch.* This could mean some infusion of the Pulitzer brand of journalism in the frontier state of Arizona.

Few of the present-day newspapers whose stories have been told date back more than 100 years. Indeed, only a little more than two and a half centuries separate the crudely printed news sheets produced in Boston by Benjamin Harris and John Campbell from the modern dailies of the mid-twentieth century. But vast changes have been recorded. The story of the growth of newspapers—and the addition of magazines, books, radio, and television to create the mass media—is the story of both the development of communications and the maturing of a nation. It is the story of journalism in American life—of the press and America.

Annotated Bibliography

Books

Berger, Meyer, *The Story of the New York Times, 1851–1951*. New York: Simon & Schuster, 1951. The best history of the *Times*.

Catledge, Turner, *My Life and The Times*. New York: Harper & Row, 1971. A readable autobiography of a capable newspaperman, reaching a climax with the struggle for "the kingdom and the power." Candid evidence given.

Conrad, Will C., Kathleen F. Wilson, and Dale Wilson, *The Milwaukee Journal: The First Eighty Years*. Madison: University of Wisconsin Press, 1964. A good newspaper history of a great daily.

Garst, Robert E., ed., *The Newspaper—Its Making and Its Meaning*. New York: Scribner's, 1945. Addresses by 12 *New York Times* staff members, describing their work.

Hart, Jim Allee, *A History of the St. Louis Globe-Democrat*. Columbia: University of Missouri Press, 1961. Tell the story of St. Louis' "other paper" in a social and political framework.

Johnson, Gerald W., et al., *The Sunpapers of Baltimore*. New York: Knopf, 1937. An outstanding newspaper history.

Kobre, Sidney, *Development of American Journalism*. Dubuque, Iowa: Wm. C. Brown Company, 1969. Traces in detail the twentieth-century histories of many leading newspapers.

Lyle, Jack, *The News in Megalopolis*. San Francisco: Chandler, 1967. Los Angeles area news media analyzed.

McNulty, John B., *Older than the Nation*. Stonington, Conn.: Pequot Press, 1964. A well-presented, readable, scholarly history of the *Hartford Courant* on its 200th birthday.

Markham, James W., *Bovard of the Post-Dispatch*. Baton Rouge: Louisiana State University Press, 1954. A discerning biography.

Merrill, John C., *The Elite Press: Great Newspapers of the World*. New York: Pitman, 1968. Forty great newspapers in terms of performance and influence include, from the U. S., the *Baltimore Sun, Christian Science Monitor, St. Louis Post-Dispatch, Los Angeles Times,* and *New York Times*. An excellent worldwide survey.

Reston, James B., *Sketches in the Sand*. New York: Knopf, 1967. The best of a leading *New York Times* editor's work.

Rivers, William L., and David M. Rubin, *A Region's Press: Anatomy of Newspapers in the San Francisco Bay Area*. Berkeley: Institute of Governmental Studies, University of California, 1971. Contemporary study with some historical material on major dailies.

Smith, Paul C., *Personal File.* New York: Appleton-Century-Crofts, 1964. Reminiscences of editor of *San Francisco Chronicle* who later headed Crowell-Collier.

Stewart, Kenneth, and John Tebbel, *Makers of Modern Journalism.* Englewood Cliffs, N.J.: Prentice-Hall, 1952. Contains extensive comment on many of the newspapers and men covered in this chapter; see index.

Talese, Gay, *The Kingdom and the Power.* New York: New American Library, 1969. Penetrating, informative recent history of the *New York Times* and study of its publishers and editors as they struggled for power.

Periodicals and Monographs

Bibliographies in the *Journalism Quarterly* annotate articles in the academic journals, in *Editor & Publisher, Saturday Review, Time, Newsweek,* and in other periodicals. See the bibliography for Chapter 27 for references to Knight, Cowles, and Newhouse.

Bagdikian, Ben H., "What Makes a Newspaper Nearly Great?," *Columbia Journalism Review,* VI (Fall 1967), 30. The paper is the *Washington Post.*

Bridges, Lamar W., and Alan Bussel, "The Fight Against Boss Crump," *Journalism Quarterly,* XLIV (Summer 1967), 240, 245. Two articles recording battles of Memphis editors Mooney and Meeman against bossism.

Brinton, James E., "Failure of the Western Edition of the *New York Times,*" *Journalism Quarterly,* XLI (Spring 1964), 170. The famed eastern paper loses out to the *Los Angeles Times.*

"The Challenger," *Time,* LXXVII (January 20, 1961), 60. Marshall Field IV, and the *Chicago Sun-Times* and *Daily News.*

Chu, Chi-ying, "Henry Justin Smith (1875–1936), Managing Editor of the *Chicago Daily News,*" Ph.D. thesis, Southern Illinois University, 1970. A teacher of writing.

DeVoto, Bernard, "Always Be Drastically Independent," *Harper's,* CCVII (December 1953), 42. The *St. Louis Post-Dispatch* is nominated as the "finest practitioner of liberal journalism."

"The Fair Lady of Milwaukee," *Time,* LXIII (February 1, 1954), 44. An extensive report on the *Journal.*

Hellman, Geoffrey T., "Profiles: Publisher," *New Yorker,* XLIV (August 10, 1968), 37. Dorothy Schiff, owner-publisher of the *New York Post.*

Mayer, Martin, "The Lady as Publisher," *Harper's,* CCXXXVII (December 1968), 90. Profile of Katharine Graham, head of the *Washington Post* and *Newsweek.*

Patterson, Alicia, "This Is the Life I Love," *Saturday Evening Post,* CCXXXII (February 21, 1959), 19. *Newsday's* story.

Price, Warren C., "The *Eugene Register-Guard:* Citizen of Its Community, 1867–1967," Ph.D. thesis, University of Minnesota, 1967. A penetrating study of a leading small daily.

Rivers, William L., and David M. Rubin, "The *Chronicle:* Schizophrenia on the Bay," *Columbia Journalism Review,* VIII (Fall 1969), 37. Analysis of an interesting paper.

Smith, Lee, "The Battle for Sunday," *New York,* IV (October 25, 1971), 34. A depth analysis of a challenge by Otis Chandler and *Newsday* to the *New York Times* and *Daily News.*

Stern, Mort P., "Palmer Hoyt and the *Denver Post,*" Ph.D. thesis, University of Denver, 1969. A field study of organizational change.

Tait, Samuel W., Jr., "The St. Louis Post-Dispatch," *American Mercury,* XXII (April 1931), 403. An analysis of editorial policy.

Tebbel, John, "Rating the American Newspaper," *Saturday Review,* XLIV (May 13 and June 10, 1961). Ratings by 125 journalism educators.

Waldrop, A. Gayle, "A Chinook Blows on Champa Street," *Journalism Quarterly,* XXIV (June 1947), 109, and "Reborn Denver 'Post' Has Prestige and Power," XXVIII (Summer 1951), 327.

White, Llewellyn, "Papers of Paradox," *Reporter,* II (January 31, 1950), 22. *Louisville Courier-Journal* and *Times* analyzed.

———, "A Good Paper Pays Off," *Reporter,* III (August 29 and September 12, 1950). Excellent reports on the *Milwaukee Journal.*

Williams, Roger M., "Newspapers of the South," *Columbia Journalism Review,* VI (Summer 1967), 26. Qualitative judgments on leading dailies.

Winter, Willis L., Jr., "The Metamorphosis of a Newspaper: The *San Francisco Chronicle,* 1935–1965," Ph.D. thesis, University of Illinois, 1968. The editorships of Paul C. Smith and Scott Newhall.

THE WEATHER
Today: Occasional light rain and warmer
Tomorrow: Occasional light rain and warmer
Detailed Report on Page 15

NEW YORK
Herald Tribune

NEW YORK HERALD TRIBUNE Established March 19, 1924
NEW YORK HERALD Founded May 6, 1835
NEW YORK TRIBUNE Founded April 10, 1841

VOL. XCII No. 31,529 — MONDAY, MARCH 13, 1933 — TWO CENTS In Greater New York | THREE CENTS Within 200 Miles | FOUR CENTS Elsewhere

Roosevelt Bids Nation Lose Fear, Join for Recovery as Banks Open; City Bankers End Holiday Today

Relief Calms Quake Zone; Rebuilding of Homes Starts

Reconstruction Is Begun as Earth Still Quivers; Many Refuse to Enter Their Battered Homes

115 Dead, 5,000 Hurt, $35,000,000 Damage

Precautions Are Taken Against Peril to Health; 'Ex-Angel of Broadway' Heads 'Spiritual Clinic'

Nazi and Empire Flags Raised by Hindenburg

Republic Drops Colors; Hitler Warns Troopers To Forego Aggression; Berlin Votes Nationalist

By John Elliott

President Paul von Hindenburg

Economy Bill Faces Fight in Senate Today

Stormy Debate Expected but Grant of Power Tomorrow to Make 500 Million Cut Predicted

Caucus Is Called To Bind Democrats

Murmuring Over 'Abdication' of Its Authority Is Growing in Congress

State, Reserve, Clearing House Officials at Work All Night on Lists of Institutions to Reopen

Lehman Appeals For the State Banks

Asks Share in New Currency; Hoarding Ban Continued; Check System Is Restored Here

President's Radio Address

WASHINGTON, March 12.—The text of the radio address delivered by President Roosevelt tonight assuring the nation that the banks, in reopening this week, "will take care of all needs," follows:

I want to talk for a few minutes with the people of the United States about banking—with the comparatively few who understand the mechanics of banking, but more particularly with the overwhelming majority who use banks for the making of deposits and the drawing of checks.

'Your Problem No Less Than Mine,' He Says in Radio Address; 'Together We Cannot Fail'

New Money Sound, Not Fiat, He Avers

Units, as They Resume, to Have Ample Supplies of Cash; Assets Will Be Intact, He Declares

By Albert L. Warner

Moscow Police Seize 4 Britons In Raid at Office

English Company's Papers Taken; 35 Russians Die for Fighting Farm Plan

By Ralph W. Barnes

Rainey Pledges Beer by Spring To Spur Upturn

$470,000,000 Business of Restoring Brews 'Entering Wedge' to Prosperity

Summary of Today's News

More Days of Grace Given to Gold Hoarders

Treasury Extends to Friday The Deadline on Returns

Radio became Franklin Roosevelt's ally; the first Fireside Chat and (*inset*) 1937 FDR.

29

Government, Publishers, and Guild

There can be no such thing as a free press and no such thing as the integrity of the news if the men and women who write the news live in fear of the security of their jobs.
—Heywood Broun

A new era in the history of the United States opened in 1933 when Franklin D. Roosevelt inaugurated the New Deal. Driven by the impact of the great depression, the nation sought for new patterns of social and economic justice and security. In doing so, it adopted philosophies concerning government participation in socioeconomic affairs extending well beyond those which arose from the Theodore Roosevelt and Woodrow Wilson eras early in the century.

The press, as a result, entered into a period of sharply intensified concern about its relationships with government. Its business operations, like those of all private enterprises, were affected by New Deal social and economic legislation. A new chapter in newspaper labor relations was opened with the rise of the American Newspaper Guild under the collective bargaining laws. And, in the turbulent New Deal era and afterwards, the question of freedom of the press was raised steadily by those who either feared or resented the strengthened hand of government.

THE 1933 ECONOMIC CRISIS

The first job of the Roosevelt administration in 1933 was to restore confidence in the country's banking system, on the verge of collapse after a wave of fear swept the nation in the winter months. This was done by emergency action, reinforced by establishment of the Federal Deposit Insurance Corporation. The second job, with some 17,000,000 persons unemployed, was to coordinate relief activities under the Federal Emergency Relief Administration, which later became the famous Works Progress Administration. By the end of 1934, one-sixth of the population was on relief. Young men were enrolled in the Civilian Conservation Corps and college students in the National Youth Administration.

But the main task of the New Deal was to stimulate recovery in industry, business, and agriculture. The agencies involved were the Reconstruction Finance Corporation, established by the Hoover administration to make credit available to businesses; the Public Works Administration, which financed job-giving construction projects; the Agricultural Adjustment Administration and the Farm Credit Administration; and, most important of all, the National Recovery Administration. The National Industrial Recovery Act, passed by Congress in June, 1933, was an ambitious effort to plan the return to prosperity. American employers were to cooperate, under government leadership, in shortening working hours, raising wages, and pledging themselves to increase employment. The act called for establishment of NRA codes of fair competition for all industries.

THE NRA AND LICENSING

Two sections of the recovery act in particular affected newspaper publishers. One was the famous Section 7-a, which guaranteed the right of collective bargaining and freedom of labor union organization. Under the shelter of its provisions the American Newspaper Guild came into being. The other was the licensing section, which gave the President power to license individual companies in an industry not cooperating under the NRA program and to revoke such licenses for continued noncompliance if he deemed it necessary and proper. Operation of a business without a license under such conditions would be unlawful. Only those who cooperated could fly the "Blue Eagle," the NRA's symbol.

Trade associations in the communications industries were called upon to write voluntary codes to which individual businesses could subscribe. The American Newspaper Publishers Association took the lead in the writing of a code for daily newspapers which would contain the safeguards and requests the ANPA leadership believed publishers wanted. The association's general legal counsel, Elisha Hanson, played a leading role in influencing the code negotiations.

The ANPA's code committee feared the licensing provisions of the NRA legislation. At the urging of Colonel Robert R. McCormick, chairman of the association's committee on freedom of the press, the publishers correctly insisted that their code deny the application of the licensing power to newspapers.

But General Hugh S. Johnson, the outspoken former cavalry officer who headed NRA, raised his eyebrows at some of the other reservations. So did some newspaper publishers, newspaper editorial workers, and others who felt that the ANPA was asking for a privileged position for daily newspapers that was not in keeping with the recovery effort.[1]

After eyeing the NRA guarantee of the right to collective bargaining, Hanson and the committee had written into their code an open-shop provision assuring any employer or employee the right to bargain individually. The code also proposed that carrier boys be exempted from NRA provisions limiting child labor. Reporters and other editorial workers who were doing "professional work" were not to be subject to the maximum hour provisions of the law. To cap their requests, the publishers insisted upon a clause stating: "Nothing in the adoption and acceptance of this code shall be construed as waiving, abrogating, or modifying any rights secured under the Constitution of the United States or of any state, or limiting the freedom of the press."

Those surrounding President Roosevelt regarded the inclusion of such a statement in the proposed code as an insulting gesture. When he approved the final draft of the daily newspaper code in February, 1934, President Roosevelt called the publishers' proposed press-freedom clause "pure surplusage," and added: "The freedom guaranteed by the Constitution is freedom of expression and that will be scrupulously respected—but it is not freedom to work children, or to do business in a fire trap or violate the laws against obscenity, libel and lewdness." This was strong medicine, and it was the publishers' turn to feel unjustly and falsely accused.

THE DAILY NEWSPAPER CODE

The final version of the daily newspaper code provided for a 40-hour week only for employees of newspapers published in cities of more than 50,000 population. Its minimum wage scale ranged from $15 a week for employees of papers published in cities of more than 500,000 population down to $11 a week in cities of less than 25,000 population. "Learners" would receive at least 70 per cent of the scale. Mechanical employees were guaranteed wages of 40 cents an hour. The minimum age for carrier boys remained at 12. The "professional worker" clause was clarified so that ordinary news-editorial employees came under the maximum hour clause. The President asked metropolitan papers to put newsmen on five-day weeks to increase employment, and most of them did so.[2]

Newspapermen received the wage and hour provisions of the daily newspaper code with little enthusiasm. The $11 to $15 weekly salary minimums did

[1] *Editor & Publisher,* LXVI (August 12, 1933), 3, carries some of the dissents, as do subsequent issues.

[2] *Editor & Publisher,* LXVII (February 24, 1934), pp. 3, 36, gives Roosevelt's executive order and the text of the code.

nothing to further the professional status of journalism, or the economic security of its workers—an obvious conclusion to which thoughtful leaders of the profession agreed. The code provisions were far from the $40 a week minimum for newsmen with two years or more experience, which New York newspapermen considered equitable at the time.

HEYWOOD BROUN AND THE GUILD

Heywood Broun

Reporters and deskmen around the country began talking about formation of collective bargaining units in the summer of 1933 when the trend of the code negotiations became apparent. Heywood Broun, the liberal and combative columnist for the *New York World-Telegram,* sounded a call for action in his syndicated column for August 7, 1933, which sparked the translation of talk into deeds. Broun deftly chastised his fellow newspapermen for not having formed a union like those of the better-paid printers, and gently chided those who feared "the romance of the game" would be lost if they organized. Then in typical Broun style he concluded:

> But the fact that newspaper editors and owners are genial folk should hardly stand in the way of the organization of a newspaper writers' union. There should be one. Beginning at nine o'clock on the morning of October 1, I am going to do the best I can in helping get one up. I think I could die happy on the opening day of the general strike if I had the privilege of watching Walter Lippmann heave a brick through a *Tribune* window at a nonunion operative who had been called in to write the current "Today and Tomorrow" column on the gold standard.[3]

[3] Broun's column is reprinted in the *Guild Reporter,* XVI (December 9, 1949), which contains several pages reviewing early Guild history and Broun's career. The early years of the Guild are examined in Daniel J. Leab, *A Union of Individuals: The Formation of the American Newspaper Guild 1933–1936* (New York: Columbia University Press, 1970).

The cautious Lippmann ignored Broun's call to arms, but the newspapermen across the country who read his column didn't, nor did they wait until October 1. Cleveland's newsmen were the first to respond, forming what became the first local of the American Newspaper Guild on August 20. The Twin Cities, Minneapolis and St. Paul, were second in line. New York, Rockford, Newark, Akron, Duluth–Superior, Cincinnati, Philadelphia, and Youngstown locals followed in rapid order. There had been newswriters' locals chartered by the American Federation of Labor and its affiliated International Typographical Union as early as the 1890s, but few had lived for any length of time. Broun himself had headed a New York effort in 1923.[4]

THE AMERICAN NEWSPAPER GUILD, 1933

New York newsmen, headed by Broun, issued the first number of the *Guild Reporter* on November 23, 1933, and called for a national convention to be held in Washington December 15. Delegates from 30 cities responded, and formed the American Newspaper Guild. Broun was elected president, a post he held until his death in 1939, and Jonathan Eddy became the first executive secretary. The newspapermen and women were seeking, they said, "to preserve the vocational interests of the members and to improve the conditions under which they work by collective bargaining, and to raise the standards of journalism."

By the time the first annual convention met in St. Paul in June, 1934, the Guild had 8,000 members. But only one of its local units had a contract with a publisher. The 1934 Guild convention called for more contracts covering minimum wages and maximum hours, paid holidays and vacations, overtime pay, sick leave, severance pay, and other usual trade union contract provisions—goals which remained to be gained by the average newspaper staff. Publishers who disliked seeing the Guild take on the form of a trade union organization were further antagonized when the convention approved a code of ethics which listed what the Guild regarded to be harmful practices of newspapers. The Guild, rebuffed in its effort "to raise the standards of journalism" on a philosophical plane, and realizing that it faced a hard fight to win union contracts, thereafter stuck closely to problems of salaries and working conditions when dealing with employers. Local units sponsored Guild discussions and competitions designed to improve journalistic practices.

[4] The early AFL efforts are summarized in National Labor Relations Board, *Collective Bargaining in the Newspaper Industry* (Washington: Government Printing Office, 1939), and in Alfred McClung Lee, *The Daily Newspaper in America* (New York: Macmillan, 1937). The most successful locals were in Scranton, Milwaukee, Boston, New York, Philadelphia, and Columbus, Ohio.

LABOR CONTRACTS AND STRIKES

The first contract to be signed by a publisher and a Guild unit included a Guild objective that was to meet determined opposition from the publishers. J. David Stern, liberal-minded publisher of the *Philadelphia Record,* signed a contract in April, 1934, which provided for a Guild-shop agreement, stipulating that all newsmen must join the Guild within 30 days of initial employment. A compromise form of the Guild shop agreement became one which required that 80 per cent of the employees covered by a contract must be Guild members. In either case the publisher was free to employ whomever he chose, without regard to prior Guild membership.

Stern guaranteed his *Philadelphia Record* employees a $20 a week basic minimum, a 40-hour week, vacation and overtime pay, and severance provisions. The second Guild contract, signed by the *Madison Capital Times* and *Wisconsin State Journal* in September, 1934, offered a $35 top minimum after two years' experience, one month of dismissal notice, a Guild shop, and a 48-hour week (down from 55 to 65 hours).[5] Vacations, holidays, and sick leave went unmentioned.

Guildsmen walked picket lines for the first time against two S. I. Newhouse papers, first in July against the *Long Island Daily Press* and then against the *Staten Island Advance*. Strike action was taken by the Guild for the first time against a major newspaper in November, 1934, when publisher L. T. Russell of the *Newark Ledger,* in New Jersey, discharged eight Guildsmen. After 19 weeks, Russell sold the paper to Newhouse, leaving the newsmen with little more than a moral victory.

In spite of what members considered as reasonable demands, Guildsmen got few concessions, and the ANG treasury was bare. Outright trade unionism was the answer of the 1935 convention which cemented a casual collection of locals into a single compact union. Then, between February, 1936, and June, 1938, Guild locals were constantly involved in one or more strikes, for a total of 16 in this period.

Head-on clashes became unavoidable. The biggest strikes were against Hearst newspapers in Milwaukee, Seattle, and Chicago. Bitterest was the 508-day strike against the *Chicago American* and *Chicago Herald & Examiner,* beginning in December, 1938. The papers were merged during the strike, which ended with an eight-month contract and a nationwide "peace formula" between Hearst and the Guild. But the formula did not apply in Chicago where the Guild lost bargaining rights at contract's end and 90 Guildsmen were fired in early 1941.

These years of peak strike activity were years of decision in many ways

[5] *State Journal* employees later withdrew from the Guild, as did some of the other early organized units.

for the Guild. In 1936 it still had only 30 contracts and 33 "bulletin-board" agreements with newspaper managements. That year the Guild joined the American Federation of Labor, only to switch in 1937 to the newly-formed Committee on Industrial Organization. The 1937 convention broadened the Guild membership base to include commercial office employees, in addition to the news-editorial and advertising personnel—a move which was opposed by quite a few Guild members and which resulted in some locals withdrawing to form independent units. Passage of resolutions on controversial topics also angered some Guild members. But as a result of overall strengthening of the national organization, the Guild had 75 newspaper contracts by 1938 and had signed its first with a press association, the United Press.[6]

THE MORRIS WATSON CASE AND THE WAGNER ACT

But the biggest Guild victory was gained in a court case involving one Associated Press staffman, Morris Watson. Watson, who had been discharged by the Associated Press in 1935, asserted he had been dismissed for Guild activities. He appealed to the National Labor Relations Board for an order compelling his reinstatement under the provisions of the Wagner Labor Relations Act of 1935, whose collective bargaining guarantees had replaced those of the NRA codes outlawed by the Supreme Court that year. When the NLRB ruled in favor of Watson in 1936, the AP carried the case to the Supreme Court, contending that the Wagner Act was unconstitutional and that in any event it did not apply to newspapers or press associations.

Elisha Hanson brought the American Newspaper Publishers Association into the case and told ANPA members to "flatly refuse to have anything to do with the National Labor Relations Board other than to notify it that it is without power under the Constitution to interfere with their business." [7] The ANPA board of directors followed with a flat statement that a publisher who agreed to a Guild shop thereby destroyed or restricted freedom of the press, arguing that unionization could only lead to biased news writing. J. David Stern, publisher of the *Philadelphia Record* and first signer with the Guild, resigned in anger from the ANPA, telling the board: "Ever since the NRA code, the American Newspaper Publishers Association has been using the pretext of protecting the freedom of the press to gain special privilege in purely business obligations. That is why I say *you* are endangering the freedom of the press, one of the most important essentials of our democracy." [8]

[6] The details can be followed in the *Guild Reporter* and *Editor & Publisher,* and are summarized in the NLRB's *Collective Bargaining in the Newspaper Industry* and in the special issue of the *Guild Reporter,* XVI (December 9, 1949).

[7] *Editor & Publisher,* LXIX (October 10, 1936), 7.

[8] *Editor & Publisher,* LXIX (December 19, 1936), 57.

The smashing reelection victory won by President Roosevelt in November, 1936, made it evident that the country had accepted the basic New Deal reform measures, including approval of the principle of collective bargaining. Newspaper publishers, recognizing the situation and desiring to abide by the majority decision, shied away from the ANPA's Guild policy in growing numbers, without awaiting the Watson case ruling. The *New York Daily News,* the country's largest newspaper, signed a contract for a Guild shop, and William Randolph Hearst ended the long *Seattle Post-Intelligencer* strike, putting President Roosevelt's son-in-law and daughter, John and Anna Boettiger, in charge of the paper. Many metropolitan papers granted higher salaries and shorter hours.

Then the Supreme Court, which had ruled adversely on key New Deal legislation in 1935 and 1936, announced a series of decisions in April, 1937, upholding the constitutionality of the Wagner Act. Among the cases decided was that of Morris Watson. Justices Hughes and Roberts swung to the liberal side to join Justices Brandeis, Stone, and Cardozo in ordering the Associated Press to reinstate Watson in his job. The five justices ruled that Watson had been illegally discharged for union activity, and it was upon that point that the case turned.[9] But the majority also observed that "The publisher of a newspaper has no special immunity from the application of general laws." Four justices agreed with the AP and the ANPA that freedom of the press was being endangered if the Wagner Act henceforth was to apply to news organizations. These were the four justices who were to become the objects of President Roosevelt's ill-fated "court-packing" plan, advanced with the intention of bringing the court back into step with the country's dominant economic and social philosophies. They were Justices McReynolds, Butler, Van Devanter, and Sutherland.

CONSOLIDATING THE GUILD, 1937–50

Upholding of the Wagner Act was a great Guild victory. It assured the American Newspaper Guild a permanent place in newspaper life. Gradually contracts were won in larger cities, including one with the *New York Times,* whose staff had long been skeptical of the Guild. But the road was still a rocky one. The recession years of 1937–39 brought widespread newspaper closings and staff prunings which left thousands of newspapermen unemployed, and made contract negotiation difficult.

The Guild, after the tragic death of Heywood Broun at age 51 from pneumonia, became engaged in a bitter fight between conservative or "pro-Guild" members and left-wing elements who were strongest in the New York City locals. Forcing an election of officers by nationwide referendum, however, brought victory to the "pro-Guild" group whose anti-Communist slate was

[9] *Associated Press v. NLRB,* 301 U.S. 103 (1937).

managed by Wilbur Bade, early editor of the *Guild Reporter*. The Guild was the first CIO union to throw out its Communist national officers. New York's locals did the same in 1947. Under the leadership of presidents Milton M. Murray and Harry Martin, and executive vice-presidents Sam Eubanks and Ralph B. Novak, the Guild remained vigorously liberal, but continued its anti-Communist policy in following years to include material and moral aid to journalists' groups in other countries.[10]

World War II brought a general "freezing" of labor relations activities. As the war ended, the Guild's goal was a $65 a week top minimum for all contracts. Then in 1946 the goal was set at a seemingly impossible $100 level. Postwar inflation made the $100 a week salary not only feasible, but reasonable, both in the eyes of Guild members and newspaper managements before 1950. Strikes broke out in 1946, however, the principal ones being against Hearst's *Los Angeles Herald & Express* and, ironically, J. David Stern's *Philadelphia Record*. Stern accused the Guild of making unfair salary demands upon him, and sold his paper to the *Bulletin* after a three-month strike. A Congressional committee investigation could not resolve later whether Stern sold because of financial distress or because he wanted to retire with a financial nest egg.

THE GUILD MATURES, 1950–70

A new strike technique was demonstrated in 1950 when 500 striking Guild employees of the *New York World-Telegram and Sun*, principal Scripps-Howard paper, were supported by 1,000 AFL mechanical unions members who refused to cross the Guild's picket lines. Such interunion cooperation ensured that a struck paper could not publish and the Guild used the threat in other cities. The Guild also became involved in major strikes begun by other unions such as the 114-day New York strike in 1962–63. AP was the first wire service to be struck—for eight days—in 1969. A replay of the Chicago showdown three decades later between Hearst and the Guild began out west in a December, 1967, strike against the *Los Angeles Herald-Examiner*, up to that time the nation's largest-circulation evening paper. Some 1,100 Guild members were affected but the paper continued to publish with employees recruited elsewhere. The Guild poured millions into supporting its demands in a new contract as the strike went into its fourth year in 1971 with the paper limping.

Too much emphasis can be placed upon strikes, however; in the main, Guild locals and newspaper managements were able to negotiate contracts at the conference table in friendly, if determined, fashion. Most Guild locals had not been on strike during the first four decades of Guild history.

[10] This subject is explored in detail in Sam Kuczun, "History of the American Newspaper Guild," Ph.D. thesis, University of Minnesota, 1970. Some other data in this account is taken from Kuczun's research in Guild archives and other documentary sources.

Although its concern for higher standards of journalism in the 1930s was shelved by necessity of economic self-preservation, the Guild revived such interest as the 1960s ended. It established the Mellett Fund for a Free and Responsible Press to finance press councils to open communications avenues between newspapers and their citizens in six communities. The Guild encouraged establishment of publications to criticise media performance and Guildsmen cautiously but increasingly sought more voice in advising newspaper management on editorial policy. Ethics, newsmen's privilege, restrictions on the press, and physical harassment of newsmen were some of the issues occupying Guild attention in the early 1970s.

Race discrimination had been noted and fought by the Guild since its inception. A resolution in 1946 laid down a seven-point program for the Guild to fight racial and religious bigotry. The biggest problem was equal opportunity for blacks throughout the newspaper industry. In 1971, ANG's Conference on Recruitment and Training of Minority-Group Employees advanced 10 proposals to break down employment barriers within the industry and pledged its resources to secure them.

There were more than 33,000 Guild members by 1971. They worked on newspapers, for the press associations and feature services, magazines, other labor unions, and specialized publications and services. In the main, the Guild was concentrated in metropolitan areas, although a good number of middle-sized dailies and a sprinkling of smaller ones were represented. More than 2,000 Guildsmen were members of a Wire Service Unit begun in 1957. A Canadian unit founded in 1951 had 3,300 members.

Salary scales continued to move upward. By 1954, the $100 top minimum goal had been reached in 90 per cent of the contracts. New goals were announced and reached until in 1970, the Guild set as new goals a $400 a week top minimum and $248 a week for beginners. The average top minimum in 130 contracts in effect April, 1971, was $207 a week. The best 1971 contract in force guaranteed $300 a week for reporters and advertising salesmen after five years of experience at the *Washington Post*. Highest top minimum in a newspaper contract was $400 at the *Washington Post,* taking effect in 1973. Nearly all contracts called for four-week vacations. Most contracts included paid sick leave, liberal severance pay allowances, paid holidays, a pension plan, and a work week of less than 40 hours.

Joseph F. Collis served as Guild president during 1953–59, Arthur Rosenstock during 1959–67, and James B. Woods was elected in 1968. William J. Farson became executive vice-president in 1955 and retired in 1969. In a 1969 reorganization, the top paid officer's title was changed to that of president. Secretary-treasurer Charles A. Perlik, Jr., was elected to succeed Farson and become president. Woods was named chairman, the top unpaid officer. Remembering the role Broun had played in making such gains possible, the Guild in 1941 established an annual award for newspaper work "in the spirit of Heywood Broun."

THE ANPA AND THE NEW DEAL

While the NRA and the Wagner Act thus had been stimulating the growth of the American Newspaper Guild as an organization of major social and economic importance, other New Deal reform proposals had become law. Some of the reform legislation affected the newspaper business directly; more of the laws affected newspapers only indirectly; and some affected newspapers not at all. But the total impact of the New Deal reform legislation of the 1930s was great upon those who preferred traditionalism to change. Conservative-minded spokesmen for the American Newspaper Publishers Association found occasion to criticise or oppose, for varying reasons, the Federal Securities Act of 1933, establishing the Securities Exchange Commission; the Social Security Act of 1935; the Wagner Labor Relations Act of 1935; the Fair Labor Standards Act of 1938, prescribing minimum wages and maximum hours; revisions of the Agricultural Adjustment Act; the Wheeler-Lea bill giving the Federal Trade Commission power to regulate unfair or misleading advertising; the Copeland pure food, drugs, and cosmetics bill; and child labor legislation.

In their many challenges to federal legislation, the ANPA spokesmen did not concentrate their opposition upon those legislative proposals which, if adopted, would seemingly jeopardize press freedom. Rather, they attempted to oppose a great variety of New Deal measures of varying potential effects upon newspapers' well-being, without balancing the extent of public interest in the measures against their own narrower interests. So the impression was left that newspaper publishers were crying "freedom of the press" because they did not want to make reasonable adjustments to new socioeconomic conditions.

THE "PRESS FREEDOM" DEBATE

Arthur Hays Sulzberger, publisher of the *New York Times*, suggested at the 1936 ANPA annual convention that perhaps the association was going too far in its campaign. He said that while safeguarding of press freedom was necessary he was not convinced that the Roosevelt administration "has or had designs upon the freedom of the press." And he reminded his listeners that the freedom of the press guarantee in the Constitution "is the statement of an essential liberty of a free people and not a grant of immunity extended to a particular trade or profession . . . the responsibilities that the franchise entails are greater than the privileges it bestows." [11]

More bluntly critical was Virginius Dabney, noted editor of the *Richmond Times-Dispatch*, who wrote in the aftermath of Roosevelt's smashing 1936 reelection victory:

[11] *Editor & Publisher*, LXIX (April 25, 1936), 4.

> The publishers association has indulged in an unabashed campaign of self-laudation; it has overemphasized the "freedom of the press" to a ludicrous extent, thereby incurring the suspicion that it is using this shibboleth as a red herring; and its members have banded together to defeat legislation, such as the Child Labor Amendment, and have thereby created the impression in many minds, whether justly or not, that they put their own private profit above the general good.[12]

Thus in a period of economic stress and social insecurity, when the press, business, and all other institutional activities were under close scrutiny, the ANPA legislative and anti-Guild activities constituted the association's public front. Little was known about the substantial work done by the ANPA as a trade association, representing 850 dailies with 90 per cent of total daily newspaper circulation. In contrast to its position on the Guild, the ANPA had sponsored an imaginative policy of voluntary arbitration in cooperation with the printing trades unions in 1900. Its Bureau of Advertising was publishing the *Continuing Study of Newspaper Reading,* in cooperation with the Advertising Research Foundation, to determine readership of advertisements and news. It had encouraged research in printing processes. And it had done a good job of defending newspapers' interests in obtaining cheap and plentiful supplies of newsprint, and in using the second-class mail privileges, although these activities brought complaints about self-interest.[13] Its New York central office operations, directed from 1905 to 1939 by Lincoln B. Palmer and subsequently by Cranston Williams, constituted capable trade association work. But all this was submerged in a "press freedom" crusade which seemed little concerned with improvement of press standards of performance.

THE "PRESS FREEDOM" CRUSADE OF THE 1930s

What were the specific complaints of the ANPA's legal counsel, Elisha Hanson, and of its committees on federal legislation? In 1933 they protested the regulation of financial advertising copy in newspapers as proposed by sponsors of the Federal Securities Act in order to protect investors from a repetition of the financial fiasco of the 1920s. And they asserted that various food and drug regulation bills under consideration in Congress "involved censorship." This contention that advertising has constitutional protection was to be persistently advanced by the ANPA, although the Supreme Court twice flatly denied the claim.[14] It was part of the general argument that business

[12] *Public Opinion Quarterly,* I (April 1937), 124.

[13] See pages 332–34, 337, 342–44, and 592–95 for earlier ANPA history.

[14] J. Edward Gerald, *The Press and the Constitution* (Minneapolis: University of Minnesota Press, 1948), p. 75.

activities of newspapers either were exempted under the First Amendment from government regulation, or should be protected against any adverse effects of Federal general business laws—an argument never recognized by the Supreme Court but sometimes accepted by Congress.

In 1934 the ANPA convention was warned about a 30-hour work week bill which did not exempt newspapers and about new proposals for child labor legislation which did not exempt newspaperboys. In 1935 the ANPA spokesmen reported on their losing battle against the Wagner Act, which was termed "one of the most obnoxious of bills." They also said they had again sought revisions in the advertising safeguards of the Securities Exchange Act, because of a drying up of financial advertising. A brief had been filed against the Copeland pure food, drugs, and cosmetics bill because amendments advocated by the ANPA and designed to modify the proposed advertising safeguards of the bill had not been included. And a suggestion was made that newspapers receive special consideration in the assessment of payroll taxes under the Social Security Act. In 1937 and 1938 the ANPA opposed, without success, the granting of increased authority to the Federal Trade Commission to regulate unfair or misleading advertising of products in interstate commerce. Newspapers, however, were released from responsibility for any false advertising the FTC might find.

In the debate over the Fair Labor Standards Act, popularly known as the Wage and Hour Law, the ANPA again contended that the First Amendment applies to the business operations of newspapers. The act looked forward to the establishment of the 40-hour week and 40 cents an hour minimum pay. Congress exempted weekly newspapers with circulations of less than 3,000 copies from the provisions of the act, but refused the exemption pleas of larger papers. Having lost the battle in Congress, the ANPA supported publishers who went to court rather than let federal investigators inspect their records. But the Supreme Court in 1946 ruled that newspapers were bound to observe the requirements of the law, like other businesses.[15] Hanson, by the mid-1940s, found this crusade unpopular; he complained that editors were giving him "plain unshirted hell for even challenging the power of Congress to destroy the press."

The end of the New Deal reform period by 1938, the coming of World War II, and a shift in ANPA leadership brought a softening of the association's voice in matters of public issue. Newspaper publishers were aroused by the press freedom implications of the suit brought by Marshall Field's *Chicago Sun* in 1943 to have the Associated Press' restrictive membership provisions declared illegal restraints of trade. But when the Supreme Court in 1945 decided against the AP, and forced it to open its membership to legitimate applicants,[16] no one found that any damage had been done. The ANPA scored a legislative victory when, after the Supreme Court had ruled in 1944 that adult newspaper

[15] *Mabee v. White Plains Publishing Co., Inc.*, 327 U.S. 178 (1946).
[16] *Associated Press v. United States*, 326 U.S. 1 (1945).

vendors came under Social Security Act provisions, it joined in persuading Congress to pass a 1948 bill removing the vendors from the protection of the law, despite two vetoes of such legislation by President Truman.

THE ANPA AND THE ITU

Passage in 1947 of the Taft-Hartley Act, replacing the Wagner Act, also pleased the ANPA leadership. But the Taft-Hartley law's outlawing of the closed shop brought newspaper publishers into a major conflict with the powerful International Typographical Union. The typographers, as a powerful traditional craft union with an organizational history running back for more than a century, were logical candidates among the closed shop unions to challenge the provisions of the Taft-Hartley law. The ANPA, with 60 years of experience in the daily newspaper labor relations field, was quick to take up the challenge.

After two decades during which all the printing trade unions and the ANPA observed the provisions of national voluntary arbitration agreements as a means of preventing labor disputes, the typographers' arbitration agreement foundered in 1922. The union refused ANPA demands that provisions of union law, including those which the publishers labeled as "featherbedding" practices, be subject to arbitration. The same year the ANPA established an Open Shop Department for the benefit of nonunion publishers; during the 1930s this department furnished crews of nonunion printers to strikebound publishers until Congress made such interstate activities illegal. While relations between the ANPA and the unions of pressmen, photoengravers, and stereotypers remained on a cordial note—the pressmen retaining their national arbitration agreement throughout the entire period—those with the typographers steadily deteriorated.

Late in 1947 the ANPA filed a complaint with the National Labor Relations Board, charging the International Typographical Union with violations of the Taft-Hartley Act. Almost immediately the ITU answered by selecting the Chicago newspaper publishers as the object of a showdown strike. The strike lasted 22 months, but the Chicago newspapers got along without typographers by substituting typewritten copy and photoengraved pages for regular makeup processes. In the end, the Chicago publishers in effect recognized the closed shop. When the NLRB finally ruled on the ANPA-ITU case in 1949, it found the ITU guilty of violating the closed shop ban, and agreed with the ANPA that union law provisions should be subject to arbitration, but upheld the union's "featherbedding" practices, including the controversial "bogus matter" rule which permits union members to reset advertising furnished the paper in ready-to-print form. The Supreme Court in 1953 upheld the union on the "bogus" setting dispute, and in 1961 approved a revised ITU version of a closed shop contract.

THE ANPA RESEARCH INSTITUTE

The publishers long had supported a mechanical department devoted to the study of improvements in the printing processes. After World War II they felt the growing pressures of a "cold type revolution" brought about by the introduction of the photographic process into printing. In 1947 a research director was named and funds were voted to establish a research center in Easton, Pennsylvania, which formally opened in 1951. It was incorporated as the ANPA Research Institute in 1954, with its own board of publisher-directors. A 1958 evaluation by a six-man committee headed by Otto A. Silha of the *Minneapolis Star* and *Tribune* gave the Institute new direction, toward experimental work in utilizing the fruits of technological innovations in printing newspapers. An annual mechanical conference for members emphasized photocomposition, offset printing, run-of-paper color printing, computerized typesetting and editing, and other advances. All concerned conceded that a breakthrough was needed in production processes which would lower costs and improve the newspaper product.

ANPA ACTIVISTS OF THE 1960s

If a change in outlook from the ultraconservative role of the 1930s was not already apparent at ANPA conventions, it was signaled in 1960 with the naming of Stanford Smith as general manager. ANPA had already joined the American Society of Newspaper Editors and other groups in backing the Freedom of Information campaign of the late 1950s, calling for access to governmental news and "the people's right to know." In the 1960s ANPA developed other trade association programs with a progressive flair.

The establishment of a Newspaper Information Service in 1960 was one such program. Through it ANPA headquarters could work with educators, students, other media, and the public. Objectives included promotion of journalism as a career; giving of awards to college and high school newspaper staffs; publication of newsletters, brochures, and booklets; and interpretation of the newspaper industry. Already ANPA had worked with other media organizations to support accreditation of journalism schools and departments, and had sponsored a "Newspapers in the Classrooms" project with the International Circulation Managers' Association to encourage young readers. In 1967 the ANPA Foundation made a $150,000 grant available through J. Howard Wood of the *Chicago Tribune* for a research study of the issue of free press and fair trial. Next year the *Tribune* pledged half of a $200,000 fund to enable black students to attend journalism schools.

ANPA's biggest legislative victory was the passage of the Newspaper Preservation Act, after three years of debate in the Congress. The act exempted from anti-trust suits the joint printing operations of 44 newspapers in 22 cities and overturned a Supreme Court decision dissolving a pooled business operation in Tucson. Opponents said the new law, signed by President Nixon in 1970, would perpetuate the status quo and militate against competitors entering major markets with new dailies. That accomplished, ANPA turned its attention to new Federal Communications Commission proposals which would bar newspaper publishers from continuing their 2-billion-dollar investment in the broadcasting business if carried out fully. Many a media enterprise depended on a balance between investment in print and broadcast operations and the issue clearly was a key one for the 1970s.

Annotated Bibliography

The most important sources are the files of *Editor & Publisher* and the *Guild Reporter,* and the proceedings of the annual meetings of the American Society of Newspaper Editors, the American Newspaper Guild, and the American Newspaper Publishers Association. Of books previously cited, Edwin Emery's *History of the American Newspaper Publishers Association* and A. M. Lee's *The Daily Newspaper in America* tell the story of newspaper relationships with the Guild and mechanical unions.

Books

Bird, George L., and Frederic E. Merwin, *The Press and Society.* Englewood Cliffs, N.J.: Prentice-Hall, 1952. Chapter 26 concerns the Guild.

Burns, James MacGregor, *Roosevelt: The Soldier of Freedom.* New York: Harcourt, Brace & Jovanovich, 1970. Pulitzer Prize-winning study of FDR, 1940–45, by the author of *Roosevelt: The Lion and the Fox* (1956), covering pre-Presidential years.

Chafee, Zechariah, Jr., *Government and Mass Communications.* Chicago: University of Chicago Press, 1947. A two-volume specific study of areas involving government and press, for the Commission on Freedom of the Press.

Hocking, William E., *Freedom of the Press: A Framework of Principle.* Chicago: University of Chicago Press, 1947. Discusses philosophical problems; written for the Commission on Freedom of the Press.

Kramer, Dale, *Heywood Broun.* New York: A. A. Wyn, Inc., 1949. Biography of the Guild's founder, a famous columnist.

Leab, Daniel J., *A Union of Individuals: The Formation of the American Newspaper Guild 1933–1936.* New York: Columbia University Press, 1970. Scholarly detail for ANG birth.

Leuchtenberg, William E., *Franklin D. Roosevelt and the New Deal.* New York: Harper & Row, 1963. Study of domestic policy.

National Labor Relations Board, *Collective Bargaining in the Newspaper Industry.* Washington: Government Printing Office, 1938. Studies both the Guild and printing union movements.

Schlesinger, Arthur, Jr., *The Coming of the New Deal.* Boston: Houghton Mifflin, 1958. Vol. 2 of his *The Age of Roosevelt,* covering 1933–34. Vol. 1, *The Crisis of the Old Order* (1957), covers 1919–33.

———, *The Politics of Upheaval.* Boston: Houghton Mifflin, 1960. Continues through the 1936 election. No further volumes had appeared by 1971.

Stern, J. David, *Memoirs of a Maverick Publisher.* New York: Simon & Schuster, 1962. Liberal publisher of the *New York Post* and *Philadelphia Record,* who tangled with the Guild.

Periodicals and Monographs

Broun, Heywood, "An Army with Banners," *Nation,* CXL (February 13, 1935), 154. The Guild president's own account.

Keating, Isabelle, "Reporters Become of Age," *Harper's,* CLXX (April 1935), 601. One of the best early articles about the Guild.

Kuczun, Sam, "History of the American Newspaper Guild," Ph.D. thesis, University of Minnesota, 1970. Comprehensive overview based upon access to Guild archives and other documentation.

Pringle, Henry F., "The Newspaper Guild," *Scribner's,* CV (January 1939), 21. A review at a turning-point time in Guild affairs.

Swindler, William F., "The AP Antitrust Case in Historical Perspective," *Journalism Quarterly,* XXIII (March 1946), 40. Scholarly analysis.

Chicago Tribune

THE WORLD'S GREATEST NEWSPAPER

SPORTS FINAL

Friday, July 16, 1971

Nixon to Visit China

President Nixon

Chou En-lai

He Will . . . . . . Visit Him

Kissinger, Chou Hold Secret Talks

BY ALDO BECKMAN

SAN CLEMENTE, Cal., July 15—President Nixon will visit mainland China sometime before next May, he told the nation tonight in a live television and radio broadcast.

The groundwork for the historic meeting was laid by Henry Kissinger, Nixon's assistant for national security, when he met secretly with Chinese Premier Chou En-lai from July 9 to July 11, Nixon said. At that time, it was announced that Kissinger was in Asia to visit Saigon, Pakistan, and India.

Chou extended the invitation for the Nixon visit during his talks with Kissinger, Nixon said. A statement that Nixon read and which was released simultaneously in Peking, said:

"President Nixon has accepted this invitation with pleasure.

"The meeting between the leaders of China and the United States is to seek the normalization of relations between the two countries and also to exchange views on questions of concern to the two sides."

Acts to Mute Criticism

... become a journey for peace, not just for our generation but for future generations on this earth we share together."

As Nixon began his three-minute statement he noted that he had pointed out on a number of occasions that "no stable and enduring peace is possible without the participation of the People's Republic of China and its 750 million people."

Kissinger Secret Well Kept

Then he revealed Kissinger's visit, which was one of the best kept secrets in the history of international diplomacy.

Midway during Kissinger's journey it was announced that he had departed from his prepared ...

Text of Speech on Page 2

Calls Security Council

Ford Sees Indochina Peace Talks Resulting from Visit

Sen. Hubert Humphrey

What China Visit Means

News Analysis

Already a Swinger

Kissinger Sure to Be a Legend

How Kissinger's Peking Parley Was Kept Secret

Formosa Protests, Others Approve Visit

Why? He Likes the Food

Features

Weather

President Nixon announced his 1972 trip to Peking on prime time television.

30

The Challenge of Criticism

Partisanship, in editorial comment which knowingly departs from the truth, does violence to the best spirit of American journalism; in the news columns it is subversive of a fundamental principle of the profession.
—ASNE Canons of Journalism

Criticism of the performance of America's mass media became particularly pointed during the liberal resurgence of the 1930s. That there was criticism of newspapers, or even extensive criticism, was nothing new; press critics had been having their say since the dawn of newspaper publishing, and public concern was widespread during such periods of major change in the American press as those which ushered in the penny press of the 1830s and the modern newspaper of the 1890s. But while much of the earlier criticism had dealt with the cultural and social values of the press, the emphasis in the 1930s was upon its political power. The press as an institution thus came under challenge more directly than at any time since the Federalist attacks upon press freedom in the 1790s.

The favorite targets for the critics were those publishers dubbed "the press lords"—notably William Randolph Hearst, Robert R. McCormick, and Roy W. Howard. Their prominence kept them at the center of an upsurge of criticism which affected newspapers generally, in a time when America was engaging in a searching reexamination of all its social, political, and economic institutions. Analysis of their journalistic roles thus becomes a factor of major importance in any study of public reaction to press performance in recent decades.

From the 1940s onward, two factors operated to widen the base of the challenge of criticism to the mass media. One, of course, was the rise of television and the attending revolution in mass communication patterns. The other was an increasing recognition of Robert E. Park's observation—"The press, as it exists, is not, as our moralists sometimes seem to assume, the wilful product of any little group of living men. On the contrary, it is the outcome of a historic process. . . ."[1] This does not mean that the Hearsts and McCormicks, the Pulitzers and Ochses, the Greeleys and Bennetts, did not exert powerful and lasting influences upon the newspaper press, or the Sarnoffs and the Murrows upon the electronic media. It does mean—as the theme of this book has stated—that social and economic forces shaping our system of values and our culture have been at least as important in shaping the mass media and in affecting their performance. In many respects, this is more true of the broadcast media than of the print media because of broadcasting's organizational structure and semipublic character.

This chapter, after examining political-based criticism of the newspapers and the roles of their "press lords" who adversely affected their images, will shift—as did public attention—to criticisms of television program content and of television's involvement in controversial issues. These criticisms came to a swelling climax in the 1960s and brought a crisis of credibility which will be examined in the succeeding chapter. Finally, the story of the growth of a professional spirit in journalism, involving extensive self-analysis and efforts to improve media performance, follows as the response to the challenge of criticism.

Much of the criticism which developed during the 1930s and later was based on issues already discussed in earlier chapters of this book. The growth of one publisher cities and of media group ownership aroused opposition among many of the critics. Decreasing opportunity for variety of expression of opinion by differing sociopolitical groups occupied the attention of others. Complaints were made that newspaper content was standardized, that there was overemphasis of entertainment and sensational material, and that there was insufficient interpretation of important news—complaints later extended to broadcasting. Certainly there was merit in general discussions of these problems. Such discussions served to warn publishers who had been slow to recognize their responsibilities to their readers. No thoughtful person would deny the validity of much of the criticism; but on the other hand, journalists would have been less than human had they not resented some of the charges leveled at them in sweeping terms and without regard for changing conditions of society which forced acceptance of conditions not to everybody's liking.

[1] Made in 1925 in his "The Natural History of the Newspaper," a chapter in Robert E. Park, Ernest W. Burgess, and Roderick D. McKenzie, *The City* (Chicago: University of Chicago Press), pp. 80–98.

THE PRESS IN PRESIDENTIAL ELECTIONS

Criticism of newspapers since the 1930s centered about, more than anything else, their editorial positions in political campaigns. Historically, a small but definite majority of daily newspapers giving editorial-page support to a presidential candidate was to be found on the side of the Republican party. As Franklin Roosevelt entered the first of his four presidential campaigns in 1932, he had the support of 38 per cent of the nation's dailies, compared to 55 per cent for President Hoover. In 1936, Roosevelt was backed by 34 per cent of the dailies, Republican Alfred M. Landon by 60 per cent. These figures are approximations gathered by *Editor & Publisher* when it launched, beginning in 1940, a comprehensive pre-election poll of dailies concerning editorial page support. Approximately three-fourths of all dailies, with 90 per cent of total daily newspaper circulation, responded to the polls until the 1960s, when the character of the contests caused the responses to drop to 60 per cent of the dailies with 80 per cent of total circulation. Table 1 shows the percentages of the responding newspapers giving editorial page support to the Republican or Democratic candidate each four years, and the percentages of circulation they represented.

The figures show that the number of dailies supporting Roosevelt declined for his 1940 and 1944 races with Wendell Willkie and Thomas E. Dewey, as did the circulation they represented. Harry S Truman reached the low point of support in his successful 1948 contest with Dewey. Dwight D. Eisenhower enjoyed the most support in 1952, for his first race against Adlai E. Stevenson.

TABLE 1 · Editorial Page Support of Presidential Candidates

Year	*Republican* Per Cent of Dailies		*Democratic* Per Cent of Dailies		*Uncommitted* Per Cent of Dailies	
		Per Cent of Circulation		*Per Cent of Circulation*		*Per Cent of Circulation*
1940	63.9	69.2	22.7	25.2	13.4	5.6
1944	60.1	68.5	22.0	17.7	17.9	13.8
1948	65.1	78.5	15.3	10.0	15.6	10.0
1952	67.3	80.2	14.5	10.8	18.2	9.0
1956	62.3	72.3	15.1	12.8	22.6	14.9
1960	57.7	70.9	16.4	15.8	25.9	13.3
1964	35.1	21.5	42.3	61.5	22.6	17.0
1968	60.8	69.9	14.0	19.3	24.0	10.5

Source: Editor & Publisher polls. In 1948, Progressive party candidate Henry A. Wallace had the support of 4 per cent of the dailies with 1.5 per cent of circulation. See *Editor & Publisher,* XCIII (November 5, 1960), 9. In 1968, American Independent party candidate George C. Wallace had the support of 12 dailies (1.2 per cent) with 159,000 circulation (0.3 per cent).

John F. Kennedy's position was improved as he defeated Richard M. Nixon in 1960. Kennedy was endorsed by 22 of 125 dailies above 100,000 circulation, while 12 endorsed no candidate. This represented more large pro-Democratic papers, with a better geographic spread, than at any time since 1944.[2]

Then came political upheaval stemming from the assassination of President Kennedy. His successor, Lyndon Johnson of Texas, became the first southerner to win the Democratic nomination in modern times. His opponent, Senator Barry M. Goldwater, represented the frustrated right wing of the Republican party. Given such a choice, newspaper publishers and editors chose to endorse President Johnson for reelection. The scales were essentially turned. Among dailies over 100,000 in circulation, Nixon had enjoyed the support of 87 to 22 for Kennedy in 1960. Johnson won 82 to his side four years later, and Goldwater only 12.[3]

Four years later came more upheaval—the assassination of Senator Robert Kennedy, the forced withdrawal of President Johnson from the Democratic race by the Eugene McCarthy crusade—and the nominations in vacuums of Hubert Humphrey and Richard M. Nixon. The scales tilted back, and the big dailies divided 78 for Nixon and 28 for Humphrey. Humphrey's percentage of the reporting circulation was better than any since Roosevelt's in 1940 on the Democratic side, save for the 1964 aberration.[4]

OTHER OPINION-MAKING FORCES

Stevenson called it "a one-party press in a two-party country." But partisan critics did not acknowledge the impact which day-by-day coverage of the news has on voter decisions, and available studies of campaign news coverage indicate at least larger dailies were essentially fair in their news columns. Research shows, too, that voters are often strongly affected by social pressures, group

[2] Among major dailies supporting Kennedy in 1960 outside the South were the *New York Times, St. Louis Post-Dispatch, Milwaukee Journal, Louisville Courier-Journal, New York Post, Newsday, Long Island Press, Pittsburgh Post-Gazette, Toledo Blade, Hartford Times, Denver Post,* and *Sacramento Bee*. The *Washington Post* did not endorse, but favored Kennedy.

[3] The 12 major dailies supporting Goldwater in 1964 were the *Chicago Tribune* and *American, Los Angeles Times, Oakland Tribune, Cincinnati Enquirer, Columbus Dispatch, Milwaukee Sentinel, Richmond Times-Dispatch* and *News Leader, Nashville Banner, Tulsa World,* and *Birmingham News.*

[4] Nine major dailies which had supported Nixon in 1960 swung to Humphrey: Hearst's *San Francisco Examiner* and *Boston Record-American,* the Cowles' *Minneapolis Star* and *Tribune* and *Des Moines Register* and *Tribune,* the Ridders' *St. Paul Dispatch* and *Pioneer Press,* and Newhouse's *Newark Star-Ledger.* Four which had backed Kennedy in 1960 now endorsed Nixon: *Newsday,* the *Toledo Blade,* Gannett's *Hartford Times,* and the Ridders' *Long Beach Press-Telegram.*

associations, and "opinion leaders." Radio and television can become highly important factors.[5]

A study of how news came to Paducah, Kentucky, made by *Fortune* magazine (August 1947), also illustrates the point that it is impossible for a single newspaper to exercise a monopoly in the realm of opinion-making. Paducah's one daily newspaper had a circulation of 12,000 copies within the city. There was also a small weekly, and the city had two radio stations, one owned by the daily paper. Outside publications came into Paducah in the following numbers: *Louisville Courier-Journal,* 1,400 copies daily and 2,400 on Sunday; New York, Chicago, St. Louis, and Memphis newspapers, 428 daily and 2,770 Sunday; weekly news magazines, 429 copies; picture weeklies, 1,968 copies; other general weeklies, 1,769 copies; monthly magazines, 13,037 copies. The public library had 110 magazines on file and circulated about 10,000 books a month. Motion pictures, public meetings, and club and luncheon gatherings also brought information to Paducah's 33,000 citizens.

CRITICISM OF THE "PRESS LORDS"

Political tension, and accompanying criticism of the newspaper's role in elections, made for extensive public acceptance of a literature of criticism of the press. Upton Sinclair's bitter book, *The Brass Check* (1919), unrealistically painted a picture of a false, cowardly press dominated by its business offices and its advertisers. While there were newspaper situations which fitted these patterns, in isolated instances of time and place, the Sinclair thesis did not ring true generally. Suspicious individuals, however, continued to quote the book as evidence of advertiser domination of the press long after that bugaboo had been exploded as a serious charge.

Caustic surveys of the "press lords" began in earnest with Oswald Garrison Villard's *Some Newspapers and Newspaper-Men* (1923). They flourished in the 1930s, which saw the publication of such books as George Seldes' *Lords of the Press* (1938), Harold L. Ickes' *America's House of Lords* (1939), and individual studies such as Ferdinand Lundberg's *Imperial Hearst* (1936). These

[5] See Bernard Berelson, Paul F. Lazarsfeld, and William N. McPhee, *Voting* (Chicago: University of Chicago Press, 1954). For studies of campaign news coverage in large cities, see the bibliography for this chapter. In his three studies of the news coverage of the presidential campaigns of the 1960s in 15 "prestige papers," as selected by the nation's editors and educators (see Chapter 28 for the polls), Guido H. Stempel found that only one deviated by more than 5 per cent from 50–50 division of space in both the 1960 and 1964 campaigns. That was the *Chicago Tribune,* whose news of the campaigns was 59.2 per cent Republican in 1960 and 65.6 in 1964. In 1968 the *Tribune* managed to give third party candidate George Wallace the lowest percentage of space (17 per cent) of any of the 15 papers. Wallace's high was 30 per cent in the *Louisville Courier-Journal,* which editorially supported Humphrey; Humphrey's high was 48 per cent in the *Los Angeles Times,* which supported Nixon; Nixon's high was 45.9 per cent in the *Chicago Tribune,* which supported him.

books were valuable as exposés, but their influence was undue in that they enjoyed wider public circulation than such counterbalancing and more constructive discussions as Casper S. Yost's *Principles of Journalism* (1924), Villard's brief *The Press Today* (1930), Herbert Brucker's *The Changing American Newspaper* (1937), Silas Bent's *Newspaper Crusaders* (1939), and such products of the growing journalism schools as Leon N. Flint's *The Conscience of the Newspaper* (1925), Willard G. Bleyer's *Main Currents in the History of American Journalism* (1927), and *Interpretations of Journalism* (1937), edited by Frank L. Mott and Ralph D. Casey.

In any event, the dynamic and intriguing personalities of some of the "press lords" provided more interesting fare for the American reading public than any other material about newspapermen and newspaper problems. To understand, therefore, the bitterness and extent of criticisms of the press since the 1930s, it is necessary to examine the roles played by the most often discussed newspaper publishers of the times.

WILLIAM RANDOLPH HEARST'S CONTRIBUTION

William Randolph Hearst, as has been suggested in previous chapters,[6] is one of the most difficult men of journalism to study and to estimate, considering the complex nature of his personality, the variegated social and political impact of his many ventures, and the length and extent of his career. Those who wrote about Hearst were never permitted access to the publisher's private papers and to the records of the Hearst empire. So the literature about Hearst ranged from reasonably fair evaluations to vehement attacks combining facts and rumors.[7] As a result, the official Hearst biography released by International News Service when the publisher's 64-year newspaper career closed in 1951 noted in its second paragraph: "And as he fashioned his vast enterprises, there grew progressively in the public mind a picture of the builder himself. It was a strange portrait, obscured by myth and legend, confused by controversy and distortion."

When Hearst had lived out his 88 years, the question became: Did he deserve the criticism which had been heaped upon him, more vehemently than upon any other publisher? There was some tendency to accord him a place in the ranks of journalistic leaders, despite the extent of criticism of him and his newspapers. The points most often made in support of the thesis that Hearst made notable contributions to American journalism are these:

[6] Chapters 19 and 20 deal with Hearst's earlier career. See also pages 457–61 in Chapter 22 and pages 626–29 in Chapter 27 for the extent of his newspaper operations.

[7] The best balanced and most analytic book is John Tebbel's *The Life and Good Times of William Randolph Hearst* (New York: Dutton, 1952). See the bibliography in this chapter and in Chapter 19 for other citations.

1. Hearst built the world's biggest publishing empire in terms of newspapers and their combined circulations. At the peak, in 1935, Hearst printed 26 dailies and 17 Sunday editions in 19 cities. The papers had 13.6 per cent of the total daily circulation in the country and 24.2 per cent of Sunday circulation. In addition, he controlled the King Features Syndicate, largest of its kind; the money-coining *American Weekly;* International News Service, Universal Service, and International News Photos; 13 magazines, 8 radio stations, and 2 motion picture companies. This, it is argued, spells a success which must be recognized.

2. Hearst's methods and innovations in newswriting and news-handling—particularly in makeup and headline and picture display—and his utilization of new mechanical processes were highly important. Hearst journalism changed the character of American journalism, it is argued, and therefore it must be recognized.

3. Hearst newspapers were edited to appeal to the mass of readers, and encouraged millions to increase their reading habits. Because of this, and because of Hearst's editorial policies and his own political activities, Hearst newspapers exercised a powerful influence in American life which must be recognized.

4. Hearst was in many ways a constructive force: stalwart in his Americanism; a believer in popular education and in the extension of the power of the people; and during different phases of his long career an advocate of many progressive solutions to national problems. These included early advocacy of popular election of senators, of the initiative and referendum, of a graduated income tax, of widespread public ownership of utilities, of breaking up of monopolies and trusts, and of the rights of labor unions.

These points, the argument runs, are in the record for all to see. Hearst's critics, and the public record, provided counterarguments. They should be prefaced, however, with this general observation:

The building of a great publishing empire does not in itself assure Hearst or anyone else a high standing in the journalistic profession. The newspapers which the craft recognizes as great are those which demonstrate their integrity and zealousness in the telling of the news, and which at the same time possess the social conscience which is acquired by their recognition of the needs of society, and by a proper and reasonable adjustment to society's desires. Honest and comprehensive coverage of the news is of course the first essential. The second is a demonstration of responsibility in community leadership. The great newspapers—whether conservative or liberal, Republican or Democrat, in their political beliefs—are those which are aroused whenever basic principles of human liberty and progress are at stake in a given situation, and which are constantly on guard against intolerance and unfairness. Operating within a consistent social framework, they do their best to be the kind of progressive community leaders America expects.

NEGATIVES IN HEARST'S CAREER

Keeping these two tests of the greatness of a newspaper in mind, then, the rebuttals to the points listed in Hearst's favor may be considered:

1. The Hearst empire, for all its one-time size, was not the roaring success which the accumulated figures would indicate. Hearst began to borrow from banks as early as 1924. In the early 1930s he had his newspapers publicize and sell a 50-million-dollar stock issue to keep themselves afloat. The intricate nature of the Hearst corporate structures makes a clear determination of the publisher's financial standing impossible. Hearst poured money into his publishing ventures from the profits of mining, ranch land, and other business operations. He also spent fabulous sums—an estimated 40 million dollars on art treasures and oddities, untold millions for his personal life—and sank more than 50 million dollars into real estate holdings which by the depression times of the 1930s became enormous liabilities. How much of this spending represents a drain on the journalistic properties, no one knows. But it is known that great sums were both made and lost in journalism; on the loss side, for example, Hearst's effort to win a foothold in Atlanta cost him 21 million dollars before he gave up.

The crash came for Hearst in 1937, when he was forced to abdicate temporarily, and watch a group of trustees liquidate a portion of his empire. Nine dailies and five Sunday editions were dropped by 1940; Universal Service was consolidated with INS; movie companies, radio stations, and some magazines were sold. Arthur Brisbane, Hearst's longtime associate who had become a front page columnist-philosopher and wealthy newspaper and real estate operator, died in 1937, and the trustees began liquidating 40 million dollars worth of New York City real estate which Brisbane had helped Hearst to accumulate. Many of the art treasures which were Hearst's pride were auctioned off by Gimbels and Macy's. Eventually even many of San Simeon's 275,000 acres were sold to help reclaim some of the 36 million dollars invested there.

Through it all, however, Hearst continued to live in regal style. The man who had bought a castle in Wales, Egyptian mummies, Tibetan yaks, and a Spanish abbey (which was dismantled stone by stone and shipped to a New York warehouse, after which Hearst never saw it again), had a truly precapitalistic attitude toward money as such. His guests at San Simeon, who were legion, continued to dive into an indoor pool from a sixteenth century Italian marble balcony, to pick flowers in a mile-long pergola stretching along Hearst's private mountain range, and to eat from kingly silver plate. Before World War II had ended, the trimming down of his empire and wartime publishing profits had accomplished the desired miracle, and the Hearst once thought to be broke was back in full command again.

When death had claimed its founder, the Hearst organization had 16 dailies and 13 Sunday editions appearing in a dozen cities. They had 9.1 per cent of the country's total daily circulation and 16.1 per cent of the Sunday total, a substantial decline in Hearst influence from the 1935 figures of 13.6 per cent daily and 24.2 per cent Sunday. The Hearst estate was valued at some 56 million dollars, based on estimated stock values, but the profit margins of the Hearst enterprises were below those of other newspapers of their size for which financial reports are available.

2. Undoubtedly Hearst editing and printing methods made their impress on American journalism. Particularly Hearst's sponsoring of mechanical innovations, and the Hearst format techniques, spurred others on. But these were contributions which were largely technical in their nature, and in the judgment of most newspapermen they were more than matched on the negative side by Hearst proclivities for sensational treatment of the news.

3. Undoubtedly, too, Hearst drew many new readers of newspapers to his fold, and held more than 5 million daily and 8 million Sunday to the day of his death. But what was the end result? Pulitzer defended the use of sensationalism in his *World* by arguing that it attracted readers who then would be exposed to the columns of his carefully planned, high-quality editorial page. The same could never be said of a Hearst newspaper.

Nor did Hearst ever exercise the powerful influence in American life which his great circulations might indicate. Among the men whom he wanted to see become president of the United States were William Jennings Bryan, Champ Clark, Hiram W. Johnson, William Gibbs McAdoo, John Nance Garner, Alfred M. Landon, General Douglas MacArthur, and William Randolph Hearst. Among the men whom he fought while they were in the White House were William McKinley, Theodore Roosevelt, William Howard Taft, Woodrow Wilson, Herbert Hoover, Franklin D. Roosevelt, and Harry S Truman. Hearst got on the bandwagons of Warren Harding, Calvin Coolidge, and Hoover in the 1920s largely because he disagreed with their Democratic opponents. He rode the Wilson bandwagon in 1912 and the Roosevelt bandwagon in 1932, but promptly got off in high dudgeon both times, even though he considered himself a Democrat. His own personal political ambitions, which bloomed strongest from 1900 to 1910, were permanently smashed in 1922. When he wanted to run for senator in New York state that year, Al Smith refused to let him on the Democratic ticket and made a bitter speech attacking Hearst's isolationist record in World War I.

4. What then of Hearst as a constructive social force? Certainly he was an advocate of Americanism. But to many his continued espousal of nationalistic policies bordering on jingoism, in a time which demanded American cooperation in international security efforts, was the most distressing feature of his newspapers. And the "Red hunts" which his newspapers fostered in the 1930s among the ranks of political leaders, educators, YMCA secretaries, labor leaders, and other citizens were based on the familiar tactics of the demagogue: those who disagreed with Hearst were "Communists." Indeed, part of the strong criticism of Hearst which developed during the 1930s centered about these

tendencies, and about his apparent admiration of the Nazi government in Germany when it first emerged. Hearst newspapers ran syndicated articles by Hermann Goering and praised the Nazi economic program, until wiser heads prevailed upon the publisher to recognize the uglier features of Hitlerism.[8] To the end, however, Hearst opposed the basic foreign policy adopted by the American people during and after World War II and distrusted the United Nations as thoroughly as he had distrusted the League of Nations.

HEARST AND THE NEW DEAL

In domestic affairs, Hearst newspapers continued to give stalwart support to public education and to the idea of public ownership of utilities. But they backslid during the 1920s and 1930s on many of the other progressive features of the Hearst editorial platform as written before World War I. The change became particularly apparent during the first years of the New Deal. Hearst had helped to obtain Franklin Roosevelt's nomination for the presidency, largely to settle an old score with Al Smith, and in the spring of 1933 his newspapers applauded vigorously as Roosevelt undertook unemployment relief, suspended exports of gold, and proposed the NRA—which, a Hearst editorial said, "embodies several basic policies long advocated by the Hearst newspapers." [9]

By 1935 the tune had changed. It was the "Raw Deal" and the "National Run Around" in both news and editorial columns. The Supreme Court decision outlawing the NRA, which Hearst papers once had proudly claimed for their own, was greeted with an American flag and the headline: "Thank God for the Supreme Court!" President Roosevelt was on his way toward establishing a "personal dictatorship," according to Hearst editorials. And a special squad of Hearst newsmen was installed in Washington, called the "smear bureau" by the cynical, whose sole duty was to unearth anti-New Deal stories for the chain's papers to run.

There are other examples in the columns of the Hearst papers of 1935 which illustrate the extent to which the earlier beliefs of Hearst had changed. The publisher who before World War I had been perhaps the most aggressive in supporting the power of labor unions said now: "The Wagner Labor Bill . . . is one of the most vicious pieces of class legislation that could be conceived—un-American to the core, violative of every constitutional principle and contrary to the whole spirit of American life. Congress in passing it is betraying the country." [10]

The publisher who had fought so long against monopolies and trusts said now: "The Wheeler-Rayburn Bill, decreeing death to the holding companies,

[8] Tebbel, *The Life and Good Times of William Randolph Hearst,* p. 256.
[9] *San Francisco Examiner,* May 6, 1933.
[10] *Ibid.,* May 29, 1935.

is PURE VENOM distilled by a PERSONAL and MALIGNANT OBSESSION, without a pretense of economic or legal justification." [11]

The publisher who always believed that he understood the common people, and was understood by them, sparked an extensive front-page coverage of WPA activities in 1936 with headlines like this one: "Taxpayers Feed 20,000 Reds on N. Y. Relief Rolls." And his newspapers warned that the Social Security Act was "A Pay Cut for You! . . . Governor Landon, when elected, will repeal this so-called security act." [12]

Hearst newspapers threw every resource of the editorial and news pages into the campaign to elect Governor Alfred M. Landon of Kansas president in 1936. When President Roosevelt was reelected by the greatest majority in history, carrying all the states but two, Hearst's enemies cried for his scalp. Liberals pointed to the obvious and heavy slanting of news column material in Landon's favor as evidence of Hearst's professional irresponsibility. Boycotts reminiscent of those carried out in World War I against Hearst papers were attempted. The Hearst name on a widely-shown newsreel was hissed. Hearst's troubles with the American Newspaper Guild added to the furor. And when it seemed in late 1937 that the Hearst empire was collapsing, his critics gleefully wrote him off as a broken-down old man.

But the triumphant liberals overreached themselves in launching the Supreme Court reorganization bill of 1937, called the "court packing bill" by those who defeated it. The New Deal reform period came to an abrupt halt. Just as the Hearst papers weathered their economic difficulties in the next few years, they weathered public attacks against them and moved into a different political climate in which they once more could go on the offensive. Vicious personal attacks on President Roosevelt continued during the war years, and when Scripps-Howard dropped columnist Westbrook Pegler because of his monotonously vituperative assaults upon the Roosevelt family, labor leaders, and Communists, Hearst welcomed Pegler into the fold of rancorous Hearst columnists. Politically the Hearst papers descended to a ridiculously synthetic, but fully publicized, boom for General Douglas MacArthur for president in 1948, giving every appearance that they believed he was a major contender for the Republican nomination that year (MacArthur received 11 votes in the party convention).

THE HEARST PAPERS CHANGE

With Hearst's death came some changes in the empire. His longtime friend, at whose home he died, Marion Davies, no longer found her wishes carried out by Hearst editors (it had been she who sponsored the Hearst papers' antivivisection campaign which harassed American medical schools). William Ran-

[11] *Ibid.*, June 21, 1935.
[12] *Ibid.*, October 30, 1936.

dolph Hearst, Jr., one of the publisher's five sons, undertook to exert leadership in toning down some of his father's policies. Local editors were given greater autonomy; they were told to "use the greatest care to avoid bias or lack of objectivity in the handling of the news"; and in other ways the new Hearst executive team sought to wipe out some of the memories of the past. The once crudely sensational *American Weekly* was completely revamped and modernized. Hearst magazine and television holdings were expanded. The younger Hearst made it clear, however, that he would not ignore "the pool of wisdom and experience accumulated by my father and his associates through the passing years." [13] Such key Hearst executives as Richard E. Berlin, president of the Hearst corporation, and J. D. Gortatowsky, board chairman for its publishing divisions, continued as advisers of the sons into the 1960s. William Randolph Hearst, Jr., took the title of editor-in-chief of the Hearst newspapers in 1955. Randolph A. Hearst became second most powerful of the brothers, as president of Hearst Consolidated Publications. Randolph's twin, David, headed West coast operations. The eldest of the brothers, George, did not choose active leadership. A fifth son, John Randolph, died in 1958.

The Hearst organization undertook a massive plant modernization program, and streamlined the papers' typography. Hearst editors sought to rejuvenate circulation in competitive city situations. Particularly in California their papers assumed independent political roles of a progressive character in selecting candidates to endorse. The Hearst Foundation gave substantial scholarships to college journalists in annual competitions designed to uncover new talent. Still, in 1971, the Hearst empire was down to 8 dailies and 7 Sunday editions with 3.3 per cent of daily circulation and 4.8 per cent of Sunday. The *American Weekly* was no more. Fabulous San Simeon became a California Historical Monument in 1958, open to bus loads of tourists. Hearst, Jr., had one major triumph: the Pulitzer Prize for international reporting went to him, J. Kingsbury Smith, and Frank Conniff in 1956 for stories from the Soviet Union. "I have a feeling that Pop and Joe Pulitzer are getting almost as big a kick out of it as we are," he told his readers.

COLONEL McCORMICK AND THE *CHICAGO TRIBUNE*

Second only to Hearst in stirring up the wrath of critics was Colonel Robert R. McCormick, publisher of the *Chicago Tribune*. McCormick was for two decades chairman of the committee on freedom of the press of the American Newspaper Publishers Association. In that role he helped newspaper publishers and editors win court battles waged in defense of constitutional guarantees. But, ironically, McCormick's insistence on perpetuating his kind of

[13] *Editor & Publisher*, LXXXV (March 22, 1952), 7.

San Francisco Examiner

Chicago Tribune

Newspaper owners William Randolph Hearst, Jr. (*left*) and Robert R. McCormick.

personal journalism—which made his newspaper distort the news picture according to the dictates of a powerful but extremely opinionated mind—was at the same time imperiling freedom of the press. Those who defended McCormick said personal journalists play important roles, as indeed some had in the history of the newspaper, and reiterated the essentials of press freedom: (1) the right to print without prior restraint; (2) the right to criticise; (3) the right to report. Those who claim these rights, however, owe society in turn a conscientious effort to criticise fairly and in the public interest, and to report the news fully and honestly. This is implicit in the contract by which the press accepts protection under our fundamental law in exchange for its valued service to the public. McCormick, by ignoring public complaints that he was not living up to his obligations, and by brushing aside similar judgments by many leaders of his profession, continued to be the kind of personal journalist he wanted to be. He also exposed the journalistic profession to the danger of loss of public confidence by providing a vast amount of ammunition to those who used the *Tribune* and similar newspapers as proof that the press was irresponsible.[14]

The quarrel with McCormick was not so much that his *Tribune* clung to an outmoded and dangerous nationalist-isolationist point of view in the face of overwhelming public support of efforts to find peace and security through international cooperation. Nor was it so much that his *Tribune* became the principal spokesman for the ultraconservative right wing in American politics, and rejected a President Eisenhower as violently as it had rejected a President

[14] For a book-length documentation, see John Tebbel, *An American Dynasty* (New York: Doubleday, 1947).

Truman. The real quarrel McCormick's critics had with him was that as he tried so hard to prove that the *Tribune* was right, and most everybody else was wrong, editorial columns became bitter personal proclamations whose prejudiced approaches to matters of public interest spilled over into the news columns. McCormick's answer, until death stilled his voice in 1955, was that his *Tribune* was the "World's Greatest Newspaper."

This claim would have had merit if newspaper greatness were measured only in terms of financial success, circulation, and mechanical excellence. In the mid-1950s the *Tribune* carried as much advertising as its three Chicago rivals combined. Its circulation, while down to 900,000 daily from a 1946 high of 1,075,000, was still the largest of any standard-sized American newspaper, and was spread through five states in an area McCormick called "Chicago-land." Its 450-man news staff, operating from the 36-story Tribune Tower, provided blanket coverage of local and area news events which was the despair of rival city editors. Its comics, sports pages, woman's pages, financial and business reporting, and advertising columns attracted readers at all levels. Technically the *Tribune* excelled in writing, editing, and typography. And what its critics called outrageously prejudiced and insufferably insulting editorials (the *Tribune* called them "the hair on our chest") had a "gutty prose" quality which commanded reader attention, if not always respect. For a venture that rated as the single most often criticised American newspaper, the *Tribune* was doing all right, and Colonel McCormick frequently reminded his critics of that fact.

MEDILL, McCORMICK, AND PATTERSON

Not all of this success was due to McCormick. The *Tribune* has a long history, beginning in 1847. The builder was Joseph Medill, who from 1855 to 1899 devoted his energies to the creation of a prosperous, powerful newspaper. In an era of personal journalism, Medill was not outdone; he belligerently stood for nationalism, for conservatism, for civic progress, and for giving a free hand to business in the days of unrestricted individualism. When he died, Medill left a financial trust which provided for the families of his two daughters—the McCormicks and the Pattersons. One son-in-law, Robert W. Patterson, and a grandson, Medill McCormick, assumed leading roles at the *Tribune*, but Patterson died in 1910 and Medill McCormick retired from the paper to become U. S. Senator from Illinois. During the period 1895 to 1914, while the family control was thus undergoing change, James Keeley rose to brilliance, first as city editor and then as managing editor. Under his direction the *Tribune* developed a crusading spirit and a community service record typical of newspapers published in those years of muckraking and reform.

The Robert R. McCormick era began in 1914. His brother Medill retired from the paper that year, and Keeley, sensing that his talents would not be appreciated by the new family representatives, joined in an ill-fated effort to resuscitate an opposition paper, the *Chicago Herald.* Sharing responsibility for the *Tribune* with the future colonel was his cousin, Joseph Medill Patterson, later the founder of the *New York Daily News.* The fourth Medill grandchild, Eleanor Medill Patterson, was to become owner of the *Washington Times-Herald.*

Building on the foundations Medill and Keeley had laid, the young cousins doubled *Tribune* circulation and advertising during the World War I period. Patterson had a particular brilliance for spotting the best comic strips and other features; McCormick proved to be an excellent businessman. Circulation was boomed, too, by the hoodlum tactics in which Max Annenberg, *Tribune* circulation boss whom McCormick thoughtfully lifted from Hearst, excelled. McCormick bought Canadian forests and built paper mills which gave him an advantage when newsprint prices soared in the 1920s.

The success of the *New York Daily News,* and the disappearance of Captain Patterson into that venture, further entrenched McCormick's position. The two papers made as much as 13 million dollars a year. The *Tribune-Daily News* feature syndicate, radio station WGN, and more Canadian paper and power investments followed. When Captain Patterson died in 1946, McCormick became the head of the *New York Daily News,* although he preferred to exercise influence by remote control. When Eleanor Patterson died in 1948, she willed the *Washington Times-Herald* to seven of her executives, but they sold it to McCormick in 1949 for 4½ million dollars. The Colonel first installed a favorite niece, Mrs. Ruth McCormick (Bazy) Miller, daughter of Medill and Ruth Hanna McCormick, as *Times-Herald* editor. But Mrs. Miller fell from grace in 1951 and McCormick took over personal control of what became the Washington "outpost" of the *Chicago Tribune.* The *Tribune* formula did not work in Washington, and in 1954, ill and weary of a paper which was losing $500,000 a year, McCormick sold the *Times-Herald* for 8½ million dollars to Eugene Meyer's *Washington Post,* which incorporated the *Times-Herald* nameplate in its own. But despite this retreat, no one except the Hearst heirs had more readers than McCormick had, with his two big dailies.

McCORMICK AND THE NEW DEAL

The memos signed "R.R.Mc." were law in the *Tribune* empire. The six-foot four-inch colonel turned eyes of ice-water blue on all aspects of the business. His private domains were the Tribune Tower and his 1,000-acre farm and estate outside Chicago, named Cantigny for the World War I battle in which McCormick participated. Those who worked for him enjoyed a paternalism which provided high salaries, health and welfare protection, and job security. They learned to follow the Colonel's lead in business affairs, in news and editorial policies, and in such McCormick specialties as military strategy and foreign relations. McCormick made a deep study of military history; but his opinions about international affairs were based upon a belief that foreigners, especially Englishmen, were dangerous. Almost as dangerous, the *Tribune* said, were New York financiers, Eastern internationalists, and educators and intellectuals.

Among the men who helped to build the *Tribune* as McCormick's aides were Edward Scott Beck, managing editor from 1910 to 1937; J. Loy Maloney, managing editor from 1939 to 1951, when he became executive editor; W. D. Maxwell, city editor who became managing editor in 1951; and sports editor Arch Ward, business manager Elbert M. Antrim, and circulation manager Louis Rose. Heading the Washington bureau were Arthur Sears Henning and his successor, Walter Trohan, who learned to shape their coverage to back up the Colonel's opinions. Such *Tribune* foreign service stars as William L. Shirer, Edmond Taylor, and Vincent Sheehan disappeared when the Colonel's personal direction of their work interfered with their coverage.

McCormick opposed President Franklin Roosevelt and the domestic policies of the New Deal with every resource. As a result the *Tribune* was voted in a 1936 poll of Washington correspondents as runner-up to the Hearst papers for the title "least fair and reliable." When the World War II crisis began to develop, the *Tribune* bitterly denounced cooperation with Great Britain, the ancient enemy; a typical eight-column banner when the lend-lease bill was under debate read: "HOUSE PASSES DICTATOR BILL." It was this combination of extreme conservatism and nationalism which incited Marshall Field to start the *Chicago Sun* as a rival morning paper (the *Tribune* having inherited the field alone when Hearst retired from it in 1939).

But McCormick's luck held. Three days after the *Sun* appeared its principal issue of isolationism *v.* interventionism was exploded by the bombs which fell at Pearl Harbor. McCormick supported the American war effort although the *Tribune* called American entrance an "FDR war plot." Marshall Field's hard-pressed *Sun*, Colonel Frank Knox's *Chicago Daily News*, and the pro-New Deal tabloid, the *Chicago Times*, opposed McCormick valiantly but without noticeably denting its readership until the merged *Sun-Times* made headway in the 1950s. The Washington correspondents again estimated the *Tribune's* standing in 1944, voting it "the newspaper . . . most flagrant in angling or weighting the news." [15]

How much the *Tribune's* activities could embarrass all American newspapers was driven home the morning after the presidential election of 1948, when reelected Harry Truman was photographed gleefully holding a home

[15] *Time*, XLIX (June 9, 1947), 68. The 1936 survey of Washington correspondents, cited above, was taken by Leo C. Rosten for his book, *The Washington Correspondents* (New York: Harcourt, Brace & Jovanovich, 1937). Cited most often as "least fair and reliable" by 93 correspondents were, in order, the Hearst newspapers, the *Chicago Tribune*, the *Los Angeles Times*, and the Scripps-Howard newspapers. Cited most often as "most fair and reliable" by 99 correspondents were, in order, the *New York Times*, *Baltimore Sun*, *Christian Science Monitor*, the Scripps-Howard papers, and the *St. Louis Post-Dispatch* (pp. 356–57).

edition of the *Tribune* whose banner line read: "DEWEY DEFEATS TRUMAN." An overconfident *Tribune* Washington bureau had let its hopes override the facts, to the delight of press critics, and to the dismay of newspapermen who had conscientiously tried to maintain news page objectivity. The *Tribune* was not embarrassed; next morning its banner was back to a more usual theme: "CONFESSES DOUBLE KILLING."

Key McCormick executives took over his *Tribune* in 1955 and continued its policies. Chesser M. Campbell, the new president and publisher, died in 1960 and was succeeded by J. Howard Wood and Harold F. Grumhaus. Clayton Kirkpatrick succeeded W. D. Maxwell as editor. The *Chicago American* was purchased in 1956 and renamed *Chicago Today*. The *Tribune's* circulation of 767,000 in 1971, down 300,000 from its top, was still 230,000 ahead of the *Sun-Times*.

Hearst and McCormick were not the only newspaper publishers who aroused the ire of those who spoke out against journalistic irresponsibility in the momentous years after 1930, when domestic and international crises demanded the best efforts of the press in obtaining and interpreting the news. Readers of other dailies than the Hearst and McCormick-Patterson papers had justifiable complaints about fairness and devotion to the public interest, although in overall perspective, American newspapermen succeeded in raising their sights during that quarter century. It was Hearst and McCormick, however, who got the spotlight.

ROY W. HOWARD AND THE SCRIPPS IMAGE

Receiving special attention, too, was Roy W. Howard, the man who by the 1930s had come to dominate the newspapers founded by E. W. Scripps. Howard was held responsible by his critics for a rightward shift in the outlook of the 20 surviving Scripps-Howard dailies, which ranked third behind Hearst and McCormick-Patterson papers in circulation. The complaints were not of the same character as those made against Hearst and McCormick; they reflected rather the disappointment and dismay of the liberals that the "people's papers" of Edward Wyllis Scripps had become in many respects conventionally conservative in tone.[16]

Robert Paine Scripps, the founder's youngest son, inherited the controlling interest in the newspapers, the United Press, Acme Newsphotos, Newspaper Enterprise Association, and United Feature Syndicate when his father died in 1926. Robert Scripps had been at the editorial helm as family representative since 1918, while Roy Howard, the architect of the United Press, had taken

[16] See Chapter 20, pages 457–61 in Chapter 22, and page 626 in Chapter 27 for the earlier Scripps story.

over business management of the newspaper chain in 1922, the year the Scripps-McRae newspapers were renamed Scripps-Howard.

The son was imbued with the philosophy of the father, although his quiet and sensitive nature kept him from exercising a firm control over policy. When editor Carl Magee of Albuquerque, New Mexico, was persecuted and driven from business in 1922 because of his efforts to expose the political machine headed by Secretary of the Interior Albert B. Fall (later convicted of bribe-taking in the Teapot Dome scandal), Robert Scripps bought the paper, the *Tribune,* and restored Magee to its editorship. In 1924 the Scripps-Howard papers supported Robert M. La Follette, Progressive party candidate for the presidency. The Scripps-Howard editors, called into session periodically to decide matters of national policy, backed Herbert Hoover for the presidency in 1928, but swung back to Franklin D. Roosevelt in 1932 and 1936.

Howard's ascendancy in Scripps-Howard affairs became apparent in 1937, when the chain's papers broke with Roosevelt over the Supreme Court reorganization bill. Lowell Mellett, editor of the *Washington News,* and other old Scripps men left the organization. Robert Paine Scripps, who had been in virtual retirement, died aboard his yacht in 1938. The Scripps wills provided for eventual distribution of the family holdings among Robert Scripps' six children and their heirs. Howard, William W. Hawkins of the United Press, and George B. Parker, editor-in-chief of the newspapers, were named trustees, to serve until the sons of Robert Scripps reached the age of 25.

Under this regime the Scripps-Howard newspapers opposed a third term for President Roosevelt in 1940 and supported Republican presidential candidates every four years through 1960. The newspaper chain was cut from 25 to 19 dailies during the depression years, with such old fighting Scripps papers as those in Akron and Toledo disappearing. Organized labor no longer found the chain's papers to be stalwart champions. The papers still reflected considerable variety in outlook and reader appeal, however, and exercise of local autonomy made outstanding such dailies as those in Memphis and the *Cleveland Press,* edited by the strong-minded and community-conscious Louis B. Seltzer. The United Press developed stature as a press association under presidents Karl Bickel and Hugh Baillie and the United Feature Syndicate became noted for its array of offerings from such capable columnists as Raymond Clapper, Marquis Childs, and Thomas L. Stokes. Liberal columnist Heywood Broun broke with Howard in 1939, but Howard also broke with extremist Westbrook Pegler in 1944. Howard's major desire was to build a powerful paper in New York City, but the result of his efforts, the *World-Telegram and Sun,* was disappointing and the paper died in 1967.

After World War II, Hawkins and Parker were replaced as trustees by Robert Paine Scripps, Jr., and Charles E. Scripps. In 1949 Charles Scripps became chairman of the trust. Neither was interested particularly in editorial matters, however, and eventual leadership in that direction fell to Edward W. Scripps II, who assumed the third trusteeship from Roy Howard when his

Milton J. Pike

Milton J. Pike

Roy W. Howard (*left*) and the grandson of E. W. Scripps, Edward W. Scripps II.

brother Samuel declined his option. One of Robert Scripps' daughters, Margaret Scripps McCabe, also showed interest in the newspapers' editorial policies, as was demonstrated when her husband, Charles R. McCabe, criticised the turn Scripps-Howard policy had taken in an introduction to a collection of E. W. Scripps' writings.[17]

Roy Howard remained powerful, however, until his death in 1964, as head of the *World-Telegram and Sun,* and his son Jack was high in the councils as president of the parent E. W. Scripps Company. In the Far West, the family of James Scripps, eldest son of the founder who quarreled with his father in 1920, was successfully rebuilding the once nearly-defunct Scripps League by developing small daily newspapers in Utah, Idaho, Montana, and Oregon. Another Scripps grandson, John P. Scripps, had built a chain of small California dailies. The name Scripps seemed certain to remain an important one in the business.

SPOTLIGHT ON BROADCASTING

As television became a dominant mass medium in the 1960s, the public attention earlier given to faults of newspapers shifted to the sins of the imagemakers. Two major areas of public activity were an ever-growing preoccupation with sex in all conceivable forms and continuing eruptions of violence—urban, racial, campus, radical, and military. What television did or did not do relative to sex and violence became a focus of public debate. Predictably, the

[17] Charles R. McCabe, ed., *Damned Old Crank* (New York: Harper & Row, 1951), p. xii.

medium was blamed for the problem in many quarters, even though sex is as old as creation and violence has been a national characteristic of American life.

Like newspapers and magazines, television had built up a list of achievements which stood it in good stead as attacks upon broadcasters mounted in the 1960s. Its ability to project the viewer into an event, and let him judge for himself, had been demonstrated during the Army-McCarthy hearings in 1954 when attorney Joseph Welch turned on Senator Joseph McCarthy for attacking a young lawyer on his staff, and again in 1960 during the Great Debates between John Kennedy and Richard Nixon. It had afforded Nixon the opportunity to defend himself when his place on the 1952 Republican ticket was threatened; it had afforded Edward R. Murrow the opportunity to unmask Joseph McCarthy in his famed 1954 documentary. It had reported magnificently the national sorrow at the assassination of President Kennedy. It had reported the onset of the Black Revolution in the 1960s and the climactic march on Washington led by Dr. Martin Luther King in 1963. . . . "I have a dream," King said. In documentaries, ABC had offered "Walk In My Shoes," a brilliant examination of the Negro's problems; NBC had produced "Same Mud, Same Blood," one of the finest documentaries from Vietnam; CBS had screened "Harvest of Shame" and "Hunger in America" as studies of economic and social inequality.

But for all this, television became the most sharply criticised of the media in the 1960s. Some thought the coverage was slanted; some thought television was creating the events; some thought that material they disliked should be suppressed. And some were justifiably criticising television for its imperfections and shortcomings.

SEX IN THE MASS MEDIA

Television was not the most advanced exponent of sexual freedom, nudity, innuendoes, and four-letter words. But it was the medium which had both a semipublic (licensed) character and an all-family audience. Motion pictures, books, and to some extent magazines enjoy individualized usage and can break social taboos which the "family" media—television, radio, newspapers, general magazines—are slow to challenge. As television became more immersed each year in the deluge of American public exposure to homosexualism, the "pill," nude fashions, movies showing explicit details of seduction and intercourse, and now-fashionable four-letter words, it reflected the new image. But the majority of the public didn't care to have television do so. Neither did television network and station executives who remain constantly sensitive to public complaints that may endanger license renewals.

The television industry's voluntary code of good practice, developed by the National Association of Broadcasters, reminds broadcasters that "television's relationship to the viewers is that between guest and host." Among its provisions is a long list of general program standards which forbid profanity, obscenity, vulgarity, attacks on religion, suicide, and condoning of crime, and which frown upon divorce, cigarette smoking, illicit sex relations, drunkenness, gambling, and bedroom scenes. When the U.S. Senate Subcommittee on Communications asked the networks to grant to the NAB Code Authority the right to prescreen any television entertainment program at will and to determine prior to broadcast whether the program violated the NAB Television Code, CBS objected. It said responsibility for evaluating and judging programs should not be centralized. All the networks agreed to consult with the NAB Code authority, to increase their own policing of programs, and to provide closed-circuit prescreening for affiliated stations, which bear the ultimate responsibility as licensees.

Yet it was CBS which suffered a public outcry of censorship when it cancelled the Smothers Brothers comedy hour in 1969 for insubordination, because the taped programs were not submitted to the network soon enough for editing and prescreening. CBS had previously censored segments of the show on grounds of poor taste, arousing the wrath of the Smothers Brothers. At issue were strongly antiwar sentiments expressed on the program and other sociopolitical content disturbing to some affiliates. One example was the singing of the anti-Marine song, "Waist Deep in the Big Muddy," by Pete Seeger, who had been blacklisted 17 years as a victim of the McCarthy era. And while the Smothers Brothers thus disappeared from prime time, Rowan and Martin's "Laugh-In" achieved high ratings for its combination of sex, satire, and borderline innuendoes, without the challenge of a "cause."

PROGRAMMED VIOLENCE

Violence has been a central theme of countless plays, novels, movies, comic books, and television scripts, from the times of the Greek dramatists to those of Matt Dillon. Television, which in the 1960s had a full quota of real violence to report from battlefields and urban riots, also loaded its programming with fantasy violence. The assassinations of John and Robert Kennedy and Martin Luther King, coupled with urban rioting and campus disorders, gave the opponents of programmed violence an opportunity.

They had the statistics in abundance. The *Christian Science Monitor* had counted 210 violent incidents and 81 killings in 78 hours of 1967 prime time; a year later the counts for 75 hours were 254 incidents and 71 killings despite network promises of reduced violence in the wake of the shootings of Robert Kennedy and Dr. King. The National Commission on the Causes and Prevention of Violence, appointed following those assassinations, logged violent incidents an average of every 15 minutes on NBC and every 10 minutes on ABC. The latter network had some incident of violence in 91 per cent of its evening programming in 1968. The Saturday morning children's cartoons had a violent incident every 3½ minutes.[18]

Senator Thomas Dodd's Juvenile Delinquency Subcommittee focused on television, throughout the 1960s, as a contributor to the increase in crime among the young. It pointed out that an impression was created that violence is a satisfying outlet for frustrations, that the fist and the gun are both manly and romantic. Most authorities agreed that seeing violence on the screen rarely directly caused criminal behavior, but they pointed out it was a needless and dehumanizing experience to watch endless destruction of human life on television. At least at the children's level, marked improvement had occurred by 1971, with the success of such educational fare as "Sesame Street" encouraging the major networks to program similar material and markedly reduce violence.

By contrast, a study of print media in the early 1960s showed a lower percentage of content portraying sex and violence than readers might suppose. An analysis of the stories in 55 newsstand magazines (family, intellectual, detective, men's, romance) showed an average of 46 incidents of violence per issue and 23 incidents dealing with sexual themes. The family magazines carried only 12 violence items and 4 involving sex. A study of 10 metropolitan newspapers showed 5 per cent of the total news space devoted to violence, less than 1 per cent to sex (except for the *New York Daily News,* which devoted a third of its space to news of violence and 3 per cent to sex).[19] Violence was defined as news of crime, war, accidents. It is apparent that prominent display of stories of sex and violence in newspapers distorts the public image of the volume of such material. The data also shows why the spotlight of public concern shifted to television during the 1960s. It had loaded its entertainment time with common denominator material—violence spiced with sex. These programs drew good ratings, but the Violence Commission reported that a 1968 Harris poll showed 63 per cent of women and 59 per cent of men felt there was too much violence on television.

RIOTS AND THE KERNER REPORT

Part of that 1968 public reaction to violence on television screens undoubtedly stemmed from reporting on news and public affairs shows of turbulence in cities and on campuses, of disorders and riots in black communities, of the tragedies of assassination cutting down such public figures as Robert Kennedy and Martin Luther King.

Watts was the scene of one great explosion in August 1965. It cost 34 lives, 898 injured, 4,000 arrested, and 45 million dollars in property damage. "Burn, Baby, Burn" was the cry of frustrated blacks angered by what they considered

[18] William Small, *To Kill a Messenger* (New York: Hastings House, 1970), pp. 80–81.

[19] Herbert A. Otto, "Sex and Violence on the American Newsstand," *Journalism Quarterly,* XL (Spring 1963), 19–26.

to be police brutality, and tortured by years of racial discrimination and white indifference. Two years later, in July 1967, the scenes of destruction were Newark and Detroit. At this juncture President Johnson appointed the National Advisory Commission on Civil Disorders with Governor Otto Kerner of Illinois as chairman. Chapter 15 of its March 1968 report dealt with the mass media and the President's question: "What effect do the mass media have on the riots?"[20]

The Kerner Commission said that the media on the whole had tried hard to give a balanced factual account of the 1967 disorders. There had been some evidence of sensationalism, distortion, and inaccuracy: most of the shooting had been done by national guardsmen and policemen, not blacks; there was no organized conspiracy spurring the rioting, but mainly hostile young ghetto blacks; property damage was exaggerated, by as much as ten times by one AP dispatch from Detroit. In many cases of error, the media had relied upon police authorities for their information. This observation by the commission was graphically reinforced in 1971 when false official statements were made that the prison guards who died at Attica in New York state had had their throats slashed. In reality they had been shot by their would-be rescuers. A courageous coroner and determined media reporters forced a prompt retraction of the false statements in fairness to the black convicts.

Television fared well in its riot coverage. The commission staff looked at 955 sequences of news and classified 494 as "calm" treatment to 262 as "emotional." Moderate black leaders were shown three times as often as militants. Because the soldiers and police were white, television scenes of actual rioting tended to make viewers think they were witnessing a black–white confrontation; actually the riots were in Negro slum areas. Overall, both network and local television coverage was cautious and restrained, the Kerner report said.

But the commission had a ringing indictment of the mass media, which was also an indictment of American society since the performance of the media largely reflected the public attitude of the times. The communications media, the commission said,

> have not communicated to the majority of their audience—which is white—a sense of the degradation, misery, and hopelessness of living in the ghetto. They have not communicated to whites a feeling for the difficulties and frustrations of being a Negro in the United States. They have not shown understanding or appreciation of—and thus have not communicated—a sense of Negro culture, thought, or history . . . When the white press does refer to Negroes and Negro problems it frequently does so as if Negroes were not part of the audience . . . such attitudes, in an area as sensitive and inflammatory as this, feed Negro alienation and intensify white prejudices.

[20] *Report of the National Advisory Commission on Civil Disorders* (New York: Bantam Books, 1968).

There has been no serious reporting of the Negro community, the commission said, with few black reporters and fewer race experts. "Tokenism—the hiring of one Negro reporter, or even two or three—is no longer enough. Negro reporters are essential, but so are Negro editors, writers, and commentators," the report declared.

The commission also recognized the problem conscientious journalists face when it commented:

> Fear and apprehension of racial unrest and violence are deeply rooted in American society. They color and intensify reactions to news of racial trouble and threats of racial conflict. Those who report and disseminate news must be conscious of the background of anxieties and apprehension against which their stories are projected.

A CBS News survey in 1968 pointed up this public fear: 70 per cent of whites responding thought the police should have been tougher in putting down riots.[21] In Watts' case, the white community later denied the area badly-needed hospital facilities even though the *Los Angeles Times* had won a Pulitzer Prize for its analysis of the Watts problem—after the riot was over.

Other studies bore out the Kerner Commission's statements about lack of black participation in the mass media. A 1969 study covering 32 of 48 major newspapers in 16 of the 20 largest U.S. cities showed that of 4,095 news executives, deskmen, reporters, and photographers, 108 or 2.6 per cent were black. Only one news executive and six deskmen were black. Negro population of the cities covered ran from 10 to 50 per cent.[22] A 1970 survey by *Time* listed the *Washington Post* as the most integrated newspaper, with 19 blacks out of an editorial staff of 222. Other numbers of 1970 black journalists: *New York Times,* 13; *Time,* 10; *Newsweek,* 10; *Look,* 5; *Life,* 5; UPI, 10; AP, 12; NBC, "about a dozen." [23] Among them were Carl T. Rowan, syndicated columnist; William Raspberry, *Washington Post* columnist; Lem Tucker, NBC Washington staff; Charlayne Hunter and Thomas A. Johnson, *New York Times;* L. F. Palmer, Jr., *Chicago Daily News* columnist, and Betty Washington, *Daily News;* William Drummond, *Los Angeles Times.* Highest ranking: William A. Hilliard, appointed city editor of the *Portland Oregonian* in 1971. Until more Negroes received college educations, and were persuaded to enter journalism as a career, the imbalance would continue, despite emergency efforts to train black men and women for the mass media.

21 Small, *op. cit.,* p. 60.

22 Edward J. Trayes, "The Negro in Journalism," *Journalism Quarterly,* XLVI (Spring 1969), 5.

23 *Time,* April 6, 1970, p. 89. See also M. L. Stein, "The Black Reporter and His Problems," *Saturday Review,* Feb. 13, 1971, p. 58.

CHICAGO 1968 AND THE WALKER REPORT

Late in 1968, after the presidential hopes of Hubert Humphrey had been wrecked by the image created during the turbulent Democratic convention in Chicago, a study of that convention known as the Walker Report was issued. Chicago attorney Daniel Walker made it for the National Commission on the Causes and Prevention of Violence. His staff took statements from 1,410 eyewitnesses and participants, had access to over 2,000 interviews conducted by the FBI. The Walker Report, referring to some events of the convention week as "a police riot," said that conditions were worse than the media had described them. Quoting from the summary:

> During the week of the Democratic National Convention, the Chicago police were the targets of mounting provocation by both word and act. It took the form of obscene epithets, and of rocks, sticks, bathroom tiles and even human feces hurled at police by demonstrators. Some of the acts had been planned; others were spontaneous or were themselves provoked by police action. Furthermore, the police had been put on edge by widely-published threats of attempts to disrupt both the city and the Convention.
>
> That was the nature of the provocation. The nature of the response was unrestrained and indiscriminate police violence on many occasions, particularly at night.
>
> That violence was made all the more shocking by the fact that it was often inflicted upon persons who had broken no law, disobeyed no order, made no threat. These included peaceful demonstrators, onlookers, and large numbers of residents who were simply passing through, or happened to live in, the areas where confrontations were occurring.
>
> Newsmen and photographers were singled out for assault, and their equipment deliberately damaged. Fundamental police training was ignored; and officers, when on the scene, were often unable to control their men. As one police officer put it: "What happened didn't have anything to do with police work." [24]

The final report of the Commission, made in December 1969, said that in Chicago police used "excessive force not only against the provocateurs but also against the peaceful demonstrators and passive bystanders. Their conduct, while it won the support of the majority, polarized substantial and previously neutral segments of the population against the authorities and in favor of the demonstrators."

If these were the documented conclusions of a distinguished national commission appointed by President Johnson—the man against whom much of the

[24] As quoted in Small, *op. cit.*, p. 211.

CHICAGO SUN-TIMES, Fri., Aug. 30, 1968 7

JIMMY BRESLIN

Kids Take A Pounding—From Police, Delegates

By Jimmy Breslin

He was running with his body too far over and he had no control of himself, so he kept stumbling into the cops in the street and the cops chopped down on his head with their clubs.

Here was this young kid running with his legs out of control and his eyes closing and hair flying each time a club came onto his head—all the way from the front entrance of the Conrad Hilton Hotel to the corner. Running, stumbling, running, staggering and then going down on his face in the middle of Michigan Av. in the city of Chicago.

The cops ran up and kicked him. A few steps away, in the gutter under the streetlight, doctors leaned over somebody who seemed badly hurt.

The crowd in the street stood with handkerchiefs over faces in the tear gas and they screamed at the cops.

The police gathered into groups and then ran into the kids and swung their clubs, cops in blue helmets and short-sleeve blue shirts. Cops with bare arms swinging in the television lights while they went for the head with their clubs, or for any place below the belt they could reach. Chicago cops who had been misdirected all day and now were completely without supervision. They were running into young kids and beating them.

They gather in groups under the lights.

"Get these bastards over there," one of them says.

"Let's get 'em."

"No, no, now wait a minute, wait a minute. Over there. There."

The Worst In 20 Years

And they ran with their clubs into the kids who are unarmed and had, for hours, infuriated the cops with their youth and their dress and their manner of talking.

In 20 years of being policemen, having policemen in the family, riding with policemen in cars, drinking with them, watching them work in demonstrations and crowds in cities all over the world, the performance of the police of Chicago on Michigan Av. last night was the one worst I ever have seen.

"My head, my head, my head, my head," a girl in a gray sweater keeps saying as she falls against the building. Her hands go to her brown head of hair, where she has just been hit by a cop.

"Get out of here," the cop shouts. He aims his club for below your midsection. He misses, changes direction and goes for somebody else.

The tear gas was everywhere and people ran into buildings with their hands over their mouths. An Ohio delegate came out of his hotel to ride to the convention and the gas hit him. He stumbled into an office building with tears streaming. The tear gas went up, and it got through the open windows of Hubert Humphrey suite.

It began in the afternoon when the kids sat on the grass in the park across the street from the hotel.

"It was a very together thing last night," a kid was saying. "We had an apartment set up and we brought in anybody who got zonked with tear gas."

A girl was on her back, blowing smoke up. "I'd tell you my name," she said. "But I can't give it. Like my parents."

Machineguns At The Ready

The National Guard had machineguns up on the bridges that cross the railroad tracks that run through the park—machineguns, machineguns on tripods. One on each sidewalk of the bridge. The cops had the kids blocked off in the park where they had gone into them with tear gas and clubs earlier.

Now the kids sat on the grass and waited for word from their leader, Sidney Peck, the professor from Case-Western Reserve who is in the militant peace movment with such people as Dave Dellinger.

As Peck is far superior to the police at the simple art of crowd movements, he waited while his kids taunted the National Guardsmen.

"Wouldn't you rather hold a girl than a rifle?" a kid said, his arms around a girl who stood inches away from the line of rifles pointed at them.

Then Peck got on the loud-speaker and told the crowd of perhaps 4,000 to break up into small groups and just walk out of the park. And the kids broke up and walked away from the police and the National Guard. Walked away and left the police and National Guard motionless. And the kids went into Michigan Av. and captured the whole street and began shouting slogans at the hotel.

To the police, however, a kid shouting a political slogan is a thing to be feared and beaten. There was no way to control them. The police of Chicago have been out of hand since April, when Mayor Daley said they should shoot young looters. Daley went over the head of his police chief when he did this. When you deal with the intelligence of the average policeman you must be very careful. Mayor Daley was not.

Voice At Convention Headquarters

So Wednesday night, rather than watch the nomination of a candidate for the office of the President of the United States, you came, crying and choking and burning from tear gas, into the lobby of the Conrad Hilton Hotel, the headquarters for the convention, and the hotel speaker called out," all guests of the hotel please go to your room immediately and stay there." And out in the street, moving through the lights, national guardsmen in gas masks pointed rifles and moved at the crowd.

There were only 4,000 kids in the streets and the treatment given them by police created a national scandal, the effect of which will be felt through the days and the weeks that they try to conduct a campaign for the Presidency. For 4,000 kids is a very small number, compared to what surely will

Turn to Page 22

Lines of policemen are strung across Michigan Av. outside the Conrad Hilton Hotel to block demonstrators trying to reach the International Amphitheatre. (Sun-Times Photo by Tom Kneebone)

The *Chicago Sun-Times* covers the climactic "police riot" in picture and story.

bitterness at Chicago 1968 was directed—how did the media come out with tarnished public images?

Here best operated William Small's warning—the public, rather than accept reality, will prefer "to kill a messenger." The messenger was primarily television. CBS anchor man Walter Cronkite found himself exploding with wrath when he saw (as did the audience) floor guards slug CBS correspondent Dan Rather to the floor—but Cronkite later found himself virtually apologizing to Chicago's political boss, Mayor Richard J. Daley, upon whom primary responsibility for using "law and order" to create disorder rested. NBC correspondent Sander Vanocur never recovered professionally from the public disfavor he incurred while covering the convention and retired from NBC in 1971. The flow of antimedia letters was so intense that the Federal Communications Commission felt compelled to conduct an investigation of the news coverage of the affair by the networks. The networks agreed to cooperate, reluctantly; by September, 1969, the FCC reported to a public that had long made up its mind the other way that the networks had been fair.

Most Americans saw a 17-minute television sequence reporting the police-crowd confrontation on Wednesday night of convention week in front of the Conrad Hilton Hotel. There, and on the side streets, police brutality reached its peak, the Walker Report said. What most viewers would scarcely believe is the fact that those 17 minutes comprised half of the time CBS used to cover the demonstrations—32 minutes out of 38 hours of network time devoted to covering the week's activities. NBC devoted 36 minutes to violence on the floor out of 35 hours of coverage, 28 minutes to demonstrations outside the hall. ABC devoted 14 minutes to the disorders. Thus only a little more than 1 per cent of network time was devoted to violence during the turbulent week, 99 per cent to events on the floor, discussions, and the boredom of political convention coverage.[25]

The public, however, criticised the media for paying too much attention to the demonstrators and for reporting too much violence. A study reported by *Broadcasting* magazine put the Wednesday night audience at 90 millions, of whom 21.3 per cent thought the police used excessive force, and 56.8 per cent thought they did not. Only 13 per cent thought the tight security measures on the convention floor were unjustified—even though one critic commented that Humphrey was nominated "in a stockade."

In Chicago that week Del Hall of CBS News was clubbed from behind as he filmed. Jim Strickland of NBC News was clubbed in the mouth when he tried to assist Hall. Claude Lewis of the *Philadelphia Bulletin* was clubbed when he refused to give his notebook to a policeman. Jim Jones of *Newsweek* was kicked in the ribs and clubbed over the head while trying to show his press credentials. Robert Jackson of the *Chicago American* suffered the same

[25] Small, *op. cit.*, p. 214.

fate. Altogether the news media suffered some 70 injuries at the hands of the police, equally divided between the electronic and print media.

But scant attention was paid to them. Eric Sevareid summed up the dilemma:

> The explanation seems obvious. Over the years the pressure of public resentment against screaming militants, foul mouthed demonstrators, arsonists, and looters had built up in the national boiler. With Chicago it exploded. The feelings that millions of people released were formed long before Chicago. Enough was enough: the police *must* be right. Therefore, the reporting *must* be wrong.[26]

It was a sobering experience for the media. It was a disastrous week for the Democratic party and Hubert Humphrey, whose campaign fell apart fatally in Chicago. For the 1972 conventions, the Democrats prudently chose Miami Beach, the safe area which the Republicans had used in 1968; the Republicans chose the law-and-order area of San Diego.

MEDIA RESPONSES TO CRITICISM

Through all of this external criticism of the media, those within the profession were responding to pressures for improvement of the press and broadcasting. They also were creating some pressures of their own.

These responses took the forms of voluntary codes of conduct, development of professional organizations devoted to the highest purposes of journalism, encouragement of education for journalism, support of studies of the press, sponsorship of the concept of press councils, demands from younger professionals for "reporter power," support of public and educational broadcasting, and the taking of advantage of improvements in technology.

ASNE, NAB, AND CODES OF CONDUCT

The American Society of Newspaper Editors was organized in 1922, under the leadership of Casper S. Yost of the *St. Louis Globe-Democrat,* to fill a long-felt need. As the group's constitution pointed out, "Although the art of journalism has flourished in America for more than two hundred years, the editors of the greater American newspapers have not hitherto banded themselves together in association for the consideration of their common problems and the promotion of their professional ideals." State and regional newspaper associations had considered news and editorial problems, but the American Newspaper

[26] *Ibid.,* p. 216.

Publishers Association had virtually excluded all but business topics from its agendas.

Membership in the ASNE was limited to editors in chief, editorial page editors, and managing editors of dailies published in cities of more than 100,000 population, a figure soon reduced to 50,000. Limited numbers of editors of smaller dailies were admitted to membership in later years.

Early meetings of the society were enlivened by a bitter dispute over the power of the group to expel a member, Fred G. Bonfils of the *Denver Post*, who stood accused of blackmailing oil millionaire Harry Sinclair in connection with the Teapot Dome scandal. At one point a vote of expulsion was taken, but the action was rescinded and the Denver editor was permitted to resign. Later the ASNE clarified its power to expel a member for due cause, but the Bonfils incident made it clear that the group did not propose to serve as a policing organization. Willis J. Abbot of the *Christian Science Monitor* and Tom Wallace of the *Louisville Times* were leaders in the fight for a stern policy, but Yost and others held to a middle course.

A code of ethics, called the "Canons of Journalism," was presented to the first annual meeting in 1923. Chief author was H. J. Wright, founder of the *New York Globe*. Some of the key paragraphs read as follows:

> The right of a newspaper to attract and hold readers is restricted by nothing but considerations of public welfare. The use a newspaper makes of the share of public attention it gains serves to determine its sense of responsibility, which it shares with every member of its staff. A journalist who uses his power for any selfish or otherwise unworthy purpose is faithless to a high trust.
>
> Freedom of the press is to be guarded as a vital right of mankind. It is the unquestionable right to discuss whatever is not explicitly forbidden by law, including the wisdom of any restrictive statute.
>
> Freedom from all obligations except that of fidelity to the public interest is vital.
>
> Partisanship, in editorial comment which knowingly departs from the truth, does violence to the best spirit of American journalism; in the news columns it is subversive of a fundamental principle of the profession.

Annual meetings of the ASNE are held each April in Washington. Proceedings are reported in a series of books, dating from 1923, titled *Problems of Journalism*, which offer in their pages some significant discussions of professional matters.[27]

Codes of conduct for the broadcasting industry were developed by its trade association, the National Association of Broadcasters. The NAB was founded in 1923 during a skirmish between the radio station owners and

[27] The proceedings of the twenty-fifth annual ASNE meeting, in 1947, contain on pages 39–53 historical reminiscences of three early members, Grove Patterson of the *Toledo Blade*, Marvin H. Creager of the *Milwaukee Journal*, and Donald J. Sterling of the *Oregon Journal*.

ASCAP over fees the latter insisted be paid for broadcasting music of ASCAP members. Paul Klugh was first NAB managing director. The role of the trade association expanded to include relationships with advertising and then, increasingly, its relationships with the Federal Communications Commission.

The NAB Code of Ethics and the NAB Standards of Commercial Practice were adopted in March, 1929, as the first voluntarily-imposed regulations on broadcasters. More detailed documents, the NAB Radio Code and the NAB Television Code, were added. About half of all commercial radio and television stations subscribed to the codes in 1970. There were other major codes and statements, particularly those of the Radio-Television News Directors Association, and the programming standards of the networks and many individual stations.

Headquarters of the NAB are in Washington, with a large staff for administration, legal problems, station services, broadcast management, government affairs, public relations, and research. The NAB Code Authority staff hears complaints concerning violations by those subscribing to the codes. There are also review boards for the Television Code and Radio Code.

NCEW, APME, AND RTNDA

Editorial-page editors and editorial writers who wanted a smaller and more vigorous "working" organization than the 450-member ASNE formed the National Conference of Editorial Writers in 1947. The idea came from a group attending an American Press Institute session at Columbia University [28] and was promoted by Leslie Moore of the *Worcester Telegram* and *Gazette,* Ralph Coghlan of the *St. Louis Post-Dispatch,* John H. Cline of the *Washington Star,* Robert H. Estabrook of the *Washington Post,* and Forrest W. Seymour of the *Des Moines Register* and *Tribune,* among others. Annual sessions were held beginning in 1947, which featured small-group critique panels in which members appraised the editorial-page efforts of their colleagues. A quarterly magazine, the *Masthead,* and convention proceedings were published. A code of principles was adopted in 1949 "to stimulate the conscience and the quality of the American editorial page." [29]

Another important national group, the Associated Press Managing Editors Association, was formed in 1931 by news executives who found the annual meetings of the ANPA and the Associated Press too little concerned with improvement of the news columns' content. The organizers in this case included Oliver O. Kuhn of the *Washington Star,* Roy Roberts of the *Kansas City Star,* Sevellon Brown of the *Providence Journal* and *Bulletin,* W. C. Stouffer of the *Roanoke World-News,* and Roy Dunlap of the *St. Paul Pioneer Press* and *Dis-*

[28] The American Press Institute was founded in 1946 through the efforts of Sevellon Brown of the *Providence Journal* and *Bulletin.*

[29] The NCEW code of principles appears in *Editor & Publisher,* LXXXII (October 29, 1949), 7.

patch. The AP news report was analyzed and criticised orally in annual meetings until 1947 when a printed report was prepared by a Continuing Study Committee. Although the studies of the different portions of the Associated Press news report were penetrating enough to arouse replies from the AP management, they were made public as the *APME Red Book* beginning in 1948.[30] Setting the pattern for the Continuing Study reports were the first chairmen, William P. Steven of the *Minneapolis Tribune* and Lee Hills of the *Miami Herald.*

The equivalent newsmen's organization in broadcasting is the Radio-Television News Directors Association. It was founded in 1946 as the National Association of Radio News Directors. First leaders were John Hogan, WCSH, Portland, Maine; John Murphy, WCKY, Cincinnati; Sig Mickelson, WCCO, Minneapolis; Jack Shelley, WHO, Des Moines; and Edward Wallace, WTAM, Cleveland. Its publication is the *RTNDA Bulletin.* The group set broadcast news standards and worked closely with journalism schools.

OTHER PROFESSIONAL GROUPS

Other professional groups were concerned with varying aspects of journalistic problems: the American Newspaper Guild, with its *Guild Reporter;* the American Newspaper Publishers Association, representing dailies; the National Newspaper Association, representing weeklies and some smaller dailies; the Magazine Publishers Association; the National Association of Educational Broadcasters; the National Press Photographers Association; the United Press International editors; and many regional organizations. Some schools of journalism joined with newsmen in sponsoring various professional conferences dealing with journalistic problems. Awards for outstanding achievement were inaugurated by Sigma Delta Chi, the professional journalism society begun in 1909 at DePauw University and expanded to include both undergraduate and professional chapters and both men and women. Research about journalism was encouraged by annual awards of both Sigma Delta Chi and Kappa Tau Alpha, journalism scholastic society founded in 1910 at the University of Missouri. Theta Sigma Phi, women's journalism society founded in 1909 at the University of Washington, stimulated interest through its annual Matrix table gatherings and its scholarship awards.

EDUCATION FOR JOURNALISM BEGINS

The ties between campus and city room were strengthened greatly in the second quarter of the twentieth century. The famous cartoon showing a city editor asking a young hopeful, "And what, may I ask, is a school of journalism?"

[30] The *APME Red Book* for 1948 opens with a history of the organization and its Continuing Study activities to that time.

no longer held true by the 1950s. It was likely that the city editor by that time was a journalism school graduate himself—or at least a college graduate with an appreciation of the necessity for sound educational training for newspapermen.

Talk about education for journalism began seriously after the Civil War, but little action resulted until the turn of the century. General Robert E. Lee, president of Washington College (later Washington and Lee University), attempted to establish training in printing in 1869, but the program languished, as did another effort at Cornell University in 1875. Kansas State College instruction in printing dates from 1873, and courses in history and materials of journalism were given at the University of Missouri from 1878 to 1884. The first definitely organized curriculum in journalism was offered at the University of Pennsylvania from 1893 to 1901 by Joseph French Johnson, a former financial editor of the *Chicago Tribune*. The University of Illinois organized the first four-year curriculum in journalism in 1904 under the direction of Frank W. Scott. The first separate school of journalism, with newspaperman Walter Williams as dean, opened in 1908 at the University of Missouri.[31]

In this first period of journalism education, emphasis was placed upon establishment of technical courses. But journalism teachers, often getting their starts in English departments, had to win academic recognition as well as the confidence of the newspaper profession. Their most successful early leader in this regard was Willard G. Bleyer, who began his journalism teaching at the University of Wisconsin in 1904. Bleyer advocated integration of journalism education with the social sciences, and through his development of this concept and his own journalism history research, established Wisconsin as a center for graduate study by future journalism teachers. Other early leaders were Eric W. Allen of the University of Oregon, H. F. Harrington of Northwestern University, Leon N. Flint of the University of Kansas, Arthur L. Stone of Montana State University, J. W. Piercy of Indiana University, Merle H. Thorpe of the University of Washington, Everett W. Smith of Stanford University, and Talcott Williams and John W. Cunliffe of Columbia University, the first two men to head the Pulitzer School of Journalism, opened in 1912 with a two million dollar endowment from the *New York World* publisher.

JOURNALISM AS A SOCIAL INSTITUTION

The second phase of journalism education saw emphasis placed upon the study of journalism history and of the press as a social institution, as well as a widening of instruction to areas other than that of the daily and weekly

[31] See Albert A. Sutton, *Education for Journalism in the United States* (Evanston: Northwestern University Press, 1945), for an historical treatment. For a current picture, see Edwin Emery, Phillip H. Ault, and Warren K. Agee, *Introduction to Mass Communications* (New York: Dodd, Mead, 1970), chap. 19. An historical analysis of trends was made by Ralph D. Casey in *Journalism Quarterly*, XXI (March 1944), 55.

newspapers. Pioneer textbooks had been written by Bleyer, Harrington, James Melvin Lee of New York University, Grant M. Hyde of Wisconsin, and M. Lyle Spencer of Syracuse. In the early 1920s the books of Bleyer in journalism history and of Flint and Nelson Antrim Crawford of Kansas State College in newspaper ethics pointed the way toward integration of technical training with analysis of the social responsibilities of the journalist. Coming into importance were the American Association of Teachers of Journalism, founded in 1912, and the Association of Schools and Departments of Journalism, established in 1917. The latter group sought to give recognition to well-established journalism curricula and thereby stimulate improved instruction in the growing number of colleges and universities offering courses.

Other newspapermen than Pulitzer aided in the establishment of journalism schools. Second in size to the Pulitzer gift to Columbia University was the endowment fund provided in 1918 by William J. Murphy, publisher of the *Minneapolis Tribune*, for journalism education at the University of Minnesota. The fund's value by the 1970's was $800,000. The owners of the *Chicago Tribune* established the Medill School of Journalism at Northwestern University in 1921 and continued to assist the school financially in subsequent years. State press associations and individual newspapermen played parts in the establishment of other schools and departments of journalism.

The 1920s saw the founding of the *Journalism Quarterly*, devoted to research studies in the field of mass communications. It began as the *Journalism Bulletin*, issued in 1924 by the teachers' group, and edited by Lawrence W. Murphy of the University of Illinois. Frank Luther Mott of the University of Iowa (later dean at the University of Missouri) became *Journalism Quarterly's* editor in 1930, followed by Ralph D. Casey of the University of Minnesota in 1935, and Raymond B. Nixon of Emory University and Minnesota in 1945, and Edwin Emery of Minnesota in 1964.

JOURNALISM AS A SOCIAL SCIENCE

A third phase of journalism education was developing by the 1930s. Fuller integration of journalism education with the social sciences was the goal, and the leading schools and departments undertook research and teaching in the field of communications as a whole. Journalism students, it was recognized, should receive a broad liberal arts education, sound journalistic technical training, and an understanding of the social implications of their chosen profession. Northwestern University established a five-year plan for professional training in 1938; the Pulitzer School at Columbia had restricted its year's course to holder's of a bachelor's degree in 1935. Graduate level instruction was expanded at other institutions, along with research in mass communications. In 1944 the Minnesota School of Journalism set up a journalism research division, the first of its kind. Among early leaders in mass communications research were Chilton R. Bush of Stanford University, Ralph O. Nafziger of Minnesota (later at Wisconsin), Wilbur Schramm of Iowa (later at Illinois and Stanford), Paul F. Lazarsfeld of Columbia University's Bureau of Applied Social Research, and Douglas Waples of the University of Chicago.

MEDIA SUPPORT FOR EDUCATION

Closer ties between newspapermen and the schools were established during the 1930s. The idea of a joint committee which would include representatives of the principal newspaper associations and the schools and departments of journalism was suggested by Fred Fuller Shedd, editor of the *Philadelphia Bulletin* who had been instrumental in the founding of the department at Pennsylvania State College (later University). Journalism educators, led by Bleyer of Wisconsin, Allen of Oregon, and Frank L. Martin of Missouri, joined in the plan in 1931. The project lapsed during the depression years but was brought into full operation in 1939 through the efforts of Kenneth E. Olson of Northwestern University. The American Council on Education for Journalism was formed by journalism educators and five major newspaper organizations—the American Society of Newspaper Editors, the American Newspaper Publishers Association, the National Newspaper Association, the Inland Daily Press Association, and the Southern Newspaper Publishers Association. The National Association of Broadcasters, Magazine Publishers Association, Associated Business Press, and Public Relations Society later joined the council's membership. The ACEJ established an accrediting program and approved work in one or more phases of journalism at 40 schools and departments in the late 1940s. The number of accredited institutions increased to 60 by 1971.

In 1949 the American Association of Teachers of Journalism reorganized as the Association for Education in Journalism. Accepting coordinate roles within the AEJ structure were the American Association of Schools and Departments of Journalism (now composed of the accredited schools) and the American Society of Journalism School Administrators, founded in 1944 by heads of other schools. The ASJSA published the *Journalism Educator*.

Serving in the American Council on Education for Journalism for long periods of time were Olson of Northwestern, Casey of Minnesota, Mott of Missouri, Fred S. Siebert of Illinois (later Michigan State), John E. Stempel of Indiana, and Alfred A. Crowell of Maryland. Active in supervising the accrediting program were Earl F. English of Missouri, Norval Neil Luxon of North Carolina, Leslie G. Moeller of Iowa, Burton W. Marvin of Kansas, Quintus C. Wilson of Utah (later West Virginia), I. W. Cole and Baskett Mosse of Northwestern, DeWitt C. Reddick of Texas, and Frank Senger of Michigan State.

Journalism schools, by the 1970s, were thus well established in the fields of teaching, research, and service. They had close ties with the profession through short courses, consultative services, and, in some states, through joint operation of a field manager service for the state press association. Their scope of interests included daily and weekly newspapers, magazines, radio and television, photography, advertising, the graphic arts, industrial editing, public relations and information writing, journalism teaching, and research in mass communications. The concept of integrating journalism education with the social sciences was fully recognized by leaders in both the schools and the profession.

A million-dollar endowment left to Harvard University in 1936 by the widow of Lucius W. Nieman, founder of the *Milwaukee Journal,* was used for a different type of educational opportunity. The Nieman Foundation, beginning in 1937, annually selected a dozen highly-qualified working newspapermen for a year of study at Harvard as Nieman Fellows, on leave from their newspapers or press associations. Louis M. Lyons, first curator of the foundation, established a thoughtful quarterly magazine, *Nieman Reports,* in 1947. Dwight E. Sargent became curator in 1964. Nieman Fellows also produced two cooperative books, *Newsmen's Holiday* (1942) and *Your Newspaper* (1947), about newspaper problems. The year at Harvard was regarded generally by Nieman Fellows as a high-point experience, giving them an opportunity to broaden their education in selected fields.

EFFORTS TO IMPROVE: STUDIES OF THE PRESS

Other attempts to study the responsibilies and the character of the American press were made in the years after World War II. Magazine publisher Henry R. Luce financed an important private study by the Commission on Freedom of the Press. The commission was headed by Chancellor Robert M. Hutchins of the University of Chicago and was composed chiefly of social science professors outside the field of journalism. Its summary report, *A Free and Responsible Press* (1947), covered newspapers, radio, motion pictures, magazines, and books, and consisted of a general statement of principles. The commission itself conducted only a limited research program in the making of its report, but it sponsored the publication of a number of books, including Zechariah Chafee, Jr.'s *Government and Mass Communications,* William E. Hocking's *Freedom of the Press,* and Llewellyn White's *The American Radio.*

The presidential elections of 1948 and 1952 brought flurries of activity in the analysis of press behavior in relation to public questions. *Editor & Publisher,* trade journal for the daily newspapers, sponsored a meeting in March, 1949, of a panel on the press, composed of 10 newspapermen and educators. The panel suggested studies for press self-improvement but an ASNE committee appointed to consider the problem came to no specific conclusions. Before the 1956 election journalism educators and Sigma Delta Chi urged a major study of press election coverage, but a group of hesitant publishers and editors vetoed action. However, effective voices were raised within the profession, in analysis of press behavior. A partial list would include J. Russell Wiggins and Alan Barth, *Washington Post;* Herbert Brucker, *Hartford Courant;* Barry Bingham and Norman Isaacs, *Louisville Courier-Journal;* James B. Reston, *New York Times;* Erwin D. Canham *Christian Science Monitor;* columnists Marquis Childs and Thomas L. Stokes; and broadcasters Elmer Davis, Edward R. Murrow, and Fred W. Friendly.

EFFORTS TO IMPROVE: PRESS COUNCILS

The example of the successful British Press Council, established in 1953 to hear complaints against newspapers under rules carefully drawn to protect the rights of both editors and citizens, led to movements to create press councils in the United States. Norman Isaacs, as president of the American Society of Newspaper Editors, argued without success for a national council. Under the auspices of the American Newspaper Guild's Mellett Fund, others established local press councils to deal with specific small communities, in the late 1960s. One effort was made on the West Coast under the direction of William L. Rivers and his associates from Stanford University; another in Sparta and Cairo, Illinois, by Kenneth Starck and others from Southern Illinois University. A media-black council, to develop a better understanding between media executives and the black community, was directed by Lawrence Schneider of University of Washington for 19 months in Seattle. In 1971, a statewide press council was established in Minnesota through the efforts of the Minnesota Newspaper Association, the Newspaper Guild, Sigma Delta Chi, and various media leaders and public officials. The council membership was divided between representatives of the media and the public, under the chairmanship of a state supreme court judge. It set about attempting to define its goals, as the first state-level council.

EFFORTS TO IMPROVE: "REPORTER POWER"

The spirit of self-criticism which accompanied the widespread feeling of dissatisfaction with and dissent to the status quo in the 1960s led to a revival of the idea of reporters' councils proposed when the Guild was organizing in the 1930s. In 1971 Guild contracts in cities from Providence to Denver were carrying clauses calling for a committee of journalists to meet regularly with management. More often, "reporter power" groups sprang up informally in city rooms, as at the *Chicago Sun-Times* and *Minneapolis Tribune* in 1970, where young staffs met to seek improvements in their professional contributions. These groups were spurred by the founding of the *Chicago Journalism Review* in October, 1968, in the wake of disillusionment among young Chicago newsmen over management and public reaction to the role of the press in the riots at the time of the Democratic national convention. Edited by Ron Dorfman, the Chicago monthly afforded an aggressive criticism of the city's press and a forum for issues of press criticism and self-improvement. Predictably the newspaper managements reacted coolly toward such public criticism. By 1971 the *Review* was a 16-page, well-printed journal. Other less well established publications appeared in other cities, including St. Louis, Providence, Honolulu, Denver, Albuquerque, Cleveland, and New York. An *AP Review* was issued periodically, written by critical staff members. The movement reflected the desire of young professionally-trained journalists to make the most effective contribution to society and to help meet some of the urgent problems of the 1970s. They expected the media to reflect a similar sense of urgency.

EFFORTS TO IMPROVE: PUBLIC BROADCASTING

A long effort to establish public broadcasting in the United States at the level of other countries was given stability in 1967 by the Congress. The Corporation for Public Broadcasting was chartered that year to dispense funds for a unified system of national and local programming. Much of the programming was done by the well-established National Educational Television (NET). The country's 202 noncommercial and educational television stations were connected through the Public Broadcasting Service, which hopefully called itself "the fourth network." The future of public financing remained to be determined; over 17 years the Ford Foundation had given the stations some 200 million dollars, a level of spending that now needed to be transferred to other sources.

Public television's best-known success was "Sesame Street," which captured the imaginations of the moppets in 1969 and 1970 and brought about some reform in children's shows by the commercial networks, which substituted educational fare for violence part of the time. Its 1971 successor was "The Electric Company," for third to fifth graders. Kenneth Clark's series called "Civilisation" was another high-level success; so were "The Forsythe Saga," "The First Churchills," and "The Great American Dream Machine." There were such innovative programs as the production of an actual courtroom trial and "The Global Village, a shared electronic experience." Two educational stations pioneering in such efforts were WGBH, Boston, and KQED, San Francisco. NET had other staple programs such as another delightful children's hour, "Misteroger's Neighborhood," "NET Playhouse," and "NET Festival."

EFFORTS TO IMPROVE: PRINTING TECHNOLOGY

Criticism of newspapers' technical performance has taken two forms: lack of sufficient research about their product and audience and failure to keep pace in technological progress. Both criticisms are valid, but recent efforts to meet them should be recognized. Since the 1930s newspapermen—as well as magazine, broadcasting, and advertising men—have paid ever-increasing attention to audience and motivational research, readership and listenership studies, readability formulas, and design and layout. Some dailies have employed their own research directors.

In technological progress, the major result has been to produce a "cold type" revolution, involving the introduction of photography into the printing process. Such machines of the 1950s as the Fotosetter, Linofilm, and Photon produced words on film and transferred them directly to a printing plate. Widely used in advertisement composition, they proceeded to make further inroads on "hot metal" typesetting. Offset printing, based upon the age-old lithography process, avoids both typesetting and photoengraving by use of pasteups photographed onto flexible printing plates. The *Opelousas Daily World* in Louisiana, begun in 1939, was the first successful daily to print by offset. It was joined by 657 other dailies by 1971 and thousands of weeklies as offset proved more economical. The Phoenix *Arizona Journal,* founded in 1962 as a rival to the jointly-owned *Arizona Republic* and *Gazette,* was the first attempt at producing an offset daily in a metropolitan competitive situation. It died in 1964 but the *Oklahoma Journal* founded that year was still printing by offset in 1971 against two established rivals.

Use of perforated tape for automatic operation of improved typesetting machines—such as the Mergenthaler Blue Streak Comet and the Intertype Monarch—brought a doubling of production during the 1950s in the traditional "hot metal" process. Engraving processes also were improved. The Fairchild engraving machine, producing plastic printing plates simply and cheaply, was a boon to smaller publications beginning in the 1940s. But these were primarily improvements on the old processes, and new ones were at hand.

Newspapers, straining as the 1970s opened to make money-saving breakthroughs in technological processes, already were using computers to set type, to store factual information, and to sort out the day's news and abstract it at the central news desks of the press associations. Editors were attending seminars where they were shown how to change headlines with a light pencil, how to dummy newspapers by keyboard, and how plastic printing plates and electronic tube typesetting would affect production.

Improvements in digital facsimile newspaper page transmission systems, announced by the ANPA Research Institute, pointed the way toward unlimited satellite-plant printing of a publication at different points inside one country, or indeed, throughout the world. Truly national or international newspapers could emerge. Another predicted development, for printing out in the home through facsimile or electrostatic technique, seemed less likely to be in the newspaper's immediate future, for cost reasons if nothing else. Delivering newspapers on film for exposure on an electronic video device and subsequent print-out might be more likely as the video revolution progresses in the world of electronics.

Annotated Bibliography

Most of the important references are referred to in the text of this chapter. Discussions involving press criticism are to be found in the American Society of Newspaper Editors' *Problems of Journalism* series, in the Associated Press Managing Editors' *APME Red Book* series, and in the periodicals *Journalism Quarterly, Journal of Broadcasting, Columbia Journalism Review, Masthead, Nieman Reports, Grassroots Editor, Editor & Publisher, Broadcasting,* and *Guild Reporter*. Bibliographies for Chapters 19 and 20 should be consulted for earlier references to Hearst and Scripps.

Books

Agee, Warren K., ed., *The Press and the Public Interest*. Washington: Public Affairs Press, 1968. Collection of 18 William Allen White lectures at the University of Kansas by leading journalists.

Arnold, Edmund C., *Ink on Paper*. New York: Harper & Row, 1963. The story of printing, emphasizing latest technology.

Bagdikian, Ben H., *The Information Machines*. New York: Harper & Row, 1971. Based on report financed by the RAND Corporation dealing with news communication methods presently and for next three decades; panel of experts project probability of technological breakthroughs. Much data.

Blakely, Robert J., *The People's Instrument*. Washington: The Public Affairs Press, 1971. Philosophical view of role public television can play.

Blumberg, Nathan B., *One Party Press?* Lincoln: University of Nebraska Press, 1954. How 35 large dailies covered the 1952 campaign; news columns found to be essentially fair.

Brucker, Herbert, *Freedom of Information*. New York: Macmillan, 1949. Able defense of press by *Hartford Courant* editor.

Casey, Ralph D., ed., *The Press in Perspective*. Baton Rouge: Louisiana State University Press, 1963. Seventeen addresses in critical vein by leading journalists and writers, in Guild Lecture series at University of Minnesota.

Clark, Wesley C., ed., *Journalism Tomorrow*. Syracuse: Syracuse University Press, 1958. A symposium on trends in the mass media.

Commission on Freedom of the Press, *A Free and Responsible Press*. Chicago: University of Chicago Press, 1947. A penetrating summary.

Drewry, John E., ed., *Post Biographies of Famous Journalists.* Athens: University of Georgia Press, 1942. Contains articles about Hearst, Roy Howard, McCormick, and Eleanor Patterson.

Emery, Edwin, Phillip H. Ault, and Warren K. Agee, *Introduction to Mass Communications.* New York: Dodd, Mead, 1970. Current status of all mass media, research, journalism schools.

Emery, Michael C., and Ted Curtis Smythe, eds., *Readings in Mass Communication: Concepts and Issues in the Mass Media.* Dubuque, Iowa: Wm. C. Brown Company, 1972. Selection of 55 articles examining current changes and debates.

Ford, Edwin H., and Edwin Emery, eds., *Highlights in the History of the American Press.* Minneapolis: University of Minnesota Press, 1954. Contains articles about Hearst, Scripps-Howard, and McCormick.

Hulteng, John L., and Roy Paul Nelson, *The Fourth Estate.* New York: Harper & Row, 1971. An informal appraisal of the news and opinion media.

Levy, H. Phillip, *The Press Council: History, Procedure and Cases.* London: Macmillan, 1967. The British Press Council examined in detail 1953–67. For U. S. examples, see Kenneth Starck, "What Community Press Councils Talk About," *Journalism Quarterly,* XLVII (Spring 1970), 20; William B. Blankenburg, "Local Press Councils," *Columbia Journalism Review,* VIII (Spring 1969), 14; Lawrence Schneider, "A Media–Black Council: Seattle's 19-Month Experiment," *Journalism Quarterly,* XLVII (Autumn 1970), 439; and Rivers (below).

Lindstrom, Carl E., *The Fading American Newspaper.* New York: Doubleday, 1960. A strong critique of trends and methods by a 40-year newspaperman (*Hartford Times*).

Mott, Frank Luther, *The News in America.* Cambridge, Mass.: Harvard University Press, 1952. An excellent discussion of news-gathering and news-distribution and of sociopolitical responsibilities.

Mott, Frank Luther, and Ralph D. Casey, eds., *Interpretations of Journalism.* New York: Appleton-Century-Crofts, 1937. The most important historical collection of statements on press problems.

Report of the National Advisory Commission on Civil Disorders. New York: Bantam Books, 1968. Chapter 15 discusses the mass media.

Rivers, William L., William B. Blankenburg, Kenneth Starck, and Earl Reeves, *Backtalk: Press Councils in America.* San Francisco: Canfield Press, 1971. By men who operated several local press councils.

Rivers, William L., and Wilbur Schramm, *Responsibility in Mass Communication.* New York: Harper & Row, 1969. An examination of the social problem, also done by J. Edward Gerald in *The Social Responsibility of the Press* (Minneapolis: University of Minnesota Press, 1963) and by John Hohenberg in *The News Media* (New York: Holt, Rinehart & Winston, 1968).

Rivers, William L., Theodore Peterson, and Jay Jensen, *The Mass Media and Modern Society.* San Francisco: Rinehart Press, 1971. Relationships between media and government; social, economic, intellectual environments of the media.

Rowse, Arthur E., *Slanted News*. Boston: Beacon Press, 1957. Analysis of how 31 large dailies reported the "Nixon fund" episode in 1952.

Schramm, Wilbur, ed., *Communications in Modern Society*. Urbana: University of Illinois Press, 1948. Contains essays on press responsibility by Paul F. Lazarsfeld, Ralph D. Casey, and Robert J. Blakely.

Skornia, Harry J., and Jack W. Kitson, eds., *Problems and Controversies in Television and Radio*. Palo Alto, Calif.: Pacific Books, 1968. Basic readings for the 1960s.

Small, William, *To Kill A Messenger*. New York: Hastings House, 1970. A prize-winning study of "television news and the real world" by the CBS Washington news manager, excellent coverage of crises of the 1960s.

Swanberg, W. A., *Citizen Hearst*. New York: Scribner's, 1961. A highly readable, detailed biography.

Tebbel, John, *An American Dynasty*. New York: Doubleday, 1947. An analysis of the McCormick-Patterson publishing empire.

———, *The Life and Good Times of William Randolph Hearst*. New York: Dutton, 1952. Best single book about both Hearst and his publishing empire.

Waldrop, Frank C., *McCormick of Chicago*. Englewood Cliffs, N.J.: Prentice-Hall, 1966. Best biography of the *Chicago Tribune* publisher. See also Jerome E. Edwards, *The Foreign Policy of Col. McCormick's Tribune, 1929–1941* (Reno: University of Nevada Press, 1971), a carefully researched analysis.

Periodicals and Monographs

"Are the Media Ready for the Seventies?" A symposium with articles by Theodore H. White, Edwin Diamond, Nicholas Johnson, Alfred Balk, James McCartney, and Stephen Barnett. *Columbia Journalism Review*, VIII (Winter 1969–70). Reaction to criticism, particularly by Spiro T. Agnew, and to media problems.

Bartness, Garold L., "Hearst in Milwaukee," Ph.D. thesis, University of Minnesota, 1968. Study of *Wisconsin News*, 1918–39, "a real Hearst newspaper."

Bigman, Stanley K., "Public Reactions to the Death of a Daily," *Journalism Quarterly*, XXXII (Summer 1955), 267. Little public concern found after merger of *Washington Post* and *Times-Herald*.

Brod, Donald F., "Church, State, and Press: Twentieth Century Episodes in the United States," Ph.D. thesis, University of Minnesota, 1968. Examines newspaper coverage of Scopes trial, Vatican relations, 1928 and 1960 elections.

"The Chicago Tribune," *Fortune*, IX (May 1934), 101. Detailed study.

Columbia Journalism Review staff, "Campaign Coverage: An Appraisal of 1960—and Implications for 1964," *Columbia Journalism Review* (Fall 1961), 6. A 14-page report on 25 metropolitan areas.

Cope, Neil B., "A History of the *Memphis Commercial Appeal*," Ph.D. thesis, University of Missouri, 1969. Story of a leading Scripps-Howard paper.

Danielson, Wayne A., and John B. Adams, "Completeness of Press Coverage of the 1960 Campaign," *Journalism Quarterly,* XXXVIII (Autumn 1961), 441. A report on a sample of 90 dailies, based on completeness of coverage of 23 campaign events.

Diamond, Edwin, "The Coming Newsroom Revolution: 'Reporter Power' Takes Root," *Columbia Journalism Review,* IX (Summer 1970), 12. Reports on internal efforts to improve.

Ethridge, Mark, "Fateful Crisis of the Newspaper," *Nieman Reports,* XIV (October 1960), 14. By *Louisville Courier-Journal* publisher.

Flanery, James A., "Chicago Newspapers' Coverage of the City's Major Civil Disorders of 1968," Ph.D. thesis, Northwestern University, 1971. Violence by police minimized in stories.

Hausman, Linda Weiner, *Criticism of the Press in U.S. Periodicals, 1900–1939: An Annotated Bibliography. Journalism Monographs,* No. 4, August 1967. What the magazines said about newspapers.

Hutchison, Earl R., "Kennedy and the Press: the First Six Months," *Journalism Quarterly,* XXXVIII (Autumn 1961), 453.

"Journalism and the Kerner Report," a special section in *Columbia Journalism Review,* VII (Fall 1968), 42. An analysis of the report's chapter 15 on the news media.

Koehler, Mary A., "Facsimile Newspapers: Foolishness or Foresight?," *Journalism Quarterly,* XLVI (Spring 1969), 29. History of a disappointment.

Liebling, A. J., "Publisher," *New Yorker,* XVII (August 2–23, 1941). Critical profile of Roy W. Howard.

Lyons, Louis M., "A Glance Backward at the Press," *Nieman Reports,* XIII (January 1959), 7. Analysis of past 20 years.

Meyers, W. Cameron, "The Chicago Newspaper Hoax in the '36 Election Campaign," *Journalism Quarterly,* XXXVII (Summer 1960), 356. Criticism of *Chicago Tribune* by the biographer of *Chicago Times* editor Richard J. Finnegan (Ph.D. dissertation, Northwestern University, 1959, "Chicago's Mister Finnegan: A Gentleman of the Press").

Nixon, Raymond B., and Robert L. Jones, "The Content of Non-Competitive vs. Competitive Newspapers," *Journalism Quarterly,* XXXIII (Summer 1956), 299. No major differences were found.

"The Press and Chicago," a group of articles on the 1968 Democratic convention, by Jules Witcover; the metropolitan Chicago press and the *Chicago Journalism Review,* by Edwin Diamond; and the Chicago suburbs by Gene Gilmore and David Beal, in *Columbia Journalism Review,* VII (Fall 1968), 5.

Sinichak, Steven, "The Chicago Journalism Review," *Grassroots Editor,* XI (July–August 1970), 10. A review of the journal's first two years.

Stempel, Guido H., III, "The Prestige Press in Two Presidential Elections," *Journalism Quarterly,* XLII (Winter 1965), 15. Study of 15 leading papers' news coverage in 1960 and 1964.

———, "The Prestige Press Meets the Third-Party Challenge," *Journalism Quarterly,* XLVI (Winter 1969), 685. Coverage of 1968 campaign by 15 major dailies.

Taylor, Frank J., "The Incredible House That Hearst Built," *Saturday Evening Post,* CCXXXII (May 9, 1959), 38. Hearst's San Simeon estate becomes a California Historical Monument.

"All the News That's Fit to Print"

The New York Times

CITY EDITION

Weather: Chance of showers today, tonight. Partly sunny tomorrow. Temp. range: today 74-94; Wed. 72-91. Temp. Hum. Index yesterday 82. Full U.S. report on Page 94.

VOL. CXX....No. 41,431 © 1971 The New York Times Company —NEW YORK, THURSDAY, JULY 1, 1971— Higher newsstand price in air delivery cities 15 CENTS

SUPREME COURT, 6-3, UPHOLDS NEWSPAPERS ON PUBLICATION OF THE PENTAGON REPORT; TIMES RESUMES ITS SERIES, HALTED 15 DAYS

Nixon Says Turks Agree To Ban the Opium Poppy

By JOHN HERBERS

Special to The New York Times

WASHINGTON, June 30—President Nixon announced today that Turkey had agreed to eliminate within a year her production of opium poppies, which account for about two-thirds of the illegal heroin reaching the United States.

Mr. Nixon, in a brief announcement delivered in the White House press room, said that as a result of negotiations between the United States and Turkish Governments, Premier Nihat Erim had agreed to ban altogether the cultivation of opium poppies by June, 1972.

He said the joint announcement, made simultaneously in Washington and Ankara, "represents by far the most significant breakthrough that has been achieved in stopping the source of supply of heroin in our world-wide offensive against dangerous drugs."

Two weeks ago, Mr. Nixon sent a message to William J. Handley, the United States Ambassador in Turkey, saying that the time for talk had passed and the United States must have action by the Turkish Government in ending poppy cultivation.

Today, the President praised Premier Erim for "courageous, statesmanlike action" and said the United States would provide money and technical assistance in helping Turkish farmers shift to other crops.

Officials would not say how much American money would be involved, but the United States has made a $3-million commitment to Turkey on the heroin problem.

Secretary of State William P. Rogers, who helped work

Continued on Page 22, Column 1

PRESIDENT CALLS STEEL AND LABOR TO WHITE HOUSE

He Asks Both Sides to Meet With Him Tuesday Before Contract Talks Start

By PHILIP SHABECOFF

Special to The New York Times

WASHINGTON, June 30 — President Nixon has called negotiators of the steel companies and steelworkers union to meet with him next Tuesday before they sit down to begin contract negotiations, a White House spokesman announced today.

It will be the first time that the President will have met with labor and management in any industry prior to nationwide contract negotiations, according to Ronald L. Ziegler, the White House press secretary.

Discussion Issues Listed

Mr. Ziegler said that the President had called the meeting to discuss general economic developments and trends in the world steel markets.

Earlier today, the chairman of the Federal Reserve Board, Arthur F. Burns, told a Congressional committee that the "first priority" should be given to a new Government move to try to moderate price and wage increases and expressed his concern over the spread of "inflationary psychology" in this country.

The Administration has repeatedly warned that excessive increases in steel wages and prices would severely retard efforts to control inflation. Hints have been dropped that import quotas that protect domestic steel from foreign competition will be eased or lifted if prices go too high.

President Nixon has been in-

Pentagon Papers: Study Reports Kennedy Made 'Gamble' Into a 'Broad Commitment'

By HEDRICK SMITH

The Pentagon's study of the Vietnam war concludes that President John F. Kennedy transformed the "limited-risk gamble" of the Eisenhower Administration into a "broad commitment" to prevent Communist domination of South Vietnam.

Although Mr. Kennedy resisted pressures for putting American ground-combat units into South Vietnam, the Pentagon analysts say, he took a series of actions that significantly expanded the American military and political involvement in Vietnam but nonetheless left President Lyndon B. Johnson with as bad a situation as Mr. Kennedy inherited.

"The dilemma of the U.S. involvement dating from the Kennedy era," the Pentagon study observes, was to use "only limited means to achieve excessive ends."

Moreover, according to the study, prepared in 1967-68 by Government analysts, the Kennedy tactics deepened the American involvement in Vietnam piecemeal, with each step minimizing public recognition that the American role was growing.

The expansion of that role, over three decades, is traced in the 3,000 pages of the Pentagon's study, which is accompanied by 4,000 pages of documents on the Vietnam era. Previous articles in The Times's presentation of this material have recounted President Johnson's movement to war in 1964 and 1965.

President Kennedy made his first fresh commitments to Vietnam secretly. The Pentagon study discloses that in the spring of 1961 the President ordered 400 Special Forces troops and 100 other American military advisers sent to South Vietnam. No publicity was given to either move.

Small as the numbers seem in retrospect, the Pentagon study comments that even the first such expansion "signaled a willingness to go beyond the 685-man limit on the size of the U.S. [military] mission in Saigon, which, if it were done openly, would be the first formal breach of the Geneva agreement." Under the interpretation of that agreement in effect since 1956, the United States was limited to 685 military advisers in Vietnam. Washington, while it did not sign the accord, pledged not to undermine it.

On May 11, 1961, the day on which President Kennedy decided to send the Special Forces, he also ordered the start of a campaign of clandestine warfare against North Vietnam, to be conducted by South Vietnamese agents directed and trained by the Central Intelligence Agency and some American Special Forces troops. [See text, action memorandum, May 11, 1961, Page 3.]

The President's instructions, as quoted in the documents, were, "In North Vietnam . . . [to] form networks of resistance, covert bases and teams for

Continued on Page 6, Column 1

The Times today resumes its series of articles on the Pentagon's secret study of the Vietnam war. The study was obtained through the investigative reporting of Neil Sheehan, and the articles were researched and written over three months by Mr. Sheehan and other staff members. The fourth and fifth articles, both by Hedrick Smith, are published today and form an account of decisions in the Kennedy Administration.

Three pages of documentary material covering the Kennedy policy begin on Page 3, and documents on the 1963 coup begin on Page 9. A summary of the three earlier articles, covering the Johnson Administration, appears on Page 15.

BURGER DISSENTS

First Amendment Rule Held to Block Most Prior Restraints

Decision, concurring opinions, dissents start on Page 17.

By FRED P. GRAHAM

Special to The New York Times

WASHINGTON, June 30 — The Supreme Court freed The New York Times and The Washington Post today to resume immediate publication of articles based on the secret Pentagon papers on the origins of the Vietnam war.

By a vote of 6 to 3 the Court held that any attempt by the Government to block news articles prior to publication bears "a heavy burden of presumption against its constitutionality."

In a historic test of that principle — the first effort by the Government to enjoin publication on the ground of national security — the Court declared that "the Government has not met that burden."

The brief judgment was read to a hushed courtroom by Chief Justice Warren E. Burger at 2:30 P.M. at a special session called three hours before.

Old Tradition Observed

The Chief Justice was one of the three dissenters, along with Associate Justices Harry A. Blackmun and John M. Harlan, but because the decision was rendered in an unsigned opinion, the Chief Justice read it in court in accordance with a long-standing custom.

In New York, Arthur Ochs Sulzberger, president and publisher of The Times, was asked at a news conference whether he thought the motto of The Times—"All the News That's Fit to Print"—had been upheld. "I think it was very much upheld," he said.

The case had been expected to produce a landmark ruling on the circumstances under which prior restraint could be imposed upon the press, but because no opinion by a single Justice commanded the support of a majority, only the unsigned decision will serve as precedent.

Uncertainty Over Outcome

Because it came on the 15th day after The Times had been restrained from publishing further articles in its series mined from the 7,000 pages of material—the first such restraint in the name of "national security" in the history of the United States—there was some uncertainty whether the press had scored a strong victory or whether a precedent for some degree of restraint had been set.

Alexander M. Bickel, the Yale law professor who had argued for The Times in the case, said in a telephone interview that the ruling placed the press in a "stronger position." He maintained that no Federal District Judge would henceforth temporarily restrain a newspaper on the Justice Department's complaint that "this is what they have printed and we don't like it" and that a direct threat of irreparable harm would have to be alleged.

However, the United States Solicitor General, Erwin N. Griswold, turned to another lawyer shortly after the Justices filed from the courtroom

Continued on Page 15, Column 1

Soviet Starts an Inquiry Into 3 Astronauts' Deaths

By BERNARD GWERTZMAN

Special to The New York Times

MOSCOW, June 30—The Soviet authorities appointed a special commission tonight to investigate the deaths of their three astronauts who perished this morning when their Soyuz 11 craft was returning to earth after the longest manned space flight in history.

News of the astronauts' deaths shocked many Soviet people. And Western specialists predicted that their deaths would retard development of the Salyut space station program. The three astronauts had spent more than three weeks working and exercising aboard the Salyut craft, described as the world's first space laboratory.

[...]ican officials said the Soviet space disaster had probably been caused by a failure in the oxygen supply. They also said the accident should not delay United States space flights. Articles on Page 30.]

Tonight, the Soviet people seemed caught up in the human aspects of the disaster and the mystery of what caused the deaths of Lieut. Col. Georgi T. Dobrovolsky, the flight commander; Vladislav N. Volkov, the flight engineer, and Viktor I. Patsayev, the test engineer.

Were their deaths caused by the weakened state of their bodies after nearly 24 days of weightlessness? Were they

U.S. and Diem's Overthrow: Step by Step

The Pentagon's secret study of the Vietnam war discloses that President Kennedy knew and approved of plans for the military coup d'état that overthrew President Ngo Dinh Diem in 1963.

"Our complicity in his overthrow heightened our responsibilities and our commitment" in Vietnam, the study finds.

In August and October of 1963, the narrative recounts, the United States gave its support to a cabal of army generals bent on removing the controversial leader, whose rise to power Mr. Kennedy had backed in speeches in the middle nineteen-fifties and who had been the anchor of American policy in Vietnam for nine years.

[...] coup, one of the most dramatic [...]es in the history of the American [...]ement in Vietnam, was a water[...] As the Pentagon study observes, [...] a time when Washington—with [...]em regime gone—could have re[...]ered its entire commitment to Vietnam and decided to disengage. [...]east two Administration officials [...]ated disengagement but, according [...] Pentagon study, it "was never seriously considered a policy alternative because of the assumption that an independent, non-Communist SVN was too important a strategic interest to abandon."

The effect, according to this account, was that the United States, discovering after the coup that the war against the Vietcong had been going much worse than officials previously thought, felt compelled to do more—rather than less—for Saigon. By supporting the anti-Diem coup, the analyst asserts, "the U.S. inadvertently deepened its involvement. The inadvertence is the key factor."

According to the Pentagon account of the 1963 events in Saigon, Washington did not originate the anti-Diem coup, nor did American forces intervene in any way, even to try to prevent the assassinations of Mr. Diem and his brother Ngo Dinh Nhu, who, as the chief Diem political adviser, had accumulated immense power. Popular discontent with the Diem regime focused on Mr. Nhu and his wife.

But for weeks—and with the White House informed every step of the way—the American mission in Saigon maintained secret contacts with the plotting generals through one of the Central Intelligence Agency's most experienced and versatile operatives, an Indochina veteran, Lieut. Col. Lucien Conein. The colonel, who is now in retirement, first landed in Vietnam in 1944 by parachute for the Office of Strategic Services, the wartime forerunner of the C.I.A.

So trusted by the Vietnamese generals was Colonel Conein that he was in their midst at Vietnamese General Staff headquarters as they launched the coup. Indeed, on Oct. 25, a week earlier, in a cable to McGeorge Bundy, the President's special assistant for national security, Ambassador Lodge had occasion to describe Colonel Conein of the C.I.A.—referring to the agency, in code terminology, as C.A.S.—as the indispensable man.

"C.A.S. has been punctilious in carrying out my instructions. I have personally approved each meeting between General Don [one of three main plotters] and Conein who has carried out my

Continued on Page 12, Column 1

[...]STATES RATIFY [...]LL VOTE AT 18

Conferees Cut Military Pay Rise As Authority to Draft Runs Out

By DAVID E. ROSENBAUM

Special to The New York Times

[WAS]HINGTON, June 30 — [...]on Administration won [...]r budgetary victory to[...] the House-Senate con[...] on the draft extension [...]

[...] conference agreement [ap]peared to represent a [...] for supporters of an [vol]unteer Army, who had [...] larger pay increases [th]ose cleared by the con[...]

[...] conferees accepted a fig[...] military pay and allow[...] that was more than $900-[...] below what both the [...] and House had ap[...] The raises voted by the [...]s would cost about [...]ion in the fiscal year [...] tomorrow and would [...] effect Oct. 1.

[...] figure approved by the [...]ce was still $800-mil[...] above what President [...]ought in his budget, but [Ho]use and Senate had [...] increases of about $1.7-[...] over the budget.

[N]ixon Administration had [...] that so large an increase [...] force severe and pos[...] dangerous reductions in [...] parts of the defense [...] Government's basic se[...] to draft men into the military expires at midnight tonight.

The conferees completed action on all provisions of the draft bill today except the Senate-passed amendment that calls for the withdrawal of United States troops from Indochina within nine months if prisoners of war are first

Continued on Page 29, Column 1

False Advertising Laid to H&R Block

By JOHN D. MORRIS

Special to The New York Times

WASHINGTON, June 30—H & R Block, Inc., which says it prepares income tax returns for eight million American annually, was accused by the Federal Trade Commission today of false advertising and illegally using confidential information supplied by customers.

The commission published similar but seperate citations against H & R Block and the Beneficial Corporation, which offers income tax services on a smaller scale through a subsidiary, the Beneficial Management Corporation. In radio and television advertisements, the name

Continued on Page 57, Column 2

ACTION BY GRAVEL VEXES SENATORS

But No Disciplinary Action Against Him Is Expected

By JOHN W. FINNEY

Special to The New York Times

WASHINGTON, June 30—Many Senators privately expressed dismay, shock and chagrin today at Senator Mike Gravel's release of parts of the Pentagon's secret study of the Vietnam war. But it appeared that no disciplinary action would be taken against the Alaska Democrat.

Last night Senator Gravel tried to read the documents to the Senate in an all-night speech and, when he was blocked for lack of a quorum, proceeded to call an impromptu meeting of his Senate Public Works subcommittee. He read from the study for three and one-half hours, with his voice sometimes breaking into sobs and tears occasionally rolling down his face.

His action incurred the displeasure of many of his colleagues, who felt that it reflected on the dignity and composure of the Senate. But in the clublike atmosphere of the Senate, there was a widespread reluctance, extending down from the leadership, to take any formal disciplinary

Continued on Page 16, Column 2

NEWS INDEX

Broadcasting

THE BUSINESSWEEKLY OF TELEVISION AND RADIO

July 19, 1971 Vol 81 No 3

Staggers headed off at the pass

Broadcasting wins apparent First Amendment victory as congressional leadership avoids showdown on CBS citation

A landmark case over broadcasters' rights under freedom of the press vs. Congress's right to legislative inquiry was sidelined last Tuesday (July 13) as the House voted 226-to-181 to recommit to the Commerce Committee a proposed contempt citation against CBS and its president, Frank Stanton. Winnerwise, it was CBS's day. Confrontationwise, it was less a bang than a whimper.

The Commerce Committee, under Chairman Harley O. Staggers (D-W. Va.), had voted two weeks earlier to recommend the citation to the House, based on the network's refusal to supply subpoenaed outtakes and other materials from *The Selling of the Pentagon* documentary (BROADCASTING, July 5).

It was the first time in memory that the House had refused to back a committee on a contempt citation. And it was the first time that a committee had tried to cite a broadcaster who, on First Amendment grounds, refused to comply with an order.

In a statement issued after the vote, Dr. Stanton said: "We are very pleased by the decisive House vote to recommit the proposed contempt citation to the Commerce Committee. As responsible journalists, we shall continue to do our best to report on public events in a fair and objective manner."

According to House Speaker Carl Albert (D-Okla.), the issue will remain privileged for the remainder of the 92d Congress. That is, it could be brought to the floor again. However, Chairman Staggers said that would not happen.

Dramatis personnae *in last week's House of Representatives drama concerning the threatened citation of CBS for contempt of Congress: onstage—Harley O. Staggers (D-W. Va.) (below), whose hope it was to force the contempt citation to a successful vote, and (picture at lower right) House Speaker*

Carl Albert (D-Okla.) (r), whose corridor conference here with Parliamentarian Lewis Deschler was one of several steps along the road to maneuvering the matter back to the Commerce Committee and apparent oblivion; offstage—Frank Stanton (top right), president of CBS, who with his news department and an important part of the future of broadcast journalism, was the object of it all.

The *New York Times* reports its victory; inset, Frank Stanton and CBS avoid censure.

31

A Crisis of Credibility

The press was to serve the governed, not the governors.
Justice Hugo L. Black

The credibility gap as an institution was painfully apparent in American life by 1970. There were gaps between President and people, President and press, press and people. To these were added gaps between old and young, black and white, intellectuals and silent majority.

One reason for the difficulties of the Presidents was the growth of a cult of disbelief. At his height, Senator Joseph McCarthy had half of the American people believing in him, which meant they believed their government was a combination of Communism and corruption—even the Army harbored treason, McCarthy said. The senator was unable to bring down war hero Eisenhower, who was less affected than were his successors by the credibility gap. John F. Kennedy inherited a Cuban crisis; news was managed and many disbelieved their government's explanations. The Warren Commission hearings proved how many Americans doubted the authoritative accounts of President Kennedy's assassination; some men made their living encouraging other versions. Senator Barry Goldwater could offer rueful testimony about the depth of disbelief he encountered in his disastrous 1964 presidential campaign. Senator Eugene McCarthy found in the winter of 1967–68 that President Johnson's public support was a hollow shell; his "children's crusade" and the reality of the Tet attacks in Vietnam shattered belief in the U.S. war effort there. President Nixon found that despite his persuasive television style he could get only a minority to believe in 1971 that he really intended to withdraw American forces from Vietnam. The credibility gap which had been attributed to the Lyndon Johnson personality persisted for Richard Nixon, partially for the same reason but also because it was a part of the American way of life.

Another reason for the difficulties of both Presidents and press was the steady diet of bad news which characterized the 1950s and 1960s, despite many years of prosperity and notable accomplishments. Americans did not want to hear they had to settle for a stalemate in Korea—"Communism, Corruption, and Korea" was a 1952 election slogan to explain the bad news, not the hard facts of a capable Chinese army opponent. A recession in the late 1950s; antagonistic receptions abroad of Vice President Nixon and even President Eisenhower; a challenge to American prestige by Charles de Gaulle; all these were unwanted subjects. They piled up in the 1960s: the Bay of Pigs, the Berlin Wall, the assassination of a President, the Vietnam war, racial riots in big cities, college campus riots, the assassinations of Senator Kennedy and Martin Luther King, the collapse of the promise of victory in Vietnam, long hair, sex and four-letter words in the open, drug addiction, Kent State, My Lai, and a near-depression. Traditionally a President pays politically for adverse news, particularly of an economic nature. But as William Small of CBS put it in a book title, the public seemed willing like the kings of old "to kill a messenger"—in this case, CBS and other networks, the *Washington Post* and other liberal newspapers, even the objectivity-seeking press associations that brought them the bad news.

The situation was ripe for demagogues. There was much bad news people did not want to believe, much reality they did not want to have exist. One group did not believe the President; another did not believe the press. And both President and press encouraged people not to believe the other. It was easy to argue, then, that reporting bad news was unpatriotic; to say that those who made bad news—as at Kent State or in the streets of Chicago—were un-American and deserving of their fates. The only solace defenders of freedom had was that such credibility gaps had existed before in history and that with determination this one also could be overcome.

In seeking to understand the development of this era of the credibility gap, one starts with the record of the relationships between the Presidents and the press, examines the overt attacks upon the press, estimates the extent of the gap between the press and the people, and also records the frictions between government and press which resulted in legislation and court decisions involving freedom of the press.

THE PRESIDENTS AND THE PRESS: FDR

No President had more effective relationships with the press than did Franklin D. Roosevelt. He met the White House correspondents informally, often in his office. He was at ease, communicative, gay or serious as the news might dictate. Like all Presidents he came to be irritated by his critics in the press, who were assigned dunce caps or iron crosses. But he met the press 998 times during his 12 years in office, an average of 83 times a year. He was known for his Fireside Chats on the radio, but in his first term he gave only eight; the same four years he communicated with the American people and won 46 states in the next election by holding 340 press conferences, most of which made solid news. FDR had capable press secretaries, of whom Steve Early was the most effective, and built a tradition of Presidential press conferences which would be hard to follow. To look ahead, President Truman dropped the average number of press conferences yearly from 83 to 42; the yearly averages later were Eisenhower 24, Kennedy 22, Johnson 25, Nixon 11 (first two years).

TRUMAN AND THE PRESS

The relationship of the President and the news media underwent drastic changes during the tenure of Harry S Truman. The Truman style, the complexity of events after World War II and the growth of the news-gathering apparatus—particularly broadcasting—during and after the war contributed to the metamorphosis.

While Truman and the newsmen around him enjoyed a cordial personal relationship—they generally liked each other—professionally they remained sharp adversaries throughout his 93 months in office. As president, he held 324 news conferences, averaging three to four a month. The president's abrupt and sometimes unpredictable comments at these sessions often appeared strangely contradictory to a period dominated by the realities of atomic energy and cold war politics.

If reporters relished the Truman news conferences for the possibility of an unexpected and sensational utterance, they came to realize also that the structure of the conferences was changing to give the administration more control over them. Truman began meeting with press secretary Charles G. Ross and others of his staff for preconference briefings and greatly increased the use of carefully prepared opening statements to which he would refer a questioning reporter when he chose not to elaborate on a matter.[1]

In the spring of 1950, the location of presidential news conferences was moved from the intimate atmosphere of the oval room of the White House to a 230-seat room in the Executive Office Building. While the change was brought about because of the growth in the number of Washington correspondents, its effect was to further formalize the presidential press conference. The move also ushered in the use of microphones and, by 1951, presidential authorization to use excerpts of recordings for broadcast news programs. As news conferences thereby became increasingly public during the Truman years, the President was obliged to exercise greater control over them, to come to them better prepared, and to respond during them with greater care. Truman's tendency

[1] Elmer E. Cornwell, Jr., *Presidential Leadership of Public Opinion* (Bloomington: Indiana University Press, 1965), p. 170.

to speak his mind, or "shoot from the hip," as some critics termed it, was not obscured entirely by the new overlay of safeguards. Salty, sometimes embarrassing slips continued despite preparation to prevent them. But the groundwork of control was laid for his successors.

Apart from the news conference, another effort at control of information created a furor among publishers and newsmen during the Korean War. Convinced that magazines and newspapers were guilty of leaking most of America's military secrets, Truman ordered all government agencies handling military information to classify it at their discretion and to restrict its use by the media. Despite a wave of criticism, the order stood.[2]

Truman responded to harsh and continuing criticism of himself and his administration by the news media with strong denunciations of the media. Particularly after his stunning election in 1948 in the face of overwhelming editorial opposition and daily news stories predicting his defeat did the President lash out at "the kept press and the paid radio." He attacked what he called the "confusion of fact with mere speculation by which readers and listeners were undoubtedly misguided and intentionally deceived."

Only when he prepared to leave office in January, 1953, did some media opponents relent. Some even saluted him affectionately. It was an unexpected pleasure for the retiring Truman who later recalled that "some editors ate crow and left the feathers on."[3]

EISENHOWER AND HAGERTY

President Eisenhower was an American hero when he assumed office, and a five-star general who maintained a reserve and a dignity in his relations with others, even though they called him Ike. He enjoyed the services of a talented press secretary, James C. Hagerty, who held office longer than any of his predecessors and who tauntingly was called by some of the newsmen he bested in professional duels, "the best Republican president who was never elected." This was unfair to both Hagerty and Eisenhower, for Hagerty prided himself on knowing how best to use the press to serve his boss, and Eisenhower exercised a basic command of the responsibilities of his office.

Eisenhower continued the large formal news conferences which had begun with Truman, having 250 correspondents at his first session and 309 at his final one, eight years and 190 press conferences later. He permitted direct quotations and taping for later television release, new gains for the press corps. Hagerty, however, had to check the material. Eisenhower made many slips of the tongue, thought faster than he talked, and skipped parts of sentences

[2] James E. Pollard, *The Presidents and the Press: Truman to Johnson* (Washington: Public Affairs Press, 1964), p. 45.

[3] See Randall L. Murray, "Harry S Truman and Press Opinion, 1945–53," Ph.D. thesis, University of Minnesota, 1972.

so that press conference transcripts had to be reworded to be intelligible. A penetrating personal question might bring a display of the famed Eisenhower controlled anger. But generally he was not too concerned with the press. He told one conference he went over the important sections of the Sunday papers that reviewed world events, and studied them carefully—"but the kind of things you talk of, cartoons and unfriendly quips, I just can't be bothered with." [4] The President was a little sensitive; Hagerty had been mobbed at the Tokyo airport, forcing cancellation of a Presidential visit, and the U-2 incident was about to bring about a debacle at the Paris Summit Conference.

KENNEDY AND TELEVISION

John F. Kennedy introduced live televising and broadcasting of Presidential press conferences, an innovation with mixed blessings. The White House correspondents found that their home offices heard and saw the presidential responses long before the news stories clattered into their news desks. The mystique of the White House press conference, in the oval room, was gone. A skillful President could use the correspondents as foils or actors, and a few correspondents became actors by choice. On the positive side, millions of Americans could see the press conferences for themselves, live at the moment or digested in the evening news. Most of Kennedy's press conferences were in the afternoons in time for Walter Cronkite and Huntley-Brinkley to feature their highlights. Kennedy handled the star role far better than any of the Presidents of his period; he was young, charming, stylish, and as disarmingly humorous or severely grave as circumstances dictated. In short, he put on a good show.

Behind this Kennedy the public knew was another figure: a President anxious for his administration's image, who gave frequent individual interviews and had correspondents as personal friends, who read a half-dozen leading papers daily and resented their criticisms so much he once banned the *Herald Tribune* temporarily. His press secretary, Pierre Salinger, took a hard line with the correspondents, as did Pentagon spokesman Arthur Sylvester, who uttered the ill-fated comment about "the government's inherent right to lie" (to save itself when faced with nuclear disaster). The press was upset about the clouded information given it about the Bay of Pigs; the administration was insisting there was a crisis between the United States and the Soviet Union so severe as to require self-control and censorship on the part of the press. The government unified its news sources, sought to manage the contacts between officials and the press, and was accused of seeking to manage the news itself. Publication of the Pentagon Papers in 1971 proved a far deeper U.S. involvement in Vietnam affairs by 1963 than the Kennedy administration

[4] *New York Herald Tribune,* May 12, 1960, as quoted in Pollard, *op. cit.*

ever acknowledged, including a share of responsibility for the assassination of President Diem, and showed the Saigon press corps had been essentially correct in vainly protesting the deepening U.S. involvement in a "quagmire." While public opinion supported the President, there was enough doubt to indicate the credibility gap had begun, even before Dallas.

LYNDON JOHNSON AND THE GAP

No President worked harder in trying to make himself available to the White House "regulars" than Lyndon Johnson. He did not care to undertake immediately the televised conferences so expertly run by Kennedy, so he called the two dozen or so regular correspondents into his office, plied them with food, and answered their questions. He took them with him to the LBJ ranch and held barbeques; he argued with them on walks in the White House rose garden; he swam with them in the pool; he even subjected himself to 135 regular press conferences, a slightly better average than Eisenhower or Kennedy. In 1964 Johnson was elected President in his own right with a record popular majority and the support of all but a dozen of the country's major newspapers. The next year his Great Society legislation consolidated the gains the country wanted to make in civil rights, aid to education, medical aid, and other social gains. Yet, for all this, the credibility gap grew as the war in Vietnam grew, until in March, 1968, the President was to use live television to announce his retirement and the start of peace negotiations.

The war in Vietnam was not the war the President and the Pentagon planned. But as Chapter 24 suggests, the newspaper and television reporters in Vietnam found not only the administration, but many of the public and sometimes their own home offices, disbelieving their stories that the war was not going as Secretary McNamara had blueprinted it. If Vice President Humphrey, an established liberal, asserted that democracy could be developed in South Vietnam, who were reporters to assert that the Diem regime and its successors were corrupt and incapable of their assignment (an estimate concurred in by Vice President Ky of South Vietnam in 1971 when he was opposing President Thieu for the highest office)? If General Westmoreland outlined plans for the clearing out of Viet Cong, who were reporters to suggest he might not find it possible?

Not until the tragedy of Tet did the extent of the quagmire in Vietnam become clear to either the President or the public. And by that time Senator Eugene McCarthy's antiwar movement was sweeping Johnson out of the presidential race. But combinations of public disbelief, disillusionment, and distaste for violence led to a stalemate in public opinion. The assassination of Senator Robert Kennedy tore the heart out of the Democratic political campaign, and opened the way for a fatal compromise in the welter of Chicago's street demonstrations and riots. The public, already recoiling from rioting and

Paul Conrad, © 1971 *Los Angeles Times,* with permission of the Register and Tribune Syndicate.

Cartoonist Paul Conrad expresses American disillusionment with the Vietnam War.

racial violence in the cities, rejected violence on its campuses and in its politics. It also rejected the "free speech" movement with its four-letter words. The Republicans, with Richard Nixon and Spiro T. Agnew, were a calm refuge for just enough voters to give them victory.

NIXON AND AGNEW

Richard Nixon had spent years studying his mistakes in the 1960 presidential race with its "great debates" on television, and in his 1962 failure in California which ended with an ill-tempered attack on the press. In 1968 he used television skillfully, appearing before controlled audiences with filtered questions rather than giving set speeches. He made a point then, and as President, of knowing the names of both friends and tormenters in the press. But he held standard press conferences only rarely, at one-half the rate of recent presidents. Instead he relied upon a technique Johnson had developed when he had dramatic news from the war to announce: request prime time network television for a brief appearance. In their first 18 months in office, Eisenhower did this three times, Kennedy four, Johnson seven. Nixon doubled the quota, to appear 14 times on maximum audience screens, according to a count made by Frank Stanton, CBS president who was under siege by Vice President Agnew. Nixon and his press adviser, Herbert Klein, arranged regional press conferences, at first for friendly newspapers only, but later for all those in the non-Establishment parts of the country.

Nixon's press conferences, averaging 11 a year his first two years in office, dropped off to seven for the first nine months of 1971. A committee of the Associated Press Managing Editors declared Nixon "does not fully accept the traditional role of the press as the judge of what is news and as an interpreter and watchdog for the public" and at most of his press conferences "has found a way to raise questions on the credibility of the press." These judgments were by executives of three conservative newspapers which had supported Nixon, the *Christian Science Monitor, Washington Star,* and *Philadelphia Bulletin.*

Agnew aroused a stormy debate late in 1969 when, in speeches at Des Moines and later, he declared that the networks and newspapers with multiple media holdings (favorite target: *Washington Post, Newsweek,* Mrs. Graham's TV stations) exercised such powerful influence over public opinion that they should vigorously endeavor to be impartial and fair in reporting and commenting on national affairs. Specifically, Agnew criticised network managements for using commentators with a preponderant "Eastern Establishment bias" and for failing to provide a "wall of separation" between news and comment. Also dominated by the "Establishment," he said, were such antiwar papers as the *Washington Post* and *New York Times* (others equally well staffed from similar social backgrounds, but conservative in tone, went unmentioned). Agnew made specific references to the dependence of broadcasting stations upon licenses, and no amount of disclaimer by him or the administration that he was threatening a censorship could calm those who assumed they would be the victims. It was undisputably true that never before had such a high federal official made such direct attacks upon those reporting and commenting on the news. Their defenders contended that the mere making of the statements by Agnew inhibited the freedom of the broadcasters suffering tongue lashes. A research study comparing random samples of newscast items reporting administration activities for one week periods in 1969 and 1970 bore out the contention that the Agnew-generated criticism had significantly affected the newscasts in the direction of "safe" handling.[5]

The Vice President went into eclipse after the Republican setbacks in the 1970 congressional elections, but CBS gave him another opening when it screened "The Selling of the Pentagon" early in 1971. Agnew attacked, and brought up again charges against the CBS show, "Hunger in America," even though the latter had been cleared by the Federal Communications Commission and had been publicly praised by President Nixon. A congressional committee attempted to subpoena all records and unused film CBS had filed in making the Pentagon film; Klein said he was opposed to such intimidation of the network; Stanton said he would go to jail rather than submit to the demand. Stanton did not have to go to jail, even though Rep. Harley O. Staggers, West Virginia Democrat, obtained the support of the Commerce Committee in requesting the House of Representatives to try CBS and Stanton

[5] Dennis T. Lowry, "Agnew and the Network TV News: A Before/After Content Analysis," *Journalism Quarterly,* XLVIII (Summer 1971), 205.

IN CAMBODIA—

IN KENT, OHIO—National guardsmen advance during clash in which four students were killed

Los Angeles Times

VOL. LXXXIX SEVEN PARTS—PART ONE TUESDAY MORNING, MAY 5, 1970 110 PAGES DAILY 10c

Troops Kill Four Students in Antiwar Riot at Ohio College

DEATH ON THE CAMPUS—

Large S. Viet-U.S. Force Opens Third Cambodia Offensive

WAR SITUATION AT A GLANCE

Guards' Gunfire Wounds 11 at Kent University

ALABAMA ELECTION

Wallace's Drive for Presidency at Stake Today

Hopes Rise for Teacher Strike Settlement by End of the Week

New U.S. Air Raids Halted Over North, but Option Remains

My Lai Disclosure Wins Pulitzer Prize

Index to The Times

TV Academy Announces Nominations for Emmys

Supreme Court Upholds Church Tax Exemptions

Witchcraft Bubbles Again —and Finds New Followers

THE WEATHER

The *Los Angeles Times* draws a parallel between Cambodia and Kent State, in 1970.

on charges of contempt of Congress. This the House refused to do, voting 226 to 181 in July, 1971, to return the request to the committee. The refusal, while encouraging to free press advocates, was more politically shocking (such turndowns by the House have been rare) than legally reassuring. A pending case involving the use of the subpoena power against newspaper reporter Earl Caldwell of the *New York Times,* to seek to compel him to testify about his news sources in a Black Panther prosecution, promised to be more definitive.

Out of it all CBS emerged with a reputation for liberal devil-may-care provocations, starting with its coverage of the Chicago convention in 1968 and encompassing its prize-winning coverage of the Vietnam war. Such an image was not deserved, and in this respect Agnew had scored a political plus. If he had a credibility gap, so now did CBS.

FREEDOM OF THE PRESS: LANDMARK LEGAL DECISIONS

Significant episodes involving freedom of the press, and the right of the people to know, became a part of the record beginning in the 1930s, along with the furor over comparatively transient matters. There were landmark cases in which newspapers appealed to the courts to uphold the historic right to freedom of expression without prior restraint and without punitive action by government. And there were revitalized efforts by newsmen to keep channels of information open by insisting upon their right of access to news.

An obscure Minnesota publisher provided a case in which the Supreme Court, in 1931 for the first time, applied the freedom of the press guarantees of the First Amendment against the States through the due process clause of the Fourteenth Amendment. The case of *Near v. Minnesota* thus served as a turning point in the battle to hold states as strictly accountable for invasions of liberty as the federal government. What was known as the Minnesota "gag law" of 1925, permitting the suppression of malicious and scandalous publications, had been applied by a court to the *Saturday Press* of Minneapolis in order to stop its smear attacks upon public officials. Calling the law a threat to all newspapers, no matter how unworthy the *Saturday Press* might be, chairman Robert R. McCormick of the ANPA committee on freedom of the press retained counsel to carry the case to the Supreme Court. There Chief Justice Hughes, speaking for the majority in a 5–4 decision, held the Minnesota law unconstitutional because it permitted prior restraint upon publication.[6] Suppression, the court said, was a greater danger than an irresponsible attack upon public officials, who in any event had proper recourse through libel action.

Huey Long, the Louisiana political boss, provided the next major case

[6] *Near v. Minnesota ex rel. Olson,* 283 U.S. 697 (1931).

in 1934. The Long machine obtained passage by the state legislature of a special 2 per cent tax on the gross advertising income of Louisiana papers with a circulation of 20,000 or more. Twelve of the 13 papers affected were opposed to the Long regime. They appealed to the courts, again with the assistance of Colonel McCormick's ANPA committee, and in 1936 the Supreme Court found the punitive tax unconstitutional. Justice Sutherland wrote a unanimous decision, holding that Long's bill was "a deliberate and calculated device . . . to limit the circulation of information to which the public is entitled by virtue of the constitutional guarantees."[7] A Baltimore city tax on advertising was voided in 1958.

Newspapers, however, often have had to appeal to higher courts for relief after they have been held in contempt by lower courts. A landmark case in giving newspapers more latitude in commenting upon judges' activities was decided by the Supreme Court in 1941. This was the case of *Bridges v. California,* with which a companion case involving the *Los Angeles Times* was affiliated. Harry Bridges, the longshoreman labor leader, had been cited for contempt because newspapers had published the text of a telegram he had sent the Labor Department threatening to call a strike if a court decision went against him. The *Times* was cited for publishing editorials deemed threatening by a court. The California Bar Association asked the Supreme Court to declare the two contempt citations unconstitutional. This the court did by applying the sanctions of the First Amendment against the state court under the due process clause of the Fourteenth Amendment, and by utilizing the clear and present danger test first applied in the Schenck case.[8] Newspapers henceforth in theory could comment upon a court action not yet closed, without fear of punishment, unless a judge could hold that press comment created so great and immediate a danger that his court could not continue to function. But state courts continued to resist this trend in thinking, and hard battles were fought by the *Miami Herald* and the *Corpus Christi Caller-Times* in 1946 and 1947 to avoid the penalties of contempt charges.[9]

THE PENTAGON PAPERS CASE

The United States government attempted in June, 1971, to impose prior restraint upon American newspapers. And for 15 days it successfully stopped the presses of two of the country's most influential dailies. For those 15 days the clock was turned back to the time of Henry VIII, who in 1534 imposed licensing upon the English press. Prior restraint ended in England in 1694 and in the colonies in 1721, to be temporarily revived exactly 250 years later.

[7] *Grosjean v. American Press Co.,* 297 U.S. 233 (1936).
[8] *Bridges v. California,* 314 U.S. 252 (1941).
[9] *Pennekamp v. Florida,* 328 U.S. 331 (1946); *Craig v. Harney,* 331 U.S. 367 (1947).

That the Supreme Court came to the rescue of press freedom and the First Amendment guarantee on June 30, by vacating its own temporary stay order of June 25 and earlier lower court orders, afforded some reassurance. But the fact that President Nixon had even instructed Attorney General John Mitchell to go to court to seek imposition of a prior restraint upon publication did great damage to the concept of liberty of the press so painstakingly developed through historical evolution and legal decisions since 1694. In the history of the Republic, no other President had so acted.

In the judgment of legal scholars, the Pentagon Papers case left little legal residue and will be remembered far longer for its political implications than for its legal stature.[10] In that respect it perhaps paralleled the Zenger case of 1735; there was no guarantee after Zenger's acquittal that another editor would not be charged in another government effort to muzzle the press—but it never seemed politically feasible for colonial administrators to try in the same manner. Possibly the next President faced with circumstances similar to those involved in the Pentagon Papers case will seek a postpublication criminal prosecution, if one seems warranted, rather than attempt again to impose prior restraint upon publication. In that sense, the case is worth detailed examination.

Sometime in March, 1971, the *New York Times* came into possession of a 47-volume study entitled "History of the U.S. Decision-Making Process on Vietnam Policy," compiled for the Pentagon at the order of former Secretary McNamara. Many copies of the study were circulating. Its contents were historical and nonmilitary in character, but highly explosive in terms of political and diplomatic interest. All documents were classified "Top Secret" under a 1953 executive order. *Times* correspondent Neil Sheehan, who had represented UPI in the original Saigon press corps and who in 1971 covered the Pentagon, was a key figure in the development of the Pentagon Papers series for the paper. Managing editor Abe Rosenthal assigned several leading *Times* staffers to weeks of painstaking work in a hotel room hideway. June 13 the *Times* printed the first installment.

Attorney General Mitchell asked the *Times* to stop the series; it refused. The government then went to a federal district judge just appointed by President Nixon and serving the first day on his new bench, with its unprecedented prior restraint order request. Judge Murray Gurfein issued a temporary restraining order June 15, forcing the *Times* to stop after the third installment. June 19 Judge Gurfein refused to grant a permanent restraining order, saying the government had failed to prove its case other than to plead a "general framework of embarrassment." But he let the temporary order stand. June 23 the U.S. Court of Appeals in New York reversed Gurfein's decision. In the meantime, the *Washington Post* had started a series of its own, and had won

[10] See Don R. Pember, "The 'Pentagon Papers' Decision: More Questions Than Answers," *Journalism Quarterly*, XLVIII (Autumn 1971), 403, whose conclusions were endorsed by other mass communications law scholars.

a clear-cut victory when Judge Gerhard A. Gesell ruled the government could not "impose a prior restraint on essentially historical data." The U.S. Court of Appeals for the District of Columbia upheld Gesell and the two cases reached the U.S. Supreme Court June 25. There, with Justices Black, Douglas, Brennan, and Marshall dissenting, the court voted 5–4 to hear testimony and continue the temporary order of prior restraint.

At this point the case collapsed as a legal landmark. The newspaper attorneys, shaken by the adverse 5–4 vote of the Supreme Court continuing a temporary prior restraint, refused to gamble on a plea that the First Amendment prohibited prior restraint under any and all circumstances. Instead, they preferred to win the immediate case on the grounds the government could not prove that national security was involved. This they did, on a 6–3 *per curiam* decision.[11] It was based on *Near* v. *Minnesota* and two more recent press freedom decisions. There were then nine individual decisions, with Justices Black and Douglas arguing that freedom of the press is absolute; Justices Brennan and Stewart declaring the government had not proved its case; Justice Marshall rejecting the contention the President had inherent power to declare a document nonpublishable in the national interest; Justice White joining the majority but inviting a criminal prosecution of the newspapermen; Chief Justice Burger and Justice Blackmun objecting to the haste shown in the case and requesting an exhaustive review of the documents; and Justice Harlan indicating he believed the President should have the power to foreclose publication of any document whose disclosure would in his judgment be harmful.

The anonymous writer of the *per curiam* decision did cite *Near* v. *Minnesota*, the landmark case of 1931 defending liberty of the press and extending the protection of the First Amendment against acts of Congress to include a ban on state action. Also cited were two quotations:

> Any system of prior restraints of expression comes to this court bearing a heavy presumption against its constitutional validity.[12]
>
> The Government thus carries a heavy burden of showing justification for the enforcement of such a restraint.[13]

The first of these quotations indicates strongly that the Supreme Court's majority stood by the landmark case of *Near* v. *Minnesota* and its basic concepts. The second reminds society that there is a loophole in the legal concept of liberty of the press—a loophole which at least Justice Harlan would have allowed the President to use unrestrainedly.

[11] *New York Times Company v. United States* and *United States v. The Washington Post Company*, 403 U.S. 713 (1971). The government soon admitted its error by selling 43 volumes of the Pentagon Papers from its Printing Office to all comers.

[12] *Bantam Books, Inc. v. Sullivan*, 372 U.S. 58 (1963).

[13] *Organization for a Better Austin v. Keefe*, 402 U.S. 215 (1971).

Chief Justice Hughes, in giving the 5–4 verdict in the 1931 *Near* case, quoted from Blackstone on prior restraint and postpublication punishment:

> The liberty of the press is indeed essential to the nature of a free state; but this consists in laying no *previous* restraints upon publications, and not in freedom from censure for criminal matter when published. Every freeman has an undoubted right to lay what sentiments he pleases before the public; to forbid this, is to destroy the freedom of the press; but if he publishes what is improper, mischievous or illegal, he must take the consequence of his own temerity.

Hughes went on to include a dicta, or observation, which weakened the case for absolute protection against prior restraint:

> The objection has also been made that the principle as to immunity from previous restraint is stated too broadly, if every such restraint is deemed to be prohibited. That is undoubtedly true; the protection even as to previous restraint is not absolutely unlimited. But the limitation has been recognized only in exceptional cases.

The Chief Justice then cited examples of military secrets, overthrow of the government, and obscenity as areas where prior restraint might apply. But he drew the line, in the following passage, on the kind of situation the Pentagon Papers case represented—disclosure of activities of public officers deemed by many citizens to be censurable:

> The exceptional nature of its limitations places in a strong light the general conception that liberty of the press, historically considered and taken up in the Federal Constitution, has meant, principally although not exclusively, immunity from previous restraints or censorship. The conception of the liberty of the press in this country had broadened with the exigencies of the colonial period and with the efforts to secure freedom from oppressive administration. That liberty was especially cherished for the immunity it afforded from previous restraint of the publication of censure of public officers and charges of official misconduct.

The question of postpublication punishment was raised in the Pentagon Papers case by Justice White and also by Chief Justice Burger, who chastised the *Times* and *Post* for not turning over the papers to the government. Here the freedom of speech cases would apply, involving the concept of "clear and present danger" evolved by Justices Holmes and Brandeis and the opposing "balancing" theory. The landmark cases include four stemming from the World War I period "red scare" and one from the post-World War II anti-Communist period.

Justice Holmes first advanced the theory that punishment be limited to political expression which constituted a clear and present danger to the governmental action at issue in the 1919 case of Schenck, a Socialist who issued a pamphlet urging resistance to the draft. Even so, Holmes concurred in upholding the conviction under the Espionage Act. In the case of Abrams, who issued pamphlets opposing a U.S. expeditionary force being sent to the Soviet Union in 1918, Holmes dissented. In this dissent, Holmes talked of the "competition of the market" of ideas.[14] In the 1925 case of Gitlow, convicted under a New York state criminal anarchy law of issuing Socialist manifestoes, the majority advanced the theory of balancing by the courts of the competing private and public interests represented in First Amendment cases. Brandeis and Holmes dissented.[15] In 1927, while concurring in the conviction of Anita Whitney under California law outlawing the Communist party, Brandeis brilliantly restated the clear and present danger theory.[16] Cold comfort, perhaps, to the convicted, that progressive legal theory was being advanced. In the 1951 case of Dennis, convicted of conspiracy under the Smith Act, the majority used the clear and present danger argument to convict Communist party members, citing the world tensions of 1948.[17] Whatever the outcomes, such postpublication trials were preferable to prior restraint mandates, for Schenck and his successors at least had their say.

A NEW "PUBLIC LAW OF LIBEL"

The historic law providing citizens recourse against defamation of character in the press always provided for fair comment on, and criticism of, those who were in the public eye when they became involved in the news. But in the 1960s the Supreme Court so clarified and extended the media's protections against libel that a new theory emerged, called the public law of libel. Under this theory, public officials and public figures cannot recover for libel unless they can prove deliberate lying or extreme recklessness in publishing without ascertaining truth.[18]

The landmark case was *New York Times Co. v. Sullivan,* decided in 1964. The *Times* had published an advertisement in 1960 protesting police actions in Montgomery, Alabama, against followers of the Rev. Martin Luther King, Jr. Sullivan, a police commissioner, sued for libel and was awarded $500,000

[14] *Schenck v. United States,* 249 U.S. 47 (1919); *Abrams v. United States,* 250 U.S. 616 (1919).

[15] *Gitlow v. People of State of New York,* 268 U.S. 652 (1925).

[16] *Whitney v. California,* 274 U.S. 357 (1927).

[17] *Dennis v. United States,* 341 U.S. 494 (1951). A subsequent decision of 1957 in the Yates case narrowed the grounds for Smith Act convictions and freed five defendants.

[18] See Donald M. Gillmor and Jerome A. Barron, *Mass Communication Law: Cases and Comment* (St. Paul: West Publishing Company, 1969), 250 ff.

damages in a state court. Reversing the judgment, the Supreme Court held that errors contained in the advertisement were not malicious and that the First Amendment protects "uninhibited, robust and wide-open" debate of public issues without any test of truth.[19]

In 1967 the Supreme Court extended this theory to cover "public figures" as well as "public officials," but drew a line concerning recklessness in not following professional precautions in checking truth when time permits. The Court reversed a $500,000 judgment which a right-wing spokesman, General Edwin A. Walker, had obtained against the Associated Press, ruling that Walker was a public figure subject to criticism. But it upheld a $460,000 judgment given University of Georgia football coach Wallace Butts for a story in the *Saturday Evening Post* accusing Butts of throwing games. The court said handling of the story "involved highly unreasonable conduct constituting an extreme departure from the standards of investigation and reporting ordinarily adhered to by responsible publishers." [20]

In *Time Inc. v. Hill* in 1967, the Court restricted the theory of right of privacy in favor of the theory of public law of libel by ruling newsworthy persons may not seek damages for invasion of privacy without proving deliberately false publication.[21] And in 1971, the Supreme Court which had "buried the common law crime of seditious libel" in *Sullivan,* extended its "actual malice" requirement from public officials and public persons to include even private individuals who have been projected into the public interest area. The case, *Rosenbloom v. Metromedia,* involved a broadcaster's references to a book dealer's "obscene" literature.[22]

OBSCENITY AND CENSORSHIP

The Post Office Department, with its power to exclude publications from the mails under certain conditions, also has at times been a threat to freedom of the press. Over the years, court decisions, administrative actions, and the sweeping use of the postmaster's power during World War I to throw Socialist publications out of the mails, built up a spirit of censorship in the Post Office. Matters came to a head in 1943 when the Postmaster General proposed to withdraw use of the second-class mailing rate from *Esquire* magazine. The second-class rate, it was contended, was a privilege, which the government could withdraw if the publication using it was not making a "special contribution to the public welfare." The Post Office thought *Esquire* was not worthy of the use of the second-class rate. The magazine's publishers, who were faced with paying a half-million-dollars a year additional in postal charges, carried

[19] *New York Times Co. v. Sullivan,* 376 U.S. 245 (1964).
[20] *Curtis Publishing Co. v. Butts* and *Associated Press v. Walker,* 388 U.S. 130 (1967).
[21] *Time Inc. v. Hill,* 385 U.S. 374 (1967).
[22] *Rosenbloom v. Metromedia,* 403 U.S. 29 (1971).

the case to the Supreme Court. There *Esquire* was upheld, with Justice Douglas commenting: "But to withdraw the second-class rate from this publication today because its contents seemed to one official not good for the public would sanction withdrawal of the second-class rate tomorrow from another periodical whose social or economic views seemed harmful to another official." [23] The decision put the Post Office Department back into its normal role of excluding publications for reasons of obscenity.

It was not an easy task to determine what was obscene, however, and society's standards on that subject were to change dramatically in the 1960s and 1970s, as they affected newspapers, magazines, books, and films. This was particularly true in the areas of four-letter words and nudity. But the Supreme Court was slow to find clear-cut guides. A landmark case came in 1957 with *Roth v. United States.* Roth, who sold distasteful material, had been convicted under the federal obscenity statute. The court upheld his conviction but set a new standard for testing obscenity: "Whether to the average person, applying contemporary community standards, the dominant theme of the material taken as a whole appeals to prurient interests." [24] To this the court in later decisions added a test of "redeeming social importance"; if this were present, the law need not apply. Under this interpretation, *Fanny Hill* was cleared. But Ralph Ginzburg, publisher of *Eros,* was not. The court ruled he had flaunted this test and had exploited erotic materials solely on prurient appeal.[25] How to define these terms remained a puzzle.

Those who are the faithful champions of freedom recognize that arbitrary action against the weak and the obscure, against the nonconformist and the radical, against the foolish and the crafty, usually leads to later arbitrary action against others. Freedom of the press, save when publication constitutes a legally determined clear and present danger to society, cannot be denied in one case without jeopardizing the constitutional guarantees of all.[26]

ECONOMIC THREATS TO FREEDOM

Freedom of the press can of course be jeopardized by a newspaper publisher. This was found true by the Supreme Court in the case of the *Lorain Journal,* an Ohio daily. When a radio station was established in the nearby town of Elyria in 1948, the *Journal's* management refused to carry the advertising of any merchant who also bought time on the radio station. The radio station obtained an injunction against the newspaper, under the antitrust laws, which the *Journal* insisted was unconstitutional. But the Supreme Court held

[23] *Hannegan v. Esquire,* 327 U.S. 146 (1946).
[24] *Roth v. United States,* 354 U.S. 476 (1957).
[25] *Ginzburg v. United States,* 383 U.S. 463 (1966).
[26] This thesis is examined exhaustively in J. Edward Gerald, *The Press and the Constitution.*

that the First Amendment was not intended to protect monopolistic practices which would destroy a competing medium and in a unanimous decision forced the *Journal* to recant.[27]

This was a clear-cut case, involving the use of boycott to destroy a competitor. Less clear-cut was the government's subsequent contention that the selling of advertising in jointly owned morning and evening papers under a unit rate plan also constituted an illegal action. A complaint brought by the *New Orleans Item* against the jointly owned *Times-Picayune* and *States* reached the Supreme Court in 1953. The court held, in a 5–4 decision, that the *Times-Picayune* and *States* were not violating the antitrust laws, but the decision was limited to the New Orleans situation alone.[28] The *Item* sold out to its rivals in 1958.

The government's next case was stronger. In 1955 it obtained a jury conviction of the *Kansas City Star* and its advertising manager on charges of monopolizing dissemination of news and advertising in the Kansas City area. The *Star*, together with its morning edition, the *Times*, and its broadcasting stations, WDAF and WDAF-TV, accounted for 85 per cent of mass media advertising income in the metropolitan area. The government charged that forced and tied-in sales of advertising and of newspaper subscriptions had brought about the death of the competing *Journal-Post* in 1942. The Supreme Court declined to review the case in 1957, and the *Star* agreed to end its combination sales and to sell the two stations, which in both instances had been pioneering efforts.[29] The *Wichita Eagle's* advertising and circulation price policies for morning, evening, and Sunday editions were brought under regulation in a 1959 antitrust suit, but the action did not save the rival *Beacon* from being forced to sell out in 1960.

FREE PRESS, FAIR TRIAL

The weighing of the rights of a free press and its readers against the rights of an accused to a fair trial became a major problem of the 1960s. In this case, the courts clearly had their way, and in the end the press generally agreed that the placing of restrictions upon reporters, photographers, and broadcasters was warranted—provided that they stemmed from cooperative agreements and not from judicial fiat.

Early action centered about the presence of photographers in the courtroom. The American Society of Newspaper Editors, the National Press Photographers Association, and the National Association of Broadcasters waged a battle through the 1950s to gain access to courtrooms for newspaper and tele-

27 *Lorain Journal v. United States,* 342 U.S. 143 (1951).

28 *Times-Picayune Publishing Co. v. United States,* 345 U.S. 594 (1953).

29 *Kansas City Star Co. v. United States; Emil A. Sees v. United States* (8th Circuit) 240 Fed. 2d 643 (1957).

vision photographers. Their argument that the photographers need not be interrupting the trials had merit, for pictures could be made without noise or light. But lawyers said the publicity stemming from photographs served to frighten witnesses and accused persons, affected juries, and offended the judicial feeling. In 1959 the American Bar Association did agree to review its Canon 35 regulating such activity in the courtroom. But no action resulted and admission of cameras remained a local decision of a judge.

Other events meanwhile vastly broadened the "free press, fair trial" debate. The assassination of President Kennedy and the haphazard conditions surrounding the killing of the accused by Jack Ruby in a press-filled area brought a plea for reform from the Warren Commission. When a Texas judge permitted television cameras into the trial of financier Billy Sol Estes, the Supreme Court reversed his conviction.[30] That 1965 decision was followed by one in 1966 ruling that Dr. Sam Sheppard had been deprived of a fair trial in Cleveland on a charge of murdering his wife because the trial judge failed to protect him from massive prejudicial "trial by newspaper" before and during his prosecution.[31]

The Reardon Report of the American Bar Association came out of the debate. Issued in October, 1966, by a ten-man committee of lawyers and judges headed by Justice Paul C. Reardon of Massachusetts, the report favored putting the responsibility on judges to curtail pretrial publicity generated either by the prosecution or the defense. The commission recommended the withholding of such information as the prior criminal record of the accused, existence of a confession, names of prospective witnesses, speculation on a possible plea, and interviews or photographs obtained without the consent of the accused. The American Bar Association adopted the Reardon Report in 1968, leaving the spelling out of specific provisions to negotiations with media representatives. By the fall of 1969 the press-bar committees of the Bar and the ASNE had found common ground for the imposition of the "fair trial" provisions without endangering the "free press." The media, in major trials of the late 1960s and early 1970s, resorted to using artists to make sketches of courtroom scenes for both print and television use, thus reverting to the artists' skills of the late nineteenth century in catching the drama of an event.

THE RIGHT OF ACCESS

The battles for freedom to print and freedom to criticise, carried on in the courtrooms, were important ones. But just as important were the fights put up for the right to have access to the news—for the right to publish news is worthless if the sources of information have been dried up.

[30] *Estes v. State of Texas,* 381 U.S. 532 (1965).
[31] *Sheppard v. Maxwell,* 384 U.S. 333 (1966).

Freedom of information campaigns were carried on beginning in the late 1940s by the American Society of Newspaper Editors, the Associated Press Managing Editors Association, the Radio-Television News Directors Association, and Sigma Delta Chi, professional journalism society. Through their efforts, and those of others, all but five states had some sort of laws requiring open public records and open meetings for conduct of public business, by 1970. Leaders of the fight included James S. Pope, *Lousiville Courier-Journal;* J. R. Wiggins, *Washington Post;* V. M. Newton, Jr., *Tampa Tribune;* and Harold L. Cross, ASNE legal counsel.

Creation of the House Subcommittee on Government Information in 1955, headed by Congressman John E. Moss of California, brought a campaign against secrecy at the federal level. Aided by the newsmen's groups, the Moss committee won revision of the 1789 "housekeeping statute" in 1958 to stop its use in denying access to records. It also won some ground in opposing the claim of executive privilege by the President and his subordinates, and reported success in 95 of 173 cases exposing undue federal censorship of information during 1958–60. Controversy between the Kennedy administration and the press flared up during the Cuban crisis and gave impetus to an effort to adopt the Freedom of Information bill, which was passed and signed by President Johnson on July 4, 1966. It provided that after one year, a citizen could go to court if a federal official arbitrarily withheld information of a public transaction other than in the areas specifically exempted under the law. These areas were nine in number including the all-important "national defense or foreign policy" one. Nevertheless, Representative Moss and others said a victory had been scored. The effect was as much to aid businessmen seeking information in federal offices as to aid newsmen.

The concept of "fairness," involving right of access to the broadcast media by persons or ideas, has already been discussed in Chapter 26. This countertheory to the right of access to the news, seeking legal protection for right of access to the media, was further advanced by law professor Jerome A. Barron in a 1967 *Harvard Law Review* article advocating access to the press as a new First Amendment right.[32] Media spokesmen, while agreeing efforts should be made to open more time and white space to individuals, minority groups, unpopular ideas, and simply nonconsensus thinking, quail at the idea of compulsory acceptance of everything offered a station, newspaper, or magazine.

Whatever the merits of such extensions of the principle of right of access, the most pressing problem in 1971 remained simple access to the facts about the affairs of government. The Pentagon Papers case illuminated the long-criticised federal custom of stamping millions of documents with "restricted" or "secret" labels. When newsmen were enabled to dig into some of those papers they found proof that President Johnson's war planners of 1964 in Washington were agreeing on a program for widespread aerial bombing of

[32] Gillmor and Barron, *op. cit.*, p. 117.

North Vietnam (to begin several months later in 1965 depending on circumstances of acceptance of such escalation by the public) on the very day the President was reprimanding White House reporters covering him on his Texas ranch for suggesting the war might be expanded. The reprimand demeaning the integrity of the press was public; the planning for escalation of the war was stamped "secret."

The great importance of a period of "crisis of credibility" is that people learn anew the lesson that all freedoms are dependent upon freedom of speech and press. These are never secure, never certain, always capable of being lost. In 1971 the United States government tried to deny its people the right to read a report prepared by their own government about a war in which they have fought and died. The rights of a citizen are only as strong as his will to defend them, and his willingness to defend those who bring him news and opinion with no other interest than his own. From James Franklin the printer to Edward R. Murrow the broadcaster, men have so tried.

Annotated Bibliography

Books

Associated Press, *Triumph and Tragedy: The Story of the Kennedys.* New York: William Morrow, 1968. Assassinations of JFK and RFK. See also United Press International, *Assassination: Robert F. Kennedy* (New York: Cowles, 1968).

Clark, David G., and Earl R. Hutchison, eds., *Mass Media and the Law: Freedom and Restraint.* New York: Wiley-Interscience, 1970. Good collection of essays in major areas of concern.

Cornwell, Elmer E., Jr., *Presidential Leadership of Public Opinion.* Bloomington: Indiana University Press, 1965. The press conference from Theodore Roosevelt to John Kennedy.

Cross, Harold L., *The People's Right to Know.* New York: Columbia University Press, 1953. Scholarly, detailed study of problems of access to news.

Devol, Kenneth S., ed., *Mass Media and the Supreme Court: The Legacy of the Warren Years.* New York: Hastings House, 1971. Presents 48 major cases, with commentaries and special notes, dealing with First Amendment questions concerning mass media.

Farrar, Ronald T., *The Reluctant Servant: The Story of Charles G. Ross.* Columbia: University of Missouri Press, 1969. Ross was a longtime *St. Louis Post-Dispatch* star before serving as President Truman's press secretary, 1945–50. A prize-winning biography.

Gerald, J. Edward, *The Press and the Constitution.* Minneapolis: University of Minnesota Press, 1948. The best source for freedom of the press cases, 1931–47.

Gillmor, Donald M., *Free Press and Fair Trial.* Washington: Public Affairs Press, 1966. Scholarly survey and analysis of critical cases, best of the literature. See also John Lofton, *Justice and the Press* (Boston: Beacon Press, 1966).

Hachten, William A., ed., *The Supreme Court on Freedom of the Press: Decisions and Dissents.* Ames: Iowa State University Press, 1968. The main historical story, with commentaries.

Hofstadter, Richard, *Anti-intellectualism in American Life.* New York: Knopf, 1963. A Pulitzer Prize-winning study of the anti-intellectual climate of the 1950s, with historical antecedents.

Nelson, Harold L., *Libel in News of Congressional Investigating Committees.* Minneapolis: University of Minnesota Press, 1961. Scholarly study of problems faced in reporting attacks on individuals.

The Pentagon Papers. New York: Bantam, 1971. Publication in paperback of the decisions and documents, edited by the *New York Times.*

Pollard, James E., *The Presidents and the Press: Truman to Johnson.* Washington: Public Affairs Press, 1964. Continues his earlier study.

Reston, James B., *The Artillery of the Press.* New York: Harper & Row, 1967. Essays discussing press influence on foreign policy.

Siebert, Fred S., Theodore Peterson, and Wilbur Schramm, *Four Theories of the Press.* Urbana: University of Illinois Press, 1956. Philosophical discussions of concepts of press freedom.

Small, William, *To Kill a Messenger.* New York: Hastings House, 1970. A prize-winning study by a CBS executive of television's troubles in the 1960s.

United Press International, *Four Days: The Historical Record of the Death of President Kennedy.* New York: Simon & Schuster, 1964. An *American Heritage* volume, includes journalistic coverage. See also The Associated Press, *The Torch Is Passed* (New York: The Associated Press, 1964).

White, Theodore H., *The Making of the President—1960. —1964. —1968.* New York: Atheneum, 1961, 1965, 1969. White covered three campaigns and their journalistic developments; most exciting was in 1960.

Wiggins, James Russell, *Freedom or Secrecy.* New York: Oxford University Press, 1964. A summation of access-to-news problems by an ASNE leader, the executive editor of the *Washington Post.*

Periodicals and Monographs

"The Assassination," a 30-page symposium on the events of November 22, 1963, in Dallas, in *Columbia Journalism Review,* II (Winter 1964), 6. Includes excerpts by leading correspondents.

Barth, Alan, "Freedom from Contempt," *Nieman Reports,* III (April 1949), 11. A study of the contempt cases of the 1940s.

Blanchard, Robert O., "The Freedom of Information Act—Disappointment and Hope," *Columbia Journalism Review,* VI (Fall 1967), 16; "A Watchdog in Decline," *Columbia Journalism Review,* V (Summer 1966), 17 (on the Moss Committee). The access to information crusade in the 1960s.

Cornwell, Elmer E., Jr., "The Johnson Press Relations Style," *Journalism Quarterly,* XLIII (Spring 1966), 3. The press got much attention from LBJ.

Cross, Harold L., "The Myth of 'Executive Privilege,'" *ASNE Bulletin,* No. 411 (August 1, 1958), 7. A documented attack.

Diamond, Edwin, "How the White House Keeps Its Eye on the Network News Shows," *New York,* IV (May 10, 1971), 45. President Nixon has television monitors, 7 a.m. to midnight.

"The First Amendment on Trial," a special issue containing 13 articles on the Pentagon Papers case, *Columbia Journalism Review,* X (September–October 1971).

Gerald, J. Edward, "Press-Bar Relationships: Progress Since *Sheppard* and Reardon," *Journalism Quarterly,* XLVII (Summer 1970), 223. Outcome of free press vs. fair trial debate summarized.

Gillmor, Donald M., "The Puzzle of Pornography," *Journalism Quarterly,* XLII (Summer 1965), 363. Traces court decisions in area of obscenity including Roth. For *Ginzburg* case and aftermath, see Kenneth S. Devol, "The Ginzburg Decision: Reactions in California," *Journalism Quarterly,* XLV (Summer 1968), 271.

Lowry, Dennis T., "Agnew and the Network TV News: A Before/After Content Analysis," *Journalism Quarterly,* XLVIII (Summer 1971), 205. Networks played it somewhat safer post-Agnew.

Murray, Randall L., "Harry S Truman and Press Opinion, 1945–53," Ph.D. thesis, University of Minnesota, 1972. A documented analysis of the influence of press opinion on Truman.

Payne, Darwin, *The Press Corps and the Kennedy Assassination. Journalism Monographs,* No. 15, February 1970. Newspaper and broadcast performance at Dallas.

Pfaff, Daniel W., "Race, Libel, and the Supreme Court," *Columbia Journalism Review,* VIII (Summer 1969), 23. Surveys Supreme Court decisions of 1960s in libel area which involved press freedom, points out connection to racial decisions. For the *Times v. Sullivan* case and antecedents see Robert M. Bliss, "Development of Fair Comment as a Defense to Libel," *Journalism Quarterly,* XLIV (Winter 1967), 627.

Pember, Don R., "The 'Pentagon Papers' Decision: More Questions than Answers," *Journalism Quarterly,* XLVIII (Autumn 1971), 403. A scholarly analysis of the Supreme Court decision upholding the *New York Times* and *Washington Post.*

Scher, Jacob, "Access to Information: Recent Legal Problems," *Journalism Quarterly,* XXXVII (Winter 1960), 41. An authoritative summary for the 1950s by a Northwestern University journalism professor who was special counsel for the Moss subcommittee.

Sigma Delta Chi, *Report of the 1970 Advancement of Freedom of Information Committee.* Chicago: Sigma Delta Chi, 1970. Access to the news summarized.

U. S. Congress, House Committee on Government Operations, *Availability of Information from Federal Departments and Agencies,* H.R. No. 2084, 86th Congress, 2nd session. Washington: Government Printing Office, July 2, 1960. A five-year summary of the trend toward secrecy. Reports with a similar title were issued every six months by the Moss subcommittee.

Index

Abbot, Willis J., 328, 392–93, 567, 723
Abbott, Lyman, 403
Abbott, Robert S., 635, 637
Abel, Élie, 607
Abell, Arunah S., 166, 173–74, 192
Abolitionist press, 211–16, 218–22
Abrams v. United States, 753
Access, right of, 757–59
Acme Newspictures, 478, 711
Adams, Frank S., 654
Adams, Franklin P., 431, 490, 574
Adams, John, and press, 80, 119–25
Adams, Samuel, 68, 70, 71, 78–81, 86n
Adams, Samuel Hopkins, 404, 432
Adams, Thomas, 126
Addison, Joseph, 13–14, 38, 44
Adler, Julius Ochs, 427
Advertising:
  agencies, rise of, 333–34
  brand names, 335, 411
  Bureau of Advertising, 337, 688
  early English, 14–15, 54–56
  in colonies, 24, 32, 44–45, 52, 54–55, 74
  in early nineteenth century, 147, 168–69
  in late nineteenth century, 316–17, 324, 333–35, 347
  intermedia competition, 445–46, 618–20
  regulation of, 405
  representatives, 337
  retail stores, 335
  revenues (1880–1910), 334–35, 337
  revenues (1929–70), 594–95, 618–20
  taxes on, 15, 748–49
Afro-American newspapers, 634–36, 639–40
Agnew, Spiro T., and press, 745–48
Agricultural news, 565
Agronsky, Martin, 607
Aitken, Robert, 89, 143
Akron Beacon-Journal, 626
Akron Press, 396, 460
Akron Times-Press, 460
Albany Evening Journal, 182–83, 340
Albany Knickerbocker, 626
Albany Times-Union, 459, 626
Albuquerque *New Mexico State Tribune,* 460, 712
Alexander, Peter W., 252–53
Alexander, Rev. William M., 635
Alford, Theodore C., 565
Alien and Sedition Acts of 1798, 120–25
Allen, Eric W., 726, 728
Allen, Frederick Lewis, 570
Allen, Robert S., 491
Alsop, Joseph, 491, 522, 536, 540, 544, 656
Alsop, Stewart, 491
Amarillo Globe Times, 661n
American Association of Advertising Agencies, 334
American Association of Schools and Departments of Journalism, 727–28
American Association of Teachers of Journalism, 727, 728
American Bar Association, 757
American Broadcasting Company:
  and criticism, 714, 715, 721
  founding, 591n
  news correspondents, 599, 606–9
  stations, 600, 602
  war coverage, 530, 545–46
American Council on Education for Journalism, 728
American Magazine, 405, 569, 631
American Mercury, 571
American Museum, 143
American Newspaper Directory, 334
American Newspaper Guild, 624, 625, 680–686, 687, 725, 730

American Newspaper Publishers Association, 332–34, 337, 342–44, 405, 592–95, 678–79, 683–84, 687–92, 706, 725, 728, 732, 748–49
American Press Association, 331, 340, 468, 489
American Press Institute, 724
American Quarterly Review, 155
American Socialist, 515
American Society of Journalism School Administrators, 728
American Society of Newspaper Editors, 436, 664, 695, 722–24, 728–30, 756–58
American Telephone & Telegraph Company, 589–91, 604
American Weekly, 359, 632, 701, 706
Anderson, James H., 638
Anderson, Paul Y., 485n, 660
Andrews, Bert, 484
Angelo, Frank, 667
Annenberg, Max, 709
Annenberg, Moses L., 454
Annenberg, Walter H., 625, 631
ANPA Research Institute, 732
Antrim, Elbert M., 710
APME Red Book, 725
AP Review, 731
Archer, Thomas, 9
Arena, 290, 403
Areopagitica, 10–11, 56, 57
Argus of Western America, 148, 158
Arnett, Peter, 539, 544–46
Arrowsmith, Marvin, 474
Arthur, William B., 579
ASCAP, 724
Ascoli, Max, 572
Ashmore, Harry S., 671
Associated Business Press, 728
Associated Negro Press, 640
Associated Press, *see* Press Associations
Associated Press Managing Editors Association, 471–72, 724–25, 746, 758
Associated Press Radio-Television Association, 472
Associated Press v. NLRB, 683–84
Associated Press v. Walker, 754
Association for Education in Journalism, 728
Atchison Globe, 430
Atlanta Constitution, 294–96, 371, 456, 490, 629, 653–54, 670
Atlanta Georgian, 459, 626
Atlanta Herald, 294, 298
Atlanta Journal, 296, 530, 589, 629, 670
Atlanta Times, 622n
Atlanta World, 634, 640
Atlantic, 403, 571, 638
Atlantic cable, 329–30
Attwood, William, 666
Audit Bureau of Circulations, 334
Ayer, N. W. & Son, 334

Bache, Benjamin Franklin, 117, 120, 124, 125
Bade, Wilbur, 685
Bailey, Charles W., 563
Baillie, Hugh, 476, 478, 712
Baker, Ray Stannard, 403, 405
Baker, Russell, 494
Baldwin, Hanson W., 483, 529, 536, 544
Baltimore *Afro-American,* 634–36, 639–40
Baltimore American, 458
Baltimore Evening News, 294, 397–98, 451, 458
Baltimore Evening Sun, 458
Baltimore *Federal Republican,* 141
Baltimore Gazette, 310
Baltimore News-Post, 458, 625
Baltimore Patriot, 197
Baltimore Post, 458, 460
Baltimore Star, 458
Baltimore Sun:
  cartoonist, 495, 496, 498
  crusading, 397–98
  foreign and Washington staffs, 482–83, 485n, 491, 528–29, 547, 563
  founding, 173–74
  news enterprise, 197–201
  recent developments, 420, 458, 625, 653, 664–66
Bantam Books, Inc. v. Sullivan, 751n
Barbour, John, 565
Barnard, Robert T., 663
Barnes, Joseph, 484, 527, 566
Barnett, Claude A., 640
Barron, Clarence W., 568
Barron's, 569
Barth, Alan, 730
Bartholomew, Frank H., 478
Bassett, James, 658
Batchelor, C. D., 498
Beach, Moses Y., 169, 199, 267
Beatty, Morgan, 607
Beck, Edward Scott, 710
Beebe, George, 664
Beech, Keyes, 484, 533–34, 536, 540
Bell, Edward Price, 483, 487, 519
Bell, Jack, 474
Bell, Phillip A., 219–20
Bell Syndicate, 493, 499
Bellows, James G., 656–57
Benjamin, Park, 172
Bennett, James Gordon:
  and *Herald,* 164, 170–73, 260
  and news enterprise, 193–94, 196–200
  and Civil War, 213, 224, 236–37, 246

Bennett, James Gordon, Jr., 433–35
Bent, Silas, 700
Berger, Victor, 515–16, 662
Berkeley Barb, 645
Berkeley Independent, 396
Berkeley Post group, 640
Berkeley *Tribe,* 646
Berkson, Seymour, 480
Berlin, Richard E., 706
Bernays, Edward L., 654
Bernstein, Theodore, 654
Berryman, Clifford K., 496
Berryman, James T., 496
Bertelson, Arthur R., 661
Better Homes and Gardens, 631
Bettey, Emily Verdery, 328
Bickel, Karl A., 478, 712
Bierce, Ambrose, 352, 389, 391, 406
Bigart, Homer, 484–85, 529, 534, 539–40, 547
Bill of Rights, 100–101
Binder, Carroll, 483, 668
Bingham, Barry, 659, 663, 730
Bingham, Barry, Jr., 663
Bingham, Robert Worth, 663
Birchall, Frederick T., 426, 483n, 488
Birmingham Age-Herald, 626
Birmingham News, 626, 698n
Birmingham Post, 460, 626
Birmingham Post-Herald, 626
Birney, James G., 214, 225
Bismarck (N.D.) *Tribune,* 661n
Black, Van-Lear, 666
Black, Winifred, 353, 358
Black newsmen, 718
Black Panther, 634, 642, 643
Black press, 218–22, 633–43
Black World, 641
Blair, Francis P., 148, 158–59
Blair, William S., 570
Blakeslee, Alton, 565
Blakeslee, Howard W., 473, 564
Bleyer, Willard G., 700, 726–28
Bliven, Bruce, 572
Block, Herbert L., 495, 498, 658
Block, Paul, 458, 462
Block, Paul, Jr., 667
Block, William, 667
Block newspapers, 482, 625, 667
Bloom, Marshall, 647
Bly, Nellie, 320
Boddy, Manchester, 459, 561
Boettiger, John and Anna, 684
Bogart, John B., 328, 432
Bok, Edward W., 290, 336, 404, 489
Bonfils, Fred G., 436–37, 457, 723
Books:
  booksellers, 9, 27
  censorship in England, 6–8
Books (*cont.*)
  in colonies, 22, 27, 38, 43n, 88, 105
  in 1820, 149–50
  first printed, 2–4
  in post-Civil War period, 288–89
  in realism period, 405–6
  paperbacks, 633
Booth newspapers, 462, 482
Boston Advertiser, 293, 457
Boston American, 390, 457
Boston *Appeal,* 219
Boston *Avatar,* 646
Boston Chronicle, 75
Boston *Columbian Centinel,* 106, 141
Boston *Evening Post,* 46, 75
Boston Gazette, 37–38, 40, 42, 79–80, 85, 87, 115
Boston Globe, 293, 319n, 341, 350, 352, 354, 458, 483, 529, 624, 661n
Boston Guardian, 634, 635, 637
Boston Herald, 293, 371, 458
Boston Herald Traveler, 483, 609
Boston *Independent Advertiser,* 79
Boston *Independent Chronicle,* 126
Boston Journal, 293, 451, 458
Boston Mercantile Journal, 161
Boston Morning Post, 161
Boston *New England Weekly Journal,* 37, 45–46
Boston News-Letter, 29–32, 37, 40, 75
Boston Post, 155, 293, 458, 661n
Boston Post-Boy, 75
Boston *Publick Occurrences,* 20, 27–29
Boston Record, 293, 457–58
Boston Record-American, 624, 698n
Boston Transcript, 161, 293, 371, 458, 624
Boston Traveler, 293, 401, 458, 624
Boston *Weekly Rehearsal,* 46
Boulder (Colo.) *Camera,* 629
Bourke-White, Margaret, 529, 578
Bourne, Nicholas, 9
Bovard, O. K., 660, 661, 665
Bowen, James, 599
Bowen, William S., 365
Bowles, Samuel, III, 183–86, 224, 260, 264–65, 400
Boyle, Hal, 473, 529, 534
Bradford, Amory, 655
Bradford, Andrew, 42, 44–45, 57
Bradford, John, 136
Bradford, William, 41–42, 56–59
Bradford, William, III, 47, 85
Bradford printing family, 46, 47n
Bradlee, Benjamin C., 660, 665
Brady, Mathew, 247–49
Bragg, Rev. George F., 635
Brandt, Raymond P., 660, 661
Brearley, William H., 333
Breslin, Jimmy, 573

Brewster, William, 21
Bridges v. California, 749
Briney, Russell, 663
Brinkley, David, 586, 607
Brisbane, Arthur, 328, 357, 359, 369, 432, 458, 491, 561, 702
Broadcasting:
  advertising, 590–91, 593, 594–95, 610, 618–20
  AM radio, 585, 587–600
  Black stations, 642
  CATV, 603–4, 610
  color, 603
  criticism of, 713–22, 738–48
  cross-media ownership, 609–10, 632–33, 692
  facsimile, 601
  fairness doctrine, 610–12, 756–59
  FM radio, 600–601, 603, 609
  government regulation of, 588, 592–93, 601–4, 609–13, 738, 746–48, 754–57
  group ownership of, 632
  Kerner report and, 716–18
  networks, 591–93, 595–600, 602, 606–9
  news, radio, 588–89, 593–94, 595–99
  news, television, 604, 606–9
  presidential press conference, 740–48
  profits, 602
  public broadcasting, 731
  regional networks, 591–92, 600, 602
  satellites and, 604
  sets in use, 590, 600
  stations on air, 590, 592, 600, 602
  television, 601–10
  time sales, 600, 602
  UHF, 602, 603
  VHF, 602, 609
  Walker report and, 719–22
  See also: American Broadcasting Company, Columbia Broadcasting System, Mutual Broadcasting System, National Broadcasting Company
Bronze Thrills, 641
Brooker, William, 37, 38, 42
Brooklyn Citizen, 624
Brooklyn Eagle, 244, 294, 498, 597, 624, 661n
Brooks, Erastus and James, 199
Broun, Heywood, 431, 493, 607, 680–81, 684, 686, 712
Brown, Cecil, 599
Brown, Sevellon, 667, 724
Browne, Malcolm, 473, 539–41, 545, 563
Brucker, Herbert, 667, 700, 730
Brush-Moore newspapers, 462
Bryan, John, 646
Bryant, William Cullen, 157, 166, 178, 225, 260, 265
Buchwald, Art, 492, 494, 666
Buckley, Samuel, 14
Buckley, William F., Jr., 493, 573, 666
Buffalo Courier-Express, 456
Buffalo Evening Telegraph, 297, 395
Buffalo News, 294, 483, 667
Buffalo Times, 460
Burck, Jacob, 498
Burdett, Winston, 607
Burnham, James, 573
Burns, John F., 564
Burrows, Larry, 546
Burt, George, 663
Bush, Chilton R., 728
Business Week, 579, 631
Butler family, 667
Butter, Nathaniel, 9
Buxton, Charles, 671

Cahn, Robert, 567
Caldwell, Earl, 748
Callender, James, 124, 133
Cameron, George T., 672
Campbell, Chesser M., 711
Campbell, John, 29–32, 37, 45
Canby, Henry Seidel, 571
Canfield, Cass, 570
Canham, Erwin D., 567–68, 730
"Canons of Journalism," 723
Canton Daily News, 661n
Capa, Robert, 538, 578
Carey, Frank J., 565
Carr, Fred, 564
Carroll, Wallace, 670
Carter, Amon G., 671
Carter, Amon, Jr., 625
Carter, Boake, 596, 597
Carter, Nathaniel, 194
Cartoonists, 494–98; *also* 51, 116, 290, 316, 340, 352, 389, 391, 400, 737, 745
Carvalho, S. S., 321, 328–29, 333, 357
Casey, Ralph D., 700, 727, 728
Caslon, William, 46, 54
Cassels, Louis, 563
Cater, Douglass, 572
Catledge, Turner, 654, 655
"Cato Letters," 15, 42
Caxton, William, 5–6, 54–55
Cedar Rapids Gazette, 661n
Censorship, *see* Freedom of the Press
Central newspapers, 629–30
Century, 290, 336, 339, 403, 569
Chafee, Zechariah, Jr., 729
Chamberlain, Sam S., 352, 358
Chamberlain, William Henry, 486
Chancellor, John, 532, 607, 608
Chandler, Dorothy, 657
Chandler, Harry, 390, 657

Chandler, Norman, 657
Chandler, Otis, 484, 627, 657, 659, 666
Chandler newspapers, 625, 627, 629, 633, 657–58, 666
Charleston Courier, 195, 196n, 200, 252
Charleston Mercury, 217–18
Charleston News and Courier, 398
Charleston *Southern Patriot,* 218n
Charlotte News, 627, 670
Charlotte Observer, 627, 669
Charney, Nicolas H., 571
Chattanooga Dispatch, 414
Chattanooga Times, 414, 485n
Chicago American, 390, 455–56, 457, 624, 682, 698n, 721
Chicago Daily News:
  cartoonist, 497–98
  under Field, 624, 653–54, 668, 718
  foreign and Washington staffs, 482–84, 487–88, 490, 494, 563–65, 667
  illustration, 543
  under Knight, 455–56, 626, 667–68
  under Lawson, Strong, Knox, 401, 455–456, 667, 710
  radio station, 589, 592
  under Stone, 260, 298–99, 338, 445
  war correspondents, 371, 519, 528–29, 533, 546
Chicago *Day Book,* 397
Chicago Defender, 634–35, 637, 639–40
Chicago *Democrat,* 203
Chicago Evening Post, 299, 455–56
Chicago Examiner, 390
Chicago Herald, 299–300, 333, 455, 457, 508, 709
Chicago Herald & Examiner, 455, 457, 624, 626, 682
Chicago *Inter Ocean,* 267, 298, 339, 340, 432, 435–36, 454–55, 496
Chicago Journal, 455–56
Chicago Journalism Review, 731
Chicago *Lado,* 644
Chicago Mail, 455
Chicago newspapers (1890–1930), 454–56
Chicago Post, 499
Chicago Post and Mail, 298–99
Chicago Record, 299, 403, 455
Chicago Record-Herald, 400, 455, 482, 490, 496
Chicago Republican, 267, 298
Chicago *Seed,* 646
Chicago Sun, 470, 528, 624, 689, 710
Chicago Sun-Times, 483, 495, 498, 500, 624, 668, 720, 730
Chicago Times, of 1854, 243–44, 300, 455
Chicago Times, of 1929, 456, 561–62, 624, 710
Chicago Times-Herald, 300, 324, 371, 455
Chicago Today, 624
Chicago Tribune:
  cartoonist, 496
  criticism of, 653–54, 699n, 706–11
  and education, 691, 726, 727
  foreign and Washington staff, 482, 485, 488, 490
  group holdings, 461, 629
  illustration, 694
  under McCormick, 455, 623–24, 698n, 706–11
  under Medill, 203, 225, 298, 340, 400
  radio station, 589, 591
  war coverage, 360, 364, 366, 371, 374, 424, 511, 519, 528, 533
  under White, 265, 271
Chicago Tribune-New York Daily News Syndicate, 499–500, 709
Chicano papers, 643–44
Childs, George W., 293, 453–54
Childs, Marquis, 492–93, 660, 661, 712, 730
Christian Century, 572
Christian Recorder, 220
Christian Science Monitor:
  founding and development, 567–68, 653–654
  illustration, 605
  and press criticism, 715, 723, 730, 746
  war correspondents, 528, 533, 540, 546
  Washington and foreign correspondence, 482–83, 485n, 486, 491, 563–64
Christianity in Crisis, 572
Christianity Today, 572
Church, Francis P., 432
Cincinnati Commercial, 203, 265, 297n
Cincinnati Commercial Gazette, 297, 456
Cincinnati Commercial Tribune, 297n, 456
Cincinnati Enquirer, 245, 297, 310, 354, 456, 511, 579, 698n
Cincinnati Gazette, 203, 246, 297n, 467
Cincinnati *Philanthropist,* 214, 225
Cincinnati Post, 297, 393, 395
Cincinnati Times-Star, 297
Civil War:
  abolitionists, 211–16
  black abolitionists, 218–22
  censorship in North, 238–45
  censorship in South, 250–51
  Copperheads, 238, 243–45
  effect on press, 231–32, 253–55
  "fire-eaters," 216–18
  northern press, 233–38, 245–47
  photography, 247–49
  reconstruction, 261–67
  sectionalism as cause, 207–10
  slavery as issue, 210–11, 222–26
  southern press, 250–53
  war correspondents, 236–37, 245–47, 250–253
Clapper, Peter, 609

Clapper, Raymond, 478, 491, 493, 712
Clark, Kenneth, 731
Clark, Robert, 609, 663
Clarke, Selah M., 328, 432
Claypoole, David C., 134
Clemens, Samuel, 204, 289, 360
Cleveland *Alienated American*, 220
Cleveland Call and Post, 640
Cleveland Herald, 297, 420
Cleveland Leader, 297, 456
Cleveland News, 297, 524, 625
Cleveland Plain Dealer, 297, 456, 482–83, 511, 529, 565, 625–26
Cleveland Press, 260, 297, 393, 395, 565, 625, 667, 712
Cobb, Frank I., 386–88, 392, 430–31
Cobbett, William, 98, 105–6, 118, 120–21, 125
Cochran, Negley D., 397
Cockerill, John A., 310, 312–13, 315–17, 321, 326, 340
Cocoa (Fla.) *Today*, 629
Coffeehouses, 24, 27, 135, 195
Coghlan, Ralph, 660, 724
Cohn, Victor, 565
Cole, I. W., 728
Coleman, William, 130, 157
Collier, Robert J., 404
Collier's, 290, 336, 401, 404, 529, 569, 631
Collingwood, Charles, 607
Collins, Isaac, 94
Collis, Joseph F., 686
Columbia Broadcasting System:
  criticism of, 714–15, 718, 721, 737–38, 740, 746, 748
  founding, 591, 593
  and news, 482, 595–99, 606–9
  stations, 600, 602
  war coverage, 529–30, 535, 542, 546
Columbia (S.C.) *State*, 398
Columbian Magazine, 143
Columbus (Ga.) *Enquirer-Sun*, 661n
Columbus (Ga.) *Ledger*, 661n
Columbus (Ga.) *Sun*, 252
Columbus (Ohio) *Citizen*, 396, 626
Columbus (Ohio) *Citizen-Journal*, 625–26
Columbus (Ohio) *Dispatch*, 625, 698n
Columbus *Ohio State Journal*, 626
Columbus *Ohio Stateman*, 244
Columnists, 298, 431, 489–94
Comics, 356–57, 359, 464, 498–501
Commission on Freedom of the Press, 729
Commoner, 511
Common Sense, 89–90
Commonweal, 572
Communications Satellite Corporation, 604, 606
Community Antenna Television (CATV), 603–4, 610
Community News Service, 641
Confederate States Press Association, 250–51
Connecticut Courant, 94, 667
Connecticut Gazette, 46n
Conniff, Frank, 480, 706
Connolly, Joseph V., 480
Conrad, Dr. Frank, 588–89
Conrad, Paul, 497–98, 658, 745
Conwell, Christopher C., 161, 173
Cook, Don, 484, 563
Cooper, Kent, 470–73
Copley, James S., 625, 630
Copley newspapers, 462
Copley News Service, 488n
Corantos, 8–10
Cornish, Rev. Samuel, 219
Coronet, 631
Corpus Christi Caller-Times, 671, 749
Corry, John, 570
Cosby, William, 58–61, 64
Cosgrave, John O'Hara, 404
Cosmopolitan, 290, 336, 401, 404, 569, 631
Cousins, Norman, 571
Cowles, Gardner, 457
Cowles, Gardner, Jr., 526, 579, 627, 633, 668–69
Cowles, John, 627, 668
Cowles, John, Jr., 570, 628, 668
Cowles magazines, 579, 633, 641, 651
Cowles newspapers, 627, 629, 633, 668–69
Cox, James M., 629, 670
Craig, Daniel, 196, 198–99, 467
Craig v. Harney, 749n
Crane, Stephen, 289, 358, 374, 406
Crawford, Nelson Antrim, 727
Creager, Marvin H., 662
Creel, George, 511–15
Creelman, James, 360, 365–66, 374
Crisis papers, 84, 90–91
Crisis, The, Copperhead, 244–45
Crisis, The, NAACP, 634, 635, 638–39, 641
Crist, Judith, 573
Criticism of the press:
  of broadcasting, 713–23
  "credibility gap," 739–48, 758–59
  of newspapers, 695–713
  responses by media, 723–33
Croly, Herbert, 405, 572
Cronkite, Walter, 586, 607, 721
Cross, Harold L., 758
Cross-media ownership, 609–10, 632–33, 692
Croswell, Harry, libel case, 133–34
Crowell, Alfred A., 728
Crowell-Collier magazines, 631
Crowley, Raymond, 661
Crusading:
  early example, 278
  by James Franklin, 38–40
  by Hearst, 359

Crusading (*cont.*)
by *Kansas City Star*, 300–302
in muckraking period, 379–407
by Pulitzer, 310–13, 315–21
Cummings, Amos J., 328, 432
Cunliffe, John W., 726
Current History, 569
Curtis, Cyrus H. K., 290, 336, 440, 453–54
Curtis, George William, 265
Curtis Publishing Company, 575, 631–32
Curtis Publishing Co. v. Butts, 754

Dabney, Virginius, 670, 687
Dale, Edwin L., Jr., 563
Dallas Dispatch, 396
Dallas News, 296, 483, 589, 625, 671
Dallas Times Herald, 625, 627, 658, 671
Daly, John, 532, 609
Dana, Charles A., 180, 223n, 232, 258, 260, 265, 267–69, 271, 326, 432
Daniel, Clifton, 655
Daniels, Derick, 667
Daniels, Jonathan, 670
Daniels, Josephus, 294, 398–99, 670
Darcy, Thomas F., 497–98, 666
Darling, Jay N., 495–96
Davenport, Homer, 352, 358, 389, 496
Davies, Marion, 705
Davis, Elmer, 425, 507, 522, 525–27, 598, 599, 730
Davis, Oscar King, 433
Davis, Richard Harding, 328–29, 358, 365, 373–74, 432–33, 487, 508, 518
Davis, Saville R., 567
Davis, Watson, 564
Dawson, Francis W., 398
Day, Anthony, 658
Day, Benjamin H., 166–69
Day, Price, 666
Day, W. H., 220
Dealey, E. M., 671
Dealey, George B., 296, 671
Decter, Midge, 570
Defoe, Daniel, 13–14, 39, 88
de Fontaine, Felix Gregory, 252–53
De Forest, Dr. Lee, 588–89
Deland, Paul S., 567
Delaney, Dr. Martin R., 219
Delaware Gazette, 46n
De Luce, Daniel, 473, 529
Democratic Review, 157
Dennie, Joseph, 132, 143
Dennis v. United States, 753
Denson, John, 656
Denver *El Gallo*, 644
Denver Express, 396, 436, 460
Denver Post, 436–37, 460, 497–98, 625, 698n, 671–72, 723
Denver Republican, 460
Denver *Rocky Mountain News*, 204, 436–437, 460, 562, 625
Denver Times, 436–37, 460
Denver Tribune, 460
Des Moines Capital, 457
Des Moines Leader, 457
Des Moines News, 396, 457, 460
Des Moines Register, 457, 483, 485n, 496, 498, 526, 565, 627, 654, 668
Des Moines Tribune, 457, 565, 627, 668, 698n, 725
de Tocqueville, Alexis, 140, 152
de Toledano, Ralph, 573
Detroit *Fifth Estate*, 646
Detroit Free Press, 297, 456, 490, 625, 626, 654, 664, 667
Detroit Gazette, 137
Detroit Journal, 340, 456
Detroit *Michigan Chronicle*, 634, 639
Detroit News, 296–97, 333, 393, 395, 456–457, 462, 483, 589, 625, 667
Detroit Tribune, 456
Detroit Times, 456, 459, 625
Deuel, Wallace, 484
Dewart, William T., 453
Dewey, Thomas E., and press, 697
de Young, Michel H., 296
Dickinson, John, 68, 76–78, 100
Dickinson, William B., 667
Dietz, David, 488, 564–65
Dilliard, Irving, 660
Dillon, John A., 310, 386
Dispatch News Service, 485n, 547
Diurnals, 10
Dix, Dorothy, 358, 390
Dixon, Frederick, 567
Don Lee Network, 592
Donovan, Hedley W., 577
Donovan, Robert J., 657
Doolittle, Isaac, 46
Dorfman, Ron, 731
Douglass, Frederick, 220–22, 635, 639
Dow, Charles H., 568
Dow Jones News Service, 568–69
Downs, Hugh, 607
Doyle, Patricia, 565
Dreiser, Theodore, 406
Drew, Elizabeth, 571
Driscoll, Frederick, 302
Drummond, Roscoe, 656
Drummond, William, 718
Dryfoos, Orvil E., 655
Duane, William, 125
DuBois, W.E.B., 635, 637, 638–39
Dudman, Richard, 546, 563
Duffy, Edmund, 495–96, 498

Duluth Herald and *News-Tribune,* 627
Duncan, David Douglas, 533, 535, 546, 578
Dunlap, John, 134
Dunlap, Roy, 724
Dunne, Finley Peter, 299, 405, 490
Duranty, Walter, 425, 483, 485–87

Early, Stephen T., 473, 741
Eastman, George, 601
Eastman, Max, 405, 515
Eaton, William J., 668
Ebony, 569, 631, 641
Eddy, Bob, 667
Eddy, Jonathan, 681
Edes, Benjamin, 79, 85
Editor & Publisher, 337, 565, 697, 729
Editorial pages, 566, 722–24; *for examples see* Greeley, 174–80; Godkin, 269–73; Watterson, 273–74; Scott, 274–75; Pulitzer, 384–88, 430–31; Hearst 392–393; Scripps, 393–95; White, 427–30
Education writers, 565–66
Edwards, Douglas, 607
Eisenhower, Dwight D., and press, 697, 739–40, 742–43
Eisenstaedt, Alfred, 578
Elliott, James, 194
Elliott, Osborn, 579
Elliston, Herbert, 658
Ellmaker, Lee, 454
El Malcriado, 644
El Paso Herald-Post, 460
Elston, Wilbur E., 668
Emery, Edwin, 727
Emporia Gazette, 427–30
English, Earl F., 728
English press:
- first printing, 5
- licensing, 5–12
- in seventeenth century, 8–12
- in eighteenth century, 13–15
- in nineteenth century, 160–61, 554–55

Environment writers, 565
Erickson, Don, 575
Eros, 755
Esquire, 575, 631, 645, 754–55
Estabrook, Robert H., 658, 724
Estes v. State of Texas, 757
Ethridge, Mark, 663, 666
Ethridge, Mark, Jr., 667
Eubanks, Sam, 685
Evans, Amon Carter, 670
Evans, Joseph E., 569
Evans, Rowland, 494
Evans, Silliman, 670
Evans, W. Leonard, Jr., 641
Evansville (Ind.) *Press,* 396
Everybody's, 401, 404, 569

Faas, Horst, 539, 546
Facsimile broadcasting, 601, 732–33
Fairchild Publications, 482
Fairness doctrine, 610–12, 756–59
Fall, Bernard, 546
Family Circle, 633
Family Weekly, 632
Fancher, Edward, 645
Fanning, Larry S., 668
Fanny Hill, 755
Faris, Barry, 480
Farmer's Weekly Museum, 132, 143
Farson, William J., 686
Federal Communications Commission, 591n, 592–93, 601–4, 609–13, 692, 721, 724, 746
Federal Trade Commission, 689
Federalist, The, series, 101
Feiffer, Jules, 645
Feldmeir, Daryle, 668
Felker, Clay, 573
Fenno, John, 105, 108, 109–12, 120, 125
Ferguson, Fred S., 477, 519
Ferguson, J. Donald, 662
Fessenden, Reginald A., 588
Fey, Harold E., 572
Field, Eugene, 298, 490
Field, Marshall, III, 566, 624, 668, 689
Field, Marshall, IV, 668
Field, Marshall, V, 628, 668
Finley, John H., 654
Finnegan, Richard J., 435, 456
First Amendment, 100–101, 748–53, 758
Fischer, John, 570
Fischer, Louis, 486–87
Fischetti, John, 497–98, 668
Fisher, Roy M., 668
Fitzpatrick, Daniel R., 495, 498, 660
Fleeson, Doris, 494
Fleet, Thomas, 46, 75
Fleischmann, Raoul, 574
Fleming, Dewey L., 666
Flint, Leon N., 700, 726–27
Flower, Benjamin O., 403
FM radio, 600–601, 603, 609
Foisie, Jack, 484, 547
Forbes, George, 637
Forcade, Tom, 647
Foreign language press, 45, 630–31
Foreign news:
- in colonial period, 28, 31
- corantos in England, 8–10
- in penny press, 181, 194–96
- post-Civil War, 326
- twentieth century, 422–26, 433, 481–88, 563

Forrest, Wilbur, 656
Fortune, 577, 631, 699
Fortune, T. Thomas, 635–37

Fort Worth Press, 460, 625, 671
Fort Worth Record, 459
Fort Worth Star-Telegram, 459, 625, 671
Forum, 290, 403, 569
Fourdrinier papermaking machine, 343
Fourth Estate, 337
Frady, Marshall, 570
Frank, Reuven, 606
Frankel, Max, 655
Franklin, Benjamin:
  and *New England Courant,* 36, 38–41
  and *Pennsylvania Gazette,* 41–45, 52, 57
  Poor Richard's Almanack, 43, 52
  postal service, 54
  and Revolution, 92, 112
Franklin, James, 38–41, 45, 57, 66n, 759
Frederick, Pauline, 607
Freedom newspapers, 630
Freedom of the press:
  abolitionists, 211–16
  Alien and Sedition Acts of 1798, 120–25
  Areopagitica, 10–11, 56, 57
  "Cato Letters," 15, 42
  economic threats to, 755–56
  First Amendment cases, 748–53
  licensing in colonies, 20, 26–29, 31, 39
  licensing in England, 5–12
  obscenity cases, 754–55
  Pentagon Papers case, 749–51
  prior restraint, concepts of, 6, 12
  right of access, 610–12, 757–59
  right to report Congress, 142
  seditious libel in England, 5–12, 15, 64
  seditious libel in colonies, 26–29, 40–41, 56, 66
  seditious libel cases, U.S., 120–25, 132–34
  tax on advertising, 15, 748–49
  tax on paper, 15, 70–73, 79
  wartime censorship, 238–45, 250–51, 515–520, 522–25, 528, 535–36, 546–47
  Zenger case, 57–66, 121
Freedom's Journal, 206, 219, 633
Freedomways, 641
Freeman, Dr. Douglas Southall, 671
Freneau, Philip, 98, 108–12, 117
Fresno (Calif.) *Tribune,* 396
Friendly, Alfred, 484, 658
Friendly, Fred W., 607, 730
Froell, Earl W., 567
Fuller, Margaret, 180, 327
Fuoss, Robert, 575

Gaine, Hugh, 93
Gales, Joseph, Jr., 142
Gallagher, Wes, 472–73, 529
Gannett, Frank E., 460–62
Gannett newspapers, 460–62, 482, 628–29
Garrison, William Lloyd, 207, 211–14, 220
Garst, Robert E., 654
Garvey, Marcus, 637
Gary (Ind.) *Post-Tribune,* 629
Gauvreau, Emile, 558–59
General Electric Company, 589, 591
George, Henry, 467–68
Georgia Gazette, 46n
Geyelin, Philip L., 660
Gibbons, Floyd, 480, 485
Gibbons v. Ogden, 151
Gibbs, Philip, 425
Gibson, Charles Dana, 290
Gilbert, Samuel, 195
Gill, John, 79, 85
Gilmore, Eddy, 473
Gingrich, Arnold, 575
Ginzburg v. United States, 755
Gitlow v. People of State of New York, 753
Gobright, Lawrence A., 240, 241, 255
Goddard, Morrill, 355–57
Goddard, William, 75
Godey's Lady's Book, 254, 255, 290
Godkin, Edwin Lawrence, 349, 372–73
Golden Argosy, 450
Goldwater, Barry, and press, 697–98, 739
Golf Digest, 633
Gonzales, N. G., 398
Good Housekeeping, 569, 631
Goodman, George J. W., 573–74
Goralski, Robert, 607
Gordon, Thomas, 15
Gortatowsky, J. D., 706
Gould, Alan J., 472
Gould, Jay, 313–14
Grady, Henry W., 294–95, 298, 326, 670
Graham, Evarts A., Jr., 661
Graham, Katharine, 579, 633, 656, 659, 660
Graham, Philip L., 484, 579, 657, 658
Grant, Harry J., 662, 665
Grasty, Charles, 294, 425, 666
Graves, Ralph, 578
Great Falls (Mont.) *Tribune,* 627
Greeley, Horace:
  during Civil War, 222–23, 233–34, 236
  and *New York Tribune,* 162, 164–65, 174–180, 182, 199, 267, 326
  presidential candidate and death, 260, 264–65
Green Duff, 158–59
Green printing family, 47, 47n
Greene, Charles Gordon, 155, 161
Greenfield, James L., 655
Gribayédoff, Valerian, 316, 340–41
Gridiron Club, 482
Gridley, Jeremy, 46
Griffith, Thomas, 578
Grimes, William H., 569
Grosjean v. American Press Co., 749

Grumhaus, Harold F., 711
Grunwald, Henry, 578
Guggenheim, Harry, 627, 666
Guild Reporter, 681, 685, 725
Gunther, John, 484
Gutenberg, Johann, 3

Hackes, Peter, 607
Hadden, Briton, 576–77
Hagerty, James C., 609, 742
Halberstam, David, 483n, 539–41, 545, 570
Haldeman, Walter N., 274, 467
Hale, David, 166, 195–96, 199
Hallock, Gerard, 166, 195–96, 199, 244
Halstead, Murat, 265, 297, 374
Hamilton, Alexander, and press, 102–4, 105–112, 121, 130, 133–34
Hamilton, Andrew, 53, 61–66
Hampton's, 404
Hannegan v. Esquire, 755
Hanson, Elisha, 678, 683, 688
Hapgood, Norman, 404
Harden, Edward, 374
Harding, Nelson, 498
Harmsworth, Alfred, 319n, 554–55
Harper's Bazaar, 631
Harper's Monthly, 181, 254, 289–90, 336, 339, 403, 570–71, 633, 645
Harper's Weekly, 184, 229, 235, 248, 252, 265–66, 271, 290, 336, 339, 496, 654
Harrington, H. F., 726, 727
Harris, Benjamin, 11, 26–29
Harris, Joel Chandler, 490
Harrison, Gilbert A., 572
Harrison, Joseph G., 568
Harsch, Joseph C., 607
Harte-Hanks newspapers, 630, 671
Hartford Courant, 667, 730
Hartford Times, 629, 698n
Harvey, George, 321
Haskell, Henry J., 669
Hawkins, William W., 712
Hayes, Harold T. P., 575
Headlines, 200–201, 254, 312, 317, 359
Hearst, David, 706
Hearst, George, 296, 351–53, 706
Hearst, John Randolph, 706
Hearst, Randolph A., 706
Hearst, William Randolph:
  biographical, 348, 351–52
  founds INS, 479–80
  and Guild, 682, 684–85
  later career, 695, 700–706, 709–11
  and magazines, 336
  in muckraking period, 388–93
  and *New York Journal,* 354, 357–60
Hearst, William Randolph (*cont.*)
  and Spanish-American War, 360, 363–71, 373–75
  and *San Francisco Examiner,* 260, 352–54
  in World War I, 511, 516
Hearst, William Randolph, Jr., 480, 706–7
Hearst Foundation, 706
Hearst Headline Service, 480
Hearst magazines, 631
Hearst newspapers, 390–91, 455, 457–62, 482, 624–26, 629, 632, 656, 667, 672, 702–3
Heaton, John L., 388
Heatter, Gabriel, 597
Hechinger, Fred M., 565
Heinzerling, Lynn, 563
Heiskell, J. N., 671
Hemingway, Ernest, 575
Hendrick, Burton J., 404
Hendrickson, Roy F., 565
Henning, Arthur Sears, 710
Henry, Bill, 530, 599, 607
Hensley, Stewart, 563
Herbert, B. B., 333
Hersh, Seymour M., 547
Hibbs, Ben, 575
Hicks, George, 599
Hicks, Wilson, 578
Higgins, Marguerite, 485, 533–35, 540
Hightower, John, 473, 563
Hill, Isaac, 158
Hilliard, William A., 718
Hills, Lee, 664, 665, 667, 725
Hinckle, Warren, 573
Hinman, George W., 435
Hoben, Lindsay, 662
Hocking, William E., 729
Hodges, Willis A., 221
Hoe presses, 160, 168–69, 201–2, 338–39
Hogan, John, 725
Hoge, James F., Jr., 668
Holden, L. E., 297
Holiday, 631
Holland, Josiah G., 185
Holt, John, 94
Honolulu Star-Bulletin, 629
Hoover, Herbert, and press, 697
Horgan, Stephen H., 341, 554
Horton, George Moses, 219
Houghton, John, 55
Houston Chronicle, 625, 671
Houston Post, 625, 671
Houston Press, 396, 625
Howard, Jack, 713
Howard, Lisa, 609
Howard, Roy W., 397, 432, 459–60, 475–478, 493, 695, 711–13
Howard, Tom, 560
Howe, Ed, 430

Howe, Quincy, 609
Howell, Clark, Sr., 295, 670
Howell, Clark, Jr., 670
Howell, Evan P., 295
Howes, Royce, 667
Hoyt, Palmer, 526, 671, 672
Hoyt, Robert, 572
Hudson, Frederic, 198, 326
Hughes, R. John, 567
Human interest news:
in *Chicago Daily News,* 298
in colonial newspapers, 28, 38, 94
in *New York Sun,* 267–69, 432
in penny press period, 167–68, 170–73
and Pulitzer, 311–12, 314–20
in tabloids, 552–62
and White and Howe, 427–30
Humphrey, Hubert H., and press, 697–98, 719–22, 744
Humphrey, Walter R., 671
Hunter, Charlayne, 718
Hunter, William, 54
Huntley, Chet, 586, 607
Huot, Louis, 597
Huss, Pierre J., 529
Hutchins, Robert M., 729
Hutchinson (Kan.) *News,* 661n
Hutchison, Paul, 572
Huxtable, Ada Louise, 565
Hyde, Grant M., 727

Illustrations:
in Civil War, 247–49
early examples, 3, 7, 47
in late nineteenth century, 290, 317, 339–341, 355–57, 365
Independent, 290, 403
Indiana Gazette, 136
Indianapolis Journal, 371
Indianapolis News, 302, 625, 661n
Indianapolis Star, 456, 625
Indianapolis Times, 460, 625, 661n
Inland Daily Press Association, 336, 728
Insider's Newsletter, 633
Intelsat, 604, 606
Inter American Press Association, 664
International Circulation Managers Association, 336, 691
International Herald Tribune, 655–56
International News Photos, 701
International News Service, *see* Press Associations
Interpretative reporting, 562–80
Irvin, Rea, 574
Irwin, Will, 391–92, 404, 432, 518
Isaacs, Norman, 625, 663, 730
Ives, Frederic, 341

Jackson, Andrew, and press, 158–59
Jackson, Robert M., 671, 721
Jackson (Miss.) *State Times,* 622n
Jacksonville *Florida Times-Union,* 626
Jacksonville Journal, 626
James, Edwin L., 426–27, 519, 654
James, Howard, 567
James, Jack, 532
Janeway, Michael, 571
Janney, Samuel, 215
Jefferson, Thomas, and press, 107–12, 122, 125–26, 129–34, 142
Jennings, Louis J., 265, 415
Jennings, Peter, 609
Jersey Journal, 626
Jet, 641
Jive, 641
John, DeWitt, 567
Johns, George S., 660
Johnson, Earl J., 478–79
Johnson, Gerald W., 666
Johnson, Haynes, 667
Johnson, John H., 616, 641
Johnson, Joseph French, 726
Johnson, Lyndon B., and press, 697–98, 717, 719, 739–40, 744–45
Johnson, Samuel, 13, 15, 55
Johnson, Thomas A., 718
Jones, Dr. Alexander, 198–99, 467
Jones, Charles H., 321, 333
Jones, Clarence B., 639
Jones, George, 181, 265, 415
Jones, Jesse, 671
Jones, Russell, 479, 537
Jonson, Broer, 9
Jordan, Max, 597
Joseph, David H., 427, 654
Journalism Bulletin, 727
Journalism education, 725–29
Journalism Educator, 728
Journalism Quarterly, 727
Journalism reviews, 731
Journalist, The, 316, 337

Kaempffert, Waldemar, 427, 564
Kalb, Bernard, 607
Kalb, Marvin, 607
Kalischer, Peter, 533, 535, 540
Kaltenborn, H. V., 529, 596–97, 598
Kansas City *Adelante,* 644
Kansas City Call, 640
Kansas City Journal, 428, 457
Kansas City Journal-Post, 457, 626n, 756
Kansas City Post, 301n, 457
Kansas City Star, 260, 300–302, 400, 428, 517, 565, 589, 654, 662, 669, 724, 756
Kansas City Star Co. v. United States, 756

Kansas City Times, 301, 340, 457
Kansas City World, 301n, 396, 457
Kaplow, Herbert, 607
Kappa Tau Alpha, 725
Karmin, Monroe, 569
Karnow, Stanley, 563
Kauffmann, John, 667
Kauffmann, Samuel H., 667
KDKA, Pittsburgh, 589, 590
Keating, Edward, 573
Keeley, James, 400, 455, 708
Keimer, Samuel, 43–44
Kellogg, Ansel N., 489
Kendall, Amos, 148, 154, 158–59, 196, 213, 214n
Kennedy, Edward, 531
Kennedy, John F., and press, 605–6, 697–698, 714, 739, 743–44, 757
Kent, Frank R., 491, 666
Kentucky Gazette, 136
Kentucky Post, 395
Keppler, Joseph, 290, 496
Kerby, William F., 568
Kerker, William C., 599
Kerner Report, 716–18
KFAB, Lincoln, Nebraska, 593–94
Kilgore, Bernard, 568
Kilpatrick, James Jackson, 493, 573
King, Larry L., 570
King Features Syndicate, 489–90, 493–94, 499–500, 701
Kingman, Eliab, 194
Kirby, Rollin, 495–96
Kirchhofer, Alfred H., 667
Kirchwey, Freda, 571
Kirk, Russell, 573
Kirkpatrick, Clayton, 711
Kirkpatrick, Helen, 484, 529
Klein, Herbert, 745
Klugh, Paul, 724
KMPC, Beverly Hills, 594
Knapp, Charles W., 333
Kneeland, Samuel, 45
Knickerbocker, H. R., 289, 480, 485
Knight, James L., 664, 668, 670
Knight, John S., 624, 626–28, 664, 667
Knight newspapers, 482, 563, 625, 629, 664–665, 667, 669–70
Knox, Frank, 456, 483, 667, 710
Knox, Thomas E., 231, 243
Knoxville Chronicle, 414
Knoxville News-Sentinel, 460
Koenig, Friedrich, 160
Koenigsberg, Moses, 480
Kohlmeier, Louis, 569
Kohlsaat, Herman, 454–55
Korean War:
  American involvement, 532–33, 536–37
  censorship problems, 535–36
Korean War (*cont.*)
  war correspondents, 473, 532–35
Kotlowitz, Robert, 570
KQED, San Francisco, 731
Kraft, Joseph, 492, 494
Kraslow, David, 484, 563
Krassner, Paul, 646
Kriss, Ronald P., 571
KRLD, Dallas, 627
Krock, Arthur, 273, 427, 483
KSD, St. Louis, 601
KSOO, Sioux Falls, South Dakota, 596n
Kuhn, Oliver O., 724
Kunkin, Art, 645
Kuralt, Charles, 607
KVOS, Bellingham, Washington, 596n

Labor news, 563–64
Labor papers, first, 155–57
Labor unions, printing, 342, 681, 690
La Brie, Henry G., III, 634, 640
LaCoss, Louis, 669
Ladies' Home Journal, 290, 336, 401, 404–405, 569, 631
Laffan, William M., 468–69
La Follette's Magazine, 404, 511
Lahey, Edwin A., 484, 564
Lal, Gobind Behari, 564
Lambert, Tom, 533
Landers, Ann, 666
Landon, Alfred M., and press, 697
Lapham, Lewis H., 571
Lasch, Robert, 660, 661
Laurence, William L., 427, 483n, 564–65
Lautier, Louis, 640
Lawrence, David, 473, 491, 579
Lawrence, William H., 609
Lawson, Thomas W., 404
Lawson, Victor, 299, 455, 468–69, 483, 667
Lazarsfeld, Paul F., 728
Leary, John, 563
Lee, James Melvin, 727
Lee newspapers, 461, 630
Leesburg (Va.) Washingtonian, 215
Leggett, William, 157
Leonard, Richard H., 662
Lerner, Max, 666
Leslie's Illustrated Newspaper, 248, 258, 290, 336, 339
L'Estrange, Roger, 11
"Letters From a Farmer In Pennsylvania," 76–78
Levine, Irving R., 607
Levitas, Samuel M. (Sol), 572
Lewis, Alfred Henry, 404
Lewis, Fulton, Jr., 493, 613
Lewis, W. H., 433

Libel, public law of, 753–54
Liberation News Service, 641, 647
Liberator, The, 211–14
Life, of 1883, 290, 336, 339, 511
Life, photojournalism, 576–78; *also* 528–29, 533, 538, 546, 569, 631, 641, 718
Lincoln, Abraham, and the press, 233–45, 249, 255
Lincoln (Neb.) *Star,* 594
Lincoln *Nebraska State Journal,* 661n
Lippmann, Walter, 405, 431, 485, 491, 492, 494, 656, 666, 680–81
Lisagor, Peter, 484, 563
Literary Digest, 290, 570, 578
Little Rock *Arkansas Gazette,* 671
Local news:
  in colonial paper, 28, 31–32, 38–41, 46, 94
  in Dana's *Sun,* 267–69
  diurnal in England, 10
  in penny press period, 167–68, 170–73
Lochner, Louis P., 473, 529
Locke, David Ross, 490
Loewenthal, Henry, 417, 420
Lomoe, Wallace, 662
London, Jack, 406, 487
London *Daily Courant,* 14
London *Diurnall Occurrences,* 10
London *Examiner,* 15
London Gazette, 11, 55
London *Guardian,* 38
London *Idler,* 55
London Journal, 15
London *Mercurius Politicus,* 11
London *Mist's Journal,* 14
London *Perfect Diurnall,* 11
London *Publick Intelligencer,* 11
London *Spectator,* 14, 38
London *Tatler,* 14
London *Weekly News,* 9–10
Long Beach Independent, 629
Long Beach Press-Telegram, 629, 698n
Long Island Press, 626, 682, 698n
Look, 546, 569, 579, 632, 651, 718
Loory, Stuart, 484
Lord, Chester S., 328, 420, 432
Lorian (Ohio) *Journal,* 755–56
Lorian Journal v. United States, 756n
Lorimer, George Horace, 290, 574–75
Los Angeles Daily News, 459, 561, 625
Los Angeles Examiner, 390, 459, 625
Los Angeles Free Press, 645, 646
Los Angeles Herald-Examiner, 625, 685
Los Angeles Herald & Express, 459, 625, 685
Los Angeles *La Raza,* 643, 644
Los Angeles Mirror, 625
Los Angeles *Open City,* 646
Los Angeles Record, 396, 459
Los Angeles Sentinel, 634, 640
Los Angeles Star, 204
Los Angeles Times:
  cartoonist, 497–98, 745
  current developments, 623, 654, 657–58, 659, 698n, 699n, 718, 749
  dynamiting of, 390
  foreign and Washington staff, 482, 484, 511, 546–47, 563, 565
  founding, 296
  illustration, 747
  radio station, 589
  Times Mirror Company expansion, 625, 627, 666
Los Angeles Times–General Features, 494
Los Angeles Times–Washington Post News Service, 657, 666
Louisiana Weekly, 640
Louisville Courier-Journal:
  in Bingham period, 662–63; *also* 589, 653–54, 659, 668, 698n, 699n, 730, 758
  in Watterson period, 273–74; *also* 260, 294–95, 338, 414, 430, 511
Louisville Herald-Post, 626n
Louisville Times, 294, 663, 668, 723
Lovejoy, Elijah, 212, 214–15
Lower, Elmer W., 606, 609
Lucas, Jim G., 488, 530, 535, 540
Luce, Henry, III, 578, 616
Luce, Henry R., 576–77, 729
Luks, George B., 357
Lundberg, Ferdinand, 699
Luxon, Norval Neil, 728
Lyon, Matthew, 116, 123–24
Lyons, Louis M., 729

Maas, Peter, 573
MacDonald, Kenneth, 669
Macfadden, Bernarr, 558
MacNamee, Graham, 590
Macon Telegraph, 250
Mademoiselle, 631
Madison, James, and press, 100–102, 108–109, 122, 139–40
Madison Capital Times, 682
Madison *Wisconsin State Journal,* 682
Magazine Publishers Association, 725, 728
Magazines:
  advertising, 335–37, 594–95, 618–20
  circulations, 150, 254, 290, 336, 450, 631n
  in Civil War, 248, 252, 254–55
  in colonies, 45, 46, 89
  in early national period, 132, 143–44, 150, 157
  groups, 631–32, 641
  in late nineteenth century, 289–90, 335–337
  in muckraking period, 401–5

Magazines (*cont.*)
news magazines, 576–79
in twentieth century, 569–79, 631–32, 641
Magee, Carl, 712
Maier, Irwin, 662
Mailer, Norman, 570–71, 575, 644, 645
"Maine," sinking of the, 367–72
Malcolm X, 642
Mallet, E., 14
Mallon, Paul, 478
Maloney, J. Loy, 710
Manifest Destiny, 361–63, 380–81
Mann, Arthur, 530, 599
Manning, Reg, 498
Manning, Robert, 571
Marble, Manton, 244, 313
Marbury v. Madison, 122
Marconi, Guglielmo, 423–24, 588, 590
Markel, Lester, 427, 579
Marlow, James, 563
Marshall, John, 122, 151
Martin, Frank L., 728
Martin, Frederick Roy, 470–71
Marvin, Burton, 728
Maryland Gazette, 46
Maryland Journal, 107
Massachusetts Spy, 86–88
Masses, The, 405, 496, 515
Masthead, of NCEW, 724
Mather, Cotton, 39–40
Mather, Increase, 27, 39–40
Mauldin, Bill, 495, 498, 530
Maxwell, W. D., 710–11
Mayflower decision, 610
McAdams, Clark, 660
McCabe, Charles R., 713
McCabe, Margaret Scripps, 713
McCall Corporation, 631
McCall's, 569, 631
McCann-Erickson, advertising agency, 594–595, 619
McClatchy, C. K., 672
McClatchy, Eleanor, 672
McClure, Alexander K., 293
McClure, S. S., 290, 336, 355, 403–5, 489
McClure's, 290, 336, 401–5, 429, 569
McCormick, Anne O'Hare, 426, 483
McCormick, Medill, 708
McCormick, Robert R., 499, 555, 624, 678, 695, 706–11, 748–49
McCormick, Ruth Hanna, 709
McCormick, Stephen J., 609
McCormick-Patterson newspapers, 461, 629
McCue, George, 565
McCullagh, Joseph B., 302, 309, 310, 669
McCulloch v. Maryland, 151
McCutcheon, John T., 400, 455, 485, 496
McDougall, Walt, 316
McEwen, Arthur, 352–53, 358
McGaffin, William, 484
McGee, Frank, 607–8
McGill, Ralph, 670
McGraw-Hill magazines, 631
McGraw-Hill World News Service, 579
McGrory, Mary, 492, 494, 563, 667
McKelway, Benjamin, 472–73, 666
McKnight, C. A. (Pete), 670
McKnight, Felix R., 671
McLean, John R., 297, 354
McLean, Robert, 472, 667, 672
McLean, William L., 453, 667
McLean family, 625, 658
McRae, Milton A., 395, 459
McWilliams, Carey, 571–72
Medary, Samuel, 244–45
Medford (Ore.) *Mail Tribune,* 661n
Medill, Joseph, 225, 298, 400, 708
Medill School of Journalism, 727
Mein, John, 75
Meinholtz, Fred E., 424
Mellett, Lowell, 712
Mellett Fund, 730
Memphis Appeal, 252
Memphis Commercial Appeal, 460, 661n, 670
Memphis News-Scimitar, 460
Memphis Press, 396, 460
Memphis Press Scimitar, 460, 625
Mencken, H. L., 571, 666
Meredith, Hugh, 44–45
Meredith Publishing Company, 631
Mergenthaler, Ottmar, 337–38
Merrill, William H., 320–21, 386, 392
Merz, Charles, 431, 654, 655
Messenger, 642
Mexican War, 190, 199–201
Mexico (Mo.) *Ledger,* 656
Meyer, Agnes E., 658
Meyer, Eugene, 658, 660, 709
Meyer, Philip, 563
Miami Daily News, 485n, 629, 661n
Miami Herald, 626, 654, 664, 669, 725, 749
Mich, Daniel D., 579
Mickelson, Sig, 725
Miller, Charles R., 415–16, 418, 426
Miller, Frank, 498
Miller, Paul, 472–73, 628
Miller, Ruth McCormick, 709
Miller, Webb, 479, 519, 529
Milton, John, 10–11, 56
Milwaukee Advertiser, 203
Milwaukee Free Press, 456
Milwaukee Journal, 662–63; *also* 302, 485n, 566, 589, 625, 653–54, 698n, 729
Milwaukee *Kaleidoscope,* 646
Milwaukee *La Guardia,* 644
Milwaukee Leader, 515–16, 630

Milwaukee Sentinel, 203, 302, 371, 456, 458–459, 511, 625, 698n
Milwaukee *Wisconsin News,* 203, 458, 626
Minneapolis Journal, 302, 404, 627
Minneapolis *Minnesota Daily Star,* 630
Minneapolis *Saturday Press,* 748
Minneapolis Star, 627, 668, 691, 698n
Minneapolis Times, 627
Minneapolis Tribune, 302, 456, 482–83, 485n, 563, 566, 627, 654, 668, 691, 698n, 725, 727, 730
Minnesota Newspaper Association, 730
Mitchell, Edward P., 432, 451–52
Mobile Advertiser and *Register,* 252–53
Modern Medicine Publications, 633
Moeller, Leslie G., 728
Mohr, Charles, 540–41
Monat, Lucia, 567
Moon, Henry Lee, 639
Moore, Fred R., 637
Moore, Herbert, 596
Moore, Leslie, 724
Morgan, Edward P., 609
Morin, Relman, 473, 534
Morley, Felix, 658
Morris, Willie, 570
Morrison, Charles Clayton, 572
Morse, Samuel F. B., 197, 249
Moss, Elizabeth Murphy, 639
Moss Committee, 758
Mosse, Baskett, 728
Mott, Frank Luther, 441, 700, 727–28
Mowrer, Edgar Ansel, 484, 487–88, 528
Mowrer, Paul Scott, 483–84, 487–88, 519
Moyers, Bill D., 666
Muckraking, 401–5
Mudd, Roger, 607
Muddiman, Henry, 11
Mueller, Merrill, 607
Muhammad, Elijah, 642
Muhammad Speaks, 634, 642–43
Muir, Malcolm, 579
Mungo, Ray, 647
Munn v. Illinois, 264
Munsey, Frank A., 290, 335, 432, 435, 440, 449–53, 554, 656
Munsey's, 290, 335–36, 401, 450
Murphy, Dr. Carl J., 635
Murphy, John, 725
Murphy, John H., Sr., 625
Murphy, John H., III, 639
Murphy, Lawrence W., 727
Murphy, William J., 302, 627, 727
Murray, Milton M., 685
Murrow, Edward R., 529, 532, 535, 553, 597, 599, 606–7, 714, 730, 759
Mutual Broadcasting System, 482, 530, 591, 597, 599, 600, 609, 613
Mydans, Carl, 533, 578

NAACP, 638, 639
Nafziger, Ralph O., 2, 728
Nashville Banner, 670, 698n
Nashville News, 396
Nashville Tennessean, 485n, 670
Nast, Thomas, 265–66, 496
Nathan, George Jean, 571
Nation, The, 260, 265, 267, 269–73, 290, 403, 486, 511, 516, 520, 571–72
National Advisory Commission on Civil Disorders, 716–18
National Association of Broadcasters, 592, 714, 723–24, 728, 756
National Association of Educational Broadcasters, 725
National Association of Science Writers, 564–65
National Broadcasting Company:
  criticism of, 714–15, 718, 721
  founding, 591, 593
  news, 482, 596–99, 606–8
  stations, 600, 602
  war correspondents, 529–30, 546, 548
National Catholic Reporter, 572
National Commission on the Causes and Prevention of Violence, 715, 716, 719–722
National Conference of Editorial Writers, 724
National Editorial Association, 333
National Educational Television, 731
National Industrial Recovery Act, 678–80
National Labor Relations Board, 683, 690
National Negro Press Association, 640
National Newspaper Association, 725, 728
National Observer, 569
National Press Club, 482
National Press Photographers Association, 725, 756
National Review, 493, 573
Near v. Minnesota, 748, 751
Negro Digest, 641
Negro History Bulletin, 641
Negro History, Journal of, 641
Negro press, *see* Black press
Negro World, 637
Nelson, Harry, 565
Nelson, William Rockhill, 260, 299–302, 359n, 400, 669
New England Courant, 36, 38–41
New England Daily Press Association, 336
New Hampshire Gazette, 46n
New Haven Register, 183
New Jersey Gazette, 46n, 94
New Journalism of 1880s, 307–21
"New Journalism" of 1970s, 570, 573–75, 644–47
New Leader, 572
New Orleans, early papers, 200n

New Orleans Daily Creole, 220
New Orleans Democrat, 294
New Orleans Item, 294, 457, 625, 756
New Orleans Picayune, 200, 252, 294, 457
New Orleans States, 294, 457, 625, 756
New Orleans Times, 294
New Orleans Times-Democrat, 364, 366, 371, 457
New Orleans Times-Picayune, 457, 625–26, 756
New Orleans Tribune, 457
New Republic, 405, 487, 520, 571–72
New York, magazine, 573–74, 645
New York Age, 634, 635–37, 638, 640
New York American, 389–90, 393, 498, 500, 558, 624
New York *Amsterdam News,* 634, 638, 639–640
New York Call, 515–16, 520
New York City newspapers (1890–1970), 449–50, 624
New York Colored American, 219
New York *Commercial Advertiser,* 105, 183, 234, 402, 452
New York Continent, 451, 554
New York *Courier and Enquirer,* 156, 166, 170, 181, 196, 199, 244
New York Daily Graphic, of 1873, 341, 554
New York Daily News, of 1855, 293, 298, 451
New York Daily News, of 1919:
  cartoonist, 498
  founding and development, 555–61; *also* 623–24, 684, 716
  group ownership, 461, 629, 709
  illustration, 552
  staff, 482–83, 485n, 494, 564
New York Daily Whig, 176
New York *Daily Worker,* 630
New York *East Village Other,* 646
New York Enquirer, 193, 219
New York Evening Call, 630
New York Evening Journal, 558
New York Evening Mail, 293, 500, 511
New York Evening Telegram, 293, 340, 433
New York Express, 199, 293
New York *Freedom's Journal,* 206, 219
New York *Free Enquirer,* 157
New York Gazette, 58–59
New York Gazette and Mercury, 93
New York *Gazette of the United States,* 105
New York Globe, 452, 635, 723
New York Graphic, tabloid, 490, 558–61
New York *Guardian,* 644
New York Herald:
  and Bennett, Sr., 170–73, 196–202, 260, 341
  and Bennett, Jr., 433–35; *also* 316, 401, 424, 511
New York Herald (*cont.*)
  cartoons, 498
  in Civil War, 224, 230, 236–37, 239, 243, 246–48, 254
  illustrations, 189, 439
  and Munsey, 452
  in Spanish-American War, 360, 364–67, 371, 374
New York Herald Tribune:
  cartoonists, 495–96, 498, 500
  final years, 624, 652–57, 659, 664, 743
  foreign and Washington staffs, 482, 484–485, 488, 491, 494, 564
  founding, 435, 452–53
  illustrations, 652, 676
  news in review, 579
  war correspondents, 527–29, 533
New York Independent Journal, 101
New York Journal:
  and Hearst, 354, 357–60, 624
  and muckraking, 388–93, 496
  in Spanish-American War, 360, 364–69, 371, 373–75
New York Journal (1770s), 94
New York Journal-American, 623–24
New York *Journal of Commerce,* 166, 195–196, 198–99, 244, 483, 627
New York Mail, 452
New York Mail and Express, 293
New York *Mechanic's Free Press,* 156
New York *Minerva,* 105
New York Mirror, 459, 558–61, 623
New York Morning Journal, 314, 354
New York *PM,* 526, 529, 566, 666
New York Post:
  and Bryant, 157, 166, 194
  in Civil War, 225, 234, 260, 265, 271
  founding, 130, 133
  and Godkin, 260, 267, 269–73, 372–73
  ownership changes, 454
  and Schiff, 666; *also* 623–24, 698n
  staff members, 403, 488, 494, 511, 516
New York Press, 388, 401, 451
New York *Ram's Horn,* 221
New York *Realist,* 646
New York *Rights of All,* 219
New York *Rivington's New York Gazetteer,* 74
New York *Royal Gazette,* 75
New York *Staats-Zeitung,* 247, 344, 627
New York Star, 451, 566
New York Statesman, 194
New York Signal, 172
New York Sun:
  and Beach, 199, 200
  in Civil War, 221, 232, 234
  and Dana, 260, 265–69, 271, 315, 432
  and Day, 166–69
  evening edition, 432, 624

New York Sun (*cont.*)
and Munsey, 433, 451–53
news in review, 579
news service, 468–69
in Spanish-American War, 360, 364–66, 371
staffing, 309, 321, 328–29, 432, 490
New York Telegram, 432, 452–53, 460, 495–496, 624, 661n
New York *Time Piece,* 121
New York Times:
cartoonist, 496
in Civil War, 223–24, 234–36, 245, 254
foreign and Washington staff, 482–83, 485–87, 494, 563, 730
illustrations, 514, 738
news in review, 579
and Ochs, 412–27; *also* 366, 371
Pentagon Papers case, 738, 746, 748, 750–753
and Raymond, 180–82, 199, 260, 265, 271
staff members, 270, 273, 333, 344, 564–66
and Sulzberger, 653–56; *also* 623–24, 627, 659, 664, 684, 687, 698n, 718
war correspondents, 525, 528–29, 533, 539, 541–46, 548
New York Times Co. v. Sullivan, 753
New York Times Co. v. United States, 749–753
New York Tribune:
in Civil War, 222–23, 233–34, 245–46
columnists and cartoons, 490, 493, 500
and Greeley, 174–80, 199, 260, 267
merger, 452
and the Reids, 272, 337–38, 341, 366, 371
staffing, 326, 328
weekly edition, 176–79
in World War I, 516, 518–19
New York *Village Voice,* 645–46
New York *Vorwärts (Jewish Daily Forward),* 630
New York *Weekly Advocate,* 219
New York Weekly Journal, 59–60
New York *Working Man's Advocate,* 157
New York World:
cartoonists, 496, 499–500
evening edition, 320–21, 432
final years, 430–32, 661
founding, 244–45
growth under Pulitzer, 313–21, 325, 328–329, 333, 340, 354–59
in muckraking period, 384–88, 394
in Spanish-American War, 360, 364–66, 369–75
staff members, 352, 563, 654
in World War I, 511, 519–20
New York World Journal Tribune, 624, 656
New York World-Telegram and Sun, 685, 712–13
New Yorker, of 1834, 176, 180
New Yorker, 544, 574
Newark Ledger, 682
Newark Star-Ledger, 626, 698n
Newfield, Jack, 645
Newhall, Scott, 672
Newhouse, Samuel I., 626, 628, 631–32, 669, 671–72
Newhouse magazines, 631
Newhouse newspapers, 482, 626, 629, 632, 669, 671–72, 682
Newman, Edwin, 607
Newport (R.I.) *Mercury,* 41n
News, early concept of, 2–4, 14, 28
Newsboys, 169, 689–90
Newsday, Long Island, 483, 497–98, 562, 623, 627, 658, 659, 666, 698n
News enterprise, 79, 191–201, 310–21, 418–426, 433–35
News letters, 3n, 4, 8, 10–11
Newspaper Advertising Executives Association, 336
Newspaper Enterprise Association, 397, 488, 711
Newspaper Preservation Act, 692
Newspaper Publicity Law of 1912, 405
Newspapers:
advertising, 594–95, 618–20, 689
black staff members, 718
business managers, 325, 332–33, 336
capital investment, 445, 455–56
circulation:
in Civil War, 237, 254
in 1820s, 135, 150
from 1880 to 1930, 442–44
national circulations, 567–68
in New Journalism era, 285, 299, 316, 355, 359, 415–16
for 1950–70, 623
in penny press period, 167, 172, 174, 176, 185
in tabloid era, 555, 561
competition, 621–22, 624–26, 692
consolidations, 442–44, 620–22
editorial staff, 325–29
evening, rise of, 292, 296
first English, 8–11
first English daily, 14
first European, 1–3
first in colonies, 26–32
first U.S. daily, 134
group ownership, 296–97, 390–91, 395–397, 457–62, 624–30
news in review sections, 579
numbers of:
in colonial period, 53, 93
in 1820s, 135, 150
from 1870 to 1900, 285
from 1880 to 1930, 442–44

Newspapers (*cont.*)
numbers of (*cont.*)
from 1930 to 1971, 620–21
in presidential elections, 697–98
profits, 622–23
qualifications for, 3
salaries, 328, 679–80, 682, 685–86
suburban, 623–24
Sunday, 316, 354–59
trade journals, 336–37
weeklies, 203–4, 285, 444, 630–31
see also: Advertising, Cartoons, Crusading, Editorial page, English press, Foreign news, Headlines, Human interest, Illustrations, Local news, News concepts, News enterprise, Sensationalism, Sports news, Tabloids
Newsprint, 47–48, 94, 343–44, 448, 622
News sheets, 2–3, 6–11, 27
Newsweek, 578–79; *also* 528, 539–41, 547, 563, 633, 656, 660, 718, 721, 746
Newton, V. M., Jr., 758
Nichol, David M., 484, 563
Nieman, Lucius W., 302, 662, 729
Nieman Fellows, 729
Nieman Reports, 729
Niles, Hezekiah, 144
Niles' Weekly Register, 144
Nixon, Raymond B., 629, 727
Nixon, Richard M., and press, 605–6, 658, 692, 694, 698, 714, 739–40, 745–48
Nixon, William Penn, 435
Noble, Edward, 591n
Norfolk *Journal and Guide,* 634, 638, 640
Norfolk Post, 460
Norris, Frank, 406
Norris, John, 333, 344, 417
North American Newspaper Alliance, 488
North American Review, 143, 150, 289–90, 403
North Carolina Gazette, 46n
Northcliffe, Lord, *see* Harmsworth, Alfred
North Star, The, 221–22, 635
Northwest Daily Press Association, 336
Notson, Robert C., 672
Novak, Ralph B., 685
Novak, Robert, 494
Noyes, Frank B., 455, 469, 472, 666
Noyes family, 294n, 666
Nye, Bill, 490

Oakes, John B., 655
Oakland Mail, 396
Oakland Post-Enquirer, 459, 626
Oakland Tribune, 459, 698n
Oberdorfer, Don, 563
O'Brien, Frank M., 453
Obscenity, 754
Ochs, Adolph S., 413–20, 423–27, 454, 654–655
Ochs, George, 454
Ogden, H. C., newspaper group, **461**
Ogden, Michael J., 667
Ogden, Rollo, 426, 654
Oklahoma City News, 396
Oklahoma City Times, 625
Oklahoma City *Oklahoma Journal,* 622n, 625, 731
Oklahoma City *Oklahoma Leader,* 630
Oklahoma City *Oklahoman,* 622n, 625
Older, Fremont, 398
Oliphant, Patrick, 497–98
Olson, Kenneth E., 728
Omaha News-Bee, 459, 626
Omaha World-Herald, 661n
O'Neill, John J., 564
Opelousas (La.) *Daily World,* 732
Orange Coast Daily Pilot, 623–24, 627
Oregon Spectator, 203
Organization for a Better Austin v. Keefe, 751n
Orlando Sentinel, 629
Orlando Star, 629
Osbon, B. S., 245–46
Otis, Harrison Gray, 296, 390, 657
Outcault, Richard F., 356–57, 498
Outlook, 290, 403
Owens, J. Hamilton, 666
Oxford Gazette, England, 11

Paine, Robert F., 395, 397, 488
Paine, Tom, 84, 88–92, 107–8
Paley, William S., 591, 606, 616
Palmer, Frederick, 487, 518
Palmer, L. F., Jr., 718
Palmer, Lincoln B., 688
Pamphlets:
in colonies, 41, 56
in England, 7, 8, 10
Panama City (Fla.) *News-Herald,* 661n
Pancoast, George, 353
Parade, 632
Paris Herald, 352, 433, 452, 554, 655–56
Park, Robert E., 696
Parker, George, 635
Parker, George B., 712
Parks, Gordon, 578
Parks, William, 46
Parsons, Geoffrey, 656
Pasadena Independent and *Star-News,* 629
Patterson, Alicia, 666
Patterson, Eleanor Medill, 624, 709

Patterson, Eugene C., 670
Patterson, Joseph Medill, 499, 555, 560–61, 709
Patterson, Paul C., 666
Patterson, Robert W., 708
Payne, Ethel L., 639
Payne, Eugene, 670
Pearson, Drew, 491
Pearson's, 404
Pegler, Westbrook, 477, 493, 705, 712
Penn, Stanley, 569
Pennekamp v. Florida, 749
Pennsylvania Magazine, 89, 143
Pentagon Papers case, 738, 749–53, 758–59
People's Voice, 640
Perlik, Charles A., Jr., 686
Perlman, David, 565
Perry, Chris J., Sr., 635
Peters, Charles, 573
Peterson's, 290
Pettit, Tom, 607
Philadelphia, *American Weekly Mercury*, 42, 44–45, 57
Philadelphia, *Aurora*, 117, 125
Philadelphia, *The Cent*, 161, 173
Philadelphia Daily News, 454, 625, 627
Philadelphia Daily Transcript, 173
Philadelphia *Distant Drummer*, 646
Philadelphia Evening Bulletin, 293, 453–54, 483, 485n, 625, 664, 667, 685, 721, 728, 746
Philadelphia Evening Item, 293, 453
Philadelphia Evening Public Ledger, 454
Philadelphia Evening Telegram, 454
Philadelphia Evening Times, 451, 453
Philadelphia *Freeman's Journal*, 93, 194
Philadelphia *Gazette of the United States*, 105, 108, 109–11
Philadelphia Inquirer, 293, 454, 625, 627, 664
Philadelphia *Journeyman Mechanic's Advocate*, 155–56
Philadelphia *National Gazette*, 109–12, 117
Philadelphia newspapers (1895–1930), 453–454
Philadelphia News-Post, 397
Philadelphia *New World*, 135
Philadelphia *North American*, 454
Philadelphia *Pennsylvania Chronicle*, 75, 76
Philadelphia *Pennsylvania Gazette*, 43–45, 52
Philadelphia *Pennsylvania Evening Post*, 93, 134
Philadelphia *Pennsylvania Journal*, 71–72, 85
Philadelphia *Pennsylvania Packet*, 84, 91n, 134
Philadelphia *Porcupine's Gazette*, 105–6, 118
Philadelphia *Port Folio*, 132, 143, 150
Philadelphia Press, 293, 454
Philadelphia Public Ledger, 173, 197, 201–2, 293, 453–54, 482, 493–94
Philadelphia Record, 293, 299, 319n, 350, 453–54, 625, 682–83, 685
Philadelphia Sun, 454
Philadelphia Times, 293, 340, 454
Philadelphia Tribune, 634, 635, 640
Phillips, David Graham, 386, 404
Phillips, John S., 403, 405
Phillips, Walter Polk, 468
Phoenix *Arizona Journal*, 622n, 732
Phoenix *Arizona Republic*, 498, 626
Phoenix Gazette, 626, 732
Photoengraving, 341
Photography, 247–49, 341, 365, 576–79, 732
Phylon, 639
Physical Culture, 558
Piercy, J. W., 726
Pittock, Henry L., 672
Pittsburgh Courier, 634–35, 637–38, 639
Pittsburgh Dispatch, 458
Pittsburgh Gazette, 136
Pittsburgh Leader, 458
Pittsburgh *The Mystery*, 219
Pittsburgh Post-Gazette, 458, 625–26, 667, 698n
Pittsburgh Press, 294, 458, 460, 625
Pittsburgh Sun-Telegraph, 458, 625
Pope, James S., 663, 758
Popular Mechanics, 631
Portland News, 396
Portland *Oregon Journal*, 626, 672
Portland *Oregonian*, 204, 260, 274–75, 593, 626, 672, 718
Portland Reporter, 622n
Postal service, 29, 37, 54, 135, 284, 329, 336
Potter, Philip, 563, 666
Powell, Adam Clayton, 640
Powell, Dr. C. B., 639
Poynter, Nelson, 670
Preetorius, Dr. Emil, 309
Presidential elections, press in, 697–98
Presidents and the press, 740–48
Press associations, 198–99, 329–32, 465–81
  Acme Newsphotos, 478, 711
  Agence France-Presse, 466
  Associated Negro Press, 640
  Associated Press:
    and broadcast news, 593, 595–96, 596n
    and Chicago *Inter Ocean* suit, 469
    of 1848–1900, 467–69
    and Guild, 683–85, 689
    of Illinois, 468–69
    leading correspondents, 473–74, 563–65
    management, 472–73
    of New York, 198–99, 239–41, 255, 330–32, 467–69

Press Associations (*cont.*)
  Associated Press (*cont.*)
    of 1900–1970, 469–72, 481, 717–18
    war correspondents, 473–74, 529, 533, 539, 541, 545, 547
    Western AP, 330, 467
    Wirephoto, 560
    World Service, 470
  Community News Service, 641
  Confederate States, 250–51
  Copley News Service, 482
  Dispatch News Service, 485n, 547
  Havas, France, 330, 466, 468, 475
  Hearst Headline Service, 480
  International News Photos, 701
  International News Service:
    broadcast news, 593, 595–96
    and Hearst, 700–702
    leading correspondents, 480
    management, 480
    merger with UP, 480
    war correspondents, 529, 533
  Liberation News Service, 640, 647
  McGraw-Hill World News Service, 482
  National Negro Press Association, 640
  Reuters, Britain, 330, 466, 468, 482, 533
  Stefani, Italy, 330
  Underground News Service, 647
  United Press, of 1882, 331, 467–68
  United Press Associations, of 1907:
    broadcast news, 593, 595–96
    founding by Scripps, 474–75
    and Guild, 683
    leading correspondents, 479
    management, 478–79
    under Roy Howard, 475–78
    war correspondents, 529, 532
  United Press International, of 1958:
    leading correspondents, 563, 565, 750
    management, 478–79
    merger of UP and INS, 478, 480
    and Negroes, 640, 718
    1970 status, 481
    war correspondents, 539, 541, 545–46
  Universal Service, 480, 564, 701
  Wolff, Germany, 330, 468
Press councils, 730
Press-Radio Bureau, 596
Price, Byron, 472, 524–25
Pride, Armistead Scott, 633–34
Printers' Ink, 337, 405
Printing:
  in colonial period, 21, 22, 26–27, 31, 41, 43–45, 46–48, 54, 94
  first Chinese, 2
  first English, 5
  first European, 1–4
  spread of, 149, 337–38
  technological improvements, 732
Printing presses:
  English Common Press, 46–48
  hand presses, 54, 160
  post-Civil War, 254, 338–39, 353, 732
  steam presses, 160, 168–69, 201
  stereotyping, 202–3
Progressive, The, 572
Providence Evening Bulletin, 294, 667, 725
Providence Journal, 196n, 294, 564, 667, 725
Providence Tribune, 626n
Public Broadcasting Service, 731
Public Relations Society, 728
Publishers' Auxiliary, 337
Publishers-Hall Syndicate, 494
Puck, 290, 336, 339, 496
Pueblo (Colo.) *Sun,* 396
Pulitzer, Albert, 314, 354
Pulitzer, Herbert, 431
Pulitzer, Joseph:
  biographical, 306–9
  in muckraking period, 384–88
  and *New York World,* 313–21, 325, 340, 430, 554, 703
  and *St. Louis Post-Dispatch,* 309–13, 660
  in Spanish-American War, 360, 364–75
  and *Sunday World,* 354–59
  and yellow journalism, 350–51
Pulitzer, Joseph, II, 431, 660
Pulitzer, Joseph, III, 659, 660
Pulitzer, Michael E., 672
Pulitzer, Ralph, 388, 431
Pulitzer prizes, lists of, 485n, 661n
Pulitzer School of Journalism, 726
Pulliam, Eugene C., 625, 630
Pyle, Ernie, 493, 529–30

Quick, 641

Radio, *see* Broadcasting
Radio Corporation of America, 589–91, 604, 606
Radio-Television News Directors Association, 611, 613, 724, 725, 758
Raleigh *Hope of Liberty,* 219
Raleigh News and Observer, 294, 399–400, 670
Raleigh *State Chronicle,* 294, 399
Ralph, Julian, 328, 358, 360, 432
Ramparts, 573
Rapid City (S. D.) *Journal,* 627
Raskin, A. H., 564
Raspberry, William, 718
Rather, Dan, 607, 608, 721
Ray, Dr. Charles Bennet, 219
Ray, E. Lansing, 669

Raymond, Henry J., 179, 180–82, 199, 223–224, 234–36, 245, 260, 265, 326
Read, Opie, 490
Reader's Digest, 569, 575–76, 631
Reardon Report, 757
Reasoner, Harry, 607–9
Redbook, 631
Reddick, DeWitt, 728
Red Lion Broadcasting Co., Inc. v. FCC, 611
Red Wing (Minn.) *Daily Republican,* 333
Reese, Benjamin H., 661
Reeves, Ben F., 663
Reid, Helen Rogers, 452–53, 656, 659
Reid, John C., 328, 415
Reid, Ogden, 656
Reid, Ogden Mills, 452
Reid, Whitelaw, 246, 272, 467
Reid, Whitelaw (younger), 656
Reitemeyer, John R., 667
Remington, Frederic, 365
Reporter, magazine, 544, 570, 572, 641
Reston, James B., 483, 494, 655, 665, 730
Reuters, Britain, 330, 466, 468, 482, 533
Revere, Paul, 86n
Review of Reviews, 403, 570
Revolutionary War:
  causes, 69–81
  and press, 84–95
Reynolds, Frank, 609
Rhett, Robert Barnwell, 216–18
Rhode Island Gazette, 41, 46n
Rhodes, E. Washington, 635
Richardson, Albert D., 246
Richardson, Donovan, 568
Richmond Civil War newspapers, 251–52
Richmond Dispatch, 251–52
Richmond Enquirer, 130n, 247, 251–52
Richmond Examiner, 124
Richmond News Leader, 671, 698n
Richmond *Southern Illustrated News,* 252
Richmond Times-Dispatch, 663, 670, 687, 698n
Ridder, Herman, 344
Ridder family, 627–29
Ridder newspapers, 462, 482
Riis, Jacob A., 328, 432
Ritchie, Thomas, 130
Rivers, William L., 730
Riverside (Calif.) *Press-Enterprise,* 661n
Rives, John C., 159
Rivington, James, 68, 73–76
Roanoke World-News, 724
Roberts, Chalmers, 563
Roberts, Charles W., 563
Roberts, Elzey, 625
Roberts, Roy A., 669, 724
Robertson, Josephine, 565
Rochester Democrat & Chronicle, 629
Rochester Journal, 458, 626
Rochester Post-Express, 458
Rochester Telegraph, 182
Rochester Times-Union, 629
Roosevelt, Franklin D., and press, 521–27, 561, 676–80, 684, 687–89, 697, 710, 712, 740–41
Roosevelt, Theodore, and press, 385–86, 389–90, 397, 400, 401–5, 428–29, 451, 637
Root, Waverly, 484
Rose, Louis, 710
Rosenbloom v. Metromedia, 754
Rosenstock, Arthur, 686
Rosenthal, Abe, 655, 750
Ross, Charles G., 660, 741
Ross, Harold, 519, 574, 577
Roth v. United States, 755
Rothstein, Arthur, 579
Rotogravure, 425
Rovere, Richard, 574
Rowan, Carl T., 494, 532, 540, 718
Rowell, Chester, 672
Rowell, George P., 334
Royko, Mike, 668
Royster, Vermont Connecticut, 569
RTNDA Bulletin, 725
Rubin, Morris H., 572
Rumor, 635
Russell, Benjamin, 98, 106, 141
Russell, Charles Edward, 404
Russell, J. S., 565
Russell, L. T., 682
Russell, William Howard, 245
Russwurm, John B., 219
Ryan, William L., 563

Saarinen, Aline, 607
Sacramento Bee, 672, 698n
Sacramento Star, 396, 460
Sacramento Union, 204
Safer, Morley, 542, 547, 607
St. Louis Chronicle, 297, 395, 457
St. Louis Dispatch, 309
St. Louis Evening Star, 457
St. Louis Globe-Democrat, 302, 309–10, 456, 625–26, 669, 722
St. Louis *Missouri Democrat,* 203, 302
St. Louis *Missouri Gazette,* 203
St. Louis *Missouri Republican,* 203, 302, 310
St. Louis Observer, 214–15
St. Louis Post, 310
St. Louis Post-Dispatch:
  cartoonist, 495
  founding by Joseph Pulitzer, 260, 302, 309–13, 321, 340, 400, 403
  news in review, 579

St. Louis Post-Dispatch (*cont.*)
  recent developments, 653–54, 659–62, 698n
  staff members, 483, 485n, 563, 565, 566, 672, 724
St. Louis Republic, 302, 333, 456
St. Louis Star-Times, 457, 625, 663
St. Louis *Westliche Post,* 265, 271, 302, 308–9
St. Nicholas, 290, 336
St. Paul Daily News, 627
St. Paul Dispatch and *Pioneer Press,* 302, 369, 398, 456, 565, 627, 698n, 724
St. Paul *Minnesota Pioneer,* 203
St. Petersburg Times, 670
Salant, Richard S., 606
Salinger, Pierre, 743
Salisbury, Harrison E., 479, 483n, 542–43, 545
Salt Lake City *Deseret News,* 204
Sampson, W. Walter, 635
San Antonio *El Rebozo,* 644
San Antonio Express, 625, 671
San Antonio Light, 459, 625
San Antonio News, 625, 671
San Bernardino Sun and *Telegram,* 629
Sandburg, Carl, 397, 405
San Diego Journal, 625
San Diego Sun, 396
San Diego Tribune and *Union,* 625
San Fernando (Calif.) *Valley Times Today,* 627
San Francisco *Alta California,* 204
San Francisco Bay Guardian, 647
San Francisco Bulletin, 204, 395, 459
San Francisco *The Californian,* 190
San Francisco Call, 204, 459, 511
San Francisco Call-Bulletin, 398, 459
San Francisco Chronicle, 296, 353, 364, 371, 395, 482, 511, 523, 565, 579, 625, 672
San Francisco *The Elevator,* 220
San Francisco Evening Post, 459
San Francisco Examiner, 260, 296, 352–54, 358, 364, 366, 390, 459, 625, 672, 698n
San Francisco News, 396, 459
San Francisco News-Call Bulletin, 625
San Francisco Oracle, 646
San Francisco *Rolling Stone,* 646
San Jose Mercury and *News,* 627, 629
San Juan Star, 626, 627
Sann, Paul, 666
Santa Barbara News-Press, 672
Sargent, Dwight E., 656, 729
Sarnoff, David, 590–91, 598, 606
Sarnoff, Robert, 606
Saturday Evening Post, 574–75; *also* 290, 336, 401, 569, 631, 754
Saturday Review, 571
Satellites, 604, 612
Savannah Republican, 252
Sawada, Kyoichi, 546
Scali, John, 609
Scanlan's Monthly, 573
Schaleben, Arville, 662
Scheer, Robert, 573
Schenck v. United States, 753
Scherer, Ray, 607
Scherr, Max, 645–46
Schiff, Dorothy, 666
Schneider, Lawrence, 730
Schorr, Daniel, 607
Schramm, Wilbur, 728
Schultz, Sigrid, 518
Schurz, Carl, 265, 271, 302, 308–9
Schuster, Marjorie, 565
Science news, 355, 359, 564–65
Science Service, 397, 488, 564
Scott, Frank W., 726
Scott, Harvey W., 258, 260, 274–75, 672
Scott, James W., 299–300, 333
Scott, Walter, 339
Scovel, Sylvester, 365, 374
Scranton (Pa.) *Times,* 661n
Scribner's, 290, 336, 339, 403, 570
Scribner's Commentator, 522
Scripps, Charles E., 712
Scripps, Edward Wyllis, 260, 296–97, 378, 393–97, 459, 474–77, 711
Scripps, Edward W., II, 712, 713
Scripps, Ellen, 297
Scripps, George, 297, 395
Scripps, James, 396, 459, 713
Scripps, James E., 296–97
Scripps, John P., 713
Scripps, Robert Paine, 459–60, 711–12
Scripps, Robert Paine, Jr., 712
Scripps-Howard Newspaper Alliance, 488, 529, 564
Scripps-Howard newspapers, 397, 432, 436, 457–62, 482, 619, 624–29, 632, 656, 664, 667, 670, 685, 705, 711–13
Scripps League of Newspapers, 396, 461–62, 630, 713
Scripps-McRae newspapers, 296–97, 395–96, 405, 459, 712
Scull, John, 136
Seaton, William W., 142
Seattle Post-Intelligencer, 459, 625, 684
Seattle Star, 396, 625
Seattle Times, 485n, 625, 627
Sedgwick, Ellery, 571
Seditious libel:
  Alien and Sedition Acts of 1798, 120–125
  in colonies, 26–29, 40–41, 56–57
  Croswell case, 133–134
  Dennie case, 132
  end of U. S. prosecutions, 134
  in England, 5–12, 15, 64

Seditious libel (*cont.*)
Zenger case, 57–66, 121
Emil A. Sees v. United States, 756n
Seigenthaler, John, 670
Seitz, Don C., 333
Seldes, George, 699
Seltzer, Louis B., 667, 712
Senger, Frank, 728
Sengstacke, John H., 628, 637, 639
Sensationalism, in news, 312, 314, 318–19, 348–75, 436–37, 552–62
Sepia, 641
Sevareid, Eric, 598, 599, 607, 608, 722
Seventeen, 631
Seymour, Forrest W., 669, 724
Seymour, Gideon, 668
Shapiro, Henry, 563
Shaw, Albert, 403
Shawn, William, 574
Shedd, Fred Fuller, 728
Sheehan, Neil, 539–41, 545, 750
Sheehan, Vincent, 710
Shelley, Jack, 725
Sheppard v. Maxwell, 759n
Sherrill, Robert, 572, 575
Sherrod, Robert, 575
Sherwood, Robert E., 522, 525, 527
Shirer, William L., 485, 529, 597–99, 710
Shnayerson, Robert, 571
Shoemaker, Vaughan, 498
Sidey, Hugh, 563
Siebert, Fred S., 728
Sigma Delta Chi, 725, 729, 730, 758
Silha, Otto A., 691
Simons, Howard, 660
Simonton, James W., 467
Sinclair, Upton, 405–6, 699
Singerly, William M., 293, 299, 319n, 453
Skillin, Edward, 572
Small, William, 721, 740
Smalley, George W., 246, 326
Smart Set, 571
Smith, Ballard, 321
Smith, Delos, 565
Smith, Everett W., 726
Smith, Henry Justin, 667
Smith, Howard K., 607–9
Smith, J. Kingsbury, 480, 706
Smith, Merriman, 479
Smith, Paul C., 672
Smith, Richard, 467
Smith, Samuel Harrison, 135, 142
Smith, Seba, 161
Smith, Stanford, 691
Smith, W. Eugene, 578
Smith, William Henry, 467
Snider, Arthur J., 565
Social Justice, 522
Soderlind, Sterling, 569
Solidarity, 515
Soth, Lauren K., 669
South Carolina Gazette, 46n
Southern Newspaper Publishers Association, 336, 728
Southern School News, 670
Sower printing family, 47, 47n
Spanish-American War, 360–75
Sparks, Fred, 484, 488, 534
Speed, Keats, 452–53
Speidel newspapers, 630
Spencer, M. Lyle, 727
Sperling, Godfrey, 567
Spokane Press, 396
Spokane Spokesman-Review, 445
Sports Afield, 631
Sports Illustrated, 577–78, 631
Sports news, early, 172, 327
Springfield (Mass.) *Republican,* 183–86; *also* 166, 224–25, 260, 265, 271, 403, 638
Springfield (Mass.) *Union,* 186
Stamp Act of 1765, 70–73, 79
Stamp Act of 1712, in England, 11, 15
Stanley, Henry M., 326, 433
Stanton, Dr. Frank, 606, 611, 738, 745–46
Star Chamber, 7
Starck, Kenneth, 730
Stark, Louis, 427, 483n, 563–64
Stars and Stripes, 519, 530–31, 547
Starzel, Frank J., 472
Staten Island Advance, 682
Stationers Company, 6–7
Stauffer newspapers, 630
Stedman, Alfred D., 565
Steele, A. T., 484
Steele, Jack, 563
Steele, John, 597
Steele, Richard, 13–14, 38, 44
Steffens, Lincoln, 402–3, 405
Steinem, Gloria, 574
Stempel, John E., 728
Stereotyping, 331, 338–39
Stern, J. David, 454, 682, 683, 685
Steven, William P., 668, 671, 725
Stevens, Edmund, 567
Stevenson, Adlai E., and press, 697
Stickney, Joseph L., 433
Stillson, Jerome B., 326
Stokes, Thomas L., 478, 488, 492–93, 712, 730
Stone, Arthur L., 726
Stone, I. F., 644, 646–47
Stone, Melville E., 260, 298–99, 468–69
Stoneman, William, 484
Storey, Wilbur F., 243–44, 300n
Storke, Thomas M., 672
Stouffer, W. C., 724
Stout, Elihu, 136

Stowe, Leland, 484, 529
Straight, Michael, 572
Stringer, William H., 568
Strong, Walter A., 455, 592, 667
Strout, Richard L., 563, 567, 572
Successful Farming, 631
Suffolk Sun, 627
Sullivan, Mark, 404, 491, 656
Sully, François, 539, 547
Sulzberger, Arthur Hays, 427, 654, 655, 659, 687
Sulzberger, Arthur Ochs, 655
Sunday supplements, 632, 641
Swain, William M., 166, 173, 197–98
Swift, Dean, 13, 15
Swing, Raymond Gram, 483
Swisshelm, Jane Grey, 327
Swope, Herbert Bayard, 431
Sylvester, Arthur, 743
Syndicates, 483–501
Syracuse Journal Telegram, 458

Tabloids, 552–62; *also* 451, 454, 456, 458, 459
Tabor City (N.C.) *Tribune,* 661n
Tacoma Times, 396
Taft, Charles P., 297
Taft-Hartley Act, 690
Talese, Gay, 575, 655
Tan, 641
Tammen, Harry H., 436–37, 457
Tampa Sentinel-Bulletin, 640
Tampa Tribune, 758
Tappan, Arthur, 166, 195
Tarbell, Ida M., 403, 405
Tatarian, Roger, 476, 478–79
Taylor, Bert Leston, 490
Taylor, Charles H., 293, 319n
Taylor, Edmond, 710
Telegraph, and news, 197–98, 203, 284, 329–30
Telephone, 284, 327, 329
Television, *see* Broadcasting
Temko, Allan, 565
Terre Haute (Ind.) *Post,* 396, 460
Territorial Enterprise, Nevada, 204
Texas Observer, 570, 647
Thackery, Ted O., 666
Thaler, K. C., 563
Theta Sigma Phi, 725
This Week, 632
Thomas, Isaiah, 68, 85–88, 106, 143
Thomas, Lowell, 597, 607
Thomas, William F., 657
Thomason, Mims, 478
Thompson, Dorothy, 493–94
Thomson, Lord, 616, 629
Thomson newspapers, 482, 629
Thorpe, Merle H., 726
Thrasher, J. S., 250–51
Time, 576–78; *also* 363, 482, 528–29, 533, 540–41, 631, 718
Time Inc., 576–78, 631, 633
Time Inc. v. Hill, 754
Times-Picayune Publishing Co. v. United States, 756n
Today, 623
Toledo Blade, 482, 490, 667, 698n
Toledo News-Bee, 396
Toledo Times, 667
Tolischus, Otto D., 483, 528
Topliff, Samuel, Jr., 195
Towne, Benjamin, 134
Townsend, Edward W., 328, 358
Transradio Press Service, 596
Tremaine, Frank, 479
Trenchard, John, 15
Triangle Publications, 631
Trohan, Walter, 710
Trotter, William Monroe, 635, 637
Trout, Robert, 607
True Story, 558
Truman, Harry S, and press, 690, 697, 710–11, 741–42
Tucker, Lem, 718
Tucson *Arizona Daily Star,* 672
Tucson Daily Citizen, 672
Tuesday, 641
Tulsa World, 698n
Turcott, John, 564
Turner frontier theory, 137–38
Turner, George Kibbe, 403
TV Guide, 631
Tweed Ring, 265–66
Typesetting machines, 337–38, 732

Underground press, 644–47
Underground Press Syndicate, 647
United Feature Syndicate, 491–94, 499–500, 711–12
United Nations Correspondents Association, 483
United Press, *see* Press Associations
U.S. News & World Report, 482, 579
United States Daily, 579
United States Gazette, 194
United States Information Agency, 532
United States v. The Washington Post Company, 749–53
Universal Service, 480, 564, 701
Urban Writers' Society, 565
Utica (N.Y.) *Daily Gazette,* 198
Utica (N.Y.) *Daily Press,* 661n
Utica (N.Y.) *Observer-Dispatch,* 661n

Utley, Clifton, 607

Vallandigham, Charles, 238–39, 244
Van Anda, Carr V., 418–26, 432, 555
Vanderbilt, Cornelius, Jr., 561
Vandercook, John, 475
Vann, Robert L., 635, 637–38
Vanocur, Sander, 607, 721
Van Valkenberg, E. A., 454
Variety, 594
Veblen, Paul, 672
Venture, 632
Vermont Gazette, 46n, 123
Veronis, John J., 571
Veseler, George, 9, 21
Vietnam War:
  Cold War background, 537–39
  criticism of, 744–48
  early Saigon press corps, 539–42
  escalation of war, 542–44
  military censorship, 546–47
  Pentagon Papers case, 738, 749–53, 758–759
  press corp changes, casualties, 545–46
  war correspondents, 473–74, 479, 539–42, 545–47
Villard, Henry, 239, 247, 271, 273
Villard, Oswald Garrison, 273, 375, 465–66, 511, 516, 571, 699, 700
Virginia and Kentucky Resolutions, 122
Virginia Gazette, 46
Vogue, 631
Voice of America, 527, 531–32
Von Eckardt, Wolf, 565

Wagner Act, 683–84, 687
Wales, Henry, 488, 519
Walker, David, 219
Walker, Gordon, 533
Walker, John Brisben, 404
Walker, Stanley, 656
Walker Report, Chicago 1968 riots, 719–22
Wallace, DeWitt, 576
Wallace, Edward, 725
Wallace, George C., and press, 697, 699n
Wallace, Henry A., and press, 572, 697
Wallace, Mike, 607
Wallace, Tom, 723
Wall Street Journal, 567–69; *also* 482, 485n, 494, 623, 653–54
Walters, Basil L., 667
Wanamaker, Thomas B., 453
Waples, Douglas, 728
War correspondents, *see* specific war
War of 1812, 138–41, 143
Ward, Arch, 710
Ward, Paul W., 666
Wardman, Ervin, 388, 401, 451
Warren Commission, 739, 757
Washington, Betty, 718
Washington, Booker T., 637
Washington, George, and press, 90, 94, 110–12, 117–18, 121
Washington, Leon H., 640
Washington *Congressional Globe,* 142
Washington Daily News, 458, 460, 485n, 562, 624, 712
Washington Free Press, 646
Washington Globe, 159
Washington Herald, 458, 624, 626
Washington Monthly, 573
Washington *National Intelligencer,* 128, 142, 233
Washington Post:
  cartoonist, 495–96, 498
  criticism of, 740, 746, 750–53, 758
  foreign and Washington staffs, 482, 484, 485n, 511, 541, 544, 546, 563, 627, 657
  founding and early years, 294, 364, 458
  Graham group holdings, 579, 633, 656, 746
  illustrations, 612
  in Meyer and Graham periods, 658–60; *also* 565–66, 624, 642, 653–54, 662, 664, 686, 698n, 709, 718, 724
  staff members, 663, 670, 730
Washington reporting:
  to Civil War, 142, 158–59, 174, 193–94
  since Civil War, 331, 481–85, 562–63, 613
  presidential press conferences, 740–48
Washington Star:
  cartoonists, 496
  foreign and Washington correspondents, 482–83, 485n, 493, 546, 563
  founding, 294
  major events at, 666–67; *also* 458, 579, 624, 654, 724, 746
Washington Times, 451, 458, 624, 626
Washington Times-Herald, 709
Washington *United States Telegraph,* 159
Wasp, The, 133
Waterbury (Conn.) *Republican* and *American,* 661n
Watson, Mark S., 666
Watson, Morris, 683–84
Watterson, Henry, 258, 260, 273–75, 430, 663
Waymack, W. W., 669
Watsonville (Calif.) *Register-Pajaronian,* 661n
WCCO, Minneapolis, 725
WCKY, Cincinnati, 725
WCSH, Portland, Maine, 725
WDAF, Kansas City, 756

WEAF, New York, 589, 590, 591
Webb, James Watson, 166, 170, 172, 181, 198–99
Webster, Noah, 105
Wechsler, James A., 666
Weed, Thurlow, 176, 181, 182–83
Weeklies, 203–4, 285, 444, 630–31
Weeks, Edward A., 571
Weller, George, 484
Western movement, and press, 135–40, 148–154, 158–59, 203–4
Western Newspaper Union, 337, 489
Western Union Telegraph Company, 330, 467
Westinghouse, 589, 591
WGBH, Boston, 731
WGN, Chicago, 591, 709
WGY, Schenectady, 589, 591, 601
WHAS, Louisville, 663
WHDH, Boston, 609
Wheelock, Joseph A., 302, 369
White, E. B., 574
White, Horace, 265, 271
White, Llewellyn, 729
White, Paul, 596
White, Robert M., II, 656
White, William Allen, 427–30; *also* 301, 404–5, 453, 521
White, William L., 429–30
White, William S., 493
Whitehead, Don, 473, 534
White House Correspondents Association, 482
Whiteville (N.C.) *News Reporter,* 661n
Whitman, Walt, 406
Whitney, John Hay, 656
Whitney v. California, 753
WHO, Des Moines, 725
Wichita Beacon, 756
Wichita Eagle, 756
Wicker, Tom, 494, 655
Wiggins, James Russell, 658, 660, 730, 758
Wiley, Louis, 417–18, 421, 427
Wilkes, John, 15
Wilkins, Roy, 639
Williams, Cranston, 688
Williams, Nick B., 657, 665
Williams, Talcott, 726
Williams, Walter, 726
Williams, Wythe, 425, 486–87, 519
Willkie, Wendell, and press, 697
Wills, Garry, 493, 575
Wilson, Quintus, 728
Wilson, Woodrow, and press, 397–400, 405, 426, 430–31, 511–17, 519–20, 637
Winchell, Walter, 490, 561
Winslow, Edward, 21
Winston-Salem Journal, 670
Wireless, 423–24
Wisner, George, 167
WJZ, New York, 591
WNBC, New York, 589
Wolf, Daniel, 645
Wolfe, Tom, 573
Wolseley, Roland E., 634
Woman's Home Companion, 631
Women journalists, early, 320, 327–28, 352–353
Wood, J. Howard, 691, 711
Woodford, John N., 642
Woods, James B., 686
Woollcott, Alexander, 574
WOR, New York, 591
Worcester Gazette and *Telegram,* 721
World's Work, 569–70, 638
World War I:
  American entry, reasons for, 507–11
  censorship, military, 518
  censorship, of press, 515–17
  civil liberties, 516–17, 519–20
  Committee on Public Information, 511–15
  Espionage Act of 1917, 515–17, 522
  Sedition Act of 1918, 516–17
  Trading with the Enemy Act, 516, 518, 522
  war correspondents, 483–85, 487–88, 518–19
World War II:
  American entry, reasons for, 520–22
  censorship, military, 522, 528
  censorship, of press, 522–25
  civil liberties, 522
  Office of War Information, 525–27, 599
  Voice of America, 527, 531–32
  war correspondents, 473, 479–80, 484, 528–31
Wright, Fanny, 156–57
Wright, H. J., 723
WTAM, Cleveland, 725
WTOP-FM, Washington, 642
WWJ, Detroit, 589

Yank, 530
Yankee network, 592
Yellow journalism, 348–75; defined, 350, 357
"Yellow Kid," 356–57, 498
Yost, Casper S., 700, 722
Young, Arthur Henry, 496
Young, P. Bernard, 638
Youngstown Telegram, 460
Youth's Companion, 290, 336

Zenger, John Peter, 53, 57–66